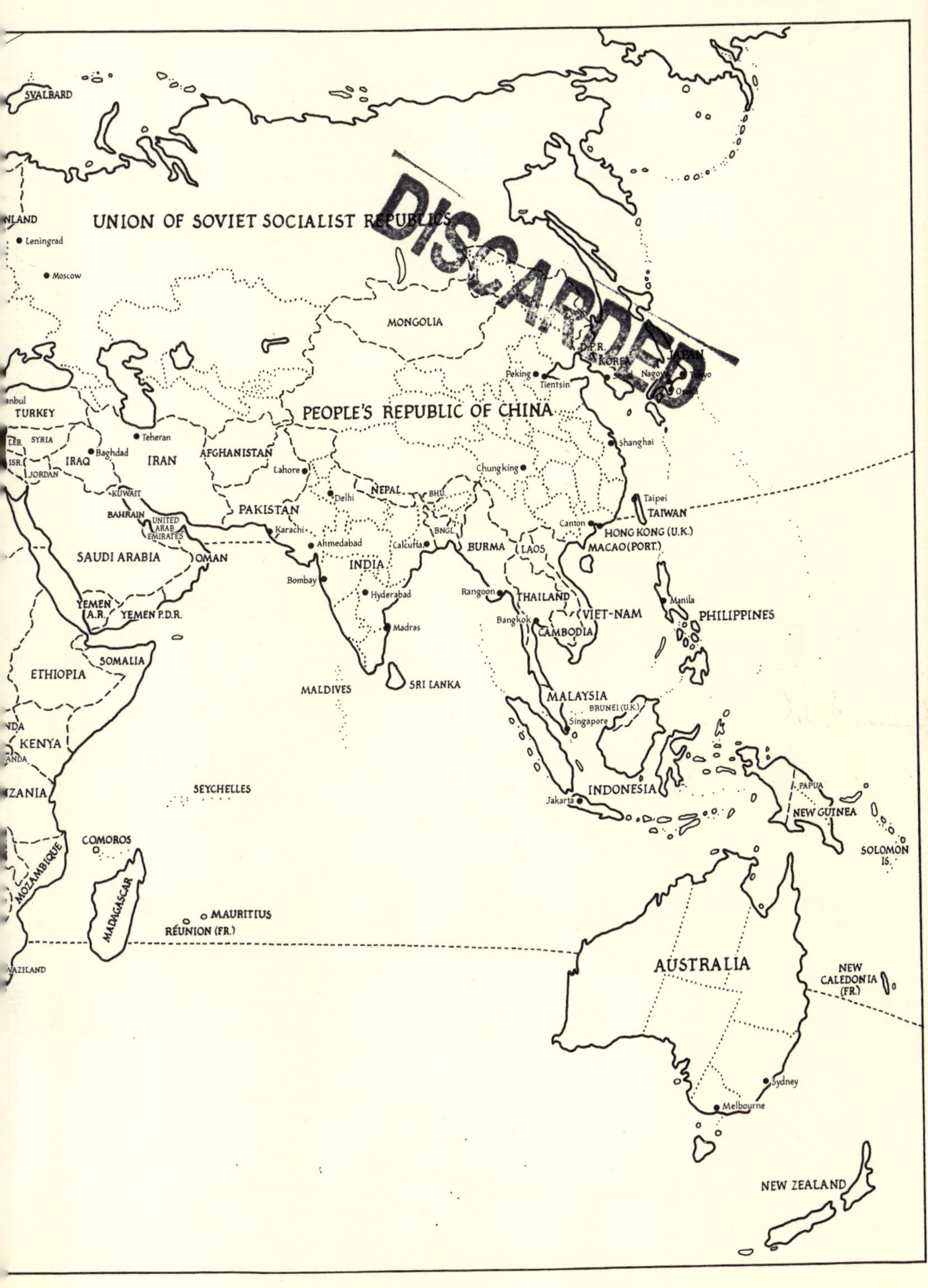
SVALBARD
UNION OF SOVIET SOCIALIST REPUBLICS
Leningrad
Moscow
MONGOLIA
D.P.R.
KOREA
JAPAN
Peking
Tientsin
Seoul
Tokyo
TURKEY
SYRIA
Teheran
PEOPLE'S REPUBLIC OF CHINA
IRAQ
Baghdad
IRAN
AFGHANISTAN
JORDAN
Shanghai
Lahore
Chungking
KUWAIT
Delhi
NEPAL
Taipei
TAIWAN
BAHRAIN
UNITED ARAB EMIRATES
PAKISTAN
Karachi
BNGL.
Canton
HONG KONG (U.K.)
SAUDI ARABIA
OMAN
Ahmedabad
Calcutta
BURMA
LAOS
MACAO (PORT.)
INDIA
Bombay
Hyderabad
Rangoon
THAILAND
Manila
YEMEN A.R.
YEMEN P.D.R.
Madras
Bangkok
VIET-NAM
PHILIPPINES
CAMBODIA
SOMALIA
ETHIOPIA
MALDIVES
SRI LANKA
MALAYSIA
BRUNEI (U.K.)
Singapore
KENYA
SEYCHELLES
INDONESIA
PAPUA
Jakarta
NEW GUINEA
COMOROS
MOZAMBIQUE
SOLOMON IS.
MADAGASCAR
MAURITIUS
RÉUNION (FR.)
AUSTRALIA
NEW CALEDONIA (FR.)
Sydney
Melbourne
NEW ZEALAND

The United States in the 1980s

The United States in the 1980s

Editors
Peter Duignan
Alvin Rabushka

Foreword
W. Glenn Campbell

Hoover Institution

Stanford University

The Hoover Institution on War, Revolution and Peace, founded at Stanford University in 1919 by the late President Herbert Hoover, is an interdisciplinary research center for advanced study on domestic and international affairs in the twentieth century. The views expressed in its publications are entirely those of the authors and do not necessarily reflect the views of the staff, officers, or Board of Overseers of the Hoover Institution.

Hoover Institution Publication 228

International Standard Book Number: 0–8179–7281–1
Library of Congress Catalog Card Number: 79–5475
Printed in the United States of America

Designed by Elizabeth Gehman

Contents

Foreword

An era of optimism prevailed in the United States from the end of the Korean War until the United States became heavily involved in the Vietnam conflict. During the 1960s it was widely stated that Americans were destined to build the Great Society at home and that poverty and racism would soon be vanquished through state agencies, massive public expenditure, and high taxes. These beliefs were also projected abroad. Nation building, massive investment, education, and foreign aid were all intended to modernize and democratize the developing countries at a rapid rate.

Now, at the beginning of a new decade, optimism is muted and it is recognized that such positive steps can and should be taken, but the means to bring about such changes are limited. Today, the prevailing public policy views of the 1960s have radically changed, and there is widespread support for policies that would restrain government involvement, lower taxation, and restrict the size of government and the scope of public enterprise. Citizens generally seek to do more for themselves; and they wish their government to do less, but to work more efficiently. Overseas, the United States has recognized that the exercise of responsible power has definite limitations. Foreign aid cannot by itself cure poverty. Modernization cannot be achieved quickly. At the same time, it has been recognized that the United States cannot export democracy to the rest of the world. Since Vietnam the limits of the nation's ability to influence world events in a constructive manner have become clearly evident.

On the other hand, coexistence and détente have not restrained Soviet expansionism. Neither has the United States won more friends among the developing countries. It has become clear that in the 1980s more must be spent on defense to face responsibly the growing Soviet military strength. Alliances must be reaffirmed and strengthened. It must be acknowledged that positive change is likely to be gradual, as opposed to the negative and often disastrous consequences of war and revolutionary upheaval. It is also evident that a sizable percentage of those who supported the concept of a Great Society have become disillusioned with the meager and sometimes negative results. At the same time, a new realism and a new sobriety have emerged that can reestablish the commitment of the United States to the defense of a free society in which individuals live at liberty and with self-respect.

As the United States enters the 1980s, Americans must deal with high taxes, increasing government regulation, inflation, fuel shortages, and enormous bureaucracies at federal, state, and local levels. Abroad, the United States appears to many to have lost the vision of how to act like a great power as well as the means to project its power and influence. In the past two decades some extraordinary changes have taken place in the United States: the gross national product has more than quadrupled; the federal budget has grown to more than $500 billion a year; hundreds of new government programs have gone into operation; government regulation of the economy has increased dramatically; dependency on foreign sources for oil has grown to almost one-half of total consumption; taxes have increased to the point where they now account for about 40 percent of personal income. In 1969, 48 percent of the federal budget was spent on defense and 30 percent on health, education, and income security. By 1977, those percentages had been reversed. In 1978, the federal government spent over $190 billion on its twelve largest income security programs—the most massive income redistribution in the history of mankind.

The next few years will present the United States with difficult choices both at home and abroad. At home, governmental over-regulation of business is diminishing the productivity of American workers. Growing inflation, brought about by tens of billions of dollars in federal budget deficits, is eroding personal savings and investment. High taxation has encouraged state tax and spending limitation movements, as voters begin to voice their views concerning the mounting cost of government. Greater government involvement in the universities threatens both the freedom and quality of higher education. Escalating costs jeopardize the availability of health care to all Americans. Price and availability of energy are uppermost in everyone's mind. The viability of the social security system is frequently questioned. And major improvements are required in our welfare, health, housing, and criminal justice systems.

In foreign affairs, a consistent and coherent strategy appears lacking. It will be necessary to counter increased Soviet aggressiveness vis-à-vis the developing countries and the Soviet strategic forces and nuclear arms that now face NATO and Western Europe. Many perceive an arc of crisis spreading across the Middle East and Africa, compounded by congressional restrictions adversely affecting the conduct of foreign affairs. The United States is no longer the dominant military power in the world, and the conduct of its foreign affairs is viewed by many abroad to be ambiguous and indecisive.

As the United States enters the 1980s amid political fragmentation, it is nonetheless clear that confidence can be restored; that a consensus in Congress can and must be rebuilt; that a rediscovery of a sense of purpose can be achieved; and that there does exist the national will required to deal effectively with the problems that confront the country domestically and internationally.

In this volume thirty-two experts have been asked to address major domestic and foreign policy questions that face the United States in the 1980s. This approach was taken in recognition of the fact that the major problems of the coming decade are interrelated, that no problem can be resolved in isolation, and that different perspectives can contribute to a clearer and more balanced understanding of problems that are often viewed as separate from one another. The primary focus is on the situation now and in the immediate future; the secondary focus is on the remainder of the decade. The authors analyze the central issues, describe the policy options open to the country, and recommend specific courses of action to deal with or mitigate the problems confronting the United States. Their findings offer a comprehensive statement for the United States to govern itself more effectively and to restore faith in the resolve of the United States as the leader of the free world.

W. Glenn Campbell
Director

Hoover Institution
Stanford University

Preface

This volume provides a review and analysis of major domestic and international issues that will face the United States in the current decade. It should be of special interest to all those concerned with the formation of public policy: to members of the academic community, to elected officials at federal, state, and municipal levels of government, to professionals of the media, to members of the business professions, and to all Americans concerned with national and international problems.

The authors were encouraged to treat their subjects from the point of view of their own perceptions of the major questions that will arise in this decade, and to view their analyses from the perspective of the United States. The essays, in general, review the origins of each issue under discussion and conclude by analyzing the choices that should be made to deal effectively with both problems and opportunities. Although they are largely based on the independent scholarly work of each author, the essays have been written so that they will be accessible to a large and varied audience, most of whom are not scholars.

All the contributions have been critically reviewed by experts, to whom the Hoover Institution is indebted for their helpful comments on the drafts. The authors were free to accept or reject the suggestions and criticisms of the reviewers. Thus, the conclusions herein represent the authors' own views and are not necessarily those of the co-editors or of the Hoover Institution.

The publication of these essays together, in one volume, emphasizes the significance of their interrelation. The individual essays are also published separately and may be obtained from the Hoover Institution.

Senior Fellow Martin Anderson, who is currently on leave, served as the project director until April 1979. At that time Senior Research Fellow Dennis Bark was appointed as project coordinator, and Senior Fellows Peter Duignan and Alvin Rabushka were named co-editors. Duignan had primary responsibility for the essays in international studies and Rabushka for those in domestic studies.

In publishing a volume of this kind, containing essays by contributors living in different parts of the United States and abroad, a great deal of effort is involved. For this reason, the book is the product of a large number of individuals who have lent their time and advice to the co-editors and the authors.

A special debt of thanks is owed the four members of the Advisory Committee of the 1980s project: George P. Shultz, President of the Bechtel Corporation and Professor at the Graduate School of Business, Stanford University; George J. Stigler, Chairman of the Hoover Institution Domestic Studies Advisory Committee and Charles R. Walgreen Distinguished Service Professor of American Institutions, the University of Chicago; Robert A. Scalapino, Robson Research Professor of Government, director, Institute of East Asian Studies, University of California, Berkeley, and editor, *Asian Survey;* and James Q. Wilson, Henry Lee Shattuck Professor of Government, Harvard University. Their advice concerning the issues to be reviewed, and the time they have taken to follow the development of the project since its inception, are gratefully acknowledged. Their association with the project, however, does not necessarily entail their endorsement of the views presented in the individual essays.

Special appreciation is extended to those who have contributed their skills to the smooth technical preparation of the manuscripts. Diane Renaud performed superbly as the project secretary. Mickey Hamilton, general manager of the Hoover Institution Press, assisted by her able staff, held the responsibility for designing and producing the volume.

For their continual and valued assistance throughout the development of the 1980s project, we also extend gratitude to Thomas G. Moore and Richard F. Staar, directors, respectively, of the Hoover Institution's Domestic and International Studies Programs. Associate Director and Senior Fellow Richard T. Burress, Associate Director and Senior Research Fellow Darrell M. Trent, and Public Affairs Coordinator and Senior Research Fellow George Marotta have been closely associated with the project from its inception, and their assistance is greatly appreciated.

Dennis L. Bark
Project Coordinator

Contributors

DOMESTIC POLICY

MARTIN ANDERSON is a senior fellow of the Hoover Institution at Stanford University. He served as Special Assistant to President Nixon and was heavily involved in the development of national welfare policy. Dr. Anderson is a graduate of Dartmouth College and received his Ph.D. from M.I.T. His most recent book is *Welfare: The Political Economy of Welfare Reform in the United States.*

MICHAEL J. BOSKIN is Professor of Economics, Stanford University. He received his M.A. and Ph.D. from the University of California, Berkeley. He is a specialist in public finance and is the author of 25 articles and the editor of several books.

JOHN H. BUNZEL is a senior research fellow of the Hoover Institution at Stanford University. He was President of San Jose State University from 1970 to 1978. He is the author of several books, including *Anti-Politics in America,* and many articles on American politics and higher education. Dr. Bunzel is a graduate of Princeton University and received his Ph.D. from the University of California at Berkeley.

RITA RICARDO CAMPBELL is a senior fellow of the Hoover Institution at Stanford University. She was a member of the National Advisory Drug Committee of the FDA from 1972 to 1975 and a member of the Advisory Council on Social Security from 1974 to 1975. A graduate of Simmons College, she received her Ph.D. in economics from Harvard University. Her most recent book is *Social Security: Promise and Reality.*

MILTON and ROSE FRIEDMAN, a husband-and-wife team of economists, are authors of *Capitalism and Freedom.* MILTON FRIEDMAN, recipient of the Nobel Prize for economics in 1976, is a senior research fellow of the Hoover Institution at Stanford University and Paul Snowden Russell Distinguished Service Professor of Economics at the University of Chicago. ROSE FRIEDMAN, in addition to other writings in economics, is the author of *Poverty: Definition and Perspective.*

ALAN GREENSPAN is President of Townsend-Greenspan and Co., Inc. in New York City. He was Chairman of the Council of Economic Advisers under President Ford. Dr. Greenspan received his Ph.D. in economics from New York University where he is Adjunct Professor of Economics. He is a member of the Board of Overseers of the Hoover Institution and serves on the boards of directors of Mobil Corporation, Morgan Guaranty Trust Company of New York, General Foods Corporation, and the Aluminum Company of America.

ALLEN V. KNEESE is a senior fellow at Resources for the Future and Adjunct Professor in the Department of Economics at the University of New Mexico. He is a specialist in environmental economics and has written extensively in the field. He is the author of *Economics of the Environment* and co-author of *Pollution, Prices and Public Policy.*

EVERETT CARLL LADD, Jr., is Professor of Political Science at the University of Connecticut and Director of the Roper Center, the largest archives of sample survey data in the world. SEYMOUR MARTIN LIPSET is a senior fellow of the Hoover Institution and holds a joint appointment as Professor in the Departments of Political Science and Sociology at Stanford University. A former professor at Harvard, he is a member of the National Academy of Sciences and the American Academy of Arts and Sciences.

JOHN McCLAUGHRY is President of the Institute for Liberty and Community and served on both President Nixon's National Voluntary Service Advisory Council and President Carter's National Commission on Neighborhoods. He has wide experience in government at local, state, and national levels, including four years as a member of the Vermont House of Representatives. A graduate of Miami University, he received master's degrees from both Columbia and the University of California, Berkeley.

THOMAS GALE MOORE is Director of the Domestic Studies Program and a senior fellow at the Hoover Institution. A former senior staff member of the Council of Economic Advisers, he was on the economics faculty of Michigan State University from 1965 to 1974. He is the author of several books, including *Trucking Regulation*, and numerous articles on the effects of government regulation on the economy.

RICHARD F. MUTH is Professor in the Department of Economics at Stanford University. Formerly on the faculty of the University of

Chicago, he is a specialist in urban economics. He is the author of several books in the field, including *Cities and Housing, Public Housing,* and *Urban Economic Problems* as well as many articles in professional journals.

ALVIN RABUSHKA is a senior fellow of the Hoover Institution at Stanford University. A former Professor of Political Science at the University of Rochester, he is the author of numerous books, including *Politics in Plural Societies* and *Caseworkers or Police? How Tenants See Public Housing.* Dr. Rabushka graduated from Washington University and received his Ph.D. from Washington University.

DAN THROOP SMITH is a senior fellow at the Hoover Institution of Stanford University. A former member of the Harvard faculty and Deputy to the Secretary of the Treasury for tax policy, Dr. Smith has a broad and varied background in the formulation of national tax policy. He is a graduate of Stanford University and received his Ph.D. from Harvard University.

MURRAY L. WEIDENBAUM is Director of the Center for the Study of American Business at Washington University in St. Louis, Missouri, and a member of the Board of Economics of TIME magazine. From 1969–1971 he was the Assistant Secretary of the Treasury for Economic Policy. His most recent book is *Business, Government, and the Public.*

FOREIGN POLICY

P. T. BAUER is Professor of Economics, London School of Economics, Fellow of the British Academy, and Fellow of Gonville and Caius College, Cambridge. He was graduated from Cambridge University. His most recent book, *Dissent on Development,* was published by Harvard University Press.

RAY S. CLINE is Executive Director of World Power Studies at the Center for Strategic and International Studies, Georgetown University. He was formerly Deputy Director for Intelligence, Central Intelligence Agency, and Director of the Bureau of Intelligence and Research, Department of State. His most recent book is *World Power Assessment 1977: A Calculus of Strategic Drift,* published by Westview Press, Boulder, Colorado, in cooperation with the Center for Strategic and International Studies, Georgetown University.

PETER DUIGNAN is a senior fellow, Lillick Curator, and Director of African and Middle East Studies at the Hoover Institution. He is the author or editor of over twenty books on African history among which is a five volume study co-edited with L. H. Gann entitled *Colonialism in Africa,* published by Cambridge University Press. His most recent book, co-authored with L. H. Gann, is *South Africa: War, Revolution, or Peace?* (Hoover Institution Press). Dr. Duignan received his Ph.D. from Stanford University. L. H. GANN is a senior fellow of the Hoover Institution. He has written widely on African history, guerrilla warfare, and contemporary world affairs. He was graduated from Balliol College and received a Ph.D. from Oxford University. His most recent work, co-authored with Peter Duignan, is a trilogy on the European rulers of Africa, published by Stanford University Press and Princeton University Press.

MARK FALCOFF is Associate Professor of History at the University of Oregon. He is co-editor with Ronald H. Doklart of *Prologue to Peron: Argentina in Depression and War, 1930–1943,* published by the University of California Press. He is a national fellow at the Hoover Institution, 1979–1980.

ALFRED GROSSER is Professor at the Institute of Political Studies and Director at the Foundation nationale des sciences politiques in Paris. He has published numerous books and articles on Germany and France. His most recent book, *Les Occidentaux,* is a study of Western Europe and the United States since 1945. The American translation will be published at the beginning of 1980 (Seabury Press).

AMORETTA M. HOEBER is a senior member of the research staff at System Planning Corporation and a graduate of Stanford University. JOSEPH D. DOUGLASS, Jr., is Director of the Policy and Strategy Analysis Division, System Planning Corporation. He received his Ph.D. from Cornell University and is the author of *The Soviet Theater Nuclear Offensive.* Douglass and Hoeber are co-authors of the book, *Soviet Strategy for Nuclear War,* published by the Hoover Institution Press.

HENDRIK S. HOUTHAKKER is Professor of Economics at Harvard University. He served as a member of the Council of Economic Advisers and is the author of numerous articles in professional journals. Dr. Houthakker received his Ph.D. from the University of Amsterdam.

FRED CHARLES IKLÉ served four years as Director of the U.S. Arms Control and Disarmament Agency and advised two Presidents on SALT negotiations. Dr. Iklé received his Ph.D. from the University of Chicago, was Professor of Political Science at M.I.T., and head of the Social Science Department of the Rand Corporation.

G. M. MEIER is Professor of International Economics at the Graduate School of Business, Stanford University. He received his B. Litt. from Oxford University and his Ph.D. from Harvard University. He has been a visiting professor at Yale University. Among his books on international economics and economic development is the third edition of *Leading Issues in Economic Development*, published by Oxford University Press in 1976.

ROBERT A. SCALAPINO is Robson Research Professor of Government, Editor of *Asian Survey*, and Director of the Institute of East Asian Studies, University of California at Berkeley. His most recent book is *Asia and the Road Ahead*. Dr. Scalapino received his Ph.D. from Harvard University.

RICHARD F. STAAR is Director of the International Studies Program, a senior fellow at the Hoover Institution, and editor of the *Yearbook on International Communist Affairs*. His most recent book, *Communist Regimes in Eastern Europe*, is in its third revised edition. Dr. Staar received his Ph.D. from the University of Michigan.

EDWARD TELLER is a senior research fellow of the Hoover Institution. A distinguished physicist and Fermi Award winner, Dr. Teller is a former member of the President's Foreign Intelligence Advisory Board and the Defense Intelligence Agency Board. He is a member of the Academy of Arts and Sciences and the National Academy of Sciences. He received his Ph.D. from the University of Leipzig.

RICHARD WHALEN is Chairman of Worldwide Information Resources, an international business consultant, and author of *The Founding Fathers, Catch The Falling Flag*, and *Taking Sides*. Mr. Whalen has broad experience in politics and business. He is a graduate of Queens College.

YUAN-LI WU is Professor of Economics at the University of San Francisco. Formerly Deputy Assistant Secretary of Defense for International Security Affairs, Dr. Wu received his Ph.D. from the London School of Economics. He is a consultant to the Hoover Institution. His most recent book is *Japan's Search for Oil*, published by the Hoover Institution Press in 1977.

Introduction

Peter Duignan and Alvin Rabushka

Two centuries ago, Thomas Jefferson is reputed to have wisely proclaimed: "That government is best which governs least." As we enter the 1980s, we in the United States would do well to remember his maxim. The 1960s and 1970s were decades of dramatic growth in legislation, government regulation, public sector spending, and bold policy initiatives in a host of social areas. We have learned by now that we cannot solve social problems by throwing money at them. Too, we have reaped a harvest of rising inflation, waste, and inefficiency in government, and of declining productivity among workers. All this is vividly reflected in ever-increasing disenchantment with and distrust of government. Special interests have come to prevail at the expense of the general interest—a theme elaborated in the opening essay by Milton and Rose Friedman.

Why do special interests prevail over the general interest? What devices can we use to stop and reverse this process? The Friedmans show that the political realities of our democratic system favor concentrated over diffuse interests. Small groups with highly concentrated interests are encouraged to spend money and work hard to get a specific program passed in Congress or attain a favorable ruling from one element in the vast government bureaucracy. Rewards to members of those groups are substantial.

To pay for any one special program, each individual is assessed only a few dollars. Thus, the great majority of taxpayers do not find it worthwhile to spend money or work hard to oppose any given program, even if they manage to find out about it. The overall result is that our democratically elected representatives vote expenditures larger than a majority of voters deem desirable. The aggregate cost of all government programs is enormous and deprives individuals of money they would otherwise have to buy goods and services of their own choice.

To halt and reverse the trend toward growing government, the Friedmans recommend the incorporation of an economic bill of rights into our Constitution to limit government power in the economic and social areas. These proposed amendments would limit total spending by the federal government, forbid government interference in the conduct of international trade, outlaw wage and price controls, preclude government abridgment of occupational freedom, replace our progressive system of personal income taxation with one flat tax rate applied to all income (in excess of business expenses and a fixed personal allowance), and fix monetary growth at an annual rate of between 3 and 5 percent to ensure sound money. Taken together, these amendments would go a long way to restoring the primacy of the general interest. They would allow the two ideas of human freedom and economic freedom, which in the past have worked together to produce the richest and freest society in the world, to again move us in the direction of economic prosperity and individual freedom—and halt our movement to ever-bigger government.

The single theme that ties together all the essays in this volume is that we have entered into an era of limits and limited government. Keynesian policies of demand management were intended to stabilize the economy and avoid both inflation and unemployment; instead, they have generated inflation and unemployment and are a major source of economic instability. As Alan Greenspan points out, inflation has become the nation's most important economic problem. If we can eliminate inflation, other policy initiatives become less important. But if we fail, the others may become irrelevant.

Inflation increases uncertainty and instability in the economy. Risk premiums for new capital investment rise, which in turn reduces capital investment, harms productivity, and leads to a decline in living standards. Thus the need to reduce inflation is imperative. Solutions to the problem entail the elimination of federal budget deficits and a long-term slowdown in the rate of growth of monetary aggregates. If we can diminish the rate of inflation and lower the risk premiums for new capital investment, the 1980s could witness an expansion in the capital goods markets with corresponding increases in productivity and living standards.

The present political consensus in America and in other industrial nations provides an opportunity for the adoption of financial policies that have a good chance of eliminating current inflationary forces. The election of Margaret Thatcher as prime minister in Britain, the maintenance of fiscal conservatism by Chancellor Helmut Schmidt in Germany, the rejection of communism by the Italian electorate, the installation of a conservative government in Canada under Joe Clark, a shift to capitalist principles in Australia, and continued dedication to fiscal conservatism in Japan signal a discernible shift to the right on the part of these electorates.

To control inflationary budget policies, Greenspan recommends that we adopt a constitutional amendment that requires a three-fifths vote on all congressional money bills as a means of restraining expenditures. Since a three-fifths vote is more difficult to obtain than a simple majority, such an amendment would restrict the present tendency to overspend in order to reward different political constituencies. Tax cuts, however, still would require only a simple majority.

Indeed, as the distinguished analysts of public opinion Seymour Martin Lipset and Everett Carll Ladd, Jr., point out, elections and polls in America from the late 1970s show a swing toward conservatism. Polls reveal that many more Americans identify themselves as conservatives rather than liberals. Opinion polls of college students indicate a definite shift from the left during the 1970s. Americans see government as wasteful and inefficient. Distrust of government has been building steadily since the Vietnam war: the percentage of people who say that the government wastes much of our tax money has risen substantially, from 48 percent in 1964 to 74 percent by 1978. Although the public still remains concerned with the plight of the poor, the indigent, and other needy segments of society, concern with inflation has come to be the overriding worry. Indeed, inflation is a major factor in breaking down the old class differences over government's economic role that had continued from Franklin Roosevelt's New Deal years. Inflation cuts across class barriers: lower social-economic groups feel that they, too, have been notably victimized by it. Thus support for measures that cut taxes and spending, or require a balanced federal budget, is found rather evenly across the populace.

Alvin Rabushka discusses the growing movement to limit taxes and spending at the federal, state, and local levels. His essay reflects Jeffersonian norms of limited government. Rabushka attributes the success of Proposition 13 in California and a bevy of movements to limit taxes and spending in more than a dozen states to the culmination of over 50 years of sustained growth in government spending, coupled with inflation and a falling off in the growth of real disposable income. Total government spending in 1929 represented about 10 percent of the Gross National Product (or 12 percent of personal income). By 1978, government spending had grown to consume nearly one-third of the GNP and more than 40 percent of all personal income.

In California the crushing burden of increased property taxes, along with the accumulation of billions of dollars in state surplus funds, produced a landslide two-thirds victory for the Jarvis-Gann Initiative. This success occasioned a variety of similar measures in many parts of the country during the 1978 election year. Moreover, interest in tax and spending limits stirred up public and congressional concern about balancing the federal budget and/or limiting federal spending, and by May 1979 some 30 states had called on Congress to invoke Article V of the Constitution and hold a constitutional convention for the purpose of requiring an amendment to balance the budget. To insure that new increases in state, local, or federal spending do not take place in the future (save in periods of emergency), Rabushka recommends the adoption of spending limits at state and federal level, along with greater reliance on users' fees, on contracting out for services, on state funding of mandated services, and on private substitution as a means of holding down costs without cutting the quality of public services.

The tax limitation campaign is part of a wider movement to reform our system of taxation. Despite recommendation by the Carter administration in 1978 to increase taxation of capital gains, Congress not only rejected the administration's proposals, but substantially reduced that taxation. Congressional consideration of the Carter proposals drew attention to the perverse effects of the existing tax treatment of capital gains; Congress concluded that a reduction in that tax more than any other would reduce tax barriers to the formation, maintenance, and effective utilization of the nation's capital stock.

The reduction in the capital gains rate in 1978 was, as Dan Throop Smith points out, a major improvement in our tax system. He recommends an extension of the existing provisions for tax-free reinvestments (rollovers) of capital gains to reduce still further the penalties against the formation and efficient use of capital. He contends that high rates of taxation discourage economic activity and investment; thus the call for lower tax rates will induce greater economic activity and investment. Smith also suggests indexing exemptions and tax brackets to reduce unintended changes in tax burdens due to inflation, and he proposes allowing for faster recovery of investments in depreciable property.

The era of limits encompasses current governmental reforms to solve important problems. In his essay on welfare reform, Martin Anderson shows that the in-kind income of welfare recipients has grown substantially since 1965, with the result that the incidence of poverty has fallen to just over 3 percent of Americans. But the welfare system has destroyed work incentives for the poor on welfare. According to Anderson, radical welfare reform is a political impossibility: he says that "no radical welfare reform plan can be devised that will simultaneously yield minimum levels of welfare benefits, financial incentives to work, and an overall cost to the taxpayers that are all politically acceptable." Anderson recommends marked changes in our welfare system, building upon what we have. Such steps include efforts to eliminate fraud, improve welfare administration, establish and enforce a clear work requirement, and, where possible, shift authority and responsibility for welfare programs to local governments, as well as encourage private charity.

The era of limits clearly applies also to the nation's single most expensive social program: the social security system. Social security provides retirement income for millions of Americans, paying out on the order of $100 billion annually. These payments have significantly reduced poverty among the elderly. But they are not cost-free. The system has had an adverse impact on the economy by lowering private capital formation. Now it confronts a long-run funding crisis that threatens its financial viability and imposes such a heavy tax burden on contributors that more than half of all American families pay more in social security taxes than in income taxes.

Can the elderly count on their promised retirement benefits? The present ratio of three and one-quarter workers for each retiree will shift, after the next generation, to a ratio of two to one. Moreover, the average length of retirement steadily increases due to greater longevity and the practice of early retirement: more workers retire at age 62 than at age 65. These trends imply a large tax increase in the future, to a rate as high as 20 percent of a worker's pay, if we are to maintain the ratio of benefits to wages that now obtains.

Michael Boskin rejects the desirability of massive tax increases on the grounds that they would seriously impede private incentives to work and save. He suggests, instead, that benefits be restructured—that the age for which full retirement benefits become available be raised from 65 to 68. He also recommends that the transfer and annuity goals of the program be separated, placing the transfer payments portion that provides income maintenance for the elderly poor into general revenues (shifting them out of the social security payroll taxes), where they would have to compete openly with other government income transfer programs. The entitlements part of the program would be converted into a genuine social insurance program by tying earned entitlements to individual worker contributions. But he also proposes that people increasingly be allowed to provide for their own retirement, in place of compulsory social security payroll taxes; for example, through more reliance on private pensions.

We have painted the decade of the 1980s as a new period of limited government in spending and taxing and limited new policy initiatives. Now is a time to balance the budget, to slow down the rate of growth in government spending, to hold and consolidate our position on public solutions to social problems. If government is limited, private activity can grow and flourish, with all the attendant benefits to the American public made possible by a rise in output and living standards.

A chief factor in declining productivity and the stagnation of real disposable income is the plethora of regulations emanating from the federal and state governments. These regulations cut across virtually all industries and activities, from the conduct of general business and the production and supply of energy to higher education and protection of the environment. Although many regulations serve the important purposes of protecting our safety and environment, excessive government regulation in general reduces savings and innovation and leads to increases in costs and prices that must ultimately be borne by consumers.

Murray Weidenbaum outlines the cost of what has become an all-pervasive set of business regulations, including not only those of the traditional regulatory agencies, but those of nearly every department of government. He calculates that direct costs of compliance (for example, mandated safety in automobiles), indirect costs imposed on business (which must change its activities to survive the regulations), and the adverse impact on innovation and development, jointly, run into the tens of billions of dollars each year. The effects are manifold: taxpayers pay higher taxes, consumers pay higher prices, jobs are eliminated, small businesses that cannot afford the burden of regulation close, and society loses from a slowdown in the rise of living standards.

What are the remedies to the deleterious consequences of over-regulation? Weidenbaum proposes that an economic impact statement accompany each suggested new regulation; this would encourage Congress not to adopt regulations when costs exceed benefits. "Sunset" mechanisms, requiring periodic review of regulations to eliminate those that no longer serve their purposes, are a second measure. But perhaps most important, Weidenbaum calls for renewed competition among business firms as made possible by diminished regulations and a reliance on market forces. As an alternative to regulation he advocates, for instance, freedom for airlines, trucking firms, railroads, and suppliers of energy to set prices.

According to Thomas Gale Moore, government regulations in fact cause the present energy crisis. When the price mechanism is not allowed to equate supply with demand, when bureaucratic judgments and allocation formulas replace the free market, the result is invariably the appearance of shortages (or surpluses). Moore recounts the history of existing energy regulations, which date back to the 1930s for natural gas and oil and to more recent decades for coal and nuclear power. Price controls on natural gas discourage conservation and encourage wasteful use because the price is set too low by government. Similarly, the entitlement program that emerged in 1973 from a rise in the price of imported oil (to protect refineries that largely process imported oil) has in effect subsidized the import of foreign oil and discouraged domestic production. Moreover, retail price controls, a hangover from Nixon wage-and-price controls, encourage wasteful use because the price is held below the market level. The reduction in production and burning of coal can be traced to the new environmental controls; the development of nuclear power, relatively a safer source of energy, is bogged down in long delays in licensing and litigation.

The solution to the nation's energy needs and to heavy dependence on imported oil is to deregulate the energy industries and let the marketplace set prices. Moore specifically recommends that the government deregulate crude oil and natural gas prices, remove all controls on the pricing of gasoline, facilitate the licensing of nuclear power plants, and carefully reduce some of the safety and environmental constraints on the mining of coal.

Some characterize the 1980s as a time when Americans must choose between economic growth and protection of the environment: that is, between reliance on the market economy and regulations. Allen Kneese shows that the price mechanism is in fact the most efficient means by which to prevent environmental deterioration. Current government practice involves the imposition of uniform standards of reduction, of both pollutants into water and emissions into the air. But Kneese reviews a number of studies that demonstrate how a given water or air quality objective can be obtained at far lower cost by the use of effluent charges or taxes instead of the regulation approach. The new method entails no major administrative burdens; all that is required is to meter the pollutants and levy a fee for each discharged unit. Firms would pursue their own interests in reducing pollution by an amount related to the cost of reduction and would thus induce new efforts to reduce pollutants. A system of effluent fees is more efficient, equitable, and effective than the present regulation and subsidization system. The key is in utilization of the pricing mechanism, for through it conservation can become good business.

The cost of health care has rapidly risen and now absorbs nearly 10 percent of the GNP. During the 1980s, we should cut costs by getting rid of unnecessary government controls and promoting competition. As Rita Ricardo Campbell shows, the federal government need not implement a comprehensive national health insurance scheme in order to make accessible adequate medical care and insurance for all. Campbell argues that most Americans, including the poor, the elderly, and minorities, have access to health care. Campbell says, "The main problem is not so much access, but rising costs—which are reflecting ever higher costs of new medical technology and a demand excess created partly by ignorance and because payment is by third parties, government and insurers, and not by consumers at time of consumption. Price does not restrain, therefore, demand to any meaningful degree." In addition the medical care industry is probably the most regulated industry in the United States. Federal and state governments exercise control over the number of physicians via grants to medical schools and licensure; over hospitals through the certificate-of-need laws under the health system agencies; over prices by various review panels; over health insurers, pharmaceutical companies, and so forth. These regulations restrict the supply of physicians, the use of less expensively trained and, thus, less costly substitute workers who are used in many other countries, and other medical products, and consequently drive up prices.

One way to control rising medical costs is to increase competition in the industry through advertising, repeal of fair trade practice laws, certification of health providers in lieu of occupational licensure, greater use and direct reimbursement of general nurse practitioners and other allied professionals, greater encouragement of health maintenance organizations, and an emphasis through consumer health education and preventive care on individuals' responsibility for their own health.

We can best solve the problems of housing and improve decaying neighborhoods by reducing government intervention in urban affairs and placing greater reliance on the price mechanism. According to the advocates of public enterprise, 1) new housing is no longer affordable by growing numbers of American families; 2) disruptions in the financial markets cause inordinate volatility in new housing construction. Richard Muth refutes both contentions. He demonstrates that real disposable incomes have risen at about the same rate as house prices and the prices of other goods and services. He argues that monetary instability, occasioned by the government's handling of the money supply, is a main cause of fluctuation in new construction and that steady, gradual increase in monetary growth would enhance the stability of new construction.

The era of limits precludes new major spending initiatives in housing programs. Muth suggests that government programs for public and rental housing that subsidize capital costs be replaced with a similar expenditure on rent certificates. Rent vouchers more closely approximate a market system in housing in which consumers seek out the best use of existing dwellings. Landlords would also have an incentive to maintain their properties in order to prevent vacancies. Such a program would house more families at no higher cost than the present system of capital subsidies to public housing and other rental programs.

On the related topic of neighborhood revitalization, John McClaughry attributes the problems of the cities to excessive and unwanted government intervention in community affairs. Neighborhoods are the starting point from which millions of citizens can check the growing power of government. To this end, ordinary citizens should gain greater control over fiscal affairs in their communities. Barriers to creative self-help must be removed by reducing the federal government's role in the community.

McClaughry recommends that local neighborhoods be empowered with fiscal authority; that a portion of taxes collected within the neighborhood be designated for the use of a local neighborhood government. Other measures include voucher payments to individual residents for expenditure on those local services that are most desired, repeal of zoning and replacement of building codes (which interfere with effective land use) with ten-year periods of builder liabilities, a shift in the burden of property taxes from improvements to land, and resistance to excessive municipal union wage claims.

A final illustration of the hazards of regulation is found in higher education, where government controls increasingly threaten academic freedom and scientific research. Higher education is already confronted with declining enrollment—which threatens to close many smaller private schools—and with the growing power of unionism among faculty members, with the reinterpretation of tenure as job security and away from its traditional interpretation as a protector of academic freedom. To maintain high standards of excellence in higher education, argues John Bunzel, universities must focus on education and not become involved in social activism that threatens to undermine the independence and primary functions of higher education. He warns that growing government regulations—for the purpose of affirmative action, for example—risk shifting the focus on skill, merit and individual promise to one of advantage for one or another racial or sexual identity.

As is true in all such surveys, we do not, in the portion of this book that is devoted to domestic issues, touch upon some important topics. These include agricultural policy, unemployment, minorities, the changing role of women in the work force and in family structure, immigration, public education, judicial intervention, and the criminal justice system: treatments of most of these subjects can be found in a related volume edited by Seymour Martin Lipset, entitled *The Third Century: America as a Post-Industrial Society,* also published by the Hoover Institution Press. Contributors to that volume contend that government intervention in these areas is likely to be more circumspect than in the past two decades. In the 1980s, all levels of government will remain within their fiscal means more than in recent years. Colossal deficits of hundreds of billions of dollars, and the inflation they produce, will not be tolerated by the American public.

To these ends, deregulation and renewed emphasis on market competition can hold down costs, create jobs, and further the individual freedoms that have been part of the American heritage. It must be recognized in government, as it is recognized in our daily lives, that the community's scarce economic resources can be efficiently allocated only through the price mechanism. In the long run, the decisions of individual businessmen, exercising individual choice (even if sometimes mistaken) in a free economy, will do less harm than government regulations and others programs; and the harm is likely to be counteracted faster. If we do not use the market mechanism to set prices, then we are left with bureaucratic and political judgments, which have failed to solve the problems of past decades.

The climate of American politics is changing at last. The New Frontier and the Great Society are receding; to the majority of Americans, the orthodoxies of the 1960s and the 1970s seem questionable. If we are to eschew our country's long-term decline, we must come to understand the proper limits of public action.

In our dealings with foreign countries during the 1980s, we likewise need to understand and accept the limits of American power. Since Vietnam, our ability to influence events in the world has contracted. We have lost military superiority to the Soviets. We have learned that foreign aid cannot by itself cure poverty, that modernization cannot be achieved quickly, and that democracy cannot be exported.

Two major foreign policy issues will continue to face the United States in this decade: how to contain Soviet expansionism and how to fulfill the expectations of modernization in the less developed countries (LDCs), where continuing instability appears inevitable.

According to Stanley Hoffman, in a special issue of *Foreign Affairs* (1979), the United States has to concern itself with three major elements of Soviet policy: the strategic-nuclear arms buildup, the size of Soviet conventional forces facing NATO and the United States, and Soviet intervention in the Third World. Soviet policymakers have proclaimed repeatedly that peaceful coexistence among states does not imply peaceful coexistence among differing ideologies; peaceful coexistence or détente are but means of intensifying the class struggle. Soviet intentions are clear and unambiguous; it is only naive Americans who explain them in terms of "convergence" or détente. Since 1974 the Soviets have entered a new period of expansion in Africa, characterized by the employment of conventional military forces—mainly Cuban—for the purpose of spreading the gospel of revolution. The West has not reacted strongly or consistently. Failure to stop Soviet-Cuban intervention in Angola has encouraged the Soviets to intervene elsewhere: for example, in Ethiopia, Yemen, and Afghanistan. Faced with a Soviet threat, NATO has agreed to spend more on arms and President Carter seems willing to rebuild U.S. military might, but it is almost too late for this. We have allowed our military strength to erode; we must act quickly, now.

Unfortunately, recent American foreign policy has lacked consistency, coherence, and a strategic sense. The issues of the B-1 bomber, the neutron bomb, the cruise missile, and the MX all show the administration's indecisiveness. Government support goes to such radical states as Algeria and Libya, but not to moderate states like Morocco.

But the major problem facing the United States in the 1980s is to gauge the intentions and strategies of the Soviet Union. Contributors to this volume see a grand design on the part of the USSR, along with preparations for a nuclear war or political blackmail. Congress, overreacting to the imperial presidency of the Vietnam war, makes it difficult for the president to exert influence overseas. Obviously, Congress must be consulted; but the president—not Congress or special interest groups—must be allowed to run foreign affairs. Unfortunately, we now have less usable power available to react to the problems of the 1980s. Department of Defense experts admitted in May 1979 that we are not at present capable of reacting quickly to a Soviet or radical takeover of the Persian Gulf or Saudi Arabia, for example. A heavily armed, mobile force of 110,000 men capable of flying to any trouble spot is only now being created.

We must make it clear to the Soviet Union that we are determined to protect ourselves, our interests, and our allies. We should tell the Soviets that we will not tolerate interruption of oil supplies from the Persian Gulf or Saudi Arabia, and that we will not allow them or their clients to deny us access to Africa's mineral supplies or to strategic choke points such as the Strait of Hormuz.

A major effort should be made to contain Soviet expansionism, to which that regime is driven by ideology and a need to demonstrate vitality and power. Although the Soviets have failed to provide a high level of material well-being for their people, they nevertheless project their power and influence around the world. Military power and aggressive military outreach seem to show the Soviets that communism is the rule of the future. American policies in the early 1980s will determine who is to win this ideological and military struggle. Given our superiority in economic production, given our vast technological resources, we should be able to win the race for survival—*if* we grasp the perils of the present and the future.

To assure U.S. survival, Fred Iklé calls for a revival of self-confidence and self-discipline, especially now, when our military situation continues to decline vis-à-vis the Soviets. American armed strength, Iklé shows, is eroding in every field, especially in nuclear armament. Even if we were to embark on a campaign of swift rearmament, the nuclear gap between the United States and the Soviet Union is increasing and will continue to increase in the 1980s. For fifteen years the Soviets have been spending twice as much on military research and development as we have; they also disburse three times as much on strategic arms. The increase in defense spending for 1980 proposed by the Carter administration, far from closing the gap, will barely keep up with inflation.

The inferiority of NATO in conventional arms might make defense of the Middle East impossible, thereby laying open a vital flank. Nuclear threats will not compensate for our weakness in conventional weapons. In the Cuban missile crisis we were able to make the Russians back down, but we now operate from a position of nuclear inferiority in relation to the Soviet Union. Tactical nuclear weapons could not be used in Western Europe without inviting a devastating response from Soviet missile forces. Western governments, subject to pressure from Soviet propaganda and their own publics and threatened by saboteurs and political agents, could conceivably collapse after only one nuclear strike.

Furthermore, as Iklé points out, U.S. and NATO military doctrine has not yet adjusted to the loss of American military superiority. We must increase our ability to retaliate against a concerted nuclear attack on the United States, besides improving our conventional fighting potential; and we must more effectively control the transfer of U.S. technology to the communists.

Amoretta Hoeber and Joseph Douglass, Jr., agree with Iklé that our ability to deter armed aggression or nuclear blackmail against ourselves or our allies is being eroded, and that we are headed for significant military inferiority in the 1980s. The Soviets believe that they can fight, survive, and win a nuclear war. American strategic thought assumes that our conventional forces could deter a Soviet attack, and that if this were not so, we could destroy the Soviet Union; hence U.S. planners think of a nuclear war as irrational and improbable. American policymakers think, mistakenly, that the USSR shares these assumptions. But Soviets proclaim in their military doctrine that they can win a nuclear war. This doctrine and their plans are designed toward surviving an initial attack and having enough missiles in reserve to force the United States to surrender. We have limited striking power; the Soviets have second and third strike capability. We cannot assess Soviet missile strength merely by counting silos. Their military literature openly tells of reserves of missiles in warehouses and depots that can be fired outside of silos: a fact that is ignored by U.S. policymakers.

The United States can no longer assume technological superiority over the Soviets. More important, they are outspending us in research and development as well as in military hardware. The trend is clear: the Soviets will overtake us in all areas. In such important fields as anti-satellite technology they are already well ahead. The Soviet lead threatens our entire intelligence and communications network. They are also superior to us in the use of reconnaissance, secrecy, command flexibility, surprise, sabotage, and in the spreading of misinformation.

The United States must reshape its strategic doctrine and restructure its fighting forces to assure their survival and our ability to fight an extended war. We must plan both for a long and a short war. Our foreign intelligence-gathering capability must be improved. The Carter administration's reforms have hamstrung the CIA, now monitored by 40 committees.

Morale in the CIA, Ray S. Cline shows, has slumped; mass resignations and firings have seriously weakened the agency, and its appropriations have been reduced. Information about foreign countries is thus hard to obtain. But the United States needs an effective intelligence agency; the Soviet Union alone employs over 500,000 agents and is supported by other communist spy networks. We must have information for self-defense.

Edward Teller writes that modern warfare is increasingly dominated by technology; here again, the United States is in danger of losing its lead over the Soviets. As we have failed to take advantage of our technical superiority, the Russians have moved ahead of us in rocketry, nuclear submarines, and anti-satellite technology. We ignore chemical and biological warfare: the Soviets do not. The United States should push ahead on producing the neutron bomb and the cruise missile—although, to inhibit escalation, we should announce that we would never be the first to use atomic weapons except within an invaded area, Teller states—and we should spend more on civil defense and research and development. But in our dealings with other nations, the USSR, for example, we should shun treaties that are based on prohibition and seek those that promote cooperation. In the free world, the elimination of secrecy should be a constant goal. The only effective antidote to military technology is a technology for peace. We cannot afford to give up the hope for a peaceful world order.

The West's military weakness is worsened by its reliance on Middle Eastern oil. By conservation and the use of other energy sources, the United States can reduce its dependence on the Middle East. The world energy market does not pose special problems to the free market mechanism, according to Hendrik Houthakker. Japan and the Western European countries permit market forces to operate, and in some cases even accentuate them, by raising domestic excise taxes. These countries have experienced no gasoline lines, no panic; they have managed to cope with their difficulties. The United States has become an exception by trying to cope with the energy problem through government intervention. United States policies have discouraged domestic production, encouraged importation from abroad, and enforced low prices for energy, thus stimulating consumption. Our policy is characterized by a reluctance to let world prices of oil prevail here in the United States, by a reliance on imports, and by a tendency to adopt short-term political expedients without regard to long-term consequences. Our energy problems have also been aggravated by high cost and by the excessive scope of environmental protection.

Excessive optimism or pessimism should be avoided regarding the Third World in the 1980s. Since World War II, the two major characteristics of the Third World have been the increased size and number of groups participating in the political system and the shrinking divisible economic surplus. Economically, these states—be they in Africa, the Middle East, or Latin America—have shown excessive population growth, neglect of agriculture, overemphasis on wasteful and duplicative import substitution industries, and unreasonable growth in public sector employment. Low productivity, the necessary import of foodstuffs, and wasteful public spending have produced chronic inflation and balance of payments deficits. Growing state socialism has depleted the resources of these societies. Most of the radical coalitions that have reached power since the end of colonial rule have brought with them economic disaster and harsh governance: Cuba, Angola, Equatorial Guinea, Vietnam, Cambodia, Ethiopia, Afghanistan, South Yemen, Algeria, and Libya, to mention only a few.

The LDCs want modernization or westernization; but their accompaniments, rapid change and societal stress and strain, they do not want. The poorer nations want to retain their own cultures and thus are ambivalent about westernization. Iran has been torn apart over this issue of westernization versus Islamic traditionalism. Syria, Iraq, and Sudan are threatened by a revival of traditional religion. Pan-Islamism is sure to be strong in the 1980s, and other Khomeinis may come to power. Similar ambivalence appears elsewhere; the Chinese, for example, alternate between welcoming the West with its technology and shutting it out; Burma and Cambodia have closed the door to the West.

We still do not know how to modernize without causing stress and strain. Clearly, the pace of change has to be reduced and impatience overcome; ambitious superplans, massive programs, and mass mobilization schemes must be replaced with more modest proposals. Fewer foreign students should be sent overseas and fewer technicians should be sent to the LDCs. In developing countries, patience may be more important than capital or technology.

In the view of P. T. Bauer, foreign aid to the Third World benefits primarily a small class of politicians and bureaucrats. It encourages socialist solutions to economic ills and promotes the power of the state and of central planning. Foreign aid operates against the interests of American taxpayers, consumers, and the poor. The West can best contribute to Third World prosperity by lowering its tariff barriers, thereby promoting world trade. Some funds now earmarked for foreign aid could be used to compensate Western business that has been damaged by Third World imports. Insofar as we give aid at all, it should be only in the form of untied cash grants, not in commodity agreements or soft loans. Aid should be confined to countries whose foreign policies do not conflict with our interests and to those that pursue liberal foreign trade policies, offer security to private investment, and refrain from undue control of their economies.

The United States is capable of alleviating the world's hunger problems. With our technology, capital, and research skills, we could teach the nations of the Third World how to become self-sufficient in food. But these nations first must lower their population growths and learn to govern themselves.

Gerald Meier sees in the 1980s the growth of protectionism, greater balance of payments deficits, and increasing instability in foreign exchange markets. The United States has lost its dominant position in the international economic system and cannot make up its mind whether to follow policies that promote our national interests or to work for a more coherent world economic system. We have shifted to protectionist policies since the mid-1970s. We need to return to free trade, to encourage competition, and to let each nation do what it does best. World trade is becoming more restricted, especially in Japan and the European Economic Community. We should coordinate our trade policies with Western Europe, Japan, and the newly industrialized countries. We must at all costs avoid defensive economic nationalism or an East-West or North-South confrontation. The United States enjoys unmatched political and economic stability and geographic security behind oceans that still provide defenses even in the missile age.

Richard Whalen writes that, if industries were led by politically aware and socially responsible businessmen, we could restore our economic primacy in the coming decade. A U.S.-centered North American free trade area to include Canada and Mexico should be more effective than rival blocs built around Japan or Germany.

Great changes took place in Asia in the 1970s. The USSR has been seeking dominance there, and Sino-Soviet rivalry has replaced the Russo-Chinese alliance, writes Robert Scalapino. He foresees grave political and economic difficulties for Asian states during the 1980s. There are three policy options open to the United States in this decade: withdraw from all of Asia except Japan; form a united front with the People's Republic of China and Japan against Soviet expansionism; or seek equilibrium by keeping relations with the USSR and the PRC in roughly equal balance. Scalapino recommends the equilibrium approach.

The United States should try to improve economic relations with Japan and give up the old patron-client relationship. We should support Taiwan and negotiate a Pacific Basin community to promote economic interests of the region. Scalapino calls for re-establishing our strategic interests in Asia, especially in India, which now dominates the subcontinent. We should try to neutralize the Indian Ocean to prevent Soviet advances there.

For the 1980s, then, we should cultivate relations with states that share our interests. We should seek accommodations with communist states only if our credibility and principles are not thereby sacrificed and if such relations are not at the expense of other ties.

Clearly, Western Europe is a vitally important area to the United States, but the United States is poorly informed about Europe and vice versa. Our isolationism is a growing danger, asserts Alfred Grosser. According to a recent poll, barely more than one-half of Americans queried would send troops to defend Western Europe against the USSR.

Western Europe is not yet an effective political unit. The smaller powers, especially Holland, fear Franco-German domination, just as France fears U.S. domination of NATO. The views of France and Germany, however, differ toward the Soviet Union. Germany supports the United States against the USSR, whereas France sometimes looks to the Soviets against the Americans. France and Britain have long tried to exercise world power with the means available to medium-size powers; Germany and Italy have made no such attempts. Germany alone in Western Europe is still shaped by World War II and the consequent partition. The USSR remains the only European great power in its own right. Neutralization of Central Europe would endanger peace because both power blocs would attempt to fill the resulting vacuum.

Important changes are taking place in Europe. West Germany has become a major economic power that on some issues challenges the United States. France is resolved to maintain and strengthen its nuclear deterrent. Even the French communists are now willing to defend that deterrent. There is increasing Euro-American tension over defense, sales of nuclear reactors and arms to the Third World, the oil crisis, inflation, and the danger of increased competition among the industrialized states—a danger aggravated by U.S. protectionism.

It is essential that American-European understanding be improved. Americans and Europeans must hold a common line toward the raw material producers of the Third World. The United States has a vital interest in the defense, the prosperity, and even the existence of the EEC. The United States should consult Europeans more, concludes Grosser; and Europeans must be willing to shoulder more of the world's responsibilities.

The 1980s may see a change in the leftward drift of states, at least in Europe. Eurocommunism has suffered reverses in France, Italy, and Spain; the far left of West Germany, Austria, and Sweden are in retreat. Why? Probably because of inflation, high taxes, poor performance of socialist economies, over-regulation, and overblown bureaucracies. Free-spending big government, which may have peaked in the 1970s, will be on the decline in the 1980s.

The public sector has failed to solve many of its major problems—a situation that calls for a return to freer enterprise and smaller government. Competitive world markets have forced Europe to tighten domestic economies, a move that has benefited the free marketeers. High taxes and inflation have been the main sparks setting off the revolution of the overtaxed and overgoverned, but conservative ideology has fueled the fire: for example, that of the older Mont Pelerin Society and the new Club de l'Horloge in France. The "new philosophers," disillusioned with the communist systems and their Gulags, have helped to pull at least Western Europe toward the center.

Soviet leadership in the 1980s will continue to be semi-educated, cynical, unscrupulous, and dedicated to the pursuit of power, in the view of Richard Staar. But the USSR will be shaken by a succession crisis that will probably involve the KGB and the armed forces. The period of temporary weakness during this crisis should be utilized politically by the United States. The new Russian leadership will face many problems: a decline in the rate of industrial growth, incipient fuel crises, a shortage of labor reserves, inefficiency, lack of discipline, and a rise of nationalism among minorities. These difficulties could induce the leadership to reduce investment in consumer goods and agriculture, but not in the military. Staar feels that the character of Russian leadership is not likely to change, and that the communist ideological campaign against the West will continue.

The Soviet hatred of America is not explained by the U.S. "threat" (which has, in fact, declined), but by the internal exigencies of Soviet power. We should analyze communist propaganda themes and expose them through our own broadcasts. We can reduce Soviet espionage by limiting the number of their diplomatic representatives in this country to the number of American diplomats assigned to the USSR. We should not provide the Soviet Union with economic assistance. Abuses against U.S. citizens in Russia should draw retaliation. No SALT treaty at all may be better than one that shackles the United States. In the Third World, we should give limited support to Peking against Moscow; and we ourselves must project our system as revolutionary in nature and capable of bringing material prosperity to impoverished nations. We must exploit the internal contradictions of the Soviet Union and use our agricultural surpluses as a political weapon. In Y. L. Wu's view, we must relearn the art of political and economic warfare, using to our own advantage the linkage between politics and economics. A coherent policy, Wu suggests, requires the existence of an adequate decision-making mechanism and a high quality of political leadership. Détente has not moderated Soviet policies; therefore, we must wage politico-economic warfare against the Soviet Union to curb its militarism and expansionism.

The Middle East will continue to play a major part in America's fortune during the 1980s. All Middle Eastern states, despite their oil wealth, suffer to a greater or lesser extent from the effects of rapid demographic growth, swift urbanization, overgrown bureaucracies, unstable governments, and internal dissensions. These troubles are not likely to be cured for a long time, according to Peter Duignan and L. H. Gann. But the United States cannot attempt to formulate a single Middle Eastern policy; here, as in all parts of the world, each country should be treated individually.

The Middle East faces the possibility of direct or, more likely, indirect Soviet intervention. Pan-Arab unity has been broken, and the Arab states need external support to keep the Soviet Union and its radical clients out of the Middle East. The United States should seek to strengthen its military and diplomatic presence in the Middle East by building up U.S. armed forces and acting in concert with NATO powers and pro-Western Arab regimes. The United States should back the Israeli-Egyptian peace settlement, subsidize both Israel and Egypt, pressure the Palestine Liberation Organization to accept peace, and work for the creation of a neutralized West Bank state to be linked, possibly by confederal arrangement, to Israel. We should work for a neutralized Lebanon, independent of Syria, structured on a confederal or possibly a cantonal basis that would eliminate the Palestinians as a political and military factor in Lebanese politics.

United States policy should aim at keeping the Soviet Union out of the Persian Gulf and strengthening Saudi Arabia. We should prepare to intervene militarily in concert with our NATO allies if oil supplies to the West are threatened. We should restore our Turkish alliance, give the Turks economic and military assistance, and if necessary opt for Turkey rather than Greece in the Cyprus issue. We should back Morocco against Algeria and Egypt against Libya. And we should be prepared in the 1980s to live with many insoluble problems in the Middle East.

During the past fifteen years of benign American neglect, suggests Mark Falcoff, Latin America has increasingly gone its own way. Again: because Latin American countries vary in size and potential, there cannot be a single U.S. policy for Latin America. Nor is there one policy or group of policies that will rapidly reverse the trends that have developed there in the past 25 years. Mexico is a potential point of friction. Its wealth will increase with new oil discoveries, but so will its population—at 3.5 percent a year. The illegal emigration of Mexicans to the United States is enormous. Should this emigration suddenly cease, Mexico would face a catastrophe.

Cuba would like to resume economic relations with the United States because the economic effects of the revolution have failed. However, there is no U.S. incentive similar to that of the USSR to subsidize Cuban sugar. Fidel Castro is unwilling to abandon his world revolutionary role. We should not make economic concessions to Cuba without receiving political concessions in return.

The United States may have to face a Marxist state in Nicaragua, as well as more trouble with Panama concerning the canal—which is important not only to our security, but also to that of Japan, Australia, New Zealand, Ecuador, Peru, and Colombia. Mistaken internal policies that have neglected agriculture and put too much emphasis on public expenditure have weakened Chile, Argentina, and Uruguay, all of which are suffering from inflation.

The United States is not the universal villain in this part of the world, and its ability to influence events is strictly limited, Falcoff argues. Brazilian government policy conflicts with U.S. policy, for example, on a variety of issues such as nuclear power and human rights. As with Chile and Argentina, we will not be able to mold events in Brazil to our liking. Overall, we can improve our relations with Latin America by providing more assistance and by changing our tariff structure, which is at present the main barrier to good relations. Latin America is closer to the United States than any other part of the Third World. We must have patience, and not expect a spectacular breakthrough; rather, we must repair a bridge that has fallen into serious disrepair.

Another aspect of Latin American relations is our dealings with Hispanic immigrants to the United States. The more than twenty million Spanish-speakers in this country today—perhaps eight million of them illegal immigrants—make up our fastest growing minority. It is estimated that Hispanics will outnumber blacks by 1990 and will dominate California around that time. Some 60 percent of them come from Mexico, but every Latin American country is represented. Their growing number and their youth (median age 21 as compared to 29 for the general population) indicate that political power may go to them in the future.

The newly independent states of Africa differ widely in size and strength. For the most part, state L. H. Gann and Peter Duignan, they are ethnically diverse, politically unstable, and subject to authoritarian rule by one-party or military dictatorships. Their post-colonial record is marked by violence and instability—though the picture is not uniformly bleak. The African continent has become a new political battlefield, and its contenders include the United States and the Soviet Union, as well as the old colonial powers, who continue to account for much of African trade. The USSR seeks to expand its influence in Africa through conventional diplomacy, front groups and orthodox Communist parties, economic contacts, naval expansion, wars of liberation designed to promote "national democratic" revolutions as stepping stones to socialism, and proletarian internationalism involving the despatch of proxy forces (East Germans and Cubans) to countries like Angola and Ethiopia. The West should not expect Marxist-Leninist regimes like that in Angola to become independent of Soviet influence and should look with distrust on Soviet attempts to gain control over such strategic areas as the Horn of Africa and the Cape. The West must be alert to Soviet designs to limit our access to valuable strategic materials, many of which (chrome, cobalt, manganese, and uranium, for example) come from Africa.

African revolutionary regimes have civil rights records that are as deplorable as their economic achievements. We should not be captivated by the progressive phraseology used by them and their supporters at home and overseas. The United States should support moderate regimes in Namibia and Zimbabwe. We should seek to cooperate with South Africa while attempting to liberalize that regime from within. We should help to stabilize the government of Zaire.

The United States must adjust its diplomacy to Africa's diversity. Our policy needs reform and reinvigoration. Some African governments want and need arms; they need assistance in building up their internal security systems. The Carter administration has refused help. This policy should be changed. More of our resources should be designated to aid in civil, military, and security matters.

To conclude, the 1980s offers both challenges and dangers. Individual initiative and responsibility must replace government controls and direction. We need more competition and less regulation. The price mechanism, not bureaucracies, must allocate our scarce economic resources. A harsher, more exacting, and more perilous age lies ahead. We do not want to turn our country into a puritanical garrison state; but we will not survive unless we save more than we spend, work more than we play, and spend more on defense and less on welfare. We must replace rhetoric with resolve and détente with a dynamic defense. The choice is ours.

Domestic Issues

PART I

The Tide is Turning

Milton Friedman and Rose Friedman

I

The failure of Western governments to achieve their proclaimed objectives has produced a widespread reaction against big government. In Britain, the reaction swept Margaret Thatcher to power in 1979 on a platform pledging her Conservative government to reverse the socialist policies that had been followed by both Labour and earlier Conservative governments ever since the end of World War II. In Sweden, in 1976, the reaction led to the defeat of the Social Democratic Party after more than four decades of uninterrupted rule. In France, the reaction led to a dramatic change in policy designed to eliminate government control of prices and wages, and sharply reduce other forms of government intervention. In the United States, the reaction has been manifested most dramatically in the tax revolt that has swept the nation, symbolized by the passage of Proposition 13 in California, and realized in a number of states in constitutional amendments limiting state taxes.

The reaction may prove short-lived and be followed, after a brief interval, by a resumption of the trend toward ever-bigger government. The widespread enthusiasm for reducing government taxes and other impositions is not matched by a comparable enthusiasm for eliminating government programs—except programs that benefit other people. The reaction against big government has been sparked by rampant inflation, which governments can control if they find it politically profitable to do so. If they do, the reaction might be muted or disappear.

We believe that the reaction is more than a response to transitory inflation. On the contrary, the inflation itself is partly a response to the

SOURCE: From *Free to Choose: A Personal Statement*, © 1980, 1979, by Milton Friedman and Rose D. Friedman. Reprinted by permission of Harcourt Brace Jovanovich, Inc.

reaction. As it has become politically less attractive to vote higher taxes to pay for higher spending, legislators have resorted to financing spending through inflation, a hidden tax that can be imposed without having been voted, taxation without representation. That is no more popular in the twentieth century than it was in the eighteenth.

In addition, the contrast between the ostensible objectives of government programs and their actual results is so pervasive, so widespread, that even many of the strongest supporters of big government have had to acknowledge government failure—though their solution almost always turns out to be still bigger government.

A tide of opinion, once it flows strongly, tends to sweep over all obstacles, all contrary views. Equally, when it has crested, and a contrary tide sets in, that too tends to flow strongly.

The tide of opinion toward economic freedom and limited government that Adam Smith and Thomas Jefferson did so much to promote flowed strongly until late in the nineteenth century. Then the tide of opinion turned—in part, because the very success of economic freedom and limited government in producing economic growth and improving the well-being of the bulk of the population rendered the evils that remained—and of course there were many—all the more prominent and evoked a widespread desire to do something about them. The tide toward Fabian socialism and New Deal liberalism in turn flowed strongly, fostering a change in the direction of British policy early in the twentieth century, and in U.S. policy, after the Great Depression.

That trend has now lasted three-quarters of a century in Britain, half a century in the United States. It too is cresting. Its intellectual basis has been eroded as experience has repeatedly contradicted expectations. Its supporters are on the defensive. They have no solutions to offer to present-day evils except more of the same. They can no longer arouse enthusiasm among the young who now find the ideas of Adam Smith or Karl Marx far more exciting than Fabian socialism or New Deal liberalism.

Though the tide toward Fabian socialism and New Deal liberalism has crested, there is as yet no clear evidence whether the tide that succeeds it will be toward greater freedom and limited government in the spirit of Smith and Jefferson or toward an omnipotent monolithic government in the spirit of Marx and Mao. That vital matter has not yet been determined—either for the intellectual climate of opinion or for actual policy. To judge from the past, it will be determined for opinion first and policy will then follow suit.

IMPORTANCE OF INTELLECTUAL CLIMATE OF OPINION

The example of India and Japan exemplifies the importance of the intellectual climate of opinion, which determines the unthinking preconceptions of most people and their leaders, their conditioned reflexes to one course of action or another.

The Meiji leaders who took charge of Japan in 1867 were dedicated primarily to strengthening the power and glory of their country. They attached no special value to individual freedom or political liberty. They believed in aristocracy and political control by an elite. Yet they adopted a liberal economic policy that led to the widening of opportunities for the masses, and during the early decades, greater personal liberty. The men who took charge in India, on the other hand, were ardently devoted to political freedom, personal liberty and democracy. Their aim was not only national power, but also improvement in the economic conditions of the masses. Yet they adopted a collectivist economic policy that hamstrings their people with restrictions and continues to undermine the large measure of individual freedom and political liberty encouraged by the British.

The difference in policies reflects faithfully the different intellectual climates of the two eras. In the mid-nineteenth century, it was taken for granted that a modern economy should be organized through free trade and private enterprise. It probably never occurred to the Japanese leaders to follow any other course. In the mid-twentieth century, it was taken for granted that a modern economy should be organized through centralized control and five-year plans. It probably never occurred to the Indian leaders to follow any other course. It is an interesting sidelight that both views came from Great Britain. The Japanese adopted the policies of Adam Smith. The Indians adopted the policies of Harold Laski.

Our own history is equally strong evidence of the importance of the climate of opinion. It shaped the work of the remarkable group of men who gathered in Independence Hall in Philadelphia in 1787 to write a constitution for the new nation they had helped to create. They were steeped in history and were greatly influenced by the current of opinion in Britain—the same current that was later to affect Japanese policy. They regarded concentration of power, especially in the hands of government, as the great danger to freedom. They drafted the Constitution with that in mind. It was a document intended to limit government power, to keep power decentralized, to reserve to individuals control over their own lives. This thrust is even clearer in the Bill of Rights, the first ten amendments to the Constitution, than in the basic text: "Congress shall make no law respecting an establishment of religion, or prohibiting the free exercise thereof; or abridging the freedom of speech, or of the press"; "the right of the people to keep and bear arms shall not be infringed"; "the enumeration in the Constitution, of certain rights, shall not be construed to deny or disparage others retained by the people"; "the powers not delegated to the United States by the Constitution, nor prohibited by it to the States, are reserved to the States, respectively, or to the people." (From Amendments I, II, IX, and X.)

Late in the nineteenth century and on into the early decades of the twentieth, the intellectual climate of opinion in the United States—largely under the influence of the same views from Britain that later affected Indian policy—started to change. It moved away from a belief in individual responsibility and reliance on the market toward a belief in social responsibility and reliance on the government. By the 1920s, a strong minority, if not an actual majority of college and university professors actively concerned with public affairs held socialist views. *The New Republic* and *The Nation* were the leading intellectual journals of opinion. The Socialist Party of the U.S., led by Norman Thomas, had broader roots, but much of its strength was in colleges and universities.

In our opinion, the Socialist Party was the most influential political party in the U.S. in the first decades of the twentieth century. Because it had no hope of electoral success on a national level (it did elect a few local officials, notably in Milwaukee, Wisconsin), it could afford to be a party of principle. The Democrats and Republicans could not. They had to be parties of expediency and compromise, in order to hold together widely disparate factions and interests. They had to avoid "extremism," keep to the middle ground. They were not exactly Tweedledum and Tweedledee—but close to it. Nonetheless, in the course of time, both major parties adopted the position of the Socialist Party. The Socialist Party never received more than 6 percent of the popular vote for President (in 1912 for Eugene Debs). It got less than 1 percent in 1928 and only 2 percent in 1932 (for Norman Thomas). Yet almost every economic plank in its 1928 presidential platform has by now been enacted into law. The relevant planks are reproduced in Appendix A to this chapter.

Once the change in the climate of opinion had spread to a wider public, as it did after the Great Depression, the Constitution shaped by a very different climate of opinion proved at most a source of delay to the growth of government power, not an obstacle.

In Mr. Dooley's words, "No matther whether th' constitution follows th' flag or not, th' supreme coort follows th' iliction returns." The words of the Constitution were reinterpreted and given new meaning. What had been intended to be barriers to the extension of government power were rendered ineffective. As Raoul Berger writes in his authoritative examination of the Court's interpretation of one amendment,

> The Fourteenth Amendment is the case study par excellence of what Justice Harlan described as the Supreme Court's 'exercise of the amending power,' its continuing revision of the Constitution under the guise of interpretation. . . .
>
> The Court, it is safe to say, has flouted the will of the framers and substituted an interpretation in flat contradiction of the original design. . . .
>
> Such conduct impels one to conclude that the Justices are become a law unto themselves.[1]

OPINION AND POPULAR BEHAVIOR

Evidence that the tide toward Fabian socialism and New Deal liberalism has crested comes not only from the writings of intellectuals, not only from the sentiments that politicians express on the hustings, but also from the way people behave. Their behavior is no doubt influenced by opinion. In its turn, popular behavior both reinforces that opinion and plays a major role in translating it into policy.

As A. V. Dicey, with remarkable prescience, wrote more than sixty years ago,

> If the progress of socialistic legislation be arrested, the check will be due, not so much to the influence of any thinker as to some patent fact which shall command public attention; such, for instance, as that increase in the weight of taxation which is apparently the usual, if not the invariable, concomitant of a socialist policy.[2]

Inflation, high taxes, and the patent inefficiency, bureaucracy, and excessive regulation stemming from big government are having the effects Dicey predicted. They are leading people to take matters into their own hands, to try to find ways around government obstacles.

Pat Brennan became something of a celebrity in 1978 because she and her husband went into competition with the U.S. Post Office. They set up business in a basement in Rochester, New York, guaranteeing delivery the same day of parcels and letters in downtown Rochester, at a lower cost than the Post Office charged. Soon their business was thriving.

There is no doubt that they were breaking the law. The Post Office took them to court; and they lost after a legal battle that went all the way to the State Supreme Court. Local businessmen provided financial backing.

Said Pat Brennan,

> I think there's going to be a quiet revolt and perhaps we're the beginning of it. . . . You see people bucking the bureaucrats, when years ago you wouldn't dream of doing that because you'd be squashed. . . . People are deciding that their fates are their own and not up to somebody in Washington who has no interest in them whatsoever. So it's not a question of anarchy, but it's a question of people re-thinking the power of the bureaucrats and rejecting it. . . .
>
> The question of freedom comes up in any kind of a business—whether you have the right to pursue it and the right to decide what you're going to do. There is also the question of the freedom of the consumers to utilize a service that they find is inexpensive and far superior, and according to the Federal Government and the body of laws called the Private Express Statutes, I don't have the freedom to start a business and the consumer does not have the freedom to use it—which seems very strange in a country like this that the entire context of the country is based on freedom and free enterprise.

Pat Brennan is expressing a natural human response to the attempt by other people to control her life, when she thinks it's none of their business. The first reaction is resentment; the second is to attempt to get around obstacles by legal means; finally, there comes a decline in respect for law in general. This final consequence is deplorable but inevitable.

A striking example is what has happened in Great Britain in reaction to confiscatory taxes. Says a British authority, Graham Turner:

> I think that it's perfectly fair to say that we have become in the course of the last ten or fifteen years a nation of fiddlers.
>
> How do they do it? They do it in a colossal variety of ways. Let's take it right at the lowest level. Take a small grocer in a country area, . . . how does he make money? He finds out that by buying through regular wholesalers he's always got to use invoices, but if he goes to the Cash and Carry and buys his goods from there, . . . the profit margin on those goods can be untaxed because the tax inspectors simply don't know that he's had those goods. That's the way he does it.

> Then if you take it at the top end—if you take a company director—well, there are all kinds of ways that they can do it. They buy their food through the company, they have their holidays on the company, they put their wives as company directors even though they never visit the factory. They build their houses on the company by a very simple device of building a factory at the same time as a house.
>
> It goes absolutely right through the range, from the ordinary working class person doing quite menial jobs, right to the top end—businessmen, senior politicians, members of the Cabinet, members of the Shadow Cabinet—they all do it.
>
> I think almost everybody now feels that the tax system is basically unfair, and everybody who can, tries to find a way round that tax system. Now once there's a consensus that a tax system is unfair, the country in effect becomes a kind of conspiracy—and everybody helps each other to fiddle.
>
> You've no difficulty fiddling in this country because other people actually want to help you. Now fifteen years ago that would have been quite different. People would have said, hey, this is not quite as it should be.

Or consider this, from an article in the *Wall Street Journal* by Melvyn B. Krauss on "The Swedish Tax Revolt" (February 1, 1979, p. 18):

> The Swedish revolution against the highest taxes in the West is based on individual initiative. Instead of relying on politicians, ordinary Swedes have taken matters into their own hands and simply refuse to pay. This can be done in several ways, many of them legal. . . .
>
> One way a Swede refuses to pay taxes is by working less. . . . Swedes sailing in Stockholm's beautiful archipelago vividly illustrate the country's quiet tax revolution.
>
> The Swedes escape tax by doing-it-themselves. . . .
>
> Barter is another way Swedes resist high taxes. To entice a Swedish dentist off the tennis court and into his office is no easy matter. But a lawyer with a toothache has a chance. The lawyer can offer legal services in return for dental services. Bartering saves the dentist two taxes: his own income tax plus the tax on the lawyer's fees. Though barter is supposed to be a sign of a primitive economy, high Swedish taxes have made it a popular way of doing business in the welfare state, particularly in the professions. . . .
>
> The tax revolution in Sweden is not a rich man's revolution. It is taking place at all income levels. . . .
>
> The Swedish welfare state is in a dilemma. Its ideology pushes for more and more government spending. . . . But its citizens reach a saturation point after which further tax increases are resisted. . . . the only ways

Swedes can resist the higher taxes is by acting in ways detrimental to the economy. Rising public expenditures thereby undercut the economic base upon which the welfare economy depends.

WHY SPECIAL INTERESTS PREVAIL

If the cresting of the tide toward Fabian socialism and New Deal liberalism is to be followed by a move toward a freer society and a more limited government rather than toward a totalitarian society, the public must not only recognize the defects of the present situation but also how it has come about and what we can do about it. Why are the results of policies so often the opposite of their ostensible objectives? Why do special interests prevail over the general interest? What devices can we use to stop and reverse the process?

The Power in Washington

Whenever we visit Washington, D.C., we are impressed all over again with how much power is concentrated in that city. Walk the halls of Congress, and the 435 members of the House plus the 100 senators are hard to find among their 18,000 employees—about 65 for each senator and 27 for each member of the House. In addition, the more than 15,000 registered lobbyists—often accompanied by secretaries, typists, researchers or representatives of the special interest they represent—walk the same halls seeking to exercise influence.

And this is but the tip of the iceberg. The federal government employs close to three million civilians (excluding the uniformed military forces). Over 350,000 are in Washington and the surrounding metropolitan area. Countless others are indirectly employed through government contracts with nominally private organizations, or are employed by labor or business organizations, or other special interest groups, that maintain their headquarters, or at least an office, in Washington because it is the seat of government.

Washington is a magnet for lawyers. Many of the country's largest and most affluent firms are located there. There are said to be more than 7,000 lawyers in Washington engaged in federal or regulatory practice alone. Over 160 out-of-town law firms have Washington offices.[3]

The power in Washington is not monolithic power in a few hands, as it is in totalitarian countries like the Soviet Union or Red China or, closer to home, Cuba. It is fragmented into many bits and pieces. Every special group around the country tries to get its hands on whatever bits and pieces it can. The result is that there is hardly an issue on which government is not on both sides.

For example, in one massive building in Washington some government employees are working fulltime trying to devise and implement plans to spend our money to discourage us from smoking cigarettes. In another massive building, perhaps miles away from the first, other employees, equally dedicated, equally hardworking, are working fulltime spending our money to subsidize farmers to grow tobacco.

In one building, the Council on Wage and Price Stability is working overtime trying to persuade, pressure, hornswoggle businessmen to hold down prices, and workers to restrain their wage demands. In another building, some subordinate agencies in the Department of Agriculture are administering programs to keep up, or raise, the prices of sugar, cotton, and numerous other agricultural products. In still another building, officials of the Department of Labor are making determinations of "prevailing wages" under the Davis-Bacon Act that are pushing up the wage rates of construction workers.

Congress set up a Department of Energy employing 20,000 persons to promote the conservation of energy. It also set up an Environmental Protection Agency employing over 12,000 persons to issue regulations and orders, most of which require the use of more energy. No doubt, within each agency, there are subgroups working at cross purposes.

The situation would be ludicrous if it were not so serious. While many of these effects cancel out, their costs do not. Each program takes money from our pockets that we could use to buy goods and services to meet our separate needs. Each of them uses able, skilled people who could be engaged in productive activities. Each one grinds out rules, regulations, red tape, forms to fill in that bedevil us all.

Concentrated versus Diffuse Interests

Both the fragmentation of power and the conflicting government policies are rooted in the political realities of a democratic system that operates by enacting detailed and specific legislation. Such a system tends to give undue political power to small groups that have highly concentrated interests, to give greater weight to obvious, direct, and immediate effects of government action than to possibly more important but concealed, indirect, and delayed effects, to set in motion a process that sacrifices the general interest to serve special interests, rather than the other way around. There is, as it were, an invisible hand in politics that operates in precisely the opposite direction to Adam Smith's invisible hand. Individuals who intend only to promote the *general interest* are led by the invisible political hand to promote a *special interest* that they had no intention to promote.

A few examples will clarify the nature of the problem. Consider the government program of favoring the merchant marine by subsidies for shipbuilding and operations and by restricting much coastal traffic to American-flag ships. The estimated cost to the taxpayer is about $600 million a year—or $15,000 per year for each of the 40,000 people actively engaged in the industry. Shipowners, operators, and their employees have a strong incentive to get and keep those measures. They spend money lavishly for lobbying and political contributions. On the other hand, $600 million divided by a population of over 200 million persons comes to three dollars a person per year; twelve dollars for a family of four. Which of us will vote against a candidate for Congress because he imposed that cost on us? How many of us will deem it worth spending money to defeat such measures, or even spending time to become informed about such matters?

As another example, the owners of stock in steel companies, the executives of these companies, the steelworkers all know very well that an increase in the importation of foreign steel in the U.S. will mean less money and fewer jobs for them. They clearly recognize that government action to keep out imports will benefit them. Workers in export industries who will lose their jobs because fewer imports from Japan mean fewer exports to Japan do not know that their jobs are threatened. When they lose their jobs, they do not know why. The purchasers of automobiles or of kitchen stoves or of other items made of steel may complain about the higher prices they have to pay. How many purchasers will trace the higher price back to the restriction on steel imports that forces manufacturers to use higher-priced domestic steel instead of lower-priced foreign steel? They are far more likely to blame "greedy" manufacturers, or "grasping" trade unionists.

Agriculture is another example. Farmers descend on Washington in their tractors to demonstrate for higher price supports. Before the change in the role of government that made it natural to appeal to Washington, they would have blamed the bad weather, and repaired to churches not the White House for assistance. Even for so indispensable and visible a product as food, no consumers parade in Washington to protest the price supports. And the farmers themselves, even though agriculture is the major export industry of the United States, do not recognize the extent to which their own problems arise from government's interference with foreign trade. It never occurs to them, for example, that they may be harmed by restrictions on steel imports.

Or to take a very different example, the U.S. Post Office. Every movement to remove the government monopoly of first-class mail is vigorously opposed by the trade unions of postal workers. They recognize very clearly that opening postal service to private enterprise may mean the loss of their jobs. It pays them to try to prevent that outcome. As the case of the Brennans in Rochester suggests, if the postal monopoly were abolished, a vigorous private industry would arise, containing thousands of firms, and employing tens of thousands of workers. Few of the people who might find a rewarding opportunity in such an industry even know that the possibility exists. They are certainly not in Washington testifying to the relevant congressional committee.

The benefit an individual gets from any one program that he has a special interest in may be more than cancelled by the costs to him of many programs that affect him lightly. Yet it pays him to favor the one program, and not oppose the others. He can readily recognize that he and the small group with the same special interest can afford to spend enough money and time to make a difference in respect of the one program. Not promoting that program will not prevent the others, which do him harm, from being adopted. To achieve that, he would have to be willing and able to devote as much effort to opposing each of them as he does to favoring his own. That is clearly a losing proposition.

Citizens are aware of taxes—but even that awareness is diffused by the hidden nature of most taxes. Corporate and excise taxes are paid for in the prices of the goods people buy, without separate accounting. Most income taxes are withheld at source. Inflation, the worst of the hidden taxes, defies easy understanding. Only sales taxes, property taxes, and income taxes in excess of withholding are directly and painfully visible—and they are the taxes on which resentment centers.

Bureaucracy

The smaller the unit of government, and the more restricted the functions assigned government, the less likely it is that its actions will reflect special interests rather than the general interest. The New England town meeting is the image that comes to mind. The people governed know and can control the people governing; each person can express his views; the agenda is sufficiently small that everyone can be reasonably well-informed about minor items as well as major ones.

As the scope and role of government expands—whether by covering a larger area and population or by performing a wider variety of functions—the connection between the people governed and the people governing becomes attenuated. It becomes impossible for any large fraction of the citizens to be reasonably well-informed about all items on the vastly enlarged government agenda, and, beyond a point, even about all major items. The bureaucracy that is needed to administer government grows and increasingly interposes itself between the citizenry and the representatives they choose. It becomes both a vehicle whereby special interests can achieve their objectives and an important special interest in its own right.

Currently in the U.S., anything like effective detailed control of government by the public is limited to villages, towns, smaller cities, and suburban areas—and even there only to those matters not mandated by the state or federal government. In large cities, states, Washington, we have government of the people not by the people but by a largely faceless group of bureaucrats.

No federal legislator could conceivably even read, let alone analyze and study, all the laws on which he must vote. He must depend on his numerous aides and assistants, or outside lobbyists, or fellow legislators, or some other source for most of his decisions on how to vote. The unelected congressional bureaucracy almost surely has far more influence today in shaping the detailed laws that are passed than do our elected representatives.

The situation is even more extreme in the administration of government programs. The vast federal bureaucracy spread through the many government departments and independent agencies is literally out of control of the elected representatives of the public. Elected Presidents and senators and representatives come and go but the civil service remains. Higher-level bureaucrats are past masters at the art of using red tape to delay and defeat proposals they do not favor, of issuing rules and regulations as "interpretations" of laws that in fact subtly, or sometimes crudely, alter their thrust; of dragging their feet in administering those parts of laws of which they disapprove, while pressing on with those they favor.

More recently, the federal courts, faced with increasingly complex and far-reaching legislation, have departed from their traditional role as impersonal interpreters of the law and have become active participants in both legislation and administration. In doing so, they have become part of the bureaucracy rather than an independent part of the government mediating between the other branches.

Bureaucrats have not usurped power. They have not deliberately engaged in any kind of conspiracy to subvert the democratic process. Power has been thrust on them. It is simply impossible to conduct complex government activities in any other way than by delegating responsibility. When that leads to conflicts between bureaucrats delegated different functions—as, recently, between bureaucrats instructed to preserve and improve the environment and bureaucrats instructed to foster the conservation and production of energy—the only solution that is available is to give power to another set of bureaucrats to resolve the conflict—to cut red tape, it is said, when the real problem is not red tape but a conflict between desirable objectives.

The high-level bureaucrats who have been assigned these functions cannot imagine that the reports they write or receive, the meetings they attend, the lengthy discussions they hold with other important people, the rules and regulations they issue—that all these are the problem rather than the solution. They inevitably become persuaded that they are indispensable, that they know more about what should be done than uninformed voters or self-interested businessmen.

The growth of the bureaucracy in size and power affects every detail of the relation between a citizen and his government. If you have a grievance, or can see a way of gaining an advantage from a government measure, your first recourse these days is likely to be to try to influence a bureaucrat to rule in your favor. You may appeal to your elected representative, but if so, you are perhaps more likely to ask him to intervene on your behalf with a bureaucrat than to ask him to support a specific piece of legislation.

Increasingly, success in business depends on knowing one's way around Washington, having influence with legislators and bureaucrats. What has come to be called a "revolving door" has developed between government and business. Serving a term as a civil servant in Washington has become an apprenticeship for a successful business career. Government jobs are sought less as the first step in a lifetime government career than for the value of contacts and inside knowledge to a possible future employer. Conflict of interest legislation proliferates, but at best only eliminates the most obvious abuses.

When a special interest seeks benefits through highly visible legislation it not only must clothe its appeal in the rhetoric of the general interest, it must persuade a significant segment of disinterested persons that its appeal has merit. Legislation recognized as naked self-interest will seldom be adopted—as illustrated by the recent defeat of further special privileges to the merchant marine despite endorsement by President Carter after receiving substantial campaign assistance from the unions involved. Protecting the steel industry from foreign competition is promoted as contributing to national security and full employment; subsidizing agriculture, as assuring a reliable supply of food; the postal monopoly, as cementing the nation together; and so on without end.

Nearly a century ago, A. V. Dicey explained why the rhetoric in terms of the general interest is so persuasive:

> The beneficial effect of state intervention, especially in the form of legislation, is direct, immediate, and so to speak, visible, while its evil effects are gradual and indirect, and lie out of sight. . . . Hence the majority of mankind must almost of necessity look with undue favor upon governmental intervention.[4]

This "natural bias," as he termed it, in favor of government intervention is enormously strengthened when a special interest seeks benefits through administrative procedures rather than legislation. A trucking company that appeals to the ICC for a favorable ruling also uses the rhetoric of the general interest, but no one is likely to press it on that point. The company need persuade no one except the bureaucrats. Opposition seldom comes from disinterested persons concerned with the general interest. It comes from other interested parties, shippers or other truckers, who have their own axes to grind. The camouflage wears very thin indeed.

The growth of the bureaucracy, reinforced by the changing role of the courts, has made a mockery of the ideal expressed by John Adams in his original (1779) draft of the Massachusetts constitution: "a government of laws instead of men." Anyone who has been subjected to a thorough customs inspection on returning from a trip abroad; had his tax returns audited by the Internal Revenue Service; been subject to inspection by an official of OSHA, or any of a large number of federal agencies; had occasion to appeal to the bureaucracy for a ruling or a permit; or had to defend a higher price or wage before the Council on Wage and Price Stability is aware of how far we have come from a rule of law. The government official is supposed to be our servant. When you sit across the desk from a representative of the Internal Revenue Service who is auditing your tax return, which one of you is the master and which the servant?

Or to use a different illustration. A recent *Wall Street Journal* story (June 25, 1979) is headlined: "SEC's charges settled by a former director" of a corporation. The former director, Maurice G. McGill, is reported as saying, "The question wasn't whether I had personally benefited from the transaction but rather what the responsibilities of an outside director are. It would be interesting to take it to trial but my decision to settle was purely economic. The cost of fighting the SEC to completion would be enormous." Win or lose, Mr. McGill would have had to pay his legal costs. Win or lose, the SEC official prosecuting the case had little at stake except status among fellow bureaucrats.

WHAT WE CAN DO

Needless to say, those of us who want to halt and reverse the recent trend should oppose additional specific measures to expand further the power and scope of government, urge repeal and reform of existing measures, and try to elect legislators and executives who share that view. But that is not an effective way to reverse the growth of government. It is doomed to failure. Each of us would defend our own special privileges and try to limit government at someone else's expense. We would be fighting a many-headed hydra that would grow new heads faster than we could cut old ones off.

Our founding fathers have shown us a more promising way to proceed: by package deals, as it were. We should adopt self-denying ordinances that limit the objectives we try to pursue through political channels. We should not consider each case on its merits, but lay down broad rules limiting what government may do.

The merit of this approach is well illustrated by the First Amendment to the Constitution. Many specific restrictions on freedom of speech would be approved by a substantial majority of both legislators and voters. A majority would very likely favor preventing Nazis, Seventh-Day Adventists, Jehovah's Witnesses, the Ku Klux Klan, vegetarians, or almost any other little group you might name from speaking on a street corner.

The wisdom of the First Amendment is that it treats these cases as a bundle. It adopts the general principle that "Congress shall make no law . . . abridging the freedom of speech"; no consideration of each case on its merits. A majority supported it then and, we are persuaded, a majority would support it today. Each of us feels more deeply about not having our freedom interfered with when we are in the minority than we do about interfering with the freedom of others when we are in a majority—and a majority of us will at one time or another be in some minority.

We need, in our opinion, the equivalent of the First Amendment to limit government power in the economic and social area—an economic Bill of Rights to complement and reinforce the original Bill of Rights.

The incorporation of such a Bill of Rights into our Constitution would not in and of itself reverse the trend toward bigger government or prevent it from being resumed—any more than the original Constitution has prevented both a growth and a centralization of government power far beyond anything the framers intended or envisioned. A written constitution is neither necessary nor sufficient to develop or preserve a free society. Although Great Britain has always had only an "unwritten" constitution, it developed a free society. Many Latin American countries that adopted written constitutions copied from the United States Constitution practically word for word have not succeeded in establishing a free society. In order for a written—or for that matter, unwritten—constitution to be effective it must be supported by the general climate of opinion—among both the public at large and its leaders. It must incorporate principles that they have come to believe in deeply, so that it is taken for granted that the executive, the legislature, and the courts will behave in conformity to these principles. As we have seen, when that climate of opinion changes, so will policy.

Nonetheless, we believe that the formulation and adoption of an economic Bill of Rights would be the most effective step that could be taken to reverse the trend toward ever-bigger government for two reasons: first, because the process of formulating the amendments would have great value in shaping the climate of opinion; second, because the enactment of amendments is a more direct and effective way of converting that climate of opinion into actual policy than our present legislative process.

Given that the tide of opinion in favor of New Deal liberalism has crested, the national debate that would be generated in formulating such a Bill of Rights would help to assure that opinion turned definitely toward freedom rather than toward totalitarianism. It would disseminate a better understanding of the problem of big government and of possible cures.

The political process involved in the adoption of such amendments would be more democratic, in the sense of enabling the values of the public at large to determine the outcome, than our present legislative and administrative structure. On issue after issue, the government of the people acts in ways that the bulk of the people oppose. Every public opinion poll shows that a large majority of the public opposes compulsory busing for integrating schools—yet busing not only continues but is continuously expanded. Very much the same thing is true of affirmative action programs in employment and higher education and of many other measures directed at implementing views favorable to equality of outcome. So far as we know, no pollster has asked the public, "Are you getting your money's worth for the more than 40 percent of your income being spent on your behalf by government?" But is there any doubt what the poll would show?

For the reasons outlined in the preceding section, the special interests prevail at the expense of the general interest. The New Class, enshrined in the universities, the news media, and especially the federal bureaucracy, has become one of the most powerful of the special interests. The New Class has repeatedly succeeded in imposing its views, despite widespread public objection, and often despite specific legislative enactments to the contrary.

The adoption of amendments has the great virtue of being decentralized. It requires separate action in three-quarters of the states. Even the proposal of new amendments can bypass Congress: Article V of the Constitution provides that "The Congress . . . on the application of the Legislatures of two-thirds of the several states, shall call a convention for proposing amendments." The recent movement to call a convention to propose an amendment requiring the federal budget to be balanced was backed by thirty states by mid-1979. The possibility that four more state legislatures would join the move, making the necessary two-thirds, has sown consternation in Washington—precisely because it is the one device that can effectively bypass the Washington bureaucracy.

Tax and Spending Limitations

The movement to adopt constitutional amendments to limit government is already under way in one area—taxes and spending. By early 1979, five states had already adopted amendments to their constitutions that limit the amount of taxes that the state may impose, or in some cases the amount that the state may spend. Similar amendments are part way through the adoption process in other states, and were scheduled to be voted on in still other states at the 1979 election. Active movements to have similar amendments adopted are under way in more than half the remaining states. A national organization, the National Tax Limitation Committee (NTLC), with which we are connected, has served as a clearing house and coordinator of the activities in the several states. It had about 250,000 members nationwide in mid-1979, and the number was climbing rapidly.

On the national level, two important developments are under way. One is the drive to get state legislatures to mandate Congress to call a national convention to propose an amendment to balance the budget—sparked primarily by the National Taxpayers Union, which had over 125,000 members nationwide in mid-1979. The other is an amendment to limit spending at the federal level, which was drafted under the sponsorship of the NTLC. The drafting committee, on which we both served, included lawyers, economists, political scientists, state legislators, businessmen, and representatives of various organizations. The amendment it drafted has been introduced into both Houses of Congress, and the NTLC is undertaking a national campaign in support of it. A copy of the proposed amendment is contained in Appendix B to this chapter.

The basic idea behind both the state and federal amendments is to correct the defect in our present structure under which democratically elected representatives vote larger expenditures than a majority of voters deem desirable.

As we have seen, that outcome results from a political bias in favor of special interests. Government budgets are determined by adding together expenditures that are authorized for a host of separate programs. The small number of people who have a special interest in each specific program spend money and work hard to get it passed; the large number of people, each of whom will be assessed a few dollars to pay for the program, will not find it worthwhile to spend money or work hard to oppose it, even if they manage to find out about it.

The majority does rule. But it is a rather special kind of majority. It consists of a coalition of special interest minorities. The way to get elected to Congress is to collect groups of, say, 2 or 3 percent of your constituents, each of which is strongly interested in one special issue that hardly concerns the rest of your constituents. Each group will be willing to vote for you if you promise to back its issue regardless of what you do about other issues. Put together enough such groups and you will have a 51 percent majority. That is the kind of logrolling majority that rules the country.

The proposed amendments would alter the conditions under which legislators—state or federal, as the case may be—operate by limiting the total amount they are authorized to appropriate. The amendments would give the government a limited budget, specified in advance, the way each of us has a limited budget. Much special interest legislation is undesirable, but it is never clearly and unmistakably bad. On the contrary, every measure will be represented as serving a good cause. The problem is that there are an infinite number of good causes. Currently, a legislator is in a weak position to oppose a "good" cause. If he objects that it will raise taxes, he will be labelled a reactionary who is willing to sacrifice human need for base mercenary reasons—after all, this good cause will only require raising taxes by a few cents or dollars per person. The legislator is in a far better position if he can say, "Yes, yours is a good cause, but we have a fixed budget. More money for your cause means less for others. Which of these others should be cut?" The effect would be to require the special interests to compete with one another for a bigger share of a fixed pie, instead of their being able to collude with one another to make the pie bigger at the expense of the taxpayer.

Because states do not have the power to print money, state budgets can be limited by limiting total taxes that may be imposed and that is the method that has been used in most of the state amendments that have been adopted or proposed. The federal government can print money, so limiting taxes is not an effective method. That is why our amendment is stated in terms of limiting total spending by the federal government, however financed.

The limits—on either taxes or spending—are mostly specified in terms of the total income of the state or nation in such a way that if spending equalled the limit, government spending would remain constant as a fraction of income. That would halt the trend toward ever-bigger government, not reverse it. However, the limits would encourage a reversal because, in most cases, if spending did not equal the limit in any year, that would lower the limits applicable to future years. In addition, the proposed federal amendment requires a reduction in the percentage if inflation exceeds 3 percent a year.

Other Constitutional Provisions

A gradual reduction in the fraction of our income that government spends would be a major contribution to a freer and stronger society. But it would be only one step toward that objective.

Many of the most damaging kinds of government controls over our lives do not involve much government spending: for example, tariffs, price and wage controls, licensure of occupations, regulation of industry, consumer legislation.

With respect to these, too, the most promising approach is through general rules that limit government power. As yet, the designing of appropriate rules of this kind has received little attention. Before any rules can be taken seriously, they need the kind of thorough examination by people with different interests and knowledge that the tax and spending limitation amendments have received.

As a first step in this process, we sketch a few examples of the kinds of amendments that appear to us desirable. We stress that these are highly tentative, intended primarily to stimulate further thought and further work in this largely unexplored area.

International Trade. The Constitution now specifies that "No State shall, without the consent of the Congress, lay any imposts or duties on imports or exports, except what may be absolutely necessary for executing its inspection laws." An amendment could specify that:

Congress shall not lay any imposts or duties on imports or exports; except what may be absolutely necessary for executing its inspection laws.

It is visionary to suppose that such an amendment could be enacted now. However, achieving free trade through repealing individual tariffs is, if anything, even more visionary. And the attack on all tariffs consolidates the interests we all have as consumers to counter the special interest we each have as producers.

Wage and Price Controls. As one of us wrote some years ago, "If the U.S. ever succumbs to collectivism, to government control over every facet of our lives, it will not be because the socialists win any arguments. It will be through the indirect route of wage and price controls."[5] Prices transmit information—which Walter Wriston has quite properly translated by describing prices as a form of speech. And prices determined in a free market are a form of free speech. We need here the exact counterpart of the First Amendment:

Congress shall make no laws abridging the freedom of sellers of goods or labor to price their products or services.

Occupational Licensure. Few things have a greater effect on our lives than the occupations we may follow. Widening freedom to choose in this area requires limiting the power of states. The counterpart here in our Constitution is either the provisions in its text which prohibit certain actions by states or the Fourteenth Amendment. One suggestion:

No State shall make or impose any law which shall abridge the right of any citizen of the United States to follow any occupation or profession of his choice.

A Portmanteau Free Trade Amendment. The three preceding amendments could all be replaced by a single amendment patterned after the Second Amendment to our Constitution (which guarantees the right to keep and bear arms):

The right of the people to buy and sell legitimate goods and services at mutually acceptable terms shall not be infringed by Congress or any of the States.

Taxation. By general consent, the personal income tax is sadly in need of reform. It professes to adjust the tax to "ability to pay," to tax the rich more heavily and the poor less heavily and to allow for each individual's special circumstances. It does no such thing. Tax rates are highly graduated on paper, rising from 14 to 70 percent. But the law is riddled with so many loopholes, so many special privileges, that the high rates are almost pure window dressing. A low flat rate—less than 20 percent—on all income above personal exemptions with no deductions except for strict occupational expenses would yield more revenue than the present unwieldy structure. Taxpayers would be better off—because they would be spared the costs of sheltering income from taxes; the economy would be better off—because tax considerations would play a smaller role in the allocation of resources. The only losers would be lawyers, accountants, civil servants, and legislators—who would have to turn to more productive activities than filling in tax forms, devising tax loopholes, and trying to close them.

The corporate income tax too is highly defective. It is a hidden tax that the public pays in the prices it pays for goods and services without realizing it. It constitutes double taxation of corporate income—once to the corporation, once to the stockholder, when the income is distributed. It penalizes capital investment, and thereby hinders growth in productivity. It should be abolished.

Although there is agreement between left and right that lower rates, fewer loopholes, and a reduction in the double taxation of corporate income would be desirable, such a reform cannot be enacted through the legislative process. The left fear that if they accepted lower rates and less graduation in return for eliminating loopholes, new loopholes would soon emerge—and they are right. The right fear that if they accepted the elimination of the loopholes in return for lower rates and less graduation, steeper graduation would soon emerge—and they are right.

This is a specially clear case where a constitutional amendment is the only hope of striking a bargain that all sides can expect to be honored. The amendment needed here is the repeal of the present Sixteenth Amendment authorizing income taxes and its replacement by one along the following lines:

> *The Congress shall have power to lay and collect taxes on incomes of persons, from whatever sources derived, without apportionment among the several States, and without regard to any census or enumeration, provided that the same tax rate is applied to all income in excess of occupational and business expenses and a personal allowance of a fixed amount. The word "person" shall exclude corporations and other artificial persons.*

Sound Money. When the Constitution was enacted, the power given to Congress "to coin money, regulate the value thereof, and of foreign coin" referred to a commodity money: specifying that the dollar shall mean a definite weight in grams of silver or gold. The paper money inflation during the Revolution, as well as earlier in various colonies, led the framers to deny states the power to "coin money; emit bills of credit [i.e., paper money]; make anything but gold and silver coin a tender in payment of debts." The Constitution is silent on Congress's power to authorize the government to issue paper money. It was widely believed that the Tenth Amendment, providing that "The powers not delegated to the United States by the Constitution . . . are reserved to the States respectively, or to the people," made the issuance of paper money unconstitutional.

During the Civil War, Congress authorized greenbacks and made them a legal tender for all debts public and private. After the Civil War, in the first of the famous greenback cases, the Supreme Court declared the issuance of greenbacks unconstitutional. One "fascinating aspect of this decision is that it was delivered by Chief Justice Salmon P. Chase, who had been Secretary of the Treasury when the first greenbacks were issued. Not only did he not disqualify himself, but in his capacity as Chief Justice convicted himself of having been responsible for an unconstitutional action in his capacity as Secretary of the Treasury."[6]

Subsequently, an enlarged and reconstituted Court reversed the first decision by a majority of five to four, affirming that making greenbacks a legal tender was constitutional, with Chief Justice Chase as one of the dissenting justices.

It is neither feasible nor desirable to restore a gold- or silver-coin standard, but we do need a commitment to sound money. The best arrangement currently would be to require the monetary authorities to keep the percentage rate of growth of the monetary base within a fixed range. This is a particularly difficult amendment to draft because it is so closely linked to the particular institutional structure. One version would be:

> *Congress shall have the power to authorize non-interest bearing obligations of the government in the form of currency or book entries, provided that the total dollar amount outstanding increases by no more than 5 percent per year and no less than 3 percent.*

It might be desirable to include a provision that two-thirds of each House of Congress, or some similar qualified majority, can waive this requirement in case of a declaration of war, the suspension to terminate annually unless renewed.

Inflation-Protection. If the preceding amendment were adopted and strictly adhered to, that would end inflation and assure a relatively stable price level. In that case, no further measures would be needed to prevent the government from engaging in inflationary taxation without representation. However, that is a big *if.* An amendment that would remove the incentive for government to inflate would have broad support. It might be adopted far more readily than a more technical and controversial sound money amendment. In effect, what is required is the extension of the Fifth Amendment provision that "No person shall . . . be deprived of life, liberty, or property, without due process of law; nor shall private property be taken for public use without just compensation."

A person whose dollar income just keeps pace with inflation yet is pushed into a higher tax bracket is deprived of property without due process. The repudiation of part of the real value of government bonds through inflation is the taking of private property for public use without just compensation.

The relevant amendment would specify:

> *All contracts between the U.S. government and other parties stated in dollars, and all dollar sums contained in Federal laws, shall be adjusted annually to allow for the change in the general level of prices during the prior year.*

Like the monetary amendment, this too is difficult to draft precisely because of its technical character. Congress would have to specify precise procedures, including what index number should be used to approximate "the general level of prices." But it states the fundamental principle.

This is hardly an exhaustive list—we still have three to go to match the ten amendments in the original Bill of Rights. And the suggested wording needs the scrutiny of experts in each area as well as constitutional legal experts. But we trust that these proposals at least indicate the promise of a constitutional approach.

CONCLUSION

The two ideas of human freedom and economic freedom working together came to their greatest fruition in the United States. Those ideas are still very much with us. We are all of us imbued with them. They are part of the very fabric of our being. But we have been straying from them. We have been forgetting the basic truth that the greatest threat to human freedom is the concentration of power, whether in the hands of government or anyone else. We have persuaded ourselves that it is safe to grant power, provided it is for good purposes.

Fortunately, we are waking up. We are again recognizing the dangers of an over-governed society, coming to understand that good objectives can be perverted by bad means, that reliance on the freedom of people to control their own lives in accordance with their own values is the surest way to achieve the full potential of a great society.

Fortunately, also, we are as a people still free to choose which way we should go—whether to continue along the road we have been following to ever-bigger government, or to call a halt and change direction.

NOTES

1. Raoul Berger, *Government by Judiciary* (Cambridge: Harvard University Press, 1977), pp. 1, 408.

2. *Law and Public Opinion* (1914 ed.), p. 302.

3. "Boom Industry," *Wall Street Journal,* June 12, 1979, p. 1, col. 5.

4. *Law and Public Opinion* (1914 ed.), pp. 257–258.

5. Milton Friedman, "Monumental Folly," *Newsweek,* June 25, 1973.

6. Milton Friedman and Anna J. Schwartz, *A Monetary History of the United States, 1867–1960,* National Bureau of Economic Research Studies in Business Cycles, no. 12 (Princeton: Princeton University Press, 1963), p. 46.

APPENDIX A

SOCIALIST PLATFORM OF 1928

Herewith the economic planks of the Socialist Party Platform of 1928, along with an indication in parentheses of how these planks have fared. The list that follows includes every economic plank, but not the full language of each.

1) "Nationalization of our natural resources, beginning with the coal mines and water sites, particularly at Boulder Dam and Muscle Shoals." (Boulder Dam, renamed Hoover Dam, and Muscle Shoals are now both federal government projects.)
2) "A publicly owned giant power system under which the federal government shall cooperate with the states and municipalities in the distribution of electrical energy to the people at cost." (Tennessee Valley Authority.)
3) "National ownership and democratic management of railroads and other means of transportation and communication." (Railroad passenger service is completely nationalized through AMTRAK. Some freight service is nationalized through CONRAIL. The FCC controls communication by telephone, telegraph, radio and television.)
4) "An adequate national program for flood control, flood relief, reforestation, irrigation and reclamation." (Government expenditures for these purposes are currently in the many billions of dollars.)
5) "Immediate governmental relief of the unemployed by the extension of all public works and a program of long range planning of public works . . . " (In the 1930s, WPA and PWA were a direct counterpart; now, a wide variety of other programs are.) "All persons thus employed to be engaged at hours and wages fixed by bona-fide labor unions." (The Davis-Bacon and Walsh-Healey Acts require contractors with government contracts to pay "prevailing wages," generally interpreted as highest union wages.)
6) "Loans to states and municipalities without interest for the purpose of carrying on public works and the taking of such other measures as will lessen widespread misery." (Federal grants in aid to states and local municipalities currently total tens of billions of dollars a year.)

7) "A system of unemployment insurance." (Part of social security system.)
8) "The nation-wide extension of public employment agencies in cooperation with city federations of labor." (U.S. Employment Service and affiliated state employment services administer a network of about 2,500 local employment offices.)
9) "A system of health and accident insurance and of old age pensions as well as unemployment insurance." (Part of social security system.)
10) "Shortening the workday" and "Securing to every worker a rest period of no less than two days in each week." (Legislated by wages and hours laws that require overtime for more than 40 hours of work per week.)
11) "Enacting of an adequate federal anti-child labor amendment." (Not achieved as amendment, but essence incorporated in various legislative acts.)
12) "Abolition of the brutal exploitation of convicts under the contract system and substitution of a cooperative organization of industries in penitentiaries and workshops for the benefit of convicts and their dependents." (Partly achieved, partly not.)
13) "Increase of taxation on high income levels, of corporation taxes and inheritance taxes, the proceeds to be used for old age pensions and other forms of social insurance." (In 1928, highest personal income tax rate, 25 percent; in 1978, 70 percent; in 1928, corporate tax rate, 12 percent; in 1978, 48 percent; in 1928, top federal estate tax rate, 20 percent; in 1978, 70 percent.)
14) "Appropriation by taxation of the annual rental value of all land held for speculation." (Not achieved in this form, but property taxes have risen drastically.)

APPENDIX B

A PROPOSED CONSTITUTIONAL AMENDMENT TO LIMIT FEDERAL SPENDING

Prepared by the Federal Amendment Drafting Committee
W. C. Stubblebine, Chairman
Convened by The National Tax Limitation Committee
Wm. F. Rickenbacker, Chairman; Lewis K. Uhler, President

Section 1. To protect the people against excessive governmental burdens and to promote sound fiscal and monetary policies, total outlays of the Government of the United States shall be limited.

(a) Total outlays in any fiscal year shall not increase by a percentage greater than the percentage increase in nominal gross national product in the last calendar year ending prior to the beginning of said fiscal year. Total outlays shall include budget and off-budget outlays, and exclude redemptions of the public debt and emergency outlays.

(b) If inflation for the last calendar year ending prior to the beginning of any fiscal year is more than three per cent, the permissible percentage increase in total outlays for that fiscal year shall be reduced by one-fourth of the excess of inflation over three per cent. Inflation shall be measured by the difference between the percentage increase in nominal gross national product and the percentage increase in real gross national product.

Section 2. When, for any fiscal year, total revenues received by the Government of the United States exceed total outlays, the surplus shall be used to reduce the public debt of the United States until such debt is eliminated.

Section 3. Following declaration of an emergency by the President, Congress may authorize, by a two-thirds vote of both Houses, a specified amount of emergency outlays in excess of the limit for the current fiscal year.

Section 4. The limit on total outlays may be changed by a specified amount by a three-fourths vote of both Houses of Congress when approved by the Legislatures of a majority of the several States. The change shall become effective for the fiscal year following approval.

Section 5. For each of the first six fiscal years after ratification of this article, total grants to States and local governments shall not be a smaller fraction of total outlays than in the three fiscal years prior to the ratification of this article. Thereafter, if grants are less than that fraction of total outlays, the limit on total outlays shall be decreased by an equivalent amount.

Section 6. The Government of the United States shall not require, directly or indirectly, that States or local governments engage in additional or expanded activities without compensation equal to the necessary additional costs.

Section 7. This article may be enforced by one or more members of the Congress in an action brought in the United States District Court for the District of Columbia, and by no other persons. The action shall name as defendant the Treasurer of the United States, who shall have authority over outlays by any unit or agency of the Government of the United States when required by a court order enforcing the provisions of this article. The order of the court shall not specify the particular outlays to be made or reduced. Changes in outlays necessary to comply with the order of the court shall be made no later than the end of the third full fiscal year following the court order.

Economic Policy

Alan Greenspan

II

The seeming halcyon days of the 1960s when economists believed they had a grasp of the fundamental forces governing industrial economies have faded in the wake of inflation and stagnation. In much of the industrial world, many of the old policy verities are gone or are going. As a consequence, the self-confidence of the economic policymaking process had been undercut.

Those who are given the mandate of their governments to create balanced, stable economic growth find themselves struggling to achieve goals that might not be achievable with the tools at hand. One must question whether economists any longer know enough about the complex dynamics of advanced industrial economies to carry out their difficult mandate. Much of what was thought to be true is not.

THE DOWNFALL OF FORECASTING

The most disturbing symptom of the undermining of our theoretical footing is the poor forecasting record of economists in recent years. Both the inflation of the early 1970s and the recession of late 1974–1975 were inadequately forecast (some would use harsher language). Since the likely impact of policy changes is evaluated from the same conceptual framework that governs our forecasts, the failure adequately to accomplish the latter raises serious questions about the efficacy of the former.

The root of the problem goes back to the early 1960s. After several years of relatively successful forecasting with the newly developed

---

The author is indebted to Dr. Annelise Anderson of California State University (Hayward) for her many helpful suggestions and criticisms.

econometric models, a general view seemed to emerge that if we could forecast the economy given certain elements of fiscal and monetary policy, we could fine-tune the levels of economic activity by calibrating the different mixes of fiscal and monetary policy. It wasn't until the mid-1970s, when our forecasting track record went badly awry, that that notion fell into disrepute.

In retrospect, the reasons for our forecasting successes in the 1960s and failures in the 1970s are clear. We had then, as now, a decidedly poor insight into the processes of inflation. The forecasting techniques for wages and prices in our models of the 1960s were clearly simplistic at best and led, when applied in the 1970s, to inaccurate predictions.

During the 1960s, however, the inflationary pressures in our economy were relatively weak. Hence, even though the structure of inflationary forces was misspecified in our econometric models, it did not surface as a problem in the aggregate forecasts of real growth and employment. It wasn't until inflation began to accelerate in the mid-1970s that the mistaken representations in our models began to create significant problems for our forecasts. By that time it became clear that the problem was not a minor technical matter that could be easily adjusted, but rather some fundamental lack of insight into the inflationary processes themselves. Regrettably, to this day our short-term forecasting capabilities still do not appropriately capture inflationary forces, as the continuous respecifying of our wage and price equations attest.

However, because economists do not know everything, that does not mean they know nothing. Despite the setbacks of recent years, there remains a vast body of tested knowledge that can readily be brought to bear on the complexity of the industrial world's economic malaise. But we must tailor our economic policy objectives of the 1980s to our economic policy capabilities. Were policy mistakes costless, then experiment could eventually find the best policy. But mistaken policies are not costless, and too often leave the economy with even more difficult problems in their wake.

DON'TS ARE EASIER THAN DO'S

We must, therefore, attempt to judge where our knowledge is secure and, hence, where policy initiatives have a reasonable chance of broad political support. Unfortunately, at the moment it would seem that if there is such a thing as a strong consensus of economic policy theory, it would be a series of "don'ts":

1) Don't run excessively large, high-employment-adjusted government deficits—they lead to inflation and recession.
2) Don't allow money supply growth to spiral out of hand, or it will create inflation; don't squeeze it too rapidly, or it will lead to recession.
3) Don't clamp rigid price and wage ceilings on a vibrant economy—they will break down.
4) Don't shut the door to your trading neighbor's goods—doing so will lead to higher prices and lower per capita real income.
5) Don't try to fix the exchange rate of a strengthening or weakening currency—a number of things can happen, none of them good.

But policy initiatives rest on the conviction of certain stable economic relationships, and when we pass to the list of policy "do's," the consensus breaks down. A stable trade-off between inflation and unemployment has become a victim of stagflation. The presumed stability of money-stock relationships with nominal income and interest rates has become increasingly open to question. In recent years, even a previously sacrosanct notion—namely, that the federal government could control the specific level of its expenditures merely by regulating its check-writing activities—has run up against mysterious outlay "shortfalls."

There is probably little argument at this stage, however, that inflation is at the base of the malaise that has afflicted the Western industrial world since the early 1970s. One senses, finally, a growing awareness that the conventional policy response to stagnation and high unemployment, that is, fiscal and monetary expansion, is somehow not working. In the communiqués following various recent world forums (Organization of Economic Cooperation and Development, summits, European Economic Community, and others), we are beginning to see a shift in the nature of the diagnosis. In the words of the 1977 Downing Street Summit, "Inflation does not reduce unemployment. On the contrary, it is one of its major causes."

This view runs counter to an inflation/unemployment trade-off, the keystone of most postwar fiscal and monetary policy initiatives. It implies that there is something in the process of inflation that undercuts investment and employment. As the evidence of the consequences of inflation on economic growth and stability mounts, the policy imperatives of the 1980s are becoming clarified. We are no longer dealing with inflation/unemployment trade-offs, but with the simple policy focus of defusing the inflationary bias in our economy. If we succeed in that, other policy initiatives are unnecessary. If we fail, other initiatives will be irrelevant.

FRAYED BUSINESS CONFIDENCE

After the sharpest economic upheaval of the post-World War II period, the world's industrial countries are struggling, so far with mixed success, to get back on the path of balanced, noninflationary growth. The United States, after recovering from the lows of 1975, still finds the achievement of full recovery elusive. After a strong burst of growth in output and employment through 1978, a sharp slowing in the rate of advance is occurring in 1979, placing the United States on a path that will still leave it short of the full employment of resources. The failure to return to a balanced, fully employed economy seems clearly to rest with inadequate private investment. It probably explains much of the stagnation in productivity that in turn is contributing to our economy's inflation bias. The cause of the investment inadequacy is all too evident—a failure of confidence. More exactly, the uncertainty that plagues the investment commitment process today is far more pervasive than a decade ago. This uncertainty is embodied in investment calculations in the form of higher-risk premiums and prevents a normal package of capital projects from meeting acceptable financial criteria.

Moreover, the investment shortfalls appear to be concentrated in long-lived investments, particularly those for which the profit expectations are especially skewed toward the later years of the investment: eight, ten, fifteen years in the future. Worst hit are investments where high-risk premiums, acting heavily to discount expected future profit, make the present value of those prospective profits minimal.

Short-lived assets, those with rapid rates of cash return, seem closer to normal levels of commitment. But long-lived assets, particularly those related to major construction projects that typically do not repay their investment costs for many years (or even decades) are still lagging badly.

As a consequence, it is not surprising to find that the average service life of capital expenditures made during the 1970s began to shorten. The life of investments made for nonresidential fixed capital during the early 1960s averaged approximately 21 years, with structures-put-in-place having a life expectancy of about 32 years, and producers' durable equipment, 13 years. Not only have the average lives of equipment and structures themselves shortened, but the mix has shifted toward equipment and away from structures. This has produced a pronounced decline in the average life of all capital investment from the 21 years plus in the late 1950s and early 1960s to under 18 years in 1979.

Long-lived equipment, such as agricultural machinery, engines and turbines, metalworking machinery, special industry machinery, general industry machinery, ships and boats, and railroad equipment, has experienced a significant relative decline, whereas short-lived equipment, such as trucks and autos, has increased its share of the producers' durable equipment market appreciably. Office equipment, especially computers, has also shown a sharp increase in its proportion of producers' durable equipment. In fact, the combination of motor vehicles and office equipment, each with an average life expectancy of roughly nine years, rose from approximately 23 percent of the producers' durable equipment market in 1959 to 40 percent of the market in 1978. The trend is less pronounced, but nonetheless evident among the various types of structures. Long-lived institutional buildings saw their share of the total structures market drop from close to 9 percent in 1959 to less than 3 percent in 1978. On the other hand, telephone and communication structures, which have somewhat shorter lives, have exhibited a marked increase in their share.

Perhaps the most important factor engendering a markedly lower average life for all capital assets has been the shift from structures to equipment. In 1959, for example, equipment accounted for only 57.4 percent of total nonresidential fixed investment. For 1978, the figure was 68.5 percent.

Part of the shortfall in construction reflects stretch-outs of utilities expansion resulting from regulatory and environmental delays. These shortfalls, of course, cannot be attributed solely to frayed business confidence. However, the very uncertainty of, for example, environmental rules is a factor in the utilities' hesitation to move ahead. Even outside the utilities area, construction has been slow in recovering. Expansion of manufacturing capacity has fallen far short of the pattern developed in earlier business cycles.

Perhaps more ominous than the foreshortening of the capital investment horizon is the shift in research and development budgets toward quick-payoff "development" projects. Industry-financed research, basic and applied, which accounted for almost 34 percent of company research and development budgets in 1960, amounted to only 25 percent of such spending in 1978.

The rise in investment risk over the past decade is also clearly reflected in the stock markets, where price/earnings ratios have fallen to the lowest levels in two decades, largely as a consequence of the increased discount rate imposed on expected earnings growth.

It is difficult to disentangle the extent to which the failure of many capital projects to pass the financial criteria for acceptance reflects a lowered expectation of earnings growth or higher-risk premiums. Both are doubtless involved. But it looks as if higher risk is by far the dominant factor. A 1977 McGraw-Hill survey indicated that approximately 25 percent of manufacturing companies required capital expenditures for modernization and replacement to "pay off in less than three years." In a similar survey taken during spring 1969, only 20 percent required a payoff in less than three years. A higher rate of return is now required, presumably to compensate for increased risk.

Although there are obviously factors other than risk that help determine capital outlays, risk premiums in and of themselves are dominantly important.

ROOTS OF UNCERTAINTY

Although the causes of this high degree of investment risk vary from country to country, at root is a profound uncertainty of the shape of the future economic environment in which new facilities might be functioning.

Although many reasons could be cited, two stand out as the key contributors to the higher level of uncertainty in the past several years in the United States. First, and by far the most important, is inflation, the fear of an increasing rate in the years ahead, and of the instability that would follow in its path. An inflationary environment makes calculation of the rate of return on new investment more uncertain. Even if overall profits advance in line with the rate of inflation, the dispersion of profits among businesses tends to increase as the rate of inflation climbs. The risk of loss rises or, at best, the attainment of profits becomes more elusive.

Thus, a much higher rate of discount is applied to inflation-generated profits than to those accruing from normal business operations. The longer the effective life of a prospective investment, the more adverse the effect, owing to the greater uncertainty attached to projections of inflation into the future. Accordingly, inflation not only introduces greater uncertainty into rate-of-return calculations, but also acts to skew the investment pattern toward shorter-lived projects in which the uncertainty is assuredly less.

A second, although somewhat smaller, contributor to higher-risk premiums is escalating business regulation. Since the rise of concern over health and the environment, the regulatory process has mushroomed. Although regulatory changes have directly increased the cost of new facilities in a major way, this has not been the crux of the risk problem. Higher costs may inhibit investment but, once specified, they at least are no longer uncertain. Far worse for capital-investment decision making is the fact that regulations may, indeed will, change in the future, and in a way that is unknowable at present. This, rather than known costs, has engendered uncertainty and hesitation among businessmen.

HOBBLING LONG-RUN CHANGE

Although investment risk has its most visible impact on capital investment and the level of economic activity, no less important is its effect on an economy's efficiency. High-risk premiums hobble the free market's ability to adjust to perceived longer-term trends. They dull the sensitivity of the supply/demand adjustment process and lead too often to brittle and unstable economic adjustments.

In particular, they are thwarting the industrial world's adjustment to sharply higher energy prices. If risk premiums were low, development of long lead-time synthetic fuels would already be well advanced (without government subsidies), and nuclear plant construction would be flourishing. Given enough lead-time and investment, expected future shortages would turn into welcome energy surpluses, but the payoffs are too far away on such projects to gain support at current levels of risk.

Under conditions of less risk, energy-saving equipment would likewise be highly profitable, and, in anticipation of large profit payoffs a decade and more hence, vast new research and development efforts in the area of energy conservation would move forward.

High-risk premiums are blunting the long-term adjustment processes, in the energy area as elsewhere, which are essential to the functioning of a free enterprise system. High-risk premiums are "blindsiding" the market system and preventing its adjustment processes from addressing the distant future. In the same way that futures prices adjust supply and demand for storable commodities for periods of one or two years, it is risk premiums that link the longer-term future supply and demand forces to the current balance.

Thus, the critical focus of economic policy in the Western world has got to be to reduce these abnormally high-risk premiums. They have created a private decision-making atmosphere that gives short shrift to long-term benefits and costs and undue emphasis to the short run.

Advanced industrial economies rest on an infrastructure of long-lived assets; unless decision making conforms to the same time frame, the economic system will lose its productive efficiency.

HOW TO GET LONG-TERM POLICIES

Unfortunately, there is no quick fix for high-risk premiums. Restoring a state of confidence will take time.

It may sometimes appear that "business confidence" is some nebulous, quasi-mystic state of mind, a neurosis that can be exorcised by some form of mass psychotherapy. It cannot. Although the exceptions are often painful history, the state of business confidence mostly reflects rational assessments. Business confidence can be improved and risk premiums lowered only by changes in the real world, changes that are perceived as presaging a less uncertain and more stable environment into which investments are committed.

This will require a significant and credible reduction in the rate of inflation, a decline that is seen as the start of a return to a permanently lower rate and, hence, of less economic instability. This means that in the longer run, high-employment budget deficits must be eliminated, and the consequent pressures on the monetary system of large federal financing lowered. A necessary condition to curbing the inflationary bias in our system is a reduction of the inflationary financial pressures that stem from overly expansionary fiscal and monetary policies.

Even with the best of intentions it would be a mistake to presume that the Federal Reserve (the Fed) alone can take the political heat required to contain inflation or confront the more difficult fundamentals of the inflation bias in the American economy. Interest rates are high because the demand for credit is high, and money supply growth in recent years has been excessive (and inflationary) because the Fed feels politically compelled to suppress interest rates by at least partially accommodating the excess credit requirements.

There is no question that the Fed has the capacity under such conditions to unilaterally constrain money supply growth, but not without pressing interest rates sharply higher in the short run. It is likely that such a rise in rates would be short-lived, and an unflinching commitment by the Fed would eventually succeed. Regrettably, our political system is unlikely to acquiesce in such a policy initiative. Thus, the only politically viable solution is to slow the monetary aggregates for a protracted period, but without engendering excessively high interest rates (even in the short run). That can be done only by reducing the demand for funds pressing on our financial system.

The marked increase in aggregate capital market borrowing has not only driven interest rates higher but, in the process, diverted an ever-increasing amount of borrowing from the capital markets (by those who were "crowded out") to the commercial banks. In an endeavor to accommodate the loan requirements of their customers, commercial banks attempted to obtain the reserves required to back up loans by borrowing in the federal funds market.

The accompanying rise in the federal funds rate has placed the Fed in its typical "no win" position. It has had to determine whether to stand aside, allowing the federal funds rate to rise, thereby thwarting some of the prospective commercial bank borrowing, or whether, by supplying reserves to the market, to hold the federal funds rate temporarily below what it would otherwise be, thereby accommodating the expanding loan demand.

That latter path, however, enlarges the monetary base, inducing an acceleration in money supply growth with inflationary consequences. The Fed as usual has straddled the issue, only partially accommodating the demand for funds. As a result, in recent years, both money supply growth and interest rates rose, but the increases in each were less than might otherwise have prevailed, at least in the short run.

Curbing the growth in federal spending and deficits is a necessary, but not a sufficient, condition to restore balance to the financial markets. If we focus wholly on the budget deficit, we are missing what may well be a far more inflationary set of credit-preempting policies fostered by the federal government.

Off-budget borrowing has risen sharply in recent years, as have mandated capital investment by business (pollution, safety equipment, and so on) that must be financed and matching grants, which have induced increased spending and borrowing by state and local governments. These demands have added heavily to capital market pressures, as has the vast expansion in credit guarantees by the federal government. The guarantees have brought borrowers into the market who in earlier times could not have met minimum credit standards.

The net effect of the increased federal intervention in the credit markets has been to decrease, at the margin, the responsiveness of credit demand to a rise in interest rates. As a consequence, interest rates must now rise higher than they would have under comparable conditions a decade ago in order to crowd out the excess demand for funds; that is, the supply and demand for funds can come into balance only at higher interest rates than previously. This would be true even in a noninflationary environment in which there was no perceptible inflation premium embodied in interest rate levels.

This explains in part the extreme difficulty the Fed has had in attempting simultaneously to dampen monetary growth while keeping interest rates at moderate levels. The heavy indirect borrowing by the Treasury has thus clearly contributed to the underlying inflation bias in the economy.

THE DILEMMA

If inflation is to be defused, the current needs of economic policy are to stretch the cost/benefit trade-off in favor of long-term gains, even if that involves short-term costs. Yet the political process that must support economic policy, if it is to succeed, has become increasingly oriented to the short range—or, more exactly, the seemingly inherent short-range focus of the political process has expanded into more and more areas of our economy. The effect has been to impart an inflation bias to economic policy through overexpansionary fiscal and monetary policies.

When decisions are reached in the private sector to build new plants or develop new markets, present and future costs are traded off against present and future benefits. Political decision making, on the other hand, tends to be short-sighted, particularly in its single-minded focus on short-term benefits. Potential longer-term problems, seen emerging from the nearsighted programs, are dismissed as something that, it is hoped, will never arise, or, if they do, can be handled by some new program (or different politician).

In recent years government's professed responsibility for every detail of economic activity, when coupled with the warped approach of the political process to cost/benefit trade-offs, has too often led to action only when crisis demanded it. However, a crisis solution by its very nature is short-range. It rarely comes to grips with anything but the immediate manifestations of a problem.

Not surprisingly, secondary crises often arise as a consequence. The price freeze of 1971 in the United States, for example, bottled up inflationary forces to be released in later years. Even when the political decision makers are aware of these later adverse consequences, they implicitly place an exceptionally heavy discount on the longer-term adverse effects. Activist economic policymakers soon build a large backlog of bridges to be crossed "when we get to them." Eventually, even the alleged short-term benefits fade as the formerly longer-term costs become current with the inexorable turn of the calendar. The cumulative costs of policy soon overwhelm the cumulative benefits.

FISCAL CONSTITUENCIES

The source of the problem is the ever-expanding number of what can be called "fiscal constituencies," that is, groups of individuals receiving payments in cash or in kind on a continuing basis under a government program. In the United States we now have tens of millions of people receiving social security, veterans' benefits, farm subsidies, public assistance, and the like, and the list is growing.

Aggravating the problem of the increasing number of these recipients is the exceptional difficulty of eliminating or even paring programs once they are under way. Curtailments do occur, but rarely. Whether a particular program actually resolves the problem to which it is addressed appears to be of little moment once the constituency has formed.

So long as government functions are general and citizens have a diffuse relationship with their government, the problem of fiscal constituencies is limited. But, as soon as strong associations with specific programs emerge, the pressure on governments to expand these programs and to create new ones has, in the past at least, seemed irresistible.

GOVERNMENT "UNCONTROLLABLES"

As might be expected, economic policy activism has led to an ever-larger proportion of the national income being absorbed by government programs. Total net government outlays at all levels in the United States absorbed a third of our gross national product during 1978. By comparison, total government before World War II absorbed less than one-fifth of GNP, and in 1929, 10 percent.

There has been some slowing in real outlays during the past year, but over the past decade America's federal outlay problem has taken on disturbing dimensions. On a high employment basis, total outlays have held steady as a percentage of GNP, but this has been solely the result of a marked decline in real defense costs. Payments for individuals (which currently comprise three-fifths of the nondefense budget) have grown at an annual rate of more than 8 percent in real terms since the mid-1950s. A large and increasing proportion of total outlays is the result of past programs. Such outlays are virtually uncontrollable without changes in the underlying legislation, which, of course, are very difficult to achieve. At present, more than three-fourths of total federal outlays are "relatively uncontrollable," up from less than 60 percent a decade ago.

In addition to the burgeoning increase in existing programs there are the inevitable new ones. The normal workings of the American government create new programs year after year. Action is the very essence of contemporary government and this produces an annual increment of new programs—another type of "uncontrollable" that makes the rise in outlays seemingly unsuppressible. It is difficult to pinpoint beforehand what money bills will be passed during the year. Recent experience, however, suggests a large, unspecified increment to outlays that is strictly the consequence of the fact that our government functions virtually all year long, creating new programs and initiatives. It should not be a surprise, then, that the large budget surpluses, whose arrival at some point usually three to five years out is regularly promised, never seem to materialize.

Some progress has been made during the past several years owing to a revision in budget procedures initiated under legislation enacted in 1974. Congress has started to review the budget as a whole, and has moved toward a procedure (not, as yet, really effective) to balance relative priorities. Nonetheless, there have not been any major new costly programs initiated during the past several years. A vast health insurance program has been sidetracked, and welfare reform, which only five years ago appeared as a large new increment to the budget, has been delayed and now appears less costly. But only the momentum of federal outlay growth has slowed; the underlying trend seems very much intact.

Though the budgetary procedures differ, much the same philosophy governs government programs in the rest of the non-communist world.

Not unexpectedly, the response in some countries in recent years to high risk and shortfalls in private investment has been an attempt to increase consumption, through fiscal expansion, in order to fill the gap left by inadequate private investment. But such policies can be nothing more than highly inflationary short-range stopgaps.

The expectation that the expansion of consumption would trigger an investment recovery, as it has in the past, has proved disappointing. This should not be surprising since increased current sales are not readily translatable into new capacity requirements when risk premiums are high.

Certainly, the substitution of government investment (and central planning) for private investment is scarcely a solution to the profound sense of malaise that confronts much of the industrial world. More disturbing still, such policies can easily become self-justifying. It can be argued that private investment is weak and therefore centrally planned government investment is needed to fill the gap. But as central planning spreads, private investment incentives atrophy still more, justifying the initial premise that more central planning is needed. At the end of this path is a regimented economy.

Fortunately, the United States has not taken that path and there are growing indications that the industrial countries of the non-communist world are looking elsewhere for solutions. It is still too soon to conclude that the postwar trend toward increasing government intervention is about to be reversed. But its momentum has certainly slowed.

A SHIFT TO THE RIGHT

The political consensus in this country and in most, perhaps all, of the major industrial nations of the world now seems to be moving toward a set of financial policies that have a reasonably good chance of diffusing underlying inflationary forces in the years immediately ahead.

In Europe, we saw Britain teeter on the edge of financial collapse in 1976, largely as a consequence of excessively stimulative financial policies. The United Kingdom has since moved dramatically in a conservative direction: first the ruling Labour party itself shifted to markedly more restrictive policies; then the electorate restored power to a Conservative government dedicated to strong fiscal restraint.

Although the ruling party in Germany is considered on the left, its chancellor and its policies clearly have been in the forefront of fiscal conservatism in the Western world. France, which as recently as spring 1978 seemed poised to be taken over by a Socialist-Communist coalition, voted in what has plainly become a far more conservative government than could have been imagined, pursuing policies that perhaps are best symbolized by the decontrol of bread prices for the first time since 1789.

As recently as 1976 the Italian Communists appeared to be on the brink of entering the government and perhaps eventually becoming *the* government. But Italy, too, has turned back this tide, and the elections of 1979 seemed to move Italy somewhat closer to the mainstream of centrist European politics. To a greater or lesser extent, the shift toward conservatism has manifested itself both in Scandinavia and elsewhere in Europe.

In the Western Pacific, the Japanese government remains dedicated to fiscal conservatism. Australia has in recent years perhaps made the most significant shift from a left-of-center government to one strongly dedicated to capitalist principles. In Canada, the recent elections brought in a conservative government, but even before that the Liberal regime of Pierre Elliott Trudeau had already moved significantly toward fiscal conservatism. In Mexico, the government has obviously moved to the right with the election of José López Portillo in 1976.

But perhaps it is in the United States where the change in political philosophy is most readily discernible. Certainly, a conclave of presumably astute political analysts in the fall of 1977 would never have attached significant probability to the political events that were to occur over the next year and a half. The odds would have appeared extremely low for a sharp cut in the capital gains tax rate and a cut in tax rates in general without further increasing progressivity in the process. Would the analysts have foreseen Proposition 13 or the phenomenon whereby virtually all candidates in the 1978 elections campaigned on planks of fiscal responsibility? Finally, could anyone have anticipated the emergent move among the state legislators to convene a constitutional convention to balance the federal budget? What is extraordinary about what has occurred in the United States is that it was not foreseen, as in fact much of what has occurred in Europe and the Pacific basin was relatively unanticipated. Nonetheless, a profound transformation in political and social values is under way.

Although there are many subsidiary reasons for what is clearly one of the major political reversals of recent history, at its root is the undeniable issue of inflation and the electorate's vociferous reaction to it. Perhaps for the first time in history, we have had middle-class-owned wealth in the context of peacetime inflation. The average households in the free societies of the Western world have reacted virulently against inflation. They see it as a force that could corrode the accumulation of assets they have been able to build and are now fearful of losing. And their reaction against inflation is largely directed at government, which is perceived to be at the root of the inflationary process.

The move toward fiscal conservatism is by no means a child of probusiness attitudes per se. The pressures for local rent control in the United States following Proposition 13 and the clear, continued majorities favoring mandatory wage and price controls make this apparent. Be that as it may, much of the fallout from this attitude of fiscal conservatism has been of assistance to the business community and is likely to foster a political environment that can be looked upon to sustain strongly increasing investment incentives during the 1980s.

THE AGENDA

However, although there is reason for optimism that the electorate's anathema of inflation will lead their elected representatives toward sound fiscal policies, there is also room for considerable skepticism. Certainly the public's stern attitude toward inflationary policies would be put to a test once the initial successes of fiscal restraint bring inflation temporarily under control. We must presume at that stage that inflationary budget policies would again begin to surface. One may hope that the recent experiences of the 1970s would put to rest concerns of reinflationary excesses in the 1980s. However, a firmer foundation is necessary for the longer run if the integrity of the dollar is to be maintained. The only approach that could insure that the current attitudes toward fiscal restraint are made permanent is a constitutional amendment.

Amendments to balance the budget seek the right remedies to the political weakness underlying our fiscal system, but they would be very difficult to implement.* Restraints on expenditure by some formula tied to other economic variables also raise technical difficulties.† In any event, the desired end of both balanced budget and expenditure limitation amendments can be met by requiring super majorities in the Congress to pass a money bill.

*The Congress cannot readily control the actual budget deficit in the short run—say, a year. Except for small parts of the budget, the levels of expenditures in the short run are determined either by entitlement programs or previously committed funds for which scheduled payments to private contractors are relatively fixed. Hence, the level of outlays in the short run is, to a substantial extent, outside the realm of executive or congressional discretion. Similarly, the Congress sets a tax rate structure that means that the level of federal receipts largely becomes a function of the level of taxable incomes generated. Notwithstanding those who believe that the federal government can finely tune the economy, taxable income levels, at least in the short run, remain outside the discretion of government. Finally, even where considerable discretion does exist, outlays often are unpredictable—the surprising outlay shortfalls in recent years being a clear case in point.

Hence, since current budget deficits largely reflect previous legislation, mandating budget balance may create contradictory law.

†Though these proposals skirt some of the obvious problems of a balanced budget amendment, they, too, have a significant problem associated with them: namely, the criteria against which budget restraint is measured. Any attempt to employ, for example, the GNP as a measure to guide expenditure growth confronts the obvious problem that the GNP is continuously undergoing redefinition with respect to inclusion and coverage. Moreover, estimates, especially preliminary estimates, are subject to revision of as much as a full percentage point. (For a $500-billion budget tied to GNP, this implies a potential shift in the ceiling of $10 billion.) A constitutional amendment must be as meaningful fifty years from now as today. Various statistical measures such as GNP or the consumer price index are not likely to live in perpetuity in their current form. One may, of course, bypass this technical problem by merely creating a generic basis for expenditure restraint in the Constitution and have congressional enabling legislation specify the elements that would guide that restraint. There is much to be said for such an approach.

For example, if 60 percent of both houses of Congress were required to pass any authorization, appropriation, expenditure, or credit guarantee bill, the underlying tendency to overcommit to fiscal constituents would be severely restricted. Such a procedure would avoid many of the problems associated with defining an appropriate balanced budget, or expenditure-limitation constitutional amendment.

It would not, however, resolve the problem of defining what, in fact, constitutes expenditures. There can be little doubt that if we restrain what is covered under the current definition of outlay or expenditure by some legal prohibition, the Congress, in its wisdom, will find alternate means to accomplish what it ordinarily would do on the expenditure side. However, such means are limited and, although we can never expect a constitutional amendment requiring a three-fifths vote on money bills to be fully effective, it clearly would have a major impact on restraining the growth of the federal sector.

Most of the areas where the Congress is apt to create expenditure-bypassing devices are on the tax side, through credits. This is not totally undesirable. We will need periodic cuts in tax rates, and any restraint on expenditure levels will probably exert additional pressure on the Congress to cut taxes in order to avoid excessive budget surpluses.

Pending the passage of a constitutional amendment requiring a three-fifths vote on money bills, we might wisely amend the Budget Act of 1974 in a similar fashion. While the three-fifths vote requirement could be rescinded by a majority of the Congress (with the acquiescence of the president), individual congressmen might well be persuaded not to vote for such a rescission since it might stamp them as less than fiscally responsible. So there is a possibility that a legislative super majority requirement could indeed hold. It is doubtful that one could rely on that for an overly extended period. A constitutional amendment mandating such a requirement appears to be the only viable long-term solution.

IN SUMMARY

The industrial countries of the non-communist world are struggling to recapture the lost momentum of the 1960s. The heavy pall of uncertainty brought the rate of private investment in many countries to virtual stagnation in the late 1970s and dampened the spark needed to push the industrial nations back on a path of sustained, noninflationary growth.

In such an environment, economic policymakers have been confronted with an exceptionally difficult mission: to find the proper mix of policies that will restore the industrial economies to the path of balanced noninflationary growth in the 1980s. Yet, at a time when successful policies are vitally needed, the tools of economic policy seem inadequate.

Partly, the dilemma that economic policymakers face is that the more they attempt to fine-tune the elements of economic growth and income distribution through conventional fiscal and monetary techniques, the more uncertain they make the environment in which private investment decisions are being made. Where policy restraint may be the most appropriate posture, our political systems, in the recent past, have seemed to press for ever-greater activism. The political climate in which policymakers must function, however, appears to be changing in a direction that will support the actions necessary to curb government programs and outlays. It is also possible that a more favorable environment will prevail for stemming the growth in investment-stifling regulation.

The short-term danger is that, in a sense of despair and frustration, policymakers will look for the short-term quick fix, such as price controls ("voluntary" or otherwise). But this need not be the outcome. Certainly most policymakers did not seek the short-term expedient when the pressures were most extreme at the depth of the 1975 recession. But in order to restore the economy of the United States to a condition of balance and growth a number of hard political choices will have to be made. Policymakers are going to have to emphasize long-term benefits, and suffer, if necessary, the short-term political costs.

Although the choices may be hard ones, the potential rewards are large. For if we are capable of defusing the underlying inflationary forces in our economy, thereby lowering risk premiums associated with potential new capital investment projects, the 1980s can usher in for the United States a period of sustained expansion in the capital goods markets. One of the consequences of the inadequacy of capital investment during the 1970s, especially in long-lived assets, has been the creation of a potential backlog that could be triggered, provided the risks and uncertainties associated with investment are lowered.

A major expansion in the capital goods markets in the early 1980s would spur renewed growth in productivity, which in turn would reinforce disinflationary fiscal and monetary policies. Standards of living largely stagnant in the 1970s would rise again and the 1980s could look a good deal more like the 1950s and early 1960s than a replay of the 1970s.

Although sensible economic policies in the United States are necessary to achieve a more prosperous next decade, they are regrettably not sufficient. As the 1970s come to an end, the balance of energy supply and demand in the industrial nations is precarious and dependent to an unprecedented extent on continued availability of Middle East oil. Failure of this vital source of energy would concentrate economic policy here, as elsewhere, into containing the damage of an energy disruption, subverting its focus on economic growth and a restoration of prosperity.

The range of possibilities for the 1980s is thus extraordinarily wide. With so much at stake, policy payoffs and costs are larger than they have been at any time in recent memory.

Public Opinion and Public Policy

Everett Carll Ladd, Jr.
Seymour Martin Lipset

III

Any effort to anticipate the way in which the American public is likely to behave politically in the 1980s must involve an awareness of the country's enduring values and commitments. To a considerable extent, two values—those of equalitarianism and achievement—have influenced our national behavior. As noted by Alexis de Tocqueville and others in the early years of the republic, equalitarianism implies that all persons are deserving of respect; that people should not bend to others because of inequality of income, position, or power; and that differences in income reflect accidental and perhaps temporary variations in social relationships. The notion of achievement is a corollary to the belief in equality. For people to be equal, they must have equality of opportunity; then they should be judged on what they actually do. Success should be attainable to all who work hard and have ability, no matter what the accidents of birth, class, or race.[1]

Although equality and achievement have reinforced each other over the course of American history, they have also led to conflict. Different policy implications have been derived from each. Equality has been associated with left or liberal forces, and implies breaking down sources of inequality and waging war on racism, sexism, and poverty. Achievement, on the other hand, has been identified with the philosophy of conservatism, as that word has been used in modern America, with a stress on individualistic or competitive values and opposition to increased state power.

Curiously, political cycles associated with the dominance of one or the other of these values have occurred during the last 60 years, in tandem with the decades. The 1920s clearly witnessed an emphasis on competition and achievement. It was succeeded by the depression decade, with the flowering of the New Deal and other movements associated with a greater stress on equalitarianism. The war dominated the 1940s, which, therefore, does not fit into the cycle. It was, of course, followed by the conservative 1950s, in which American students and adults sought self-enrichment and largely ignored equalitarian forces. The 1960s gave birth to the equalitarian war-on-poverty concerns of the New Frontier and the Great Society, and even more strikingly to a variety of mass movements designed to combat diverse forms of racism and sexism. The 1970s produced the great calm on the college campuses, and a return to serious study. Increasingly, in the larger public, there have been more conservative anti-government views, and the decade came to a close with Proposition 13 in California and the nationwide tax revolt. Not surprisingly, the partisan coloration of each decade has corresponded to these cycles. The Republican 1920s were followed by the New Deal 1930s. Eight years of the 1950s were Dwight Eisenhower's. John Kennedy and Lyndon Johnson, of course, presided over most of the 1960s. The presidencies of Richard Nixon and Gerald Ford formed the majority of the 1970s, and the Republicans might well have retained the White House in 1976 were it not for Watergate.

Fitting the cycles of American values and politics—equalitarianism-achievement, liberal-conservative, Democratic-Republican—into ten-year boxes is obviously a bit too neat. Looking back on the decades and the changes, social scientists and historians note many beginnings and declines that fall outside the ten-year formula. The realignment of American politics in the 1930s, which made social class and urbanization more salient sources of party support, was preceded by the election of 1928, in which Al Smith increased the Democratic vote in urban areas and among less privileged groups.[2] The campus and civil rights militancy of the 1960s had its origins in protests during the last years of the preceding decade, while the Democrats made striking gains in the 1958 congressional elections. Campus disturbances and antiwar protest had begun to slacken off in 1969 (although the Cambodian incursion of 1970 created what proved to be a short-lived massive revival).[3] Should the 1980s follow the cyclical pattern of past decades and sustain a new emphasis on equalitarianism and liberalism, latter day political analysts will be able to point to the overwhelming popularity in the polls in the late 1970s of one of the most liberal politicians in the country, Sen. Edward Kennedy. They will be able to note that in spite of approval of tax cuts and complaints about government waste and inefficiency, the public was showing support for liberalism in the areas of health care, opportunities for minorities, and education.

How seriously should we take the rough indication that political cycles, reflecting varying value emphases, are seemingly associated with decades? It may be that our perception of time in these categories encourages us to give decades a significance, much like birthdays or New Year's Day. There are also statistical quirks, highly improbable patterns occurring in a regular sequence, without logical explanation. One such is the inexplicable fact that every president elected after 1820, in a year divisible by twenty, has died in office, while only one other president has died while incumbent.

The presumed association of values and political cycles with the decades, of course, can be interpreted more plausibly than regularities in presidential mortality. Americans, committed both to equalitarianism and achievement, periodically turn away from what appears to be an excessive concentration in one direction. After a span of something like a decade, the inadequacies of one particular emphasis become evident and there is a shift to the other.

The history of value and political cycles implies that the 1980s will be more equalitarian, liberal, and possibly more protest-prone than the 1970s. An examination of a somewhat different pattern of political interaction suggests, however, that the opposite may be the case. There is some evidence that shifts toward the left or right on the political spectrum occur at about the same time in most Western countries. William Rees Mogg, editor of the London *Times,* has noted that in "the years 1945 to 1978 the roughly matching parties, Labour and Democrat, Conservative and Republican, have been in power simultaneously for three-quarters of the time. . . . Even more interesting is that the change of party has been synchronized. Whichever country changed was followed by a change of party in the other country at the first following election." (*The Christian Science Monitor,* September 12, 1979, p. 22.) Exposure to common broad experiences—recession or inflation, international tensions, Soviet aggression, the oil crisis, and the like—has similar effects on the electorate of most industrial societies. The argument can be made for the existence of international ideological currents. In recent national elections, from 1977 to 1979, in nations as diverse as Israel, Spain, Portugal, France, Britain, Italy, Japan, Canada, Australia, Finland, and the European Economic Community, more conservative or bourgeois parties have won over labor, socialist, and communist parties. In 1979 only Austria stood out against this trend, while the Swedish elections witnessed a gain for both the Social Democrats and Communists producing a near deadlock in Parliament. Although the shifts in popular voting have been small in many cases, there can be little doubt, as the 1970s came to an end, that voters in many countries were shifting support away from the collectivist, laborite, and more equalitarian-oriented parties to those that placed greater emphasis on free enterprise, competition, and less state intervention.

Although both American historical and comparative international political experiences offer clues about the 1980s in America—whether more equalitarian or more achievement oriented, more liberal or more conservative—these clues are tentative and limited. To try to estimate where the United States is going, therefore, we turn to a more direct source of evidence: trends revealed by public opinion polls, as well as voting behavior and partisan choices. But even these more quantitative data are not without their contradictions.

PUBLIC OPINION

It has become something of an article of faith as the 1970s end that Americans are moving away from liberal values and perspectives, toward commitments decidedly more conservative than those that prevailed in the past. The passage of California's Proposition 13 in June 1978 by a two-to-one margin, together with the strong campaigns in other states across the country to impose limits on taxing and spending, are the most frequently cited evidence for this presumed swing to the right. Buffeted by high taxes and inflation, people are turning away from the liberal, big-spending social programs first initiated in the United States under Franklin Roosevelt and greatly elaborated during the 1960s. Lewis Uhler, a political conservative who heads the National Tax Limitation Committee, argues that the new resistance to government spending has stimulated a general inclination to challenge the drift toward governmental, as opposed to private, market-centered solutions to social problems.[4] And Walter Heller, a political liberal who chaired the Council of Economic Advisors under John F. Kennedy, laments Proposition 13 and its many counterparts as a "blind, self-interest-motivated lashing out at the government."[5]

The sense of a swing toward conservatism does not rest simply on the evidence of a tax revolt. Polls inquiring about attitudes toward defense spending, an issue that generally separates liberals from conservatives, have found a steady increase since 1974 in the proportion favoring higher appropriations for the military. Americans have exhibited generally greater support for a firmer foreign policy.

The 1978 elections revealed some modest conservative victories. Some liberals went down to defeat within the primaries of both parties. Donald Fraser, the head of Americans for Democratic Action, lost to a conservative in his primary bid for the senatorial nomination of the Minnesota Democratic Farmer Labor party. In Massachusetts, liberal Democratic Governor Michael Dukakis was defeated for renomination by a tax-cutting conservative, Edward King. Clifford Case, one of the most liberal senators, was beaten in the New Jersey Republican primary by an arch-conservative, Jeffrey Bell. In the November elections, Republicans gained 3 seats in the Senate and 16 in the House, plus 310 legislative seats across the country.

Surveys of the ideological identification of samples of Americans, asking respondents to state whether they consider themselves liberals, conservatives, or moderates, find more self-identified conservatives than liberals. Thus, in a poll taken by Gallup in August 1978, 43 percent described their political position as "right of center," whereas 20 percent classified themselves as "left of center." Earlier in the year a CBS News/*New York Times* poll reported that the ratio of self-described conservatives to liberals was 42 to 23 percent. A Roper survey in March 1979 found almost identical results, conservatives outnumbering liberals by 44 to 23 percent. Caution is needed in the interpretation of these data because people mean many different things when they employ the terms liberal and conservative. In the relatively conservative 1950s, polls occasionally found self-described liberals outnumbering self-proclaimed conservatives. In 1955, for example, a Gallup poll showed the United States public divided 53 percent liberals and 41 percent conservatives.

A shift toward greater conservatism is evident on the college campuses—the center of left-leaning protest during the 1960s and early 1970s. During the Vietnam years, American universities were awash in protest demonstrations; now the campuses are quiet, as career-oriented students concentrate on grades and securing jobs. Opinion polls of college students indicate a definite shift away from the left in political opinions in the 1970s. In 1970, 37 percent of first-year college students identified their political beliefs as liberal or far left; by 1978, that proportion had dropped to 26 percent. Interest in politics had also declined sharply, as only 37 percent reported in 1978 that it was essential or important to keep up-to-date with political affairs, compared to 53 percent in 1970.[6]

Opinion surveys have documented broad popular concern with various consequences of the rapid social change of the last two decades (such as the perceived deterioration of the family) and some reassertion of support for traditional values. For example, a 1978 Yankelovich study found 84 percent of Americans indicating that they would welcome "more emphasis on religious beliefs."[7] The public, concerned with the high incidence of crime, now takes a tougher stance toward punishment than it did ten years ago. Support has risen for the death penalty for persons convicted of murder. Only in 1966, in the period for which survey data are available, did a majority (53 percent) of Americans come out against the death penalty. By 1978, support had risen to a point near the post-1930s high: 70 percent endorsed use of the death penalty for convicted murderers, whereas just 30 percent were opposed.[8]

It is not hard, then, to see why so many politicians and others who attend closely to election results and public opinion data see the United States as moving to the right. Yet other happenings in the political arena furnish contradictory signs. Although more people identify themselves as conservatives than as liberals, the Democrats have a considerable advantage over the Republicans in party registration figures and party identification distribution in opinion polls. In 1978, two areas that Republicans have long dominated in party registration—Orange County, California, and the state of Maine—shifted to the Democratic camp, the latter for the first time in its history. But according to the Louis Harris organization, the number claiming to be Democrats in opinion surveys has steadily declined since Jimmy Carter was elected, from 51 percent in 1976 to 38 percent in 1979. This result, however, does not offer solace to Republicans, for their proportion has remained constant at 24 percent over the three years, whereas independents have increased from 23 to 33 percent. These changes in party identification largely reflect a shift away from the Democrats by self-identified liberals, presumably because Jimmy Carter is viewed as having become conservative. In 1976, 74 percent of the liberals described their party affiliation as Democratic, but by 1979 only 41 percent did so. During this time, the percentage of independents among the liberals jumped from 15 to 39 percent.

Polls inquiring in 1979 about the presidential preferences of Americans invariably found that the most popular choice for 1980 was the most liberal one, Edward Kennedy. Kennedy is clearly a strong advocate of big government. He is the sponsor of the most extensive government medical care program ever advanced by a major American political figure. And he is an ideological opponent of big business, as reflected in his position on corporate taxes and his strong support for legislation restricting corporate mergers. Not surprisingly, a national survey conducted for the *Washington Post* in May 1979 found that a large proportion of Kennedy supporters have much more conservative views on various issues than he does. These supporters could turn against him, should they discover the contradiction between their political stance and his in the course of a campaign. Still, it should also be noted that the polls show that Kennedy is perceived by the electorate as more of a liberal than other contestants for the 1980 nominations of both parties. In trial heats among Democrats, Kennedy runs far ahead of both Carter and Jerry Brown. When Americans were asked in 1979 whether they would prefer each of the three leading Democrats against a variety of Republicans—

including Ronald Reagan, Howard Baker, John Connally, and Gerald Ford—Kennedy invariably had a substantial lead over various Republicans. Carter and Brown did much more poorly, frequently running neck and neck with, or behind, prospective Republican rivals.

POLITICAL LABELS

Part of the problem in trying to determine the direction in which the country is moving lies in the ideological categories we employ: liberalism and conservatism. Students of American politics know that these categories have been recently used with so many different, and often conflicting, meanings that they have been robbed of much of their clarity and hence usefulness. Such labels have been so loosely employed that one cannot make easy, confident assertions about liberal or conservative trends in U.S. public opinion.

The problem of using the traditional terms is compounded by the fact that liberalism-conservatism has probably never been a single-dimension continuum. There are a series of distinct dimensions, and an individual can occupy quite different positions, relative to the entire public, on each of them—liberal on domestic economic policies, centrist in foreign affairs, conservative on some cultural and life-style issues, and so on. Given the multidimensionality of liberalism-conservatism, it is possible for an individual to move in opposite directions at the same time—toward the liberal end of one continuum and the conservative end of another.

It should also be noted that terms like liberal and conservative are ideological categories; opinion analysts have shown that people simply do not hold views that are as coherently packaged or constrained as ideology implies.[9] Individuals are not liberal just because they answer a given question in the liberal fashion. They may be appropriately described as liberal only if they employ some larger conceptual dimension—some variant of liberalism—to order their responses to a variety of issues. Put another way, there is a lot of opinion change in the United States and other countries that is not really ideological at all, but which is mistakenly described as evidence of ideological shifts.

Academic commentators on the ideological divisions in the United States since the 1930s have found it useful to differentiate between economic and noneconomic liberalism-conservatism.[10] The first polarity basically refers to attitudes toward issues associated with New Deal reforms. Economic liberals have generally endorsed the extension of the welfare-planning state, and have backed government policies and expenditures to improve the lot of the less privileged, the poor, the unemployed, the elderly, and the sick. They have favored a progressive income tax, hitting harder at the wealthy and at corporations. They have supported trade unions and the regulation of business. Economic conservatives have generally opposed such policies. The noneconomic or social dimension, as it has come to be called in recent years, encompasses questions of civil liberties for unpopular groups and perspectives, the rights of criminals, the claims of minority groups and women, new social and cultural values, and, most recently, environmental issues. On this dimension those called conservatives, though not overt opponents of the rights of political and social minorities, or of efforts to improve the environment, have tended to be less enthusiastic about involving the government actively. They have been more hardline on issues of law and order and have been unhappy about changes in conventional morality.

The Great Depression, as implied earlier, brought about a fundamental change in the attitudes of Americans toward welfare state policies, government economic planning, progressive income taxes, and labor unions. In large measure, popular reactions to such issues were strongly correlated with social class. The less privileged overwhelmingly backed them. The higher a person's income, the less favorable his attitude toward economic liberalism. By electing and reelecting Franklin Roosevelt and Harry Truman, the majority of Americans voiced approval for such policies. By the time the Republicans returned to control of the White House in 1953 under Dwight Eisenhower, they had come to accept these policies as institutionalized, and only sought to modify their scope and administration. Still, these issues continue to separate economic liberals and conservatives and, to some extent, Democrats and Republicans.

Changes in attitudes involving noneconomic liberalism-conservatism, in general, occurred following World War II. Polls taken during the 1930s and during the war showed that large numbers of Americans had negative attitudes toward Jews and blacks, and that most people believed women should remain in their traditional roles, as nonemployed housewives and mothers. Prejudice against minority racial and religious groups, as reflected in opinion surveys, dropped strikingly in the years immediately following the end of the war.[11] These shifts were reflected in changes in institutional policies toward Jews. Jews were admitted in large numbers to universities, which had had restrictive quotas both on student and faculty levels, as well as to various professions and businesses from which they had been barred. The improvement in popular feelings about blacks may have been reflected in the Supreme Court decisions in the 1950s outlawing segregation in schools as well as other public institutions. The populace moved in a more conservative direction, however, with respect to civil liberties for dissident political groups. Public unwillingness to allow equal political rights to communists and other unpopular ideological minorities, high during the 1930s, increased during the late 1940s and early 1950s. In addition, the cold war was developing, along with the hot war against North Korea and the People's Republic of China, events that encouraged repressive measures against groups identified with the enemy.[12]

Attitudes toward civil liberties for unpopular, particularly leftist groups, as well as civil rights for minority groups and women changed strikingly during the 1960s and 1970s. Public attitudes favoring equal rights increased sharply during this period. This change in the public's response spurred the passage of a variety of civil rights laws, beginning with voting rights and extending to the implementation of affirmative-action programs. During the 1960s, there was also a strong liberal shift regarding the death penalty, abortion, extramarital sex, the status of homosexuals, and the rights of political radicals.

Economic and social liberalism-conservatism are correlated. Some people, however, are economic conservatives and social liberals, others are conservative on social issues and liberal on economic ones. The first group has tended to be disproportionately composed of well-to-do, well-educated persons; the second has drawn strength from less affluent and poorly educated whites.[13]

The politics of the 1960s—which emphasized noneconomic issues, including attitudes toward the Vietnam war and American foreign policy generally—identified many well-educated persons with left-of-center politics. This pressed them to favor as well a liberal orientation: support for government policies on behalf of underdog elements in society, including minorities, women, and the underprivileged. They also became hostile to establishment institutions generally, especially big business. As a result the liberal wing of the Democratic party gained greatly in ideological coherence and in support from well-to-do, well-educated people. Conversely, many less affluent whites, who belonged to or favored trade unions and supported welfare-planning state redistributionist policies, turned against liberalism. This they identified with support for minorities, for integration, busing, and affirmative-action policies giving special preference in employment and education to blacks and women; as well as with the coddling of criminals; with a rejection of traditional concepts of morality regarding sexual and family matters; and with the challenge to authority and patriotism reflected in campus and other protests of the 1960s and early 1970s.

The concerns of lower-status whites were particularly evident in the support given George Wallace in Democratic party presidential primaries from 1964 to 1976. The enthusiasm for him was expressed in the polls, in his high approval rating, in the 25 percent who indicated a preference for him for president as a third party candidate early in 1968, as well as in the 13 percent of the vote he received as the American Independent party candidate.[14] These feelings were also apparent in the sizeable votes for law and order and anti-busing candidates in local elections in such cities as Boston (Louise Day Hicks), Philadelphia (Frank Rizzo), Los Angeles (Sam Yorty), and Minneapolis (Charles Stenvig).

The position of the Democratic party as the majority party was strengthened. Its ranks were reinforced by an infusion of support from well-educated middle- to upper-class elements for whom the social and foreign policy issues became salient. At the same time, poorer and less educated whites, who had identified with the Democrats as the party representing economic interests of persons like themselves, remained linked to the party, for they continued to see the Republican party as the instrument of big business, uninterested in the common man.[15] Many, of course, were unhappy with the Democrats' association with the cause of minorities, campus protests, and cultural change, a fact reflected in the low votes received by Hubert Humphrey and George McGovern in 1968 and 1972, respectively. This group, however, generally continued Democratic in contests for congressional, state, and local offices, remained registered Democrats and in polls identified themselves as Democrats and conservatives. In 1976, many of them voted for Jimmy Carter, whom they regarded as a moderate or conservative Democrat. It is notable that he lost support during the campaign as some voters began to perceive that he was more liberal than they had earlier believed.[16]

However, the backlash against the newer dimensions of social liberalism among less affluent whites did not involve an increase in the proportion expressing prejudice against minorities. Since World War II, there has been increasing acceptance of the equalitarian values of the American creed. Most Americans have come to recognize the rights of minorities and women to equal treatment. The social conservatives typically object, not to the direction, but to the pace of the change. And they are generally less willing to support government policies that give the deprived special advantages. The majority of the population favors fair employment legislation, the legal right to equal treatment in securing employment, and the right of blacks to attend any school they desire or live where they want. But most oppose giving special preference to minorities or women; policies that require white children to attend schools they do not wish to attend; and government programs designed to move blacks into white neighborhoods. The upshot of these developments is an electorate that has become increasingly liberal on social issues, while remaining essentially committed to the New Deal welfare policies.

The picture has become complicated in the last years of the 1970s by the emergence of sustained high inflation. By eating away at savings and retirement plans and reducing the real income of some, inflation has produced a sharp reaction. The public has come to see large-scale government spending as a major source of inflation and now supports policies that promise to bring inflation under control. Tax protests have been fueled by escalating taxes, produced by the inflationary increase in home prices, and by the movement of many into higher tax brackets as their dollar, but not their real income, increases. Hence, when people have the opportunity to vote for lower taxes in referenda, or when they are queried about taxes in the polls, they opt for lower taxes and reduced government spending.

This behavior has been intepreted as a conservative reaction. But the same citizens, when offered the chance to vote for rent control, a "liberal" measure, do so. And since the middle of 1978, most Americans have expressed support for wage, price, and profit controls. Particularly incensed by the sharp increase in the price of oil, they express much hostility to the oil companies and strong support for price control of petroleum products. In June 1979, a CBS News/*New York Times* poll reported a decisive majority (60 to 29 percent) in favor of rationing gasoline as an alternative to allowing prices to rise. Americans have also become increasingly angry toward both big business and trade unions, which they identify as powerful, self-seeking institutions that pursue unwarranted profits or high wages at the expense of the public—and hence contribute to higher prices.

This analysis suggests that recent changes in public opinion do not reflect a consistent move to the right. Most Americans have remained or have become committed to liberal orientations in the economic and social spheres. But their reactions to specific electoral and policy alternatives will be determined by larger events in the domestic and economic spheres. Much as we could not have anticipated the political impact of Vietnam and Watergate at the start of the 1960s, it is impossible to know what major happenings will structure the way Americans will respond in the 1980s. Still, a detailed examination of American attitudes at the start of the new decade will give us some indication of the parameters of both opinion and action.

THE GROWTH OF SOCIAL LIBERALISM

The increased support for social liberalism is evident in a variety of areas, including civil liberties, civil rights, and personal morality. Americans have become notably more supportive of pro-civil liberties positions. They are now more inclined to endorse the freedoms of speech, press, employment, and the like for unpopular minorities than at any time since the polls began inquiring into this area. This trend is particularly clear in a comparison of the replies to identical questions asked first in 1954 by Samuel A. Stouffer and his colleagues and then repeated in the 1970s in the General Social Surveys of the University of Chicago's National Opinion Research Center (NORC).[17] Should someone who favors "government ownership of all railroads and all big industries be allowed to teach in a college or university?" Just 33 percent said yes in 1954. A quarter of a century later, a clear majority, 57 percent, agreed that this leftist teacher should have a right to a job. Similarly, the proportion who feel that a person who wants "to make a speech in your community against churches and religion" should be allowed to speak, moved up from 38 percent in 1954 to 62 percent in 1977.

Questions of civil rights—for blacks, other ethnic minorities, and women—show much the same sort of progression. The trends reported by Gallup on whether people would cast a presidential ballot for candidates of certain status or ethnic background are typical of such findings. The proportion who would vote for a woman rose from 32 percent in 1937 to 54 percent in 1955, to 69 percent in 1971, to 81 percent in July 1978. Those giving the same response for a Jewish candidate increased from 46 percent in 1937 to 62 percent in 1958 to 82 percent in 1978. For a black nominee, the favorable percentages shot up from 42 percent in 1958 to 57 percent in 1967 to 84 percent in 1978.

Voting for a black for president does not involve a major change in personal behavior. It is, therefore, important to note that the number of whites reporting that they have no objection to sending their children to schools in which half or more than half the students are black has also steadily increased. Among northern whites, individuals who object to children attending half-black schools have declined from 33 percent in 1963 to 23 in 1978. Over the same period, southern whites have also become much more liberal, moving from 78 percent opposed to their children going to half-black institutions in 1963, to just 28 percent in 1978.

One of the most severe attitudinal tests of white racial liberalism is racial intermarriage. As recently as 1965, more than half the American public endorsed legislation prohibiting marriages between blacks and whites. By 1977, however, nearly three-fourths of the population maintained that there should be no laws against racial intermarriage. Not surprisingly, these attitudes, like others in this area, correlated strikingly with education and age. The better educated and the younger the person interviewed, the more liberal he is.

Americans have become generally more supportive of equal rights for women. Just over half (51 percent) in 1970 stated that they favored "most of the efforts to strengthen and change women's status in society today." By 1979, with such efforts expanded, well over two-thirds of the populace (70 percent) indicated their approval.[18] The propriety of a married woman not in financial need holding a job was supported by only 22 percent of the public in 1938, by 63 percent in 1970, and by 73 percent in 1978.

It must be noted, however, that the majority of Americans are not willing to approve of certain kinds of affirmative-action programs. These include programs that appear to give minorities or women special preference (for example, job or educational quotas) or that involve compulsory integration in schools (busing) or housing. Americans continue to favor equality in the context of equality of opportunity for individuals but oppose programs equalizing outcomes.[19]

There are increasingly liberal reactions to a wide assortment of social, cultural, and life-style issues. There has been, for example, a weakening of many of the old codes of personal comportment—meaning that there is now less opposition to premarital sex, abortion, the use of marijuana, and so on. In 1969, 13 percent of the public wanted the use of marijuana legalized; nine years later 31 percent held this view.[20] Only 15 percent of the adult population in 1969 favored legalized abortions in the case of a woman who is married and simply does not want any more children; nine years later the proportion had risen appreciably to 40 percent.[21]

The way surveyors phrase their questions in some ways gives the clearest sense of the amount of liberalizing that has occurred in views on personal comportment. In 1978, NORC interviewers asked, "If a man and a woman have sex relations before marriage, do you think it is always wrong, almost always wrong, wrong only sometimes, or not wrong at all?" Roper interviewers 39 years earlier had posed the same question quite differently: "Do you consider it all right, unfortunate, or wicked when young girls have sexual relations before marriage?"

MILITARY SPENDING AND FOREIGN POLICY

Attitudes toward foreign policy and military spending link in many ways with the social questions. In the post-World War II years, a hard-line foreign policy has implied opposition to Soviet policies and to the expansion of communism. Thus, it is not surprising that research on the factors correlated with support for increased U.S. military spending find that such views are associated with a generally conservative political ideology. Polls taken by NORC during the 1970s show that self-identified conservatives and those who favor capital punishment for convicted murderers are disproportionately for increased military expenditures.[22]

Shifts in attitudes toward defense spending have closely paralleled international developments. In 1960, Gallup reported that 18 percent said we were spending "too much," as contrasted to 21 percent replying "too little." As opposition expanded to the Vietnam war and American entanglements abroad, the proportion who believed that American defense spending was excessive grew steadily until, by 1969, it comprised a majority, 52 percent; only 8 percent thought we were not spending enough. The Vietnam effect lasted through 1974, when the ratio of too much to too little was 44 to 12 percent. From then on, apparent concern with Soviet expansionist policies and the weakness of the American response brought about a change in public mood. Gallup surveys showed that, by 1977, more people replied too little (27 percent) than too much (23 percent), and by 1978, too little had a decisive lead (32 to 16 percent).[23] Similar findings were reported by NORC in annual surveys taken from 1973 to 1978.[24] Comparable shifts in opinion occurred between 1974 and 1978 with respect to support for sending American troops abroad. An analysis of factors related to these changes by the Chicago Council on Foreign Relations "suggested that the principal reason for increased support of both defense spending and willingness to commit troops in selected areas was the perceived growing influence of the Soviet Union."[25]

Because attitudes toward foreign policy and defense spending are linked to liberal or conservative self-identifications, the growth of hard-line attitudes in these areas should strengthen conservatism in public opinion. This trend may be related to the small but steady increase in proportion of those who describe themselves ideologically as conservatives in the same 1973–1978 NORC polls that inquired into attitudes toward military expenditures. This change may parallel the shift to the left in public mood with the growth of anti-military attitudes during the Vietnam war. It should be noted, however, that such attitudes do not correlate with party identification. Curiously, Republicans are no more likely to favor greater spending on armaments than Democrats.[26] And according to a May 1979 CBS News/*New York Times* poll, party identification does not differentiate supporters from opponents of the SALT II treaty, although self-identified liberals are much more pro-SALT than conservatives.

ECONOMIC LIBERALISM

Support for economic or New Deal liberalism continues at a high level. In spite of the widespread speculation about a swing to the right, spurred by concerns about the level of government spending, there is as yet no indication of a widespread inclination to cut back substantially on the liberal, interventionist state. In some instances, the move is in the opposite direction. For example, 64 percent of those polled in a 1964 survey agreed that "the government in Washington ought to help people get doctors and hospital care at low cost." In 1968, the proportion was about the same—66 percent. But in 1978, 85 percent of those surveyed in another national study wanted the national government to assume this responsibility.[27]

"In all industries where there is competition," the Opinion Research Corporation has asked, "do you think companies should be allowed to make all the profit they can or should the government put a limit on the profits companies can make?" In 1946, 31 percent wanted government to limit profits; 25 percent took this position in 1962. But in 1977 an all-time high of 55 percent endorsed this form of government intervention.[28] Admittedly, this question touches on two separate opinions: views of business corporations and their profits, and judgments about the appropriate role of government. Still, the jump in support for a governmental role in this area is consistent with the generally expansive views of contemporary Americans on government responsibilities.

When asked whether the federal or state governments should cut back on spending for public services, the public today overwhelmingly favors sustaining or increasing current spending. (There are only isolated exceptions, such as welfare, which seems to connote a dole for people unwilling to work.) When questioned by the Survey Research Center of the University of Michigan in November 1978, whether they would trade off key government services for two major tax reductions, over three-fifths rejected the cut. Specifically, when asked whether "Federal income taxes should be cut by at least one-third even if it means reducing military spending and cutting down on government services such as health and education," 62 percent replied no, while 27 percent favored the proposal. People in all social classes, in all regions of the country, and of all political persuasions now consistently endorse high levels of public expenditures for most social services, according to National Opinion Research Center polls. For example, 91 percent who refer to themselves as upper class maintain that we are either spending too little or the right amount "to improve educational systems." Ninety-four percent of professional and 95 percent of unskilled workers take these pro-spending positions on "improv[ing] the nation's health." Seventy-three percent of grade-school-trained Americans and 81 percent of college graduates want to maintain or increase expenditures "to improve the condition of blacks."[29]

DISSATISFACTION WITH GOVERNMENT

This discussion is not intended to imply that every facet of contemporary American public opinion comes closer to sustaining the idea of economic liberalism than of conservatism. Americans are unhappy about welfare spending. Above all, they reject some features of the big government apparatus that has been established since the New Deal—even as they are profoundly supportive of a high level of public service. Government is now viewed as wasteful and inefficient.

The distrust of government is an attitude that has been building in America since the country became divided over the wisdom of the Vietnam war. It has been sustained through the various misfortunes that have occurred since: massive civil disobedience by students and minorities in the late 1960s, Watergate, recession, and inflation. One of the most widely noted shifts has been in the level of political trust expressed by the American public. The Survey Research Center (SRC) of the University of Michigan has asked four "political trust" questions in national surveys from 1958 to 1978. Confidence changed little between 1958 and 1964; in that six-year period the average increase in "mistrust" as measured by the four questions was only 4 percent. In the subsequent six-year period, 1964–1970, mistrust increased by an average of 17 percent on the four items, and the increase exceeded 20 percent on three of the four. In that six-year period of intense political controversy and polarization, the percentage of Americans saying that "the government wastes a lot of money we pay in taxes" rose from 48 to 69 percent. The percentage maintaining that "the government is pretty much run by a few big interests looking out for themselves rather than for the benefit of all the people" climbed from 30 to 52 percent. And the percentage who felt that "you can trust the government in Washington to do what is right . . . only some of the time or none of the time" (rather than "always" or "most of the time") rose from 22 to 45 percent.

Political cynicism did not increase markedly during this period on one of the SRC's political trust questions. The percentage who felt that "quite a few of the people running the government are crooked" rose from 30 percent in 1964 to 33 percent in 1970—an increase hardly comparable to the enormous jump in cynicism measured by the other items. In 1972, the perception that most government officials are crooked again increased only modestly, to 38 percent. But as one might guess, the Watergate affair soon corrected the noticeable lag in this political trust item. By the end of 1973, the first year of the Watergate revelation, the proportion who agreed that most government officials are crooked rose to 57 percent. At the time of the 1974 election, a few months after President Richard Nixon's resignation, this figure fell below a majority, but remained high, at 45 percent. It was slightly lower, 42 percent, in 1976, and fell to 39 percent in 1978, back to its pre-Watergate level.

The earlier increases of the other "distrust attitudes," which mounted so markedly between 1964 and 1970, were sustained by the Watergate experience and have continued to move up since then. From 1970 to 1978, the percentage of Americans claiming that the government wastes a lot of money rose from 69 to 77. The percentage with the view that the government is run for a few big interests increased from 45 to 67 percent.

DISSATISFACTION WITH INSTITUTIONS

Although the focus here is on attitudes toward government, it is important to note that the lowering of confidence after the mid-1960s has been general and is not limited to political institutions. As one major pollster, Daniel Yankelovich, noted in 1977:

> We have seen a steady rise of mistrust in our national institutions . . . Trust in government declined dramatically from almost 80% in the late 1950s to about 33% in 1976. Confidence in other institutions, the universities, the unions, the press, the military, the professions—doctors and lawyers—sharply declined from the mid-60s to the mid-70s. More than 61% of the electorate believe that there is something morally wrong in the country. More than 80% of voters say they do not trust those in positions of leadership as much as they used to. In the mid-60s a one-third minority reported feeling isolated and distant from the political process, by the mid-70s a two-thirds majority felt that what they think "really doesn't count." Approximately three out of five people feel the government suffers from a concentration of too much power in too few hands, and fewer than one out of five feel that congressional leaders can be believed. One could go on and on. The change is simply massive. Within a ten to fifteen year period, trust in institutions has plunged down and down, from an almost consensual majority, two-thirds or more, to minority segments of the American public.[30]

The conclusion that there has been a drastic decline in confidence in almost all American institutions is sustained by the findings of many pollsters, among them Gallup, Harris, Yankelovich, Roper, NORC, and

SRC. Louis Harris is probably the opinion analyst most widely cited on trends in public confidence because he has asked a continuing series of questions. In 1966, Harris for the first time posed this question: "As far as people in charge of running various institutions are concerned, would you say you have a great deal of confidence, only some confidence, or hardly any confidence at all in them?" In 1966, the average percentage voicing "a great deal of confidence" in the leadership of nine different institutions was 47 percent. Five years later, in 1971, the average percentage replying "a great deal" had fallen to 28 percent. The important point is that confidence fell in the leadership of every institution named by Harris.

It appears that Americans became increasingly distrustful of all the major institutions of society as the Vietnam war became a hopeless quagmire and as protest movements over the war and over minority rights disrupted national stability. Confidence in military leaders fell most precipitously between 1966 and 1971, from 67 percent expressing "a great deal of confidence" in the former year to a mere 27 percent in the latter. Confidence in the Congress declined from 42 to 19 percent, and confidence in the executive branch of the government fell from 41 to 23 percent. The schools, another institution at the focus of controversy during the late 1960s, suffered considerable loss of public support: from 61 percent expressing "a great deal of confidence" in the people in charge of the educational system in 1966 to 37 percent in 1971.

Private institutions were not immune to the prevailing trend of increasing distrust and cynicism. Harris asked Americans how much confidence they had in the leaders of major companies. Business leaders declined in public esteem from 55 to 27 percent from 1966 to 1971. Religious leaders also lost standing, falling from 41 to 27 percent. Confidence in the leaders of two institutions that were not highly regarded to begin with—the press and organized labor—deteriorated further, from 29 to 18 percent expressing high confidence in the press, and from 22 to 14 percent for labor. Two institutions well regarded in 1966 continued high, relatively speaking, in 1971: confidence in leaders of medicine fell only from 73 to 61 percent over the span, whereas confidence in the leaders of science dropped from 56 to 46 percent. Thus science and medicine, the two institutions most remote from the social turmoil of the late 1960s, showed the smallest decline in public confidence, although neither escaped the prevailing trend, and medicine caught up to the general decline pattern in the late 1970s.

During the 1970s, many polls analyzed confidence in institutions. The various surveys tend to concur that relatively little change has occurred since 1970, other than small-scale variations that probably reflect the effects of short-term events, sampling variations, or both. Table 1 shows that the average high confidence level for the nine institutions in Harris polls from 1966 to 1979 remained largely in the mid to high twenties from 1971 to 1979.

The low percentages reported by Harris as expressing high confidence in different institutions should not be interpreted as demonstrating that the overwhelming majority of Americans have little or no confidence in American institutions. It has been argued that the question Harris uses is phrased so as to discourage favorable responses, since he presents his respondents with one very positive and two negative choices. George Gallup, who did not begin inquiring into confidence in institutions until 1973, offers his interviewees four possible answers: a great deal, quite a lot, some, or very little. When the question is posed this way, a much larger percentage choose Gallup's two favorable replies than opt for Harris' single positive choice. Gallup inquired about confidence in the same five institutions—religion, the Supreme Court, organized labor, Congress, and big business—between 1973 and 1979. The average percentage reporting a great deal or quite a lot of confidence in these was 42 in 1973, 46 in 1975, 44 in 1977, and 42 in 1979. Clearly, Gallup's formulation produces results that suggest that many more Americans feel positively about national institutions than is indicated by Harris's results. They also indicate little variation in rates of confidence during the seventies.

The variations in reported absolute levels of confidence do not negate our interpretations, since what concerns us is trends. In this regard, the various surveys using different questions agree. We have reported Harris's findings in greater detail because he is the only pollster who has inquired about many institutions from 1966. It is clear from the Harris findings, as well as the more discrete results of other surveyors cited by Yankelovich, that a large drop in overall confidence in American institutions occurred during the second half of the 1960s and that there has been no recovery during the 1970s.

THE PROBLEM OF GOVERNMENT

The sources of public discontent with government performance have been thoroughly probed. As we have seen, they do not involve opposition to liberal policies—to those designed to aid the underprivileged; to control aspects of the economy; or to improve the leisure, home, and work environments. Rather, what seems to disturb many

TABLE 1

Decline of Confidence in Primary American Institutions

Question:

A. As far as people in charge of running ________ are concerned, would you say you have a great deal of confidence, only some confidence, or hardly any confidence at all in them?

(Percentages of those expressing "a great deal" of confidence)

	1966	1971	1973	1974	1975	1976	Feb. 1977	Nov. 1977	1978	1979
National, State, and Local Government										
Executive branch, federal government	41	23	19	28	13	11	23	23	14	17
Congress	42	19	29	18	13	9	17	15	10	18
State government*	—	—	24	—	—	16	18	19	15	—
Local government*	—	—	28	—	—	19	18	21	19	—
Other Institutions										
Medicine	73	61	57	50	43	42	43	55	42	30
Higher education	61	37	44	40	36	31	37	41	41	33
Organized religion	41	27	36	32	32	24	29	34	34	20
The military	62	27	40	33	24	23	27	31	29	29
Major companies	55	27	29	21	19	16	20	23	22	18
The press	29	18	30	25	26	20	18	19	23	28
Organized labor	22	14	20	18	14	10	14	15	15	10
Average	47	28	34	29	24	21	25	28	26	23

SOURCE: Louis Harris Associates, latest survey February 1979.

*These institutions are not included in the averages since they are not asked about in every poll.

people is a sense of government incompetence and waste, as well as, in recent years, the inability of government to handle the number one problem, inflation. Virtually every major survey on the latter documents the exceptional emphasis voters place on government waste and inefficiency. Many people feel that tax dollars are not being efficiently used, and that property and income taxes could be sharply reduced without significant service reductions. Votes for tax-cutting measures do not reflect a desire for less government, but for less wasteful and more effective government.[31]

This perception of a highly inefficient government is so strong that just after Proposition 13 mandated a 57-percent property tax cut in June 1978, two-thirds of Californians from public employee households said that it was not likely many of the state's public service workers would lose their jobs. There was, of course, the special California circumstance of a huge state surplus—the existence of which had led State Treasurer Jesse Unruh to describe Gov. Jerry Brown as the "father of Proposition 13." But it is also clear from extensive survey inquiries that California voters of all persuasions believed government was wasteful concerning their tax dollars. It cannot be ascertained how much people think waste can really be pared, and how much they are simply permitting themselves a symbolic slap at perceived malperformance. It is clear that most voters are not embracing tax limitations with the intent of reducing public services. In late June 1978, a CBS News/*New York Times* poll asked a special sample of Californians whether they were willing to see various services "cut back a lot, or only a little, or not at all" in the wake of passage of Proposition 13. At the same time, a cross-section of all Americans was asked a variant of this question. As Table 2 shows, the great preponderance of all voters, including heavy majorities among Proposition 13 proponents, rejected significant service cuts.

About the only service most people want to reduce is welfare. But detailed explorations of what people mean by the welfare programs they would like to reduce, strongly suggest that they have "welfare chiselers" in mind. Many people believe that the welfare rolls are grossly inflated by the presence of able-bodied persons who should be required to take jobs. But the same polls that find that the public would like to reduce welfare also report that they oppose cuts for the elderly and for special education or services for blacks, the poor, the handicapped, or the needy. Seemingly, many of the same people who object to welfare (read "welfare chiselers") continue to back the welfare state.

The public, as noted earlier, has reacted to inflation in diverse ways. People want to cut taxes, but they give solid endorsement to controls over wages, prices, rents and profits. A clear majority say they would

TABLE 2

Willingness to Cut Local Government Services in the Wake of Proposition 13

Question:
"Now that Proposition 13 has passed, are you willing to see ________ cut back a lot or only a little or not at all?"

Question:
"If taxes were reduced in your community, would you be willing to have ________ cut back a lot or only a little or not at all?"

	California Voters (percent)				*Voters Outside California (percent)*			
	All Respondents		*Backers of Proposition 13*		*All Respondents*		*Backers of Proposition 13*	
	Cut a lot	Cut only a little or not at all	Cut a lot	Cut only a little or not at all	Cut a lot	Cut only a little or not at all	Cut a lot	Cut only a little or not at all
Police services	3	97	2	98	6	94	7	93
Library hours	13	87	16	84	18	82	21	79
Fire protection	1	99	1	99	3	97	3	97
Garbage collection	5	95	6	94	7	93	8	92
Public transportation	9	91	13	88	16	84	19	81
Street repair and improvements	7	93	10	90	9	91	11	89
Welfare and social services	44	56	57	43	43	57	51	49
Park maintenance	16	84	14	86	21	79	28	72
Schools	6	94	13	87	7	93	11	89

SOURCE: CBS News/*New York Times* poll, June 1978.

prefer a pay increase lower than the cost of living if there were assurances that inflation was in fact being brought under control. Taxes are felt to be too high and relief is desired, but the public is far more anxious about halting inflation than that taxes be cut. Surveys by CBS News/*New York Times* in 1978 showed that roughly two-thirds of Congress were in favor of some rollback of the social security tax increase mandated by the Ninety-fifth Congress—apparently an anticipatory response to voters' presumed anger—while two-thirds of voters wanted to keep the new taxes as they are. About 90 percent of the public maintained that "controlling inflation is more important than cutting taxes." Americans, in fact, in 1978–79 came to see it as something of an either-or proposition, that is, they were convinced that governmental actions in the areas of taxing and spending are a major contributor to inflation.

Government is responsible for inflation, but people doubt government can take the necessary correctives. As of 1979, most people felt that no president and no unit of government outside the presidency could "keep prices from going up all the time." Two-thirds of Americans similarly believed in 1979 that a balanced federal budget within the next few years is unattainable, no matter who the players. During the 1974–75 bout with double-digit inflation, about two-thirds of the populace did not agree that inflation was "one of the facts of life and here to stay," maintaining instead that it would be halted after a while. By summer 1978, however, high inflation was viewed as certain as the proverbial death and taxes. By an extraordinary 9–1 margin, Americans felt that high inflation would continue. Inflation is the prime reason for the public perception that big government, though essential, seriously lacks competence. Should either party be able to convince the American people that it can be counted upon for a competent, coherent response to inflation, it would reap large electoral dividends.

Still, many of these same people are willing to turn to the inefficient government to solve social ills. Government regulation to deal with air and water pollution, to assure product safety, and to protect the environment wins majority support in various polls. To fight inflation, most people endorse rent control, wage and price control, and gas rationing. Such a response may appear contradictory, but it may also reflect that the populace has become accustomed to the idea that the way to solve a problem is to have the government deal with it. And if many problems, such as those referred to here, result from the self-interested, income-enhancing motivations of people and institutions, as many believe they do, then the only force potentially available to control or regulate the problems produced by self-interest is the government—inefficient, incompetent, and wasteful as it appears to be.

THE DECLINE OF NEW DEAL ERA DIVISIONS

Today, the big economic issues—such matters as the appropriate role for government in economic life, business versus labor, taxation, and spending for social programs—no longer display any coherent class division. It was different 30 and 40 years ago, when lower socioeconomic groups espoused a liberal political economy while the preponderance of the middle class held to a conservative approach. All manner of groups—auto workers, public employees, farmers, blacks, and so on—still make economic demands, of course, and differ one with another. But there is nothing as all-encompassing and persistent as the great working class/middle-class split of the New Deal era.

This reduction of class conflict on economic issues came about as widespread agreement developed on two basic propositions. First, there is no alternative to a large and sustained role by government in regulating the economy, providing social services, and assuring economic progress. Second, inflation is the fundamental economic problem in the United States, and government, through escalating spending and deficits, bears prime responsibility for it. This combination of views is neither liberal nor conservative; measures taken in response to it in such terms are highly misleading.

The salient differences between upper-income and lower-income Americans during the 1930s is frequently overstated..We know, in fact, that each of these broad strata was internally divided on all major issues and that the country was far from undergoing class warfare. Still, the events of the time produced a split between business and labor, or between the middle class and the working class, that seemingly was more distinct than it ever had been. The Great Depression had created general economic hardship. Grave doubts had been cast about the capacity of the old business leadership. In response, government assumed broad new responsibilities. The balance of political and economic power between business and organized labor was greatly altered. In a climate where economic issues dominated the political agenda, working-class Americans regularly found themselves on the opposite side from those in business and professional occupations.

The nationalization of business firms was seriously argued in the 1930s, and this issue split the population along class lines. As Table 3 indicates, two-thirds of unskilled workers in 1937 favored government ownership of the banks, which was the stand of less than one-third of people in business and professional jobs. A clear majority of lower-

TABLE 3

Attitudes on Economic Issues By Occupational Stratum, 1936–37

	Business/ Managerial Workers	Skilled Manual Workers	Unskilled Manual Workers
Government Ownership of Banks (Percentage favoring government ownership)	29	45	65
Government ownership of the Electric Power Industry (Percentage preferring public ownership versus private ownership)	42	68	77
Greater Federal Regulation of Business (Percentage favoring centralizing this regulating power in Washington)	33	51	55
Enactment of a Second National Recovery Act (Percentage who think a second NRA should be enacted)	45	59	72
Federal Government Takeover of All Business and Industry in War Time (Percentage favoring federal takeover in war time)	38	48	64
Limitation by Government of Private Fortune Size (Percentage believing government should have limiting power over private fortune size)	38	44	60
Fairness of Big Business to Their Employees (Percentage disagreeing that big business is usually fair)	28	36	51
Profits Made by Big Business (Percentage who think that big business profits are too big)	46	62	74

SOURCE: Information obtained from a combined set of twenty 1936–1937 American Institute of Public Opinion (Gallup) surveys.

income Americans then wanted limits on the size of private fortunes; large majorities of the upper-income groups opposed any such intervention. The trend toward more government regulation of business was supported by the working class and strongly opposed by the middle class. Three-quarters of unskilled workers, but less than half of professionals and managers, maintained in 1937 that business profits were too large.

Looking at survey data from the 1930s, every measure of class produced the same strong relationships. The higher the economic status, the more likely individuals were to reject a bigger role for labor, to support business, to resist government intervention, and to oppose new social welfare programs. Americans with below-average incomes were consistently more inclined to liberal stands than those with incomes around the national average; the latter in turn were more liberal than their more prosperous fellow citizens. Unskilled manual workers gave more support for liberal programs than artisans, who were more liberal than business managers, and so on.

The reason for such neatness is not hard to uncover. Liberalism and conservatism spoke to contrasting interests and perceptions of upper- and lower-status Americans. An effort was under way to change the balance of power in society, especially to strengthen workers and organized labor vis-à-vis the old middle class and business. This effort required that government get into the act on labor's side. Something of an us-against-them mentality developed in each stratum. The United States did not have class consciousness of the English variety, but enough developed to fire the business-labor animus and to produce clear and consistent differences between middle-class and working-class Americans on a variety of discrete issues. Liberalism involved efforts to employ the state on behalf of new claimants for power and recognition, and to secure a redistribution of economic resources. It was disproportionately backed by the beneficiary economic class. Conservatism, in contrast, formed the resistance to the new and a defense of the old order. It received solid support from the more privileged segments of the populace.

Looking at issues outside the economic realm, there are few consistent patterns. Higher-status Americans in the 1930s were more internationally minded than the working class. They were less likely to voice prejudicial attitudes toward religious and racial minorities. But when it came to position on social issues, 1930s class differences were modest indeed. On some matters the upper-status groups were even a bit more conservative than the less privileged. For example, the death penalty for convicted murderers was backed in 1936 by 69 percent of businessmen and professionals and 63 percent of unskilled and semiskilled workers. Just one-quarter of those in business and professional jobs said they would vote for a fully qualified woman for president; wage workers were slightly more progressive on this question. But in any case, the social issues were not salient during the 1930s. Liberalism-conservatism was an ideological division located largely in economic policy and in the divergent interests of the working and middle classes in the face of the momentous changes of the depression decade.

ECONOMIC ISSUES IN THE 1970s: BEYOND LIBERALISM

Over the 1940s, 1950s, and 1960s, new economic controversies arose and old ones faded, but the New Deal pattern held. But at the end of the 1970s, the old class divisions are in extraordinary disarray. The current efforts to restrict the growth of government—through measures stipulating balanced budgets or limiting growth in public spending to the rate of growth in the GNP—have as much support among the most economically disadvantaged as among the most privileged segments of American society. In 1978, 87 percent of manual workers told Gallup interviewers that they favored a constitutional amendment mandating a balanced federal budget—a proportion higher by 12 percent than the support among business and professional people. Backing for big tax cuts, along the lines of Proposition 13, reached almost identical proportions across the various occupational and income groups. Stemming the steady growth of government taxing and spending is now a central concern, and it is an issue unrelated to the kind of systematic class differences of the New Deal years.

It is hard today to find much of the us-against-them perceptions involving business and labor that loomed so large in the old liberal-conservative division. For example, the proportion of Americans in the highest income positions holding favorable views of union leaders matches exactly that within the lowest income group. Identical proportions of those earning $25,000 a year and more, and those from families with annual incomes of $7,000 or less, profess favorable opinions of business corporations. On the question whether the growth of big business is likely to pose a threat to American society over the next two or three decades, high-income people, and those in business and professional jobs, in a complete reversal of the historical pattern, are actually more troubled by large business enterprise than blue-collar workers and those with low incomes.

Various new economic issues have emerged, notably involving environmental questions, energy, and economic growth. Such matters typically lack any real connection with the historic economic liberal-conservative axis. What is the liberal response on a trade-off question of environmental protection versus economic growth? Upper and lower economic groups split only on highly proximate interests. For example, Table 4 shows that lower-income Americans give more backing for the elimination of pollution-control devices on cars to save gasoline than do people with high incomes. At the same time, low-income individuals

TABLE 4

Attitudes on Economic Issues by Income Level, 1978

	Under $7,000	$ 7,000–14,999	$15,000–24,999	$25,000+
Energy Conservation: Elimination of Pollution Control Devices to Conserve Gasoline (Percentage favoring elimination of pollution control devices)	51	52	42	39
Labor Union Leaders: Reasonable and Responsive (Percentage who feel that few labor union leaders are reasonable and responsive)	52	49	47	52
Future Threat from Big Business (Percentage who think the development of big business may be a threat to society and life in the United States over the next 20–30 years)	27	34	36	51
Opinion of Big Business Corporations (Percentage whose opinion of most big business corporations is unfavorable)	34	36	32	32
Trade-Off: Increase Police Protection, Despite Higher Taxes (Percentage favoring more police protection even if it means higher taxes)	35	32	35	36
Proposition 13: Lower Property Taxes to 1% of Market Value (Percentage who would vote against a similar proposition in their community)	30	30	31	35
Tax Cut of All Taxes by One-Third (Percentage feeling that cutting all taxes by one-third would be a good thing)	46	49	49	49
Control Inflation: Increase Corporate Taxes, Despite Resultant Increased Prices (Percentage willing to see corporate taxes raised, even if prices increased, because of long-term control of inflation)	25	29	31	33
Control Inflation: Freeze all Salaries and Wages (Percentage willing to see all salaries and wages frozen even if some injustices result)	39	42	45	39
Control Inflation: Limit Income Increases to 5% (Percentage willing to legislate for no income increase more than 5% annually)	41	39	37	37

TABLE 4 (continued)

	Under $7,000	$7,000–14,999	$15,000–24,999	$25,000+
Cost of Living Exceeds Income (Percentage who feel that cost of living has gone up more than their income)	90	79	70	52

SOURCE: Surveys of the Roper Organization, as cited in *Roper Reports*, 1978.

are less willing to see special taxes instituted on gas-guzzling cars. The common thread here, of course, is that the less affluent are less prepared than their more affluent fellow citizens to pay the price of environmental cleanup through higher car prices and greater gasoline consumption.

THE NEW IDEOLOGICAL ADMIXTURE

Even as they endorse measures to restrict the growth of government spending and taxation, Americans remain extraordinarily supportive of a high level of government services in virtually all sectors. There are no longer significant class differences in this commitment. Thus, almost identical proportions of business managers and unskilled workers, of high-income people and those in the lowest income brackets, want to maintain or increase current spending for environmental problems, health, urban needs, education, improving the position of blacks, and so on.

But though Americans rich and poor overwhelmingly approve the "service state," by equally formidable margins they view inflation as Public Enemy Number One. Without any notable differences relating to economic position, they want to curtail the growth of taxing and spending and deficit spending, which they hold responsible for inflation. An extraordinary three-fourths of all Americans—three-fourths of both business and professional people and of manual workers—described inflation as the nation's most important problem in various polls taken in 1978 and 1979.

Had the big increases in taxation that have occurred over the past two decades been distributed disproportionately on upper-income groups, the divisions that had earlier prevailed with regard to public-sector activity might still have persisted. But instead, as Table 5 shows, between 1953 and 1977 the proportion of income paid in taxes doubled

TABLE 5

Proportions of Family Income Paid in Taxes, 1953–1977

	1953	1966	1977
Families earning around the average income	11.8%	17.8%	22.5%
Families earning twice the average income	16.5%	19.3%	24.8%
Families earning four times the average income	20.2%	23.4%	31.4%

SOURCE: Advisory Commission on Inter-Governmental Relations, *Significant Features of Fiscal Federalism—1978–1979* (Washington, D.C.: Advisory Commission on Inter-Governmental Relations, 1979), pp. 30–31.

for the average family, while increasing by only half among families earning four times the national average. The costs of government were brought home forcefully to a broad range of the populace.

When Franklin Roosevelt's administration dramatically expanded the role of government, it encountered strong opposition of a philosophical sort. The upper classes of the New Deal years opposed the interventionist programs of Roosevelt, not only because they viewed them as threats to their ascendancy and as economic costs, but also because they believed that private solutions were intrinsically preferable to public ones. Philosophical disagreements over the proper scope of government were deep and widespread. Today, though some continue to oppose all government intervention as a matter of principle, the New Deal state has achieved general acceptance. In the years after World War II, more and more groups came to find that they could use government to advance their own interests.

A number of developments, then, served gradually to erode the once reasonably robust class differences over government's economic role and programs. But it is the high inflation of recent years that has delivered the coup de grace to the old class conflict and, for the moment at least, to economic liberalism-conservatism. Whether or not the perception squares with reality, lower socioeconomic groups feel they have been notably victimized by inflation. Thus, 90 percent of those earning $7,000 a year or less, 79 percent in the $7,000 to $15,000 range, 70 percent of those earning $15,000 to $25,000, but only 52 percent of those with incomes over $25,000 claimed in late 1978 that increases in the cost of living were exceeding the growth of their incomes.

This sense of inflation as a democratic enemy, striking everyone but especially the little people, has had a profound impact on attitudes toward government. Support for various measures—from tax cuts, to spending curbs, to requirements that budgets be balanced, whatever may help to control or mitigate the impact of inflation—can be found rather evenly across the populace. And, since they see themselves especially burdened by inflation, the lower income and occupation groups support anti-government actions to control inflation at least as strongly as the upper-middle class. At the same time, of course, lower income groups also endorse increased government intervention to stabilize wages, rents, and prices. Although economic divisions remain, they are vastly more fragmented. Specific groups pursue policies designed to advance their interests. But the great class struggles of the New Deal era are gone.

The general acceptance of government responsibility to redress assorted perceived social problems—particularly to aid the underprivileged elements in the society—does not mean that the belief in individualism and achievement has disappeared from American society. The same public opinion surveys that report approval of specific proposals to aid the deprived also indicate a preference for individuals improving their own situation, rather than relying on the government for assistance. These surveys also reveal a strong suspicion of increased state power. But the same Americans who often reject a remedial role for government on the ideological level, when reacting to specific social and economic problems, support federal intervention. It seems evident that American egalitarianism—sympathy for the underdog—leads people to endorse proposals for government action designed to increase opportunity, while at the same time they continue to adhere to anti-government, individualistic, and meritocratic values. Americans appear to want a society in which each individual is self-supporting and is able, through competition on an equal basis with others, to improve his situation without outside assistance. Because they are aware that such equal opportunity does not exist, they also endorse remedial programs by the state. As a result, in spite of their continued adherence on an ideological level to individualistic anti-state values, when asked to approve various proposed federal programs, their commitment to equal rights and opportunities leads them to support such proposals by sizeable majorities.

Many of the inconsistencies point up a deep contradiction between the two values that are at the core of the American creed—individualism and egalitarianism. Americans believe strongly in both values and, as the earlier discussion suggests, the history of social change in the country reflects a shifting back and forth between them. One consequence of this dualism in the American value system is that political debate often takes the form of one consensual value opposing the other.[32] Liberals and conservatives do not typically take alternative positions on issues of equality and freedom. Instead, each side appeals to one or the other core value. Liberals stress the primacy of egalitarianism and the social injustice that flows from unfettered individualism, while conservatives enshrine individual freedom and the social need for mobility and achievement. Both sides treat the entire American public as their natural constituency. In this sense, liberals and conservatives are less opponents than they are competitors, like two department stores on the same block trying to draw the same customers by offering different versions of what everyone wants.

The contradiction between these core values is especially apparent in racial attitudes. Gunnar Myrdal concluded back in the 1940s that most Americans put their beliefs about race and their often inconsistent beliefs about equality and achievement into separate mental compartments: "Few liberals . . . are without a well-furnished compartment of race prejudice"; those most "violently prejudiced against the Negro" also have "a whole compartment in . . . their valuation sphere housing the entire American creed of liberty, equality, justice and fair opportunity for everybody."[33]

Much of the progress in the early years of the civil rights movement was made by breaking down the compartmentalization of the American mind and forcing the public to see that the country's attitudes and institutions fell outrageously short of our equalitarian ideals. It is the equalitarian element in the American creed that created the consensus behind the civil rights revolution of the past thirty years. But the more recent focus of the movement on substantive equality and forced integration has pushed it up against the individualistic, achievement-oriented element in the American creed. As this has occurred the consensus has broken.

On every issue, the public opinion data show a positive, pro-civil rights majority when only equalitarian questions are at stake but a negative view when an issue pushes up against basic notions of individualism. Thus, on central issues involving compulsory inequality, American sentiment is powerfully against discrimination. Trends on these issues have been consistently liberal, and now the white South concurs with the national mood. The consensus breaks down, however, when compulsory integration is involved. Affirmative action policies have, therefore, forced a sharp confrontation between equalitarian and individualistic values. White Americans look favorably on compensatory action because compensation for past discrimination is consistent with the equalitarian creed. Such action essentially makes the conditions of competition fairer without violating the notion of a competitive system. But most Americans, including many blacks, oppose the notion of preferential treatment, as such treatment violates the notion of open and fair individual competition.

IMPLICATIONS FOR THE 1980s

Although, as noted earlier, a simplistic cyclical approach to American politics would suggest that the 1980s will witness a revival of liberalism in reaction to the moderate or conservative predominance in the 1970s, it would be an error to rely heavily on the cyclical analysis. In looking back over the decades since World War I and at what seemingly has dominated their ideological character, the role of big events is impressive: postwar reaction and prosperity in the 1920s; the Great Depression in the 1930s; the cold war, Korea, and prosperity in the 1950s; Vietnam and mass protest in the 1960s; and affluence, assorted high-level scandals, growing international tension, and inflation in the 1970s. To predict the basic character of the 1980s, therefore, would require, at minimum, a prophet's ability to foresee the state of the economy and of international relations. Should the long-anticipated recession persist, economic liberalism could revive as a major force. Conversely, continuation of high inflation will reinforce current demands to curtail government expenditures. A further curtailment of oil supplies will probably produce increased support for rationing as an alternative to soaring gas prices and lines at the service stations. Increased international conflict will likely result in greater support for increased military expenditures, which would probably mean demands for curtailment of social programs. A revived anti-Communist mood would probably strengthen conservative sentiments generally.

The actions of various groups will also play a role in determining social policy. In recent years, pressure from groups affected by inflation has forced many liberal politicians to refrain from pressing to expand the welfare function of the state. But a revival of militant protest by blacks and other underprivileged groups as a reaction to declining income and/or increased unemployment rates could have a powerful impact on the national agenda, much as such behavior did in the 1960s.

Whatever the events that determine the outlook of the 1980s, Americans will probably continue their support for activist policies designed to implement the assumptions of equalitarianism—preferably perceived in the context of enhancing individual opportunity. Though Americans will continue to voice a preference for individuals improving their situation through their own efforts, they will readily turn to the state when it appears that individuals do not have a fair chance acting alone.

These contradictory values leave abundant room for leaders and political forces of diverse orientations to maneuver to attain majority support among the electorate. Leadership, a role not discussed here, can still be a major factor in determining policy outcomes. In the recent past, Democrats and liberals have shown a greater capacity for appealing to the electorate because they have emphasized both the equalitarian and achievement values. The Kennedy-Johnson war on poverty program was presented as a way of equalizing the race for success, by giving the underprivileged the means they lacked to compete in a race among individuals. Conservatives and Republicans, on the other hand, while appealing strongly to the individualistic and anti-government sentiments of Americans, have shown less ability to demonstrate their commitment to equalitarianism. They have been viewed, therefore, as being less compassionate than their rivals, and as favoring preservation of the established order in areas that most Americans perceive as requiring reform. Essentially, the Republicans have been viewed largely as conservative defenders of the status quo, whereas the Democrats have managed to be both liberals and conservatives at the same time—advocates of equalitarianism and achievement, of welfare and individualism.

Public opinion is clearly not the sole or even the main determinant of public policy at the national level. Many of the specific reactions that are voiced to pollsters reflect weakly held views. Opinion surveys have reported sharp reversals in popular sentiment following decisive actions by the president and Congress. What the polls reveal is the general mood of the electorate; their results are not the equivalent of referenda held following campaigns in which arguments on both sides have been presented to the electorate.

What can be said about the larger state of opinion in domestic matters is that, since the 1930s, the large majority has been socialized by developments to look for government as a solution to both national and a variety of personal problems. Although events of the past decade and a half have resulted in considerable distrust of big institutions, including government, and most people would like to cut them back in size and power, there has not been an equivalent reduction in the propensity to turn to government. When this orientation is put in the context of the continuing desire of Americans to improve the situation of the underprivileged and minorities, it is likely that the political system will continue to seek to produce solutions to expressed social needs. A policy of "benign neglect" will not be popular, even when warranted.

NOTES

1. For an analysis of the shifting value emphases, see S. M. Lipset, *The First New Nation: The United States in Historical and Comparative Perspective,* rev. ed. (New York: Norton Library, 1979).

2. James L. Sundquist, *Dynamics of the Party System* (Washington, D.C.: Brookings Institution, 1973), pp. 171–182; and David Burner, *The Politics of Provincialism: The Democratic Party in Transition, 1918–1932* (New York: Alfred A. Knopf, 1968).

3. On campus protest, see S. M. Lipset, *Rebellion in the University* (Chicago: University of Chicago Press, Phoenix Books, 1976).

4. Interview with Lewis Uhler, conducted by Everett C. Ladd, Jr., January 9, 1979.

5. Walter Heller in Walter Heller and Arthur Burns, "Tax Revolt: The Lady or the Tiger?" *Public Opinion,* 1 (July/August 1978): 13.

6. "College Students," *Public Opinion,* 2 (June/July 1979): 32.

7. Survey by Yankelovich, Skelly, and White for *Time,* March 1978.

8. These data are from surveys by the American Institute of Public Opinion (Gallup). The 1978 data are from a survey conducted March 3–6.

9. See, e.g., Philip Converse, "The Nature of Belief Systems in Mass Publics," in *Ideology and Discontent,* ed. David Apter (New York: Free Press, 1964), pp. 206–261.

10. For a discussion of these concepts and evidence, see S. M. Lipset, *Political Man* (Garden City, N.Y.: Doubleday, 1963) pp. 92–97.

11. Charles Stember, *Jews in the Mind of America* (New York: Basic Books, 1941); Harold E. Quinley and Charles Y. Glock, *Anti-Semitism in America* (New York: Free Press, 1979) (this book summarizes changing attitudes toward blacks, see pp. 131–157); Rita James Simon, *Public Opinion in America: 1936–1970* (Chicago: Rand McNally, 1974) pp. 55–103; and S. M. Lipset and William Schneider, *From Discrimination to Affirmative Action: Public Attitudes 1935–1980* (Washington, D.C.: American Enterprise Institute, forthcoming).

12. See Samuel Stouffer, *Communism, Conformity, and Civil Liberties* (Garden City, N.Y.: Doubleday, 1955).

13. S. M. Lipset and Earl Raab, *The Politics of Unreason: Right Wing Extremism in America, 1790–1977* (Chicago: University of Chicago Press, Phoenix Books, 1978), pp. 457–459; and William Schneider, "Democrats and Republicans, Liberals and Conservatives," in *Emerging Coalitions in American Politics,* ed. S. M. Lipset (San Francisco: Institute of Contemporary Studies, 1978), pp. 190–192.

14. For a detailed analysis of the Wallace support, see Lipset and Raab, *The Politics of Unreason,* pp. 378–406.

15. Everett C. Ladd, Jr., *Transformations of the American Party System* (New York: W. W. Norton, 1975), esp. pp. 226–331; and Everett C. Ladd, Jr., *Where Have All the Voters Gone* (New York: W. W. Norton, 1978), esp. pp. 2–14, 38–45.

16. Gary N. Orren, "Candidate Style and Voter Alignment in 1976," in *Emerging Coalitions,* ed. Lipset, pp. 142–145.

17. Survey by Samuel A. Stouffer, reported in his *Communism, Conformity, and Civil Liberties*; and National Opinion Research Center, General Social Surveys, latest survey of 1977.

18. Surveys by Louis Harris and Associates, latest survey of June 27 to July 1, 1978.

19. S. M. Lipset and William Schneider, "The Bakke Case: How Would It Be Decided at the Bar of Public Opinion?" *Public Opinion*, 1 (March-April 1978): 38–44.

20. Survey by the American Institute of Public Opinion (Gallup) in 1969; and National Opinion Research Center, General Social Survey, 1978.

21. Ibid.

22. Louis Kriesberg and Ross Klein, "Changes in Public Support for American Military Spending" (paper, Department of Sociology, Syracuse University, 1979).

23. "Support for More Defense Spending at an 18-Year High," *Public Opinion*, 2 (March–May 1979): 25.

24. Kriesberg and Klein, "Changes in Public Support."

25. The Chicago Council on Foreign Relations, *American Public Opinion and U.S. Foreign Policy 1979* (Chicago: Chicago Council on Foreign Relations, 1979), p. 26.

26. Kriesberg and Klein, "Changes in Public Support."

27. Surveys by the Survey Research Center of the University of Michigan, 1964, 1968; survey by CBS News/*New York Times*, January 8–12, 1978.

28. Surveys by the Opinion Research Corporation, latest survey of 1977.

29. These data are from the National Opinion Research Center's General Social Surveys, 1973–1978 merged dataset.

30. Daniel Yankelovich, "Emerging Ethical Norms in Public and Private Life" (paper presented to Columbia University seminar, April 20, 1977), pp. 2–3.

31. S. M. Lipset and Earl Raab, "The Message of Proposition 13," *Commentary*, 66 (September 1978): 42–46; and S. M. Lipset, "The Public Pulse: What Americans Really Think about Inflation," *Taxation and Spending*, 2 (April 1979): 32–33.

32. This discussion is taken from Lipset and Schneider, "The Bakke Case," pp. 43–44.

33. Gunnar Myrdal, *An American Dilemma* (New York: Harper and Brothers, 1944) p. xiv.

Tax and Spending Limits

Alvin Rabushka

IV

No issue is more salient in contemporary American politics than limiting taxes and controlling government spending. Landslide passage of Proposition 13 on June 6, 1978, highlighted public outrage over rising taxes and the seemingly uncontrollable runaway growth of government spending. Proposition 13 was a contagious phenomenon. On election day in November 1978, eight states approved new tax limitation measures, and three additional states authorized spending limits.

Nor is Proposition 13 the end. Paul Gann and the "Spirit of 13" Initiative movement have collected 900,000 signatures to place a spending limitation measure on the California ballot that would tie increases in state and local government spending to increases in the consumer price index (CPI) and population. If this amendment is adopted, California will be required to balance its budget and to limit its spending. Moreover, in April 1979 Howard Jarvis announced a campaign to place on the ballot a measure to halve California's personal income tax, index the income tax to the CPI, freeze the state sales tax at its present level, and eliminate the inventory tax on business. Another group has begun an initiative campaign to eliminate the sales tax over a period of three years. Proposition 13 is not the end of limiting taxes and governmental spending in California.

Movements are under way in other states and localities to roll back or freeze taxes and to place caps on government expenditures. Election day in 1980 will probably witness another dozen or more statewide referenda on issues of tax and spending limits.

Nor is the movement to limit taxes and spending confined to state and local governments. Several organizations and individuals have launched campaigns to restrain federal spending. The National Taxpayers Union has worked with many state legislatures to petition Congress to invoke

Article V of the Constitution and call a constitutional convention to draft an amendment requiring a balanced federal budget. Another organization consisting of prominent academics and public officials, the National Tax Limitation Committee, has drafted an amendment to limit federal spending (known as the Friedman amendment after Professor Milton Friedman). Howard Jarvis, co-sponsor of Proposition 13, has launched his own nationwide American Tax Reduction Movement. His plan seeks to reduce taxes by $50 billion, set a 15-percent limit on the capital gains tax, cut $100 billion from the federal budget over a four-year phase-in period, and retire the national debt by reducing spending more than taxes.

Hundreds of members of Congress have sponsored joint resolutions to require a balanced federal budget, place a limit on the share of gross national product (GNP) that the federal government can spend under normal circumstances, reduce the share of national income that the federal government can spend, or require that the federal government be constrained both by a spending limit and a balanced budget requirement. No issue commanded more congressional attention in spring 1979 than the balanced budget/spending limit movement.

Congressional interest in the balanced budget amendment will probably increase as the number of states petitioning Congress nears the two-thirds required by the Constitution, but is likely to shift to more pressing business if the movement begins to die. Whatever the outcome of the various campaigns, voters in more and more states will undoubtedly place constraints on taxes and spending.

Public opinion polls reveal a growing consensus that government must be restrained, that the direction of government spending, regulation, and taxation must be reversed in order to preserve our democratic processes and free enterprise economy. Public opinion no longer supports further expansions in public spending. Now more than ever, higher percentages of Americans say that taxes are too high, that the government wastes tax money and can no longer invariably be trusted to act correctly. Sixty percent of Americans regard inflation as the most important national problem, and, according to Gallup, 80 percent favor a constitutional amendment to require a balanced budget.

Proposition 13 may have inspired the current tax revolt, but opposition to taxes is firmly rooted in American history. The notorious Stamp Act of 1765 was repealed by the English Parliament in 1766 because of colonial protest and opposition. A substitute tax on glass, paint, paper, and tea, imposed on the colonies in 1767, met equally vociferous opposition and was subsequently repealed in 1770. The infamous 1773 Tea Act gave rise to the Boston Tea Party. Historians record the revolutionary war cry as "No taxation without representation!" but I suspect that "No taxation!" may be closer to the truth.

Despite these early tax revolts, government spending and taxes were not burdensome until well into the twentieth century. In 1902, for example, federal spending constituted less than 3 percent of GNP, and government spending at all levels accounted for only 8 percent of GNP. In 1978, in contrast, the respective shares had risen to 22 and 33 percent, an eightfold increase for the federal government and a fourfold increase for all levels of government. In a few years, the national debt will exceed one trillion dollars, mostly because of deficit spending in normal, peacetime circumstances.

THE GROWTH OF AMERICAN GOVERNMENT IN THE TWENTIETH CENTURY[1]

As just noted, government spending in 1902 constituted only a modest share of GNP or personal income. Between 1902 and 1913, total government spending as a share of GNP remained almost constant at 8.8 percent. But then began an incredible burst in public spending. Between 1913 and 1932, government revenues doubled as a percentage of GNP, and government spending more than doubled. This growth was due in part to passage of the Sixteenth Amendment (the income tax) and World War I with its related expenditures.

In 1929, the date for which national income and product accounts are first available for the United States, total government spending was about 10 percent of GNP and about 12 percent of personal income (see Table 1). These percentages grew steadily and reached nearly one-third of GNP and 40 percent of personal income by 1978. The composition of this spending has also shifted; the federal share has increased from about one-quarter to just over two-thirds.

The increase in federal spending has outpaced the growth of federal revenues, resulting in a massive deficit. Before World War I, the federal debt stood below $2 billion. It grew to $24 billion after the war, increased to $43 billion during the New Deal–depression years, and exploded to $260 billion by the close of World War II. About $23 billion was added to the federal deficit between 1947 and 1965. In the next decade, the total was $148 billion. Between 1976 and 1979 alone, the deficits exceeded $200 billion.[2]

By the end of fiscal year 1980, gross federal debt is expected to reach $899 billion, of which $690 billion will be held publicly. This latter sum is equal to $3,100 per capita. Interest on the federal debt is projected at $57

TABLE 1

Growth of Government Spending (billion $)

Year	GNP	Personal Income	Federal Spending	Total Government Spending*	Total Government Spending as Percentage of GNP	Total Government Spending as Percentage of PI
1929	103.4	84.9	2.6	10.3	10.0	12.1
1939	90.8	72.4	8.9	17.6	19.4	24.3
1949	258.0	205.6	41.3	59.3	23.0	28.8
1959	486.5	382.1	91.0	131.0	26.9	34.3
1969	935.5	745.8	188.4	285.6	27.6	38.3
1978	2,106.6	1,707.3	461.0	684.2	32.5	40.1

Source: *Economic Report of the President* (Washington, D.C.: Government Printing Office, 1979): Table B-72, p. 267; Table B-17, p. 202; Table B-18, p. 203.
Note: *Includes federal, state and local governments.

billion, or $260 per capita. Interest payments are the third largest item in the federal budget and consume 9¢ of every budget dollar.

Large and accumulating budget deficits make limiting monetary growth more difficult. The greater the amount of money issued to finance the deficit, the higher the subsequent inflation. Between 1947 and 1967, an era of only modest budget deficits, the inflation rate averaged just 1.6 percent; in contrast, the average rate from 1967 to 1977 was 7 percent, and has accelerated to better than 9 percent in 1978–79.

Until 1973, the growth in government spending was accompanied by a steady rise in real private income. Since 1973, growth in real private income has fallen off dramatically. As a result, the public is increasingly concerned over its total tax burden and the aggregate amount of government spending.

What are the facts?[3] Between 1947 and 1973, real disposable income per capita grew on average 2.5 percent per year (and nearly doubled during this period). In contrast, between 1973 and 1977, the rate fell to 1.3 percent per year. But this growth figure of 1.3 percent is somewhat misleading as a measure of private economic well-being because it omits both the rapid increases in the labor force participation rate and the enormous government deficits that accumulated in this five-year period.

The 1970s have seen rapid growth in labor force participation. Although real disposable income per worker grew by an annual rate of 3 percent between 1947 and 1973, the corresponding figure for 1973 to 1977 is 0.3 percent (five million more workers joined the labor force in this period). And if we construe the issuance of debt as a postponement of taxes, real disposable income less increased federal debt per worker fell by 0.3 percent per year. Since 1973, real economic growth has slowed substantially, and virtually all real economic growth has gone into increased government spending—trends that readily promote a taxpayer revolt. It is inconceivable that taxpayers want all of this modest growth to be spent by government.

The growth of government spending has been accompanied by declining public confidence in government. Surveys conducted by George Gallup, Louis Harris, the Institute of Social Research at the University of Michigan, and CBS/New York Times reveal major shifts in public opinion between 1957 and 1978, the year of the tax revolt.[4] The percentage of respondents who said that government wastes money rose from 46 to 80. But the number of those who said they trust Washington to do what is right most of the time declined from 75 to 34 percent. Although Americans have never been enthusiastic about paying taxes, compared with ten years ago, higher percentages today feel that their income and property taxes are too high.

Americans are increasingly feeling the effects of inflation. Between 1958 and 1973, for example, the number of Gallup's respondents naming inflation as the nation's most important problem was always less than 20 percent. Since 1974, the percentage has ranged from a low of 25 to a high of 79. Complaints about taxes and government waste have escalated as taxpayers endure rising rates of inflation and stagnant real income. The movements to limit taxes and spending are visibly rooted in reason, not caprice.

CALIFORNIA: BLUEPRINT FOR THE FUTURE

Proposition 13 exploded on the American political scene. Given California's modest initiative requirement and its lively political culture, it is not surprising that the tax revolt should surface there. Briefly, Proposition 13 limits taxes to 1 percent of market value, computed initially on the basis of the 1975–76 assessment rolls, with a maximum 2 percent assessment increase annually. At time of sale, the property can be revalued based on actual market price. Proposition 13 immediately decreased local governments' property tax receipts by $7 billion, or 57 percent. It also requires a two-thirds vote of the state legislature to increase state taxes, and local governments may impose special taxes (except property taxes) only after approval by two-thirds of the jurisdiction's voters.

However, the Jarvis-Gann initiative to gain property tax relief and "send the politicians a message" followed a decade of unsuccessful initiatives to reduce property taxes or government spending. What changes, then, brought about Proposition 13's overwhelming success?

Property tax reform and spending limits have been part of California history since the mid-1960s.[5] A bribery scandal in 1965 prompted reform to ensure a uniform statewide ratio of 25 percent between a property's assessed value and its market value. This reform actually increased the burden on single-family housing since commercial properties had previously been paying a disproportionately high burden of the tax bill. The resultant increase in homeowners' tax bills motivated the Watson Initiative, or Proposition 9, on the November 1968 ballot. This amendment proposed limiting taxes to 1 percent of a property's current market value for property-related services (public safety, general government, etc.) and also gradually eliminating the use of property tax revenues for people-related services (education and welfare). Opponents of Proposition 9 forecasted massive increases in income and sales taxes to offset declines in property tax revenues. Meanwhile, the state legislature passed a more moderate tax relief alternative, California's first homeowner's exemption. Watson lost by more than two-to-one, and the homeowner's exemption passed by a slight majority. Analysts of the vote concluded that California voters felt the 1960s were good years and thus were not predisposed to vote against taxes.

Subsequent measures fared no better than the Watson initiative. In 1970, for example, Howard Jarvis failed to obtain the necessary signatures to place a somewhat standard tax limitation initiative on the ballot. But in 1972, Watson qualified a second initiative (Proposition 14) for the ballot. It proposed to substitute increases in sales, liquor, cigarette, and corporate income taxes and state funding of education and welfare to compensate for property tax relief. Despite the deteriorating economic climate and the beginnings of steady increases in assessed values for single-family housing, Watson again got only one-third of the vote.

In November 1973, Governor Reagan proposed a limitation on public spending (Proposition 1). The proposed amendment linked growth in state expenditures with the growth rate in personal income and required that future increases in tax rate schedules receive a two-thirds vote of the legislature. Governor Reagan proposed this spending limit after raising the maximum tax rate on personal income from 7 percent in 1967 to 11 percent in 1971, with somewhat smaller 2 percent increases in the tax rates for corporations and banks.

Proposition 1 lost by a 56–44 percent margin. Analysts of the election believe that the proposal was unclear and cast in difficult technical language and that public dissatisfaction with the level of government spending was still low.

After 1973, California's tax climate, especially property taxes, changed dramatically.[6] A period of rapidly accelerating housing prices sharply increased property taxes. Between 1973 and 1978, the year of Jarvis-Gann, housing prices in California grew more rapidly—often two to three times as fast—than in most other major urban areas. Thus, many families were paying property taxes well in excess of what they had anticipated. Property tax bills increased far more rapidly than homeowners' disposable income.

Not only were property taxes accelerating, but by 1976–77 California ranked third after Alaska and New York in state and local tax collections per $1,000 of personal income. In all, California governments took 15.5 percent of their residents' personal income in 1976–77 (compared with 9.3 percent in 1957). The state's property tax receipts per $1,000 of personal income were 41 percent above the national norm, and the share of property taxes accounted for by single-family dwellings rose dramatically after 1973.

Still, two attempts to place property tax limitation initiatives on the 1976 ballot, one by Watson, one by Paul Gann, could not obtain the necessary number of signatures.

Rapidly rising assessments meant that local governments could enjoy rising property tax receipts without raising tax rates—indeed, the average combined tax rate for homeowners fell by nearly 5 percent between 1974 and 1978, but assessment increases more than doubled. Throughout the mid-1970s, local government spending, fueled by the tax yields of rampant housing inflation, grew about 10 percent per year. In the early 1970s, legislation to set maximum tax rates was ineffective in holding down tax bills since it was rising assessments, not rising tax rates, that increased the tax burden.

But perhaps the most interesting elements in the chronicle of Proposition 13 were the state budget surplus and the legislature's inability to produce a major tax relief program. When Governor Brown took office in 1975, the state had a surplus of less than $400 million. By June 1978, this had grown to $6 billion, with prospects of passing the $10 billion mark by fiscal year 1979–80 if Proposition 13 were not passed. Since the state's personal income tax is steeply progressive, increases in personal income due to inflation translate into even larger proportionate increases in state tax receipts. Every 1 percent rise in personal income increases income taxes by 1.7 percent. With taxable income typically rising 10 percent per year during the late 1970s, state tax receipts rose 16 to 17 percent per year. Thus, high rates of inflation coupled with a strong statewide economy generated an enormous surfeit of tax receipts and a budgetary surplus fast approaching unreasonable dimensions. Despite the surplus and rising taxpayer resentment, the state legislature did not pass a meaningful tax relief program. Howard Jarvis and Paul Gann were able to qualify their initiative petition in one month.

In early 1978, the state legislature proposed a less drastic rival measure, but it was too little, too late. Proposition 8, which would have separated the rolls for residential and commercial property taxes, but provided less current or future tax relief, failed to gain a simple majority in the June primary election. Proposition 13 won by an overwhelming 65 percent majority.

What was the message of Proposition 13? Was it, as some authors claim, simply a lashing out against inflation? Was it a protest vote against big government? Was it a complaint against government waste? Or was it simply a desire to cut taxes?

The California Poll, conducted by Mervin Field, revealed that voters believed that both taxes and waste could be cut with no serious reductions in the provision of essential services.[7] Seventy-three percent of the California electorate rated the state government as "very" or "somewhat" inefficient, and majorities labeled county and city governments and school boards equally inefficient. A majority of voters even said that small budgetary cutbacks would have no effect on the provision of local services.

In view of the escalating state surplus, many Californians not surprisingly believed that property taxes could be cut without jeopardizing public services. Even so, 41 percent wanted less spending on public housing, and 62 percent wanted cuts in welfare. Fifty-eight percent of those polled in June 1978 said that in place of the present budgetary system, they wanted to set a limit on state spending.

Support for Proposition 13 encompassed partisan, ideological, and social class differences. Majorities in virtually every class of the population voted for the measure. The public services that voters want cut back most are income redistribution programs that provide few benefits to middle-income taxpayers; those services voters want maintained or expanded serve middle-income taxpayers. Proposition 13 can be interpreted, at least initially, as an anti-tax, anti-government, anti-inflation, anti-income-redistribution gesture of taxpayers, and of homeowning taxpayers in particular.

FALL 1978: THE TAX REVOLT SPREADS

Forty-seven states, Puerto Rico, and the District of Columbia have either a constitutional or statutory prohibition or restraint on state deficit financing, some dating from the nineteenth century.[8] These provisions either restrict the ability to incur debt, require balanced budgets or appropriations, or provide for the management of an impending or already incurred deficit. However, these constitutional and statutory prohibitions on state deficit financing have not prevented rapid growth in state taxing and spending, due largely to inflation and progressive tax rate schedules.

Although 1978 is recognized as the year of the tax revolt, movements to limit state spending and taxing began to appear on state ballots during America's bicentennial year, 1976. Five states (Michigan, Utah, Colorado, Florida, and Montana) had propositions to limit taxation. Despite failure in every case, these movements presaged the vastly greater number of tax and spending limits that surfaced in 1978.

Tennessee voters were the first to adopt an explicit limit on spending; on March 7, 1978, its voters approved by a two-thirds majority an amendment limiting the rate of growth of state spending to the state's economic growth rate. (Perhaps New Jersey deserves credit as the first state to adopt stringent limitations on state and local government spending. In 1976, the state legislature limited increases in state spending to the annual per capita increase in wealth [about 10 percent per year] and set local government caps at 5 percent per year. Adoption of these limits did not require voter approval. In 1977 the Colorado legislature enacted a statute that limited spending increases to 7 percent per year until 1983.) Then the dramatic and highly publicized success of Proposition 13 inspired a number of similar initiatives in more than a dozen other states.

Although twenty states voted on some form of tax or spending measure, the issue in six states was not so much limiting as shifting the burden of taxation or changing the rules for assessments. In Illinois, for example, the property tax ceiling referendum was purely advisory. Massachusetts voters authorized cities and towns to tax residential property at lower rates than commercial property. Missouri voters, in anticipation of property reassessments, authorized their legislature to require local governments to reduce tax rates to hold down property taxes. Montana voters rejected a plan to transfer assessments for property taxes from the state to local governments.

South Carolina, which already operates under a balanced budget requirement, now manages its fiscal affairs under an additional constraint: its voters authorized the establishment of a "rainy day" reserve fund equal to 5 percent of the general budget to be used for emergencies only after a two-thirds vote of the legislature. Finally, in Colorado, voters rejected a plan to liberalize the 7 percent statutory spending limit with one tied to inflation, which at the time exceeded 7 percent.

Table 2, the box score for the 1978 state referenda, is divided into spending limits and tax limits. A similar pattern of voting emerges from both tax and spending limitations. Majorities favoring tax and spending limitations exceeded, on average, majorities rejecting limits. Oregonians flirted with adoption of a Proposition 13–type limitation on property taxes. Other No votes in Oregon and Arkansas won by modest majorities. In contrast, the percentages approving new tax limits ran as high as 84 percent in Texas, and in only two instances were less than 55 percent.

Overall, the voters' message was clear: runaway government spending and taxing must be limited. But due to variations in the limits imposed and in the perceived efficiency of public spending, the availability of surpluses, and the effectiveness of interest groups, it is difficult to draw general conclusions about the measures that failed, save to note their small margin of defeat.

Organized efforts are under way to put tax and spending limits on the 1980 ballot in other states. These proposals will differ among states, reflecting local goals and economic conditions. Most measures will appear in states that already have constitutional or statutory requirements for balanced budgets. State and local governments thus begin the 1980s bound under fiscal constraints that may affect the quantity and quality of public services, but definitely limit their powers to tax and spend. Government growth in the 1980s will not rival that of the 1970s.

1979: A YEAR OF BALANCED FEDERAL BUDGETS AND SPENDING LIMITATIONS

Before 1900, the government of the United States was rarely troubled with budget deficits. Rapid economic growth throughout the nineteenth century generated sufficient revenues, primarily from customs duties, to finance federal spending. Although deficits sometimes occurred due to economic decline or war, budgetary surpluses in good years quickly restored the overall balance. These infrequent deficits were clearly viewed as exceptions from the principle of fiscal balance, and corrective measures were invariably promised and soon taken to restore normal conditions. As a result, the real value of government debt per capita in 1891 was about the same as in 1791.

The philosophy that government should be self-supporting implied a practice of balanced budgets. In the event, the frequent surpluses made federal borrowing a rare event. Revenues and expenditures were not incorporated into an overall official federal budget until 1921, but the presence of a budgetary surplus each year during the 1920s suppressed debate on a statutory or constitutional requirement for a balanced budget.

During the past 50 years, however, the federal budget was balanced only nine times and only once in the past 20 years. The outcome is one-sided: $626 billion in deficits and only $34 billion in surpluses. In 1977, real debt per capita was 23 times greater than at the start of the century.

Although President Roosevelt campaigned in 1932 on a balanced budget platform and several bills were introduced in Congress in 1936 to balance the budget, national interest lay dormant until 1975 (with the exception of the Eisenhower years). In that year the Senate Judiciary Committee held hearings on balancing the budget, from which arose the movement led by the National Taxpayers Union to mobilize state

TABLE 2

1978 State Limitations

Part One: Spending Limitations

Approved				Defeated			
Arizona (state spending limited to 7 percent of total personal income; half of state money to be exempt from the limit; emergency increases allowed with approval of two-thirds of legislature)				Nebraska (local governments and school boards can increase spending by more than 5 percent per year only if four-fifths of state legislature approves or population or enrollment increases by more than 5 percent)			
	Yes	382,031	78.2 percent		Yes	203,474	44.8 percent
	No	106,684	21.8		No	250,357	55.2
		488,715	Turnout = 29.8 percent			453,831	Turnout = 40.6 percent
Hawaii (state spending can increase only at rate of increase of state economy; limitation on state bonded indebtedness; tax refunds or credits made if general fund has a surplus exceeding 5 percent of revenues for two consecutive years)							
	Yes	168,508	66.8 percent				
	No	83,718	33.2				
		252,226	Turnout = 39.6 percent				

Part Two: Tax Limitations

Approved	Approved	Defeated
Alabama (restricts increases in all kinds of property taxes in any county to 20 percent; different kinds of property assessed at different rates) Yes 313,577 60.4 percent No 205,782 39.6 519,359 Turnout = 19.9 percent	North Dakota (reduces income tax rates for individuals, increases them for corporations; new tax rates would require approval by two-thirds of legislature) Yes 127,280 65.1 percent No 68,215 34.9 194,495 Turnout = 42.4 percent	Arkansas (repeals 3 percent sales tax on food and prescription drugs) Yes 223,004 45.0 percent No 272,086 55.0 495,090 Turnout = 32.3 percent
Idaho (limits property taxes to 1 percent of current market value; two-thirds vote of legislature required to impose any new tax) Yes 162,486 58.4 percent No 115,737 41.6 278,223 Turnout = 46.6 percent	South Dakota (two-thirds vote of legislature required to raise sales tax on real property tax) Yes 113,901 52.9 percent No 101,207 47.1 215,108 Turnout = 44.4 percent	Michigan ("Tisch Amendment" to limit annual property tax increases to 2.5 percent) Yes 1,025,824 37.3 percent No 1,723,968 62.7 2,749,792 Turnout = 42.9 percent
Michigan ("Headlee Amendment" to limit taxes to current percentage [9.5 percent] of state personal income; ties property tax increases to level of inflation; requires voter approval of all new tax increases and bond issues) Yes 1,444,456 52.5 percent No 1,307,989 47.5 2,752,445 Turnout = 43.0 percent	Texas (increases homestead exemptions, reduces taxes on the elderly, reduces farm and timberland taxes) Yes 1,550,234 84.1 percent No 293,233 15.9 1,843,467 Turnout = 20.3 percent	Oregon (legislative referendum on more relief to homeowners and renters, but no relief for business) Yes 382,280 45.1 percent No 465,746 54.9 848,026 Turnout = 48.5 percent
Nevada (limits property taxes to 1 percent of current fair market value, prohibits assessment increases of more than 2 percent per year) Yes 140,310 77.8 percent No 40,109 22.2 180,419 Turnout = 39.1 percent	West Virginia (allows school taxes and bonds to pass by simple majorities instead of present requirement of 60 percent) Yes 141,743 43.8 percent No 181,906 56.2 323,649 Turnout = 24.1 percent	Oregon (limits property taxes to 1.5 percent of market value) Yes 422,139 48.3 percent No 451,985 51.7 874,124 Turnout = 49.9 percent

Source: *Public Opinion*, November/December 1978, p. 28.

legislatures to call a constitutional convention to require a balanced budget. Five state legislatures approved balanced budget resolutions in 1975. By May 1979, the number had grown to 30, four short of the two-thirds required.

Economic trends and the political temper of the times have made the balanced budget an issue with tremendous popular appeal. The public believes that chronic deficit spending causes several harmful consequences: inflation, decreases in private spending and investment, and increases in interest rates, with reduced investment in capital goods.

Another movement seeks an amendment limiting federal spending. In July 1978, a number of distinguished economists and public servants formed the National Tax Limitation Committee to work on a proposed constitutional amendment to limit federal spending. A draft of the amendment was released in Washington, D.C., on January 30, 1979, and offered in Congress by Senators John H. Heinz and Richard Stone several months later. The amendment seeks to limit increases in total government outlays to the percentage increase in nominal GNP of the last calendar year preceding the current fiscal year. If inflation exceeds 3 percent, the permissible increase in total outlays is reduced by one-fourth of the excess of inflation over 3 percent. The amendment further stipulates that fiscal surpluses be used to reduce the public debt of the United States. It also permits declarations of emergency, allows increases in total outlays if approved by a three-fourths vote of Congress and a majority of state legislatures, prevents reductions of grants to state and local governments, and contains an enforcement provision.

THE BALANCED BUDGET AMENDMENT: PROS AND CONS

Proponents of a balanced budget amendment couch their support in normative, economic, and political terms. The moral benefits of a balanced budget are not to be overlooked. A balance between taxing and spending means that society must live within its collective means. A balanced budget is analogous to the financial circumstances of an individual household or firm. The balanced budget thus conceptually links governmental finance and the average family's budgetary practice.

A balanced budget amendment would solidify the link between spending and revenue. It would compel public officials to determine first what resources are available to government and, against that constraint, choose among the many competing claims on public spending. It would ensure that the people know exactly how much it will cost in terms of taxes to finance federal programs.

What are the economic consequences of a balanced budget amendment? It is generally acknowledged that spending programs are more popular with the voters and Congress than higher taxes. Thus, a balanced budget requirement forces Congress to weigh the costs of expenditure programs while allowing Congress to take credit for the benefits these programs provide. An amendment is deemed necessary because such modest reforms as the Congressional Budget Act of 1974 only marginally curbed the federal government's propensity for deficit financing.

Most important, a prohibition of deficits will reduce inflation. It will, as well, contribute to price stability and to increased spending by the private sector, increase after-tax returns to capital and labor, slow depreciation of the dollar in foreign exchange markets, and prevent massive new outbreaks in spending except in emergencies. A balanced budget will be excellent therapy for national inflationary psychology; it will help end the bias toward borrowing and spending.

Under the amendment, if politicians voted new spending programs, they would have to eliminate old programs or raise additional taxes. Resistance to the elimination of existing programs or to tax increases would discourage many new spending proposals and eliminate the current bias towards overspending. It would end future deficits and eliminate the inflationary effect of new money creation, which has in past years financed these deficits.

Although some regard any tax increase as inherently undesirable, a balanced budget amendment still permits an increase in public spending if there is an overriding democratic consensus. In practical terms, however, and in the current era of tax revolts, few politicians will want to campaign on a platform of higher taxes to finance more spending. The balanced budget will require that tax increases be explicitly voted, rather than implicitly imposed by deficit spending and inflation—this will effectively constrain new government spending.

Political values and perceptions are important determinants of government action. For this reason, a balanced budget amendment is especially attractive. It is easy to understand—every housewife understands the need for living within her means. It is also widely supported. Polls show overwhelming support for a balanced budget, often by margins of six-to-one.

Most supporters of the balanced budget amendment are keenly aware of practical difficulties in its implementation. Every proposed amendment contains an emergency escape-hatch clause, based on some declaration of emergency and a two-thirds or greater vote by Congress, to suspend the requirement in the event of war or serious economic downturn. Some proposed amendments suggest the creation of a "rainy day" reserve fund from budgetary surpluses for periods of temporary deficit. Others suggest that a small unplanned excess of, say, 2 percent be permitted under the balanced budget requirement and that any sum over 2 percent be treated as outlays of the next fiscal year.

Although practical difficulties are acknowledged, most proponents regard continuation of present fiscal policy—deficits and concomitant inflationary pressure—to be far more dangerous than grappling with the implementation of a balanced budget constraint.

Opponents of a balanced budget amendment fall into two camps: those who prefer a spending limitation and those who oppose a constitutional restraint on fiscal flexibility.

Professor Milton Friedman exemplifies the first view. He contends that drafting a technically satisfactory amendment in order to achieve a balance over a period of good and bad years is difficult. What would happen if any reserve fund ran out in the face of unforeseen deficits? A constitutional limitation on spending, in his view, avoids this pitfall and effectively achieves his target of limiting the future growth in government spending.

Professor Paul Samuelson takes the second position and argues that economics is an inexact science and that it would be unwise to freeze policy rules for the indefinite future and thereby limit the flexibility required to deal with future problems.[9] Moreover, in his view, the present system of American democracy can cope with any national trend toward unreasonably large government. And if the escape clause is too lenient, the amendment becomes only a pious resolution cluttering the Constitution.

Other criticisms of a balanced budget highlight its conceptual difficulties. What does "outlays" mean? How does one prevent the emergence of "off-budget" spending or the separation of current and capital expenditures now found in several state budgets? How does Congress cope with the general unreliability of economic forecasts? What are the appropriate enforcement provisions if a projected balanced budget becomes unbalanced in the course of the fiscal year? How and by whom will the budget subsequently be made to conform to the constitutional prohibition?

My purpose is not to consider the pros and cons of a constitutional convention. But the passage of such resolutions by 30 states by May 1979 makes the issue of a balanced budget pressing.

A SPENDING LIMITATION AMENDMENT: PROS AND CONS

Proponents of a spending limitation often advance the same arguments as those who advocate a balanced budget. The fundamental defect in present budgetary procedure is that Congress considers spending programs on a piecemeal basis and the public cannot express its views on the size of the budget.

The major objective of a spending limitation amendment is to link the growth of government to growth in the private economy, either in terms of GNP, personal income, or changes in the CPI. Specific clauses could allow for upward or downward adjustments in the level of government spending to cope with emergencies.

Advocates of the National Tax Limitation Committee amendment (the Heinz-Stone amendment) emphasize its feasibility for limiting government. The amendment adeptly avoids the major pitfall of the balanced budget. Since outlays are based on the calendar year preceding the current fiscal year, spending growth is based on actual data and not economic forecasts. The 21-month difference between the fiscal year and the calendar year on which it is based incorporates, in the view of its advocates, an automatic countercyclical element in federal spending. Slow economic growth will slow federal spending 21 months later when the economy may be booming. Conversely, rapid economic growth will increase government spending 21 months later when the economy will most likely be slowing down.

The Heinz-Stone amendment also contains a strong incentive to reduce inflation. A rate of inflation above 3 percent cuts into the share of government spending. Thus, to maximize its real spending, the government would attempt to minimize inflation. The link between real economic growth and government spending would encourage more federal interest in promoting economic growth.

Critics of a spending limitation are again of two minds. One group opposes any constitutional limitation on federal fiscal policy or flexibility. The second claims that a balanced budget amendment is superior to a spending limitation.

There is nothing inherent in a spending limit that prevents future deficits. Projections showing that inflation or economic growth will produce a balanced budget under a spending limitation (because under our progressive tax structure, tax revenues increase faster than GNP) will prove false if Congress votes tax reductions. Thus, the pressure on monetary inflation would not necessarily be eliminated.

Another defect of many of the proposed spending limitation measures is their complexity. Typically complex proposals lose support as ratification nears. Moreover, some critics object to the inflexibility of these measures, which would prevent desirable increases in expenditures unless a state of emergency is declared.

TRENDS IN THE 1980S

Tax and spending limits are the culmination of the past fifteen years of high inflation, rising taxes, runaway government spending, and the simultaneous recognition that higher and higher levels of public spending do not readily solve social problems. All levels of government grew rapidly in the past few decades; in the 1980s, in contrast, they will face both growing public pressure against and new constitutional constraints on government growth. Forty-seven states already enjoy some constitutional or statutory prohibition of or restraint on budgetary deficits. More than a dozen states must operate under tax or spending limits. After election day 1980, the number will reach or surpass several dozen. Future increases in state and local taxes or spending will be linked to increases in such indicators as personal income, the CPI, or population increase.

The new limits on spending or taxing mean that state and local governments cannot practice deficit finance or raise new taxes to pay for new spending programs. If inflation, coupled with progressive personal income tax rates, increases state revenues more rapidly than personal income or the CPI, taxpayers in those states will enjoy tax refunds or cuts in tax rate schedules, subject to provisions regarding accumulated budgetary surpluses.

Economic circumstances vary widely across states, and, as we have seen, tax and spending limits assume a variety of forms and extremes—no one limit fits all circumstances. Nor is it necessarily desirable that standardization should be imposed.

Still, the trend of tax or spending limits raises some general questions. As in California, Proposition 13-type property tax limitations may lead to state funding as a substitute for reduced property tax collections. But the catch is the accompanying prospect of greater centralization, with possible loss of local autonomy. This prospect troubles enthusiasts of local democracy and community control. Unless state assistance is free of strings (for example, block sharing of sales taxes with local government, without categorical stipulations), local influence and authority may wane.

Curiously, the concern about autonomy of state and local governments has not prevented or even slowed the enormous increase in intergovernment grants. Federal grants-in-aid to state and local governments have grown from the modest total of $7 billion in 1960 to $80 billion in 1980. Federal grants to state and local governments are equivalent to 32 percent of locally collected tax receipts and have doubled in the past twenty years. The rhetoric calls for state or local autonomy; in reality localities seek more state aid and the states, in turn, more federal aid.

What is the likely impact of spending or tax limits on shared government programs? Some say that spending limitations will force financially strapped local governments to maintain their grant-in-aid matching money and further cut their support of conventional services. Others say that the effects will be minimal because local governments share state and federal priorities. Moreover, should the federal government maintain current levels of aid to states and cities that voluntarily cut their expenditures for matching funds?

The entire system of intergovernmental grants rests on the premise of continued public sector spending; it was not designed to work smoothly in an era of declining state and local government spending. We are thus likely to see greater attention to analyzing the impact and equitability of intergovernmental grants and matching funds. We will also see increased pressure on the states and federal government to pay the full costs of programs and policies imposed or initiated from above. Indeed, the entire system of intergovernmental grants will be called into question, especially if a tax or spending limit becomes national law.

Trends at the national level are more difficult to forecast. However, only the federal government has the power to print money and sustain indefinite budget deficits.

The congressional movement to eliminate budget deficits should continue to grow. As of April 1979, some 238 lawmakers sponsored either constitutional amendments or laws requiring the government to balance its budget except in time of war or other national emergencies. Another 108 senators and representatives, led by Congressman Jack Kemp and Senator William Roth, proposed a 30 percent tax cut over three years, equal to about 170 billion dollars. Still another 131 lawmakers favor an automatic adjustment of tax brackets each year to account for inflation.

However, no one issue dominates national politics for long. If the number of states calling for a constitutional convention fails to reach 34, Congress will probably continue to hold hearings and talk of the need for a balanced budget or spending limitation, but is unlikely to do more than deliberate. But as the 34th state prepares to pass a resolution, Congress will move with alacrity to offer its own amendment. Thus, the movements to limit taxes and spending are more likely to succeed at the state than the federal level.

RECOMMENDATIONS FOR THE 1980S

Most states have some limitation on deficit finance. However, these bans have not prevented a steady growth in state spending and taxes. Tax or spending limits are necessary to halt, and perhaps reverse, the trend to increased government spending.

Every state should enact a statute or constitutional amendment that links increases in taxes or spending to an appropriate measure of individual economic gain. These measures should include procedures for emergency overrides, but by no less than a two-thirds vote of the state legislature or of the voters in a local jurisdiction. (Gann's proposed "Spirit of 13" amendment is an excellent model.)

At the same time, to cut taxes and spending without cutting public services, the following strategies can be adopted.

1) Let users pay. This policy puts the burden of support for services on users, rather than on taxpayers in general. It therefore cuts costs by discouraging casual use of limited resources. This policy would apply to recreation programs, parks, golf courses, camping permits, swimming pools, libraries, cemetaries, housing developers, utility fees, airport fees, bridge and ferry tolls, school lunch charges, and other areas. Consumers of these "public" services pay privately for bowling, movies, and other recreational activities. There is no reason why many more publicly provided services cannot be supplied on a commercially viable basis. The general principle of charging for a commodity what it costs ensures that someone who is content with an economical supply of it does not subsidize someone else who wastefully luxuriates in it.
2) Contract for services. Increasingly cities and counties have realized tax savings by turning to outside contractors. A study completed at the Columbia University Graduate School of Business found that refuse-removal firms under contract to medium-sized cities cost nearly 30 percent less than similar public municipal programs. Another example is the innovative fire service protection based in Scottsdale, Arizona; a private company services thirteen communi-

ties at about half the expense of neighboring fire departments of equal quality. Urban landscape maintenance costs in Lynwood, California, fell by one-third when a private landscape firm took over tree trimming from the city.[10]

Other examples of contracting out include food preparation (fast-food franchising) in high school cafeterias, data processing for government records, security guards for public buildings (at lower cost than municipal police), golf course maintenance, vocational education, child day-care (which has been provided in Dade County, Florida, for half the per capita cost of county services), maintenance of municipal vehicle fleets, and even private provision of bustop shelters (which derive their revenue from the sale of advertising space). In the past decade, perhaps 500,000 municipal jobs have been transferred from the public to the private sector, at great savings to taxpayers.

3) Fund mandated services through the state. This strategy requires a state to fund, from within the state's spending or taxing limit, the total cost of programs it mandates on local governments. Otherwise, a state could shift spending to local units of government and thus free funds for new spending programs without violating the limit. Local governments would then have to raise new taxes (unless the limit applied to each unit of local government as well) or cut back services that residents may value more highly than those imposed by the state.

4) Emphasize private substitution. There is no inherent reason that Americans should look to government for those goods and services that can be individually acquired. For example, each of us can make a more determined effort to install double dead bolt locks, smoke alarms, and fire extinguishers and take other preventive measures to reduce security or fire risks. These private actions and expenditures may be more effective than spending a similar number of dollars in public police and fire programs.

   There is no reason that individuals cannot provide for their own recreational activities, education, medical care, and housing and pay utility rates that fully support the cost of private provision. Of course, at least for the foreseeable future, that small minority of Americans whose limited incomes preclude some minimally acceptable level of consumption of basic goods and services will remain. But the current mix of welfare and income transfer programs addresses this community of people. It is neither necessary nor appropriate for the general taxpayer to support the provision of goods and services that the overwhelming majority of Americans can afford to provide for themselves.

At the national level, I recommend that Congress propose the following constitutional amendment, which requires a balanced budget and limits federal spending:

A PROPOSED CONSTITUTIONAL AMENDMENT TO BALANCE THE FEDERAL BUDGET AND LIMIT FEDERAL SPENDING

Section 1. To promote responsible fiscal and monetary policies, the government of the United States shall be required to balance its budget.

a) Total outlays in any fiscal year shall not exceed total revenues. Total outlays shall include budget and off-budget outlays and exclude redemptions of the public debt and emergency outlays.
b) When, for any fiscal year, total revenues received by the government of the United States exceed total outlays, the surplus shall be used to establish a reserve fund up to but not exceeding 5 percent of total annual outlays, which may be used to cover a temporary deficit in any one year. All other surplus revenues beyond this 5 percent reserve fund shall be used to reduce the public debt of the United States until such debt is eliminated.
c) To permit orderly implementation, the requirement for a balanced federal budget shall be phased in over a period not exceeding four years, beginning with the first fiscal year following ratification. Any deficit on that date shall be reduced by no less than one-fourth in each of the four succeeding fiscal years.

Section 2. To protect the people against excessive governmental burdens, total outlays of the government of the United States shall be limited. Total outlays in any fiscal year shall not increase by a percentage greater than the percentage increase in nominal gross national product in the last calendar year ending prior to the beginning of said fiscal year.

Section 3. Following declaration of an emergency by the president, Congress may authorize by a two-thirds vote of both Houses a specified amount of emergency outlays in excess of the total outlays limit for the current fiscal year, and it may suspend for that emergency period the balanced budget requirement by a specified amount in excess of the reserve fund described in Section 1b.

Section 4. The government of the United States shall not require that state or local governments engage in additional or expanded activities without compensation equal to the necessary additional costs.

Section 5. The Congress shall enact all necessary legislation to implement this article.

Section 1 mandates a balanced budget and limits total federal outlays to federal revenues. The amendment aims at attaining a balance over a period of years; it is somewhat flexible on a year-to-year basis. The principle of the annuality of revenue and expenditure estimates is necessary if the Congress is to exercise its responsibilities and powers, but it is wrong to look strictly at each year separately. On average, taxes and spending should even out, and the existence of reserves should permit steady implementation of agreed-on programs in the event revenues fall short of projections. Note finally that the requirement of balance is phased in over a gradual period to minimize disruptions in the conduct of the public finances.

Section 2 follows the Heinz-Stone amendment and limits increases in spending to the percentage increase in GNP of the calendar year preceding any fiscal year.

Section 3 allows the president and Congress to suspend the balanced budget and spending limit provisions for one year. Simultaneous conduct of the Vietnam War and the Johnson administration income transfer programs could not have been possible under this amendment without three successive declarations of emergency. An explicit declaration of emergency, in turn, may have restrained the massive deficits or wartime spending between 1966 and 1968 and stimulated public debate on these two important national policies.

Section 4 prevents the federal government from circumventing a constitutional spending limit by mandating that states or local governments engage in new or expanded activities without full federal funding. Finally, Section 5 leaves to the Congress responsibility for enacting legislation to implement the details and procedures of the amendment.

The proposed amendment is, I think, not so long as to clutter the constitution, but sufficiently detailed to ensure consensus on its meaning.

If my proposed amendment is adopted, federal finances would be conducted in the same manner as in those states with both balanced budget and spending limit provisions. The balanced budget requirement means that new spending programs must be funded by levying new taxes or by terminating old spending. It also means that federal budget deficits will no longer be the inflationary force they have been since the mid-1960s.

But since a balanced budget clause does not prevent government spending as a share of national output from rising (as has taken place in many states), only the inclusion of a spending or taxing limit ensures that the size of government can be stabilized (perhaps decreased), save in emergency years. Together the two provisions will compel fiscal responsibility on the part of the federal government for the first time in

50 years. It is the American people who will benefit in the decade of limits—the 1980s.

NOTES

1. The title of this section is taken from Roger A. Freeman, *The Growth of American Government* (Stanford, Calif.: Hoover Institution Press, 1975).

2. These totals are calculated from the *Economic Report of the President 1979* (Washington, D.C.: Government Printing Office, 1979): Table B-69, p. 263.

3. See Michael J. Boskin, "Some Neglected Economic Factors Behind Recent Tax and Spending Limitation Movements," mimeographed (December 1978).

4. *Public Opinion*, July/August 1978, pp. 29–31.

5. For a history of California's experience with property tax reform and spending limits, see Frank Levy and Paul Zamolo, "The Preconditions of Proposition 13," Urban Institute Working Paper 1105–01 (October 1978), pp. 4–17.

6. See William H. Oakland, "Proposition 13: Genesis and Consequences," *Economic Review of the Federal Reserve Bank of San Francisco*, Winter 1979, pp. 7–24.

7. Mervin Field, "Sending a Message: Californians Strike Back," *Public Opinion*, July/August 1978, pp. 3–7.

8. *Limitations on State Deficits* (Lexington, Ky.: Council of State Governments, 1976).

9. *AEI Economist*, April 1979, pp. 4–6.

10. Mark Frazier and Jim Lewis, "New Ways to Cut Your Local Taxes," *Readers Digest*, March 1979, pp. 159–62.

Issues in Tax Policy

Dan Throop Smith

V

INTRODUCTION

The purpose of this summary statement is to describe briefly the major issues in federal tax policy that must be resolved, for better or worse and by intent or neglect, during the 1980s. No attempt will be made here to break new ground in theoretical analysis or even to summarize recent work in tax theory. Although much of that work is brilliant, it is based on assumptions so restrictive that the results have little bearing on actual decisions in public policy. Here, the focus is entirely on the principal alternatives confronting the public, the Congress, and the administration.

Tax policy arises from the interplay of economic, political, and social forces. Each of these is composed of various facets that are just as likely to conflict with as to reinforce each other. Advocates of specific provisions or changes in the law selectively choose among the diverse objectives of tax policy those that support their proposals. The most difficult task for those making or analyzing policy is to maintain perspective. Without adequate perspective, one can be swayed by an analysis that is not only plausible but valid as far as it goes.

All taxation is inherently repressive. This means that the higher the percentage of national income taken by taxation, the greater the likelihood that taxes will discourage and distort personal and investment activities. This general proposition seems self-evident. But it also follows that the higher the percentage of national income taken by taxes, the more important it is to design the tax structure to minimize the damage that inevitably arises from a large total tax burden. The worst of taxes will not do much harm if the total is small and tax rates are low. But even the "least bad" taxes—there are no "good taxes"—will do some harm if the total is large and tax rates are high, and inevitably have social and political as well as economic effects.

Discussions regarding critical levels of total tax burdens are gross oversimplifications. As guides to public policy they may even be dangerous. Excessive emphasis on the total amount distracts from the essential political decisions regarding the structure of the tax system—the specific taxes, and the rates and definitions that determine who pays what and under what circumstances.

It is easy to think of extreme examples to illustrate the importance of specific taxes and tax rates. An increase of one percentage point in a sales tax or in the basic income tax rate—though a burden to taxpayers as it reduces the funds available for private use—will not significantly affect decisions to work, to save, or to invest. Though a new tax of 100 percent on all increases in income over the prior year's income might well bring in even less revenue, it would greatly discourage and distort work, savings, and investment. The United Kingdom shortly after World War II actually had a tax of over 100 percent on certain increases in income. Without going to that extreme, our tax system has many unnecessarily destructive aspects.

This general analysis is on a quantitative basis and does not include revenue estimates. When the secondary effects of changes in tax laws are taken into account the effects on revenues often become quite uncertain; some reductions in rates may reasonably be expected to increase revenues. Recommendations for specific proposals would of course have to include estimates of probable immediate and longer-term effects on tax receipts. Changes involving short-term revenue losses can be phased in over several years. Laws reducing tax disincentives can stimulate economic activity even before the laws are fully effective.

The purpose of taxation is to transfer funds, in one way or another, from individuals and families to pay for government activities. As the government assumes a larger role in the nation's economy, people have to give up a higher proportion of their private income in taxes. Ideally, the division between private and government spending arises from a consensus, reached through the governmental process, on the best and fairest use of a country's total output of goods and services.

The benefits of wise government expenditures should offset the adverse effects of taxation, with a net improvement in productivity, consumer satisfaction, and the quality of life. But people do not directly associate the benefits of government services with the taxes they pay, as they do in justifying the efforts and risks involved in earning income to pay for private expenditures. The familiar phrases about working a certain fraction of one's time for the government and then working the balance of one's time for oneself reflects this point of view.

Taxation is repressive in that it reduces the direct personal rewards for all forms of economic activity—effort, entrepreneurship, savings, investment, and the productive use of natural resources. There really are no "tax incentives." So-called incentives simply reduce the inherent disincentives of all forms of taxation.

BALANCED BUDGETS OR DEFICIT SPENDING

The first major issue regarding tax policy is whether tax revenues and government spending should be currently balanced. Attitudes and policies regarding deficits in national government budgets have changed several times in the past half-century. The principal changes are merely noted here before turning to the major issues regarding the tax system itself.

Before the 1930s, any deficit was universally regarded as imprudent and irresponsible except in war periods when a deficit was accepted as inevitable but regrettable. During the 1930s deficits became respectable based to a considerable extent on Keynes' *General Theory* that developed the proposition that a low level of economic activity might not be self-correcting.

World War II made large deficits inevitable on a scale that was universally recognized as inflationary, but inflation was viewed as one of the social and economic costs of war. In the immediate postwar period, with the rapid decline in military expenditures, the deficit was automatically reduced. The traditional assumption that continuing deficits were unjustified was again put forth.

Balanced budgets became a national policy in 1953 with a new president and new Congress. But in contrast to the attitude prior to the 1930s, it was generally recognized that in a recession increases in taxes or reductions in expenditures would have perverse economic effects and that a temporary deficit might be acceptable to offset some of the reductions in private spending.

During the 1950s, the theoretical concept of a full employment balanced budget developed. This provided a rationalization for continued large-scale deficit spending, as long as the economy operated at less than an idealized, and perhaps unattainable, level of full employment. Though advanced in theoretical writing, the idea of deficit spending, while the economy is operating at less than an idealized full capacity, was not adopted until 1961 under a new administration. Throughout the Kennedy, Johnson, Nixon, and Ford administrations, there were repeated avowals of intent ultimately to balance the budget. But spending persistently ran ahead of revenues in both good and slack times.

In the 1960s, new theoretical support for deficit financing came from the Phillips curve, a statistical analysis that indicated a trade-off between inflation and unemployment. The idea that elimination or reduction of inflation would lead to increased unemployment was irresistible to those who favored increased government spending without increased taxation. No longer was it necessary to deny that continued deficit financing was inflationary. Inflation was accepted as a necessary price to pay to avoid unnecessary unemployment. But the belief in this trade-off has been responsible for more social, economic, and political harm than any other economic fallacy of the last half-century.

The error in the conclusion drawn from the Phillips curve arose from a failure to recognize that both unemployment and changes in prices are dependent on other, more fundamental, factors such as cyclical fluctuations. They are not causally related to each other. In boom times, prices rise and unemployment falls. In slack times, prices fall or rise less rapidly, while unemployment increases.

By the mid-1970s the long-term fallacy of the Phillips curve became widely recognized by economists. Simultaneous economic stagnation and inflation is well described by the new word stagflation. But the idea of a perpetual trade-off between unemployment and inflation has persisted in popular and political circles. It has been routinely raised by those who object to any curtailment of government spending. A popular obsession with short-term economic buoyancy at the expense of more inflation and a greater risk of a major crash is a problem in many countries. Misguided pressures for recurring injections of fiscal and monetary stimuli have been particularly strong in the United States.

A new sentiment developed suddenly in this country in 1978–79, involving a complete reversal of public and political attitudes regarding continued deficit financing. The change reflected dissatisfaction with two aspects of the country's economic, political, and social life—continuing inflation and the increasing size and extent of government intervention in private and business affairs. Each of these was viewed as feeding on and reinforcing the other.

At the federal level, two alternative constraints have been proposed. One would require balanced budgets and the other would impose limitations on total spending. It has been presumed that either limitation would automatically achieve the other. But each would require escape clauses. A limitation on expenditures would not prohibit tax reductions, even if this led to continuing inflationary deficits. And a requirement for balanced budgets would not prohibit excessive growth of expenditures under escape clauses to deal with defense or other emergencies. Both constraints are needed, with necessary escape clauses on each.

CONFLICTING OBJECTIVES OF TAX POLICY

The second major issue of tax policy involves determining the balance among the various objectives and consequences of taxation. The general proposition that taxation should be used simply to raise revenue ignores the basic fact that taxes inevitably affect economic activity, investment, consumption, and relative prices.

In the past half-century, the simple and traditional objective of raising revenue—with minimum public complaint and minimum economic damage—has been complicated by a succession of additional explicit objectives, some of which have received only brief but concentrated attention. These include: fluctuations in revenue that help to counteract business cycles; reduction of impediments to economic growth; favorable balance of payments; economic neutrality; administrative simplicity; and differing concepts of equity, including programs for the redistribution of income. And since there are no accepted standards of equity, considerations on the fair distribution of the tax burden involve perennial controversy.

The objectives of tax policy are frequently contradictory. Elements that are conducive to economic growth may be regarded as inequitable by some people. Economic neutrality may be incompatible with economic growth. Refinements to increase equity are likely to be administratively complicated. And policies that are considered equitable by those whose goal is maximum redistribution of income may be considered inequitable and vindictive by others.

Each individual strikes his own balance among the many objectives of tax policy. Through the political process, the country will also strike a balance, which, in theory, represents an approach to a consensus. But, in reality, this balance represents whatever combinations of abstract principles, special interests, and demagoguery have influenced the political coalitions responsible for enactment of the ever-changing laws.

Equity

The single objective of fairness, or equity, in taxation has resulted in endless controversy and has produced a vast literature. An equal tax for each person, each adult, or each family would be simple and comprehensible. But since it would impose a disproportionately heavy burden on those with small incomes, it was not used to any extent even in early colonial days.

Renewed interest in welfare economics has recently expanded the breadth of the discussion. The phrase "ability to pay," so often asserted in discussions of specific tax legislation, is so subjective that it is essentially meaningless.

Since the ability to pay taxes depends on the potential taxpayer's economic well-being, a simple distribution of the total tax burden in proportion to economic well-being would seem fair. But the question immediately arises as to whether economic well-being is measured by income, wealth, or some combination of the two. And, more fundamentally, doubts arise regarding the fairness of proportionate taxes, in view of the large disparities in income and wealth. Ten percent of a large income is generally thought to represent less want-satisfying power than the same percentage of a small income. Those with larger incomes should thus pay proportionately more, and those with smaller incomes should pay proportionately less. Acceptance of this proposition leads to support of progressive taxation, with the rate rising with the size of the income or wealth. But once adopted, there is no objective way to determine what degree of progression is fair.

In recent years, many people have advocated progressive taxation, not simply as the fairest way to finance government expenditures, but for the avowed purpose of redistributing income and wealth. Direct transfer payments to beneficiaries of various government programs, which have grown faster than traditional government purchases of goods and services, provide a vehicle for redistribution under a progressive tax system.

The words inequality and inequity are frequently used interchangeably in both tax and popular literature. Inequality is presumed to be inequitable. Accordingly, any combination of expenditures and tax policies that reduces inequality is presumed to be equitable. Consideration of the validity of these presumptions carries one into concepts of justice that space does not allow us to pursue here. For many people inequality of result in contrast to equality of opportunity does not necessarily represent inequity. Attempts to secure equality of result may, in fact, represent an inequity, especially if they arise from the politics of envy, or a misplaced sense of social guilt.

Difficulties with Progressive Taxation

Two recurring errors are made in the application of a policy of progressive taxation in tax legislation. It is often argued that any tax that is not progressive is unfair and, hence, unacceptable. But this argument ignores the fact that to raise the total revenue required, our tax system must inevitably involve many different taxes. Fairness should be measured by the distribution of the total burden, not by each component.

The second error in the application of progressive taxation is the presumption that any increase in taxation should also be progressive, even when applied to a tax that is already progressive. Actually, a proportional increase in a progressive tax is itself highly progressive. A simple example illustrates this point dramatically. A 50-percent increase in the individual income tax rates, which range from 14 to 70 percent, might be thought of as unfair because it is only proportional. But a 50-percent increase raises the bottom rate only from 14 to 21 percent, reducing the previous net income by less than 9 percent from 86 cents to 79 cents on the dollar, while the top rate is raised from 70 to 105 percent, reducing the net income by more than 100 percent from 30 cents to a negative 5 cents on the dollar. A failure to recognize that an increase in tax should be appraised in terms of its effect on the amount remaining after an existing tax has led to unexpected results. One of these is noted in the discussion of the development of individual income taxation.

One other general proposition should be kept in mind when appraising the fairness of a tax system. Taxation represents only one aspect of the government's financial activities. The benefits of government spending are distributed unevenly among income classes. Though analyses of the distribution of benefits are imprecise and, inevitably, made on uncertain assumptions, conclusions generally indicate that benefits per capita are disproportionately large for those with smaller incomes. As programs involving transfer payments increase, this disproportion rises. With benefits tilted in favor of those with lower incomes, the combined effects of expenditure and taxation would involve redistribution downward, even if the tax system were proportional. Progressive taxation thus compounds the redistribution that would exist under proportional taxation.

INDIVIDUAL INCOME TAXATION

The modern individual income tax in the United States was introduced in 1913, immediately after the adoption of the Sixteenth Amendment authorizing income taxation. Income taxation had previously been declared unconstitutional as a direct tax. Policy issues regarding individual income taxation can be grouped under two major headings: tax rates and the definition of taxable income.

Tax Rates

The normal tax rate in 1913 was 1 percent on income above $3,000, with a surtax starting at another 1 percent on income above $20,000 and rising to 6 percent on income above $500,000. In the congressional debates, no one challenged the statement by one of the proponents that a combined tax above 10 percent was unimaginable. By 1917, the top rate had risen to 67 percent under the combined pressures for revenues and resentment against potential profiteers during World War I. The top rate was gradually reduced by 1926 to 25 percent, where it stayed until 1932. In that year, in a vain and misguided attempt to balance the budget, the bottom rate was raised from 1.5 to 4 percent and the top rate to 63 percent.

The increase from 25 to 63 percent in the top rate might be thought of as roughly proportional to the increase in the bottom rate from 1.5 to 4 percent—an increase of something over 150 percent. But the 150-percent increase in the bottom rate reduced net income by less than 3 percent from 98.5 cents to 96 cents on the dollar. At the same time, net income at the top was reduced from 75 cents to 37 cents, or by more than 50 percent. The absurdity of appraising the impact of changes in tax rates only in terms of the rates themselves is apparent when one thinks of the subsequent increases in the bottom rate from 4 to 20 percent, or by 400 percent. An increase in the top rate of equal proportions would have pushed that rate to 315 percent.

When rates are reduced, the impacts on net income operate in reverse. A reduction in the top rate from 90 to 80 percent doubles the net income from 10 cents to 20 cents on the dollar, while the full elimination of a bottom rate of 20 percent would increase the net income from 80 cents to a dollar, or by 25 percent.

During World War II, rates were increased drastically, the top rate rising to 91 percent and the bottom rate to 20 percent. It was recognized that only in the bottom brackets could significantly more revenue be obtained. After the war, the range of rates settled back to the present range of 14 to 70 percent. In 1969, the top rate was reduced to 50 percent on so-called earned income, such as wages, salaries, and commissions.

The House Ways and Means Committee Report on that tax reduction noted the perverse effect of high tax rates on earned income. All of the reasons stated there are equally applicable to investment income. Apparently only political considerations prevented a general reduction to the 50 percent maximum. Senator Russell Long, chairman of the Senate Finance Committee, has stated that he favors a maximum rate of 33 percent on any sort of income. Thus, it has become politically acceptable to consider a reduction of high-income-bracket rates.

Tax Base

Taxable income conforms generally to the popular concept of income. It includes wages and salaries, interest, dividends, royalties, individual shares in the net profits of unincorporated businesses, and agricultural activities. But the general conformity is modified by a large number of additions and subtractions, each of which has some justification but around each of which there is endless controversy.

Additions: fringe benefits and imputed income (income-in-kind). Many forms of employment involve working conditions that increase the effectiveness of the employees, while giving them pleasure and perhaps saving them personal expenses. Meals in company cafeterias and dining rooms provide good examples. They can increase a sense of identification with the company and with fellow workers; and they can save time. But, in addition, they can also save money for employees when sold at less than full cost. The same reasoning applies to the dining rooms for members of Congress, cabinet officers, and those entitled to eat in the White House mess. Should the employer's net costs be allocated to employees as taxable fringe benefits? To do so is regarded as harassment by those subject to the additional taxation. But failure to do so may be regarded as negligence by conscientious tax officials, and may disturb other taxpayers who read of abuses of tax-free fringe benefits.

A distinction should be made between those fringe benefits that are provided in the ordinary course of business, and those designed primarily to save or postpone taxes. In general, tax administration seems to have gone too far in taxing fringe benefits merely on the grounds that they give pleasure to the recipients. Wherever the line is drawn, however, there will be borderline cases covering such diversities as the use of company cars, attendance at conferences in congenial surroundings, or free health clinics and company housing.

The Congress has specified that the employer's costs for health insurance and pension plans should not be taxable to employees, though pensions are fully taxable when received in years after retirement. A condition for postponement of taxation to beneficiaries is that the plans must be broadly applicable. They must not be of primary benefit to upper-income-bracket individuals who would gain the most from tax exemption or tax postponement. The reasons for the special treatment of pension and health plans are probably a combination of avoidance of administrative complications, encouragement of private provisions of socially desirable arrangements (medical insurance and retirement income), and avoidance of taxpayer resentment if they were taxed on imputed income determined by actuarial calculations. But there are recurring proposals to extend the concept of taxable income to include such items as elements in a comprehensive tax base.

Imputed income may also arise from a personal investment. Owner-occupied houses constitute the favorite example. A tenant pays rent from his after-tax income. A homeowner, by investing part of his capital in a home, gets his return by the right to occupy his home, and this return-in-kind is not taxed. Advocates of the broadest possible tax base argue for inclusion of the rental value of owner-occupied homes in taxable income. Others support our existing treatment on the grounds that it conforms to ordinary concepts of income. They note that the imputed income approach, if adopted, should be equally applied to those who own private automobiles instead of leasing them or own dress clothes instead of renting them for special occasions.

Deductions. The costs of earning income constitute the first category of deductions. They are similar to business expenses, except that they are personal in nature. The costs of work clothes and safe deposit boxes are good examples of expenses related to earned and investment income, respectively. Although they seem simple, there are many borderline situations. For example, work clothes may be appropriate for regular use and used as such. Safe deposit boxes may be used for memorabilia as well as investment securities. A trip to check on a large agricultural investment may be a prudent expense, but it may also provide a splendid vacation.

Tax administrators must be vigilant to prevent abuses that bring the tax system into disrepute. But they must be equally vigilant to avoid harassment that brings themselves into disrepute. There will always be honest differences of opinion as to where the lines should be drawn. Senior officials should refrain from attempts to modify the law administratively to make it conform to their ideological preferences.

A second category of deductions from taxable income includes catastrophes of various sorts, from losses by fire to major medical expenses. The tendency has been to restrict allowable deductions to amounts above a certain level, usually specified as a percentage of income. These restrictions simplify administrative details for both taxpayers and tax administrators, and seem consistent with the underlying goal of equity. Routine medical expenses and minor casualty losses are a part of life.

Deductions for charitable contributions have led to perennial controversy. Support for deductions is based on several propositions: donors do not benefit personally; private donations support activities that would often have to be supported by tax revenues; in a pluralistic society, it is useful to have a diversity of educational and charitable institutions; and, in the absence of allowable deductions, income taxation would dry up the source of charitable gifts. Opponents of such deductions argue that this practice permits private decisions concerning the use of what would otherwise be government funds. Opponents also argue that such deductions give greater benefit and incentive to high-income-bracket than to low-income-bracket taxpayers.

These differences of opinion raise a fundamental issue of political theory, regarding relations between the people and the government. Many thoughtful people believe that a deductible contribution represents private use of what should properly be regarded as government funds. Deductible contributions are thought of, in a loose sense, as government expenditures. But those who support the deduction of charitable contributions contend that the people grant the government specified sums in taxes. What is not taken away in taxes remains in private hands as a matter of right. Decisions concerning the appropriateness of deducting charitable contributions should be made on the basis of this fundamental issue. I strongly support the principle that the people provide limited funds to the government, and oppose the concept that what individuals have left in some way represents a government expenditure.

Opinions also differ on whether deductibility gives an incentive for charitable contributions. Income taxation shifts the balance between the net cost of personal use of income and that of a charitable donation. At a 70 percent rate it "costs" only 30 cents to give away a deductible dollar; the higher the tax rate the less the "cost" of a gift. But, more fundamentally, the higher the tax rate, the less income is left for personal use and charitable contributions combined. Deductibility merely neutralizes the restrictions previously imposed by progressive income taxation. Even after deductions, the higher-bracket taxpayer has a smaller proportion of his total income to use for all purposes than lower-bracket individuals. In economic terms, the net results of progressive income taxation and deductibility of charitable contributions will depend on the relative elasticity of satisfaction resulting from consumption, savings, and contributions. It is not unreasonable for some people to feel that the deductibility of charitable gifts does not fully offset the reduction in income for all uses resulting from highly progressive taxation.

Vigilance is necessary to prevent charitable contributions from being used for personal benefit. "Scholarships" for which only one's own children qualify, or reciprocal scholarships with a friend for the children of both, are obvious examples long since outlawed. Private foundations also have been misused for personal benefit.

Capital Gains

The appropriate tax treatment of capital gains is highly controversial. Many countries do not tax capital gains at all. No country taxes capital gains at the same level as ordinary income. Trust law, corporate law, national income accounting, and, traditionally, people thinking about their own financial affairs all distinguish between capital and income. But for over half a century, one well-supported theory in tax policy—the net accretion concept—has held that the net appreciation in the value of one's assets should be considered and taxed in the same way as wages, interest, rent, and business profits. As a concession to practicality, most advocates of taxing capital gains as income agree somewhat regretfully that taxation must be delayed until gains are realized. But, in their theory, postponement of taxation until that time represents a sort of interest-free loan from the government. Full taxation of capital gains is a major element in the proposed comprehensive income tax, which would also include many elements of imputed income.

Congress has never accepted full taxation of capital gains, recognizing that capital and income should be treated separately. The differential tax treatment usually has been given by including only one-half of capital gains in the tax base. For many years there was also an alternative maximum tax of 25 percent on some or all capital gains.

In 1978, the administration recommended a much higher taxation of capital gains. In probably the most dramatic event in the history of tax legislation insofar as relations between the executive and the legislature are concerned, the Congress not only rejected the administration's proposals, but substantially reduced the taxation of capital gains. Congress raised to 60 percent the amount of gain excluded from the tax base, and waived several ancillary taxes that had pushed the effective rate to over 49 percent. As a result, the top 70-percent rate applied to 40 percent of a gain produces a maximum effective rate of 28 percent. Some felt that the action of Congress was prompted by the administration position. Congressional consideration of the administration proposal directed attention to the perverse effects of the existing tax treatment of capital gains. Congress concluded that a reduction in that tax, more than any other, would reduce the tax barriers to the formation, maintenance, and effective utilization of the nation's capital stock.

Sentiment in Congress indicates the possibility of additional constructive relief in the taxation of capital gains. One possibility is allowance for a tax-free rollover by which capital gains would not be taxed if they were reinvested in other assets. This tax-free treatment is now available on the sale and purchase of a principal residence and directly or indirectly on pension funds, investment real estate, and individual retirement accounts.

As is true whenever differential tax rates apply, there have been numerous attempts to convert ordinary income into capital gains. The treasury, the Congress, and the courts must be on guard to prevent abuses. And those who most strongly support making a distinction between capital gains and income should be among the first to decry new abuses to protect the integrity of this fundamental principle. Unfortunately, these same individuals often resist any amendments, no matter how artificial or contrived a pretended capital gain may be.

INCOME TAXATION FOR INDIVIDUALS OR CONSUMPTION TAXATION

During the 1980s there will be much discussion and very likely some legislative action aimed at changing our traditional concept of taxable income for individuals from amounts received to amounts spent on consumption. The concept, though startling on first acquaintance, is really very simple.

If one were asked whether he would favor a deduction for savings in an individual income tax the answer would probably be yes. If one were then asked whether he would agree to have withdrawals from savings taxed as income to the extent that they were used for consumption, the answer, after a little hesitation, would probably again be yes. These two changes in the income tax would essentially make it into a consumption, or expenditure, tax.

The concept of consumption as a measure of individual income goes back to the early part of this century. It is as logical and theoretically defensible as the prevailing concept of taxable income. And it has the great advantage of removing the existing tax barriers to the formation, use, and maintenance of capital. Now that capital is recognized as having great economic value to society, as well as to individual owners, postponement of taxation until savings are consumed seems to be in the national interest.

To the extent that people save for later consumption and eventually consume their savings, a consumption tax would provide a closer approach to lifetime averaging. This goal is often advocated on equity grounds, and allowed to a limited extent in the complicated averaging provisions of the law. To the extent that inherited wealth or realized capital gains are used for consumption, a consumption tax would apply to these sums the full level of taxation.

CORPORATION INCOME TAXATION

The incidence, that is, the actual burden, of the corporation's income tax, imposed on the net income of corporations, is uncertain. Neither statistical nor theoretical analyses have provided definitive answers regarding the extent to which the burden of corporation income taxation ultimately rests on stockholders, on consumers, or, through a process of diffusion, on owners of all capital. In conventional theory, a tax on profits reduces profits by the amount of the tax, and the burden rests on stockholders in the form of lower dividends, lower corporate retained earnings, or both. But newer price theories and the opinion of many businessmen support the belief that corporation income taxes are treated as an element of cost. Ultimately, these taxes are reflected in the prices charged by the price leaders in many industries. And many of those who still believe that the tax rests on profits argue that through the operation of "efficient" capital markets, the returns to all forms of investments will adjust to each other. According to this line of reasoning, differential rates of return will be re-established. The substantial original reduction in return to stockholders because of taxation will be diffused to become a minor reduction in returns on all investments.

Uncertainty regarding the incidence (the actual burden) of the corporation income tax makes it acceptable—even attractive—politically. It produces a great deal of revenue. It is generally thought of as resting on business, which in turn is presumed to have limitless funds. Or, if the tax is thought of as resting on stockholders, they are presumed to be wealthy and hence proper subjects of additional taxation. The general public is pleased because it believes business is bearing the burden. Businessmen believe the tax is shifted to an appreciable extent, and stockholders do not feel directly the impact of the double burden on dividends.

But, in fact, wherever the burden of the corporation income tax finally rests, it is a bad tax. To the extent that it is shifted to consumers, it is a capricious excise tax falling on various commodities and services to unknown extents but in ways that would not be chosen by either a rational or a political process.

To the extent that the tax rests on the corporation and its stockholders, it discriminates against equity capital—the base for all corporate financing. This, in turn, is part of the base for increased national production and productivity.

Definition of Taxable Income

The definition of taxable corporate income is, with a few important modifications, the same as the definition of net income that appears in financial reports and is used by management. An equally good description of both taxable and business income is: net sales minus the cost of goods sold, general and administrative expenses, interest, and all state and local taxes.

For tax purposes, it is always desirable to take a deduction as soon as possible. An immediate savings in taxes, even if offset by a later payment, allows a company the use of the funds in the interim. Conversely, prompt collection of taxes gives the government the use of the funds that much sooner. Differences in the attitudes toward timing of deductions lead to continuing controversies on such matters as the speed of depreciation, and decisions as to whether research and development expenditures, promotional outlays for new products, and interest during major construction projects should be treated as current expenses or capital outlays. Conversely, taxpayers want to postpone the realization of income on such matters as prepaid subscriptions, while the treasury gains from immediate realization. Establishment of definite standards by legislation or regulation would be helpful for reducing controversy and litigation. For financial reports, business managements usually prefer exactly the opposite of what they seek for tax purposes. At least in widely owned companies, it is more desirable to show good near-term earnings, especially if there is hope that growth in later years will offset effects of prior postponements of recognition of expenses or early recognition of income.

The tax law has permitted the use of "last-in, first-out" (LIFO) inventory accounting since 1937. This method, by which the costs of the most recently acquired goods are presumed to be the cost of those currently sold, was adopted to minimize anticipated fluctuations in income over a business cycle as prices rise and fall. It has turned out to be vastly more important to insulate businesses from artificial increases in profits as prices rise permanently during subsequent inflation.

Inventory profits arising during inflation do not represent disposable funds; they are automatically tied up in inventory. They give a false sense of high profitability for individual companies and for business generally, with adverse effects on both wage claims and on public attitudes regarding price policies. The Department of Commerce and other agencies regularly adjust aggregate reported profits to eliminate inventory profits. It is regrettable that LIFO accounting was not generally adopted at the start of World War II.

Under continuing inflation, the Financial Accounting Standards Board may require LIFO accounting as one of the modifications necessary to reduce the overstatement of profits. If this is done, LIFO would be much more widely used for tax purposes.

Depreciation. The proper treatment of depreciation is the most important issue in the determination of taxable business income. It is also the most difficult on which to obtain agreement. Since there is no theoretically correct way to write off investments in industrial plant and equipment, the tax law should be based on whatever treatment is in the public interest.

Prior to the introduction of the corporate income tax in 1909, a variety of accounting conventions were used for depreciation. Conservative New England manufacturing companies depreciated their plants on their financial records down to one dollar as quickly as possible; it was a sign of prudence to do so. Railroads wrote off the cost of improvements on roadbeds only as they were replaced. Postponement until that time helped to permit the railroads to show profits in the earlier years after construction until traffic developed. Neither of these extreme treatments, nor any method between them, represented absolute truth.

With the coming of income taxation, the treasury took an interest in depreciation deductions for tax purposes. Rapid write-offs would be at the expense of current revenue. And business firms that had been postponing deductions for business purposes could not afford to pass up the immediate tax deductions. Write-offs spread in equal amounts over the expected life of individual items or groups of similar items of property was a simple rule, commonly used by companies attempting to avoid erratic fluctuations in reported income. Straight-line depreciation was thus the obvious method for general use for tax purposes. It continued to be almost the only method for 45 years.

In 1954, fundamental improvements were made to reduce the tax impediments to investments in plant and equipment. One of these involved authorization for the use of declining-balance depreciation, at double the rate used for straight-line depreciation. Faster depreciation would decrease the period in which funds were at risk, and it would increase the availability of funds for reinvestment. And the law recognized that less depreciation in the later years of use would be balanced by less productive use and higher maintenance expenses to give a smooth annual cost over the entire period of use.

After considerable deliberation, the treasury and Congress decided not to make adoption of declining-balance depreciation for tax purposes conditional on its application in a company's financial records. It was not anticipated that the difference between faster tax depreciation and slower book depreciation would come to be treated by the accounting profession as a "reserve for deferred taxes." This implied that companies had been granted a temporary respite in paying their taxes, which they would have to make up for in subsequent years.

For a company that continues operating indefinitely, and that continues retiring and replacing capital equipment, "deferred taxes" constitute a revolving account. For a growing company, deferred taxes is a constantly increasing account. The treasury and the Congress intended the faster depreciation write-offs to reduce taxes in the years when the charges were made. There was no intent to make a temporary or continuing interest-free loan to any company as critics have charged—and as the accounting rule implicitly indicates.

The introduction of the asset-depreciation-range presumption established acceptable estimates for useful lives in 1971. It was a major improvement in two respects. It reduced and largely eliminated controversies regarding life estimates, and it substantially shortened the periods over which the cost of depreciable property could be written off for tax purposes. An investment tax credit introduced in the same year has been popular with business, in spite of many changes. It was originally introduced on a temporary basis for "fine tuning" the economy. After a series of on-again, off-again changes, it seems to have finally settled at 10 percent for longer-lived assets. To the surprise of some of its proponents, it, too, is treated by accountants as a deferral rather than an immediate reduction in taxes.

In 1979, there was substantial bipartisan interest in adopting a simple set of capital recovery allowances to replace the traditional, but much-modified, system of depreciation allowances. A few broad categories of property would be established and given arbitrary write-off periods, with no reference to actual service lives. Ten years for buildings, five years for heavy equipment, three years for light equipment, and one year for tools and investments required to meet environmental standards would be reasonable.

The most useful single change in the rules for determining taxable business income would involve establishment of arbitrary and rapid capital recovery allowances. This would, of course, have to be matched by a provision for full taxation as ordinary income, rather than as capital gain, of any recovery of prior write-offs on sales of property up to the original purchase price. This is already done for most depreciable property. Faster capital recovery would bring our tax laws more in line with those of other countries. It would substantially reduce the tax impediments to capital investments, in part by increasing the availability of internal funds and reducing the periods over which invested funds are at risk.

Income from foreign subsidiaries. Among the subjects omitted because of lack of space is the taxation of business income earned abroad. Proposed changes intended to give a theoretical symmetry in our tax law would damage, if not destroy, the viability of much of our business investment abroad.

INTEGRATION OF CORPORATION AND INDIVIDUAL INCOME TAXATION

Dividend income is taxed twice. Corporate income is taxed to the corporation regardless of its retention or distribution to stockholders, and dividends are taxed in full to individual stockholders. No other form of income arising through corporations is subject to double taxation. All wages, salaries, interest, rents, and royalties are deductible in computing taxable corporate income. No other major country fails to give relief for some or all of the double tax.

The sentiment for some relief is widespread. This is based, to a considerable extent, on recognition of the need for more investment by corporations, as well as the adverse effect of the prevailing low level of stock prices in relation to earnings. Relief can be given at either the corporate or the stockholder level. At the corporate level, a deduction could be allowed for some or all of the dividends paid, making dividends comparable to interest. In the European Common Market relief is provided at the stockholder level, by allowing taxable stockholders to treat part of the corporate tax as a credit against their individual taxes on dividends received.

Good arguments can be made for and against each method of relief. A deduction for dividends paid would do away with the present penalty against equity financing, as opposed to debt financing, at the corporate level. It would be simpler than relief at the stockholder level. But it would mean that established companies in a position to distribute substantial dividends would be subject to lower taxes than companies that had to retain all of their income. These would in many instances be new or small companies. A higher tax rate applied to them would impede new enterprises and the continued independent existence of small companies. And to the extent the corporation income taxes are treated as costs, differential taxation on the basis of the extent of distribution of earnings is unjustified.

Relief at the stockholder level would remove or reduce the double taxation at the point where it is, in fact, doubled. In view of the uncertainty concerning the incidence of the corporation tax, a credit for only part of the corporation tax would seem reasonable. Relief at the stockholder level would have an immediate and commensurate effect in increasing stock prices, thereby decreasing the cost of new equity financing and reducing the inducement for one corporation to buy another or to retire its own stock. Furthermore, it would make American companies less of a bargain for foreign purchasers. The principal argument against relief at the stockholder level is that it can be more complicated if a perfectionist attempt is made to identify both the corporate earnings from which dividends are paid and the corporate taxes paid on those earnings. As a practical matter, a few rules of thumb can provide a reasonable balance between equity and simplicity.

Chairman Al Ullman of the House Ways and Means Committee has placed relief from double taxation high on his list of priorities. Some relief might have been adopted in 1978 if various business groups had not argued so vigorously about which method was preferable and for special provisions of particular importance to each. The general idea of relief from double taxation of dividends is a controversial one. Those interested in relief should have the good sense to let congressional leadership determine what is feasible and agree to support whatever method is preferred in Congress. Otherwise, relief may be postponed indefinitely, to the detriment of the groups that might benefit directly, as well as the economic well-being of the nation as a whole.

VALUE-ADDED TAXATION

During the last decade, a completely new tax on business has been universally adopted in the European Common Market. Value-added taxation (VAT) deserves all the attention it is receiving in this country. With sympathetic comments from the chairmen of the two congressional tax-writing committees and interest from the secretary of the treasury, consideration of VAT will almost certainly become the most important and far-reaching issue in tax policy for the 1980s.

This is not the place to analyze the numerous alternative forms and administrative aspects of VAT. European experience and the evolution of the laws in Europe can be helpful in decisions regarding the desirability of adopting a VAT and in formulating one if it is established.

One point deserves emphasis at the start. If one is asked what is good about a value-added tax, the answer must of course be "nothing"—except that it may be less bad than the present and prospective alternatives. But first, a simple description. A value-added tax is imposed as a percentage on a company's total sales, with a credit for the taxes incurred in the prices it has paid for its purchases from other companies. Stated more briefly, the base for a VAT is a company's sales less purchases.

The most frequently noted attribute of a VAT is the fact that it is neutral in virtually all respects. It is neutral with respect to capital-intensive and labor-intensive industries. In this respect, it differs from business income taxation, which discriminates against the use of capital in industry, and from payroll taxes, which discriminate against employment of labor. It is neutral with respect to all goods and services subject to the tax; there are no differential taxes depending on the particular products. A VAT is neutral with respect to vertically integrated business companies and those operating independently at successive stages in a long chain of production. In this respect, unlike a turnover tax, VAT does not penalize small, independent companies.

The VAT is always rebated on exports, thereby making a country's goods more competitive internationally. By contrast, the payroll tax and the income tax on business profits cannot be rebated on exports. And a VAT is imposed on all imports, which can have a positive influence on a country's international position.

A VAT is self-policing when collected on the basis of specific itemization on invoices. Each purchaser expects to have the full VAT shown on invoices paid to establish the credit he is entitled to against the VAT that he in turn must pay. The familiar controversies involved in determining the base for business net income taxation do not arise. When something is bought and paid for, the VAT included in the price is a current credit, whether the item goes into inventory or is sold immediately, and whether the item is a machine with a long or a short life. There is no need to guess the future use or life of the item purchased.

There are four principal objections to value-added taxation. The first is simply that it is new. The adage that "any old tax is a good tax and any new tax is a bad tax" has some real merit, as well as psychological insight. Any new tax involves shakedown problems. But those problems and fear of innovation as a matter of principle, if overemphasized, can prevent adoption of changes that in a short time will be recognized as improvements.

A second objection to a value-added tax is that it is not an income tax. For those who idealize income taxation for purposes of redistribution, any tax that is not inherently progressive is unsuitable. This point of view is based on value judgments, which involve inevitable differences of opinion. But since top-bracket tax rates do not and cannot produce a major part of the total required revenue, some other taxes must be relied on. Thus, it becomes a matter of comparing VAT to its alternatives. There is uncertainty as to what, in fact, would be the alternative to a new VAT. On this point no assurance can be given. Even a specific substitution of VAT for increased payroll taxes would not preclude subsequent increases in VAT as an alternative to other taxes or to finance larger expenditures.

The third objection to a VAT is also based on the distribution of its burden. Whether it would constitute a heavier burden on those with lowest incomes depends on what it replaces. But, in any case, to the extent justified or politically required, credits can be allowed against income taxes for the amounts presumptively paid in VAT. And the credits can be made refundable for those not subject to income taxation.

The final objection, and this is a fundamental one, is that the revenue yield of a VAT is so great that its availability will make restrictions on government expenditures less probable. A VAT is estimated to yield around $10 billion for each percentage point of tax, and the yield would rise automatically with inflation. Whether the chances of controlling expenditures would be worse with a VAT in place involves a political judgment based on relative risks and dangers.

PAYROLL TAXES

The original plan for financing the social security system, established in 1937, was for contributions (taxes) of equal percentages of payrolls up to a specified amount per capita to be paid by employers and employees. The funds were to be accumulated in a social security trust fund analogous to the reserve fund of a life insurance company. On an actuarially sound basis, the fund at any time would be sufficient, along with interest earned on the funds from the government securities in which they were to be invested, to pay the retirement benefits specified in the plan. Retirement benefits were based on income earned up to a specified maximum amount, with no additional benefits for a spouse or other dependents. Since benefits constituted much higher percentages of lower incomes, there was from the beginning a redistribution of income downward.

The original plan for accumulation of a fund to cover prospective liabilities for benefits has failed spectacularly. Rather than full funding, the reserve fund has come to be measured in terms of the number of months of current benefits it can cover. In spite of the fact that the tax rate has risen from 1 percent initially to 5.85 percent in 1977 for both employers and employees, changes in benefits have increased much more rapidly than taxes.

The redistribution feature of the system had been increased. In 1977, the earnings base on which taxes were to be paid was set to rise from $16,500 in 1976 to $42,600 by 1987, with the tax rate rising to 7.65 percent for both employers and employees. But, according to one calculation, only 15 percent of the additional revenue from that increase in the tax base is to be returned in increased benefits related to larger segments of income. Dissatisfaction with the financing of the social security system reached a high point in 1978, based on the prospective increases in tax rates and the large increases in the tax base.

Fundamental changes must and will be made in the financing of social security. Payroll taxes have apparently reached a politically acceptable upper limit. Alternative proposals include reduction of benefits, and financing part or all of the costs from other or general revenue sources. General revenue will come from either income taxation or a new form of taxation or more deficits. (The facetious phrase "take it out of the deficit" is too frequently a valid but ironic way of describing the result of reliance on general revenue.)

Value-added taxation, as universally used in the European Common Market, is the most reasonable and frequently mentioned new form of taxation to finance some or all social security payments. The present payroll tax increases the cost of labor, thereby falling more heavily on labor-intensive industries and thus shifting the balance in favor of the use of capital rather than labor in production processes. This fact should logically make labor groups prefer the value-added tax, which is neutral in its impact on labor and capital. But the traditional objections of labor to any broad-based tax have not yet been widely overcome in this country.

ESTATE AND GIFT TAXES

Estate and gift taxes are more important for their economic and social effects than as a source of revenue. The tax, at rates ranging from 18 to 70 percent, amounted to $5.3 billion in 1978. Its impact in limiting the amounts of property that can be transferred to succeeding generations within a family and in influencing the forms of investment is disproportionately high.

Estate taxation is paid out of capital to a greater extent than any other tax. It seems doubtful that prospective decedents increase their savings to any great extent to leave a contemplated net sum to their heirs or that heirs increase their savings in order to restore a net bequest to its pre-tax level. In this respect, estate taxation differs from income taxation that ordinarily reduces both consumption and savings. From an economic standpoint, estate taxation thus reduces the capital in the country below what it would be otherwise by almost the full amount of the tax. Also, in spite of several relief provisions it forces the sale or merger of many family businesses and farms of substantial value.

From a social standpoint, estate taxation reduces the inequality of wealth and income. Opinions on the desirability and fairness of taxation for this purpose are based on many differing value judgments. Estate taxes encourage the use of trusts extending beyond one generation. Beneficiaries of trusts are likely to have different activities and attitudes, for better or worse for both themselves and society, than those who own their capital outright. From an economic standpoint, property in the hands of trustees is likely to be invested differently than it would be in the hands of individual owners.

Estate taxation influences the timing of transfers of property between generations. The need to pay a tax at the time of a lifetime gift discourages transfers before death because the family immediately foregoes the income on the capital used to pay the tax. But the fact that the tax paid on a lifetime gift is not in the estate that is subject to the transfer tax at death works the other way. A step-up in the tax basis of property received as an inheritance has a freezing or lock-in effect for existing owners, discouraging sales of appreciated assets before death to avoid the capital gains tax. But the carry over of basis of inherited property continues the lock-in effect, as heirs are induced to postpone the capital gains tax indefinitely.

In brief, no other tax has so many economic and social ramifications in proportion to the revenue received as the estate and gift tax. An appraisal of the tax, and of any proposed changes in it, should take account of its many far-reaching consequences.

EXCISE TAXATION

Before the introduction of income taxation, the principal sources of federal revenue had been excise taxes, customs duties, and, for some periods, the proceeds from sales of public lands. During the past half-century, the latter two of these have withered away, and excise taxes, though continuing in absolute importance, have ceased to be of major relative importance. The continuing excise taxes on liquor and tobacco have been acceptable on sumptuary grounds. Aside from pro forma protests by representatives of the industries involved, there is little objection to them. Since most of them are at specific amounts per unit, rather than as a percentage of value, it would seem reasonable to convert them to a percentage basis at rates that would maintain the tax, in a period of continuing inflation, as at least a constant percentage of the retail price.

Aside from sumptuary taxes and excises appropriately levied on the benefit principle to pay for particular expenditures, there is little justification for selective excise taxes.

Gasoline taxes have been used to finance highway construction through the highway trust fund. That fund was established to prevent the cost of highways from becoming a charge on the general revenues. The tax receipts have moved ahead of expenditures, and there are various proposals to use some of the payments in the fund for mass transit. This diversion would be, to say the least, a distortion of the benefit principle that the highway trust fund represents, but it is probably less bad than placing an additional burden on income taxation.

IMPACT OF INFLATION ON TAX BURDENS

Inflation has led to unintended distortions in the distribution of the tax burden on individuals, as well as unintended absorptions of capital from business. The inequities and perverse economic effects are widely recognized. Fortunately, partial remedies are readily available for the problems; relief should not be postponed in hopes of finding ideal solutions.

A progressive income tax automatically takes proportionately more revenue from incomes as they rise in nominal amounts with inflation. The government thus gets in tax revenue a higher fraction of a constant level of real income. This built-in tax increase is no less inequitable because it is unintended. It permits the government to finance through increased taxes government expenditures that constantly rise as a fraction of the gross national product without having to vote higher taxes. The situation is bad from all standpoints, except for those who want to conceal the increasing burden of an expanding government.

The simple remedy is obvious. The brackets and personal exemptions in the individual income tax should be increased in proportion to inflation, thereby keeping them constant in terms of real income. Canada has successfully adopted this relief measure. Though it may be less than ideal, it provides a semblance of justice and would be a vast improvement over the present situation, which gives no relief at all.

Unfortunately, there is widespread confusion over the effects of inflation on the distribution of tax burdens at various income levels. It is frequently presumed that progressive taxation makes the increased tax burden proportionately heavier on those with smaller incomes. This is a false conclusion, based on superficial analysis. Actually, those with larger incomes are more likely to be proportionately more heavily penalized by progressive taxation if pre-tax incomes rise proportionately as a result of inflation. It is the essence of a progressive tax that for everyone at all income levels the top bracket (marginal) tax rate is always higher than the average rate. And it is the spread between a person's top bracket rate and a pre-inflation average tax rate that determines the proportionate burden from an inflationary increase in income.

Consider two extremes. A person just below the taxable income level has an increase in wages. This increment income is taxed at the lowest rate of 14 percent—an infinitely large increase in the rate of tax. But this person can keep 86 cents for each dollar of new income, in comparison with the pre-inflation situation with no tax, when he kept 100 cents on the dollar. If his income rose by $1.17 instead of one dollar, he would keep even with inflation after a tax of 14 percent.

But a person already in the 70-percent bracket, subject to an average tax rate of 50 percent, would keep only 30 cents of each dollar of new income. Previously he kept on the average 50 cents, on his pre-inflation income. Thus, even though he would stay in the same tax bracket, his income would have to rise by $1.67 to keep even with inflation under the same 70-percent rate that he was already paying. And a person with a marginal rate of 50 percent and an average rate of 30 percent needs $1.40 more income under inflation to keep even, though the marginal rate does not change.

It is the percentage spread between the pre-inflation average and marginal tax rates that determines the increasing burden of progressive taxation under inflationary income increases. A large increase in a marginal rate, when the average rate is still small, represents a smaller increase in burden than a substantial increase in a high average rate even though the marginal rate does not change.

Progressive taxation under inflation will drastically reduce the spread of net incomes after taxation unless larger incomes rise proportionately more than smaller incomes. Although this may be an intended result, we should at least recognize the actual result. At present, there is still a widespread mistaken belief that the burden of progressive taxation under inflation is proportionately heavier on those with lower incomes.

Increases in tax brackets and exemptions in proportion to inflation will remove unintended and disproportionate tax burdens on those whose incomes rise in proportion to inflation. But they will do little for those on fixed incomes. These are the real victims of inflation. It is they, mostly retired people, who suffer most and justify the well-known statement that inflation is the cruelest tax of all. Little thought has been given to special tax relief for those whose incomes have failed to keep up with inflation. Thus a distinction must be made, not between those with low and high incomes, but between those with substantially fixed incomes and those whose incomes have kept even with or run ahead of inflation.

Perhaps some sort of "reverse averaging" against a base of pre-inflation real income could be devised. Or, selectively, it could be recognized that interest and typical annuities provide little or no real income. It seems particularly unjust to tax the interest on treasury savings bonds when the full pre-tax interest would not be sufficient to offset the fall in the real value of the principal. The problem is large and will become even more serious. Relief will be difficult and expensive in terms of revenue. But for those trying to live on fixed incomes, the tax system is truly a cruel addition to the basic injury of inflation.

The final point to note is the well-known fact that, as prices rise with inflation, depreciation on original costs falls short of providing funds to replace plant and machinery at higher costs. The Financial Accounting Standards Board and the Securities and Exchange Commission are both attempting to modify accounting procedures to adjust for distortions in business income caused by inflation. Some of the proposed procedures are extremely complicated, requiring considerable judgment in their application, and with results that would not be readily comprehensible.

Quite apart from inflation, there is a strong case for allowing more rapid capital recovery under the tax law, as previously noted. The rates contemplated under these new rules would give sufficient relief to make it unnecessary to develop special and more complicated tax adjustments to take account of replacement or current costs of depreciable property. Inflation provides another reason for adopting relatively rapid tax allowances for capital recovery.

SUMMARY

Of the many current issues regarding federal tax policy, the following are of major importance for the 1980s. This summary includes recommendations on each topic.

1) Public revulsion against the total tax burden, the size of the government, and continued inflationary deficits have all come to a head in 1978–79. Proposals to limit total government spending or to require balanced budgets are sometimes thought of as alternatives, either one of which would achieve both results. But since each would have to have escape clauses, a combined constraint is desirable to secure the intended result.
2) Overemphasis on the total tax burden distracts attention from the importance of the structure of the tax system. The higher the total, the more important the structure. Some taxes that are not particularly repressive at low rates become very bad at high rates.
3) Taxation at high levels inevitably has many consequences in addition to raising revenue. It is necessary to maintain a balanced perspective among the many economic, political, and social consequences of taxation.
4) High rates of individual income tax have particularly perverse effects on economic activity and investment.
5) Taxable income generally corresponds to the ordinary understanding of income. A comprehensive tax base to include various forms of imputed income such as the rental value of owner-occupied homes and the actuarial value of employers' contributions to pension plans is advocated by some theorists. Extension of the tax base in this manner by statute or administration would be regarded as harassment by most taxpayers.
6) The advocates of a comprehensive tax base argue for full taxation of capital gains, preferably on the basis of changes in value even when gains are not realized. Probably no single change in the tax law would do so much damage to the economy. The reduction in the capital gains rate in 1978 was a major improvement. An extension of the existing provisions for tax-free re-investments (rollovers) of capital gains would be desirable to reduce the tax penalties against the formation, maintenance, and efficient use of the nation's capital.
7) Proposals to shift the base of individual income taxation to taxation on consumption deserve favorable consideration. Though the concept in the abstract seems strange and even formidable, a consumption base would simply involve a deduction for savings and inclusion in the tax base of withdrawals from capital for consumption.
8) The burden of the corporation income tax is uncertain. To the

extent that it rests on stockholders, it discriminates against equity capital, which is the base for business investment, which in turn is a principal base for increasing productivity. To the extent that the corporation income tax constitutes a business cost, it is shifted forward to consumers and constitutes a capricious excise tax. In either case, it is a bad tax, though the uncertainty regarding its incidence makes it politically attractive.

9) Tax allowances for more rapid recovery of investments in depreciable assets are desirable to reduce the tax penalties against investment in capital equipment and to bring our tax laws more nearly in line with other industrial countries.

10) Some form of relief from double taxation of corporate dividends is long overdue to reduce the tax barriers against investment in the private sector. No other major country still imposes full double taxation. Relief at the stockholder level would be preferable to relief at the corporate level, but whatever form is more acceptable politically should be widely supported.

11) Our tax treatment of income from foreign subsidiaries of U.S. parent companies puts them at a serious competitive disadvantage. Our tax law and regulations should be kept in line with those of other industrial countries.

12) Value-added taxation, as generally adopted in the European Common Market, is the most neutral form of taxation. It has neither the tax penalties against labor that exist in the payroll tax nor those against equity capital in the corporation income tax. It would be preferable to either of these taxes, as a partial substitute or as an alternative to a further increase in either.

13) Inflation has made more urgent the case for faster recovery of investments in depreciable property.

14) Inflation has shifted the burdens under the progressive individual income tax. Contrary to the popular presumption that those with lower incomes are more adversely affected, it is generally those in middle and upper income brackets who are hardest hit. Indexing of exemptions and tax brackets is urgently needed to reduce unintended changes in relative tax burdens and unlegislated increases in the total tax burden.

15) Those on fixed incomes suffer most under the combination of inflation and individual income taxation. It is almost unconscionable to treat as taxable income interest and annuities that, under inflation, do not constitute real income. In terms of equity, in-

come tax relief for those on relatively fixed incomes is by far the most important issue in federal tax policy.

Some of the foregoing recommendations would save revenue. Others would lose revenue in the short run. The latter could be phased in over a few years. But most of those that appear to forego or to lose revenue in the short run would increase the vitality of the economy and improve taxpayer morale in ways that would assure higher tax receipts within the near future.

Welfare Reform
Martin Anderson

VI

POVERTY IN THE UNITED STATES

In the early 1960s the United States, after eight years of peace and steadily increasing prosperity, roused itself and threw its considerable resources into two mighty efforts—bringing freedom to the people of South Vietnam and prosperity to the poor in America. At first the efforts on both fronts were tenuous and tentative. Then the tragic death of John Kennedy thrust Lyndon Johnson into the presidency. With characteristic force and impetuosity, and eager to establish himself as one of our great presidents, Johnson rapidly and dramatically escalated both wars.

We are all too familiar with the consequences of the war in Vietnam. Thousands of Americans were killed or maimed, billions of dollars were spent, and the Vietnamese people now live under a totalitarian regime with fewer freedoms than before. But most of the nation has lost sight of Johnson's other war. Our deep ignorance concerning what happened in the war on poverty is matched only by our acute awareness of all that happened in Vietnam.

As the war on poverty began to gain momentum in 1965, federal, state, and local governments together were spending over $77 billion a year on social welfare programs. Most of this government spending was for social security benefits and education. Just slightly over $6 billion was being spent on direct welfare. The task of eliminating poverty was viewed as extraordinarily difficult, if not impossible. At that time, some 33 million Americans were officially classified as poor. The poverty line

---

This essay draws on Martin Anderson's, *Welfare: The Political Economy of Welfare Reform in the United States* (Stanford: Hoover Institution Press, 1978).

was then a little over $3,000 a year for a family of four. Each year it was adjusted upwards to account for inflation. Tens of billions of dollars would have to be given to all those below the official poverty line if they were to catch or surpass that ever upward-moving standard that divided the country into the poor and the nonpoor.

And the money was given. An almost bewildering array of Great Society programs was launched, all with the central purpose of transferring tax dollars from the middle- and high-income classes to the low-income class. Millions of government checks, for tens of billions of dollars, were printed and mailed and cashed. The most ambitious attempt to redistribute income ever undertaken in the United States had begun.

As the efforts to combat poverty accelerated, a peculiar thing occurred. The harsh criticism of government efforts to reduce poverty that were prevalent in the early 1960s did not diminish. In fact, after the federal government officially declared war on poverty, the criticism of welfare seemed to grow in step with the proliferation of antipoverty programs. Welfare programs were denounced as stingy, unfair, demeaning to recipients, contributing to the breakup of families, and so narrow in their coverage that many poor Americans were destitute, some of them actually starving. Even the specter of hunger in America was raised on the evening television news. The people most knowledgable about our welfare programs denounced the entire welfare system, calling it a dismal failure, bankrupt, a mess in need of total reform. The more government seemed to do, the worse the situation seemed to become.

The most serious charge was that the war on poverty, in spite of the billions being spent, was not achieving its main goal: to raise poor people's incomes above the poverty line. As the monetary costs of waging wars both at home and abroad mounted, inflation began to take its toll. The official poverty line was adjusted upwards each year for inflation. But as the economy grew and welfare programs expanded and poor people's incomes increased, it appeared that the line they had to cross moved ahead of them at about the same pace.

According to the official government statistics, there has been virtually no change in the poverty level since 1968. For the entire period from 1968 to 1975 the proportion of Americans in poverty apparently hovered around 12 percent. In fact, the Census Bureau reports that there were 500,000 more poor people in 1975 than there were in 1968. Essentially we have been told that while some progress was made in reducing poverty during the early 1960s, little, if any, progress has been made since 1968.

Most of us, not having the capability or the desire to conduct our own census, accept what we have been told.

Yet one wonders. The United States is the richest nation in the world. Its citizens are, by and large, uncommonly generous and benevolent. Individuals contribute billions of dollars every year in small, private acts of charitable giving. Private charitable institutions spend billions more. Federal, state, and local governments spend tens of billions of dollars every year on welfare and income transfer programs. The economy has been growing steadily, creating more and more jobs. Is it possible that some 26 million people still live in abject poverty, having "extremely low incomes"; that one-eighth of this great nation is literally poor?

In 1970 Edward Banfield, professor of government at Harvard University, wrote:

> Some statisticians believe that most figures used considerably exaggerate both the number of persons whose incomes are low year after year and the lowness of their incomes. The poor (and the nonpoor as well) generally underreport their incomes, perhaps because they do not always know how much they receive or perhaps they are unwilling to tell. Also, every survey catches some people who at that particular time are below their normal incomes. (Thus, in 1960 it was found that in the large cities consumers with incomes under $1,000 were spending $224 for every $100 of income received . . .) Even if one takes the reported incomes as given, questions of interpretation arise. One economist, using the same figures as the Council of Economic Advisers, cut its estimate of the amount of poverty in half—from 20 percent of the population to 10 percent.[1]

In early 1975, Roger Freeman, senior fellow at the Hoover Institution at Stanford University, wrote,

> The annual income surveys of the Bureau of Census materially underreport income and . . . cash (money) income omits income in kind . . . Low-income persons get food stamps, housing subsidies, medical benefits, etc., none of which are counted as income . . . This makes income appear lower than it actually is . . . In other words, an unknown number of persons and families have a money income below the official poverty level in a particular year but may not be poor in any meaningful sense of the word.[2]

The welfare experts have all known this, probably for the last fifteen or twenty years. But few, if any, have had a clear idea of the extent of the understatement of income and how it varied from the rich to the poor. The Census Bureau continued to publish its erroneous statistics, all the while giving itself deniability by pointing out in some obscure part of the text that "the underreporting and nonreporting" should be taken into account when using its statistics.

Back in 1965, the in-kind income of welfare recipients was relatively small, and even with the acknowledged underreporting of income the degree of overstatement of poverty was perhaps negligible. But as the value of in-kind income grew over the years, and as the level of actual poverty fell, the total amount of in-kind income not counted and income not reported accounted for a larger and larger percentage of what was officially reported as poverty.

Over the years, the discrepancy between what was actually happening to the poor in America and what the statisticians in Washington were telling us grew wider and wider. Finally the "poverty gap" in the official Census Bureau statistics became so apparent that it was almost embarrassing to use the numbers. Almost—for virtually without exception everyone went on using them.

There have been sporadic attempts to correct the numbers. Academicians, and even the Census Bureau itself, attacked parts of the problem. In 1972, for example, the bureau reported that it had obtained only "87.0 percent of all wage and salary income, 81.7 percent of all social security benefits, and 65.5 percent of all public assistance benefits."[3] But the results of such studies, though helpful, never gave any clear indication of the order of magnitude by which the official government statistics overstated poverty.

Some analysts began making educated guesses. In 1976 John Palmer and Joseph Minarik of the Brookings Institution, two acknowledged welfare experts, speculated that "a definition of household income that both includes the recipients' cash valuation of in-kind benefits and adjusts for underreporting of cash income would probably reflect a current poverty rate close to 5 percent rather than the official level of 12 percent."[4]

But guesses, even by prudent experts, can't be used as a sound basis for national policy. Finally, in frustration, Congress, using its newly formed research arm, the Congressional Budget Office (CBO), decided to answer for itself the question, How much poverty is there in the United States?

The results were startling. Using exactly the same poverty line as the venerable Census Bureau, the fledgling CBO reported in mid-1977 that its analysis showed less than 14 million Americans in poverty in fiscal 1976—only 6.4 percent of the population.

There are two reasons why these new figures differ so radically from the traditional ones of the Census Bureau. First, the new congressional study counts the value of noncash welfare benefits in determining the yearly income of poor people. Over $40 billion a year is spent by the federal government alone on food stamps, day care, public housing, school lunches, medicaid, and medicare. The Census Bureau statistics ignore these billions in benefits; the Congressional Budget Office statistics do not. Any income statistics that ignore the gigantic sums spent by government on welfare and income transfer programs that provide in-kind benefits are simply not valid. As Alice Rivlin, the director of the CBO, has said, "You can argue whether the line for determining poverty ought to be higher or lower . . . But you can't argue that because benefits don't come in the form of cash, they're not benefits."[5]

The second reason involves the underreporting of income. The Census Bureau acknowledges it, and has some rough estimates of what it is for various categories of income, but they are not reflected in the final statistics. The Congressional Budget Office, using the estimates of underreporting, makes adjustments that are reflected in its final estimate of poverty.

In late 1977 Morton Paglin, professor of economics and urban studies at Portland State University, refined the poverty corrections even further. In addition to the kind of corrections made in the CBO study, he corrected for the fact that the Census Bureau neglects to account for households because it unrealistically assumes "that there are no economies of scale and no income sharing unless the persons making up the unit are all related by blood or marriage."[6] The simulation model used by Paglin to estimate the effect of in-kind welfare benefits on the poverty level is similar to the one used by the CBO—with one further refinement. The empirical data base was used to allocate benefits by program and household size, and the simulation was not performed until "the last stage when assumptions about multiple benefits must be made."[7]

Paglin's more refined, more recent estimates of poverty are even more startling than those of the CBO. By his calculations *only 3.6 percent* of Americans were poor in 1975.[8]

Whereas the official level of poverty reported by the Census Bureau has been essentially constant since 1968, the revised poverty estimates by both the CBO and by Professor Paglin agree that (1) there has, in fact, been a *steady decline* in the poverty level since 1968, and (2) the degree of poverty had shrunk to very low levels by 1975.

And this is what one would expect as a result of the massive amount of welfare spending. As Paglin notes, "The [welfare] transfers have been on a sufficiently massive scale to effect a major reduction in the poverty population. It would have been amazing if they had not done so. What is surprising is the lack of recognition of this accomplishment. Social scientists have generally accepted and have given wide currency to the official poverty estimates. It is time for the statistical veil to be lifted so that the poverty problem can be seen in its true dimensions."[9]

Some welfare experts are beginning to change their minds about the extent of poverty in the United States. Reflecting on the revised CBO statistics, Alice Rivlin commented, "The nation has come a lot closer to eliminating poverty than most people realize."[10] Sar Levitan, a professor of economics at George Washington University who has written extensively on the welfare programs of President Johnson's Great Society, concluded in early 1977 that "if poverty is defined as a lack of basic needs, it's almost been eliminated."[11]

The results of the studies by the CBO and Paglin should not be surprising to anyone familiar with the growth of our economy and the increase in our welfare and income transfer programs over the past decade or so. Ever since Lyndon Johnson declared a war on poverty in 1964, two powerful forces have been pushing more and more Americans out of poverty.

The first, and perhaps most important, force is the strong, sustained economic growth of the private sector. The gross national product more than doubled from $688 billion in 1965 to $1,710 billion in the third quarter of 1976. This gain of over $1 trillion in GNP was accompanied by 18 million new jobs. Over 89 million Americans were employed at the end of 1976. The growth in family income was equally dramatic: from about $7,700 in 1965, the average family income more than doubled to $15,546 in 1975. Even after making allowances for inflation, higher taxes, and a sharp increase in restrictive government regulation, the private economy produced millions of new jobs and significantly higher wages and salaries. Many of these new jobs and higher paychecks undoubtedly went to people classified as poor when the war on poverty began and to others who would have become poor in the meantime.

The second major force removing people from poverty is the vast and growing array of government welfare and income transfer programs. Since the war on poverty began there has been an explosive growth in social welfare spending. Total government spending on all social welfare programs increased from $77 billion in 1965 to $286 billion in 1975, close to a fourfold increase in a decade. Spending on direct welfare programs has grown even faster. In 1965 the combined spending of federal, state, and local governments on public welfare was just over $6 billion. By 1975 it was over $40 billion, almost seven times greater.

When President Nixon took office, 48 percent of the fiscal 1969 federal budget was being spent on defense and 30 percent on health, education, and income security. In fiscal 1977, after eight years of Republican administration, the percentages were *exactly reversed:* 30 percent of the federal budget was spent on defense and 48 percent on health, education, and income security.

The number of people remaining in poverty is very small and it grows smaller every day. The growth of social welfare programs—Aid to Families with Dependent Children (AFDC), Supplemental Security Income (SSI), food stamps, child nutrition, day care, public housing, medicaid and medicare, tuition aid, and social security—has been so comprehensive and diffuse that virtually all people who cannot truly care for themselves or their families are eligible for a wide variety of cash grants and services that provide a decent and adequate standard of living.

As surprisingly low as the revised estimates of poverty are, the actual figures may be considerably lower. The poverty statistics still contain large numbers of undergraduate and graduate students, some wealthy people living off assets who report no income, recipients of income from illegal activities such as robbery, drug traffic, prostitution, and gambling who obviously aren't eager to report to any government agency, and other people who simply don't like to tell anyone what their true level of income is. Workers who enter or leave the labor force sometime during the year may have substantial earnings that would place them well above the poverty line. Yet they may be counted as officially poor. When the census count is made early in the year, those questioned are asked how much income the family had during the last calendar year. Someone beginning work on, say, October 1, with an annual salary of $12,000 would be able to report actual earnings of only $3,000 during that calendar year, and thus would be included among the poor. And there are even a few people who deliberately choose not to earn more, even though they are capable of doing so, in order to enjoy a particular life-style that requires a good deal of free time.

As Robert Haveman, fellow of the Institute for Research on Poverty at the University of Wisconsin, wrote in 1977: "The day of income poverty as a major public issue would appear to be past . . . A minimum level of economic well-being has by and large been assured for all citizens."[12]

The war on poverty has been won, except for perhaps a few mopping-up operations. The combination of strong economic growth and a dramatic increase in government spending on welfare and income transfer programs for more than a decade has virtually wiped out poverty in the United States.

There will be isolated instances where a person is unaware of being eligible, or is unjustly denied aid by a welfare bureaucrat, or simply chooses not to accept the social stigma of being on welfare. But these cases are the exceptions. In fact, just the opposite concern—those getting welfare who have no right to it—is the one that seems to be growing.

When the policymakers were passing and implementing the welfare programs that are currently on the books, their deliberations, it must be remembered, took place in the context of a deep and widely held belief that poverty was widespread and highly intractable to their previous efforts. The welfare and income transfer programs now in place have developed a momentum of growth that is unlikely to slow down in the near future.

We have built up an array of programs and resources to attack a poverty "army" of 25 to 30 million poor people. The "enemy" is no longer there, but the attack goes on unabated. We have built up such a large arsenal of welfare programs, and their momentum of growth is so strong, that we may soon pass into an overkill capability with regard to government measures to combat poverty. Perhaps we already are there.

The main goal of welfare in the United States, at least as perceived and understood by the vast majority of Americans, is to provide a decent, adequate level of support, composed of both cash and services, to all those who truly cannot care for themselves. The key criteria by which to judge the efficacy of welfare programs are two: the extent of coverage and the adequacy of support.

Coverage of the eligible welfare population is now almost universal—if one is sick, or is hungry, or cannot work, or is blind, or has small children to care for, or is physically disabled, or is old—then there are dozens of welfare programs whose sole purpose is to provide help.

And the level of help is substantial. The average mother on AFDC with three children qualifies for about $6,000 a year. In some rare cases in high-paying states, this amount can go so high as to be equivalent to an annual before-tax income of over $20,000. Virtually all people who are eligible qualify for government checks and government-provided services that automatically lift them out of the official ranks of poverty.

The "dismal failure" of welfare is a myth. There may be great inefficiencies in our welfare programs, the level of fraud may be very high, the quality of management may be terrible, the programs may overlap, inequities may abound, and the financial incentive to work may be virtually nonexistent. But if we step back and judge the vast array of welfare programs, on which we spend tens of billions every year, by two basic criteria—the completeness of coverage for those who really need help, and the adequacy of the amount of help they do receive—the picture changes dramatically. Judged by these standards our welfare system has been a brilliant success.

The war on poverty is over for all practical purposes. We should now begin thinking about how to revise our welfare strategies to deal with the problem of preventing poverty, to make programs more effective and efficient, to eliminate unnecessary programs, and to focus more on the social problems that widespread welfare dependency will bring.

THE POVERTY WALL

The virtual elimination of poverty in the United States has not been accomplished without costly social side effects. The most important and potentially troublesome effect is the almost complete destruction of work incentives for the poor on welfare. The nature of our new welfare programs and the massive increases in welfare payments have combined to sharply reduce, and in some cases eliminate altogether, any financial incentive for welfare recipients either to get a job or to attempt to increase their current low earnings. The welfare system has so distorted incentives to work that people on welfare now face higher effective marginal tax rates on earned income than even those making $100,000 a year or more.

This destruction of work incentives is a direct and necessary consequence of the drive to eliminate poverty. All our major welfare programs are "income-tested," meaning that the amount of welfare received in cash or in services is dependent on the amount of money the welfare recipient earns. When someone on welfare begins to earn money, or increases his or her earnings, it is assumed that the need for welfare declines, and the amount of welfare payments or services is reduced according to a formula appropriate to the welfare programs providing benefits.

If a welfare recipient is receiving money and services from two or more programs, the earning of additional income has a multiplier effect on net take-home "pay." If a person is receiving benefits from three different programs, there will be three separate benefit reductions as soon as the new income is reported.

Most of our welfare programs were designed and developed to take care of the needs of a particular poor segment of the society, and often little or no thought seems to have been given to the effect of their interaction with other welfare or public assistance programs. The result is a cumulative negative effect on a poor person's incentive to work that is devastating.

For example:

> In New Jersey an unemployed man with a wife and two children receiving public assistance and food stamps would add only $110 to this net monthly income if he took a full-time job paying $500 a month. In addition, he would lose eligibility for medicaid, which pays an average of $52 a month for the medical bills of an AFDC family in New Jersey. A Tennessee father who is eligible for food stamps and the unemployment insurance maximum gains only $4 a week by taking a part-time job paying $75 a week. A New Jersey mother of three receiving benefits from medicaid, aid to families with dependent children, food stamps, and public housing would gain only about 20 percent of the total income derived from taking a full-time job paying as much as $700 or even $1,000 a month.[13]

A reduction in the amount of one's welfare check has the same effect on one's net pay as the payment of taxes. The amount of the welfare reduction, when expressed as a percentage of new or additional earnings, is equivalent to a marginal tax rate on earned income. Perhaps it should be called a "welfare tax." In the first example cited above, the effective marginal tax rate is 88 percent; in the second it is 95 percent; and in the third, 80 percent.

In 1972 the Joint Economic Committee of Congress conducted a comprehensive review of welfare programs in the United States. Martha Griffiths, chairman of the Subcommittee on Fiscal Policy that conducted the study, made this comment on the results of some of its studies: "Current government programs can discourage work effort and result in intolerably little improvement in the income of the beneficiaries . . . These are the equivalent of confiscatory tax rates."[14]

The incredibly high marginal tax rates paid by those on welfare are a serious and direct disincentive to work. Why should someone work 40 hours a week, 50 weeks a year for, say, $8,000 when it would be possible not to work at all for, say, $6,000? People on welfare may be poor, but they are not fools. Any rational calculation of the net returns from working by someone on welfare would discourage any but the most doggedly determined.

To further compound the problem, poor people are subject to regular federal, state, and city income taxes when their earnings move over the poverty level. For instance, in 1976 they had to pay 5.85 percent of their earnings in social security taxes. And when the typical family of four had earnings of over $6,900 a year it had to begin to pay federal income taxes. Many states have income taxes that start at fairly low levels of income. And then, of course, there are a number of cities with income taxes, especially those with high welfare populations like New York City. These tax rates are combined with the tax rates resulting from welfare reduction, and they all apply at the critical range of income where a person is just beginning to feel self-sufficient. The tax rates are not directly additive, because welfare programs such as AFDC and food stamps compute benefits due on net earnings after income taxes have been deducted.

Little can be done about the problem. The elimination of all federal, state, and local taxes up to, say, $10,000 of annual income would be prohibitively expensive in terms of lost tax revenues, for—to be fair—taxes for everyone earning income within that range, including those not on welfare, would have to be eliminated.

There are only two ways to eliminate the high tax rates implicit in our current array of welfare programs. One is to sharply reduce the basic welfare payment; the other is to hold the basic payment where it is and simply lower the rate at which welfare benefits are reduced as income rises. There are serious problems with both alternatives. The first, lowering the welfare payments, is politically impossible today. The second, lowering the welfare reduction rate, would increase the cost of welfare to taxpayers by such phenomenal sums—tens of billions of dollars a year—that it has no better chance of becoming a political reality than the first.

For better or worse, high marginal tax rates are a necessary and enduring part of our current welfare system. The policymakers had no other choice. As the extent and level of welfare escalated rapidly during the last decade, they had to keep the marginal rate of taxation on welfare and public assistance very high in order to avoid massive increases in the number of Americans eligible for welfare and the spectacular cost that would have followed.

But the acceptance of these high, incentive-destroying tax rates has had an unforeseen cost. With scarcely anyone noticing it, the poor people in this country have been deeply entangled in a welfare system that is rapidly strangling any incentive they may have had to help themselves and their families by working to increase their incomes.

Few deny the depressant effect high marginal tax rates have on the incentive to work and earn more money. Partly in recognition of this fact, the top federal tax rate on earned personal service income was recently lowered from 70 to 50 percent. But as tax disincentives were being reduced for the nonpoor, our welfare programs moved in the opposite direction. In the headlong rush to help poor people, we have created a situation where the poor of America are subjected to significantly higher rates of taxation than the nonpoor.

We have, in ironic consequence of our massive effort to eradicate poverty from the land, virtually destroyed any financial incentive that the poor may have had to improve their economic condition. We have, in effect, created a *poverty wall* with our tax and welfare system that, while assuring poor people a substantial subsistence level of income, destroys their incentive to work and sentences them to a life of dependency on the government dole.

The gross disparity between the tax disincentives faced by welfare recipients and by working people not on welfare is shown graphically in Figure 1. The working head of a typical family of four pays three major taxes on earned income—social security tax, state income tax, and federal income tax. The heavy solid line in Figure 1 represents the total marginal tax rate that such a family pays on wages and salaries as a result of these three taxes. The total marginal tax rate attributable to the combination of these three taxes in 1976 begins at a little below 6 percent, increases to over 19 percent at $6,100 of income, then climbs steadily to

FIGURE 1

Marginal Tax Rates for Welfare Recipients and for Wage Earners

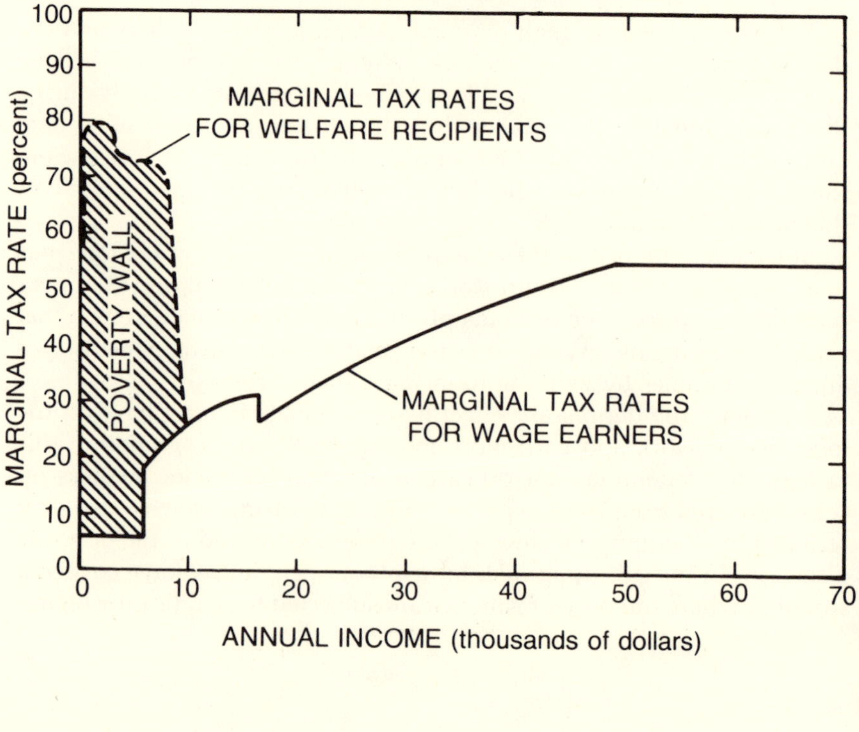

almost 32 percent at $16,500. At this point it drops by 5.85 percent because of the income limitation on the social security tax. Then it begins to climb once again until it peaks at 61 percent for $49,800 of annual income. For any additional earned income over $49,800, the marginal rate remains constant at 61 percent.

The tax burden facing the poor person on welfare is dramatically different. The poverty wall effectively prevents many of the poor from ever leaving that status. Perhaps even sadder, it may even take away the hope of doing so.

The nature of the poverty wall that confronts any particular welfare family is determined largely by where the family lives and the number of welfare programs it benefits from. The various combinations possible are almost endless, but a typical case can effectively illustrate the order of magnitude of the marginal income tax rates these families are subject to when welfare benefits are reduced because of increased family income. One such example was recently constructed by Henry Aaron of the Brookings Institution to show the nature of the tax rates faced by an AFDC family of four that also received medicaid benefits, food stamps, and housing assistance.[15]

As Aaron points out,

> The marginal tax rates are high and capricious. On all earnings from $576 to $8,390 per year, the family eligible solely for AFDC and medicaid faces a tax rate of 67 percent. Eligibility for food stamps and housing assistance raises the tax rate as high as 80 percent, and brings it to 73 percent over the income range from $4,000 to $8,300. When earnings reach $8,390, the family is removed from the welfare rolls and at that instant loses $1,000 medicaid benefits and, if eligible, a $288 food stamp bonus.[16]

The dotted line in Figure 1 traces the course of the effective marginal tax rates that face a typical welfare family thinking either about going to work or about trying to increase earnings. Although the nature of the marginal tax rates will vary widely from family to family, depending on the welfare programs they receive benefits from, the relative order of magnitude of the tax rates they face compared with those of nonwelfare workers is clearly shown. Up to earnings of approximately $8,400 a year, welfare recipients typically face effective marginal tax rates that are far, far higher than those faced by the typical working family, in that same range, not receiving welfare. In fact, the tax rates are substantially higher than for all workers not on welfare, regardless of income. It is only when the earned income of welfare recipients reaches about $10,000 a year that they achieve the same tax status as other working Americans.

There is one additional tax rate complication that should be noted here. In 1975 an *earned income credit* was added to the federal income tax code. Its basic purpose was to increase the financial incentive to work for the heads of low-income families by giving them money as a reward for working. Past changes in the deductions, exemptions, and credits of the federal income tax have given massive financial relief to poor families by eliminating all federal taxes on incomes of less than $6,100 a year. This special "credit" eliminated federal taxes on all incomes up to $6,900 and added a new twist.

The earned income credit applies only to earnings up to $8,000 a year. A family with no income receives no "credit." But, beginning with the first dollar earned, a family gets an earned income credit equal to 10 percent of all earnings up to $4,000 a year. If earnings are $1,000, the "credit" is $100; the maximum "credit" is $400 for earnings of $4,000. Because there are no federal income taxes to be paid within that income range, the "credit" is translated into a federal payment. If a family earns $1,000 and files a federal tax return, the federal government will mail it a check for $100. If the earnings are $4,000, the check will be for $400. For earnings between $4,000 and $8,000 the amount of the earned income credit declines. For earnings of $5,000 the "credit" is reduced to $300; for earnings of $6,000 it is $200; for earnings of $7,000 it is $100; and at $8,000 the "credit" is phased out completely.

The earned income credit is, in effect, a separate welfare program run through the Internal Revenue Service. The federal government now pays low-income workers a bonus of 10 percent on all earnings up to $4,000, and then decreases the size of the bonus by 10 percent as earnings increase to $8,000. In 1976, "$1.3 billion was transferred to 6.3 million low-income tax units" through this so-called tax credit.[17]

One notable result of the earned income credit is a *negative* total marginal income tax rate of 4.15 percent on all earned income of less than $4,000 a year. But once the family passes the magic $4,000 level, the marginal tax rate leaps dramatically by 20 percent to just under a positive 16 percent. At $6,100 of income the normal federal income tax comes into play, and the result is an additional sharp increase: between $6,000 and $7,000 the total marginal income tax rate is 29.2 percent; between $7,000 and $8,000 it is 31.8 percent.

The range of earnings from $4,000 to $8,000 is a critical one in terms of work incentives. For many people it is here that the struggle to escape from poverty and welfare will take place. Unfortunately, the earned income credit has instituted a potentially destructive barrier that low-income workers must now deal with. Over a $2,000 span of income, the marginal income tax rate increases over 33 percentage points—from a negative 4.15 percent to a positive 29.2 percent. Instead of facing the kind of gradually rising marginal tax rate shown in Figure 1, many low-income workers, because of the earned income credit, must now cope with an abruptly steep "tax wall" that is similar to the one confronting their more unfortunate brothers and sisters on welfare.

The earned income credit will probably not become a permanent part of the federal income tax, but until it is removed it will severely distort the financial incentive effects of the federal income tax. When the effects of the earned income credit are combined with those of social security taxes and state income taxes, the path of the total marginal tax rate is wondrous to behold, resembling the profile of a roller coaster far more than a sober financial chart.

Thus, while poverty was being virtually eliminated during the last decade or so, a poverty wall of high taxation was erected in front of millions of Americans. As more and more reliance was placed on using financial incentives to work to induce people to leave the welfare rolls, government welfare policies themselves raised an effective psychological barrier to their gainful employment. As one staff study prepared for the Joint Economic Committee's study of welfare put it, "In contrast to the rhetoric of Government officials exhorting recipients to work for their income, the Government itself imposes the largest barrier to work."[18]

In effect we have created a new caste of Americans—perhaps as much as one-tenth of this nation—a caste of people free from basic wants but almost totally dependent on the state, with little hope or prospect of breaking free. Perhaps we should call them the Dependent Americans.

THE CLAMOR FOR WELFARE REFORM

As the number of welfare programs multiplied and the number of people receiving welfare checks and benefits grew, as the amount of the welfare payments increased, as the number of people living in poverty dropped precipitously, one might have reasonably expected to hear a round of cheers for this unprecedented attack on poverty. But this did not happen. The voices of praise were silent. Instead the welfare system was denounced by nearly all those who cared enough about what was going on to comment and write about it. The more money that was transferred from the taxpayers to those without incomes, the more the criticism grew.

Books were written about welfare reform. President Johnson made the war on poverty his major domestic concern. President Nixon proposed a "Family Assistance Plan" as his domestic policy centerpiece.

George McGovern tried to get his campaign moving in 1972 by proposing $1,000 a year for everyone. Hundreds of academic studies poured forth. President Ford tried to develop a plan in 1974, and President Carter, on taking office in 1977, quickly made welfare reform one of his first domestic priorities.

Yet in spite of the powerful pressures for welfare reform, the wonderfully detailed plans that were put forth, and the support of the media, little was accomplished in the way of major, substantial change. The welfare system grew and prospered along traditional lines, almost immune to the mounting chorus of criticism. It is surprising that no radical change took place and that so little credit was given to the system for what it was accomplishing. Perhaps the answer to this anomaly lies in the nature of the several philosophical approaches to welfare that exist in this country, and in the relative power of the groups that hold these views.

There are essentially three philosophical approaches to welfare in the United States. The first is the **private charity** approach. Holders of this view maintain that the state has no business appropriating other people's money to give to those deemed poor. They believe that private charitable organizations and acts of private giving could do the job effectively and with a greater sense of personal caring than the government, and that these private efforts would increase to the extent that government diminished its role in welfare. In today's society the private charity view is held seriously by only a small percentage of the population, and, except for the important supplemental role of private charity, has little effect on government policy.

A second philosophical view, the **needy-only** approach, holds that persons who, through no fault of their own, are unable to care for themselves or for their families should receive help from the government. The role of government is seen as a limited one. Welfare payments should go only to needy people, and the amount of the payment should be in proportion to their need. If someone is able to work, welfare should be denied. People on the welfare rolls should be helped and encouraged to become self-sufficient by whatever reasonable means are available and effective. Being on welfare is viewed as a state of dependency, an acknowledgment that one is not able to take care of oneself without help from others. The needy-only approach is taken by the overwhelming majority of Americans. It has been the traditional approach to welfare in this country for many years, and support for it is widespread and deep.

The third philosophical approach is a relative newcomer to the United States. Only within the last two decades or so has it been discussed seriously and gained support. Its premises are that everyone has a right to a basic level of income, that the government should guarantee to every citizen a level of cash income high enough for him or her to live in moderate comfort, and that no restrictions whatsoever should be placed on the use of the money. This is the **guaranteed income** approach to welfare. Some holders of this view seem to believe that people basically like to work, that they will do so whenever they are sufficiently rewarded, and that even mild incentives will encourage them to leave the welfare rolls and improve their standard of living.

At the heart of the guaranteed income approach is the premise that people have a *right* to a certain level of income completely independent of their ability to earn. Under a guaranteed income there is no attempt to differentiate between those who cannot help themselves and those who can. The system automatically provides benefits to everyone. It is assumed that no stigma can be attached to those who cannot take care of themselves, as everyone would have the same minimum level of income by right. In special cases of extreme need, the basic income guarantee can be augmented. What distinguishes this view from the traditional view of welfare in the United States is its assumption of starting with a base income guarantee for everyone, and then building up and out from that base.

Although these three approaches to welfare exist side by side, only two of them—the needy-only approach and the guaranteed income approach—are serious contenders for the hearts and minds of welfare policymakers. Private charity is almost universally approved, but few support it as the total answer to poverty. One can make a logical, theoretical case for the private charity approach, but it is not politically viable at this time.

The clamor for welfare reform and the controversy surrounding it stem largely from a deep conflict in the philosophical views of the two remaining groups. The first group—supporting the needy-only approach—contains the large majority of the American people. They believe there is a clear role for government to play in providing cash benefits and services to the poor, especially to the blind, the disabled, and the aged, but they reject the concept of a guaranteed income by large margins in poll after poll. Their views on welfare, however, are passive. They don't demonstrate; they don't study the welfare system; they don't write or make speeches about it. Their power lies in their votes, at the polls. They will tolerate and even enthusiastically support a political candidate who pledges to improve welfare—who pledges to see that the really needy get adequate help and to end the welfare abuse and fraud they suspect permeates the entire welfare system.

But they will turn on the candidate who proposes to guarantee an annual income, with their money, to someone who is capable of working and doesn't feel like it. They have a realistic, traditional view of life. They believe there are many people, perhaps even themselves, who, if guaranteed an income, would simply cease working and loaf. And they do not understand, and probably never will understand, why they should work to support someone who prefers not to work.

The advocates of a guaranteed income are different. The number of advocates and supporters of this philosophical approach is small, but as a group they are very influential. They come from the universities, the welfare agencies that administer the programs, the media, and the government. Some of them are welfare recipients. What they lack in the raw political power of votes, they make up for with the effectiveness and persistence of their advocacy. They study the welfare system, they develop the programs and draft the legislation, they administer the programs and then they criticize them. They write and speak and make their views known, both to the media and to policymakers. On occasion they have been known to demonstrate.

Almost without exception, the calls for sweeping "welfare reform" over the past fifteen years or so have come from the supporters of some form of a guaranteed income. What they consider to be reform, however, differs markedly from what the holders of the needy-only approach consider to be reform. The advocates of a guaranteed income want to radically change the current welfare system from welfare for the needy only to a guaranteed income for all. Almost everyone else sees welfare reform as something that will ensure that those who need help get help, as something that will remove from the welfare rolls those who are defrauding the system, and will make the programs more efficient and less costly to the taxpayers.

The greatest difficulty faced by the proponents of a guaranteed income is the fact that the vast majority of the American people don't accept the idea. Most Americans cannot understand why they should work and support others who, though capable, are not working. They feel it is morally wrong. As Henry Hazlitt once stated, "If you claim a 'right' to an income sufficient to live in dignity, whether you are willing to work or not, what you are really claiming is a right to part of somebody else's earned income. What you are asserting is that this other person has a duty to earn more than he needs or wants to live on, so that the surplus may be seized from him and turned over to you to live on. This is an absolutely immoral proposition."[19]

As far as the American public is concerned, the idea of a guaranteed income has been crisply rejected in every known public opinion poll that has dealt with the issue. There is little popular support for the principle of a guaranteed income and a decided lack of interest in the subject. As Aaron Wildavsky and William Cavala stated in 1970, "Policies that provide unearned income run counter to widely held and deeply felt American values, such as achievement, work, and equality of opportunity. The large tax increase or drastic reallocation of public funds required to guarantee income has few supporters."[20]

THE EFFECT OF WELFARE ON WORK

One of the most important questions that should be asked about any radical welfare reform plan that promises to guarantee incomes is: What effect will it have on the work effort of the poor? Most Americans still believe strongly in the work ethic. If millions of low-income Americans "retired" from the labor force to live on their income guarantees, there is little question that intense political controversy would follow. Those receiving the guarantee could become a powerful political force, demanding and getting ever-increasing benefits. There would certainly be some negative effect on the economy if large numbers of people stopped working or reduced the number of hours they worked.

A major reduction in the work effort of the low-income population would have endless ramifications—socially, economically, and politically—and the speculation on what the consequences of these ramifications might be is also endless. There seems to be little disagreement with the proposition that any substantial reduction in the work effort of the low-income population would pose the danger of profound, far-reaching social and economic consequences. There is, however, a great deal of uncertainty about whether guaranteeing incomes would really cause the recipients to stop working en masse. And speculation on the possible consequences is idle unless we have sufficient reason to suspect that it might, in fact, happen.

Most people have what, to them, seems a common-sense view of a guaranteed income. If someone has the option of working or not working to obtain the same or virtually the same amount of income, all other things being equal, he will choose not to work. In some cases, of course, social factors such as the work ethic, pride, and what his neighbors might think will induce him to keep on working. But what if a guaranteed income plan should become so widespread that many of his fellow workers in the same income bracket choose not to work, and the social pressure directed against him becomes a pressure not to work? In recent years we have seen such a change in our welfare system. Partly because of the sharp increase in the number of people on welfare, and partly because of the efforts of "welfare rights" groups, the stigma of being on welfare seems to have been substantially attenuated. Many on welfare today feel no compunction whatsoever about receiving it, often asserting that they have a right to it. Some workers, who gain great psychological satisfaction from their work, may choose to continue what they are doing in spite of the guarantee. But how many low-income jobs provide that kind of satisfaction? Without actually trying a nationwide guaranteed income, and relying on what we know (or what we think we know) of human nature, it seems reasonable to assume that the fears of large numbers of people quitting work to live off the dole are not unfounded, and that such a possibility is fraught with dangers for our society.

We know that if we raise the effective tax rate closer and closer to 100 percent, a person's incentive to work diminishes. At 100 percent he gets nothing but whatever psychological pleasure there is in the work. Conceivably, under certain circumstances he might continue to work as the rate surpassed 100 percent. But this would be an unusual case.

What happens when a person is guaranteed the same amount of income, or some amount close to it, whether he works or not? A priori, we would expect that as the amount he received moved closer and closer to the amount he would receive if he worked, he would work less and less. If the amount of guaranteed income surpassed the amount he could earn by working, the disinclination to work would be even greater. The higher the guarantee relative to the amount he could earn by working, the less inclined the person would be to work—except, of course, for the psychological benefits involved.

The effect of increased income on a person's work effort has been studied intensely by economists for many years, and among them there is almost unanimous theoretical agreement that a guaranteed income would cause significant numbers of people to cease working or reduce the number of hours worked. But no matter how convinced we may be in our own minds that many people would gladly swap the cacophony of an alarm clock at 7 o'clock every morning and the necessity of doing what someone else wants them to do 40 hours a week, 50 weeks a year, for a leisurely rising time and the freedom to pursue their personal interests, we are still not completely sure what would happen if a real guaranteed income should come to the United States.

Advocates of a guaranteed income themselves have few qualms about the possible adverse affects on our society. Commenting on the psychological aspects of a guaranteed income, psychoanalyst Erich Fromm, an ardent advocate of such a plan, acknowledges that "the most obvious question is whether a guaranteed income would not reduce the incentive to work," but then quickly lays this concern to rest as he continues, "Man, by nature, is not lazy, but on the contrary, suffers from the results of inactivity. People might prefer not to work for one or two months, but the vast majority would beg to work . . . Misuse of the guarantee would disappear after a short time, just as people would not overeat on sweets after a couple of weeks, assuming they would not have to pay for them."[21]

In spite of such enthusiastic professional opinion, a few nagging doubts do remain. Have the economists been wrong in their theory all these years? Are the common-sense instincts of the average American in error? Will a large segment of our society, perhaps as many as 30 or 40 million people, now on welfare or earning relatively low incomes proceed much as they did before they discovered that a reasonably high level of income is guaranteed, whether they work or not? Or will they stop working in substantial numbers?

As with all social policy there is no sure answer. There is no foolproof way to know what the social and economic consequences of a new, radical social welfare plan will be until many years after we implement it. When the military draft was ended by President Nixon in 1971, many people feared that our military strength would be sharply reduced as both the number and the quality of recruits dropped. They also predicted an all-black army, an army composed of the children of the poor, or one made up of the misfits of our society. Fortunately, their predictions were wrong. When a national urban renewal program began back in 1949, many scholars, politicians, and social commentators confidently predicted the rebirth of our nation's cities. But no one predicted that urban renewal would scarcely renew a city block, let alone a city, that it would worsen housing conditions for the very people it set out to help, that it would destroy four homes, most of them occupied by blacks, for every home it built—most of them to be occupied by middle- and upper-income whites.[22]

In the case of the guaranteed income, we are more fortunate. During the last decade or so an impressive body of data has been painstakingly accumulated by scholars and government analysts that allows us to predict the consequences of a guaranteed income with far more confidence than was possible for other social policies in the past. These studies concern the behavior of people, in particular welfare recipients and low-income workers, under conditions that simulate to some degree the conditions that would exist under a guaranteed income. Individually, their results are rather tentative and inconclusive. Taken together, their findings are inescapably clear—and alarming.

There have been three major types of research studies that attempt to estimate the effect of radical welfare reform plans on the work effort of the poor and the near-poor. The first type is based on an analysis of existing welfare programs, of how people now on welfare have changed, or not changed, their attitude toward work. The second type, called the "cross-section" study, is essentially an economic and statistical analysis of large quantities of survey data showing how people tend to behave when faced with cash transfer payments and increasingly high marginal tax rates. The third type is composed of a series of direct experiments in which selected families were "given" a form of a guaranteed income and their actions were closely observed and analyzed. All three types of studies have the same goal: to judge the effect of guaranteed welfare payments on the work effort of those who would receive them.

The ultimate purpose of the studies and experiments is to predict what would happen if a guaranteed income were established in the United States. Making such a prediction is fraught with difficulties and uncertainty. The studies and experiments cover different groups of people, under different circumstances, in different parts of the country, at different times. The specific nature of any guaranteed income can vary depending on the level of the basic income guarantee and the tax rate imposed on income earned by recipients of the basic guarantee. A precise prediction of what would happen if such a radical social scheme were tried is impossible, but it is entirely feasible to construct an "order of magnitude" prediction that can give us a reasonably accurate idea of the direction and approximate extent of the social consequences that would flow from a guaranteed income.

As to the direction that these changes would take, the studies and experiments are all in agreement. Regardless of whether it is a study of an existing welfare program, or an economic and statistical analysis of survey data, or a controlled guaranteed income experiment; regardless of whether one considers the work response of husbands, or of wives, or of female heads of families, the results are consistent: a reasonable level of a guaranteed income causes low-income workers to *reduce* the number of hours they work, and the larger the amount of the guarantee relative to their income, the more they tend to stop working. The high tax rates that would be a necessary part of any politically feasible guaranteed income plan would also cause low-income workers to reduce the number of hours they work; and the higher the marginal tax rate the more they would tend to stop working. As the report on the results of experiments in Seattle and Denver concludes, "The empirical results indicate that both disposable income and net wage changes induce husbands, wives, and female heads of families to reduce their labor supply. These results are statistically significant, are consistent with economic theory, and are relatively large, indicating that behavior is influenced by changes in incentives."[23]

What many people have suspected for some time is true. Poor people, like those with higher incomes, make rational economic decisions. If their income is little affected by working more, they will not work very much more. If their income is little affected by working less, then they will work less. This is not to say that the poor value idleness, but they do value leisure, just as much as the nonpoor. Whether they will spend that leisure time profitably or not we do not know. But it seems fair to say that bowling, fishing, working around the house, writing poetry, or, in some cases, just loafing for awhile, are clearly more attractive than many low-income jobs. The question is not will low-income people reduce their work effort if guaranteed an income with large implicit tax rates; the question is how much they will reduce it.

The actual amount of work reduction that would occur as a consequence of a guaranteed income will never be known for sure unless we implement one and live with it for a decade or so. But based on the best evidence we now have—from studies of existing welfare programs, from economic and statistical analyses of survey data, and from six major guaranteed income experiments—we can be reasonably sure that the institution of a guaranteed income will cause a substantial reduction (perhaps as much as 50 percent) in the work effort of low-income workers. As long feared by the public, and recently confirmed by independent research studies, such a massive withdrawal from the work force would have the most profound and far-reaching social and economic consequences for our society.

THE IMPOSSIBILITY OF RADICAL WELFARE REFORM

For over fifteen years a number of economists and social science theorists have put forth plans for radically altering our welfare system from its current purpose of helping needy people to guaranteeing incomes for everyone. The long string of specific proposals includes Milton Friedman's negative income tax (1962), Robert Theobald's guaranteed income (1965), James Tobin's guaranteed income plan (1965), R. J. Lampman's subsidy plan (1967), Edward Schwartz's guaranteed income (1967), the negative income tax plan of President Johnson's Income Maintenance Commission (1969), President Nixon's Family

Assistance Plan (1969), George McGovern's $1,000-a-year plan (1972), Great Britain's credit income tax (1972), and HEW's Income Supplementation Plan (1974). The plans provided for minimum income guarantees ranging from $1,500 to $6,000 a year for a typical family of four. The effective marginal tax rates ranged from 50 percent to well over 100 percent. The costs of the plans ranged from several billions to over $50 billion a year. All would have added tens of millions of people to the welfare rolls.

A common thread running through each of these plans is the planner's dream of simplification. The welfare system we now have is difficult to understand and difficult to administer. It has multiple programs, varying payments, and regulations that vary from state to state. It is very complex. The radical reform plans would replace it with a single system that purportedly would be easy to understand and easy to administer, with the same payments and regulations applying to the entire country.

The current welfare system can be likened to a rugged terrain of hills, mountains, and valleys, a wonderfully complex array of programs, payment levels, and eligibility rules that change as one moves from city to city, from state to state. It can be argued that this is as it must be, a complex welfare system dealing with the very complex problem of the poor in America. This view is shared by a small, but influential group of welfare experts. One of them, Senior Fellow Richard Nathan of the Brookings Institution and formerly Deputy Undersecretary for Welfare of HEW, asserts flatly, "The existence of a 'welfare mess' tends to be overstated. Any system that provides aid to people in the lowest-income groups, who are highly mobile and often have limited job and literacy skills, is going to be difficult to administer."[24]

All of the radical welfare reform plans would like to level the hilly and mountainous terrain of the current welfare system, replacing it with broad, flat plains. One critical element in all these plans is the height of the plain that would replace the hills and mountains. If it is set lower than any of the hilltops and mountain peaks, welfare payments will be reduced for hundreds of thousands, perhaps millions, of Americans. If the new welfare plan is raised to the highest peaks and all the valleys are filled in, welfare payments will be sharply increased for millions of Americans and the costs will be extraordinarily high. There is no way out of this dilemma.

But the demography of low-income America has not hindered the quest for a guaranteed income plan that will work. Like medieval alchemists searching for the universal solvent, some modern social scientists continue to search for a feasible guaranteed income plan—a plan that will simultaneously provide a decent level of help for the poor, guarantee a basic income for all, have a reasonable cost, and be acceptable to the voting public. All would agree that such a plan is difficult to find; perhaps a more interesting question is whether such a plan is possible.

All radical welfare reform schemes have three basic parts that are politically sensitive to a high degree. The first is the basic benefit level provided, for example, to a family of four on welfare. The second is the degree to which the program affects the incentive of a person on welfare to find work or to earn more. The third is the additional cost to the taxpayers.

There are many other important aspects of welfare programs and the plans to reform them, but each of the above three is critical to the chance of any particular reform plan passing Congress and being signed into law by the president. To become a political reality the plan must provide a decent level of support for those on welfare, it must contain strong incentives to work, and it must have a reasonable cost. *And it must do all three at the same time.* If any one of these parts is missing or deficient, the reform plan is nakedly vulnerable to anyone who wishes to attack and condemn it.

The typical welfare family of four now qualifies for about $6,000 in services and money every year. In higher-paying states, like New York, a number of welfare families receive annual benefits ranging from $7,000 to $12,000, and more.

There is no way that Congress, at least in the near future, is going to pass any kind of welfare reform that actually reduces payments for millions of welfare recipients. Even the most hardy welfare skeptics in Congress will shy away from this possibility. The media response would be virtually unanimous: the "reform" would be denounced as cruel and mean-spirited. Countless documented case examples would soon drive the point home to everyone watching the evening television news. Even if Congress were to pass a cut in welfare benefits for millions of Americans, no president could resist vetoing the bill.

Any radical welfare reform plan has to ensure that virtually no one now validly covered under any of our welfare programs would suffer any loss or reduction in benefits. This is especially true of programs for the blind, the aged, the disabled, and those on AFDC. The minimum level of support provided for a family of four by any reform plan must approach the level of payments in states like New York and California, where a large segment of the welfare population lives, a level that averages approximately $6,000 a year.

A second major consideration concerning the political feasibility of any radical welfare reform plan is the "welfare tax rate." All current welfare programs that are income-tested provide for a reduction in the amount of the welfare payment when the recipient of those payments begins either to earn money or to earn more money. And all of the proposed radical welfare plans incorporate some schedule of welfare payment reductions as a function of increasing income—the more you earn, the less you get from the taxpayers.

This welfare tax rate has the same effect on the financial incentive to work as normal taxes. As noted earlier, the financial incentive for a welfare recipient to get a job, or to earn more money, is directly related to how much the person earns and how much welfare benefits are reduced because of those earnings. If a welfare recipient earns an additional $1,000 a year and his welfare check is reduced by, say, $200, the result is precisely the same as if he had to pay $200 in federal income taxes on $1,000 of income. In both cases the effective tax rate would be 20 percent. If welfare benefits are reduced $500 for every $1,000 increase in earnings, the tax rate would be 50 percent; if they are reduced $700 for every $1,000 increase in earnings, the tax rate would be 70 percent, and so on.

A person's desire for additional income is unquestionably diminished when he realizes that he can keep only half or a quarter of it for himself. To make the financial incentive to work the main instrument for inducing potentially self-sufficient people to leave the welfare rolls and rise out of poverty, and then to impose on those people incentive-destroying rates of taxation far above that of the average worker, is unconscionable and clearly contrary to the expressed goals of welfare reform.

Any radical plan for the reform of welfare that does not ensure a strong financial incentive to work is vulnerable to the same charges that were leveled at President Nixon's Family Assistance Plan by the Senate Finance Committee with such devastating effect in 1969.

Exactly what constitutes a strong financial incentive to work is open to debate, for a marginal tax rate that may discourage one person from working could easily have little or no effect on someone else. But in general terms we can say that low marginal tax rates, from zero to, say, 15 or 20 percent, seem to have a relatively minimal effect on work effort; that as tax rates move up into the region of 40, 50, or even 60 percent, an increasing number of people are adversely affected; and that as tax rates approach the confiscatory levels of 80, 90, or even 100 percent and more, the work disincentive becomes very powerful.

Plans containing truly effective financial work incentives would entail tax rates not exceeding 15 or 20 percent. Tax rates as high as 50 percent might be politically tolerable in today's context, but would not be effective in motivating people on welfare to work. Any radical welfare reform plan having tax rates that begin to stray up into the category of 70 and 80 percent and above has practically no chance of gaining political acceptance. All some enterprising senator or congressman would have to do to demolish the plan would be to construct a few charts showing how welfare recipients' take-home benefits changed as they began to work and earn more money. It would quickly be proven that the financial incentive to work was almost nonexistent.

A third major consideration affecting the political feasibility of any radical welfare reform plan is the cost. The amount of money that any welfare reform plan can add to the federal budget and still be politically acceptable is a function of many factors and changes constantly. Among other things it is a function of whether people believe the amount now spent on welfare is sufficient or not, of how high welfare reform is on the public's list of spending priorities, and of the fiscal condition of the federal budget.

The current circumstances and the prospects for change are not encouraging. A 1976 nationwide Harris poll indicated that 58 percent of the public felt that spending on welfare could be cut by one-third without serious loss. The danger of double-digit inflation and high unemployment threatened by the huge budget deficits being incurred by the federal government is causing every new spending proposal to come under the strictest scrutiny. A major radical welfare reform plan could be financed only by increasing taxes, cutting expenditures on other federal programs, or borrowing money—or some combination of these.

The politically acceptable cost of welfare reform is difficult to estimate with precision. But given the public's attitude toward welfare spending in particular, and the widespread opposition to higher taxes in general, to spending cuts in other federal programs, and to increased federal budget deficits, there seems to be little hope of mobilizing the public support necessary for a substantial increase in welfare spending. In fact, any increase in federal spending for welfare reform may be out of the question in the near future.

For any radical welfare reform program to succeed politically—to be passed by the Congress and signed into law by the president—three necessary major conditions must be met: 1) total welfare benefits for a typical family of four cannot fall much below $6,000 a year; 2) the total effective marginal tax rate on welfare recipients' earnings should not exceed 50 percent, and cannot exceed 70 percent; and 3) there should be no substantial additional cost to the taxpayers.

The three basic elements involved in any radical welfare reform plan—the level of benefits, the marginal tax rate, and the overall cost to the taxpayers—are *inextricably linked to one another*. If the level of benefits is increased, and the tax rate is held constant, the overall cost must increase; if the overall cost is held constant, the tax rate must increase. If the tax rate is decreased, and the overall cost is held constant, the level of benefits must decrease; if the level of benefits is held constant, the overall cost must increase. If the overall cost is decreased, and the level of benefits is held constant, the tax rate must increase; if the tax rate is held constant, the level of benefits must decrease.

It is impossible to change any one of these three main variables without affecting the others. Setting the values for any two of them automatically determines the other one. There is a direct mathematical relationship among all three variables—minimum benefit levels, tax rate, and cost—that is fixed for any particular radical welfare reform plan, a relationship that cannot be broken.

When any two of the three basic elements of radical welfare reform are set at politically acceptable levels, the remaining element becomes unacceptable. For example, if both the minimum welfare benefit level and the tax rate are set so they will be acceptable in today's political context, the cost of radical welfare reform balloons into tens of billions of dollars, adding millions of Americans to the welfare rolls. On the other hand, if the welfare benefit level is set at a politically tolerable level, and the overall cost is held down, the result is a tax rate that approaches confiscatory levels and destroys the financial incentive to work. And, finally, if the cost is acceptable and the tax rate is low enough to create a strong financial incentive to work, welfare benefits must be reduced to such a low level that the plan would have no chance whatsoever of being enacted. *There is no way to achieve all the politically necessary conditions for radical welfare reform at the same time.*

As long as Americans believe that poor people who cannot help themselves deserve a decent level of welfare support, that people's incentive to work should not be taken away from them, and that to increase their taxes to give money to someone who may not feel like working is unthinkable, the kind of radical welfare reform being discussed in some of today's best and brightest intellectual circles is going to remain an ideological fantasy, bereft of friends in the hard world of politics.

In addition to the three major determinants of political feasibility just discussed there are other factors that reduce the chances for political success of any radical welfare plan that attempts to guarantee incomes. First, any such plan would add millions of Americans to the welfare rolls. The lower the welfare tax rate, or the rate at which welfare benefits are reduced as earned income increases, the higher the annual income a person can have and still remain on welfare. Because of the existing distribution of income in the United States, even slight increases in the level of income a person can have and still qualify for welfare would make millions of additional people eligible. As Leonard Hausman has pointed out, "It is impossible, under any scheme, to maintain low cumulative tax rates while extending substantial cash and in-kind transfers to the working poor without also extending the coverage of these programs to middle-income brackets."[25]

Second, as indicated earlier, any form of a guaranteed income would cause a substantial amount of work reduction among low-income workers that could easily run as high as 50 percent, and possibly be even higher. While scarcely appreciated now, this could well turn out to be the most politically damaging aspect of a guaranteed income.

And finally, there are certain to be unanticipated social effects. For example, one striking result of the guaranteed income experiments was a sharp increase in the number of broken marriages for the low-income families who took part in the experiments. This unexpected phenomenon is ironic, as one important virtue often claimed for a guaranteed income is the strengthening of the family. The measured results of the Seattle-Denver guaranteed income experiments revealed that the incidence of marriage breakup for whites, who had been given an income guarantee of $3,800 a year, increased 430 percent during the first six months of the experiment. Over the entire two-year period studied, family breakup—relative to the control group—increased 244 percent for whites, 169 percent for blacks, and 194 percent for Chicanos.

Apparently many low-income women had been dissatisfied with their marriages but had remained with their families because they were unable to support themselves. When a guaranteed income gave them a sufficient degree of financial independence, even though only for a few years, they left.

One could argue that these marriage breakups were a good thing: the couples were unhappy together, and the guaranteed income made it possible for them to separate or get divorced. On the other hand, there may be quite a few taxpayers who won't understand why their tax money should be used to subsidize the breakup of marriages, especially those that involve children.

If the insoluble conflict among the goals of adequate welfare benefit payments, low marginal tax rates, and low budget cost is ignored—as it can be—there still remains a delicate task for the politician who supports such radical welfare reform. In the next election, he is the one who will have to answer his opponent's charge that he voted for welfare "reform" that lowered welfare benefits for hundreds of thousands, or even millions, of poor people, or that subjected welfare recipients to higher tax rates approaching confiscatory levels, or that added billions of dollars to the welfare budget. He is the one who will have to explain why so many more Americans went on welfare, why so many of them stopped working, and, perhaps, why so many of their marriages broke up.

Politically, it's all very risky.

WHY PRESIDENT CARTER'S PLAN FAILED

Congressional leaders informed President Carter on June 22, 1978 that his proposed welfare reform plan was dead for that session of Congress. There was not even enough support in the House to pass a compromise bill costing less than half the $20 billion price of the original bill.

Why did this much-heralded "reform" plan fail? The core of any valid welfare reform is the number of people affected and how they are affected. One of the first items the Congressional Budget Office tackled when it began its analysis of President Carter's Program for Better Jobs and Income (PBJI) was what it called the program's "distributive impact," namely: 1) how the program would affect "the distribution of [welfare] recipients and benefits by income level," and 2) "the number and types of families that would gain or lose benefits relative to the current welfare system."[26]

The preliminary results were astonishing. According to the estimates of the CBO, approximately 44 million Americans currently receive some form of welfare aid from such programs as Aid to Families with Dependent Children, Supplemental Security Income, state general assistance, the earned income tax credit, and food stamps. Carter's welfare reform plan would have increased this number by almost 22 million,[27] so that some 66 million Americans would have been receiving welfare. That is just about one-third of the nation.

The massive increase in welfare spending over the past ten to fifteen years has dramatically reduced poverty in the United States—so much so that there are few poor people left. Would Carter's plan, by adding $20 billion to the annual welfare budget, have substantially increased welfare payments to these poor? The answer is no.

The welfare changes proposed by President Carter would have had an unexpected effect. As Table 1 shows, the vast majority of those who

TABLE 1

Distribution of Welfare Recipients by Pre-Welfare Family Income Classes under Current Welfare Policy and under President Carter's Welfare Reform Plan (PBJI)

Family Income Class	Number of People Receiving Benefits under Current Welfare Policy[a]	Number of People Receiving Benefits under Carter's Reform Plan	Number of People Added by Carter's Reform Plan	Percent Increase
Less than $5,000	25,600,000[b]	26,900,000	1,300,000	5
$5,000 to $9,999	12,000,000	16,300,000	4,300,000	36
$10,000 to $14,999	3,600,000	15,200,000	11,600,000	322
$15,000 to $24,999	2,600,000	6,600,000	4,000,000	154
More than $25,000	600,000	1,000,000	400,000	67
TOTAL	44,400,000	66,000,000	21,600,000	49

Source: Robert D. Reischauer, Assistant Director for Human Resources and Community Development, Congressional Budget Office, statement to Task Force on Distributive Impacts of Budget and Economic Policy, Committee on the Budget, "Preliminary Analysis of the Distributional Impacts of the Administration's Welfare Reform Proposal," October 13, 1977, page 13, Table 2(a). Preliminary estimates as of October 12, 1977. Based on earlier CBO studies, an average family size of 2.824 was used to convert numbers of families to people.

[a]Includes Aid to Families with Dependent Children, Supplemental Security Income, state general assistance, food stamps, and the earned income tax credit.

[b]Number of people rounded to nearest 100,000.

would have received welfare checks for the first time were in the middle-income group; and a few were in the upper-income group. The number of people from families with pre-welfare incomes of less than $5,000 a year would have increased only slightly (5 percent), under the proposed reform. As we move up into the higher-income classes, however, Carter's welfare reform would have a greater impact. The number of people included in families earning between $5,000 and $10,000 a year would have increased by 36 percent.

But the greatest impact was to be in the income brackets between $10,000 and $25,000. Carter's plan would have given welfare benefits, including earned income tax credits, to 11.6 million more Americans who come from families earning between $10,000 and $15,000 a year, an increase of 322 percent in the number of families. And 4.3 million Americans who now receive no welfare and come from families with incomes between $15,000 and $25,000 a year would also have benefited—a 154 percent increase (see Table 1).

The CBO's analysis of how the distribution of welfare benefits would have changed under Carter's proposed welfare reform clearly and dramatically shows that most of the new beneficiaries under PBJI would have come from America's middle-income class. There was to have been a minimal effect on people in poverty. Of the almost 22 million additional people who would have received welfare, 74 percent would have come from families having incomes of over $10,000 a year, and more than 94 percent from families with incomes that exceed $5,000 a year. Carter's welfare plan, in its broad thrust, would have focused on aiding people not now receiving any welfare.

In summation, the welfare reform that President Carter originally proposed in 1977 would have probably cost somewhere in the neighborhood of $20 billion a year more than our current welfare system. Nearly 22 million more Americans would have received some form of welfare. Effective marginal tax rates would have remained very high and acted as a serious disincentive to work. The administrative complexity of welfare would have been compounded and more welfare workers would have probably been needed to handle the increased caseload. The problems caused by the separate existence of medicaid, day care, and housing assistance programs were ignored. An examination of the gainers and losers under PBJI shows clearly that those who need welfare the least would have gained in the greatest numbers; those who truly cannot care for themselves and are now on welfare would have benefited little. The thrust of Carter's plan was to further the idea of a guaranteed income, expanding welfare into the heart of the middle class of America. This was not welfare reform. It was a potential social revolution of great magnitude, a revolution that, had it come to pass, could have resulted in social tragedy.

Those who followed past efforts at radical welfare reform were not surprised that President Carter's plan failed like the rest. From past experience, however, one can with some confidence predict that new plans will soon spring, phoenix-like, from the intellectual ashes of the old ones.

WHAT CAN BE DONE

There are two ingredients necessary to a successful program of welfare reform. First, it must be built on a clear and accurate perception of the current nature of the welfare system in the United States; and, second, it must be guided by a deep appreciation for the attitudes of Americans toward caring for people who cannot care for themselves. A plan for radical welfare reform that assumes the current system is virtually a total failure and does not take into account the public's hostility toward any form of a guaranteed income will ultimately fail, if not in the halls of Congress, then later, during its implementation. But if the reform plan builds on the strengths of our current welfare system and embraces a philosophical approach that is familiar to and accepted by the American people, its chances of success are high.

The experience of more than a decade clearly shows that the American public will accept changes in the welfare system if they move in the direction of reorienting the system toward the needy-only approach to welfare. A program of reform that increases benefits to the truly needy, controls costs to the taxpayers, eliminates fraud and abuse, and provides strong encouragement for people on welfare to become self-supporting is entirely feasible—socially, economically, and politically. The legislative details of such a plan would be numerous and complex, matching in size and complexity the array of welfare programs we now have. The welfare system is constantly changing in small ways as the regulations governing its implementation are adjusted by the welfare bureaucrats. Any reform specifics would depend on the current state of each of the programs.

There are, however, some relatively timeless principles that could guide the detailed development of any national welfare reform plan. If we begin with the premise that any serious plan for welfare reform must be politically, economically, and socially feasible, we are forced to operate within certain constraints: the plan must be consistent with what most Americans believe welfare should do, it must have a reasonable cost, and it must efficiently and effectively provide an acceptable level of welfare benefits to the truly needy.

There are at least seven guiding points for such a program:

Point One: Reaffirm the needy-only philosophical approach to welfare and state it as explicit national policy. A welfare program can succeed only if it is basically in line with what most people believe is right. In the short run it might be possible to pass legislation that would institute a guaranteed income for all or, at the other extreme, simply eliminate all government welfare programs over a period of time and allow private charitable efforts to take care of people in need. But neither of these approaches will work unless preceded or accompanied by massive changes in deeply held public beliefs. A major change in either direction is possible, but until such change begins to occur any move to reform welfare that is not based on the needy-only approach will be inherently unstable and destined to fail.

Further, there must be a clear statement of national welfare policy as a guide for those who formulate the specific laws and regulations governing the welfare system. With no clear, well-defined principles the criteria for judging specific changes in welfare programs are murky, leaving advocates, pressure groups, government officials, and politicians relatively free to support or oppose specific changes, guided only by their own personal philosophical views on what our welfare system should ultimately be. The mere promulgation of a national welfare policy would not eliminate this, but the presence of clear principles against which specific actions could be judged by outside observers would certainly attenuate such tendencies.

Point Two: Increase efforts to eliminate fraud. Perhaps the one single thing about our current welfare system that most infuriates the typical American is the flagrant fraud perpetrated by a sizable percentage of welfare recipients.

The extent of fraud and dishonesty has been clearly and irrefutably documented numerous times in recent years. For example, a HEW study of New York City in 1973, corroborated by a parallel study conducted by the General Accounting Office, showed that in the AFDC program alone, over 10 percent of the recipients were ineligible for any payment whatsoever and 23 percent were being overpaid (8 percent were underpaid). A California study, conducted in 1972, revealed that 41 percent of the state's welfare recipients were either ineligible or overpaid. Admittedly, some of these welfare irregularities are due to administrative error on the part of the welfare bureaucracy. But there is no question that hundreds of millions, probably billions, of dollars are taken from taxpayers every year and given to people who have no legal right to receive them.

Few Americans begrudge a truly needy person the money and services that our welfare programs provide, but most are enraged at the thought of someone who is fully able of caring for himself smugly cashing a government welfare check at the local supermarket. For many Americans welfare reform means only one thing—apprehend those who are defrauding the system and remove them from the welfare rolls.

Perhaps no other single issue has contributed more to the low status of welfare recipients than the public's conviction that a high percentage of those on welfare don't deserve it. Because there is no practical way to identify welfare cheats, a certain portion of the hostility generated by those who abuse the welfare system gets directed at all who receive welfare. As long as fraud is widespread, anyone on welfare is suspect to some degree in the minds of many people. A substantial reduction of welfare fraud would result in large cost savings and would greatly help restore confidence in and respect for the system. And it would wipe away the stigma of cheating from those who validly receive welfare.

Point Three: Establish and enforce a fair, clear work requirement. A welfare system based on the needy-only approach requires some means of ensuring that only those who truly cannot help themselves receive aid. During the last decade or so we have come to rely heavily on financial incentives to induce people on welfare to work if they are able to do so. Unfortunately, this has produced the dilemma of the poverty wall. There is no feasible way that the very high effective marginal tax rates imposed on the poor by our current welfare system can be reduced. The radical welfare reform plans proposed would only exacerbate the problem. Any significant reduction in welfare tax rates, significant enough to create an effective financial work incentive, would either be prohibitively expensive or result in a very low basic welfare payment.

We have gotten ourselves into the position of relying on a work incentive technique that is *unworkable*. Financial work incentives are fine in theory, but in the current welfare situation the constraints of cost and benefit levels have rendered them virtually useless. As a practical matter the financial work incentives produced by marginal tax rates of well over 70 percent are negligible—and there is no politically feasible way to decrease the rates enough to make them effective.

There is a way out of this dilemma, but it requires that we reexamine our commitment to using financial incentives to encourage people to remove themselves voluntarily from the welfare rolls and find work. The idea of using financial incentives to induce people to get off the welfare rolls is faulty in principle. It attempts to persuade people to do something they should be required to do. If we assume that our welfare system is to provide help to the needy only, it then follows that either a person has a valid need for welfare payments and should be on the welfare rolls or that person does not have a valid need for welfare payments and should not be on the welfare rolls. If persons are capable of self-support, both for themselves and for their families, they should not expect to receive any money from other members of the society who work and pay taxes. There is no reason people should be given financial incentives to do what they rightfully should be doing anyway.

The basic principle involved here is one of independence versus dependence. If a person is capable of taking care of himself, he is independent and should not qualify for any amount of welfare. To the extent that a person is dependent—that is, to the extent that he cannot care for himself—to that extent he qualifies for welfare. If he can earn part of what he needs, then he has an obligation to work to that extent.

The major difficulty with such a principle is its implementation. For someone must judge whether or not the welfare recipient is capable of work. But difficult as this may be, it can be done. As in all judicial-type decisions, there are things that reasonable persons can reach agreement on. It will, however, require a shift away from the growing trend toward a more automatic, check-mailing type of welfare operation to a more personalized, people-oriented kind of welfare administration that emphasizes both the authority and the responsibility of local government.

In sum, we must abandon the idea of depending on financial incentives to induce people to leave the welfare rolls. Instead, our welfare programs should be guided by the simple principle that a person gets welfare only if he or she qualifies for it by the fact of being incapable of self-support. If they don't qualify, they have no right to welfare. Rather than being encouraged to find work, they should be given reasonable notice and then removed from the welfare rolls.

Point Four: Remove inappropriate beneficiaries from the welfare rolls. There are certain categories of welfare recipients whose eligibility, while legal, is questionable. With the needy-only principle as a guideline the welfare rolls should be examined carefully and the regulations changed to exclude any groups who fail to qualify. Two prime candidates for disqualification would be workers who strike and then apply for welfare benefits claiming loss of income, and college students who queue up for food stamps.

Point Five: Enforce support of dependents by those who have the responsibility and are shirking it. Too often we fail to ask why people are on welfare. In many cases the answer is simple: a father deserts his family with the clear knowledge that because of the way the law works there is little chance that he will ever be called to account. Today a high percentage of families receiving welfare payments have an absent parent who could contribute to their support. Although increased efforts have been made in recent years to remedy this situation, it is time to reassert strongly the old idea that both the father and the mother have a responsibility to care for their children.

This kind of child support enforcement could substantially lower welfare costs. During 1976, the first year the federal government made any serious effort to track down runaway welfare fathers, the Department of HEW collected some $280 million. It is estimated that such collections could mount as high as $1 billion a year by 1980.

For every absent parent who can be required to contribute to the support of his or her spouse and children we could remove, on the average, three or four people from the welfare rolls. If only as a matter of justice, parents who desert their families should be tracked down, across state lines if necessary, and required to provide a reasonable level of support.

Point Six: Improve the efficiency and effectiveness of welfare administration. Almost everyone seems to agree that the administration of the welfare system could be greatly improved—in effectiveness, efficiency, and responsiveness. The necessity for major improvements in countless areas of administration has been repeatedly documented. Reports and tales of gross mismanagement have become almost commonplace; shocking revelations no longer seem capable of rousing a benumbed public. For example, in 1976 New York State's welfare inspector general estimated that "nearly $1 billion, or almost one-sixth," of welfare-related costs in New York, were "being dissipated through recipient and vendor fraud, administrative error or unnecessary and overbilled services."[28] A billion dollars a year being lost through bad management in one large state would have been a page one scandal not too many years ago. The *New York Times* carried the story on page 29.

Administration is perhaps the most unexciting, intractable area in which to initiate welfare reform. People's eyes glaze over at the first mention of reorganization, revised regulations, and improved personnel administration. But dull as the area may be to most, it is of critical importance to any effective welfare reform plan. Welfare reform cannot succeed until and unless administrative reform is made a matter of top national priority, unless clear standards of performance are set, and until those standards are rigorously enforced by rewarding those welfare managers who succeed and penalizing those who fail.

Point Seven: Shift more responsibility for welfare from the federal government to state and local government and to private institutions. The question of which level of government—federal, state, or local—is best able to perform a particular function, or indeed whether the function should not be attended to by government at all but instead be left to private initiative, is one that has perplexed scholars and policymakers for a long time. When President Eisenhower took office in early 1953, one of his first acts was to establish a national commission of distinguished Americans (among them Oveta Culp Hobby, Clark Kerr, Hubert Humphrey, and Wayne Morse) to study this problem and recommend to him a set of specific actions. The commission worked intensively for almost two years and concluded:

> Assuming efficient and responsible government at all levels—National, State and local—we should seek to divide our civic responsibilities so that we leave to private initiative all the functions that citizens can perform privately; use the level of government closest to the community for all public

> functions it can handle . . . [and] reserve National action for residual participation where State and local governments are not fully adequate, and for the continuing responsibilities that only the National Government can undertake.[29]

Public opinion polls now indicate strong support for such a shift. A 1976 nationwide Harris survey posed a number of propositions and asked whether the statement applied more to the federal government or to state government. The results revealed that the majority of the American people felt that state government was "closer to the people" (65% to 12%); state governments could "be trusted more" (39% to 15%); state governments "really care what happens to people" (36% to 14%); the federal government "is more out of touch with what people think" (56% to 12%); and the federal government "gives the taxpayer less value for the tax dollar" (44% to 23%).[30]

Another national Harris poll, designed expressly to determine how the American public feels about the role of state and local governments, produced results more directly relevant to the issue of welfare. When asked what level of government—state, local, or federal—should make key policy decisions in regard to welfare, the American public favored state and local governments over the federal government by a margin of 56 percent to 39 percent. Five percent were undecided.[31]

I can think of no more appropriate place to apply the progressive principles of decentralizing government than to our welfare system. It has been argued, and fairly so, that a good deal of the waste and inefficiency in our welfare programs, the growing impersonalization, and the strong desire to automate the whole thing, is directly linked to the increased federal role in welfare. As authority over welfare has become centralized in Washington, the policymakers have become increasingly remote and isolated from the welfare recipients. As government, at all levels, has taken a greater and greater role in welfare, people seem to have become more reluctant to contribute to private charitable institutions.

We can arrest this trend toward a centralized, impersonal welfare bureaucracy by moving on two fronts. First, we should encourage people to take a more active role in charitable endeavors by allowing them a tax credit for charitable contributions, perhaps with some limit as to the maximum credit that could be taken. If it is considered good to use a tax credit to finance political campaigns, wouldn't it be even better to use one to encourage the growth of private charity? In addition, the current limit on the amount of charitable contributions that is deductible in computing taxable income should be raised significantly. If pursued properly, such a combined policy of credits and deductions for charitable contributions would gradually reduce government's role, while at the same time increasing the total resources available for welfare.

Second, for the continuing, large role in welfare that would remain for the government in the near future, an effort should be made to transfer both authority and responsibility for welfare programs, and the resources used to fund those programs, from the federal government to state and local governments. On balance, the closer the level of government is to the people, the more efficient and effective our social welfare programs are apt to be. As Dan Lufkin concluded, after serving for two years as Connecticut's first commissioner of environmental protection, "The more the administration of policies and programs is brought down to the state and local level, the better the people will be able to judge who is fair, who is honest, who is creative, and who is productive and efficient."[32]

A comprehensive welfare reform plan that hewed to these seven basic principles could go far toward restoring equity and efficiency to our welfare system. Its cost would be minimal and, in fact, could even lead to reductions in welfare expenditures. The latent public support for such a plan is clearly there. What is missing is the strong national commitment for this kind of welfare reform that can come only from a White House initiative.

Practical welfare reform demands that we build on what we have. It requires that we reaffirm our commitment to the philosophical approach of giving aid only to those who cannot help themselves, while abandoning any thoughts of radical welfare reform plans that will guarantee incomes. The American people want welfare reform that ensures adequate help to those who need it, eliminates fraud, minimizes cost to the taxpayers, and requires people to support themselves if they can do so.

NOTES

1. Edward C. Banfield, *The Unheavenly City: The Nature and Future of Our Urban Crisis* (Boston: Little, Brown and Co., 1970), pp. 115–116.

2. Roger A. Freeman, *The Growth of American Government: A Morphology of the Welfare State* (Stanford: Hoover Institution Press, 1975), pp. 143–144n.

3. John L. Palmer and Joseph Minarik, "Income Security Policy," in *Setting National Priorities: The Next Ten Years*, ed. Henry Owen and Charles L. Schultze (Washington, D.C.: Brookings Institution, 1976), p. 525.

4. Ibid.

5. Quoted in Mark R. Arnold, "We're Winning the War on Poverty," *National Observer*, February 19, 1977, p. 1.

6. Morton Paglin, "Transfers in Kind: Their Impact on Poverty, 1959–1975" (Paper presented at the Hoover Institution, Conference on Income Redistribution, October 1977), p. 14.

7. Ibid., p. 32.

8. Ibid., Table 8.

9. Ibid., p. 38.

10. Quoted in Arnold, "We're Winning the War on Poverty," p. 1.

11. Quoted in ibid.

12. Robert H. Haveman, "Poverty and Social Policy in the 1960's and 1970's—An Overview and Some Speculations," in *A Decade of Federal Antipoverty Programs: Achievements, Failures, and Lessons*, ed. Robert H. Haveman (New York: Academic Press, 1977), p. 18.

13. U.S. Congress, Joint Economic Committee, Subcommittee on Fiscal Policy, press release, Washington, D.C., December 22, 1972.

14. Ibid.

15. Henry J. Aaron, *Why Is Welfare So Hard to Reform?* (Washington, D.C.: Brookings Institution, 1973), pp. 32–35.

16. Ibid., pp. 33–34.

17. U.S. Congress, Congressional Budget Office, *Welfare Reform: Issues, Objectives, and Approaches* (Washington, D.C., July 1977), p. 15.

18. U.S. Congress, Joint Economic Committee, Subcommittee on Fiscal Policy, *Income Transfer Programs: How They Tax the Poor*, prepared by Robert I. Lerman, Studies in Public Welfare, Paper no. 4 (Washington, D.C., December 22, 1972), p. vi.

19. Chamber of Commerce of the United States, *Proceedings of the National Symposium on Guaranteed Income* (Washington, D.C., December 9, 1966), p. 13.

20. Aaron Wildavsky and William Cavala, "The Political Feasibility of Income by Right," *Public Policy* 18 (Spring 1970), p. 321.

21. Erich Fromm, "The Psychological Aspects of the Guaranteed Income," in *The Guaranteed Income: Next Step in Economic Evolution?*, ed. Robert Theobald (Garden City, N.Y.: Doubleday and Co., 1965), pp. 177–179.

22. Martin Anderson, *The Federal Bulldozer: A Critical Analysis of Urban Renewal, 1949–1962* (Cambridge, Mass.: M.I.T. Press, 1964), pp. 228–230.

23. Michael C. Keeley, Philip K. Robins, Robert G. Spiegelman, and Richard K. West, *The Labor Supply Effects and Cost of Alternative Negative Income Tax Programs: Evidence from the Seattle and Denver Income Maintenance Experiments*, Part I: *The Labor Supply Response Function*, Research Memorandum 38 (Menlo Park, Calif.: Center for the Study of Welfare Policy, Stanford Research Institute, 1977), p. 26.

24. Richard P. Nathan, "Modernize the System, Don't Wholly Discard It," *Los Angeles Times*, February 27, 1977, sec. 6, p. 3.

25. Leonard J. Hausman, "Cumulative Tax Rates in Alternative Income Maintenance Systems," in *Integrating Income Maintenance Programs*, ed. Irene Lurie (New York: Academic Press, 1975), p. 40.

26. Robert D. Reischauer, Assistant Director for Human Resources and Community Development, Congressional Budget Office, statement to Task Force on Distributive Impacts of Budget and Economic Policy, Committee on the Budget, "Preliminary Analysis of the Distributional Impacts of the Administration's Welfare Reform Proposal," October 13, 1977, p. 11.

27. Ibid., p. 13, Table 2(a).

28. *New York Times*, September 30, 1976, p. 29.

29. Commission on Intergovernmental Relations, *Commission on Intergovernmental Relations: A Report to the President for Transmittal to the Congress* (Washington, D.C., June 1955), p. 6.

30. *Current Opinion* (Roper Public Opinion Research Center), September 1976, p. 89.

31. Dan W. Lufkin, *Many Sovereign States: A Case for Strengthening State Government—An Insider's Account* (New York: David McKay Co., 1975), p. 225, Table 15.

32. Ibid., p. 194.

Social Security and the Economy

Michael J. Boskin

VII

The social security system—perhaps the most popular, and in many ways the most successful, government income-security program in the United States—is in serious trouble today. Although it is the major source of retirement income for millions of Americans, and an important source for millions more, it also imposes the largest part of the tax burden for many American families. Since its inception in the economic disruption of the Great Depression, social security has grown much more rapidly than virtually any other government program. Social security taxes account for about a quarter of all federal government revenues, and social security benefit payments amount to over $100 billion per year.

The social security system has provided substantial income security and relief from poverty for the elderly, and it annually transfers billions of dollars from the younger, wealthier generation of workers to the older, poorer generation of retirees. Despite these accomplishments and some attempts at gradual reform, the system has not kept up with rapidly changing economic, social, and demographic conditions. It is having substantial adverse, and probably unintended, effects on the overall economy; it faces a long-range funding crisis of stunning proportions; it is being charged with unfair treatment by many groups in the population; and it is being abandoned by many state and local governments and nonprofit organizations. Social security is therefore at a crossroads in its history. A variety of commissions, the Congress, and the administration have all been considering various proposals to change the system, but most of these suggestions are only stopgap

---

This essay updates material contained in Michael J. Boskin, *The Crisis in Social Security* (San Francisco: Institute for Contemporary Studies, 1977).

solutions to social security's short-term problems; they do not begin to deal with the basic issues of adverse incentives and the long-term funding crisis.

HISTORY OF SOCIAL SECURITY

At the time of social security's enactment during the severe economic depression of the 1930s, as much as one-quarter of the labor force was unemployed, very few families had two wage earners, real wages were much lower than today's, and there were no widespread government antipoverty programs; hence the economic situation of a family whose primary earner was unemployed was often desperate.

Many of the elderly were particularly hard hit. It is common for families to accumulate wealth over their working lives to finance their retirement, but during the Depression, many of the elderly were forced to liquidate their assets early because of unemployment and short-term income needs. Thus, the social security system appeared to be able to achieve two goals in the 1930s: providing income support to the elderly; and inducing them to leave the labor force, thus opening up jobs for the rest of the population.

The original Social Security Act set up a more or less genuine trust fund along the lines of private insurance: funds were to be accumulated through mandatory withholding of a portion of a worker's wages throughout the period of his employment, then repaid to him with interest during his retirement; and retirees were to be paid back principal plus interest out of the accumulated reserves. It soon became apparent, however, that the first few cohorts of retirees would receive back very little in social security benefits, and therefore would have little incentive to leave the labor force and very little income support.[1] The initial contributions, or taxes, to social security were levied on employer and employee at a rate of 1 percent each up to the first three thousand dollars of earnings, a total of sixty dollars per year. A person who retired after paying into the system for only a brief period, therefore, would be entitled to a very small annuity, as little as one or two dollars per month. Since taxes substantially exceeded benefits during this period, it was perhaps to be expected that the system would have to be shifted to a pay-as-you-go basis, to avoid the need to finance minimum income support during retirement from general revenues. Thus, by 1939 the goal of a fully funded social security system was abandoned and replaced by a program in which current taxes were to be used to pay current benefits, and a small cash reserve, euphemistically entitled a trust fund, was to be accumulated.

In the years since 1939, coverage has been extended, taxes and benefits have increased, and other modifications have been made; but the system's essential features have remained unchanged. The original legislation provided for compulsory coverage for nonrailroad employees in commerce and industry. By the late 1970s, almost 90 percent of employees in the United States were covered by social security; the remaining 10 percent were primarily employees of federal, state, and local governments. The original tax of 1 percent on each employer and employee on earnings up to three thousand dollars has now been increased to more than 12 percent on earnings to more than twenty thousand dollars. (The tax rate has more than doubled and the taxable ceiling has been raised considerably since 1960 alone. More than half of American families already pay more in social security taxes than in income taxes.) Furthermore, the 1977 Social Security Act Amendments legislated tax increases that would bring the tax rate to more than 15 percent by 1990, and the current ceiling on taxable earnings to almost thirty-two thousand dollars by the early 1980s, and thereafter it will increase as average earnings in the economy increase.

THE NATURE OF THE SYSTEM

The relationship between taxes and benefits in the social security old-age survivors program reveals its basic nature.[2] As I have already noted, social security taxes are levied at a flat rate on both employees and employers on all covered earnings up to a maximum ceiling. Since this ceiling will be rising to almost thirty-two thousand dollars by 1982, more than 90 percent of total earnings will be covered. In computing total contributions, the contributions of employer and employee must be combined, since even though the employer nominally pays half of the tax, most economists agree that the employee eventually bears this tax burden in the form of lower wages. Because social security payroll taxes are levied on labor earnings only up to a ceiling, and because no deductions or exemptions are allowed, they are often described as being extremely regressive. In fact, low- and middle-income families do pay a higher share of their income in social security taxes than do the wealthy, but the program has many features that tilt its benefits distinctly toward the low-income population, and its basic form of financing is enormously progressive.

Social security benefits are paid to beneficiaries partly on the basis of past earnings, and they do increase as past earnings and social security taxes increase—but not in direct proportion. Thus, the benefit formula is heavily weighted toward low-income workers. The so-called replacement rate—the ratio of social security benefits to average covered monthly earnings during work years—decreases with these earnings, and benefits replace a larger fraction of lost earnings for the retired poor than for retired middle-income and wealthy individuals. Since 1960, benefits (including disability and hospital as well as old-age benefits) have approximately quadrupled after adjusting for inflation. Retirement benefits currently average two hundred sixty-five dollars per month for a retired worker.

To determine benefits, a primary insurance amount (PIA) based on average monthly covered earnings (AME) is calculated. (AME is derived from earnings subject to taxation over the worker's lifetime.) Current legislation uses taxes paid since 1950 or after age twenty-one, whichever is later.[3] Survivor benefits are paid for spouses and for children under eighteen, those still in school under age twenty-two, and dependent parents. The dependent child benefit is 50 percent of the worker's PIA for each dependent up to a maximum dollar amount; the surviving spouse's benefit is equal to the deceased spouse's PIA. Thus, benefits are paid on a *family* basis. Indeed, if both spouses have work histories in covered employment, survivor benefits are available only when they are larger than the amount each worker could collect on his or her own account.

In addition, workers may opt for early retirement: they may retire with permanently reduced benefits at any age between sixty-two and sixty-five (sixty-five being the age at which they may begin to receive their full PIA). Currently, more social security beneficiaries receive their first check at sixty-two than at sixty-five.

Perhaps social security's most important feature is its pay-as-you-go financing. As I have already noted, current benefits are paid almost exclusively out of current taxes. Therefore, in the absence of any offsetting private behavior, social security would be paying almost $100 billion annually to the retired population from taxes paid by the younger working population. Since real economic growth averaged approximately 2.5 percent per year in the United States until the last five years or so, real income almost doubled between generations. In transferring such a large sum from the current generation of much richer workers to the older generation of much poorer retirees, the system, therefore, is actually extremely progressive.

GOALS OF SOCIAL SECURITY

The old-age component of social security is intended to achieve two major goals: to replace income lost at retirement and to provide minimum income support to the aged. The second of these, sometimes called the transfer or welfare goal of the system, aims at providing some socially adequate level of support; the first is an attempt to provide social insurance against the vagaries of macroeconomic fluctuations, imperfections in private insurance markets, and imperfect foresight regarding future income, inflation, life expectancy, health, and the like. These conditions may lead many citizens to undersave for retirement, forcing them on the public as general charges via welfare or other government transfer-payment programs. Each of these goals enjoys wide public support, but in attempting to meet both with a single program, the social security system is not doing the best job possible in achieving each.

Although the system attempts to provide social insurance against undersaving for retirement through compulsory tax contributions, it is difficult to determine the extent to which individuals do undersave. Accurate information at the individual and family level on private savings and intergenerational transfers is not easily obtainable and most of the information we do have covers the period since the massive growth of the social security system, and hence is conditional upon the actual tax and benefit situations of individuals and families and on their perception of their future taxes and benefits. Thus, if social security had substituted for private transfers, we would expect to observe small amounts of such transfers, and we would need to be able to compare the current levels with those before the imposition and growth of the social security system. Various studies have shown, however, that as a result of poor planning or unanticipated events, a large proportion of the elderly might find themselves destitute in the absence of the social security system.[4]

What sort of return can each generation expect from this implicit forced-saving program? The pay-as-you-go nature of the system prevents the development of a real trust fund and the formation of real capital. Tax contributions by current workers are used to pay benefits to current retirees, with an implicit promise that the next generation of workers will pay taxes to finance the retirement years of the current generation of workers. Even if the social security tax rate remains constant, as the base upon which taxes are levied grows, because of increases in the working population or in real per-capita income (perhaps as a result of technological change), retirees will obviously receive much more than they paid in taxes when they were working. The ratio between the value of the total benefits received and of the total taxes paid discounted to the present can be regarded as an implicit rate of return on social security taxes.[5] The tax base grows roughly at a rate that is the sum of the growth rates of the population and of real wages—about 3 to 4 percent on the average over the last half century—but the annual rate of return earned on investment in private capital has apparently substantially exceeded this return. This has led several critics of social security to argue that social security is a bad deal for the young.[6] It is clear that the current slowing in the rate of population growth and the substantial decline in the rate of growth of productivity will make the expected return for current young workers much smaller than it has been for previous generations; and that in the absence of other consequences, the younger population might be better off investing in private capital. However, given the pay-as-you-go nature of the system, we are in a fundamental dilemma: if we decide to shift to a fully funded system or to some other method of financing the retirement benefits of the elderly (for example, from other taxes), the population working at that time will have to pay twice—once to finance their own retirement and once to take care of the current retirees.

In brief summary, social security as a forced-saving program has been a mixed success; the benefits are tied only loosely to past earnings and a variety of changes in the economy make the implicit return lower than could be obtained on alternative investments; but there is evidence that some of the elderly would undersave in its absence, and therefore that a forced-saving program of some sort is required. I shall return to this issue in my discussion of policy options.

The second goal of social security, that of achieving minimum income support for the elderly, has also met with mixed, but greater, success. Research has shown that social security benefits account for about one-third of the money income of elderly individuals and families.[7] Many social security recipients would be destitute without social security, and many more would have their standard of living substantially impaired if social security benefits were drastically reduced. It is not necessarily true, however, that the total income of the elderly, as a group, or as individuals, has increased by amounts equal to total, or per capita, social security benefit payments. This is because social security does not take place in a vacuum, but occurs in a broader context of private intrafamily and intergenerational transfer payments and may merely substitute for other income sources (for example, continued earnings and private transfers of income).

There are two major forms of private intrafamily or intergenerational transfers: private bequests from parents to children, and private support of elderly parents by children. As I have said, it is extremely difficult to obtain data on either of these forms of private transfer. Whether because of embarrassment, imperfect memory, or some other reason, many respondents to household surveys simply refuse to answer such questions or ignore them; and where internal checks are available, the answers prove to be inconsistent. It is clear that Americans as a whole are spending a much larger fraction of their income on public education than they did before the enactment of social security legislation, and that this is a social bequest from taxpaying parents to children in the form of knowledge and skills that will increase future earnings. Simultaneously, a steadily declining proportion of the elderly are living with their children. Therefore, social security may be viewed, at one extreme, simply as a system for the socialization of private intrafamily or intergenerational transfer payments and rearrangements of wealth. Such a system would represent no small accomplishment, since it would presumably increase the sense of certainty that the transfer payments would be received and perhaps decrease the psychological dependence across generations within families. It is by no means clear, however, that social security benefits have offset private intrafamily transfers dollar for dollar. At the other extreme is the view that social security has not displaced private intrafamily transfers at all, but has simply supplemented these other sources of income. In my opinion, the truth lies somewhere between these two extremes, but a definitive answer must await the development of better techniques to gather and analyze data on private intrafamily transfers.

Other problems also make it difficult to assess the needs and resources of the elderly. For example, a number of public in-kind transfer payments, such as subsidized medical care and housing, are now available to the elderly.[8] Senior citizens consume goods and services in very different proportions from the general population; thus the consumer price index provides a rather poor measure of their cost of living. In addition, the elderly are doubly poor in a sense: they are making less income than they received during their years of employment, and they are receiving far less than the current working population, since real economic growth makes the lifetime income of each new generation substantially greater than that of its predecessor.

It is clear that social security has at least partially filled a substantial void in our income-security system. But it has done so at a substantial cost, as I shall show in the following section.

THE CHANGING ECONOMY AND THE ADVERSE EFFECTS OF SOCIAL SECURITY

Since the inception of the social security system, the economy of the United States has changed drastically. Perhaps the most important of these changes has been the rapid growth of real per-capita income (until the early 1970s); the enormous growth of government, especially of income-security programs in addition to social security; a substantial increase in the ratio of employed adults to the total adult population, particularly in the participation of married women in the labor force; an enormous shift toward smaller families and one-person households; the growing popularity of early retirement; an enormous increase in life expectancy for the elderly since 1960; and a sharp decline in the birth rate following the post–World War II baby boom. Each of these changes, and others, had important effects on social security, particularly on the way it interacts with the economy as a whole. For example, the age structure of the U.S. population is changing rapidly. Today there are 3.25 workers for every retiree; however, this ratio will fall to only 2.0 workers for every retiree when the post–World War II baby boom generation retires. To maintain the same ratio of social security benefits to wages, social security tax rates will have to rise sharply, to well over 20 percent. This will dwarf even the substantial increases voted in the 1977 amendments that are due to take effect in the 1980s and 1990s.

Largely as a result of the changing age structure of the population, social security's long-term funding position is precarious; currently legislated benefits exceed currently legislated taxes by more than three-quarters of a trillion dollars—an amount considerably higher than the privately held national debt of the United States. Therefore, taxes will have to increase substantially, benefits will have to drop sharply, or other sources of revenue will have to be found.

The effects of the shift in the age structure have been exacerbated by an increase in the average length of the retirement period, an increase of approximately 30–35 percent since World War II. Two factors have caused this rise. First, the trend toward early retirement, which began at the turn of the century, has accelerated considerably in the last three decades. In 1948, 50 percent of all men over age sixty-five were in the labor force; today only 20 percent are. Second, at the same time there has been a large increase in life expectancy. Before 1960, gains in life expectancy were caused primarily by declines in infant mortality and in deaths among younger people. Since that time, however, these gains have mostly come from prolonged life spans among the elderly—about 1.5 years for men and 3.0 years for women. These increases, combined with earlier retirement, have lengthened the average period from retirement to death by approximately four or five years. Thus we are faced with the prospect of a larger fraction of our population needing support in old age for substantially longer periods. Future trends in retirement and life expectancy are not easy to extrapolate, particularly given the rapid changes in the labor force in recent decades. Will the increased labor-force participation of women result in lifetime careers? Will it level off? Will the increased stress of work lead to a greater incidence of diseases that shorten life among these women? Will we cure major diseases, such as certain forms of cancer, in the years ahead, thereby lengthening life expectancy? Each of these questions is difficult to answer, but it is clear that any additions to the average length of the retirement period will substantially increase the long-term deficit in social security funding and that any decreases will have the opposite effect.

The sharp decline in the labor-force participation of the elderly may be due, in part, to the social security system itself. As I noted above, there was an enormous transfer of wealth to the first few cohorts of retirees under the pay-as-you-go system. In addition, social security benefits are reduced by fifty cents for every dollar earned beyond a modest amount. A growing body of evidence suggests that these features have made social security a prime contributor to the startling increase in early retirement.[9]

Perhaps even more disturbing, the social security system may well be in competition with private saving and bequests and may thus serve as a substitute for private savings. Since it is financed on a pay-as-you-go basis, however, no real capital accumulation occurs. Although the issue is still in dispute, substantial evidence has been accumulating that social security may well reduce the supply of private capital.[10] If the promise of future social security benefits has led people to save less privately for their own retirement, and if the amount of this decrease has not been offset by adjustments in private intrafamily intergenerational transfers, then social security has substantially reduced private saving in the United States over the last several decades. Indeed, if the substitution of unfunded government implicit debt for real assets has been dollar for dollar, as one study has suggested,[11] the net effect on the private capital stock has been to reduce it by trillions of dollars.

If, however, as I mentioned earlier, social security is in part simply a medium for the socialization of private intrafamily intergenerational transfers, then its effects on private savings may be less severe; and if the system has encouraged longer retirement periods, this may lead to increased saving for retirement. Unfortunately, current information and data simply do not provide a definitive measure of the offset to the large decrease in saving.

If social security has indeed affected saving in any of these ways, as I believe it has, a variety of measures could be adopted to deal with this problem; I will discuss these later in this essay. It is clear, however, that there is a saving crisis in the United States today. Despite the rapid spread of the ownership of capital to the general population, the national rate of saving has fallen sharply in recent years. By the end of 1978, personal saving was less than 5 percent of personal income compared with an average rate over the preceding half dozen years of almost 7 percent. Our investment rate has not fallen off nearly so sharply, since it has been propped up by increased imports of foreign capital. How long we will be able to continue to finance even this modest level of private investment with foreign capital imports is not clear. Advanced or mature economies have financed their investment and growth out of foreign capital much less often than less developed economies have (including the United States in the nineteenth century). Personal saving rates in Japan, France, and West Germany are three or four times the U.S. rate.

There are many possible explanations for the decline in private saving in the United States: the changing age structure of the population; the growth of government programs, including social security; the heavy taxation of income from capital, especially when our unindexed income-tax system is combined with our high rate of inflation; and inflation itself. Consensus is growing, however, on the importance of increasing the private saving rate in the United States in the decade ahead, and reforming the method of financing for social security may be one vehicle for doing so.

In short, the enormous benefits of the social security system have been partially offset by its drawbacks. Workers in state and local government or nonprofit enterprises are opting out of the system in many cases, and millions more young employees are wondering whether they are getting a fair deal from it. The elderly, on the other hand, are nervous about the financial integrity of the system and its ability to continue to provide support for their retirement income.

In addition, many groups in the population believe that they are being treated unfairly. For example, working women whose benefits do not exceed those of their spouses contend that they receive no more return from their contributions than women who neither work nor pay taxes. Thus, there is a movement to change the tax or benefit treatment of dependent spouses.[12] Groups with life expectancies different from those of other groups are not now treated separately in the social security system. Similarly, men complain that women, whose life expectancy substantially exceeds their own, and who make the same total tax contributions, receive the same *annual* benefits, and therefore receive far more *total* benefits than men, on the average. Efforts to remove such inequities go beyond economic policy and economic decision making; they may well fall in the realm of interpretation of constitutional law.

Nevertheless, pressures from these groups may impede any attempts to reform the system.

POSSIBLE SOLUTIONS

Three types of problems plague the social security system: the adverse incentives it creates, its long-term funding deficit, and its apparent inequities. Although each could be dealt with in a variety of ways, I will present my own general analysis of the problem and suggestions for improvement.

The long-term funding deficit, the system's most critical present problem, is intimately related to each of the others. For example, increases in taxes or decreases in benefits designed to ameliorate the deficit might affect private saving and retirement decisions. The 1977 Social Security Amendments, which caused the greatest negative outpouring of mail in the history of Congress, legislated huge tax increases throughout the 1980s and 1990s, but these will hardly begin to reduce the gap between tax revenues and benefit payments. If we wait until the baby-boom generation retires and then raise tax rates to finance benefits at their current relative levels, the tax burden imposed on the working population at that time will create a crisis; indeed, a sharp polarization of society on the basis of age will be almost unavoidable. Tax rates would have to be increased to more than 20 percent of salaries, and such a burden, on top of federal, state, and local income taxes, would severely impede incentives to work for much of the population (even though workers in some Western European countries are already operating under even greater tax burdens.)

Obviously, some combination of tax increases and benefit decreases is required to reduce the deficit, particularly if the trends toward early retirement and greater life expectancy continue or grow even stronger. Enormous curtailment of benefits alone, in my opinion, is not the answer. What is necessary is a restructuring of benefits that will take into account the twin goals of social security, as well as the rapidly changing nature of our economy and the economic situation of the current and future elderly.

For example, a sharply dwindling proportion of our population works in physically demanding and dangerous jobs; moreover, increasing numbers of people are entering the labor force later in life because of substantial increases in college enrollment. In the years ahead, therefore, a larger and larger segment of retirees will have worked for shorter periods in less physically demanding jobs. This development, combined with the increase in life expectancy, may well make it desirable to increase the age at which full social security benefits are obtainable. I suggest gradually increasing that age over the next several decades to sixty-eight. Workers would be permitted to opt for earlier retirement at an actuarially fair reduction in benefits; indeed, if my suggestion (discussed below) for separation of the transfer and annuity goals of the system is adopted, they should be able to retire at any age and receive an actuarially fair reduction in their earned entitlements. Decreasing the number of years over which individuals collect social security may be more politically acceptable than decreasing the annual level of benefits.

A second major goal of social security reform ought to be the separation of the transfer and annuity goals of the system. We are simply not doing as good a job in meeting either of these goals as we should. Continuing to try to achieve them both in one program with one method of finance will continue to lead us into conflicts that prevent us from achieving either. The transfer-payment part of the system ought to be gradually shifted out of payroll taxes and into general revenues, where it should compete openly with other government income-transfer programs, spending programs, and tax reductions. A separate minimum-income-support or transfer-payment program for the elderly, financed out of general revenues, would also do much to meet the arguments of groups who argue that they are treated unfairly. Such problems have no place in earned-entitlements, social-insurance, or forced-saving programs. The current social security program already embodies one such program: Supplemental Security Income (SSI), which is funded from general revenues and supplements social security benefits for some two million elderly persons. Since the current benefits received under the regular social security program are almost all an intergenerational transfer, in the sense that the benefits received by current retirees average roughly five times their contributions plus interest, the program I recommend involves a much more fundamental reform than mere expansion of SSI. Further, as each new cohort of retirees collects benefits, this intergenerational transfer component will decrease (due to longer covered earnings histories, higher covered earnings and tax rates, and so on); but the transfer component will exceed the earned entitlement component for several more decades.

It is important to stress that these transitions must be made gradually. Many individuals have already made retirement plans; capital markets have adjusted to the current set of expectations about major social security benefits and taxes, and any rapid unexpected changes would result in large windfall gains and losses for various groups of the population.

The entitlements portion of the program should also be gradually strengthened to begin to provide genuine social insurance, in which individual benefits paid are precisely tied to lifetime individual contributions or taxes, plus interest.[13] Such a move would also reinstate the insurance goal of social security, which has been continuously eroded by a variety of redistribution devices within the system. As I have already noted, there are valid reasons for requiring individuals to provide, during their working years, for their own retirement. There is no reason, however, that such insurance must be provided publicly. Although the period of transition to a new system would be painful, we should begin to open up more ways in which individuals can prove that they have provided for their retirement, either privately or publicly. We also need to reconsider whether the forced-saving program should be based on a fixed percentage of payroll or earnings up to a certain ceiling, or whether people should be permitted to guarantee that they would achieve a given level of annuities; under the latter system, they might be able to cease contributing after they had reached their goal, or tax rates might be varied inversely according to income.

The severe problems facing social security—apparent inequities, adverse incentives, and funding crises—can be ameliorated if we begin to pay attention to the purposes of the program and to gradually unravel the disincentives it has created. Changing the age structure on which benefit entitlements are based and the form of financing of the program should be among the first goals. We should separate the transfer and annuity goals into separate programs; gradually raise the age at which full retirement benefits are paid; and begin to build a genuine trust fund in the earned-entitlements part of the program. But these changes would require one generation of workers to pay general revenue taxes to support the benefits of the current retirees, in addition to paying for their own retirement. I would offer a more modest proposal, therefore: gradually moving toward partial fulfillment of the goal of complete funding. If it turns out that the problems I envisioned do not materialize when the baby-boom generation retires, we can use the partially accumulated trust fund to pay benefits during the baby-boom generation's retirement. This will enable us to smooth the rise in tax rates necessary to fund the baby-boom generation's longer period of retirement and avoid the crisis early in the next century of a tax increase several times the largest peacetime increase in U.S. history.

Moreover, we must begin to deal with these problems soon. Some of the unintended adverse consequences of the current system are continuing year after year and the day of reckoning is rapidly approaching, but even more important, millions of individuals are presently trying to plan their retirement-income needs and sources. The uncertainty surrounding the social security system today makes this task even more difficult. A comprehensive reform of social security must be begun before the crisis of the baby-boom generation's retirement is upon us, or our options for dealing with these problems will be severely limited.

NOTES

1. See the excellent discussion in Rita Ricardo Campbell, *Social Security: Promise and Reality* (Stanford: Hoover Institution Press, 1977).

2. Throughout this essay I am discussing basically the old-age and survivors' part of the social security system. The disability insurance program and the hospital insurance program are each important in their own right and have grown rapidly in recent years, but I will discuss them only in passing.

3. A more detailed description is provided in Campbell, *Social Security*.

4. See, for example, Peter Diamond, "A Framework for Social Security Analysis," *Journal of Public Economics* 8, no. 3 (December 1977): 275–298; and Larry Kotlikoff, "Essays on Capital Formation and Social Security, Bequest Formation, and Long-run Incidence," (Ph.D. diss., Harvard University, 1977).

5. For the first generation of retirees after social security was adopted, of course, the rate of return was extremely high; its members either were not taxed or paid taxes only over a short period of earnings while they were young, but received a substantial transfer during their retirement.

6. See Martin Feldstein, "Social Security, Induced Retirement and Aggregate Capital Accumulation," *Journal of Political Economy* 82, no. 5, (September/October 1974): 905–926.

7. See James Schultz, "Income Distribution and the Aging," in Robert H. Binstock and Ethel Shanas, eds., *Handbook of Aging and the Social Sciences* (New York: Van Nostrand Reinhold, 1976).

8. See Schultz, "Income Distribution."

9. See Michael J. Boskin, "Social Security and Early Retirement," *Economic Inquiry* 15, no. 1 (January 1977): 1–25; and Michael J. Boskin and Michael Hurd, "The Effect of Social Security on Early Retirement," *Journal of Public Economics* 10, no. 5 (November 1978): 361–377.

10. See Feldstein, "Social Security"; and Alicia Munnell, *The Effects of Social Security on Personal Saving* (Cambridge, Mass.: Ballinger, 1974). For a contrary view, see Robert Barro, "Are Government Bonds Net Wealth?" *Journal of Political Economy* 82, no. 6 (November 1974): 1095–1117.

11. Feldstein, "Social Security."

12. A variety of proposals to deal with inequities between women working in the market and women in the home are discussed in Campbell, *Social Security*. A particularly appealing possibility that Campbell proposes is to allow several years per child (perhaps limited to a certain number of children) to be excluded from the AME calculation. (Currently, for women who drop out of the labor

force, five years can be excluded, but additional years enter as zeros in calculating AME).

13. Thus, the earned entitlements portion would provide a consistent unit of account on both the tax and benefit side: the individual. So would the transfer program: the family.

Government Power and Business Performance

Murray L. Weidenbaum

VIII

The massive encroachment of government power over private business in recent years has been, in the main, self-defeating. Despite the noble intentions of its proponents, increasing government intervention has inhibited the ability of the typical business enterprise to meet the consumer's needs. This intervention has tended to minimize, rather than maximize, achievement of the basic social objectives that have provided the motivation for expanding government involvement in private decision making.

The point to be developed here involves far more than mere identification of the waste and inefficiency that often occur in the process of governmental regulation. If the problem were simply one of cost, it would be serious but manageable. Rather, the rapid and pervasive growth of government regulations and requirements is increasingly preventing the private enterprise system from delivering to the public the rising standard of living and employment level that is expected and that provides the basic political support for the future of the business system.

Variations of this theme have been sounded by a number of observers. For instance, Harold M. Williams, chairman of the Securities and Exchange Commission (SEC) and formerly dean of the Graduate School of Management of the University of California at Los Angeles, has warned that, to the extent that the regulatory presence becomes pervasive, it tends to undermine the foundation of the private sector: "the qualities of will and initiative and self-sufficiency which are

---

This essay draws on the author's book *The Future of Business Regulation* (New York: Amacom, 1979).

essential to the growth and preservation of private enterprise."[1] Although some critics of this trend are inclined to view the expanding governmental presence as a conspiracy to eliminate the capitalistic system, that is not an accurate assessment of the motives of most proponents of the trend. Holders of the interventionist approach are typically oblivious to the full range of effects of their proposals, seeing the benefits and ignoring the costs of their actions. The purpose of this paper is to increase the general understanding of the consequences of detailed governmental regulation of business—to the end that the government's objectives can be reached more effectively and with less of the powerful, though unintended, side effects on the business system.

That purpose will involve describing the fundamental problems that arise from the proliferation of governmental activity, then showing the desirability of a change in the tendency toward it. Surely, at least in the short run, the future holds more, not less government regulation of business. But the trend will be uneven. In fact, it would not be surprising if the prospects for the private enterprise system in the United States were more favorable a decade from now than they are today. That pleasant state of affairs, however, will not come about effortlessly. The first step toward it is to understand the long-term effects of continuing these recent trends—and to communicate that understanding to a wide audience of voters, taxpayers, and public and private decision makers.

It is important to appreciate the direct connection between extensive regulation by government, in the first instance, and the pleas that result for more detailed government intervention in business. When government policies add to the cost of private production and thus to the prices charged to consumers, those policies can result in strong pressures for even greater government involvement in wage and price decisions. When excessive government regulation of business reduces the ability and incentive of business to engage in technological innovation and the development of new products and markets, the economy suffers a further reduction in its capability to achieve such important national objectives as greater job opportunities, rising standards of living, and an improved quality of life.

Moreover, when government policies sharply curtail the ability of the private sector to generate adequate savings to finance economic growth, not only is the government viewed as the banker of last resort, but the basic vitality of the business system is called into question. Public dissatisfaction with business performance increases greatly. This, in turn, sets the scene for another round of government involvement, ranging from proposals to nationalize specific industries to the subsidizing of others (always, of course, with the imposition of still more restrictions and regulations). Energy is a clear example of this phenomenon; and the automotive, pharmaceutical, and health care industries are about to provide more vivid illustrations. It is a truly vicious circle, because the expansion of government involvement is self-reinforcing. The result is often a downward spiral in the economy as a whole.

To be sure, not all government interference is undesirable, nor can all the shortcomings of the American business system be attributed to it. It must be recognized that impetus for expanded government action is being provided by a variety of citizen groups truly concerned with various shortcomings in our national life. In many cases, the new wave of regulation reflects public and congressional knowledge that traditional federal and state or local programs have not been effective. It is also promoted by the belief that the private sector itself is responsible for many of the problems facing society: pollution, discrimination in employment, unsafe products, unhealthy working environments, misleading financial reporting, and so forth. In that view, voluntary responses by business have not been and will not be entirely satisfactory.

Nevertheless, the rising tide of regulation has become a barrier to productive economic activity. The costs of government regulation are pervasive: 1) to the taxpayer for supporting a galaxy of government regulators, 2) to the consumer through higher prices to cover the added expense of producing goods and services under government regulations, 3) to the worker in the form of the jobs eliminated by government regulation, 4) to the economy as a result of the loss of smaller enterprises that cannot afford the onerous burdens of government regulations, and 5) to society through a reduced flow of better products and a slower rise in the standard of living.

IMPACTS ON BUSINESS

It is hard to overestimate the rapid expansion and the variety of government involvement in business occurring in the United States. Governmental intervention is not limited to such traditional independent agencies as the Interstate Commerce Commission, the Civil Aeronautics Board, and the Federal Communications Commission. Rather, the operating bureaus of government—the Departments of Agriculture, Commerce, Energy, Health, Education and Welfare, Interior, Justice, Labor, Transportation, and Treasury—are all involved in actions affecting virtually every firm in every industry. It is truly archaic to refer to regulated industries in the United States. During the 1970s every industry became regulated, at least to some important degree.

Most changes influencing business-government relations in recent years have been in the direction of greater government involvement in many aspects of life: environmental controls, job safety inspections, equal employment opportunity enforcement, consumer product safety standards, and energy restrictions. Indeed, when we look at the emerging business-government relationship from the business executive's viewpoint, a considerable public presence is evident in what historically have been private matters.

No business, large or small, can operate without obeying a myriad of government rules and restrictions. Costs and profits can be affected as much by a directive written by a government official as by a management decision in the front office or a customer's decision at the checkout counter. Fundamental entrepreneurial decisions—such as what lines of business to go into, what products and services to produce, which investments to finance, how and where to make goods and how to market them, and what prices to charge—are increasingly subject to government control.

Virtually every major department of the typical corporation in the United States has one or more counterparts in a government agency that controls or influences its internal decision making. There is almost a "shadow" organization chart of public officials matching the organizational structure of each private company. The scientists in corporate research laboratories now do much of their work to ensure that the products they develop are not rejected by lawyers in regulatory agencies. The engineers in manufacturing departments must make sure the equipment they use meets the standards promulgated by Labor Department authorities. Sales and marketing staff must follow procedures established by government administrators in product safety agencies. The location of business facilities must conform with a variety of environmental statutes. The primary thrust of many personnel departments has shifted from serving the staffing needs of the company to meeting the standards of the various executive agencies concerned with employment conditions. Finance departments bear the rising burden of paper work imposed by government agencies who treat information as a free good—or, in any event, who assume that more is always better than less.

Because of the complexity and immense degree of governmental involvement, it is difficult to grasp its totality. But, quite simply, there are few aspects of business that escape some type of government review or influence. Most important, the impacts of regulation go far beyond general requirements for corporate performance: more and more they permeate every facet of consumer activity, ranging from the purchase of breakfast food to the programs available on television.

As would be expected, a variety of important adjustments to government intervention is taking place in the structure and operation of the typical American corporation. Each major business function is undergoing important transformations. Some are merely reacting to government actions. Others reflect an effort to anticipate or obviate further government activity. All the changes tend either to increase the overhead costs of doing business or to deflect management and employee attention from the conventional tasks of designing, producing, and distributing better or cheaper goods and services. As Arthur F. Burns has stated, "as things stand, many corporate executives find so much of their energy is devoted to coping with regulatory problems that they cannot attend sufficiently to the creative part of their business."[2]

The role of top management is undergoing a metamorphosis as it responds to the changing external environment. The outlook of corporate executives is shifting from primary concern with conventional production and marketing decisions to coping with a host of external and often strange policy considerations, frequently motivated by groups with nonbusiness and noneconomic priorities. Members of senior management groups may become as attuned to the desires of those new interests as to their traditional accountability to shareholders. Some corporate annual meetings seem to be devoting as much time to the politics of South Africa as to the economic needs of Middle America.

Not surprisingly, numerous chief executives report that one-third or more of their time is now devoted to governmental and public policy matters: dealing with the many federal, state, and local regulations that affect a company, meeting with a variety of special interest groups that make demands on the organization's resources, and participating increasingly in the public policy arena. A survey by the Conference Board, a highly regarded business research organization, revealed that 43 percent of the chief executives who responded devote one-fourth or more of their time to external relations and 92 percent devote more time to this than they did three to five years ago.[3] A chief executive very different from the popular stereotype is emerging in American corporations. The metamorphosis of the modern corporation at its highest levels is clear: corporate executives are less private entrepreneurs in a free enterprise system than they are unelected quasi-public officials in an amorphous and complex system that includes both private and social concerns.

Some of the most fundamental impacts of governmental intervention are discernible in the corporate research and development area, although the ramifications are likely to unfold only over a long period in the form of a reduced rate of product and process innovation. A rising share of corporate research and development budgets is being shifted to so-called defensive research, that is, to meeting the requirements of government regulatory agencies, rather than to designing products with greater customer appeal. This trend is most advanced in the automotive industry, where the head of the General Motors research laboratory has stated: "We've diverted a large share of our resources—sometimes up to half—into meeting government regulations instead of developing better materials, better manufacturing techniques, and better products . . . It's a terrible way to waste your research dollars."[4] There is a similar trend in the chemical industry in response to a plethora of new laws and regulations, all ostensibly designed to yield a cleaner or safer environment.

It must be discouraging to the innovative instincts of American business to undergo experiences like the recent one of Monsanto, a major chemical company, with its Cycle-Safe plastic bottle for soft drinks. According to John W. Hanley, Monsanto's president, shoppers in the test markets liked the product because it was lightweight and shatter-resistant. It was also recyclable. But the Food and Drug Administration (FDA) banned the new product because it was made with acrylonitrile (a chemical that had been used in food contact applications for more than 30 years). The regulators say that if the bottles were filled with acetic acid and stored for six months at 120° F, an infinitesimal amount of the chemical could leach into the solution. But in fact, a carbonated beverage stored at 120° would burst the bottle in a few weeks. Nevertheless, Monsanto has had to close all plants making Cycle-Safe bottles.[5] The government, via the regulatory process, is building a "legal envelope" around existing technology.

The aggregate impact of the rulings of the FDA, the Environmental Protection Agency (EPA), the Occupational Safety and Health Administration (OSHA), and the Consumer Product Safety Commission (CPSC) are also altering the manufacturing function of the typical American business firm. One result of the pressures for production processes to meet government environmental and safety requirements is that a larger share of company investment (about one-tenth at present) is being devoted to these required social responsibilities, rather than to increasing the capacity to produce a higher quantity or quality of material output, at least as conventionally measured. Coupled with the many factory closings due to regulation, these requirements are resulting in a smaller productive capacity in the American economy than is generally realized.

The combined effect of a lowered stock of productive capital and more expensive and elaborate production and review processes can only result in a decline in the ability of the American economy to deliver to the public the rising standard of living that has become a hallmark of the private enterprise system. And when the resources are available to produce new products, it is becoming far more difficult to market them. A powerful feedback effect occurs, of course, in terms of increasing the uncertainty of new investments, thus reducing their desirability. In the words of Arthur F. Burns, "Such uncertainties and frustrations cannot be brought under a dollar sign; but they have a telling effect on a nation's business."

In addition, virtually every aspect of the marketing function of business is affected by government. Government regulations increasingly restrict the options available to the marketing manager. Advertising is now subject to basic regulation by the Federal Trade Commission (FTC), which has been broadening its area of concern with reference to "misrepresentation" by business firms. The details of product warranties are controlled by the Magnuson-Moss Act of 1975. Packaging and labeling are regulated by the FTC, the FDA, the CPSC, and the Department of Agriculture. Motor vehicle producers must include mileage ratings in advertising; cigarette packages must display statements about their probable link to cancer; appliances must be labeled according to energy usage; and processed foods must list ingredients in specified order. The most severe restrictions, however, relate to the growing power of government agencies to refuse to permit the production of products that do not meet their standards, or to require the recall of such products already sold.

As one astute observer of the Washington scene points out, the adverse though unintended impact of the regulatory activities in the personnel area is this: "It has become considerably more expensive to employ anyone."[6] In an analysis of the impacts of the 1973 consent decree in which the American Telephone and Telegraph Company pledged to carry out an equal employment program, Carol J. Loomis concluded that the favoring of women and minorities required by the decree has "necessarily also required some lowering of employment standards, and this combination had produced bruising side effects."[7]

Ironically, many existing federal, state, and local regulatory policies discourage companies from taking such "socially responsible" actions as locating manufacturing operations in central cities. Rulings that generally favor rural or suburban areas include zoning, noise limitations, and environmental restrictions on air and water use. As the Campbell Soup Company wrote in response to an inquiry by the Committee on Banking, Finance, and Urban Affairs of the U.S. House of Representatives, rural locations generally make it easier to minimize any adverse effects a facility may have on the local environment and to meet or surpass government environmental requirements, all at considerably less cost than would be the case in the city.[8]

The most direct company response to the widening role of government in business is often through expansion of selected staff operations. Every company is creating some capability to inform itself about and evaluate present and future government developments relating to its activities. Firms of substantial size generally maintain headquarters planning staffs and Washington offices; smaller companies rely primarily on their trade associations and on Washington-based attorneys and consultants. In some cases, substantial changes are made in the corporate organizational structure. A company may establish a major headquarters office on government relations, with direct ties to each of its operating departments—as well as offices in Washington and in state capitals.

Professor Douglas North, of the University of Washington, contends that the key margin of decision making in our society is access to government influence. The predictable result "is to shift the locus of the investment of resources into attempts to favorably influence the strategic government official or to prevent the enactment of governmental policies that will adversely affect the interest of groups."[9] North's point may be overstated. Many opportunities for new private undertakings still exist. Moreover, the adverse public reaction to the massive use of business resources in politics would, under present circumstances at least, be overwhelming. Nevertheless, he is indicating an important emerging development, especially in the case of larger business organizations.

Government regulation hits small business disproportionately hard, often unintentionally: the standardized directives typically do not distinguish companies by size. In practice, forcing a small firm to meet the same requirements as a large company with highly trained technical staffs at its disposal places a significantly greater burden on the smaller enterprise. This general point is supported by data and examples from such different governmental regulatory programs as the EPA, the OSHA, the Employee Retirement Income Security Act of 1974 (ERISA), the National Labor Relations Board, and the SEC.[10]

What may not be apparent is the basically anti-competitive nature of the federal regulations. The problems faced by the larger companies should not be underestimated. But it is realistic to expect that most of them will be able to adjust to the expanded regulatory environment, although at higher cost and with reduced output. Surely it is not the intent of groups favoring an expanded role of government to single out the smaller firm. In fact, those groups typically focus their criticism on the industrial giants. But the result is often the reverse of what they intend—a weakening of the role of small and new firms in the American economy and a more concentrated industrial structure. These developments have led Lee Loevinger, who has been both FTC chairman and Assistant Attorney General for Antitrust, to state, "Thus small enterprises are slowly squeezed out and barriers to entry are established by government fiat that would make an old fashioned monopolist either envious or embarrassed."[11]

MEASURING THE EFFECTS

Examining the entire process of government intervention, it is clear that business is the quintessential middleman. The consumer must bear the ultimate effects. Government imposition of socially desirable requirements on business may appear at first to be an inexpensive way of achieving national objectives, and it would seem to represent no significant burden on the consumer. But the public does not get a free or low-cost lunch when government imposes requirements on private industry. In large measure, the costs of government regulation show up in higher prices of goods and services: a hidden tax. Thus the real level of federal taxation, in terms of the government burden imposed on the public, is higher than generally realized.

This phenomenon is clearest in the area of automobile regulation. The newly produced automobile in the United States carries a load of equipment mandated by the federal government, ranging from the catalytic converter designed to reduce air pollution to such seldom-used safety equipment as seat belts and shoulder harnesses. There was approximately $666 in government-mandated safety and environmental control equipment in the typical 1978 passenger automobile. Ten million cars were sold that year, so that higher auto prices paid by American consumers totaled $6.7 billion.

Further hidden are the regulatory expenses embedded in the price of a new home: the costs of the many inspection permits, licensing fees, and environmental impact statements, and the extra financing required during the inevitable delays. These costs have been estimated conservatively at over $2,000 for an average new home. With almost two million new residences built annually, the hidden tax of regulation to homeowners comes to about $4 billion a year.[12] Therefore, the final direct link in the cause-and-effect chain of reaction to government regulation is not the business enterprise, but the consuming public.

But examination of these visible costs to the motorist and the homeowner provides only the initial or "first-order" effects of government intervention. It is the indirect, or second-order effects that are huge: the various efforts involved in changing the way a company conducts its business in order to comply with federal rulings. One such cost, in time and money, is the growing amount of paper work imposed on businesses: reports, applications, questionnaires, and replies to orders and instructions. The most serious second-order effect is the sometimes dramatic loss of productivity resulting from various federal restrictions. In 1976, coal production in the United States averaged 13.6 tons per worker per day, a 32-percent decline from the 1969 figure of 19.9, and a sharp reversal from the growth in labor productivity during the preceding seven years. It is widely agreed that the basic cause of this decline was the changes in mining procedures made by the coal companies in complying with the Coal Mine Health and Safety Act of 1969.

In a pioneering study, Dr. Edward Denison, of the Brookings Institution, estimated that business productivity in 1975 was 1.4 percent lower than it otherwise would have been, due to the total costs of meeting governmental pollution and job safety requirements.[13] One percent may not seem like much until we realize that the total annual gain in productivity experienced by the American economy may only be 2 to 3 percent. That productivity loss leads to a reduction of over $20 billion in the annual level of the gross national product. Government regulation can also have strongly adverse effects on employment, as demonstrated in the minimum wage area, where teenagers have more and more often been priced out of labor markets. One study shows that the 1966 increase in the statutory minimum wage resulted in a lowering of teenage employment in 1972 by 225,000 from what it otherwise would have been.[14]

It is difficult, of course, to obtain an aggregate measure of the total cost of complying with government regulations. An effort to do so has been made at the Center for the Study of American Business at Washington University in St. Louis. Robert DeFina culled from the available literature the more reliable estimates of the costs of specific regulatory programs. Using a conservative procedure, he put the various dollar figures on a consistent basis and aggregated the results for 1976. The total annual cost of federal regulation was found to be approximately $66 billion: $3 billion of taxpayer costs to operate the regulatory agencies, and $63 billion (twenty times as much) for business to comply with the regulations.[15] Thus, on average, each dollar that Congress appropriates for regulation results in an additional $20 of costs imposed on the private sector of the economy.

Applying the same multiplier of twenty (between the operating and compliance costs) to budget figures available for more recent years, the costs arising from federal regulation of business in the United States (including both the expenses of the regulatory agencies and the costs induced in the private sector) total $102.7 billion for 1979, or almost $500 per capita. That is a substantial hidden tax imposed by federal regulation.

Yet, the most fundamental impacts of governmental intervention are the third-order, or induced effects on the corporation. These are the actions taken by a firm to respond to the direct and indirect effects of regulation. Such responses often include negative effects like cutting back on research and development and on new capital formation because of the diversion of funds to meet government-mandated social requirements. The basic functioning of the business system is adversely affected by the cumulative impacts of the government actions, notably in a firm's pace of innovation, ability to finance growth, and, ultimately, capability to perform its central role of producing goods and services for the consumer. These induced impacts, which are difficult to measure, may in the long run far outweigh the more measurable direct costs resulting from the imposition of government authority over private-sector decision making.

Government regulation affects the prospects for economic growth and productivity by levying a claim for a rising share of new capital formation. This claim is most evident in the environmental and safety areas. In late 1978, as the OSHA concluded work on a proposed general carcinogen regulation, the cost of compliance with that new standard was estimated to exceed the cumulative cost of meeting OSHA standards to date.[16] And that by no means exhausts the future regulatory possibilities. With reference to the Labor Department's proposed noise standards, the troubled steel industry estimates that conversion to the engineering controls desired by OSHA would cost approximately $1.2 million for each affected steelworker. The industry also maintains that it can provide better protection for only $42 per employee: $10 for ear protectors, $12 for noise monitoring, and $20 for audiometric testing.[17]

The governmental decision-making process can also have adverse effects on capital formation by introducing uncertainty about the future of regulations governing the introduction of new processes and products. It is becoming more and more difficult for American companies to move ahead with building conventional energy facilities. It took the Standard Oil Company of Ohio (Sohio) more than four years to obtain the 703 permits, plus approval by the voters in a local election, required to construct a delivery terminal and a pipeline from Long Beach,

California, to Midland, Texas. Many of the requirements were environmental, from air quality approval to California Coastal Zone permits. Whenever changes in the project were made in order to meet a particular agency's regulations, the company had to resubmit applications to agencies that already had approved other aspects of the project. Sohio discovered that three different agencies required that all other permits be granted before they could consider the company's application. Fortunately, Sohio was able to negotiate a compromise.[18] But as of mid-1979, it seems unlikely that the company will be continuing with this project.

In newer high-technology areas, the adverse impact of regulation on new undertakings is even more striking. Here is the conclusion of an analysis of the regulatory experiences of an electric utility attempting to build a nuclear power plant:

> The current uncertainty which surrounds the nuclear licensing process is a major factor contributing to the deferral of many utilities' decisions to build such facilities. Due to the lead time necessary for planning bulk power facilities and the vast amounts of capital involved, it is not surprising that utilities are increasingly apprehensive about making a commitment to a nuclear plant as long as there is no certainty that it will ever be licensed.[19]

After noting that 42 different federal, state, regional, county, and municipal agencies regulate his new aquaculture company, George S. Lockwood, founder and president of Monterey Abalone Farms, states in a paper presented to the American Association for the Advancement of Science that direct costs imposed by regulatory bodies are not the major problem. At issue, rather, is "the great uncertainty" about whether any new activity will meet rapidly changing regulatory standards.[20] Another small research and development-oriented company, Nutrilite Products, reported similar negative experiences. After repeated efforts to obtain approval for a new "biological" form of insect control (instead of a more environmentally difficult "chemical" approach), the company concluded, "We're going back to making vitamin supplements and trying to stay as far away as possible from the Environmental Protection Agency."[21]

Where the impact of government is less dramatic it may be no less profound. A significant but subtle bureaucratization occurs in the corporate activity being undertaken, to the extent that management attention is diverted from product development, production, and marketing concerns to meeting government-imposed social requirements.

In the employee pension area, for example, the Employee Retirement Income Security Act of 1974 has shifted much concern on the part of the management of pension funds from maximizing the return on contributions to minimizing the likelihood that fund managers would be criticized (or even sued) for their investment decisions. It thus becomes safer, though not necessarily more desirable to the employees covered, for pension managers to keep more detailed records of their deliberations, to hire more outside experts (in order to dilute responsibility), and to avoid innovative investments. The federal rules also tend to make the pension fund manager unwilling to invest in anything but blue-chip stocks, thus depriving smaller, newer, and riskier enterprises of an important source of venture capital.[22]

From the experience with pension fund regulation, we can see that the nation is paying yet a further price for the expansion of government power: attenuation of the risk-bearing and entrepreneurial characteristics of the private enterprise system that have contributed so effectively to rapid rates of innovation, productivity, growth, and progress. Thus, the ultimate negative impact on the business system that results from government intervention is the termination of specific products, as is occurring increasingly in the chemical industry, and the abandonment of entire enterprises, as is frequently the case in the foundry industry.

Viewing together the three categories of regulatory effects set forth here, it is difficult to dispute a statement by Lee Loevinger that regulation is now so complex that it is possible for the staff of any regulatory agency to find any person or firm engaged in the field of its authority to be in violation of some regulation.[23] The first-order effects of regulation—the direct costs incurred by American businesses in complying with the directives of regulatory agencies at all levels of government, which now amount to billions of dollars annually—are becoming larger and more obvious. The second-order effects—indirect costs incurred by private companies as they change their basic ways of doing business in order to survive in the expanding labyrinth of government regulations—are even more burdensome. The vast amount of time and energy poured into paper work and the subsequent slowdown of productive effort are so pervasive that they are difficult for the average citizen to comprehend.

And on top of all this, there are the third-order effects—the cumulative adverse results of regulation on industry's pace of innovation and development, its ability to finance growth, and its capability to perform the basic function of producing goods and services. Moreover: American business does not operate in a closed society, and it finds itself more and more handicapped in competing at home and abroad with foreign companies that do not bear similarly heavy regulatory burdens. The ultimate costs of excessive government involvement in the economy can be seen in the factories that are not built, the jobs that are not created, the goods and services that are not produced, and the incomes that are not generated. The approach being presented here should not be misinterpreted. There is little basis for objecting to the use of government power to achieve a cleaner environment, a safer work place, or other social objectives. Rather, the point to be made is that ignoring the costs and other adverse side effects of regulation can often result in carrying such government activity far beyond the sensible point where the benefits are at least equal to the costs.

ANOTHER WAVE OF REGULATION?

It is easy to develop enthusiasm for proposals that would streamline regulatory programs and economize on the use of such governmental power. But many of the existing pressures for change, which have obtained varying degrees of public support, demand and would produce opposite results. They range from altering the basic organizational structure of the modern corporation to adopting a national planning mechanism.

Many so-called corporate activists would use the government's power to charter corporations in order to alter their basic function and organization. Specific suggestions range from restructuring corporate boards of directors to include large numbers of representatives of designated interest groups, to mandating public reporting of various business functions deemed as involving "social responsibility."

Ralph Nader has developed numerous ambitious and far-reaching proposals to restructure the American corporation.[24] To achieve what he terms the "popularization" of the corporation, he would have the government rewrite the rules that govern its chartering. He advocates assumption by the federal government of the chartering power from the individual states. The federal government would then broaden the current disclosure requirements of the SEC to cover "the whole impact of the corporation on society." Nader would require each company to establish a procedure for handling complaints, which, in some versions of his proposals, would be categorized and fed into a national computer system, where they would be instantaneously available to all citizens. Although he acknowledges that "this sounds like Buck Rogers," he also urges the establishment of a mass information system that would cover such areas as the research being conducted by every company. He also would open corporate tax returns to public inspection, for "a corporation does not have the right of privacy, like an individual."

For corporations beyond a certain size, or having a "dominant" position in a market, Nader would require that approximately one-fourth of the board of directors be chosen in national elections. Individual directors would be assigned responsibility for specific areas of concern, such as the environment or employee relations. He has also urged a mandatory mail plebiscite of shareholders on all "fundamental" transactions. The result of his reforms, Nader acknowledges, is a concept of "social bankruptcy" whereby a company would be thrown into receivership if it failed to meet its "social" obligations. What he does not acknowledge is the massive scale of public involvement and private expense that would result from his reforms. All this, moreover, is apart from the technical impracticality of carrying out his visionary schemes.

More modest proposals for change in the structure of the American corporation have come from other sources. Harold Williams, SEC chairman, contends that the ideal board of directors would include only one company officer, the chief executive. All other board members, including the chairman, would be from outside the company and would exclude bankers, lawyers, and anyone having business dealings with the company. In his view, outside-dominated boards could do a better job of representing the stockholders' long-term interests than can executives who are responsible for day-to-day management.[25]

A third set of proposals was developed by a group of business, academic, and professional leaders convened by the American Assembly in April 1978. This group urged that corporations take the initiative in responding to the changing environment facing business, minimizing the need for government action. The assembly focused on the corporate board as having a primary role in interpreting society's expectations and standards for management. The majority of board members, it urged, should come from outside company management, unencumbered by relationships that limit their independence. The report recommended that key internal managers, in addition to the chief executive, remain eligible to serve. It also pointed out several of their strengths, which include bringing the perspectives of the board into the discharge of their regular duties, and helping outside members evaluate possible successors to the chief executive. Moreover, the assembly recommended that a corporation's chief executive officer not serve as chairman of the board. It also pointed out that effective self-regulation requires oversight mechanisms to set standards, monitor compliance, and ensure that the self-regulation does not become self-serving in restraint of trade.[26]

All three proposals for restructuring American corporations share a strong notion of public accountability. Each takes the fundamental approach of changing both the composition and the function of corporate directorships; each to a varying degree would make some aspect of "private" management more "public." In the case of Nader's proposals, corporations would become quasi-nationalized public holdings run by elected officials, which would alter much of what we have come to know as free enterprise. Although the proposals of Williams and the American Assembly can be described as working in the same direction, they would proceed in a more moderate way and with an eye toward the corporations' own capabilities for self-regulation. Although it is unlikely that any current set of proposals—Nader's or Williams' or those of the American Assembly—for the reform of corporate governance will be adopted in its present form, it would not be surprising if some significant portion of these proposals were put into effect, either by force in the form of government regulation, or voluntarily to avoid such overt action by government.

Numerous other proposals exist for new federal undertakings that are not intended to alter the basic relationships between government and business, but that would nevertheless have the effect of producing great changes. An obvious example is the plans to establish a comprehensive national health insurance system operated by the federal government. These plans focus on the expanded delivery of health care to the entire American population and inevitably attempt to deal with the sharp escalation occurring in medical costs. The proposals are generally intended to rectify the cost problem by enforcing detailed control mechanisms, not only over health care professionals, but also over the industries that supply health care products and services.

Dissatisfaction with continuing high levels of inflation and unemployment has led to a rising chorus advocating what are called "incomes" policies. This type of government intervention in business decision making has been used widely in Western Europe and occasionally in this country. Unlike the traditional tools of monetary and fiscal policy, which tend to affect the economy indirectly, incomes policy means that the government is participating directly in those private business decisions that eventually determine how much income individuals receive from their economic activities. Incomes policies cover a broad spectrum of alternatives, ranging from presidential "jawboning" against individual wage and price increases, to voluntary adherence to federal guideposts on wages and prices, to government control over specific wage and price changes. The free market can be viewed as one end of a spectrum of incomes policies, comprehensive and compulsory wage and price controls as the other end.

In fall 1978, the Carter administration embarked on one such experiment in incomes policy, though it claimed that the wage and price standards established were voluntary. Enforcement was to be indirect, via publication of the names of companies violating the standards, and the withholding from them of large government contracts. As an indication of how truly voluntary the wage and price restraint effort really was, in early 1979 it was very difficult to identify any company that had indicated it would not go along with the "voluntary" standards. As in the case of more overt regulatory efforts, the standards are accompanied by more and more paper work and by a proliferation of detailed rules and procedures.

If the federal government were to launch a long-term program of control over private wage and price decision making, this would represent yet another expansion and complication of government involvement in internal business operations. It is likely, but not inevitable, that government will exercise a growing influence on the business system of the United States in the years ahead. This will depend both on business reactions to the underlying situation and on the changing views of the many other interest groups involved.

There are indications, nonetheless, that public attitudes toward government regulation are shifting. As recently as 1976, a plurality of the public that was sampled advocated more government regulation of business (31 percent versus 27 percent). By fall 1978 the plurality went the other way: 30 percent favored less regulation, 24 percent more. Significantly, when asked whether the complaints of business about excessive regulation are justified, 44 percent responded yes and 32 no.[27]

POSSIBILITIES FOR IMPROVEMENT

In theory, government can attempt to impose on business a vast array of social responsibilities. The proper public concern, therefore, is with the ability of the corporation to take on these added duties while continuing to serve society's basic economic purposes.

We must be mindful of the serious problems faced by government itself. This is a period in which public disenchantment with government is growing rapidly. The approach suggested here is a constructive response to that citizen concern through forcing government to act more sensibly and reasonably. The result would be to shore up some badly needed public faith in government and public support for the things that government does do. Of course, substantial tension between business and government is inevitable. As historian Paul Johnson has pointed out, active, interventionist government should be expected to view private enterprise with hostility because the latter constitutes a countervailing power in the state.[28]

Nevertheless, there is a compelling case for restraint in the exercise of the great power of government over business, especially in imposing social burdens on business. Those social burdens do not necessarily improve the public attitude toward government; instead, they invariably interfere with the ability of the corporation to perform its basic job for society: the economic function of producing goods and services, and the creation of jobs and income in the process. As we have seen, there are limits to the ability of the business firm to take on a variety of ancillary responsibilities. Many of those who urge business to assume an array of social burdens simply have not stopped to consider the adverse effects of such well-meant actions.

With these points in mind, let us consider an approach to regulatory reform that departs from the ordinary, one that involves the Congress more than the bureaucracy. At the outset, it is helpful to emphasize the compelling case for reform of government regulation. First, as has been demonstrated on numerous occasions, the regulatory apparatus is cumbersome and costly. Second, government regulation generates numerous adverse side effects: higher inflation, more unemployment, lower productivity, reduced capital formation, and a slowdown in technological innovation. Third, the primary objection to regulation is that, by and large, it is not working. It is not a question of begrudging a "few" more billion dollars for job safety, consumer health, and so on. Rather, the point is that the typical regulatory program is not effective in reaching these worthy objectives. Virtually every study of the regulatory process reaches that conclusion.

The solution to these problems surely is not to redouble the existing regulatory effort. That method only resembles a typical hangover remedy. Nor is the main answer the obvious one of berating the bureaucracy—though, to be sure, much nonsense emanates from the regulatory agencies, and silly regulations should be revised or eliminated. Instead, we need to recognize that the fundamental source of the problem is statutory. Every regulation is promulgated under authority of a statute passed by Congress, and every regulator is paid via congressional appropriation. In general, Congress has set up too many regulatory agencies, passed too many regulatory laws, and established too many unrealistic regulatory objectives. Table 1 attempts to put into historical perspective the recent expansion of federal regulation. Clearly,

TABLE 1

Chronology of Federal Regulatory Agencies

Field	Prior to 1930	1930s	1940s	1950s	1960s	1970s	Total
Consumer safety and health	1	2	1	0	1	6	11
Job safety and other labor conditions	0	2	0	0	2	5	9
Environment and energy	2	0	0	0	1	2	5
Finance	2	2	0	0	0	3	7
Industry	3	5	1	1	2	2	14
General business	4	0	0	1	0	2	7
Total	12	11	2	2	6	20	53

Source: Compiled from data contained in Marsha Wallace and Ronald Penoyer, *Directory of Federal Regulatory Agencies* (St. Louis: Center for the Study of American Business, Washington University, 1978).

the burst of new regulatory activity during the 1970s dwarfs the highly publicized growth of such action during the New Deal period of the 1930s. Moreover, more than half of the existing regulatory agencies have been established since 1950.

But given the wide range and complexity of government regulation, there are no simple approaches to reform. The sensible question is not whether we are for or against regulation of business. A substantial degree of governmental intervention is to be expected in a complex, modern society. And many of the objectives sought by regulatory agencies are worthy of continued public support. Indeed, it is the means used rather than the ends pursued that merit criticism. The need is to identify those sensible changes that can be made in the regulatory process so as to achieve the desired social goals—less pollution, fewer product hazards, and so on—with a minimum adverse impact on such other important goals as more jobs and less inflation. Ultimately, the relevant question is whether, in view of the many aims of our society, government regulation in a particular instance is doing more harm than good.

Four approaches hold promise for long-term reform in the regulation of business by government. First, an information base must be developed: specifically, an economic impact statement should be required prior to issuing each new regulation. The notion that policymakers should carefully consider the costs and other adverse effects as well as the benefits of their actions is neither new nor revolutionary. The Ford administration did institute a form of economic impact statement for new regulations, and President Carter has recently made some changes in the procedures.[29] Unfortunately, neither the Ford nor the Carter approaches are up to the task.

Merely requiring a reluctant agency to perform cost-benefit analyses is not enough. The key action needed is for Congress to pass a law limiting regulations to those instances where the total benefits to society equal or exceed the costs. Over-regulation, the economist's shorthand for regulation for which costs exceed benefits, should be avoided. Obviously, failure to take those costs into account has resulted in the problem of over-regulation facing the United States today. Benefit-cost analysis itself is a neutral concept, giving equal weight to a dollar of benefits as to a dollar of costs. In fact, effective regulatory programs—those that show an excess of benefits over costs—would be given a new and strong justification for their continuation.

From time to time a glimmer of hope arises from the operations of the judicial process. In October 1978, a three-judge panel of the Fifth U.S. Circuit Court of Appeals set aside OSHA's new benzene exposure standards because the agency failed to show a reasonable relationship between anticipated benefits and costs. The court pointed out in its decision that, although OSHA would not have to conduct an elaborate cost-benefit analysis, it would have to determine whether the benefits expected from the standards bear a "reasonable relationship" to the costs imposed.

The second approach to regulatory reform is to subject all existing regulatory activities to a "sunset" mechanism. Each agency should be reviewed by Congress on a strict timetable, to determine whether it is worthwhile to continue it in light of today's needs or whether the sun should be allowed to set on it. The existence of many government programs, regulatory or otherwise, is prolonged far beyond their initial need and justification. In a world of limited resources, the only sensible way to make room for new priorities is to eliminate or periodically cut back older, superseded priorities. A sunset evaluation, for example, might reveal that pollution taxes could achieve higher levels of air and water purity than the existing standards approach—at the same total costs.

The third approach is to focus the federal budget process more directly on regulatory activities. As a start, it would be helpful to include a section on the total cost of government regulation in the special analyses volume accompanying the annual budget. This would be similar to the existing analyses of other extrabudgetary activities, notably federal credit programs and tax expenditures. Such a special analysis would be an initial step toward a federal regulatory budget, which would cover both government and private costs of meeting regulatory requirements. To the federal budget maker, the $4.8 billion for operating the 55 regulatory agencies may seem a paltry sum, unworthy of much attention. But the $100 billion of annual compliance costs imposed on the private sector by those agencies surely merits closer scrutiny than it has been given to date.

The fourth and perhaps the most fundamental approach to regulatory reform does not involve regulation at all: it is to focus on alternatives to regulation. Many regulatory activities simply are not needed. In the case of the traditional one-industry type of regulation—of airlines, trucking, railroads, and natural gas—a greater role should be given to competition and to market forces. In other cases, the more widespread provision of information to consumers on potential hazards might be far more effective than banning specific products or setting standards that require expensive alterations in existing products. The information approach takes account of the great variety of consumer desires and capabilities. Interestingly, many surveys show that this is the alternative preferred by the consuming public—although not by some of the consumer organizations that claim to speak for the public.

Recent progress toward deregulation of airlines, however, should not be taken as indicative of a basic shift in government policy toward less regulation in general. The facts support the reverse view. The overall pace of regulation of business continues on an upward trajectory. The number of agencies, regulatory programs, and authorizing statutes—and the budgets to carry them out—are all growing.

Basically, therefore, it is attitudes that need to be changed, in a shift away from what Kenneth Shepsle calls "the regulative tendency."[30] Experience with the job safety program provides a cogent example. Although the government's safety rules have resulted in billions of dollars in public and private outlays, the basic goal of a safer work environment has not been achieved. Days lost due to job accidents rose from 51 per 100 full-time workers in 1973 (when OSHA was established) to 60 in 1977, the latest period for which data are available.[31]

A more satisfying answer to improving the effectiveness of government regulation of private activities requires a basic change in the approach to regulation, and one that is not limited to the job safety program. Indeed, that program is merely an illustration. If the objective of public policy is to reduce accidents, then public policy should focus directly on the reduction of accidents. Rather than issue citations to employers who fail to fill out forms correctly, emphasis should be placed on the regulation of employers with high and rising accident rates. But the government should not be much concerned with *how* a company achieves a safer working environment. Some companies may find it more efficient to change work rules, others to buy new equipment, still others to retrain workers. Choosing among these options is precisely the kind of operational business decision that government is not good at and therefore should avoid.

The overriding point to all these recommendations should not be lost sight of: the purpose of reducing the regulatory load is not to lighten the burden on business. Rather, it is to improve the ability of the business system to meet the needs of the consuming public. Paradoxically, that is the general justification for most regulatory activities established by the government. But it is clear in governmental matters as elsewhere that the heart is not a thinking instrument. Well-meaning intervention in private-sector decision making should not automatically be justified by the nobility of its proponents' motives.

Clearly, any dispassionate examination of business-government relations in the United States reveals that the public welfare now requires the policy pendulum to swing in the direction of less government intervention in private decision making. Congressman John B. Anderson of Illinois has drawn a parallel between the "interventionist mentality" toward regulation and American foreign policy a short time ago. "The federal government has to stop making war on every problem. Just as Vietnam taught us we can't be the policeman of the world, so the present quagmire of regulation should teach us that we can't police every nook and cranny on the domestic front."[32] My proposals are not a recipe for dismantling the regulatory apparatus; they would provide an opportunity to increase the effectiveness of regulatory actions that the government does take.

NOTES

1. Harold M. Williams, "SEC and Mutual Funds: Hands-Off Regulation To Be Given College Try," *Money Manager*, August 14, 1978, p. 6.

2. Arthur F. Burns, *The Condition of the American Economy* (Washington, D.C.: American Enterprise Institute, 1979), p. 8.

3. Phyllis S. McGrath, *Managing Corporate External Relations* (New York: Conference Board, 1976), p. 49.

4. "How GM Manages Its Billion-Dollar R&D Program," *Business Week*, June 28, 1976, p. 56.

5. John W. Hanley, "The Day Innovation Died," *Vital Speeches of the Day*, November 1, 1978, pp. 55–58.

6. Lee Loevinger, "The Impacts of Government Regulation," lecture at New York University, October 25, 1978 (p. 9).

7. Carol J. Loomis, "AT&T in the Throes of 'Equal Employment,' " *Fortune*, January 15, 1979, pp. 45–57.

8. U.S. Congress, House, Committee on Banking, Finance, and Urban Affairs, *Large Corporations and Urban Employment* (Washington: U.S. Government Printing Office, 1978), pp. 54–55.

9. Douglas C. North, "Structure and Performance: The Task of Economic History," *Journal of Economic Literature*, September 1978, p. 969.

10. Kenneth W. Chilton, *The Impact of Federal Regulation on American Small Business* (St. Louis: Washington University, Center for the Study of American Business, 1978).

11. Loevinger, "Impacts," p. 32.

12. Murray L. Weidenbaum, *The Costs of Government Regulation of Business*, a study prepared for the Joint Economic Committee (Washington: U.S. Government Printing Office, 1978), pp. 2–3.

13. Edward F. Denison, "Effects of Selected Changes in the Institutional and Human Environment upon Output per Unit of Input," *Survey of Current Business*, January 1978, pp. 21–44.

14. James F. Ragan, Jr., *Minimum Wages and the Youth Labor Market*, Publication no. 14 (St. Louis: Washington University, Center for the Study of American Business, 1977), pp. 1–12.

15. Robert DeFina, *Public and Private Expenditures for Federal Regulation of Business*, Working Paper no. 22 (St. Louis: Washington University, Center for the Study of American Business, 1977).

16. "Identification, Classification, and Regulation of Toxic Substances Posing a Potential Occupational Carcinogenic Risk," *Federal Register*, October 4, 1977, pt. 6, pp. 54149–54247.

17. Donald Ubben, "OSHA Noise Standards Stir Debate," *Washington Report*, December 19, 1977, p. 3.

18. F. G. Garibaldi, "Government Procedure and Our Energy Future," speech prepared for Indianapolis Contemporary Club, January 18, 1978, pp. 6–9.

19. Milton R. Copulos, *Confrontation at Seabrook* (Washington, D.C.: Heritage Foundation, 1978), p. 44.

20. George S. Lockwood, "Some Causes and Consequences of Declining Innovation," address to the Third Annual Colloquium on Research and Development Policy, American Association for the Advancement of Science, Washington, D.C., June 21, 1978, p. 6.

21. William Tucker, "Of Mites and Men," *Harper's*, August 1978, pp. 43–58.

22. Shoya Zicky, "How Small Funds Are Coping With the New Pension Law," *Institutional Investor*, September 1975.

23. Loevinger, "Impacts," p. 47.

24. Eileen Shanahan, "Business Change: Nader Interview," *New York Times*, January 24, 1971, sect. 3, pp. 1, 3. For a more detailed analysis of the case for

federal chartering, see Ralph Nader et al., *Taming the Giant Corporation* (New York: W. W. Norton, 1976). For a contrary view, see Robert Hessen, *In Defense of the Corporation* (Stanford, Calif.: Hoover Institution Press, 1979).

25. Harold M. Williams, "Corporate Accountability," address to the Fifth Annual Securities Regulation Institute, San Diego, Calif., January 18, 1978.

26. American Assembly, *Corporate Governance in America*, New York, Columbia University, 1978.

27. "Less Government Regulation Favored," *St. Louis Globe-Democrat*, October 16, 1978, p. 5A.

28. Paul Johnson, "Has Capitalism a Future?" *Wall Street Journal*, September 29, 1978, p. 24.

29. See U.S. Office of Management and Budget, *Evaluation of the Inflationary Impact of Major Proposals for Legislation and for the Promulgation of Regulations or Rules*, Circular no. A107, January 28, 1975; "Improving Government Regulations," Executive Order 12044, *Federal Register*, March 24, 1978, pt. 6, pp. 12661–12670.

30. See Kenneth A. Shepsle, *The Private Use of the Public Interest*, Working Paper no. 46 (St. Louis: Washington University Center for the Study of American Business, 1979).

31. For additional detail see, "BLS Reports on Occupational Injuries and Illnesses for 1977," *U.S. Department of Labor News*, November 21, 1978, p. 5.

32. John B. Anderson, "Regulation and Rationality," address to the National Governors Conference, Boston, Massachusetts, August 28, 1978, p. 7.

Energy Options

Thomas Gale Moore

IX

Government mismanagement of our energy resources has created a situation that is serious, but not catastrophic. During the 1970s, government regulation of the energy industries has been inefficient, inequitable, and inappropriate. Although presidential statements have emphasized energy independence from foreign sources, government policies have made us more dependent on the Organization of Petroleum Exporting Countries (OPEC). The government has called for greater production of coal, and yet has discouraged its mining. The Carter administration has given only half-hearted support to nuclear power, one of the cleanest, safest, and most economical forms of energy. During the decade, the petroleum industry, like the natural gas and nuclear power industries, became regulated. This leaves only the coal industry free from government control of prices and output.

EXISTING ENERGY REGULATIONS

The federal government regulates all major forms of energy resources in the United States. In some respects, both the oil and the natural gas industries can trace the origin of government controls back to the 1930s. In the late 1930s and early 1940s, minimum prices and working conditions of coal miners were regulated. Nuclear energy has been under strict government administration since its origin.

Natural Gas Regulation

In 1938 Congress passed the Interstate Pipeline Transmission Act, which gave the Federal Power Commission (FPC) authority to control rates charged by interstate pipeline companies. The act explicitly excluded the control of natural gas prices at the wellhead. Nevertheless, in 1954 the Supreme Court held in *Phillips Petroleum Company* v. *Wisconsin* that the FPC was required by the act to regulate the interstate selling price of natural gas. With some reluctance, the FPC assumed the task of trying to fix rates and terms of sale of some 4,000 independent producers of natural gas to the interstate market. Initially, the FPC attempted to regulate the rates of return of each of these producers. But it soon became evident that this was an impossible, herculean task.

With the Permian Basin Area Rate Proceeding (1961–1965), the FPC applied the concept of area base rate regulation. In this approach, costs are averaged for a particular field and arbitrarily allocated between oil and gas. A single rate is then established for all sales from that field. Since the Permian Basin proceeding, the FPC has used area rate regulation and vintaging. Vintaging means that the ceiling price of gas depends on the particular time gas from a well is first sold under contract in interstate commerce.

Regulation of an essentially competitive market creates shortages. Fundamental economic principles dictate that supply and demand are responsive to price. That is, at higher prices suppliers will explore, discover, manufacture, or produce more of a given product than at lower prices. The more profitable it becomes for the suppliers to produce a product, the more will be offered for sale. On the other hand, price affects demand inversely. Higher prices encourage consumers to seek alternatives, to economize, and to conserve. Lower rates encourage greater use, the substitution for other products, and careless consumption. These propositions imply that there is some market clearing price at which the amount consumers want to buy equals the amount suppliers wish to sell. If price is held below this level by government fiat, consumers will seek to buy more than suppliers want to sell, producing shortages. This fundamental economic truth cannot be repealed by wishful thinking, appeals to patriotism, or statements about the inequities of higher prices. This law applies, whether the subject is rent controls, price controls on gasoline, or ceilings on natural gas prices.

The workings of supply and demand in the natural gas market are complicated by the nature of the institutional arrangements. Natural gas is normally sold on long-term contracts between the producer and the purchaser, usually involving a natural gas pipeline. Such multi-year arrangements are important from both the buyer's and the seller's points of view. The well owner wants to contract for disposal of the natural gas that he will be producing over the next decades. The buyer wants to be assured of a supply for his pipeline in order to serve the distributing companies with whom he has contracted to provide gas.

Another difference between natural gas markets and many other markets is that natural gas reserves are in the nature of inventories. Producers and pipeline companies do not want to hold unlimited inventories. They will seek to find additional gas supplies only when inventories (that is, reserves) fall below a desired level. Once found, however, the inventories are, with some qualifications, freely available for sale. After the wells are in place, the cost of continuing to produce natural gas remains low until the field begins to be depleted. When this happens, additional capital expenditures may produce larger supplies.

These peculiarities of the natural gas market imply that if price controls are imposed, shortages do not occur immediately. However, in other industries price controls result quickly in demand exceeding supply. For example, if the retail price of gasoline is fixed below the market clearing level, there will soon be shortages. When controls were imposed on natural gas, however, well owners continued to produce from existing reserves. The only noticeable effect was a decline in the completion of new gas wells, starting in 1962. But since that period shortages of natural gas have become more and more evident. In numerous parts of the country, gas companies have had to turn away new customers because of a lack of supplies. Some parts of the country have never been able to obtain natural gas, or have never had enough to permit industrial use. Large manufacturers have been increasingly told that natural gas is available only on an interruptable basis. In winter 1977, because of both price controls and controls on natural gas at the state level, some states, in particular Ohio, suffered acute shortages of natural gas, so that many firms had to curtail operations.

Regulation has led to some rather bizarre results. Some natural gas is still priced as low as 25 cents per thousand cubic feet. Until fall 1978, the highest natural gas price permitted by the government was $1.45. Though the Natural Gas Act of 1978 has raised the ceilings on natural gas, maximum rates still differ greatly depending on when the gas was first marketed. Vintage pricing of natural gas bears no relationship to any physical differences between supplies. Prices to consumers are thus based on average costs, not on the incremental price for additional supplies.

The Natural Gas Act of 1978 has defined at least eight different types of natural gas for pricing purposes. Each of these types has a base price, and an escalation clause permits charges to increase with inflation. In addition, for some categories of natural gas, such as "new natural gas," an escalation factor permits prices to increase annually 3.5 percent faster than inflation until April 1981.* After that date, the ceiling rises 4 percent faster than inflation. For example, new natural gas as defined in the act had a basic price of $1.75 per million British thermal units (BTUs). But with inflation and escalation it could sell for $2.18 in May 1979. Gas from wells selling in interstate commerce prior to 1973 had a ceiling price of only 34 cents in May 1979. The following will eventually be deregulated: most gas defined as new natural gas, gas from new onshore production wells, gas selling for more than one dollar under intrastate contracts or under expired contracts for intrastate gas that has been renegotiated, and high-cost natural gas.

Other categories of natural gas are expected to remain under price ceilings indefinitely. Thus, gas that is indistinguishable to the consumer will sell for widely differing prices depending on when it was first marketed. Moreover, the Natural Gas Act of 1978 imposed the first controls on intrastate sales of natural gas. Prior to this act, producers of natural gas could sell their product to consumers or distributors within the state free from controls. Numerous firms and petrochemical plants thus moved to gas-producing states to take advantage of the availability of plentiful natural gas. Before fall 1978 and after shortages began to occur at the interstate level, intrastate natural gas sold for more than the interstate ceilings. The new controls on intrastate gas limit price increases in many cases. The immediate result has been an increase in the gas available for interstate sales. This appears to be due to the higher price that interstate gas now receives and the elimination of the uncontrolled intrastate market.

The continued regulation of natural gas prices creates problems for both supply and demand. By holding down prices, regulation discourages production. Although the act requires that after 1984 most new natural gas will be exempt from controls, producers may be reluctant to invest in natural gas exploration until deregulation becomes a fact. As has happened in the past, Congress may extend controls. Moreover, the gradual phaseout of price regulation may deter exploration and development. Since the price that a producer will receive in the future will go up faster than inflation until prices reach the free market level, it may be in the entrepreneur's interest to wait. Depending on the producer's discount rate and how soon prices reach market clearing levels, it may be

*New natural gas is defined by law as gas produced from wells drilled after April 19, 1977, 1) on the outer continental shelf, 2) 2.5 miles from the nearest "marker" well or, if closer than 2.5 miles, 1,000 feet deeper than any within 2.5 miles, and 3) from new onshore reservoirs.

more profitable for the producer to hold off production until the maximum price increases.

For those producers who will be controlled indefinitely, incentives to invest in further production are minimal. Depending on bureaucratic decisions, it may not be profitable to increase production by using new technologies or investing in secondary recovery (that is, techniques designed to augment output). The concept of keeping the price of "old" natural gas down (no increase permitted in real terms) is based on an erroneous belief that the quantity of such gas sold is independent of its market price. Actually, the higher the final price, the stronger the incentives to find ways of increasing gas production. No matter what the price, all the gas cannot be removed from the ground. But higher incentives will result in more gas.

The partial decontrol mandated in the 1978 act will not expand production as much as would total deregulation. Since consumers pay an average of "old" and "new" gas prices, and since supply will be limited, "new" natural gas prices will actually be higher than if "old" gas had also been decontrolled. Of course, if regulation is ever totally removed, the gas that is not currently being produced because of regulation will become available. Even the limited benefits of this act, however, will not be fully realized until August 1987, when deregulation is extended to new onshore wells of less than 5,000-foot depth.

On the demand side, continued regulation will result in prices that are artificially low. Even after 1987, consumer prices will be based on an average of old natural gas prices and unregulated prices. The result is that consumers will continue to waste gas by using more than they would if they had to pay the true cost. Congress partially accounted for this for industrial users by devising an incremental pricing scheme. This system provides for protection of residential consumers by imposing the higher costs of the deregulated new natural gas on large industrial users of the fuel needed to generate steam or electricity. Schools, hospitals, electric utilities, small industrial boiler fuel facilities, and agricultural users are exempt. Thus, not only will there be a multiplicity of prices for producers, there will also be a variety of prices for users. Large boiler fuel users will have to bear the costs of all gas sold above $1.48 per million BTUs (adjusted for inflation after March 1978), except for Alaskan gas, and only up to the point that the BTU cost of gas equals the BTU cost of fuel oil. Due to incremental pricing, favored consumers will, therefore, actually pay less than the true average cost of natural gas. As a consequence, wasteful use will continue. Congress, as a gesture toward offsetting the improvident use of underpriced gas, banned the use of natural gas for decorative outdoor lighting.

If all gas were allowed to rise to the market price, then all users would pay the costs of the most expensive cubic foot of natural gas produced. Such a policy would also provide maximum incentives for producers to find more natural gas and for consumers to economize.

In summary, then, it might be said that the New Natural Gas Act was a weak step in the right direction. It provided some additional incentives over the long run to find new natural gas for sale in interstate markets. But this is at the cost of discouraging the production of natural gas for intrastate markets. During the last half of the 1980s, this act will result, if not amended, in complete decontrol of new and high-cost gas. This will provide maximum incentives to find new sources, even though additional old gas production will continue to be discouraged. At the same time, the act will provide for higher prices for some users but lower prices for others. The result is that the heating of swimming pools by gas will be encouraged at the expense of industrial uses.

Continued controls on natural gas prices implies that average prices to consumers will continue to be below the cost of new gas. Thus, wasteful uses will persist. Nevertheless, the 1980s may see a recognition that this nation will not exhaust its supplies for decades. Large quantities of natural gas exist in Alaska and northern Canada that currently appear too costly to pipe to the lower 48 states. If price goes high enough, this gas will become economic. Vast quantities of natural gas lie in Mexico that could be imported if we were willing to pay the cost.

Some geologists have claimed that there are 60,000 to 80,000 trillion cubic feet of gas beneath the Gulf Coast region. It has been estimated that this gas contains ten times the energy value of all the other known coal, oil, and gas in the United States. This 60,000 to 80,000 trillion cubic feet should be compared with the presently known reserves of natural gas of approximately 200 trillion cubic feet. Of course, the gas under the Gulf Coast is expensive and difficult to reach. Only when the price of natural gas rises enough will it be profitable to exploit this.

It may, of course, never be profitable to drill for this gas. As gas companies exhaust cheap sources of fuel, the free market price will rise. Consumers and other users will be induced to conserve and to substitute other energy sources. Thus, it is quite possible that alternative energy supplies and conservation may prevent it from ever being economic to tap this gas. Nevertheless, it should be recognized that physical exhaustion of the supplies of natural gas is both a technical impossibility and an economic absurdity.

For the 1980s, though, the principal problems will not involve availability of natural gas, as long as decontrol of new gas is permitted, but rather the waste engendered from too low an average price to users. This may result in inefficient investments, such as a natural gas pipeline from the arctic that would not be able to pay for itself if the gas were priced to users at cost. The low pricing might also encourage the importation of liquified natural gas that also would not sell if it were priced at cost. Large-scale facilities for coal gasification might be built that would be uneconomical if the cost were not averaged with cheaper fuel.

To prevent this potential waste, either old gas should be deregulated or regulation of investment in other supplies of gas will be necessary. It seems likely that old gas will remain regulated so that average gas prices are below the cost of new gas. If that is the case, the Department of Energy will either have to permit uneconomic investments to produce more gas or establish a rationing scheme to limit demand to the supply. The Natural Gas Act of 1978 essentially legislates such a rationing scheme by classifying users according to priority, such that the most favored are residential customers.

It is quite possible that during the 1980s the average price of gas under regulation would be higher than the price in a free market, but that it would include cheap old gas averaged with expensive other gas. This result depends on how the supplies of gas from old wells and from new sources relate to price. If output from old wells is more responsive to price than that from new sources, then the average price will exceed the free market level. Even if this is not true, the additional cost of new gas will be greater than the value consumers put on it, and wasteful uses will be common.

Oil Industry Regulation

The oil industry first became regulated in 1930, when states, mainly for conservation reasons, established prorationing. Prorationing was ostensibly intended to prevent overly rapid development of oil fields. In the early 1930s, with discovery of the large east Texas field, the price of oil plummeted to about ten cents per barrel. This low price did not discourage production because of the common-law principle of the law of capture: whoever extracts the oil owns it. Consequently, producers tried to pump oil as fast as possible; any oil left would be taken by their neighbors. The net result was an inefficient exploitation of a valuable resource. Although prorationing was designed to prevent this, it also led to higher prices and more profits for crude oil producers, which explains the strong industry support for prorationing.

Proration was a regulatory system designed to control output from individual oil wells and to limit the drilling of new wells in known fields.

Each state operating a prorationing scheme would estimate the "appropriate" output for its state on the basis of estimated demand at the prevailing price. The state would then allocate output among the prorated wells and the exempt wells.

The Congress, to support state control over production, passed the Connally "Hot Oil" Act, prohibiting the interstate movement of oil produced illegally under state laws. The Bureau of Mines aided the state government regulatory commissions by making estimates of the monthly demand for petroleum, based on existing stock and on desired stocks, as reported by oil companies.

Prorationing kept oil prices in the United States above the free market level. It has been said with some truth that the world price of oil was set by the Texas Railroad Commission from the 1930s through the early 1950s. As cheap oil from Saudi Arabia and Venezuela began flooding the world market in the early 1950s, the U.S. price began to diverge from the world price. With prices abroad lower than in the United States, our oil imports began to grow. By 1957, imports were threatening the prorationing system, and President Dwight D. Eisenhower called for voluntary import quotas on oil. When it became apparent in 1959 that voluntary quotas had failed, Eisenhower imposed mandatory restrictions. These quotas, which were constantly changed, restricted imports until the early 1970s. Companies that had been allocated quotas found them valuable. On average, import tickets sold for around $1.25 a barrel. Small refiners were given extra tickets for each barrel of oil they refined that was produced from U.S. wells. Such tickets could not be sold openly, but they could be traded for larger quantities of domestic oil, with the consequent gain to the recipient.

By the early 1970s, world oil prices began to rise sharply, and increased U.S. imports were necessary to satisfy domestic demand. In 1971, under legislation passed the previous year by Congress, President Richard Nixon imposed a wage and price freeze. After the freeze, controls were continued but increasingly relaxed.

By August 1973, regulation of petroleum prices had become complex. There was old oil and new oil, released oil and stripper oil. Old oil was defined in terms of a base production control level, which was the volume of oil produced from reservoirs during 1972. New oil was oil from reservoirs discovered after 1972. Released oil was defined as that oil produced from old reservoirs in excess of the 1972 base production control level, plus an equal amount of old oil. Since the price of released oil was uncontrolled, the value of a barrel produced in excess of the base production level exceeded the world price by the difference between the old oil price and the world price. Prices for old oil were defined in terms of the price existing in May 1972 plus 35 cents. Stripper oil was petroleum from wells producing less than ten barrels per day. New and stripper oil sold at world prices.

The oil embargo of fall 1973 and the subsequent fourfold increase in the prices of crude in world markets resulted in the passage of the Emergency Petroleum Allocation Act of 1973. Under this act, old oil prices were increased to an average of about $5.05 per barrel and new, released, and stripper crude were allowed to rise with world prices.

After some agonizing, and for what many people thought were political reasons, President Gerald Ford signed the Emergency Policy and Conservation Act at the end of 1975. This act extended controls over crude oil prices for 40 months, expiring officially on May 30, 1979. The act redefined oils in terms of lower tier, which was the old oil; upper tier, which was new oil; and stripper oil. Released oil was no longer a defined category. The bill provided that the weighted average price of both upper and lower tier oil be equal to an average level, set initially at $7.66. In effect, the price of upper tier oil was lowered to achieve this average price. The average has been permitted by law to rise with inflation, plus an escalation factor, and is now well over $9 per barrel. Stripper oil prices have been subsequently completely deregulated. As of March 1979, for example, old oil sold for $5.82 a barrel, new oil for $12.84, Naval petroleum reserve oil for $13.97, stripper oil for $14.88, and Alaskan oil at the well head for $6.66 a barrel.

With this variety of prices and the confusion caused by such a bizarre system, the government had to devise a way to equalize prices for all refiners. The resulting equalization scheme, called the Entitlements Program, required a refiner using cheap crude (that is, old oil) to buy an entitlement from a refiner importing or using expensive crude. For example, suppose that 40 percent of the oil refined is lower tier selling for $5.50 and 60 percent is upper tier selling for $14.00. The average cost of oil is then 0.4($5.50) + 0.6($14.00) = $10.60. A refiner using old oil would have to pay $5.50 to the producer and buy an entitlement for $5.10 for each barrel. An importer would receive $3.40 in entitlements for each barrel imported, reducing his cost to $10.60. In practice, this scheme taxes old oil and gives the proceeds to purchasers of expensive crude, such as imported oil. In other words, government policy subsidizes the import of foreign oil. As a consequence, the act that perpetuated this sytem has often been referred to as the OPEC Relief Act of 1975.

As pointed out above, under the import quota scheme of the 1950s and 1960s, smaller refiners were given access to more cheap imported oil than they would qualify for had they been normal-sized refiners. This policy subsidized small refineries. These benefits have been continued under the Entitlements Program. The smallest refineries—those under 10,000 barrels per day capacity—received the largest subsidies. Such refineries are very inefficient, yet they receive bonuses that have been estimated as equal to $2 on each barrel of crude processed or about $20,000 a day extra from the program alone. Not only are such refineries wasteful, but they cannot produce as large a proportion of light products such as gasoline as the large refineries. With this windfall, it is not surprising that since 1976 over 40 new small refineries have been built and more are under construction. Total subsidies run over a billion dollars a year.

The objective of the small refinery bias is unclear. Some believe it is intended to aid small business. Certainly it is not because the owners of such plants are poor; on the contrary, they are often millionaires. These refineries have revenues of 50 to 60 million dollars a year. Even though the average income of an Exxon stockholder is considerably less than the average income of an owner of one of these small refineries, Congress insists on this small refinery bias.

President Jimmy Carter has accepted the option provided in the 1975 act of decontrolling crude oil prices over a 28-month period starting after June 1, 1979. However, he has asserted that he would not veto a bill extending controls. He has announced a 28-month phaseout of controls that would move domestic crude oil prices to world levels by September 1981. The White House plan to phase out the control of crude oil prices in this country is a major step in the right direction. But it would have been better to shorten the time period. During this phaseout, producers may hold back on the production of crude, in order to secure a higher price. Why produce oil now at $6 a barrel, when in 28 months producers can get $15 to $20? Of course, some crude will be produced, since oil wells cannot be shut off like faucets. Nevertheless, over this interim period, production may fall rather than rise. A quick transition, therefore, while leading to an immediate jump in the price of gasoline and home heating oil, would have the beneficial effect of encouraging domestic production immediately, rather than after September 1981.

To complement his phaseout of price controls on crude oil production, President Carter proposed two taxes, one on windfall profits, which amounts to an excise tax on old oil. This tax would expire in 1981 when all oil is deregulated. If world oil prices rise above 1979 levels, the White House also wants a tax on that higher price for all domestically produced crude. This will, of course, discourage domestic production and increase imports. It may be that the Congress will not adopt the tax; in that case, if decontrol of oil goes forward, supplies should be ample and prices as low as technically possible. Decontrol will also reduce the subsidy on imported oil. But if Carter's proposed tax becomes law, more oil will be imported and foreign production will be greater, resulting in higher world oil prices.

Currently, there is a short-term energy crunch in the United States stemming from regulation of petroleum products. In much of the nation gas stations are closing on weekends, reducing their hours and their service. The Department of Energy regulates both the wholesale price of gasoline and the retail price, but until recently the regulated price was above the market clearing price and had no impact. In a free market, price would rise, encouraging increased supply and reducing the quantity consumers wish to buy. But because of the controls, this market response has not been permitted to occur. Naturally, the result has been shortages. Moreover, the shortages have not been uniform across the nation, but have been concentrated in certain areas, no doubt due to the unanticipated effects of Department of Energy regulations.

Although the regulation of the price of other refined products has been abolished, price controls on refined gasoline have continued. There is some dispute over whether these controls have actually been binding. Until 1979, actual prices were generally less than the maximum permitted prices. Competition was more effective than price controls in keeping costs down.

The sheer complexity of the regulation of refining prices has made enforcement difficult, if not impossible. The controls specify that a refiner or a reseller may charge the May 15, 1973, price, plus any allowable cost increases. These cost increases include dollar-for-dollar hikes based on increases in crude oil prices or the price of products. Nonproduct costs such as labor, fuel, utility, pollution-control costs, interest, marketing, and so forth, could also be passed on. Increased capital expenses, however, could not, thus reducing incentives for investment. The allowable costs have changed over the life of the program. Filling station dealers are restricted to a cents-per-gallon limitation on nonproduct costs, which partially explains the shortages in 1979. The profit for dealers was essentially fixed in terms of cents-per-gallon, which in real terms after inflation has been decreasing.

Sellers could "bank" cost increases if market conditions did not permit pricing to fully cover allowable costs. That is, if a dealer did not charge the maximum allowable, he could later make up for the less than maximum price by charging more. The rules dealing with the banking of costs, how past costs could be recouped, and how to treat deregulated products have grown increasingly complex. It is virtually impossible to determine definitively the maximum legal price. Thus the oil companies are constantly subject to allegations of overcharging. Since each of the regulations produces distortions, the government is continuously modifying and adding to the regulations.

A presidential task force concluded that the government

> had not . . . fully audited base period figures for refiners' sales to each class of purchaser in 1973 . . . Additionally, the current "banking" regulations for refiners are so complex that it is extremely difficult to determine, at any given point in time, the appropriate price ceiling for a particular product . . .
>
> The Task Force . . . also found . . . that very few resellers are in compliance with price regulations . . . [I]f not all retailers have appropriate price records and do not have an audited base period price, it is simply impossible for meaningful price controls.*

The continued controls of gasoline prices became effective in 1979. Gasoline became in short supply in spring 1979, with the escalation of world oil prices; the increased shortage of light crude most suitable for gasoline due to the Iranian shutdown; the entitlement program, which reduced the possibility of recovering the cost of purchasing oil in the spot market at above average cost; and a government policy of encouraging heating oil production over gasoline refining.

Until spring 1979, refineries were required to assign costs of production in proportion to output. If 50 percent of the output was gasoline, then half of any increase in costs could be added to gasoline prices. But gasoline, especially unleaded gasoline, costs more to produce than other refinery products. Since other refinery products had been decontrolled, refineries had an incentive to produce those products, and not gasoline. In particular, refineries had little incentive to invest in costly equipment to produce unleaded gasoline. Thus, the capacity of refineries to produce unleaded gasoline did not increase. Yet, as the proportion of cars needing unleaded gasoline increased, the shortage of unleaded grew.

Early in March 1979, the Department of Energy authorized refiners to charge five cents more for every gallon of gasoline produced. Though this tilt in the pricing scheme was ordered to encourage the production of gasoline, it did nothing to stimulate investment in the production of unleaded gasoline.

One potential solution would be to deregulate gasoline prices. However, the Environmental Protection Agency is concerned that a free

---

*Paul W. MacAvoy, ed., *Federal Energy Administration Regulation Report of the Presidential Task Force* (Washington: American Enterprise Institute, 1977), pp. 142–143.

market in gasoline might aggravate problems. In particular, the comparative shortage of unleaded gasoline would result in its price rising relative to the cost of leaded gasoline. Many drivers would then use leaded gasoline for their recent model cars, even though it would damage catalytic converters.

There are two possible solutions to this dilemma. One is to impose a tax on leaded gasoline. This is opposed by many consumer groups and liberals because it would raise the cost of gasoline to the drivers of old cars, who are often the less wealthy members of society. The alternative, which has not been given much consideration, is to reduce the taxes on unleaded gasoline. While this would reduce funds for the highway trust fund, it would diminish and perhaps even eliminate the disparity between the price of leaded and unleaded gasoline.

The costs of these regulations are not confined to this misallocation of resources, or to the wastes and shortages. A presidential task force estimated that the petroleum industry had to file 600,000 forms a year with the Federal Energy Administration (the predecessor of the Department of Energy), and that the costs to refineries of simply filling out and filing these documents were as much as $79.5 million per year, but total compliance cost was estimated to be as much as $570 million annually. In addition, the administration of these regulations by the Department of Energy is budgeted at $160 million for fiscal 1980.

Notwithstanding government claims designed to justify these regulations, there is no prospect that the United States or the world will physically run out of crude oil. However, it does seem likely that few, if any, new fields as big as Saudi Arabia and Mexico will be found in the future, and that most increases in reserves will come from smaller, less accessible fields. This implies a rising real cost for petroleum. As the price goes up, users will find that other sources of energy, or even using less energy, is cheaper. At a high enough price, oil will simply be priced out of the market, even though supplies will still exist.

For example, current oil recovery techniques never take all of the oil in the ground. At a price, more oil can be pumped out. Thus, existing oil fields in the United States can supply a diminishing quantity of crude for the indefinite future at higher prices. In addition, the oil contained in the shale of the Rocky Mountains is vast, and contains enough oil to run our economy for hundreds of years. However, shale oil is expensive, and extracting it would create major environmental problems.

The petroleum prospects for the 1980s are good, provided that crude oil is deregulated. While the United States may never again be self-sufficient in crude, the elimination of the entitlement program will make us less dependent on foreign sources than we would be with a continuation of controls. In fact, the share of the market accounted for by imports might even decline from the current level of about 50 percent.

While 1979 gas lines are likely to be temporary, as long as controls are maintained on the price of refined products, the possibility of future shortages is very real. If this country is to establish a rational energy policy, these controls must be abolished. If not, the 1980s will see periodic shortages of gasoline; long queues at filling stations; black markets; and a considerable waste of energy, gasoline, and other resources in an effort to circumvent the shortages.

Coal Production

Except for a period in the late 1930s and 1940s, when the government attempted to establish a cartel for the coal industry, it has basically been an unregulated and competitive industry. Starting in the 1960s, the government has increasingly intervened to regulate mine safety. More recently, environmental controls have been imposed on strip mining, on problems of land subsidence from mining, and on mine drainage. The use of coal as a fuel has been subject to environmental restrictions that increase its cost. And although the government has been imposing these controls on coal production and coal use, it has been calling for greater production and more dependence on coal. The Carter administration has emphasized that coal is our most abundant source of energy.

Coal, however, is a dirty fuel: it pollutes the atmosphere. Most coal contains sulphur, which adds to air pollution. Even low-sulphur fuel produces ash. To deal with this, the government has required power plants and other industries that burn coal to use low-sulphur fuels with dust collectors, or to install scrubbers to remove the sulphur oxides from the smoke. Scrubbers are expensive (a recent installation cost $400 million, or about one-third the cost of the power plant), their reliability has been questioned, and their use sharply increases the cost of using coal. The Clean Air Act Amendment of 1977 requires that scrubbers or the "best technological system" be installed, even for plants using low-sulphur fuels. This provision is counterproductive, in that it discourages the use of low-sulphur fuels, and was enacted to protect the market position of high-sulphur coal from the East and Midwest.

If the aim is to reduce air pollution in the cheapest manner, a more efficient approach would be to tax sulphur-oxide emissions. Power companies and other users of coal would then seek the methods that reduce air pollution at the lowest possible cost. These might involve using low-sulphur fuels, scrubbers, desulphurizing the coal, or currently unknown techniques. However, the government has not accepted this approach and is mandating "the best available technology" designed to reduce sulphur emissions.

The coal mine Health and Safety Act of 1969 imposed stringent requirements on underground mine safety. These provisions have sharply reduced not only mine fatalities, but also the long-term gain in productivity that the coal industry had enjoyed since the 1940s. Average tons mined per day per man fell from a high of 19.9 in 1969 to 14.3 in 1977, while fatalities per man-hour were reduced about 60 percent. Figure 1 shows the impact of the 1969 act on coal prices. Based on an index of 100 for the prices of coal, oil, and natural gas in 1969, the chart shows that coal prices moved up sharply before the other fuels. The big jump in all fuel prices occurred after 1973 and the Arab oil embargo.

Figure 1 also shows that natural gas prices have continued to increase because of the growing shortage, and regulation has permitted increasingly higher prices in order to create incentives to locate new gas. The picture portrayed by Fig. 1, however, is somewhat misleading. Though natural gas prices have risen more sharply than the prices of coal or oil, the actual cost of fuel per million BTUs is just the reverse. In 1977, average natural gas prices at the well head were roughly half the price of crude oil for the same BTU content. Coal was somewhere in between. However, the regulated price of new natural gas, which in May 1979 was $2.18 per million BTUs, is equivalent to $12.63 per barrel of crude oil. Upper tier crude sold for $13.06 per barrel in May 1979, imported oil at about $16, and world spot prices were reported as high as $30.00. Natural gas is still underpriced in relation to oil; but coal, which in spring 1979 was selling for the equivalent of less than $7 per barrel of crude oil, is an even greater bargain. Coal prices have fallen about 30 percent between 1978 and the spring of 1979.

Known coal reserves are huge and can last for hundreds of years. The question does not concern supplies of coal, but whether the consumer and industry are willing to pay the price to mine it safely and burn it cleanly. The chief impediments to cheap coal lie in the regulation of its use and its mining. Final regulations on strip mining have not yet been adopted, and the requirements for scrubbers for power plants have not been issued. To the extent that these environmental and safety controls are relaxed, coal will be cheaper and more plentiful and will more adequately satisfy our energy needs. The requirement of scrubbers for all plants and the limitation on strip mining will reduce the use of low-sulphur fuel, which in many cases would be the cheapest way to reduce pollution.

The public and the administration must recognize the trade-off between a cleaner environment and cheaper energy. It would seem that

FIGURE 1

Relative Price Changes for Major Fossil Fuels

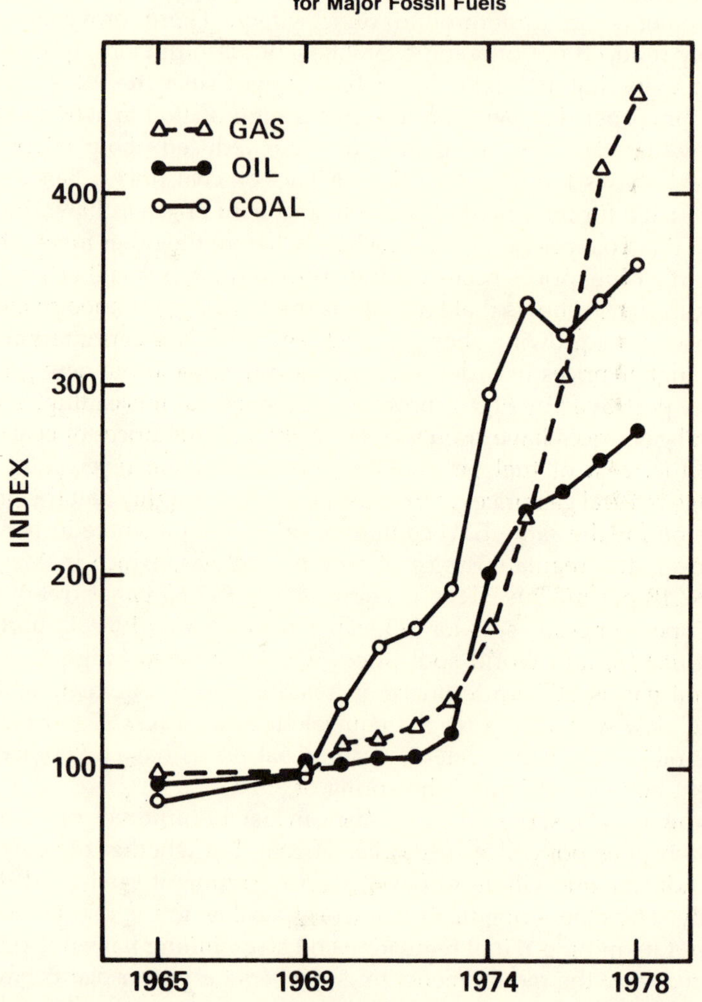

neither extreme is appropriate. No sensible person would advocate a pristine environment without the consumption of any fossil fuel. Such an environment might be good for some animals and plants, but the present population of the world could not be sustained. At the other extreme, no sensible person would advocate the abolition of environmental controls. Dirty, smoke-filled air can sicken and kill. Thousands have died due to air pollution inversions in the past and could again in the future.

Should strip miners have to return the land to a condition close to the pre-mined condition? The major justification for doing so is that surface mining disfigures the landscape, and it takes a long time to recover. Strip mining may also lead to erosion of neighboring land. If stripped land is remote and in an unpopulated area, there is less justification for large expenditures to return the land to its primitive beauty. On the other hand, if strip mining will produce a scar that many will witness, then controls to reduce the visual damage may be warranted. Erosion problems may also justify regulation.

Expenditures for pollution abatement should be extended to the point where the last dollar spent reduces the cost of pollution to the public by one dollar. For example, controls or taxes should be imposed on air polluters up to the point that the marginal cost of reducing sulphur oxides and particulates equals the marginal benefit in terms of longer and healthier life, better aesthetics, and less damage to plants and buildings. Of course the measurement of the value of a longer and healthier life presents great difficulties, but can be estimated by how much people will pay to increase their life expectancy by a month or how much they will pay to avoid ill health. Valuing better aesthetics also depends on what the public will pay.

The desirability of restricting strip mining and requiring mining companies to expend large sums on returning the land to something close to its previous condition depends upon the value to consumers of that action. The relevant question then becomes how much consumers are willing to pay to see that land returned to something close to its prior condition.

Nuclear Power

Nuclear power now produces about 13 percent of the nation's electric power. This percentage cannot increase greatly during the 1980s, since licensing restrictions and long construction times foreclose any quick new projects. In the United States, it now takes nearly twelve years from the time a power company decides to build a nuclear facility until it is on-line. In Japan, on the other hand, where licensing restrictions are much less, it takes only a third of that time. After the accident at the Three Mile Island plant in Pennsylvania, delays will undoubtedly be greater than they have been in the past. Thus, only those power plants already under construction will be able to come on-line during the 1980s.

There are currently 88 nuclear plants under construction, with 11 projected to be finished in 1979, 12 in 1980, 12 in 1981, 17 in 1982, and 15 in 1983. These plants will add 101,000 megawatts of power, tripling the capacity of the currently licensed nuclear power stations. There are another 28 units under construction permit review, but it is unlikely that much of the 32,000 megawatts of power planned could come on-line before the late 1980s or early 1990s. In recent years it has taken an average of over 8 years from the time a construction permit is issued until a full power operating license is granted. Table 1 represents data on the licensing of nuclear power plants in the early 1960s and the 1970s. As can be seen, the major change has been an increase in the length of time needed to secure a permit to start construction and obtain a license to operate the plant.

A combination of factors has resulted in a major slowdown in the growth of the nuclear power industry. In 1972 and 1973, 29 and 32 new plants were ordered for a total of about 70,000 megawatts of capacity. But in 1974, after the oil embargo and a slowdown in the demand for electricity, there were as many plants canceled as ordered, and in 1975 no new plants were ordered. In 1976, 1977, and 1978, 2, 4, and then 2 plants were ordered. To a large extent, the precipitous drop in the number of new plants ordered has been caused by the deceleration in the growth of demand for electric power. In the postwar period prior to 1973, the demand for electric power grew at the rate of about 7 percent a year. After 1974, the rate fell to about half that. In addition, the environmental movement and antinuclear groups have pressed for delays in the installation of new nuclear power plants. Antinuclear forces are launching a major offensive to shut down American nuclear power and prevent the construction of more such plants. It seems unlikely that they would be successful in shutting down existing power plants, since this would lead to blackouts and brownouts, and would create major power shortages in many parts of the country, especially the midwest. But it is likely that such opposition will delay the construction and licensing of new plants.

The Carter administration proposed legislation in 1978 to reduce licensing delays, but neither the industry nor environmentalists supported it. Even after the Three Mile Island accident, the Department of Energy still asserted that they were going to submit a new bill to expedite licensing. It is highly uncertain whether such legislation will be passed by Congress. There will certainly be a battle between environmentalists and antinuclear forces on the one side and pronuclear power groups on the other. If the legislation does pass and does significantly reduce licensing times, it will contribute to alleviating possible power shortages.

TABLE 1

Average Months to License Nuclear Power Plants

	Average Months to Secure Construction Permit	Months between Construction Permit and Filing for Operating License	Average Months to Secure Full Power License	Average Months Elapsed from Initial Filing with Government to Full Power License
Plants Initiated Prior to 1964 (16 plants)	11.4	23.6	19.8	54.8
Plants Fully Licensed After 1974 (17 plants)	20.3	26.7	53.4	100.3
Percent Change in Decade	+78.1	+13.1	+169.7	+83.0

Source: *Program Summary Report.* U.S. Nuclear Regulatory Report NUREC-0380, vol. 3, no. 3, March 16, 1979.

Opposition to nuclear power is ironic. From an objective point of view, nuclear power is one of the cleanest methods of generating electricity, one of the safest, and one of the least environmentally degrading. All fossil fuel plants produce carbon dioxide, which many scientists believe will result in an increased percentage of carbon dioxide in the atmosphere. It is feared that this will create a greenhouse effect on earth that would warm the earth and melt the polar ice caps, raising the oceans and flooding major coastal cities. All fossil fuel plants, except natural gas facilities, yield other significant air pollutants. Coal is especially dirty, generating sulphur oxides, ash, and carbon dioxide. Coal is also an unsafe fuel to use. Coal miners die routinely; over one hundred miners are fatally injured every year. Large quantities of coal must be shipped long distances to power plants, tying up valuable resources in freight transportation. Expensive scrubbers and other devices must be attached to clean the exhaust from coal power plants.

Oil plants are only somewhat better, since they can be a major source of pollution. If high-sulphur oil is used, sulphur oxides are emitted. In addition, the transportation of oil can be highly damaging to the environment. Oil spills are now common around the world. Oil globlets have been reported in the middle of the Atlantic. Many beaches in the Mediterranean are no longer attractive for swimming because of oil. Oil also has other disadvantages. It is highly dangerous; oil fires occur and explosions kill workers. Moreover, the production of crude oil is concentrated in the hands of a group of rather unstable Third World countries located in the Middle East. The Iranian lesson should not be lost. Future steady supplies of oil from the Middle East are clearly uncertain and problematical.

On the other hand, nuclear power is comparatively safe. No member of the general public has been killed from nuclear power anywhere in the world. No U.S. atomic power plant worker has been killed due to an accident in a nuclear power plant. Since less uranium needs to be mined than coal to generate electricity, there are fewer deaths due to mining of uranium fuel than there would be from coal mines to provide the same electric power. Table 2 presents some rough calculations concerning the relative risks of generating electricity by various means. As can be seen, nuclear power is one of the safest: it is clean; and besides occasional radiation leaks, it produces no air pollutants.

Nuclear power does have two significant disadvantages. First, it releases a small amount of radioactivity into the environment. However, this background radiation is negligible, and even fervent antinuclear power advocates do not consider it dangerous. But there is the possibility of a major accident that would release a considerable amount of radioactivity. A core meltdown, for example, could result in a major release of radioactivity. This could, under some weather conditions, affect large numbers of people. The probability of such an occurrence is very small.

Apparently, the accident at Three Mile Island was created by a series of mistakes by operators, together with equipment failure. Even then, the public was not obviously harmed. Although some environmentalists claim that we were lucky at Three Mile Island, it might be more accurate to acknowledge that Three Mile Island was an example of bad luck. It is highly improbable to have that many mistakes, one after another. Moreover, we have learned from Three Mile Island, which reduces the risk of another such accident.

Nevertheless, accidents will occur in the future. Sooner or later, with virtual certainty, there will be a major nuclear power plant accident with a major release of radioactivity into the atmosphere. Where and when it will happen is unknown, but it is just as inevitable as a major earthquake in the San Francisco Bay area that will kill thousands of people. Even recognizing the inescapability of an accident with a release of radioactivity, nuclear power is still safer than coal and oil (see Table 2).

The second major drawback to nuclear power is the problem of waste disposal. Nuclear power plants produce highly radioactive wastes. There are a number of possibilities for dealing with these wastes. One is to recycle them through a reprocessing plant that will extract plutonium, the remaining uranium, and other nuclear products, leaving a residual of highly radioactive, concentrated waste, to be stored. Alternatively, the original waste, including plutonium, and the remaining uranium can be stored without processing. One advantage of reprocessing is that the plutonium can be used as a fuel for generating electricity in other power plants. Moreover, the residual uranium can be enriched and recycled, providing more atomic fuel. Another advantage is that reprocessing results in a smaller physical bulk of waste that must be stored.

TABLE 2

Estimated Range of Deaths for a Specific Energy Output (10 GWy)

Coal	50–1,600
Oil	20–1,400
Wind	120–230
Solar, space heating	80–90
Uranium	2½–15
Natural Gas	1–4

Source: Data from Dr. Herbert Inhaber, associate scientific adviser to Canada's Atomic Energy Control Board, as revised and reported in the *Wall Street Journal*, April 24, 1979, editorial page. These estimates include total costs, from mining or extracting fuel to the actual generation of electricity.

A major disadvantage of reprocessing is that plutonium is produced in a form that could be used to create bombs by other countries, or even by sophisticated terrorist groups. There has been considerable debate over the desirability of reprocessing because of its production of plutonium. It is uncertain whether this plutonium can be adequately safeguarded. Certainly, the fear that unstable foreign governments would secure this plutonium seems unwarranted. Foreign governments can acquire plutonium from foreign reprocessing plants; the existence of an American reprocessing plant will not significantly affect their ability to acquire plutonium. A number of countries have built or are building processing plants. There has been talk of reprocessing plants in Taiwan, Korea, Iraq, and Pakistan. Unfortunately, the nuclear genie is out of the bottle and there is no way to put it back. Trying to stopper the bottle in the United States will have little impact on the world at large.

Although a nuclear reprocessing plant in this country might be the target of a terrorist group attempting to secure plutonium, we could guard against this. In any case, it would be more effective for a terrorist group to steal an atomic bomb directly from an air force arsenal than to try to steal raw plutonium from a reprocessing plant. Since it requires expertise and expensive equipment to handle the plutonium safely and to convert it into a usable bomb, terrorists would gain little by stealing plutonium.

The major problem with reprocessing plants is not plutonium, but that they are not economic. Considering the current and expected future cost of mining new uranium, reprocessing—an expensive, cumbersome, and highly radioactive process—does not produce sufficient economic benefits to warrant a major investment.

Whether there is reprocessing or not, the wastes (which would be less with reprocessing) must be stored. Thus far, the Department of Energy has failed to come up with a long-run solution to the waste disposal problem. The antinuclear forces have made this their most telling argument. Many states, including California, have passed legislation barring the construction of new power plants until the waste disposal problem has been satisfactorily handled. The Department of Energy has proposed burying wastes deep in salt mines, but to date there has been little experimentation to determine the feasibility of this plan. Moreover, no state or community wants to have highly radioactive garbage stored in its area. The major nuclear power question facing the government in the 1980s is what to do with the spent fuel from reactors. Most experts and most studies have concluded that a satisfactory solution is technically possible. Some suggest that burying the wastes under the deep sea bed is both feasible and would protect the elements from contaminating the environment for thousands of years. However, a safe and sure method of storing the wastes for centuries has not yet been proven. The federal government must proceed with a demonstration project to show the feasibility of long-term storage. It might have been desirable at one time to have the private sector handle wastes, but the issue has become so political that only the government can provide the public with a convincing demonstration.

Nuclear fusion uses hydrogen as a fuel. If developed, atomic energy is potentially inexhaustible. Though some people fear that uranium reserves for fission plants might be exhausted, this does not appear likely for some time to come. Although the easiest and most accessible supplies of uranium have already been exploited, mining and prospecting for uranium is still a relatively new industry, and there are undoubtedly large deposits that have not yet been found. Even existing deposits can be mined more thoroughly and lower grade ores tapped. In addition, as mentioned above, reprocessing of spent fuel can produce plutonium, which can be used to power reactors.

A number of countries, including France, West Germany, the United Kingdom, Japan, and the Soviet Union, are working on breeder reactors, designed to produce more fuel than they consume. The United States is spending hundreds of millions on breeder research and development, although the administration has wisely decided not to continue with the uneconomic Clinch River breeder reactor.

Nevertheless, the 1980s may experience a decline in the importance of nuclear power. Not only is the environmental movement attempting to block new construction, but economic regulation of electric utilities may make new power plants unprofitable for utilities. For example, the Pennsylvania Public Utilities Commission, in the Three Mile Island case, has taken the approach that the cost of the accident should be borne by the company's stockholders. On the other hand, any reduction in costs due to a nuclear plant must normally be passed on to ratepayers. As a consequence, regulation imposes the cost and risks of accidents on stockholders and passes on the gains to customers. This is not a formula designed to encourage nuclear power. This bias may be partially offset if a nuclear plant produces electricity at lower than average cost for the company. Since rates are based on average cost, the utility may find that it is still economical to proceed with nuclear power, providing it is the lowest-cost source, although the asymmetry biases utilities against atomic energy. It would be better if ratepayers and stockholders shared the costs of accidents, depending on any show of negligence by the utility. The cost of "acts of God" would fall mainly on ratepayers, and the cost of carelessness would be borne by stockholders.

The Three Mile Island accident was an absolute disaster for the nuclear power industry. It has crystallized in the public mind the dangers of nuclear power, even though no one was known to have been harmed by the accident. The recommended evacuation of pregnant women and small children added to fears, as did the public discussion of a general evacuation and of a core meltdown. The fact that no one was killed and no evacuation was necessary may not be as important as the confusion and hysteria of the media reports. Certainly, Three Mile Island has strengthened the antinuclear forces.

The environmental movement has attempted to stop not only nuclear power, but all major new power plants. For example, after nine years of effort, a group of utilities led by Southern California Edison Company abandoned an effort to build a huge coal-fired plant on a barren part of the Kaiparowits plateau in southern Utah. The Sierra Club, the Audubon Society, and other environmentalist spokesmen ignored the overwhelming evidence by federal scientists that the impact would be minimal. This led the utilities to give up in 1976, when, after the cost of the project had increased sevenfold, they still needed 220 permits from 42 federal, state, and local agencies. At the moment, a consortium of utilities, headed by Los Angeles Department of Water and Power, is attempting to secure a building permit for a huge 3,000-megawatt, coal-fired plant in Utah designed to burn low-sulphur fuel. Environmentalists are bitterly opposed to the Intermountain Plant, even though the utilities will install $600 million worth of control equipment on the $3 billion facility.

It has become increasingly difficult to build any kind of power plant. A public more and more sensitive to environmental matters objects to dirty, coal-fired plants and is scared of nuclear power plants. Oil power plants have been discouraged by the government because their construction would increase our dependence on foreign suppliers of oil. Environmentalists also object because oil power plants produce air pollution. Natural gas-fired power plants would be acceptable both from a safety and environmental point of view, but until recently it was widely believed that the shortage of gas precluded its use for boiler fuel. However, the partial deregulation and increased availability of natural gas can supply power for generating plants if the government permits.

Alternative Energy Supplies

A number of politicians, environmentalists, and others have urged the government to promote conservation and alternate energy sources. In particular, solar energy has been recommended as a source of continuous nonexhaustible, nonpolluting energy. Critics have argued that the government has emphasized too heavily traditional forms of energy and nuclear power while ignoring solar and other newer types of technology.

Table 3, drawn from the 1980 federal budget, gives the expected and forecast government expenditures for developing major energy sources and for promoting energy conservation. In fiscal year 1980, the government will be spending the largest proportion of its energy budget on conservation. Nearly $1.5 billion will go to promote conservation, either in the form of research on technical developments or on grants and tax credits to encourage private and state conservation efforts.

This huge outlay for conservation is unnecessary. If the price of energy were allowed to rise to a market clearing level with deregulation, there would be no need to promote conservation. Consumers would

TABLE 3

Major Government Outlays and Tax Credits for Energy Supply and Conservation (Millions of $)

	Fiscal Year	
	1979	1980
Research and development		
Nuclear power		
Fission	1,095	970
Uranium enrichment	121	16
Fusion	339	364
Total nuclear	1,550	1,350
Fossil fuels		
Coal	671	658
Petroleum	99	68
Gas	40	40
Oil shale	2	5
Other	0	6
Total	812	777
Other and new technologies		
Solar: outlays	551	730
tax credits	88	74
Total	639	804
Geothermal	135	132
Energy conservation		
Technology development	204	232
Conservation grants	286	427
Tax credits	935	825
Total conservation	1,425	1,484

Source: Budget of the United States, fiscal year 1980.

have a strong incentive to economize if fuels were priced at replacement costs. Businesses and industry would devote efforts to waste reduction if energy were priced at free market levels. But, as indicated above, the government, through a series of regulatory measures, has attempted to keep the price of both oil and natural gas well below market clearing levels.

In the past, not only have oil and gas been underpriced, but nuclear energy has been heavily subsidized. The research and development of nuclear energy has been mainly supported by the government. From 1970 to 1978 alone the federal government spent over $7 billion (in 1978 dollars) on research and development of nuclear power. In the 1980 budget the total projected outlay for nuclear power is greater than for any other form of energy. Of that expenditure, most will be spent on fission, a source of energy that is already in commercial operation.

The nearly $1 billion to be spent on nuclear fission is devoted to four aspects of the industry: 1) the light water reactor technology and fuel cycle research and development, 2) the commercial waste management program to deal with spent fuel from nuclear power plants, 3) breeder reactors, and 4) high temperature gas cooled reactors. The justification for the large expenditure on nuclear power is not clear. It is a commercially available source of energy at the moment. There are incentives by manufacturers and industry to develop the industry. It would be appropriate for the government to let the private nuclear power industry compete without federal aid. Critics of nuclear power are right when they assert that it has been unwarrantably subsidized by the government. It is probably true that if it were not for government research and development, the private sector would have taken longer to develop the industry. It is quite likely that the return from investment in nuclear power has not been positive. Nevertheless, since the investment has been made, the technology should be used. It is still a cheaper source of energy than most other alternatives, although coal may have the edge in certain parts of the country.

Opponents of nuclear power are also right when they argue that utilities are not paying the full cost for nuclear power. Projected costs of nuclear power facilities have probably underestimated outlays for spent fuel disposal. The costs of nuclear accidents apparently have not been included.

Another subsidy provided to nuclear power producers is the congressionally enacted Price-Anderson limit of liability to $560 million in any nuclear disaster. Any residual cost from a major nuclear power disaster must be borne by the public. The objective of the Price-Anderson Act was to encourage nuclear energy, when there was little experience with it. But now that it is commercial and well developed, there is no justification for this limit. The Price-Anderson Act should be repealed, and utilities should face the cost of a nuclear power accident. Ratepayers and utility company stockholders should ultimately be responsible.

The second most heavily subsidized source is solar energy. For fiscal year 1980 the federal government plans to spend $730 million on solar energy research, with another $74 million in tax credits to encourage the use of solar energy. There are basically two forms of solar energy. One is passive, in which water or other substances are heated directly by the sun, and that heat is then used for space or water heating. This form of solar energy has been employed ever since man first walked. Solar water heaters used in Florida and in other parts of the country with sunny climates are nearly competitive with other energy sources. Properly built houses can be warmed in the winter and kept comfortable in the summer.

The other proposed use of solar energy is to convert sunlight into electric power. Fuel cells that convert sunlight to electricity use a variety of approaches. Single-crystal silicon cells were developed for the space program but are too expensive for mass use. Thin film cells, though cheaper to manufacture, are too inefficient. Other approaches are being developed, but it is apparent that the cost of photovoltaic cells is currently several orders of magnitude higher than more traditional methods of generating electricity. It has been estimated that a fuel cell electric plant would require vast acres of space for solar collectors. These would be unsightly and undoubtedly would produce opposition. Moreover, the cells themselves must be manufactured and any waste disposed of. They are not necessarily pollution-free. In light of these considerations, spending nearly three-quarters of a billion dollars on research is unwarranted. The private sector has incentives to find a cheap source of solar energy.

The third largest category of government spending on research and development of energy is in coal research. Since coal is one of our most plentiful sources of fossil fuels in this country, and since existing environmental standards make it increasingly difficult to burn coal directly, the government is devoting resources to developing clean sources of energy based on coal. But just as for solar and nuclear power, it is probably more efficient to leave the research to the private sector. Since there are large profits available for developing cheap and clean fuels, there is no necessity for the government to spend hundreds of millions of dollars on research in these areas.

If the government is to support research on energy, it seems strange that the Department of Energy is spending over $600 million on coal research and only $5 million on oil shale. Actually, oil shale is one of the most plentiful sources of fuel oil that exists in this country. It is expensive, but with the right technology it could be extracted. It would seem that if the government is going to put money into energy research, it would be worth spending a somewhat larger proportion of the federal research and development budget on shale and less on coal. The coal industry is already populated by a number of firms with large enough resources to carry on their own research.

The Energy Tax Act of 1978 exempted gasohol (gasoline containing at least 10 percent alcohol) from the 4-cent per gallon federal excise tax. To receive this tax break, the alcohol must come from agricultural products or wastes. Lobbyists, congressmen, and senators from farm states have been strong supporters of this subsidy. Iowa has gone further and exempted gasohol from its state taxes of 6.5 cents per gallon.

For the moment, these subsidies are terribly inefficient. It takes more oil and gas to ferment grain into alcohol than is saved. The federal and state subsidy in Iowa amounts to the equivalent of $44.10 per barrel of alcohol, a rather high price to pay to save even $30 a barrel oil. President Carter has promised the Iowa farmers that the government will spend $11 million to help build small-scale alcohol fuel plants.

President Carter has also proposed a federally chartered Energy Security Corporation to develop and subsidize the production of 2.5 million barrels of oil by 1990 from synthetic sources such as shale, tar sands, coal, and alcohol. This corporation would direct the investment of $88 billion between 1979 and 1990. As indicated above the expenditure is likely to be very wasteful and, since the corporation has little incentive to keep costs low, it is likely to be very inefficient.

POLICY PROPOSALS

It seems unlikely that the government will get out of the energy business entirely during the 1980s. The government is already deeply involved in subsidizing, promoting, regulating, berating, and researching the energy industries. Certain guidelines, however, are desirable. The first priority is the deregulation of crude oil prices. President Carter has asserted that he will deregulate these prices over the next 28 months, with the result that by 1981 they will be completely free of regulation. However, even in 1981, if his policies are followed, a tax will continue to be imposed on any increase in crude oil prices above the spring 1979 level, whether a result of market forces or OPEC manipulation. The tax would simply discourage domestic production and encourage foreign production. The tax, therefore, should not be enacted. Together with the dismantling of the controls on crude oil prices, this would be the most important step toward reduction of our dependence on imports and the lowering of world oil prices.

The second priority is the deregulation of natural gas prices. The 1978 act does not go far enough in removing controls. According to the act, only new natural gas and a few other unimportant categories would be free to sell at world market prices. All control on natural gas should be removed in order to promote supplies to the fullest. Since natural gas is one of the safest and cleanest fuels available, maximum production should be encouraged.

The third priority facing this nation is to facilitate the licensing of electric power plants. Both nuclear plants and fossil fuel plants have been subject to increasing regulatory and bureaucratic delays in government authorizations. This has led to an abandonment of plans for the construction of major power plants, both fossil fuel and nuclear. Although it is important to keep the environment clean, it is also important to facilitate new power plant construction. To do this, the Congress must restrict the ability of environmentalist groups to contest the construction of power plants. The public should be given an opportunity to make its point, to be heard, and to be duly considered; but once a ruling has been made, the plant should be permitted to go forward. Under existing law, it is possible to appeal again and again and to subject the plants to endless delays. Most of this cost is not borne by the litigants, but by the public utilities and eventually the ratepayers. A step in the right direction might be to make protesters subject to liability for the costs of delay if the protests are found to be without merit.

President Carter has proposed an Energy Mobilization board that would have the power to designate selected energy projects as "critical" for the nation. For those projects the board could set deadlines for issuance of local, state, and federal permits and could waive procedural requirements such as public hearings and environmental impact statements. Rules of the board could be appealed directly to the U.S. Court of Appeals to reduce the time spent in litigation. This proposal has considerable merit if the principal problem of successive regulation cannot be addressed directly.

If these three priorities are followed, the United States will face a decade of adequate but higher priced energy supplies. There would be no chance of running out of fuel, and there would be no chance that the country would face major shortages. Not all energy problems, however, would be eliminated by these steps. Controls on the pricing of gasoline should also be removed. These controls can create temporary shortages at filling stations and unbalanced supplies nationwide. In addition, the environmental and safety constraints on the mining of coal should be reduced. Safety should be decided by the wishes of miners and their willingness to trade off wages for safety. Restrictions on strip mining should be lowered, and, in fact, federal controls should be abolished. Since the environmental costs of strip mining are of a local nature, it should be up to the localities or, at most, the states as to what regulations should be imposed on strip mining. The federal government need not be involved. If Wyoming, for example, prefers the income generated from strip mining of coal to an empty, but beautiful, plateau, then that choice should be Wyoming's. These steps, coupled with the ones suggested above, would lead to higher prices for natural gas and oil and lower prices for coal. The abolition of subsidies for nuclear power will raise its costs, but quicker licensing will reduce costs. The net impact is unpredictable.

In any case, the higher cost for oil and natural gas will encourage the substitution of coal for the other fuels. As long as environmental constraints exist on the burning of coal, however, industry will be faced with the cost of cleaning up the coal either before or after it is burned. This will provide industry with strong incentives to develop ways of turning coal into a pollution-free resource. With these steps there would no longer be the necessity for the federal government to subsidize research and development on coal. Nor would there be the necessity of spending nearly $1.5 billion on conservation efforts. Higher prices for oil and natural gas would in themselves encourage conservation.

The $1.5 billion that the federal government spends on conservation is only the tip of the iceberg. The government has mandated more fuel-efficient automobiles and fuel-efficient appliances. These costs will be borne by consumers even though they were government-required. In any complete accounting they should be added to the governmental sector. If oil were allowed to rise to world market prices, as suggested above, there would be no need for mandating fuel-efficient automobiles. And if electricity were priced at the marginal cost of generating it, there would be no necessity for requiring fuel-efficient appliances. Thus, the deregulation efforts suggested could reduce government spending by billions, while achieving the aims of conservation and coal gasification.

As a final recommendation, the federal government should turn the nuclear fission industry over to the private sector entirely. The development and disposal of waste could be handled by private firms, with utilities contracting with other companies to handle their wastes. The

Price-Anderson limits on liability should be eliminated, provided utilities are permitted to benefit as well as bear the cost of nuclear power. Government ownership and operation of the uranium enrichment plants should be abolished and the plants sold to the private sector. Research and development of nuclear fission should be borne by the private sector. These steps would guarantee that if nuclear power continues to exist and flourish, it would have to do so in competition with other energy sources and on a full-cost basis. It would also guarantee that research and development would not be wastefully spent, and would be targeted toward the most promising technologies.

Throughout the 1970s, government officials have alleged that it is necessary to develop a national energy program. However, they have never explained why this is important. Private sector incentives, following the dictates of Adam Smith's invisible hand, will provide energy at the cost of finding and developing it. If the cost of energy rises because it is becoming more scarce, then consumers will face incentives to conserve and to substitute capital or labor for energy. Conservation will be practiced by those who find it most economical, not by those whom the government thinks it is most expedient to coerce. Those energy technologies that are cheapest, least polluting, and least troublesome will be developed and offered to the public. Billions of dollars of government money and private sector resources will be saved if we depend on the free market and not on the public sector. It should be the primary goal of the 1980s to return this country and the energy sector to the free market. As a side benefit, we would be less dependent upon foreign oil supplies and, as a consequence, would put pressure on world oil prices.

Unfortunately, a major obstacle to our moving in this rational direction is an inordinate fear of some politicians that a few individuals will receive great benefits from deregulation, while others will have to pay higher costs. It cannot be denied that this will occur. Yet it seems a small price to pay for a rational energy policy. At least half the gain that will go to the oil producers from deregulation will actually be sent to Washington in the form of higher tax receipts. If some consumers are hurt badly by deregulation, then larger efforts for income redistribution might be required. However, as others in this volume point out, poverty has been virtually abolished in this country, and most poor are fairly well insulated from inflationary factors. Perhaps gas stamps or energy stamps, like food stamps, could be given to the poor. It would take political courage to deregulate, but the consequences of not deregulating are persistent shortages, prolonged economic inefficiency, and continued waste. Rich as we are, we cannot afford to continue our current policies. We must have a rational energy policy, the free market.

Environmental Policy

Allen V. Kneese

X

That environmental problems are not new is shown by environmental conditions in relatively modern and even medieval cities. The history of the city of London is especially well documented. In the fourteenth century, butchers had been assigned a spot at Seacoal Lane near Fleet prison. A royal document reports: "By the killing of great beasts, from whose putrid blood running down the streets and the bowels cast into the Thames, the air in the city is very much corrupted and infected, whence abominable and most filthy stinks proceed, sickness and many other evils have happened to such as have abode in the said city, or have resorted to it."[1] Five centuries later, Charles Dickens reported, "He knew of many places in it unsurpassed in the accumulated horrors of their long neglect by the dirtiest old spots in the dirtiest old towns, under the worst old governments of Europe."[2]

It seems clear that in developed countries environmental conditions that directly and immediately affect the daily lives of the mass of citizens have improved immensely—at least until the middle of the twentieth century. Why then has environmental pollution become one of the most important problems of the day for many people? Several factors appear to be involved.

First, immense increases in industrial production and energy conversion have occurred in recent decades. The associated flow of materials and energy from concentrated states in nature to dispersed states in the environment have begun to alter the physical, chemical, and biological quality of the atmosphere and hydrosphere on a truly massive scale. Furthermore, we now have the means to detect even small changes in these natural systems.

Second, exotic materials are being introduced into the environment. Applications of modern chemistry and physics have exposed the world's biological systems to strange materials to which they cannot adapt (at least not quickly) or to which adaptation is highly specific among species and therefore disruptive.

Third, the mass of people have come to expect standards of cleanliness, safety, and healthfulness in their surroundings that were the exclusive province of the well-to-do in earlier times.

These considerations also suggest the increasing importance of viewing environmental issues as part of the general natural-resources problem rather than in isolation. In this context the present state of our natural resources policy is, to say the least, not encouraging.

I will return to this theme in a moment, but first, a few comments on the structure of this essay. The next section discusses the nature of environmental problems in the context of broader natural-resources issues. Following that I will review briefly the policies we have developed in the United States to try to deal with our environmental problems. Next, an alternative set of policies is presented, discussed, and evaluated. To this point I will be discussing the "mass" pollutants (for example, oxygen-demanding organic residuals in water and sulfur compounds in the air). These have received by far the greatest amount of legislative and administrative attention. But as the decade closes, efforts to deal with substances in the environment that are small in amount but highly toxic are moving to the center of attention and will greatly challenge our ability to manage the environment over the next several years. The essay concludes with a discussion of policy with respect to this new set of environmental problems.

NATURAL RESOURCES POLICY AND ENVIRONMENTAL ISSUES*

In my view the present state of natural resources in the United States, including policy at the national level with respect to them, is a matter for deep concern. Our policies are fragmented, suffering from multiple schizophrenia, and grossly overdependent upon direct regulation rather than on modification of the defective system of economic incentives, which is a primary source of our resource problems in the first place. To begin to remedy the deficiencies of our resource policies it is necessary to understand that our resource problems, from the energy crunch to the state of our watercourses, from landscapes shattered by surface mining to the often deplorable quality of our urban air, are interrelated issues. To

*This section draws heavily on Allen V. Kneese, "Natural Resources Policy 1975–85," *Journal of Environmental Economics and Management* 3, no. 4 (Dec. 1976): 253–288.

come to grips with this web of national problems we need a coherent program of resource policies rather than the scattershot, one-resource-at-a-time approach to legislation that exists today.

To some extent the present situation results from the fact that our policymaking processes are in a state of transitional stress. Policy artifacts such as depletion allowances and many other favorable tax treatments of extractive industries are remnants of a time when encouragement of rapid use of our natural resources was regarded as unquestionably desirable and the discharge of residuals to the environment could be, or at least was, neglected. We have federal oil and gas price regulations that reflect the abundance of another day. At the same time we ration the end uses of some of our fuels. We have in our legal and regulatory structure a number of biases against recycling, but we also have on the books laws that, if successfully implemented, would place strict controls on the use of environmental resources. Our policymakers are trying to come to grips with an inherited policy structure that, although fragmented and often internally contradictory, was largely constructed in an era of resource abundance. For the most part it reflects that context, but it now contains bits and pieces that mirror more recent events.

One aspect of the situation is more distressing, however. Current policy efforts, especially at the congressional level, do not give any evidence of a clear understanding of the basic nature of our resource problems and the associated integration and redirection of policies and modification of the policymaking process that they demand. Nothing could illustrate this more clearly than Congress' confused attempts to develop an energy policy over the past few years. At the most basic level, many of our most severe problems stem from several kinds of failures in the set of incentives that our market system, as it presently functions, generates. In more than a few instances, these misdirected incentives are further aggravated by public policies. Rather than altering perverse incentives, the inclination of Congress has been to move steadily in the direction of establishing more and more complex regulations. Many of these regulations are now coming to be widely recognized as arbitrary and capricious in application. Moreover, they usually fail to achieve their objectives, or if they do achieve them they do so only at great, and often unnecessary, cost.

I will elaborate on this theme. But first it will be helpful to take a look at what economic theory sees as the operation of an ideal market and what the most salient departures of actual markets, especially with respect to environment-resource issues, are from the functioning of this model. This brief digression will provide a somewhat abstract but reasonably coherent framework for the development of a broad perspective on our environmental problems.

The Ideal Market

When economists speak of the market they usually have in mind a particular type of intellectual construct. This conceptual model is the product of an evolutionary intellectual process going back at least as far as Adam Smith's *The Wealth of Nations*. The model grew out of the observation of a very special phenomenon. Economic activities—farming, mining, industrial production, selling, and finance activities—were unplanned and, on the surface at least, seemed entirely uncoordinated, and yet in the end order could be seen in the results. Smith saw with great clarity that the powerful signaling and incentive forces of prices determined by free exchange in markets were at the core of the process that, via many independent economic units, transformed resources into products and distributed them to consumers in accordance with their demands. Hence, his famous phrase "the invisible hand of the market."

In usual circumstances markets do produce an orderly and directed production process. But economic theorists have also been very interested in finding out whether this order was just orderly or whether it might have other desirable or normative properties. Theorists found that the results of an ideal market process may be regarded as desirable or normative if a basic value judgment is accepted and if the market-exchange economy displays certain structural characteristics.

The value judgment is that the personal wants and preferences of the individuals who constitute the present members of a society should guide the use of that society's resources. This is also the premise that is at the root of Anglo-American political theory.

The three structural characteristics are:

—All markets are competitive; this means that no specific firm or individual can influence any market price significantly by decreasing or increasing the supply of goods and services offered by that specific economic unit. A good example is an individual farmer. He can sell or hold his crop as he wishes and yet affect the market price for corn not at all. Competition must extend to all markets, including those for money.

—All participants in the market are fully informed as to the quantitative and qualitative characteristics of goods and services and the terms of exchange among them.

—All valuable assets in the economic system can be individually owned and managed without violating the first assumption—that

> is, that of perfect competition (this has usually been implicit). Individual ownership of all assets plus competition implies that all costs of production and consumption are borne by the producers and consumers directly involved in economic exchanges. A closely related requirement is that there must be markets for all possible claims. This becomes particularly pertinent when one considers questions on conservation and the role of future markets. I will discuss this matter in a little more detail later in connection with policies regarding nonrenewable natural resources.

If all these conditions hold, it can be concluded that the best social solution to the problem of allocating the society's scarce resources is to limit the role of government to deciding questions of equity in income distribution, providing rules of property and exchange, enforcing competition, and allowing the exchange of privately owned assets in markets to proceed freely.

Market exchange, with each participant pursuing his own private interest, will then lead to a "Pareto optimum" (named after Vilfredo Pareto [1848–1923], a prominent Italian economist and social theoretician). The proof that ideal markets can achieve a Pareto optimum may be regarded as one of the basic theorems of modern theoretical economics. Perhaps the most straightforward way of intuitively grasping the meaning of a Pareto optimum is to regard it as a situation in which all possible gains from voluntary exchange of goods and services have been exhausted and no participant is willing to make further exchanges at the terms of trade that have come to exist. Money is the medium of exchange and prices are the terms of exchange, but behind them lie exchanges of real goods and services of all kinds. Under the conditions postulated, an exchange takes place only when both parties feel they benefit by it. When no more beneficial exchanges can be made, the economic welfare of one individual cannot be improved without damaging that of another—in other words, unless a redistribution of assets favorable to him occurs. When no one can be better off without someone else being worse off, Pareto optimality has been reached. In economic parlance, an efficient balance has been obtained.

The connection between such a market exchange and the real working economy has always been tenuous at best. But the idealized model has served as a standard against which an actual economy could be judged as a resource-allocation mechanism for meeting consumer preferences. I shall use it in this way in considering the current state of our resource problems and policies, especially with respect to environmental resources. But, as I hope this discussion will make clear, questions of resource supply are closely interlaced with environmental considerations. The connection is revealed by considering the conservation of mass.

Pollution Problems in a Market System

With this background, it is easy to see the nature of the malfunction of real markets vis-à-vis the workings of the ideal market: the fundamental cause of pollution problems in market systems. We start with a simple concept from physics.

When materials—minerals, fuels, gases, and organic material—are obtained from nature and used by producers and consumers, their mass is essentially unaltered. Material residuals generated in production and consumption activities must therefore be about equal in mass to the materials initially extracted from nature. Similarly, all energy converted in human activities is discharged to the atmosphere or watercourses.

Conservation of mass-energy, taken together with the peculiar characteristics of environmental resources, has important implications for the allocation of resources in a real market system as contrasted with the ideal one. Although most extractive, harvesting, processing, and distributional activities can be conducted relatively efficiently through the medium of exchange of private ownership rights as the idealized market model envisages, the process of returning the inevitable residuals generated by production and consumption activities makes heavy use of common-property resources.

The term common-property resources refers to those valuable natural assets that cannot, or can only imperfectly, be held in private ownership and that therefore cannot be exchanged in markets like ordinary commodities. Important examples are the air mantle, watercourses, large ecological systems, landscapes, and the auditory and electromagnetic spectrums. When open and unpriced access to such resources is permitted, it is apparent what must happen. Careful study of particular common-property or common-pool problems such as oil pools and ocean fisheries has shown that unhindered access to such resources leads to overuse, misuse, and degradation of quality. Environmental degradation takes the form of discharges of large masses of materials and energy to watercourses and the atmosphere, lowering their quality. The less massive but highly destructive dispersal of litter and junk into urban and rural landscapes stems from the same roots. Furthermore, resource-extraction processes themselves can cause visual and other forms of pollution: clear-cut forests, mine tailings, unreclaimed strip-mine land, and acid mine drainage are just a few examples.

Costs associated with the destructive effects of these situations are of no consequence to the enterprises involved because they are imposed on, or transmitted through, common-property resources. The impacts of these effects, referred to as external costs, are imposed on society as a whole. Pareto optimality is not gained through exchange because private ownership of natural assets must be incomplete. Without ownership, the market can generate no incentive to protect environmental resources.

Conservation of mass-energy tells us that as economic development proceeds and as the flow of the mass of material and energy through the economy increases, provided that environmental resources remain in their common-property status, environmental conditions must display a tendency to get systematically worse as the economy grows.

Another result of looking at environmental pollution problems in terms of the concept of mass balance is that it reveals the interdependencies that must exist among different streams of residuals. For example, treatment of a residual does not reduce its mass: indeed, mass is increased because the treatment process itself requires the input of materials whose mass is also conserved. The result is that pollution control programs aimed at reducing the pollution in one medium often aggravate the problem in another. The incineration of sludge from waste-water treatment plants and the emission of additional gases into an already polluted urban atmosphere is a classic example. Wise environmental policy must provide some means of dealing with quality problems in all the media simultaneously.

As I have indicated, the main source of our environmental problems is the inability of market exchange as it is presently structured to allocate environmental resources efficiently—that is, to price their destructive use appropriately. But if we could stretch our minds and envisage a situation where these common-property resources could be reduced to private ownership in pieces small enough to be exchanged in competitive markets, then, distributional issues aside, the market could function just as efficiently to allocate them as it can to distribute any other resource. Prices would be generated, for example, for the use of air and water for the (usually destructive) activity of waste disposal. These prices would be signals and incentives reflecting the cost of the opportunity to use these resources for waste disposal and would affect the whole complex of decisions about their use—the design of industrial processes and the kinds of raw materials used, the nature of the final products produced, and the modification (not elimination—conservation of mass and energy prevents this) of streams of residuals before the purchaser paid for the privilege of discharging what was left. Conservation would suddenly become good business.

Instead, I have already shown, throughout history these resources have largely remained as open access common property. Moreover, it is so difficult to define rights to environmental resources that the desirable effects of market exchange affecting them must remain merely theoretical. However, explicit pricing of these resources through the medium of government administration could go far toward making environmental protection more efficient and effective than do the policies we now have. Before developing this theme, let us look more explicitly at what the ideas developed so far suggest in terms of the interrelationships between problems in the use of environmental and other resources.

Environmental Market Failure and Resource Commodities

The combination of two simple but illuminating concepts introduced in the previous section, conservation of mass and common-property resources, provides considerable insight into the basic nature of environmental-pollution problems in a market system. But the implications are not limited to environmental matters. When the use of certain (environmental) resources is not priced, the entire price structure gets distorted. Thus the prices of extractive resource commodities, which are exchanged in markets, deviate substantially from the actual social costs of their use. This comes about in two main ways.

First, the removal and processing of extractive resource commodities involve particularly heavy use of environmental resources. Strip mining, the processing of copper, the conversion of coal, the making of steel, and the refining of oil are obvious examples. In the ordinary course of market exchange the social costs associated with any damage to these environmental resources are not reflected in the costs incurred by the private producers of resource commodities and by the ultimate users of the products produced from them.

Second, when such commodities are devoted to their end uses they further generate social costs that the market does not reflect. Junkyards, litter in the countryside, and the combustion of fuel in automobile engines are obvious examples.

Thus the unfettered market generates a systematic bias, the result of which is essentially to subsidize the production of extractive resource commodities. The larger the impact on environmental resources in the extraction, processing, and use of resource commodities, the larger the subsidy. Furthermore, as environmental resources become increasingly scarce and valued, and as the production of environmentally destructive resource commodities increases, the societal subsidy to such production correspondingly increases.

The natural tendency of markets to work in this unfortunate manner is bad enough. But policies formed to stimulate the production of resource commodities during the euphoria of extreme abundance and in the interest of rapid economic growth aggravate the situation. Special tax treatment of extractive industries in relation to ordinary industries abounds. Depletion allowances, capital gains treatment, and expensing of various kinds of capital investments and operating expenditures are obvious examples. Superimposed on all this are policies that favor production from virgin materials rather than use of secondary materials. Railroad rate discrimination and discriminatory labeling requirements are often-cited examples.

The ultimate result of malfunctioning of the market and the biases of policy is excessive use of materials and energy in general, excessive use of virgin materials in particular, too little recovery and reuse of materials and energy, and excessive environmental deterioration. These miscarriages are not isolated and random events: they are a systematic result of the way our market and governmental institutions have operated.

In the context of the conceptual framework I have just developed, I will briefly review pertinent aspects of our efforts to deal with environmental problems in the United States.

Evolution of Environmental Policy

Over the post–World War II period, at all levels of government in the United States, numerous laws have been passed attempting to come to grips with the degradation of environmental quality. The rationale for such laws has been totally unrelated to the concepts I have developed in previous sections of this essay. In this process of policy formation, the role of the central government has gradually become increasingly dominant. It is worth reviewing the history of federal legislation in a little detail because it clearly highlights the pitfalls of exclusive reliance on efforts to impose direct regulations and on subsidy approaches. A summary review of the complete set of air and water laws is found in Table 1. I will select some of the more pertinent acts for brief discussion in the text.[3]

With respect to both air and water, the early federal legislation (in the 1950s) established enforcement action against individual sources of residuals discharges as the principal policy tool for controlling those discharges. These actions could be brought by the federal authorities against residuals dischargers if specific interstate damage could be demonstrated to have resulted directly from discharges at a particular

TABLE 1

Outline of Major Federal Legislation on Air and Water Pollution Control

Date of Enactment	Popular Title and Official Citation	Key Provisions
	Water	
March 3, 1899	1899 Refuse Act (30 Stat. 1152)	Required permit from chief of engineers for discharge of refuse into navigable waters.
June 30, 1948	Water Pollution Control Act (62 Stat. 1155)	Gave the federal government authority for investigation, research, and surveys; left primary responsibility for pollution control with the states.
July 9, 1956	Water Pollution Control Act Amendments of 1956 (70 Stat. 498)	Established federal policy for 1956–1970 period. Provided 1) federal grants for construction of municipal water treatment plants; and 2) complex procedure for federal enforcement actions against individual dischargers. (Some strengthening amendments were enacted in 1961.)
October 2, 1965	Water Quality Act of 1965 (79 Stat. 903)	Sought to strengthen enforcement process; provided for federal approval of ambient standards for interstate waters. (Minor strengthening amendments were enacted in 1966 and 1970.)
October 18, 1972	1972 Water Pollution Act Amendments (86 Stat. 816)	Set policy under which federal government now operates. Provided 1) federal establishment of effluent limits for individual sources of pollution; 2) issuance of discharge permits; and 3) large increase in authorized grant funds for municipal waste treatment plants.
	Air	
July 14, 1955	1955 Air Pollution Control Act (69 Stat. 322)	Authorized, for the first time, a federal program of research, training, and demonstrations related to air pollution control. (Extended for four years by the amendments of 1959.)

TABLE 1 (continued)

Date of Enactment	Popular Title and Official Citation	Key Provisions
December 17, 1963	Clean Air Act (77 Stat. 392)	Gave the federal government enforcement powers over air pollution through enforcement conferences—a method similar to 1956 approach for water pollution control.
October 20, 1966	Motor Vehicle Air Pollution Control act (79 Stat. 992)	Added new authority to 1963 act, giving the Department of Health, Education, and Welfare power to prescribe emissions standards for automobiles as soon as practicable.
November 21, 1967	Air Quality Act of 1967 (81 Stat. 485)	1) Authorized HEW to oversee establishment of state standards for ambient air quality and of state implementation plans; and 2) for the first time, set national standards for automobile emissions.
December 31, 1970	Clean Air Amendments of 1970 (84 Stat. 1676)	Sharply expanded the federal role in setting and enforcing standards for ambient air quality and established stringent new emissions standards for automobiles.

SOURCE: Allen V. Kneese and Charles L. Schultze, *Pollution, Prices, and Public Policy* (Washington, D.C.: The Brookings Institution, 1975) p. 31–32.

source. Laws providing for modest federal subsidies for construction of municipal waste-water treatment plants and for certain water quality planning activities were also introduced early in the postwar period. It is now generally agreed that these first federal legislative enactments had little or no positive effect on the quality of the nation's environment.

Succeeding legislation was passed in an effort to strengthen enforcement provisions of earlier laws and, in a series of steps, the number of federal subsidies authorized for construction of municipal waste-water treatment plants was increased. Beginning in the mid-1960s, in the Water Quality Act of 1965, Congress began trying to circumvent the necessity for showing actual interstate damage in federal enforcement actions in the water quality area. This was to be accomplished by requiring the states to set water quality standards for interstate and boundary waters and to develop plans for attaining these standards. After many delays, the states finally complied in the late 1960s.

Watercourse standards were set by the state agencies on the basis of more- or (usually) less-informed consideration of potential water uses. The idea embodied by the law was that violations of water quality standards as a result of failure by a discharger to conform to the plan were to be regarded as prima facie evidence of interstate impact, without the necessity to show that direct damage had resulted in one state from a specific discharge in another.

A similar approach was legislated a few years later for air quality. But in this case nationally uniform ambient standards were set that were supposed to represent a threshold below which no health damage would occur—a politically convenient fiction. In addition, new sources of atmospheric emissions were supposed to be equipped with the best available control technology, and federal law, following the lead of California, began to specify stringent effluent limitations on automobile emissions.

The ambient standards implementation plan was no more effective as an approach to the water quality problem than the previous law had been. By the end of the 1960s it became apparent that nearly all the implementation plans were so loosely related to the water quality standards that the law would be unenforceable. Furthermore, the subsidy programs for the construction of waste-water treatment plants not only had been relatively ineffective but also had resulted in serious inefficiencies of various sorts. I will return to this point a bit later. At about the same time, an ancient piece of water legislation, the 1899 Refuse Act, was rediscovered. This law required that all industrial waste dischargers have permits from the U.S. Army Corps of Engineers. The provision was clearly intended to protect navigation, but it was now interpreted to extend to all forms of residuals discharged to watercourses. Enforcement of the law was started, and the Corps of Engineers received a large number of applications and began to issue some permits. But shortly before the process of issuing permits began, Congress passed another environmental law, the National Environmental Protection Act (NEPA). This law, among its various provisions, required that all federal, and federally supported, actions having a potentially significant impact on the environment must be preceded by an environmental impact statement. The courts ruled that permit-issuing activities of the Corps of Engineers fell under the provisions of the act. Consequently, the corps abandoned the hopeless task of issuing permits for which tens of thousands of environmental impact statements would be needed.

Following these events, Congress passed a new water quality law in

1972. Among its provisions was the requirement that permits be issued for all point-source waste discharges to watercourses. This time the permit issuing was not subject to the provisions of the NEPA and was to be done by the Environmental Protection Agency (EPA) and the states. Although the current law is notoriously ambiguous, the intent of its supporters seems to have been to make uniform across the nation the permit requirements for particular industries and municipalities. These requirements are to be based primarily on considerations of technical feasibility rather than on the uses to which receiving waters are to be put. However, stream standards established under the 1965 act are still to be the controlling ones if discharges under the permit system should result in poorer water quality than they required (one-third to one-half the stream miles in the country may fall into this category). The permit stipulations are also intended to become stricter in a succession of steps until a national goal of zero discharge is achieved in 1985. Subsidies for construction of municipal waste-water treatment plants were increased mightily by the 1972 laws, and under provisions of other laws, industries can benefit from rapid write-off of pollution control equipment against taxes and from low-interest municipal bond funding of facilities.

The pattern then, applying to both air and water and culminating in the most recent water quality legislation, has been toward increasingly heavy federal subsidization of certain kinds of pollution control facilities, greater and greater centralization of control efforts increasingly based on emission standards that are in turn based on some sort of concept of technical feasibility, and an effort to make emission standards as uniform nationally as possible.

There are several reasons for having deep reservations about the pollution control program that has evolved in the United States. The federal subsidies that have been provided bias the choice of control technologies toward end-of-the-pipe treatments rather than toward the use of processes that reduce the generation of waste in the first place. In practice, the municipal subsidies have tended to slow down construction as municipalities have queued up to await federal funds whose availability has always been less than authorized, or, more recently, as municipalities have striven to obey the letter of the law in planning requirements.

The imposition of uniform standards (for instance, among waste dischargers)—the objective of the federal legislation—implies that discharges from sources where control costs are high have to be controlled as much as those from sources where control costs are low. Accordingly, any level of ambient environmental quality attained is accompanied by higher costs (research suggests that these are higher by a multiple) than would be associated with a least-cost set of control efforts. Specifying particular "best available" technologies to be used in pollution control may have a serious dampening effect on the development of new pollution control technology. It puts firms in a quandary: if they innovate, they hand the regulatory authorities the means of imposing on them new and more stringent standards of pollution control. With respect to automobile emissions, for example, present control efforts appear to have locked us into a technology (reliance on modification of the internal combustion engine) that many scientific reports conclude is a very poor long-run approach to the problem.

Finally, the history of efforts to enforce the federal government's pollution laws, together with the vast short-term cost implications of recent legislation (should it be successfully implemented), elicit deep doubts about whether the federal program can ever be effectively enforced, much less whether it can produce efficient results. Even though an objective of recent legislation, especially of the Water Quality Act, was to make enforcement easier and more effective, there is still room in the actual statutes for staggering amounts of litigation and all the attendant delays. Large-scale litigation is in process. Many informed students of the permit-issuing process believe that the result will be to force permit requirements, for those permits that are issued, down to the lowest level of accepted practice, and that substantial environmental improvement will not be the result. Legislation for control of air pollution from stationary sources is still largely untested, but there are some major cases in the courts, and those reductions in emissions that have occurred by means of fuel substitution show signs of disappearing in the wake of the energy crisis as the nation shifts to greater emphasis on the utilization of coal. The automotive emissions provisions of the Clean Air Act have produced tinkering with the standard internal combustion engine rather than a shift to basically low-emission engine technologies.

A basic problem with the present program is that enforcement, especially since it involves criminal penalties, must leave ample room for due process: this means that there are many possibilities for delays or variances while the free-of-charge use of common-property resources continues. The economic incentive for users is to hire lawyers rather than to get on with discharge control. The recent report of the National Commission on Water Quality is implicitly a devastating indictment of the regulatory approach by a commission and commission staff basically sympathetic to that approach.[4]

ALTERNATIVE STRATEGIES

In this section I examine alternative strategies based explicitly upon the recognition that pollution problems, at their core, result from the failure of the market system to generate the proper incentives for the allocation and management of a particular type of resources: those with common-property characteristics. I begin with water and air pollution and then consider the failure of incentives in environmental management in general.

Effluent Charges and Cost Minimization

The overall costs of control are minimized by concentrating the reduction in pollution most heavily among those firms and activities whose costs of reduction are least.* An efficient approach to pollution control, therefore, requires different firms to reduce pollution by differing amounts, depending on their costs of reduction. Moreover, besides applying conventional waste treatment methods, each firm should take advantage of a wide range of control alternatives—modifying its production processes, recycling its by-product wastes, and using raw materials and producing varieties of its product that cause less pollution.

In theory, a regulatory agency could devise an efficient regulatory plan for reduction of pollution. Effluent limitations for each type of polluting activity could be designed to achieve the minimum-cost solution. In practice, however, the need to tailor limits to each firm and to consider for each the cost and effectiveness of all of the available alternatives for reducing pollution would be an impossible task. There are up to 55,000 major sources of industrial water pollution alone. A regulatory agency cannot know the costs, the technological opportunities, the alternative raw materials, and the kinds of products available for every firm in every industry. Even if it could determine the appropriate reduction standards for each firm it would have to revise them

*This is an oversimplification. The impact on water quality from the wastes of any firm depends on the firm's location along the river basin and on the hydrology of the stream. A least-cost solution for achieving any given level of ambient water quality would therefore have to take into account both these factors. Each firm's effluent would have to be weighted according to its impact on water quality along particular reaches of the watercourse. In a least-cost solution, each firm would then have to cut back its effluent to the point where its marginal cost per weighted unit of effluent reduction was the same as that for every other firm. But a study of the Delaware Estuary performed in the mid-1960s by the federal government shows that a fairly simple system of effluent charges could come close, in terms of costs, to the more complicated least-cost solution for the whole system.

frequently to accommodate changing costs and markets, new technologies, and economic growth.

Effluent charges, on the other hand, tend to elicit the proper responses even in the absence of an omniscient regulatory agency. Each source of pollution would be required to pay a fee for every unit of pollutant it discharged into the air or water. Faced with these effluent charges, a firm would pursue its own interest by reducing pollution by an amount related to the cost of reduction.

Each firm would be faced with different removal costs, depending on the nature of its production processes and its economic situation. For any given effluent charge, firms with low costs of control would remove a larger percentage of pollution than would firms with high costs—precisely the situation needed to achieve a least-cost approach to reducing pollution for the economy as a whole. Firms would tend to choose the least expensive methods of control, whether these involved treatment of wastes, modification of production processes, or substitution of raw materials that had less serious polluting consequences. Furthermore, products whose manufacture entailed a lot of pollution would become more expensive and would carry higher prices than those that generated less, so consumers would be induced to buy more of the latter.

The effluent-charge approach has another characteristic that makes it superior to the regulatory approach. Under the present system a firm has no incentive to cut pollution further once it has achieved the effluent limitation specified by regulation. Indeed, it has a positive incentive not to do so, since the additional reduction is costly and lowers profits. Because under the effluent-charge plan penalties would have to be paid for every unit of pollution firms had not removed, they would have a continuing incentive to devote research and engineering talent to finding less costly ways of achieving still greater reductions. This continuing incentive is important. The quantity of air and water available to the nation is fixed, roughly speaking. But as economic activity grows over time the volume of pollution discharged into the air and water will rise unless an ever-increasing percentage of pollutants is removed.

Economic research has tended to support the practical value and effectiveness of an effluent charge or tax approach. In the most pertinent case study, it was found that effluent charges could achieve a given water quality objective in the Delaware Estuary area for about half the cost of a regulatory approach aimed at uniform reductions. The efficacy of charges is also supported by the response of industrial firms when they become subject to municipal sewer surcharges, geared to the pollution content of waste waters. Even though such charges were much lower than a true effluent charge would be, the amount of wastes discharged to the municipal sewer system usually fell dramatically.[5]

Regulation versus Effluent Charges

Governmental folklore has it that regulation and enforcement are direct, effective, and dead-sure means for attacking market failures. Studies of how the regulatory process has worked in general, coupled with the earlier review of its operation with respect to pollution problems, reveal that it is instead cumbersome, corruptible, and arbitrary and capricious in its impact.

Lawmakers have exhibited skepticism about the effectiveness of market-like devices such as effluent charges. But the knowledge we have about the impacts of price changes, and the limited evidence specifically about effluent charges, provides strong arguments for their superiority over regulation. They constitute a relatively neutral device whose enforcement could be incorporated into the body of precedent and experience already surrounding the nation's tax laws. The imposition of charges or taxes would require that effluents be metered at each outfall. But regulations also call for metering. From that point on, the payment and collection of effluent taxes involve no major administrative burdens; more important, they raise no specter of court battles such as the case-by-case struggles over regulatory decisions. (Even though there is much tax litigation, the great bulk of taxes—especially excise taxes, which most resemble effluent charges—are paid without legal struggles.)

Effluent charges have another strong advantage over regulation, one that is especially important in times like the present when much of the national program of air pollution control seems to be falling victim to the energy crisis. That advantage is that the responses they call for can be flexible, but they always call for some sort of response. When tough restrictions are relaxed or eliminated, the continuing social costs of the pollutant discharges are in no way reflected in the discharger's decision making. He is "home free." Furthermore, whatever effectiveness the enforcement approach may have is entirely dependent on constant, vigorous enforcement, which can easily give way before the shifting enthusiasms, fears, and perceptions of problems by the public and its representatives. In a government that proceeds from crisis to crisis, as ours often does, this is an extremely important problem for the enforcement approach.

Instituting Effluent Charges

Despite the apparently compelling reasons for favoring a system of effluent charges as one of the cornerstones of effective and efficient national and regional water quality management, it would be difficult for particular states and regions to pioneer such a marked departure from previous practice. Indeed, as I showed in previous sections, states may find it difficult or impossible to institute even the more conventional controls. Although several states and regions have taken initiatives recently, the federal government's greater insulation from powerful local interests gives it the opportunity for leadership.

There is much to recommend a national minimum charge that would establish the principle universally and blunt industry's threats to move to more permissive regions. Moreover, the charge could provide an immediate across-the-board incentive to reduce discharges into the nation's watercourses. Unlike the strategy embodied in the 1972 amendments, such a charge would affect every waste discharger immediately, unavoidably, and equitably. Had such a charge been levied at an adequately high level when it was first seriously proposed to Congress in the sixties there would surely have been a great improvement in water quality nearly everywhere, rather than the stabilization or continued deterioration that has actually occurred.

The national charge could be considered a minimum that could be exceeded by state and regional agencies responsible for water quality management at their discretion and according to their own objectives. Revenues obtained by the federal government could supplement funds from general tax sources and be made available for financing the federal program, with the excess turned over to other governments of general jurisdiction. As an illustrative calculation, if the charge for BOD (biochemical oxygen demand) was set at 30 cents per pound (a strong incentive to reduction because it is well above the costs of higher-level treatment except at the smallest outfalls, and far above the cost of process changes in many industries), the annual revenues would be about $4 billion to $6 billion. On the assumption that charges for other substances would yield similar amounts, total annual revenues would be $8 billion to $12 billion.[6] But the amount would fall rapidly once the incentive took effect, probably to less than $1 billion after several years. Also, it might be preferable to implement the charges in stages, increasing them annually until they reach full scale.

In emphasizing effluent charges, I do not mean to imply that administrative rulings and legal remedies are unimportant in water quality management. Indeed, as I discuss in the concluding section, the discharge of some substances (primarily heavy metals and persistent organics) should probably be prohibited entirely; Joseph Sax, among others, has suggested ways in which the courts could take a more constructive part in environmental management.[7] But I am persuaded that economic incentives and regional management are the central elements in effectively and efficiently coming to grips with the problem of water quality management, in the long term as well as the short term.[8]

Air Pollution Alternatives

Just like the formation of national policy, economic research in the air pollution area and policy proposals stemming from it lagged behind similar activities related to water pollution by several years. The central ideas, methodology, and main results of the research were quite similar in the two areas. The efficiency advantages of emissions charges, and of greater or lesser degrees of regional planning and management, turned out to be even more spectacular for air than for water. The first such study, in the Memphis metropolitan area, compared the uniform-cutback approach with the cost-minimizing systems that would be induced by emissions charges, and found the latter method significantly less costly.[9] A later notable study, in preparation for the president's proposal of what was to become the Air Quality Act of 1967, involved construction of a composite model embodying elements from several major U.S. cities that had severe problems associated with the discharge of sulfur oxides and particulates. It was found that cost-minimizing programs could achieve the same environmental objectives with only 10 percent of the costs of the uniform-cutback method.[10] These results do not even include the more indirect efficiency effects, which I have discussed in connection with water and are equally valid here.

Sulfur Oxides Tax. After further study by the Council on Environmental Quality, the Treasury Department, and the EPA, these considerations of efficiency, efficacy, and equity led President Nixon to propose the Pure Air Tax Act of 1972 in February 1972. The president had great difficulty in getting congressional attention for the resulting bill, but he supported it again in his 1973 environmental message. A strong approach was especially needed in this area because some studies had shown severe health implications of discharges of sulfur oxides.

To date, the switch from high- to low-sulfur fuels has been the primary reason for reduced emissions of sulfur oxides. As the events of late 1973 amply demonstrated, such a switch can readily be reversed—and its gains easily lost—especially if no economic penalties remain for emitting large quantities of sulfur oxides. The technologies for removing sulfur from fuels (especially coal) before burning, or from the exhaust streams, are on the drawing boards, but the past five years have seen little movement toward development of these alternatives. Here is a situation ripe for the application of a strategy based on economic incentives.

The bill proposed by President Nixon would have levied a charge beginning with calendar year 1976 on emissions of sulfur into the atmosphere. The initial tax rate was calculated to induce curtailment of sulfur emissions sufficient to meet the 1975 air quality standards established by the Clean Air Amendments. In the years after 1976 the tax rate would depend on the quality of a region's air in the preceding year; it would be fifteen cents and ten cents per pound, respectively, where primary and secondary standards were violated, and zero where all standards were met.

One problem with this proposal is that it would encourage existing firms to move operations from "dirty" regions to "clean" ones, and new plants to settle there in the first place, to avoid paying a charge. In time, therefore, shifts in industrial location would degrade the quality of air in the cleaner regions and bring the entire country down to the lowest common denominator.

This problem is at least partially dealt with in identical bills later proposed by Rep. Les Aspin (H.R. 10890) and Sen. William Proxmire (S. 3057) that would levy a flat national tax. Three main points of these bills are particularly worth noting. First, a target level of twenty cents per pound of sulfur would have been reached in five cent increments between 1972 and 1975. The target charge was greater than the then-estimated costs of high-level abatement but less than the estimated average cost of damages across the nation (put by EPA at about thirty cents per pound). Second, the tax would be uniform across the nation, both to insure administrative simplicity and to avoid creating havens for polluters. Finally, because Congress rather than an agency would set the level of the tax, the debate would be out in the open. Since these proposals were made, the only major action taken to levy emissions fees has been by the Navajo tribe. In 1977 the Tribal Council enacted a sulfur-emissions fee. The resulting legal situation is considerably more complex than it would be with respect to a national or state fee, and the matter is now in litigation.

Alternatives for Automobile Pollution. Even with today's relatively simple systems, maintenance of pollution control devices on automobiles is a very serious problem. Cars are tested before they are sold to see that they meet the emissions standards already imposed on the manufacturer; but no follow-up assures that they continue to meet the standards, though a number of studies have shown that few can do so after as little as 10,000 to 15,000 miles of use. For example, results released by EPA in 1973 showed that more than half the vehicles tested after on-the-road service had higher emissions than the standards applicable to their model years permitted.[11]

How can we solve the twin problems of insuring maintenance and stimulating technology? Twenty years ago economists at Rand Corporation proposed an answer—a smog tax.[12] In one possibly very powerful version of this tax, cars would be tested periodically and assigned a smog rating, indicated by a seal or coded device attached to the car. Then, when the driver purchased gasoline, he would pay a tax, over and above the basic gasoline taxes, that would vary with his smog rating. The virtue of levying the tax at the level of the individual automobile is that it can elicit responses all the way from the driver (by driving less) to the manufacturer (by manufacturing cars that pollute less).

I feel that a scheme of this type has many attractive features and should be tried. But short of its full implementation, some of its incentives could be incorporated into the present law.

A study by Henry Jacoby and others recommends one way of accomplishing this goal that would essentially extend the deadline for achieving emissions-reduction goals and apply an economic incentive to innovation in the interim.[13] It would preserve the pre-1975 standards, which are essentially the same as those still in effect, and postpone the mandatory incorporation of stricter standards for several years. A fine equivalent to 5 to 10 percent of a car's cost would be levied on a model whose emissions fell between interim standards and the final goals.

I would propose to make different changes in the present law. The first would be a slight reduction in the existing standards so that no catalytic converters would be needed to achieve it. Then I would institute a smog tax on automobiles that would increase progressively over the remainder of this decade and into the next until in the mid-1980s the rate for a car still emitting at the 1974 new-car level would exceed the several hundred dollars per car associated with the catalytic system. A few urban areas with severe smog problems would be targeted for special treatment. I believe this strategy would almost certainly lead to the large-scale introduction of inherently low-emission and thermally efficient engines within the next few years.[14] It would clearly be second best since it would not influence behavior the way an emissions tax levied on the motorist would; but I believe it would be a vast improvement over the current system.

Fees for Atmospheric Emissions. Emissions fees would have to be set on a number of different air pollutants. In calculating the appropriate fees it would be important to set them in the proper relationship to each other, to prevent the adoption of processes that reduce one type of pollutant only to increase another. One such scheme is the "pindex" method of weighting according to toxicity; a sample fee has been determined for California on this basis.[15] It starts with a fee calculated on the basis of an estimate of damage or the control cost to reach a target level of removal, and it deduces, on the basis of their relative toxicity, the implied fees for other substances for which no direct measures of harmfulness have been calculated.

Concluding Comments on Effluent Fees

Enough work has been done on the use of effluent fees and regional management devices for water and air quality management to provide a firm basis for a strategic alternative to the way we have been attacking these problems at the national level. Although any practicable program will necessarily contain many crudities and arbitrary elements, I feel that workable legislation based on this alternative not only is possible, but also would be much more efficient, equitable, and effective—in both the short run and the long run—than the legislation Congress has adopted. The proposals I have reviewed share the difficulty of the present approach in that they treat closely related problems in isolation, but they would mark a start toward the comprehensive and effective environmental management that we must ultimately achieve as part of a coherent natural resources policy.

TOWARD AN ENVIRONMENTAL-NATURAL RESOURCES POLICY FOR MASS RESIDUALS

As I indicated earlier in this essay, the conservation of mass implies that all of the materials and energy flowing through the economy must show up as residuals to be returned to the various environmental media. Accordingly, efforts to reduce discharges into one medium will increase the burden on others unless the processes used permit the material to be recycled. For example, the sludge from waste water treated in the usual kind of plant is often incinerated, and a favorite way of removing particulates from stack gases is to scrub them with a stream of water. These considerations suggest the need simultaneously to bring all the various residuals under management in an integrated, coherent program. These relationships present tangled complexities for any approach to emissions-control policy.

At the moment, economists and engineers are actively developing comprehensive models of a residuals management program that systematically deals with all the major residuals from production and consumption activities.[16] Until such models become routinely applicable, and until appropriate regional institutions can be created to use them for formulating fully coherent management programs for all the media simultaneously, it is highly important that our national legislation at least recognize the basic nature of the problem.

A systematic attack on perverse incentives should proceed on two fronts. First, we should remove the incentives that have been built into our system to aid rapid exploitation of virgin materials; they have encouraged excessive use of materials in general and attached false economic advantages to the use of virgin as opposed to recycled materials.

Removing these incentives will mean higher prices, but these should be carefully distinguished from inflationary increases. They reflect the embedding in prices of the social costs of particular goods and services—costs that now fall upon consumers whether they consume the polluting commodities or not.

The most important area for such reform is depletion allowances. Producers of most mineral products, such as lead, zinc, copper, and bauxite, can deduct from their gross incomes a substantial allowance for depletion, thereby reducing the effective tax rate they pay. This practice provides a major subsidy to producers in the form of lower prices of a number of resources, and thus encourages the excessive use of virgin materials as well as of all other materials. It appears not only that depletion allowances are entirely inappropriate to our current circumstances, but also that much can be said for federal efforts to strengthen the hands of the states in instituting or raising severance taxes.

To open a second front in the war on perverse incentives, we should directly and systematically encourage conservation of environmental media. As I have indicated, a fully coherent set of effluent charges is not possible at the moment, but levying such charges on a broad front would recognize the interdependencies among the environmental media and promote processes that consume fewer materials or that are more conducive to recycling, as well as treatment of residual materials where appropriate.

A very promising start in this direction was contained in a bill several years ago by Rep. John H. Heinz III of Pennsylvania. The bill would amend the Internal Revenue Code to levy "a tax on the discharge of taxable items . . . by any stationary or non-stationary source of pollution into the atmosphere or into or upon the navigable waters of the United States, adjoining shorelines, the contiguous zone, or the ocean."[17] The bill sets up a procedure for determining the tax rates to be set by Congress and calls for review at intervals. While it needs considerable elaboration, its direction is clearly right.

Eliminating subsidies for exploiting virgin materials and imposing across-the-board effluent charges could have a powerful effect on conservation of resources and improvement in environmental quality. Such actions would also have the desirable efficiency effects that I have previously discussed.

Present legislation tries to deal with all these problems, and to influence the whole vast array of decision makers involved, solely through direct regulation and subsidies. If this approach stands, it will, I believe, open a field day for lawyers, result in heavy costs, require a huge bureaucracy to give it any chance of success, impose ad-hoc and capricious impacts, and involve far-reaching intrusion of the government into decisions about the design of industrial processes.

I do not suggest that an incentive-oriented approach alone could deal with all of the sticky problems that arise in achieving environmental control objectives. As I discuss in the next section, the discharge of highly toxic substances would still have to be prohibited by law and prevented through regulation. Schedules of effluent and emissions charges that truly minimized the costs of pollution control would be too complex for practical application; the consequent simplified schedules would inevitably introduce some inefficiencies into the system. Because current production techniques and locations of industrial firms are based on a world in which effluent and emissions charges do not exist, the introduction of charges would probably have to be gradual to avoid excessive disruption. Some allowance for temporary relief might be needed for hardship cases; thus decisions of a regulatory type might have to be reintroduced during an interim period.

The advantage of the incentive approach is not that it is free of administrative problems nor that it can fully duplicate a theoretical least-cost solution, but that it is, in my judgment, far superior to the regulatory alternative on both of these counts.

THE PROBLEM OF HAZARDOUS MATERIALS

So far I have discussed what might be called the mass pollutants. These are the voluminous residuals produced by human activities of production and consumption. The concepts of mass balance and common-property resources are quite illuminating with respect to the origin of, and possible remedies for, pollution from these types of residuals. In addition the appropriate role of changes in economic incentives as part of the policy structure to deal with them seems clear.

There is however, another class of pollutants, some of which are deliberately introduced into the human food chain as additives; for these such concepts are less revealing and economic incentive changes are possibly less pertinent. These are materials emitted into the environment that are generally small in quantity but present large, although usually very uncertain, threats to human health or life-support systems. These are what are often referred to as hazardous materials.

The dangers of man-made hazardous materials in the environment and their potential impacts both on life-support systems and directly on human health represent the new generation of environmental problems. These problems present one of the most important and complex sets of public-policy issues currently facing modern society. Hundreds of new chemicals are introduced each year for beneficial use in society, but their adverse impacts on the environment and on human health are virtually unknown and may remain highly uncertain for many years to come. Other potentially serious problems include the hazards associated with nuclear power, coal combustion, coal gasification and liquefaction, carcinogens in drinking water, ozone depletion, the buildup of carbon dioxide, pesticides, and toxic chemicals generally.

Clearly, all of the foregoing problems pose some, mostly unknown, risks to human health. But the alternatives of reducing substantially or even stopping all technological progress until we are certain of all the impacts, or of drastically reducing consumption with no concomitant changes in technology, would impose enormous costs on society both now and in the future. Thus, the heart of the public-policy issue is how to strike an appropriate balance between, on the one hand, ways of providing the needed goods and services to human society, including the use of new technology and the development of new products, and, on the other, ways to eliminate or reduce the environmental and health risks associated with the use of these products and their processes of production. The policies that have so far been developed depend upon direct regulation to try to achieve this objective. Some regulation is essential in this field, but even here the possible important role of changes in economic incentive has largely been ignored. I will return to this topic after a brief review of the various laws pertaining to that set of hazardous materials usually referred to as toxic substances.[18]

Hazardous-Materials Legislation

Federal Water Pollution Control Act. The federal Water Pollution Control Act contains a section specifically about the control of toxic pollutants. Under section 307 the administrator is directed to compile a list of "toxic pollutants or combination(s) of such pollutants," to publish proposed effluent standards for the pollutants within 180 days, and to publish final standards within another 180 days of the proposal of such standards and the hearings that follow them.

While EPA has issued no final effluent standards for hazardous pollutants as defined in section 307, the standards, when designated, will be based on best-available technology—to be determined on an industry-by-industry basis. Discharge standards have been proposed for the pesticides aldrin, dieldrin, and DDT and for endrin, toxaphene, benzidine, and PCBs.

Section 208 of the act requires area-wide planning for the control of water pollution. In principle this includes planning and associated regulation for control of non-point sources such as pesticide residues in agricultural runoff.

Federal Insecticide, Fungicide, and Rodenticide Act. Pesticide laws initially were designed to insure honesty in packaging and safety in use, but they have evolved to enhance environmental quality and protect public health as well. The Federal Insecticide, Fungicide, and Rodenticide Act (FIFRA) and the Federal Environmental Pesticide Control Act that amended it now provide, among other things, for the registration of all pesticides and the uses to which they are put, the certification of individuals who apply certain restricted pesticides, and premarket testing of all new pesticides.

All pesticide registrations expire every five years and must be renewed. If the registration of a particular pesticide or pesticide use is denied, the administrator of EPA must publish reasons for denial in the federal register. The EPA has suspended the registrations of all crop uses of DDT, aldrin, and dieldrin, and most uses of heptachlor and chlordane because of evidence of their carcinogenicity as well as their persistence in the environment. Recently, EPA has also moved against pesticides containing kepone, chloroform, endrin, and chlorobenzilate.

Toxic Substances Control Act. The Toxic Substances Control Act (TOSCA) became law in 1976. Generally speaking, it is intended to fill the gap between the regulation of pesticides by EPA under FIFRA (as amended) and the regulation of food, drugs, and cosmetics by the Food and Drug Administration. It is expected to play a major role in federal toxic-substance policy.

The TOSCA gives EPA the following wide authority: to require testing of any new chemical or new use of an existing chemical when it "may present an unreasonable risk of injury to health or the environment" (the cost of the tests are borne by the manufacturer); to control the manufacturing, distribution, and sale of chemical substances through sanctions ranging from relatively mild labeling requirements through strict prohibitions and extending to seizure or recall of "imminently hazardous" substances; and to require proponents of a new chemical to provide information on that chemical's name, properties, structure, intended levels of production and use, and by-products created. The EPA is directed to carry out research, testing, and monitoring necessary to implement the provisions of the act; this is to include the development of a system by which data on toxic substances are collected and can be retrieved and under which government research and information on toxics—from whatever source—are coordinated.

Resource Conservation and Recovery Act. Subtitle C of the Resource Conservation and Recovery Act of 1976 deals with hazardous-waste management. Because this act, like TOSCA, is so new, the government has had little experience with toxic-substance control under this subsection of the law. Nevertheless, many feel that the act may play an important role in toxic-substance policy.

Section 1004 (5) of the act defines hazardous waste as ". . . a solid waste, or combination of solid wastes, which because of its quantity, concentration, or physical, chemical, or infectious characteristics may a) cause, or significantly contribute to an increase in mortality or an increase in serious irreversible, or incapacitating reversible, illness; or b) pose a substantial present or potential hazard to human health or the environment when improperly treated, stored, transported, or disposed of, or otherwise managed."

Within eighteen months of passage of the act, the administrator of EPA was to have established standards governing the generation, transportation and treatment, storage, and disposal of hazardous wastes. These guidelines have now been published.

Clean Air Act. That portion of the Clean Air Amendments most relevant to the control of chronically toxic substances is section 112, which provides for national emissions standards for hazardous air pollutants to which no ambient air quality standard is applicable.

The administrator of EPA is directed to issue a list containing each hazardous pollutant for which he intends to publish standards; he is then to publish the proposed emissions standards for each pollutant and hold hearings on them within 180 days from the time they are put on the list. The final standard is to be published within another 180 days unless the hearings provide information that convinces the administrator that the pollutant is not hazardous.

Transportation Regulation*

Transportation regulation lags behind even the regulation of other sources of toxic materials. The main reason is the fragmentation and lack of clarity of the present statutory and administrative program. The ambiguity of the situation can hardly be overemphasized. Practically speaking, existing rules under the Occupational Safety and Health Act (OSHA) and the Clean Air Act apply to transportation of toxic materials only while rail tank cars, tank trucks, or tank vessels are on the premises of industrial plants for loading and unloading. Five statutes apply to the control of risks from transportation of toxic materials outside the plant premises: the 1975 Hazardous Materials Transportation Act, the 1972 Ports and Waterways Safety Act, the Dangerous Cargo Act, the Federal Railroad Safety Act, and OSHA. The first four statutes are administered by agencies within the Department of Transportation, and the last by OSHA, in the Department of Labor. Some modes of transport are potentially subject to more than one statute. Although the scope of some of these statutes is well defined, it is unclear whether several others authorize regulations meant to protect transportation workers alone, only the general public, or both.

Economic Incentives and Hazardous-Materials Policy

The set of laws pertaining to toxic-substance regulation requires the generation of an enormous amount of information by both industry and the government and massive bureaucratic interventions into the market. The problem of regulation in this area is shot through with uncertainties of all sorts, and the magnitude of the task seems appalling when one considers the thousands of new substances advertently and inadvertently introduced into the environment each year.

Although there is no evidence that Congress specifically considered the role of changes in the economic incentive system when it enacted the existing set of laws to regulate toxic substances, in practice, the alteration of incentives associated with these laws may be their most important impact over the long run. For example, the expenses required by the reporting and premarket-testing provisions of TOSCA will significantly increase the cost of introducing a new substance that is potentially hazardous. Similarly, certification requirements for applications of certain pesticides that are considered dangerous but have no known good substitute will increase the cost of using those pesticides.

*For a more complete discussion see David D. Doniger, *The Law and Policy of Toxic Substances Control* (Baltimore: Johns Hopkins Press for Resources for the Future, 1979).

Another legal area that affects economic incentives is liability rules. Although liability is often hard to establish in the area of environmental risk, there has been a tendency in the past to bail out those who have engaged in an activity that later turns out to have produced such risk, and the well-known Price Anderson Act, which limits liability of utilities in the event of nuclear accident, is still on the books. In the past it was perhaps justifiable for the public to assume some of the liability for the environmental risks produced, since because of lack of testing and information generation risks were often discovered long after the fact. The Price Anderson Act was part of a program—misguided in the view of some, including myself—to introduce quickly a large new technology that might have some rather extreme environmental risks associated with it. But in the new situation, where testing is done to try to anticipate possible ill effects, a clear imposition of liability on the entity introducing the substance should go far to assure that the tests are done carefully and the results interpreted cautiously.

Another type of incentives policy that might produce better results than regulation in some instances is the imposition of a tax or fee on the potentially hazardous substance. In the case of pesticides, for example, Congress has chosen, or gives the EPA administrator discretion to choose, in certain instances, to require certification of applicators and restrictions on the kinds of crops to which a pesticide may be applied. It is at least arguable that a stiff fee on such a pesticide would result in the use of that pesticide only for purposes where there is no substitute of lesser hazard, and in its careful application. This would avoid most of the cost of the present approach, and it might be more effective, since the present provision would seem, on the face of it, to present very difficult enforcement problems.

One cannot say that study of the role of economic incentives in hazardous-materials policy is in its infancy: it is not yet born. It is, however, one of the most important, even urgent, areas for research by environmental economists.

NOTES

1. Quoted in B. Lambert, *History and Survey of London,* vol. 1 (London, 1806).

2. These statements are from *The Public Health as a Public Question: First Report of the Metropolitan Sanitary Association* (address of Charles Dickens, Esq., London, 1850).

3. For a relatively full discussion of the history of federal environmental legislation see Allen V. Kneese and Charles L. Schultze, *Pollution, Prices, and Public Policy* (Washington, D.C.: Brookings Institution, 1975).

4. *Staff Draft Report: National Commission on Water Quality* (Washington, D.C.: U.S. Government Printing Office, April 1976).

5. Further discussion of these results and citations is found in Allen V. Kneese and Blair T. Bower, *Managing Water Quality: Economics, Technology, Institutions* (Baltimore: Johns Hopkins Press, 1968).

6. BOD has been emphasized here because it is the single most common water-borne waste material and often a good indicator of other pollutants; but other substances should also be included in the charges scheme. Various weighting methods to establish equivalences have been suggested, but perhaps the best starting point would be the systems that have long been in effect in the Ruhr. See Kneese and Bower, *Managing Water Quality*.

7. Joseph L. Sax, *Defending the Environment: A Strategy for Citizen Action* (New York: Alfred A. Knopf, 1971).

8. The engineering, legal, and political aspects of charges systems are explored in depth in Frederick R. Anderson et al., *Environmental Improvement Through Economic Incentives* (Baltimore: Johns Hopkins Press, 1978).

9. See Azriel Teller, "Air-Pollution Abatement: Economic Rationality and Reality," *Daedalus* 96 (Fall 1967): 1082–1098.

10. See Jack W. Carlson's "Discussion" of a paper by Allen V. Kneese entitled "Environmental Pollution: Economics and Policy," both appearing in American Economic Association, *Papers and Proceedings of the Eighty-third Annual Meeting, 1970, American Economic Review* 61 (May 1971): 153–166, 169–172. A more complete discussion is found in U.S. Department of Health, Education, and Welfare, Office of the Assistant Secretary (Planning and Evaluation), "An Economic Analysis of the Control of Sulphur Oxides Air Pollution" (HEW, 1967, mimeograph).

11. CALSPAN Corporation, *Automobile Exhaust Emission Surveillance: A Summary*, APTD-1544 (Research Triangle Park, N.C.: U.S. Environmental Protection Agency, Air Pollution Technical Information Center, 1973) pp. 4–40.

12. D. M. Fort et al., "Proposal for a Smog Tax," reprinted in *Tax Recommendations of the President, Hearings before the House Committee on Ways and Means*, 91st Cong., 2d sess., 1970, pp. 369–379.

13. Henry D. Jacoby et al., *Clearing the Air: Federal Policy on Automotive Emissions Control* (Cambridge, Mass: Ballinger, 1973).

14. Such engines can almost certainly be developed. See, for example, Graham Walter, "The Stirling Engine," *Scientific American* 229 (August 1973): 80–87.

15. See A. M. Schneider, "An Effluent Fee Schedule for Air Pollutants Based on Pindex," *Journal of the Air Pollution Control Association* 23 (June 1973): 486–489.

16. See Clifford S. Russell and Walter O. Spofford, Jr., "A Quantitative Framework for Residuals Management Decisions," in *Environmental Quality Analysis: Theory and Method in the Social Sciences*, ed. Allen V. Kneese and Blair T. Bower (Baltimore: Johns Hopkins Press for Resources for the Future, 1972). See also Allen V. Kneese, Robert U. Ayres, and Ralph C. d'Arge, *Economics and the Environment: A Materials Balance Approach* (Baltimore: Johns Hopkins Press for Resources for the Future, 1970).

17. U.S. Congress, H.R. 635, January 1973.

18. For a more complete discussion see Paul R. Portney, "Toxic Substances Policy and the Protection of Human Health," in *Current Issues in U.S. Environ-Environmental Policy*, ed. Paul R. Portney (Baltimore: Johns Hopkins Press for Resources for the Future, 1978).

Your Health and the Government

Rita Ricardo Campbell

XI

Public interest in health has been steadily increasing as the costs of medical care have risen. These now absorb nearly 10 percent of the gross national product. The rise in costs for medical care is a worldwide phenomenon among industrial countries, which are using ever more expensive medical technology.

Saving an individual's life at one age makes that individual susceptible to future diseases. Expensive treatment for a heart attack saves an individual possibly for cancer, and successful treatment of that cancer may save him for pneumonia, which antibiotics cure, only for the patient to endure another type of cancer, possibly induced by the treatment for the first cancer. The costs of medical treatment over a lifetime for each individual have on the average become increasingly higher.

Our society is aging. Life expectancy at age 65 increased by 1.4 years between 1965 and 1975. Life expectancy for white women increased by 1.8 years and for all other women by 2.0 years. The comparable data for men are 0.8 and 1.1 years respectively. Medical costs of saving additional years of life at older ages are usually higher than at younger ages.

The economic implications of the discovery of life-saving antibiotics in the 1940s and later expensive life-saving technology was not understood by the general public until the late 1970s.

Because of space limitations, this chapter does not cover all aspects of government involvement in your health. There is no explicit consideration of public policies about medical schools, medical research, and nursing homes. These are very complex matters which cannot be discussed within part of a single chapter.

HEALTH AND ECONOMICS

Medical care is purchased in the hope that it will improve health. More money spent on medical care may not improve health and in some instances may even worsen it. In the United States the utilization per person of medical care is high relative to that in other countries. This raises the question of whether additional dollars spent on medical care will yield additional health benefits in the 1980s that are worth the cost. The answer depends on the kinds of medical care, how extensive the care, and which groups of persons receive it. Although additional care may make patients more comfortable, medical care for minor illness and in many cases for chronic illness will not necessarily improve health.

The level of medical care provided cannot be the best available for everyone. The word best implies comparison with less than the best. Today although everyone is promised access to adequate care, adequate is not always defined. A 1965 British National Health Service Report specified adequate as "the best service possible within the limits of the available resources."[1] This definition may give small comfort to Americans in the 1980s because of the public reaction against high taxes. Moreover, there is disagreement within the medical profession as to the technological meaning of adequate, or even optimal, care in a given medical situation. Thus, the level or quality of adequate medical care may vary depending on who uses the term.

The distribution of medical care will affect the total health benefits received. More medical care to the rural poor will because of manpower shortages in rural areas which limit access, yield on the average a higher total health benefit per dollar spent than an additional dollar spent for medical care of suburban, middle-income families.

The populations of the world who live longest are those who live at high altitudes, do physical work, and eat sparingly. Although there is general agreement that the level of one's health is greatly influenced by genetic inheritance, nutrition, and living habits, this knowledge did not affect the daily life of the average person in the 1970s. Greater emphasis on consumer education can probably improve American health habits. Some persons value a more active but shorter life over a longer but less productive one. Health education may yield a higher payoff than increasing expenditures for medical care.

Improvement of the environment, including prevention of air and water pollution, can improve health. This chapter does not discuss these matters further except to point out that this is an area of increasing expenditures because of the much higher incremental costs of removing

5 percent of pollution, when a purity level reaches 90 percent than when it was 60 percent. In 1977, $14.1 billion in public and private funds were spent on air pollution controls.[2] Although these expenditures improved health, they were not available to spend for medical care.

Economics is concerned with the allocation of scarce resources to various needs in the most cost-effective manner. The demand for medical services in this country has been increasing steadily for many reasons:

1) The higher level of technology is anticipated to give more comfort or more cures
2) Older persons today have a much greater life expectancy
3) Our culture does not honor the aged as do many other cultures
4) Physicians are to a degree substitutes for ministers
5) The consumer's out-of-pocket expense is far less than the cost of the resources received for medical care.

The last point is the most significant. For most other goods and services that the consumer buys, he pays at least the cost of the resources. The low out-of-pocket price of medical care makes it a great bargain. Third parties, including the government, employers, and insurance companies, pay for 94 percent of the hospital bill and 61 percent of physician services. Thus, most medical costs are not paid by the consumer at the time of consumption.

Education about the limitations of medical care is rare; glamorization of the new, spectacular medical technology is common. Enormous advances in medical science and technology have resulted in far larger benefits to acutely ill patients than 35 years ago. As our population ages, chronic disease, which requires periodic medical care, has become more widespread. This, as well as social and economic changes in the family, creates greater demand for long-term nursing care facilities and innovative home-care programs for the elderly. But, although life expectancy has been extended, the quality of the extra years may be so diminished that the patient and the patient's family may question whether there has been an overall gain. Moreover, medical care has become so pervasive that everybody tends to be a patient in some respect.

Individuals are to a degree responsible for their own health. The professional medical health care practitioner is not the sole, or necessarily the most important, influence on an individual's level of health. The authoritarianism of medical practice has become increasingly questioned, especially by feminists. The trend toward lay involvement with health care during the 1970s will continue with greater diversity in the 1980s.

MEDICAL CARE POLICY

When government policymakers make decisions about the nation's health, the decisions are in most instances directed toward medical care: containment of costs and maintenance of quality of medical care; entry control via requirements of licensing of physicians and other suppliers of medical care; accreditation of existing hospitals and proof of need for new or expansion of old hospitals and nursing homes; financing of medical care; and regulation of insurers, advertisements, and organization of medical care. Government policymakers debate whether consumer demand for medical care should be restrained, and how this best can be done since price no longer serves to allocate medical care.

The two large government programs, Medicare for the aged and Medicaid for the poor, which became effective July 1, 1966, pay 40 percent of all personal health expenditures. These programs continue to stress symptomatic care, because of limited funds and the long feedback time needed to prove whether preventive care is cost-effective. However, during the 1970s the Early and Periodic Screening, Diagnosis and Treatment Program for children was established under Medicaid. And in 1975, $70 million was earmarked to provide dental care, the most under-used type of health care for poor children. New legislation in 1976 provided about $40 million over a three-year period for immunization against communicable disease. By the late 1970s, commercial health insurance companies and Blue Cross and Blue Shield were using advertisements in the media to encourage individuals to maintain good health through better living habits. Large business firms were stressing fitness programs. The long-run hope is that these policies will help restrain medical care and premium costs.

The political antecedents of national health insurance include the comprehensive Wagner-Murray-Dingell bill, which was debated in the Senate in 1939 and 1940, and President Harry Truman's continuing push for a comprehensive program until its defeat in 1950. President Truman wrote later that "I have had some bit of disappointment as President but the one that has troubled me most, in a personal way, has been the failure to defeat the organized opposition to a National compulsory health insurance program. But this opposition has only delayed and cannot stop the adoption of an indispensable Federal health insurance plan."[3] Yet despite this prediction, tremendous positive support from labor unions, and a 1942 *Fortune* magazine poll showing 74 percent of those questioned in favor of government health insurance and a 1943 Gallup poll showing 59 percent in favor, no national, comprehensive compulsory health insurance was enacted in the United States then nor do I foresee such a development in the near future.

Rather, analysis of legislative proposals made in 1979, and the scarcity of federal tax revenues for domestic programs indicate that a limited form of federal health insurance for catastrophic or major medical expenses to cover all persons might be passed. As early as 1952, I stressed the importance of this form of health insurance, as opposed to the financially disastrous, comprehensive, first-dollar coverage now prevailing under Medicaid and many private health insurance plans.[4] The hospitalization portion of Medicare is more akin to catastrophic health insurance because of its deductibles; its cost-corridor of 20 percent, paid by the consumer after 60 days of in-hospital care; and other exclusions. In fiscal year 1977, Medicare paid for 74 percent of hospital care expenses and only 56 percent of physicians' services, and 3 percent of nursing-home care for the aged. The latter type of care has been replaced in small measure by reimbursed home health care.[5]

Many persons assume that passage of a federal catastrophic health insurance plan would be an initial or continuing step toward comprehensive coverage of all medical care costs. But others, including myself, feel that it could well be the final step in the series of partial health insurance measures already enacted. The main need is development of more competitive medical-care markets and gradual decrease in regulation of costs until the competitiveness in these markets is sufficient to contain the costs. The latter would take many years.

MEDICAL CARE AND THE POOR

The political drive for compulsory national health insurance (read correctly "national medical insurance") financed at least in part by the federal government, continues. The deputy assistant secretary (as of writing, 1979) of the Department of Health, Education, and Welfare (HEW) wrote in 1977:

> In 1976 an estimated 24 million people received services covered by Medicaid—a number similar in size to the poverty population, which was estimated at 25 million that year [which] adjusting for movements in and out of Medicaid suggests that perhaps no more than half of the poor population is covered by Medicaid at any one time . . . [and, therefore,

> there is needed] a major reform of the current network of financing programs, public and private, which can best be accomplished by the introduction of national health insurance . . . if the low-income population is to have access to adequate health care.[6]

That only half of the poor population is estimated to receive Medicaid assumes that every poor person needs to see a physician at least once a year. But about one-fourth of the total population does not see any physician during a given year. The poor who may eat less well and live in relatively inadequate housing, are believed to need more medical care than the non-poor. However, some correction downwards of the estimate that no more than half of the poor population are covered by Medicaid at a point in time still should be made. Labor unions and others continue to press through Senator Ted Kennedy for some form of comprehensive national health insurance.

In the opinion of many well-informed economists, the poor under Medicaid do have access to adequate medical care, with the exception of some rural poor and children of relatively few urban poor.[7] Their analyses emphasize barriers to access to medical care other than level of income. For example, Myron Lefcowitz and Michael Grossman emphasize the greater significance of low level of education, which is correlated with low income. Lefcowitz also states that "the share of income required for medical care is greater for the poor. Any policy which picks up the tab . . . is more income-distributive than health improving."[8]

Data on access to medical care by the poor prior to 1970 is not very pertinent to the 1980s. Lu Ann Aday and Ronald Andersen have updated to 1976 the University of Chicago's 1963 and 1970 survey data. They define family incomes in 1976 below $8,000 as "low income." In 1976, 73 percent of all such low-income persons had seen a physician during the previous year. The proportion is 77 percent for urban blacks; rural, southern blacks and low-income, Spanish surnamed persons in the Southwest were less likely, each at 65 percent. Only 68 percent of all rural farm inhabitants had seen a physician during the previous year. Rural versus urban, not low versus high income, appears to be the most important variable.* Unpublished 1976 data of the federal government's Health Interview Survey also show a continuing decline in the number of poor who made no doctor visits during the previous two years: 1964, 28 percent of poor below $3,000 annual family income; 1973, 17.2 percent below $6,000; and 1976, 15.1 percent below $7,000.[9]

---

*Because of the interrelationship among the variables of income, education, ethnic background, and place of residence, and because, as of writing, only a summary of Aday and Andersen's new book is available, a more precise statement cannot be made at this time.

Low-income persons continue to use dentists far less than high-income persons. About 61 percent of the latter saw a dentist during the previous year, as compared to only 33 percent of low-income persons. Unpublished 1976 data of the Health Interview Survey state that 67 percent of those earning $7,000 or more and 47 percent of those earning less, had not used a dentist in the previous two years.[10] There has been a slight increase in private health insurance coverage for dental care over this period.

Sociologists such as Thomas Bice and Diana Dutton argue that once Medicaid and Medicare were fully implemented, education, cultural factors, and the impersonal, mass-produced technology of hospital outpatient clinics and emergency rooms act as a greater barrier to physician care than income.[11] There is general agreement that poor persons are more likely to receive medical care from lesser-trained medical personnel, general practitioner rather than specialist, resident and intern rather than established physicians, and in outpatient clinics and other settings less accommodating than offices of private physicians.

Lack of medical facilities in rural areas may act as a special barrier to the rural poor. Individuals whose native language is not English usually do not communicate well with English-speaking persons knowledgeable about medical care. Individuals who have a usual source of medical care—86 percent of the low-income population in 1976—use more medical care than those persons who do not have a customary source of care.[12] U.S. Health Survey Interview data about self-perceived barriers to medical care in 1974 find that the highest percentage in their population sample cite "trouble getting appointment" and only one-half of that percentage state that the care would "cost too much." Among families with incomes less than $5,000 annually, the percentage who have "trouble getting appointment" was identical with the percentage who state that the care would "cost too much." Only 10.4 percent of all families interviewed cited any barrier to receiving medical care.[13]

There are probably several million poor people just above the Medicaid cutoff, who do not have access to adequate medical care because they are not employed by a company with a health insurance benefit package. In addition, there are thousands of younger people, aged 22 to 25, who are no longer covered under their parents' health insurance plans. They do not yet realize that if their employment does not automatically cover them, they should seek such health insurance coverage. Many of these individuals may be graduate students who have relatively low-priced options available to them. Similarly, many other young people who work and live outside the system, such as those who barter handcrafts, workers in agricultural communes, and self-employed who evade taxes are also unlikely to purchase health insurance. The Congressional Budget Office estimates that 18 million persons have no government or private health insurance coverage.

The percentage of poor without access to adequate medical care in 1980 is likely to be in the range of 10 to 15 percent. Fifteen years after implementation of Medicaid the important barriers are other than financial. No one in the United States today would deny needed medical care to ill people. The definition of "medical need" is debatable but it is used here in a broad sense. The fact that a small percentage of the population may not have ready access to medical care other than emergency care is not an argument for federal government, comprehensive health insurance.

The above data of Aday and Andersen indicate that underutilization of medical care is centered in the rural farm areas, whether the residents are white or nonwhite. In every country of the world there is a dearth of physicians in rural areas. Some of these countries have more physicians per capita than the United States, and many have comprehensive national health insurance. Increasing the total number of physicians does not make medical practice in rural areas more attractive to well-educated physicians and their families. Such areas lack specialized medical facilities, and have few museums, theaters, or other cultural centers. The federal government may be too far removed from rural areas to solve these regional and local problems. Specific solutions tailored to specific problems may be far more helpful. For example, grants and loans made to small towns by wealthy foundations, such as the Robert Wood Johnson Foundation, and by large companies, such as Sears, Roebuck, have had success in attracting physicians.

Regional groups can play an important role. The Western Interstate Commission for Higher Education (WICHE) established a regional network of continuing education for physicians serving rural areas in the West. WICHE also increased airlift ambulance service from rural mountain areas to the nearest university medical center, and encouraged communication networks to link rural paramedics to physicians who supervise medical care at a distance.

By 1979 there were 1.8 physicians per 1,000 population in the United States and this ratio can be anticipated to increase to nearly 2.5 by the end of the 1980s. However, physicians are not evenly distributed throughout the country. Rather, they are centered in urban areas, as in the Soviet Union, the United Kingdom, and other countries with national health insurance. Thus the financing of medical care by the federal government alone cannot solve the problem of distribution of medical services.

MAJOR POLICY OPTIONS

There are four major policy options supported by different groups within the United States. They are discussed in the sections that follow.

The Status Quo

This option is usually a composite of voluntary restrictions suggested by medical care providers, health insurers, and government officials concerning the prices of medical care, the organization of delivery of services, and the utilization of surgical beds and expensive medical technology. Medical care is already a heavily regulated industry and most providers would prefer voluntary rather than more compulsory regulation.

The costs of medical care are determined by the price of an item or service multiplied by the number of units consumed. Medical care items sold by a provider usually have four prices: price resulting from the costs reimbursed by Medicare; price resulting from costs reimbursed by Medicaid; price negotiated with Blue Cross-Blue Shield; and price charged to the commercial insurer. The provider may refuse to accept Medicare's price, and then bill the patient for the difference. The provider has the option to refuse Medicaid patients, but once committed must accept Medicaid's price. The commercial insurer is charged the highest price in order to make up the price deficiencies in the government-financed plans. The "Blues" receive a discount price for large volume buying. Some taxpayers who become ill pay higher taxes on earned income to supply general revenues for Medicaid and part of Medicare and also pay higher prices for their medical care if it is covered by commercial insurance than would exist without these government programs. Some nationwide insurance companies, for example Travelers, have been refusing in some instances to pay total surgical and other fees being billed as not "reasonable and customary" in a geographic area. They are offering in some cases 80 percent or less, amounts from which is then further deducted the cost-corridor payable by employees covered by major medical insurance. Travelers sued Blue Cross of western Pennsylvania as monopolists, but the U.S. district court ruled that Travelers had failed to prove that Blue Cross domination resulted from illegal coercion.

Proposed restraints on medical charges are directed usually toward hospital costs, which constitute 40 percent of the total health care bills; physicians' bills are 20 percent. Almost $200 billion, or about 9 percent of the gross national product (GNP) was being spent by 1980 annually on health, including dental care, drugs, nursing home care, research, construction, and administrative health insurance costs. This percentage has been steadily increasing from less than 4 percent in fiscal year 1929 to 6 percent in 1965, 9 percent in 1976, and the author's estimate, to 10 percent in 1982.

From 1950 to 1965 the average annual rate of growth in per capita health expenditures was 5.5 percent. After the passage of Medicaid and Medicare, per capita expenditures rose to an annual rate of increase of 10 percent during 1970. After the price freeze of August 1971 and price control regulations beginning in November of that year, the annual rate of increase in prices of medical care services was reduced to 4 percent. After controls were lifted, the annual rate of increase peaked at 14 percent for the 12 months ending April 1975. The annual rate of increase leveled to about 10 percent in 1976 and 1977. Meanwhile the GNP has been rising at a lesser annual rate. These two trends in tandem lead to the conclusion that 10 percent of the GNP will be spent on health care in the 1980s (See Fig. 1).

FIGURE 1

Total Hospital Costs Rose More Than 2 Times Faster Than the CPI (All Items)

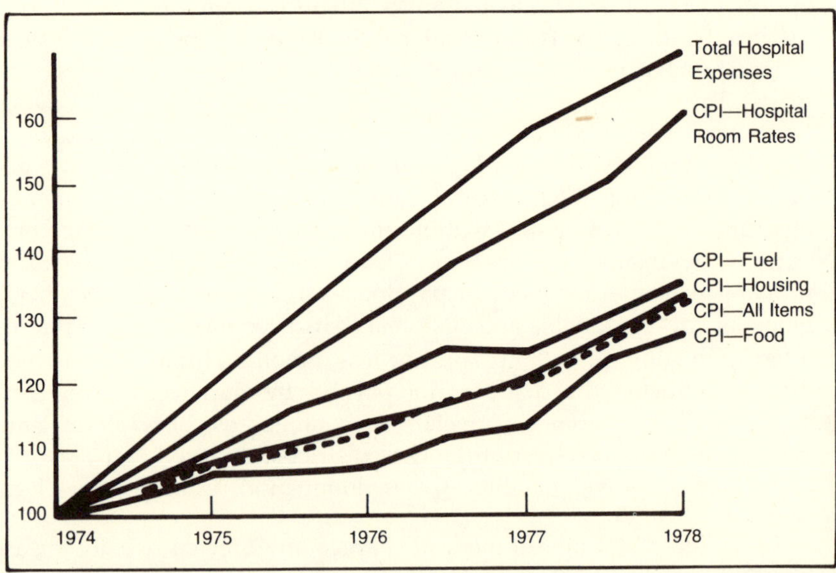

Source: *Congressional Quarterly*, July 21, 1979, p. 1461.

Voluntary Restraints. Voluntary controls do not have long-run viability. Even in their early stages in the late 1970s not enough momentum was achieved to cut costs substantially. The Congressional Budget Office (CBO) estimated that without voluntary restraint hospital expenses would have increased by 14.5 percent in 1978, and that they actually increased by 12.8 percent. The comparable CBO estimates for 1979 were 15.5 percent and 13.9 percent respectively. The respective differences in rate of increase were merely 1.7 percent and 1.6. During the period of compulsory controls, from the freeze of August 1971 through Phase II, April 1974, the rate of increase of medical, dental, and drug expenditures was successfully cut for that two-and-one-half-year period to 6 percent, or half of the former annual rate of increase of about 12 percent. However, when price controls were lifted, medical care prices, as well as some utilization rates soared so that no long-run effect could be observed.

A proposed 1979 voluntary ceiling of 9.7 percent on hospital expenditures would have exempted 57 percent of the nation's hospitals. It is unlikely that voluntary controls of this nature can be successful in the 1980s. Even the compulsory control of Phase II in the health sector was "successful only in a limited fashion and viable only as a short-run device. Its success was because of two conditions which cannot be anticipated to hold in the long run: voluntary compliance by providers and a conscious use of delay in decision-making by regulators."[14]

In the surgical area, voluntary restraint on costs is aimed primarily at the utilization rate, not at the level of the fees. Trade unions, insurance companies, other large companies, and various Blue Cross and Blue Shield plans now encourage individuals to obtain second opinions if an operation is suggested and then to refuse surgery if the consulting physician does not concur with the first opinion. As a safeguard, the consultant may not perform the surgery. The rationale is that the United States has been experiencing an annual increase in all surgical rates over twice the rate of increase in population. Moreover, the United States has higher surgical rates for elective operations, such as hernia and elective hysterectomy, than in the United Kingdom and other countries where most surgeons are not paid on a fee-for-service (FFS) basis, but are usually salaried. Also, surgical rates in prepaid group practice in the United States are lower than in FFS practice. A congressional subcommittee stated that in 1978 there were "two million unneeded operations last year with a loss of more than 10,000 lives . . ."[15] Voluntary, second-opinion programs for elective surgery exist under Medicaid in some states. And HEW (the Department of Health, Education, and Welfare) has established a national, toll-free hotline to help consumers find qualified surgical consultants. Long-term evaluation is still needed to establish whether second opinions provide savings or whether in an undue number of cases operations are merely postponed but possibly to a more appropriate time. Large business firms are increasingly supporting second-opinion programs.

The "Blues," and other insurers are refusing to reimburse automatically the routine battery of tests on hospital admission. They now recommend that in order to obtain reimbursement approval, each test be specifically ordered as needed. This practice has already been adopted by many hospitals. Third-party payers have also refused to reimburse for use of the expensive computerized tomography (CT) scanners, which are not always approved because they are judged unnecessary by regional Health Systems Agencies. These reimbursement controls by third parties will increase because of the high costs of new medical technology. Because the CT permits a noninvasive, more accurate diagnostic procedure than invasive arteriography to determine whether a brain tumor exists, it has great benefits for some individuals. There are other types of noninvasive, diagnostic methods, such as gamma scans and ultrasound exams, which are less expensive and may, in some cases of suspected cancer, be as effective in making a differential diagnosis. Because of the profusion of new medical technology, there is need for reliable information for physicians, patients, and the general public. This could decrease the number of diagnostic tests given. Although third-party payers would restrict the purchase of CT scanners as too expensive ($300,000 for brain scanners; $460,000 for full-body scanners in 1978), the public might view it differently. Brain scanners are generally considered far more cost-effective than the full-body scanner. The latter is more expensive and replaces a less-invasive technology. The crux is who pays the bill. Although third-party payers are the direct mechanism of payment, the public through taxes and premiums are the final payers. The public may have more confidence than government policymakers that continued innovation and price competition among private companies that manufacture medical devices will occur if sales are allowed to increase. Estimates for 1985 indicate that prices of scanners will not rise with the general inflation, and may even fall.

The role of large companies in negotiating group health insurance premiums and benefits is sometimes overlooked. Industry pays 75 percent of all group health insurance premiums, and is actively seeking cost containment measures. Mobil Oil amended in the late 1970s its company plan for medical, ambulatory care costs. Mobil now pays 100 percent instead of 80 percent of costs for second surgical opinion, ambulatory surgical care, and home health care agencies. Where Mobil previously did not pay for care in extended care facilities and alcoholism and drug abuse facilities, it now pays 100 percent of these costs.[16] Mobil has also developed an unique cash bonus plan that annually pays each employee in their Comprehensive Medical Expense Benefit Plan "the difference if any, between the company contribution and the total cost of the plan coverage." Eighty percent of their employees are in the plan. Other large corporations are working with providers as well as insurers in order to restrain medical cost increases.

Financing. The *status quo* option is a combination of private and government financing in which almost all personal hospital care is paid by third parties: 55 percent by government, 37 percent by private health insurance, and 2 percent by charities. Only 61 percent of physicians' care, mostly surgical, is paid by third parties. To the degree that a third party, not the consumer, pays the bill at the time of consumption, the consumer or patient has little concern about the price and, therefore, will act to demand medical care as if it were "free," 100 percent reimbursement. The purchase of medical care is complicated further because at times the physician and not the consumer makes the decision about what to purchase. Until recently most physicians have been unaware of the prices of the x-rays and tests which they order.

Most private health insurance is group insurance in which tax-subsidized premiums are expensed and paid by the employer. Since the premiums are not considered part of wages, they escape both corporate and personal income taxes. If the *status quo* of financing arrangements is maintained during the 1980s, there will be further government regulation, especially of hospitals. Because there is almost total cost reimbursement for hospital beds, the incentive for hospital-based physicians to hospitalize patients, invent new surgical techniques, and adopt new high technology that requires hospitalization, is high. At the same time, when consumers do shop, they shop primarily for quality. Only those without third-party coverage shop for price.[17] Hospital costs absorb more scarce resources than would occur if there were a lower level of automatic third-party reimbursement of hospital bills more in line with ambulatory care reimbursement. The argument for a cost-corridor or co-insurance, usually set at 20 percent of the hospital (or surgeon's) bill, and paid by the consumer, is based on theoretical analysis and empirical data indicating that co-payment restrains demand.

As private catastrophic or major medical expense coverage became more widespread in the 1970s, there was also an increase in the percentage of physicians' services reimbursed by third parties. The 40 percent that is not reimbursed permits price to act in part (or at "the margin'' by consumers who do not have coverage) as an allocator of physicians' services. Because 80 percent of surgical care is reimbursed by a third party, the percent of costs of reimbursed out-of-hospital ambulatory office visits is much lower. Demand by employees for these services is sensitive to deductibles of $50 to $100. Their dependents who do not work, and thus probably place a lower cost on their time, are sensitive to deductibles up to $500.[18] A study of Stanford University's employees enrollment in a Palo Alto Medical Clinic group plan before and after imposition of a 25 percent cost-corridor indicates a cutback in demand for physicians' services of about 25 percent.[19]

By the close of the 1970s Blue Shield of California was advertising catastrophic expense coverage policies in the Los Angeles area with deductibles of $500, $1,000, $1,500, and $2,000, thus placing deductibles for private health insurance in the same range as those of federal legislative bills. Blue Shield policies also have a 20 percent corridor up to either $15,000 or $20,000, and then pay 100 percent of all covered services.

For political reasons I do not anticipate a shrinkage in the favorable federal tax treatment permitting exemption from personal and corporate income taxes all employer-paid premiums that result in several billions in direct subsidy. Without some reduction in 100 percent cost reimbursement under Medicaid and first-dollar coverage in many private plans, hospitals will continue to offer the most expensive technology, surgeons who are paid a fee-for-service will operate more often, and individuals will overutilize ambulatory care.

Through education of the consumer, demand for physician office visits could become increasingly responsive to market incentives. The number of annual physicians' visits per capita has been falling slightly for over thirty years: in 1958 there were 5.3 visits per capita; in 1970, 5.0; in 1976, 4.9; and in 1977, 4.8. During this period the number of physicians per 1,000 population increased, as did the number of diagnostic and radiological procedures. The latter partly reflects a change in methods of practice, more defensive medicine in apprehension of malpractice suits, and not merely a target income approach to compensate for fewer visits.

''Since 1950, physician' fees have increased about 80% more than all prices, and expenditures for physicians' services have increased about 80% more than our Gross National Product.''[20] Because the fees used are not reimbursed costs but an average of private fees to insurers, they are higher than an average that includes charges paid by Medicaid and Medicare where physicians accept the assigned fee as the total fee. The increase in physicians' fees partially reflects an increase in quality and the level of technology, as well as the cost increases of labor and other inputs. Greater per capita utilization of medical services is not always desirable. Excessive elective surgery and medically unnecessary medical tests amount to several billion dollars annually. Although any estimate is hard to defend because there are no accepted norms, it is important to recognize the problem. One estimate is that the annual costs of "excess radiology, excess pathology and unnecessary hospital stays," may exceed three billion dollars.[21]

Excluding insurance premiums, the real, net out-of-pocket expense to consumers for medical care has been steady during the 1970s, though the real costs of other goods have been rising. Although personal health care expenditures for the aged more than tripled from 1966 (the beginning of Medicare) to 1977, out-of-pocket expenses by the aged about doubled. This is despite the fact that in 1977 Medicare paid only 74 percent of their hospital care expenses and 56 percent of their physicians' services. In view of these data, the decline in per capita physician visits shows some restraint by consumers and physicians; the latter, who in cases of chronic disease propose the timing of check-up visits, which the patient may or may not observe.

Most economists emphasize the importance of the physician in the determination of demand for medical care. I believe that this may be overemphasized in the case of ambulatory care. There are no accurate, empirical data on the degree of physician-induced demand in the United States and the econometric analyses of this issue make fairly rigid assumptions. The prices that economists use in these analyses do not include the costs of travel time and waiting to the consumer/patient nor are the prices usually patients' out-of-pocket prices at time of consumption. The consumer initiates the first visit for a medical problem, but the physician suggests the timing of the return visit. Although much of the demand for physician services, laboratory tests, x-rays, and many complex medical procedures which require medical expertise are physician-induced, patients affect demand for physician care by delay and refusal to initiate and to continue care. Mark Pauly estimates that "reasonably-informed" purchases of total personal health care are "perhaps one fourth" and are "at least half of the ambulatory care visits."[22]

Clearly some physicians are imperfectly informed and in cases of chronic disease patients accumulate experience that helps them to evaluate medical care. Moreover, the patient may purposely seek medical information. It is the patient and not the physician who knows best the patient's unique set of values which determines his or her evaluation of the potential benefit from a given treatment, which the physician may describe, as well as the risk of that and alternative treatments.

The National Health Survey estimated that in 1975, 18 percent of all general surgeon visits and 29 percent of internists' involved cases were "serious or very serious." Although the patient's and physician's perception of seriousness may differ, these data indicate that there are still a large percentage of instances where the patient can delay initial or return visits to physicians.

Patient adherence to drug regimen in hypertension is only 50 percent. Although compliance is higher for more symptomatic diseases, it is still low enough to create problems for designers of controlled clinical drug trials. Physicians can increase acquiescence by patients if they explain why they wish the patient to follow particular procedures. Patients in the 1980s will continue the trend of the 1970s to become more knowledgeable, questioning, and assertive about their own medical care. However, this trend may be weakened if third-party payments cover a greater percentage of ambulatory medical care.

Medicine's successes have increased the need for medical care in old age. If physicians had as much influence on demand for their services as credited, one would anticipate, in view of their numbers and the prevalence of third-party payments, that per capita visits would have increased. The consumer who must give up time as well as money for medical care may be more discerning than usually acknowledged. Among other explanations, it may be that some physicians do not like treating chronically ill older persons who are incurable, given the current level of knowledge.

Regulation. The medical care industry is probably the most regulated industry in the United States. The trend to regulate more will continue during the 1980s, despite efforts to increase competition. Because of the high level of third-party payments, increased competition cannot become effective for several years. Meanwhile, medical care prices will continue to rise; tax revenues will have to increase to meet higher Medicare, Medicaid, and other government-paid medical care bills; and the costs of regulation will continue to add to the size of these bills. The costs of compliance in acute care hospitals in New York with the regulations of 164 agencies was estimated at $1.1 billion, or one-fourth of their total acute general hospital care bill.[23]

Although regulation already exists in the health sector, some individuals view more regulation as a viable alternative to national health insurance. This is despite regulation's failure to contain costs and to assure achievement of the goals of equity that proponents of national health insurance attribute to their proposal. It can be argued that regulation has decreased equity. MediCal (Medicaid in California) reimburses about 60 percent of California's physicians' usual charges, and on the average reimburses much less than Medicare reimburses. As a result, prices to private insurers are much higher to cover losses and sick taxpayers pay twice: once that part of medical bills higher than their insurance companies allow, and again in taxes on earned and other income, which support Medicare and Medicaid. Piecemeal, planned deregulation along with increased competition seems preferable to more government regulation and interference, which result in no better rationale for the resulting allocation of resources.

The American Hospital Association has fairly consistently favored government regulation benefitting hospitals. The American Medical Association (AMA) initially opposed much of the health legislation, including Medicaid and Medicare, which have greatly benefitted its members in recent years. However, the AMA, with increased sophistication , has varied its policies to maximize its gains. The AMA opposes some types of regulation, deliberately influences in its favor implementation of existing regulation such as the Peer Standards Review Organizations [PSRO], and supports only regulation that benefit its members. The 1976 federal evaluation of PSROs in Medicare was that they spent more than they saved. The 1977 rating indicates that there are considerable differences in quality of leadership and performance, but older PSROs appear to be more effective than new ones. Increasingly, the capture theory of regulation appears to be applicable to medical care industry. Instead of the government protecting the consumer of medical care, regulation has served largely to benefit providers. The picture is one of health care absorbing an ever-larger percentage of the GNP and resulting in contraction of other, worthwhile sectors of the economy.

Federal and state governments have exercised control over an extensive area: the number of physicians, by per capita grants to medical schools and licensure; physicians' medical practices via PSROs and new drug approvals; hospitals, by the Hill-Burton Act and Health Systems Agencies' control of certificates-of-need; prices, by federal wage and price control and hospital charges by various states' review panels; structural organization, by limitations on prepaid group practice and on retail stores' provision of health services; health insurers, by regulation of the level of their reserves, composition of their boards, and level of their premiums; and pharmaceutical companies, by regulation of research methods and marketing.

In recent years regulation of the marketing of pharmaceutical drugs by the Food and Drug Administration (FDA) and by some state governments has increased. The original 1906 Food and Drug Act gave a broad mandate to FDA to prevent "the manufacture, sale, or transportation of adulterated or misbranded or poisonous or deleterious foods, drugs, medicines, and liquors, and for regulating traffic therein . . ."[24] Even today many of FDA's decisions are still made under the broad mandate of that initial Act. The 1938 revised Act expanded the area over which FDA could regulate and in 1962 it was amended to require that new drugs be tested prior to marketing not only for safety but also for "efficacy."

The administration of the statutory law emphasizes anticipated, biological risk to gain anticipated biological benefits. This is a risk-benefit analysis which does not take into account potential benefits other than biological, as for example, enjoyment of a more active life and higher income from earnings because of better health from taking a new drug. Under the statutory law, FDA has a negative mandate, to protect the public from harm. In accordance with that mandate, it has emphasized biological risk and has ignored to some degree potential biological benefits which might accrue to small sub-groups of the population.

FDA has interpreted the statutory law's requirement of "substantial evidence" of safety and efficacy of a new drug to mean with rare exceptions two controlled, double-blind clinical trials which meet their administrative standards. Epidemiological data are rarely accepted as substantial evidence. These requirements make it more expensive to market drugs in the United States than in most other countries of the world. Research on new efficacious drugs to treat diseases for many of which there is no treatment, has moved abroad within the last decade. By 1974, 50 percent of the new chemical entities studied in humans by large U.S. pharmaceutical firms were first studied abroad. But in 1963, only one year after the additional requirement of efficacy, none of the 15 large innovative U.S. pharmaceuticals conducted its initial human studies abroad.[25]

In 1976 the Medical Devices Act was passed by Congress and regulations under that Act have been implemented. These have resulted in a substantial increase in the cost of developing and marketing new medical devices in the United States. In 1978 far-reaching, new legislation to regulate the marketing of new drugs was proposed in Congress and although that legislation failed, it is anticipated that it will be pushed for passage during 1979 and 1980. It is easier to regulate a few large pharmaceutical firms than to regulate effectively thousands of hospitals and physicians, and it is also easier to sell the public regulation which purports to protect the public's health than known ineffective regulation over costs.

The most important negative effect of the proposed drug amendments, as written in 1979, is that they would permit the FDA to become the final arbiter of the scientific methods, the experimental and statistical techniques used in the beginning of the investigational, research stage of testing a new drug. To require use of specific, formal scientific methods, experimental and statistical, would manacle innovation. Guidelines for research come from past research. Innovation *per se* means seeking new ways of research.

There are many other parts of the 1978 and 1979 proposed legislation which would add to the costs of pharmaceutical research and thus delay development and marketing of new, beneficial drugs but there are space limitations which prevent me from discussing these. The American Society for Clinical Pharmacology and Therapeutics proposes that the existing criterion of substantial evidence be replaced by a weaker one of significant evidence and to retain the efficacy requirement.

Some argue against the efficacy requirement because individuals differ biologically and that a few patients will respond to a new drug when they have not responded to an older drug. How many such patients are needed to demonstrate the superior efficacy of a new drug? There are some legislators who believe that relative efficacy of a drug is best determined for the patient by the physician and the patient, not by administrative regulation at the point of market access.

From the consumer's point of view any new legislation should speed up, not reduce, the innovation of new drugs which are therapeutically beneficial. Such legislation should also encourage in each dispensed prescription drug package information about the risks and anticipated benefits of the drug, written in language which the patient can understand. Spelling out of the anticipated benefits within a given time frame would help the patient to judge whether the drug is effective. Benefits are too often assumed as known. In most European countries more drugs are sold over-the-counter (without prescription) than in the United States. In Italy the same descriptive package insert is given to the patient as is given to the physician. Why are the residents of the United States assumed to be less capable of making their own judgments than the residents of other countries?

The National Center for Health Care Technology was established in November 1978 to recommend for which new technologies Medicare should not reimburse payment, as well as which older technologies they consider obsolete. Governmental decisions of this nature will slow diffusion of new medical technology and its costs, but will also depress the medical device industry and delay more beneficial, new therapeutic innovation in this area. If competent physicians set standards of medical need for different technologies and agree on guidelines, they would guard against inappropriate use of the newer technology and high concomitant costs from duplication. Cost-benefit and cost-effective studies of new medical devices are badly needed, but a governmental agency cannot be an impartial expert. If physicians make available the needed biological information, economists can spell out costs and benefits under different sets of value judgments and consumer/patients will have more information on which to base decisions.

A 1979 committee report of the National Academy of Science on medical technology does "not deal with the issues of ethical and social choices now made possible by the availability of medical equipment to prolong life or the financial costs of such technology . . . [nor its] . . . implicit power to redistribute wealth in the society and to confer benefits upon some of the most underprivileged . . . The committee's main focus has been on the costs and effectiveness of the process of technological change, not on the equity of its consequences."[26] After five meetings, four closed and one open, and a few commissioned papers, the committee issued its recommendation. These are followed by a significant dissenting opinion, part of which is quoted here. "[The] approach ignores . . . (1) how development of technology relates to advances in the sciences and medicine, (2) who made each item and why, (3) what medical purposes they are intended to serve, and (4) how other technological innovations not directed to the concept of large scale address the same medical problems."[27] Physicians and consumers who either are or will be patients should be aware of the problems, the ethical issues, and the need for full cost-benefit analysis and not leave decisions of this nature entirely in the hands of experts and/or a government agency.

Regulation to control costs, either prices or utilization, has not worked in the past, and there is no promise that more of the same will work in the future. Some proponents of regulation argue against making the market more competitive because they object on grounds of equity to the distribution of medical care that could occur under a perfectly competitive market. But a perfectly competitive market is not really attainable. Even close approximation probably will never exist in the health sector. Moreover, equity can be better obtained through taxation and public spending than by piecemeal regulation.

Increase Competition

A second national policy option is to increase deliberately the amount of competition among all kinds of medical care providers. This option also has a large component of voluntary action. For example, the AMA made 47 recommendations in the report of their National Commission on the Cost of Medical Care. Many of its proposals fit equally into this category and into maintaining the status quo.

Advertising. The AMA has gone a long way in recognizing the changing socioeconomic climate of opinion, as well as legal realities, when they stated in their "Task Force Report on the Marketplace," that "Physicians should be able to advertise prices for rather well-defined procedures just as lawyers can now. Such advertising could also include length of time required to obtain an appointment, willingness to accept new patients (or Medicare/Medicaid patients), institutional affiliations, and whether the physician is Board-certified."[28] This detail is not repeated in the 47 recommendations of their national commission. However, the AMA's House of Delegates approved directories in December 1978, thus reversing their position of the early 1970s when they opposed listing meaningful information about each physician except for advanced degrees, university, and specialty board examinations passed. Because most large public libraries purchase the existing directory of specialists, and the *Physicians' Desk Reference* (PDR) on prescription drugs, I believe they will also purchase the proposed, more meaningful, directories. During the 1980s, consumers' knowledge about medical care services will continue to increase. Competition will become more common as the supply of physicians increases from 1.8 in 1975 to about 2.5 per 1,000 population by the end of the decade of the eighties.

To increase competition in medical care delivery, the Federal Trade Commission (FTC) is using the federal antitrust law to rule against professional associations that bar, as a matter of "professional ethics," advertising about prices of medical care, dental care, eyeglasses, contact lenses, hospital care, and health insurance. The American Dental Association (ADA) consented in April 1979 to an interim two-year FTC order that bars the ADA from restraining dentists from the use of truthful advertising under its "principle of ethics." A similar FTC consent order is likely to be accepted by the AMA.[29] According to an agreement with the FTC, the final outcome for the ADA and the AMA will be identical. The AMA has appealed a 1978 FTC administrative law judge's ruling that the AMA's advertising prohibitions violate antitrust law.

The FTC had argued in 1979 that comparative advertising in a particular industry, not health, should be allowed because it "maximizes one of advertising's greatest consumer benefits, viz. reducing the time it takes to obtain sufficient information to make a rational purchase decision."[30] The FTC interpreted its "eyeglasses rule" in a letter to the Illinois attorney general as preempting state laws and permitting advertisements to state "whether an advertised price includes single vision and/or multifocal lenses, refers to hard and/or soft lenses, includes an eye examination, includes all dispensing fees and includes both frames and lenses."[31] In 1979 the FTC also issued a consent order to require the California Medical Association to stop producing and publishing their commonly-used, medical care-pricing schedules, Relative Value Schedules, "to withdraw those already published and 3) to stop giving instructions for their conversion factors."[32] It does permit them to provide reimbursers lists of procedural terminology and historical prices.

At the state level, repeal of fair trade practice laws is creating a more competitive climate. Substitution by pharmacists of generic drugs for trademark prescription drugs, when available* are increasing but advertisements of prices of generic drugs are rare in practice. During the 1980s advertisement of prices in the various health care markets will increase.

Sears, Roebuck and Company has established 280 optical departments in the 39 states that permit direct or leased operations. It also has a pilot program of leases to a management firm hiring dentists to practice in some of their stores. Sears is testing the feasibility of prepaid dental clinics throughout its U.S. operations. Other large, retail chains have also had optical departments for many years. The entry of profit-oriented business into the delivery of health care is increasing.

FTC is also requiring that the majority of boards of health institutions must not be persons at-interest. Physician domination of 44 of the 69 Blue Shield organizations of physicians has been challenged on grounds of conflict of interest. The FTC has also publicly noted that competition from alternative providers has been reduced by AMA's lobbying "against payment of federal health benefits for health care services by clinical psychologists and other non-physicians unless the patient was referred to the non-physician by a physician."[33]

Occupational Licensure. Competition among professional suppliers will remain limited by state licensing practices during the 1980s. State licensing boards usually have a majority of those persons whose occupation is being licensed or who are competitors of the proposed new licensees. The level of difficulty of a licensing examination is

*Single source prescription drugs whose patents have not run out limit this market. Some generic forms, whose effective ingredients are the same as the trademark drugs, may not have equal bioavailability and, therefore, may not be approved as substitutes. Although the active chemical ingredients of two drugs may be identical, the bioavailability of the drugs to the body over time may differ because the inert "carriers" (flavoring, color, solvents, etc.) differ. Savings in this area, in practice, have been small.

controlled by persons in that occupation, who have an economic interest in keeping the difficulty level high. All persons who might pass the examination are not automatically licensed in each state.

An interesting example is a class action suit by those who applied for the dental examination after August 1, 1974 and those who "may be denied dental licensure . . . in the future," in Hawaii (*Pekarsky, et al.*, v. *Ariyoshi, et al.*, civil no. 76–0455) in which "the plaintiffs claim that they were illegally denied their dental licenses because they were either of Caucasian ancestry or new/non-residents of Hawaii."[34] It was claimed that during a two-year period 30 out of 35 Orientals, and only 28 of 74 non-Orientals passed the dental board examinations. Six of the seven members of the licensing board in Hawaii were of Asian ancestry.[35] This illustrates how an at-interest licensing board can keep outsiders from receiving a license to follow an occupation for which they have received training at accredited schools. The fewer the dentists per 1000 people the higher the fees if advertising and other requisites of a competitive market are present.

National licensing, rather than state licensing, or a switch to certification, which is more supportive of competition, is unlikely. Certification, as compared to licensure, supplies the information that an individual has met a minimum level of competence by passing a test or completed a course program. Certification does not bar noncertified persons from following an occupation, but permits those persons who are certified to advertise this fact. Noncertified persons generally charge less and do work of a lower quality than certified persons. Licensing eliminates the availability of lower-quality care, as measured by the ability to pass an examination—and, concomitantly, lower-priced services. To the degree that consumers might wish to purchase these, consumer choice is reduced. The price is higher and the quality may be higher than the consumer may prefer to pay.

When third-party payment is at a high level, freer entry alone will not insure free competition among suppliers, because the consumer is less concerned than normally about the price. However, over 50 percent of physicians' bills for nonsurgical, ambulatory care are paid by the consumer. In this area freer entry would increase competition.

It is traditionally argued that with respect to physicians, the social costs of no licensure are higher than private costs. For example, unlicensed incompetent physicians could by poor treatment let an epidemic develop unchecked. Although this may have been plausible before the use of powerful antibiotics, this seems an unlikely scenario in the United States in the 1980s.

With an average 50-percent third-party reimbursement of a licensed physician's bill for ambulatory care, it is uncertain whether the average of the remaining 50 percent would exceed the total out-of-pocket price of a nonlicensed physician to the consumer at the moment of purchase. The unlicensed practitioner and other lesser-trained persons who are not reimbursed can be competitors, especially in the care of aged persons. Lonely individuals may prefer and thus be willing to pay for more care if they are chronically ill with an already diagnosed incurable disease.

There are over 60 licensed health occupations, including physician, registered nurse, inhalation therapist, X-ray technician, and laboratory technician. Exceedingly capable physicians can differentiate themselves from all licensed physicians by taking specialty board examinations and writing and lecturing in their specialty. Therefore, they do not need the protection of a license to assure an ample number of patients. It is the far greater number of less capable professionals and nonprofessionals where the more capable cannot set themselves apart, who are so strongly in favor of licensure.

The number of allied health jobs that are licensed has grown steadily. Licensure means that a specific function can be performed only by licensed personnel under the states' Nurse and Medical Practice Acts. This has made the manpower structure in health care very rigid. Licensure increases costs of medical care, because only large hospitals can keep busy all the licensed personnel they hire.

A recent experimental health manpower program in California (AB 1503) trained existing health care professionals for expanded roles. It also established career ladders so that whatever an individual had learned at a lower level could then be considered part of training for a higher occupational level. Creation of career ladders had been proposed for many years because it would act to reduce costs of training. However, the anticipated, expanded roles for registered nurses, physicians' assistants, and pharmacists to prescribe, dispense, and administer drugs (allowed until January 1, 1983, under the amended 1977 California Nurse Practice Act) have been opposed primarily by physicians, not by consumers. Even though the University of the Pacific School of Dentistry's initial project demonstrated increased productivity by use of assistants supervised by dentists, the project was not continued. Opposition was again voiced by the competitive supplier, the dentist.

In May 1977 a survey of pilot projects was made under AB 1503 to educate trainees for expanded roles. Table 1 illustrates that although many persons had completed their training, not all trainees were employed at the higher levels.

TABLE 1

Utilization of Trainees in Expanded Roles (May 1977, California)

Health Profession	Completed Training	Utilized Trainees (estimated)
Medical Auxiliaries	298	202
Nursing	2,201	1,073
Pharmacy	91	51
Dentistry	210	64
Mental Health	4	0
	2,804	1,390

Source: Dick Howard and R. Douglas Roederer, *Health Manpower Licensing: California's Demonstration Projects* (Lexington, Ky: Fourth Annual Report, the Council of State Governments, April 1978, p. 17).

Licensing of occupations is often defended on the grounds "that society is a better judge than the individual concerning what is good for him."[36] If the licensing board is dominated by the group being licensed or its competitors the temptation is to restrict entry in order to maintain demand for their services. The greater the supply of a service, generally speaking, the lower the total income of the suppliers. "The median of income of self-employed physicians—$63,000 in 1976—had risen by 1975 to equal four times the earning of the census-defined, broad group of 'professional and technical workers.' " But in 1939, their earnings were less than twice as great as the earnings of that group.[37] Physicians' appreciation of limited entry was illustrated by the standing ovation given by members of the Association of American Medical Colleges, October 24, 1978, to former HEW Secretary, Joseph Califano when he announced that HEW wanted medical schools to "gradually reduce the size of their classes" over the next few years because physician oversupply was threatening runaway costs. Califano's simplistic elaboration was that "every additional physician over the average career of 40 years adds $12 million in health care costs to the economy. By the year 2000, health care costs will reach 1000 billion—about 12 percent of the Gross National Product."[38]

If licensing boards perform well they can serve to maintain quality and give quicker administrative, as compared to judicial, redress in view of our crowded court calendar. However, such boards are restricting entry into health occupations, thus restricting competition from equally and also lesser-trained, and thus less expensive, personnel who could substitute services at lower prices. One facet of quality—and quality is part of the service being purchased—that the physician provides is confidentiality or privacy. There are some who argue that an unlicensed professional would not provide this to the same degree as the licensed lawyer and licensed physician. However, this claim has not been tested.

In February 1978, the federal government acted to increase competition through the supply side of the market by directly reimbursing under Medicare less-expensively trained personnel than the physician, such as the general nurse practitioner. As these lesser-trained persons, educated at one-fifth of the cost of educating a physician, increase in number, it is feasible that they could relieve shortages of primary care practitioners, as in rural areas. Costs to the consumer will be lower, however, only if the savings are passed along to the consumer and do not become a type of profit to the physician or the group that hires him or her. In some instances use of physician assistants or "extenders" may complement rather than substitute physician care.

Consumers during the 1980s will complain more about the high costs of medical care than they have in the past. They may also switch in greater numbers to substitutes for physicians outside the medical hierarchy: lay midwives, homeopaths, use of self-care books, and self-labeled healers. Over one million copies of a decision-tree analysis approach paperback, *Take Care of Yourself: A Consumer's Guide to Medical Care*, have been sold, mostly to insurance companies and Blue Cross and Blue Shield, which have distributed them to policyholders.[39] This book has been so successful that a similar one was written about children's health for parents. Evaluations conflict on whether the use of decision-trees (or step-by-step analyses by a consumer) to judge if a complaint is significantly serious to see a physician actually reduces the number of physician visits. Although Blue Cross and Blue Shield support that this approach reduces the number of visits, a recent academic article reports the reverse.[40]

If general nurse practitioners were directly reimbursed by all insurers, as now under Medicare, their use would be greatly expanded, especially in home care visits to the chronically ill. Individuals would then hire and pay general nurse practitioners in rural areas, as is being done in Colorado.[41] This development would postpone, and in some cases eliminate, use of nursing homes, generally a more expensive and less desirable option. Of a total of one million registered nurses, there are about 15,000 nurses in independent practice. About 2,000 are midwives, some are public health nurses serving chronically ill in their homes, and others the poor in health clinics. Although the nurses' new independence is being challenged, primarily by physicians, upgrading nurses for expanded roles will increase during the 1980s.

Health Maintenance Organizations. Subscribers to health maintenance organizations (HMOs), or someone else on their behalf, pay a given amount per month, determined a year ahead, for medical care. The amount is determined per capita, not per service. The physician may be paid per capita, a salary, or fees for services rendered. Most are paid a salary, usually with a bonus. The lower the costs of tests, x-rays, hospital days and physician visits charged to the accounts of their patients, the higher the bonus. One successful HMO in a community encourages the formation of other HMOs, especially the independent practice type.

HMOs are a special hybrid form that serves as both insurer because they bear a large degree of financial risk, and as a medical organization to deliver medical care. Their per capita costs are lower than fee-for-service practice because of strict review of use of hospital days and medical services, and emphasis on using those resources most appropriate or least costly, to the problem presented. The Kaiser-Permanente prototype owns hospitals and its savings are primarily through reduction in use of hospital days. In 1973 federal loans were authorized to those HMOs which provide a very broad range of benefits. In 1976 amendments to decrease the range of mandatory benefits were passed, but the requirement of community-rated charges was retained. Most commercial insurers set premium levels in accordance with the claims experience of a group, as of a company's employees, in the previous year. Many Blue Cross and Blue Shield plans set premium levels in accordance with the claims experience of the geographical community served during the past year. The HMO Act provides for loans to both prepaid groups which have salaried physicians and Independent Practice Associations (IPAs), which are organized groups of physicians who are reimbursed on a fee-for-service basis by the IPA, with which they contract. IPAs are sometimes called Foundations. The IPA charges subscribers a per capita fee. Large amounts of capital are not needed by IPAs because they do not usually own a hospital, but rather use existing facilities. IPAs depend on in-house peer review of utilization to contain costs.

If the per-capita fee of the HMOs were experience-rated, as are premiums of most commercial insurance plans, this would relate choice of provider to the level of cost. More employers are offering the option of HMOs in addition to those of private health insurance, which usually include community-rated Blue Cross and Blue Shield plans. Where there are no HMOs in a geographic area, some employers have become involved in starting one.

Consumers do not usually pay the per capita amount to the HMO but rather, their employers or the government pay. It is consumers, however, who select their HMO or a fee-for-service physician on the basis of anticipated health needs in the coming year. Young, healthy, unmarried individuals are less likely to select an HMO, and more often choose the least costly, commercial plan, which offers fewer benefits. Because employers pay 75 percent of health insurance premiums,[42] consumers are less concerned with total medical costs than with their costs at the time of consumption, which may be nil. Convenience and facets of quality dominate individual decisions: During what hours are services available? How long are waits for appointments? What is the level of quality of the physicians, including referred-to specialists, who provide the services?

For consumers who place a high value on their time, waiting acts as a barrier to medical care. Rationing by waiting does not assure distribution of scarce resources in accordance with medical need because that implies "a high correlation between a low opportunity cost of other uses of time and need for medical care."[43] Married women who have children and who work outside the home place a relatively high value on their time. This is also true for self-employed individuals, professionals, and blue-collar workers who lose wages when not at work.

The government and some employers may prefer their employees to enroll in HMOs because the government or company can then more easily budget costs for medical care a year ahead. This makes planning easier. The government as a large buyer of medical insurance can usually negotiate lower per capita costs with a smaller HMO than insurance companies would offer for a comparable benefit package. Insurance companies, including Blue Cross and Blue Shield, are usually larger than HMOs with the possible exception of Kaiser-Permanente. Contracts offered by insurers, including Blue Cross and Blue Shield, do not cover all hospital and physician care costs and a lower premium for a smaller package of benefits is a common option. Insurers are helping physicians to organize prepaid groups, including IPAs, are providing some underwriting, and are lending physicians marketing and management expertise.

Increasing numbers of physicians are refusing to accept a government-assigned fee under Medicare for their total fee, and thus bill patients for the excess. Insurance companies offer contracts to cover out-of-pocket payments by the elderly, but many of these do not adequately fill the gaps in Medicare coverage. Elderly patients, who are the heaviest users of medical care, may, therefore, prefer HMOs.

Some physicians are refusing to accept new Medicaid patients.

Others limit the number of Medicaid patients whom they will treat because various states are reimbursing 75 percent or less of their customary charge. In California, "Medi-Cal payments currently [1978] represent approximately 60 percent of billed charges."[44] Lower-than-cost reimbursements increase per capita fees, non-HMO fees, and health insurance premiums to other consumers. Some commercial insurers are refusing to pay all of the fee charged by the physician. When this is done the consumer must pay the bill first. The consumer may resent the insurance companies' apparent lack of faith because the employer's summary of the plan may not always state that medical charges are judged as to whether they are "reasonable" and at the "customary" level in the geographical area. By reducing reimbursable amounts, insurance companies are acting to contain their costs but not necessarily the health care cost of the country. They are creating incentives for consumers to police charges of both physicians and insurers and to join prepaid groups. This may increase competition. Increasingly, states are negotiating with HMOs for care of Medicaid patients.

During 1975, $245 per person was spent out-of-pocket for all types of health care, including $63 for health insurance premiums.[45] The percentage increase in out-of-pocket expense 1970–1975 was 36 percent, while all personal health care expenditures rose 84 percent during the same period. Personal health care expenditures since 1970 have been increasing at an annual rate of 16.8 percent. This reflects the open-ended costs reimbursed under FFS by some private health insurers and the government, as well as the higher prices paid by individuals who do not have third-party insurers nor government to contain costs through their large buying power. Insurers and government also refuse in the name of cost containment to reimburse hospitals for purchase of expensive equipment that is not approved as needed by the Health System Agency (HSA) in their region. Costs to some consumers are rising faster than to others. Should the insurers make the decisions about allocation of resources in our society? HSAs are quasi-government groups often dominated by traditional suppliers. Should they make these decisions? The consumer, if the marketplace worked, would be far preferable. Companies who pay the premiums must, and many have, become involved.

In prepaid groups, individual per capita charges are not related to individual utilization. But neither are annual premiums under group health insurance, which comprises most health insurance in the United States. Per capita cost reimbursement on a prospective basis is not in itself a cost-containment method, but creates a lag in adjustment of per capita charges to changes in utilization of services and in costs of providing services.

Data indicate that HMOs have lesser overall per capita charges than FFS charges computed on a per capita basis for comparable populations. In the case of HMOs which own their own hospitals, per capita costs are lower because they use less hospital days—fewer admissions and shorter length of stay for persons of similar age, sex, and diagnosis who use FFS.

HMO physicians to whom annual bonuses are given have an incentive to contain costs. If a physician's patient's costs to the HMO are lower than the average costs of all the HMO's patients, the physician in some groups receives a bonus. Control over referrals includes peer reviews and these are stricter if the referral is to specialists who are outside the group. Only physician initiated referrals are paid for by most HMOs. This practice saves the group money, but it may be at the expense of both quality for the patient and costs to the individual and society. Subscribers who self-refer to purchase what they believe are more capable physician services, pay for the out-of-plan fees in addition to the monthly per capita charges. Commercial insurers generally exercise no control over self-referrals or referrals by FFS practitioners, except by refusing to reimburse the higher charges of some specialists.

Large employers are large buyers, and can, like federal and state governments, exert pressure on the levels of insurance premiums and per capita charges. Additionally, large companies have the alternative of self-insuring. National policy has recently encouraged employers to offer employees a choice among several modes of medical care delivery, including HMOs. An employer may decide to limit financial responsibility for health care of employees to the lowest cost among the competing plans offered by HMOs and insurers. Employees who want the more expensive options pay the difference. Relative economic strengths of the company, which may be unionized, and the insurer—the two negotiating parties—will differ, as will the age and sex distribution of employers' labor forces. Age and sex are important variables in determining the utilization of medical services by an employee group. Different companies will strike better bargains with different types of suppliers. Employees should be informed in any summary of plans, the precise medical benefits which are reimbursed, and whether actual charges or a percentage determined by the insurer are reimbursed. Labor unions may consider that any savings negotiated are a potential source of future wage increases.

The consumer finds that group practice, whether prepaid or not, will tend to transfer all costs of waiting to the patient. It is not economical for physicians paid by a group to have a less than full schedule. Thus, the group will not hire an additional physician until it is reasonable to assume that he will be carrying almost a full load. Thus, waiting for an appointment and waiting in a physician's office is part of the price the consumer pays, but his employer does not pay, except insofar as the employers' costs are higher because of the number and length of absences from work to obtain medical care. These may be greater when employees obtain medical treatment from groups than from non-group practice. Reduced hospitalization under prepaid group practice may offset the otherwise greater costs because of waiting. These costs are not small. One large multinational company that provides in-house, complete medical care to 75 percent of its employees claims that their additional costs over costs of more traditional insurance packages are more than offset by reductions in absenteeism. Time otherwise spent traveling to and waiting for medical care and travel time to return to work are avoided.

In recent years Kaiser-Permanente has questioned the cost-effectiveness of their annual presymptomatic screenings, except as a method to separate the worried well from the sick (that is, triage), and then to direct the former to less costly trained personnel for health education and advice. Through triage, large HMOs and large multispecialty FFS groups of any type can handle more consumers per physician, and physicians can concentrate on those who are truly sick. Whether quality of care is thus reduced is not proven one way or the other at this time. Savings from greater use of general nurse practitioners and physician assistants can be partially passed on to consumers through lower per capita payments. Savings can also be retained to invest in hospitals or to provide larger bonuses or retirement income to physicians.

Kaiser has decreased the frequency of its previous annual, multiphasic health checkups because they are not cost-effective over the long run, except among older men, "45 to 54-year old male participants after 5–7 years," as measured by the number of days of work lost because of disability and chronic illness.[46] Some claim that HMOs use more preventive procedures, which are cost-effective in the long run. It is unknown whether this is true, and if so, whether it is because of the organizational structure or because the price of preventive care in HMOs is lower. One economist's study suggests that "when people have full coverage for 'preventive' ambulatory visits, they have at least as many, if not more, services under the FFS system than in an HMO."[47]

Not all HMOs, nor all groups in general, have maintained an adequate level of quality. Physicians, both in groups and under the FFS system, have been subject to malpractice suits—the last resort to maintain quality of care. "A physician in non-solo practice has a 2.8 percent higher probability of a [malpractice] claim than a solo practice physician."[48] The question of quality of medical care is a difficult one because there are no norms for surgical rates and hospital days, both of which are less in HMOs than for comparable patients in FFS. Qualifications of providers, diagnostic procedures, prescribing practices used, and health outcomes, life or death, sick or well, are the usual proxies to meaure quality of care. Los Angeles County had a significantly lower death rate in January and February 1976, when surgery dropped by 40 percent because of a physicians' slowdown to protest the level of malpractice premiums. This suggests the level of difficulty involved. There are no clear-cut measures of quality of medical care, and consumers rarely have adequate information to judge the level of care they are receiving. However, this is also true in other areas, such as the servicing of automobiles or purchasing hi-fi equipment. Consumer feedback and final outcomes are more quickly realized in areas other than medical care. However, consumers of medical care do make some judgments, whether they are well-informed ones or not. Prepaid group structure, however, limits the application of that judgment.

Out-of-plan use of medical care by prepaid group subscribers may be fairly substantial. In 1972, almost one-third of New York City's Health Insurance Plan (HIP) Medicare enrollees had out-of-plan physician services reimbursed by the government.[49] About one-fourth of East Baltimore Medical Plan's Medicaid enrollees, 814 individuals, voluntarily left that plan between November 1971 and September 1973.[50] Data are rare in this area. Interviews of persons who leave an HMO are needed to find out what percentage might have moved away (possibly low in Medicare and Medicaid populations); travel a great deal; disliked long waits; or were dissatisfied with the perceived quality of the medical care because they did not see a physician, did not like their physician, did not select a particular physician, found diagnosis or treatment decisions unacceptable, or did not wish to use the specialists to whom they were referred.

When referral by an HMO physician is made to a specialist outside the HMO, the HMO pays the bill. Tertiary-care specialists cannot be efficiently utilized even on a part-time basis by any but the largest HMOs, and even they must negotiate a contract for care as needed with some tertiary-care specialists. In most instances, self-referrals are paid by the subscribers or by third parties on their behalf, such as the Social Security Administration for Medicare patients. The New York HIP study found that "out-of-plan users tend to be more seriously ill than those receiving all their services within the plan" and they are also more likely to have been hospitalized.[51]

The authors of the HIP study appear most concerned about the implications of self-referrals for society's diminished cost containment if HMOs were to become the major source of medical care. The study does not explore why patients initiate referrals. Rather, the extent of out-of-plan use becomes an argument for even more comprehensive and widespread HMOs under an integrated national health insurance program, with limits on enrollment transfers. It seems unwise to recommend a national health insurance program in which HMOs through incentives to providers will become the dominant mode of delivery of care when it is not known why people leave HMOs. Although large HMOs have more board-certified specialists proportionately than FFS, this is no guarantee that their quality of care is higher in practice than that of older and lesser-trained physicians in the FFS sector. A summary by one economist who has reviewed the literature on HMOs and quality concludes in his book to be published in 1980 that " . . . the quality question remains unresolved . . . The specific financial incentives of HMOs seem to have little direct effect on quality . . . considerable variation in quality exists among HMOs."[52]

The low 3 percent of population enrolled in HMOs acts as a warning signal. To make it more difficult for consumers to switch providers in the face of these unknowns makes a mockery of the concept of quality of care. As a first step, a number of small HMOs over a large geographical area might explore how they could informally cooperate to contract tertiary specialists, at least part-time. This, plus greater use of contracts for a limited amount of time of other specialists outside the HMO, would improve quality of care for HMO subscribers.

Like any form of group practice, HMOs can utilize allied health personnel and expensive equipment more effectively than a physician in solo practice. This is an attribute to all groups, not just prepaid groups. Many advantages exist for group practice. Prepaid group practice in the United States is a minuscule part of all group practice. Although by 1969 there were over 6,000 group practices, employing 18 percent of active, nonfederal physicians, only 85 of the 6,000 groups had more than half of their business in prepayment plans. By 1975 there were almost 8,500 groups employing 24 percent of all active, nonfederal physicians, but only 142 groups earned 50 percent or more of their gross income from prepaid practice.

Lack of marketing experience has been costly to many HMOs. Individuals who have established satisfactory physician-patient relationships do not tend to join a group practice that will break up that relationship. Young, highly mobile individuals are more likely to enroll in group practice. A survey made in 1973 in Rochester, New York, indicates that economic reasoning dominated the decision not to join prepaid groups: "Two thirds of the non-joiners gave high cost as a reason for not joining."[53] In other words, healthy individuals are reluctant to commit sizeable, monthly amounts for a service that may benefit them only far in the future. Noneconomic reasons, "greater access, availability, comprehensiveness" and the promise of 24-hour availability (which is important to parents who travel), dominated the choice of the joiners for the new, prepaid groups in Rochester.

There is no conclusive evidence that HMOs can provide the same quality of care at lower prices than other groups or FFS practice to all persons, not primarily employed persons. Subscribers to HMOs are mainly people who work, as well as their families. Employed persons are at least healthy enough to hold down a job. It is the sick person, one who is not completely well and who has difficulty working full-time, who is the high user of medical care. These persons are underrepresented in HMOs. To the degree that dependents of employed persons are not as healthy as the employed person, the argument of self-selection of the more healthy into HMOs is somewhat weakened. Some HMOs have provided Medicaid patients care at lesser per capita cost than FFS. The high percentage of fraud and abuse in Medicaid may account for some of this differential, and differences in quality of care for another part.

FTC officials speculate that HMOs, encouraged by HEW's guidelines of November 1977, will likely increase in number and impact in the coming years. Thus competition for patients will help hold down costs in the FFS sector. Yet by early 1979 only 88 of 203 HMOs qualified for government loans. Although enrollment in HMOs increased 14 percent in 1978 over 1977, as reported by Inter-Study, the year-end total enrollment was 7.4 million, of which 47 percent were in the six Kaiser plans. Kaiser HMOs were well established prior to legislation. Their success may be due to their in-house availability of large amounts of start-up monies; that initially the company's employees had no access to other health care providers; and to very competent management, which has enabled Kaiser to earn capital to invest in their own hospitals.

If HMOs are to cut costs through less hospital utilization, they need to own or control a hospital. Many towns believe that if they have no hospital, they lack status and therefore are unwilling to sell an existing hospital. Health Systems Agencies (HSAs), created by the federal government, require a hearing to demonstrate a need for more beds in a given geographical are. Because of government regulation, a certificate-of-need must be obtained before one can build a hospital, add to an existing hospital, or purchase expensive equipment. Hospitals compete on the basis of the range of services they offer and their expensive, high technology equipment that attracts prestigious staff. Competition among hospitals is not price competition; indeed, with over 90 percent of their bills met by third parties, it need not be. The closing of a hospital was almost unheard of until the late 1970s. Even though some hospitals made no money and many had a bed occupancy below 50 percent during price controls 1971–74, these hospitals stayed open.

Decisions about whether to permit hospital expansion are often political. Government regulation by HSAs and reimbursement rules under Medicare prevent new capital to be used for better quality hospital beds and equipment, while at the same time government continues to reimburse costs of older, failing hospitals whose occupancy rates may be below 50 percent, thus shoring them up against failure. The normal shrinkage of obsolete capital does not occur.

Established hospital beds, whether occupied or not, require continuing financial support. Local tension among hospital administrators and physicians is being created by decisions about who is to pay for an increasing number of empty, standby beds, or which beds are to be phased out. The National Institute of Medicine estimates that in the late 1970s there were 100,000 excess beds.[54]

The growth in subscribers of HMOs from 2 percent to 10 percent of the population in seven years[55] in Minneapolis and St. Paul is often cited as indicative of future trends. One reason for a recent spurt in growth has been the 1976 legislation that relieved HMOs from providing many expensive kinds of benefits required by 1973 legislation and which private insurance plans do not usually provide. In addition, there has been a tremendous increase in the percentage of physicians who are specialists and who find that there are not enough referrals from primary care physicians to keep them busy practicing only their specialty. In 1940 77 percent of all "patient care physicians" were general practitioners and 24 percent were specialists, but by 1975 the distribution was reversed to 17 percent and 83 percent, respectively.[56] By joining a group, physicians may increase their referral practice because their colleagues will refer their patients to them rather than those outside the group.

Established HMOs, such as the Kaiser-Permanente groups, are still flourishing. The Group Health Cooperative of Puget Sound, Washington, a successful 31-year-old HMO, has bought the first federally funded model HMO, Sound Health Association. However, a part must also have been played by the competition of the four-year-old United Healthcare Plan, organized by Safeco Insurance Company, an unique open-panel IPA of 610 primary care physicians that uses tighter control over referrals to specialists and hospital use than is customary even in most closed panels. Each primary care physician, including pediatricians and internists, is rewarded for keeping costs low by receiving one-half of any surplus in the account of any patient for whom he is the financial medical manager and penalized 5 percent of the capitation fee and 10 percent of an FFS, if there is a deficit. Unlike the usual IPA, " . . . the accounts and incentives are kept at the individual primary-care physician level, [and] his accountability is not diluted among any group of doctors, not even among the partners in group practice."[57] Thus there is no dilution of a physician's savings as exists in the usual IPA. The primary-care physician is paid to manage the financing of specialist care, but also "More problems are managed initially by the Primary Care Physician without the need for referral to specialists."[58] It is unknown to what degree the latter reduces quality of care.* However, it is unlikely that the majority of patients of this IPA fully understand the cost-containment system under which these physicians work and the potential impact of its incentive system. Prepaid group practice does not replace FFS practice in the eyes of all consumers. Prepaid group practice, which uses multiphasic screening to separate the sick from the worried well, does not usually provide for the worried well to see a physician. Some prepaid groups use other than physicians for 25 percent or more of ambulatory visits. Although this is cost-effective, it may be at a sacrifice of satisfactory patient-physician relationships.

The economic climate of the 1970s also discouraged growth of HMOs. In any inflationary period:

> A prepaid group has the disadvantage of a fixed monthly income, whereas a fee-for-service group has a steadily increasing income resulting from an increasing number of services sold in response to rising demand and at higher prices. Thus, one would expect prepaid groups to increase during deflation and fee-for-service groups to increase during inflation. In recent years, inflation has created a more favorable climate for fee-for service groups than per capita groups.[59]

Difficulties of the newer HMOs may stem from lack of available administrative talent, especially in the marketing area. This need is partially met by the more experienced "Blues," commercial insurers, and large companies that pay health insurance premiums. The requirement of community rating rather than experience rating the per capita

*There is inhouse review to find any substandard care, and two physicians are on probation, as of writing.

charge of HMOs to qualify for a federal loan does not encourage many large firms to supply management and promotion expertise to new HMOs, unless the company has a large percentage of all workers in the geographical area being served. It is claimed that if several HMOs form in a community and in total penetrate the market by 20 percent, they will offer sufficient competition to FFS providers to restrain increases in the level of fees and possibly utilization of hospital days, as well.

The largest HMO, Kaiser-Permanente, is concentrated in the Far West with "substantial market penetration in Seattle, Portland, San Francisco, Los Angeles, and Honolulu." It is claimed that they have "brought about a positive response from the predominant fee-for-service sector."[60] But physician fees are among comparable urban populations, the highest in Los Angeles and New York City, where the large prepaid group, the Health Insurance Plan (HIP) dominates.* Thus, there is a need to document whether HMOs do by competition lower the fees of physicians who are not in HMOs. More data is also needed to establish clearly whether HMOs substitute more office visits for in-hospital patient care.

Large companies, such as General Motors, which pays 1.3 billion dollars annually for medical care premiums for its employees, encourage employees to become members of hospital boards, insurance company boards, and boards of Blue Cross and Blue Shield. General Motors holds seminars for these individuals in order "to help them become expert at asking what and why." After 25 years' experience with HMOs, the vice-chairman of General Motors states, "It seems to us that group practice is not for everyone . . . We hope that it will grow and become an economical alternative to the traditional health care delivery system."[61]

Other Competitive Approaches. Because prepaid group practice has experienced slow growth, has contained costs mainly via lesser use of hospital days, rather than via lower fees charged by other providers, it is desirable to look at other complementary and alternative methods of increasing competition in health care. I have already discussed the increased latitude for professionals to advertise and potential changes in licensure boards which govern entry across the spectrum of occupations in health care. Additionally, the use of ambulatory surgi-centers serves to increase competition because they save dollar costs of the payer, as

*According to Zachary Dyckman, "The most noticeable difference from the undeflated [by cost-of-living] conversion factors is that surgical fees are no longer highest in New York, but in Los Angeles . . . Deflated conversion factors are higher in several localities in California than they are in the New York City area." (*A Study of Physicians' Fees*, Council on Wage and Price Stability, March 1978, p. 101.)

well as time costs of the patient. There are also an increasing number of clinics which offer alternatives to traditional practice. Some clinics specialize in management of specific symptoms of ill health by methods not traditionally used by physicians, such as biofeedback for stress-related disorders, and acupuncture. By the end of the 1970s, biofeedback had already received acceptance by a large number of physicians. Both inside and outside the traditional medical structure, abortion clinics have multiplied. Other clinics are built around relief of a single problem, such as management of pain. Geriatric clinics treat persons of a particular age-group. Ambulatory mental health centers treat persons who have a particular set of disorders.

For centuries, many persons have traveled to health spas to take the medicinal waters, which were, in many instances, substitutes for medical care. In the 1980s persons will also use spas, attend encounter sessions, other types of therapy groups, weight-reducing clinics, and clinics to stop smoking. Substitutes for medical care are myriad and include self-help books, which have multiplied in number of titles and copies sold, over-the-counter or nonprescription drugs, vitamins, and numerous health foods. Some individuals will combine traditional and nontraditional health care into their own personalized packages.

The Occupational Safety and Health Administration (OSHA) agency and environmental concerns have blurred the distinction between so-called occupational medicine and personal medicine. In most large companies, medical care is offered to employees only for treatment of accidents and disease related to the workplace. Increasingly, it is recognized that occupational disease may be more widespread than was believed. A few companies provide in-house, primary medical care for all health problems of their employees and even fewer provide in-house specialists' care. Of these, a small number also provide coverage for their employees' dependents. Some company plans have been accepted as a desirable fringe benefit, which increases employee loyalty to the company; others view such a plan as an intrusion of employee privacy. Trust, and therefore success, depends primarily on the administrator of the company plan.

This type of medical care in a company can act as an alternative for employees, but not usually for their dependents. It, therefore, cannot substitute entirely for fee-for-service medicine or an HMO. The latter provides comprehensive care for all members of the family if they so desire, and usually near their place of residence, rather than at the workplace of the employee. However, one argument sometimes expressed by fee-for-service physicians in the area where a company's complete primary care plan operates is that this is unfair competition. Is it possible that a complete primary care plan of a large company will keep physicians' fees lower in a given geographical area than they would otherwise be?

Catastrophic Expense

A third major national policy option debated in Congress for many years is government-financed or government-sponsored catastrophic or major medical, health insurance coverage for all persons. The main argument for this type of insurance is that everyone, including those who are working or have any source of income, dread the often unexpected, large treatment costs of a chronic disease, such as cancer, kidney failure, or injuries from a severe accident. The permissible deduction from federal income taxes of those medical expenses above 3 percent of adjustable gross income does not help persons who pay no income tax, but does help those with higher incomes. In 1970, this medical deduction, plus the exclusion from taxes of health insurance premiums paid by employers and the $150 individual itemized deduction for health insurance premiums, equaled an indirect subsidy of $4.4 billion.[62] Yet "six percent of all taxpayers had remaining out-of-pocket medical expenses exceeding 10 percent of their income in 1970."[63] By 1979 this subsidy had increased to $13 billion.[64]

A line of demarcation between high health expenses and catastrophic medical expenses is hard to draw, whether expense is defined in terms of total dollars spent out-of-pocket (costs above payments by third parties) or as a percent of income spent out-of-pocket. The insurance concept of catastrophic expense as it is being debated in Congress implies that persons have the means to pay routine medical care expenses, either by other insurance, or from a high income or large assets. Some young, healthy persons may purposely avoid first-dollar insurance coverage as a self-perceived waste of their money and utilize preventive care as a partial substitute.

Persons covered by Medicaid have virtually complete catastrophic coverage in most states. Under Medicare, individuals pay a deductible equal to one hospital day of charges, receive 60 hospital days without payment, and then for the sixty-first through the ninetieth day, pay 20 percent, and after the ninetieth day, 100 percent. They have only a limited form of catastrophic insurance. Part B of Medicare reimburses physicians, again after a deductible, but many physicians charge more than the reimbursed amount.

By 1977, 147 million persons had some form of private major-medical coverage and an additional 7 million had such coverage under prepaid groups. This is almost one-half the population. Most of the premiums for private catastrophic coverage are paid for by employers. Unless the tax laws change, private major-medical insurance will grow.

Private, major medical plans have dollar deductibles of $300 to $2,000, a continuous cost-corridor, and an overall lifetime limit, some as high as one million dollars. Even with these restraints, costs higher than the insurer anticipates may occur. Insurers are imposing their own standards of "reasonable and customary" charges in a given area. Thus in periods of rapidly rising prices protection of the privately insured is decreasing as is that of those under Medicare. This result becomes an argument for government involvement in catastrophic health insurance protection.

Many of the private plans, including those of HMOs, exclude some types of health care, such as unlimited ambulatory mental health services and nursing home care, which each alone can account for extraordinary expenses. However, most proposed national legislation also does not cover these items.

Fortunately, about 75 percent of all hospital stays are less than 10 days. More than 90 percent of hospital stays end before 30 days, and less than 1 percent exceed 100 days.[65]

Catastrophic expense insurance applies only to those amounts which the individual pays. If a $5,000 deductible is used, about 2.5 million non-institutionalized persons would exceed that amount; if $2,500, about 7 million. With lower deductibles, the persons affected rise rapidly; there are 20 million, or about 10 percent of that population with total annual medical expenses over $1,000.[66] In fiscal year 1978, 7 million families had out-of-pocket medical expenses above 15 percent of their gross income, while if their total health expenditures were used, the number of families would be about 20 million. Government benefits based on percent of income, rather than dollar amounts spent will, if tax financing remains the same, redistribute income to the poor. The 15 percent of income appears to be more liberal than a $5,000 requirement. On the basis of the Congressional Budget Office (CBO) estimates used here, the 15 percent cutoff is comparable to an absolute dollar amount of $2,500.[67]

A major argument against mandating any type of national catastrophic health insurance or provision for it by employers is that it rewards overutilization of expensive technology, once the deductible is spent and that, therefore, the most expensive equipment will be commonly used to keep persons alive, some in a state of a "living death" at high dollar and emotional costs to them and their families; and also, at health care costs higher than otherwise to the taxpayer. The federal government's experience with the pilot, catastrophic expense coverage of kidney dialysis and transplants, effective July 1, 1973, points to the rapid growth of providers, a switchover from less expensive home dialysis to more expensive hospital dialysis, and other cost-increasing trends that forced legislative amendments in 1978 to control costs. Because the program enacted in 1972 permitted patients using hospital dialysis rather than home dialysis to pay less dollars out-of-pocket, home dialysis patients dropped in a 5-year period from 40 percent to 10 percent of the treated population. Home dialysis is far less expensive. In April 1974 HEW estimated the first-year costs of this program at $240 million. The total cost of the program in 1979 was over one billion dollars annually for 40,000 patients. Until the legislation was amended, costs were expected to reach $6 billion for 75,000 patients by 1992.

This experience clearly points to a problem of containing costs when all catastrophic expenses are paid after a deductible, even with a cost-corridor. Therefore, proposals for a sizeable cost-corridor or other forms of copayment can be expected to be included in such plans. Even if copayments do not substantially restrain demand, they cut government's expense by the amount the consumer pays under a government plan. In all tax-supported government health programs, abuse and fraud of substantial amounts have been reported. One estimate is as high as $1 for every $6 spent on health care.[68] There is no reason to believe that any new program will be an exception. Development of methods to reduce fraud is needed.

Costs of any new government catastrophic health insurance program are estimated to be several billion dollars additional per year. Senators John Danforth, Robert Dole, and Pete Domenici introduced a bill (S. 748) in March 1979 that would provide coverage for all out-of-pocket payments above 15 percent of family income. The sponsors estimate that it would cost the government about $3 billion in the first year. Revenues to finance these costs are to be raised by a tax increase of 10¢ per package of cigarettes (S. 801). The proposal is based on a user-tax rationale: smokers will require higher catastrophic health expenses on the average than nonsmokers.

The Carter administration would mandate minimum catastrophic expense coverage to be paid for by employers. For employers who do not already pay for such insurance this would, under the tax laws of 1979, increase their payroll taxes for that part of the costs above the reduction in their corporate profit taxes resulting from expensing larger premiums. To increase employers' payroll taxes at the beginning of the 1980s even more than the 1977 social security amendments already require will depress the economy. Employers shift payroll taxes forward in the form of higher prices, thus fueling the already existing inflation. In some instances employers will in the short run adjust to higher payroll taxes by reducing the number of employees. This will increase unemployment. Alternative forms of financing are possible, but space limitations do not permit in-depth analysis of them.

Whether one supports catastrophic medical expense coverage for all depends on how it is financed and one's value judgments. What are its potential benefits in an equity sense of the well paying for medical care of the very ill? Can employers substitute premiums for catastrophic health insurance for some part of the health insurance premiums which they already pay, by increasing the copayment for which the consumer is responsible? Can cost containment through consumer education, living wills, and other measures offset the technological imperative to keep terminal patients alive by artificial means even when, given the current state of technology, they have no hope of recovery? Patients have always had the right to refuse treatment, but in an increasing number of cases, patients can become comatose before they have made a decision. Nine states have passed living-will laws to give individuals greater control over whether or not they want extreme life-support measures used to prolong their lives. The legislatures of 27 additional states have similar bills on their agendas. The 1980s will see an increase in legislation of this type.

In this debate, my value judgments are that the well should pay in part at least for catastrophic expense of the very ill. This judgment does not, however, rule out concomitant use of the tax system to decrease unhealthy habits, cost-effective measures to encourage prevention of disease and accidents and to improve audit of government spending. The growth of courses on medical ethics in medical schools is encouraging, as is the increasing number of courses at all levels of university education on the economics of health.

Comprehensive National Health Insurance

Almost all of the traditional, explicit arguments for compulsory comprehensive national health insurance have already been discussed and many rebutted. The major ones are:

1) The poor do not have access to adequate medical care
2) Prices are high, partly because medical care markets are not competitive and consumers are ignorant about services they purchase, and partly because of the costs of government regulation
3) Private health insurance markets do not eliminate for everyone the potential risk of financial hardship of catastrophic expense, nor do

> they cover the unemployed, or provide coverage at reasonable fees for those individuals not in groups, such as the self-employed.

Implicit is that the well, because they are able to work, have higher incomes; they, like all high-income persons, should pay through taxes for care of the unwell, and for part of the medical training costs involved in teaching hospitals. Although there is some evidence that substitution of interns' and residents' cheaper labor for established physicians' more expensive labor offset training costs in terms of loss of quality and price of training, there is not agreement on this matter.

Proponents of national health insurance can be divided into two major groups: those who would concomitantly seek to control costs of medical care by restructuring the organization of delivery to favor HMOs, and those who do not seek also to restructure the medical care delivery system. Proponents and opponents alike seek to contain costs by reducing fraud and abuse in existing government health programs, by increasing competition among suppliers and also by reducing demand through consumer education about the limits of medical care in maintaining or improving personal health. Most also encourage advertising, use of private insurers as fiscal intermediaries, and would require all companies of a given size to provide health insurance benefits for their employees and their dependents.

Individuals differ about the effectiveness of prospective, negotiated fees and of government and quasi-government reimbursement controls to contain costs. Although all agree that the total costs spent for health especially for ambulatory medical care will increase under any new federal government health-financing plan, there is considerable disagreement about the level of future costs of any specific plan. Estimates of amounts are not given here because the benefit packages and their financing change as compromises are sought in Congressional committees. Political tradeoffs are made. Probably the only clear-cut statement about future costs that can be made, and is supported by experience, is that all such estimates are always below the actual costs.

Compulsory national health insurance does not mean, as it is proposed and being discussed in the United States, that government will provide health care services but rather, the government will finance personal health care services in addition to the 40 percent which they already do finance under various government programs. To compel employers to pay for a mandated, benefit package is in essence to increase payroll taxes, which Social Security already requires. Opponents stress that if government pays for all costs of all medical care for everyone, then price cannot allocate medical care. Other methods, such as waiting, which already plays a role in rationing medical care, and administrative rules will fill this role.

Even the most ardent proponents of comprehensive health insurance leave out some health care benefits, most notably in the areas of mental health and nursing-home care. Mental health costs are very unpredictable, and nursing-home care as life expectancy increases have become per person exceedingly high. Dental care, except for children, and prescription drugs, except for the chronically ill (and then only drugs on a list or formulary), are also usually not included.

Opponents of national health insurance point out that the federal budget is in deficit, and any new program which requires additional billions of tax dollars is primarily a redistribution of income program.

> In 1975 the *lower one-half* of the population (persons with adjusted gross incomes of $8,930 or less) paid 7.1% of total federal personal income taxes, while 55% was paid by the top 5% of the population (persons with adjusted income of $29,272 or more). Obviously, if more than half the people and I say more than half because these are *adjusted* income figures, pay only 7% of the federal personal income taxes, any national program that needs more tax money is, above all else, a program to redistribute income. The taxpayers' revolt indicates that those persons in the upper one-fourth of the population (those with adjusted gross incomes of $15,898 or more) who pay 72% of total federal personal income taxes will not support an expensive, compulsory national health insurance program.[69]

Although legislative bill numbers and sponsors of various types of health insurance bills may change over the years, the issues will not. Not all the data are available to answer such questions as: What effects do deductibles and cost-corridors have on demand for different types of medical services? To what degree do physicians control demand for medical care, including x-rays, tests, office visits, hospital days, and drugs? With rapidly rising costs due in large measure to new, expensive medical technology, and incentives structured for most providers not to save money, but rather to spend and compete on a status basis, does regulation have a place? Will membership of HMOs increase sufficiently to provide effective price competition to physicians who charge patients, a fee-for-service, whether in group or solo practice? Can demand for medical care be restrained by educating consumers and also physicians about the cost-effectiveness among medical procedures, about preventive methods and substitutes for medical care? Does the American public acknowledge that waiting as well as price is already allocating medical care? Would the public accept the explicit rationing rules such as those of the British National Health Service (NHS) in place of existing, implicit rationing?

For example, kidney dialysis and transplants are not available after age 50 under the NHS. The American public is likely to reject this type of allocation by regulation, but they have already accepted some degree of allocation by government induced decrease in supply and by waiting. The method of determining who gets what and when is important because whenever resources are scarce, there has to be some method of rationing the items in short supply. Within the United States, 1974 law established Health Systems Agencies, which by denial of certificates disapprove building new hospital beds and purchasing expensive medical equipment. This method implicitly rations by reducing supply, a system the British have followed for years. Rationing by age and by the type and value of a person's work has been used in some countries when the waiting lists become long. Other less obvious forms, including allowing no pain killer for routine childbirth and dental care, are also used, but are less effective. If medical care is viewed as a right, different from all other goods and services, and that by some magic everyone is entitled to unlimited quantities of the best, costs cannot be controlled. There is a growing movement to educate and to deregulate and use tax revenues to give the poor cash vouchers with which they can directly purchase medical care or medical insurance.

Prevention and Consumer Health Education

"It is recognized today that the individual's state of health or illness is a continuum, ranging from optimum adaptation to environment and no disease to maladaptation with various levels of disease. This concept puts stress on prevention and early detection of disease—as well as on the care of symptoms and, if possible, rehabilitation.[70]

Because of shortages of natural resources, medical care has treated primarily symptoms except for a few proven methods of preventive care, such as vaccines and immunization against such diseases as polio and diphtheria and the prophylactic use of some drugs.

Recently, screening for early presymptomatic disease, followed by health education, has been proposed as a method of delaying symptomatic disease, increasing the quality of life, and even prolonging life. Screening for a specific disease among older persons may be cost-effective if the disease is relatively common, if it can be effectively treated, and if persons take the treatment. Screening of infants at birth for hypothyroidism at an incremental cost of one dollar per infant (over costs of screening for all amino acid metabolism disorders) also is cost-effective because medical follow-up is assured, and medical treatment is virtually assured to prevent otherwise ensuing mental retardation.

But these examples may be representative of exceptions to a general rule. Screening for many other specific diseases has not been cost-effective, even when directed at targeted populations that are most at risk. This is because at the beginning of the 1980s not all diseases can be effectively treated, follow-up medical care cannot be always assured, and there are often reported a large number of "false positives," which indicate that persons have a disease that they do not have. This creates anxiety and the need for retesting. The anxiety costs from false positives can transform an otherwise positive benefit into a negative benefit. Sometimes when follow-up care is given, the lifetime costs are higher than otherwise would have occurred without early screening; benefits from improvement in morbidity and mortality may or may not offset these higher costs.

The technique of screening for prevention may be oversold. For example, the "pap smear" is used to detect cervical cancer, a disease of relatively low incidence. Those most at risk (those with multiple sexual partners) are not usually screened, and no decline in deaths from cervical cancer in the non-targeted population, which has been screened can be documented.[71] The pap smear generally detects a precursor to a type of cancer that takes at least 15 years to develop. Screening for cervical cancer has also turned up many "false negatives." These give a false belief to persons who have been screened that they are well. On the other hand, some researchers maintain that annual screening for cervical cancer "can reduce the incidence and mortality rates of invasive cervical cancer."[72]

Screening targeted population groups for genetic disease has had some success. For example, tests are made to detect the probability of Tays Sachs disease occurring in future births to women at risk and for pregnant women at high risk. This is a severely disabling disease for which there is no treatment, and which leads to early death of the child.

Screening is a viable technique to allocate, but only in part, scarce medical resources. Consumers at entry to the medical care system can be given a battery of tests by a paramedical staff under physician direction. This method is used primarily by Kaiser-Permanente and other prepaid groups to direct only the sick to the physician, and to direct other persons as the worried well to health education personnel.

This is not a technique accepted by all physicians. Its importance to the economist is that because of the size of third-party payments, price does not allocate medical care. Because resources are scarce in relation to wants, some method of allocation is needed. "Waiting," which is a form of price, and regulations can also allocate medical care.

Whether multiphasic screening allocates scarce resources optimally in relation to medical need is still being debated. The larger the number of tests, the greater their costs and there is no agreement for every test about which criteria indicate abnormalities that need treatment.

Kaiser-Permanente after a one-year trial in Oakland, California, states that screening to sort new patients has "achieved increased physician accessibility to new patients by 20 times, reduced the waiting time for new appointments from 6 to 8 weeks to a day or two, saved physician time and costs for entry work-up by 70 to 80 percent, reduced total resources used throughout the year by $32,500 per 1,000 entrants, and proved very satisfactory to patients and generally so to staff."[73] Although Kaiser's method saves money—"one physician can adequately supervise nine nurse practitioners in the health-evaluation service," their "Medical Department physicians . . . were equally divided" about preferring the traditional or the new entry system.[74] Although the patients were happier than the physicians about multiphasic entry screening, it is possible that some Kaiser physicians believe that quality may suffer or that their workload has been changed unfavorably because of triage by nonphysicians, to sort the sick from the worried well. It is also revealing in respect to quality that the first time a patient sees a physician, the appointment is scheduled for only 30 minutes.[75]

Some believe that there should be mass screening to detect specific asymptomatic disease in its early stages, such as hypertension, which is very common. However, "there is no hard evidence that any therapy will change the natural history of the disease"[76] and adherence to prescribed therapy is low. There is also some evidence that asymptomatic persons labeled as hypertensive have a diminished feeling of well-being, and may even increase significantly their number of days absent from work.[77] Government policy to encourage mass screening for this disease seems unwise given the information available at the beginning of the 1980s.

Some argue that health education of the consumer can be used to change life styles so that mortality and morbidity outcomes will improve. There is increasing evidence to support this. Mortality from heart disease, the leading cause of death in the United States, has declined over 20 percent since the mid-1960s, while in Sweden and in some countries behind the Iron Curtain there has been an upturn in heart disease deaths for males.

It is not clear what part of the decline in the United States can be attributed to a change in life-style, more exercise, less smoking, lower weight, decrease in Type A personality, or possibly less job-related stress because both spouses work. Not all of the decline is usually attributed to better medical care immediately after a heart attack, but better medical care has contributed to the decline. Among suggestive data is an earlier decline in terminal myocardial infarctions in California than in the United States as a whole. Both jogging and biofeedback relaxation techniques are identified with the California life-style. Although fatal heart attacks have declined, there is no definitive data over a given period of time on the incidence of nonfatal heart attacks. If these too have declined, it would be clear that the individual's way of life, through prevention, plays an important role in decreasing cardiovascular illness. If nonfatal heart attacks have increased, the role of better medical care would be the more important factor than health education and prevention in explaining the recent decline in mortality due to heart attack.

As early as 1952 there was testimony in the Senate that "there is evidence which suggests that, dollar for dollar, spending on visits to doctors and on drugs may not be as effective in increasng the health of low-income groups as spending on housing and food."[78] Almost thirty years have passed and evidence to support the above has accumulated, despite the slow growth of nutrition as an accepted science. Patient education is being performed in the physicians' offices, hospitals, clinics, and schools. But the media and especially television have had a greater impact through spots, regularly scheduled question and answer programs with a physician-expert, and story lines with medical content. "Personal behavioral decisions, such as smoking and dietary patterns, appear to have dramatic effects on health and mortality. Public policy appears to be better directed toward inducement of such health-producing behavior than inducement of further medical preventive procedures."[79]

Many large companies that self-insure health benefits and have in-house education programs to change health-related ways of living—smoking, nutrition, and exercising—also believe in long-run cost containment from such programs. Such companies often provide in-house physical fitness facilities. However, as life expectancy at age 65 increases, economic adjustments and increased costs can be anticipated. It is important for companies and individuals to review their retirement plans.

PROBABLE DIRECTION OF THE 1980s

Cost containment was the primary problem of the 1970s. I foresee two probable developments during the 1980s, neither of which will successfully contain costs. One is continuance of present financial arrangements, small growth of HMOs, and increased government regulation. Those who continue to support costly government regulation of new capital health expenditures argue that otherwise medical technology will snowball needlessly under third-party payments. Although reduction of the level of percentage reimbursed of bills for medical care would be a more rational restraint on costs because it would reduce demand, this does not seem politically feasible unless catastrophic health insurance coverage is used as a tradeoff.

The other route involves an increase in all facets of competitive marketing, with big business and possibly trade unions taking the lead as counterweights to control increases in costs of medical care and health insurance premiums. The most effective act of large companies to control health care costs may be the use of their buying power leverage in negotiating health insurance premiums for specific benefit packages and also directly, prices charged by providers of care, such as HMOs and hospitals. Additionally, companies can increase through active programs the number of HMOs and also make available accurate information about health care through employee newsletters.

On the supply side, industry should recognize that a major cause of high costs is "the complex of perverse incentives inherent in our dominant financing system for health care . . . that rewards providers of care with more revenue for giving more and more costly care, whether or not more is necessary or beneficial to the patient."[80] If employers pay the lowest available alternative among health insurance premiums and HMOs per capita charges for a given set of benefits, the employee selecting more costly financial arrangements would pay the excess. If employers follow this route, then they have a responsibility to give full information about the low cost alternative which they select, including what the arrangements are for review of quality and the rules to reduce the percentage reimbursed if providers are claimed to overcharge. It is desirable that employers also provide information about the alternatives for which they do not fully pay.

There will be more involvement of consumers in their own health care. If these directions are successful there will be a gradual deregulation of the health industry, now overregulated by government, and an increase in competition. Either route is likely to be accompanied by short-run cost increases, but the second route holds out greater promise for long-run cost containment.

Some observers view expenditures on cost-effective preventive care to be limited in the near future. But Blue Cross, Blue Shield, and the federal government believe that though there is not an immediate payoff from consumer health education and preventive medicine, that a cost-containment effect will occur in the not-too-distant future. For example, Blue Cross has been exploring the possibility of marketing cancer-screening insurance policies. Such policies would cover costs of primary prevention through health education, screening for early pre-symptomatic treatable cancer, and finance follow-up medical care. Their goal is to detect treatable cancer while it is still localized and has not yet spread to other parts of the body. Although there is currently no cure for cancer, long remissions of leukemia and Hodgkin's disease can occur, and are sometimes assessed as cures. The purpose of this screening is to control the spread of cancer and to induce such remissions. Whether such screening insurance is cost-effective depends partly on whether the patient delays in seeking definitive diagnosis and treatment and partly on the availability of effective treatment. Such insurance policies are likely to be marketed primarily to middle- and high-income persons who appear to be at lesser risk to cancer than low-income, low-occupational status persons.

Detection of cancer-inducing environmental factors and food additives is also part of prevention. There is need, however, to quantify the probability of risk from all sources and then to select rationally how government monies should be allocated for the greatest payoff per dollar spent. Cost-effective preventive health measures will be sought and implemented by the government and private parties in many areas during the 1980s.

It is likely that the only increase in government insurance during the next decade will be to cover catastrophic expenses of medical care, a proposal which has been debated for several decades.

In the 1980s, competition among suppliers will increase. The FTC's efforts of the late 1970s and early 1980s will increase acceptance that medical care is a service much like other services. This will be despite physician protests against a commodity view of medicine. More information will become available to those consumers who seek it. Books and articles on various aspects of health care will be widely distributed. As HMOs increasingly use triage by multiphasic screening to sort out the worried well, fewer consumers will see physicians nor expect to see physicians when they perceive themselves to be ill.

Consumers will seek information, compare, and shop around. Two recent articles support the contention that individuals in the 1970s "shopped for medical services as they did for other commodities and that they are showing more discrimination in their choices than evidenced in the past."[81]

As government regulation and government control over financing of health care has increased, the problem of protecting the patient's privacy increased. When federal and state governments pay for the delivery of medical care, they bear a responsibility to assure that they are getting their money's worth. Computer records of utilization and costs by provider and patient are kept by hospitals, clinics, and group practices in order to provide more easily the government and other third-party payers the information requested before making payment. Many patients' health records are thus likely to be in a computer data bank, and relatively few will remain in the files of a physician in solo practice, who may not use a computer. However, patients in many states do not have a "general right to see their own records, either before the data is released to third parties or as a matter of patient interest during regular care."[82]

The author concurs with the *Report of the Project on Medical Records and Citizen Rights* that:

> As a general matter, patients should have a right to full information about their health conditions. Where health data is to be used to make judgments about service payment and claims, or in any non-medical social and governmental programs, the individual should have an absolute right to inspect what is to be released from his/her record. In chronic and acute care, patients should also have a right to see any part of the medical record, including the medical professional's working notes, if they insist upon this after the medical professional has had a chance to explain directly to the patient why he or she feels that such disclosure would not be in the patient's best medical interest. A special procedure is suggested for patient-access problems in psychiatric care.[83]

AUTHOR'S RECOMMENDATIONS

1) Of the recommendations that follow, the most important is education of consumers about what medical care can and cannot do, and about what they can do to improve their own health. More dissemination of information through advertising; directories of physicians by specialties, and of hospitals with representative charges, staffs, and tertiary care specialists are needed. Most public libraries purchase the national directories of physicians by specialties and manufacturers' descriptions (FDA approved) of prescription drugs, which intelligent consumers can use. But most persons apparently do not know about these informational sources. There is also a need for new compilations about HMOs, hospitals, nursing homes, health insurance benefits, and alternative medical technologies, written in language consumers can understand.

Unless consumers are knowledgeable about what they buy, the market cannot approach a competitive market.

2) Certification should replace licensing of all allied health manpower jobs. The majority of any licensing board should not consist of either those persons who already hold that license or those practicing an occupation competitive with the one being licensed. Substitution for physicians and dentists by less expensively-trained personnel should be encouraged through direct reimbursement to them by third-party payers. Then those who wish to can work independently of an employer, and consumers who wish to purchase less expensive and lesser quality care can do so. Reimbursement to these certified persons would be at a lesser rate than if the physician or dentist had performed the task. When group practices and hospitals submit charges for work done by lesser-trained persons, their accounts should indicate it and reimbursement should be made at the lower prices.
3) Federal and state governments should encourage growth of new HMOs, profit and nonprofit, through loans for start-up capital costs, but with legal assurances of repayment. Quality controls within HMOs remain a problem. Business, through its established Washington Business Group on Health and similar groups organized to combat the runaway costs of their health benefit plans could contribute specialized knowledge in the areas of effective quality controls and cost containment.
4) Elimination of 90 percent of the fraud and abuse in existing government programs is necessary. To eliminate the other 10 percent might cost more than it is worth.
5) Medicaid and Medicare should be retained, but with some modifications. Data indicate that introduction of small copayments among Medicaid patients may reduce ambulatory care but increase inpatient hospital care. Further research is needed. Copayments among other income groups reduce demand. Insurance coverage for out of hospital surgicenters and health care received at home should be more widely available.
6) The federal government should require all employers who have more than a minimum number of employees to provide some form of catastrophic health expense coverage for their employees and dependents. This should not be enacted until abuse in existing government programs has been virtually eliminated. To help pay for these premiums, companies might increase the existing size of the deductible and/or the cost corridor in their health plans or in-

troduce new ones. Unions will fight this, but if the United Auto Workers are willing to discuss this, and they were in 1979, then other unions should. Government and private catastrophic health insurance by disease category, kidney disease and cancer, should be replaced by general catastrophic health insurance.

7) For those who are self-employed or otherwise uncovered by private and government plans, a minimum level of catastrophic expense benefits, government-determined, should be made available by insurers who bid competitively on the benefit package.

8) The federal government should limit the level of health insurance premiums that employers can continue to expense and which employees also do not count as income. This is an open-ended subsidy which distorts consumer spending and allocation of resources.

9) Congress should, after debate, spell out the meaning of the requirement of "substantial evidence" of efficacy to market a new drug or remove efficacy as a criterion. Knowledgeable and rich Americans can now obtain proven beneficial drugs from abroad, while the poor can not.

10) Deregulation, rather than increases in regulation, is desirable. The experience of the health sector with price control and its aftermath should discourage any new attempts in this direction. FTC antitrust actions should continue, but with political discretion in view of changing court interpretations of permissible antitrust action in nonprofit industry and the insurance sector. Only as the markets become more competitive can deregulation occur without undue price increases.

NOTES

1. *Report of the Committee of Enquiry into the Cost of National Health Service* (Guilleband Report), Her Majesty's Stationery Office, London, 1965, p. 50.

2. *Congressional Quarterly*, March 17, 1979, p. 463, Council on Environmental Quality estimate.

3. Harry S. Truman, *Memoirs: Years of Trial and Hope*, vol. II (New York: Doubleday, 1956), p. 23.

4. R. R. Campbell and W. G. Campbell, "Compulsory Health Insurance: The Economic Issues," *Quarterly Journal of Economics* 66 (1952); R. R. Campbell and W. G. Campbell, "Reply," *Quarterly Journal of Economics* 67 (1953): 126. "and the large, unexpected non-recurring expenses for hospitalization, major surgery, etc. It is for the latter category that insurance means of payment are both needed and desired. This is also the area in which voluntary insurance plans have been expanding at a rapid rate."

5. R. Gibson and C. Fisher, "Age Differences in Health Care Spending, Fiscal year 1977," *Social Security Bulletin* 42 (1979): 12.

6. Karen Davis and Cathy Schoen, *Health and the War on Poverty* (Washington, D.C.: Brookings Institution, 1978), pp. 53, 54, 213.

7. See, for example, 1976 update of the University of Chicago survey of 1963 and 1970 data in "A New Survey on Access to Medical Care," Special Report no. 1 (Princeton, N.J.: Robert Wood Johnson Foundation, 1976), pp. 10 ff. Hereafter referred to as "Aday and Andersen, 1978" (to be published in book form) Chicago, Ill.

8. Myron J. Lefcowitz, "Poverty and Health: A Re-Examination," *Inquiry*, March 1973, p. 12.

9. Ronald Wilson and E. L. White, "Changes in Morbidity, Disability, and Utilization Differentials between the Poor and the Nonpoor; Data from the Health Interview Survey: 1964 and 1973." *Medical Care* 15 (1977), p. 640; and unpublished data for 1976 from Health Interview Survey, National Center for Health Statistics received by author May 1979.

10. Unpublished data for 1976 from the Health Interview Survey, National Center for Health Statistics, received by author, June 1979.

11. Diana Dutton, "Explaining the Low Use of Health Services by the Poor: Costs, Attitudes, or Delivery Systems?" *American Sociological Review* 43 (1978): 348–368.

12. Aday and Andersen, 1978.

13. U.S. Department of Health, Education, and Welfare, *Health: United States*, pub. no. HRA 77–1232, p. 209.

14. R. R. Campbell, Remarks at Regulatory Reform Conference, Hoover/American Enterprise Institute, Washington, D.C., Sept. 10, 1975, typed p. 45.

15. Jane Brody, "House Panel Calls for More U.S. Control of Surgery," *New York Times*, December 27, 1978, p. 1.

16. R. H. Egdahl and D. C. Walsh, *Containing Health Benefit Costs: The Self-Insurance Option* (New York: Springer-Verlag, 1979), p. 61.

17. Sandra Greene, Dennis Gillings, and Eva Salber, "Who Shops for Medical Care in a Southern Rural Community—How Much and Why," *Inquiry*, Spring 1979, pp. 62–72.

18. Joe Newhouse and Maureen Murphy, "An Estimate of the Impact of Deductibles on the Demand for Medical Care Services," mimeographed (Santa Monica, Calif.: Rand Corporation, May 1978), p. 19.

19. Ann Scitovsky and N. McCall, "Coinsurance and the Demand for Physician Services," *Social Security Bulletin*, May 1977, p. 19.

20. Zachary Dyckman, *Physicians: A Study of Physicians' Fees*, U.S. Council on Wage and Price Stability, Staff Report, March 1978, p. 43.

21. *Ibid.*, p. 92.

22. Mark Pauly, "Is Medical Care Different?" in *Competition in the Health Care Sector*, Proceedings of the Federal Trade Commission, March 1978, p. 25.

23. *Enterprise*, National Association of Manufacturers, October 1978, p. 16. Estimate of Hospital Association of New York.

24. Gilman G. Udell, Compiler, *Federal Food, Drug and Cosmetic Act With Amendments,* House of Representatives, U.S. GPO, Washington, D.C., 1970, p.1.

25. Louis Lasagna and William Wardell, "The Rate of New Drug Discovery," in Robert B. Helms, ed., *Drug Development and Marketing,* AEI, Washington, D.C., 1975, p. 157.

26. *Medical Care Technology and the Medical Care System* (Washington, D.C.: National Academy of Sciences, 1979), p. vii.

27. *Ibid.,* p. 99. By William Yamamoto.

28. AMA National Commission on the Cost of Medical Care, 1976–77, *Summary Report,* vol. 1 (Monroe, Wisconsin: American Medical Association), p. 42.

29. *Wall Street Journal,* April 30, 1979, p. 8.

30. *FTC News Summary,* no. 19, March 30, 1979, p. 3.

31. *FTC News Summary,* no. 30, June 15, 1979, p. 2.

32. *Ibid.,* p. 3.

33. Burt Schorr, "FTC Rules Against AMA in Case Pivotal to Health Care Antitrust Effort," *Wall Street Journal,* November 29, 1978, p. 10.

34. *Honolulu Advertiser,* June 4, 1979, p. A5.

35. *New York Times,* December 3, 1978, p. 36.

36. Thomas Moore, "The Purpose of Licensing," *Journal of Law and Economics* 55 (1961): 103.

37. Dyckman, *Physicians,* p. i.

38. *Science,* November 17, 1978, p. 726.

39. Donald M. Vickery and James Fries, *Take Care of Yourself* (Reading, Mass.: Addison-Wesley, 1976).

40. Alfred Berg and James P. Logerfo, "Potential Effect of Self-Care Algorithms on the Number of Physician Visits," *The New England Journal of Medicine,* March 8, 1978, pp. 535–537.

41. R. R. Campbell, "The Effect of Emerging Health Roles on Financing and Health Payment Plans," (mimeographed paper given at AAAS, New York City, January 31, 1975). Also microfilm, University of Michigan, Ann Arbor.

42. Robert Gibson and Charles Fisher, "National Health Expenditures Fiscal Year 1977," *Social Security Bulletin,* July 1978, p. 5.

43. R. R. Campbell, comments in *The Role of Health Insurance in the Health Services Sector,* Richard N. Rosett, ed. (New York: National Bureau of Economic Research, 1978), p. 209.

44. Michael Jones, "Physician Reimbursement Under the Medi-Cal Program," *Socio-Economic Report* April/May 1979, California Medical Association, San Francisco, Calif., p. 3.

45. U.S. Public Health Service, *Personal Out-of-Pocket Health Expense,* 1975, Series 10, no. 122, p. 2.

46. S. Ramcharan, *et al.,* "Multiphasic Checkup Evaluation Study," *Preventive Medicine* 2 (1973): 216.

47. Harold Luft, "Why Do HMOs Seem to Provide More Health Maintenance Services?" *Milbank Memorial Fund Quarterly,* Spring 1978, pp. 163, 164.

48. Kathryn M. Langwell and Jack L. Werner, "A Probability Model of Malpractice Claims," mimeographed, American Medical Association, June 1979, p. 13. (Space limitations prevent in-depth discussion of malpractice and its intricate relationship to quality of care.)

49. Carol Greenfield, *et al.*, "Use of Out-of-Plan Services by Medicare Members of HIP," *Health Services Research*, Fall 1978, p. 256.

50. Lloyd Wollstadt, Sam Shapiro, and Thomas Bice, "Disenrollment from a Prepaid Group Practice: An Actuarial and Demographic Description," *Inquiry*, June 1978, p. 145.

51. Greenfield, *et al.*, "Use of Out-of-Plan Services," pp. 259, 251.

52. Harold Luft, "Quality," Chapter 10 of *Health Maintenance Organizations: Dimensions of Performance* (New York: Wiley-Interscience, 1980), typed draft, p. 44.

53. Klaus Roghmann *et al.*, "Who Chooses Prepaid Medical Care," *Public Health Reports* 90 (1975): 523.

54. *Controlling the Supply of Hospital Beds*, Policy Statement, Institute of Medicine, National Academy of Science (Washington, D.C.: 1976), p. 7.

55. Michael Pertschuk, The FTC and Health Care: The Role of Competition." Speech, Washington, D.C. June 7, 1979, p. 2, mimeo.

56. Dyckman, *Physicians*, p. 42.

57. Stephen Moore, "Cost Containment Through Risk-Sharing by Private Primary Care Physicians," mimeographed, 1979, pp. 6, 7. (Also *New England Journal of Medicine*, vol. 300, no. 24, June 14, 1979, pp. 1359 ff.)

58. *Ibid.*, p. 13.

59. R. R. Campbell, *Economics of Health and Public Policy* (Washington, D.C.: AEI-Hoover, 1971), p. 26.

60. *Health Maintenance Organizations: Toward a Fair Market Test*, Policy statement by a committee of the Institute of Medicine, PB—239 505, (Washington, D.C.: National Academy of Sciences, 1974), p. 13.

61. Victor Zink, Statement to the U.S. Senate Subcommittee on Health, mimeographed, April 19, 1976, p. 6.

62. Bridger Mitchell and Ron Vogel, "Health and Taxes," *Southern Economic Journal* 41 (1975): 667.

63. *Ibid.*, p. 670.

64. Alain C. Enthoven, "Health Care Costs: Why Regulation Fails, Why Competition Works, How to Get There From Here," *National Journal*, May 26, 1979, p. 888.

65. U.S. Congress, Congressional Budget Office, *Catastrophic Health Insurance*, Budget Issue Paper, January 1977, pp. 2, 3.

66. *Ibid.*, p. 6.

67. *Ibid.*, p. 8.

68. "Medicaid Abuse: Even Worse Than Feared," *U.S. News and World Report*, June 4, 1979, p. 43.

69. Rita Ricardo Campbell, "Proposition 13 and National Health Policy," *FORUM on Medicine*, April 1979, p. 277.

70. R. R. Campbell, *Economics of Health,* p. 26.

71. Anne-Marie Foltz and Jennifer L. Kelsey, "The Annual Pap Test: A Dubious Policy Success," in *Health and Society, Milbank Memorial Fund Quarterly,* 56 (1978): 432–435.

72. Jonathan E. Felding, "Success of Prevention," *Health and Society, Milbank Memorial Fund Quarterly,* 56 (1978): 284.

73. Sydney Garfield, *et al.*, abstract of "Evaluation of an Ambulatory Medical-Care Delivery System," in *The New England Journal of Medicine,* Feb. 19, 1976, p. 426.

74. *Ibid.*, p. 429.

75. *Ibid.*, p. 427.

76. *Science,* December 15, 1978, vol. 202, p. 1175.

77. R. B. Haynes, *et al.*, "Increased Absenteeism from Work after Detection and Labelling of Hypertension Patients," in *The New England Journal of Medicine* 291 (1978), pp. 741–744.

78. U.S. Congress, Joint Committee Subcommittee Hearings, *Low Income Families,* 81st Cong., 1st sess., 1952, p. 162, as cited in R. R. Campbell and W. G. Campbell, "Compulsory Health Insurance," p. 3.

79. Charles E. Phelps, "Illness Prevention and Medical Insurance," *The Journal of Human Resources,* vol. 13, supplement 1978, p. 183.

80. Enthoven, "Health Care Costs," *National Journal,* p. 885.

81. Greene, Gillings, and Salber, "Who Shops for Medical Care," p. 68.

82. Alan F. Westin, "Patients' Rights: Computers and Health Records," *Hospital Progress,* April 1977, p. 57.

83. Alan F. Westin, *Computer, Health Records and Citizen Rights,* Columbia Univ., New York and U.S. National Bureau of Standards, monograph no. 157 (Washington, D.C.: Government Printing Office, 1978), pp. xviii–xix.

National Housing Policy

Richard F. Muth

XII

Housing has long been an area of special concern for Americans. A home represents for most of us the biggest single purchase we ever make, and we are more likely to go into debt to buy a home than for any other reason. Much of our other consumption takes place in the home, and our home is the most visible manifestation to others of our affluence and social standing, or lack of them. Many important events such as a marriage or the birth of a child may be associated in our minds with our home. In taking on a significance that is much greater than for any other consumer good, housing has given rise to innumerable economic, political, and social questions. In selecting a manageable number of them for this essay, I have been helped considerably by the article "Neighborhood Revitalization" in this volume, which discusses several I might have tackled. I have narrowed my attention still further by concentrating on four issues that seem especially important in both professional and popular discussion. Two of these, the affordability of housing and fluctuations in new residential construction, affect the whole of the U.S. economy more or less simultaneously. I have followed the common terminology of economics by calling them macro-issues. The other two questions—urban growth limitations and low-income housing programs—I call micro-issues by way of contrast. Though of interest to us all in the same sense macro-issues are, they relate more to specific areas, to groups of the population, and to the best way to make use of scarce resources. After discussing each of the above, I conclude with a brief section on what I perceive to be a common mistake in discussions of housing issues.

MACRO-HOUSING ISSUES

Affordability

Over the past decade and a half the prices of new houses have risen rapidly along with other prices. In some parts of the country, among them the Washington, D.C. area and coastal California cities, these rises have been particularly dramatic. For instance, in Santa Clara County, at the southern end of San Francisco Bay, house prices have climbed at a rate of 15 to 20 percent per year through the 1970s. Almost anyone who contemplates buying a home today must wonder, "How can anyone afford it?" Many have concluded that fewer and fewer Americans can and have suggested a variety of measures governments might take to correct the situation.[1]

What is perhaps the best measure of house prices is shown in Table 1. This is the Census Bureau's estimate of the market price of the typical new house sold nationally in the year 1974. The rise in house prices shown is indeed dramatic—from under $25,000 in 1965 to over $50,000 in 1977, an increase of about 125 percent. But most of this increase can be accounted for by the decline in the value of the dollar. The second column of Table 1 shows the average of all prices as measured by the Bureau of Labor Statistics (BLS) Consumer Price Index (CPI). Between 1965 and 1977 the CPI almost doubled.

When compared with the behavior of consumer prices generally, the rise in new house prices seems much less dramatic. The third column of Table 1, where the average sales price in column one is deflated or divided by the CPI, shows that in terms of dollars of constant purchasing power, new house prices rose from about $25,000 to $29,000 over the twelve-year period, or at the rate of around 1.5 percent per year.

TABLE 1

New House Prices: 1965–1977

Year	Average Sales Price House Sold 1974 (Thousands of Current Dollars)	Consumer Price Index (1967 =100)	Deflated Average Sales Price (Thousands of 1967 Dollars)	Average Sales Price/ Disposable Income per Household
1965	23.3	94.5	24.7	2.83
1970	29.1	116.3	25.0	2.67
1973	35.6	133.1	26.7	2.69
1977	52.4	181.5	28.9	2.97

Source: Calculated from *Statistical Abstract.*

Elsewhere I have estimated that housing prices rose relative to other consumer prices at a rate of about 1.4 percent per year from 1915 to 1941.[2] The recent rise in housing prices therefore again seems much less striking. The fourth column of Table 1 compares new housing prices with disposable income per household. The ratio was somewhat higher in 1977 than in 1965, though not dramatically so. Indeed, the ratio actually fell somewhat until the early 1970s. Real disposable income per household, after rising from $8,700 in 1965 to about $9,900 in 1973, fell sharply to $9,500 with the recession of 1974–1975 and remained there until 1976. Yet in 1976 (not shown in Table 1), the ratio of average sales price to disposable income per household was about the same as in 1965. There is no clear indication, then, that housing prices are rising faster than incomes.

So far the evidence suggests that during the past fifteen years house prices have risen somewhat faster than prices generally and at about the same rate as incomes. But what about the cost of living in a house? This cost depends partly, of course, on the cost of buying the house, though the two by no means move strictly together. The cost of living in a house, or its implicit rental value, depends in addition on interest rates (the cost of financing its purchase), property taxes, wear and tear by the occupants, and the costs of maintenance and repair. These costs have risen as well. From 1965 to 1977 the average interest rate paid nationally on conventional first mortgages used to finance new home purchases rose from 5.83 to 8.95 percent per year. Property tax rates on new houses financed by the Federal Housing Administration (FHA) likewise rose from 1.43 to 1.84 percent annually over the same period.[3]

One important offset to all these cost increases is the appreciation of the value of a house while it is lived in. The average American household moves perhaps once every five years. If during the five years between the time a family buys a house and resells it the house rises in value, this increase in value serves to offset the other expenses of living in it. Under noninflationary conditions, the items enumerated in the paragraph above would probably amount to about 8 percent of the market value of a house once the income tax advantage of living in a house is considered,[4] or $2,000 per year on a $25,000 house. But if housing prices are rising at the rate of 1.5 percent per year, a $25,000 house will bring about $26,900 when sold five years later, and the cost of living in it is reduced by around $400 annually. The appreciation of house prices has had a particularly strong impact on the cost of living in a house in the 1970s. In the five years preceding 1973, the average sales price of the typical house sold in 1974 had risen at a compound annual rate of 6.3 percent; between 1972 and 1977 it rose at a 9.9-percent annual rate.

The net effects of all these factors are summarized in the first column of Table 2. This column shows my estimate of the number of dollars necessary to live in the typical house sold in 1974. In deriving this estimate I have included the offset for appreciation of market value during the preceding five years, and have deflated the current dollar cost by the CPI. The resulting series is an estimate of the current dollar cost of living in the typical 1974 house relative to the current dollar cost of all consumer goods. The first column indicates that, relative to the cost of other consumer goods, the cost of living in the typical 1974 new house decreased somewhat between 1965 and 1970, fell more sharply till 1973, and fell precipitously by 1977. In 1977 the estimated real cost of owner-occupied housing was only one-third as great as it was in 1965.

Now, I readily grant that these specific numbers are subject to considerable doubt, for there is no strong basis for making the specific allowance for the appreciation in house values that I have used in calculating the real implicit rental value of home ownership. But some corroborating evidence is provided by the second column of Table 2 which gives the rent component index of the CPI relative to the CPI itself. It suggests that, like my real implicit rental value of home ownership in column one, the rental cost of tenant-occupied dwellings has fallen relative to consumer prices generally over the twelve-year period 1965–1977. The reason, I suspect, is much the same as with the implicit rental cost of home ownership. The rise in the value of rental dwellings serves to offset other costs of providing rental housing, and landlords are forced by competition to raise their rentals less than prices of other commodities. Still another piece of evidence is shown in the third column of Table 2, housing expenditures made from the national income accounts relative to

TABLE 2

Rental Values of Housing: 1965–1977

Year	Implicit Rental Value of House Sold 1974 (Thousands of 1967 Dollars)[a]	Deflated Bureau of Labor Statistics Rent Component Index (1967 = 100)	Space Rental Expenditures/ Disposable Income
1965	1.93	102.5	.139
1970	1.80	94.7	.137
1973	1.39	93.4	.137
1977	0.64	84.6	.142[b]

Source: Calculated from *Statistical Abstract* and *HUD Statistical Yearbook*.
[a]Calculated as described in text.
[b]1976.

disposable incomes.[5] The ratio has remained remarkably constant over recent years, despite the rise in house prices. Taken as a whole, there is little reason from Table 2 to conclude that the cost of occupying housing has risen faster than other prices in recent years. Quite the contrary: there is a strong presumption that the cost of occupying housing has actually fallen relative to other consumer prices over this period.

Though the real cost of occupying any given-size dwelling has probably declined over the past fifteen years or so, the cost of financing the purchase of the typical house sold in 1974 could conceivably have risen. For those who are already home owners, of course, the appreciation in current market value of the current home provides a source of funds for making the down payment on another home should the family move. But what about first-time home buyers? Table 1 indicates that disposable incomes per household have risen at about the same rate as house prices. However, a family might typically save for several years to acquire the down payment to buy its first house. Although during an inflationary period many short-term interest rates rise to reflect the increase in prices, the rates that the typical family can receive on its savings are limited by federal regulations to 5.25 percent per year for savings accounts at commercial banks and to 5.5 for shares in savings and loan associations. Only if a family is sophisticated enough to invest in shares of recently developed money-market funds, which pay returns equal to those of treasury bills and other short-term securities, might it hope to keep the real value of its accumulated savings intact. Even so, that part of the interest return that merely compensates for the decline in the value of the dollar is subject to federal, state, and local income taxes. Given the existence of federal deposit insurance, ceilings on the interest rates that thrift institutions may pay do not protect the safety of the depositor's accounts. Rather, their effect is simply to increase the earnings of the institutions themselves. In my judgment, such ceilings ought to be abolished. If this were done, first-time home buyers would have much less trouble accumulating the down payment for their purchase.

With the exception of the difficulties in the costs of acquiring a first house in recent years, the above suggests that living in one's own home has not become more expensive relative to other things. Nevertheless, complaints that housing is too costly are perennial. There are, of course, many things that governments might do to make it cheaper for the average family to occupy its home. But for the efficient use of our nation's resources, housing would be "too costly" only if the returns to resources used to produce it were higher than the returns these same resources might earn elsewhere in the economy. There appears to be little reason to believe this to be the case. In some instances, local building codes may prevent cost-saving innovations in home building, and it would appear that trade unions have secured higher wages for skilled construction workers than similar workers earn elsewhere. Careful economic studies concur, however, that the impact of such factors raises housing prices only on the order of 5 percent.[6] Arrayed against these are numerous factors discussed below that have reduced the cost of housing to large numbers of American families. We have, in my view, probably made housing too cheap relative to other things that we as Americans buy and consume. I see no reason, therefore, further to reduce the earnings of resources used to produce housing relative to their productivity in providing other goods and services.

New Construction

The building of new homes has long been one of the more volatile sectors of our economy. New residential construction fell continuously from 1925 to the depths of the depression in 1933. During the late 1940s and 1950s there were three pronounced downturns in residential construction activity. More recently, we experienced declines of roughly 20 percent in new residential construction in 1965–1966 and again in 1969–1970, and 50 percent from the first quarter of 1973 to the second quarter of 1975. Such fluctuations are thought to cause financial hardship for construction workers and firms, making housing more expensive than it might otherwise be, and deprive the nation of much-needed housing when new construction declines. In order to appraise fluctuations in new residential construction and their effects, it is first necessary to inquire into the reason for them.

Since the downturn in 1965–1966 it has been popular to attribute declines in new residential construction to so-called disintermediation. This dreadful word is derived from the fact that thrift institutions serve as intermediaries between savers and borrowers, in effect pooling the savings of a number of persons to make mortgage loans to buyers of houses. When the interest yields on treasury bills and other short-term securities rise above the maximum rates thrift institutions are allowed by law to pay on accounts, the process of pooling is disrupted. Rather than opening or adding to accounts in thrift institutions, some savers purchase these short-term securities instead. Others may draw down their accounts for the same purpose. The net inflow of funds into thrift institutions is thus reduced, giving these institutions fewer funds to invest in new residential mortgages. For this reason, it is alleged, new residential construction declines.

Before the construction downturn of 1965–1966, short-term interest rates were considerably lower, and disintermediation was not the perceived problem. (Indeed, to my knowledge, the term had not then been invented.) Yet we experienced downturns in new residential construction similar to those we have experienced lately. In the earlier period, interest rate ceilings on mortgages insured by the FHA were the popular culprit. As yields on alternative securities rose, so the argument ran, FHA mortgages became less attractive to lenders because their yields were prevented from rising, and lenders reduced the number of the FHA loans they made. What this argument overlooked was widespread discounting of FHA loans.[7] Just as the effective yield on a bond is increased by selling it at a price below its face value when market yields are above the bond's coupon rate, FHA mortgage lenders advanced borrowers less than the full amount of the loan to be repaid. Despite the ceilings on contract interest rates, therefore, the yields lenders received rose enough to induce them to make FHA loans.

Arguments about the effects of disintermediation are similarly incomplete. For if deposits at thrift institutions fall below what they otherwise would have been and the proceeds are used to purchase, say, treasury bills, their yields fall because of the increase in demand for bills. In like manner, if thrift institutions make fewer mortgage loans than they otherwise would, the yields on mortgage loans rise. Mortgage loans, then, become more attractive to other lenders, perhaps life insurance companies and pension funds. Likewise, because their yields have fallen, treasury bills become less attractive to other holders of financial assets. Why, then, don't other lenders use funds that might have been invested in other securities to purchase mortgage loans instead?

The answer, I submit, is that the rise in mortgage yields reduces the number of mortgage loans borrowers wish to make, given the prices of new houses. As noted earlier, interest costs are an important component of the costs of living in an owner-occupied house. Given the prices of new houses, a rise in mortgage interest cost increases the cost of living in such a house. Indeed, given the level of income and other factors determining the position of the demand curve for housing, the available stock of housing fixes house rentals. A rise in interest rates thus means that potential buyers will buy only if house prices fall. The fall in house prices that results from the rise in interest rates makes house building less profitable. As a result, the rate of new construction falls.

The current situation provides an interesting illustration of the argument just made. Recently, commercial banks and savings and loan associations have been permitted to offer money market accounts to their depositors. These accounts offer essentially the same yields to their depositors, are of the same minimum size, and require savers to invest funds for the same period as do treasury bills. Consequently, there is little or no incentive for depositors to withdraw their funds as treasury bill yields rise above the maximum rates payable on regular thrift accounts. New construction remained at relatively high levels throughout 1978 but fell sharply from around 2 million units at seasonally adjusted annual rates to about 1.6 million units in the first quarter of 1979. As this is being written (April 1979) it is too early to know whether the decline in housing starts will persist. Most forecasts anticipate a decline in housing starts of about 20 percent in 1979. If this decline in fact occurs, disintermediation clearly will not have been responsible for it.

The reasons for downturns in residential construction are especially important when considering the desirability of stabilizing new construction. If rate ceilings on accounts at thrift institutions were the cause of downturns in residential construction during times of rising interest rates, arguments for stabilizing construction would have more cogency. Though I argued earlier that such ceilings ought to be abolished, they do not appear to me to be responsible for fluctuations in residential construction to a significant extent. I would judge that new construction activity declines during periods of rising interest rates because potential buyers of houses value housing less highly during such periods. Rather than eager buyers being denied the opportunity to purchase much needed housing by impediments to flow of funds through our financial system, we have downturns in new construction precisely because buyers find the purchase of new housing less desirable when interest rates are rising.

In appraising the desirability of stabilizing levels of new construction activity it is important clearly to understand the nature of fluctuations in residential construction. The residential construction sector of the economy seems inherently countercyclical, although with a lag, and was so earlier in the postwar period.[8] During prosperous periods, the real returns on other forms of real capital investment are high and rising. Accompanying the increase in demand for real capital investment is an increase in demand for loanable funds to finance their purchase, so interest rates rise. Given relative stability in other factors determining the demand for new housing, rising interest rates reduce the amounts buyers are willing to pay for new housing. Since resources move into and out of new residential construction fairly easily, the effect of falling prices is principally to reduce the rate of new home building.

The sequence of events is precisely the reverse when other demands for funds are declining. Falling interest rates increase the amounts buyers will pay for new houses. As a result, new residential construction becomes more profitable and housing output increases. Fluctuations in new construction of housing tend to offset fluctuations in investment demand in other sectors of the economy. The economic system as a whole is thus more stable, and aggregate output fluctuates less than it would if new residential construction were less subject to fluctuation.

Fluctuations in new construction admittedly affect the costs of housing, though to my knowledge no one knows to what extent. It is by no means clear, though, that construction workers or firms suffer as a result. Because employment in construction is less regular and subject to more frequent periods of seasonal and cyclical unemployment, workers and firms receive higher earnings when employed to compensate them.[9] Consequently, buyers of houses pay higher prices for them than they would if new home building were more regular. It is altogether appropriate that the market impose a surcharge on new houses, owing to the conditions under which they are produced. To take a somewhat similar situation, accountants and others who assist persons and firms in preparing tax returns probably receive a bonus in higher than average earnings because their work is concentrated at certain times of the year. Such persons work extra hours in March and early April because buyers value their services more highly then and are willing to pay a premium to have tax advice available when they want it. In much the same way, the demand for new construction is especially heavy at certain times within the business cycle because, interest rates being lower then, new homes are worth more to their buyers at these times.

All this is not to say that we should do nothing about fluctuations in new construction. In my view we have experienced greater fluctuations in new construction than we should, especially since 1965, because of monetary instability. Throughout the last fifteen years we have had excessive monetary growth, with such consequences as inflation and higher nominal mortgage interest rates than during the 1950s and early 1960s. Moreover, the rate of monetary expansion has been highly irregular. Early in the expansion of the nation's output and employment from the low point of preceding recessions, the Federal Reserve System allowed the money supply to grow at especially rapid rates. Consequently, nominal interest rates have remained lower and levels of new construction higher than if monetary expansion had been more moderate. Ultimately, however, the monetary growth rate has been cut back sharply, as it was in 1966, 1969, 1973 and, most recently, in the fourth quarter of 1978. Such cutbacks have in each case caused sharply rising nominal interest rates and falling rates of new home building. Unlike the declines in residential construction that result from rising demands for other forms of investment, the declines in new construction since 1965 have not been stabilizing. Rather they are part of the instability, part of the cost, that an unstable monetary policy has imposed on the economy. Insofar as I can discern, there are no compensating benefits from monetary instability. High on the agenda for any program for the 1980s should be the achievement of greater monetary stability, one of whose important benefits would be a reduction in fluctuations in new residential construction activity.

MICRO-HOUSING ISSUES

Growth Limitations

Ever since we first became aware of the vast growth and decentralization of population and economic activity in major metropolitan areas following World War II, writers on urban and national affairs have asked whether we should limit urban growth. During the late 1960s and early 1970s there was considerable interest at the national level for formulating and enforcing a national growth policy. Since that time, the focus of attention has shifted to the local level. Many communities have enacted measures to limit their growth, one of the best known being Petaluma, California. As is so often the case, there are several substantive issues connected with the limitation of urban growth. First I will take up those of lesser quantitative importance and then consider those of greater impact.

Lesser problems. One of the most frequently voiced concerns over urban growth is that it uses up valuable farm land. Yet to anyone who has driven across the country recently, such a complaint obviously lacks substance. And, paradoxically, since 1975 we have also begun to worry about agricultural surpluses once again. The fact is that urban areas take up surprisingly little of our land. In 1970, the 248 urbanized areas defined by the Bureau of the Census contained about 60 percent of our nation's population and occupied roughly 35 thousand square miles of land, only about 1 percent of the U.S. total of about 3.5 million square miles. We could continue to convert nonurban to urban land for many more decades without appreciably affecting our available nonurban land area.

Quite apart from the magnitudes involved, public discussion frequently overlooks the market's built-in corrective mechanism for urban expansion. If the expansion of urban land has an appreciable impact on the supply of agricultural land, the rental value of agricultural land would tend to rise as would farm prices. The rise in farm prices would reduce somewhat the quantity of farm products people would want to buy. At the same time, as the rental value of farm land rose, more intensive agricultural techniques would be utilized, so that output per acre would tend to increase. Both would tend to reduce or eliminate the "shortage" of farm products urban expansion initially produced. Furthermore, the rise in the rental value of farm land would make further conversions to urban uses more expensive and hence reduce them. Only if there were some aspect of farm land that farmers don't sell would the market fail properly to adjudicate our division of available land between urban and other uses.

Such an aspect of farm land is what is often called open space. Unlike the food and fiber he produces, the farmer does not sell the right to enjoy the open space his farm provides to neighboring urban dwellers. Hence the benefits his land provides as open space is not taken into account in the farmer's decision as to whether to continue to farm his land or to sell it for urban development. Thus, one might expect that too much land would be converted to urban uses in the vicinity of urban centers.

For this as well as for other reasons, local governments have resorted to moratoriums on development, large-lot zoning, and a variety of devices to limit further urban expansion into the surrounding countryside. Doing so results in the converse problem: too little conversion of land. Almost all such devices to preserve open space seemingly cost the local taxpayer nothing. As with anything else, the less open space costs us, the more of it we would like to have. Yet the opportunity cost of limiting urban growth to society as a whole is clearly not equal to zero. Rather it is the difference between the rental value land would earn in urban uses less that actually earned in nonurban ones. Though the local taxpayer may think he is getting something for nothing, society as a whole pays a price.

By using one of several devices, it is possible for the value of farm land as open space to be taken into economic calculation and for the consumer of this open space, the local taxpayer, to be made to face up to the opportunity cost of the land as open space. Local governments, for example, might buy up the development rights to the farm land. The farmer would then collect the payment for the benefits of open space he produces from the interest earned on the sum received for these rights. Alternatively, a city or a regional park district might buy the land outright from the farmer and lease part of it back to him or to other nonurban users such as cattle grazers. In either case, the local taxpayer would pay for open space through higher taxes to pay the interest and repay the principal on bonds issued to buy the property or its development rights.

Another important reason for the popularity of growth limitations is that existing local taxpayers believe that further development of their communities will lead to an increase in their taxes. They may be correct for two reasons. First, existing taxpayers in the community may have paid taxes to retire debt issued to acquire still serviceable capital assets such as school buildings and water and sewer systems. As the community grows, more such assets may need to be acquired and paid for. If existing as well as new residents are charged for these improvements by levying taxes on all residents to pay off new bond issues, taxes on existing residents will rise relative to the services they receive from local government. Moreover, new residents will receive services more cheaply in existing communities than in newly established ones. The best remedy for this situation is to levy development charges on land newly converted to urban uses equal to the present value of the additional future capital charges required to service the new residents.

The imposition of appropriate development charges would solve what some perceive to be another problem related to urban growth. It is frequently complained that new urban growth is not always contiguous to already built-up urban areas. There are several good economic reasons why urban development might proceed this way. When such is the case, however, the installation of new water and sewage disposal facilities may be more costly, and the new residents may be more costly for the municipality to service in other ways. If the community were to impose appropriately higher development charges for dispersed as opposed to contiguous new growth, these higher costs would be covered without raising taxes for existing residents. Moreover, developers would then have the incentive to take the higher costs of municipal services in scattered development into account in planning new residential developments.

The other reason why taxes on existing members of the community may rise with urban growth is that new residents may have lower incomes. For certain services such as police and fire protection, property taxes to support them are roughly equivalent to the value of benefits different families receive. But for public education, the largest single category of municipal expenditure, the benefits received per child are probably pretty much independent of the value of the residence his family inhabits, and thus of the property taxes or even sales taxes it pays. So long as public education is locally financed, then, families have an incentive to move into communities where existing residents are wealthier than they are, and the latter will try to keep newcomers out. Indeed, local finance of public education has other disadvantages, principally that expenditure on a particular child's education varies to an important degree with the wealth of the community he lives in. To overcome these difficulties, taxes for the support of public education might well be levied and collected by a higher level of government, such as the state government. Doing this would also cope with the *Serrano v. Priest* and other recent state court decisions that have found that local financing of public education violates state constitutions. Payments for support of a child's education could then be made to the school district in which he resides by whatever formula is deemed equitable. (Better still, such payments could be made directly to the child's parents in the form of an educational voucher to be spent on a school of their choice.)

More important problems. There are two principal reasons why the land area occupied by metropolitan centers are too big: the underpricing of freeways and other roads used for rush-hour commuting and federal programs that have stimulated the growth of home ownership. Limiting future growth of urban areas would, of course, help undo the mischief these have caused. But even if our urban centers were to grow no larger, we would still be faced with serious problems of rush-hour congestion and air pollution. Our problem is not merely one of preventing these problems from becoming worse by limiting further growth. Rather, we should direct our attention to proper pricing of roads and the waste disposal capacity possessed by the atmosphere, whatever size our urban centers may become. If this were done, growth would not be a problem.

The use of public roads may seem free, but in fact motor vehicle operators pay for them through taxes on gasoline and tires. During morning and evening rush hours in most cities these roads are congested. By congested I mean not merely crowded, but rather that an additional vehicle entering the highway system slows down traffic. The reduction in the speed of travel caused by a single additional vehicle is quite small; but because large numbers of vehicles are affected by it, the aggregate increase in travel time by all highway users and the increased money costs they incur is by no means small. Any driver entering the road system experiences whatever delays in travel are dictated by current conditions and can be expected to take those costs he incurs into account in his travel decisions. But he is not required to pay for the delays he imposes on other drivers. It is in this last sense that urban roads are underpriced during commuter rush hours. Not surprisingly, if urban roads are underpriced they will be overused.

The situation with regard to air pollution is similar to that of congestion. Any commuter has the incentive to consider the money and time costs to him of choosing a particular time of day and mode of travel for the journey to and from work. He does not, however, have to consider the costs of the wastes his vehicle discharges into the atmosphere. Although the amount of such discharges by any one vehicle may be small, just as is the case with the additional congestion it produces, the total effect on all persons within the area may be appreciable. Just as commuters are not charged for the additional congestion costs that their commuting produces, neither are they charged for their contribution to air pollution.

The underpricing of urban roads during rush hours affects the spatial distribution of population within the urban area. The cost of commuting is an important determinant of how far workers are willing to commute. The less they have to pay for commuting, the farther from their jobs they will live. Consequently, if the use of roads for commuting is underpriced, the land area occupied by an urban region will be larger than if commuting is correctly priced.

How high should charges for peak-hour vehicle travel be? A recent investigation suggests that appropriate charges might be substantial. This study of the San Francisco Bay area concluded that peak-period commuting charges would be of the order of 3 to 6 cents per mile per commuter in the less heavily traveled parts of urban areas and perhaps as high as 12 to 22 cents in the more congested central city.[10] Charges of only 3 cents per commuter per mile could increase the cost of traveling an additional mile by as much as 50 percent. My own calculations suggest that, had commuter charges been appropriate, the typical American city in 1950 would have been 40 percent smaller and the value of all land up to its city limits, including that which would be used for agriculture instead if it were smaller, would have been 32 percent greater than it actually was.[11] Rough as these figures may be, they certainly suggest a substantial overexpansion of urban areas from the failure to price commuting properly.

There are a variety of ways in which higher charges on rush-hour commuting could be imposed. One of the simplest would be to require drivers to purchase and display a vehicle sticker for the use of certain streets and freeways during peak travel periods. Such a plan was actually adopted in Singapore several years ago. According to a report in the *San Francisco Chronicle*, charges of $1.65 daily or $34 monthly were imposed for vehicles using a central zone of the city from 7:30 to 10:15 A.M. Central-zone auto traffic decreased 74 percent during this period and car pools increased 82 percent, though public transit ridership increased only 10 to 15 percent. Obviously, appropriate commuting charges can reduce rush-hour congestion.

The other principal contributor to excessive urban land use is the federal government itself. Through both the structure of the personal income tax and federal mortgage programs, the federal government has led more families to inhabit owner-occupied dwellings, principally in single-family detached houses. Under the federal personal income tax, a home owner is not required to declare the rental value of his home as income. At the same time, he can deduct mortgage interest and property taxes paid. Consequently, his taxes are lower if he is a home owner than if he rents the same dwelling. Similarly, under a variety of programs but especially under FHA and Veterans Administration mortgage programs, some families have been able to finance the purchase of houses more cheaply than they otherwise could have.

Single-family detached houses whose occupancy these programs have stimulated typically use more land than other types of dwellings. Furthermore, they are cheapest to build in the outer parts of urban areas, where land is cheaper, than in the more central parts. Consequently, these federal programs have increased the total amount of urban land and encouraged residence in suburban as opposed to central city areas. My calculation of the effects of the federal income tax advantage to home ownership, though also rough, suggests that it has increased the land area occupied by cities by about 15 percent.[12]

The tax exemption of income from owner-occupied housing exacerbates another problem, namely, that our system of taxation allows capital invested in owner-occupied housing to produce only about half the before-tax return that capital employed in the corporate sector does. The principal culprit, however, is the corporate income tax. The income from equity investment in the corporate sector pays a tax of about 50 percent. (For simplicity and brevity, I abstract here from capital gains and other features of our tax system such as accelerated depreciation and investment tax credits.) Suppliers of equity capital would have to earn a before-corporate income tax return of 17 percent to receive the approximately 8.5-percent return that suppliers of borrowed funds receive. Since roughly two-thirds of corporate capital is equity capital, corporations must earn about 14 percent per year per dollar of invested capital to pay after-corporate income tax returns of 8.5 percent to suppliers of both debt and equity corporate capital. On the other hand, there is no corporate income tax on owner-occupied housing and no personal income tax on income from capital invested in owner-occupied housing. Hence, if the typical taxpayer pays federal income taxes at the rate of 20 cents per dollar, capital yielding 6.8 percent in owner-occupied housing yields the same after-personal income tax return as corporate capital yielding 8.5 percent before the personal income tax.

The upshot of the above is that each dollar's worth of capital invested in owner-occupied housing adds only about half as much to the national income as a dollar's worth of capital invested in the corporate sector. In essence, our tax system makes owner-occupied housing too cheap and reduces the national income by shifting capital from more productive to less productive uses. There is no room in this essay to enter the thicket of tax reform, nor am I especially qualified to do so. Tax reform is a perennial issue, however, and will still be one in the 1980s. Any program for tax reform must take into account the waste of resources induced by the differential taxation of capital invested in owner-occupied housing. Indeed, because of this waste I find it hard to take seriously any proposal for making owner-occupied housing cheaper still.

Low-Income Housing

Since the low-rent public housing program was established in the late 1930s, the United States has experimented with a variety of programs that have sought to improve the housing occupied by lower-income families. Generally known by the section numbers of the various housing and other acts which authorize them, they are far too numerous to describe here. Moreover, most of them have fallen into disrepute and disuse because of widespread public dissatisfaction. Apparently, many anticipated that better housing would somehow magically transform the lives of its occupants, which it clearly hasn't done. Paradoxically, lower-income families by their behavior appear to view housing programs as highly successful. Waiting lists for admission to public housing projects are long—typically of the order of the number of occupied dwellings. This strongly suggests that lower-income families view public housing as a means for increasing their well-being. In order to make any progress at all in improving our lower-income housing programs, it is absolutely necessary that we see them for what they can be—not as a panacea for urban ills, but rather as a device for bettering the lot of the lower-income population.

Judged from this perspective, our previous efforts have been seriously deficient. Though we have changed name and number repeatedly, new lower-income housing programs have generally been but new mixes of old program elements and mistakes. We have repeatedly subsidized the capital cost of housing at the expense of current expenditure for maintenance and operation, and we have repeatedly provided lower-income housing in newly built housing instead of in existing dwellings.

Finally, we have repeatedly failed to realize that providing assistance to lower-income families in the form of specific commodities—whether more housing, more food, or even more medical care—does less to improve their well-being than providing them with the money equivalent in the form of additional income to spend as they wish. In the remainder of this section I elaborate on what I see as past mistakes in our lower-income housing programs and suggest what I think is a superior alternative.

For some reason which I, as a mere economist, have never been able to understand, public programs usually provide subsidies to the production of various commodities by subsidizing the capital costs of producing them. To take but three examples, the federal government subsidizes capital used in producing rural electricity, subsidizes urban transport through cash grants for the purchase of buses and rail systems, and subsidizes higher education by providing funds for the construction of dormitories and other college buildings. It is therefore not surprising that we have tended to subsidize lower-income housing by subsidizing the capital cost of building it.

This has been the case in particular in the public housing program. Under it, the federal government has paid at least 90 percent of the debt-service on bonds issued by the Local Housing Authority (LHA) to finance the building of public housing projects. These bonds in turn, as obligations of local governments, have carried interest rates that are about half the market rate of interest since the interest paid on the bonds is exempt from federal personal income taxation. Moreover, local governments excuse public housing projects from the payment of property taxes (although payments in lieu of taxes at 10 percent of rentals are made). All told, then, capital invested in public housing "costs" the LHA only about 5 percent of what it would cost a private developer. By costs I mean, of course, that the LHA must collect only five cents from public housing dwellers for each dollar a private developer would have to collect for the same dwelling from his tenants in order to cover the cost of the capital invested in the unit. It is in this way that the rental payments made by occupants of low-income public housing are reduced or subsidized. Prior to 1969 the rental payments tenants made covered the whole of the cost of maintenance, repairs, and operation of the dwellings they occupied. To cite another example, under the Section 235 program, low down-payment loans were made to lower-income households carrying interest rates of about 1 percent per year to purchase housing on the private market. At the time most loans under the program were made, interest rates on conventional first-mortgage loans were about 8 percent per year. Thus, the interest cost component of what I have called the implicit rental cost of home ownership was only about 12 cents for lower-income persons purchasing homes under the program for each dollar of cost that another buyer would incur.

The large number of abandonments under the Section 235 program is well known. Though these difficulties are often attributed to fraudulent or other illegal activities on the part of local FHA officials and others, they really quite graphically reflect the problems of capital cost subsidies. Only the capital costs of acquiring a dwelling, not the costs of maintaining or operating it, were subsidized. Therefore when heating, plumbing, or electrical systems required major repairs, or temporary declines in income occurred, it was cheaper for the lower-income family simply to default on the mortgage and give up its house than to attempt to remain in it. In like manner, certain difficulties of the low-rent public housing program may well be due to the nature of the subsidy to housing produced under it. That public housing projects frequently consist of massive, high-rise structures that are poorly maintained and in disrepair reflects, at least in part, the fact that the capital costs of such projects are heavily subsidized but expenditures for maintenance and repair are not.

Quite generally, when the costs of one input but not others in production are subsidized, more of that input relative to others will be used. But the opportunity cost that society as a whole bears is given by market rather than subsidized prices. Because capital cost subsidies increase the use of capital relative to current expenditures in producing housing for lower-income persons, the cost of providing that housing is higher than it would otherwise be. I have estimated that the resource cost to the economy of providing low-rent public housing was increased by roughly 20 percent by subsidizing capital but not current costs.[13] Stated differently, for every five public housing units that were produced, six could have been provided at the same total cost to the economy, had capital and current expenditure been equally subsidized.

Housing for lower-income families under various public programs has often been provided in newly built rather than in existing structures. In order to obtain sites for building new structures, existing dwellings that house lower-income families have frequently been demolished. Since the sites plus their existing structures must be acquired at fair market value, the site costs for such units are unusually high. Indeed, I have estimated that construction on cleared slum land has meant that the resource costs of the public housing program have also been about 20 percent greater than they would have been if all public housing had been built on other sites.[14] Moreover, the demolition of existing structures has meant that their occupants were displaced and their lives disrupted.

Certain later modifications of housing programs have partially corrected the mistakes just described, and the scheme I will propose later would completely correct them. One vital shortcoming of housing programs cannot be eliminated short of replacing subsidies with general income subsidies or their equivalent. This is the fact that an increase in the consumption of a single commodity such as housing is never worth more and is generally worth less to the recipient than a cash sum equal to the cost of providing the subsidy that the recipient can spend as he wishes. Stated as simply as possible, a 20-cubic-foot refrigerator without additional food to put in it is not worth much more than an 18-cubic-foot one. When additional housing is provided by a housing program, only part of the subsidy actually increases the well-being of the recipient. The remainder merely serves to reduce the valuation the recipient places on housing relative to other kinds of consumption. But if the subsidy recipient receives cash that he can spend as he chooses, the dilution of the value of the subsidy is avoided. As in the example above, an additional cubic foot of refrigerator space together with more food to fill that space is worth more than two additional cubic feet without any more food.

The dilution of benefits of housing subsidy programs has probably been greater than in the case of many other programs. In most subsidy programs, of which the food stamp program is a good example, benefits are potentially available to all individuals the law makes eligible. Housing programs have worked quite differently. Under them perhaps no more than one in ten eligible families has actually received additional housing. For those who have benefited, the increases in housing consumption have been relatively large. Consequently, the benefits of housing subsidies have, in large part, been dissipated. Had the same total increase in housing consumption provided by our housing subsidy programs been equally divided among all eligible families, the aggregate benefits of this additional housing would have been far larger.

Now, of course, so long as housing under government programs is provided primarily by building new housing, it would be quite difficult to do what I have just suggested. There is an alternative way, however, in which the additional housing provided for lower-income families could be packaged into a larger number of smaller-size bundles. This is by providing each eligible family with a housing allowance or rent certificate that could be used for the payment of rent. Families or individuals could use these certificates, along with such of their own resources as they would desire, to purchase housing on the private market. Landlords would redeem the vouchers received for cash. Such a program would be much like the food stamp program, under which lower-income families receive stamps that are "spent" along with part of their incomes for food in private grocery stores.

The proposed subsidy program would not only correct what appear to be the principal shortcomings of previous housing subsidy programs but would have subsidiary advantages as well. With a subsidy applied to rental payments rather than to capital costs, private landlords would have the monetary incentive to use capital and current expenditures in the right combinations. Indeed, I suspect that under the program I am proposing, most of the rental subsidy would be used to improve existing dwellings. It would thus work to slow the deterioration of inner city neighborhoods and, unlike the low-rent public housing program, lead to increased property tax collections by central city governments. The high cost of acquiring existing dwellings and demolishing them to provide sites for new units and the forced relocation of the lower-income residents of these dwellings would also be avoided.

Above all, the value of the direct benefits of the program would be higher than under current programs. Early in the Carter administration, the food stamp program was converted from a food price subsidy to what is essentially an income subsidy. This was done by dropping the requirement that families pay, say, 30 cents for stamps worth one dollar for the purchase of food and simply giving each family a fixed allotment of stamps. Since families typically spend more on food than the value of their stamp allotment, the food stamp program in effect if not in name became an income subsidy program. Congress is unlikely to vote more funds for housing programs than low-income families would spend on housing if free to spend as they wish. Even an annual expenditure of ten billion dollars would provide the bottom fourth of households (by income) an average subsidy of only about $50 a month. Thus, a rent certificate program under which certificates were given to all lower-income families would have precisely the same effect as an income subsidy program of the same size. As such, the diminution of benefits that would result from giving, say, 10 percent of the families certificates ten times as large would be avoided.

Such a rental certificate program would have a number of other advantages. One is administrative simplicity. Since no new public housing would be built under the program, there would be no plans to approve and no financing to arrange. Since no minimum standards would be set for dwellings occupied by subsidy recipients, no dwellings would have to be inspected for compliance. Indeed, setting minimum standards would increase the size of required subsidy to induce families to take part and limit the number of families that could receive subsidies under the program. All that would be required administratively would be verification of eligibility and the issuing and redeeming of certificates. Such a program would also tend to promote freedom of residence for lower-income families. Beneficiaries of the program could seek privately produced housing anywhere they wished. Their residential choices would not be limited to the single vacancy opening up for them when they come to the top of the waiting list, as is now the case. Finally, beneficiaries of the program would not be stigmatized as project residents may now be. Few would know that their neighbors have paid part of their rent with a rent certificate.

Some may object at this point that we already have such programs in the leased public housing and Section 8 (of the Housing and Community Development Act of 1974) programs. Under both, LHAs in effect lease housing on the private market and sublease it to lower-income families. Such programs have indeed done much to correct the shortcoming of earlier programs. Of particular importance is that these programs subsidize rental payments, not capital costs. The Section 8 program, however, does make provision for interest rate subsidies for newly constructed or substantially rehabilitated housing for lease under the program. Both programs are administratively more complex than the one I am suggesting and limit the choices open to eligible families. Perhaps most important is that, as in earlier housing programs, relatively few families receive benefits, which reduces the value of the program.

The only serious objection I have heard to subsidizing rental payments made by lower-income families is that the principal effect would be to line the pockets of landlords. At the crude level at which it is generally made, the objection is simply fallacious. Though any given landlord would indeed like to increase the rental he charges without improving the accommodations he provides, competition among landlords would prevent this. At a more serious level, the allegation implies that the private market housing supply is highly inelastic. If this were the case, of course, the leased public housing and Section 8 programs would also merely raise lower-income rentals without improving housing. But two pieces of evidence strongly suggest that the private market housing supply is relatively elastic. First, despite widespread perception to the contrary, the average quality of central city housing has improved markedly in the postwar period as incomes and thus housing expenditures have risen. Census data indicate that the fraction of substandard dwellings—that is, dilapidated or lacking plumbing facilities—fell from about 20 percent in 1950 to 10 percent in 1960 to around 5 percent in 1970.[15] Second, in city-wide housing allowance experiments conducted during the past five years in Green Bay, Wisconsin, and South Bend,

Indiana, no evidence whatsoever of price increases attributable to the payment of the housing allowances was found.[16] The objection that housing allowances would not improve housing seems to lack force.

A POSTSCRIPT

One theme common to most of the issues discussed above lies largely submerged, like the proverbial iceberg. Most discussions of housing problems are aimed at the specific area of concern, such as the affordability of housing or whether cities are too big. Proposed solutions are often suggested for making housing cheaper or cities smaller. Yet what I think is a more important question—namely, whether resources devoted to housing are wisely used—is all too frequently neglected, even in professional discussion of housing problems.

Consider, for instance, the issue of the affordability of housing. The evidence discussed earlier suggests that houses have become more expensive to buy but less expensive to live in over the past fifteen years or so. But are houses too expensive? Too expensive relative to what? In any ultimate sense, comparing today's house prices with those of fifteen years ago is not a sensible answer. For there is no assurance that houses were in any sense correctly priced earlier and that what was correct has not changed in the interim. The question that should be asked is whether resources used to produce houses are more valuable or less valuable than they would be if used in other ways. Stated differently, does shifting more resources into the production of housing make us better off? For by using more resources to produce housing we must give up something else of value. Is that something else worth more or less than the additional houses we get instead? Judged from this perspective, it would appear that, as noted earlier, housing is too cheap. It is too cheap in the sense that an additional dollar invested in the corporate sector earns over twice as much as an additional dollar invested in owner-occupied housing. By investing less in owner-occupied housing and more in the corporate sector, the value placed by consumers on the nation's output would be increased.

Other housing issues should be addressed in the same fashion. Are our cities too big? The answer depends very little on how much they have grown since 1950 or whenever. Rather, the question to ask is, how much does an additional acre of urban land add to the national income compared with an additional acre of nonurban land? Because of both our failure to price automobile transportation correctly and our subsidies to owner-occupied housing, we have shifted land from more valuable nonurban uses to less valuable urban ones. Do lower-income families have enough housing? Certainly not, if by enough we mean housing of middle-class standards. Yet, by providing lower-income families with better housing, we have withdrawn resources from uses that lower income families value more.

Admittedly, the assigning of appropriate values to alternative uses of resources is often difficult. In many cases, of course, the market valuation of resources provides the correct answer. For many issues of housing policy, however, nonmarket considerations may be especially important. I submit that we shall make more progress in solving economic and social problems by asking the right questions than by asking easily answered but meaningless questions.

NOTES

1. In particular, Bernard J. Friedan et al., *The Nation's Housing: 1975 to 1985* (Cambridge, Mass.: MIT-Harvard Joint Center for Urban Studies, 1977).

2. Richard F. Muth, "The Demand for Non-Farm Housing," in *The Demand For Durable Goods*, ed. Arnold C. Harberger (Chicago: University of Chicago Press, 1960), pp. 29–96.

3. As calculated from data on average property tax expense and sales prices of new homes in *HUD 1977 Statistical Yearbook*.

4. The income tax advantage, discussed more fully below, means that the typical family pays only about 80 percent of the interest and property tax cost of living in a house. The 8 percent cited in the text is based upon interest rates of 6 percent, property tax rates of 2 percent, depreciation of 2 percent, and maintenance and repair expenses of about 1.5 percent per year. See Muth, "Demand for Non-Farm Housing."

5. Since the numerator of this ratio refers to the rental expenditures actually made for housing, it would reflect any tendency for people to live in smaller dwellings generally if the cost of occupying a given-size dwelling were rising faster than other consumer prices or vice versa.

6. Sherman J. Maisel, *Housebuilding in Transition* (Berkeley: University of California Press, 1952), and Richard F. Muth and Elliot Wetzler, "The Effect of Constraints on House Costs," *Journal of Urban Economics* 3 (January 1976), 57–67, though using quite different methods for different periods, reach remarkably similar conclusions on this point.

7. See William W. Alberts, "Business Cycles, Residential Construction Cycles, and the Mortgage Market," *Journal of Political Economy* 70 (June 1962), 263–281 and Jack Guttentag, "The Short Cycle in Residential Construction," *American Economic Review* 51 (June 1961), 275–298.

8. See Alberts, "Business Cycles."

9. Evidence on this point is provided by Stephen P. Sobotka, "Union Influence on Wages: The Construction Industry," *Journal of Political Economy* 61 (April 1953), 127–143.

10. Theodore E. Keeler and Kenneth A. Small, "Optimal Peak-Load Pricing, Investment, and Service Levels on Urban Expressways," *Journal of Political Economy* 85 (February 1977), 1–25.

11. Richard F. Muth, "Numerical Solution of Urban Residential Land-Use Models," *Journal of Urban Economics* 2 (October 1975), 307–332.

12. Ibid.

13. Richard F. Muth, *Public Housing: An Economic Evaluation* (Washington, D.C.: American Enterprise Institute, 1973).

14. Ibid., pp. 12–13.

15. Changes in urban housing quality between 1960 and 1970 are analyzed by Otto A. Davis, Charles M. Eastman, and Chang-I Hua, "The Shrinkage in the Stock of Low-Quality Housing in the Central City," *Urban Studies* 11 (February 1974), 13–26.

16. See *Executive Summary: Fourth Annual Report of the Housing Assistance Supply Experiment*, R-23-2/I-HUD (Santa Monica, Calif.: Rand Corp., March 1978), esp. pp. 18–19.

Neighborhood Revitalization

John McClaughry

XIII

To the extent to which American urban policy since World War II has been consciously defined, it has constantly sought a focus, an organizing concept for its specific policy recommendations. In the early fifties, that concept was urban renewal. By the early sixties, "poverty" had come to the fore, followed by "reorganization" for efficient service delivery. Then came enhanced fiscal capacity, the concept behind the community development revenue-sharing legislation of 1974. By the late seventies, these policy concepts had, to put it as gently as possible, lost their allure. The time was clearly ripe for the emergence of a new organizing concept.

It now appears that the concept for the eighties will be neighborhood revitalization. And it is interesting to note that the idea of the neighborhood as a focus for urban policy is, of all the concepts yet advanced, the only one with a respectable claim to a grass-roots origin. It was not invented in Washington or in city hall. It welled up naturally from the desires of urban dwellers, of all races and ethnic origins, who instinctively recognized what Aristotle and Lao-tzu knew so well: that the immediate neighborhood is and should be the center and focus of human life in the city.

It is also highly significant that this renewed emphasis on preserving and revitalizing urban neighborhoods springs in no small measure from a realization among urban residents that most if not all of the previous urban wonder drugs had the effect of nearly killing the patient. Urban residents have thus become, at best, justifiably wary of government programs and, in not a few instances, bitterly hostile to them. This wariness or hostility to government help is a particularly salient factor that all too many politicians, eager to get on the "save the neighborhood" bandwagon, do not yet fully appreciate.

The older cities of America have been, for more than a decade, in deepening trouble. Many of their middle-class residents, encouraged by better transportation and Federal Housing Administration (FHA) home mortgage guarantees, have departed to the suburbs. The central cities have been left with rising proportions of the poor and their social and economic problems. The older cities have suffered a steady deterioration of economic base, as industries have relocated to more congenial surroundings.

Unfortunately, many city governments have continued to implement traditional policies that at best have failed to reverse the trend and at worst have become major contributing factors. Encouraged by federal programs, cities have attempted solutions that only made the problems worse or shifted problems from one area to another. Urban renewal, land use controls, code enforcement, excessive licensing, property taxation, and rent controls have had a predictably negative effect on the city's image as a place of opportunity, growth, and enterprise. The preservation of ossified and costly municipal bureaucracies, frequently coupled with fiscal mismanagement and corruption, has compounded the problems.

But government intervention has not been the only problem facing the inhabitants of large cities. Too many city halls have seemed to dread spontaneous citizen activity. They have in many cases appeared fearful of allowing any governmental powers to devolve back to the people from whom they were taken. Too often they have concentrated on distributing political and economic rewards, on maintaining institutionalized service bureaucracies, on stifling public choice in favor of approved monopolies, and on keeping their citizens under control. Too many city governments have allocated their scarce energies to campaigns of creative begging from Washington.

Nor have city and state governments distinguished themselves in lowering the barriers to "people power" posed by the structure of laws, ordinances, and government practices within which urban residents must operate. Despite the problems of the older cities, there is considerable evidence that neighborhood residents can achieve remarkable successes through creative self-help. Indeed, this fact is of central importance to the encouragement of an urban renaissance in the 1980s. Create an environment where citizen leadership can flourish at the grass-roots level, where more resources can be creatively employed under the control of the people who produced them, where the barriers posed by governmental practices, edicts, and monopolies have been swept away; and many of the seemingly intractable problems of urban America may well begin to shrink to far more manageable proportions.

The themes of this essay can be simply and clearly stated.

First, the urban neighborhood is a vitally important focus for the lives of millions of urban Americans.* It is a place of familiarity, of belonging. It does much to define a resident's perception of his or her relation to the larger society beyond its boundaries. It often boasts a rich tradition accumulated over many generations, perhaps even dating back to the days when the neighborhood was an independent village or borough.

But a neighborhood is not merely a place that affords psychological benefits and gives social support to its residents. It is also an arena for civic action and creative self-help. Its preservation and evolution is a matter of shared concern among its residents. Human beings can readily relate to the scale of their neighborhood. That human scale encourages them to exercise leadership or invest their talents, energies, and resources in making their neighborhood a more satisfying place to live.

The importance of the neighborhood and similar human-scale mediating structures lies not only in the sense of accomplishment and direct benefit its residents may achieve through their mutual efforts. The neighborhood is one of the key social institutions that must be strengthened if the growing power of large institutions—notably the government—is to be checked.

A second theme deals with the perennial problem of resources. People with no financial resources can occasionally accomplish great things, but insisting on heroic sacrifice is not sound policy. People need some modest level of resources to act effectively on a sustained basis to advance the interests of their neighborhoods.

Even in the poorest of urban neighborhoods, the amount of resources is surprising—not enough to finance massive centrally planned solutions, but often enough to support significant citizen initiatives. As much of these resources as possible should be left under the control of

*Much scholarly effort has been expended in formulating a precise definition of neighborhood. For the purpose of this essay, a neighborhood is defined as a predominantly residential area of a city that is 1) characterized by its own economic, cultural, and social institutions (schools, churches, police and fire stations, shopping districts, community centers, and fraternal and charitable organizations); 2) typified by some tradition of identity and continuity; and 3) inhabited by people who perceive themselves to be residents of the neighborhood and participants in its common life.

those engaged in citizen-initiated self-help. For the poorest groups in society, it will be necessary for government to augment these indigenous resources. The wise policymaker will recognize, however, that such redistribution should be carried out not in the name of reducing statistical inequalities, but in the name of providing a reasonably secure base from which lower-income people can begin to move forward under their own power.

A third recurring theme is the pressing need for ending government intervention that has little prospect for assisting neighborhood residents. The federal urban renewal program, with its "federal bulldozer," typifies the kind of government intervention that has fueled outspoken antigovernment attitudes among those whom the intervention is, at least theoretically, supposed to benefit. Time after time neighborhood leaders implored the National Commission on Neighborhoods to tell those who made federal urban policy in Washington to simply leave their neighborhoods alone. That is not the kind of appeal that is well received in Washington, but it is an appeal that can be ignored only at considerable political risk.

Finally, and perhaps most important, there is the recurring theme of lowering the barriers to creative self-help. These barriers result from thoughtless government laws, ordinances, and practices that have been devised over the years to permit more efficient centralized control over the population, or to protect certain privileged groups in society, or to replace citizen action with well-meaning but stifling government paternalism.

A chief task of urban policy in the 1980s must be to design and implement a compatible set of subpolicies aimed at stimulating the creative energy of the people themselves. This will mean radical changes in government organization, in legal precepts, in taxation, and in the shape of long-accepted institutions.

POLICY RECOMMENDATIONS

It is one thing to state bold principles, but quite another to translate them into a well-coordinated, sensible public policy. This problem, however, is much less serious in the case of these principles than in the case of principles advanced in support of the usual massive government-dominated solutions to urban problems because the recommendations based on these principles restore maximum initiative, resources, and opportunity to the people themselves. They do not require the construction of a complex administrative machine, whose various cogs and levers must be perfectly synchronized to produce the desired results. If the end result of a "people power" neighborhood policy seems chaotic and diverse to the professional planner, that may tell us more about the biases of professional planners and managers than about the vitality of the people, the neighborhoods, and the cities.

The following recommendations are offered as representative of what is needed to carry out the principles and themes set forth above. In any given state and city, conditions will of course dictate the precise combinations, sequences, and adjustments of recommendations to be implemented.

Restructuring Urban Government

A principal goal of restructuring urban government is to counter what Richard Goodwin a decade ago termed "the most troubling political fact of our age: that the growth in central power has been accompanied by a swift and continual diminution in the significance of the individual citizen, transforming him from a wielder into an object of authority."[1] The task today is to devolve political power in the direction of the small-scale human community and the individual citizen.

Designing a proper and effective division of responsibilities among individuals, families, mediating structures, and the various levels of government is admittedly an extremely difficult task—a task complicated by conflicts among vocal economic, social, and political interests. The general direction of needed reform, however, now seems increasingly clear.

It lies in the direction of the "federated city."[2] Governmental functions that involve substantial economies of scale, or must be performed uniformly over large territories, or involve sizable investments of capital would be managed by a metropolitan-level government. Other government functions would be devolved to "mini-governments," which might be boroughs, community service districts, or neighborhood governments. As many functions as possible would be left to neighborhood self-help organizations, church parishes, fraternal societies, and individuals.

There are several more or less clearly defined steps in devising a federated city. The first is administrative decentralization: municipal decision making is decentralized to district or community levels, subject to overall supervision by city officials. New York's district managers were a celebrated example of limited administrative decentralization. In Dayton, Ohio, six elected neighborhood boards allocate a large portion of revenue-sharing funds to meet neighborhood priorities. The boards also enter into performance contracts with city department heads in which the departments agree to provide specified levels of services to each neighborhood. Birmingham, Alabama has adopted a similar decentralized administration: 86 neighborhood citizens committees work together to allocate all of the city's community development revenue-sharing funds. In Atlanta, an exemplary program of neighborhood advocacy planning, where city-paid planners are detached to serve as neighborhood advocates in the city planning process, has been developed.

Robert K. Yin and Douglas Yates have analyzed 215 case studies of urban decentralization, including both decentralization of choice to service clients and decentralization of functions to subcity entities.[3] Although they do not entertain utopian visions of the uses of such techniques, they do conclude that such techniques can lead to improved citizen understanding and participation, increased human-service orientation, better accountability of service bureaucracies, and more street-level sensitivity to service delivery programs. The studies of Vincent and Elinor Ostrom at Indiana University, Duane Elgin at Stanford Research Institute, and the Advisory Commission on Intergovernmental Relations have shown that the supposed economies of scale in urban service delivery are frequently little more than a persistent myth.[4] It may well be good economics to decentralize a great many labor-intensive public services to the neighborhood and small-community levels.

Beyond administrative decentralization, on which much experience has now accumulated, lies the concept of a neighborhood body as the administrator. Under this concept, the neighborhood council, borough, ward, or service district is the prime provider of services. The services are still financed by transfers from higher levels of government, since the providing bodies do not have revenue-raising powers of their own, but within broad guidelines they are performed by a body under the direct control of local citizens. The most common version is a contract arrangement in which neighborhood organizations operate mental health outreach programs, youth recreation programs, or community centers.

The next step—considerably less common—is that of an accountable neighborhood-level body not only entering into contracts with the city to perform certain services, but also making the decision, familiar to all large manufacturing concerns, of "make or buy." For example, a neighborhood corporation responsible for refuse collection or street repair could decide to establish its own service company or purchase the service from private vendors. The practice of governments purchasing services—even to the extent of an entire public works department—

from private contractors has been highly developed under California's well-known Lakewood plan. Lakewood and many other newer California cities are involved in an elaborate network of service contracting, both with other cities, counties, and special districts and with private contractors. There would seem to be no real reason, other than the ever present legal and political barriers, why organized urban neighborhoods of 10,000–20,000 people could not emulate independent cities of the same size, at least in matters that are not necessarily the province of a metropolitan or regional body.

The final step in the process of creating a federated city is to create a true federation, with a sizable number of neighborhood-level components, each enjoying its own tax base. Since there are some functions that must be administered on the metropolitan level, that level must also have its own independent taxing power. And since there would necessarily be a disparity of taxable resources among rich and poor entities, a revenue-sharing formula would be necessary, perhaps along the lines of the Twin Cities metropolitan plan in Minnesota.

To date, no city has dared to move much beyond cautious administrative decentralization and limited experimentation with neighborhoods as contract providers of services. North America's most celebrated federated city, metropolitan Toronto, is not a true federated city. Its large urban core, the city of Toronto, contains 35 percent of the population of the metropolitan area and necessarily dominates the metropolitan organization. Were Toronto to divide itself into boroughs the populations and influence of which approximated those of the suburban partners, its claim to being a true federated city would be far stronger. Although the city-county of Indianapolis has had enabling legislation to begin becoming a true federated city since 1972, it is now clear that opposition from elected officials has brought the process to a halt.

The manifold political and legal problems faced by those seeking a reorganization of metropolitan government are well known and prodigious. It is unlikely that any blueprint for radical change will so capture the hearts and imaginations of urban voters as to persuade them to opt enthusiastically for the change. Consequently, the stages leading toward the federated city are not likely to be organizationally neat. What is important, however, is not the neatness of the product, but the devolution of real power from centralized bureaucracies to democratic bodies closer to the people and from government generally to the nongovernmental sector. As agonizing and halting as the process may be, the price of not moving in this direction is the ultimate erosion of the liberties and opportunities of the people by the faceless and all-powerful state.

Neighborhood Fiscal Empowerment

The basic premise of neighborhood fiscal empowerment is that it is desirable to encourage neighborhood improvement efforts which are organized and carried out by neighborhood residents themselves. These efforts require resources and such other factors as information, expertise, organization, and realistic opportunity, but tangible resources must be at the disposal of local residents in amounts proportional to the magnitude of the problems to be overcome.

Neighborhood fiscal empowerment is a generic term for a public policy that seeks to place, or to leave, within the hands of neighborhood residents sufficient financial resources to permit them to undertake a wide range of cooperative neighborhood improvement activities with a reasonable chance of success. It scarcely needs be said that the major obstacle to neighborhood fiscal empowerment in middle-income neighborhoods is the depression of incomes of the inhabitants through government's continual demands on income in the form of taxation. This obstacle is currently the target of numerous proposals for tax limitation. Until these attacks succeed, however, the existing level of government taxation and economic mismanagement will continue.

Within the narrower framework of neighborhood fiscal empowerment, there are a number of essential criteria. The particular technique adopted must generate sufficient resources to allow neighborhood residents to achieve worthwhile results. It should operate with a minimum of nonproductive middlemen so that the great bulk of the resources are available for productive use. It is almost inescapably necessary that some element of income redistribution be involved in any program that attempts to assist the people of lower-income neighborhoods. The technique must thus contain some device for assuring taxpayers that the funds are being wisely expended in the public interest.

Furthermore, the neighborhood fiscal empowerment technique must promote the maximum self-sufficiency feasible at the neighborhood level, consistent with the level of available neighborhood resources. It should minimize the specter of co-optation of neighborhood initiatives by higher levels of government that control the flow of funds. It should be administratively practical and capable of implementation in a wide variety of neighborhood situations. Finally, the technique should emphasize the legitimacy of the neighborhood-level organization involved in the eyes of the neighborhood residents.

From the standpoint of the organized (political) neighborhood movement, the most popular form of neighborhood fiscal empowerment is direct funding from Washington. This was the original mechanism for the Office of Economic Opportunity's community action programs until they were brought under the effective control of city halls by the 1967 Green Amendment. Direct funding is the mechanism of the Neighborhood Self-Help Development Fund, a small but highly touted item in President Carter's national urban policy. Under this latter provision, enacted by Congress in 1978, the Department of Housing and Urban Development (HUD) will make grants to selected neighborhood organizations with approved track records, "with the concurrence of" city governments. This program—practically all that survives of President Carter's loudly proclaimed "national urban policy"—began in 1979 with a modest authorization of $15 million.

Similar to direct funding is indirect funding in which the federal government makes a grant to city hall, which in turn makes a grant to the favored neighborhood organization. Community Development Block Grant funds, authorized by the Housing and Community Development Act of 1974, can be and have been so used in a number of cities.

Judged by the criteria for neighborhood fiscal empowerment discussed above, both direct and indirect funding have little to recommend them. Consider the question of the legitimacy of the receiving organization. Does the favored group truly command the support of the great majority of neighborhood residents? Who is to pass judgment: city hall? HUD? During field trips in 1978, the National Commission on Neighborhoods saw many cases of neighborhood organizations, funded by or with the approval of city hall, that seemed to have far more rapport with the political leaders of the city than with the citizens of the neighborhood. Neighborhood residents may, of course, give their tacit support to an organization of accomplished grantsmen on the grounds that it might do some good for the neighborhood. This is not, however, a compelling argument for the direct funding approach.

Then there is the question of accountability. In any direct or indirect funding approach, some provision must be made for proper use of the funds to accomplish the stated public interest goals. Thus such programs inevitably come burdened with numerous rules, regulations, inspections, and audits. Compliance puts a serious burden on the receiving organization. The regulation makers and auditors can be expected to use every technique available to prevent embarrassing developments at the local level. They want to forestall scandal, bad publicity, and the loss of public and congressional support for the program. The receiving organization must therefore be ever mindful of its relations with its government benefactor, especially if it hopes to obtain more funding in the future. This tends to orient the grantee toward satisfying those who provide the funding or approve its disbursement, which can lead to debilitating political and bureaucratic intrigue.

Direct and indirect funding both carry the threat of co-optation. A major strength of a neighborhood organization should be its responsiveness to neighborhood residents and its willingness to defend their interests against outside institutions. Often neighborhood organizations cannot oppose outside institutions without jeopardizing their very existence, which depends upon continued funding from Washington or city hall. These approaches give the strong impression of having markedly low efficiency in terms of application of funds to actual productive use. There are simply too many political and bureaucratic snouts in the trough. And the chance of maximizing self-sufficiency in the neighborhood is small.

An alternative device for neighborhood fiscal empowerment is the creation of a subcity governmental structure that can more readily be controlled by neighborhood residents and relies primarily (though not exclusively) on its own tax resources to fund its efforts. A full-blown neighborhood government would presumably have a relatively independent revenue base. This base could be developed in several ways, the most direct by giving the neighborhood government the statutory power to levy property, sales, or income taxes upon neighborhood property and residents, in addition to existing citywide taxes. A less far-reaching and perhaps more efficient method would be to earmark a portion of various taxes collected within the neighborhood for the use of the neighborhood government. This would of course diminish the revenues available to the higher levels of government that perform the administrative duties. Finally, a variant of tax-increment financing for neighborhood fiscal empowerment is possible. Under this technique, any increase in the property tax base that results from an improvement campaign sponsored by the neighborhood government is deemed to have resulted from that campaign and is paid over to the neighborhood government by the city.

Where a full-fledged neighborhood government is not politically possible, a more limited community services district may be a reasonable alternative. Such districts, supported primarily by property taxation, have long been used in California and Florida to finance a broad range of public improvements and services. Perhaps the most highly developed example is the Reedy Creek Improvement District in Florida. This special district has the powers of owning and leasing property and eminent domain (even outside its boundaries!) and controls drainage and reclamation, irrigation, water and sewers, flood prevention, waste disposal, mosquito abatement, airport and highway construction, parking, recreation, fire protection, utilities, mass transit, and land use. The district is also exempt from county building controls. Police protection appears to be the only normal governmental power that Reedy Creek lacks. The district is governed by a five-member board, elected by landowners on the basis of one vote per acre owned. The district is better known as Disney World.[5]

An alternative to both the direct/indirect grant system and the creation of governmental or quasi-governmental bodies at the neighborhood level is the public choice system built around tax subventions or voucher payments to individual neighborhood residents. The tax credit version, long advocated by Sen. Mark Hatfield, would allow taxpayers to take a credit against their federal income tax liability for contributions made to nonprofit neighborhood corporations certified by the secretary of the treasury.[6] The credit would vary from 10 percent for higher-income taxpayers to 80 percent for lower-income taxpayers. This device could be used at state or municipal levels by allowing neighborhood residents or businesses to claim credits against property, income, or possibly even sales tax liabilities.

The voucher alternative is embodied in bills sponsored in 1978 and 1979 by Congressmen Joel Pritchard and James Blanchard, members of the National Commission on Neighborhoods.[7] Under the Pritchard-Blanchard approach, HUD would conduct a pilot program to test the feasibility of a neighborhood improvement credit (voucher). Each adult in a neighborhood would receive a voucher that he or she could assign, along with a required matching contribution, to the neighborhood improvement program most favored by the citizen. The programs could be public, such as a police foot-patrol fund or a community school program; or private, such as a community credit union, community development corporation, Neighborhood Housing Services, church athletic league, or senior citizen center.

Both the tax credit and voucher plans involve a redistribution of resources by some level of government. But unlike the direct and indirect grant programs or the neighborhood government alternative, the tax credit and voucher approaches afford a citizen a real choice about the use of his or her money to benefit the neighborhood. The plans avoid the lethal problems of legitimacy, accountability, and co-optation, since no collective choice is involved. The organizations to which the funds are assigned must compete for the patronage of citizens. They must look to these citizens, and not to a government, for continued financial support.

Urban Economic Development

The economic health of the nation's cities depends on their capacity to attract and hold wealth-producing industries offering income-producing jobs. The great cities arose because they had that capacity. Today, many question whether the older eastern cities, in particular, have a viable economic future. As George Sternlieb has pointed out, between 1970 and 1974 selective migration into and out of the nation's central cities led to a disastrous loss of some $30 billion in urban incomes.[8] The fiscal calamities of New York and Cleveland are well known.

But even as pundits lament the terminal decline of New York, there is a building boom of impressive dimensions under way, and revitalization of many formerly declining neighborhoods is proceeding at a pace so rapid as to produce anguished cries of "gentrification." Indeed, T.D. Allman, writing in *Harper's*,[9] argues persuasively that policymakers are still trying to find solutions to urban problems that are fast disappearing. The coming crisis, he believes, will occur not in the central cities but in the suburbs.

It is nonetheless clear that much must be done to make the older central cities more productive of real wealth and income. The first key ingredient is municipal fiscal integrity. Wealth producers (other than those whose wealth depends mainly upon manipulating city bureaucracies) will naturally avoid cities that continue to engage in fiscal mismanagement. Sound city management means staunch resistance to the clamoring of public employee unions, now second only to the Teamsters in national membership. It will require honest accounting for pension funds and a refusal to pay current expenses from capital budgets. Cities must recognize that there are limits on what they can do for their residents.

Prudent city management must entail a re-examination of exemptions from the city's property tax base, with the aim of broadening that base to the maximum feasible limits, as well as a re-examination of the city's licensing and regulatory activities to identify those that impose needless costs on wealth creators. It also requires prudent investment in the maintenance of infrastructure (sewers, highways, bridges, water systems) essential to industrial and commercial activities. And, as pointed out previously, the city will need to consider a host of techniques like private contracting and user charges to secure real economies in service programs, create new economic opportunities in the marketplace instead of continuing to feed municipal monopolies, and redirect the costs of special benefit programs to those who enjoy the benefits.

The private sector union problem is a particularly difficult one, since it is more or less beyond the control of city government. Many urban-based unions—such as the construction trades and manufacturing unions—have, not surprisingly, become extremely defensive in the face of urban economic decline. Instead of re-examining their own practices, which might have contributed to the disappearance of jobs for their members, they have sought to prevent layoffs of their members, limit entry, and extract ever higher and more restrictive contract settlements from the remaining employers. There is something profoundly self-defeating about this. The more unions persist in defensive operations, the less likely that a city can attract the kind of employers that the unions most fervently want to attract.

From a national perspective, much needs to be done to expand opportunities for small- and medium-sized businesses generally, including relief from the outrageous government paperwork burden, a rollback of excessive regulatory edicts under the Occupational Safety and Health Act, improvements in the securities and patent laws, and the encouragement of investment in small- and medium-sized businesses through tax devices like the proposed individual enterprise account. Measures to encourage employee ownership of small businesses and profit sharing also offer possibilities for strengthening small business.

One intriguing idea for promoting economic development in depressed urban centers is the enterprise zone concept, developed independently by Sir Geoffrey Howe, the Conservative party spokesman on economic affairs in the United Kingdom, and Rep. Louis Jenkins of the Louisiana House of Representatives.[10] In the enterprise zone, government regulation would be reduced to the bare minimum necessary to protect public health and safety. There would be no zoning, no building codes, no rent control, no minimum wage, no closed or union shop, and no unexpected increases in the minimal level of taxation. On the other hand, there would be no government loans or subsidies to business or any other form of government assistance. The enterprise zone could be combined with a free port area in which there would be no customs duties, no exchange controls, and no other government impediments to economic activity. As Prof. Peter Hall—curiously, a socialist—has pointed out, the free port area would be based on "fairly shameless free enterprise."[11] Within it would be a real-life example of what could be done in wealth creation and income generation when the heavy hand of government is removed. Implementation of such an idea will come over the dead bodies of a large number of municipal officials, union leaders, and even businessmen in areas not eligible for the same benefits. Nonetheless, if the situation in South Bronx and Lawndale worsens, sooner or later this idea will gather strength as a last desperate alternative.

Redesigning Urban Systems

Yet another group of tasks falls under the rubric of redesigning urban systems, that is, changing the rules of the game by which urban life is played.

A prime candidate for reform is the property information system in effect in many older cities. Although it varies from city to city, the usual property information system is a direct descendant of the old English parish land records, and is about as easy for the layman to penetrate. Simply ascertaining the ownership of an abandoned building has proven a staggering problem to more than a few neighborhood improvement groups, especially where the system is as Byzantine as in Chicago. Neighborhood groups need accurate and readily available information about properties. They cannot survive protracted delays and frustrations and the necessity to spend their meager resources on battalions of experts to discover what is supposed to be public knowledge. Forsyth County, North Carolina, has pioneered the development of a model computerized land records and urban information system that, when complete, will readily display all relevant information about titles, encumbrances, mortgages, pending judgments, zoning classification, tax valuation and assessments, and even the incidence of auto accidents, arson, and crime in the block.

Even where the basic information about the status of a given parcel of property can be readily obtained, the neighborhood improvement group faces formidable problems with the tax delinquency and property recycling systems in most older cities. It is generally no simple matter to acquire an abandoned, tax-delinquent hulk. Barring herculean efforts and special influence at city hall, the time needed to acquire and begin to restore an abandoned building can run from three to ten years in many cities. A process requiring this amount of time is poorly suited to meet the needs of citizen self-help groups, since long delays quickly lead to discouragement and disintegration of enthusiasm and leadership.

Space does not permit a detailed discussion of a desirable model for recycling dilapidated and tax-delinquent properties back onto the market.[12] There are a host of administrative and legal improvements that have now been field-tested (notably in St. Louis) that provide clear title to a new purchaser with considerably less delay and expense than under earlier procedures. An effort should also be made to experiment with the adaptation of the carried interest concept, familiar to students of petroleum law, to the acquisition and rehabilitation of declining urban properties.[13]

Another urban system crying out for reform is zoning. It is now clear to even the advocates of zoning that in practice zoning has prohibited constructive changes that could lead to revitalization. At the same time, zoning has forced sterile planning concepts upon happily intermixed urban neighborhoods, to the detriment of the community and its residents. The simplest remedy for zoning is its repeal and replacement with a modern private-nuisance enforcement system along the lines advocated by Prof. Robert Ellickson.[14] Another alternative is a workable system of transferable development rights (TDRs) in which the area where rights are transferred is a substantial section of the city and the government makes no locational decisions beyond initially apportioning the TDRs and defining the schedule of TDRs required for various kinds of development.[15] The private covenant system, once discredited because of its use to effect racial exclusion, can also be institutionalized and streamlined to permit effective action against property owners who create genuine nuisances.[16]

Building codes pose a serious obstacle to inner city rehabilitation, as numerous witnesses before congressional committees, national commissions, and expert conferences have testified. In perhaps its most signal and original contribution to public policy, the National Commission on Neighborhoods recommended the scrapping of the traditional building code enforcement system in favor of an essentially privatized system drawn from the French experience.

In France, with only a few, limited exceptions, there is no public enforcement of building codes. Instead, the French Civil Code imposes on all builders a liability of up to ten years for major structural defects. To protect against possible malpractice claims, a builder purchases warranty insurance. To protect their reserves, companies hire private inspectors to check that a building is safely built and thus unlikely to cause warranty claims. Mortgage lenders and property insurers generally require warranty insurance as a condition of making a mortgage loan or writing property insurance, except in the smallest projects. The system is essentially self-enforcing and places the responsibility for public safety on the builder, not the government.

The traditional building code enforcement system in the United States is clearly nearing a dead end in the matter of urban rehabilitation. The certainty of black and white rules defeats technological advances and often imposes unconscionable costs when old buildings are being restored. On the other hand, introducing added flexibility at the point of inspection exposes the inspector to both legal liability and the temptations of corruption. Since even experts in the field can adduce no clear evidence that building codes have any net benefit to the public, it seems clear that the time has come to reprivatize building codes, thus removing them as an obstacle to urban revitalization.

Finally, cities need to re-examine their licensing laws. All too often licensing laws are a device for excluding competition in the skilled trades and professions, rather than for weeding out incompetents. Professors Robert Gaston and Sidney Carroll at the University of Tennessee have shown that strict licensing laws for electricians and plumbers result in *less* net protection for the public.[18] By limiting the supply and hence inflating the costs of electricians, the laws encourage property owners to let problems slide, make jerry-built repairs, or hire fly-by-night operators to patch things together. Licensing laws are also notorious, as the Urban League has long recognized, for barring entry to minority youths seeking to fill a market gap in neighborhoods where licensed (white) tradesmen do not care to venture. The appropriate solution to this problem is to switch from mandatory licensing to voluntary certification. This should be coupled with registration of contractors so that consumers can review the track records of those who offer needed services. The most competent providers could advertise their successful completion of advanced competency examinations offered by private organizations like Underwriters Laboratories, and less competent practitioners could compete on the basis of lower price. It might be necessary to have some system of required financial responsibility to allow consumer recovery in case of negligence and injury.

Reinvestment

In the past five years, a great deal of political rhetoric has been lavished on the problem of redlining. This is a practice engaged in by some financial institutions in which certain areas (redlined on a map) are deemed off limits for mortgage and business loans. Neighborhood groups, particularly those allied with the Chicago-based National Peoples Action movement, have protested long and loudly against lending institutions that have redlined the neighborhoods inhabited by their depositors. One result has been a spate of federal laws, such as the Home Mortgage Disclosure Act of 1975 and the Community Reinvestment Act of 1978, that put pressure on lending institutions to reinvest their depositors' funds in the declining or struggling neighborhoods previously shunned by the institutions. California, Illinois, and several other states have passed stiff anti-redlining statutes. Whether these acts fulfill the expectations of their advocates remains to be seen, however.

Unfortunately, the thrust of the organized neighborhood movement has been to persuade the government to force reluctant institutions to take an action that holds every promise of increasing their lending losses, jeopardizing their depositors' accounts, and involving them in untold miseries. On sober reflection, it is hard to be critical of a bank that makes the highest-quality loans it can.

The real answer to the bank that siphons its depositors' funds out of their declining neighborhood is greenlining: an organized withdrawal of depositors' funds, which can then be deposited in another institution that is sufficiently responsive to neighborhood needs. If no such institution is available, then the complainers should be afforded a realistic opportunity for creating a new institution to serve their needs, such as a community credit union. Present regulatory barriers to the entry of such new institutions—which have been kept as high as possible at the insistence of existing lending institutions—should be reduced to an absolute minimum.

The same principle applies to the related subject of property insurance redlining. Instead of trying to pressure the state insurance commissioner to force reluctant companies to extend coverage against their judgment or to offer policies at a loss that other policyholders must subsidize, the victims of insurance redlining should organize their own mutual insurance fund. The existence of a strong neighborhood organization almost automatically increases the insurability of property within the neighborhood. In an insurance industry with so many well-developed techniques for reinsurance, there is no valid reason why a neighborhood of even 10,000 people cannot create a functioning property insurance pool once the basic procedures for its creation have been simplified. The first neighborhood to discover the potential of this idea may well find itself the creator of a neighborhood-oriented mutual insurance company serving urban neighborhoods all across America.

Another useful step toward spurring reinvestment in urban neighborhoods is to reprivatize the Federal Housing Administration. Created in 1935 to stimulate investment in the stagnant housing industry, the FHA pioneered the low down-payment, level-payment home mortgage. Today, however, there are at least eight private mortgage insurance companies operating throughout the United States and several others operating on a regional basis. Instead of maintaining its expensive and frequently ossified national field organization, the FHA should recast itself as a reinsurer of the reserve funds of private mortgage insurance companies that take above-average risks.

Under this program, the new FHA would reinsure the reserve fund of a private insurer against losses exceeding some mutually agreed normal level. For this it would charge an insurance fee. The prime lender and the private insurer would carry out all the lending and insuring functions, and the FHA would be called upon only if a wave of abnormal losses occurred. Instead of bearing risk at the third position, after the mortgagor and the lender, the FHA would retreat to the fourth position, after the private mortgage insurer. Such a program was carried out with complete success by the Wisconsin Indemnity Fund in 1971, working with the Mortgage Guaranty Insurance Company of Milwaukee. Its adoption at the national level would be a major step in reducing unnecessary government expense and bureaucracy while increasing opportunities for a more flexible response to mortgage insurance needs by free-market actors.

Any program for stimulating urban reinvestment must deal decisively with the recurring problem of rent control. A large number of otherwise knowledgeable people seem to believe that rent control leads to desirably low rents for tenants, with few or no adverse effects upon "greedy landlords." But the evidence is about as overwhelming as such evidence can be that rent control accelerates urban decay and abandonment, assists the wrong people, misallocates housing space, creates housing shortages, depresses the construction industry, aggravates municipal fiscal problems, and produces heightened social conflicts that defeat efforts for rational accommodation of competing interests.

Before concluding these suggestions in the area of reinvestment, it would be worthwhile to mention perhaps the one government-inspired program that has had an outstanding positive effect on improving urban neighborhoods: the Neighborhood Housing Services (NHS) program, launched in 1973 at the initiative of the Federal Home Loan Bank Board (rather than HUD, which has openly opposed the program on more than one occasion). Under NHS, a concept first tried in Pittsburgh's central north side beginning in 1969, a local organization comprising neighborhood citizens, local government officials, and lending industry representatives is formed. The federal Urban Reinvestment Task Force (URTF) provides this local organization with a trained field executive for a period of eight to ten months. It also provides a one-time matching grant of $50,000 for a neighborhood improvement housing loan fund. After this, the hand of Washington is seen no more.

The NHS model has now spread to over 35 cities and is achieving real results. As the Senate Banking, Housing and Urban Affairs Committee pointed out in reporting the legislation to convert the URTF into a Neighborhood Reinvestment Corporation in 1977, "the NHS is a local program. The program is nongovernmental . . . nonbureaucratic . . . a self-help effort. The program is not a giveaway. . . "These characteristics do much to explain the success of the NHS despite the welter of failed and discredited government programs for achieving many of the same ends. Whether the NHS can maintain its essentially private-sector, local, self-help orientation in its new incarnation as the Neighborhood Reinvestment Corporation remains to be seen, but to date its leaders have carefully avoided the most serious pitfalls.

Property Taxation

Property tax increases in American cities have been a source of municipal alarm and taxpayer outrage. For over a decade in older urban areas, property tax rates have been rising—in absolute terms, in comparison with suburbs, and in comparison with the newer growing cities. At least until 1973, expenditures rose more rapidly in the older urban centers, and much faster than assistance payments from federal and state governments. Thus local property taxes had to be increased to raise more money. Since 1974, however, expenditures have actually been increasing more slowly in the older cities, most of which are losing population. Yet tax rates and assessments have continued to increase.

A prime reason for this is the shrinkage of the property tax base. This is in turn caused by several factors. One is the disappearance of ratables as buildings are abandoned and businesses leave the central city. Another is the rise in abatements, exemptions, and other tax-related subsidies produced by desperate city efforts to maintain an industrial base. Yet another is the prevalence of nonprofit tax-exempt institutions.

It should be borne in mind that high property taxes are not produced by the compulsion of city fathers to hoard money. Taxes are raised to cover expenditures. In the twenty years between 1957 and 1977, the unit cost of state and local government increased 179 percent in real dollars, whereas the price of goods and services purchased by consumers increased only 108 percent. This increase was largely due to increased wages paid to public employees. Did taxpayers obtain added benefits from these increased expenditures? There is no consensus on measuring the quality of benefits received, but it is hard to find a taxpayer who thinks these two decades of increasing taxes were a bargain.

Property taxes provide about 53 percent of the revenues of the nation's largest 59 cities. Both the level of taxation and the specific form that it takes has a real—and negative—impact on much self-help activity. The high levels of taxation pre-empt private resources for public programs that may not be viewed as beneficial to the taxpayer as an alternative allocation of his resources. And the structure of the property tax itself has long been suspected of inequities and economic fallacies.

Municipalities can leave more resources in their citizens' pockets by making urban government more efficient. Putting more "free" services on a user charge basis, and contracting with private or public vendors for the provision of many traditional municipal services, are two major steps in the right direction. Many sound recommendations for improving the property tax administration process, which cities are slowly and sometimes grudgingly attempting to implement, have been made.

Another important step for relieving pressure on a narrow property tax base is for a city to reconsider its policy toward exemptions and abatements. In Newark, for instance, two-thirds of the city's land area is tax-exempt, and some 55 percent of the total value of taxable property is simply not part of the tax base. It is sound policy to make hitherto exempt institutions, including those operated by the state and federal governments, pay more of their share of the cost of operating a city.

Similarly, instead of offering outright tax abatements for industry—thus shifting the property tax burden in the direction of homeowners and apartment dwellers—the city should enter into a contract that provides for the repayment of any tax subvention out of subsequent profits of a business, if there are any. If the venture proves unprofitable, of course, the abatement would not be repaid.

A strong case has been made for shifting more of the property tax burden—or even all of it—away from improvements and onto the land itself. Such a shift would encourage improvements and discourage the speculative holding of undeveloped land. It would concentrate development in areas of high land values, with beneficial effects on the problem of urban sprawl. And it would recover for society as a whole much of the value of sites that were created by taxpayer-financed investment, while leaving more profits in the hands of those who invested in construction and rehabilitation of improvements.

Unfortunately, the common practice in urban America is to tax improvements more heavily than land. This is pronounced in the case of New York City, according to studies made by Prof. Philip Finkelstein of Adelphi University.[19] The time is clearly ripe for, at the very least, a shift of the tax burden equally to land and buildings. Pittsburgh has led the way toward site-value taxation by adopting a 1979 revenue program that taxes land at 97.5 mills and improvements at 24.75 mills. When the overlapping taxes of Allegheny County and school district are added, the Pittsburgh property taxpayer will pay 147.5 mills on land and 74.75 mills on buildings, a ratio of almost 2:1. This difference should be enough to permit economic assessment of the effects of the site value taxation tilt.

With improvements in administrative procedures and in the system for recycling delinquent parcels back into the marketplace, the property tax system promises to continue as a mainstay of local government finance. With a steady shift toward site value taxation, property owners will have more incentive to make improvements, and speculators will suffer greater penalties for keeping land out of productive use. It is difficult to see how this can be anything but beneficial to the revitalization of inner-city neighborhoods.

Income Taxation

Given the complexity of the Internal Revenue Code, it would be possible to concoct an infinite number of tax provisions to benefit neighborhood revitalization and self-help activity. Senator Hatfield's neighborhood corporation tax credit plan, discussed earlier, is an example. Two provisions dealing with incentives for neighborhood-based housing improvement, both developed by the author and recommended by the National Commission on Neighborhoods, are set forth below.[20]

The first provision would create a favorable tax position for a developer who agrees to build or rehabilitate rental housing, depreciate it over a ten-year period, and then convey it to a neighborhood organization that had in the interim gradually assumed the responsibilities of property management and upkeep. The object of this proposal is to attract profit-seeking investors to create decent housing and then to transfer that housing to neighborhood-based ownership and management after the tax shelter benefits have substantially diminished.

Because of changes in the tax code in 1969 and 1976, tax shelter investors have become increasingly concerned about so-called "back-end penalties," tax benefit recovery provisions that come into effect when the original owner disposes of a property. The aim of the commission's proposal is to relieve these back-end penalties under carefully defined circumstances. Namely: when, after a ten-year holding period, the building is sold to a qualified neighborhood improvement corporation, the so-called "back end penalties" (liability for the recapture of accelerated depreciation over straight line and the effect of that excess on the minimum and maximum tax provisions) shall be deferred for a period of five years. So long as the building is satisfactorily maintained throughout that five-year period, the original owner will be forgiven 20 percent of the back-end penalties otherwise due and may claim a charitable deduction of 20 percent of his equity in each of the five years. There are more qualifying details, including standards for proper maintenance, but the thrust of the proposal should be clear. Note that the proposal gives the conveyor a continuing incentive to work with the new owner both before and during the five-year period to assure proper management of the property.

A second meritorious proposal of the commission is the community reinvestment trust (CRT). The CRT is a modified form of the real estate investment trust (REIT), which has been a part of the Code since 1960. The CRT would be organized along the same lines as a REIT to make investments in neighborhood construction, rehabilitation, or commercial improvement. Neighborhood residents would be eligible to claim a 10-percent federal income tax credit on any investment made in the CRT operating in their neighborhood. The CRT would, however, be forbidden to use accelerated depreciation of their real estate investments, partially counterbalancing the revenue loss caused by the tax credit. The commission recommended that HUD be authorized to insure the first $5,000 of an individual investment, but a better solution would be for HUD to reinsure private investment insurance against excessive losses. Where the properties to be built or improved are insured under an FHA-type program, the risk of loss of investment by the CRT would of course be minimal.

These two tax law changes would not be earthshaking in their application. But over time they would have the effect of making neighborhoods with good neighborhood organizations more attractive places for real estate investment, by both residents and outsiders. In addition, the CRT would offer neighborhood residents a vehicle designed to facilitate their own investment in their own neighborhood, giving them a chance to protect the value of their prior investment in a home by stimulating the improvement of the neighborhood around it. These two recommendations may not be the final solution to neighborhood reinvestment incentive, but they are a modest and responsible beginning.

The foregoing recommendations, though necessarily sketchy, illustrate the kinds of suggestions that, taken together, can stimulate a renaissance of the inner city and its neighborhoods. They are not intended to serve as a blueprint. Experience has shown that those who invent blueprints are disappointed by the results—as are the people who suffer the implementation. The important thing here is to firmly establish the principles of human-scale, grass-roots self-help initiatives, the restoration to taxpayers of the resources needed to deal with their own problems, the reduction of institutional and legal barriers to public choice and creative self-help, sound economic policies in the macroeconomy and staunch resistance to the temptation to create yet another government program, bureaucracy, special privilege, monopoly, or institution, where a dose of freedom and spontaneity will do better. If these principles are faithfully adhered to, the prospects for urban neighborhoods in the 1980s may well become the brightest in recent history.

NOTES

1. Richard Goodwin, "The Shape of American Politics," *Commentary,* June 1967.

2. This term is appropriated from Joseph F. Zimmerman, *The Federated City: Community Control in Large Cities* (New York: St. Martin's, 1972).

3. Robert K. Yin and Douglas Yates, *Street Level Governments: Assessing Decentralization and Urban Services* (Santa Monica, Calif.: RAND Corporation, 1974).

4. See Elinor Ostrom, "Size and Performance in a Federal System" (Workshop in Political Theory and Policy Analysis, Indiana University, 1976); Robert L. Bish and Vincent Ostrom, *Understanding Urban Government: Metropolitan Reform Reconsidered* (Washington, D.C.: American Enterprise Institute, 1973); Duane Elgin et al., *City Size and the Quality of Life* (Washington, D.C.: Senate Subcommittee on Rural Development, 1975); and Advisory Commission on Intergovernmental Relations, *Size Can Make a Difference,* ACIR bulletin 70–8 (Washington, D.C.: ACIR, 1970).

5. See Note, "New Community Development Districts," *Houston Law Review* 9 (1972): 1032.

6. The most recent version is S.2502, introduced October 1, 1973 (*Congressional Record,* p. S18133 [daily ed.]. See Hatfield's "Bringing Political Power Back Home: The Case for Neighborhood Government," *Ripon Quarterly* (Summer 1974): 19–26.

7. See H.R.13894, introduced August 16, 1978, and H.R.2128, introduced February 13, 1979.

8. See testimony of George Sternlieb in "Rebirth of the American City," hearings before the House Committee on Banking, Currency and Housing, September 22, 1976, 1: 353–55.

9. T. D. Allman, "The Urban Crisis Leaves Town," *Harper's,* December 1978.

10. See *Enterprise Zone: A Solution to the Urban Crisis?* (Washington, D.C.: Heritage Foundation, 1979).

11. Peter Hall, ibid. at 9.

12. A condensed list of useful recommendations may be found in *People, Building Neighborhoods,* Report of the National Commission on Neighborhoods (Washington, D.C.: U.S. Government Printing Office, 1979), pp. 39–40.

13. Ibid., pp. 181–183.

14. See Robert C. Ellickson, "Alternatives to Zoning: Covenants, Nuisance Rules, and Fines as Land Use Controls," *University of Chicago Law Review* 40 (1973): 683.

15. See Jerome G. Rose, ed., *Transfer of Development Rights* (New Brunswick, N.J.: Center for Urban Policy Research, 1975).

16. See Bernard Siegan, *Land Use Without Zoning* (Lexington, Mass.: D.C. Heath, 1972); and Note, "Land Use Controls in Metropolitan Areas: The Failure of Zoning and a Proposed Alternative," *Southern California Law Review* 45 (1972): 335.

17. See *Report of the National Commission on Neighborhoods,* pp. 204–208.

18. Sidney L. Carroll and Robert J. Gaston, "Occupational Licensing and Service Quality in the Building Trades: Electricians and Plumbers," Unpublished National Science Foundation report, University of Tennessee, Department of Economics (1975?).

19. Philip Finkelstein, *Real Property Taxation in New York City* (New York: Praeger, 1975).

20. See *Report of the National Commission on Neighborhoods,* pp. 187–194.

Higher Education: Problems and Prospects

John H. Bunzel

XIV

There was a time when the world of higher education never had it so good. The past, of course, was not really as we now remember it, but American academics who began their careers after World War II and in the 1950s or even early 1960s can remember when the university was a community of relative peace, stability, and continuity. It was a period not without problems and tensions, but those who had chosen the academic way of life felt they belonged to a fine and important profession. Their relationships with students and colleagues were marked by a kind of civility and reason that not only enhanced their commitment to the values of merit and achievement but generated a high degree of personal satisfaction in their teaching and scholarship. This is not to suggest that the spirit of competition and rivalry was absent, for more than a few professors (then as now) were fully skilled in the art of political infighting and, above all, of protecting and cultivating their own turf. (Some wag, obviously an insider, has remarked that the reason academic politics are so petty and vicious is that the stakes are so low). It is only to say that there was still a widespread feeling that the university was made up of self-governing individuals who shared responsibility and authority for achieving mutually held goals and for maintaining the fragile understandings of a professional community on the campus. The consensual processes that served its needs had yet to be shattered by the new and powerful forces of populism and fragmentation and the emotional excesses of ideological politics.

It is no secret that the experiences of the middle and late sixties left their mark indelibly. It was not merely a question of a bruise or two: the academic world will never be the same again. The dramatic increase in race consciousness sometimes intermingled with a new awareness of the peoples of the Third World; the rise of an increasingly aggressive civil rights movement frequently torn by conflict, and of a drug culture hostile to discipline and constraints of any sort; the tormenting frustration centered on Vietnam that ravaged our national life; the large numbers of young faculty and new students who were often added hastily in a dramatically swelling labor market, none of whom was socialized to accept the internalization of the standardized academic norms—these were but a few of the developments of the 1960s that changed the campuses and their educational climate. Further, in the last ten years our cultural values have shifted, and with that has come a shift, inevitably, in university standards.

Today, in spite of the unquiet quiet on the campuses, higher education is confronted with many different but serious and complicated troubles. The whole society is now in transition—but to what? It is a paradox of our times, Clark Kerr has observed, that as more and more Americans from all walks of life are able to obtain an education at some postsecondary institution, knowledge has come to be seen "as less of a source of good and more a potential source of evil." Besides, many people no longer believe that going to college will improve their prospects of getting a job. One reason educators do not know what our colleges and universities will look like in ten or twenty years is that there is little agreement among them about what education should be or do. We exalt education throughout the land, but are we developing the kinds of knowledge and attitudes of mind we want to see passed on from one generation to another? Is vocational training a substitute for education? What is our idea of an educated person?

The future of the university will depend on how it adapts to a society that is in the process of redefining itself. It will also depend on what it conceives its basic mission and purposes to be. In the most practical terms, our institutions of higher education have a dual obligation: to expand the principle and practice of equal access and to preserve standards of excellence. The university's future will depend on how it accommodates both. In the words of former University of Chicago president Edward Levi, we must reach more minds without deserting the mind.

The issues discussed below are neither exhaustive nor definitive. They are intended to suggest the diversity of problems and concerns facing higher education in the next decade.

THE DEMOGRAPHICS OF ACADEMIA: ENROLLMENT TRENDS AND PROBLEMS

For most of the past 25 years higher education has prospered in a climate of expansion. For a time student enrollments grew rapidly, and this growth provided bigger budgets, which in turn made it possible for colleges and universities to hire thousands of new faculty members.

Now the bubble has burst. Enrollment is slowing down, and tighter budgets have become a stubborn fact of life. Not only has the academic job market leveled off, but a further downward turn lies ahead in the 1980s. Very simply, the optimism that characterized the beginning of the 1970s has turned to worry and even disenchantment at the end of the decade, with the academic world at the mercy of a declining birth rate that is now at an all-time low of 1.9 births per woman. The baby boom that followed World War II, which increased the number of school-age children by 70 percent between 1950 and 1970, has become the baby bust of the 1970s. Down 11 percent since 1970, the number of students in elementary and high schools is expected to fall another 10 percent in the next decade. The 18–24-year-old group presently in decline is not expected to return to normal until the late 1990s.

Many educators believe that the unexpected enrollment drop in 1979 means that the downward trend long forecast for the 1980s has arrived. Apart from the effects of inflation, rising tuition costs and other mounting educational costs, college age students are uncertain about the economy and generally apprehensive about the economic health of the nation. For example, there has been a substantial slowing in the growth rate of the enrollment of women, and in 1979 women's gains failed to offset the continuing decline in men's enrollment, as they had the year before. According to Garland Parker, director of the University of Cincinnati's Office for Enrollment Policy and Educational Research, most of the gains in women's attendance in 1979 at four-year institutions were in part-time enrollment. Overall, counting part-time and full-time students, women's enrollment rose 1.7 percent and men's fell 2.2 percent. Among full-time students, women's enrollment was up 0.9 percent and men's down 2.4 percent. Enrollments of part-time women students were up 3.5 percent, and those of part-time men students were down 1.5 percent. A decrease in full-time enrollment is important, Mr. Parker points out, because this category provides most of the nation's trained business leaders, clergy, doctors, engineers, lawyers, teachers, and other professionals.

There were other changes in campus enrollment in 1979. The growth rate for enrollment in professional schools slowed. However, enrollment in independent law and medical schools still climbed 7 percent, and at engineering, technological, and business schools it rose 0.9 percent. As Mr. Parker says, demand for places in such career-oriented schools may be outstripping the colleges' ability to provide them. At private universities such as Harvard and Yale there has been a 1 percent enrollment gain (and it could be much larger). But enrollment at big unitary public state systems slipped 0.8 percent, and at other large public universities such as Ohio State enrollment fell 1.7 percent.

The uncertain future of higher education is depressing to many small, private colleges that do not have the money to make prudent or necessary changes. George Washington University has been able to construct new buildings on its valuable downtown property, which it has leased to businesses. Grinnell College in Iowa has purchased a commercial television station in Dayton, Ohio. But hundreds of campuses have no solid endowments and cannot turn to state legislatures to bail them out if they get into financial trouble. Depending heavily on tuition to make ends meet, they face a more difficult future than public institutions, major private research universities, and the elite four-year colleges, which generally have greater resources. For many schools it is a question of getting through the difficult period immediately ahead. By the year 2000, enrollments in higher education are expected to grow again.

There are other problems. Between now and 1985 college graduates are more likely to be employed below the level of skill for which they were trained, resulting in job dissatisfaction, high occupational mobility, and perhaps (for the first time) unemployment. A Labor Department study has also shown that colleges and universities are overproducing in many areas, resulting in a surplus of chemists, food scientists, meteorologists, oceanographers, physicists, political scientists, psychologists, and teachers. Further, public confidence in higher education (as well as in all the other major institutions of society) has dropped in this country some 40 percent from its high point in the early 1960s, when the importance and accomplishments of education were viewed with much more enthusiasm.

The matter of numbers of students and their impact on higher education has raised some important questions about whether decent standards of student achievement are being upheld. One of the great accomplishments in this country has been the movement from elite to mass higher education and subsequently to a system of universal access. But what should be the minimum requirements of acceptable performance at a college or university to which there is universal access? At other kinds of institutions faculty members are also asking, once again, what the role of a liberal arts education should be in the modern world. What values, skills, and intellectual habits should be developed before a student can be properly certified as liberally educated? The debate has a special urgency at a time when significant increases in enrollment have occurred in such vocationally oriented programs as business and engineering, while at the same time students are turning away from the social sciences and the humanities and arts. The difficult problem is to find a way to make any of the reductions in faculty and staff that are necessitated by budgetary cutbacks, with the least possible disruption of the whole academic program. For example, campuses facing the possibility of faculty layoffs confront painful decisions when 90 percent of the faculty of a school of social sciences is tenured. The simple truth is that many institutions are finding their options severely limited by the large numbers of tenured academics on their staffs.

COLLECTIVE BARGAINING

First, the recent past: within the last dozen years or so, faculty unionism has emerged as a major movement in higher education. Not surprisingly, collective bargaining has staked out a firmer beachhead and grown more rapidly in the publicly funded sector, claiming its earliest and most aggressive support among faculties of two-year community colleges. But the movement honors no boundary between public and private institutions. Today faculties on about 500 campuses, one-fourth of all college professors, belong to or are represented by a union, most often the American Federation of Teachers (AFT) or the National Education Association. Although faculty unionization has gained a large amount of strength in state colleges and universities, the principle of collective bargaining has widespread backing in every sector of higher education. However, there are differences in the degree and intensity of support by academics. Thus professors at the elite, doctorate-granting research universities are less interested in joining a union than their more teaching-oriented, nonpublishing counterparts. Instructors and assistant professors are much more anxious to organize collectively than full professors. The more politically liberal faculty are far more predisposed to unionization than those who describe themselves as conservatives. There are also differences between the various academic fields, with social scientists and humanists far more pro-union than their colleagues in the so-called business-applied disciplines.

The future of collective bargaining in the 1980s is a matter of speculation. In recent years faculty unionization has slowed down, with the exception of the "sleeping giant" of California, which came awake in 1979 after the passage of a state law granting all public employees the right to join a union. But collective bargaining could accelerate once again in the next two decades, though most likely without following a fixed or consistent course. Much will depend on, for example, the health of the economy and whether many other states pass legislation that permits organizing activity. The pace will quicken if organized labor is successful in getting Congress to pass federal legislation extending collective bargaining rights to nonfederal public employees not now covered by state legislation. But perhaps more than anything else, the unorganized educators throughout the country will be watching to see if collective bargaining has made a significant difference on campuses that have gone union. Major gains by these faculties will be the greatest spur to expanding unionism in the academic world, especially in the public sector. For the moment, however, it appears that the union movement is in the doldrums.

Some trends are already evident. The academic model of university governance, which was based on the ideal of faculty colleagues and administrators sharing a sense of purpose, has all but disappeared on an increasing number of campuses. Apart from the battle for the buck that is at the root of all union activity, the erosion of trust and collegiality that has led to faculty unionism has interjected an adversary quality into the relationship. Whether collective bargaining will ever redistribute power on the campus in a radical or fundamental way is a matter of opinion and perspective, but there is no doubt that it introduces qualities of formalism and rigidity into faculty-administration relationships that militate against the formulation of policy and the resolution of issues in the traditional collegial spirit. Decisions are arrived at more in the spirit of trading (a quid for a quo) than from a mutual exploration and evaluation of the merits of issues. This change in emphasis is not free of cost to a university.

Other changes can be anticipated. Presidents, for example, will continue to lose their ability to make policy decisions on the campus as leadership becomes more administrative than executive and discretionary judgment is replaced by the formalism of rules and regulations designed to locate power and authority in explicit terms. Presidents and chancellors of statewide systems of colleges and universities will have almost no role in collective bargaining negotiations but will be expected to carry out the provisions of union contracts. This clearly represents a shift of power to the faculty—not to individual professors working through the traditional network of informal processes of accommodation and decision-making, but to a union confronting management through a body of labor professionals who may be insufficiently knowledgeable about the academic world and insensitive to important academic considerations. Furthermore, the traditional authority of boards of trustees will probably be diminished, because faculty unions will lead to the gradual transfer of power from the local campuses to outside parties such as statewide coordinating boards and ultimately to political agencies of the state, which will find it necessary to sit at the bargaining table when contracts are negotiated. These developments can easily lead to more rather than less intrusion into all aspects of university affairs by legislators and others who control funds and who will monitor more and more closely the higher education community, insisting on records of classroom usage, faculty contact hours, faculty-student ratios, percentages of students in particular groups who graduate, and other statistical and cost-benefit analyses of the academic process. As Emeritus Professor Dael Wolfle of the Graduate School of Public Affairs at the University of Washington has noted, two results seem inevitable: more emphasis on what can be objectively measured and stated in concrete terms about an institution's performance, and a diminution of campus authority over academic matters. Procedural details, of course, can be dealt with at the bargaining table. But the hard-won principle that a university should be free from outside control will be further undermined as the bargaining table for public institutions moves from the campus to the political arena, or the state capitol. There is a touch of irony here: those on the faculty who have pressed for collective bargaining have also been among the most vociferous in denouncing the pronounced tendencies toward centralization in higher education.

Through the 1970s, private universities such as the Ivy League institutions in the east and Stanford in the west have been subject to the requirements of the National Labor Relations Act, the same law that covers private employers. But in none of these universities has the faculty chosen to bargain collectively. With few exceptions this is also true in states that have enacted collective bargaining legislation covering higher education. Although nonacademic employees in various categories do bargain collectively, the faculties of the major elite universities have not turned to faculty unionism. In 1977 the University of California (UC), one of the country's most prestigious public institutions of higher education, opposed a collective bargaining bill pending in the state legislature. During the following year UC withdrew opposition after it was agreed in committee that key sections of the amended legislation would apply only to the nineteen campuses of the California State Universities and Colleges system (CSUC). For example, political representatives of the governor, the speaker of the assembly, and the Senate Rules Committee will sit only at the CSUC bargaining table. Fearful of political interference, UC insisted on preserving its own academic autonomy.

But UC also had other concerns. Its prominent faculty is committed to a culture of scholarship and high academic standards; this is one reason why UC professors have been much less supportive of faculty unionism than those who teach in the community colleges and the CSUC system. They are unenthusiastic about some of the "faculty union types," such as those in the AFT who went on strike at San Francisco State in 1969 (even though two-thirds of the faculty disapproved of their tactics and goals). These activist union members spend many hours a week trying to organize their colleagues into the kind of union that has wider appeal in the least professional sectors of higher education: two-year colleges and other institutions of lower scholarly standing. Faculty members at UC have felt that this kind of unionism is incompatible with the long-range interests and status of university professors who have always valued highly their independence, self-regulation, and freedom as professionals.

One of the principal reasons UC wanted to keep its distance as much as possible from the CSUC system was the conviction that decision making under collective bargaining dominated by an AFT-type union is likely to have a leveling effect on the application of professional standards to faculty review and performance. The UC faculty would never choose to go in that direction for several reasons. One is that where this kind of unionization is established, meritorious accomplishment and scholarly achievement become less important in individual tenure and promotion decisions than seniority and other generalized but less discriminating standards of competence. The impact of collective bargaining puts in sharp focus the collectivist outlook and egalitarian norms that are inherent in unionization. Qualitative distinctions in individual performance become less important than objective standards such as seniority and longevity, leading to the flattening out of individual differences. In short, when it comes to academic standards the unions would discount individual quality in favor of equity for the group. But colleges and universities are in the business of making discriminating judgments, which is one reason that some institutions have excelled and others are only ordinary. One would like to purchase equity for our campuses, but (to borrow a phrase from University of Oregon President William B. Boyd) at a price less than excellence.

It remains to be seen whether the new management-labor model of academic governance will make a college or university a better educational institution. Will students get better teaching and learn more in the classroom? Will faculty scholarship and research be more effectively advanced? Will the much-heralded sense of community between faculty and students be deepened? Will excellence be pursued with more dedication and commitment? Will the new power relationships within the university provide wiser leadership for American society in the years to come?

Will these questions receive any attention as union contracts are negotiated at the bargaining table?

TENURE—OR WHAT?

The debate about tenure goes on—between those who feel it has created "a rigid and carefully defined class structure" within our colleges and universities and is "one of the chief causes of intellectual cowardice,"[1] and those who claim the essence of tenure is "wholly in the complement of reliable procedural requirements it affords as protection against summary, unilateral, unexplained, and unreviewable nonrenewal."[2] The fact is that practically all of the familiar assertions about the system of tenure are true, but there is an additional truth that whatever one sees in tenure is, like virtue or sin, in the mind of the beholder.

There is still a need for candor about some of the merits and demerits of tenure. Does tenure protect incompetent professors on the faculty? Yes—unqualifiedly. Tenure has been a shield for indifference and laziness, and has provided a lifetime position with a comfortable salary for people who should not be in the classroom. But the protection of incompetents is the price paid for a system that, on balance, is sound because it has added stability and strength to the academic profession.

Can a college get rid of a professor who is incompetent? One would be hard pressed to think of a single instance where the charge of incompetence was made formally and publicly, a hearing held with academic due process, and a verdict returned that the individual was indeed incompetent and should be dismissed. Professor Nathan Glazer has observed that no faculty has ever moved against a fellow faculty member to take away tenure for any reason. Even the American Bar Association and the American Medical Association, he points out, have a better record than that.

Is tenure too easy to get? Except in the academically outstanding institutions, the answer is very often yes. In the process by which tenure decisions are made, policy does not always require that only those who have demonstrated the highest capacity for professional excellence and future promise should be assured continuing appointment. A college or university at which nineteen out of twenty receive tenure every year is likely to be an institution at which tenure is a reward for average or satisfactory work rather than a mark of distinction. A self-respecting university will subscribe to a higher standard. The question it will ask is, has the candidate demonstrated such evidence of competence and potential that the university cannot live without him or her? If the answer is yes, tenure will be granted. If doubt exists or the evidence is weak, tenure will be denied.

The controversy over tenure today differs from the same issue in the past in several important respects. For one thing, it is taking place at a time when tight money and a tight job market have led fiscally conscious trustees and legislators to worry about how operating costs can be reduced when the number of tenured faculty is rising and faculty salaries consume at least 75 percent of total budgets. Campus administrators who wrestle with these problems know that the next ten years will be ones of consolidation, of self-evaluation, and of learning to live with dwindling resources. They also know they face a particularly serious problem that is new to higher education: namely, the discouraging outlook for young scholars and teachers hoping to receive permanent faculty appointments, especially if student enrollments decline and faculty members continue full-time teaching until age 70. In every field of knowledge it is the young scholars and researchers who are not only essential for the future but also (to quote the president's biomedical research panel) "indispensable for the work that has to be done today." If something is not done to address this problem, "we will discover sometime in the late 1980s that we have skipped a generation." A college or university whose faculty is incapable of self-renewal faces a potential disaster.

As a result of the move to unionization, perhaps the most significant difference in the system of tenure as the academic world has known it is its shift in emphasis from a concern about academic freedom to a demand for some form of simple, if not almost automatic, job security. The tradition of tenure is giving way to the language of contract as the unions hold out the promise of better protection and more permanent security, not only to all members of the faculty, but also to more people in the bargaining unit such as librarians, counselors, admissions officers, registrars, and others. Richard Chait, director of Harvard's Institute for

Educational Management, believes that tenure will gradually become obsolete and anachronistic as strong contracts are negotiated and others are renewed.

The big question is whether traditional tenure practices and ironclad union contracts can exist together on the same campus. No one really expects tenure to be bargained away. It is much more likely, says Chait, that tenure will simply disappear because tenure and unions are not philosophically congenial. Tenure may become "a superfluous second coat of armor" with a union contract. State legislators will soon see no need for tenure when job security is won at the bargaining table. Furthermore, possible federal legislation "may open up tenure as a term or condition of employment, thus making it negotiable."

Those who have been calling for an end to tenure may wish to temper their opposition when they consider whether the approach of unionism to job security is less compatible with academic quality than is tenure. It is not remarkable that lifelong job security for elementary and high school teachers is achieved not only more quickly but also with less searching and independent evaluation of a person's quality than is tenure under a system of rigorous review. In the leading universities, tenure review by peer evaluation involves careful weighing of a person's competence and productivity: this is why an affirmative decision is not made lightly. Although the whole process has been abused in some institutions, it is still much more rigorous than the way unions recruit job holders (no one is excluded). With all its inequities it has served the academic profession reasonably well, and if more colleges and universities paid more attention to its qualitative use it could be the kind of system that allows one to say, "Two cheers for tenure."

MORAL-PROFESSIONAL ISSUES AND CONFLICTS

Perceptions of the extent to which moral problems exist in higher education vary according to personal values and judgment. Academics frequently differ about whether a given issue really involves an important moral dimension or (at the other extreme) is simply a minor conceit that is annoying and time wasting. Nonetheless, colleges and universities are faced today with choices and decisions that can have far-reaching consequences. Following are but a few of the problem areas affecting faculty, students, and administrators, though not always equally.

1) In an interview with *behavior today* in January 1979, Professor David Riesman pointed to a problem that he says constitutes part of "a great moral crisis in education." Anticipating a projected decrease of 5 to 30

percent in full-time enrollments from a peak of about seven million in 1980, state colleges and universities will be battling frantically for scarce students in the next two decades, with heavy emphasis on recruiting older students. Some institutions are already doing things that, in more prosperous times, they would have considered educationally unacceptable. These "compromises of integrity" or "shady practices" include exaggerated or false claims to prospective students about the vocational benefits of their programs, continued recruiting of graduate students in fields where the job prospects are dim, deliberate inflation of grades by faculty members to encourage high enrollments in their courses or departments, and pressuring of faculty members by administrators (in the words of one observer) "to give students what they want, whether this involves less complex readings, vocational programs, credit for life experience, or impressive-sounding new programs empty of significant academic content."

If one adds to this "Darwinian combat" the parallel struggle for tenure slots, Riesman says, the end result must often be characterized as "a demoralized faculty and an immoral one." Some schools now routinely cancel courses when enrollments drop below a certain level, thus opening the door to "politicization and possible corruption as instructors seek to keep the number of students in a class above the danger point." As the sovereignty of the consumer rapidly becomes the governing doctrine, colleges are increasingly trying to sell themselves to students, with the result that "the long-run nature of esoteric scholarship is in question." Whole fields and academic majors may be jeopardized if their lack of popularity threatens an institution's fiscal condition. The moral crisis, Riesman believes, with its overtones of heightened competition, comes at a time when many "involuntary students" continue to be "bribed to go to college," and when such possible alternatives as apprenticeship or the opening of a small business continue to be rejected by most of those who can afford to meet tuition costs.

2) The number of foreign students is growing so large so that it, too, will be a factor in shaping the future of higher education. Now only 2 percent of the nation's 11.4 million college students, foreigners are expected to make up 10 percent by 1990. Meanwhile, the approximately 235,000 foreigners who are believed to be attending postsecondary schools today, as the *Washington Post* has observed, are getting more than their share of good grades and advanced degrees, requesting and obtaining shifts in curricula that suit their needs. For many small colleges hoping to guard against closing, foreign students are an obvious way to try to hang on until the resurgence of American students in the 1990s. But as these colleges become dependent upon foreign students for their

survival and other colleges recruit them to bolster their own sagging enrollments, how far will these institutions be prepared to go to change their curricula to fulfill the needs of students from abroad? The Carnegie Council on Policy Studies in Higher Education has cited evidence of the proliferation of off-campus programs of dubious quality and "hucksterism" in the recruiting of nontraditional and foreign students. The director of a National Association of Foreign Students Affairs project says that things are already getting out of hand as some schools think up programs of dubious academic value to attract international students. Others promise to begin a program if students who can pay their way will enroll, even if what they end up studying turns out to be of little use when they return home.

The Carnegie Council's concern is that unless corrective actions are taken, "this situation is likely to lead some students to take even greater advantage of the situation," and to make some colleges "even more reluctant to insist on ethical conduct by students and even more likely to engage in improper conduct themselves."

3) Claiming to represent the moral conscience of the university, student activists have recently been demonstrating against trustees' or regents' policies of investing funds in American companies doing business in South Africa, where apartheid is practiced by that nation's white minority. Apartheid, they insist, is a moral issue that calls for the right and moral course of action—namely, complete divestiture of all university stock holdings. Any other policy, they claim, would contaminate the university with the virus of South African racism.

In their single-minded focus on the issue of apartheid (or on other social issues that students have used to demand that the university sever connections on moral grounds with individuals, corporations, and even governments), they have overlooked or minimized another issue—that is, whether colleges and universities in this country have either the responsibility or the obligation to act as institutions of political action and social reform. The protestors have no doubts at all about what actions and reforms are necessary. They also believe a university should use its total resources for political goals and should be a base of decisive action for those of high moral purpose.

But there is another view of a university. It has as its primary focus the life of the mind in the pursuit of truth and transmission of knowledge. The university is not to be mistaken for an institution concerned with social activism to achieve particular purposes, and it will resist those who want it to become an instrument of political action. In the next ten years it may well be that the relative serenity of the seventies will be broken by those who continue to press colleges and universities to become involved, as centers of higher learning, in new and complex political questions. As they have in the past, these pressures and demands will raise fundamental questions about the nature of a university and its moral obligations as an institution.

4) There are important moral and ethical considerations arising out of a special kind of problem that has emerged with particular force in recent years in the biological and medical sciences. The general question is how freedom of inquiry can be maintained in the face of an increasing tendency to regulate in ever greater detail the course of research and the application of its findings. The more specific issue concerns the protection of human subjects in the research process and the steps that must be taken to ensure that moral or ethical norms are not violated or an individual's privacy invaded in the attempt to acquire more knowledge.

5) Both Congress and the academic community have been addressing urgent questions about current and future relations between colleges and universities and the intelligence community. There is no disagreement over the need of the United States to have an effective system of foreign intelligence. The issue is whether the integrity and professional standards of an institution of higher education are compromised when faculty members are covertly employed as consultants or researchers, are used to gather intelligence in foreign countries in the course of their academically supported travel, or are asked to identify and recruit American and foreign students on U.S. campuses. Are the academics who render services to the Central Intelligence Agency (CIA) guilty of a breach of professional ethics, or (as Adm. Stanfield Turner, director of Central Intelligence argues) are they acting in good faith and from laudable motives—without compromising the integrity of the academic profession—in assisting these endeavors? Or should universities make it clear that faculty members who engage in covert activity for any outside agency, government or private, violate their academic and moral commitments and should be censured or dismissed?

6) There is the related question of so-called academic moonlighting: should college professors be free to do consulting work for whomever they choose—the United Farm Workers, big growers, the CIA, or General Motors—or is it the business of the university or the legislature to forbid or force disclosure of those activities of a faculty member above and beyond full-time work done for the university? It has been estimated that in recent years the percentage of American academics practicing their skills after hours has grown from 37 to 44 percent, mostly in such fields as business administration, education, and engineering. Members of the faculty who have been consultants maintain that their direct contact with business and government keeps them in touch with the outside

world and enriches their teaching capabilities. But many legislators argue that financial disclosure requirements should be imposed on academics on the grounds that they are state employees and that disclosure is in the public interest: the public has a right to know. In 1978 a committee of the California legislature passed supplemental language that said, among other things, that disclosure statements of individual faculty members and administrators shall be public and shall be available to students participating in classes taught by the respective faculty members. On the other side of the issue, as one professor put it, is disclosure of all consulting connections "a typical example of a solution searching for a problem?"

LEGISLATIVE CONTROL VERSUS INSTITUTIONAL AUTONOMY

One reason the University of California is a great and distinguished public institution of higher education is that it was chartered separately and thereby granted autonomy under the state constitution, subject only to the policy decisions of the board of regents. But in recent years the state legislature has been looking for ways to gain more control over the university. In 1977 it almost succeeded, in unprecedented fashion. At the last minute, however, the senate-assembly conference committee on the state budget reversed itself and voted to let UC make its own decisions about student registration fees.

The central issue was not student fees. The fundamental question was and is today whether the university (or any college or university) will continue to be removed from politics and free from political interference. It is no secret that public institutions are threatened in many states by an increasing number of political initiatives in the form of more red tape, constitutional amendments, legislation, and budgetary controls by the state. Boards of regents and trustees believe as a matter of principle that a university should govern itself rather than become the servant of social and political opinion in the legislature. It is a principle that has frequently been compromised in the past by legislators (and others) determined to intervene in the university's affairs. In the Joe McCarthy days of loyalty oaths and other demands from the political right, the liberals fought to keep the campuses free and independent. Is the principle they were defending any less sound today because many of the university's allies are now on the right, though many liberals have done an about-face?

The liberals of today, of course, have concerns and objectives different from those that aroused the more conservative-minded interventionists in the past. In California many of them have their own priorities, which they are prepared to impose on UC (and the nineteen institutions that make up the CSUC system)—affirmative action, new admissions criteria, a de-emphasis on faculty research (or control over what sort of research at the UC faculty should do), using the university as an instrument of social transformation, and so on. The political agendas of many liberal legislators are also crowded with ideas about how to democratize the university to meet the basic needs of human beings—and they often want those basic needs defined in Sacramento rather than at UC. The question is whether state governments are constantly reaching beyond their grasp when they try to tell the regents, the administration, and the faculty what to do and how to do it.

Consider some language in the California state budget that, had it been accepted, would have ordered the university to promote a certain number of faculty members on the basis of criteria developed by a committee of the assembly. Under the state constitution decisions about tenure and promotion have traditionally been left to the university. Certain legislators wanted to change that because, they said, research was being emphasized at the expense of classroom instruction. Therefore, they drafted some control language that appropriated funds for 22 new undergraduate faculty positions only if faculty members were to be tenured and/or promoted primarily on the basis of teaching ability. In the university's view this was an attempt by the legislature to intrude into the internal affairs of the campus. It rejected the notion that state legislators are qualified to pass judgment on the adequacy of university teaching and research.

Another issue aired in a subcommittee on education involved farm workers who had been displaced by agricultural mechanization developed through university research projects. They came to the legislature for help. The assembly subcommittee inserted supplemental language directing UC to devise a procedure for determining how all future research projects are socially related to agricultural mechanization. By applying pressure, the university in this instance was ultimately able to have the control language deleted and thereby maintain its budget autonomy for another year.

Or consider a bill signed into law in 1978 by Governor Brown that, as the American Council on Education agreed in its amicus curiae brief, will cripple the accuracy of peer judgments and evaluations by requiring UC to make available to faculty members the confidential documents upon which employment, tenure, promotion, and termination decisions are based. In the post-Watergate climate of today, the politicians' position is simple: confidentiality is equivalent to secrecy, secrets are bad, and honest people do not need secrets and do not like them. Thus they want a policy of open files. What they do not understand is that academic peer judgments are not secret in any invidious sense of the word. They are professional evaluations available to faculty committees who weigh their worth in reaching a decision about the person under review. Far from being secret, these evaluations are the subject of intensive scrutiny by faculty, deans, and administrative officials, all of whom have a common interest in seeing to it that this self-correcting, self-balancing review mechanism works professionally and fairly. Furthermore, confidentiality of peer judgment is the best way to assure candor and honesty in assessing faculty performance and, in turn, to maintain the high standards of the university, which by its very nature cannot give consent or legitimation to anything less than the pursuit of excellence.

The growing problems of UC with the legislature exemplify what is happening (to one degree or another) in many states throughout the country. Over the years there have been angry words as the budget for higher education in California has been negotiated in the legislative process. The basic struggle in each session has been over the legislators' efforts to muster enough votes to attach control language to the budget, language that, in effect, would have established policy for the university. As the *California Journal* has pointed out, the risks are great for both sides in a legal showdown. The university does not want a court to say that the legislature may establish policy through the power of the pocketbook, and the legislature does not want a court to say that it has little or no voice in how the board of regents spends taxpayers' money. Thus some form of negotiations obviously must take place, and controls are inherent in such a process.

Those who push hard each year to have control language inserted in the budget argue that the legislature has the responsibility for making certain that (in the words of one of the most hostile critics of UC) "the money taxpayers have authorized us to appropriate is going for the taxpayers' purposes, not just for some private ego trips of academics or intellectuals or an institution in an ivory tower." From the university's point of view, the board of regents—not the legislature—speaks for the public interest: this is why the governor and other state elected officials serve on the board. University executives feel it is "improper for a small group of legislators to sit as a court of appeals and hand down decisions in the form of budgetary control language."

The debate will continue indefinitely, not only in California, but in any state where colleges and universities must go to the politicians in the legislature for financial support and, one might add, as long as there are lawmakers who believe that their ideas about how to run a university should prevail.

FEDERAL REGULATIONS AND ENFORCEMENT: AFFIRMATIVE ACTION

With the exception of stable or declining enrollments, rapid rates of inflation, and budgetary cutbacks, the major challenge facing higher education in the next decade and beyond will be its relationship with the federal government. Campuses see their autonomy slipping away as the result of increasing federal intervention, through what academics regard either as ordinary government employees carrying out the requirements of public policy or as power-wielding bureaucrats bent on enforcing a particular principle or law. Although descriptions and perceptions of the bureaucratic infection may vary, the academic community is virtually of one mind in opposing the transfer of more and more authority and decision making from educational institutions to government officials.

Perhaps the single most controversial undertaking of the federal government has been the move to increase the hiring of minority and women faculty members by the approximately 3,000 colleges and universities in the United States. If the institutions fail to take affirmative action in recruiting more women, blacks, and other minorities for faculty positions, they face the possibility of a cutoff of federal research and other grants. Put simply, enforcement of this powerful requirement has increased the government's role and has dramatically changed hiring and employment procedures on the campuses. Anyone looking for an example of how such university goals as self-governance, academic excellence, individual judgment, and local decision making have become entangled in the web of the federal regulatory process could do no better than to focus on the impact of affirmative action rule-making and enforcement in the academic world.

The crucial problem has been how to interpret and then apply federal regulations that prohibit discrimination on grounds of race or sex but also require affirmative and corrective action on behalf of certain minority groups and women. Apart from the confusion caused by overlapping jurisdictions and the conflicting views of different enforcement agencies of the government about what procedures to follow in their investigations of employment patterns and personnel practices in higher education, there has been no clear agreement either on or off campus on what constitutes discrimination. At one time, a ruling that discrimination had occurred turned on whether an employer took racial considerations into account in making employment decisions. Now discrimination can take place even if the employer does not intend to discriminate in this way. The new test is whether an employer's hiring procedure has a discriminatory or adverse impact on certain (but not all) minority groups. In other words, the effects of a university's employment practices are what now constitute discrimination. If the effect of these practices is to disadvantage blacks in relation to whites, the burden is on the campus to show that it is not guilty of discriminating on grounds of race, reversing the ordinary requirements of legal procedure.

A cause of grief and mischief for heads of academic departments, as well as for deans and other administrators who are responsible for faculty appointments, is the increasing tendency of the government's compliance agencies to regard numbers (of women and minorities hired or promoted) as ends in themselves. But educators have long believed that the important goal for a college or university is and should be "equality of opportunity for every individual and the appointment of the best qualified person in every instance." They feel that government officials who investigate hiring and promotion practices often make a bad mistake in relying heavily on a numbers definition of discrimination. The implication is that the real, though unstated, aim of federal policy is not to promote equal opportunity but to bring about an equalization of results for certain groups through preferential hiring and proportional representation—what has been called a charade of numbers in the quest for statistical parity.

It is important to point out that if the basic goal of affirmative action is to assure as much as possible that members of both sexes and of all races and ethnic groups are accorded genuinely equal employment opportunities in higher education, then a numerical analysis of the circumstances of different groups can be helpful. Colleges and universities can strengthen their recruitment efforts and procedures if they are able to compare more precisely, through detailed analysis, the proportions of women and members of minority groups among those recently hired with their proportions in the various pools from which faculty candidates are drawn and appointments made. Thus numerical analysis can serve a useful purpose if that purpose is not simply a particular numerical result, but instead the fairest and most vigorous effort to reach out for women and minorities (because this is the best guarantee of equal access and opportunity on a nondiscriminatory basis) and the ultimate appointment of the best qualified person (because this is the only way to guarantee that the university's continuing search for excellence will not be compromised).

Higher education's problem with goals and timetables, as they are customarily understood by the compliance agencies, is that they are not clearly and unequivocally tied to selection of the best-qualified individual regardless of race or sex. The setting of goals has tipped the balance away from providing equal opportunity for every individual; the agencies imply that unless a particular numerical goal has been reached there has been under-utilization, which in turn means unequal treatment and discrimination. But this preoccupation with numbers and statistical parity suggests that the primary objective of a university in its hiring procedures should be to use goal setting as a way of favoring applicants on the basis of race or sex, when "the aggregate numbers of groups of people," as Princeton's president William Bowen has stated, "should be seen as expected by-products of affirmative action efforts, not as the goals themselves." In short, the manipulation of dubious figures and statistical data—the numbers game—cannot make genuine equality of opportunity "more of a reality than it has been" and can never be a substitute for "improving the lot of real people."[3]

Goals and timetables, it must be remembered, are consequent upon the concept of under-utilization and the requirement to eliminate it. One can argue that goals are really quotas (even if merely soft or benign quotas). The Department of Health, Education, and Welfare (HEW) has said that a university's attainment of specific numerical goals according to the timetables in its affirmative action program will not be the single test of compliance or noncompliance. Nonetheless, these goals are perceived as a clear commitment by various groups on campus, which then hold the university accountable. The HEW insists it is not advocating rigid or inflexible quotas that must be met. But the problem with applying numerical goals in a flexible manner is that there is no way of predicting how this method will work out in practice. Furthermore, the implication in the word goal that the number is something to be aimed at is precisely what gives a goal the character of a quota and allows it to be used as an instrument of administration and enforcement.

Based on the affirmative action results achieved in higher education during the 1970s, it is fair to say that no dramatic changes have occurred in the ethnic and sexual composition of the faculties and staffs at most colleges and universities—if the only real way to measure progress (as the compliance agencies insist) is by the dexterous management of statistics and numbers.[4] Instead, affirmative action has proved to be a case study of the costs that institutions as complex as universities can suffer as a result of the government's attempts to bring about social change through elaborate regulatory mechanisms, heavy-handed investigatory techniques, and a frequently undisguised built-in adversarial bias. The university's efforts to turn its energies and resources to legitimate and high-priority programs that will assist women, minorities, and the handicapped are severely reduced when administrators and faculty members find themselves caught up in a constantly shifting and complex succession of procedures that require even more elaborate campus policies and guidelines. In the words of a UC (Berkeley) study: "Federal laws breed regulations; Federal and state laws and regulations and University regulations breed campus regulations; All regulations breed reports; Reports breed further reports; Reports and regulations provide excellent evidence that one is doing something when one is not."[5]

A special set of problems arises when charges of racial or sexual discrimination are filed against a university and are then carried to a campus grievance hearing or a court (or both), or to the Office for Civil Rights (OCR), the Equal Employment Opportunity Commission (EEOC), or the state's Fair Employment Practices Committee. Most colleges are not found guilty of purposive or systematic discrimination in such cases. This is neither an argument for complacency nor an attempt to suggest that the process of liberating America's women and minorities has been completed. That is certainly not the case. But many administrators and faculty members feel there is something wrong with the method of investigating all complaints of discrimination (including those of a frivolous or deceitful nature) when the investigative agencies of the government come onto the campus with the starting assumption that discrimination has actually taken place, thereby forcing the institution to prove its innocence. In practice, EEOC or OCR usually operates as an advocate of the person or group bringing the complaint, rather than as a neutral arbitrator, essentially because under the law that is the role the agency must play. Yet why should the university always be cast in the role of a defendant seemingly trying to hide something?

There is a point on which the investigative agencies and the universities agree: both are dissatisfied with the whole complaint procedure, though for different reasons. The only real enforcement power an agency has is to cut off federal funds, which is like trying to kill a gnat with a bowling ball. Therefore, an agency's true power lies in its ability to harass—a weapon it can and does use effectively regardless of the merits of an individual complaint. As UC has learned, the agency must take advantage of the opportunity provided by a complaint to use that power. In fact, Berkeley's requests that the harassment stop are regarded by the agencies as a move to "strip them of the most useful means at their disposal to carry out their responsibilities." From the perspective of a college or university, the time and money spent in responding to demands for information and data simply show how progress toward legitimate affirmative action is sacrificed to the agencies' insatiable appetite for forms and files—for racial profiles (of all applicants in the past two, four, or maybe even ten years), copies of job announcements and descriptions, written and unwritten procedures, "name, title, sex, ethnicity, and role of each member of the selection committee," telephone notes, special computer runs, and "any additional information that would assist us," all to be submitted "in no more than thirty (30) days from the date of this letter."[6]

Other problems are posed by the government's approach to affirmative action and by the expansion of federal authority that has allowed the bureaucracy to intrude into the nooks and crannies of academic employment and practice. Some clarifying steps would help. For example, there should be an explicit disavowal of any intention to establish proportional representation in employment. Under-utilization should be treated as an evidentiary problem and the government obligated to show in a particular case that the under-representation in question is the result of deliberate discrimination. Only then should the government or the courts be permitted to impose the remedy of goals, timetables, and, in rare cases, racially preferential treatment.

Similarly, there should be clarification of the extent to which a compliance agency or court should second-guess professional judgments regarding standards of appointment, retention, and promotion. Academic peer judgment is a sound tradition grounded in long-standing practice. If HEW or EEOC can substitute its judgments for those of the faculty and administration, then critical issues of academic freedom are raised. Furthermore, many factors taken into consideration in academic hiring inescapably depend upon subjective, evaluative decisions. In their unrelenting search for objective criteria of measurement, the regulators and rule makers have too often failed to understand that professional judgments cannot be measured with statistical precision because there is no simple litmus test for availability, no single objective test of quality, and no clearly quantifiable marketplace. Thus when it deals with higher education (and with other professions), the government should tread softly. A soft tread would mean, among other things, that the burden would be on the government to demonstrate that a university standard or practice had been discriminatory. It would also mean that adverse or differential impact would not be allowed as prima facie evidence of discrimination.

What, then, should federal law and policy require of colleges and universities in the 1980s in the area of equal educational opportunity?

—Higher education should be expected to exhibit and foster an attitude of cooperation with the national policy of equal opportunity at all levels without regard to an individual's race, religion, color, or national background.

—Higher education should be expected to oppose all practices that give persons any advantage, or impose upon them any disadvantage, because of anything extraneous to their own merits, that is, their skills, abilities, achievements, and promise. At the very least, any preference or disadvantage based on race or sex should be sustainable only upon a showing, by clear and convincing proof, that it is essential to an over-riding public purpose that can be attained in no other way.

—Higher education should concentrate its efforts on its essential mission: education. It should not be asked to compromise those efforts by favoring experiments or policies that jeopardize them. Government regulations or guidelines that affirm the principles of nondiscrimination and equal opportunity are fundamentally in error in that they establish as the major goal an immediate increase in the numbers of women and minorities on faculties and staffs and in student bodies. Colleges and universities must continue to seek a more cosmopolitan membership, but this effort should be viewed as an expected and desirable by-product of proper policy rather than as a primary, if not exclusive, goal. An affirmative action program should clearly state that an academic institution serves society best by providing quality education to all eligible students on the basis of equal access and equal treatment. That is its primary function. It is also the principal way it can contribute to the mitigation of inequalities in the country and should be emphasized in any policy statement on equal opportunity. If the educational mission were regarded as paramount, many of the ambiguities and contradictions of affirmative action regulations and enforcement would be avoided.

—Higher education needs to do more to reach effectively people who have been denied the benefits of higher education, or who have had special barriers placed in their way. Any erosion in the quality of academic programs cheats them and is inconsistent with broadening the opportunity for quality education.

—Congress can help secure these objectives by well-conceived programs of financial support. The greatest hope lies in a combination of long-term efforts that range from introducing minority high school students at the earliest age possible to the opportunities available to them in medicine, law, teaching, and so on—to motivating those with potential as college undergraduates to pursue careers at the professional level so that the ranks of the truly qualified will be legitimately expanded. There should be guidance and assistance for people before they become incapacitated students. We need to rescue good minds at the high school level before they become dulled and ill-equipped to go on to college. The federal government, state legislatures, and private foundations, as well as business and industry, should make available the necessary resources as further confirmation of our active commitment to provide increased employment opportunities for women and minorities in higher education in fact as well as in legal theory.

—Congress should insist on adjudicatory procedures that accord with due process and that permit colleges and universities to receive a quick and fair (and independent) determination on issues of pertinency and privilege with respect to demands for files and records. This is an area where the usual rule of very broad delegation under a generally stated statutory policy is not good practice. Congress should be explicit about what it expects and what it does not expect.

—Everyone—schools, students, employees, citizens, and federal agencies—should be able to determine from a regulation or statute what constitutes compliance. Nothing so vague that it requires guessing should be subject to enforcement. Nor should there be grossly overlapping areas of enforcement among the federal agencies working in the same area, with the predictable conflicts among them over interpretations, patterns of enforcement, and the like. This, of course, is nothing more than the standard jurisprudential rule about clarity in law making.

—Basic objectives should not be drowned in an administrative maze of requirements and reports, or in rules so arcane or impractical (or both) that compliance becomes impossible or so many resources must be diverted to achieve it that the basic objectives are defeated. What is at issue is a theory of limits—more precisely, the need to impress upon the federal government that it must define its proper role in the affairs of higher education by setting realistic and necessary limits to the regulatory process and to the imposition by the bureaucracy of comprehensive and cumbersome rules. Many legitimate social goals could be more responsibly and effectively achieved (and at far less administrative cost) if the critical decisions in education were left to those on the campus whose judgment and informed intuition are guided by long years of experience rather than to government officials who are unfamiliar with the major academic functions of a university.

NOTES

1. R. Keith Miller, "Tenure: A Cause of Intellectual Cowardice," *The Chronicle of Higher Education*, April 30, 1979, p. 72.

2. William W. Van Alstyne, "Tenure: A Conscientious Objective," *Change*, October 1978, p. 45.

3. William G. Bowen, testimony before the U.S. Department of Labor, September 30, 1975.

4. Individual campuses vary in the degree and quality of impact of affirmative action. For example, some institutions have hired large numbers of women, and some women have moved up the academic and administrative ladders. Antinepotism policies and maternity-leave regulations have been loosened at many colleges and universities. Perhaps the largest gain for the academic women's movement is the gradual recognition that women have often been discriminated against in many (and frequently subtle) ways. But apart from the fact that shortages of women and minority candidates still remain in many fields, the most serious problem is getting worse: the bottom has fallen out of the job market.

5. Albert H. Bowker and Patrick M. Morgan, "The Impact of Federal Regulations on the University of California, Berkeley" (unpublished study, Berkeley, September 19, 1977), p. 406.

6. Ibid., p. 70.

Foreign Affairs

PART II

Arms Control and National Defense

Fred Charles Iklé

XV

To prevent catastrophe in the years ahead, America's defense and foreign policy requires, first of all, a renaissance of self-confidence and self-discipline at home. Without greater coherence and resolution at the center—both in the executive branch and in Congress—the United States cannot marshal the effort needed to arrest the ongoing decline in its power. Without a revitalization of its convictions, the United States will not be able to present its case, let alone support it. Without the courage of its convictions, America will not be prepared to withstand prolonged and painful pressure in a deadly crisis.

To assure the survival of the United States as a free nation is, of course, the first priority for America's defense and foreign policy. Other goals—to work toward a peaceful and democratic world order, to enhance American trade and access to resources, to foster humanitarian action and moral values consistent with American traditions throughout the world—are largely supportive of this task. It is the overarching objective—America's physical and political survival—that has come to make such demands on American statecraft today. In the next decade, the dangers will loom even larger, while the capability of the United States to cope with a major trial of strength will be increasingly in doubt.

A wide and varied range of other issues, to be sure, confronts American foreign policy. Many can be traced to historical developments that have been transforming this century: the closer social and political proximity of all nations because of modern technologies of communication, transportation—and warfare; the demographic revolution that gives an increasing weight to Asia, Latin America, and Africa; and the rapid dissolution of the European colonial empires after World War II.

But in the next five to ten years, three new challenges clearly will endanger America's security—either singly or, more likely, in combination. First, given present trends, the Soviet Union will continue to gain in military power relative to the United States. Second, the dependence of the United States and its principal allies on Middle Eastern oil creates a political and military vulnerability that will contribute to the weakness of the West and is likely to precipitate major crises. Third, the nuclear strategy of the Western alliance is beset by fundamental problems that will be sharply aggravated by the adverse trends in the global military balance and remain insolvable for years to come.

THE ERODING FOUNDATION OF STRENGTH

Like harbingers of a long hard winter, the news of Russia's relentless military buildup has been reaching us in bits and pieces. We have long been misled by those Indian summer days—slight improvements here and there and all sorts of ambiguities—that gave us warmth and cheer. Only in the late 1970s did the recognition gain ground in the United States that Russia's military might has steadily grown relative to ours for at least fifteen years. Yet the trend began in the early 1960s when the United States decided to curtail its investment in strategic forces because it was thought that, given the substantial American nuclear advantage, greater expenditures on conventional arms were more useful—a valid view at that time.

But the United States continued to reduce its budgets for strategic forces beyond the time when a substantial margin of superiority made it safe to do so. This policy of retrenchment was based on the belief that Soviet leaders did not want to match, much less to overtake, the United States in strategic nuclear power. This mistaken belief was articulated, in particular, by Defense Secretary Robert McNamara, but it was held by many other senior officials and was not seriously debated or challenged, even by those who had doubts. It derived from the American strategic theory, prominent in the early 1960s, that U.S. and Soviet strategic nuclear forces could be used only to ensure a stalemate. Beyond the requirements of mutual deterrence there was nothing to be gained from additional nuclear forces, and—so this belief went—the Soviets had no reason not to accept this doctrine as we did and act accordingly.

From that time until the early 1970s, the buildup in Soviet missile forces was underestimated eight times in a row in the official intelligence process in Washington—an extraordinary repetition of the same mistake. This intelligence failure—only brought to light thanks to the careful research of Professor Albert Wohlstetter[1]—disastrously misled American force planners and Congress. It gave them a comfortable justification to prepare for a future far more benign than the one they finally had to recognize. This series of underestimates also led American plans for strategic arms control astray. Proposals for a freeze in missile launchers were advanced by the United States in the late 1960s in the belief that the growth in Soviet missile numbers was about to taper off.

Perhaps the consequences of these errors would not have been so lasting if our military resources and political attention had not been diverted by the war in Vietnam. We might then have halted the continuing decline in our budget for strategic forces and Soviet leaders might have been less tempted to achieve an advantage and more interested in equitable arms limitations and reductions.

Some warning voices were raised early on. Certainly in the late 1960s and the early 1970s, several experts argued that the Soviet Union was trying not only to match the United States militarily, but to overtake us—views ridiculed as "paranoid" or "alarmist." Today, with so much additional evidence at hand and the dissension of Vietnam largely behind us, a new consensus that finds it necessary to accept the "alarmist" views of yesterday has emerged. Now "doves" and "hawks" widely share a calm but grim appreciation that the Soviet Union is indeed building up its military strength at a rate much faster than the United States, with no abatement in sight. Today's disagreements are no longer about the arms trend, but about its political meaning.

Although the Soviet Union attained parity in strategic arms in the early 1970s, its vigorous buildup continues. Given the delayed and restrained response by the United States, the shift in the strategic balance will continue to the Soviet Union's advantage during the next five years, if not longer. Not even an immediate, massive crash effort by the United States could halt this shift in the strategic balance. The Soviet Union has several strategic missiles coming off the production line in the early 1980s, while the Carter administration delayed the initial deployment of a new land-based missile until 1985. And the new American submarine-based missiles are being produced more slowly than planned. Of course, certain improvements in U.S. strategic forces have proceeded more rapidly; for instance, equipping the Minuteman III missile with a more powerful warhead and more accurate guidance and arming part of the old B-52 bomber force with new air-launched cruise missiles.

The growing Soviet strategic advantage can be described in many ways: by "static" measurements—the number and quality of their existing forces compared with ours; or by "dynamic" assessments—how their forces would perform and interact with ours in a campaign. The bottom-line question for the United States is what would happen to the American deterrent in the event of different types of large-scale nuclear attacks by the Soviet Union. One such contingency is a Soviet first strike by perhaps half of the increasingly formidable Soviet ICBM force, a strike designed to destroy nearly all U.S. land-based missiles and bombers not on alert, but to leave American cities largely undamaged. The massive Soviet ICBM force still unlaunched, threatening American cities, might then deter the United States from retaliating with its submarine-based missiles. The political-military implications of such a sequence have been widely discussed and heatedly debated.

Comparisons of military forces are inevitably uncertain and shaped by doubtful assumptions. The geographic and political constraints on a conflict, the actual performance of men and equipment, the element of surprise, efficacy of tactics and intelligence—these factors and many others would help to determine the outcome of a campaign. In peacetime such factors are imponderables; in a war they might favor an enemy as readily as our side. The strength and composition of ready armies and their arsenals, in contrast, are givens. They not only cast their shadow on the political arena, but the greater any disparity in tangible peacetime strength, the greater the likelihood that the advantage in such an imbalance will offset the imponderables of war. Hence, in looking ahead, it becomes highly important to gauge any definite trend in the ratio of forces. Here we face a bitter truth. Inexorably and unmistakably, the trend favors the Soviet Union—the imbalance in military forces is steadily growing to the disadvantage of the United States.

The Soviet military buildup has not been confined to strategic arms. The Russians have strengthened and augmented their army, adding more tanks, artillery, and men, and they are building more ships for their navy than is the United States. But the most comprehensive picture of the shifting military balance emerges if we look at trends in overall military spending by the two superpowers. According to CIA estimates, overall Soviet military expenditures exceed ours by about 40 percent. But for the acquisition of arms and for military research and development, the Soviets spend more than twice as much as the United States, and for strategic arms alone they spend about three times as much. These comparisons provide the most ominous portent for the future military balance. They mean that the gap in military capability between the United States and the Soviet Union will widen; Russia will become stronger—unless these trends change radically. No such change is in sight. The Carter administration's proposed increase in defense spending in the 1980 budget will come nowhere near eliminating the 100 percent difference in military procurement and research—indeed, it may barely keep pace with inflation.

By spending twice as much as we do for military procurement and three times as much for strategic arms alone, the Soviets will, moreover, achieve a cumulative gain. Unlike operating or personnel expenditures, arms bought this year will be usable in future years. Military research, too, is largely a cumulative effort. Such investments will add more military assets to the Soviet arsenal than are being added to ours—a disparity in military power that grows steadily, year by year.

THE GEOPOLITICS OF OIL: THE WEST'S NEW VULNERABILITY

Almost as important as the military balance is the geopolitical balance—the geography of territories and resources that are hospitable or available, either to the United States or to the Soviet Union. Although the military balance has been shifting against the United States over the past fifteen years, the geopolitical balance has deteriorated primarily in the past five years.

The two shifts are, of course, related. On the one hand, Soviet geopolitical expansion strengthens the reach and power of the Soviet military establishment by acquiring positions throughout the world: access to port facilities, overflight and landing rights, and intelligence posts. On the other hand, the growing might of the Soviet military establishment helps the geographic expansion of Soviet influence. Greater military strength may once have been a precondition for geopolitical expansion; now these two dimensions of power are mutually reinforcing.

Today, the increasing preponderance of Soviet military forces casts a shadow of influence and intimidation well beyond the region of past Soviet military interventions, that is to say, beyond Eastern Europe. This shadow protects aggressive actions by Soviet allies, such as Cuba and Ethiopia, or by other countries opposed to the United States, such as Libya, enabling them to fight for the installation of totalitarian regimes in the Third World unfriendly to the United States. For example, in Africa and Asia seven pro-Soviet Communist parties have seized power or territory since 1975.[2] Moreover, the shadow can intimidate governments that are basically pro-American, making them unwilling to oppose Soviet policies and to cooperate with the United States.

Any deterioration in America's position in the geopolitical balance not only affects the military security of the Western alliance in the narrow sense of facilitating the adversary's deployment and movement of military forces throughout the world. Increasingly, this deterioration also undermines the economic base that the West would need to prevail in a major crisis or in an armed conflict. Most critical is the growing Soviet capability to deny Middle Eastern oil to Western Europe, Japan, and the United States. The non-Communist world now receives some 40 percent of its oil from the Persian Gulf alone—more than double the American capacity for oil production. For Western Europe, oil from the Persian Gulf supplies 60 percent of total consumption.

The vulnerability of so much of the West's energy supply is dramatic. Pumping stations, pipelines, and tanker routes are susceptible to small military attacks and sabotage. Moreover, many oil-producing countries, even beyond the Persian Gulf region, are susceptible to political inducements or pressures that could turn them against the United States. This risk is not confined to an Arab-Israeli conflict in which the Arab states—from Libya to Saudi Arabia—might oppose with their "oil weapon" those who support Israel. In other conflicts as well, the Soviet Union and its allies could organize an anti-American front of most oil-producing countries in the Middle East and Africa, whose governments would be driven to support this front, either because of ideological conviction (for instance, Libya) or because of fear of internal unrest and Soviet coercion.

Thus, the denial of oil to Western Europe, Japan, and the United States could become a means of pressure in a variety of contingencies. For example, the pressure might be applied against the United States and West European nations if such a Western group sought to support its friends in Africa in repelling an aggression by Soviet-backed forces. In a more direct use of violence, the stoppage of oil through political pressure might be reinforced by physical destruction of critical facilities. Most damaging would be to interrupt by such physical destruction the oil flow from producing countries siding with the West combined with political control of the oil exported by countries siding with the Soviet Union. As the interruption would bring about a massive shortage, the available exports could be used to bribe this or that European country to cooperate with Soviet policy.

Use of the oil weapon against the United States is, of course, most likely in a conflict where the United States supports Israel, for example with military supplies, in a war against Arab nations. The idea has occurred to the Soviet Union before. In the Arab-Israeli War of 1973, it beamed propaganda into the Middle East exhorting countries to support the oil embargo. In any conflict in the 1980s, the Soviet position would be far stronger than in 1973. Unless the geopolitical situation in the

Middle East and the Horn of Africa changed dramatically, Soviet military forces, or Cubans, would be able to make use of bases in Afghanistan, Ethiopia, South Yemen, and perhaps Iran. Given present trends in the region, moreover, Pakistan's and Turkey's ties to the West would be weaker than in 1973. And above all, both the worldwide and the regional military balance would have shifted substantially in favor of the Soviet Union.

Hence, in a future crisis affecting the Middle East, America's position would be much inferior to what it had been in past crises. Until the mid-1960s, the British maintained a strong military position east of Suez, primarily through their naval deployments in the Indian Ocean. The British fleet could use the port of Aden—now available to the Soviet Union. When the British gradually withdrew, the Johnson administration—absorbed by the demands of the war in Vietnam—decided not to replace them. Subsequently, in the Nixon administration, the ties with Iran were strengthened and the Shah's armed forces, with their modern American equipment, were regarded as a stabilizing force in the Persian Gulf—as indeed they were for a number of years.

Today, the Soviet navy has a larger presence in the Indian Ocean than in the 1960s, and Soviet airlift capability to the region of the Persian Gulf exceeds ours. Unless the adverse trends can be unexpectedly reversed, a future American president will simply not have enough instruments of power to thwart a Soviet, or Soviet-sponsored, attack on the oil fields of those Middle Eastern countries that still dare to produce for the West in defiance of an embargo directed by Moscow.

The denial of petroleum is, of course, not a new method of economic warfare. The Second World War made the "oil weapon" part of the historical experience of Germany and Japan; for the United States the new dependence on imported oil is a radical change. In contrast, during the Suez crisis of 1956, the United States was still producing so much oil that it could, by stepping up production, make up much of the shortfall suffered by France and Great Britain from the blockage of the Suez Canal. This was made easy because in the 1950s the flow from oil wells in the United States tended to be restricted by government policy in order to sustain prices. In Texas, the largest oil-producing state, the Texas Railroad Commission was the public body that controlled the level of oil production. When Western Europe was threatened by an oil shortage in the 1956 Suez crisis, the Texas Railroad Commission could simply decide one morning to turn up production, and the shortage was largely eliminated.

The contrast in 1979 is stark. In 1956, a quaintly named and all but unknown regulatory body in Texas could by fiat enable the United States to replace a large portion of the Mideast oil. In 1979, the power to relieve an oil shortage suddenly has passed to foreign governments—primarily, Saudi Arabia. Furthermore, blocking the passage of tankers through the Strait of Hormuz would deprive the West of an amount of oil more than twice as large as all the oil produced in the United States. It would take only minimal military action to close off that narrow strait.

Several implications of the geopolitics of oil stand out. The Persian Gulf has become an area of great strategic importance for the West—the "Ruhr" of the 1980s. Yet it lies outside the perimeter of the Western alliance system. In several respects, this area is as exposed and as vulnerable as West Berlin. But the implications of such vulnerability are much worse. Unlike Berlin, the Middle East is not only politically or symbolically important; it is crucial for the economic functioning of the West. Furthermore, West Berlin could be successfully protected by the United States and its allies because two conditions were met: the population in the divided city courageously and unequivocally opposed the Soviet encroachments and America's military position in Central Europe was backed up by superior nuclear forces. Neither of these conditions will obtain in the Persian Gulf area.

The West would be economically crippled by a cutoff in the Middle Eastern oil flow, yet almost powerless—in the short run—to prevent it. Some Western democracies might be susceptible to political blackmail if threatened by a prolonged oil denial. In the long run—over ten or twenty years—the dependence on oil imports could probably be overcome, and measures might be worked out to reestablish friendly and economically viable relations with the major oil producers.

But over the next several years, the United States would find it hard to stop a determined drive by the Soviet Union to expand its potential power over the West's oil supply. Soviet influence in the area can build on many assets: the virtual incorporation of Afghanistan into the Soviet empire; a hold on South Yemen through Soviet advisers, East German police experts, and Cuban combat troops; the turbulence in Iran with its strong Communist undercurrent; and the instability of other Persian Gulf nations. If military force were applied gradually and discreetly here and there, Soviet reach could be further extended. Counterintervention by the United States would be risky, for in the event the conflict flared into an open and expanding war, America's conventional military strength would be insufficient to defeat the forces that the Soviet Union could easily commit in the region.

At this point, could American nuclear strength be brought to bear?

THE SHRINKING USEFULNESS OF OUR NUCLEAR DETERRENT

Military theory, like any other intellectual endeavor, is always much wiser in hindsight. Before June 1950, the idea that American forces might fight major battles in another war without using the atomic bomb seemed unworthy of serious attention to all but a few farsighted strategists. But the Korean War remolded our theories about the usability and usefulness of nuclear arms. Since that war, it has seemed plausible that the United States would have strong reasons to refrain from using its most powerful weapons when fighting an adversary who possesses only conventional arms.

But the Korean experience did not altogether end American plans for fighting conventional aggression with nuclear weapons. The sudden military buildup in the United States and Western Europe that had been provoked by the North Korean attack included a vast expansion in nuclear armaments. And a large array of these nuclear weapons was developed with the idea that they would be used not to deter *nuclear* attack on the United States and its allies, but to deter or to counter *conventional* aggression by the Soviet Union or perhaps even by other powers. The notion that these "tactical nuclear arms" provided a powerful and useful complement to conventional arms was stressed. In December 1953, President Eisenhower said: "Atomic weapons have virtually achieved conventional status within our armed service." In 1954, President Eisenhower's message to Congress stated: "A wide variety of atomic weapons—considered in 1946 to be mere possibilities of a distant future—have today achieved conventional status in the arsenals of our armed forces." Similarly, in 1954, Secretary of State Dulles said: "The present policies will gradually involve the use of atomic weapons as conventional weapons for tactical purposes. If that occurs and there is a replacement of what is now known as conventional weapons by a different type of weapons, they will, of course, be used." As late as 1957, Secretary of Defense Charles Wilson testified before Congress: "The smaller atomic weapons, the tactical weapons, in a sense have now become conventional weapons."

During the Vietnam War, however, the idea of using nuclear arms received scarcely any serious attention within the U.S. government or in public discussions. President Johnson, of course, clearly rejected it. President Nixon reaffirmed this rejection in 1971, when he stated, in response to a press conference question regarding the use of air power in Indochina, that he was "not going to place any limitation upon the use of airpower except, of course, to rule out a rather ridiculous suggestion that is made from time to time that our airpower might include the use of tactical nuclear weapons."

The idea expressed by Secretary Dulles in 1954—that nuclear weapons would replace conventional weapons and would "of course, be used"—turned out during the Vietnam War to be a "ridiculous suggestion" that was "of course" to be ruled out. This contrast should be attributed less to the passage of time than to the impact of reality—the reality of an ongoing war—which always plays havoc with military theories. To be sure, between the mid-1950s and the mid-1960s, U.S. policy had moved away from the cavalier reliance on "tactical" nuclear arms as substitutes for conventional forces. Even for the region where plans and preparations for tactical nuclear warfare were taken most seriously—the North Atlantic Treaty Organization's (NATO) central front in Germany—a new doctrine had gained ground that envisaged a strengthened conventional defense so as to permit a "pause" in a conventional war before NATO had to use nuclear weapons.

Thus, the contingencies in which the United States envisages that it might initiate tactical nuclear warfare to cope with conventional attack have progressively become more circumscribed. Two developments account for this. The first has been a growing recognition of the military uncertainties and the political costs of initiating nuclear warfare. Since nuclear weapons had never been used on a battlefield, military officers had to rely on largely untested calculations to predict their effectiveness. If the United States had introduced this new weapon in a conventionally fought campaign, it would have ventured into new territory. Adverse political reactions could have been expected throughout the world. In the long run, as the Soviet Union and perhaps other nations built up nuclear arsenals, the United States would become increasingly exposed to nuclear attack. Hence, long-term American interests seemed to dictate that nuclear arms be reserved for the most dire emergency. This was the lesson of the Korean War, at times contradicted by official U.S. statements. The Vietnam War, however, cemented this lesson firmly in American thinking.

More recent trends contributed to the decreased American reliance on nuclear arms. The growing nuclear capability of the Soviet Union made it increasingly plausible that if the United States introduced nuclear arms into a conventional conflict, the adversary, assisted by the Soviet Union, would respond in kind. In contrast, in the early stages of the Korean War, the danger of a Soviet nuclear response was not imminent since the Soviet Union had only started to build its nuclear arsenal.

Today, by far the most important and perhaps the only remaining contingency for which American defense policy contemplates initiating the use of nuclear weapons is a large-scale conventional attack against Western Europe that cannot be stopped by NATO's conventional forces. An important question for the 1980s is how the continuing growth of Soviet nuclear capabilities will affect Western attitudes toward this idea of relying on nuclear arms as a backup to conventional defenses. Precisely in this central contingency, the vastly increased Soviet nuclear capability would pose the greatest danger.

We face several contradictions here. The war in Korea led to the discovery that the United States has powerful reasons not to use nuclear weapons when fighting a conventional war, even where it is not confronted with Soviet nuclear might. Yet new technological possibilities for building less destructive, more accurate nuclear weapons in large quantities encouraged military theories that called for using nuclear arms to redress a possible American weakness in a conventional campaign. This development, in combination with the institutional interest of the U.S. army in playing a role in the "nuclear future," led to a massive buildup of nuclear arms in Europe. Some were enormously destructive (especially in light of the dense population in the region), others were of much lower yield than the Hiroshima bomb. But all were called "tactical" or "theatre" nuclear weapons, regardless of their destructiveness, to distinguish them from "strategic" nuclear arms that were predominantly based in the United States or at sea. Production of "tactical" nuclear arms and their deployment in Europe continued until the mid-1960s. Today, most of these weapons, or in some cases newer ones, are still deployed overseas.

American views on the introduction of nuclear weapons in a conventional war have thus developed on two separate tracks. The experience of Korea and Vietnam led to a diminishing belief in America's ability to rely on tactical nuclear arms outside of Central Europe. But for Central Europe, theoretical planning and actual preparations for tactical nuclear warfare continued, thriving in a sheltered existence. For this region, neither the European nor the American attitudes towards tactical nuclear war have been forged on the anvil of reality. By viewing the Central European case as unique, Western strategists could continue to speculate on the use of nuclear weapons to redress the relative weakness of the West's conventional forces.

Over the last decade or two, these speculations may have served a useful purpose for NATO. Officials within the alliance and Western military scholars could argue—with some plausibility—that NATO's threat to use nuclear weapons to stop a conventional attack, given the large number of nuclear arms deployed in Central Europe, made any Soviet plan for a conventional attack more risky and so helped deter it.

NATO's threat to introduce nuclear arms in a conventional battle has long reassured the countries of Western Europe, especially the Federal Republic of Germany. It is still seen as the ultimate cure for the West's inferiority in tanks, artillery, and men. Moreover, the idea that a massive conventional attack would surely lead to the United States using nuclear weapons bolsters the confidence of Germans and other West Europeans.

This confidence stems not only from the belief that the threat of American nuclear intervention serves to deter the Soviet Union. It also arises from a psychological paradox. A conventional war, experienced by Europe twice in this century, is all too real a disaster. It can be visualized in detail as an unfolding, long, drawn-out calamity, its horrors vividly remembered. Nuclear war, in contrast, is an abstract idea. Its instantaneous dreadfulness is so unimaginable that people tend to think about it in all-or-nothing fashion: either no nuclear weapons will be used, or aggressor and defender will be totally destroyed. By imagining that conventional war in Europe would trigger the use of "tactical" nuclear weapons if the attack could not be stopped by conventional arms alone, a conventional war seems linked to the nether world of nuclear holocaust and hence deterred.

Or so it seems before the day of crisis. The danger is that an adversary could exploit the fear of nuclear war to force the West to yield in some important conflict. Several factors would work against the NATO countries in the event of a major contest of will with the Soviet Union.

First, the global strategic balance will favor the East in the 1980s in most of the important measures of power. Second, the Soviet Union could probably destroy nuclear arms deployed in Western Europe by a "preemptive" attack with its SS-20 missile force. The NATO governments, knowing this, would have good reason to be extraordinarily reluctant even to discuss the use of tactical nuclear weapons. They would have to keep in mind that the enemy might learn of such an impending decision—say through a spy in the highest councils—a melodramatic but uncomfortably realistic concern. They might recall, for example, Willy Brandt's experience as German chancellor, when his closest assistant turned out to be a Soviet spy.

Third, and perhaps most important, Western governments would be far more subject to the pressures of public opinion than the Soviet government. To appreciate these possible pressures, one must remember that a vast chasm now exists between the destructive power of existing nuclear armaments, on the one hand, and the human comprehension of this gruesome potential, on the other. At the beginning of the nuclear era, this chasm was much narrower. The destructiveness of the atomic bomb had not yet been outstripped by the thousand times more powerful thermonuclear weapons. The devastation of Hiroshima and Nagasaki, which had produced a deep emotional reaction throughout the world, was still a vivid and detailed impression, particularly in the West where people had fuller access to the facts.

Over time, however, this reality—mankind's only experience with massive nuclear devastation—receded into the past. There were still the grim drama and emotional impact of weapons tests and their radioactive fallout, until the partial nuclear test ban in 1963 put an end to American and Soviet tests in the atmosphere. So today, even the emotional impact of tests is muffled. Although people in Western countries can inform themselves easily about the vastness of nuclear arsenals and their immense destructiveness, the nuclear threat has become a subterranean ghost in our lives. To keep the ghost exorcised, we rely on a curious kind of priesthood—the strategists, arms control experts, and defense analysts—who talk about "deterrence", "stability", and "nuclear exchange" as if offering a reassuring liturgical incantation.

As long as the exorcism works, the comforting distance between everyday life and the nuclear reality is maintained. Yet this chasm between the nuclear world and the here and now of our lives might suddenly close, bringing the nether world to our doorsteps. In the context of a conventional war, it would take but one nuclear detonation somewhere—which might be a "warning shot" or an accident—to propel the horror of nuclear destruction into public consciousness in every Western country. And if a large-scale conventional war in Central Europe broke out, it might not even require the emotional impact of a nuclear detonation to bring into our consciousnesses the terror of nuclear war. Enormous pressures would be mobilized and brought to bear on government leaders—through parliaments, the media, and other channels—to avoid at almost any price the risk of large-scale nuclear war.

Such a reaction could shatter the political foundations of NATO. The long-standing reliance of NATO governments on the nuclear backup to a conventional defense would suddenly turn from an asset into a liability. In peacetime this reliance is reassuring since it seems to banish the risk of war—any war. But in an acute crisis when nuclear destruction is no longer an abstract fear but a concrete vision of terror, the same reliance on nuclear arms may make NATO governments afraid of their own military capability. Almost any step in military plans and operations that might bring the alliance closer to the threshold of nuclear war would be fiercely resisted by at least some governments. Far from bolstering a full-scale conventional defense, NATO's nuclear threat could turn inward to unravel the alliance in the hour of crisis.

The more firmly NATO leaders expected that a conventional war in Europe would develop into a nuclear war, the more anxious they would be to terminate the fighting if a conventional war actually broke out. Every day, every hour, the conventional campaigns were being fought would seem to prolong the risk of imminent nuclear war.

In negotiating a termination of such a conflict, the West would suffer from a threefold handicap. First, the Western democracies would be politically less well equipped than their adversary to sustain the pressures from such a wrenching crisis. They would contemplate the risk of nuclear destruction with more fully articulated fears and would seek to negotiate with a more humane sense of proportion. Moreover, the corrosive effect of the horrible prospect of nuclear war on statesmen and the public in the West would undoubtedly be stimulated by Soviet propaganda and Soviet-inspired political agitation. The political structure of Communist totalitarianism—and this must be recognized—gives the Soviet Union (and other Communist powers) an advantage in a conflict during which civilian populations could be terrorized by the threat of nuclear destruction.

Second, without strategic superiority, the United States loses the fundamental advantage that compensated for the lack of martial discipline and single-mindedness in the Western alliance. In the 1950s, President Eisenhower could brush aside Khrushchev's nuclear threats as a hollow bluff. (Yet even in that period the United States was, at times, quite hesitant in defending its rights in Berlin.) In the Cuban missile crisis in 1962, President Kennedy could bargain hard enough to obtain the essential American objectives. (Yet even in that crisis senior American officials agonized over the nuclear risks and possible catastrophic outcomes.) But in the 1980s, the extra reservoir of strength that has helped the United States through prior doubts and crises will no longer exist.

Third, military doctrine in the United States and other NATO countries has not been adjusted to the loss of American superiority. Indeed, given the differences in the political structures of Western democracies and Communist totalitarianism, it is unclear how and to what extent such an adjustment could be made. Soviet nuclear strategy (as Douglass and Hoeber show in their essay in this volume) prepares the military and political leaders of the Soviet Union to exploit Western weaknesses. Soviet strategy envisions the use of nuclear weapons not as a measure of retaliation but as a means of achieving political ends—either complete victory, or a compromise favorable to the Soviet Union, or at least an outcome that minimizes damage to the homeland.

In contrast, the overarching purpose of Western nuclear strategy is to prevent nuclear war by threatening a potential aggressor with nuclear destruction—a threat that would, when carried out, be purely an act of revenge. Western strategic thinking has increasingly regarded nuclear weapons as psychological instruments, the means to dissuade the adversary from attacking, not as military instruments to fight an adversary if deterrence failed.

Intermittently, the U.S. Defense Department has tried to plan and prepare for militarily meaningful nuclear strikes. But these efforts have not been followed, by and large, with the necessary improvements in command and control structures and with other measures needed to permit a rational termination of such a war. As a result, nuclear strategy and military planning in the West still focus predominantly on an image of nuclear war that consists of a single campaign: the attack and the immediate response. The second half of this single campaign—the response—has only one objective: averting the first half. In our anesthetizing jargon, this cataract of horrors is given a pretty name—"nuclear exchange"—as if it were a transaction in foreign trade. Thus the potentially most painful event in history is rendered strangely painless. All too comfortably, an eschatology has become strategic theory.

But in the test of a real armed conflict, the comforting imagery would dissolve. Ominous intelligence data, frightening news bulletins, and harrowing battle reports would paint a new reality in glaring light. At this point, initiating the use of nuclear weapons would have to serve some purpose other than revenging the attack. The overriding objective for every politically responsible government would be to minimize nuclear destruction to its homeland. As the choice became real—no longer a paper exercise—military and political leaders would be overwhelmed by what they had quietly known all along: that NATO's strategy for "first use" has not been adjusted to the loss of America's nuclear superiority. NATO's doctrine would be silent on how the destruction unleashed by initiating the use of nuclear weapons could be brought to an end in ways that served our political purposes. At the gates of hell, the old eschatology would offer little solace.

THE DYNAMICS OF THE CRISIS

The Soviets "will never be superior to us in national strength, nor in overall military strength," said President Carter in a revealing interview. "They spend more than twice as much of their gross national product on military matters, but we are still much stronger, and we will always be stronger than they are, at least in our lifetime."[3] Those who share this view tend to regard the balance of power in the world as essentially stable. They hold that the changes that have occurred or that may occur in the future do not constitute a shift in military power large enough to jeopardize America's security.

Besides, according to this view, America's most powerful potential military challenger is not sufficiently motivated to exploit his military strength. "There is no doubt in my mind that the Soviets want peace," President Carter said in another interview.[4] "In nuclear weapons . . . we both accepted the concept of equivalency."[5] Thus, an enduring harmony in ultimate military objectives and a stable balance in overall military strength is seen to prevail between the world's two largest powers.

This equilibrium in the world is further buttressed—according to this view—by the close symmetry in the outward thrust of both superpowers. "As is the case with us," President Carter said, "[the Soviets] would like to expand their influence among other people."[6] And again, Carter opined, "the Soviets take advantage, I believe, of opportunities throughout the world to enhance their own influence . . . I have to say we do the same."[7]

Since the Soviet Union is estimated to spend three times as much as the United States on strategic arms and is increasing this effort by 4 to 5 percent each year, while the much smaller American arms effort will grow by scarcely 3 percent, it seems puzzling that President Carter should consider that "we will always be stronger than they are, at least in our lifetime." Perhaps the trends in global military power have neither shocked nor stimulated political thinking in the United States and in the Western world at large because the resulting change has been gradual, its implications concealed, and its impact postponed. The fundamental flaws of NATO's nuclear strategy—as we have seen—can be painlessly ignored as long as NATO is not put to test. And the shift in the East-West military balance has occurred gradually. To appreciate the peril of this decline in American strength, one has to see it in its totality over a ten- or fifteen-year period and weigh the possibility of a similar, further decline over the next decade.

Geopolitical changes, too, have crept up on us, with a far greater cumulative impact than is apparent from events in a single year. And the larger trend is further obscured by the setbacks the Soviet Union has suffered. It lost its alliance with Egypt, and more importantly, it is now confronted with a hostile China. Yet added together, the geographic expansion of Soviet influence since 1944 has been a process of one step backward, two steps forward.

In contrast, the United States entered the postwar period with large reserves in terms of geopolitical assets and military advantages, which have been eroding rather steadily. For example, in the mid-1950s it would have seemed alarmist, even outlandish, to predict that a Caribbean nation might fight American interests in the Middle East and Africa while Soviet pilots and modern Soviet aircraft replenished the air force of that Caribbean nation at home. In the mid-1950s, the United States maintained a base in Libya and military facilities in Ethiopia (where the Soviet military are now ensconced); our British ally had a naval base in Aden (now used by the Soviet navy); and Singapore was a major British naval base, while today the Soviets can use Cam Ranh Bay in Vietnam.

Because of this gradual erosion in geographic assets and in relative military strength, the West's capability to cope with a crisis is becoming progressively weaker. And each future setback will be more dangerous since it will impact on a weakened position. The power balance—having gradually shifted to one side—might suddenly tilt at an accelerating pace, and at some point, the world's political structure would be decisively transformed. The deterioration will feed on itself, mounting to a crisis that engulfs all nations.

Such a crisis might start to unfold, for example, if the United States retreated in the face of a major challenge from the Soviet Union. The more apparent it became that the global military balance was the main cause of the retreat, the more serious its consequences. The repercussions would be particularly painful if the United States had actually tried to maintain the status quo through force, but was militarily defeated in a local war. (The American defeat in Indochina was different because other nations attributed it to inadequate American staying power in an unpopular war, not to overall military weakness.) After the shrinkage of American power had thus been dramatically revealed, many nations would seek to rearrange their positions relative to the United States, the Soviet Union, and other powers. Some American allies would move to neutrality; unaligned nations would move closer to the Soviet Union.

We have become overly habituated during the last 35 years to a world in which a bipolar balance of power has limited the scope and speed of change. But history reminds us that political and military changes may suddenly accelerate at meteoric speed and explode into a global sweep once the military relationship among the major powers is shattered. In an era when communications and travel were immeasurably slower than today, Napoleon completed the expansion of his vast empire, from Spain to Russia, within some seventeen years. Hitler's achievement of power, the collapse of the collective security system of the League of Nations, Hitler's rearmament of Germany, his annexation of territories, and the world war which he unleashed occurred within the span of less than thirteen years. The British policy of appeasement lasted no more than five of these thirteen years.

In the present era, by contrast, the American involvement in the war in Vietnam dragged on for 13 years. The SALT negotiations, too, have lasted for 13 years. The Arab-Israeli conflict has continued for 30 years. The division of Europe between East and West has been maintained by the presence of military forces for 35 years.

The particular course that a major world crisis might take is, of course, unpredictable. But the dynamic that would deepen and accelerate the crisis can be seen today. The triggering event might occur almost anywhere and could take various forms. For example, an effort by the United States to help its friends in the Middle East or to protect the flow of oil against Soviet-backed disturbances or armed attacks could lead to a contest between American and Soviet strength in that region. For valid reasons, the United States would see its vital interests at stake. The Soviet Union, on the other hand, might see an opportunity to bring to bear the superior military might on which it had lavishly expended its resources for so many years. Confident of the righteousness of its cause and its historic destiny and aware of the various advantages of its military potential, the Soviet Union's leaders might decide to press ahead. The United States would try to maintain resistance. But if the Soviet Union persisted, as well it might, an unequal contest would ensue. American arms assistance and military advisers would be pitted against Soviet proxy forces (e.g., Cubans) and against Communist political action and subversion. The airlift capabilities of both sides and ultimately American and Soviet combat forces might become directly involved.

The fact that America's military preparations and spending have lagged behind Russia's for so many years would begin to tell in such a confrontation. In such a local war, the United States would be pushed into retreat by superior conventional forces, and globally it would confront Soviet nuclear capabilities in many respects more formidable than its own. Now the notion that America's nuclear forces could somehow deter the Soviet Union from fully exploiting its conventional military advantage would suddenly be revealed as a delusion. If such a crisis reached this point, where and how could the United States and those of its allies who remained steadfast halt the retreat? What remaining resources—military, economic, and political—would prevent a follow-up offensive to subjugate what would be left of the Western world? Napoleon and Hitler did not halt while they were victorious.

In the Second World War (as in the First), the military might of Germany was finally overcome because the United States could mobilize its strength to restore the global military balance. In both World Wars I and II, the reserves of American strength were, in fact, far from being exhausted. Particularly in the Second World War, these reserves represented the ultimate stabilizer, the means for rebuilding and guaranteeing a world order in which those Western democracies that had been militarily too weak to protect themselves could survive and where new democracies could emerge. In the present era, however, there is no such "ultimate stabilizer" since the military capabilities of the United States are already an integral part of the Western alliances. If these capabilities should prove insufficient, there is no "arsenal of democracy" to come to the rescue.

WHAT CAN BE DONE?

The new and mounting threats to America's security cannot be easily met. A determined effort requiring broad political support and some sacrifices will be needed if in a future crisis the United States is to withstand the grim, triple pressures: Soviet military preponderance, a flawed nuclear strategy, and the acute vulnerability of the West's oil supply.

Moreover, other foreign policy problems clamor for attention. In fact, many who are influential in America's foreign policy consider these other problems more important. They hold that miliary threats can be kept in check if the United States pursues present arms control policies and continues its present defense effort—give or take a 3 percent increase. They feel that instead of spending more on defense, higher priority must be given to such problems as the gap between the rich and the poor nations, the growing worldwide demand for natural resources, and the risk that more nations will acquire nuclear arms. Supporters of this perspective often argue that the United States must adapt to a changing world and, indeed, has reasons to welcome many recent changes; that instead of pining for its old supremacy and an obsolete international order, America must move with the tide.

But where will this tide carry us? It is fatuous to argue that the United States should accept all these changes or stand convicted of rigidly clinging to the status quo. Over the past 35 years, America has been in the vanguard of most successful and salutary changes in the world: economic development in poorer countries, a huge expansion in the world economy, technological and scientific innovation, the creation of stable democracies in Japan and West Germany, the establishment of international institutions, the transformation of European colonies into independent nations.

Another argument for a relaxed approach to the shift in the global power balance contends that the Soviet Union would never take full advantage of its superior military might by exploiting its growing margin of strength to expand its empire. This confident prediction of Soviet self-restraint is reminiscent of another forecast in vogue in Washington ten to fifteen years ago: that the Soviet Union would not try to achieve full parity in strategic arms, let alone seek to surpass the United States. American foreign policy should be prepared to welcome and seek to encourage Soviet self-restraint, but it should not count on it.

In foreign policy, perhaps more than in any other field of government policy, we must allow for much uncertainty and be prepared for misfortune as well as good luck. We must neither turn our hopes into wishful thinking nor let our fears become self-fulfilling prophecies of doom. Efforts to stem a further deterioration in America's relative military power must not assume that an indefinite continuation of the Soviet military buildup is foreordained and hence can be answered only by an indefinite American buildup. On the contrary, by recognizing the ominous sweep of the present trends (instead of wishfully thinking that stability had arrived), chances for meaningful arms control and mutual restraint are much improved.

And an effort to prevent further losses in our geopolitical assets is not a desperate remedy, a last ditch stand that assumes our every setback abroad results in a permanent loss, that every shift in a country toward closer ties with the Soviet Union equals a permanent expansion of the Soviet empire. By pursuing an assertive and self-confident foreign policy, we will be better able to absorb some losses because we are better prepared to make some compensating gains. It is precisely a passive and indifferent attitude toward the political color of the world map that provokes an accelerating erosion of the realm of freedom.

What specifically can be done? The answer leaves room for hope if we assume that the United States will summon the conviction and perseverance to make the necessary efforts.

These efforts can be grouped into three "tiers." The first tier has been the most basic American security requirement for the last 25 years or so: a deterrent against a concerted nuclear attack on the United States. In essence, this means the United States must maintain a nuclear capability to threaten convincingly a response to such an attack that inevitably deprives it of any possible rationale. Agreement on the essentiality of this requirement is nearly universal, but considerable disagreement prevails among experts on how best to meet it in the future. Nevertheless, specific measures that appear to be technically feasible have been proposed and—provided the executive branch leads the way confidently and presents a good case—will be supported by Congress and the people.

In contrast, greater intellectual and political complexities confront us at the second tier: the efforts needed to cope with a conflict in which the Soviets made full use of their superior conventional forces. While their conventional superiority was growing over the past decade, the old answer—"first use" of U.S. nuclear weapons to stave off defeat—has become obsolete because of the changed nuclear balance. Indeed, as I argued above, it has become a dangerous trap. Moreover, simply strengthening the conventional forces of the United States—the remedy that first comes to mind—will not and cannot be sufficient. An improvement in conventional strength is clearly necessary and useful, not only for NATO's central front (which the Carter administration has made its priority), but also for other regions. Yet the disparity in quickly mobilizable conventional strength, particularly manpower, is too wide to be overcome by the kind of buildup that the United States might muster under peacetime conditions. Even in prior decades when the United States spent more than twice as much as it does today for defense and the draft kept manpower costs far below present levels, the United States could not match the Soviet Union in ground forces.

Only in wartime or during a provocative and widely recognized national emergency will the United States generate a significantly larger conventional force and only if the president, Congress, and the majority of the people are united in determination and willing to make sacrifices to save the country. As a result of the war in Korea, the fraction of the gross national product the United States spent on defense increased from 4.5 percent (about the present level) to 13 percent within less than four years. In World War II it increased from 1.3 percent in 1939 to 45 percent in 1944. No doubt, when people complacently refer to America's greater economic strength as a counterweight to Russia's military establishment, they have in mind this capability to expand defense production. Yet the thought is usually left implicit, as if a war could be won or deterred by the mere existence of a plethora of American consumer goods, without converting this economic capacity into military strength.

The U.S. capacity to expand its defense effort many times over the present level—given the necessary time and political determination—is perhaps the most important deterrent to a major conventional attack.

Moreover, it is a highly stabilizing deterrent and serves to discourage a repudiation or major violation of arms control agreements (provided they are verifiable). Yet this capacity has been badly neglected, and its implications tend to be misunderstood.

American military doctrine clings to the assumption that a large-scale conventional war would be short, particularly if Soviet forces were involved. This assumption derives from the canonical view of a NATO–Warsaw Pact war, according to which either NATO forces would quickly stop the aggression and restore the status quo or—in the short-circuiting jargon—"the war would go nuclear." In the present era, this shaky assumption clearly no longer justifies neglecting preparations for expanding defense production. The assumption is particularly unconvincing for theaters of conflict other than Central Europe.

We should harbor no illusions, however, that "American ingenuity" and our economic prowess could readily duplicate the feat of American mobilization after Pearl Harbor. In 1941 and 1950, the proportion of unused industrial capacity was considerably larger than it is today, weapons technology required shorter lead times between the decision to produce and delivery to the troops, and (with a few exceptions) the United States had an advantage in access to raw materials. Moreover, America's overall industrial capacity is now much less superior to that of its adversaries than in 1941 or 1950, and the Soviet Union presently has a much larger ongoing arms production program than the United States—and hence a headstart for a competitive expansion. But this is all the more reason to take certain steps today that would place the United States in a better competitive position.

Several measures could be taken to improve the American capacity to expand defense production rapidly: the preparation of prototype designs specially suited for emergency production, carefully updated stockpiling of long-lead items and raw materials, and administrative preparations. Compared with the total defense budget, these would be low-cost measures. Some of these measures are being undertaken today, but are given a low priority and guided by obsolete concepts.

It is curious that our latent capacity to expand defense production has not received more scrutiny and attention.[8] Given Russia's continuing three-to-one edge in strategic arms spending and its two-to-one edge in overall military purchases and in military research, this capacity—America's potential for expanding its military might—is, after all, our only counterbalancing reserve of military strength.

Many other new efforts are needed to protect the United States and to help avoid war apart from the requirements for nuclear and conventional arms—both ready and mobilizable. American foreign policy must be invigorated on a third tier: political action abroad; aid, foreign trade, and intelligence; and information, words, and ideas.

Repairing U.S. intelligence capabilities is a high-priority task for the administration and Congress. As a result of the political turmoil in Washington in the mid-1970s, members of Congress initiated legislation and inquiries into American intelligence operations. Parts of this legislation, along with the publicity that was stirred up, seriously damaged our intelligence organizations. Some who favored the changes wanted merely to correct past abuses, effect necessary reforms, and strengthen legislative supervision. Others were motivated by their search for publicity—lambasting the CIA seemed to be the popular thing to do. And perhaps a few wanted to hobble American intelligence capabilities because they felt the United States had too much power.

Additional damage was done by other legislation that favored certain civil rights at the expense of the government's investigative capabilities (and thus, in the last analysis, at the expense of other civil rights). Finding the necessary compromise between government powers and individual liberties requires a sense of proportion and sound judgment. During the politically turbulent 1970s, the balance shifted too far toward the public's right to know to the detriment of the legitimate secrecy essential for foreign intelligence operations. And the laudable effort to protect privacy has resulted in restrictions on government surveillance that hamper the discovery of criminal activities and foreign espionage.

A more sensible balance must also be struck in restricting and controlling nonmilitary, unpublicized actions that the United States could usefully take abroad—so-called "covert operations." Today, congressionally imposed restrictions are so onerous that the United States is almost unable to give "quiet support to a friend"—Ray Cline's description (in this volume) of the essential purpose of "covert operations."

In the years to come, much more so than in the past, the United States must be in a position to use a broad and varied range of instruments to exert influence abroad. As I have argued, the United States will have to rely heavily on its capability to expand defense production massively since its ready military forces are becoming increasingly outnumbered. But this ultimate dependence on American industrial strength requires the retention of geopolitical assets—that is to say, a margin of safety in terrain and resources. Hence, the United States must be able to protect its influence and its interests in many areas of the world without having to resort to military intervention. Indeed, the very purpose of our nonmilitary instruments for exerting influence abroad is to reduce the likelihood and intensity of conflicts, without retreat, and to preserve America's assets, without a confrontation of arms.

Additional policy changes are needed if the United States is to protect its assets when it faces difficult trials of strength. The U.S. government must control the transfer of advanced technology to foreign countries, particularly to the Soviet Union, more consistently and effectively. The commercial gains from such transfers are usually short-lived and frequently amount to only a pittance compared with the development costs that American firms or our government initially invested. On the other hand, the military disadvantages to the United States from technology transfers can be substantial since many transfers either help some specific weapons program or enhance an adversary's military resources in general. The position of those who are complacent about this risk is inconsistent. On the one hand, they argue that we need not worry about the Soviet arms buildup since the United States is ahead in technology; on the other hand, they maintain that nothing is to be lost militarily from the transfer of advanced technology.

Last, we must marshal a resource that we have been neglecting too much. We must pay more attention to the weight of words and ideas. The term "propaganda" has long had a derogatory meaning in American usage, but that should not blind us to the fact that our adversaries have been conducting propaganda on a large scale—and often successfully.

America's case is much stronger than that of its Communist adversaries. Yet we have far too readily permitted our adversaries to provide the agenda and the vocabulary for the global contest of ideas. We should be on guard against "semantic infiltration"—the insinuation of the opponent's vocabulary into our own. When during the war in Vietnam an American secretary of state described what American soldiers were opposing as a war of *liberation*—without placing liberation in quotation marks—he inadvertently supported the image of that war that our enemies tried to cultivate. And we paint an upside-down image of political change when we call "progressive forces" those who seek to replace an authoritarian regime with a totalitarian one—more efficient in its police control and censorship, and more suppressive of human rights. Again, we should not refer to prison or concentration camps as "re-education camps" when they are located in Vietnam. Tracking down such semantic infiltrations provides us with an instructive gauge of our own intellectual flabbiness.[9]

Most American officials who are on the firing line in the battle of words and ideas—our Foreign Service officers, senior officials of our information service, delegates to international conferences—are highly skilled. These men and women can meet the challenge if properly guided. Perhaps if the State Department were more closely linked to the electorate, the strength of conviction and values of the vast majority of the American people would be more effectively heard abroad.[10] But this leads us to the pivot for America's role in the global contest of beliefs and ideas. It is the president who must have the strength of intellect and eloquence to lead the government and the people and to present America's case to the world.

NOTES

1. Albert Wohlstetter, "Racing Forward or Ambling Back?" *Survey* no. 314 (Summer/Autumn 1976): 163–217, and "Optimal Ways to Confuse Ourselves," *Foreign Policy* no. 20 (Autumn 1975): 170–98.

2. Donald S. Zagoria, "Into the Breach: New Soviet Alliances in the Third World," *Foreign Affairs* (Spring 1979), p. 733.

3. Interview with President Carter by Bill Moyers (WNET, New York) November 13, 1978.

4. Don Oberdorfer, *Washington Post*, February 1, 1979.

5. Interview by Bill Moyers (see n.3).

6. Ibid.

7. Don Oberdorfer (see n. 4).

8. An exception is the article by Paul Bracken, "Mobilization in the Nuclear Age," *International Security* 3, no. 3 (Winter 1978/79): 74–93.

9. For some further telling examples of "semantic infiltration" see Daniel Patrick Moynihan, "Words and Foreign Policy," *Policy Review* (Autumn 1978), p. 69.

10. Laurence H. Silberman, "Toward Presidential Control of the State Department," *Foreign Affairs* (Spring 1979), p. 882.

Soviet Approach to Global Nuclear Conflict

Amoretta M. Hoeber
Joseph D. Douglass, Jr.

XVI

The primary U.S. objective vis-à-vis the Soviet Union is twofold: first, to deter direct acts of war by the Soviet Union against the United States and, second, to deter other potential Soviet actions that are contrary to U.S. interests, including the use of the threat of war against the United States or its allies to gain political concessions. Although the United States continues to deter Soviet threats, its ability to deflect Soviet political thrusts is clearly decreasing. Soviet challenges are increasing in both frequency and boldness, and confidence in the long-term U.S. capability to deter or even to influence any Soviet actions short of direct attack on the United States appears less and less certain.

The deterioration of the U.S. ability to deter and influence Soviet actions has been both a function and a reflection of the tremendous buildup in Soviet military capabilities during the past decade. This buildup is projected to continue and can no longer be dismissed as merely defense oriented. The United States is visibly headed for a position of significant inferiority in the early 1980s, with no real prospect of reversing the trend. Not only has the United States not responded to the buildup, but U.S. inaction during the past decade may well have encouraged Soviet pursuit of such superiority. Exacerbating this inaction has been the considerable effort of the U.S. government to downplay the importance of the Soviet buildup and to sell the current

The sources cited in this article are but a small sample of the books and articles used in our research. For a fuller discussion, see our *Soviet Strategy for Nuclear War* (Stanford: Hoover Institution Press, 1979).

military balance as equivalence, despite overwhelming evidence to the contrary. Even less openly recognized by the U.S. government than the Soviet buildup, however, has been the relation of that buildup to Soviet military doctrine and the Soviet interest in encouraging, if not coercing, the United States to remain inactive. Soviet insistence on U.S. assent to the Strategic Arms Limitation Treaty (SALT) II as it is currently drafted, without any senatorial advice, a treaty that clearly codifies Soviet military strategy and superiority, is one clear example of such Soviet efforts.

The success of Soviet tactics is due in part to the lack of interest in and understanding of the nature and meaning of Soviet military thought. Increasing numbers of Americans, however, are beginning to question the validity of both the U.S. doctrine that led us to the current dilemma and our understanding of Soviet motives and intentions. Perhaps the clearest indication of this concern is the fact that leading political figures are shifting the blame to previous administrations and to other parties (for example, Congress).[1] This is, however, an oversimplification. The decisions being criticized should not be viewed as having stemmed solely from the character of certain administrations. Rather, the current predicament results more from decisions based on a broad set of assumptions that have guided U.S. strategic concepts and U.S. military and political behavior for several decades.

This same set of assumptions has also constrained our understanding of the Soviets. Further, the U.S. view of Soviet concepts and consequently our interpretations of Soviet actions are severely affected by two closely intertwined problems. First, a perceiver tends to see what he wants to see or to find what he is looking for. For example, because we believe that no rational man would contemplate nuclear war, we tend to believe that the Soviets have reached or will reach the same conclusion. Second, because U.S. policy and planning are based on this belief, we find it difficult to conceive that the Soviets are building a capability—and indeed think it is possible to build a capability—to fight a nuclear war. This second problem exacerbates the first because if the policy and planning of the United States—based on its view of the impossibility of nuclear war—are to the advantage of the Soviet Union, then the Soviets have a strong incentive to feed or substantiate the U.S. view. Because of these problems, much of the development of U.S. military and arms control policies appears to have been pursued in a context that has not seriously considered the extent of Soviet planning for global nuclear conflict, the Soviet concepts and criteria for strategic decision making, the importance of surprise in Soviet doctrine, and the value and uses of superiority in Soviet eyes.

Rather than developing a clear understanding of our adversary, the United States has tended to mirror-image its own judgment; more specifically, its dedication to the theory that deterrence is best achieved by threatening unacceptable damage and its concept of forces prepared only for fighting a nuclear war—should deterrence fail—by devastating the Soviet Union. United States planning for strategic retaliation in the event of general war with the Soviet Union has therefore been strongly influenced by the notions of spasm war and the force requirement needed to destroy industrial and unprotected military targets. Conceptually, U.S. policy holds that there would be no victor in a nuclear war. Consequently, nuclear war is irrational, unwinnable, basically unthinkable, and *cannot* occur; neither American nor Russian leaders can therefore use nuclear weapons for political ends. Not only is nuclear war or the threat of nuclear war an unusable instrument of politics, but nuclear forces and even military power generally can thus be separated from the economic and political competition between states. In the view of U.S. leaders, these conclusions mean that the basic rule of the game between the United States and the Soviet Union is that mutual strategic deterrence has been and will continue to be in effect.

Because of the dangers of inadvertent or accidental nuclear use—or even because of the danger of untoward escalation if non-nuclear forces become enmeshed with each other—another fundamental U.S. belief is that the only road to stability and safety in the nuclear age is arms control that leads, eventually, to nuclear disarmament. In this view, it is essential to rid the world of nuclear weapons. This belief has been one of the driving factors behind arguments that the SALT process is important because it could eventually lead to disarmament even if particular agreements along the way do not further this basic objective. According to this logic, the United States must exercise self-restraint and play the leading role in arms reduction since we have enjoyed superiority in strategic nuclear capability, both in material aspects and in intellectual understanding of the strategic nuclear problem, for a considerable time. In contrast, the Soviet Union's position has been considerably inferior, and this condition is exacerbated by what can be called a traditional Soviet sense of insecurity. In the early days of SALT, Soviet inferiority was seen as hampering their ability to negotiate on so important an aspect of their forces as nuclear weapons. Thus, it was seen as necessary to permit the Soviet Union not only to achieve parity in nuclear strength, but perhaps even to surpass the United States, so that they could become secure and in this security increase their comprehension of deterrence. Then, it was assumed, Soviet political leaders could and would reduce the influence of their military-industrial complex and channel decisions on military procurement in the desired direction. The United States, accordingly, was to be patient and avoid actions that might upset this natural and inevitable process.

Further, this logic holds that pursuing arms control and reduction, even unilaterally, involves little risk because of the enormous overkill that even a small collection of nuclear weapons represents. Because one cannot win a nuclear war and indeed because any type of protracted fighting with nuclear weapons is impossible, it is necessary in this view only to assure that the United States retains a minimum deterrent capability. Most recently, in the 1979 State of the Union address, President Carter suggested that this minimum is perhaps as low as "just one of our relatively invulnerable Poseidon submarines."

For all practical purposes, this set of beliefs has existed as more or less official national policy for over a decade. The basic flaw of these concepts is that they depend on the other side's holding the same beliefs. And the Soviets do not. United States refusal to recognize this is a serious error that may well place the nation irretrievably in mortal danger. Basic Soviet beliefs regarding nuclear war and stability diverge sharply from the Western positions. In contrast to the United States, the Soviets firmly believe in a logic for competition between states that encompasses political, economic, and military power.

For two decades the United States has effectively ignored the available evidence on Soviet concepts, motivations, and intentions that would have shown that the Soviet Union does not subscribe to the logic ascribed to them. Authoritative Soviet writings and pronouncements on military doctrine and strategy have been dismissed as either mere propaganda or military confidence building. Official statements of Soviet military doctrine and strategy have been denigrated because, like their counterparts in the United States, they have been seen as military and driven by the Soviet version of the military-industrial complex. As such, they are not considered to reflect the broader and more sensible political considerations of the civilian politicians who are in control and who would make the basic military-strategic decisions regarding how and when to go to war, or to threaten to go to war, even if they placate the military by allowing continuing increases in defense expenditures. This view overlooks the unity of Soviet political and military thought. Soviet thought centers around one basic point, a point that is contrary to Western concepts: that military strength, including nuclear and even intercontinental nuclear forces, can in fact be used for political purposes—even to the extent of engaging in global nuclear war. The Soviets believe that nuclear weapons per se have not altered the fact that war is primarily a political act. Further, they seem convinced that the active export of their revolutionary efforts can proceed most effectively and with relative impunity if buttressed by overwhelming military capability. Consequently, their strategic objective (and they are attaining this objective) is to acquire a combination of offensive and defensive capabilities that not only will support their expansionism, but will permit, should war come, a Soviet victory. The most important aspects of this strategy are superiority, surprise, survival, and clear and coherent goals.

QUANTITATIVE AND QUALITATIVE SUPERIORITY

Quantitative and qualitative superiority in nuclear forces is the first goal. *"Now not only quantitative superiority, but also qualitative superiority over the opponent has become a matter of prime importance."*[2] This goal is both general and specific. One primary aspect is to achieve military-technical superiority, which includes both quantity and quality:

> The basic condition for the proposed buildup of economic potential, effective economic mobilization, and the support of the war is now the achievement of military-technical superiority, which is understood to be superiority over the enemy in the quantity and quality of armaments and in the technical equipment of troops.
>
> Using the achievement of Soviet economics, sciences, and technology, the *party and state* are doing everything necessary to bring about our constant qualitative and quantitative military and technical superiority over the armies of the leading capitalist states.[3] (Emphasis added.)

And, more specifically: "No lags will be allowed in the military field: maintaining reliable military-technical superiority is a task conditioned by the international duties of the Soviet Union."[4] The task of achieving and maintaining military-technical superiority is not just a military one; the "party and state" are equally involved. The party, says General Yepishev, "constantly is concerned that the Soviet Army and Navy have military-technical superiority over the armed forces of our probable enemies, the imperialist aggressor states."[5]

On the quantitative side, according to Soviet military writings, reserve forces that are unaccounted for in Western perceptions of the Soviet threat are considered extremely important. The Soviets traditionally organize their forces into three strategic echelons. In addition, there are active forces and reserves. This differentiation does not apply merely to ground forces, as is often thought. In the Soviet literature, it refers to all forces, including nuclear missiles of all categories—tactical, operational-tactical, and strategic. The Soviets consider all strategic echelons and reserves as important and view them as playing distinctly different roles.

The first strategic echelon is manned at full strength (90 percent day-to-day), is fully equipped, and is to be ready for combat within a few hours, or in even less time in the case of the Strategic Missile Force Command. (One dichotomy between Soviet strategy as written and force posture as observed relates to the readiness of the first strategic echelon of intercontinental forces. It is well recognized that in peacetime these forces are kept at a readiness level considerably below that discussed as a requirement in the Soviet literature. This may reflect either a Soviet assumption that there will be a period of threat; a prioritizing of resource allocation; the current state of Soviet technology, for example, missile gyroscopes; or some combination of these factors.) The second strategic echelon is manned at appreciably lower levels (as low as 20 percent overall and 50 percent for officers and critical personnel), is completely equipped, and is to be able to mobilize and be ready for combat within a few days. The third strategic echelon is essentially unmanned, except for critical command elements that may be independently located or in peacetime possibly integrated into second or perhaps first strategic echelon units. At the onset of mobilization, these command personnel would split off and form units of the third strategic echelon, which is to be mobilized and combat ready within three weeks. All three strategic echelons have reserves of both people and materiel. These reserves are used to replace losses and to provide for the mobilization of the second and third strategic echelons.

In contrast to the first and second strategic echelons, the third strategic echelon, which can be viewed as a strategic reserve or which is constituted out of such reserves, has no immediate mission assigned to it and is an extra force for use by the Supreme High Command when and as necessary. The strategic reserve, as a generic category of forces, has a special meaning to the Soviets. The Soviets represent the German failure to recognize the existence of such reserves as a critical error in German planning and view these reserves as having provided the superior correlation of forces that enabled them to defeat the Germans in World War II. Such a completion of victory is also the role assigned to the reserves in contemporary warfare:

> The increasing scale of armed conflict requires strong reserves for augmenting the efforts of the first strategic echelon which will hardly be in a position to execute alone the great number of important strategic missions in the path to achieving the goals of war.

> Thus, to carry out modern armed conflict successfully it is necessary to have, in addition to a strong first echelon, strong and well-trained subsequent strategic echelons and the peacetime establishment of powerful state reserves.[6]

The concept of reserves of nuclear weapons and means of delivery specifically refers to those forces remaining after the initial nuclear exchange or battle. This postexchange balance is viewed as the primary measure of the correlation of nuclear forces. In fact, an important scenario in Soviet strategy has the war continuing until one side exhausts its stock of nuclear weapons. If the other side still has a sufficient quantity (which appears to be measured at least in the hundreds), it then wins by default. A notable aspect of both the second echelon and the strategic reserves is their concealment. This is critical because neither takes part in the initial exchange, and hence, to survive they must be hidden from the enemy.

A number of sources make it clear that the concept of reserves applies to strategic missiles:

> No matter how high the level of military-technical progress, the basic, objective law of war, formulated by Lenin, will not cease to operate: "He will gain the victory in war who has the greatest reserves, the greatest sources of strength, and the greatest support among the masses of the people." (*Collected Works*, vol. 30., p. 55) . . . the expression "sources of strength and reserves," includes, along with human resources, *all types of the latest combat equipment, including nuclear-rocket weapons* . . . without military-technical superiority over the enemy, achieved before the beginning of the war and maintained throughout its progress, victory in modern war cannot be assured. (Emphasis added.)

> The combat actions are represented as a series of consecutive strikes, as a result of which both sides suffer losses. The losses may be partially recovered by means of reserves, and undamaged missile sites are reequipped with missiles during the course of combat.[7]

Further, statements concerning the role of civil defense units in assisting in the "transportation of munitions, armaments, and other material and supplies to strategic missile troops" in a period of mass enemy nuclear strikes have also been identified.[8] Thus, the missiles visible to satellites may well be primarily the first strategic echelon, and there may be stores of strategic missiles and warheads in warehouses or depots (that is, not in silos, which would reveal their locations and which are unnecessary because the required combat readiness is measured in hours, days, and even weeks rather than in minutes as is the case with the first strategic echelon).

The existence of such missiles, as of some other items, is extremely difficult to prove, and there is insufficient public evidence available to enable one to state with certainty that the Soviets have implemented their doctrine in this respect. However, the existence of the principle and its logic in authoritative, internal Soviet literature is clear, and implementation would imply a significant store of reserve intercontinental ballistic missiles (ICBMs). The possibility of such missiles is an important issue because of the political and military implications. Two major aspects of U.S. strategic policy are challenged. The first is the validity of the Western discussions and calculations of force balances on which many of the rationales for the Carter administration's arguments in support of SALT are based, which may simply leave out a possibly significant component of the Soviet forces and a significant factor in the internal Soviet assessment of the balance. The second is the relevance of the U.S. approach to arms control verification of strategic missile forces. The approach appears to have been to impose limitations on what can be verified (in the case of ICBMs, silos) even if they are perhaps relatively meaningless items, rather than to attempt to limit missiles.

Because of the extent to which the Soviets focus on reserves, including nuclear missile reserves, and because of the Soviet propensity to retain older systems even though they are being replaced with new systems, the total size of the Soviet intercontinental missile force may well be (and these authors believe is) considerably larger than that indicated by the conventional approach that just counts silos. Given the consistent case that can be made for Soviet interest in concealing such reserves, considerable caution should be observed in relying on the assumption that what we do not see does not exist.

It is in the context of calculation of the correlation of forces that the Soviets appear to carry out actual assessments of relative force capability and actually consider war and the special role of *qualitative* factors. "Calculating the correlation of forces," according to a 1969 Soviet article,

> is not an end in itself. It is connected with many functions of strategic planning and the military-political leadership both during the prewar period as well as while a war is in progress. Obviously it is extremely important not only to establish the correlation of forces of the sides, but also on the basis of this to work out the most correct political and military decisions. From the established correlation of forces of the sides depend the elaboration of the plan for the war and for operations, the purposefulness of strategy and operational art, and the determination of ways to change this correlation to achieve victory in armed combat. Deficiencies

> in revealing the actual military capabilities of the sides lead, as experience shows, to a stratification of errors: the plans worked out for a war are unrealistic, instead of an offensive strategy a defensive strategy is used and vice versa, the military efforts are incorrectly distributed in regard to operational directions, time, etc.[9]

Nuclear weapons are of primary importance in the calculation: "[Results depend] . . . on the presence and distribution of nuclear weapons among the various branches of the armed forces and the combat arms, on the power of the available nuclear warheads and the capabilities of their carriers, and the effectiveness of the systems for air defense and the control of troops."[10] It is important to note here, in contrast to the manner in which the strategic balance is assessed in the West, the explicit inclusion of air defense and command and control. These capabilities—and others—are often encountered in Soviet discussions of the correlation of forces, where both qualitative and quantitative factors are considered explicitly. The principal measure of the quantitative factors in the nuclear portion of the correlation is equivalent megatons. The most important qualitative factors that enter into the calculation include assessments of command and control; reconnaissance; readiness; secrecy (including cover and deception); and missile accuracy, survivability, and support. Command flexibility is considered an especially important qualitative aspect of the Soviet nuclear force development objectives. This flexibility does not refer to options available on the eve of war, from which the Soviet leadership can select, but rather to the capability to shift efforts, redirect strikes, and alter the sequence of missions during a war. That is, flexibility means nuclear battle management at the strategic level. This is the rationale behind the importance in Soviet calculation of such factors as command and control, reconnaissance, and technical support, including the supply of new missiles from reserves. This is also one reason why the ability of leaders to use forces is regarded as a major contributing factor in victory.

SURPRISE AND THE ONSET OF WAR

The Soviets attach considerable importance to surprise and to the role of deception and disinformation in achieving surprise. Surprise, as is expanded on below, is regarded in the Soviet literature as a vital if not the single most important condition for success in war: "A more important condition for achieving victory than overall superiority in weapons and manpower is the ability to use concealment in preparing one's main forces for a major strike and the element of surprise in launching an attack against important enemy targets."[11] In the mid-1950s, the Soviets extensively analyzed the impact that the nuclear weapon would have on future warfare. Their stark conclusion was that nuclear weapons necessitated a revolution in all aspects of military affairs—equipment, training, tactics, doctrine, strategy—but that they especially increased the importance of surprise. Under Stalin, surprise was regarded as a temporary factor whose importance was more tactical than strategic. In the nuclear age, however, it was decided that this was no longer true because of the potential decisiveness of the first nuclear strike and the enormous difficulty that would be involved in regaining the strategic initiative if it were ever lost.

As explained by then Defense Minister Marshal Grechko in 1975:

> When there is a threat of aggression it is necessary to follow the military preparations of the enemy especially vigilantly, reveal his intentions in time and take the necessary steps to repulse a hostile attack. Any omission here provides the aggressor with the chance of taking the initiative, and it will be extremely difficult to get it back subsequently. This situation plays a greater role as the armies of warring sides possess more powerful means of warfare.
>
> Now high combat readiness has even greater significance. The nature of contemporary warfare is such that, in case the imperialists unleash it, too little time will remain for organizing retaliatory actions. This means that the problem of surprise today has acquired a particular keenness. Therefore, the importance of a proper and timely estimate of the situation before the war begins and adoption of appropriate decisions increases to the very same extent as did the role of surprise.[12]

Surprise, in the Soviet view, ensures success. It makes it possible to inflict heavy losses in short periods of time, to paralyze the enemy's will, and to deprive him of the possibility of offering organized resistance. These are repeatedly stated by the Soviets as their immediate strategic objectives in nuclear war. "Any aggressor," the Soviets explain,

> risks unleashing a nuclear war only with confidence of achieving victory. Any confidence in the success of a nuclear attack can occur in conditions whereby there is a sufficiently high guarantee that nuclear strikes will be delivered to the objectives of destruction, that a mass launch of ballistic missiles and takeoff of aircraft will occur for a relatively long time undetected by the country against which the attack is being carried out, and that the armed forces, and above all the strategic nuclear means of the enemy, will suffer such destruction that they will be incapable of carrying out a powerful retaliatory nuclear strike.[13]

Among the means to be employed in achieving surprise are misleading the West about Soviet intentions, safeguarding the security of operational plans, and unexpectedly using nuclear weapons and means and methods with which the enemy is unfamiliar. Surprise is considered a strategic factor, and all techniques—secrecy, cover, deception, disinformation—are to be actively employed to achieve it. A major element of Soviet diplomacy, emphasized by all Soviet leaders beginning with Khrushchev and a probable component of Soviet motivations in SALT, has been an attempt to convince the West that they do not seek superiority and that they oppose the concept of striking first. This enhances the Soviet capability to achieve superiority and surprise. Thus, the problems of interpreting statements of Soviet leaders directed toward the West regarding critical elements of their strategy, particularly the utility of nuclear forces, the value of superiority, and issues surrounding surprise first strikes, is or should be clear.

The Soviets emphasize the need to prepare for several variants of global nuclear war. These variants are distinguished mainly according to the way in which the war begins and to a lesser extent by the ordering of and the speed with which the various goals are pursued. The principal variants most often discussed in their literature are a surprise attack from the West and a Soviet surprise attack on the West. Both of these variations can occur either directly or in a situation in which the war begins as a local war and then escalates. The Soviets assume that both sides will attempt to achieve surprise when the situation calls for war. However, the Soviets expect that there will be a period when the surprise attack is in preparation. Determining the onset of that preparatory period—that is, the beginning of the period of threat—is considered an especially important military task since correct determination of that can eliminate the surprise. This concept suggests that, in general, the Soviets do not expect a surprise, out-of-the-blue attack from the United States. This should not be misconstrued to mean that such a surprise attack by the West is not of concern to the Soviets, however. On the contrary, the primary assumption underlying the Soviet approach to combat readiness is the possibility of a surprise attack: "The danger of nuclear world war is now connected not only with a possible sudden attack by the imperialists on the socialist camp as a whole but also with the possibility that a local conflict will develop into a world war."[14] This is a basic point of Soviet military doctrine: "Soviet military doctrine proceeds from the standpoint that if the imperialists unleash another world war, it may begin with a surprise nuclear attack by the imperialist powers against the socialist nations or may escalate from a local conflict."[15] Although Soviet plans encompass the variant of a surprise attack from the West, this is thought by the Soviets to be an unacceptable way for war to begin. Accordingly, considerable efforts, including strategic espionage, analyses of the enemy (U.S.) capabilities, exercises, plans, doctrine (national security policy), and leadership personalities and abilities are considered by the Soviets to be of major importance. Technical warning sensors are also important, but only to enable a launch-on-warning response, which, while better than being completely surprised, is considered a poor second-best way for a war to start.

According to Soviet writings, the initiation of strategic nuclear operations, if it occurs, is to be a rational decision. The emphasis is on victory, on objective, scientifically based, well-substantiated decisions, and on taking all evidence into account for the initial strike, that is, at the very outset. The Soviet measure of success of the initial strike is a combination of the superiority gained in the process (the probable nuclear correlation of forces that would exist after the exchange of nuclear strikes) and of the force of the strike that the enemy (mainly the United States) would be capable of returning. The most important immediate objectives of a Soviet first strike would be 1) to disrupt the U.S. capability to organize a response, thus preventing an immediate Western counterstrike, and 2) to destroy the total Western military capability, beginning with the nuclear component. The first would occur before the second, but the second would receive the weight of the attack.

The first nuclear strikes would be those with the most difficult (from the U.S. point of view) associated warning problems, such as submarine-launched ballistic missiles and launches from unknown ground launch facilities, and would be directed against U.S. command and control. This character of the first strikes would be the last step taken to maximize surprise. It likely would be accompanied, possibly slightly preceded, by highly selective sabotage acts designed with the same goals—surprise and decapitation.

The major portion of the Soviet attack would be timed to arrive immediately following the initial strikes, perhaps within five to fifteen minutes, and coordinated attacks—nuclear, combined arms, assault, and sabotage—would be initiated in all strategic regions of the world. The nuclear strike might involve several successive salvos and extend over several hours. The principal targets of this strike and of coordinated sabotage activities would be the immediate military potential of the United States—nuclear capabilities and reserves; forces of all designations; command, control, and intelligence/reconnaissance; political and administrative control; communications, transportation centers; and electric power. (The Soviets regard the last as the basis of military potential, and it may be the single target class whose destruction the Soviets assess would have the most major and immediate impact on the capability of a nation to recover and on the morale of its population.) The notion of preserving strategic leaders and leaving communications intact for negotiation purposes appears to be a Western concept alien to Soviet thought. More likely, the Soviets would strive to destroy the government—"the aggressive leaders who unleashed the war"—so that realistic or progressive elements can accede to power.

Although the Soviet literature stresses the concept of the simultaneous mass strike, it should not be inferred from this that the Soviets think only or even principally in terms of one massive blow or one spasm exchange involving only strategic nuclear forces:

> Nuclear war . . . should not be thought of as a gigantic technical enterprise alone—as a launching of an enormous number of missiles with nuclear warheads to destroy the vital objectives and manpower of the enemy, or as operations by the armed forces alone. Nuclear war is a complex and many-sided process, which in addition to the operation of the armed forces will involve economic, diplomatic and ideological forms of struggle. They will all serve the political aims of the war and be guided by them.[16]

The Soviets see a war as proceeding in a phased fashion, where one performs missions in accordance with the priorities accorded them. The initial period of the war is even described as extending only until the short-term strategic goals have been attained. Hence, the Soviets talk of a first strike and subsequent strikes and of sequences of strikes and sequences or "series" of strategic missions, rather than of a simultaneous all-at-once strike.

The overall purpose of this total coordinated attack, as most typically stated in the Soviet literature, would be to inflict such immense casualties and vast destruction that the economic, moral, political, and military capabilities collapse, making it impossible for the West to continue and thus presenting the United States with the clear fact of defeat. This likely is the Soviet strategic goal for the initial period of the war. This is not the end, however. The war would continue, both to locate and destroy the remnants of U.S. and other capitalist military capabilities and to consolidate Soviet military gains in other parts of the world, most notably Western Europe and the Middle East.

These Soviet ideas on war initiation and progression have two important implications. First, Soviet superiority would not, from their point of view, lessen the likelihood or risk of war—strength provides the Soviets with many significant advantages (for example, flexibility), but not with security. From their point of view, as the West grows weaker, the risk of war and the possibility that the West would initiate a war actually grow greater. Second, the Soviets, in launching a first strike, would employ all means and tactics—diplomatic, undercover agents, technical—to achieve surprise. The Soviets would strive to attack at that time least expected by the West and in a manner determined to be most difficult for the West to detect and assess. As part of this strategy, the Soviets should be expected to undertake—and, in fact, to have been undertaking for some time—active measures specifically intended to deceive or mislead the United States and to forestall any efforts by the United States to increase its own readiness. Both diplomatic and nondiplomatic efforts are considered appropriate, not only to produce constant evaluations of U.S. political and military readiness for war, but also to engage in deliberate deception aimed at seriously disrupting U.S. decision-making capability. Diplomatic efforts are not considered to be outside of the strategy of war, but rather considered an integral part of that strategy. It is in this light that SALT ought to be examined.

WAR SURVIVAL MEASURES AND POSTWAR GOALS

In planning a war, the Soviets focus on the outcome, particularly on the postwar political environment. In contrast to the U.S. view, nuclear war is not seen as the inevitable end of civilization. Closely coupled with the notion of nuclear war as a continuation of politics and the need to prepare for such a war is the Soviet disagreement with Western beliefs that not only would nuclear war be the end of politics, but also that there can be no victor in such a war: "There is profound error and harm in the disorienting claims of bourgeois ideologues that there will be no victor in a thermonuclear world war. The peoples of the world will put an end to imperialism, which is causing mankind incalculable suffering."[17] An integral aspect of Soviet military strategy is the belief that under favorable circumstances, despite the unprecedented destruction, they can indeed win. The depth of this belief is difficult for many in the West, given our concept of such a war as the end of humanity, to understand and accept as a legitimate view. Further, according to Soviet thought, nations could recover from such a war, especially if they were prepared, as the Soviet Union expects to be. Not only does the belief that the war can be won emerge clearly in their writings, but the criteria for winning are specified in statements on strategy and are reflected in the steady growth of their capabilities.

Further, in statements like the "annihilation of the enemy and the seizure of his territory," the "enemy" is capitalism and the main enemy is the United States. Soviet military and political planning has to consider this up front:

> The chief military stronghold of imperialism is the United States. This is the result not only of the leading role of this country as the main power of the capitalist world, but also by the proportion of American armed forces in the overall system of the armed forces of imperialism. The United States now has more than 50 percent of the total number of armed forces of all the NATO countries, more than 90 percent of the ICBMs and missile-firing submarines, more than 80 percent of the strategic and 60 percent of the tactical aircraft, about 40 percent of the naval forces, and up to 50–60 percent of the conventional types of armament.[18]

The Soviet Union is clearly impressed with the economic and military potential of the United States when aroused. It is most important to the Soviets that they recover first and that the United States not be given the opportunity to recover and strike back as it did following Pearl Harbor. This is one rationale for the Soviet view that global war requires total victory and total defeat.

Hence, critical aspects of the Soviet preparation for global nuclear war include developing and implementing war survival measures to ensure as rapid a recovery of the economic and military potential of the Soviet Union as possible and establishing specific plans for postwar occupation and control for each of the probable theaters of military operations, both continental and intercontinental. Although the Soviets believe that a mass initial nuclear strike can "predetermine the subsequent course of the war,"[19] can accomplish major strategic missions, and can ensure total defeat, it generally is viewed as insufficient to complete the victory. Maintaining the strategic initiative through to and including occupation and control is considered essential for victory. This thought sequence has been consistently voiced for many years in the Soviet military literature, which emphasizes that "combat operations will continue for the purpose of the final defeat of the enemy on his own territory"[20] and that "ground forces, using the results of strategic nuclear strikes, will complete the defeat and annihilation of the enemy and the seizure of his territory."[21] Statements such as these and the following are generally considered to apply to Europe:

> Under conditions where nuclear rocket weapons are used . . . that side which manages during the first days of the war to penetrate more deeply into enemy territory naturally acquires the capability for more effectively

> using the results of its nuclear attacks and disrupting the mobilization of the enemy. This is especially important with respect to European theaters of operations with their relatively small operative depth.[22]

If, however, occupation and control are especially important in Europe, perhaps they are also important with respect to the intercontinental theater. Although it is often difficult to distinguish between the continental and intercontinental theaters in Soviet discussions and between Soviet discussions of their strategy and of U.S. strategy, statements on occupation and control in Soviet writings are believed to apply to the United States almost as much as they apply to Europe, but for somewhat different reasons and perhaps involving some vastly different approaches or options. Thus, "rendering aid to the people to free them from the yoke of imperialism" may apply to the United States in a "new world war"[23] as much as it applied to Poland, Hungary, Czechoslovakia, East Germany, and the Baltic states after World War II. The destruction of capitalism as a form of government and the installation of governments favorable to the development of Soviet communism are seen as prerequisites of complete victory. The destruction of an enemy's military forces and potential and the seizure of strategic areas are means to facilitate these ends. Hence, consideration of occupation and control appears to enter into the planning of the war effort from the beginning.

This is not to argue that intercontinental occupation is necessarily part of current Soviet plans, or to argue that they now have the capability to occupy and control the United States, or to suggest that the task would even be feasible immediately following a nuclear battle. Rather, the point is that occupation and control are an integral part of Soviet strategy. The Soviet scenario for global nuclear war is not the Western scenario where, following a spasm nuclear exchange, both sides retreat homeward to lick their wounds and begin the long and arduous task of recovery in isolation from the rest of the world.

IMPLICATIONS FOR THE UNITED STATES

The differences in Soviet and U.S. concepts of the utility of nuclear forces combined with the shifting force balance and, even more important, the decisions that need to be made on SALT and on the U.S. strategic posture make it imperative that the U.S. assumptions be reassessed.

The major conclusion that has emerged from this rather modest survey of Soviet internal literature is that they appear to take seriously their doctrine that communism and capitalism are irreconcilably locked in conflict and that this conflict encompasses all aspects of national power. The Soviet objective is to destroy capitalism and replace it everywhere with their brand of socialism. Their strategy is to subvert noncommunist nations and assist national liberation movements and revolution. This is one of the major rationales behind the growth in the Soviet armed forces and particularly in their ability to project power overseas. This is explicitly discussed in the Soviet literature as the external role of the army, a role whose importance has been greatly expanded in the 1970s.

The expansion is directly coupled with the growth in Soviet strategic nuclear capabilities, which serves two basic objectives. The first objective is to prevent U.S. interference in the Soviet export of revolutionary movements. The second is to fight and win a nuclear war should the West decide to interfere. The results of the first are already being felt, for example, in the Middle East and Africa. Although the second objective is not currently operative, the reluctance of the West to address the possibility seriously may have considerable impact in the 1980s. The lack of seriousness is demonstrated by the following example. In an effort to explain SALT to "confused citizens," the *Washington Post* presented the following "theoretical" scenario of the treaty critics:

> In response to some political or military crisis, the Soviet Union fires a sufficient number of its SS-18s and SS-19s to destroy our land-based missiles. This might result in 20 million American deaths. The U.S. could retaliate with thousands of airborne and submarine-borne missiles. But instead of retaliating we would, in effect, surrender.
>
> Why? Because the only targets we could hit would be cities and industrial complexes, and that would bring down on the United States mass destruction from the remaining Soviet weapons. In short, it would be better to lose 20 million than 160 million Americans.[24]

This scenario is then dismissed by the *Washington Post* as an "intellectual game"—pure speculation. And it is. In no sense does it reflect how complete a Soviet surprise first strike would be if designed and executed to present the country with the clear fact of defeat, which is precisely the objective of Soviet military strategy. Further, the factors that most ensure the success of a surprise attack are not technical systems, but rather mental attitudes. That is, a nation is most vulnerable when it believes such a war is impossible, an underlying assumption of the current strategic thought in the United States.

In contrast, global nuclear war, in the Soviet view, is not the unthinkable end but the continuation of politics, and the goals of war would be the same as the goals of Soviet peacetime policy, namely, the worldwide destruction of capitalism. In a typical statement, the goal of Soviet military doctrine and strategy "is described as total destruction of the enemy. Lenin stated that in conducting combat 'we must not "knock down" but rather *destroy* the enemy . . . ' "[25]

The dangers in the U.S. failure to recognize and deal with the true rather than the imagined motivations of the Soviet Union are more than the continued growth of a simple strategic imbalance. Considering the interrelations among military, political, and economic power, along with the nature of the external threat over and beyond that of nuclear war, the United States may indeed be reaching the position where even if it wanted to, it would be unable to reverse the trends. Even more ominously, this condition might not even be publicly recognizable. The Soviet Union has dedicated immense resources and intellectual capability to understanding the United States, its political processes, its locations of power, and the mechanisms for influence and control and is not likely to stand by and watch should the West seriously attempt to reverse its current course of action and attempt to regain its position. Their actions during the recent neutron bomb fiasco may be an indication of what to expect in the future at home as well as abroad.

After World War II, the United States enjoyed overwhelming superiority in nuclear weaponry and an initial postwar monopoly on nuclear technology. Later the United States retained general superiority even though the Soviet Union had entered the field. United States planners could reasonably assume that the threat of a strike against the enemy's population and industrial targets was sufficient to deter attacks both against the United States itself and to a significant degree against the United States's principal allies, as well as deter other activities contrary to U.S. interests. Given U.S. superiority at that time, it is probable that any threatened U.S. response would have deterred the Soviets. However, to compete effectively with the Soviets today and in the future, the United States must understand that not only does it no longer determine the rules, but it must now deter—if at all—according to Soviet rules, whether they are right or wrong.

Although over the past 30 years the United States has not agreed and may well continue not to agree with Soviet beliefs, the loss of U.S. superiority in the nuclear arena as well as changes in other aspects of the relative U.S. and Soviet posture means that the United States's attitudes and beliefs are to some extent irrelevant. Having surrendered the initiative to the Soviet side, the United States has no choice but to revise both its posture and its strategy to compete on Soviet terms. Given a Soviet strategic posture designed to provide a war-winning capability, the definition of an inferior U.S. strategic posture is obvious—one that would permit the Soviets to anticipate victory.

The first step in developing a capability and a corresponding strategy and doctrine to compete on Soviet terms is understanding the Soviet strategy and doctrine in detail in order to know the rules of the game. The second step is setting and fulfilling specific objectives for the U.S. posture and strategy that will achieve appropriate goals within the context of the Soviet ground rules both for deterrence and in the event deterrence fails.

The views presented in this article are an attempt to understand Soviet strategy. As for the second step, the Soviet view of the objectives of war implies that the United States must develop a strategy and capabilities to implement such a strategy, which would result in U.S. domination in the event of a conflict, rather than simply depending on an increasingly incredible threat of spasm punishment. With substantial fractions of the U.S. strategic force increasingly vulnerable to surprise attack and antiballistic and antibomber defenses and U.S. surviving elements likely to be committed to preplanned strikes, the present U.S. strategic force posture and strategy have been, we believe accurately, described as both brittle and thin. If deterrence fails and the preplanned retaliation by residual forces is implemented and fails to have a decisive effect on the course of the war, present plans envision that little will be available to improve the situation. From a military standpoint, a sizable commitment of residual strategic forces in a large-scale retaliatory attack would effectively disarm the United States and leave the Soviet Union with a large reserve capability for strategic delivery, given the force balance today and in the future. The use of surviving U.S. strategic weapons even against war-related industries would probably not influence the outcome of the Soviet offensive aimed at victory with ready and reserve military power in hand. It would probably be a wasteful use of scarce residual capability.

A strategy to manage effectively scarce resources in a post-initial attack environment, rather than just a spasm punishment response strategy and a capability to support such a strategy not only could, if successful, add to deterrence, but could in fact potentially determine the outcome of the conflict. Such a U.S. strategy can be credible, however, only if the United States has a reliable ability to absorb any Soviet attack and a strategy and capability then to wage an effective war-fighting campaign against remaining Soviet military power over an extended period of time. The Soviet perception that the United States possessed such a war-fighting capability could accomplish two tasks—it would in effect frustrate Soviet attempts to gain a war-winning capability at all levels, and in addition, it could inject an unacceptable degree of uncertainty into Soviet calculations of mission success and hence contribute to their reluctance to pursue courses counter to U.S. interests.

However, implementing such a strategy will not be easy, either in terms of force posture or in terms of political acceptability, unless the issues of SALT are settled in such a way as to encourage rather than discourage necessary actions. To implement such a strategy, the United States needs a considerably larger and more effective force posture than at present, and one that has survivability, striking power, mobility, flexibility (in the Soviet use of the word), and significant endurance of properly developed, deployed, and usable strategic and general purpose forces suited for operations in an extended war-fighting campaign against the full spectrum of Soviet military power. The ability to maintain—and especially to reconstitute—essential command, intelligence, surveillance, and communications capabilities in an appropriately timely fashion is also critical if the surviving capability is to be effective.

Survival of forces is critical. The current vulnerabilities, particularly of land-based ICBMs, provide Soviet leaders with an opportunity to create a critical postattack imbalance of strategic forces. One option might well be for a small force of alert missiles in launchers that might be constrained by SALT and a large store of ICBMs that could either be held whole or disassembled in dormant conditions safe from surprise attack and available for use as required through an extended postattack period of time. Such a store of ICBMs would not be prohibited by even the severely unbalanced SALT II treaty now under consideration, as it limits only launchers and not missiles.

Real flexibility in use of U.S. systems is also an essential component of such a posture. Many important Soviet military targets in known locations will be worth counterattacking immediately; so preplanned targeting is relevant in the initial postattack period. However, Soviet planners can anticipate the more likely preplanned responses and prepare to cover those potential losses with hidden reserves and dispersed mobile systems that are not vulnerable to preplanned attack and which must be found. Thus, as time passes, the Soviet target system will become less well known and perhaps widely scattered so that flexible capabilities for ad hoc targeting will increase in importance.

A capability for reuse of certain types of systems over a considerable length of time is also of considerable value. If the loss of fixed U.S. land-based missiles is heavy, the primary residual U.S. strategic power today and through most of the 1980s would be carried by escaped bombers and alert ballistic-missile-carrying submarines (SSBNs) at sea. However, once the bombers and SSBNs are stripped of their modest numbers of bases, ports, or tenders, the passage of time in itself will reduce their effectiveness. Without extensive prior preparations, those bombers that escape, deliver their weapons, and return cannot be recycled. Further, the reliability and accuracy of missiles at sea are likely to degrade over time, and in the end the submarines themselves may face supply and crew exhaustion. A large Soviet reserve of unexpended hidden or mobile land-based missiles of long and intermediate range could simply outlast U.S. power and remain to attack or intimidate with impunity. Unfortunately, the modest postattack endurance of residual U.S. strategic forces today not only does not achieve such a purpose, but on the contrary might well compel their hurried, misdirected, or ineffective use.

All these improvements require decisions not necessarily incompatible with the SALT treaties, but extremely difficult to make in an environment where SALT has been approved with enthusiastic accolades. Although the mistaken beliefs discussed above have contributed to the current predicament, it is important not to lose sight of the fact that this is only one part of the problem. A great deal of the credit belongs to the Soviets, who have worked hard to achieve their desired result, namely, U.S. complacency and reduced competitive position. This has, after all, been one of the primary goals of the Communist party since its inception. Through the use of deception, disinformation, subversion, and propaganda, the Soviet Union has engineered and actively pursued an aggressive foreign policy designed to bring exactly these results into being. And at the same time, it is not difficult to understand why many key individuals have apparently been able to dismiss explicitly stated Soviet intentions and motivations. The Soviet mind set and political mechanisms are totally alien to Western thought processes. Even a rudimentary comprehension of them requires hundreds, if not thousands, of hours of reading and analyzing what the Soviets say to the outside world and to themselves and comparing this with what they do. For anyone in government office, such time is not easily available. However, in light of the watershed decisions relating to SALT and needed improvements in our strategic posture, it is truly time to allocate the necessary resources to this task. Serious questions need to be asked about Soviet activities, and serious answers must be found.

NOTES

1. See, for example, "Kissinger's Critique," *Economist*, February 3, 1979, p. 17.

2. B. Byely et al., *Marxism-Leninism on War and Army (A Soviet View)*, trans. U.S. Air Force, Soviet Military Thought Series, no. 2 (Washington, D.C.:

Government Printing Office, 1974), p. 259. Emphasis in original.

3. Col. A. Gurov, "Economics and War," *Voyennaya Mysl'* 1965, no. 7 (July), FDD 962, trans. 5/25/66, p. 7, and Marshal of the Soviet Union S. S. Biryuzov, "The Lessons of the Beginning Period of the Great Patriotic War," *Voyennaya Mysl'* 1964, no. 8 (August), FDD 904, trans. 4/23/65, p. 29.

4. Maj. Gen. Ye. Nikitin and Col. S. Baranov, "The Revolution in Military Affairs and Measures of the CPSU for Raising the Combat Might of the Armed Forces," *Voyennaya Mysl'* 1978, no. 6 (June), FPD 0005/69, trans. 1/16/69, p. 7.

5. Army Gen. A. Yepishev, "The CPSU and the Soviet Armed Forces," *Voyennaya Mysl'* 1968, no. 1 (January), FPD 0093/68, trans. 5/22/68, p. 10.

6. Maj. Gen. K. Sevast'yanov, Maj. Gen. N. Vasendin, and Capt. 1st Rank N. V'yunenko, "Comments on the Article 'Augmenting Strategic Efforts in Modern Conflict,' " *Voyennaya Mysl'* 1964, no. 9 (September), FDD 896, trans. 3/2/65, p. 35.

7. Capt. 1st Rank V. Kulakov, "Problems of Military-Technical Superiority," *Voyennaya Mysl'* 1964, no. 1 (January), FDD 939, trans. 8/4/65, p. 10; and V. I. Varfolomeyev and M. I. Kopytov, *Design and Testing of Ballistic Missiles—U.S.S.R.*, trans. Joint Publications Research Service, JPRS—51810 (Washington, D.C.: JPRS, November 19, 1970), p. 318.

8. Lt. Col. Ye. Galitskiy, "The Coordination of Civil Defense with Units of the Armed Forces," *Voyennaya Mysl'* 1968, no. 4 (April), FPD 0052/69, trans. 5/27/69, p. 48.

9. Col. S. Tyushkevich, "The Methodology for the Correlation of Forces in War," *Voyennaya Mysl'* 1969, no. 6 (June), FPD 0008/70, trans. 1/30/70, p. 26.

10. Ibid., p. 31.

11. Col. A. Postovalov, "Modeling the Combat Operations of the Ground Forces," *Voyennaya Mysl'* 1969, no. 3 (March), FPD 0101/69, trans. 10/30/69, p. 29.

12. Marshal A. A. Grechko, *The Armed Forces of the Soviet State (A Soviet View)*, trans. U.S. Air Force, Soviet Military Thought Series, no. 12 (Washington, D.C.: Government Printing Office, 1975), p. 72.

13. Maj. Gen. N. Vasendin and Col. N. Kuznetsov, "Modern Warfare and Surprise Attack," *Voyennaya Mysl'* 1968, no. 6 (June), FPD 0005/69, trans. 1/16/69, p. 46.

14. Maj. Gen. K. Stepanov and Lt. Col. Ye. Rybkin, "The Nature and Types of Wars of the Modern Era," *Voyennaya Mysl'* 1968, no. 2 (February), FPD 0042/69, trans. 4/25/69, p. 68.

15. Gen. Maj. A. S. Milovidov, ed., *The Philosophical Heritage of V. I. Lenin and Problems of Contemporary War (A Soviet View)*, trans. U.S. Air Force, Soviet Military Thought Series, no. 5 (Washington, D.C.: Government Printing Office, 1974), p. 100.

16. Byely, *Marxism-Leninism on War and Army*, p. 12.

17. Milovidov, *Lenin and Problems of Contemporary War*, p. 17.

18. Army Gen. S. Ivanov, "Soviet Military Doctrine and Strategy," *Voyennaya Mysl'* 1969, no. 5 (May), FPD 0017/69, trans. 12/18/69, p. 55.

19. Byely, *Marxism-Leninism on War and Army*, p. 304.

20. Gurov, "Economics and War," p. 5

21. A. S. Zheltove et al., *Methodological Problems of Military Theory and Practice*, trans. U.S. Air Force, Foreign Technology Division, Wright-Patterson Air Force Base, FTD-MT-24–87–71 (Dayton, Ohio: December 18, 1971), p. 127.

22. V. D. Sokolovskiy, *Soviet Military Strategy*, ed. Harriet Fast Scott (New York: Crane, Russak & Co., 1968), p. 312.

23. Ibid., p. 187.

24. Richard Harwood, "SALT: Straight Answers for Confused Citizens," *Washington Post*, June 10, 1979, p. D4.

25. Milovidov, *Lenin and Problems of Contemporary War*, p. 106.

The Future of U.S. Foreign Intelligence Operations

Ray S. Cline

XVII

The prognosis for intelligence operations in the United States must be guarded. Reliable information about foreign situations and trends has never been more needed than it will be in the 1980s. There is a recent historical base and an existing functional framework for an intelligence effort of top quality in this country. Yet at the approach of the next decade the Central Intelligence Agency (CIA) and the other agencies in coordination with it are operating at a lower state of effectiveness and morale, and with less public confidence, than at any time in the past 25 years. The future of U.S. intelligence is a crucial policy issue. The president, the Congress, and the people of the United States ought to give the highest priority to providing the kind of data collection and analysis capability that an open society must have to survive and prosper in a volatile, often dangerous world.

The value of secret intelligence in wartime has been clearly appreciated by American political leaders since the time of George Washington, who personally directed espionage operations during the Revolutionary War, but the concept of a central, coordinated intelligence system to support national decision making did not become clearly articulated until World War II. The wartime Office of Strategic Services (OSS), the precursor of CIA, was promptly abolished when hostilities ended in 1945.

The embodiment of a peacetime central, coordinated system in law and bureaucratic reality dates only from 1947, when the National Security Council (NSC) for strategic decision making and the CIA were established. The literature and doctrine of U.S. intelligence is only beginning to crystallize in forms adequate to provide the foundation for a consensus on what kind of intelligence machinery is needed and how it should operate within our free political process.

In his pioneer historical analysis *Strategic Intelligence for American World Policy*, veteran OSS and CIA officer Sherman Kent pointed out that:

> Although there is a good deal of understandable mystery about it, intelligence is a simple and self-evident thing. As an activity it is the pursuit of a certain kind of knowledge; as a phenomenon it is the resultant knowledge . . . and strategic intelligence, we might call the knowledge upon which our nation's foreign relations, in war and peace, must rest. If foreign policy is the shield of the republic, as Walter Lippmann has called it, then strategic intelligence is the thing that gets the shield to the right place at the right time. It is also the thing that stands ready to guide the sword.[1]

In this sense, the overwhelming importance of intelligence activity, the actor or agency, and of the "resultant knowledge" seems self-evident. The United States, nevertheless, was almost totally unprepared for the dangers and stresses of the 1940s in the field of intelligence, as in so many other areas.

Now, once again, the United States stands on the brink of tragedy because it has not yet restored the damage done to the whole, coordinated intelligence machine in the mid-1970s, when CIA's flaws and abuses became the center of a news media and political circus. The flaws and abuses had been reviewed and largely corrected internally more than a year before the public investigation began, but this was hardly mentioned by the critics. The solid achievements that vastly outweighed the mistakes have been comparatively little noted. Partly as a result, the dynamic thrust of accomplishment has not been sustained under the onslaught. The intelligence agencies have gradually wound down to a slow speed and a defensive posture, and in some areas they have come to a complete halt. Where we go from here, up or down, is the pressing question.

In its narrowest context, intelligence is simply information. It can be collected in some clandestine manner, that is, secretly and often at some personal risk because the facts sought are being deliberately withheld. In a broader sense, intelligence on foreign affairs includes such additional categories as press reports, foreign radio broadcasts, foreign publications, and, in the government, reports from foreign service officers and military attachés.

In the world of international affairs, intelligence is only useful to the United States if it is subjected to evaluation and analysis to put it into the context of our ongoing national security and foreign policy concerns. It must be evaluated for accuracy and credibility in the light of its source or its collection method, for the validity and significance of its content after it is collated with other available data, and for its impact on U.S. interests, operations, or objectives. The result of this total intelligence process is a report intended to assist policy and operational officers in making decisions.

Such analytical findings can suggest the pattern of future development in foreign affairs and provide the evidential base for making estimates about these developments, including estimates of the probability of particular scenarios of foreign actions. The future estimate is the subtlest and most difficult kind of intelligence. If objectively and imaginatively worked out, it builds an indispensable floor under prudent policymaking.

The collection of intelligence and its evaluation or analysis are seldom any longer questioned as legitimate and essential parts of the Washington bureaucratic process. Sometimes moral scruples are expressed about stooping to clandestine and illegal techniques of getting information, but generally Americans feel it is only fair game to try secretly to obtain data that other nations are hiding from us—on the assumption that this data is likely to affect our relations with those nations and might indeed affect the security of American institutions or lives. Similarly, the need for analytical research to reduce raw data to meaningful ideas is usually regarded as a normal function of government, although it is often overlooked as a result of fascination with the details of espionage and the technical collection of electronic signals or photographic images. If national decisions are to be made, national efforts to provide a sound and carefully articulated data base are clearly worthwhile.

CREATION OF THE CENTRAL INTELLIGENCE AGENCY

The birth of CIA stems from recognition of the need for establishment of a procedure for orderly deliberation and decision on military and diplomatic policy. It is linked with one of the truly creative innovations in American government in our time: the setting up of the NSC under the chairmanship of the president, with the secretary of state and secretary of defense as key members. A crucial element in this structure was that the Joint Chiefs of Staff reported directly to the NSC on military policy and the CIA reported directly to the NSC on foreign situations, trends, threats, and opportunities. Thus an objective data base was available to the president along with a technical evaluation of military risks and requirements. On this foundation the NSC could blend foreign policy aims and defense policy programs into a realistic, coherent national strategy. President Harry Truman considered the building of the NSC system one of his great accomplishments.

The National Security Act of 1947 gave CIA a line of command to the NSC because the NSC was presided over by the president. Since the duties of the cabinet officials designated as members of the NSC could only be advisory, in that they simply shared the chief executive's power, the effect was to give CIA the direct channel to the president that the advocates of central intelligence had always sought. The act recognized that peacetime problems could not be dealt with by a separate department of peace and an isolated department of war but should be examined as political-military issues.

Section 102 of the act established CIA for "the purpose of coordinating the intelligence activities of the several Government departments and agencies in the interest of national security," and directed it "to correlate and evaluate intelligence relating to the national security, and provide for the appropriate dissemination of such intelligence within the Government using where appropriate existing agencies and facilities." The concept was clear that the new CIA was intended to be a central coordinator, a first among equals in the older community of intelligence agencies, and a central evaluator of information relating to the national security. The act plainly prohibited CIA from exercising policy, subpoena, law-enforcement powers, or internal-security functions so that it could in no way become a secret police force on the model of the Soviet KGB. The head of the new central agency was specifically assigned unprecedented but indispensable responsibility for protecting intelligence sources and methods from unauthorized disclosures. With these provisions the National Security Act of 1947 gave CIA a charter that has served it well for more than 30 years. When the CIA formally came into existence on September 18, 1947, the United States for the first time in its history had the foundation for developing a comprehensive peacetime intelligence system.

The agency grew rapidly in the two decades following its creation, building organizational structure and capabilities to inform policymakers. The CIA analysts concentrated on publishing a current intelligence "daily" for the president, alerting him to dangers, problems, or opportunities affecting the nation's strategic posture, its foreign relations, and international economic interests. Information from all sources poured into CIA, from newspapers and magazines, radio broadcasts, signal intercepts of wireless messages or of electronic characteristics of weapons, reports of diplomatic and military officers stationed abroad, foreign agents, and liaison counterparts in friendly countries. By 1956 CIA had developed its own high-altitude U-2 aircraft and was collecting detailed photography of advanced Soviet weapons by overflying the USSR above the range of anti-aircraft guns. In the 1960s the agency's computer-programmed satellites were circling above the earth every 90 minutes at a height of approximately 100 miles, taking precision photographs and also capturing whole new families of electronic signals. Putting together evidence from all these sources required CIA to master new techniques in the essentially scholarly job of collecting and sorting data, keeping files, and doing research. From all these processes CIA became increasingly skilled at piecing together a reliable picture of the international environment with which all of our lives are intimately entangled in the shrinking, complex, troubled political world.

COVERT ACTION

Although CIA's clandestine intelligence collection and intelligence analysis were definitively authorized in the National Security Act, the function of covert psychological and political action was only elliptically referred to in the catch-all clause about "duties related to intelligence affecting the national security." This clause was later cited as giving authority for all CIA covert action programs. Clark Clifford, later chairman of the President's Foreign Intelligence Advisory Board and also secretary of defense under President Lyndon Johnson, said in 1975 that he considered covert action to have been authorized by this elastic clause.[2]

The responsibility for covert action, not a responsibility sought by the agency, was fated to play a crucial role in coloring perceptions of CIA. The CIA entered into covert action operations under pressure from leading U.S. officials of the day to support basic U.S. foreign policy. In the light of Josef Stalin's activities in Central Europe and Berlin in 1947–1948, there was great pressure by many thoughtful, patriotic men to find ways to forestall Soviet use of local communists or nearby military forces to intimidate and dominate the governments of Western Europe.

Those officials who argued that the United States had to fight back covertly against widespread political subversive efforts sponsored by the Soviet Union in Germany, France, and Italy in 1947–1948 were: Secretary of State George C. Marshall, probably the most distinguished statesman to emerge from World War II; Secretary of War Robert Patterson; Secretary of Defense James Forrestal; and George Kennan, then director of the State Department's Policy Planning Staff. President Truman concurred in their recommendations, and every subsequent president endorsed the wisdom of trying to frustrate Soviet—or other communist—subversive political activities by giving covert assistance to those who would oppose communist aims.

It is hard to remember how menacing the Soviet encroachments appeared. In February 1948 the communist coup in Czechoslovakia succeeded, and in March the popular and well-known Foreign Minister Jan Masaryk jumped or, probably, was pushed from a window to his death. The shock in the United States was tremendous. Many American officials, such as General Lucius Clay, commander of U.S. forces in Europe, anticipated a military attack on Berlin and Western Europe. It was common in Washington to hear predictions that war would come as soon as the Soviet Union succeeded in manufacturing an atomic bomb, thus neutralizing the only U.S. weapon that could stop the massive ground forces which Stalin kept poised along what Churchill had christened the iron curtain.

The American strategic response was the Kennan strategy of containment, which reasoned that the Soviet police state would mellow and its outward thrusts for dominion would diminish if the USSR's external aggression did not pay off. Hence the Marshall Plan was adopted to give economic incentives to the threatened states of Western Europe, and a substantial American military force remained in place to provide security. Between economic assistance and military protection, a middle zone of low-intensity conflict short of war arose. This was the zone in which the United States would use covert political and psychological efforts to counter Soviet influence, supplementing U.S. diplomatic efforts by assisting moderate noncommunist groups.

Opinion in 1948 in Washington was that this effort to stabilize Western Europe against the threat of Soviet assaults on Italy, France, and Germany would fail unless Soviet support of local communist parties could be exposed and countered. To expose the threat of subversive takeover from within, intelligence was needed about the USSR, its intelligence system, and Communist party ideology and tactics and the inroads they had made into Western European political, labor, cultural, and journalistic circles. To counter these inroads, noncommunist political parties had to be provided with information about Soviet efforts so that they could win electoral support. Newspaper stories, radio broadcasts, and political pamphlets had to be financed, written, and disseminated to let the public know the dangers of the situation.

With respect to Italy in particular, which had an election scheduled for April 1948, Americans with knowledge of Italy, especially Americans with family connections or religious ties to the Catholic hierarchy, were sought to carry the message to Italian voters that association with the United States would save Italy, whereas communist rule would destroy it. The methods employed were psychological and political. They mainly involved teaching American electoral techniques to Western Europe and providing money for local political groups to organize, counter communist propaganda, and get out the vote. From the viewpoint of U.S. officials, the aim was entirely democratic—in the tradition of our own often hard-fought state elections—and totally for the good of the country concerned, as well as for the benefit of U.S. interests in Western Europe. Christian Democratic party leader Alcide De Gasperi, then prime minister, and Pope Pius XII showed great anxiety lest the parliamentary parties be decisively outvoted as a consequence of communist strength, discipline, and militancy. American officials shared this concern. Shortly after it was created, the NSC approved a directive, NSC 4/A, dated December 19, 1947, which gave CIA authority to carry out covert psychological warfare in support of American political, economic, and diplomatic efforts in Italy.

The NSC clearly intended to prevent the communists from winning the April election by authorizing covert actions of a kind that could not be directly engaged in by diplomats. Financial and technical assistance to the Christian Democrats and other noncommunist parties, as well as efforts to split off socialists from the united front group dominated by the communists, had to be covert. Italian party leaders could not afford to let communists obtain evidence that they were supported by foreigners because it would blunt public anger at the Communist party for its own financial and policy dependence on the Soviet Union. Hence CIA got the job of passing money and giving the technical help needed to get out the vote and win the election.

These covert action programs in Italy were viewed simply as part of diplomatic and military policy by U.S. officials. George Kennan took an active role in support of all aspects of implementing the Italian policy. His view, never belligerent from the military viewpoint though firmly in favor of containing further Soviet advances in Europe, is revealing. On March 15 he cabled:

> I suspect that many of the European Communists, partially victims of their own propaganda, are excited by recent successes and by prospect of seizing rich prizes in western Europe. On the other hand, the savage abruptness and cynical unconcern for appearances of recent action in Czechoslovakia leads me to feel that Kremlin leaders must be driven by sense of extreme urgency . . . As far as Europe is concerned, Italy is

> obviously key point. If Communists were to win election there our whole position in Mediterranean, and possibly in western Europe as well, would probably be undermined.[3]

In May 1948, Kennan advocated the formal creation of a permanent covert political action capability. As a result the NSC issued a new directive sanctioning CIA's continued conduct of covert activities as worked out in a consultation and review procedure with State and Defense officials. The CIA was to be an instrument of policy, not an instigator. It was instructed to propose specific information programs and other political action that would negate communist efforts to expand Soviet political influence in Western Europe.

State and Defense guidance was general, and the responsibility appeared to belong to CIA for meeting the Soviet challenge in those secret back-alley battles. The operations themselves, or at least the foreign policy program within which they were carried out, were remarkably successful. A lot of credit went to CIA, credit which it only partly deserved; and much later it received most of the blame when covert action programs got out of hand—blame that also largely belonged to the policymakers, not to the instrument of covert action, CIA.

Covert action is the controversial element in intelligence activity that is most difficult to explain openly and defend persuasively. Reasonable men differ about whether it is right for the United States to intervene secretly in order to influence the course of events in other countries to American advantage—even if it appears that this will also be to the advantage of the people of the country concerned. Many critics of CIA consider covert political action of a subtle, nonviolent kind to be legitimate, but they draw the line at paramilitary operations and believe that CIA simply overdid the covert role. Some observers support covert intervention in the democratic, parliamentary societies of Western Europe but not in the politically less mature developing nations; others argue exactly the opposite. It was probably foreordained that a major public hue and cry over secret activities of this kind would cause alarm and tend to inhibit the activities and damage the morale and effectiveness of the agencies responsible for carrying them out.

THE WATERGATE ERA: PRESS AND CONGRESSIONAL INVESTIGATION OF CIA

The crisis from which our intelligence system has not yet recovered began in the overheated Washington atmosphere of the Watergate scandal and the resignation under threat of impeachment of President Richard Nixon.

The close of the Nixon era was a bad period for the whole federal bureaucracy. The end of the Watergate episode was followed by a wave of press and congressional investigation and criticism that fully occupied Bill Colby, the director of Central Intelligence from July 1973 through 1975. Colby acquitted himself as well as anyone could in the circumstances, but it was a no-win proposition. For CIA this period was a disaster.

In light of the Watergate inquiry in mid–1973, Colby reviewed all of CIA's operations over the past years, asking every CIA officer to identify anything irregular or questionably legal that CIA had ever done. The resulting summary report including 683 possible violations of directives or law was dubbed the "Family Jewels." Colby quietly changed procedures where he felt they were wrong, advised the congressional oversight committee chairmen in the Senate and House what he had done, and hoped for the best. But the atmosphere of Washington in the aftermath of Nixon's downfall was hostile to any form of secrecy. The leaks began occurring, first from Congress to the press, and then from everywhere to the *New York Times* in particular, which set out to make a name for itself in investigative reporting. The *Times* released a sensational year-end account in December 1974 alleging massive wrongdoing over the years by CIA, all plainly based on CIA's own self-correction studies. Both houses of Congress got into the act with official inquiries, and 1975 was virtually a lost year for CIA. It took over a year for the tales of misdeeds, nearly all taken from CIA's own "Family Jewels" report, to become public.

At the end of 1975, President Gerald Ford tried to soothe the storm, during which CIA was castigated for things it never did as well as for many things it had done under direct order from several different presidents of the United States. Senator Frank Church, chairman of the Senate select committee investigating CIA, opined that the agency might have been a "rogue elephant" running amok, a charge so thoroughly refuted in his own investigation that his final report retracts it.

Most Americans who lived through the Nixon administration would agree that its later years constituted a very unhealthy period in American political life. A fever of intellectual and social change swept through the country in the late 1960s and early 1970s. It was catalyzed by the tragedy of the fruitless military struggle in Vietnam that resulted in protest demonstrations against the government. By June 1972, the tawdry, bungled Watergate break-in brought the crisis of presidential authority to a head; the Nixon inner circle set out to cover up their illegal action and in doing so nearly destroyed the political fabric of U.S. society. Nixon's resignation on August 4, 1974, marked the end of an era.

In many ways CIA was a victim, caught in the tide of paranoia and cynicism about public service that had built up during the Nixon-Watergate experience. Naturally the painstaking inquiry into CIA's activities turned up mistakes. For one thing, it emerged that one of the stumble-prone "plumbers" whom the White House had hired to track down leaks and do other domestic political intelligence work for the 1972 election was a retired clandestine operator of CIA's earlier, more expansive overseas period: Howard Hunt. Despite his personal acquaintance with Richard Helms, DCI at the time, Hunt had been eased out of CIA. With an unerring instinct for the machismo image adopted by many clandestine operators, the White House picked up Hunt and teamed him with a similar eccentric, Gordon Liddy, a retired employee of the Federal Bureau of Investigation (FBI). Hunt used his White House connections to get CIA to provide him with an "ill-fitting wig" and a voice-disguise device.

Although these things were done with the clear endorsement of the White House, CIA should not have let itself be drawn into them. It was revealed later that Nixon had pressured Helms and his principal deputy, General Vernon Walters, to have CIA call the FBI off the track of the laundered money paid to the Watergate burglars. In response, after a few days of hesitation, CIA decisively indicated that its operations provided no ground for diverting the FBI from the Watergate investigation.[4] This unwillingness to cooperate in the White House cover-up probably cost Dick Helms his job five months later, after the 1972 election. Nevertheless, the episode raised suspicions—never confirmed—that CIA had more to do with Watergate than ever surfaced.

At this point, in 1973-1974, the Senate and House intelligence subcommittees began to take closer notice of CIA covert action, particularly in Chile, which was then under study by separate Senate and House foreign relations subcommittees dealing with multinational corporations and inter-American affairs. It is now clear the CIA's covert action program in Chile in the 1970s was undertaken under express orders from President Nixon and National Security Assistant Henry Kissinger. Both CIA and the Department of State were reluctant to become so deeply involved in what appeared to be an unfeasible program to keep President Salvador Allende out of office after he had won a plurality in the September 1970 election. At one point, President Nixon and Dr. Kissinger even took matters out of the hands of the 40 Committee (the covert action review group) of NSC and directed CIA, against the judgment of many of its officers, to try to stage a military coup—a project that never came to anything. CIA continued to provide large sums of money, evidently around $8 million, to support parliamentary opposition (especially to keep alive an opposition press) to Allende's increasingly arbitrary and socially disruptive rule. All CIA's efforts were unsuccessful. The military coup that overthrew Allende on September 11, 1973, was not in any way under U.S. sponsorship or control, though it may well have been facilitated by U.S. anti-Allende pressures. These facts on CIA's covert action in Chile were investigated and confirmed by the Church committee, which concluded that the agency was not *directly* involved in the 1973 coup. Its clandestine operators had gathered information from the Chilean military officers who plotted and carried out the coup but did not give them assistance.[5]

The covert action programs of earlier years had dwindled in number and scope by the end of the 1960s. Aside from the big paramilitary and counterintelligence operations in Laos and Vietnam, where U.S. military forces were engaged, no covert action projects of any significance were then in operation. There were numerous lesser covert action projects of a psychological-cultural sort, but the last two major political interventions in foreign election processes had ended.

The advent of a communist-supported political front in the western hemisphere in 1970 plunged CIA back into covert action on a massive scale—too massive to remain covert for long. Nixon and Kissinger, beset by problems in Vietnam and the Middle East, quickly and inexpertly set out to win covertly their strategic battles. Money was pumped into Chile once again and hastily and clumsily invested in Italian politics, where communist electoral gains had continued. The White House used CIA for what it conceived CIA was good for: fighting covert military campaigns in Southeast Asia and large-scale intervention in political elections in Chile and Italy. These efforts were the only big covert programs of the 1970s. They all came to grief. They also nearly destroyed CIA.

Advice from professionals on covert intelligence work should have been heeded on the key questions of feasibility, risk, and the possibility of withdrawal in the event of failure. Covert support to the democratic opposition forces in Chile made sense, to help them survive in an increasingly polarized, brutal competition with revolutionary activists spurred on by the Cuban secret intelligence staffs working for Allende. To change the results of the elections by bribery *after* they had taken place was not feasible, however, and the attempt was counterproductive.

There was plenty to criticize in this bizarre performance. The more it surfaced, the more emboldened became CIA's critics, who not only questioned specific areas where policy was thought to be wrong but wanted to shut down the whole covert action capability of CIA. Indeed, in some cases critics wanted to shut down the whole CIA on the grounds that secrecy is inherently immoral and incompatible with democracy. The fat was in the fire; CIA could not possibly defend itself publicly in so sensitive a matter where White House decisions were involved.

THE CASE AGAINST CIA

As if the Chile affair were not enough, Seymour Hersh of the *New York Times* attracted worldwide attention at Christmas 1974 with an exposé of CIA. The accusation was that the CIA, "directly violating its charter, conducted a massive illegal domestic intelligence operation during the Nixon Administration against the anti-war movement and the other dissident groups in the United States." This would have been a serious indictment, if it had proved true.

The presidential (Rockefeller Commission) and the congressional (Church and Pike) inquiries began immediately to sift through the evidence on which the charges were based. In the process of the investigations other allegations were made, so that a great deal of information emerged that had not been public before about specific CIA activities. In this atmosphere, criticisms of CIA multiplied, and their moral tone suggested that the CIA had come close to being an American gestapo. However, detailed analysis of the facts by these official boards of inquiry proved that illegal CIA activity was entirely in domestic fields, mostly where the White House had pushed the agency into dubious enterprises. The findings state that the actions were not massive; the *Times* stories had been exaggerated.

It is a simple matter to outline what CIA actually did in its conduct of intelligence operations in the United States that has been criticized as beyond the margins of its legitimate functions. First, CIA set up in its computerized information storage-retrieval system a special file with a name and organization reference index that included about 7,200 files on Americans associated in some way with anti-war or dissident groups.

There are millions of names in CIA files, and many thousands of American names among them have turned up over the years in correspondence, routine administrative business, or intelligence reports. Most of the dissident names were entered in the CIA reference index because the FBI had requested a check on whether CIA had evidence that they were in contact with foreign intelligence agents or were receiving funding from foreign sources. In the majority of these so-called dossiers there was only one piece of paper. Most references in the others resulted from information reported from abroad citing evidence—not necessarily firm—that the individuals in question were thought to be in contact with foreign intelligence agents. The recording of these names was not a large effort in terms of total CIA name reference files. The existence of a file did not indicate active CIA surveillance of any kind except in cases where there was evidence suggesting that a person was in contact with foreign intelligence agents abroad.

It is not illegal for CIA to record foreign intelligence reports or to file and reference official queries about Americans suspected of working for foreign intelligence agencies. Whether the FBI acted legally or wisely in determining that someone was suspect and should be checked by CIA is another matter. Some of the FBI internal security operations labeled as counterintelligence against dissidents and demonstrators were probably illegal and were certainly politically ill-advised. Yet there was a climate of lawlessness among the anti-Vietnam protest specialists, and the FBI has a legal charter to investigate foreign agent activities and to prevent crime, including foreign espionage. In any case, the inquiries found that CIA did not arrest, harass, or abuse anybody in connection with this or any other of its programs.

The CIA also established contact with foreigners in the United States to facilitate the conduct of clandestine operations abroad. This activity is in direct pursuit of the function of foreign espionage, which is assigned to CIA by the NSC directive that spells out the intent of the National Security Act of 1947. It is not illegal to recruit foreigners for this purpose, although some reformers would like to outlaw such recruitment.

Cover positions in U.S. organizations were established by CIA for its officers to use in funding or conducting clandestine operations abroad. Such cover is essential for the support of legitimate foreign intelligence operations. No illegal acts in the United States were involved. No domestic intelligence target was involved.

Individual Americans already holding positions abroad were recruited by CIA to collect information or disseminate views in the interests of U.S. policy. Their cover included positions in cultural, educational, labor, and youth enterprises. The CIA had used agents in these groups to collect information about Soviet propaganda efforts, to counter these efforts with objective information, and to sponsor the formation of U.S.-oriented organizations abroad. Gradually, under the pressure of news media protests, CIA severed contacts with most of these people, and in mid-1976 it announced it would no longer use the services of U.S. journalists for clandestine work. Most contacts between

CIA and American journalists had been mutually beneficial, harmless news-gathering exercises. The danger of "contamination" of the American press by false information put out abroad by CIA was grossly exaggerated. CIA never deliberately tried to mislead the U.S. news media, who were in any event capable of editorially checking against error.

Counterespionage information was collected *abroad* by CIA on possible links between foreign governments or agents and U.S. dissidents; CIA specifically targeted, in its counterintelligence *abroad*, organizations or American individuals named by the FBI as suspected of illegal foreign contacts. This counterespionage activity was authorized expressly by NSC directive. Explicit orders for this information came from the White House and the FBI. Solid evidence about American citizens working for foreign intelligence groups would have provided basis for criminal charges under the Espionage Act. Naturally, the information and the operations carried out to obtain it had to be secret, to permit collection of data that foreign intelligence would try to hide. This secrecy also protects any American from injury by public revelation of reports that could be substantiated. No other U.S. agency except CIA could pursue this kind of inquiry overseas.

In this borderline gray area, where CIA linked some of its work with FBI internal security investigations, the record becomes less favorable. Presidents Johnson and Nixon felt sure that the anti-war protestors were being financed from abroad. Both J. Edgar Hoover and Richard Helms were persuaded to do things that in retrospect seem unwise and probably illegal. For one thing, CIA employed Americans to join dissident groups in the United States so that they would become attractive targets when they traveled abroad, where it was hoped they could obtain information on foreign intelligence activities and interests.

Fewer than 30 individuals were involved in this activity, and they were originally intended strictly as bait for foreign agents. Nevertheless, the procedure brought CIA to the margins of an internal security penetration program. In response to insistent demands from the White House for data on the dissidents, CIA provided the FBI with reports on dissident group meetings collected as a by-product of these operations. There is a legitimate argument in favor of CIA bait operations of this kind as an essential preliminary step for successful counterespionage abroad. In this sense these activities were not strictly in violation of the charter, and no illegal acts occurred.

It now seems clear that CIA should not have authorized these special penetration cases. The agency knew it was in dangerous waters. The whole program for consolidating information on U.S. dissidents was organized into a special section, ultimately employing 52 people, that disseminated reports to the White House. The unit responsible for what was code-named operation CHAOS reported directly to Helms; he handled it gingerly but clearly thought that he had to comply in some fashion with direct orders from Johnson and Nixon. With hindsight, he no doubt wishes he had refused the task.

During this period, CIA felt an obligation to protect itself from what might be foreign-directed criminal activity. Theoretically, at least, activities of a domestic internal security nature were justified by CIA legal counsel under the National Security Act provision that gives the director responsibility to guard "intelligence sources and methods." This was a period of raids, file burning, and "trashing" in American cities and universities, and as a result the agency undertook several types of precautions.

For a short term the Security Office of CIA penetrated Washington area dissident organizations to check reports that these groups threatened the security of CIA personnel, installations, and files. Twelve agents were involved, and their effort continued for less than two years. It was terminated when the Washington Metropolitan Police Department developed its own resources. In this case the agency should have relied on the FBI and other law enforcement agencies to protect it, despite the fact that Hoover was uncooperative with CIA.

In addition, CIA carried out a dozen break-and-enter operations of a counterintelligence nature against the homes of CIA employees or ex-employees suspected of violating security regulations. These operations, which took place in the United States, were illegal, although they were related to a legitimate counterintelligence function and to the responsibility to protect intelligence sources and methods. The operations should not have been authorized without a judicial search warrant and assistance from law enforcement authorities.

Telephones were tapped where CIA suspected violations of security regulations by its employees or thought other citizens were receiving intelligence information. Legitimate counterintelligence concerns led to these taps—32 in all. Many were not illegal at the time they took place. The law has since changed, reflecting greater public emphasis on privacy rights. In the future, new legislation will make it more likely that too little, rather than too much, electronic surveillance will be allowed.

The most flagrantly illegal act of the CIA was to survey and open selectively the mail of U.S. citizens, mainly to and from the Soviet Union, in a program going back to 1953, when American contacts with communist countries were infrequent and the United States was still in what amounted to an undeclared state of war in Korea. This mail intercept should probably have been done by the FBI, which did some mail interception. The record does not show that the interception was ever properly and unambiguously cleared with higher authorities.[6] In many bureaucratic matters, a procedure of long standing seems to carry on under its own momentum without careful review or authorization. The operation was terminated in 1973, for opening mail in time of peace was clearly against the law.

When all the evidence was reviewed by the official boards of inquiry, it appeared that CIA was mainly guilty of vigorously pursuing espionage and counterespionage targets leading to foreign agents or to information on foreign activity needed for U.S. security. In most of these cases, it was following White House orders, perhaps too obediently, but not as irresponsibly as suggested by its critics.

REBUILDING THE CENTRAL INTELLIGENCE SYSTEM: AN IMPERATIVE FOR THE 1980s

Against such a background of inquiry and criticism, there is no doubt that the performance of the U.S. central intelligence system has deteriorated. What went wrong has been discussed thoroughly for more than five years in the halls of Congress, in the press, and on many street corners. The question now before the nation is what must be done as the United States approaches the 1980s. Morale has dipped in every agency, especially CIA. Foreign governments and foreign agents no longer provide information as willingly as when CIA was viewed as an elite organization capable of protecting its secrets forever. There has been a major exodus of experienced professional intelligence officers from government. To compound the difficulties, CIA has suffered from a shrinkage of cooperation and cover from American institutions that have a natural common interest with CIA in the "knowledge industry": the news media, universities, big business.

It is imperative that our central intelligence machinery be rebuilt and its capabilities reinvigorated. We cannot delay, for the world around us is dangerously volatile. Violence is widespread, and the openness of American society is a tempting target. Changes inside and among nation-states are endemic. The interest of the United States is in orderly change and restraint of violence, particularly undiscriminating terror, totalitarian revolution, and war. There are many opponents of this interest; only 20 percent of the four and a quarter billion people in the world live in relatively free, politically pluralist societies.

The balance of political and economic power depends on the relative influence of the Soviet Union, the United States, and other major nations in the zone of conflict around the periphery of Eurasia. The nations in this area are linked by sea to the international trading system in which the U.S. economy is dominant, but they are also subject to overt and covert meddling by the Soviets and the Chinese that is designed to increase the influence of the USSR and the People's Republic of China (PRC).

Soviet intelligence forces, some 500,000 strong, and such other Soviet-controlled national intelligence services as those of Cuba and East Germany, continue their activities worldwide. Their objective is to collect intelligence, particularly on the economic and technological advances on which the future strength of free societies depend, and to use this information covertly to influence economic, military, and political developments everywhere, including in the United States, to their strategic advantage.

At the same time the Soviet Union, as well as all of the East European communist powers, conceal within their borders as prime state secrets nearly every aspect of national policy and behavior. Policymakers in the United States cannot afford to face this kind of international environment in the 1980s without knowing what developments may be encroaching upon our security.

The United States must reassume a role of greater responsibility in the intelligence field worldwide. Our activities should focus on giving our leaders sufficient information to protect our security, to promote our international interests, and to develop foreign policies supportive of democratic values and institutions in nations that wish to maintain an alliance with the United States in the decades ahead. To do otherwise in the face of hostile and secretive adversaries would be to engage in unilateral disarmament in the sphere of gathering and evaluating information—a sphere that should be a strong point in a free society.

Owing to the special focus of recent congressional investigations, it has become clear that the operations of a national intelligence agency sometimes place considerable strain upon the American ethos of honesty and fair play. At other times those operations can be characterized by excessive zeal in the name of national security. These findings raise a host of issues that must be addressed: questions of fundamental American traditions and basic rights; how to protect those rights without shackling the intelligence organization; questions of command and control of intelligence operations; executive responsibility and congressional oversight; questions of secrecy and covert activity in an open society. In brief, the apparent anomaly seen by many in the very concept of an "American" national intelligence agency must be examined and resolved.

The presidential and congressional inquiries have brought to the surface numerous questions pertaining to lines of authority, chain of command, responsibility, and response. What has seemed in the past to be exclusively a function of the executive branch, along with foreign policy and the prosecution of war, is now perceived as rightfully responsive to congressional needs and even to the public at large. The authority to be assigned to the director of the national intelligence entity and the place his agency ought to occupy in the national structure must be made clear beyond any doubt. The internal structure of the intelligence organization and the quality of the persons who fill key positions must be judged in terms of effectiveness in contributing to the nation's security. All of these issues remain to be settled and the capabilities of the intelligence system urgently restored to the highest level permitted by U.S. resources and talents.

THE CHALLENGE OF THE 1980s

Research, analysis, and estimates. It is the CIA's job to foresee and prepare policymakers for disasters like the collapse of the government in Iran, with the concomitant cut in oil for the advanced industrial nations. If the shah's government had been alerted in time, CIA covert advice might even have stabilized and saved it. This did not happen during the winter of 1978–79. The bankruptcy of American intelligence was clearly revealed in this case.

In broad terms, it is essential to meet the challenge of the 1980s by providing the intelligence input in the form of information and analysis that we need to develop a coherent strategic concept on which to base our foreign policy. Strategic coherence has been almost totally lacking in the Carter administration. Only when our foreign policy is based on precise and consistent strategic thinking and is responsive to warning signals from the intelligence community can intelligence effectively play its role—described by Sherman Kent in *Strategic Intelligence* as the thing that gets the shield to the right place at the right time.

For example, President Jimmy Carter at the end of 1978 began touting the PRC as a friendly, peace-loving quasi-ally of the United States, just preceding its plunge into war with Vietnam early in 1979. The result of the Chinese attack was that the Soviet Union increased its presence—

and influence—in Vietnam by moving into former American air bases at Danang and former American naval facilities at Cam Ranh Bay. The sea lanes of Southeast Asia are now much more vulnerable to Soviet interruption than before, and both Japan and South Korea are more liable to Soviet pressure because of their dependency on oil and other trade commodities that reach them via these sea lanes. How could the United States have better assisted our enemies at the expense of our friends in that part of the world?

Apparently CIA was cautious, whereas the White House was reckless in its flirtation with Peking. Advance warning by CIA about the Chinese intentions to attack Vietnam was solid. The agency was unable, nevertheless, to forecast the consequences of "playing the China card" forcefully enough to prevent the White House from making what in hindsight seems a gross strategic miscalculation. Only a reinvigorated intelligence system with real prestige and clout can do the job of influencing national policy planners to take longer-range, more sophisticated views of the strategic issues at stake in decisions like the sudden move regarding China, especially in the context of the Sino-Soviet conflict.

The work of drafting national estimates on strategic situations and the probable consequences of various options in U.S. policy ought to be a first-priority task for CIA. It need not be a clandestine activity. In our open society the scholarly, legal enterprises of the central intelligence system ought to be recognized as part of the normal political process and be separated institutionally and administratively from the more controversial field of clandestine operations. The research analysis functions now carried by the National Foreign Assessments Center should be viewed as a critically important and unique element of government—having a fiduciary responsibility to the whole fabric of national security policy. The president should consult the experts in this area systematically and disregard their estimates at his own peril. The substance of the findings ought to be available to the congressional intelligence committees and made public in as much detail as the security classification permits. No effort or expense should be spared in attempting to employ the very best talent at every level of the staff responsible for reporting current research findings and assessing future strategic trends. The generation of expertise created in the past 40 years is now almost entirely gone from the intelligence agencies. Replacing them and consulting the wisdom of some of those still active in research in international strategic developments is vital to success in the 1980s.

Creating an independent agency for the research, analysis, and estimates staffs would set apart the work of this service, whose written reporting, for the most part, could be openly acknowledged as a legitimate element of national decision making. Although sources and intelligence methods and perhaps some politically sensitive findings ought to remain secret, much could be revealed for the benefit of public understanding of the issues dealt with. The analytical scholars within the intelligence community could have closer contact with those in universities and think tanks, and much of their research data could be made available to anyone interested. Institutions of learning, their teachers, and their students would have opportunities to cooperate with intelligence insiders, and it is to be hoped that mutual respect would grow. In time of need, excellence, objectivity, and research skills in the intelligence agencies would be generally assumed, and the erroneous impression that research analysts are engaged in illegal and immoral activities could be dissipated. Then the quality of intelligence and the inclination of policymakers to rely on it could be restored to the optimum levels of the 1950s and early 1960s.

Clandestine collection. In today's world, open or semi-official sources are sometimes not sufficient for wise defense and foreign policy decisions. Our major adversaries, like the Soviet Union and the PRC, try to conceal from the United States all facts that are pertinent to their plans, programs, or ambitions in world affairs. The most important data about these matters in such countries can only be studied in secret by men who can penetrate their societies. The clandestine operators should be few in number, and their administrative management should be separate from the research, analysis, and estimates staffs. The separation would free the analytical elements of the community from the controversies bound to arise when the pros and cons of secret activities abroad are debated. In the meantime, espionage and the secret technical collection of data could be carried on as a quasi-military function under authority of the president as commander-in-chief.

Laws reflect national and cultural customs, and what appears right for one group of people at a given time often appears wrong to others. It is not against the law for American agents to look at what is going on in foreign countries except where special areas are declared off limits; and eliciting information from friendly foreign nationals is commonplace. Real espionage begins with controlled penetration into subjects that are legally restricted in order to prevent outsiders from learning anything. Nearly every country sends representatives abroad to discover what can be learned in other places, overtly if possible, clandestinely if necessary. In the latter case bribery, deception, or blackmail are employed in collecting intelligence on which the security of the United States depends. Many people feel these acts are unethical, but prudent regard for the common defense should be cited in support of secret operations in foreign countries, and a select service responsible for espionage should be established under the NSC.

Covert action. Infrequently, but when national interests abroad are judged by the president absolutely to require it, the clandestine service unit responsible for espionage ought to be tasked to operate in foreign countries to influence opinion, change political allegiances, or alter the course of events. Covert U.S. operations, especially those of a paramilitary kind, are plainly illegal in the view of the people likely to be disadvantaged by them, as well as by many others who are morally scrupulous.

Can CIA's illegal activities, particularly covert political intervention in other nations, be morally justified? The answer must be "yes," and limited covert action capabilities should be revitalized so that secret activities can be undertaken in self-defense—in protection of the security of Americans at home and abroad. The main justification is that many other governments have extensive clandestine intelligence services, and some are avowedly interested in overthrowing representative governments and establishing dictatorships in free societies. Most Americans do not have much trouble in tolerating clandestine counterintelligence at home by the FBI under appropriate legal restraints established by Congress and the Department of Justice. Nor are they disturbed by U.S. clandestine intelligence collection in closed, hostile societies, or even in more innocent countries where hostile secret services are trying to make penetrations and influence political events in ways unfavorable to U.S. interests.

Still, leaving prudent and pragmatic considerations aside, serious-minded observers argue that a free society cannot engage in secret activities, particularly covert political operations, without violating its fundamental ethical values. The answer to this criticism is that the security of American citizens and the survival of our political and economic institutions are part of the American value system. When they appeared under real threat, the citizens of the United States fought for these values in World War II; and for the most part they believed that their participation in that costly conflict was thoroughly justifiable.

In a sense, CIA's operations in what we loosely call peacetime, that is, when conflicts are of a lower intensity than total military combat, are the moral equivalent of military combat in war. Clandestine intelligence collection and covert political action are both extensions of diplomacy and instruments of policy designed to prevent resort to war. As former DCI Colby said, CIA's covert operations are designed to provide effective action at a middle level, supporting our defense and foreign policy without surrendering important points on the one hand or sending in military troops on the other. Decisions and actions by the U.S. government in the field of intelligence ought to be judged by the same ethical standards as decisions about peace or war.

Here the responsible citizen has help from a large body of philosophical literature on the doctrine of "just war" as part of the Western Christian tradition. The theory of just war contends that political authority must be judged by whether an act of war 1) is directed toward a morally justifiable end, such as self-defense, 2) employs means appropriate to the end and not excessive or destructive to the ultimate goal, and 3) has a reasonable chance of success. These main principals of just war are described by contemporary writers including Ernest W. Lefever, Paul Ramsey, and Robert W. Tucker. Except for that minority of Americans who believe that our military forces and civil police are more dangerous to American society than the crimes and hazards they are charged with protecting us against, intelligence operations seem to be an essential, warranted element of the apparatus of national authority set up in the U.S. Constitution to ensure domestic tranquillity, provide for the common defense, and promote the general welfare. If these are morally sound objectives of governmental policy, then—in light of the international dangers that could impinge on our tranquillity, defense, and general welfare—conducting secret operations in support of security of an open and free society is prima facie ethical. The task is to ensure, as in the case of war, that intelligence activities are indeed aimed at ends contributing to our security, that the means employed are defensible, and that the chances of success are reasonably good. In fact, these are the judgments that the president, the NSC, the CIA, and the congressional oversight committees must make in establishing policy that governs intelligence programs and in approving specific plans for action. Perfecting these instruments of internal governmental accountability is among the most urgent jobs that need to be done so that clandestine and covert actions can be conducted to meet the dangers of the 1980s.

Budget. The amount of money spent annually on all the U.S. intelligence agencies together is now only approximately $5 billion. This is probably a rock-bottom price for the minimum effort commensurate with American security requirements. It should increase from now on for several years at least as rapidly as defense expenditures and, for a time, perhaps even more rapidly. At present we are budgeting too little, in view of the cost of satellite reconnaissance systems and their fundamental importance in monitoring strategic weapons, not to mention the cost of rebuilding an espionage network of human sources that will operate at least as widely and as well as it did at the height of CIA's successes in the 1950s and 1960s. In a sense, our need for an espionage network is greater now than then because our relative military strength has decreased and political structures worldwide are more unstable.

When other people try to conceal their intentions, particularly when they appear to be establishing relationships potentially hostile to the United States and its allies, espionage is the only way to discover behavior patterns, trends in thinking, and future plans that may jeopardize American interests. The resignation or forced retirement of experienced personnel, the chilling atmosphere of restrictions proposed in legislation before the Congress, and the lack of good cover arrangements abroad all have reduced the effectiveness of human source collection. These trends must be reversed.

Technical intelligence collection. Electronic intercepts and photographic reconnaissance, including the collection of signals and images by aircraft and satellites, provide the basic background of what can be seen or overheard, against which the reports of human agents take on maximum meaning. Electronic data transmission and surveillance and detection systems reach into every critical facet of the military, industrial, and economic activity of all countries, especially the technologically advanced nations. The gadgetry for handling information flow is ballooning in cost and numbers of personnel required. The whole intelligence collection effort must keep expanding with the state of the art. In addition, great care must be exercised to ensure that intelligence analysts are of such high quality that they can process images and signals in a timely and sophisticated way in order to answer policy questions, rather than flooding the system with raw, undigested items of evidence.

Failure to exploit both human and technical collection systems on a comprehensive scale means that many opportunities to avert crises will be lost. Awareness of the possibility of an impending hostile act allows flexibility in meeting the threat to national security and, in fact, may deter or prevent the act altogether. The mix of human and technical source collection needs to be finely tuned and the balance adjusted, with greater emphasis on the difficult task of establishing reliable human sources to find out what is going on inside people's heads—where pictures do not help.

Counterintelligence. Effective counterintelligence is necessary to ensure, inasmuch as possible, that intelligence operations can be pursued in secrecy and with confidence that the product will be reliable. Guidelines by the White House must be explicitly established to regulate the collection of information about U.S. citizens—whether by wiretap, mail opening, or direct surveillance when circumstances justify it. It should be permissible, with appropriate guidelines, for some agency of the government to follow up on incomplete information that suggests U.S. citizens' involvement in espionage, without requiring the strict evidence concerning the probable commission of a crime that is needed to procure court warrants under existing procedures. The courts are not a good place to settle upon a balance between the benefits of following up fragmentary evidence of a foreign intelligence penetration in the United States, on the one hand, and the risks of suggested intrusive intelligence operations against American citizens, on the other. The NSC and the attorney general ought to make such determinations subject to policy review by the congressional oversight committees. The judgments are political, not legal.

Restrictions in regulations in this regard should focus on the retention and dissemination of the information collected, not on prevention of the collection of information that could result in major dangers to American internal security. This counterintelligence function should mostly devolve on the FBI within the United States and in any case should never involve the CIA in law-enforcement activities, domestic intelligence, or internal security. The CIA's clandestine capabilities must be adequate, however, to provide raw information, when available, from its sources abroad to assist the FBI, the Secret Service, and other security agencies. These domestic security intelligence agencies also need strengthening, training in sophisticated intelligence methods, and safeguarding against hostile penetrations. An intelligence system that does not take effective precautions against hostile infiltration is not worth having.

Intelligence reporting. It should be noted that data collected by clandestine means is nearly useless unless collated and studied analytically along with the mass of overtly available data accessible to scholars in university and professional research organizations. Historical continuity, interdisciplinary analysis, and rigorous professional training in strict objectivity must be essential judgmental ingredients of every intelligence conclusion that is of any consequence. The mass of incoming data must be reduced to manageable form with appropriate caveats concerning reliability of source and credibility in the light of established knowledge. When clearly relevant to national security or foreign policy, intelligence reports that summarize or describe the evidence available must be distributed in forms suitable for both working intelligence analysts and policymaking officials: copiously to the former and sparingly to the latter. Current intelligence briefs must be supplemented by in-depth research reports on many areas of the world, in politics, economics, technology, and military affairs. In some cases, speculative estimates need to be prepared, peering into probabilities for the future. At some levels it is crucial to make "net" estimates, where the give-and-take between U.S. military, economic, and political capabilities to influence foreign situations can be analyzed. In all cases, procedures must be evolved to ensure that reliable and objective information is understood and actually used by policymakers with appropriate guidance from senior intelligence analysts.

The talent bank that exists in CIA's National Foreign Assessments Center, the Defense Intelligence Agency, and the Department of State's Bureau of Intelligence and Research is a national asset that needs refreshing and enlarging. The development of these analysts' skills to the highest possible levels is a prime requirement. There is no use in having good evidence unless it can be put into a form that can be comprehended and acted upon by top government officials. To perform this task is the job of intelligence analysts. One important way to supplement and sharpen their capabilities is for the CIA, the White House, and the Congress to encourage close rapport between intelligence analysts and the scholarly community of universities and think tanks, as well as the more serious journalists. With better public understanding and approval of the importance of research and analysis, morale will improve in this part of the intelligence community and new talent will be attracted. Achieving this result is essential.

Legislative guidance and executive regulations. Finally, legislation and regulations ought to provide for selective, secretly planned, and carefully monitored covert action. When CIA programs have encompassed political and economic action, propaganda, and paramilitary activities, they undoubtedly have overstepped reasonable bounds for a time. The Bay of Pigs operation was too military, the Chilean political intervention of the 1970s too hastily contrived and crude. But covert action now is almost nonexistent. It should be resumed, though with great care. The passage of analytical intelligence reports, operations reports on technical and agent findings, and counterintelligence data is especially useful in building rapport with political action assets in foreign countries. Nothing illegal is involved. Covert action is best described as quiet support for a friend, providing help in ways not attributable to the formal apparatus of U.S. diplomacy and not requiring the use of overt military force.

Covert action must be used wisely and sparingly. According to present legislative provisions, any covert action plan must be cleared through seven congressional committees. This provision makes it virtually impossible to organize any major plan without some word of it leaking to the press. Access to information on plans for covert action should be restricted to the Senate and House oversight committees. It is ridiculous for 150-odd congressmen to hear what covert actions the president is considering.

Legislative and executive orders must be drafted to allow some latitude of judgment on the part of intelligence officials under general policy guidelines. These orders should also provide more stringent controls on unauthorized access to secret intelligence, as well as appropriate penalties for unauthorized disclosures by officials in the intelligence community, the policymaking elements of government, and the Congress and congressional staffs.

Congressional oversight mechanisms are useful for providing general policy guidance on the conduct of all intelligence missions, but they should not be employed for direct managerial control of the executive functions of government—among which covert action is one of the most sensitive and delicate.

There are many factors to be considered in restructuring our intelligence system in line with these principles. In essence, however, what is needed is for the officials of NSC, the Congress, and the concerned public to realize just what contribution a central, coordinated intelligence system makes to the security and effective policymaking of an open society. If they reach this realization, they will jettison most of the legislative strictures spelled out so laboriously in the mammoth draft bill S. 2525.

It is quite possible that the nation would be better served if Congress passed no new legislation at all. The controls and protection against illegal or improper practices embodied in Executive Order 12036 (January 26, 1978) are adequate—if not excessive—for any reasonable critic. This kind of administrative detail belongs in an executive order that can be changed quickly when the need arises, rather than in concrete legislation.

If Congress proceeds with new legislation, it should write into law simple, positive instructions not unlike the operative sections of the National Security Act of 1947. The president should then increase the budget by 5 percent a year in real dollars for five years. He should make a nonpartisan search for outstanding leaders of each element of the intelligence community, then allow the whole intelligence system and its leaders a period of about five years of benign neglect. Under general NSC and congressional oversight, the DCI could then get on with rebuilding the intelligence system, bringing in high-quality new talent and insuring that all employees are carefully indoctrinated about the critical importance of basic intelligence functions, as well as the requirement of operating within the legal and moral context of our open society.

No comprehensive legislation or managerial legerdemain can accomplish this rebuilding of CIA and the other elements of the intelligence community. Only enlightened leadership at all levels, from the White House and the DCI down, can do the job. It must be done, and promptly, if our security and world power position are to be protected.

SUMMARY

From all this history and all these arguments, the only possible conclusion is that the United States has allowed its intelligence agencies to be savaged by excessive criticism, demoralized within their corps of indispensable professional staff, and drastically reduced in capability. It is therefore essential to revitalize a sophisticated, secret, central American intelligence system. There is nothing more critically important in our whole political process.

The intelligence function can only meet the challenges of the uneasy peacetime of the 1980s if it is strengthened substantially in budget, manpower, and talent and if it is asked to collect information on all foreign situations, trends, threats, and opportunities relevant to U.S. interests abroad. This broad mission must be carried out with great skill, self-confidence, and objectivity. Techniques of collection should be multiple and employed with flexibility based on analysis of the target personalities, the target countries, and the risks of using the various methods available for the purposes envisaged.

In the end, everything important about intelligence depends upon the kind of people who do the work and the kind of people who use the knowledge produced in the decision-making process, a process that must favor realism and intellectual honesty. Only the most competent and responsible men and women will do, especially at the top. The conclusions reached by the Rockefeller Commission in its *Report to the President*[7] made this point clear in discussing the appointment of the DCI:

> In the final analysis, the proper functioning of the Agency must depend in large part on the character of the Director of Central Intelligence.
>
> The best assurance against misuse of the Agency lies in the appointment to that position of persons with the judgment, courage, and independence to resist improper pressure and importuning, whether from the White House, within the Agency, or elsewhere.

NOTES

1. Sherman Kent, *Strategic Intelligence for American World Policy* (Princeton, N.J.: Princeton University Press, 1951), p. vii.

2. U.S., Congress, Senate, Select Committee to Study Governmental Operations with Respect to Intelligence Activities, *Supplementary Detailed Staff Reports on Foreign and Military Intelligence*, 94th Cong., 2d Session, bk. 4 (Washington, D.C.: Government Printing Office, 1976), p. 31.

3. For NSC papers and related documents on Italy, see U.S. Department of State, *Foreign Relations of the United States*, vol. III: *Western Europe* (Washington, D.C.: Government Printing Office, 1974), pp. 724–789.

4. *Report to the President by the Commission on CIA Activities within the United States* (Washington, D.C.: Government Printing Office, June 1975), pp. 199–202; hereafter referred to as the *Rockefeller Commission Report to the President*.

5. U.S., Congress, Senate, Staff Report of the Select Committee to Study Governmental Operations with Respect to Intelligence Activities, *Covert Action in Chile: 1963–1973*, 94th Cong., 1st Session, December 18, 1975, p. 2 and passim.

6. *Rockefeller Commission Report to the President*, pp. 20–21, 101–115.

7. Ibid., p. 17.

Technology: The Imbalance of Power

Edward Teller

XVIII

HISTORICAL BACKGROUND

The Torrent of Time

In the second half of the past century Friedrich Engels, an advocate of radical changes in society, predicted that no change was to be expected in weapons of war. His argument, though limited, was rational: The rifle could shoot as far as a man could see and as fast as he could take aim; nothing else would be necessary. A single technological development tore his prophecy to shreds. The machine gun did not take aim; it committed wholesale slaughter; it seemed to stop any attack. It has been said of this weapon, "Of all the hideous 'engines of war' produced in the twentieth century, none has exacted a more dreadful toll of human life than the machine gun."[1]

Engels, a student of the economic consequences of technology, was unable to foresee the intense acceleration of military developments resulting from technology's growth and influence. This swift change is also irreversible. Once new tools enter upon the stage of history they rarely exit, but remain and interact with all that entered before. The action inexorably accelerates with the passage of time.

Today all on earth are close neighbors: the First World, which is liberal; the Second World, which is dictatorial; and the Third World, where changes are rapid and often violent. The fate of all hinges on the development and use of technology. If we want to understand and influence the future, we should review and understand humankind's new tools.

Some say the generation just past accomplished more in technology than all generations before it. Probably the same will be said of the generation to come. Comparisons of past accomplishments with contemporary ones can be misleading; more important than comparisons of quantity are comparisons of quality. If we compare the horse and buggy with a rocket to the moon, quantitative comparisons become arbitrary.

Similarly, old and new methods of warfare are neither analogous nor easily comparable. But in all cases we are talking about conflict, about tests of strength, resolve, and, above all, ingenuity; unfortunately but inevitably, we are talking about violence.

The Napoleonic wars were hardly affected by new technology. The nineteenth century saw some relatively minor changes. In our century, technology entered warfare in full force. In part, this was due to a new style of linking scientific ideas with technology.

A revolution of ideas occurred in science in the first thirty years of this century, a revolution so great that the vast majority of highly educated persons has not yet grasped the new ideas. To most of us the word relativity signifies, at best, a maze of mathematical formulas—which relativity is not. Terms such as atomic theory, or the more specific quantum mechanics, to most people mean nothing; yet from these two sets of ideas, occurring entirely within one generation, have emerged developments stranger and vastly more important than the once revolutionary idea that our earth is not the whole universe, or even its center.

From the scientific revolution of ideas sprang consequences of a totally different kind. Science and technology have become twins. As a result, applied science is developing rapidly and in unexpected ways. With each new practical scientific application, new technologies emerge that can be used in warfare. There is no separation between technology for peace and technology for war, and I believe the two will remain inseparable.

Public awareness is more advanced in the case of scientific applications, since all of us are exposed to some ramifications of the applications—in computers, for example. Exposure, however, does not guarantee comprehension. The consequences of widespread lack of understanding often manifest themselves as deep-seated fears.

We should strive to eliminate some common misunderstandings. The new events and possibilities are surprising, frightening, and large in scale. When confronted with something greater than ever seen before, the human mind frequently jumps to the conclusion that it is facing something infinite, something limitless. That conclusion is mistaken. When we are overly impressed by progress in any given development we lose our sense of proportion; we then enter the realm of what is called the unthinkable.* But thinking is the distinguishing mark of a human being. Thinking and decision making allow us to influence our future.

A variety of new situations will be described here; what cannot be provided is a roadmap. Only by considering all the new weapons—those in the recent past with its rapid changes, those now being deployed or planned, and those we can presently perceive only dimly—can we begin to grasp the practical necessities of defense and military preparedness.

The torrent of time will not be stopped. By action based on understanding, it could ultimately be guided into peaceful channels.

First Shocks of Technology

The nineteenth and twentieth centuries have produced an astounding variety of innovations in the technology of warfare, and they will produce more. The undesirable side of human character remains unchallenged as a primary motive force of history. It is a terrible fact that political tensions in Europe once over-rode shared heritage and common humanity. At the outbreak of war in 1914, feelings of patriotism were so strong as to be described by the word euphoria; many people, especially in Germany, behaved as though peace had been painful.

But technological innovations have had almost as great an effect on military conflicts. The machine gun, for instance, which evolved from the primitive Gatling gun demonstrated in the American Civil War, was important in bringing about the dreadful stalemate and trench warfare of World War I.

The role of the railroad, which should not be under-rated, illustrates an important facet of the impact on warfare of technological change: the unpredictability both of the likelihood of armed conflict and of its resulting course. This is not to say that technological changes are the basis of conflict; they simply limit the value of predictions about warfare. The most decisive single factor in the Russo-Japanese War probably was that the trans-Siberian railroad had not yet been completed.

As Germany prepared for war its strategists carefully studied Gen. William Tecumseh Sherman's use of railroads in the American Civil War. They expected their own mobilization speed to be decisive and Russian mobilization to be slow. An extensive, efficient German rail network was organized into four major trunk systems. Thirty-six army corps were deployed; a corps consisted of 35,000 men, 8,000 horses, 150

*"Greek fire," consisting of the irreconcilable elements of fire and water (actually a mixture mainly of unslaked lime, sulphur, and naphtha), which stopped the first Muhammadan onslaught on Constaninople, was such an unthinkable weapon. It was secret, and it was outlawed by the pope. The secret was kept much better than that of the atomic bomb.

artillery pieces, 50 machine guns, and all supplies. Deployment of each army corps took 180 trains.

This major *Aufmarsch* was accomplished between August 2 and 16, 1914, with trains moving at closely timed intervals, some as slowly as 20 miles per hour, 24 hours a day. Approximately 1,260,000 men were transported. Yet the initial impact of the railroad did not end the war, as the German General Staff had anticipated. In the first decisive battle of the Marne, the French managed to stop the onslaught with a surprise: transport by the taxis of Paris.

Another important surprise in World War I was the submarine—not its existence, but its role. No Allied strategist anticipated that the submarine would counteract the British blockade and enable Germany to establish a partial counterblockade.

The use of gas warfare could have become an important surprise. Fritz Haber proposed the use of chlorine, but even though German General Staff members accepted gas, they did not really believe in it. They used gas not in shells, as Haber had suggested, but from fixed canisters in their own lines; its use was dependent on favorable winds and meteorological conditions to carry it to Allied troops. Gas was used at the Ypres salient, and its effect was greater than expected. The Germans had not anticipated important results; for once they had not planned carefully; they did not exploit the success of their first attack on April 12, 1915. The Allies' total lack of preparation for gas attacks is remarkable, since Germany had earlier used gas against the Russians on the eastern front, and routine interrogation of captured German soldiers indicated preparation for a gas attack.

The British, with astounding speed, developed gas masks—very simple devices using activated charcoal. A few weeks later when Germany, recognizing the effectiveness of gas, used it again, the Allies were prepared for it. It was no surprise and there was no panic.

Many attempts were made to break the long and agonizing stalemate of World War I by innovation. Besides submarines and gas, tanks and aircraft were developed and used in battle, as well as sound-ranging equipment for locating distant artillery. When the war began neither France nor England had hand grenades or mortars, both of which became indispensable to trench warfare upon their speedy and effective development.

Nevertheless, World War I was decided not by technological change but by exhaustion: hunger in Petrograd and unavailability of fresh troops in Germany. Incidentally, one of the last men temporarily blinded by an Allied gas attack was Adolf Hitler.

Naval Power

Naval warfare probably has made fewer headlines in recent years than most other phases of real or expected conflicts. Consequently, its role may appear to have diminished from that played in historic events of the past. In both world wars, however, naval warfare figured importantly, and in the years between the two conflicts its methods changed thoroughly. It continues in a state of transition and perpetual uncertainty. Naval power presents some of the United States' most worrisome problems.

During World War II the naval forces of the Allies were successful, not only in American battles in the Pacific, but in defeating a renewed and powerful counterblockade in the Atlantic that spawned new types of mines and techniques for countering them, submarine detection by sonar, and, most notably, radar. Together with intelligence, radar played a major role in Allied success in the Atlantic. By the end of the war, 785 German submarines had been sunk, mostly in the Atlantic; 300 were destroyed in an eleven-month period between the introduction of new airborne shortwave-length radar on Allied patrol planes and the German installation of appropriate detectors on their submarines.

Despite heavy casualties, U.S. naval successes resulted in a confidence in our technical military superiority that for years made anything beyond ordinary efforts seem unnecessary, even militaristic. This danger was overcome, at least partially, by the sustained initiative of one man, Hyman Rickover. Rickover's proposal that a true submarine be built—one that need not surface for air—was not readily accepted by the U.S. Navy. The proposal appeared daring, and in fact Rickover was proceeding with his nuclear submarines before a suitable reactor, capable of generating electricity sufficient to propel a submarine, had been perfected. Submarines, which are hard for potential enemies to locate or destroy, perform vital tasks in our defense, probably the most important of which is to carry nuclear rockets.

Other technological innovations have influenced naval power since World War II, and an extensive program for building new ships (which has not been approved by Congress) is currently proposed.

But Russia has fully realized the significance of naval power and has caught up with us and moved ahead in several areas of naval operations. The United States leads Russia only in number of aircraft carriers. We have thirteen; Russia, by Americans standards, has none. The Russians may be building one carrier at present. They also have three ships that can launch aircraft that do not need a long runway, but the aircraft have limited performance. Aircraft carriers of the American type may have priced themselves out of the market, however, costing more than $2 billion. Ambitious plans for ships that carry effective "vertical" or "short" takeoff and landing aircraft are being developed, but they are bogged down in Congress.

Russia is superior in cruisers 36 to 28, in destroyers 89 to 69 (with 27 in the U.S. reserve), in frigates 103 to 65; in the category of small combatants (small but carrying ship-to-ship missiles) the USSR has 105, the United States none. The United States has 77 attack submarines and 41 ballistic missile subs; Russia has 252 attack and 86 missile submarines.

When did we lose our naval superiority?

According to the chairman of the Joint Chiefs of Staff, the USSR built up its operational surface fleet slowly and steadily, while ours declined rapidly in number of units between 1969 and 1975.[2] A detailed comparison of 1968 and 1976 shows: aircraft carriers in the U.S. fleet declined 23–13, cruisers 34–26, destroyers 221–69.[3] Only frigates increased: 50–64. Our ballistic missile submarines remained constant at 41, nuclear attack submarines increased 33–64, and diesel attack submarines decreased 72–10.

Despite impressive numerical discrepancies, we comfort ourselves with the superior quality of our naval forces. Two points should be emphasized, however: first, the Russian navy has modernized greatly in recent years, continues to do so, and now possesses many sophisticated weapons. Performance of their ship-launched missiles is impressive. Second, Russian equipment, though far from sophisticated and certainly not modern in World War II, was serviceable and effective. Russian military equipment functions well in battle conditions; when used in quantity and with determination it is effective.

The United States observes on Russian ships equipment we cannot fully evaluate; it may be significantly innovative. But even by counting the Soviet ships we cannot avoid the conclusion that the United States is no longer in the position, in the event of war, to guarantee freedom of the seas to her own shipping and that of her allies.

Russia's trend of forging ahead toward control of the seas continues, a trend uniquely disquieting in view of U.S. reliance upon imports. Russia is nearly self-sufficient. Among imports the United States needs petroleum is probably first, although we keep a strategic domestic reserve in the ground (that could suffice for a year) against possible hostilities. Still, a blockade of trans-Atlantic shipping could be exceedingly painful, and it is difficult to assess when we could start to resist the blockade militarily—particularly if we knew we were militarily inferior.

The American public is justifiably sensitive about the vital freedom of the seas. Too few people realize that the United States has retreated from a position of confidence that we could enforce this freedom. That position seems to have passed into Russian hands in an undramatic way through hard work, modernization, sound judgment, and a consistent long-term plan based on singleness of purpose.

Even now the Soviet navy is attuned more to act as a spoiler than to dominate open sea lanes, though the Russians may try to attain that goal in the future. Russian naval growth indicates a clear shift in their perception of their role, from a continental power to a global force. This is particularly clear in the writings of Admiral Gorshkov.[4]

In view of these facts, it is remarkable that many American policymakers still consider Russian military preparedness purely defensive. Of course, it is impossible to prove that the men in the Kremlin have definite plans to use their navy for conquest. It is more likely that they are building a flexible force, its application not yet determined. But in considering our policies for the 1980s we must ask ourselves two questions. Is the U.S. Navy powerful enough to counteract, if need be, the Russian fleet, which is becoming the strongest in the world? And what are the technological developments and surprises that could either destroy or maintain the freedom of the seas?

Blitzkrieg

One consequence of technological development has been, and continues to be, acceleration of the pace of warfare. It was in World War II that the true speed of mechanized warfare was demonstrated for the first time. The melding of technological innovations for warlike purposes culminated in the German blitzkrieg. A few people in several countries had recognized that the combination of good communications, fast and powerful tanks, motorized infantry and artillery, and close air support would drastically accelerate the speed of attack. But only the country determined to dominate made an effective effort to utilize that combination.

The blitzkrieg was first seen clearly in Poland, but its effectiveness was discounted. The Poles' lack of strength and Russia's attack upon them two weeks later were assumed to be the reasons for Germany's speedy victory—until the same thing happened to the French, despite British support. With the invasion of France and the Low Countries there remained no doubt that something qualitatively new had evolved. A synergism resulted whereby combined elements such as mobility, mechanization, and speed created an effect different from and greater than the mere sum of the individual factors. This product of new developments is particularly difficult to anticipate or predict.

Hitler was determined that there should be no repetition of the trench stalemate of World War I; whatever happened must happen fast. In France it happened fast and with full effect. The fate of Germany's offensive on the eastern front was probably sealed by the four to six weeks delay in the attack on Russia that began June 22, 1941. Before fatal blows could be delivered, the hard Russian winter set in. The blitzkrieg became a prolonged slugging match.

The destruction wrought by the Nazis in Russia was on a grand scale, but no grander than the scale of their folly. They moved into territories, such as the Ukraine and the Baltic states, that had suffered under both tsarist and communist oppression, where they might have been greeted as saviors. But Hitler's regard for their peoples as subhuman activated the will to resist. Further, by indiscriminate over-reaction to guerrilla acts, the Nazis intensified resistance in occupied territories. This resistance, plus great distances and Russian winters, proved too much for German technology. The human element remains important and may well be decisive even in the age of technology.

Russia's remarkable rapid evacuation of population and industry also figured prominently in its withstanding the German assault. We will do well to recall this phenomenon when considering Russian ability to manage a massive relocation of its people before threatening to use their nuclear arsenal.

Rockets

Rockets are old, but rockets are new. The Chinese enlivened special occasions with rockets many hundreds of years ago; "the rockets' red glare" was familiar in 1776. Unlike airplanes, however, rockets do not rely on a supporting atmosphere, consequently they are obvious instruments of space travel.

The principle of rocket function is simple. Its fuel, liquid or solid, is ignited and turns into a gas that is expelled backward, with resultant forward propulsion of the rocket. The rocket has one severe limitation: its speed is related to that of the gases expelled at the rear.

It is not difficult to obtain rocket velocity equal to that of the expanded gas, provided the *payload,* the mass to be carried by the rocket, is approximately equal to the mass of the fuel. Difficulties are encountered when greater rocket velocities are sought. These difficulties are dealt with by accelerating the rocket in stages, each stage carrying additional fuel as well as the payload. By utilizing such superior rocket fuels as liquefied hydrogen mixed with liquefied oxygen, plus multi-stage acceleration, rockets are lifted, at speeds up to twelve kilometers per second, beyond the gravitational field of earth. Unfortunately, each stage doubles the total weight because each stage must lift all subsequent stages; with increasing speed the size of the rocket increases exponentially.

It may be desirable to return the rocket and set it down gently on earth. Re-entry uses atmospheric friction for braking action, and much of the re-entry vehicle may be burned away in the process. Thus we may start with a rocket half as tall as the Empire State Building; as it is launched, brilliant flame is created and thunder heard for miles. The great structure rises slowly, majestically; soon it vanishes from sight, leaving the earth and all its vapors behind. When the rocket returns from its adventure only a capsule remains, containing three astronauts in Spartan accommodations.

American military rockets, Minutemen, use premixed solid fuel, circumventing the complexities of careful handling and pumping of volatile fuels. The Minuteman is fueled and ready for action, but that advantage has its price: the gases emitted from a solid fuel have a lower velocity; more stages are needed, and more weight. Furthermore, a Minuteman rocket must be transported as a fueled unit.

Rockets demand great emphasis on engineering. Their science is elementary, but the job of the engineer is fantastic. Hundreds of thousands of parts go into a functioning rocket, and all must be reliable. By comparison, assembling an atom bomb is simple (though the story of a clever student producing a nuclear bomb in an attic remains a fable).

Among the engineering feats of rocketry is rocket guidance. A manned rocket lands gently on the moon, more than 200,000 miles away. It returns, splashing down within a mile of ships ready to pick up the space travelers. The entire procedure is done blind. No eyes, no external signals steer the rocket. Instead, it is internally directed. An apparatus on board registers with astounding accuracy any change in direction, acceleration, deceleration. From its preflight rest until splashdown, information is available at any moment on its speed and direction. A relatively simple computer calculates and reveals, instant by instant, where the rocket is located. The modern rocket is one object that always knows its place.

Our sophisticated modern rockets evolved from the relatively simple rockets massed by the Russians to encircle Nazi attackers of Stalingrad in World War II. That rocket bombardment was devastating. But the Nazis, in the final months of the war, made even more impressive use of rockets. German technologists moved rapidly with rocket development for weapons of war. They produced the devastating V-2, *Vergeltungswaffe* 2, the second in a series of weapons designed for reprisal against the British. The V-2 left the atmosphere and re-entered at a speed faster than that of sound: first came the impact, then the noise following behind the rocket. This ballistic missile came too late, by a few months, to change the course of World War II. It was the surprise that barely failed in its mission.

Russians after 1945, fully conscious of the potential power of rockets and continually worried about an attack from the west, step by step increased their rocketry. They used German experts, squeezed them dry, then sent them home. In the United States we pursued more ambitious goals with less success. Germans who came to this country stayed.

Round one of the cold war rocket race was won by the success of Sputnik. Suddenly America, in at least one respect, was no longer number one. The shock was resounding. Efforts were made to upgrade the teaching of science. President Kennedy—opposed by many scientists—determined that by 1970 we must get to the moon. In 1969 that plan became reality. People around the world stayed awake and watched, millions upon uncounted millions. Interest in science and technology was stimulated in many young people. The greatest show in the solar system became, briefly, the greatest show on earth.

The success was ephemeral. The triumph of American technology met with strong resistance: Why go to the moon? Instead, why not solve the troubles on our domestic space ship? But nay-sayers to the moon substituted no positive program for the earth.

In the 1960s, evidence was accumulating of Russian missile strength, though this secret information was not shared with the American people. Not until 1972, with the Strategic Arms Limitation Treaty (SALT I), did the American public become aware of Russia's real advantage in possessing many large missiles that could carry hydrogen bombs across an ocean.

It was during the 1960s that the Minuteman missiles were deployed. The vast potential strategic importance of intercontinental ballistic missiles (ICBMs) was beginning to be understood by many. Missile-carrying nuclear submarines were concurrently developed, which, together with the Minuteman, were joined with the tightly directed Strategic Air Command capability to carry atomic and hydrogen bombs, to present an impressive deterrent force. The existence of this force played an important role in the 1962 Cuban missile crisis.

At that time, the United States could initiate talks with Russia for the purpose of limiting arms, and the initiative apparently would not involve great risks because we negotiated from a position of strength. That strength was further enhanced by an ingenious invention, the multiple independently targeted re-entry vehicle (MIRV), whereby a single rocket could carry several nuclear explosives each of which could seek out a predetermined target.

By 1972, however, most of the advantage had been lost, a fact revealed to the public by the terms of the SALT I treaty. Russian strength in nuclear weapons and the systems to deliver them had steadily increased, and it increases still. Today Russia has far more than enough power to deter the United States from a first strike—which we, indeed, have never contemplated. Russia has more and heavier rockets than the United States; it is developing the largest nuclear submarine fleet; it has caught up with us in MIRV technology. It is also on the verge of introducing an excellent intercontinental bomber called the Backfire, claiming that it will be used only for tactical purposes. The United States is now negotiating from a position of weapons inferiority.

One element in the present comparison of Russian and American rocket forces is particularly disturbing. Seeking a viable treaty, we placed emphasis on what we can see—counting only submarines and well-prepared emplacement of intercontinental ballistic missiles. How many missiles may be in reserve, how fast silos can be reloaded, whether firing facilities exist in places not accessible to our inspection—all these questions are difficult to resolve. Our intelligence community may imagine that it could discover big numbers of additional Russian missiles; but it failed (for example) to discover the Cuban missile emplacements until almost too late.

In military terms, what counts is the weight that can be lifted and delivered over a distance of 5,000–6,000 miles by a rocket. We know that today Russia has the advantage in this throw weight. Their payload is five times as big as ours. In only a few years the ratio could increase to tenfold without our noticing it.

The element of surprise has always been important. In our age of technology its importance has become paramount. If the Soviets obtain an overwhelming quantitative advantage, however, American deterrent power could become ineffective.

Unused weapons are instruments of the cold war. By depriving an opponent of any hope of escape, they may enforce winning decisions. Among today's unused weapons, rockets that can deliver warheads in half an hour, and that can wipe out civilian and military targets alike, may well be the most terrifying and the most decisive.

Airplanes

Between the two world wars the airplane came of age. Before 1939, Germany knew the next decisive developmental step: the turbojet. In a turbojet, instead of utilizing a free propeller, air is compressed by a small shielded propeller and fuel is injected, burned, and then expanded through a second propeller in the rear that works on the same shaft as the initial compressor. Had the Germans pursued this development they might well have maintained air superiority; but Hitler believed he would win with what he already had. Jets were introduced by the Nazis toward the end of the war, but the effort was too little and too late.

Aircraft played a vital role in World War II, both in battle and in massive bombing raids against cities and production facilities. Their use then continued in conflicts less widespread. Israel's air superiority, for instance, figured decisively in the Six-Day War of 1967.

Jets, meanwhile, were developed further. They reached sound velocity, then crossed the sound barrier. A swept-back wing design was adopted in order to avoid excessive air resistance from shock against the wing's leading edge. But the swept-back wing, although effective in near-sonic and supersonic flight, is less so at the slower speeds of takeoff and landing. Consequently, airplanes were designed with a variable wing configuration. The variable wing, perpendicular to the fuselage at takeoff, is moved on pivots to the swept-back position in flight. The difficulties of achieving a pivot neither too heavy nor too fragile, however, threaten to offset the advantage of the variable wing design.

Airplane development has served peaceful purposes and wartime requirements with equal efficiency. Planes have speeded mankind's tempo in peace and in war. They well exemplify the statement that peacetime and wartime technologies cannot be separated.

Chemistry in War and Peace

Before World War I, chemistry had developed an important military tool: high explosives, in which chemical reactions propagate with supersonic velocity. Developed for use in mining, quarrying, and construction, high explosives were, by their nature, obviously slated for importance in warfare.

A peaceful development that proved a significant influence in World War I was the discovery by Fritz Haber, in Germany in 1912, of a solution to the old problem of obtaining plentiful nitrogen compounds inexpensively. Nitrates obtained by the Haber process were quickly turned to the manufacture of gunpowder. Germany had met this elementary wartime need by utilizing nitrogen obtained from guano, which came chiefly from South America, but access was disrupted early in the war by the British naval blockade.

To those who would emphasize the differences between peaceful and military uses of sciences, it might be well to point out that the Haber process, besides helping to prolong the catastrophe of World War I, served greatly for good. From the start Haber had made, the Kellogg Company in the United States developed, in the 1960s, techniques for producing ammonia and converting it cheaply, effectively, and on a large scale into fertilizers. The needs of a rapidly expanding population could not have been met without such mass production of inexpensive fertilizers.

A similar pattern has been repeated again and again in more recent applications of chemistry. Nylon, for example, developed as an inexpensive substitute for silk, went to war in parachutes. Germany met a wartime gasoline shortage by developing the Lurgi process for coal gasification and liquefaction, which produced a petroleum-like fuel. Cut off from natural rubber supplies in World War II, the United States developed artificial rubber. The contrast is remarkable between the past stories of success and our present inability to solve the energy problem during a period of several years.

Nuclear Weapons

Nuclear weapons inspire awe, fear, anxiety. Nuclear weapons, nonetheless, are among today's realities. Good sense dictates at least a modicum of fear of any weapon, a fear customarily identified as caution. But the fear of nuclear weapons, already great, is exacerbated by general lack of knowledge about them.

Obtaining information about nuclear weapons is hard for most people. Facts seem to be tangled among dark threats of ultimate destruction; our innate distrust of the unknown interferes with our ability to comprehend; respected voices are raised, but often their words conflict. Had we succeeded in ending World War II with a mere demonstration of an atomic bomb, without killing many thousands of civilians, relevant questions could now be discussed with more clarity.

Nuclear explosives produce four effects: heat, shock, prompt radiation, and fallout. For big strategic weapons the effects of shock and heat are most important. Prompt radiation, most of which is delivered in a fraction of a second and ceases within minutes, acts only at the short range, where destruction is total in any case. Fallout is more widespread, but it claims fewer victims.

The damage to Hiroshima, not worse in overall destructive effects than that to some other cities such as Dresden, Hamburg, or Tokyo, was particularly significant because it came from a single bomb. That bomb's intense heat burned people who were more than two miles from the point of explosion. Heat was followed swiftly by a shock wave that flattened buildings all over the city. A fire storm quickly ensued—spontaneous conflagrations from the bomb's heat plus thousands of individual fires ignited as the shock wave overturned hibachis filled with glowing coals. Most of Hiroshima's victims died by fire: many by the blast of the bomb, more by the explosion's radiated heat, and even more trapped under collapsing and burning buildings.

In the years after 1945, stories proliferated of an uncontrollable force that could wipe out the world or produce a population of genetic monsters. Fallout and radiation became words common in our lexicon but ill defined in our minds. Today, after 35 years, nuclear after-effects can be evaluated. Major surveys and studies, carried out jointly by the Japanese and U.S. goverments, were started between 1947 and 1950 to determine genetic as well as bodily effects of the bomb. A summary of the studies states: "Thus far, there is no evidence of genetic changes attributable to the A-bombs."[5]

The studies, on the other hand, do indicate certain delayed effects of ionizing radiation. Significantly increased incidence among survivors of certain cancers, notably leukemia, correlates with the amount of exposure. In the human lifespan the fetus is the most vulnerable to radiation damage, and effects are most pronounced in children whose mothers were in their first eighteen weeks of pregnancy at the time of the Hiroshima bombing: their mortality rate, especially as infants, increased with the intensity of the mother's exposure to radiation. But no increase of inheritable genetic changes or increased congenital malformations have been detected among offspring of survivors.

Damage from nuclear weapons is severe and should not be underestimated. Doomsday prophecies, however, are unfounded.

Work with atomic fusion followed logically after the fission bomb. Atomic energy is based on the release of energy that accompanies rearrangement of the building blocks of nuclei. Fission releases the energy in big, heavily charged nuclei; among the lighter nuclei, energy is released by fusion. The fusion process is the basis for the hydrogen bomb. Some work on the hydrogen bomb concept had been done during World War II but was abandoned in the United States after the war's end. But a pronouncement by Stalin showed that Russia intended to develop everything the United States had—and more.

It was generally believed that, having produced the atomic bomb, the

United States should relax, that American weapons superiority was assured forever. Suddenly, only four years later, Russia had the atomic bomb. The existence of atomic bombs meant that oceans were no longer significant barriers. An intercontinental attack could become real, swift, and terrible—the most important of these truths being that the action of war could be immensely accelerated. No longer was the United States in the position in which it had found itself throughout its history, with time and distance in its favor. By September 1949 technology had developed to the point that the United States was effectively no more isolated than Poland had been at the start of World War II.

Reasons for the United States to delay its fusion development no longer seemed valid. A bitter debate ensued, however, over the development of a new and bigger bomb. In January 1950 President Truman made the decision to go ahead, but considerable opposition to actual development and implementation continued. Coupled with the Oppenheimer controversy, the opposition caused a deep and lasting alienation of much of the scientific community from work for national defense.

One positive effect of the hydrogen bomb debate was the establishment, in addition to Los Alamos, of a second weapons laboratory, in Livermore, California. As a consequence of stimulating competition and mutual checking between the two laboratories, both fission and fusion weapons developed rapidly. Soon they were adapted not only for aircraft-borne bombs but also for explosives carried by rockets that could be fired either from American land-based sites or from nuclear-powered submarines. Thus, in the 1950s, the United States established a truly formidable force that made effective retaliation certain.

Near the end of President Eisenhower's administration, an attempt was made to limit further nuclear arms development by prohibiting the testing of such weapons. A moratorium was entered into, a "gentlemen's agreement" whereby Russia and the United States concurred that nuclear testing be halted until further notice. The moratorium ended abruptly when, upon a two-day notice given by Premier Khrushchev, Russia resumed testing in 1961 with two highly successful test series. The United States hastily put together one test series. Some analysts are convinced that the balance of nuclear power was tipped in favor of Russia at that time.

A comparison of those particular tests by the two countries is still prohibited in the United States today by security laws. It seems peculiar that rules of secrecy will not permit the American people to know the facts that lead analysts to their conclusions.

Following the 1961 tests there were vigorous negotiations to prohibit further nuclear testing. Test ban proponents claimed that fallout was assuming dangerous levels. A second argument in favor of a test ban was our continued assumption that we were ahead of the Russians, leading to the belief that by prohibiting tests we could freeze Russia in an inferior position. The truth seems to have been the opposite—that we were the ones frozen in an inferior position—although it was not so obvious then as it is today.

The third and perhaps most powerful argument for entering into a test ban agreement was that in so doing we would somehow slow down the arms race. But such an agreement is a symbolic act through which a nation, instead of really decreasing the probability of war, tries to convince itself that something has been achieved toward security.

What actually occurred was that nuclear testing in the atmosphere was banned. The consequences of that ban were not fully foreseen. Great ingenuity was shown in performing tests underground. When testing had gone on in the atmosphere, the products of explosions dispersed; they could be collected, and they yielded information about the nuclear activities of any country. Once testing was limited to underground, this source of information was lost.

The present state of nuclear weaponry is very different from what the majority of the people believe it to be. It is generally held that both the United States and Russia have an "overkill" potential. For Russia this may well be true, but it is not so for the United States. The Russians have placed great and increasing emphasis on civil defense. Should the international situation become tense, they are prepared to evacuate their cities, removing civilians at a time of the government's choosing. They have established secure food storage; they have prepared shelters for the portion of the population that would remain in cities. They could launch an attack feeling secure against ravages from retaliatory bombings. The United States has done virtually nothing toward effective civil defense.

Our country may find itself in the situation where it has to give in to Russian demands or face the end of the United States. Our retaliation, should it be delivered, would damage Russia's population less than did World War II. Furthermore, Russia could defeat the United States with only a fraction of its nuclear weapons. With the rest it could coerce whatever peoples it chose and force them to deliver machinery, goods, or labor.

Official Russian policy proclaims that they will win a nuclear exchange. Today this statement may or may not be justified. But, extrapolating past trends, it is apt to become true. The men in the Kremlin do not like to take risks. However, the time seems to be approaching when Russians will be able to count on success in a nuclear exchange. Our own plans for the 1980s must seek to prevent this awesome possibility.

Radiation: Radar, Lasers, and Beyond

Radiation—energy radiated in the form of waves or particles—was identified in our century as a tool of humankind. Radio telegraphy and broadcasting had widespread peaceful applications before World War I. In that conflict, along with other methods of transmitting messages, they were adapted to military needs.

The great potential of electromagnetic waves was recognized by British scientists in 1935 when, forseeing a Nazi air attack, they worked to develop and refine radar, the shortwave radiation that could detect and track airplanes. Their product was a powerful instrument of warfare, essential in winning the Battle of Britain. It followed ships at sea, even the periscopes of submarines; later it was used in large-scale bombing raids on Germany.

Radar developed in Germany was, at least initially, superior to that of the British, a fact that is not generally known. In Germany, however, liaison was poor between technical people and the military command. Furthermore, the Germans failed to develop the ingenious apparatus that emitted shortwave radar and was small enough to be carried in airplanes.

Radar was emitted and received during and after World War II in the parabolic dishes that can still be seen rotating near airports. These dishes, unlike reflectors of light, need not be solid; a metal framework suffices, so long as its interstices are smaller than the wavelength it handles. Developed as a decisive instrument of war, radar has proved a benefit to civilian aircraft navigation and safety.

Phased-array radar, a new, more powerful type, was deployed after World War II. In phased array, radar beams are emitted from a multiplicity of relatively small sources. Appropriate timing of the emissions, with accuracy of a small fraction of a micro-second, insures that all waves emitted will reinforce each other in a selected direction, while canceling in other directions. It is thus possible to obtain much more powerful radar beams than through older techniques; also the beam is redirected electronically, increasing speed and flexibility. Furthermore, the equipment is "harder," meaning that it will stand up better under a bombing attack than the older radar dish. In modern air defense and in any possible missile defense, phased-array radar plays a crucial role.

The wavelength of radar is shorter than that of radio; the wavelength of lasers is far shorter still. Lasers consist of extremely intense and well-directed light beams. When appropriately modulated, they can be used to transmit information at an astounding speed. Indeed, each separate wavelength can carry a "yes" or "no" message by being "on" or "off," therefore signals can be sent as fast as wavelength follows wavelength. The speed with radar is a billion signals per second; with lasers it can be many trillions.

Microwaves, extra-short-length radar, can penetrate heavy clouds that block lasers. Thus it is possible to maintain two-way communication between an operator and remotely guided vehicles by means of a reliable system of electronics available in lightweight, small packages.

During World War II the Japanese tried to produce a death-ray based on radar, a premature attempt that was unsuccessful. In laser beams today energy can be so concentrated as to destroy structures, particularly light structures such as airplanes or satellites.

It is also possible to use particle beams for destructive purposes. Particle beams can consist of electrons or of atomic nuclei, especially protons (the nuclei of the lightest of atoms, hydrogen). There are claims that particle beams are effective over vast distances, but such claims seem premature. There is real hope, however, that particle beams could aid in defense against incoming missiles that are as close as a few miles.

Of the various radiation forms, lasers have been the most flexible. Even prior to their military applications they had a growing peaceful potential. Laser applications range from intricate eye surgery, through replacement of telephone wires by glass fibers guiding laser light from speaker to receiver, to use of lasers in the controlled fusion of atomic nuclei. It should be re-emphasized that development of a variety of lasers, differing in frequencies, power levels, pulse lengths, and exquisitely precise directionality, can serve equally well to destroy an attacker or to measure the distance from the earth to the moon.

A PROGRAM FOR THE 1980s

Causes of a Hidden Imbalance

Charles de Gaulle wrote in 1932 that, following a conflagration such as the world had never experienced, its peoples were in a mood to detest the very thought of war. His statement, unfortunately, did not apply to rulers like Hitler or Stalin. After 1933 Hitler quickly rearmed his country; Stalin acted similarly in 1945. In both cases, the great flexibility of modern technology accelerated the shift in power.

Rearmament continued in Russia after Stalin's death. It is still progressing, and the end is not in sight. An even greater danger is that Russian strength is underestimated in the United States. There are several reasons for this, and they must be understood; otherwise, it is impossible to realize the threat of Russian military supremacy.

In 1945 American military power stood unchallenged. Victorious in World War I and World War II, we suffered losses that were great but that were incomparably less than the havoc wrought by those wars upon the other combatants. Russia in particular emerged with a strong army, but it had tasted defeat, and that memory would not be forgotten. It is not surprising that the USSR continued to place great emphasis on military preparedness. The decision to arm was made by Russia's leaders; its people had neither the means nor even a strong wish to oppose that decision.

To the American observer, Russian civilian development appears slow and inefficient. (Even so, the Russian standard of living has greatly improved in the past 35 years.) It is hard to believe that the Russians have done much better in military matters than in the civilian sector. An observer cannot adequately compare the two because one is basically open and the other strictly secret. Our military intelligence has obtained glimpses of great progress in Russian weaponry, but this information is not available to the American public. It sometimes seems that we keep Russian secrets better than we keep our own. Furthermore, the false alarm of a "missile gap" in 1960 made our intelligence overcautious about crediting the Russians with great and growing military strength.

It is also important to understand what we can and what we cannot find out about Russia's secret weapons. The Communists have a truly closed society. We obtain fragments of information, but we are in difficulty when we try to get a comprehensive view. The indications we obtained about the Russians' progress probably produced a valid picture when they were catching up with the free world and to some extent following the technological trail we had blazed. But in recent years we find more and more developments, or rather indications of developments, that we do not understand. All too easily we explain them away with: "The Russians are crazy." We forget that novel technology nearly always appears crazy.

We in America want to maintain the status quo. The Russian leadership has a mission. In this situation, the natural inertia of a large military organization hampers progress on our side of the Atlantic, while in Russia, military matters retain the highest priority.

Technology is all-important in modern warfare. It is axiomatic that America is pre-eminent in technology. Does this axiom still hold at a time when many of our young people consider technology irrelevant?

But the main reason the present imbalance is hidden lies in man's reluctance to believe negative news about himself or his own. We resist the suggestion of inferiority.

The imbalance can be overcome if we have some time, considerable ingenuity and, above all, determination. Development of the imbalance has been described earlier in this essay; in the portion following, suggestions are made for dealing with this difficult situation.

Secrecy

Shortly after the end of World War II, Niels Bohr, the founder of atomic theory, made a statement I shall never forget: "In the coming cold war it would be reasonable to expect each side to use the weapons it can handle best. The best weapon of a dictatorship is secrecy, but the best weapon of a democracy should be the weapon of openness." In my opinion openness is a necessary weapon. Without it, we shall not realize our danger until it is too late. If we use it with care and with reason, we can rally American defenses, unite the free world, and preserve peace.

Secrecy, unfortunately, is habit-forming. We can scarcely imagine how we could get along without it. We should remember, however, that secrecy was actually of greater advantage to us when we had secrets to keep. Today, when Russia almost certainly knows all of our technical military secrets and is apt to have many secrets of which we are ignorant, secrecy has to be re-evaluated.

Of course, if we reveal our secrets the Russians will not reciprocate. Are we not, therefore, speaking of unilateral disarmament? The answer is: in our hands secrecy boomerangs—instead of hurting our opponents with it we hurt ourselves.

Let us compare two developments: nuclear weapons and electronic computers. In the former we had stringent government secrecy; the Russians quickly overtook us and have probably passed us by. In the latter we are still the leaders. The Russians may take as much as ten years to catch up. If we continue to work vigorously, we are apt to stay ahead indefinitely. Part of the explanation for this is that our consumer-oriented society favors computer development. But another reason is that the unhampered flow of information has generated new ideas in computer research and accelerated their implementation, whereas in our nuclear development, secrecy tied our own hands.

The boomerang of secrecy is also at work in our relations with our allies. Annoyance about secrecy was a strong motive for de Gaulle to terminate full French participation in NATO.

Perhaps the main reason for eliminating secrecy is that most of secrecy is make-believe. It does not work in a free society. It affects our own law-abiding scientists, even deters them from participating in the development of weapons. But secrecy puts almost no obstacle in the way of foreign governments determined to learn or rediscover the secret. To put it simply: a secret known to a million people is, in fact, no longer a secret. In Russia's closed society secrets can be kept longer and more effectively.

When arguing for openness in technology, I do not mean to actually throw open our laboratories to all foreign observers. The type of secrecy practiced by America's private companies does work. But the principles of discoveries should be open. There are no secret formulas, though the alchemists sought them. (The one fact the alchemists proved was that science and secrecy are hardly compatible—except, perhaps, under the iron heel of a dictator.) What can be kept secret, at least for some time, is what we call "know-how."

It would not be realistic to propose that secrecy should be abolished forthwith. We can, however, greatly reduce it. Today we are smothered by millions of "classified" documents. A determined move toward openness is firmly recommended. Its purpose is threefold: to stimulate research on military technology within our scientific community; to promote cooperation with our allies in the same field; and to inform the American public of the true state of military preparedness in the West, in the East, and elsewhere, so far as such knowledge is available to our intelligence.

A more detailed proposal is difficult to make, especially since we want it to be realistic and acceptable. Yet such a proposal is made here, both to give an example of what could happen and to begin a concrete discussion on this important topic. We could continue "classification" of documents and, therefore, secrecy in its present form. But we could impose the condition that all classified documents should be published within two years of issue. That would fully preserve tactical secrecy but exclude strategic and technological secrecy. A small number of documents might need to be kept secret for longer periods, but in those cases a few highly responsible persons would have to certify, year by year, that continued secrecy is required. The rule should be: when in doubt, declassify. Today the opposite is practiced.

We could go further, and we should persuade our friends and allies to follow our example. Our goal must be to make the free world an open world. These actions, if successful, will lead to military strength. Cooperation in the sharing of know-how, and extension of the "most favored nation status," should in all respects be restricted to those countries that open up. The existence of secrecy can not be kept a secret.

All this could bring about military strength and increased security in the short term. In the long term, even the Russians might join the open world when they perceive the practical advantages. And an open world would not be so very different from a free world. Admittedly, these are dreams. But they could inspire concrete and detailed proposals that will allow us to escape from the snare of secrecy in which we have been caught for too many years.

Military Research

We are not engaged in an arms race, but rather in a race of technology. The former emphasizes the quantity of arms, the latter their quality and particularly the element of novelty. Comparisons of quality would be difficult even in the absence of secrecy. Since secrecy prevails, and since it is effective on the side of Russia, comparison becomes virtually impossible.

It is widely believed in this country that American and Russian military preparedness are roughly equivalent. In greater detail, it is stated that Russia is ahead in quantity and we are ahead in quality. It is somewhat disquieting that the Russian advantage lies in the area that is more easily checked, while we are supposedly ahead in those respects where verification is most difficult.

One individual familiar with military technology and with intelligence, Dr. John S. Foster, Jr. (director of defense research and engineering for the Department of Defense for seven years, under both Republican and Democratic administrations), estimates that in 1960 the United States and the USSR spent equal percentages of their military budgets on research and development, while in 1974 that percentage was three times as high in Russia as in the United States. The quality of future weapons depends more on research and development than on any other factor; the obvious recommendation is that we should spend more on it. Today we spend approximately 10 percent, so this recommendation does not seem too difficult to implement.

Actually, more money is necessary but not sufficient. First, a rapid budget increase is apt to lead to low efficiency. The change must be gradual. Second, more money can be spent well only if more scientific talent is available. Military research is unpopular among scientists, partly on account of secrecy. (In regimented Russia, where scientists are not free to choose their careers, this latter argument is less valid. Actually, the Russian leadership seems wise enough to add inducement to coercion.) This is one reason why we should abandon or at least reduce secrecy.

But our scientists will not turn to national defense unless they perceive an actual danger to the United States. A danger was perceived in 1939, only two years before Pearl Harbor. It is vital that scientists should perceive the danger now, before it is too late. What is at stake is not only the prevention of defeat, but the prevention of war. Nevertheless, convincing the American scientific community that military research is necessary is a most difficult undertaking.

Defense Against Nuclear Weapons

What have Russia, China, Sweden, and Switzerland in common? They all have placed great emphasis on civil defense as a countermeasure to nuclear attack. Anyone who seeks reliable and complete defense against nuclear attack will search in vain, but the two large totalitarian countries and the two small free countries just mentioned have found it worthwhile to take some precautionary measures.

In the United States a counterforce strategy, presently favored by many, is supposed to destroy enemy military targets, including nuclear weapons before they are launched. Implementation of this strategy would be exceedingly difficult, particularly if our nuclear forces are numerically inferior to those of, say, the Russians. Furthermore, our bombs would be apt to hit empty Russian silos after the missiles had left. Worst of all, preparation for a counterforce strategy could dangerously resemble the preparation for a first strike.

The idea of deterrence by retaliation is generally accepted, and I believe it should be continued. We actually have deployed a triad—bombers, submarines that carry nuclear rockets, and land-based nuclear missiles—in the expectation that at least one of these instruments of retaliation will work. Recognized Russian superiority in missiles delivered by rockets has led to discussions about insuring the continued effectiveness of our land-based missiles.

One suggested solution is to "fire on warning." This means that when we have clear indication of a massive Russian attack, we launch our rockets before the Russian missiles arrive. This is a particularly unfortunate proposal. It is conceivable that the alarm could be false. There might even be situations in which the Russians would simulate an attack to draw our fire. Above all, to fire on warning is apt to destabilize a situation that already possesses much too little stability.

Our strategic airplanes are apt to run into stiff defense. By comparison, we have practically no air defense. In view of the proliferation of Russian "Backfire" bombers (which can take off from Russia, deliver their bombs, and land in Cuba), we should re-establish effective air defense. Finally, our missile-submarines should be deployed under the arctic ice, where they are hard to detect and close to their targets. This could delay retaliation but would make it more certain.

An alternative method of retaliation, the counterpopulation strike, is obviously unacceptable. The only choice remaining is the "countervalue" option—to retaliate by destroying Russian industry after the people have left, a plan made all the easier by concrete USSR preparations for evacuation.

In the late 1960s and early 1970s anti-ballistic missiles (ABMs) were discussed, and the United States began to deploy them. Under SALT I, deployment of ABMs was limited to two locations, both for the United States and for Soviet Russia. Research on ABMs was not prohibited and is difficult to verify. Today the United States has abandoned ABM deployment, together with research on improved, more effective, and less expensive active defense systems. Russia continues to maintain ABM defenses around Moscow, and we have reason to believe that research continues.

It is strongly recommended that the United States place emphasis on this type of active defense; progress along these lines would be crucial. The strength of our electronics industry raises the hope that ABMs could become truly effective. A vigorous research program on ABMs would not be too costly, since research is generally cheap compared to deployment.

If we took civil defense measures, including counterevacuation, Russia would not be able to count on a complete and early victory. This may be the best strategy to deter aggression, particularly in view of the Russian leadership's tradition of conservative planning. Adventurism is a crime in the communist vocabulary. Plans for evacuation need not be expensive, and indeed, such plans are needed in order to reduce casualties from natural disasters. People are routinely evacuated when there is danger from flood or hurricane, both of which have become more predictable. In the future, even large earthquakes might be forecast in a reliable manner. The new Federal Emergency Management Agency, which has no significant budget thus far, has been set up for the twofold purpose of disaster preparedness and civil defense. If we spent $1 billion per year on it, it could pay for itself in connection with natural disasters. Flexible management, with no sharp boundaries between peacetime disasters and war, could be advantageous.

SALT I, II, III, ∞

(*The last sign in the heading is the mathematician's symbol for infinity*)

"Our troubles are due to modern weapons. Let us prohibit them."

"Death is caused by the passage of time. Let us stop time."

These two proposals are equally realistic. Yet the first one was the basis for U.S. policy for more than twenty years. If it continues to be our policy in the 1980s, the consequence may be that in the 1990s we shall have lost our freedom to make policy decisions.

We started serious negotiations with the Russians with the Baruch Plan, which would have effectively established international control over nuclear energy. The plan came many months after Hiroshima, and it came too late. By the time we submitted it, our wartime armies had been disbanded and lend-lease to Russia had been stopped. First we threw away our stick and carrot, then we told the mule to move.

Resuming talks about disarmament, we negotiated from a position of strength; today we continue to negotiate, but from a position of weakness. The negotiation process itself may have contributed to our present inferiority. At any rate, does it pay to continue negotiations with a country that holds the upper hand and is determined to extend its power or its ideological beliefs, which are two faces of one political fact: Russia and communism?

One past treaty, SALT I, had some advantages for the United States. We promised not to build the weapons for which Congress (in 1972) would not have appropriated the necessary funds. Also, SALT I revealed a fact that the American people needed to know: that Russia was ahead of us in large missiles carrying nuclear explosives.

With SALT II, the burning issue at this writing, the situation is reversed. Congress and the people are beginning to realize the need for better defense. SALT II is now signed. If it is ratified, whatever sense of urgency now exists is apt to be lost. The need is to wake up—but instead we are offered a tranquilizer.

Several details of SALT II are dangerous in a specific sense. One is connected with the cruise missile, the other with verification. The cruise missile is a first step toward an important fighting arm of the future: the remotely piloted vehicle, a topic to which we shall return. This line of development holds some promise for an American effort to catch up militarily with Russia. In the SALT II negotiations, the emissaries of the Kremlin placed great emphasis on restricting the cruise missile. Additionally, efforts were made to prevent cooperation with our allies, or even exchange of information, on the cruise missile. To drive a wedge between NATO partners is a prime goal of Russian policy.

The desire for verification led to the logical conclusion that only limitations that can indeed be verified should be in the treaty. Consequently, the limitation was placed on the number of silos, rather than rockets. If missiles, together with relatively simple ejection equipment, were secretly stored in warehouses, in numbers greatly exceeding the number of silos permitted, the spirit of the treaty would certainly be violated. Even if we tried to prohibit such deployment, verification would be all but impossible.

Should we, therefore, avoid all future treaties? That is not my recommendation. We should avoid treaties with prohibition as their substance. Such treaties breed distrust; they automatically serve the purposes of a closed society and place an open society at a disadvantage.

We should seek treaties that promote cooperation. Our treaty with China is such a treaty (excepting the regrettable negative clauses relating to Taiwan). With Russia we could, for instance, agree to develop jointly the peaceful uses of nuclear explosives. Engineering, production, and execution would all be jointly undertaken. Provision should be made for other nations to participate in this cooperation.

When carried out in common, success due to contributions from all participants is a hopeful approach to peace. Indeed, the main point in peace is not absence of arms (which can be hidden), but the development of positive personal and national relationships.

Proliferation

A discussion of negotiations on nuclear weapons would be incomplete without considering the nightmare of nuclear proliferation. It is fortunate that today the "nuclear club" has only six members.

We have tried to prevent proliferation by treaty; but it is not clear that this treaty will be more effective than the Kellogg-Briand Pact that, in 1928, outlawed war. For one thing, many states important to the success of the nonproliferation treaty have not signed or ratified it.

The Carter administration has stopped work on nuclear reprocessing plants in the United States, hoping the action will be imitated abroad and that consequently less plutonium, an important material for nuclear explosives, will become available abroad. In fact, that action has stimulated the planning and building of reprocessing plants abroad, accelerating proliferation. Furthermore, the building of small reactors, to which it is easy to attach small reprocessing plants, remains unlimited and unsupervised. Finally, nuclear explosives can be made with the light isotope of uranium instead of plutonium, and each year sees more publication of methods for inexpensively separating the relevant isotopes. South Africa, which feels abandoned by its natural allies, will almost certainly use its fully developed isotope-separation facilities to produce atomic explosives.

Russia prevents nuclear proliferation in its own sphere of influence by exercising complete dominance. We could slow down the spread of nuclear weapons in the free world through generous cooperation. South Africa could use nuclear explosives to destroy entry points through which arms deliveries could be made in support of an attack on it. If South Africa could buy conventional arms from us, it could be persuaded against developing nuclear weapons. Because of friendship with the United States, Taiwan has abstained from development of nuclear weapons, which it could use against an invasion from the mainland. Now it is highly likely that Taiwan, no longer able to count on American help, will soon acquire nuclear arms.

Another way in which the Carter administration is attempting to prevent the spread of nuclear weapons is through a comprehensive ban on nuclear testing. Even if such a ban came into being, it would not prevent states from developing and stockpiling untested weapons. More dangerous than nuclear weapons is their secret existence in various countries. To the element of destruction would then be added the element of surprise. Today relatively primitive, but nonetheless highly effective, nuclear weapons can be produced with ease by governments (though certainly not by small terrorist groups). Testing is needed for the refinement of nuclear weapons and for the functioning of the more advanced ones. A ban on testing would not prevent the proliferation of nuclear explosives. Instead, it would deprive us of the knowledge that nuclear proliferation has occurred.

It would be a great help if, after reducing or eliminating the main functions of secrecy in our own country, we could induce our allies to open up. In that event, nuclear proliferation could not occur in the free world without general knowledge of the fact. Governments then could be more easily dissuaded from establishing nuclear arsenals.

We are trying to accomplish the right purpose by the wrong means. It will prove easier to reduce the motivation for developing nuclear weapons than to impose prohibitions—for all of the latter can be circumvented. Establishing a feeling of partnership in the free world remains the best way to prevent nuclear proliferation, as well as numerous other dangers.

NATO: A Step Toward Unity

I vividly remember the time when unity of Europe seemed a beautiful, impossible dream. In a way, this dream has now come true. National hatreds, rooted in cruel conflicts of centuries, are no more—with one exception. The exception proves the rule, or, more precisely, puts the rule to a difficult and valid test. The Russians do not hate their fellow Europeans; it is clearly their totalitarian government that prevents peace and unity.*

We have come a long way. In 1914 the virus of nationalism infected almost all of Europe; in 1939, despite the heritage of hatred represented by Hitler, all of Europe, including Germany, was plunged into gloom at

*I would like to forget another exception, the conflict between Greece and Turkey.

the outbreak of war. Now in NATO and the European Common Market, emotional conflicts have dwindled to a scale scarcely greater than is found among the states of our union. The way to this limited peace was long and terrible. But we are not at the end of the road.

NATO must be defended. Finlandization of Europe must be avoided. In this regard the United States has behaved without fanfare, committing some mistakes, but still establishing a good record. Important measures have been taken toward distributing the responsibility for the common defense more equitably. Recent progress has been made to spread arms production among more of the allies and to make more equipment interchangeable. Credit for this progress goes to many, among them, certainly, U.S. Secretary of Defense Harold Brown and NATO Commander Alexander Haig. These policies should be continued and perfected. The reduction and where possible elimination of secrecy could and should bring the Atlantic allies more closely together.

The Russians have not forgotten the blitzkrieg, or their reaction to it. They have built up a formidable armament of tanks, rockets of all sizes, and other instruments of invasion. We should counter this by unity and ingenuity. The situation has one hopeful aspect: the Warsaw Pact includes one hundred million people who are the last colonial subjects on our globe. If Western Europe is invaded and holds out under attack, the Russian colonial empire will crack. If we plan appropriately, the danger of rebellion in Eastern Europe may well serve as a deterrent to Russian invasion.

Can Western Europe resist? How can it resist? Answers are complex, but three elements of defense can be emphasized. First, inconspicuous but strong defenses in depth are desirable. The Maginot Line itself was not a mistake, but reliance on it alone was. Defense in depth must be supplemented by mobile forces and by the home defense of each city. Second: among the modern instruments of war, the Russians rely far more than we do on rockets. Rockets, with good guidance, are more effective than the artillery still favored by our conservative military establishment.

Third, and most important, we must come to grips with the proper use of nuclear weapons. In this regard the United States has chosen an easy but dangerous road: procrastination.

Genuine need exists for the development of small nuclear explosives—that is, for tactical nuclear weapons. Work in this field has been neglected in the United States for the last two decades. Of the four effects of nuclear explosives—heat, shock, prompt radiation, and fallout—prompt radiation alone is practically the only significant effect from small nuclear explosions of a kiloton or less. This holds for those explosives that have become known as neutron bombs.

The neutron bomb, actually a nuclear warhead, is essentially a small, enhanced radiation weapon designed to be exploded a few hundred feet above the surface of the earth. Its shock, heat, or fallout on the ground are negligible; virtually all structures remain undamaged by it. People in the open within a radius of a thousand feet would be killed by its prompt radiation, which then rapidly dissipates. If the nuclear warhead were aimed at troops, planes, or tanks whose armor does not provide protection, those military forces would be destroyed. Noncombatants could be safe at a distance of half a mile or more, or in a deep cellar. The dreadful side effects of war that threaten civilians are less from the nuclear warhead than from other methods of defense. For example, neutron bombs are less destructive for the defended and more effective against the invader than an artillery barrage. Small nuclear warheads could blunt or stop massive aggression against Western Europe by strong forces of the Warsaw Pact, which consist chiefly of Russian armament and Russian manpower. Nuclear mines of various yields could be deployed at bottlenecks of expected invasion. Evacuation should, of course, take place before they are used. Here cleanliness (minimal residual radioactivity) is desirable and also attainable.

To inhibit escalation we should announce that we would never be the first to use any atomic weapons, including neutron bombs, except within an invaded territory. An aggressor would then have to make the choice between marching against a nuclear defense without using nuclear weapons, or employing nuclear weapons in his attack. In the latter event, nuclear retaliation against the aggressor's territory would ensue. But, in the dreadful event of a third all-European war, such retaliation should avoid inflicting damage on the civilian population of Eastern Europe. In case of Russian aggression those peoples will prove to be our allies; the Russian armies could suffer in Eastern Europe as the Nazi invaders suffered from the resistance movement in Russia.

Ultimately, the NATO alliance should be extended. But the important problem for the 1980s is to save Europe. This can be done. If the alliance is strong, the attack on it will never materialize. The way will then be open for extending the area of peace, freedom, and security by gradual and peaceful means.

CCC: Communication, Command, and Control

Our policy of deterring a nuclear attack is based on the assumption that our counterblow would cause unacceptable damage. This policy has a weak point. The United States cannot use nuclear weapons except by order of the president (or his authorized representative). Such an order will not be issued except for the gravest reasons. On the other hand, the first blow of the enemy could destroy our central command authority or its means of communications.

There is a technical way out of this difficulty. We could and should adopt it, yet we have not done so. Nuclear weapons can be rendered unusable by certain devices governed by reliable electronic signals. The president should be in control of these signals. Arrangements can be made (using the difficult art of electronics and computers) so that only the president or his representative can issue these signals for all American nuclear weapons. When presidential power is broken by force of arms, he can no longer issue the signals. The nuclear system "fails armed," which means that when the signals do not arrive, the weapons can be launched.

The system as envisioned would actually move gradually. In a situation where the president can no longer act, lower-ranking military commanders automatically take over his responsibility of restraint; but each commander can restrain only part of the force. If he, in turn, is put out of action, the authority descends and becomes even more fragmented. Since a general plan will have been drawn up, this is not a serious disadvantage.

One advantage of this system would be that it would be in the interest of an aggressor not to interfere with it. As long as the president can act, he can negotiate. If he is killed, with this system, retaliation becomes more certain.

In some appropriate form the system can and should be extended to NATO. Nuclear weapons, including small tactical ones, can be distributed, ready for action. But, according to one proposal, the weapons cannot be used unless both the NATO commander-in-chief and the head of the invaded country lift the restraint. Again, in case of incapacity, the decision descends to lower echelons. In this way the needed military action, both responsible and reliable, could be assured.

It should be emphasized that years of careful work have gone into development of the system. It has many variants, and a well-considered choice will have to be made from among them.

At any rate, CCC is today the Achilles' heel of our military force. This vulnerability must be eliminated, either as described above or in some other manner.

The Role of Space

Space already plays important roles in military affairs, particularly in communications and intelligence gathering. Both of these functions are apt to become increasingly important in the future. An extension of our information gathering, including continuous surveillance of the oceans, should have high priority.

The most disturbing circumstance about our use of satellites is that the Russians are developing systems to destroy them. It probably would not, and in fact should not, be reason for us to go to war if they deprived us of our satellite "eyes." Yet we could be left in a dangerous situation, should war follow within a few weeks or a few months. We have, therefore, ample reason for making adequate preparation to ensure our continued presence in space.

This can be done in two ways. One is to increase our ability to launch satellites of all needed varieties within a short time. The other is to provide decoys in space, thereby multiplying the number of targets the Russians would have to knock out. A combination of these two procedures could, indeed, prevent the Russians from ever attempting to eliminate our space vehicles. A third possibility is to prepare retaliation against such a Russian move by destroying their space vehicles. But, at least in regard to the important item of information gathering, the Russians rely on their spacecraft less than we do; therefore emphasis on the first two approaches is recommended.

At considerable cost we have developed an admirable instrument: the space shuttle. Making full use of the facilities developed, we could launch 70 shuttles per year. If such great numbers were deployed, the cost per firing would be moderate (approximately $20 million). Unfortunately, we are planning to launch no more than a half dozen shuttles per year. This is a waste of invested capital. If we launched more shuttles, possibly in cooperation with other countries, particularly our allies, a great variety of additional uses for shuttles would emerge. One of the most important consequences of numerous launchings would be that we could promptly replace instruments that the Russians might destroy.

In preparing decoys for space vehicles, the main objective would be for the decoys to look like functional space vehicles. On the whole, this is not too difficult. Usually the main problem with a decoy is its mass. In order for a decoy to be inexpensive it must be light, but usually the light weight gives it away—for instance, in meeting air resistance, a lighter vehicle is more easily slowed down. Exceedingly little air resistance is encountered by space vehicles. Therefore, lightweight decoys for space vehicles are more feasible than decoys for almost any other application.

There can be no question that the military use of spacecraft will continue to increase. There are many possible extensions of present uses, for example, as effective aids in navigation, and in the prompt reporting on battle situations and distribution of enemy forces. As we shall see, spacecraft can serve importantly in connection with remotely controlled vehicles. Spacecraft could emit laser beams or be used to carry nuclear weapons. In the latter case, it is less likely that these weapons would ultimately be used near the ground, which requires expensive deorbiting. More likely—by use of lasers, other forms of beams, or nuclear weapons—spacecraft will be equipped to destroy enemy spacecraft. In addition, nuclear weapons exploded in a spacecraft would have a great influence on the high layers of the atmosphere, especially the ionosphere. Thus, normal means of communication would be disrupted.

The development of technology is hard to predict, particularly in a new field such as the conquest of space. It is a virtual certainty that the military uses of space will be more varied and more ample than we at present imagine. It is, therefore, strongly recommended that the space shuttle program should be fully exploited and that its possible applications to national defense should not be neglected.

RPVs

Remotely piloted vehicles (RPVs) have been mentioned. Radiation, with its continuing refinements, promises sophisticated remote-control weapons. If satellites are used to transmit information, an operator and his weapon could be on different continents; sensory information, pictures, accelerations—anything that can be noticed—could be transmitted from the vehicle to the decision-making operator.

If control is to be exercised over shorter distances, high-flying planes could be used instead of satellites. For these planes, speed may not be so important; it might be more essential to equip them with means of self-defense. Indeed, RPVs could play the role of small fighter planes or small rockets to defeat an attack on the mother ship.

It is probable that these weapons of the future, designed for information gathering, fighting, or bombing, will become smaller, cheaper, more flexible, and more expandable. It is important to note that such weaponry will not necessarily result in greater damage inflicted upon an adversary, but may instead result in damage inflicted where it counts militarily, with minimal injury to noncombatants.

The possibility of RPVs exists for Russia as well as for us. But in this special category, there is one reason why we may be able to outdo the Russian effort by a great margin. That reason is that RPVs require electronics, and in this respect our technology is still superior to that of any other country. Further emphasis on electronics is therefore recommended.

The use of RPVs was first explored by the U.S. Air Force. It can also be applied to small naval vehicles and to small but effective tanks. The cruise missiles developed by the Air Force represent an important step toward RPVs. They must be considered as primitive, however, because they are not under continuing control but, instead, are pre-programed.

An ingenious new airplane design is now in experimental stage. A single wing is used in this design, pivoting at its center at the fuselage. The wing is at right angles to the plane at takeoff and landing, but at high speed the entire wing unit is pivoted; then what appears as the right wing points forward while the left points backward. Peculiarly enough, this asymmetric configuration works. Because the torques cancel at the pivot and effective pivots are easier to design, this compares favorably with present variable-wing planes where the needed pivot is under considerable stress.

This new design has been flown only as a small-scale experimental model and is not yet capable of carrying a man. It could easily be launched as a small RPV that could fly at both subsonic speeds and, with the wing at an angle, at velocities as high as 1.7 times the velocity of sound (roughly 1,000 miles per hour). This plane could also be developed into a full-scale passenger carrier, again demonstrating the close connection between wartime and peaceful technology.

The RPVs, using advanced American electronics, may represent the speediest way to re-establish rough equivalence with Russian military preparedness.

Innovations in the U.S. Navy

It is of the highest importance for the United States and the free world to prevent the developing Russian predominance on the world's oceans. Indeed, we need a navy that can stand up to the threat of nuclear warfare.

Among the innovations that could be considered is that of numerous small U.S. naval bases in the middle of an ocean. With the shift in international balance moving consistently against us, the United States is losing naval bases abroad. Mobile naval bases could be very valuable, and a model for such a base exists. The base would consist of a platform above wave action, supported by hollow buoyant cylinders that reach well below wave action. Such a platform would be stable even in heavy seas. One important but difficult variant would make the whole structure submersible to a shallow depth, so that it could not be observed from space. It would provide room for a significant amount of equipment and military personnel. Though its speed might not exceed five knots, the base would be capable of moving toward areas of threatened conflict.

A mid-ocean naval base would be vulnerable to destruction by nuclear attack, but this is true of any base. Furthermore, the mobile base could be defensively equipped, including anti-ballistic missiles. The supporting buoyant tubes should be shock-resistant (possibly using titanium surrounded by porous shock absorbers). The question of minimum cost and maximum utility needs the greatest attention. The base would supply and repair naval vessels and could launch missiles and play the role of an aircraft carrier. It would unambiguously be under the flag of the United States, moving in international waters.

The mobile base would be only one element in a rather elaborate weapons system. Valuable auxiliary craft would include a large number of small seaworthy ships, most of them submersible, probably carrying few personnel and considerable electronics—though they could carry *no* personnel and only electronics (RPVs). As with other remote-control vehicles, human bodies and brains can remain far from the actual firing line.

Power for the base probably would best come from nuclear means, though some energy could well be derived from wave action. The small craft would probably not be driven by nuclear energy—not that reactors would be too big, but because the small craft would then become too expensive. We must reverse the trend toward fewer and fewer weapons that are ever more valuable and no less vulnerable.

Probably the small craft would be powered by petroleum. But here nuclear energy could also assist, for it would be possible to construct big submarine oil tankers with nuclear propulsion that carry as much as 200,000 tons. These tankers would be difficult to track and, consequently, could supply the mid-sea bases and their small craft. The result would be an active, agile navy with a striking radius up to a thousand miles.

Large submarine tankers would be expensive, but their cost could be offset by their valuable service both in war and in peace. They need not be restricted to carrying oil for the navy; they could carry oil or other supplies to our allies and to our own personnel abroad; able to move under polar icecaps, they could be a link to northern Alaska. The U.S. Navy could support development of vessels that have a dual role since, in an emergency, the vessels would immediately be assigned to the Navy. Freed from the resistance of surface waves, large submarine tankers are capable of great speed, moving much faster than a surface vessel of equivalent capacity and power. For these tankers, as well as for some other submarines, titanium hulls might be considered.

Together the three interrelated components—floating naval bases, fast small vessels, and large supply submarines—would possibly be less expensive, more practical, and more effective than the remarkable ships we have heretofore constructed.

Future Weapons

In thinking about future weapons, most people envision a magnification of existing weapons. This unimaginative view has not been borne out by developments during recent decades in which technology has become ever more important in military affairs.

Because the Hiroshima bomb exceeded the power of the largest high-explosive bomb more than a thousandfold and because, a few years later, the hydrogen bomb increased the yield by an additional factor of one thousand, it was natural for people to conclude that no end to destruction is in sight.

Yet at present the development of large nuclear explosives has reached a point where further increase in size may have no purpose. Too large an explosion would force the atmosphere within a ten-mile radius to disperse into space. Local damage would be enormous, but horizontal propagation into wider areas would be difficult to accomplish. Also, most of the additional radioactivity created in so immense an explosion would leave the earth and the atmosphere. Arguments that much larger explosions may be needed do not seem convincing. Similarly, an extension in the range of particle beams has been widely predicted. But upon careful investigation, this development has proved so difficult technically that it is unpromising.

There is a possibility that chemical and biological warfare may be used in future conflicts. The fact that these forms of warfare have been outlawed may not be meaningful, since verification appears impossible. In the special case of biological warfare, the Soviets are at a disadvantage. Due to Lysenko's initiative, they not only rejected the Mendelian theory of mutations, but they practically exterminated a whole generation of highly able Russian researchers. Yet the effectiveness of biological warfare depends on the study of mutations in micro-organisms. Such research, of course, must be supplemented by investigation of the corresponding immunology.

Problems of verification, plus the close link between research on biological warfare and most beneficial medical research, make practical recommendations exceptionally difficult. My fervent hope would be that, instead of outlawing biological warfare, we outlaw secrecy in biological science. If we can bring about close worldwide cooperation in the arts of healing and preventive medicine, the secret development of biological weapons would become very difficult.

New weapons, however, pose a more general question of utmost difficulty. If one claims to foresee future technologies, one lays claim to equaling the genius of all the outstanding researchers who will work in the foreseeable future. To predict the future is difficult; to predict the technological future is impossible. The one recommendation I can make is that strong support be given equally to research in applied science and to research in pure science, which can become applied in a rapid and unexpected way.

Fortunately, the anti-technological and anti-scientific trend of the 1960s has come to an end, but we have not yet regained the momentum in research for which America was once famous. If the United States and the free world will forge ahead in research, with all its peaceful and military applications, this will be the only defense against surprises that otherwise are apt to destroy our country and the great progess in freedom accomplished in the past several centuries.

Technology: Influence for War or for Peace

The belief is widespread today that modern weapons are vastly more destructive than those of earlier eras. But throughout history the term "ultimate weapon" has been used again and again; just as frequently, that ultimate weapon has been replaced by a new candidate. In reality, the limits of damage from weapons have always been set, not by weapons, but by the intentions of those who wield them.

Perhaps the primary conclusion to be drawn about the interaction of technology and weapons is that its chief product is surprise. The Israelis were caught by surprise in 1973 when new kinds of anti-tank and anti-aircraft weapons were used by the Arabs. Their surprise may be minor compared to what could occur in future wars. An arms race dealing with quantities of weapons has been supplanted by a technological race with goals of novelty, ingenuity, and speed. Advancing technology also tends to shorten the duration of a conflict, so that it has become imperative to prepare well in advance for the possibility of conflict.

The United States, long protected by its ocean barriers, is now a near neighbor to all in a closely-knit world—a circumstance demanding adaptation on our part. Adaptation is usually a slow, difficult process. But no nation, not ours or any other, can exist in isolation. A desire to turn back the clock is unrealistic.

The only effective antidote to military technology is technology for peace. Technology's influence intensifies the need for a stable world order. The horrors of war, great throughout mankind's tumultuous history, could hardly become more horrible. What has become worse is uncertainty, and with it an increasing feeling of insecurity.

In an age of instant communication and rapid travel, the world will not continue to exist one-quarter rich and three-quarters wretchedly poor. We participate and watch as the Industrial Revolution encompasses the planet; its spread brings danger and opportunity. A conjunction of the symbols for danger and opportunity, in Chinese calligraphy, means *crisis*:

danger	opportunity
危險	機会

Every reasonable person wishes that technology be used to insure peace. Implementing that process requires a measure of worldwide order, a fact that can be illustrated by two examples.

A short-term imperative is to find more food for the world's growing population. One obvious source is ocean cultivation, which would yield protein now lacking in diets of the poor around the globe. The technical means for producing food from the oceans are developing rapidly. Our knowledge of ocean life is justly said to be primitive, but the bottleneck is not apt to be continuing lack of knowledge. The very existence of enhanced scientific and technological expertise intensifies the need for reliable international cooperation in using the oceans for the common good.

The second example is the influence that could be exercised upon the weather. Presently we watch the weather from our satellites; soon we will be able to predict it more accurately; thereafter we shall begin to modify it. The result of meteorological modification is a potential source of great benefit, but also a potential source of conflict.

There appear to be only two paths toward a viable world order. One, well tested, is the way of conquest and domination, the manner in which empires always have been built. The Kremlin seems prepared to pursue this approach. The other is a novel way and almost untried: the way of consensus and cooperation. This path was followed by the United States when it aided its recent enemies, Germany and Japan, in their postwar recovery.

It is essential to remember that, although a wrong step can be taken in a hurry and on a large scale, right steps are made gradually, one by one, demanding patience. Even weapons play a role in taking the right steps, inasmuch as we live in a world where the will to dominate is far from extinct. Facing many contemporary divisions, ranging from ideological to racial, we can hardly imagine that peaceful cooperation can be established in the absence of substantial force to back up this cooperation. There must be a sufficient counterforce to keep the peace, to allow time for the slow but essential development of a viable world order that promotes the coexistence of widely varying societies.

Progress toward such an objective, since the end of World War II, has occurred in discouragingly small steps. Even so, we cannot afford to give up hope; we cannot afford to stop taking small steps. It should be possible to establish a peaceful world order based on cooperation but backed by military power. Then, with a peaceful family of nations established, we can hope that military power would wither away.

NOTES

1. Peter Chamberlain and Terry Gander, *Machine Guns* (New York: Arco, 1974), p. 1.

2. Paul J. Murphy, *Naval Power in Soviet Policy,* Studies in Communist Affairs, vol. II (Washington, D.C.: U.S. Government Printing Office, 1978), p. 110.

3. Norman Polmar, *Ships and Aircraft of the U.S. Fleet,* 11th ed. (Annapolis: Naval Institute Press, 1978).

4. "Admiral (Sergei G.) Gorshkov, the commander in chief of the Soviet navy, spelled out very clearly the meaning of all this in 1968 when he said: '. . . The flag of the Soviet Navy flies over the oceans of the world. Sooner or later the United States will have to understand it no longer has mastery of the seas.' If these present trends continue, Admiral Gorshkov's boast will be reality long before 1985." Quoted from John S. Foster, Jr., *"Power and Security,"* in Edward Teller, Hans Mark and John S. Foster, *Critical Choices for Americans,* vol. IV (Lexington, Mass.: D. C. Heath, 1976).

5. Iwao M. Moriyama, "Capsule Summary of Results of Radiation Studies on Hiroshima and Nagasaki Atomic Bomb Survivors: 1945–75," Radiation Effects Research Foundation, Technical Report RERF TR 5–77 (1978), p. 1.

World Energy Sources

Hendrik S. Houthakker

XIX

Viewed in strictly economic terms, the world energy markets present no problems that the price mechanism could not deal with. The progressive exhaustion of mineral fuels, so often viewed with alarm, can in principle be resolved by progressively higher prices; this enables costlier materials to be put into production and demand to be curtailed according to the supply available at those prices. Indeed, to an economist the intense concern about running out of oil appears distinctly naive; the world is merely running out of cheap oil. The man in the street may think that oil, once "cheap and abundant" (to use the obligatory cliché), has suddenly become expensive and hard to obtain. But anybody familiar with elementary economics should know that all commodities are scarce to some degree. It is only when prices are not permitted to match supply with demand that shortages become visible.

The domination of the world oil market by a cartel strong enough to determine the world price is also untroubling to economic analysis. Cartels have existed in many commodities for short or long periods; their inner workings and external effects are not particularly mysterious. In the case of a ubiquitous mineral such as oil, it is unlikely that a cartel will be completely comprehensive. Acceptance of the cartel price will not only reduce demand for the commodity, but will lead to increased production outside the cartel, thus bringing about a new equilibrium in which the cartel may or may not survive. When the cartelized commodity is as important as oil, there may also be macroeconomic effects on employment, inflation, and the international monetary system. But none of these pose insuperable difficulties. When the Organization of Petroleum Exporting Countries (OPEC) quadrupled the price of oil early in 1974, there were widespread fears of an international financial collapse, which have not been realized so far.

If pure economics provides us with so much reassurance about the ability of the price mechanism to cope with these problems, why does the energy problem appear to have worsened rather than improved in the last few years?

Before answering this question it is worth pointing out that many countries have indeed permitted market forces to play their part. Most European countries, as well as Japan and those developing nations that are not members of OPEC, simply accepted the higher oil prices, and in many cases even accentuated them by raising domestic excise taxes. In these countries there have been no gasoline lines or other signs of panic. Although their economic growth was somewhat reduced, they have by and large taken the adverse developments in their stride. They have learned to live with lower energy consumption, facilitated in many cases by increased production from alternative energy sources such as nuclear power. It is mostly in the United States, where the cartel price was not accepted and where excise taxes were not raised, that the energy markets have been severely disrupted. Recurrent shortages and the establishment of a large bureaucracy are the main symptoms of this disruption, which in turn has adversely affected other countries.

Why is it that the United States, usually considered the bastion of free enterprise, has not been prepared to let market forces take their course? To put it differently, why are we relying so heavily on the political process to solve what would seem to be essentially an economic problem? Presumably it is not because our political system is so much better at dealing with economic difficulties than the market; the results to date hardly suggest that explanation. The call for an energy policy has been loud and clear, but politicians and bureaucrats have only managed to produce several frequently contradictory policies that add up to chaos.

The reason for our heavy reliance on the political process is not its efficiency, but rather that a pure market solution has been perceived as unacceptable by influential pressure groups. Unlike other countries, the United States has a long history of government involvement in the energy markets. Until the early 1970s most of this involvement was undertaken at the behest of the oil and gas industry. State control of oil production, special tax treatment, and import restrictions have been with us for many years. The economic justification for these measures was often questioned. But since public interest in energy matters was negligible until 1973, the industry generally had the votes in Congress to sustain and extend such measures.

Another form of energy, nuclear power, has had heavy government involvement from the start, particularly through the Atomic Energy Commission and the Price-Anderson Act, which restricts the liability of utilities using nuclear power. Hydroelectricity has also long been the responsibility of federal agencies, especially in the Tennessee Valley and in the Pacific Northwest. Among the various energy sources, only coal did not initially rely on federal intervention, and indeed became the principal target of environmental and occupational safety concerns when they emerged in the late 1960s.

From a historical standpoint, therefore, the reaction of the administration and the Congress to the sharp rise in world oil prices is not surprising. A fairly elaborate, though not well coordinated, complex of energy policies was already established, and its continued operation was threatened by forces outside the control of the government and of interested parties. Concern over the inflationary impact of expensive oil products made the administration and the Congress even more reluctant to let market forces prevail. More important, a rise in the domestic oil price to the world level would have created large windfall profits for domestic producers. These were widely considered to be undeserved, especially in view of the special favors the industry had previously enjoyed. In other countries, especially those in which domestic energy production is insignificant, government involvement in the energy sector is largely confined to levying excise taxes, and there is no outcry about windfall profits.

Before the 1970s, the level of U.S. energy prices was mixed compared to those prevailing elsewhere in the world. The import quota scheme established in 1959 served to keep the U.S. price of crude oil well above the world price. Because of relatively low excise taxes, however, the retail price of gasoline in the United States was much lower than in Europe and in most other countries. The excise tax revenue here was dedicated to highway building, which in turn encouraged driving. The price of natural gas, held down by price controls, was low by international standards. Coal was also relatively cheap and, in conjunction with cheap hydroelectricity, permitted low-cost electricity. On balance the United States was a country of low energy prices at the consumer level—one reason why per capita energy consumption here is so much higher than on other continents. (Energy consumption in Canada is generally similar to our own.)

Long before the cataclysmic events of 1973–74, there were indications that the U.S. combination of relatively low energy prices and high energy consumption might not be sustainable. The first sign of trouble appeared in the oil industry. In response to growing demand, U.S. oil output increased from 7 million barrels per day in 1960 to 9.6 million barrels per day in 1970. But imports also increased as the quotas were liberalized. Not enough new oil was discovered to sustain the increase in production, and output declined after 1970.

In retrospect there was considerable justice in the accusation leveled against the oil policies prevailing at the time (particularly the import restrictions): namely, that they amounted to draining America first. With oil so much cheaper abroad, it was contrary to economic efficiency to deplete high-cost American oil prematurely. Yet much of the domestic industry in effect insisted on this. The Cabinet Task Force on Oil Import Control, convened by President Richard Nixon early in his administration, recommended the replacement of the quota by a tariff, but this recommendation was initially rejected and was not adopted until 1972. By that time the quota system had virtually broken down as the demand continued to grow while domestic oil output fell. The growth in oil demand was stimulated further by government-mandated substitution of oil for coal in the electric power industry for environmental reasons, enacted with little consideration of the impact on the energy markets. Shortages began to appear in natural gas, since price controls encouraged consumption while discouraging production. With the introduction of wage and price controls in 1971 the price of oil also became a matter of direct federal responsibility.

The inevitable result of these developments was a sharp increase in U.S. oil imports, which doubled between 1969 and 1973. In 1973 oil imports accounted for more than one-third of the total supply. Until the early 1970s the United States was not a major factor in the world oil market, since it drew mostly on Western Hemisphere sources in Venezuela and Canada. As the U.S. demand for imported oil increased, these sources became insufficient, and additional imports had to be bid away from the Middle East and Africa, the main suppliers to Europe and Japan. The balance of power in the world oil market shifted to the exporting countries, which had already established a framework for cooperation in the form of OPEC. The worldwide inflation that had begun in 1972 provided an added incentive for the exporters to show their muscle, as did political developments in the Middle East. Nevertheless the $10 per barrel world oil price set by OPEC at the beginning of 1974 came as a surprise, not only to the general public, but also to most of the presumed experts in the industry and elsewhere.

It should not be inferred from this brief history that the oil price increase of 1973–74 was attributable largely to U.S. oil policies. Even if these policies had been different, the demand for imported oil would probably have increased. However, the United States might have been in a better position to deal with OPEC if there had been spare capacity in our oil industry. After thirteen years of import quotas this spare capacity had vanished.

The preceding historical summary shows that U.S. energy policies did not begin in 1973, as is commonly believed. Although these policies did change after 1973, there were important elements of continuity, including:

1) strong reluctance to let the world price of oil prevail within the United States
2) reliance on imports rather than on domestic measures to cover the increasing oil deficit caused by prevailing policies
3) a tendency to adopt short-term expedients without regard to their long-term consequences.

These three points add up to inadequate attention, until recently, to the effect of increased U.S. demand on the world oil market. In effect we have acted as if the supply elasticity of imported oil is infinite—that is, as if unlimited quantities are available at the prevailing price. To be sure, the effect of increasing oil imports on the U.S. balance of payments has been recognized for some time, but this consideration has nothing to do with the supply elasticity of imported oil. In any case, the government left the solution to that problem to the foreign exchange markets, where the dollar duly depreciated, rather than establishing an effective oil import policy.

The United States is a member of the International Energy Agency, one of whose purposes is to coordinate the oil import policies of the industrial countries, but little has been accomplished along those lines. One reason for this is that the United States has given priority to domestic considerations, particularly to holding domestic oil prices down; our only approach to OPEC has been of a diplomatic nature. Although other members have not made effective use of the International Energy Agency either, their oil imports did not increase after 1973, so their responsibility was somewhat less. This subject will be further discussed later in this article.

THE INNER WORKINGS OF OPEC

As mentioned earlier, OPEC, founded in 1960, had been established well before the events of 1973–74. It passed its first test of strength in 1971, when negotiations in Tehran over the price of oil led to a humiliating capitulation by the United States and the major oil companies. It appears, however, that OPEC had not yet realized the full extent of its power over the world price. During the Arab oil embargo of the United States and other countries in fall 1973 the spot price of oil went as high as $17 per barrel. This gave OPEC a better idea how far it could go: not as high as $17, since the spot market is somewhat erratic, but certainly much higher than the $2.50 level prevailing at that time.

As it turned out the $10 figure was well chosen from OPEC's point of view. For nearly five years the world price, expressed in constant dollars, remained close to that level. The demand for imported oil outside North America was relatively weak because of widespread recession, the depressing effect of high prices on consumption, and the growing production in the North Sea. These factors were largely offset by the increase in American imports; consequently, OPEC had no need for large cutbacks in production to maintain the price, and all members experienced substantial increases in revenue. Some of them, notably Saudi Arabia and Iraq, actually produced more during this period than before 1973; others such as Kuwait and Venezuela produced considerably less.

There have only been occasional strains within the cartel, of which the split price in the first half of 1977 and again in the second half of 1979 were the most conspicuous manifestations. Generally, however, OPEC has operated successfully. As a result there has been no great pressure to tighten its rather loose structure. Unlike more highly organized cartels, OPEC has no formal mechanism for allocating output among the members. Each member is free to sell as much as he wants provided the cartel price, adjusted by certain differentials, is not undercut. While these differentials are in theory equivalent to output quotas, and have often been on the agenda of OPEC meetings, they do not appear to be subject to formal agreement. Member countries that are dissatisfied with their share in total output have on occasion changed the differential unilaterally. By avoiding undue rigidity in its internal structure, OPEC has so far managed to overcome the internal difficulties that tended to weaken past cartels.

This relative cohesion is especially remarkable because the members have widely divergent interests. Those on the western side of the Persian Gulf (principally Saudi Arabia, Kuwait, and the United Arab Emirates) have large reserves but small populations. Their economic base outside the oil sector is negligible. These countries do not need large oil production to satisfy the current needs of their residents. The main determinant of petroleum output in those countries is their attitude toward economic development and its political concomitants.

Although these countries, unlike the present regime in Iran, have considered development to be desirable in itself, they have been worried in varying degrees about the influx of foreign workers that would accompany it. To the extent that foreign workers have radical political opinions, they are a threat to the stability of the conservative monarchies that control the western side of the Gulf.

Another consideration affecting desired oil output in these countries is their stake in the prosperity of the industrial countries. Having invested much of their oil revenues in the West, they have a considerable interest in prosperity there. On the other hand, variations in oil output can be used to gain political leverage, as was attempted during the Arab oil embargo of 1973–74. Although that effort was not successful, the idea of another such attempt in the future has probably not been abandoned.

The three countries along the western Gulf have reconciled these considerations in various ways. Saudi Arabia, the largest and most powerful of them, has settled for a fairly high rate of oil production, exceeding the pre-1973 level, but certainly not straining its enormous reserves. It has gone heavily into economic development, to the point where its initially large current account surplus had almost disappeared by 1978. The United Arab Emirates with their tiny population have much less scope for development, but have also maintained a sizable rate of output. Kuwait, on the other hand, has chosen to keep much of its available oil in the ground.

In sharp contrast to these three countries is Indonesia, the OPEC member with the largest population. Faced with severe financial pressures, it has generally produced at capacity, in effect paying little attention to its membership in OPEC. Indonesia has not only been unable to accumulate assets abroad, but has gone deeply into debt.

Until the fall of the shah, Iran's strategy was more similar to Indonesia's than to that of Kuwait. The shah's heavy emphasis on industrial development required a high rate of oil output, but the social consequences of this development policy brought about a revolution. The new regime in Iran significantly reduced the rate of oil production, thus incidentally strengthening the market power of the cartel. It is not clear at present to what extent Iran's ultraconservative policies coincide with the economic aspirations of the Iranian people. Any attempt to turn back the clock is likely to engender tension, but the situation in Iran still is too unsettled to allow informed speculation on the subject.

There is no need to discuss the oil policies of the individual OPEC members further, except to note that they can generally be divided into three groups. The hawks, who insist on higher prices, have generally been led by Iraq and Algeria, countries that are also radical in their political outlook. Saudi Arabia and the United Arab Emirates, under traditional rulers, have been prominent among the doves. Venezuela and Kuwait have often served as mediators between the two, while most other members have tended to support the hawks. As mentioned already, the hawks and the doves have not always been able to compromise on a single price, causing the cartel members to "agree to disagree." This happened most recently in early summer 1979, when Saudi Arabia and its allies decided on a price of $18 per barrel, while the other members committed themselves only to a maximum price of $23.50 per barrel. A gap of this magnitude probably cannot be maintained for more than a few months. It is worth noting, however, that the agreed split price is better from the cartel's point of view than the chaotic situation prevailing in early 1979, when members were free to add surcharges to the cartel price. Spot prices as high as $35 per barrel were reported at that time.

Presumably the present split within OPEC reflects different perceptions as to the future of the world oil market. Since their reserves are large in relation to their populations, the Saudis and their allies can take a longer view than most other cartel members. The doves are probably concerned that an unduly high cartel price will lead their customers to adopt more stringent conservation measures and to develop alternative energy resources. If successful, such measures could lead to a permanent reduction in the world demand for oil. Fears of a recurrence of the 1973–74 recession may also influence Saudi thinking. The hawks, it would seem, are not only less interested in these long-term considerations, but may also feel that they can sell their oil even in a weak market by going down to the Saudi price. Although the world oil market is likely to remain turbulent for some time, the survival of OPEC is not seriously threatened by the split price.

OPEC'S EXTERNAL RELATIONS

The success of OPEC as a cartel is due not only to its flexible internal arrangements, but also to its external policies, particularly with respect to the developing countries. The price rise of 1974 was widely hailed as a triumph for the Third World, which at last was standing up to the imperialists. Indeed, there was much talk at the time about formation of other commodity cartels, but little has come of it. Actually the non-OPEC developing countries were seriously harmed by the oil price increase, which forced them to borrow heavily from industrial countries in order to maintain their economic growth rates. By a skillful combination of rhetoric and financial aid the OPEC countries nevertheless managed to retain the allegiance of their less fortunate brethren. As a result, the division of the noncommunist world between the industrial and the developing countries has become deeper than ever.

To some extent the industrial countries are to blame for this development, which has made it even more difficult to deal with OPEC. One manifestation of the confusion generated by the oil crisis was the Conference for International Economic Cooperation, known also as the "North-South dialogue." The idea of solving the international oil problem by diplomatic means may have had some merit, but unfortunately the industrial countries came to the conference without any clear strategy. The original idea was that there would be three sides to the dialogue: the industrial countries, OPEC, and the non-OPEC less developed countries (LDCs). Since the North (that is, the industrial countries) had nothing concrete to offer either to OPEC or to the non-OPEC LDCs, the cartel soon succeeded in presenting itself as the champion of the Third World as a whole. The resulting confrontation between the North and the South was a prolonged exercise in futility, which could hardly be described as a dialogue.

THE INDUSTRIAL COUNTRIES AND OPEC

It is not surprising that OPEC has treated the industrial countries, its principal customers, with thinly veiled contempt. Although some OPEC members are aware of Western interests, even they can see no need for a serious discussion. The Europeans and the Japanese are at least responding in the right direction, albeit passively, by allowing the world price to prevail inside their countries. But the United States, preoccupied largely by domestic political considerations, has played straight into the hands of the cartel by relying heavily on oil imports. At the Tokyo summit in early summer 1979, there were some indications of a greater sense of urgency among the leaders of the industrial countries. But the development of a concrete plan of action still lies in the future.

Let us consider what the West could usefully do. The oil problem is primarily an economic one, and secondarily a political one. Since the use of military force can be ruled out for practical purposes, a political approach to OPEC must rely on diplomatic means. Such an approach has been attempted for several years. It involves reminding the Saudis, the Iranians, and any other OPEC nations that will listen, of their interest in Western prosperity, their dependence on the West for protection against the Soviet Union, and so on. The results of this approach in terms of cartel policy have not been impressive.

More recently, the inability of the United States and its allies to influence developments in Iran has severely weakened the credibility of diplomatic persuasion by the industrial countries. Although the shah was generally of little assistance in oil matters, his departure has further reduced the number of OPEC leaders who are willing to listen to Western arguments. Those leaders who remain in power are now more vulnerable to internal and communist pressures.

In these circumstances there is not a great deal the United States can do on the political side. Events in Iran hardly suggest that the United States can protect the rulers of the Western Gulf states against domestic upheavals. Proposals for a stronger military capability in the Persian Gulf are probably justified in view of our vulnerability to interruptions in oil supplies from that area. It appears, however, that even the Western-oriented governments in the area are not enthusiastic about such proposals, since they might lead to greater Soviet involvement. Thus their value as a bargaining tool is small.

Having sponsored a separate peace between Egypt and Israel, the United States is unable to deliver another item of great interest to Saudi Arabia and its neighbors: the establishment of some kind of Palestinian homeland. The Arab governments want this not merely on grounds of ethnic solidarity, but also because it would give them a place to repatriate their Palestinian workers if they became too troublesome. By now these governments have no doubt realized that a Palestinian political entity is at best a remote possibility.

The potential benefit of a purely diplomatic approach to the problem of OPEC is therefore hard to see. In fact, there is little evidence that such an approach was fruitful in the past. Between 1974 and 1978 the cartel price remained unchanged in constant dollars, not because of Western diplomatic pressures on leading oil exporters, but because it served the perceived economic interests of most OPEC members. During that period the only countries that were unhappy about their share of OPEC output were Venezuela and occasionally Nigeria, neither of which was a prime target of Western diplomatic pressure. Saudi Arabia, on which the pressure was concentrated, suffered no economic hardship by producing as much as it did. Perhaps the Iranians feel in retrospect that they produced too much oil. But that was the result of a deliberately chosen development strategy and not of persuasion by the industrial countries. If the intense diplomatic activity during that period had been successful, some OPEC countries would have produced more than they really wanted. In fact, nearly all of them had considerable spare capacity that they hastened to bring into production when the oil market turned strong during the Iranian revolution. This suggests that their previous output was below the desired level.

Any attempt by the consuming countries to influence OPEC's policies must therefore emphasize economics rather than diplomacy. This does not mean that diplomacy should be abandoned, but that it should be reinforced by a conscious use of the economic power the industrial countries possess. Actually, the industrial nations could exercise considerable power in the world oil market. Total oil consumption in the Organization for Economic Cooperation and Development (OECD) area (excluding Australia and New Zealand) amounted to about 42 million barrels per day in 1978, compared to total production in the noncommunist world of about 49 million barrels per day. (The communist countries as a group are only a minor factor in world oil trade.) Since the OECD countries themselves produced about 12 million barrels a day, their net imports were about 29 million barrels per day, roughly the same as total OPEC exports. Not all OECD imports came from OPEC, and not all OPEC exports went to OECD countries, but the remaining oil movements are relatively small. If we look only at trade volumes, therefore, it would seem that the market power of the industrial countries as a group is potentially as large as the market power of OPEC.

By themselves trade volumes are not a good indicator of market power. Under present circumstances it would be much more painful for the industrial countries to cut consumption by one million barrels per day than it would be for OPEC to cut production by the same amount. The weakness of the industrial countries is that they are highly dependent upon oil; expressed more technically, their price elasticity of demand for imported oil is low. This elasticity is low because oil consumption as a whole is not very sensitive to price when the stock of oil-consuming equipment is fixed (as it is in the short run). In addition, oil production in some of the industrial countries has not been permitted to respond to higher prices. Not much can be done to increase the short-run price elasticity of oil consumption; this is primarily a matter of improving the energy efficiency of vehicles, machinery, and other oil-using equipment, a necessarily slow process in which some progress is being made. Another important factor affecting demand is substitution of other energy sources for oil, a matter to which we shall return.

The main reason oil production in the OECD countries does not presently respond to higher prices is simply government policy. The bulk of this production is in the United States, with most of the remainder divided between Canada, the United Kingdom, and Norway. For reasons discussed earlier, the United States has had price controls on crude oil for a number of years. Although these controls distinguish between "old" and "new" oil, the net effect has been to let production from old wells decline sharply without doing enough to stimulate output from new discoveries. Recognizing the failure of these policies, President Jimmy Carter announced a program by which domestic oil prices will gradually reach world levels by the end of 1981. Although this is an important step forward, the difficulty inherent in gradual decontrol according to a prescribed schedule is that it encourages the owners of resources to postpone new production until the world price is actually attained. Immediate decontrol would have been preferable from an economic point of view, but this would probably have engendered still more of the shortsighted opposition to windfall profits that has bedeviled our energy policies until now. Perhaps the windfall profits tax presently under consideration in Congress will help defuse this essentially irrelevant issue.

The main question raised by decontrol is how much additional oil it will produce compared to the steadily declining output that is likely if controls are maintained. Since the United States has been producing oil for more than a century, and has been explored more thoroughly than any other part of the world, the prospects for major onshore discoveries are not bright. However, higher prices will make less prolific and deeper wells profitable. Ultimately, these could be quite significant, especially if further progress is made in enhanced recovery. Offshore exploration has been disappointing so far, but a number of promising areas have not yet been opened for leasing. Although a large increase in U.S. production is improbable, raising the domestic crude price to the world level should make it possible to maintain present production levels for the remainder of this century. Since higher prices will also slow the growth in consumption, they should make it easier to moderate or reverse the rapid growth in U.S. oil imports that has had such adverse effects on the world oil situation, and is likely to continue under current controls.

Canada has also kept domestic oil prices below the world level, but it has reduced the harm to some extent by providing tax incentives for exploration. Since Canada became an important oil producer only recently, the potential for increasing production is greater than in the United States, and significant discoveries continue to be made. Canada also has vast reserves of oil-bearing tar sands and heavy oils, whose production costs, though high, are no longer prohibitively so. As in the United States, energy policy has been complicated by domestic considerations. In particular, there have been disagreements between Alberta and the federal government, whose approach tends to reflect the short-term interests of consumers in Ontario and Quebec. The recent victory of a new government more oriented toward the western provinces may lead Ottawa to adopt less restrictive oil policies. Although Canada is a net oil importer at present, it has the potential of becoming a net exporter again, provided domestic prices are high enough.

The United Kingdom and Norway are the most recent additions to the list of substantial oil producers. In these countries the scope for further discoveries is even greater than in Canada. Moreover a number of small fields have already been discovered that are not commercial at present prices, but would become so at higher prices. Great Britain made a good beginning in its oil industry, which started to produce only in 1975 and is now approaching two million barrels per day. The Labour government, however, slowed down new exploration starting in 1975, and also adopted financial measures that tended to discourage production in the future. The recently elected Conservative government is likely to be more open to production, and may indeed push for further expansion. An important consideration may be that the British treasury will capture a large portion of the proceeds from North Sea oil. This could make it easier to proceed with a reduction in direct tax rates, which is a cornerstone of the new government's program.

Norway, on the other hand, has proceeded slowly in the development of its sector of the North Sea. At present only one major field is in production, compared to about a dozen in the British sector. A second and larger one may come onstream in 1980 or 1981. Like the previous British government, the Norwegian government has been concerned about the impact of increased oil revenues on the remainder of the Norwegian economy. But the go-slow policy in oil production has not prevented strong inflationary pressures and a large deficit in the balance of payments. At some point the Norwegians, like the British, may well conclude that the North Sea is the best thing they have going for them. Large deposits are believed to exist in the area north of the sixty-second parallel, which has not yet been opened to exploration. While it would no doubt take some years to bring any deposits that are found into production, a more aggressive Norwegian oil policy would still be valuable from the point of view of the industrial countries. As a constraint on OPEC price increases, potential oil production would be as effective as actual production.

There are still other industrial countries that could conceivably supply additional oil. The German, Danish, Dutch, and French sectors of the North Sea and surrounding waters have until now been explored only lightly. Australia, which until recently followed a policy of low domestic oil prices, may also be able to increase its already sizable production. Even if higher oil prices in the industrial countries added only a few million barrels per day to the supply, this quantity would be helpful in keeping their oil imports under control.

For the purpose of changing the balance of power in the world oil market, it is not only supply and demand in the industrial countries that matters. Since transportation costs are relatively low, the market is worldwide. Supply and demand outside of OPEC and OECD are just as important, barrel for barrel, as supply and demand within these regions. The countries that belong neither to OPEC nor to OECD can be divided into two groups: the non-OPEC developing countries and the communist-dominated nations.

The non-OPEC developing countries, unable to afford the foolishness practiced by the United States, have had to accept the world price. Consequently they must be presumed to be conserving as much oil as their circumstances dictate. On the supply side, however, much remains to be done. Several countries in this group have the potential for increasing domestic production. Some of them, notably Mexico, are becoming substantial exporters. But even countries that have no prospect of net exports can still help stabilize the world oil market by supplying a larger fraction of their demand from domestic sources. Exploration in these countries is often impeded by lack of domestic capital and by nationalistic policies, although neither of these has seriously impeded Mexico's success. Provided nationalist sensitivities are taken into account, greater efforts by the industrial countries to encourage exploration in the non-OPEC LDCs could be quite rewarding. Some countries, particularly Argentina and Egypt, are already more or less self-sufficient and could become net exporters on a significant scale. Others, such as Brazil and India, are too large to have much prospect of self-sufficiency, but their production could be substantially increased by more active exploration. Encouragement of the oil industry in these countries, through technical assistance, suitable financing, and possibly by tax incentives, should be considered a high priority by the industrial countries.

The communist countries present a special problem. Here, too, any change in net oil imports will affect the industrial countries, but political factors clearly constrain the ability of the West to influence the oil policies of these countries. The Soviet Union is now the world's largest oil producer, but its output shows signs of reaching a peak. A large part of its exports now goes to Eastern Europe and is a vital element in Russian control of that area. The Soviet Union has been forced to reduce exports because of growing domestic demand, obliging Eastern Europe to compete in the world market and adding to that area's severe economic problems. The Soviet economy is not noted for efficiency and probably wastes a great deal of oil; despite the theoretical ability of central planning to deal with such matters, it is not clear that the Soviet government can do much in practice. It should be recalled, in this connection, that the Soviet Union is also the world's largest wheat producer; yet it has become increasingly dependent on imports. The Central Intelligence Agency has predicted that the same will happen with oil, with disturbing consequences for the world oil market. Indeed, it is not inconceivable that an oil deficit will lead the Soviet Union to adapt a more aggressive policy toward the Middle East, where in recent years it has been relatively passive. Iran, in particular, must be an inviting target for the Russians, which is a major reason for strengthening U.S. military capability in the Indian Ocean. Contrary to the situation in non-OPEC developing countries, it is not in the interest of the West to facilitate greater Soviet oil production, even if there were means of doing so. Oil is too significant a factor in Soviet military strength to be viewed strictly in economic terms.

The case of China is somewhat different again. Under its present regime, China does not appear to present an important military threat to the West, and indeed has become a useful counter-threat to the Soviet Union. China does have considerable potential in oil, but because it has a huge domestic market it is unlikely to become a net exporter on a large scale. Plans for Western participation in exploration are well advanced, but the attitude of the Chinese leaders toward economic involvement with the West has varied considerably over the years, and these plans may not be fully realized. It is probably wise not to count much on China for alleviation of the world oil situation.

OTHER FOSSIL FUELS

The discussion so far has focused almost entirely on oil, an emphasis that is appropriate because oil presents the most immediate problems in the energy field. However, oil is not without substitutes. One of these, nuclear power, will be discussed in greater detail later in the article. As explained there, nuclear power is not a close substitute for oil at present prices. More immediate substitution possibilities are offered by natural gas and coal.

Natural gas is a relative newcomer to the world energy market, and its worldwide potential at present market prices is far from being attained. In the United States, where natural gas first became important in the 1950s, exploration was long held down by price controls even more restrictive than those on crude oil. In 1978, legislation was enacted that will ultimately allow natural gas prices to be determined by market forces. Unfortunately the idea of gradual decontrol, whose defects have already been noted in connection with oil, is even more prominent in the natural gas law. As a result the United States will have to wait until the late 1980s for the potential of natural gas production to be more fully realized.

The natural gas picture abroad is more encouraging. Large discoveries have been made in Canada, not only in remote Arctic regions, but also in the more accessible Rocky Mountain area and in the offshore Atlantic. Mexico has found much gas along with its recent oil discoveries. In Europe natural gas first became an important factor after the discovery of a huge accumulation in the Netherlands. Since then the United Kingdom has developed large gas fields, and some of the North Sea oil fields also contain large amounts of gas. Other areas where gas has been discovered in recent years include Algeria, the Persian Gulf, Thailand, Malaysia, Indonesia, Australia, and New Zealand.

Compared to oil, the main problem with natural gas is its high transportation cost, which is to some extent offset by lower processing costs and more favorable environmental characteristics. Because of continuing discoveries in Europe and North America, it is unlikely that long-distance gas transportation by special tankers will become as important as was expected some years ago. Nevertheless, the existence of potential natural gas supplies in more distant areas provides an important constraint on the rise in oil prices. So far natural gas has been used mostly for heating and industrial processing, but it may be possible to develop technologies that will convert it into a motor fuel. This would provide competition in the area of transportation, where oil has reigned virtually supreme.

Coal is the stepchild of the energy markets. Not many years ago it was used widely in transportation, in manufacturing, and in homes, but by now its use is mostly confined to the generation of electricity. In North America coal production has been stagnant, and in Europe and Japan it has actually declined. Environmental and labor problems are a major cause of this performance. This is particularly unsatisfactory, because (at least in the United States) coal is the cheapest form of energy on a BTU (British thermal unit) basis. Whereas coal can cause serious pollution unless properly utilized, the environmental restrictions applicable to coal appear to be sometimes excessive. For instance, under present U.S. law, scrubbers must be installed in coal-fired electric power stations even if the coal has a low sulphur content. Since scrubbers are both expensive and unreliable, the net effect is to reduce the demand for coal well below the capacity of existing mines.

There is currently much talk about the use of coal as a raw material for synthetic oil and gas, but the economic and environmental aspects of the required technologies are little known. Indeed, the lack of interest in the private sector for such projects casts serious doubt on their economic feasibility. The only country where coal is being converted into oil on a substantial scale is South Africa, which is prepared to subsidize this industry in order to reduce the country's dependence on foreign (and mostly hostile) oil supplies.

No doubt a capacity to produce oil from coal at, say, $40 per barrel would provide some protection against soaring oil prices. But it is likely that additional oil could be obtained from conventional sources by secondary or tertiary recovery at a lower cost. Although the construction of pilot plants for coal conversion is probably justifiable as a means of obtaining more accurate economic and environmental data, it would be irresponsible to embark on projects involving tens or even hundreds of billions of dollars without adequate investigation.

In the meantime, existing restrictions on coal use should be reviewed to determine an appropriate balance between environmental protection and the need for reduced reliance on imported oil. Until such a review is successfully completed, coal cannot play the major role in U.S. energy supply that its relative abundance warrants. But it is quite possible that other countries, particularly in Latin America, may become large users of U.S. coal, especially if further growth of nuclear power is interrupted. Electricity is the fastest growing energy sector, and for much of the world the choice of fuel is between coal and uranium. For developing countries, coal-fired stations have the advantage of being less capital-intensive than nuclear stations.

ADDITIONAL MEASURES BY THE INDUSTRIAL COUNTRIES

The preceding discussion implies that the OECD countries could strengthen their influence on the world oil market merely by allowing market forces to operate, particularly in the United States and Canada. Their position may be further strengthened by going beyond market forces. Since OPEC is by its very nature anti-competitive, the importing countries need have no compunction about concerted measures if these promise to improve the performance of the world oil market—to the benefit not only of the industrial countries, but also of the non-OPEC developing countries. The first and most essential step, no doubt, is to let the market operate in North America, but it is necessary to look beyond this first step.

A concerted policy toward OPEC would involve some method of

reducing oil imports below the level corresponding to the world price set by the cartel. In principle, there are two methods, one involving import quotas and the other a tariff. Oil import quotas have a long history, particularly in the United States. The conclusions reached by the 1979 Tokyo summit also appear to point in this direction.

The main difficulty with import quotas is that they are simple in intention but difficult to implement. Under import quotas, the right to import oil must be subject to a government license. The allocation of these licenses among importers is the Achilles' heel of any quota scheme. To give away the licenses, as was done under the earlier U.S. quota scheme, is in effect to subsidize the recipients regardless of their need or merit.

A better idea is for the government to sell the licenses, either by auction or at a fixed price. Under an auction scheme the number of licenses sold is fixed so that the quantity of imports can be strictly controlled, but the domestic price will depend on the price of the license. The sale of import licenses at a fixed price is tantamount to a tariff, discussed below. In either case the government gets the revenue from the import licenses; it can then decide whether to add the proceeds to general revenue or to use them for some special purpose, such as subsidies for conservation or new energy sources. Actually there is no particular merit in setting aside these revenues. The case for subsidizing conservation or new sources should not depend on the fortuitous availability of certain revenues, but should be valid even if the subsidies must be financed from general revenues. Dedication of revenues to trust funds weakens the budgetary process and can lead to misallocation of government expenditures.

There is a difference of opinion over whether it is more important to fix the quantity of imports through quotas or their landed price via a tariff. A tariff is easier to administer, and gives greater certainty to domestic producers—an important consideration in industries with long lead times for investment. The following discussion will, therefore, focus on the tariff, though most of this applies equally to a quota system in which the licenses are sold at auction.

The main purpose of a tariff is to capture some of the monopoly profits that OPEC is now enjoying at the expense of importing countries. More particularly, the purpose is to forestall further increases in the cartel price, which are a distinct possibility in the absence of concerted action by the industrial countries. It is unlikely that a tariff would either force OPEC to roll back its cartel price or break up the cartel, though these outcomes are conceivable under certain circumstances. The higher domestic prices in the industrial countries resulting from a tariff will encourage conservation in oil use and expansion of domestic oil production: in that respect the tariff would reinforce ordinary market forces. In addition, it will generate substantial revenues, the magnitude of which depends on the level of the tariff and the elasticity of demand for imported oil. By raising its price, the cartel achieves much the same effect but keeps the profits to itself. In order to be fully effective, a tariff would have to be levied by the industrial countries together, possibly with preference to exports from non-OPEC countries.*

There are four main objections to a tariff (as well as to import quotas):

1) *The resulting rise in domestic prices will be unpopular.* Although this is true, the resulting revenue can be used to provide offsetting reductions in direct and other taxes.
2) *A further price increase will be inflationary.* Perhaps so, but in the case of the United States and Canada the reduction in oil imports to which a tariff will lead should strengthen the value of the dollar, thereby reducing inflationary pressures in other traded commodities.
3) *Most of the benefits will go to the oil companies.* This depends on the tax system, including any windfall profits taxes that may be enacted. In any case this distributional argument, which has done so much to confuse energy policy in the United States, overlooks the fact that most of the windfall profits would otherwise go to OPEC. There is no way such profits can be captured by domestic consumers without a tariff.
4) *A tariff might lead OPEC to raise prices even more than it would otherwise have done.* This is most unlikely. OPEC will fix oil prices within a range consistent with the economic interest of its members, just as it has done in the past. As argued above, there is no reason to believe that diplomatic pressure has caused OPEC to set a lower price than it otherwise would have.

These four objections, therefore, are not convincing. A more serious question is whether the industrial countries are prepared to act together. At present they probably would not be, since the United States and Canada have not yet allowed their domestic prices to rise to the world level. Once this hurdle is overcome and the long-run outlook for oil prices is more carefully evaluated, joint action seems possible. The

*For further details and quantitative estimates, see Hendrik S. Houthakker, *The World Price of Oil* (Washington, D.C.: American Enterprise Institute, 1976); also Theodore H. Moran, *Oil Prices and the Future of OPEC*, (Washington D.C.: Resources for the Future, 1978).

substantial revenue generated by a tariff, or by a quota system with ticket sales, could be an important inducement. Moreover, there are few alternatives open to the OECD countries if they decide to adopt a more active posture with respect to OPEC.

In fact there appears to be only one other proposal that has been seriously advanced for dealing with the cartel. This proposal, made by Professor Morris Adelman of the Massachusetts Institute of Technology, envisages a system by which the United States would set up a central buying agency to which exporting countries would submit secret offers of oil. The idea is that the cartel members would then undercut each other in order to gain access to the large market provided by the United States, thus breaking up or significantly weakening the cartel. However, this purpose is not likely to be realized. It would be necessary for OPEC merely to set up a central selling agency of its own, which would submit a single offer on behalf of its members, or tell the members how much to offer. The most likely outcome of this proposal, therefore, is greater cohesion in the cartel—the opposite of what is intended. The tariff, on the other hand, would not challenge the existence of OPEC as such; it would merely transfer some of OPEC's future monopoly profits to the importers.

NUCLEAR POLICY

Other than the problems raised by OPEC, the problem of nuclear power is the most important one in international energy policy. It is more truly a political problem, since it involves matters of life and death, whereas oil in the final analysis is merely a question of money.

As it happens, oil and nuclear power are not very closely related sources of energy. Nuclear power can be used only to generate electricity, whereas oil is no longer a major factor in the electric power market. Many existing power generating stations, of course, consume oil, but new stations are generally being designed for other fuels since oil has become too expensive. Although some oil-fired stations can be converted to coal at considerable expense, they cannot be converted to nuclear fuels.

The basic economics of nuclear power is fairly straightforward. Nuclear power plants are very capital intensive, and will therefore be competitive with plants using fossil fuels only if uranium is cheap enough to offset the higher capital costs. Like fossil fuels, uranium is a depletable resource, though it can be supplemented to some extent by thorium, a more abundant mineral that so far has had only limited application. As the supply of uranium is depleted its price will tend to go up because deeper and leaner ores will have to be brought into production. Although uranium is one of the most widely dispersed elements in the earth's crust, at any time only the higher concentrations and more accessible deposits can be profitably produced. There is consequently no danger of running completely out of uranium, but the price may become prohibitively high once the better ores are exhausted.

The principal economic and political complication of nuclear power is that uranium consumption depends not only on the output of nuclear power, but also on the nuclear fuel cycle. In the simplest case the nuclear fuel cycle involves mining uranium in the form of an oxide known as yellowcake, enrichment of the uranium to enhance the portion of an isotope that can be split, and use of the enriched mixture in a light-water reactor, where it decays gradually into spent fuel and radioactive waste. (The enrichment step is omitted in heavy-water reactors, which need not be considered separately here.) The disposition of the spent fuel is the central problem. When nuclear power was first conceived, it was anticipated that the spent fuel would be recycled to yield not only reusable uranium, but also plutonium, another radioactive element. As far as uranium is concerned, this reprocessing stage would complete the nuclear fuel cycle.

Unfortunately, plutonium can be used not only to generate electricity in breeder reactors, but also to manufacture atomic bombs. Unless reprocessing is strictly controlled, therefore, it could lead to the twin dangers of proliferation (the production of atomic bombs by nations that do not yet have them) and diversion (the use of atomic explosives by terrorists).

Obviously the risks of proliferation and diversion cannot be taken lightly; it is no exaggeration to say that the future of humanity depends in part on the effectiveness of control over reprocessing. Shortly after taking office, President Carter decided that the United States would forego reprocessing and would discourage it in other nations. He also attempted, with less success because of congressional opposition, to halt the construction of a breeder reactor fueled by plutonium.

Without reprocessing the nuclear fuel cycle is incomplete. If the spent fuel from light-water reactors is not recycled, the demand for virgin uranium is increased, the available supply is more rapidly depleted, and the price of uranium rises more quickly to a level where more advanced forms of nuclear power, such as the breeder reactor, become competitive. The Carter administration, however, would also end the breeder reactor, thereby making the future of the industry uncertain.

The current U.S. policy with respect to reprocessing and the breeder has met with considerable resistance abroad. Most European countries are strongly committed to nuclear power, despite some vocal domestic opposition. They do not want to return to coal for their electricity production, since the European coal supply is limited and expensive, and would have to be supplemented by imports from Eastern Europe and the United States. Those countries that have made considerable investments in the breeder, particularly France, also have no desire to abandon it for what they see as exaggerated fears that ignore economics. Because some Europeans have had high hopes of selling nuclear reactors and reprocessing plants abroad, they interpret the new American policy as unfair competition, though in fact its impact on the American nuclear equipment industry has been equally adverse. The official European position on reprocessing is that it can be effectively controlled by international organizations. This view appears to be shared by the developing countries, many of which consider nuclear power the most promising answer to their rapidly growing energy demands.

This dispute among the industrial countries has led to a joint study known as the International Nuclear Fuels Cycle Evaluation (INFCE), which is supposed to resolve these issues. No report from INFCE has yet been published, and it is not clear that a compromise between the American and the European views can be found. In the meantime the Europeans are proceeding with both reprocessing and the breeder reactor, though pressure from the United States has stalled European efforts to sell reprocessing equipment to developing countries.

The adamant European attitude can be explained in part by the huge potential of the world market for nuclear equipment, where projected sales over the next twenty years could run into trillions of dollars. At present, however, this market is anything but brisk. This is attributable not only to the dispute over reprocessing and the breeder, but also to weakness in the demand for light-water reactors. Apart from concerns over safety, which will be discussed further, the main reason is that until recently the future demand for electricity was widely overestimated. In most countries, including the United States, the electric power industry is more sophisticated in engineering than in economics. In particular, it has traditionally rejected the notion that the demand for electricity depends on its price, despite abundant econometric evidence to the contrary. In recent years the real cost of producing electric power has increased due to both higher fuel prices, including uranium, and higher interest rates. The real price of electricity has gone up and the growth of demand has slowed down considerably. As a result, there have been many cancellations and postponements of construction projects. The fact that these have particularly affected the nuclear side of the industry suggests that nuclear power is not competitive in large parts of the world, though it still appears to be so in Europe. One can argue, however, that the recent rise in real electricity prices is transitional and that the industry will resume a high growth rate in the 1980s, especially in the developing countries.

Concerns over the safety of nuclear power have also become more intense, and have led to the formation of a widespread anti-nuclear movement. Although the safety record of nuclear power has been exceptionally good so far, this has not convinced the critics. They interpret the Three Mile Island accident as grist to their mill, even though there were no immediate casualties. The disposal of the radioactive waste generated by nuclear reactors also awaits a permanent solution.

The main weakness of the anti-nuclear movement is that it has no realistic alternative. At the present level of technology, solar energy does not appear to be a serious possibility for electricity production, especially since its environmental implications (for instance, in land use and the spatial distribution of industry) have not been adequately explored. Some opponents of nuclear power argue that the world can do quite well with much less energy than is usually projected for the future. This proposition is defensible, but it leads to the further question of how the necessary conservation is to be brought about. The only proven way of inducing conservation is through higher prices, to which the public at large is opposed. To keep energy consumption in the United States at the present level, some calculations suggest, prices may have to quadruple in real terms between now and the early years of the next century. Though there is some doubt whether such a policy would be consciously adopted, it could come about without an explicit decision if American energy policies are allowed to drift further along the lines criticized in the beginning of this article.

The most likely effect of the present concern over nuclear safety is that it will lead not to the abandonment of nuclear power, but rather to the required installation of additional safety devices that will raise its capital cost. As a result coal-fired stations will become more competitive, provided the environmental problems can be satisfactorily resolved. A slowdown in the construction of new nuclear stations will have a favorable effect on uranium prices, making the need for reprocessing and the breeder reactor less urgent. In the developing countries, where much of the growth in demand for electric power is likely to occur, there will be a shift to hydroelectricity where it is available, or to coal, some of it imported from the United States.* If these various shifts cannot be

*For quantitative projections of the world's energy production and consumption by fuel and region, see Hendrik S. Houthakker and Michael Kennedy, "Long Range Energy Prospects," *Journal of Energy & Development*, Autumn 1978.

accomplished within a reasonable time, the growth rate of the world economy will be adversely affected.

CONCLUSIONS

1) OPEC is firmly in control of the world oil market; its market power has been greatly reinforced by the reluctance of the United States and Canada to allow their domestic oil prices to rise to the world level set by the cartel.
2) A concerted policy by the industrial countries, particularly a common tariff on imported oil, could transfer some of OPEC's future profits to the importers.
3) Nuclear power will become relatively more expensive, primarily as a result of heightened concerns over safety, but it will continue to expand. A decreased growth rate will make it possible to postpone difficult decisions concerning reprocessing and the breeder reactor.
4) Any shift in electric power production away from nuclear reactors is likely to increase foreign demand for American coal.
5) Except possibly in the nuclear area and in dealing with OPEC, market forces are capable of bringing about the necessary adjustments in the world's energy markets.

Foreign Aid and the Third World

P. T. Bauer

XX

Do not attempt to do us any more good.
Your good has done us too much harm already.

Sheik Muhammed Abduh,
an Egyptian in London, 1884

THE THIRD WORLD AND FOREIGN AID

Since the end of World War II, Westerners have widely come to accept the concept of a Third World. It is a strange notion, harder to define even than terms like the Third Rome and the Third Reich with which it shares certain dialectical characteristics. The term lacks a clear geographical definition—the Third World includes most of the globe: Asia except Japan and Israel, Africa except South Africa and Rhodesia, and Latin America. In practice, the term denotes the non-Western or non-Westernized parts of the globe. Also called underdeveloped, less developed, developing, or known as the global South, the Third World comprises two-thirds or more of mankind.

The inhabitants of the so-called Third World have little in common. They range from Stone Age hunters to members of industrialized and highly advanced groups and societies, from poor countries to the very rich. Since World War II, Third World countries such as South Korea, Thailand, the Ivory Coast, Mexico, and Brazil have progressed much more rapidly than Western countries such as the United States and Britain. The Third World is not a grouping of politically nonaligned countries; many of its rulers, such as Kwame Nkrumah, Indira Gandhi, and the present leaders of Vietnam and Mozambique, have often been bitterly hostile to the West. Thus neither poverty nor stagnation nor political neutrality provide a unifying characteristic of the Third World. What is there, indeed, in common between Papua New Guinea and Mexico, Malaysia and Lesotho, Afghanistan and Chile?

The concept of an underdeveloped world, eventually to become the Third World, was forged after World War II, largely under United Nations auspices and leadership. From its inception, the unifying characteristic has been that Third World countries demand and receive Western aid.[1] Both the Third World and foreign aid are Western inventions. Foreign aid is certain to remain central to economic relations between the United States and the Third World in the 1980s.

The fictitious unity of the Third World has made it possible and apparently sensible for the United Nations and its affiliates to organize concerted action for the purpose of obtaining aid. Opposition to the West has become a source of political and financial benefit to Third World leaders and to influential groups in the West. By presenting a sharply divided world—a rich and developed West versus a wretchedly poor Third World—they promote international wealth transfers.

The ideas of the underdeveloped world and foreign aid were even born simultaneously, coupled in President Truman's Point Four Program of 1949, which proposed that the fruits of Western economic progress be used to help the underdeveloped countries where over half of mankind was living in misery. Large-scale wealth transfers from the West and the concept of the Third World are thus inseparable. There will be U.S. aid to the Third World as long as the concept survives. At issue are only the amount, direction, methods, and repercussions of the aid.

AID AS AXIOM

In its early days, the advocates of aid argued that a few years of limited support would ensure the material progress of the recipients. Some 30 years and hundreds of billions of dollars later, indefinite extension of massive international wealth transfers is taken for granted. Foreign aid is perhaps the only form of state spending rarely criticized in principle. Aid programs may at times be criticized for having been wasteful or misdirected, but this criticism then becomes a basis for revising and increasing aid. Aid is desirable—this seems to be the starting point, not the conclusion, of all discussion on the subject.

Giving more means doing better; "increase" and "improvement" have come to be used interchangeably. We read in a 1972 report by the

Organization for Economic Co-Operation and Development (OECD) that "in these GNP terms, the biggest *increases* were made by Sweden, Portugal, and Denmark; France with the United Kingdom *also doing well*. Belgium, Germany, Italy, Norway, and the United States also improved their performance" (italics added). This practice, which equates benefits with costs, has become so common that we no longer notice how perverse it is. Of course some benefits may result, but not necessarily. Moreover, the beneficiaries, if any, may not be the peoples of the Third World but their governments or some other groups.

Just as the validity of the axiom is unrelated to reality, the provision of aid is unrelated to its results, to the circumstances of the donors, and to the conduct of the recipients. Whatever happens in the recipient countries can be adduced in support of more aid. Progress is regarded as evidence of the aid's efficacy and becomes an argument for its expansion; lack of progress is evidence that the dosage has been insufficient and must be increased. Some aid advocates argue that it would be unwise to deny aid to the speedy, those who progress, and cruel to deny it to the needy, those who stagnate. Aid is like champagne: in success you deserve it, in failure you need it.

Because aid is taken for granted, substantial sums continue to flow during times of financial adversity for the donors. Large-scale British aid has continued through the sterling crises of the 1960s and 1970s, even with devaluations and severe restrictions on British state and private spending, including foreign investment and travel. Recent U.S. experience is also instructive. In 1977–78 the weakness of the dollar caused much anxiety among Western governments, including at times the U.S. government. The U.S. current-account deficit, caused in substantial part by foreign aid, was a major cause of this weakness. Yet official bodies, including the OECD, kept urging the U.S. government to expand aid.

Because the dollar and the pound are the two principal reserve currencies, there are worldwide repercussions to large-scale U.S. and British aid. A fall in their exchange rates inflicts large losses on those, including many in the Third World, who were prudent enough to build up reserves but foolish enough to hold them in dollars and pounds. Aid can also contribute to international inflation. It can do so if, as a result of aid, the government deficit in the reserve-currency countries is larger than it would be otherwise, though the inflationary effect would depend on fiscal and monetary policies in these countries. The periodic International Monetary Fund gold auctions, the proceeds of which are given to Third World governments, are inflationary in a minor way because this form of aid converts accumulated reserves into current spending. But all these consequences of aid are ignored; aid is by definition virtuous and so is any policy designed to increase it.

The conditions of recipient countries and the conduct of their governments have produced a rich crop of anomalies. Thus in the 1960s and 1970s Western aid went to countries of the Organization of Petroleum Exporting Countries (OPEC), including Bahrain, Kuwait, and Saudi Arabia, whose oil revenues often exceeded their spending and whose per capita incomes were much higher than those of many donor countries. In other cases coercive governments have received much support. India, for instance, was given much Western aid in 1975–1977 while Mrs. Gandhi condemned thousands of poor villagers to compulsory sterilization; and President Idi Amin of Uganda received substantial Western aid as late as 1978. In April 1978 a new World Bank loan was announced to Mengistu's Ethiopia at a time when large-scale slaughter, of political opponents and also of ordinary people, was reported in reputable Western newspapers.[2] President Nyerere of Tanzania has received Western aid for years while in his country millions of people have been forcibly herded into primitive collective villages. Those trying to resist have had their homesteads destroyed and lost their civil rights. Large numbers of people have been forced to leave Tanzania, and there have been political executions and killings.[3] Western aid has been described as indispensable for President Nyerere's political survival. In August 1978 the World Bank announced an interest-free loan of $60 million to Vietnam at a time when the Hanoi government suppressed private economic activity and persecuted large numbers of people to the point where they became desperate to escape.

By now, both donors and recipients have come to agree that aid is a matter of right; to examine the conduct of the recipients would improperly infringe on their sovereignty. The American and British governments can examine the conduct of their own local authorities who receive taxpayers' money but should apparently not do so with foreign governments.

Firm forward commitments several years ahead represent another corollary of the axiom that aid is desirable. For Britain, bilateral commitments alone now exceed £750 million. No one knows what kind of governments will be in power in the recipient countries, let alone what their policies will be. In 1977 the British foreign secretary expressed regret that European Economic Community aid to Amin's Uganda could not be terminated because of past commitments.

Axiomatic acceptance has developed into virtually unlimited commitments. The World Bank member governments have large contingent liabilities in the form of the bank's uncalled capital. The scale of the bank's future activities is unpredictable, and even if some governments wish to limit them, which is doubtful, they may not be able to do so. (The U.S. government tried unsuccessfully to veto a loan to Vietnam in August 1978.) The bank will likely press Western governments to increase their contributions in order to cover its expanding obligations.

Western governments have widely accepted open-ended commitments, such as the Pearson Commission's proposal for sufficient aid to raise the growth rate of developing countries by one-fifth. Aid is commonly seen as an instrument of worldwide equality, the elimination of absolute poverty, and the establishment of a guaranteed minimum income everywhere. The acceptance of such vague objectives implies a totally open-ended commitment to aid. Yet such aims cannot be secured from outside but depend on the policies, attitudes, and conduct of the Third World governments.

Aid supporters will question the conduct of recipients only to protect their other precepts, notably advocacy of comprehensive economic planning or the expropriation of the assets of productive or prosperous people. But the inclination to impose these conditions does not offset the anomalies of the aid fetish; as we shall see shortly, it often compounds them.

RATIONALIZATIONS

Arguments in support of aid are often advanced for the benefit of audiences not yet regarded as firm supporters. The most familiar arguments are that aid is indispensable to development, that it relieves poverty, that it is an instrument for international redistribution of income, that it is restitution for Western exploitation, that it serves the interests of the donors, and that it will help control the unprecedented population growth in the Third World. But these arguments are mere rationalizations; they shift in accordance with the vagaries of intellectual and political fashion.

Development

In the early days of foreign aid, the prime argument was that aid was indispensable because the incomes of underdeveloped countries were too low to generate the capital required to raise incomes: the vicious circle of poverty. If this notion were valid, countless people and societies in all parts of the world could never have emerged from poverty without alms—material progress could never have started from the one universal state of poverty.

It is obviously false that poverty is self-perpetuating, that poor people cannot improve their lives without alms. The West progressed without aid and so did large areas of the Third World; for instance, Southeast Asia, West Africa, and Latin America. Moreover, Western societies faced conditions far more difficult than those facing the Third World, which can draw on huge external markets, an abundant supply of capital, and a vast range of modern technology and skills. Official aid is not indispensable to progress. And even if it were true that the Third World could not progress without doles, it is not clear why Western taxpayers should be the ones to pay.

According to a variant of the vicious-circle argument, aid is required because external payment difficulties are inherent in the early stages of development. Gunnar Myrdal wrote in 1956 that something must be wrong with a developing country that does not have foreign exchange difficulties. Yet payment difficulties cannot possibly be concomitants of development; all Western countries and many Third World countries have progressed rapidly without experiencing them. Both rich and poor countries encounter such difficulties when governments promote monetary demand in excess of available resources, or, in short, live beyond their means.

It is sometimes argued that while the West could advance without alms, the Third World cannot do so because external economic conditions are much less favorable now than when the West developed. This argument is spurious: many Third World countries have progressed rapidly in recent years without aid or payment difficulties, and external conditions today are far more favorable to economic development than in the history of the West.

If the prospects of many Third World countries are less favorable than were those of the West, this has nothing to do with external factors. Economic achievement depends on people's attributes, attitudes, motivations, mores, and political arrangements. In many Third World countries the prevailing mores and attitudes are uncongenial to material progress; witness the reluctance to kill animals, preference for a contemplative life, opposition to paid work by women, and widespread torpor and fatalism. And the policies of many Third World governments are plainly damaging to economic achievement.

If attitudes or policies run counter to economic development, doles from abroad will not promote it. The argument that aid is indispensable runs into a Morton's Fork dilemma: if conditions for development other than capital are present, capital will either be generated locally or be made available commercially from abroad to governments or to business. If the required conditions are not present, infused capital will be wasted.

It might be argued that while aid is not indispensable to progress, it is required to accelerate what would otherwise be very slow progress. This contention is also invalid. As we have seen, many Third World countries progressed rapidly without aid. Official aid cannot significantly promote development in the sense of the rate of increase in the national income. Although often substantial compared to other economic magnitudes in both donor and recipient countries, it is usually a small fraction of the national income of the recipients, particularly in large countries to which goes most aid. For instance, for Nigeria the figure is 0.3 percent, for India 1.5 percent, for Indonesia 3 percent, for Zaïre 5 percent. These percentages are in fact large overestimates because they are based on national income statistics which, for most Third World countries—particularly the large countries in Asia and Africa—greatly understate the national income. Such understatement is now widely recognized; in some cases it amounts to several hundred percent, as has been noted for India in the World Bank's *World Development Report: 1978.*

The maximum contribution of aid to the current national income of the recipients is the percentage of the national income it represents. This percentage is much less than appears from the conventional statistics because of their understatement of the national income of Third World countries. The benefit is reduced further by various adverse repercussions of aid. Altogether, the maximum favorable impact is generally too small to be discernible in the statistics of national income, both because these are subject to wide margins of error, which do not remain constant over time, and because the national income is affected by many factors other than aid.

The maximum contribution of aid to the promotion of development in the sense of the *rate of growth of the national income,* as distinct from its impact on the *current national income,* is even smaller. This contribution is determined by the productivity of aid and the cost of alternative sources of finance. A hypothetical example illustrates the magnitudes. Assume that aid amounts to 3 percent of the conventionally measured national income of the recipient country. Assume further a generous economic return of 15 percent on the aid funds, a return that incidentally would certainly attract private investment. If this aid is a gift, then 3 percent of the national income that yields a 15-percent return would increase the rate of growth of the national income by less than .5 percent.

Governments that can use capital productively can borrow abroad. It is for this reason that the maximum contribution of aid to the rate of growth of the national income can be no more than the avoided cost of borrowing the funds represented by aid. In our hypothetical example, these funds represented 3 percent of the national income. If the cost of borrowing is 10 percent, the maximum contribution of unrestricted aid to growth of income is then less than one-third percent of the national income. If this aid is not free but takes the form of a soft loan or is tied to exports from the donors, its cost is increased and its maximum net contribution correspondingly reduced.[4]

Even before the various adverse repercussions are taken into account, the contribution of aid to the rate of growth of income is certain to be so small as to be statistically insignificant. And this maximum contribution will remain too small to be discernible in the statistics even if more generous, but not wholly impossible, assumptions are substituted for those employed here.

Although it can alleviate immediate shortages, aid thus cannot materially assist long-term development. This is so even when development is its declared objective and is obvious when its declared objective is relief of poverty, restitution, redistribution, or some other purpose.

Aid is not expected to yield a commercial return; it is therefore not adjusted to market factors or to general local conditions, as is commercially supplied capital. Official gifts and loans can be written off at no cost to aid administrators whose fortunes do not depend on productive use of the funds supplied but on the amount of spending they advocate and administer. Aid therefore is often not deployed productively. And, of course, when investible funds are highly productive, they will be generated locally or made available commercially from abroad.

In any event, development does not depend on large amounts of capital. Major categories of capital formation are often similar to consumer durables: they are items on which income is spent, rather than instruments for its increase. This is evident in housing and other forms of public investment that require substantial monetary saving. Moreover, a large proportion of so-called investment spending—made by the government or directed by it—often does not represent capital formation but is merely spending on various activities and projects that the government deems politically useful.

Therefore, aid is at best a small reduction in the cost of investible funds, which are small in relation to the national income and which are not basic to development. And aid brings about a host of repercussions that adversely affect the basic determinants of development, a matter that I shall examine below.

Poverty

Relief from poverty seems at first a simple and irreproachable goal of aid. But the apparent simplicity conceals major pitfalls. As objectives of aid, poverty relief and development differ in much the same way as assistance to invalids and scholarships for promising students. The criteria of allocation and expectations of repayment are altogether different.

Official aid is quite unsuitable for the relief of persistent poverty. Consider again the magnitudes involved. As official aid is normally a small fraction of the total national income of recipients, it cannot substantially raise the general level of incomes or living standards. If, however, there are groups who are very poor relative to the rest of the society, this suggests a political and social situation in which the governments receiving the official aid are unable or unwilling to help such groups. Attempts to channel official aid directly to the poorest often pose intractable problems.

Official aid goes to governments, not to poor people. Its expenditure is governed by the personal and professional ambitions of politicians and civil servants. Much is spent on politically inspired prestige projects: airlines, inefficient industries, Western-type universities the graduates of which cannot find jobs, and construction of new capitals at vast cost (Brasilia, Islamabad, Dodoma in Tanzania). These projects often have to be subsidized by local taxes, including those on the poor. State spending in Third World countries, including that supported by aid, benefits the relatively well-to-do rather than the poor.

Aid in its present forms is not calculated to relieve Third World poverty. But if it were reorganized specifically for this purpose, it would pose a problem familiar to social reformers: if they dispense aid and do nothing more, they risk transforming poor people into dependent paupers. Entire societies can be pauperized in this way. The Navajos, heavily assisted by the U.S. government for many decades, are a familiar example. Less known is the large-scale pauperization in the U.S. Trust Territory of Micronesia, described in the *Washington Post* (July 27, 1978), where many people have abandoned agriculture and fishing because they can live comfortably on government handouts. The outcome is persistent poverty, which in turn provides rationalization for perpetual aid.

Donors cannot avert pauperization by instilling in the recipients the requirements for economic achievement. This would involve far-reaching coercion to uproot the supposed beneficiaries' deep-seated mores and values. Many aid-recipient governments, as well as their populations, would refuse aid on such conditions.

Few Third World governments are interested in the relief of poverty. The poor, especially the vast mass of rural poor, are politically ineffective and thus of little interest to the rulers. State relief of poverty does not generally accord with local mores. The most indigent groups in the Third World, for instance, the aborigines, pygmies, and desert people, are largely outside the orbit of aid.

Many of the policies regarded as aid, such as commodity agreements and debt cancellation, benefit the poor only by chance, if at all. Countries that export primary products—Malaysia, the Ivory Coast, Brazil—are among the most prosperous Third World countries. Within these nations it is the well-to-do, especially the established producers, politicians, and administrators, who benefit from commodity agreements. These agreements raise the prices of necessities and restrict supplies by forcibly excluding potential producers, doubly harming the poor.

Debt cancellation, too, is quite unrelated to relief of poverty. Many of the countries that have had their debts reduced or cancelled are relatively well off, Argentina, Peru, and Turkey among them.

Finally, many aid-recipient governments have pursued policies that have both reduced per capita incomes and aggravated the lot of the poorest. The suppression of private trade and the expulsion of traders have had such results—the traders have above-average incomes and their elimination has led to a partial breakdown of the exchange economy in countries such as Burma, Uganda, and Zaïre. By the criterion of poverty, such governments qualify for more aid. The adoption of poverty of the population as criterion for aid to the government encourages policies of impoverishment.

Aid to the Third World is often conceived as a discharge of moral obligation to help the less fortunate. But, as we have seen, aid often aggravates the position of the weak. Even if it helped the poorest, it would still differ radically from the discharge of a moral duty. The donors are, in effect, the taxpayers who have to contribute whether they like it or not and often do not even know that they contribute.

Redistribution

Egalitarianism, or redistribution of world income, has become an increasingly prominent dimension in aid discussion. But the phrase is misleading because nowhere is there a fixed income to be redistributed.

Redistribution means that part of some people's income is confiscated for the benefit of others. But redistribution is more than a simple transfer from rich to poor, as evident from the heavy taxation of the poor in the Western countries, including Britain and the United States, where much of the fiscal process is directed at curtailing the freedom to dispose of incomes rather than at redistributing them from rich to poor.

Unlike progressive taxation, aid is a transaction between governments and is in no way adjusted to the personal and family circumstances of donors and recipients. Many people in donor countries are far poorer than some in recipient countries. Redistributive taxation on the basis of conventional international income comparisons produces such anomalies as the transfer of resources from American welfare recipients to wealthy Indian landowners and African chiefs.

Differences in social institutions and political arrangements undermine the usefulness of international comparisons. Most Indians, for instance, object to killing cattle. Apart from its direct effect on the food supply, this attitude restricts the scope of animal husbandry and obstructs progress in agriculture. In India, cattle compete with people for food rather than contribute to the supply. Why should Westerners be taxed to equalize their incomes with those of people whose religious and social practices keep them poor? Why should American and British men and women be taxed for the benefit of societies whose poverty is partly caused by forbidding women to take paid work?

Income statistics, generally subject to large margins of error, are vitiated by problems of concept and measurement. For instance, the proportion of children is much higher in the Third World than in the West. As incomes and requirements of children are lower than those of adults, statistics which are not adjusted for differences in age composition inevitably exaggerate Third World poverty. Professor Dan Usher's estimate that the various errors and biases amount to several hundred percent has not been seriously disputed; indeed, it has been commended by Professor Paul A. Samuelson, and by Miss Phyllis Deane, pioneer of national income accounting in tropical areas. Yet, fifteen years after Usher first published his findings, advocacy of aid for redistribution still relies on statistics that claim to estimate Third World incomes within a few percentage points.

The need to contain the widening income gap between rich and poor countries is sometimes adduced to support international wealth transfers. This particular argument exhibits all the defects of international income comparisons and several others as well. If international income comparisons involving the Third World are largely meaningless, this applies even more to estimates of a gap between arbitrarily chosen aggregates of such incomes. Further, while aid certainly removes resources from the donors, it does not necessarily, or even generally, raise incomes in the recipient countries. The argument prejudges its results.

Changes in the degree of equality or in the extent of poverty come about through a variety of causes that invite different responses. Incomes can become more equal as a result of regrettable or objectionable factors, such as increased mortality among the poor, their forced sterilization, expulsion or massacre of the relatively rich, and enforced large-scale reversion to subsistence production. Conversely, the distribution of income can become more equal as a result of, say, an increase in the supply of productive capital relative to unskilled labor. Such differences in experience are clearly pertinent to both domestic and international economic policy. If an epidemic reduces the number of poor in a society, this is hardly a ground for withholding aid; nor is a reduction in incomes as a result of the persecution of productive minorities a reason to grant more aid. These evident but basic considerations are too often ignored because egalitarian discourse, including that on aid, focuses on the results of economic processes to the neglect of the processes themselves.

There is, however, one gap between the Third World and the West which is more significant and precise than the nebulous gap in incomes or living standards: the difference in life expectancy. This gap has narrowed sharply in recent years. In less-developed countries, life expectancy rose from an average of 30–40 years in 1950 to 52 years by 1970. By comparison, in the developed world it increased from 62–65 years to 71 years over the same period. The difference has dropped from approximately 26 to 19 years—a large improvement over such a short period.

Like the idea of a vicious circle of poverty, the notion of a widening gap is an effective slogan—not an argument helpful for understanding or sensible action. Policies of world redistribution are usually based on the tacit assumption that people's capacities, values, and mores are fundamentally uniform and that differences in income and wealth result from accident or exploitation. If that were so, redistribution, or confiscation, would be just and relatively painless, and it would not significantly reduce the aggregate income of all the groups affected, though the process would remove some individual incentive. In reality, however, attitudes, motivations, and policies differ greatly in different societies. The visible gap in international incomes and living standards is the result of these differences.

Three conclusions follow. First, the effects of wealth transfers to promote international equality will be purely temporary. The underlying factors of the gap between the rich and poor will continually reassert themselves. Income will be equal only when its production is equal.

Second, once it is realized that visible income differences reflect differences in economic performance, the leveling process would have to be extended to the underlying determinants, involving far-reaching coercion to eliminate international differences in attitudes and values. It would amount to attempted remolding of people. The coercion would certainly have to include much higher taxation in Western countries and additional taxes on the relatively prosperous Third World groups. Such far-reaching policies cannot be attempted by national governments; they postulate international authority with totalitarian powers.

Third, international wealth transfers reallocate resources from more productive users to the less productive. Wealth transfers reduce total world income. International redistribution may reduce national and world incomes, but it cannot realize its stated aims.

Restitution

Because of the notion that income differences result from exploitation, redistribution and restitution are often closely linked in the advocacy of wealth transfers. Logically, however, they are quite distinct. In what follows, I shall summarize my arguments from earlier publications and supplement them with recent information and observations.[5]

Progressive clergy, Marxist-Leninist writers, and Third World leaders are vocal exponents of the view that the West has caused the poverty of the Third World. Their belief extends far beyond these numerically restricted groups: many in the West believe that Western prosperity has been secured at the expense of the Third World, that "we have climbed on the shoulders of the rest," in the words of a pamphlet distributed by a Third World group in Cambridge, England, a few years ago. Professor Ronald J. Sider, a prominent American clergyman, has written in *Christianity Today* (July 14, 1976) that it would be wrong to suggest that 210 million Americans bear sole responsibility for all the "hunger and injustice in today's world. All the rich developed countries are directly involved . . . We are participants in a system that dooms even more people to agony and death than the slave system did."

Such views are not simply unfounded but false. Throughout the Third World the most advanced and rapidly advancing regions are those with which the West has established the widest commercial contacts, such as Singapore, Malaysia, West Africa, and Latin America. Conversely, the poorest and most backward are those with the fewest such contacts—the aborigines, pygmies, and desert peoples being extreme cases. The idea that aid is restitution for past and current Western misconduct also flatly contradicts the suggestion that it should be given to the poorest countries, as they have little or no external commercial contacts.

Commercial contacts extend people's range of choice. To suggest that this is damaging is to say that people in the Third World do not know what they are doing when they trade with other countries. This condescension, which originates in the West, is often welcome to Third World rulers who can tighten the grip on their subjects by restricting external commercial contacts.

The notion that economic contacts with the West somehow damage the Third World is often supported by the allegation that the West manipulates terms of trade against the Third World. But in reality, the terms of trade have in recent decades been highly favorable to Third World countries, particularly the factoral and income terms that are the ones pertinent to economic development. But even if the terms of trade were unfavorable by some criterion, this would not mean that Western commercial contacts are harmful to these societies—only that they are not quite as beneficial as they could be.

These allegations about the terms of trade often envisage the West as a monolith, its members somehow acting in concert to impose themselves on the Third World. But the terms of trade emerge from innumerable market transactions. The confusion of the diverse collectivity of Western countries with a single decision-making unit derives in part from the naive suspicion that anyone who succeeds in an impersonal market system must somehow have manipulated it to his own advantage.

Another allegation, widely heard in the United States, is that high Western consumption deprives the Third World of too much of the world's resources. But Western consumption is paid for by Western production, which in addition finances both aid and exports of commercial capital to the Third World.

The various allegations of Western responsibility for Third World poverty are all based on the patronizing suggestion that the economic fortunes of the Third World are determined by the West or its forebears. These allegations divert attention from the real causes of poverty, and therefore from the possibilities of mitigating it. They serve to reinforce the widespread feeling of guilt in the West—a feeling that inspires policies directed at its own relief rather than at improving the lot of the Third World poor. Exponents of this guilt are more concerned with their own emotional condition than with the fate of people at the receiving end.

Self-Interest

We are often told that aid serves the economic and political interests of the donor. When advocates of aid address politicians, labor leaders, and businessmen, they often say that aid promotes Western exports and employment because it is used to buy our products. This was in 1979 perhaps the most widely used argument for aid. But as aid is provided by the people of the donor countries, it normally reduces the domestic demand for goods and services in these countries. To argue that aid helps our domestic economy is like saying that a shopkeeper benefits from being burgled if the burglar spends part of the loot in the victim's shop. Direct subsidies to export industries would generate more employment.

Aid is often advocated, particularly in the United States, as a political instrument for keeping the Third World outside the Soviet orbit. But to serve Western political interests, aid would need to be geared to the significance, location, and conduct of the recipients—a form of political or military subsidy with clear conditions attached. However, much U.S. aid goes to countries of no military, political, or economic significance, and no political conditions are imposed on the recipients, as is evident from Western aid to Angola, Ethiopia, Mozambique, Tanzania, and Vietnam. Multilateral aid, a substantial and increasing proportion of total aid, is widely supported on the ground that the interests of the donors do not influence its allocation.

In practice, Western interests are ignored also in bilateral aid. Wholesale expropriation of Western enterprises has not stopped aid to Algeria, Ethiopia, Ghana, Mozambique, Sri Lanka, Tanzania, Zaïre, Zambia, Vietnam, and many other countries. And when the governments of India and Pakistan sought external mediation in the Kashmir dispute in 1965, they turned to the Soviet Union, although they had received American and British aid for years. Aid was never seriously envisaged as an instrument of Western political strategy. If it had been, it would be administered by the political sections of foreign ministries and the defense departments of the donors, not by special aid agencies.

The Western donors' baffling disregard of their own interests arouses suspicions in the recipient countries. It suggests that aid is a covert attempt to buy influence, that it is only partial restitution for past wrongs, or that it is an instrument for dumping unsalable goods. Such allegations are frequently advanced even by friendly aid recipients.

Population Control

The suggestion that aid will reduce population growth to the benefit of both donors and recipients straddles several of the above arguments for aid. This suggestion is sometimes behind financial and technical assistance for birth control programs. But these can be financed by the recipient governments themselves. A more popular version envisages a beneficial spiral where aid raises incomes, higher incomes lead to smaller families, and reduced population growth in turn leads to higher incomes.

Each stage in this reasoning is inconclusive. As we have seen, aid does not necessarily raise incomes; indeed it is more likely to retard their growth. Nor do higher incomes as such reduce population growth. True, higher incomes and reduced birth rates often go together; both reflect greater interest in higher living standards. A rise in the cost of bringing up children, which often accompanies a general rise in living standards, also reduces family size. But a rise in income without a change in the basic determinants of economic performance raises population growth even more because of the higher life expectancy. If people are better off, they will generally have more children unless their higher incomes are accompanied by changes in motivation. Higher income per se, therefore, will not reduce population growth.

Slower population growth does not normally increase incomes appreciably; a family's income level depends largely on personal, social, and political factors, not on physical resources. This is evident in most of Africa and Latin America and much of Asia, where some of the poorest groups live in fertile yet sparsely populated areas, such as Borneo, Sumatra, and parts of Brazil. The great economic differences between ethnic and religious groups inhabiting the same regions are also pertinent. Compare the differing performances of Chinese, Indians, and Malays in Malaysia; Asians and Africans in East Africa; Ibo and others in Nigeria; and Greeks and Turks in Cyprus.

REPERCUSSIONS

The inflow of aid has major adverse repercussions that are likely to far outweigh any tiny contribution of aid to development. In considering these repercussions, we must remember that contribution of aid to development is limited by the difference between the cost of commercial capital and the relationship of aid to Gross National Product (GNP). Adverse repercussions are caused by amounts of aid which, although small relative to GNP, are substantial relative to government revenue, to the volume of imports or exports, or to the size of the exchange sector.

The inflow of aid tends to raise the exchange rate, to support overvalued exchange rates, and to increase domestic money supply. These effects depend on the financial policies of the recipients. Aid thus weakens the international competitive position of the recipients, something that can be offset only by an increase in real productivity as normally accomplished by commercial capital. But aid is not linked to productivity and is more likely to reinforce inflationary tendencies in recipient countries.

Many Third World governments favor balance-of-payments crises for securing aid even though such crises encourage inflationary policies. Inflation is an effective instrument of taxation, and it also provides excuses for imposing controls. Inflation will result also in the West, brought about by growing government spending. The increasing multilateral component of aid also works in this direction because the inflationary consequences, at home and abroad, are now much less likely to be taken into account.

Official wealth transfers go to goverments, not to the people at large. They encourage the disastrous politicization of life in the Third World. The handouts increase the power, resources, and patronage of governments, reinforced by preferential treatment of governments trying to establish state-controlled economies.

Academic and official development literature insists that comprehensive planning is indispensable to development, thus promoting state control. Yet extensive planning has played no part in the progress of the West or of many Third World countries. Third World countries with relatively free economies, such as Hong Kong, Singapore, Malaysia, and the Ivory Coast, have progressed much more in recent years than have those with closely controlled economies, such as Burma and Ghana. This is not surprising: comprehensive planning does not augment resources, it only concentrates state power. State controls promote wasteful deployment of resources, restrict the range and variety of foreign and domestic contacts, and inhibit the spread of new ideas and methods. They intensify the fight for political power, especially in racially and culturally mixed societies.

Egalitarian policies favored by aid supporters work in the same direction. Because of the ethnic and cultural heterogeneity of many Third World countries, egalitarian policies imply more intense coercion there than in the more homogeneous societies of the West.

Third World rulers favor state controls, not as instruments of development or equality, but because controls make it easier to defeat opponents, to reward supporters, and of course to divert resources to themselves. Such use of state controls is taken for granted throughout the Third World. It is criticized in the West only when the critics dislike a regime for other reasons. Mountains of evidence confirm that the pursuit of power, not development or equality, lies behind the mistreatment of Chinese in Indonesia and Malaysia, of Asians in East Africa, Indians in Burma, Tamils in Sri Lanka, and Ibo in Nigeria—the claims of aid-recipient rulers notwithstanding.

Hostility to the free market, which is rife in international and domestic aid agencies, also favors aid recipients who try to strengthen state controls. Indeed, it has often been suggested that the establishment of collectivized economies in the Third World is the prime objective of many aid administrators. Foreign help, including expatriate personnel financed by aid, is often indispensable to Third World state controls.

When social and economic life is extensively politicized, political power may become a matter of life and death, as in Ethiopia, Indonesia, Iran, Pakistan, Tanzania, Uganda, and countless other countries. Politicization diverts attention, activities, and resources from economic activity to politics and public administration, sometimes because this is profitable and often because it is necessary for economic and physical survival. All this provokes tension and even civil war. The history of the Third World in recent decades cannot be understood without considering these relationships between state controls and political conflict.

Beside politicizing life, aid has also facilitated the pursuit of barbarous policies by enabling the governments to conceal from their own people some of the adverse economic consequences of their policies, and by conferring respectability on these policies through continued support from abroad.

Economic and social change in poor countries has been uneven, in that it has affected certain groups, regions, and activities more than others and in that some groups have adjusted to change more rapidly than others. Hostile reactions to change vary from sullen apathy to violent rejection. Insistence on the need for donations from abroad obscures the necessity for the people of the Third World themselves to develop their faculties and attitudes and to adopt the conduct and mores required for sustained material progress—that is, if they indeed prefer higher incomes to their established ways. (This proviso is necessary because people may reasonably prefer to retain their traditions and remain poor; they might welcome material well-being, but not at any cost.)

Official aid is much more likely than commercial contacts to create acute social strains. Commercial ventures are usually geared to local conditions; economic return depends on correct assessment of conditions, while taxpayers' funds are directed from afar and are under no such constraint. The uprooting effects of Western commerce is gradual and tentative. In contrast, many influential aid advocates and administrators propose to completely remold societies, by force if necessary. Aid recipients are thus subjected to total and abrupt change rather than gradual initiation into new ways. In such circumstances, large groups of people decline into an apathetic, inert mass, and they may well be less able than before to take advantage of economic opportunities. Yet such sequences are likely as long as aid places resources in the hands of rulers who, in order to consolidate their authority, wish to destroy traditional modes of life. Former Ugandan president Milton Obote overthrew the popular *kabaka* (traditional ruler) with a large force of tanks amid much bloodshed. Aid money is usually controlled by representatives of the new, centralizing bureaucracy, and, in the absence of an (unstable and fortuitous) alliance between them and the traditional rulers, it promotes enforced disintegration of traditional society.

Aid is neither necessary nor sufficient for material progress. It often supports or even underwrites policies that retard material progress. But it cannot be established conclusively that aid can never promote development—that is, that its adverse repercussions always offset any very small positive contribution of the inflow of resources, even though the adverse effects touch on the basic factors behind development while the marginal benefits do not. It should be noted that the effect of aid on development cannot be inferred from conventional national income statistics: the biases and errors of these statistics (which do not remain constant over time) will necessarily dwarf any positive contribution that aid could possibly make to development. Moreover, the difficulties of establishing causal relationships on the basis of statistical data are particularly pronounced when we try to connect the changes in the economic condition of a society with one particular variable—in this case the inflow of aid. Even according to the Pearson Commission, "The correlation between the amounts of aid received in the past decades and the growth of performance is very weak."[6] The difficulties arise, of course, because the changes depend on many factors operating with different and varying time lags, ranging from quite short periods to generations. For instance, the prosperity of the OPEC countries in the 1970s can hardly be attributed to the Western aid they received in the 1960s.

It should be amply clear from the above that the positive contribution of aid to development is at best only marginal and is likely to be offset by major adverse repercussions. Any general presumption about its net effect on development is therefore adverse. This adverse presumption is underlined by the pronounced shift in emphasis in the advocacy of aid from promotion of development to relief of poverty as the principal ground for aid. The adverse presumption is supported also by the plight of many recipients after decades of aid, including recurrent famines, breakdowns in the economy, persistent balance of payments problems, and difficulties in servicing even very soft loans, the costs of which have been reduced by inflation. Either these soft loans have not increased incomes and taxable capacity, in which case the aid has been wasted, or the aid recipients simply refuse to service these loans. Both interpretations justify the conclusion that aid, though it may bring some benefits, does more harm than good to the peoples of the recipient countries. But even if it did promote development, it is still questionable whether aid could justify the further politicization of life and the barbarous policies it has helped bring about.

PROSPECTS

The Third World and foreign aid are inseparable. If there is a Third World in the 1980s, the United States will give aid. What kind of aid should we give?

The record of the advocacy of foreign aid is one of intellectual failure and political success. The implications and results of foreign aid make it clear that it should be terminated—but at present this is not feasible.

The momentum of existing commitments and the forces behind them preclude early termination, even though other policies could better contribute toward the declared—and generally accepted—objectives of aid. The resulting dilemma is evident: the longer wealth transfers continue, the more difficult it becomes to change course, to question the principles behind them—especially in the face of formidable vested interests. "After spending $221 billion in 31 years to help other countries, the United States finds it is a habit hard to break," wrote *U.S. News and World Report* in 1976. As early termination is impossible, the immediate task is to examine how certain declared objectives of official transfers can best be attained and the worst anomalies contained—all by measures that erode rather than reinforce the interests behind them.

Relief of Distress

This aim of many generous aid supporters should be left to voluntary agencies, with exceptions such as emergency assistance to disaster victims. Ordinary citizens voluntarily contribute large sums for this purpose, and if governments made it clear that this was the province of voluntary charities, the contributions would probably increase greatly. There are other advantages to leaving relief work to charities, particularly those charities that are not politicized: they know far more than Western governments about conditions in the countries in which they operate. Genuine charities are also usually more interested than are Third World governments in assisting the poorest and most distressed. Their activities do not directly promote the politicization of life, increase the stakes of political power, exacerbate political tension, or sustain oppressive policies. Indeed, insofar as they provide an alternative source of help to Third World peoples, such agencies may even reduce the power of governments.

Voluntary aid is financed by people who give to help their fellows. Official aid, in contrast, is tax money extracted from the contributors without their personal consent. A Swiss government proposal to provide substantial funds to the International Development Association was taken to the voters in 1976. The proposal was unanimously supported by the media and the churches, universities, and schools. Yet, in this first-ever popular vote on foreign aid, the proposal was heavily defeated. At the same time, the Swiss voluntarily contributed great sums to a fund for the victims of an earthquake in Italy, as well as to many Third World charities. Clearly, the public can distinguish official aid from voluntary charity.

International Political Strategy

In our context, this key matter can be, and should be, dismissed with only a brief comment. Official Western economic aid has nothing to do with political strategy. This is self-evident for multilateral aid, which is advocated explicitly on the grounds that it is unaffected by the political interests of the donors. But it applies to bilateral aid as well. The suggestion that Western economic aid serves the political strategy of the donors is merely transparent rationalization of the advocacy of aid rather than an argument of substance. If official wealth transfers can promote the political interests of the donors, their appropriate forms are political and military subsidies, which have nothing to do with routine aid.

Third World Development

Official Western policy can best contribute to Third World development by lowering its trade barriers against Third World exports. These barriers restrict markets and external contacts, inhibit productive investment, exacerbate unemployment, and contain the spread of skills. Their partial or complete removal could do much to accelerate material progress in many Third World countries, particularly those in South Asia and Latin America. However, these barriers, familiar obstacles to liberal trade policies, are likely to become stronger in view of the growing competitive strength of many Third World industries, the growing difficulties of internal adjustment, and the apparently ever-increasing effectiveness of pressure groups. We should keep in mind that Western consumers and taxpayers will continue to pay for the benefit of workers, managers, and owners of protected industries.

It might be sensible to lift some of these restrictions and simultaneously to redirect some aid expenditures to compensate Western groups damaged by cheap Third World imports. Such a course would involve drawbacks: why should the victims of one kind of economic change be compensated and others not? Still, if found feasible, such a policy might be a lesser evil than the indefinite continuation of ever-expanding import restrictions and ever-increasing aid.

Possible trade liberalization invites the more difficult question of liberalizing the immigration policies of donor countries. I cannot here develop this issue, which clearly involves wide-ranging political, social, and cultural matters. But should trade liberalization make substantial headway, one could then consider the conditions under which freer immigration could be implemented and financed, possibly by aid funds, so as to benefit both the present donors and Third World countries without serious upheaval in the former.

Aid Reform

Official aid will continue, even if all these changes were to take place. The immediate political task, though a second-best solution, is therefore to try to improve aid while working toward its eventual termination.

Aid should take forms that make it possible to identify its costs and benefits. Commodity agreements must be ended; apart from damaging the interests of the poorest, both in the West and in the Third World, and thus creating demands for more redistribution and more wealth transfers, this form of aid bypasses even the semblance of legislative control. Its overall impact is impossible to assess, though we know that it usually triggers political tension within and between the participating countries.

Aid should take the form of untied cash grants. Tied aid confuses assistance to Western export interests with assistance to the Third World recipients, suggesting that it is only a means for exporting unemployment or dumping unsalable surpluses. Subsidized loans confuse handouts with investment and create tensions because the donors see them as gifts and the recipients as burdens. The aid element in subsidized loans is often difficult to compute because this requires assessment of the commercial terms and because the servicing of such loans is open to all kinds of manipulation. Such loans also lead to demands for debt cancellation, which, among other perverse results, does nothing to help the poor.

Should untied cash grants be bilateral or channeled through multinational organizations? Supporters of the multilateral approach claim that their method removes aid from the political arena and generally makes aid allocations more objective and conducive to development. These claims are unfounded: transfer of taxpayers' money to foreign governments is inevitably political; the multilateral approach achieves only the further replacement of the already modest legislative control with control by those running the international organizations.

International aid administrators have distinct personal, political, and professional interests. Most of their constituents are Third World governments, and they increasingly regard themselves as spokesmen for the Third World. They persistently favor the expansion of aid and the preferential treatment of governments trying to impose extensive state controls. These priorities please their constituents and create more influence, power, and jobs for the administrators. Moreover, these people—especially the most influential and active—tend to be hostile to the market system and to the internal arrangements of Western society.

The prospects may be menacing. Multilateral aid has become part of the campaign to equalize world incomes and living standards. Such international equalization involves large-scale coercion. The greater these attempts and the greater the distance between the victims and those who exercise control, the more intensive, ruthless, and lasting will be the process.

Multilateral aid eliminates the last vestige of contact between the recipient governments on one side, and donor taxpayers and their representatives on the other. This further reduces the contact between suppliers and users of aid. This is likely to reduce whatever productivity these funds may have because contact between supplier and user of capital promotes its productivity. Finally, multilateral aid makes it impossible for donor governments to restrain even the most wasteful and barbarous policies of the recipients.

For this reason, aid should take the form of bilateral cash grants. This form can be most easily controlled by the elected representatives of the taxpayers. Such grants should be given for strictly limited periods, and donors should refuse long-range commitments, as it is impossible to foresee who the eventual recipients will be and what they will do.

Who should receive the grants? Not governments whose external policies conflict with the donors' interests. The allocation should also favor governments that pursue liberal foreign trade policies and offer security for private investment, both foreign and domestic. Such conditions encourage foreign trade and investment and would benefit the peoples of the recipient countries by reducing their dependence on their governments.

The donors can, and should, go even further. In allocating aid they should favor governments that, within the bounds of human and financial resources, try to perform the indispensable tasks of government but refrain from close control of the economy—governments that govern rather than plan. This criterion would promote liberal economic systems, minimize coercion, reduce political tensions, and favor material progress.

Should such aid, even when it goes to governments pursuing liberal economic policies, be a general budget supplement, or should it be directed to specific projects? The latter course seems generally preferable; it places greater restraint on the politicization of life and government patronage than do simple cash grants. It is also likely to contribute more directly to economic productivity. The donors should also make it clear that these transfers do not represent restitution for misconduct, nor are they an instrument for global redistribution or for securing specified growth rates and income levels. If this is not made clear, the donors will be subject to sustained blackmail and pressured to accept completely open-ended commitments.

Beside removing some of the anomalies of aid, these criteria would simplify its administration and remove some of the mystique surrounding it. They would reduce the cost of administering aid, lessen the influence of the international and domestic aid organizations, and in turn make it somewhat easier to eventually phase out the whole system of official wealth transfers.

These constraints in the allocation of aid are not unreasonable. If public spending is controlled by representatives of the taxpayers, why should taxpayers' funds going to foreign governments not be subject to such control?

The above criteria merely replace the current bias in favor of state-controlled economies with a liberal influence. Thus, they go counter to the frequent suggestions that aid should be used to promote redistribution (confiscation) and planned economies in the Third World.

Aid represents gifts of scarce capital; the demand necessarily exceeds the amount available. Aid to one recipient not only diminishes the resources of the donors, it also reduces the aid available to others. If aid is used ineffectively by some recipients, aggregate future requirements will be increased. And if some recipients pursue damaging economic policies, they will harm the prospects of other recipients, add to the unpopularity of aid within donor countries, and increase future aid requirements. So both donors and recipients have an inescapable interest in the productive use of aid.

There is ample scope for reforming the methods and criteria of Western aid. The entire aid system, including the commitments of the donors and the criteria of allocation, must be reconsidered. Despite appearances, now may be the time to begin. In the last year or two some of the more bizarre results of aid have been noted even in publications that support aid, including the *Washington Post* and the *Economist*. If the system is not reconsidered, the West, including the United States, will be drawn into further unlimited commitments, the system will continue to promote totalitarian collectivism in many poor countries, Western taxpayers will continue to underwrite inhuman policies, and the objectives of many generous aid supporters will continue to be frustrated.

The aid reform suggested here ought to be acceptable to those aid supporters who seek to improve the economic conditions of Third World peoples. If other objectives are deemed more important—more jobs for aid administrators, greater power for international organizations, more state control of Third World economies, or the pursuit of worldwide equality—my proposals will not appeal. But when were such objectives approved by Western voters and taxpayers, let alone chosen by them?

NOTES

1. Unless otherwise indicated, all references to aid are to official economic aid, either bilateral or channeled through official international economic organizations.

2. For instance, the *Times* (London), March 22 and 23, 1978.

3. See the *Times* (London), November 28, 1969, and March 8 and 19, 1973.

4. It has even been argued that the maximum contribution of aid to development is smaller still, namely, the *return* on the avoided cost of borrowing. But we are now in the realm of second or third differentials of the impact of aid on the level of income. Of course, this method of calculation only reduces further an already negligible figure.

5. See P. T. Bauer, *Dissent on Development* (Cambridge: Harvard University Press, 1976); and "Western Guilt and Third World Poverty," *Commentary* (January 1976), esp. sec. 5.

6. *Report of the Commission for International Development* (New York, 1969), p. 49.

U.S. Foreign Economic Policies

G. M. Meier

XXI

As the 1970s witnessed the disintegration of the Bretton Woods regime, so must the 1980s see innovative policies to raise the standard of international economic conduct among nations. For a quarter century, the Bretton Woods system imposed some order on the world economy through the International Monetary Fund (IMF), the World Bank, and the General Agreement on Tariffs and Trade (GATT). But a liberal economic order becomes increasingly difficult to sustain as each nation finds it more onerous to achieve simultaneously the multiple objectives of internal balance (a tolerable level of unemployment and inflation), external balance (avoidance of imbalance in international payments), and trade liberalization (a reduction in trade restrictions). When conflicts within a nation intensify, so too do the tensions and conflicts among nations.

These conflicts stem from an intensification of the "internationalization process," and the re-establishment of order in the world community depends on their resolution. Three recent changes complicate their resolution, however: 1) the politicization of economic issues; 2) the linking of trade, monetary, and development issues; and 3) the loss by the United States of political hegemony and status as a supereconomy.

TOWARD PUBLIC ORDER IN THE WORLD COMMUNITY

The consequences of increased internationalization are already visible, but no authoritative international process for establishing standards and rules of conduct in international economic affairs exists. The result is that every nation practices suboptimal policies that conflict with the policies of other nations. The challenge of the 1980s is to raise the quality of public decisions in the international economic area, both in the choice of objectives and in the use of policy instruments. Protectionism, the Organization of Petroleum Exporting Countries (OPEC), the depreciation of the dollar, and the calls for a new international economic order are only immediate manifestations of the more general global economic challenge.

Much has been written recently about interdependence. But it is not a new phenomenon; for centuries, world economic integration has been increasing, and nations have become more sensitive and vulnerable to external events. In the past quarter century, however, the pace of integration has accelerated. The consequences of interdependence have also become more pronounced; the duration of international economic conflicts has lengthened, the extent of economic gains and losses has grown, and the inadequacy of policy measures to resolve conflicts has increased.

Interdependence might be better interpreted as the result of the internationalization of the economic system. In the broadest possible sense, the problems of the 1980s will stem from the consequences of internationalization. An outstanding feature of this process has been the increase in the international flow of commodities, factors of production, management, technology, and financial capital, which have consequently become more responsive—or more elastic—to differences between domestic and foreign variables. The stocks of foreign factors within a country are also much larger now.

Another aspect of this process has been the internationalization of institutions. Beyond the nation-state, a number of intergovernmental institutions have arisen—ranging from international organizations such as the GATT, the World Bank, the IMF, and the United Nations Conference on Trade and Development (UNCTAD), to regional arrangements such as the European Economic Community (EEC), the Andean Group, and the Organization for Economic Cooperation and Development (OECD). Interest groups, such as labor unions, employer associations, and foundations, have also expanded across national borders. Above all, the growth of multinational corporations has been remarkable, and a greater number of larger firms operate an expanding number of foreign subsidiaries.

To an economist, the internationalization of markets is commendable because it promotes efficiency, specialization, and competition. To a national policymaker, however, internationalization has a negative side: it heightens the vulnerability of a nation to external developments. Domestic autonomy in policymaking is subordinated to international policy considerations. International economics is opposed by national politics. When the economic objectives of two or more nations clash, international tension and conflict result. This has been especially noticeable when the structure of world production and the distribution of the world product have altered, with the resultant re-allocation of benefits among nations and groups within nations.

The conflicts can be grouped in three categories: 1) those that arise because a nation seeks to acquire a larger share of the gains from trade or foreign investment; 2) those that arise when a country tries to avoid being damaged by developments in another country; and 3) those that arise because a country wants to maintain its domestic autonomy in policymaking when confronted with an international event.

More specifically, the major conflicts tend to concern the following issues:

1) Markets: the attempt of each nation to have greater access for its exports to the markets of other countries and ready access to imports of needed resources from the markets of other countries.
2) Terms of trade: the attempt of each country to improve its terms of trade by raising export prices relative to import prices.
3) Terms of foreign investment: the attempt by host governments to raise the benefit-cost ratio of foreign capital inflows.
4) Adjustment costs to imports: the attempt of each nation to minimize market disruption or domestic injury from greater imports.
5) Costs of balance-of-payments adjustment: the attempt of each nation to minimize the cost of adjusting to a disequilibrium in its balance of payments by avoiding remedial policies or by trying to place some of the burden of adjustment on other countries.
6) Stabilization policies: the attempt of each nation to exercise national economic autonomy in stabilizing its own economy without subjecting its policies to external conditions.

The most important policy issues raised by these conflicts relate to international trade policy, international monetary policy, and international development policy. In searching for a normative order that might resolve these conflicts, many policymakers have sought more effective management of the internationalization process in the hopes of establishing an economic order with less discord. "Managed" or "orderly" trade has been hailed as an objective as has "managed floating" or "orderly arrangements" of foreign exchange rates. Some have advocated "collective management" by a small group of OECD countries.

And the management of economic relations (trade, investment, debt) between the more and the less developed countries is a continual request in international forums. But each request for more management of the international economy must evoke a cautionary response: Avoid mismanagement!

POLICY CHOICES IN TRADE POLICY

Since fostering the reciprocal trade agreements program of the 1930s, the United States has advocated trade liberalization in a series of multilateral trade negotiations. Following the sixth round of GATT negotiations in the late 1960s (the Kennedy Round), the weighted average tariff for the major trading nations was reduced to less than 8 percent on all industrial products and 2 percent on raw materials. The ratio of tariffs to dutiable imports was as high as 53 percent in 1930–1933 but by 1974 declined to 8 percent. At the start of the 1970s, the greater part of international trade was substantially free of restrictions, and exporters and importers enjoyed a considerable degree of certainty and stability. But this changed after the oil crisis and world recession of 1974–75 as nations retreated from a liberal trading system toward a "new protectionism"—new both in form and severity. Nontariff barriers were increasingly applied to imports, in the form of quantitative restrictions, orderly marketing agreements (OMAs), and voluntary export restraints (VERs), which all imposed some type of quota on imports and paralyzed the operation of the price mechanism internationally.

Outside the market price system, the United States pursued these quantitative limitations on footwear, textiles, and color televisions. Although in 1977 the U.S. International Trade Commission (ITC) recommended the imposition of tariff quotas applicable to imports of nonrubber footwear from all sources, the president decided instead to negotiate OMAs with the principal supply nations (Taiwan and Korea), applicable until 1981. Again, instead of following the ITC's recommendation of an increase in tariffs, the president negotiated an OMA covering U.S. imports of television sets and parts from Japan for the period 1977–1980. This OMA limited imports to 1.75 million sets a year, a 40 percent reduction from the 1976 level of imports.

"Buy national" policies in government procurement and antidumping regulations also spread protectionism. Subsidies on exports became more suspect, and countervailing duties were increasingly applied, without the necessity of proving any domestic injury. The vexing problems of textile imports was met with a Long-Term Textile Agreement (1962–1973) and then the Multifiber Agreement (1974–1981), which expanded coverage of quotas to man-made fibers and wool as well as cotton textiles and imposed a maximum annual rate of increase in imports in the interest of orderly trade and the avoidance of market disruption. Although the Multifiber Agreement set a 6 percent annual rate of growth for exporting countries, it also leaves considerable scope for importing countries to set lower limits through bilateral agreements. Accordingly, the United States reached agreements with Hong Kong, Korea, and Taiwan to limit their 1978 exports of textiles and clothing to the United States at the 1977 level and to increase the exports of a number of sensitive items at a rate substantially less than 6 percent thereafter. The particular problem of steel imports was met by the U.S. Treasury initiating a "trigger price" mechanism in 1978 that established minimum prices at which steel mill products could be imported, with dumping penalties for any sales of imported steel at prices below the trigger level.

The causes of the new protectionism are several and extend beyond the traditional objective of protecting a particular industry against a sudden upsurge of competing imports. True, the problem of excess capacity in the textile and steel industries supported protectionism in these industries. Political pressures from import-sensitive industries also influenced substantive provisions of the Trade Act of 1974 and the voting on the act. Subsequently, in complaints filed with the ITC, many American firms succeeded in having imports controlled through escape clause actions that claim domestic injury or through the imposition of antidumping or countervailing duties. During the 1970s, there were over one hundred such actions.

Beyond the traditional pressures for protectionism, however, socio-political concern with economic security and "fair shares" has increased, leading to selective interventions in the economy in support of particular interests. The reluctance to adjust to economic change became more widespread, even if at the expense of economic efficiency or growth. The cliché that "imports are responsible for the loss of jobs"—though demonstrably wrong for the aggregate economy—gained more supporters in an economy suffering from both unemployment and inflation. Although import restrictions to maintain jobs in import industries adversely affect jobs in export industries, and though the loss of jobs from completely duty-free imports would be less than the normal annual displacement of workers through technological change, nonetheless in an economy already suffering 6 or 7 percent unemployment, the desire to perpetuate existing employment—even in senescent industries—is strong. A government concerned about creating jobs without inflation may view protection as superior to an expansionary fiscal policy. Organized labor, which earlier supported a liberal trade policy, also became increasingly protectionist, and many AFL-CIO unions favored import quotas during the 1970s.

Protectionist forces also grew stronger as the U.S. trade deficit worsened during the 1970s. With American imports greater than exports and Japan and Germany maintaining large surpluses in their trade balances, the popular appeal of controlling imports to reduce the trade deficit was considerable. Instead of turning to the alternative remedial policies of deflation or exchange rate depreciation, many interest groups simply advocated direct controls over trade.

Finally, controls on American exports or imports were instituted to achieve other objectives of American foreign policy. For instance, exports of enriched uranium were controlled as part of the nonproliferation issue. Relations with the Soviet Union also dictated some trade restrictions. More generally, so did the issue of human rights.

As protectionist forces gained strength, the consequences of protectionism—the sheltering of high-cost, inefficient domestic producers, an increase in the domestic price of sheltered commodities, a reduction in domestic consumption of the commodities, and a restriction of import volume—became more widespread. Although both tariffs and quotas have these effects, the tariff is relatively genteel in comparison with the physical control exercised by a quota. Though the tariff raises the price for consumers, it still allows consumer choice between domestic products and imports. A quota, in contrast, restricts consumer choice and limits competition between domestic and foreign producers in a direct, specific, physical manner. The market power of domestic producers is increased, and domestic importers may increase prices. These price increases are then passed forward through other stages of the production process. A quota also prevents future changes in relative costs and shifts in comparative advantage from affecting the structure of production; the quantitative control freezes factors of production in low-productivity activities and delays any transformation in industrial structure, forestalling the desired reallocation of resources from lower- to higher-productivity sectors. There are thus no incentives to become more productive or adjust to competitive pressures. Discretionary decision making supplants the dictates of the market, with uncertain and arbitrary results.

Trade restrictions also create uncertainty, and the threat of the imposition of an OMA or VER has a chilling effect on exporters. This is especially significant for the newly industrialized countries (NICS), such as Korea, Taiwan, Hong Kong, and Singapore, that are rapidly expanding their exports of manufactures and semimanufactures to the more industrialized countries. The claims of market disruption and domestic injury cause the older industrial countries to invoke not only tariffs, but the more restrictive nontariff barriers of quotas, OMAs, and VERs—through unilateral or bilateral policies undertaken outside GATT.

Unfortunately, the recently concluded multilateral trade negotiations (Tokyo Round) did little to ease the problem of nontariff barriers. Although overall tariff cuts were some 33 percent, applying to about one-fifth of world trade over an eight- to ten-year period, the agreements on reducing nontariff barriers were not as significant. Some reforms of arbitrary practices in customs valuation, procedures for setting technical standards for imports, competitive international bidding for supplying goods to governments, and limitations on the use of government subsidies to encourage exports were accomplished. A major failure of the Tokyo Round was the lack of regulation of market safeguards. This will continue to be a crucial issue for future negotiation. Without action on market safeguards, the force of the new protectionism will not be diminished.

During the 1980s, as in recent years, a sharp increase in imports, whether induced by a tariff reduction or simply occurring autonomously, will evoke requests by domestic producers of import-competing products, and workers in these industries, for some form of market safeguard to limit imports. Complaints of domestic injury will be frequent. When the costs are more visible to a government than the benefits, the policy reaction is likely to be to raise a previously lowered tariff, impose quantitative restrictions on imports, apply countervailing duties or antidumping restrictions, or resort to OMAs and VERs.

The terms market disruption and domestic injury are attempts to define the social damage from imports—but the terms are as narrow or broad as some social decision maker cares to make them. The terms can be interpreted to refer to dislocation costs that result from imports that are not fully calculated by the market—namely, the cost of unemployment, the cost of transferring the displaced resources to new activities, and the value of the output forgone until resources move to new productive activities.

As an expedient means of restraining imports, the OMAs and VERs deserve special attention. They bypass the GATT and avoid the conditions specified by Article XIX of GATT for using a quota or increasing a previously reduced tariff. The GATT conditions are more restrictive—namely, the imports must be due to a prior tariff reduction, the country that imposes a market safeguard must do so on a most-favored-nation basis, and it must offer in return some compensation by way of another tariff reduction or else face retaliation.

Similarly, an OMA or VER avoids the restrictions on import relief stipulated in the U.S. Trade Act of 1974 (Section 201). Instead of following most-favored-nation treatment, the OMA or VER can be applied in a discriminatory fashion to a specific country. Further, as with any quantitative restriction, there is none of the unpredictability about the amount of imports that characterizes a tariff; regardless of the differential between domestic and foreign prices, imports are restricted to a definite quantity.

The U.S. Trade Act of 1974 gave a broad mandate to seek revision of GATT during the Tokyo Round, including an explicit call for "the revision of Article XIX of the GATT into a truly international safeguard procedure which takes into account all forms of import restraints countries use in response to injurious competition or threat of such competition."[1] Although the United States viewed a new safeguards agreement as one of the objectives of the Tokyo Round, no success was achieved. In the immediate future, therefore, efforts must still be made to revise Article XIX of GATT. This is necessary from the standpoint of negotiation strategy to achieve trade liberalization, to prevent more serious protectionist legislation from being enacted, and to reduce pressure on countries to solve their trade problems outside the multilateral framework of GATT. It is also necessary to approach more closely the conditions of economic efficiency.

How might Article XIX be revised? In resorting to OMAs, the determination of serious injury is too often based on national political pressures instead of economic analysis. It would be desirable if bilaterally negotiated agreements could be brought under multilateral surveillance by some international review body. Although it may initially be difficult for nations to agree on a standard of serious injury, the international review body would serve a useful function by attempting to harmonize national procedures, provide an international forum for additional consultation, and eventually establish more definitive criteria for the use of market safeguards. Moreover, in the event a national finding of injury was found internationally unacceptable, the safeguard-invoking country might then be compelled to offer equivalent compensation to or suffer corresponding retaliation by its trading partners. If, however, the finding is accepted, then trading partners could be asked to waive their right to compensation or retaliation.

Moreover, it would be desirable if countries could be given an effective assurance of a continually growing access to the protected market and a foreseeable removal of the market safeguard. This is especially vital for the NICs that are entering export markets. To this end, the right to invoke Article XIX might be conditioned by requirements that 1) the protection afforded by the safeguard measure be degressive over a certain number of years (such as a diminishing tariff rate or enlarged quota over time) and terminal within some designated time period; 2) the invoking country be obligated to promote adjustments that will reduce the dislocation cost; and 3) the use of the safeguard measures and the adjustment efforts be open to multilateral surveillance.

If the situation of "serious injury" is to be ameliorated and dislocation costs reduced, governments must pursue adjustment policies. Otherwise industries that prefer protection to adjustment will continue the pressure for retention of the market safeguard. The international review body should therefore insist that the market safeguard mechanism be coupled with appropriate policies of adjustment assistance. In various ways, efforts could be made to limit the use of safeguards and promote adjustment assistance. For example, the incentives to adopt policies of adjustment assistance would be intensified if retaliation were permitted or additional and proportionately larger concessions were required whenever the safeguards were not removed or reduced after a designated time period. Any protective measure could also be required to be sharply degressive over a fairly short time span. If countries would agree to use production subsidies rather than tariffs or quotas, the fiscal cost might also induce speedier adjustment policies. At the least, methods of international surveillance could be instituted to disclose the types of adjustment policies being used and to monitor their progress.

Market disruption can be defined as simply the inability or unwillingness to make adequate adjustments to imports. The problem of market safeguards must therefore be analyzed in conjunction with measures of adjustment assistance. In the U.S. Trade Act, adjustment assistance takes various forms: direct compensation to workers and firms in industries suffering serious injury from imports, retraining and relocation allowances for displaced workers, employment and marketing information, technical assistance, financial assistance and tax relief to firms, and assistance to affected communities. The objective of these measures, however, should be to provide transformation assistance—that is, promote the movement of resources out of the industry that is losing its comparative advantage—not to perpetuate the retention of inefficient resources in the depressed industry.

Adjustment assistance and market safeguards are complementary, not alternate policies. Whereas market safeguards slow down the speed of the change that has to be absorbed, the adjustment assistance should be designed to increase the speed with which change can be absorbed. The justification for market safeguards is that they reduce adjustment cost by extending the transformation process in time. The justification for adjustment assistance is that it hastens the removal of trade restrictions. Otherwise the case for assistance to an import-competing industry has no more merit than assistance to exporters injured by competition from other exporting countries or assistance to any domestic firm injured by economic changes. The removal of trade distortions must be the ultimate purpose of adjustment assistance. From the viewpoint of the American economy as a whole, empirical studies have shown that the cost of adjustment assistance to affected workers and firms is much less than the benefits from imports. These benefits are reduced prices for consumers, a more efficient allocation of domestic resources, and the avoidance of retaliatory protectionist action by other countries that would adversely affect American exports.[2]

To make the transformation assistance more effective, the conversion of resources to higher-productivity uses should be promoted as early as possible. Instead of delaying an investigation and an adjustment assistance program until serious injury has been determined, it may be more sensible to shift to an "early warning" approach that makes it possible both to anticipate probable difficulties and to deal with these at an early stage. In essence, the problem is to devise an anticipatory, comprehensive approach that will be harmonious with the changing character of the international division of labor and facilitate the movement of resources in the direction of more efficient international resource allocation.

This problem of dislocation will become more acute—and the time for adjustment shorter—as technology is diffused more rapidly to the less developed countries (LDCs), transnational corporations expand, and the developing countries accelerate their industrialization process. As the LDCs acquire a wider comparative advantage in the well-standardized, labor-intensive manufacturing industries, they will become increasingly competitive with the older labor-intensive, import-sensitive industries of the more developed countries. To facilitate this change, incentives are needed for speedier adjustment policies as the protectionist effects of market safeguards are continually reduced and ultimately eliminated.

In the immediate future, the resort to nontariff barriers will continue to place the free trade versus protection debate in a context wider than the old-fashioned tariff debate. The nontariff barriers are closely linked to issues of fair trade as ambiguous as they are controversial. Especially needed now is a clarification of international rules that will define legitimate actions to protect fair competition and abuse of these actions for protectionist purposes.

Finally, it is apparent that it is even more difficult for the United States to institute efficient trade policies when it has a balance-of-payments problem. Trade protection is often balance-of-payments protection in the absence of an effective adjustment mechanism for international payments imbalance. Appropriate policies for international trading arrangements therefore require, in turn, appropriate policies for international payments problems.

POLICY CHOICES IN INTERNATIONAL MONETARY POLICY

Beyond complicating trade policy, balance-of-payments problems must be addressed in their own right. American policymakers now confront complex decisions about the role of the dollar as the leading international currency, the respective degrees of flexibility and intervention in foreign exchange markets, and the future course of international monetary reform. Since the United States ended the convertibility of dollars into gold in 1971, the international monetary system has changed markedly. Most major currencies have been floating in international currency markets—but not freely. Monetary authorities choose to intervene on currency markets to hold the rate at a value different from what would be determined in freely flexible exchange markets.

Although the United States has wanted flexibility in exchange rates to correct an imbalance in international payments, it also has wanted stability in the value of the dollar to sustain its acceptability as a reserve currency, willingly held by foreign monetary authorities. But whereas the accumulation of dollars by other nations and their use as reserve assets are now voluntary instead of mandatory as before 1971, the dollar has declined in value since 1978 relative to such other major currencies as the yen, deutsche mark, and Swiss franc. If Japan and West Germany do not adopt measures to remove their trade surpluses, it then becomes all the more imperative that the United States strengthen its own trade position by becoming more competitive. This requires, in turn, both disinflationary policies that a government is reluctant to sponsor when there is already a high rate of unemployment, and measures to increase productivity that may take a long time to be effective. As long as there is internal imbalance—through governmental deficit spending and inflationary pressures—there will be external imbalance, and the dollar will depreciate relative to the stronger currencies of less inflationary countries.

The Existing Regime

As with the GATT, the IMF has been superseded by unilateral action. The task of the 1980s is to reconstitute a code of conduct in international monetary affairs. Since 1973, the international monetary system (some critics may say "nonsystem") has become one of floating exchange rates—but with discretionary official intervention to manage the float (again, some critics might say a "dirty float"). The managed floating regime contrasts with the previous system of pegged-but-adjustable exchange rates established by the IMF after World War II and enduring under the gold-convertible dollar standard until 1971. Since the collapse of this system, there have been many proposals for international monetary reform. But, at the same time, the foreign exchange markets have necessarily had to continue functioning daily in some manner. Countries have determined their exchange rates under the new international paper dollar standard in varous ways: some have chosen to peg their currencies to a single currency, some to a basket of currencies, some have joined in a currency area with limited margins of fluctuations in the exchange rates between partner countries (European Monetary System), and some float independently.

If rates were freely floating, there would be no need for international reserves; all the balancing would be done through exchange rate movements until supply equalled demand on the foreign exchange markets. But if countries intervene on the markets to prevent their exchange rates from moving beyond a limited range, the monetary authorities will again need internationally acceptable monetary assets with which to intervene to hold the rate within the desired range.

Now suppose exchange rates were freely flexible. If, for example, the United States imported more from Japan than it exported to Japan, the dollar would depreciate in terms of yen—the rate changing, say, from ¥215 : $1 to ¥200 : $1. The export prices of American goods would then fall in terms of yen, and this should cause the quantity of exports to increase. The prices of goods imported by the United States would tend to rise in terms of dollars, and this would reduce the amount imported. If the response in demand to changes in prices is sufficiently high, the exports of the country with a depreciating currency will rise relative to its imports, and the incipient deficit will be avoided by the price changes caused by movement in the exchange rate.

In contrast, if the exchange rate is held fixed, then the balance-of-trade deficit requires a loss of international reserve assets from the deficit country or the imposition of restrictive controls on trade or the sufferance of deflation in income and output until the demand for imports falls sufficiently. The merit of a freely fluctuating exchange rate is that it allows a country to escape the costs of direct controls or deflation. But this assumes that 1) governments allow the rate to move freely, 2) the depreciation of the deficit country's currency will be effective in removing a deficit, and 3) the country is willing to endure the costs of depreciation.

What are the costs of adjustment through depreciation? Depreciation has a general effect on all prices in the foreign trade sector, acting as if a subsidy had been given to all exports and a tax imposed on all imports. A government may want, however, to be selective and alter only some prices of specific exports and imports. Depreciation may then be costly because it is selective and not general in its impact.

Depreciation also requires a shift in resources when the demand for exports increases, the demand for imports falls, and the demand for import-substitutes produced at home rises. Resources must then be transferred into the export- and the import-competing sectors unless excess capacity already exists in these sectors. These readjustments in resource allocation are neither frictionless nor timeless; they involve costs of transfer.

Further, depreciation entails a change in the distribution of income. Those who consume imported commodities suffer a rise in their cost of living and a fall in their real incomes. Exporters, in contrast, reap a windfall because foreign currency is now worth more in exchange for home currency. The factors of production employed in export- and import-competing sectors are also likely to benefit as demand shifts toward these sectors.

Because depreciation is itself inflationary and exacerbates inflationary forces, it is especially costly during an inflationary period. The increase in exports and decrease in imports diminish the available supply of goods at the same time as the aggregate demand for commodities rises. In addition, there may be a cost-push type of inflation since import prices are rising. Domestic firms may also raise their prices of competing substitutes when import prices rise (the price of American cars may rise when the price of imported Japanese cars rise). Wages also rise as the cost of living increases and labor seeks to maintain real wages. To offset these inflationary forces, the country may need to impose contractionary monetary and fiscal policies or find other instruments by which a depreciation-inflation spiral can be halted.

Finally, if depreciation is effective in increasing the volume of exports and reducing the volume of imports, it must reduce the total amount of resources available for home consumption, investment, and government expenditure. The rest of the world gains greater command over the depreciating country's resources, and the depreciating country has less command over foreign resources. The ultimate consequence of depreciation is that the deficit country's real expenditure must decline. The availability of resources must expand relative to the competing demands for the resources.

When a country suffers a balance-of-payments deficit, no mechanism of adjustment is without its burden. The central policy problem is to determine which of the alternative adjustment mechanisms is least burdensome and how the burden of international adjustment is to be shared among deficit and surplus countries.

The United States has wanted to avoid the alternative burdens of a more general and deeper deflation in income and employment and the costs of direct controls on trade and capital movements. Flexibility in the exchange rate gives the government another policy instrument that might allow the country to avoid surrendering national autonomy over its domestic economic policy objectives (internal balance) or the gains from trade (trade liberalization). At the beginning of the 1980s, however, the problem for the United States appears more acute. Depreciation has not quickly removed the trade deficit, and its costs are being felt more keenly. Moreover, the large fluctuations of the dollar threaten its acceptability as an international paper-dollar standard.

By the end of the 1970s, governments had revealed through their policy actions that they do not desire full flexibility of exchange rates. The permissible fluctuation under the managed floating system has been wide at times with substantial short-term fluctuations, but still considerably within the range that would have occurred if there had been no market intervention.

Conditions in financial markets, rather than the demand and supply of foreign exchange for commodity transactions, may now be more important for determining short-run exchange movements. Interest rate differentials between countries induce large international movements in short-term capital. Current rates of return, risk factors, and expected future rates of return are significant in determining the prices of foreign currencies. When these returns and risks change substantially, so do exchange rates—unless governments intervene to manage the fluctuations in exchange rates. And this they have done. Governments have been attempting to put upward or downward pressures on their currencies not only by direct intervention in the exchange markets, but also indirectly by influencing foreign borrowing, imposing capital controls, and pursuing monetary policies that affect short-term capital movements. In view of competitive nonrevaluations (the reluctance of Japan and West Germany to appreciate their currencies) and dirty floats, the essential question in practice has been what degree of flexibility is feasible—what is the acceptable and desirable range of limited flexibility? Furthermore, if a managed floating system is to continue, should not the floating rates be managed internationally rather than nationally? The central policy issue is to determine the optimal degree of flexibility and then devise guidelines or rules for multilateral surveillance by the IMF.

Policy decisions regarding exchange rates are in turn closely related to phenomena of international liquidity—that is, the sources, amounts, and distribution of the means of settling international accounts. As governments intervene in the foreign exchange markets, they affect their foreign reserve holdings. At present, official international liquidity is composed of the monetary authorities' holdings of gold, foreign exchange, drawing rights at the IMF, and special drawing rights (SDRs). The total stock of international liquidity has become highly responsive to the volume and incidence of official intervention in foreign exchange markets and to the amount of borrowing by governments in private international financial markets, such as the Eurocurrency market (where deposits denominated in dollars are held in banks outside the United States).

It is striking that world reserves rose almost sixfold from 1959 to 1977, but that world monetary gold holdings contributed scarcely at all to this huge expansion, and allocations of SDRs and IMF lending contributed barely 10 percent to the global increase.[3] Most of the increase was foreign exchange holdings, of which traceable dollar and Eurodollar holdings accounted for more than 80 percent, having risen nearly twenty times, from $10 billion in 1959 to $81 billion at the end of 1972 to $197 billion at the end of 1977.

The global change in official exchange holdings raises two essential questions. Should any future rise in reserves take the form of even larger dollar balances or should any increase be in other forms of international liquidity (gold, IMF quotas, or SDR allocations)? And will the surplus countries continue to find the dollar an acceptable reserve asset? If the international community agrees to create reserves from sources other than the dollar or surplus countries become reluctant to hold a shrinking paper dollar, then the United States will confront greater pressures for balance-of-payments adjustment.

The Near-Term Outlook. Although the deficit in the trade and services accounts of the United States is expected to decline in 1979 from the $17 billion deficit in 1978, concern about pressure on the dollar remains. Depreciation of the dollar will stimulate exports and reduce imports—but with some lags. Although depreciation raises the prices of imports and lowers the prices of exports, the physical volume of imports and exports may change only with a time lag because of fixed buying habits and long-term contracts that alter only over a longer period. By 1979, however, some of the positive effects of the previous depreciation of the dollar were appearing; the U.S. trade deficit was smaller. But even though the yen had appreciated, Japan's trade surplus with the United States still increased in 1979. Clearly, currency depreciation and appreciations alone are not enough to right international imbalances. Domestic management of fiscal and monetary policies are equally important. Unless inflationary pressures are removed in the United States and more expansionary pressures instilled in the Japanese and German economies, the variations in exchange rates cannot be fully effective. Any deflation through a decline in money wages is politically unacceptable. Consequently, more emphasis must be given to a contraction of aggregate demand in the American economy—to the management of credit and fiscal policies. Unless growth in the money supply is slowed and the fiscal deficit reduced, the pressure of high aggregate domestic demand will continue to spill over into a deficit in the balance of payments. And the dollar will depreciate. It would certainly be retrograde policy to attempt to improve the balance-of-payments position by import surcharges, quantitative restrictions, and controls over capital outflows instead of by domestic monetary and fiscal restraint.

It is striking that despite the floating rates of the past several years, the broad pattern of previous disequilibria among the major trading countries has scarcely changed. The countries that experienced the largest surpluses before the increase of oil prices have about doubled them despite the strong appreciation of their currencies, and the countries then in deficit have seen their deficits more than triple in the past six years despite the depreciation of their currencies.[4] Again, this points up the need to couple exchange rate changes with domestic policies—contractionary in the United States and expansionary in Europe and Japan. As long as the United States continues to have a higher rate of growth and to exhibit a higher rate of inflation than do its industrial trading partners, the American trade balance will suffer, and the dollar will continue under pressure. The "made in America" causes of the U.S. deficit must be treated at home. Monetary restraint, credit contraction, and a reduction in government expenditures must be realized in order to disinflate the domestic economy and stabilize the dollar. A more stable dollar, in turn, will help stop inflation from accelerating.

Longer-Term Considerations

The dollar problem must be considered as part of the wider problem of international monetary reform. The persistent issue is whether a national currency—the dollar—should be the major international reserve asset. Germany, Japan, and Switzerland have not encouraged the increased use of their currencies as reserve currencies, and some 80 percent of foreign exchange reserves continue to be held by central banks in the form of dollars. A second important issue—demonstrated by the experience with floating rates—is whether floating rates should be allowed to be managed, either nationally or internationally.

These issues would, of course, be of less concern if there were more policy coordination among nations. In a sense, international policy coordination and national adjustment mechanisms for balance-of-payments problems are alternatives. If the coordination of monetary, fiscal, wage, and commercial policies were 100 percent effective, there would be no need for a nation to endure the burden of adjustment to international imbalance. But 100 percent effective begs the question. And, despite the pronouncements of economic summits, the implementation of the policies implied by economic summitry has yet to be realized.

Policy coordination, however, may mean some act of collective management in the world economy to provide a more effective framework for the pursuit of international policies. The collective decision of the Rio Agreement in 1969 to create SDRs is an example of this type of policy coordination. The SDR facility provided for the creation and distribution of reserve certificates (SDRs) as the result of deliberate and concerted decision by the members of the IMF. It was their international acceptability—not any intrinsic worth—that bestowed the function of money on SDRs. This mechanism of reserve creation was the first time in monetary history that the control of the volume of reserves was governed by international law and determined by the exercise of reason within the framework of law, instead of as previously by such random and uncoordinated influences as the deficits of a reserve currency country (the United States) or the volume of gold production.

This type of policy coordination is needed if reliance on the dollar as the major source of liquidity is to decrease. International monetary arrangements must provide other sources of reserves. This can be done most expeditiously by extending the international credit facilities of the IMF. A growing number of economists advocate that the SDRs become the major portion of global reserves. The SDRs (now valued in terms of a weighted average of sixteen currencies) might become a substitute for gold and foreign exchange holdings, as long advocated by Professor Robert Triffin. The American negotiators of the original SDR agreement tried to shape it so as to make it "better than gold, but not as good as the dollar." Instead of viewing the SDR as an addition to, rather than a substitute for, foreign exchange holdings, Triffin has emphasized the need to demonetize gold and control the flood of dollars in the world reserve pool.[5]

This highlights the central task of world monetary reform—the upgrading of the IMF since its downfall in 1971. One means would be to have the IMF establish a "substitution account" to issue SDRs in exchange for outstanding dollar and gold reserve balances. This creation of international reserve deposits with the IMF would relieve the dollar of its particularly vulnerable position as a reserve asset that must maintain stability to remain an attractive asset for foreign official and private holders. An inconvertible, fluctuating, and shrinking dollar has already led to the creation of the European monetary system in the EEC. This regional currency bloc is a first step toward the use of a parallel currency as an alternative to dollars and Eurodollars. For European nations, it could become a significant departure from their hitherto unlimited acceptance of dollar overflows. In the future, the conversion of foreign dollar claims into a substitution account at the IMF might even be denominated in European Currency Units as well as SDRs.

Many advocate that the IMF should also undertake some type of international surveillance of exchange rates. Under managed floating, governments intervene in exchange markets for a variety of objectives—some of which are of a beggar-thy-neighbor character. By undertaking surveillance, the IMF would discourage as "illegitimate" those exchange-market interventions that cause conflict among nations, such as intervention to gain a competitive advantage in foreign markets or to maintain employment or profits in export- or import-competing industries. The IMF should coordinate the objectives of international intervention and the actual practice of intervention so that two countries do not work at cross-purposes on the same exchange rate. A start in this direction might be realized by establishing some presumptive guidelines on the maximum permissible change in the rates. These would emphasize two objectives: 1) assuring orderly markets by avoiding rapid rates of change unless the changes in the rates are clearly necessary because of rapid and unexpected changes in underlying conditions, and 2) linking intervention policies to some desired national levels of international reserves to assure that exchange rates are not allowed to deviate very far from the rates that would clear the market without intervention over a period of time.

A third important function of the IMF can come through its "provision of conditional liquidity." By establishing the right of a nation to draw upon the credit branches of its quota and the right to share in any increase in reserve assets that may be forthcoming, the IMF can exercise considerable influence over domestic policies that affect exchange rates and the level of reserves, as well as influence the impact of one country's policies on another country's economy.

The challenge of international monetary reform throughout the 1980s and the correlative role of the IMF will ultimately be to seek ways of preserving the benefits of the internationalization process by reducing the detrimental restrictions on international transactions while minimizing the costs of having to give up national autonomy in policymaking. To achieve this, it is in the United States' interest to promote a revitalized IMF, with stronger financial and consultative functions—even if the Fund will still fall considerably short of being a "world central bank."

POLICY CHOICES IN INTERNATIONAL DEVELOPMENT POLICY

Monetary problems link the United States mainly to Western Europe and Japan, but the problems of international development compel the United States to pay attention to Africa, Asia, and Latin America. The easy optimism of earlier decades is gone. Foreign aid is no longer considered to be either a necessary or a sufficient condition for development.[6] A quick takeoff into development remains a possibility only in Rostow's *Stages of Growth*; in reality the success stories of development are few. And yet, the challenge of development will be even more persistent in the decade ahead.

The proper response to this challenge does not lie in succumbing to the rhetoric of the new international economic order (NIEO). The need is neither "new" (the demands have long been voiced), nor "international" (but rather national "delinking" and "self-reliance"), nor "economic" (but political and ideological), nor "order" (but a North-South confrontation). The more realistic approach is to recognize that the demands for a NIEO reflect the consequences of the internationalization process with its attendant tensions and conflicts. But the adversary national interests are being given a particular North-South coloration.

The problems of development must therefore be factored into the solutions of the problems of conflict that arise from the internationalization process. This means that economic independence cannot be simply legislated in response to the demands of UNCTAD or the NIEO as if the metropolitan country were legislating political independence. Economic independence must be attained through a structural transformation of the developing economies in which industrial production becomes a larger proportion of total production and manufactured exports become a larger proportion of total exports. A few countries have achieved this transformation (South Korea and Taiwan are leading examples). It is instructive that in doing so, these small countries went through a period of reliance on external capital; without the capital inflow, the transformation would have been long delayed, and these countries would have been condemned to the lower level of per capita income that only primary production can support.

The emergence of the newly industrialized countries (NICs) reflects a new *international* industrial revolution based on the transfer of capital and technology from advanced countries, worldwide sourcing by multinational corporations, the production of semimanufactures and manufactures in the developing countries, and the provision of markets in the advanced countries. To realize the potential offered by this combination of elements, the advanced countries must allow market access for the new exports from the NICs. The developing countries, in turn, must undertake self-help measures and effective national economic management to take advantage of the opportunities provided. Especially important are the removal of price distortions in their economies and a liberalization of their foreign trade regimes. The transition from a regime of import substitution to export promotion may, however, have to be underwritten with support from the advanced countries.

More than ever, the 1980s are likely to demonstrate the mutual needs of the more developed and less developed countries. This will be seen in a number of ways. Already a large proportion of U.S. exports—more than one-third—are directed to LDCs. In contrast with an overall trade deficit in 1979, the United States had a substantial trade surplus with LDCs. Exports of manufactured goods from the United States to LDCs have been rising by some 15 percent a year. It is striking that the United States exports more manufactured goods to the developing countries than it does to Western Europe, Japan, and the Communist countries combined. Moreover, the rate of growth in American exports to LDCs is appreciably higher than to the developed countries. When the 35 countries that imported more than $500 million worth of American exports are ranked in terms of growth of such exports during the 1970s, the first twelve places are taken by LDCs. Among the LDCs, those that import the most from the United States are those that are developing the most rapidly. Clearly the United States gains from overseas development. American labor can benefit only when U.S. exports of manufactured goods to the LDCs increase much more rapidly than imports of manufactured goods from the LDCs, as has been the case.

In addition, almost two-thirds of the improvement in the United States service account (income on foreign investment, royalties and fees, insurance and banking, and other invisible items in the balance on current account) during the 1970s is attributable to transactions with LDCs. More than one-half the United States' service receipts are now from the LDCs.

The economic expansion in Asian and Latin American countries has helped maintain growth in the American economy. Even though more than a "Marshall Plan for the Third World" may be needed to reflate the world economy, it is nonetheless true that the more rapid rates of growth in developing countries have lessened the costs of slumpflation in the advanced countries by stimulating exports from these countries.

Although complaints about "cheap" manufactured imports from the NICs preoccupy the International Trade Commission, these imports do lessen inflationary pressure. Lower-priced imports, plus the competition that free trade gives to domestic monopoly, should be welcomed by an inflationary economy. The resulting minor job displacement must be placed in proper perspective, and temporary adjustment assistance policies may reduce the costs of transformation to higher productivity jobs. It is striking that Robert McNamara, president of the World Bank, stated at UNCTAD V that the consumer cost per job protected was more than $50,000 per year in sugar, carbon steel, meat, television sets, and footwear.[7] If protection is seen as a temporary political response to the employment problems created for a small group of workers, then clearly there are less inflationary and less costly forms of income support available. Moreover, if the LDCs cannot export to the United States, then the United States cannot continue its rapid expansion of exports to the LDCs.

Access to raw material supplies is also clearly in the interest of the United States. Our dependence on foreign supplies of minerals is well known—for example, of bauxite, nickel, zinc, chromium, manganese, cobalt, and tin.

Beyond this, the response to demands for international commodity management should be cautious and skeptical. It is true that nonfuel primary-commodity exports account for some 25 percent of total trade revenue for the LDCs, and this revenue is subject to considerable fluctuation. International commodity agreements to stabilize prices, however, have had a dismal history. An international commodity agreement should be considered only if it assumes adequate supply, moderation of price fluctuations, and nondistortion of the resource allocation of prices. Instead of these commodity controls, it is more efficient and equitable to deal with commodity price fluctuations through domestic stabilization programs and support of the IMF's compensatory financing facility for a shortfall of export receipts. Additional measures to expand the IMF's capability to even out foreign exchange earnings from the export of foodstuffs and industrial raw materials should be considered. Such measures may avoid the inefficiency of price stabilization agreements, but still encourage investment in natural resource industries.

During the past decade, it has become apparent that the United States has turned toward LDCs not only in export and raw material markets, but also in international financial markets. The net flows of private capital to middle-income developing countries increased 30 percent a year between 1970 and 1975. The bulk of this external capital came from commercial banks that syndicated Eurocurrency loans to the governments of the developing countries. Although in its projections of the future growth of these middle-income developing countries the World Bank assumes that the flows will grow at a lower rate of 12 percent a year, even this reduced growth in lending will mean that net flows from private sources will rise considerably, from $26 billion in 1975 to $80 billion in 1985. This in turn means that outstanding balances would increase from $84 billion in 1975 to $350 billion in 1985.[8] Corrected for inflation, the 1985 figures at 1977 prices would only be half as large, and in real terms the growth in net disbursements would be only about 5 percent a year. But the fact remains that the magnitude of external indebtedness is large and growing. The debt servicing of this large capital inflow is of prime importance to the entire international financial community.

Private capital inflow allows a developing country to acquire resources from abroad through a deficit on merchandise trade. To service the debt, however, both effective national economic management and export-oriented policies are required, as are self-help measures to raise the levels of domestic saving and taxation so that a larger proportion of investment can be financed from domestic sources. Growth in export revenue is also necessary to provide the foreign exchange for imports and to pay the interest and amortization on the external capital. Given the large volume of commercial bank lending to developing countries, it is essential that debt servicing be maintained lest confidence in the international financial system be shaken. There need be no fear of a debt crisis as long as all sources of external financing are sustained—not only commercial bank loans, but also private direct investment, private portfolio investment, and official lending. Expansion of resources available to the IMF will also help maintain confidence of private lenders. So too will the growing volume of exports from the borrowing countries.

As long as the system of international financial intermediation through commercial bank lending is sustained, both developing and developed nations will gain. Savings from the richer countries can be transformed into productive investment in the developing countries. More significant than the profit to financial institutions are the resulting increase in income in the borrowing countries and the additional demand for exports from the more industrialized countries. As a "region of recent settlement," a significant part of the United States' economic history was written in terms of growth-cum-debt. The future history of growth in newly developing countries might also come to be written in terms of American foreign investment.

For reasons of enlightened self-interest, the United States should therefore support policies more conducive to the acceleration of international development. A distinction in policy strategy may be made between low-income developing countries (less than $250 per capita) and middle-income developing countries (above $250 per capita). In low-income countries, the need is for concessional finance and policies like those pursued by the World Bank devoted to the eradication of absolute poverty. The quality of the World Bank's professional staff and its success with project loans have made the World Bank the leading international development institution. The case for periodic increases in the authorized capital of the World Bank is compelling enough to allow its lending program to expand to countries that do not qualify for commercial loans. Similarly, the soft-loan window of the Bank—through the International Development Association (IDA)—must be expanded through replenishment of IDA's resources. The United States cannot afford not to give the World Bank its fullest support.

For the middle-income countries, more reliance can be placed on private loans from commercial banks. These countries are capable of accelerating their structural transformation from primary production into industrial production and can expand their production for export of manufactures—but only if the transformation process is underwritten with sufficient external capital. This has been done for South Korea and Taiwan; it can be done for other countries.

To assure proper debt servicing, however, the United States should support the IMF's programs of conditionality when imposed on nations seeking standby arrangements with the IMF. By stipulating the conditions under which a nation may have access to higher credit tranches in the IMF, the Fund is able to impose conditions of effective national economic management in a way and to a degree that no nation alone could do. In supporting the IMF and the World Bank, the United States would in effect also be supporting debt servicing for private lenders to developing country borrowers. Any measure that improves the general financial position of the developing countries will also enhance their ability to borrow from private markets.

For all developing countries, outward-looking strategies of development that will promote exports are to be supported. The limitations of inward-looking import-substitution policies have been exposed. A few success stories have been written in terms of export of manufactures and semimanufactures. But more countries in the future must share the success of South Korea, Taiwan, Hong Kong, Singapore, Brazil, and Mexico. To allow this to happen, the United States and other industrialized nations must not resist the importation of manufactures from the developing countries. The World Bank estimates that if all tariff and nontariff barriers on manufactures were eliminated, the annual export earnings of the developing countries by 1985 would increase by almost $25 billion.

This brings us back to the problem of market safeguards, discussed above. To facilitate trade liberalization or prevent the imposition of more severe orderly marketing agreements, the United States should provide more adjustment assistance to its senescent industries that are being outcompeted by industries in the developing countries. Domestic aid to these industries may be more effective than foreign aid if the transfer of resources out of these low-productivity, high-cost industries would allow greater market access for exports from the developing countries. Developing countries must be allowed to realize their comparative advantage in the labor-intensive industries, while American production specializes in high-skill, capital-intensive, and research and development-intensive production.

SUMMARY: UNDERLYING THEMES

This discussion has centered on three major international economic policy issues: reversal of the nontariff barriers of the new protectionism, international monetary reform, and recognition of the mutual needs of the more developed and less developed countries. There are also other policy areas of importance—East-West relations, energy problems, and the role of multinational corporations—but other papers in this volume examine these related topics. In this paper, we have recommended measures by which American foreign economic policy—challenged as it is by the collapse of the Bretton Woods system—must be directed during the 1980s to reduce the new international economic disorder.

In the three major problem areas of trade, money, and development, nations have revealed through the policy choices that they have adopted that they will not submit to free trade, freely flexible exchange rates, or a significant transfer of concessional finance. American foreign economic policy must therefore foster trade liberalization, promote guidelines for exchange rate interventions, strengthen the role of private international finance, and expand the opportunities for exports from developing countries.

In each of these policy areas, the United States must now consider policy coordination with Europe, Japan, and the newly industrialized countries. American foreign economic policy must operate in the context of a multipolar power structure.

It is also clear that the three policy areas are linked to each other. The solution of one depends on the solution of the others. A consistent policy "package" is required since trade, money, and development issues have become interrelated.

Foreign economic policy is, of course, shaped by the state of the domestic economy. Unless the domestic economy can lessen inflation and unemployment, there will be continual pressures for controls over foreign trade and even capital movements. But it must be realized that an open, competitive world economy can contribute more to domestic economic expansion.

Further, policies must be pursued in a way that will assure that internal interests do not conflict with external interests. The disarray of the international economy has had adverse effects on the domestic economy. The overall policy goal for the 1980s—how to pursue domestic economic goals of full employment and economic stability without sacrificing the gains from trade liberalization or enduring the costs of external imbalance—remains more distant than it was at the start of the 1970s. Any answer must now avoid a continuation of defensive economic nationalism, or an East-West or North-South confrontation.

Neither market forces, as would be represented by free trade or freely floating exchange rates, nor international codes of conduct are now ascendant in establishing world economic order. There is always a danger that the regulation of international economic conduct will be abandoned to either simple unilateral action or ad hoc negotiation dependent on bargaining power. In such an environment, the traditional "liberal" beliefs in a harmony of interests, mutual gains from trade, foreign investment as a non–zero-sum activity—all the beliefs that support internationalism over nationalism—would be submerged. To avoid the dangers of nationalism and policy competition among nations, policy coordination is needed.

Many of the policies recommended in this paper depend on international coordination for their effectiveness. Trade liberalization, coordination of international monetary policies, and cooperation between the IMF, World Bank, and commercial banks, all require a diminution in competition among national policies and more cooperative international action. This is especially neeeded between Western Europe, Japan, newly industrializing countries, and the United States. The political system must conform more harmoniously with the character of the international economic system.

The need for multinational policymaking is simply a corollary of the principle that the level at which a decision is made should be high enough to cover the area in which there is an impact. In order that the decisions regarding necessary policy instruments be optimal, there must not be "external" effects—that is, the influences exerted on the well-being of groups outside the jurisdiction of those who make the decision should be weak. The area in which the impact of the instrument will be felt determines what decision level will be optimal. For many policy issues in the world economy, the nation-state is clearly an inappropriate economic decision-making unit. Decisions taken at the national level are often far too low to be optimal.

In the last analysis, therefore, not American foreign economic policy alone, but policy coordination and supranational decision units will be required to reduce the tensions and conflicts created by the internationalization process. Some system of functional federalism among nations,[9] with different economic functions handled at different levels of government, will be necessary to provide the international economy with some decision-making powers comparable to those in the national economy. In this wider approach to policymaking, more progress can be made toward international deregulation and the greater enjoyment of full and efficient use of global resources.

NOTES

1. Trade Act of 1974, Sec. 121 (a) (2), 19 U.S.C. sec. 2131 (a) (2).

2. Stephen P. Magee, "The Welfare Effects of Restrictions on U.S. Trade," *Brookings Papers on Economic Activity* (1972), pp. 645–708; Ilse Mintz, *U.S. Import*

Quotas: Costs and Consequences (Washington, D.C.: American Enterprise Institute for Policy Research, 1973); and Thomas B. Birnberg, *Economic Effects of Changes in Trade Relations between Developed and Less Developed Countries* (New York: Overseas Development Council, 1978).

3. Robert Triffin, *Gold and the Dollar Crisis: Yesterday and Tomorrow*, Essays in International Finance no. 132 (Princeton: Princeton University, International Finance Section, 1978), pp. 4–5.

4. Ibid., p. 13.

5. Ibid., p. 8.

6. In this connection, see the essay by Peter Bauer in this volume.

7. Robert S. McNamara, "Address to the United Nations Conference on Trade and Development" (Manila, Philippines, May 10, 1979), p. 12.

8. International Bank for Reconstruction and Development, *1978 Annual Meeting of the Board of Governors: Summary Proceedings* (Washington, D.C., September 25–28, 1978), pp. 20–21.

9. Richard N. Cooper, *Economic Mobility and National Economic Policy*, Wicksell Lectures (Stockholm, Sweden: Almqvist & Wiksell, 1974), p. 59.

U.S. Foreign Economic Policy: Politico-Economic Linkages

Yuan-li Wu

XXII

As the 1970s draw to a close, U.S. foreign policy is beset by many problems. This essay deals with one such problem area where there appears to be considerable disarray: the linkages that make foreign economic policy an integral part of foreign policy. By focusing on the interconnection between the political and the economic spheres, my discussion will cut across the traditional divisions of foreign economic policy, including commercial, investment, monetary, and balance of payments problems. My purpose is to identify the principal incongruent politico-economic relationships in U.S. policy, to explain how they have come about, to present the choices available to policy makers, and to suggest the fundamental elements of a viable policy and program.

SOME PERPLEXING QUESTIONS

First, the economic and noneconomic aspects of a coherent foreign policy should be mutually compatible even if they cannot be mutually supporting. If apparent inconsistencies are tolerated, they should be explained, perhaps in terms of consciously contrived tactics. U.S. policy falls considerably short of this criterion.

Second, an optimum policy is by definition one that will best serve America's long-term objectives. Those objectives, therefore, need to be defined as unambiguously as possible. We often speak of national interest or national security without defining the substance and scope of either term. Our choices might vary widely—from survival as a nation-state and an independent economic entity (a bare minimum) to worldwide hegemony. In the post–Vietnam War years, the interest of the

United States has fluctuated between maintaining the postwar international status quo and modifying it. However, faltering attempts to determine what degree of modification the United States can tolerate have resulted in confusion and uncertainty.

Management of Politico-Economic Relations with Adversaries

The U.S. approach to East-West trade and economic relations has been a perplexing issue. Previously, our policy has varied with time. After the outbreak of the Korean War, we elected to impose a complete economic embargo on North Korea and the People's Republic of China (PRC). A similar tack was taken in the sixties with respect to Cuba and North Vietnam.

The logic of this approach, which also governed U.S. economic relations with the Soviet Union, is simple: an acknowledged adversary should be denied every advantage derived from the import of goods, services, or technology. In practice, there was a gradual shift from total denial to the selective control of "strategic trade," according to both a common COCOM (Coordinating Committee) list of controlled "strategic goods" and a more stringent set of controls enforced by the United States.

Long before Kissinger's appointment as secretary of state, the list of strategic goods had been whittled down. During his term of office, however, the idea that the Soviet economic structure could be influenced through trade held sway. It was thought that by deliberately fostering Soviet economic interdependence with the West, we could introduce a new constraint on Soviet behavior.[1] From this viewpoint, the 1972 U.S.-Soviet trade agreement and the first Strategic Arms Limitation Talks (SALT) agreement in the same year were a single package.

Under the Carter administration, U.S. policy has oscillated between strategic-trade controls and issue-by-issue bargaining. An example of the bargaining approach is permitting or denying the sale of a sophisticated computer to the Soviet Union depending on Soviet policy in Africa. This technique undermines any idea that the strategic nature of the particular computer can be evaluated on an objective basis.

Prior to the passage of the Jackson-Vanik amendment to the 1974 trade act, official U.S. policy appeared to favor expansion of nonstrategic trade with the Soviet Union through the extension of credit. This was prompted partly by a growing desire to increase our exports. The granting of most-favored-nation (MFN) status to the Soviet Union, augmented by Export-Import Bank credit, was regarded as a first step.

Since December 1978, when the United States announced its full diplomatic recognition of Peking and the termination of its defense treaty with Taiwan, the same approach has been taken in U.S.-PRC trade. The United States apparently hopes to follow the May 1979 U.S.-PRC commercial treaty by granting MFN status to both China and the Soviet Union as a token of political evenhandedness. This economic favor will be indirectly tied to Soviet restraint in other negotiations, including perhaps the final version of the SALT II agreement. We again find ourselves face to face with the issues of the Kissinger period.

For the purpose of this paper, the important question is whether such an approach toward economic relations with an adversary, actual or potential, is the optimal one from both the economic and the noneconomic points of view.

In the Soviet case, neither selective relaxations of U.S. exports controls nor promises of increased trade and credit appear to have had a noticeably moderating effect on Soviet policy in Africa, the Middle East, or Asia, or on the continuous Soviet military buildup. Only in the case of Soviet policy toward the emigration of its own citizens can one credit the Jackson-Vanik amendment with some impact.

In the case of Peking, which may no longer be regarded as an adversary by many Americans, present U.S. policy is not wholly consistent with our policy toward other developing countries exporting labor-intensive products.[2] We cannot justify attempts to increase protection against imports from nonadversary developing countries at the same time that we are easing the way for imports from adversary developing countries like the PRC and the Soviet Union. An economic argument—that we need to balance our trade with the Communist countries—is a retreat toward bilateralism, which is against the principles of free trade we profess.

Practically speaking, there is no valid basis for countervailing duties in the event of suspected dumping of products when domestic costs in nonmarket economies are what Communist state planning and exporting agencies say they are. Nor can one easily define "market disruption" or "equivalent concession" on the part of the nonmarket economies that receive tariff favors. On the other hand, if we claim that our purpose is entirely manipulative, there is little evidence that we can manipulate better than the Communist countries can. In fact, we do not seem to possess an adequate administrative staff to engage in such manipulation. Finally, in 1978, U.S. two-way trade with the Soviet Union (totaling $2.8 billion) and with the PRC ($1.1 billion) was far too small to be economically significant.

Managing Politico-Economic Linkages with Allies

In contrast to the minimal level of bilateral U.S.-Soviet and U.S.-PRC trade, the sheer volume of our trade with the developed economies of Western Europe and Japan has made it a central focus for American foreign economic policy. The case of trade between the United States and Japan illustrates the intertwining politico-economic relationships between us and our allies especially clearly.

Japan is customarily described as the lynchpin of American policy in the Western Pacific, and official Japanese spokesmen often claim to view our country in the same way. Yet the 1970s have been replete with major economic disputes between the two. An increasing volume of bilateral trade and a large Japanese surplus since 1971 have generated louder and increasingly acrimonious debates over rising U.S. balance of payment deficits.

A dispute over Japanese textile exports to the United States in the 1960s, a 10 percent import surtax imposed by the United States in 1971, a temporary ban on U.S. soybean exports in 1972, charges by U.S. businessmen of Japanese dumping on the American market, and U.S. insistence on "voluntary" export controls, or orderly marketing, by Japanese exporters of many products are but a few of the more celebrated cases. Scarcely veiled threats of more restrictive U.S. import legislation[3] have accompanied demands that Japan appreciate the yen, lower its nontariff barriers, open government purchasing to U.S. suppliers, and increase the purchases of U.S. goods at a rate commensurate with faster Japanese domestic economic expansion.

Japan, for its part, has nurtured an impression that the United States has deliberately singled it out as the black sheep of the international economic community and has tried to punish it for the prudence and alertness of its government and business community, which it claims Americans have been unable to match.

The soybean embargo of 1972, though triggered by confusion among analysts between firm sales and option contracts, many of which were held by Japanese importers themselves, was interpreted in Japan as a callous blow aimed at the Japanese consumer. In spite of joint U.S.-Japanese calls for a coordinated policy on oil importing at the 1979 Tokyo summit, Japanese critics of U.S. policy like to point out the American failure to reduce the ability of the Organization of Petroleum Exporting Countries (OPEC) to raise crude oil prices by curbing American consumption and importing.

Also on the energy front, the Japanese fear that the United States may eventually retreat to the Western Hemisphere for its supplies and leave its Japanese ally to the mercy of the Middle Eastern oil producers. Other U.S. deficiencies frequently cited by the Japanese include an unwillingness to make domestic adjustments to restore economic equilibrium and the exertion of political pressure to force surplus trade partners (countries with a trade surplus) to make adjustments, with all their attendant economic and political risks.

Another fundamental Japanese argument is that its ability to pay for future imports must be safeguarded by first building up overseas investments. This can be done only through the maintenance of an export surplus over a long period. In Japan's view, export surpluses are essential to the future economic survival of Japan, even though the size of its present surplus may appear excessive.

Many of these comments are also applicable to relations between the United States and Western European nations. Among the European NATO powers, West Germany, a surplus country like Japan, has also been most successful in weathering the worldwide international payments problems caused by OPEC's price increases.

A determination of the adjustments that countries with deficits and surpluses should make to restore equilibrium in international payments involves yet another political argument. The economic recovery of Western Europe and Japan after World War II was made possible by U.S. defense guarantees. The smaller defense burden they have had to bear has contributed to their economic growth.

Even after allowing for their greater present expenditures on defense, these nations obviously have the economic capacity to do more, both for themselves and for their American ally. The problem is complicated by three facts: a) not all the allies have exactly the same adversaries or perceive the same degree of threat from them; b) active economic relations are maintained by all allied countries with the principal potential, if not actual, adversaries; and c) these relations have contributed to the growth of the adversaries' power in the past.

Economic ties are especially important between the Soviet Union as a supplier of natural resources and Western Europe and Japan as exporters of capital equipment, technology, and credit. A critical question, therefore, is whether economic quarrels between allies will cause lasting adverse political effects on the cohesiveness of the alliance. Allied differences on trade and defense matters center on what all the countries involved will accept as an equitable distribution of burden. One consistently unresolved issue is how to assign the proportional responsibility for restoring equilibrium to the balance of international payments of individual countries. Some of these countries, according to others, have helped to create these disequilibria, both in their own economic affairs and in those of other nations. Another basic issue, even though it is not at the forefront today, is the distribution of the defense burden among all the allies. Until an acceptable formula has been developed to allocate this responsibility equitably, we can hardly expect a common allied policy on East-West economic relations.

To other countries it seems that the United States, in its attempts to unravel these perplexing problems, may be placing more economic burdens on some of its allies at the same time it is courting its potential or actual adversaries. To the United States, the situation seems exactly the opposite. Not surprisingly, most nations seek national solutions for their own problems, as well as for certain common problems, such as the impact of OPEC price increases, while ignoring the difficulties of other nations. The conduct of a country's economic policy toward its allies is tied to the way it manages its relations with its adversaries. A skeptic might well wonder how in the world one can distinguish between an adversary and an ally: some of us in fact make no such distinctions.

Ad Hoc Politico-Economic Interrelations

Many countries are neither adversaries of the United States nor major allies, like the European NATO powers or Japan, with whom the propriety and desirability of alliance are beyond question. Politico-economic relations between the United States and this large third group of countries encompass a wide range of divergent developments and practices.

Politically, some of these nations, like South Korea, though associated with the United States by mutual defense arrangements, may view their real relationship with this country as a little tenuous. Others, like Malaysia and Singapore, are considered nonaligned or neutral wherever their real sympathies lie.

A majority of the countries in this large group are non-Communist nations in which economic assistance, sometimes accompanied by military sales and grants, continues to serve the traditional purpose of promoting development and political stability. Some are economically client states of the United States; others, mostly in Africa, are more closely associated with other European powers whose colonies they were previously.

The real concern of countries in this group is their own physical security and economic well-being. Most of the developing nations among them still have to grapple with the traditional problems of poverty and/or income instability produced by fluctuations of either world demand for, or domestic supply of, a small number of exports. A few of these developing nations, however, have made remarkable progress in recent years in both non-oil exports and general economic development.[4] Furthermore, the ranks of rapidly expanding developing economies are progressively being increased by later starters. To this group a dominant common concern is whether their large export markets in the developed countries may be gradually closed as a result of the protectionist proclivities of the latter.

The Tokyo round of multilateral trade negotiations, when ratified by the major trading nations and the decisions of the June 1979 Tokyo summit on energy, will be of vital concern to these rapidly growing trading nations. For a few that are caught up in the flux of international political realignments, like South Korea and Taiwan,[5] continuation of economic expansion and political survival are really one and the same.

Still another group within this same subset of developing nations consists of the oil exporters whose efforts since 1973 to redistribute income and wealth globally have met with unusual success. Discussion of their special case will be postponed to a later section.

From time to time, in dealing with some of these countries, the United States has tied trade to political and ideological preconditions. On occasion the purpose has clearly been to bring about compliance with U.S. objectives of the moment. At other times, the purpose has been much less clear; sloganeering has replaced purposeful policy. A few examples will suffice.

a) Under the Carter administration, human rights have ostensibly been made a general condition in determining U.S. relations with certain countries that are not avowed adversaries. A presidential determination of the condition of human rights in a country and approval from the Congress are needed before the Export-Import Bank can grant it credit.

b) Because of the U.S. government's concern about nuclear proliferation, the administration has sought to renegotiate safeguard agreements with a number of countries that had previously contracted to import enriched uranium from the United States to fuel their power reactors. These negotiations are still continuing at this writing. In one case, U.S. aid to Pakistan was stopped on the ground that Pakistan had tried to acquire the capability to reprocess nuclear-reactor spent fuels.

c) The United States has reportedly threatened to discontinue supplying uranium to Taiwan's power reactors. This threat was said to have been made in the course of negotiations in early 1979 on how to continue bilateral relations after the United States switched its diplomatic recognition from Taipei to Peking.

d) In a more extreme case of economic warfare against a nonadversary, the United States has been participating in a trade embargo against Rhodesia sponsored by the United Nations (U.N.). The objective is Rhodesian acceptance of the specific formula of black majority rule favored by the U.N. and supported by the United States and Great Britain prior to the election of the Thatcher government.

e) In a recent example of the long-standing U.S. practice of using economic aid as a positive inducement to foreign acceptance of policies favored by this country, the United States promised economic assistance to both Israel and Egypt in negotiations at Camp David. This led to the signing of the peace treaty between the two belligerents in March 1979.

The wisdom of U.S. policy in the specific instances cited above is not within the scope of my analysis at this point, but certain basic issues that the examples illustrate are. Among the questions raised are the internal consistency of U.S. foreign political and economic policies and the mutual compatibility of conflicting objectives. Discussion of the implications of several such issues follows.

The Proliferation Issue. One still unresolved question is whether independence from unreliable energy imports for U.S. allies is more (or less) important to the United States than the risk of proliferation of nuclear weapons in the absence of stricter safeguards. Can proliferation really be averted and stricter safeguards enforced if countries possessing the technical and financial capability to produce nuclear weapons feel desperately insecure? Is the importance of nuclear power overestimated? To this author, at least, the correct answer to both questions is no.

The Human Rights Issue. The two sides of the human rights question can be simply stated: On the one hand, there are those who hold that human rights in a foreign country should not be the concern of the United States in determining foreign economic policy. On the other, there is the view that human rights are our concern, but the important issue is how that concern should be expressed.

Each view can be defended. The first holds that one power has no right to interfere with another power's treatment of its subjects. The second considers human rights to be absolute values. Its supporters put themselves into the position of those whose rights are to be safeguarded. The second view seems truer to the American tradition, except that in actual application the original proposition has been distorted. The best way to promote human rights has too often been determined from the perspective of the country applying the pressure, and not from the viewpoint of those whose rights have been denied.

Application of the human rights proposition, however, is a phase of a wider problem: should economic pressure on foreign countries be restricted to those most vulnerable to it? This approach may seem cost-effective to the country applying the pressure and may therefore appear attractive to those whose mission is to look for the most expeditious method to accomplish a given high-sounding objective in the short run. It creates obvious inconsistencies, however—for example, when the United States criticizes smaller nations like South Korea but remains silent on the PRC's large-scale trampling of human rights over the course of several decades.

Arms Aid. The use of foreign aid as an inducement to foreign countries to pursue a course preferred by the United States has declined in recent years. An exception has been the export of arms. Foreign military sales in 1970 totaled about $1 billion; foreign military-assistance grants in the same year amounted to a little over $2 billion. These totals increased substantially in later years. According to the Defense Security Assistance Agency, total formal and informal military-assistance requests transmitted to Congress between May 18, 1977, and August 2, 1978 (including some expired offers and some military construction and spanning two fiscal years) amounted to $23.6 billion. Of this total, requests for $7.4 billion, $8.0 billion, $1.7 billion, and $0.3 billion came for Saudi Arabia, Iran, Israel, and Egypt, respectively.[6] Where the transfers represented sales, they contributed to U.S. balance of payments. Arms transfers such as those to Iran under the shah, however, were hardly consistent with the objective of promoting human rights in that country.

Administrative Discretion and the Soviet Threat. We cannot fail to notice in the preceding examples the important role discretionary power plays in diplomacy. Whether the carrot or the stick was used in any instance seems to have been based entirely on an assessment of the relative strengths of the United States and the opposing party. The actions of the United States do not appear to have been guided by any general principle except one: if the matter involves the Soviet Union in any way, its effect on Soviet capability or behavior must be a dominant concern. Policy makers in the United States evidently believe that the threat to U.S. security comes from the Soviet Union as a nation-state; in their view international communism no longer constitutes the greater danger, as it did in the 1950s.

OPEC's Test of the U.S. Response to Foreign Initiatives

The policy of the United States should also be examined from the perspective of American response to foreign initiatives. Nationalism and self-assertion have become common traits among the developing countries that have gained new political status since World War II. The almost universal desire of these countries for economic development is frequently tinged with more than a little xenophobia.

With the exception of a few foreign-trade-oriented, non-oil-exporting countries, most developing nations do not seem to have left the nineteenth-century specter of economic imperialism behind them. Many profess, through the U.N. Conference on Trade and Development (UNCTAD) and other forums, to see the need for redress of past economic and political wrongs, both real and imagined, through tariff concessions, special financing facilities, and outright assistance from the more developed countries, and through protection of their own domestic industry.

This attitude affects U.S. foreign investment and the traditional U.S. support for worldwide economic development and free trade. Since many multinational firms are based in the United States, we cannot be aloof to the treatment these firms receive in their host countries. Nor can we be indifferent to the performance and conduct of the multinationals. American firms must seek not only to be competitive, but also to sell the idea of private, free enterprise. However, domestic attempts to regulate business conduct and insure environmental protection have not always helped.

At a different level, the policy issues are even more serious. Since 1973, the United States and other oil-importing countries, both developed and developing, have been under active economic attack by the oil producers. Although this economic warfare was initially an attempt to influence the attitudes of the developed countries in the historical Arab-Israeli conflict, it has evolved into a concerted effort to redistribute income and wealth globally. Although the United States is by no means the lone target of OPEC's economic offensive, U.S. economic capability and leadership have been tested and found wanting.

From the last quarter of 1973 to June 1979, crude oil prices (using the standard reference price of Saudi Arabian light crude) rose from $3.01 a barrel to a minimum of $18.55. This increase has challenged the post-Vietnam assumption that even though the United States might lower its profile in foreign political and military affairs, it could increase its economic activity whenever it had to. It was taken for granted that the traditional tools of economic presence—trade, foreign investment, and aid—would sustain our foreign actions. Policy makers little thought that an unfavorable balance of payments would in time become a stumbling block.

The share of liquid fuels in the energy the United States consumes has become greater since the 1973 oil crisis. The proportion of imported fuels has also increased, again with emphasis on liquids. An import surplus of $10.6 billion was registered in U.S. trade with OPEC in 1974, when the overall U.S. trade deficit was $5.4 billion. By 1976, our trade deficit with OPEC had risen to $12.5 billion, although our overall trade deficit was $9.3 billion.

In 1977, before the latest round of oil price increases, the U.S. trade deficit for the year was projected at $23.5 billion (compared with $28.5 billion in 1978). In 1979, after the minimum oil price increase of 21.5 percent agreed to by OPEC in June, and assuming an 8.5-million-barrel daily import rate and an average price of $21 a barrel, our oil bill will rise to $178 million a day. In comparison, total U.S. exports in 1979 were projected in May 1979 to be $165 billion, or $450 million a day.

In addition, whereas three militant Arab states (Libya, Iraq, and Algeria), supplied 14.4 percent of U.S. oil imports in September 1973, their share had risen to 22.7 percent three years later. In 1978, 10 percent of U.S. crude oil imports came from Libya, one of the most militant of Arab oil-exporting states.

A few of the consequences of this situation for U.S. foreign economic policy can be enumerated. First, the continuing oil payments deficit has greatly aggravated the overall balance of payments deficit. Second, the massive additions to the large dollar balances already in nonresident holdings have limited the degree to which the floating exchange rate can be safely employed as an option to correct the disequilibrium in the U.S. balance of payments. Third, on the domestic front, the cost-push inflation brought on by higher energy prices has aggravated the long-standing inflation generated by other forces and made the conflict between the adoption of stringent fiscal and monetary anti-inflationary measures and fear of an increase in unemployment a difficult issue for many politicians.

The need to tackle immediate issues at home and the increasing constraints on U.S. policy abroad vie with each other for the policy makers' attention. Finally, our declining ability to secure a crude oil supply at its source has exposed our vulnerability on the oil front for all to see. It follows that if any major foreign country should plot to maximize its own national advantage at the expense of the United States or its allies, both a breach of allied unity and economic conflict would become more likely.

U.S. Balance of Payment Difficulties and the Alliance

The failure of the United States to meet OPEC's challenge promptly and energetically has not meant that other countries even more dependent upon imported oil, including members of the Atlantic alliance and Japan, have also stood idly by. On the contrary, our sluggish and ineffectual performance, together with the greater success of some of our allies in meeting the same challenge, has enabled those allies to shift a portion of their oil-created trade deficits with OPEC to those who have been less successful. In Japan and West Germany, trade deficits with OPEC have been more than offset by surpluses earned elsewhere, especially in the large U.S. market. This development has contributed to the exacerbation of economic and political relations between the United States and its allies.

Our failure to deal effectively with OPEC has to be understood in the context of our balance of payments dilemma. First, fixed exchange rates would require unpopular deflationary measures to deal with chronic balance of payments deficits. Direct control over foreign trade and exchange transactions, even if limited to specific segments of the balance of payments, contravenes a basic U.S. commitment to the liberalization of all international transactions. For both these reasons, the United States has opted for floating exchange rates during the last several years.

Depreciation of the dollar has had worldwide economic and political consequences, however. As a reserve currency and a vehicle used by the world in external transactions, the dollar has been acquired by non-U.S. owners in large amounts. Surplus countries (including the members of OPEC) holding large dollar balances and other assets denominated in dollars are reluctant to allow the dollar to depreciate indefinitely, which it could very well do under floating exchange rates.

This rational concern notwithstanding, there is a distinct possibility that the continuous depreciation of the dollar and increasing U.S. deficits could at some point trigger a precipitate decline in its market value through speculative sales of dollars and attempts by individual holders of dollar balances, especially smaller countries among the more militant OPEC members, to switch to non-dollar assets. A headlong depreciation could be stopped only by massive market intervention. (Intervention by the United States on the foreign exchange market during the quarter November 1978–January 1979 came to $6.9 billion, according to the Federal Reserve Bank of New York.) Other nations must be willing to provide the necessary foreign currencies, either through a swap arrangement or through loans in foreign currencies. The accumulated dollar holdings, or dollar overhang, growing larger from OPEC earnings each day, restrict the corrective effect of a floating exchange rate on the chronic U.S. balance of payments deficit. Foreign financing of the U.S. deficit requires foreign confidence in the United States and foreign willingness to bail out the U.S. economy. The foreign countries may legitimately ask why they should continue to do so.

A major objective of the United States in the years after the 1973 oil crisis has been to strengthen political-military relations with Saudi Arabia and, before the fall of the shah, also Iran, the two largest oil producers in the Persian Gulf. By bolstering the military capability of those nations through arms sales and by encouraging a conviction that their security depends primarily on U.S. support, the United States was successful until the 1978–79 Iranian political crisis.

The two major oil suppliers had been convinced that they should continue to supply oil to the United States and other Western powers and reduce their pressure on the U.S. balance of payments by purchasing dollar securities, moderating their demand for oil price hikes, and selling oil for dollars. This eased the U.S. payments problem, helped to maintain the dollar as an international medium of exchange, and discouraged other dollar owners from disposing of their holdings. Ironically, our policy of lowering our military presence and substituting economic power has come full circle if it has not actually been reversed. Military power has now become a primary prop of the U.S. balance of payments. The United States had fallen back on the politico-military option for lack of a better cure for our balance of payments disequilibrium that policy makers could devise and for political reasons would accept.

Is There a "Soviet Option"? Cohesiveness of America's Alliances

The lackluster performance of the United States in attempting to meet OPEC's continuing challenge follows a string of failures to support its allies. Vietnam, Taiwan, and Iran cannot be ignored by the NATO countries, Japan, Saudi Arabia, Israel, or other nations in their assessments of the future.

How cohesive are America's alliances? At this juncture, let us suppose for argument's sake that the objective of Soviet foreign policy is maximal progress toward eventual global domination. In that case, it would regard the United States, supported by its NATO and Japanese allies, as the principal opponent in its path. Aggressive Soviet foreign economic planners would then seek to bring about the disintegration of U.S.-led alliances by converting the allied countries into mutually antagonistic economic entities and by reversing the trend toward international economic interdependence in the West.

Under normal conditions, the Soviet Union and the other CMEA (Council of Mutual Economic Assistance, also known as COMECON) members as a group are not in a position to divert any significant portion of trade away from market economies to themselves. These countries simply cannot provide a sufficiently large and varied supply of goods to the rest of the world; market economies can find these goods better among themselves. However, OPEC's insatiable desire for a larger share of the world's output and wealth has created a new economic climate. Developments such as the Iranian political turmoil or Khadafi's threat to cut off Libyan oil supply to the West might present the Soviet Union with opportunities it would not otherwise dream of.

The West and Japan may now be more ready than before to contribute to the development of Soviet resources in exchange for Soviet promises of future supply. In order to speed Soviet economic development, the USSR must import foreign technology and capital for the exploitation of its domestic natural resources. (Capital movements in both directions take place between the Soviet Union and other members of CMEA. Some Western capital flows in to offset the outflow of Soviet capital to other CMEA countries.)

Repayment for foreign credits from the market economies is financed from export sales of products from the development projects. This is a program of selective interdependence with the West. It is questionable, however, that this interdependence could reach a level at which it would act as an effective restraint on the conduct of Soviet foreign policy, as some U.S. policy makers have hoped. Concern about the risks of such interdependence is mutual. Soviet procrastination in providing the necessary information for quick agreements is matched by reluctance and delays on the part of some potential creditor countries.

The mounting size of the outstanding Western credit, now estimated at around $50 billion, has increased the economic as well as political risks to the creditors. The magnitude of single projects has been a major factor in the breakdown of some negotiations, for example, the Tyumen oilfield proposal immediately after the 1973–74 oil crisis. The lenders' resistance may be lowered, however, if their unfulfilled demands for energy must be satisfied and if they are unwilling to let an energy shortage trigger a serious recession. Trade could well be diverted to CMEA for this reason.

To promote economic integration within CMEA, the Soviet Union has to honor its commitment to export energy and other raw materials to other CMEA members. In an eventual confrontation between the West and OPEC, the Soviet Union could try to divert energy and other raw material supplies from OPEC and other countries to CMEA countries. Such a redirection of trade would be in the Soviet interest. This would be consistent with my previous suggestion that the Soviet Union may appear to be a more promising future supplier to the developed countries. The cohesiveness of U.S.-led alliances may soon have to face this additional test.

Suboptimal Performance

The existing U.S. balance of payments deficit is worse than it has to be, given the real external demand and export supply functions of this country, because of our failure to operate at the "efficiency boundary." Persons experienced in U.S. export operations and business activities overseas have suggested the following underlying reasons for this suboptimal performance: Interest in supplying the export market may be inadequate on the part of some business firms. Where that interest is insufficient, export marketing does not command support at the decision-making level within the corporate bureaucracy.

This organizational shortcoming is not usually found in large multinational companies or in export firms run by individuals who have had a long-term personal interest in the foreign market. Medium-sized and smaller firms, on the other hand, frequently reflect it. The size of the U.S. market, years of high-level economic activity at home, and low interest in foreign affairs on the part of large segments of the population, including even a portion of the opinion-making elite, have reduced any sense of urgency about export expansion. Government regulation has also increased the cost of export marketing for many firms.

A corollary of these conditions is that the United States possesses a less comprehensive and efficient commercial intelligence and information network than those of Japanese trading companies. Insufficient timely market information, especially at the detailed, micro level, can put U.S. firms at a handicap in competition with other major exporting countries. A second corollary is that the United States has come up with a smaller supply of innovative ideas, for example, concerning local marketing and representation in potential export areas and cooperative ventures with foreign personnel and capital.

Another set of factors that has contributed to less than full exploitation of the export market by American firms consists of the many noneconomic disincentives and barriers in this country to export. These include the effect of antitrust laws on cooperative foreign operations by individual firms, especially in dealing with state trading countries; the legality issue of public relations and promotional expenditures; opposition from stockholders who disapprove of business operations in particular countries, such as South Africa and Chile; and even the requirement for environmental impact reports on certain exports to foreign countries.

U.S. FOREIGN ECONOMIC POLICY AND ITS SHORTCOMINGS

The many perplexing issues involved in U.S. foreign economic policy and its apparent inconsistencies with U.S. foreign policy can be explained through the following simplified recapitulation of certain developments since World War II. Needless to say, a rational explanation of shortcomings is not an argument in their defense, but it will highlight the key areas where change will be necessary.

If international disequilibrium, once it has set in, continues to worsen, rejection of the adjustments necessary to restore equilibrium will eventually result in the collapse of the international system. Reconstitution of that system will then be necessary, but to make a new equilibrium stable, adjustments to either basic policy objectives or the traditionally preferred modes of adjustment will be necessary.

Immediately after World War II, the United States was the unquestioned leader in the non-Communist world. It was to the net political and strategic advantage of all non-Communist-aligned countries to cultivate American goodwill and to secure U.S. support. On the American side, fear of Stalinist expansion beyond Eastern Europe and of a Sino-Soviet Communist monolith made automatic U.S. support of other non-Communist countries appear to be politically and strategically advantageous. The basic ingredient for a cohesive alliance, a fear of Communist aggression, was felt by all the non-Communist nations.

The United States was for many years the only major developed country with an economy large enough to export merchandise and capital. A new outflow of U.S. resources to aid in the reconstruction of the economies of numerous aid recipients was accepted uncomplainingly by U.S. domestic interests. As the world economy recovered and expanded, our share in it increased. The United States was for a long time the source of increasing international liquidity to finance worldwide economic expansion.

For both economic and (in the nuclear field) technological reasons, the United States was for many years also the principal source of support for global defense. Both within NATO and in the Pacific, U.S. forces and defense expenditures provided the mainstay of defense against all contingencies. Neither the United States nor its allies questioned this arrangement. No thought was given for some years to relating the cost of collective defense to either ability to pay or benefit derived.

As economic recovery and modernization occurred, most conspicuously in, but by no means limited to, Western Europe and Japan, countries outside the United States became increasingly able to compete. Those nations benefited from higher rates of capital accumulation than in the United States, transfers of technology from the United States, and expanding domestic research and development, plus sheer hard work.

In the United States, on the other hand, the economic success and affluence that enabled us to emphasize such noneconomic values as compassion, sensitivity to suffering, and environmental concerns also spared the younger generation from learning about the virtues of hard work, thrift, and self-discipline. These diverging trends caused productivity in Western Europe and Japan to increase steadily and at faster rates than in the United States.[7] Other events, not directly connected with long-term economic developments, contributed to a worsening of the same trends. These included the involvement of the United States in the long-drawn-out Vietnam War and economic commitments to worldwide defense that became increasingly costly.

These underlying changes in the world economy did not receive sufficient recognition in the United States until the late sixties and early seventies. By then, the outflow of U.S. dollars had gone far beyond the liquidity requirements of global economic expansion, and a chronic deficit in the U.S. balance of payments had set in. However, the role of the U.S. dollar as a reserve and vehicle currency and the growing magnitude of dollar holdings abroad limited the options available to correct the external payments problem.

At the same time, having recovered economically, both Western Europe and Japan were eager to expand trade and investment with foreign countries, including the Communist powers. Since the countries that benefited from their trade and other relations with Communist nations are not necessarily those who pay the costs of defense against those same nations, a uniform allied economic policy has become virtually impossible.

In this context, the high cost of all types of modern military equipment, the pre-eminent role of the United States in the nuclear field, ever-increasing manpower costs in defense, and the psychological costs of the Vietnam conflict contributed to a reassessment by the United States of its military role since World War II.[8] Radical changes in the military capability of the Soviet Union, together with a widening Sino-Soviet ideological and political split, made it practical to consider different approaches toward the two major Communist powers.

This led to two very important shifts in American thinking: a) An almost imperceptible shift took place in our interpretation of national security, from security for our own country and our allies to maintenance of the international status quo, provided that the Soviet threat, which had become dominant, could be minimized. An armed Soviet state, rather than international communism, became the primary source of external threat. b) U.S. military commitments around the world were to be lowered, first through disengagement from Vietnam and then through a general decrease in involvement, especially where previous U.S. commitments were no longer regarded as essential in meeting the Soviet threat or were actually perceived as a hindrance.

The dual effect of these changes was a growing realization that we needed to redefine our alliance system, and the emergence of a trading system, in which we continued to profess international economic liberalization as an ideal, separate from the alliance system. The second effect was an outcome of the first. We were, in effect, trying to persuade ourselves that we should act as if political and economic linkages played no part in foreign policy. The truth is that we had given up an old definition of an alliance system based on common adversaries without formulating a generally accepted new definition that would help retain the alliance's cohesiveness.

A series of events, beginning about 1973, has further reduced the "expected value," in foreign perceptions, of American support and the American military presence abroad. These were: our precipitate withdrawal from Vietnam, an ally; the establishment of closer relations with the PRC at the expense of Taiwan, a former ally; the announced reduction of American ground forces in Korea, still an ally; our apparent inability to save the shah's regime as an ally in the Middle East; and our inability to produce an energy policy that would reduce our economic vulnerability and help secure an oil supply for our European and Japanese allies. Our inadequate response to OPEC's challenge has contributed to an increasing rate of domestic inflation, a worsening balance of payments, a depreciating dollar that must be supported with external help, and an increasing perception by foreign nations of our growing economic and military weakness.

The expected value of U.S. goodwill has declined at the same time that U.S. domestic economic difficulties and the adverse impact of external deficits on the U.S. economy have risen. Not surprisingly, the need to redress the balance of payments deficit and meet a demand for protection by industries reeling under the onslaught of imports from some politically allied countries has increased precisely when the noneconomic value of U.S. goodwill to those allies has declined; the demand for more trade and economic relations with Communist countries has also risen precisely when the Soviet Union, at any rate, has become a potentially more formidable adversary.

Each of the above incongruencies in policy has been aggravated by other developments involving other countries. The sharp increase in the price of oil has affected many trading nations simultaneously, and the number of large trading nations has increased. Some of these trading nations are quite small measured by other standards. The oil price increase, therefore, initially presented a much greater threat to their economic, or even political, survival than it did to that of the United States. Although this does not explain why our response to the oil crisis has been less than exemplary, it does explain the alacrity with which the smaller countries have made their responses. As pointed out in the last section, their successful responses, in addition to those of developed countries such as West Germany and Japan, mean that at least a portion of their trade deficits has been shifted to the United States and other importing countries that have responded more slowly.

Conflict and mutual recriminations appear more pronounced between the United States and Japan than between the United States and the European Community (EC). This discrepancy may be explained by a) a more rapid rate of decline in the expected value of U.S. goodwill to Japan than to the European NATO powers and b) the size of Japan's trade surplus with the United States, compared with that of EC countries.[9]

As for U.S. economic relations with the Communist countries, as U.S. balance of payments difficulties have worsened, the short-run net economic advantage of expanding trade with these countries has increased from our point of view. On the other hand, as Soviet power has increased, the political and strategic risks of inadequately controlled East-West trade have also increased.

The cases of both the Soviet Union and the PRC are shrouded by uncertainties about their future leadership successions. Since spring 1979, the ability of the PRC to make effective use of Western trade, capital, and technology has also become increasingly doubtful. In assessing the overall net advantages of economic relations with these two Communist nations, different U.S. administrations—and even different policy makers in the same administration—can arrive at divergent conclusions regarding their desirability and what adequate control means.

What seemed in the last section to be incongruencies between U.S. foreign policy in general and U.S. foreign economic policy can be explained logically. Nevertheless, a logical explanation is not a justification. The present U.S. policy obviously is not an optimal one. Nor is it acceptable to other countries. Perhaps one of our most immediate practical problems is that we are not capable of sustaining our present politico-economic measures to deal with the nation's external economic disequilibrium. Besides, the political effects of our present policy on the integrity of our surviving alliances could be devastating.

POLICY CHOICES FOR THE 1980s

Finally, I shall discuss several questions concerning future U.S. policy:

—What basic decisions must be made about U.S. foreign economic policy?

—What are the choices available?

—What choices should be made in the light of my analysis of past experience?

—What would constitute a viable program, as distinct from preferred choices based on principle?

The Ultimate Choices

All policy decisions require a choice of goals. An optimal policy must first of all define the long-term national interest that is to be optimized. Theoretically, the following choices are available: a) The "maximand" (or objective to be optimized) may be limited to national security (including in this context both physical security and economic well being) for the United States alone. b) At the other extreme, it may be the maximization of security for the United States *and all* other countries except avowed adversaries of the United States. c) Finally, we may define the maximand as national security for the United States and a smaller group of other countries than in alternative (b). The smaller group under the last alternative could include, for example: i) only the market economies, ii) only certain political and military allies of the United States that can be enumerated, iii) market economies that are also U.S. military allies, or iv) an unspecified group of countries. The present publicly stated U.S. policy aimed for the maximization of physical security is best approximated by (c-ii), and our policy to maximize economic well-being is closest to (c-i), but the real position of the United States in both cases is actually closer to (c-iv).

The United States can hardly retreat to *Festung* America, which is alternative (a), if for no other reason than that the policy would not be viable in the long run. Alternative (b) is not acceptable to many other countries. Thus, in practice, we are left with alternative (c). Furthermore, discussion in the previous sections has shown that both foreign economic policy and foreign policy in general should be aimed at achieving maximum security and well-being for the same group of countries; many past incongruencies in U.S. policy have arisen when these two groups have differed. Accordingly, the United States must select as its associates countries satisfying two conditions. They must be countries that in time can fully liberalize their external economic relations; this rules out the nonmarket economies. They must also be countries that share common political values with the United States, including a commitment to freedom, because a common set of enemies no longer exists.

Having defined as our policy objective the maximization of physical security and economic well-being for the United States and a group of affiliated nations—market economies aspiring to safeguard the independence and personal freedom of their peoples—a series of additional decisions has to be made on a) how members of the group should deal with one another; b) how to deal with nonmembers; and c) whether the group is to be expandable.

On the first point, since membership in the group is based on shared values, members must not resolve conflict among themselves by coercion in any form. They must not restrain trade or discriminate against one another, economically or otherwise, but should move continuously toward total nondiscrimination.

Furthermore, since membership is voluntary, its attraction should consist of mutual long-term economic benefit and noneconomic support. Starting from where the United States now finds itself, the following elements would have to be included in U.S. foreign economic policy: a) further liberalization of trade and movement of capital and persons; b) correction of the existing balance of payments disequilibrium through a mixture of exchange-rate variations, increases in productivity, and internal economic adjustments; c) curbing of domestic inflation, also through internal economic measures; and d) maximum use of the market mechanism to bring about necessary structural changes in the economy called for by exogenous developments, including OPEC's economic warfare. It then follows that controls on foreign trade and exchange or economic adjustments forced on other members through the use of political and economic leverage must be ruled out. The last point is a departure from current practice.

In dealing with nonmembers, members must act as a group in negotiating concessions toward international economic liberalization. If nonmembers act as a cartel seeking special economic advantages, as

OPEC has tried to do, a confrontation through collective bilateral bargaining to settle the bilateral terms of trade will be necessary. In dealing with nonmembers that are nonmarket economies, state or private collective trading agencies may have to be organized. If the nonmembers are adversaries posing physical threats to one or more members, the cost of defense must be shared by the threatened members and others in proportion to the benefit derived from the maintenance of economic relations with the adversaries. This is also a break with present policy.

Finally, membership in the proposed affiliated group must be open-ended. Any nation that satisfies the two basic conditions of membership and is prepared to accept the preceding rules of conduct in dealing with both members and nonmembers may apply for membership. The proposed concept does not require radical changes in existing international economic and other institutions such as the International Monetary Fund (IMF) and the General Agreement on Tariffs and Trade (GATT), although it does present a new outlook. It is in a sense a further broadening of the concept of the EC and could well include those nations as members. The pivotal idea is the restoration of a few basic rules for international political and economic conduct that have been allowed to lapse.

In return for self-restraint, the affiliation will bring its members nondiscriminatory economic relations and group support. A real departure from practice of the recent past is the proposed treatment of adversary or nonmarket economies, against which there will be a united front for both negotiation and control.

Preconditions for a Viable Program

What has been proposed so far constitutes a set of long-term adjustments designed to reverse the trends that past policies have produced. These adjustments will necessarily meet objections from advocates of protectionism and uncontrolled East-West economic relations. It would be unrealistic to move toward such long-term changes without first establishing several preconditions. These are domestic policies a) to make the United States more competitive internationally; b) to increase the value of U.S. noneconomic support to foreign countries; and c) to improve coordination of the political, military, and economic aspects of our foreign policy.

First, emphasis must be placed on internal economic and attitudinal adjustments to increase productivity; curb inherently inflationary tendencies; promote research and development, innovation, and new investment; and, in general, encourage private initiative.

Purely domestic macro- and micro-economic measures are outside the scope of this paper. Nevertheless, mention should be made that certain steps can be taken to improve the U.S. trade balance even in the short run by removing various disincentives to export. Among these are the adoption of more reasonable standards of conduct consistent with practices in specific foreign markets and a relaxation of restrictions on business operations that have little bearing on domestic antitrust or environmental policy. Other positive measures could include better commercial intelligence and tax incentives for American expatriates.

Above all, the pressure on our balance of payments exerted by the surplus dollar holdings of oil producers can be reduced if a cooperative effort is made to invest these surpluses in developing, oil-importing countries using U.S. technological and managerial help as well as U.S. equipment. Multilateral cooperative ventures involving the oil exporters, the developing countries themselves, and other nations will contribute to lowering the oil exporters' aggregate payments surplus as well as to reducing the burden of adjustment for countries with large deficits, including the United States.

Second, the United States will have to increase its military capability to deal with a potential political use of superior military power by the Soviet Union aimed at further lowering the credibility of the United States as a dependable ally. Unless this credibility is greatly increased, other countries will be progressively less willing to agree to economic and other concessions to further liberalize trade. They will also be reluctant to share the cost of collective defense and to regulate economic relations with the nonmarket economies on a common basis with the United States. Assuming that the U.S.-Soviet nuclear balance does not deteriorate to the point of permitting Soviet first use of strategic weapons in a crisis, the United States will have to strengthen its conventional forces during the forthcoming decade so that U.S. support will again become a valuable intangible asset.

Finally, the most important of all preconditions for an intelligent and coherent policy is the existence of an adequate decision-making mechanism, together with high-quality of political leadership and that leadership's understanding of the politico-economic linkage appropriate to the existing situation.

A recent study of foreign policy mechanisms and coordinating agencies in the United States[10] suggests that although the existing U.S. government machinery has its deficiencies, those defects can be corrected more readily than can the traditional attitudes of some policy makers within the bureaucracy. In these traditional attitudes, economics represents low diplomacy and security matters in the narrower sense constitute high diplomacy. As long as the political and economic spheres are not thoroughly intermeshed in both thought and deed, it is hard to see how the economic and noneconomic aspects of foreign policy can be properly integrated with each other or with domestic policy.

In the final analysis, the most important single element is the quality of the leaders, including their grasp of the politico-economic linkages of foreign policy beyond the purely tactical and manipulative aspects. If this leadership can successfully arouse public opinion and impress upon the voters that certain critical decisions can no longer be postponed, the prospects for a coherent, successful foreign economic policy in the 1980s will be infinitely better. If this occurs, then the performances of the more petulant and grasping members of OPEC in Geneva in June 1979 may turn out to have provided the United States and other oil-importing countries with a clear view of the steps they must take and the leadership they will need.

NOTES

1. Similar views had been expressed by other government officials. See U.S., Congress, Senate, Subcommittee on International Finance of the Committee on Banking and Currency, *Joint Resolution 169 Concerning East-West Trade* (Washington, D.C.: Government Printing Office, 1968), part 2, pp. 628–629.

2. A re-examination of its import procurement plans was ordered by the PRC in spring 1979, one of the reasons being insufficient income from exports. Oil and raw material exports alone will apparently be inadequate to meet the projected demand for foreign payments. They must be augmented by exports of labor-intensive goods, to be manufactured and marketed abroad with foreign cooperation.

3. See the testimony of Robert S. Strauss, special representative for trade negotiations, in U.S., Congress, Senate, Subcommittee on International Trade of the Committee on Finance, *United States/Japanese Trade Relations and the Status of the Multilateral Trade Negotiations*, 95th Cong., 2d sess., February 1, 1978 (Washington, D.C.: Government Printing Office, 1978), p. 8.

4. During 1965, seven countries registered world trade totaling 10 percent or more of the value of U.S. world trade ($48.9 billion) in that year. The number of countries rose to fifteen in 1977, when U.S. trade was valued at $273.8 billion. Similarly, the number of countries whose world trade was 5 percent or more of the value of U.S. trade increased from nineteen in 1965 to thirty-four in 1977. Of those thirty-four, nine were oil exporters; five were non-oil-exporting developing countries (Brazil, South Korea, Taiwan, Hong Kong and Singapore); three were socialist countries (the USSR, the PRC, and Yugoslavia); and the remaining seventeen were European countries plus Canada, Australia, South Africa, and Japan.

5. In 1977, the total trade of South Korea, Taiwan, Singapore, and Hong Kong amounted to 52.1 percent of Japan's trade and 27.2 percent of U.S. trade.

In the same year, Australia and South Africa, both major non-oil mineral exporters, together accounted for 46.4 percent of Japan's overall trade and 24.2 percent of U.S. world trade.

6. The amounts delivered would, of course, be much smaller. See "U.S. Arms Sales Abroad, A Policy of Restraint?" *AEI Defense Review* 2, no. 5 (1978).

7. The following comparative data on annual percentage changes in labor productivity (measured by output per man-hour) are illuminating:

	1960–1973	1973–1977
United States	3.0	2.2
Japan	10.2	3.7
West Germany	5.5	5.6
France	6.1	4.8
United Kingdom	4.0	0.1

SOURCE: U.S. Dept of Labor, Bureau of Labor Statistics, USDL 78-443 (Washington, D.C.,May 12, 1978).

8. See a discussion on this subject in Yuan-li Wu, *U.S. Policy and Strategic Interest in the Western Pacific* (New York: Crane & Russak, 1975).

9. In 1977, the United States had a deficit current account balance of $8.1 billion with Japan, versus a $2.5 billion deficit with West Germany and a $2.7 billion surplus with all Western Europe. In 1978 the U.S. deficit with Japan was $11.6 billion.

10. See Stephen D. Cohen, *The Making of United States International Economic Policy* (New York: Praeger Publishers, 1977).

International Business

Richard Whalen

XXIII

The French researcher Louis Armand has coined the phrase "planetarization of our world" to describe the revolutionary, technology-driven shrinkage of the space within which leading contemporary businessmen live, work, think, and plan. As the new breed of *Concorde* commuters symbolize, there is a single, unified global business environment and financial system.

But most of the world's population, especially politicians, move at a much slower, earthbound pace and still think in more constrained and parochial terms. Thus, the new economic cosmopolitanism uneasily coexists and sometimes clashes with a truculent nationalism. What economics and technology unite, politics, alas, continues to tear asunder.

Therefore, although essentially similar trends are evident throughout the advanced industrial nations that constitute the transnational global economy, each country's political response is quite different, based on the special characteristics of the local environment and the balance of forces and interests within it. These factors must be understood by businessmen if they are to survive and perhaps prosper.

In the United States, a uniquely rich and fortunate nation for most of its brief history, businessmen and politicians long have been able to coexist without understanding much about the specifics of each other's daily work. For the most part, they ignore each other—or worse, when offended, they ignorantly denounce each other, often in abstract ideological terms.

It is astonishing but true that in European nations with leftist and outright socialist governments, leading politicians and businessmen share an intimate, informed awareness of national economic interests and broad agreement on the political measures needed to pursue them that is entirely absent among their counterparts in the capitalist United

States. Much as they may despise each other, these Europeans cooperate because they recognize that their small, vulnerable countries simply cannot afford to deny the crucial relations between politics and economics in the modern world. We Americans are virtually alone in indulging ourselves in this destructive self-delusion, and we are dangerously late in recognizing that we too are vulnerable.

It is not at all difficult to see how this self-indulgence and self-deception became habitual. The generation of Americans who entered business after World War II and rode the long curve of the global boom to unprecedented heights, has a great deal of cumulative positive experience behind its instinctive optimism, its straight-line upbeat projections, and its assurance that all will be well. This approach, after all, has met the test; for decades, it has produced ever-higher profits. Is it any wonder that those middle-aged Americans who have guided corporate business enterprises through an era of expanding mass prosperity should believe in happy endings? They have directly experienced that seeming lesson of history.

But during the first generation after World War II, American business enjoyed competitive advantages that were certain to be narrowed and eventually lost as the rest of the world recovered. American business expanded rapidly and profitably in international markets because of the matchless assets represented by our nation's across-the-board primacy: our intact industrial base and our enormous technological leadership, our vast military superiority and, most important for businessmen, the commanding position of the dollar as the world's key trading and reserve currency. In the early 1960s especially, the overvalued dollar made foreign growth cheap and easy.

Now, inevitably, these assets are eroding. America's overall margin of advantage has dwindled and in some fields has disappeared entirely. American business faces formidable foreign competition for continued expansion in a low-growth global economy dominated by political forces that most businessmen have not yet begun to grasp. For example, the Tokyo Round of the General Agreement on Tariffs and Trade (GATT) marks a new era of negotiated and regulated "fair trade" involving expanded government monitoring of competition according to the rules set by various codes of acceptable international trading behavior. Foreign governments will become ever more deeply involved in export promotion and subsidy, including export financing, to the increasing disadvantage of U.S.-based multinational enterprises, while Washington struggles to adjust outmoded laws, institutions, and practices to the way the new global economy actually works.

In the new global economy linked by instant communications and readily available technology, as Philip Caldwell, the thoughtful president of the Ford Motor Company, has observed:

> There is almost no time lag between the introduction of a new product or idea in one country and a demand for something like it in others. We producers of durable goods are not much better off now than the makers of women's clothing—good designs can be copied and put into production very quickly . . .
>
> Rising expectations are just as evident when it comes to governments. It has been said that every emerging nation wants first and foremost a steel mill and a national jet airline of its own. At last count there are now at least 30 new steelmaking facilities and more than 50 national airlines in countries that did not have either as recently as 25 years ago.

But, Caldwell noted, the goals of emerging nations extend beyond steel mills and airlines. Using their natural resources as bargaining chips, emerging nations can

> insist that foreign manufacturers use a high percentage of locally produced components, thus creating more jobs and more auxiliary industries within each country, and to further demand arrangements for the export of a substantial share of their output. This has greatly affected the balance of automotive production worldwide and has had a strong impact on the industrialized nations.
>
> The "have not" nations possessing natural resources want all the benefits of industrialization—more jobs, greater work skills, higher incomes, better education for more people and a generally higher quality of life. There has been remarkable progress in that direction all around the globe, and especially in Latin America and Asia. In too many cases, however, this progress has been accomplished through high levels of protection for home industries and a disproportionate emphasis on exports. This has created major new competitors in our export markets and in the U.S. itself.

This phenomenon is not restricted to Latin America and Asia, however. Caldwell pointed out that the communist nations of Eastern Europe have entered the European car market and warned that China may soon follow the lead of Japan.

> Trade is a two-way street. If China is successful in achieving full industrialization, we might in 20 or 30 years have to compete against Chinese manufacturers just as hard as we compete today against the Japanese.

> And if 20 or 30 years seems far in the future, consider what Japan, with a population not much more than half of ours, has accomplished in less time. For the Kennedy round of the GATT negotiations beginning in 1962, Japan was treated as a developing country. Only 15 years later, she was producing 8 1/2 million cars and trucks annually compared with 12 1/2 million in the U.S.; 113 million tons of raw steel to 125 million; 10 million color television sets to 7 million. Japan used the protection of severe import quotas, high tariffs and prohibitions against foreign investment to develop industries of world scale.

In short, Japan used political economics to stage its miracle and so did every other U.S. competitor, but we are still pretending that the two are separate and distinct.

Mr. Caldwell grimly concluded:

> The fact is that the U.S. has become essentially a service economy, with too little emphasis on expanding manufacturing capacity to serve developing hard-goods markets abroad. Our civilian employment has increased by 15 million, or 20 percent, over the past 10 years, but nearly all of this increase has been in service industries and government. Manufacturing now accounts for less than 25 percent of all U.S. jobs.
>
> In effect, we have become an economic colony for much of the industrialized world, exporting agricultural products and raw materials, and importing manufactured goods. If we continue in that direction, we will not have the sinews for a vigorous well-balanced economy.[1]

Of course, every businessman can make a self-serving case for reducing government "interference," and of course, a relative decline in the towering American economic position after World War II was both inevitable and welcome. We needed to put our foreign competitors back on their feet so they could again be our customers. Moreover, the extremely rapid growth of U.S. foreign investment (it more than doubled during the 1960s) could not continue indefinitely. The rest of the world was bound to catch up.

But that catch-up phase ended at least a decade ago. By 1974, several industrial countries had closed the per capita income gap and achieved the same relative living standards as the United States. Since then, in a period of worsening strategic and military reverses, mounting political instability and economic crisis marked by the rise of the Organization of Petroleum Exporting Countries (OPEC) oil cartel, and the worst global recession since the great depression of the 1930s, a profoundly worrisome new trend has appeared.

The United States is falling further behind its major trading partners and competitors, both in the developed and the developing nations. Behind this trend lies a major shift in new industrial plant capacity to the advanced developing countries (Brazil, Mexico, Korea, Taiwan), affecting the competitive prospects of the United States and other advanced industrial nations. This politically disruptive issue sharply delineates the conflict between established political-economic interests in the countries of the Organization for Economic Cooperation and Development and their low-wage competitors in the developing countries, which claim a moral as well as an economic right to belong to the free world economic community as full-fledged industrial members. This claim is backed by their urgent need to earn the money to repay massive debts owed to the private banks of the West.

But the United States is not losing ground solely because brand-new factories (many of them U.S.-owned) are springing up in low-wage countries. The root of our difficulty lies within ourselves. We are abandoning the values, attitudes, and business methods that formerly made us preeminent. We have forgotten the sources of our prosperity and strength. Once, we believed in the work ethic, thrift, investment, and risk-taking private enterprise. Now, after decades of encouraging, merchandising, and subsidizing radically opposing values and forms of behavior, our resulting weakness shames and indicts us.

WORLD TRENDS CHALLENGING AMERICAN SOCIETY AND BUSINESS

As a nation, we Americans are rather like spendthrift heirs who fritter away a position of great wealth and advantage. We have overspent and overborrowed until we have virtually exhausted our credit. Meanwhile, we have neglected to use resources potentially at our command to drive better bargains abroad. Now we find ourselves forced to roll up our shirt sleeves and get back to work as citizens before we are businessmen.

We confront the following trends, ranging from the merely adverse to the truly ominous:

1) A continuing shift in the American-Soviet military balance, strategic as well as conventional, to the visible disadvantage of the United States, causing further erosion of the U.S.-centered alliance structure.

An American journalist living in Moscow and writing under a protective pseudonym reported in early 1979 on a long conversation with the prominent Russian historian and leftist dissident intellectual

Roy Medvedev. Medvedev said the Soviet Union

> is moving in one direction—toward the strengthening of our military might. By the end of the century Russia will be the strongest country on earth, there is no denying that. Of course our country has many problems—we're poor, we dress badly and eat badly. But in the key sectors of the economy we are growing and growing, and the United States cannot stop us. We are going to overtake the United States and that is inevitable . . .
>
> Our country is a military machine. We are continuing now as we did in World War II . . . We won because our system allowed the spending of colossal resources for one purpose alone—military strength. We may be primitive, but we will take over . . .
>
> Americans are fools. They come to Russia, stay in our hotels, eat in the restaurants and find out that everything here is badly run. Then they return to the United States with the conclusion that since Russia can't run a hotel, it can't build a rocket either. They don't realize that we put everything into rocketry, that the government does not care whether or not anything is left over for the population.

The reporter noted Medvedev's explanation of America's chief weakness, which he had heard frequently from Russians:

> Americans cannot keep up with this kind of a system. In the United States everything is based on private interest, and it is impossible to get anything accomplished there. People talk about Soviet bureaucratism, but it's really America that is plagued by this problem. If the Pentagon wants to build a new fighter or bomber, it has to pay Lockheed twice as much as the plane costs in order to get private industry to do the job for the government . . .
>
> Americans care too much about their standard of living to build an army to match ours. Everything is ruled by private interests. There's no unified command. Nixon couldn't beat tiny Vietnam because the country was too divided to win a war. We send a few thousand troops down to Angola and we took over the place in just a few weeks.

Contemplating the Russian's words, the American reporter concluded:

> The mood within the Soviet Union is clearly one of war. Medvedev's statements are unusual only because they were articulated by a distinguished intellectual. I have heard many other Russians express the same view . . . The frightening thing to realize is that Russians perceive a weakness in America, because this perception of weakness is what promises international instability in the years to come.[2]

Those words bear repeating: *This perception of weakness is what promises international instability in the years to come.*

2) A continuing and deepening foreign distrust of the American government's resolve to control runaway inflation and protect the international value of the dollar as the world's central currency.

The American dollar has been dethroned as the world economy's sole trading, reserve, and official intervention currency. The consequences of the end of the era of U.S. global economic and financial dominance will unfold in the next decade and beyond as other nations seek a more broadly based and secure monetary system. No agreed alternative is in sight, and the danger exists that regionally based competitive trading and currency blocs will emerge. The first, the European Monetary System, was launched in early 1979.

The primary cause of the dollar's decline and America's loss of competitive vigor can be summed up in a single word: inflation.

During the first decades of the postwar era when the dollar was strong, the United States was, comparatively speaking, a low inflation country. Between 1951 and 1970, the average annual price rise in the United States was 2.4 percent (compared with 2.2 percent for West Germany, the least inflationary industrial nation). Since 1970, the inflation rate has risen dramatically, and, the United States now stands above even the United Kingdom on the inflation ladder.

Since the end of World War II, the portion of the nation's output absorbed by expanding government has doubled: from 16 percent in 1947 to 27 percent in 1962 to 32 percent in 1977. At all levels of government, the public sector has grown more rapidly than the private sector, which, of course, must bear the costs of the entire economy. Quite simply, we have paid for our expanding public sector and soaring budget deficits by printing more dollars and engaging in a worsening devaluation of the dollar. By saving less and consuming more, we have gravely undermined our competitive position in world trade.

America's competitive performance is abysmal. In 1978, U.S. productivity improved at a rate of less than 1 percent. Japan's productivity grew ten times faster. This was a significant factor in Japan's $11.5 billion trade surplus with the United States.

For our cumulative inflationary excesses, we are likely to pay a heavy price in the future in terms of lost jobs, products, and markets. Technological innovation in the United States is slowing down markedly, according to studies made by the American Productivity Center, while leading foreign competitors, such as Japan and Germany, are making greater efforts in research and development. They are doing so because business and government are long-term partners in high-risk innovation and because they recognize the grim challenge posed by the suddenly competitive industrialized Third World. Meanwhile, in the United States, the situation and results are entirely different. As Union Carbide Corporation's director of corporate technology complained not long ago: "Government officials keep asking us, 'Where are the golden eggs?,' while the other part of their apparatus is beating hell out of the goose that lays them."[3]

3) The persistent imbalance of trade and payments between the United States and the rest of the world is symptomatic of deep-seated structural weaknesses in the U.S. economy.

These unprecedented U.S. deficits are poorly understood by the American public. Politicians and the news media continually link the falling dollar and rising U.S. oil imports. Indeed, the temptation is strong to blame it all on OPEC.

In reality, no connection exists between a country's level of oil imports and the strength or weakness of its currency. Japan and West Germany import almost all of their petroleum requirements, yet the yen and the mark are the strongest major currencies in the world.

According to a 1978 study by the staff of the Saint Louis Federal Reserve Bank, the chief cause of the dollar's weakness is an excessive increase in the U.S. domestic money supply relative to the growth in the money supplies of other key currencies. Says the study: "A cutback on oil imports without a cutback on excess money growth in the United States (relative to excess money growth abroad) could not have a marked effect on the U.S. balance of payments or the foreign exchange value of the dollar."[4]

Domestic inflation has sapped the competitive vigor of American industry abroad. According to an August 1978 analysis by the Cleveland Federal Reserve Bank, which closely monitors the U.S. industrial heartland, "a massive deterioration" has occurred in the overall U.S. trade position since 1975.[5] In the 1975–1978 period, total exports rose by almost 24 percent, while total imports soared more than 72 percent, causing a swing in the U.S. position from a record $11 billion surplus in 1975 to a $34.1 billion deficit in 1978.

The causes of this vast trade gap are numerous, the study finds, and cannot be traced to any single major influence like rising oil imports. Of the $45 billion trade swing since 1975, fuel imports accounted for only $15.4 billion or about 35 percent. Even if oil imports had remained flat since 1975, the United States still would have run a record $24 billion trade deficit in 1978.

The long-term nature of these unfavorable trade trends is evident when non-oil imports are measured as a percentage of the United States's gross national product (GNP). From the early postwar years through the mid-1960s, except for a brief upsurge during the Korean War, non-oil imports remained stable at about 2.5 percent of GNP annually. An uptrend developed around 1966, as U.S. inflation began to worsen. Now, the non-oil import penetration of the U.S. economy is more than 6 percent of GNP. And the degree of penetration is increasing.

In its study of 1975–1978 trade data, the Cleveland Federal Reserve Bank noted that the machinery and transport equipment category, although the largest in dollar terms and still running an $8.9 billion surplus in 1978, experienced a $13.3 billion erosion in its cumulative surplus for the three-year period. After energy, this is the second worst swing in the U.S. position, a significant sign of eroding competitive strength. Manufactured goods classified chiefly by material show the third largest negative swing for the 1975–1978 period: $12.1 billion. In 1978, the category showed a $15.9 billion deficit. Even food and live animals, long an export mainstay, recorded a $2.6 billion decline for the 1975–1978 period.

A longer-term Commerce Department analysis of 1965–1976 trade data revealed several far-reaching changes:[6]

a) The United States is becoming more dependent on exports to non–market-oriented developing countries and Eastern Europe, including the USSR. The hoped-for "China boom" illustrates this trend.

   From 1965 to 1976, the share of U.S. exports to developed countries declined from 68 percent to 63 percent, while exports to developing countries doubled to 10 percent over the same span. Western Europe led the decrease in U.S. overseas markets. Exports to Eastern Europe rose from less than 1 to almost 4 percent. The net result is that the United States directly and indirectly subsidizes more exports that earn less hard currency.

b) From 1965 to 1976, as the share of U.S. imports from developed countries decreased sharply (from 67 percent to 54 percent) imports from developing countries soared from 33 percent to 45 percent over this period. Japan proved an exception, boosting its share of U.S. imports from 11 percent to 13 percent. Lower-cost competitors, sending steadily upgraded goods into U.S. markets, are making big inroads.

c) The share of U.S. imports from OPEC tripled between 1965 and 1976, hitting 22 percent. Measured in constant dollars, the oil component in total U.S. imports rose from 7 to 12 percent. Significantly, the U.S. propensity to consume nonpetroleum imports, such as capital goods, automotive products, and consumer goods, soared during this period. In 1965, these three groups were 29 percent of nonpetroleum imports, and in 1976, a stunning 51 percent.

d) Always reliable U.S. agricultural exports reached a peak of 25 percent of total exports in 1973, but declined to 20 percent in 1976. In constant dollars, agricultural exports continue to account for one-fifth of total exports.

These form a disproportionate share of bilateral U.S. trade with Japan, however. The United States is cast in the disadvantageous role of raw material exporter vis-à-vis the Japanese economic superpower. Japan is not merely a difficult market for American businessmen to penetrate; the United States is often a second-best Western competitor. For example, Japan's machinery imports from Western Europe are growing more than twice as fast as those from the United States.

As these trends attest, the United States has lost the enormous technological superiority of a generation ago, and European and Japanese competitors now can offer many comparable or better products. Seen in long-term perspective, enormous U.S. trade and payments deficits are external signs of internal economic imbalances: excessive government stimulus to consumer demand and neglect of expanded productive capacity; obstacles to business innovation and risk taking; declining investment returns on capital since the mid-1960s; increasing disincentives to work, production, and capital formation; stagnant productivity per worker; and—the all-encompassing negative factor—the relentless growth for two generations of public sector spending at the expense of the tax-burdened private sector.

4) As the dollar-centered world financial system slowly comes apart and inflation-driven international debts pile up, especially among poor oil-importing countries, the interrelated U.S. and foreign banking systems are exposed to growing risks of major default, originating in the unregulated Eurodollar markets.

In mid-June 1979, David Rockefeller, chairman of the Chase Manhattan Bank, publicly warned that surging oil prices and greatly increased financial surpluses were creating unbearable pressures on the world's private banking system. The banks would no longer be able to play the recycling role—reinvesting petrodollar deposits—that had eased the burden of OPEC's quadrupled prices since 1974. Rockefeller said it was "imperative" that international government-backed lending institutions, such as the International Monetary Fund, assume the leading role in lending to oil-importing nations, especially the less developed countries.

In equally blunt terms, then Treasury Secretary W. Michael Blumenthal acknowledged in a speech that the new strains imposed by explosive OPEC price hikes would endanger not only overextended individual banks, but also the entire international financial system. And most outspoken of all was the scholarly, soft-spoken chairman of the House Banking Committee, Congressman Henry S. Reuss, who said: "Without wanting to cry havoc or shout fire in a crowded theater, I think the ability of the financial system to pyramid inflationary loans to developing countries is limited and those limits are being approached."[7]

Thus, Rockefeller, Blumenthal, and Reuss at last broke the public silence that had disguised rapidly increasing private concern among leading bankers and senior officials throughout the industrialized world. The ultrasensitive secret let out in the open was that some unknown number of loans were worthless and would never be repaid. As a result, some lending institutions and their central banks would be forced to deal with the consequences of these defaults before cumulative debt liquidations and bankruptcies were unleased.

Something more valuable than money could be swept away by a debt landslide, according to Leslie C. Peacock, vice-chairman of the Texas Commerce Bank.

> The debt of less developed countries constitutes a potential threat to the stability of the international financial system. If that potential threat is transformed into actual damage, it will not be because of massive debt repudiation arising out of the profligacy of less developed countries and/or out of the excessive amounts of credit extended to them by U.S. and European banks. It will be because the debt burdens assumed by these countries are justifiable and supportable only in a world of relatively free trade, which is within the capacity of industrialized nations to preserve. There is every reason to believe that the debt burden of LDCs is a manageable problem in a world of liberal trade policies and reasonably high private investment, but there also is no doubt that the same debt burden could become a serious problem if the world retreats into protectionism and economic isolationism.[8]

5) The United States is becoming more like other industrial nations and therefore must adjust policies and public attitudes to changed circumstances. Attitudes appropriate to a vanished era of national self-sufficiency are now extremely serious obstacles to effective domestic and international policies.

Since the beginning of 1979, the world has been rudely shaken from the complacency caused by the seeming oil glut and the steady decline of real oil prices as the result of inflation and the dollar's weakness. New disruptions in oil supplies, especially from strife-torn Iran, and skyrocketing oil prices in a market suddenly become anarchic have profoundly altered public psychology and the economic outlook in the major import-dependent consuming nations, especially the United States.

Local shortages of gasoline and soaring prices have had an especially heavy impact on the consumer-oriented, automobile-centered U.S. economy, which occupies a position of central importance in world trade. Although the potential amount of energy available in the United States and the rest of the world is almost unimaginably enormous, its *timely* availability is highly uncertain. This is the question mark that overshadows the world economy.

American vulnerability to OPEC is the consequence of an intolerable lack of foresight in the world's putative leading power, a stumbling into the future as the result of seeing only the short run and the quick, easy buck. Despite enormous actual and potential sources of energy in the United States, the American economy, with its unique emphasis on the automobile, has become increasingly dependent on imported energy resources, which has major impact on the world energy supply and demand balance and on other import-dependent consumers. In the early 1950s, net U.S. oil imports accounted for less than one-tenth of U.S. consumption. These imports now approach one-half of U.S. consumption.

In the 1980s, the growing dependence on imported oil will have major implications for America's trade and current account balances. In 1978, U.S. oil imports cost $42 billion, compared with less than $8 billion in 1973. In 1979, they are expected to soar to more than $60 billion. Somehow, like other countries, the United States must earn or finance its imports, which means the United States must swiftly regain its export vitality and competitiveness.

The severe worldwide economic recession during 1974–1975 aroused protectionist sentiment throughout the industrial nations, and so could the downturn that began in the United States in mid-1979. The Tokyo Round of GATT is an attempt to keep the world on the course of trade liberalization by codifying various export subsidy and promotion techniques ("the rules of the game") in order to avert outright trade wars. The attempt is by no means certain to succeed, especially since OPEC's price gouging compels oil consumers to expand their export earnings by any means possible in a stagnant world economy. If the new trading system is to succeed, the former one-sided dependence on the United States to absorb imports and maintain both economic expansion and currency stability must be replaced by a multifaceted system marked by more equal sharing of burdens and responsibilities.

As economies become more open, however, they also become more susceptible to external developments affecting the supply and prices of the goods that they import. Over the long term, the major industrial economies have become increasingly dependent on imported raw materials. Even the United States, which once was more self-sufficient in many raw materials than other countries—a source of American strength and influence—has increased its reliance on imports of these commodities. By 1978, net imports accounted for over half of U.S. consumption of twenty important metals and other minerals.

The magnitude of U.S. oil imports relative to the total economy is not significantly smaller than for most other industrial countries. In 1978, U.S. oil imports represented 2 percent of GNP, a share equal to that of Germany and only slightly lower than the 2.6 percent of Japan, which is generally viewed as the most oil-dependent country. Moreover, U.S. oil imports were 25 percent of total merchandise imports in 1978, compared with 10 to 17 percent for the three major European oil importers (Germany, France, Italy) and 32 percent for Japan.

By 1990, according to Morgan Guaranty Trust Company, under the assumption of drastic conservation efforts and of a reduction in the growth of U.S. oil consumption by more than half the rate of 1975–1978, the value of U.S. oil imports could reach $175 billion. Such an import bill would be more than three times the 1979 level and would equal the *total value* of merchandise imports in 1979.

This scenario is based on oil imports of 11–12 million barrels per day by 1990 and average annual oil-price increases of 4 percent in the next decade, with world inflation at 7 percent. It implies effective energy policy measures in the United States that have not yet been adopted.

To say the least, as the Morgan Guaranty analysts declared, the prospect of continued heavy oil-import dependence suggests that the United States must increase its export efforts. It must develop new products, widen its export markets, and become as aggressive an exporter as other major oil-importing industrial countries. To achieve this, the United States must remain internationally competitive by improving its productivity performance and maintaining a stable and realistic dollar exchange rate. Finally, all this implies that the United States must give greater recognition and priority to international considerations in the formulation of domestic economic policies.

Simultaneously, the need for new investment in energy-efficient capital equipment to replace obsolete and unproductive capacity will become critical. If this unprecedented recapitalization does not occur in timely fashion, the United States, like other oil-consuming nations, faces the prospect of prolonged stagflation and declining living standards.

BUSINESS IS A POLITICAL ACTIVITY

If America's actual and perceived economic, military, and political weaknesses continue uncorrected, the chances of a worldwide financial and economic crisis or a major war, or both, will increase because the political and economic order held together since 1945 by America's real and perceived strength will come apart. To be sure, it does not have to be shattered all at once by economic chaos or military catastrophe. It can as easily be destroyed (and it is being destroyed) by national defaults and retreats, actual and symbolic, and by countless individual denials of faith in the future of our system and the vitality of its values.

It is cruelly ironic that although the dissident Medvedev and his Russian countrymen are poor and oppressed by a regime they despise, they nonetheless feel genuine patriotic pride. Quite humanly, they respect national strength. In America, amid boundless freedom and plenty, we find public disrespect verging on contempt for a weak government that dares not offend voters by telling them unwelcome truths. The irony is crowned by this fact: the people are in closer touch with reality than their timid leaders; and they are waiting to be told what ails America and how it can be cured, in plain language free of false promises.

The editors of *Business Week* have offered a brief, accurate diagnosis:

> Between the fall of Vietnam and the fall of the Shah of Iran, the U.S. has been buffeted by an unnerving series of shocks that signal an accelerating erosion of power and influence. Although the shocks themselves have occurred primarily in the military and foreign policy arenas, they have deep-seated economic and monetary roots. That erosion of power is the product of the failures of U.S. leaders to recognize the connections between political, military and economic events and to develop coherent approaches that deal with them in an integrated fashion.[9]

These connections, the essential threads of policy continuity, social stability, and national security, have been broken not only by foolish politicians but also by neglectful businessmen who assumed that someone else would shoulder these responsibilities. In countries, such as England, with a traditional aristocracy and highly visible establishment, such duties are more clearly assigned and less easily shirked. But in America's mass democracy, with its largely anonymous and competitive elites and adversary politics, the call to duty seems only a call to the rough-and-tumble debate and legislative battle that businessmen instinctively shun.

In the first generation after World War II, America scarcely needed a policy; we were supreme, the richest and most powerful nation in the world by the widest margin in human history. The U.S. economy became the engine of the entire world economy. The universal acceptance of the dollar as the world's money symbolized an era that could be called the *Pax Americana*.

Now, that era is fading. We are suddenly aware of the connections we took for granted, the decisive interdependence of political and economic forces in maintaining world order and growth. We see that as the U.S. economy weakens, so does American prestige and influence abroad and our ability to shape events.

What does all this mean to American businessmen active in the world economy? Simply this: they are caught in a political process that they must understand and influence on behalf of larger objectives, beginning with their own personal survival in freedom, or they will be destroyed by this process that is beyond their comprehension and control. In short, they have no choice but to think, plan, and act politically.

Dr. George P. Shultz, a rare individual who combines political, academic, and commercial talents (he was secretary of the treasury and now serves simultaneously as president of Bechtel Corporation and professor of management and public policy at Stanford University's Graduate School of Busness), has described the energy crisis in terms that illustrate my point. In a 1977 lecture, he said: "What we have here is a case where the political process is simply unable to face up to economic and strategic reality. I believe that our problem in the energy field today is not a geological one; it is not a scientific one. It is a problem in political economy of government and how government has arranged things."[10]

Businessmen, especially those who are experienced and knowledgeable in the energy business, have been almost entirely excluded from the process except as whipping boys and scapegoats. And they, with few exceptions, have counted themselves lucky to be excluded and victimized, for they thus were spared responsibility for the tragicomical outcome of the search for an energy policy on Capitol Hill. Of course, as knowledgeable citizens, they should have fought, hard and publicly, for the right to put their practical wisdom at the service of the national interest, but energy company lawyers and public affairs executives (who are increasingly the same cautious people) would not think of wading into a debate uninvited and sticking it out. Moreover, our system of democracy cannot depend on ordinary men and women to behave in extraordinarily heroic fashion. We must so arrange things that ordinary citizens doing their self-interested best can pull our country through. Alas, corporate patriotism is simply inadequate. The closest thing to political initiative by the energy industry was Mobil's tax-deductible corporate advocacy advertising, which was slightly more provocative than the gray pages of the *Congressional Record*.

As George Shultz has pointed out, the typical businessman and politician reflect entirely different ways of thinking. The businessman, faced with a problem, tends to seek the most efficient solution and relies on the market mechanism to allocate resources by price. The politician seeks the most equitable solution—one that seems "fair"—and he relies on balancing and compromising interests. The businessman is patient and waits for the market to deliver good results. The politician is impatient and fearful; his time horizon extends no further than the next election.

Politicians often complain bitterly about the narrow-mindedness of businessmen, their lack of scope and imagination, and there is some justice in their complaint. A few years ago, I gave a luncheon speech to a group of Swiss bankers and businessmen in Zurich. Afterward, one of them asked my opinion of a research project his firm had undertaken. The aim of the inquiry was to determine what changes this modest-sized company would have to make in its business operations after the Soviet Union overran the rest of Europe.

The gentleman in Zurich was, to say the least, highly selective in his assumptions and narrowly focused in his concerns. He assumed that the Swiss traditions of free-market capitalism and political neutrality could survive anything, including a possible thermonuclear war; and further, that after some adjustments the Soviet conquest of Europe would not interfere with business as usual behind the Alps. His like-minded American cousins in, say, Kansas City, make the same unwarranted assumptions, as I can personally attest. They assume, all these transnational bourgeois superoptimists, that they can prosper in this complex, unstable world on their own nonpolitical terms. Something worse than the Russians may await them: swift obsolescence in the emerging postcapitalist and postindustrial societies that politically mandate their economic satisfactions.

Survival is the politician's working definition of success, and the businessman, reared in a more forgiving environment in recent years, might well adopt it. To survive, the politician typically must manage multiple interests and loyalties, keeping his commitments few, hedged, and short-term. If successful businessmen as a class took enough time to learn the politician's trade, they might well be attracted to its high personal ego risks and rewards, far more stimulating than the stock market, and they might compensate society for their ego tripping by bringing valuable practical experience to bear on problems that are too important to be confined to the level of amateur, academic theorizing.

What is profoundly wrong with American business performance in the new global political economy is its unrealistic divorce from practical political experience, and vice versa. The solution, quite simply, is to enlist more retired astute politicians in the senior ranks of American business as corporate executives and directors and give them a broad charter to do well for themselves by doing better for the country in international bargaining at every level. By the same token, successful businessmen attempting to become politicians should be encouraged to use their entrepreneurial daring and their self-promotional skills on behalf of the nation's objectives, with the prospect of being recognized as other nations honor their commercial and financial go-getters.

Only the combined motives of patriotism and egotism can draw a financially independent American into his country's service, but these should be reinforced to get from the business elite the "best and the brightest" that the academic sphere has recently produced to the national detriment. Academics alone cannot run anything, including a college. If it were possible within the American culture to bring together brilliant academics and superlative entrepreneurs, all in their mid-40s, the U.S. government might enjoy in its upper-level policymaking positions at the State, Treasury, and Commerce departments the same extraordinary solidarity that characterizes Japan's senior bureaucracy. Of course, it is possible if we all believe it is important and necessary and so organize ourselves in the next generation.

Politics in a democracy is always messy, disorganized, contradictory, and completely nonideological. It is redeemed only by the promise of results. America has abundant, perhaps excessive democracy, but it urgently needs concrete results.

BUSINESS MUST WIN THE COMMUNICATIONS BATTLE

The crucial prerequisite to achieving results is to arrange a permanent cease-fire in the civil war between Washington and the corporate business community. This means identifying and exposing to public censure those who have acquired a selfish vested interest in perpetuating the outmoded and socially destructive adversary relation between business and government. These range from the tin-god bureaucrats of the Securities and Exchange Commission and the Federal Trade Commission and the mercenaries in the trade associations who live well lobbying against anything government attempts, to the insidiously influential, overpaid, and underworked congressional staffers who spend their days dreaming up antibusiness investigations, hearings suitable for television, and legislative proposals that will get their bosses' names in the newspapers. The list could be extended, but my point is obvious: we have ritualized and institutionalized conflict between business and government, which now must cooperate systematically for the sake of the nation's survival.

Many of those in government who oppose and hamstring business at every opportunity are not merely ill-informed or misguided, as some businessmen naively assume. On the contrary, as Irving Kristol has cogently explained, these representatives of the university-bred "new class" are motivated by contempt for businessmen and their values as well as the desire for personal power to reorganize society around morally suitable leaders, namely themselves.[11]

To win cooperation from this "new class," business must summon the will and resources to confront and conquer them in a sustained exercise in democracy: a communications battle for the minds of ordinary citizens who trust neither bureaucrats nor corporate executives, but who do not want to see their living standards steadily eroded. Business can win this battle by sincerely identifying its interests with those of the society as a whole.

Throughout the industrialized world, the large modern corporation is being redefined as a socially created and socially regulated entity entrusted with satisfying economic needs and fulfilling responsibilities to the total society of which it is an integral part. Basically, the changing nature and function of the corporation reflect changing public values. General Electric's Ian Wilson has called the large corporation "a microcosm of society," an entity bound to reflect that society's shared values—social, cultural, moral, political, and legal, as well as economic. Inevitably, there will be disagreement over how to measure corporate performance and responsibilities against this new yardstick, but businessmen should seek every opportunity to reassert their sincere concern for and involvement in the rest of American society.

American business cannot survive, much less prosper, apart from the rest of society, and this fundamental mutuality of interest must be accepted and communicated by every corporate businessman who aspires to influence public opinion.

As my former colleague on *Fortune*'s Board of Editors, John A. Davenport, wrote a few years ago:

> In one way or another, businessmen must learn to become more effective defenders of the whole political economy, and the moral values which support it, than is the case today. We are not asking here that busy executives become overnight accomplished orators and philosophers. We do suggest, as Walter Lippmann reminded us in his *The Public Philosophy*, that the deepest issues of our day are philosophical and that 'ideas have consequences.' The ideas and ideals that have shaped what we know as Western civilization are now at issue.
>
> It is time for businessmen to bring to their defense a fraction, at least, of the energy and money now being dissipated on the sale of widgets.[12]

If business prevails in this struggle to mobilize the voter-consumer's self-interest, indignation, and common sense, Congress will quickly respond by legislating overdue reforms: a comprehensive revision of the tax laws to offset the impact of inflation on corporate earnings, depreciation, capital formation, and investment to improve productivity; a coherent and effective export promotion effort; tax incentives for exports as well as for domestic capital investment; modernization of our antique antitrust laws, which are completely out of scale with the global economy and global competition; and creation of a "Department of International Trade and Industry" and vast expansion of export-financing facilities. This list is by no means exhaustive; it merely illustrates the scope of our unfinished legislative business relating to improved U.S. participation in the world economy.

As George Gilder has written: "Abstractions everywhere are confused with things." Under the tutelage of the moral imperialists of the new class, the United States exports fewer things, but vastly increased numbers of words. For example, under the Foreign Corrupt Practices Act of 1977, we export abstract moral standards, imposing ex post facto punishment on U.S. corporations that made "improper payments" abroad—that is, payoffs and bribes to obtain orders. The only result of the Act is that our foreign competitors now sell more things abroad while we sell fewer. They are content to operate according to local standards of business ethics and morality. We insist on our own, to our unilateral disadvantage, an incredible position for a nation whose share of world exports has shrunk by one-third since 1960.[13]

Or consider the moral-ecological imperialism of a group of so-called public interest lawyers who sued the U.S. Export-Import Bank, demanding that it be required to file an environmental impact statement before making a foreign loan. The only practical effect of this legal mischief is to erect yet another barrier to U.S. exports. While our competitors lavish favors and subsidies on their export-oriented industries, we do everything to discourage them. The self-indulgent, self-aggrandizing new class and its legions of lawyers who amuse themselves at the expense of the national interest are anachronisms left over from the affluent sixties. We can no longer afford them, and the same Congress that gave them such an intolerably long leash should now shorten it.

In a properly functioning free, democratic, and sane society, one not ruled by petty bureaucrats, legal vigilantes, and anonymous congressional staffers, the popular priorities are clear: material progress and plenty come ahead of pseudomoral uplift. Once this all-important order of priorities is reasserted, the prescription for a more dynamic American presence in the world economy is self-evident. Indeed, there is encouraging evidence the domestic political economy is already beginning to recover.

In late 1978, business economist Alan Greenspan revised his long-term projections along surprisingly optimistic lines, anticipating several similar bullish analyses since published. Said Greenspan:

> Over the course of the last year and, particularly, of the last six months, a political-economic shift has emerged which has significantly increased the probabilities that the 1980's will be a period of lower inflation and stronger economic activity than perceived previously. The American people, who had for years been becoming increasingly disenchanted with the growth and ubiquitousness of government, have finally 'revolted' . . . Proposition 13 brought the shift to national attention. For the first time voters said they want taxes cut and they want this even if it means some services might have to be forgone. More important, perhaps, than Proposition 13 were the instructions brought back to Washington by Congress from their constituents.
>
> Business needs a freer rein. Taxes that are stifling incentives for investment must be eased. Economic growth must be spurred. Taxes must be cut and government spending must be curbed.[14]

Greenspan's encouraging projections, as he candidly recognizes, are clouded by many uncertainties, but he is surely right about the changing mood at the grass roots and the response on Capitol Hill. It is laying the groundwork for the United States to exploit some unappreciated economic and geopolitical strategic assets in the 1980s. As *Business Week* has reported, "profound changes . . . are working to increase the competitive advantage and economic power of the U.S. over its traditional rivals in the industrialized world, Western Europe and Japan," arising chiefly from the transformed economic relations between the industrial and the less developed countries. "For the multinational corporation and big international investors, North America has again become the area where potential profitability is greatest, at least among the developed areas of the world."[15]

It will not do to idealize the typical American businessman who, in the words of an impatient senior Republican member of the House Ways and Means Committee, "is often as ignorant of how our economy actually works as any welfare worker." Ignorance, indifference, personal and corporate inertia, deep-rooted cynicism—these crippling defects among businessmen (and their fellow citizens) will not disappear overnight. But the clearcut challenge to our nation's competitive ability in every sphere ought to trigger our instinct for survival and revive our will to excel. Led by politically aware and socially responsible businessmen, America in the coming decade can restore its primacy in the new global political economy and thereby protect all that depends on American strength and leadership.

NOTES

1. Philip Caldwell, "US Becoming Economic Colony for Failing to Meet World Changes," *Financier*, February 1979, p. 21 (excerpts of speech before the Los Angeles Council of World Affairs).

2. Robert Herr [pseud.], "Spengler in Moscow," *New Republic*, March 31, 1979, p. 15.

3. "Vanishing Innovation," *Business Week*, July 3, 1978, p. 46.

4. "Oil Imports and the Fall of the Dollar," *Federal Reserve Bank of St. Louis Review*, August 1978, p. 5.

5. "Changing Patterns in U.S. Trade," *Cleveland Federal Reserve Economic Commentary*, August 1978.

6. U.S., Department of Commerce, Bureau of Economic Analysis, "Long-term Trends in U.S. World Trade," October 1977.

7. *Washington Post*, June 14, 1979. See also William J. Quirk, "The Bankers' Dilemma," *New Republic*, January 27, 1979.

8. Leslie C. Peacock, "International Financial Issues: The Views of a Banker," *National Journal*, June 3, 1979.

9. "The Decline of U.S. Power," *Business Week*, March 12, 1979, p. 36.

10. George P. Shultz, "Energy and the Market Place," speech before the Center for the Study of American Business, Washington University, St. Louis, November 7, 1977.

11. See Irving Kristol, *Two Cheers for Capitalism* (New York: Basic Books, 1978) for a comprehensive statement of his influential arguments.

12. Quoted in George Hammond, *Business Has Failed to Explain Itself,* Future of Business Pamphlet no. 11 (Washington, D.C.: Georgetown University Center for Strategic and International Studies, 1979). Hammond, the chairman of Carl Byoir & Associates, Inc., the international public relations firm, provides a lively personal history of corporate image making during the past four and a half decades.

13. The *New York Times* (June 26, 1978) reported that as a result of the new anti-bribe laws, American businessmen in Asia claimed that they had lost sales "worth millions of dollars" to European and Japanese competitors who were not encumbered by such laws.

14. Alan Greenspan, *Long-Term Projections* (Townsend-Greenspan & Co., Inc., 1978).

15. "New World Economic Order," *Business Week,* July 24, 1978, p. 68.

Asia
Robert A. Scalapino

XXIV

As we enter the 1980s, extraordinary changes have taken place within the Pacific-Asian region and in the relation of the United States to this significant half of the world. If one uses 1950 as a benchmark, the dimensions of these changes become readily apparent. Three decades ago, the Sino-Soviet alliance appeared likely over time to dominate the Eurasian continent. Today, the Sino-Soviet cleavage is so deep and pervasive that it shapes Pacific-Asian interstate relations more than any other factor. No nation escapes its impact, an impact both beneficial and dangerous. When the definitive history of our era is written, the radical transformation of the Sino-Soviet relationship in the mid-twentieth century will quite possibly be recorded as the most significant political development, even if subsequent reduction of the current intense hostility occurs.

Meanwhile, trends involving two major Communist states have been complex and in some respects contradictory. The Soviet Union has signaled that it intends to be a major power in Asia, and in comparison with 1950, its presence—military, political, and economic—has increased. But Soviet foreign policies in Asia, with several notable exceptions, have been unsuccessful, and its influence as opposed to its presence in the region is currently less than at certain earlier periods.

China also has a considerably greater presence compared with its early years, when the principal policy of the United States and its allies was containment by isolation. Moreover, its regional influence appears to be growing through eastern Asia. But the serious internal problems confronting the People's Republic of China (PRC), especially economic problems, limit its power and authority and raise the issue of priorities acutely.

Changes in the U.S. position are equally great. Earlier commitments of the United States in Asia were acknowledged by friend and foe to be extensive and powerful. Now, all Asian governments are affected by the sharp decline in American presence and influence. It is less that U.S. military power in the region has diminished, although that has happened, but more that the United States appears to lack a coherent strategy, reflecting the absence of an American foreign policy consensus and a firm American commitment. To Asians, the United States, while still the world's most powerful nation, has become unpredictable.

The broadest trends relating to the major states thus suggest a balance of weakness despite steadily increasing military capacity. A combination of internal problems and the intolerable costs of a major war limits the ability of the large powers to control or influence developments outside their territories. Here lies the basic paradox of Pacific-Asian international relations. However, a balance of weakness is no more stable than a balance of power. Hence, uncertainty and fluidity, particularly regarding American and Soviet policies, dominate Asia.

These trends have enhanced the roles of the "inner" states of the region, including China, which is part of the inner region as I am using this term. In 1950, the indigenous voice of Asia was weak: decolonization was just beginning; Japan remained under occupation; the PRC had been established in 1949, inheriting a massive populace disunited and impoverished by multiple wars; Kim Il-song was attempting to unify the Korean peninsula under communism; in Southeast Asia, a series of guerrilla wars disrupted governments and blocked economic development; southern Asia was gripped by deep political and economic crises.

Western dominance over Asia has been relegated to history. Colonialism, however, is far from dead. Asian nations control other Asian nations. Ethnic, religious, and regional groups are subjugated by dominant national groups. But the power emanates from Hanoi, Peking, Manila, or Jakarta, not from Paris, London, Washington, the Hague—or Tokyo.

Interstate and civil wars continue to be a part of Asian politics, but in recent years, the major powers, specifically the United States and the Soviet Union, have avoided direct involvement. The conflicts have thus been regional, not global in scope. To be sure, the specter of a Sino-Soviet conflict continues to haunt the scene. Indeed, such a conflagration seemed dangerously close during the 1979 Chinese invasion of Vietnam. The task of containing Asian wars while seeking to prevent them from becoming cumulatively adverse to our interests and those of our Asian allies is one of the primary tasks of the 1980s.

The increasing importance of independent Asian states in regional and global politics makes a critical evaluation of political and economic trends within these states vitally important. At present and for the foreseeable future, the relation between domestic and international politics promises to be very close.

Nearly four decades after World War II and the subsequent upheaval within Asia, political stability remains elusive for many Asian states. There are, however, some positive signs. Second and third generation leaders are generally less ideological, more pragmatic, and more committed to internal development than to foreign adventurism. Nation building has made some progress and, through trial and error, political institutions attuned to indigenous needs are emerging in various states.

Only in Japan, however, do political institutions mesh effectively with the socioeconomic system, yet have the evolutionary potential to provide future stability. Elsewhere, institutional development is rudimentary and slowed by antiquated socioeconomic foundations and numerous crises. The stability of many Asian states depends upon an individual leader, a dominant party, or a governing military establishment. Although this situation may reflect the needs and nature of the society, it makes the future less predictable. Succession crises are inevitable in most instances. If the political system proves rigid, moreover, a growing gap with societal needs will ensue, creating pressures that may ultimately erupt in violence.

We must assume, therefore, that the 1980s will be a volatile period for many Asian nations. Nationalism will continue to be the primary political expression, but even at the end of the 1980s, nation building will be far from complete throughout most of Asia. The majority of these societies will have relatively shallow political institutions, still experimental in nature and incapable of garnering deep allegiance from the citizenry. "Law and order" will be maintained largely through authoritarian means, and although this will provide stability for some societies, others will slip into recurrent violence. In any case, the typical Asian polity will continue to be quasi-authoritarian, possessing elements of pluralism and political openness but diverging considerably from the Western parliamentary model.

In the political continuum, such states will constitute the vital center. The Asian Communist states, despite periodic tremors, will likely remain close to the one-party dictatorship/heavily statist model of their origins. Pluralism and privatism will be scarce and in their fullest expression clustered at one end of the political spectrum, in a few states reflecting the classic Western liberal system. Currently, this group includes only Japan, India, Bangladesh, and Sri Lanka. The immediate future of democracy in Asia is problematic due to its fragility and the contrary cultural heritage and unresolved developmental problems of most Asian states.

Political variations are matched by economic ones. A widening gap has developed between the relatively affluent states and those still struggling with widespread poverty resulting from persistently low or uneven growth rates. Japan, Taiwan, South Korea, and Singapore are economic leaders. Each of these societies has sprung historically from the Sinitic culture with its propensities for education, complex organization, and a work ethic. But the PRC demonstrates that these advantages can be dissipated or limited by factors of scale and political-economic weaknesses, man-made but systemic in character. Among the non-Sinitic cultures, a considerable range can also be found, with Thailand and Malaysia at the upper and Burma at the lower end of the spectrum.

The variables governing Asia's economic future are necessarily many and complex, encompassing domestic politics and foreign policies as well as resources and economic decisions. For some states, indeed, the former factors will be more telling than the latter. Taiwan, Thailand, and Malaysia, for example, face uncertainties in the political realm that could offset the currently favorable economic trends. In varying degree, the primacy of political variables also applies to many other Asian states, including China, India, Pakistan, the Philippines, and Indonesia, to signal the most obvious cases.

On the positive side, the extraordinary scientific and technological advances of recent decades promise to continue, providing potential improvements in such vital fields as agriculture, population control, and industrial production undreamed of ten years ago. Moreover, new technological-managerial elites are emerging in many Asian societies that are increasingly equipped to accept and utilize these new opportunities effectively. On the other hand, some problems, such as population, are not susceptible to quick or easy control. Nor is it clear that the newly emerging managerial and scientific elites will be able to operate with maximum effectiveness and overcome political and cultural obstacles.

In sum, there is no reason to believe that past political and economic variations will disappear during the coming decades. Asia will continue to be marked by great diversity both in systems and performance. Within such large states as India variations will be extensive, both economically and geographically. In general, the states already acculturated to economic development will continue to advance, and within most of these societies the gap between urban and rural sectors will gradually narrow. Meanwhile, societies currently lagging will advance unevenly but fail to gain on the leaders, and here the urban-rural gap will become more pronounced before it begins to shrink. Millions of Asians will continue to live close to the minimal subsistence level through the rest of the twentieth century, but they will live—and live longer—thus making rapid advances in standards of living more difficult to achieve.

Finally, the current focus of most Asian states is first on domestic issues and second on regional relations. This was not always the case. Earlier, a first generation revolutionary leadership, typified by such diverse figures as Nehru and Sukarno, Mao Tse-tung and U Nu, often shirked the tasks of economic development and political consolidation at home in favor of global postures. Now, for the most part, foreign adventurism has been de-emphasized, as have grandiose plans to launch the Third World as an entity and principal actor on the international stage. The situation in Indochina and with special reference to Hanoi and Peking currently runs against this trend in some degree. But the struggle to control Indochina is essentially a regional conflict, although one with far-flung international consequences. Japan, with its global economic concerns, is also a partial exception, but in Tokyo too, regionalism is receiving increasing attention.

Current developments suggest that the future Asian international order will be a complex aggregation of regional accommodations. These and a few critical bilateral ties will constitute the matrix from which the Pacific-Asian region will take its political and economic form. In the construction of the new order, the role of the major powers will be considerable. Both their actions and inactions will govern the broadest trends. Increasingly, however, the policies of secondary powers will assume importance, singly and via such groups as the Association of Southeast Asian Nations (ASEAN). And in the final analysis, the linkage between major power relations and the more independent policy decisions of Asia's medium-sized states will determine the future of this vital sector of the world.

U.S. STRATEGIC ALTERNATIVES

As we enter the 1980s, three broad strategic alternatives confront the U.S. government and the American people. In their pure form, they can be labeled the strategies of withdrawal, united front, and equilibrium.[1]

The true minimalist position argues that neither America's national interests nor general considerations of global security require our strategic presence in Asia. Most minimalists have advocated a gradual withdrawal of all American military forces and installations. And to some extent, American policies in the 1970s accorded with their desires. Massive forces, including naval forces, were removed during the last stages of American involvement in Indochina. Moreover, in accepting defeat there, an act that astonished many Asian leaders including Mao Tse-tung, the U.S. government appeared to signal a profound shift in its post-1945 policies of a direct and intensive strategic commitment to Western Europe and East Asia. This policy shift was further evidenced in the Guam Declaration of 1969. After the Indochina defeat, moreover, we pledged to withdraw ground forces from Korea, a pledge made unilaterally with no commitments from the Communist side. Finally, in conjunction with the diplomatic recognition of the PRC in 1979, the United States announced the termination, after one year, of the Mutual Security Treaty with the Republic of China on Taiwan.

The latter action did not necessarily bear the same connotations as other evidences of strategic withdrawal, given the full circumstances surrounding it. Indeed, as is noted later, some ardent exponents of PRC recognition were prepared to substitute Peking for Taipei as an American ally. By 1978, moreover, the Carter administration had commenced a re-evaluation of its Asian policies because of the heavy decline in American credibility throughout the Pacific-Asian region and the consequent repercussions on events and policies within the area. The official rhetoric changed. Administration spokesmen began to insist that the United States intended to remain a major power in the Pacific-Asian region. More significantly, the Korean troop withdrawal decision was reopened, the lengthy negotiations with the Philippines over renewal of base rights were successfully concluded, and there was even some suggestion that our Pacific-Asian military forces might be augmented in the future.

These and other developments indicated that for the Carter administration, strategic withdrawal from Asia had been excessive, requiring adjustments in earlier policies. Withdrawal, however, has not been eliminated as a strategic alternative. Its exponents remain active and count upon extensive public support. If they cannot achieve total victory, they hope to exercise continuing influence. Since they come to their position from varying perspectives and pose a by no means negligible appeal, that hope is not unreasonable.

In their most complete form, the arguments underlying the withdrawal strategy extend to political and economic as well as to strategic considerations. These arguments are dissimilar since they reflect varying emphases, diverse ideological positions, and differing levels of concern about Asia. The central theses, however, are these. First, it is asserted that the primary threat to the United States comes from the Soviet Union at present. The world's other superpower is the sole nation that can damage the American continent physically. The central arena of the Soviet threat, it is further argued, is not in Asia but in Europe, and secondarily, in regions like the Middle East. Thus, American forces should be withdrawn from Asia, enabling the nations of that region to find their own strategic balance—one likely to be directed against Russia given present trends.

It is further asserted that it is illogical for the United States to have military forces in East Asia and to contemplate participation in a war involving this region, given the limitless manpower available there and the radically different cultural values, political objectives, and military capabilities. Both civil and military figures have opposed the use of major American ground forces in Asia since the Korean War, and that issue has seemingly been settled at this point by the Guam Declaration and subsequent American policies. The minimalists, however, would outlaw *all* military involvement in East Asia, including naval and air support. By extension, the same arguments are advanced with respect to South Asia, with the additional thesis that this is neither a region of great strategic significance to the United States, nor one in which the United States can hope to play a major political or economic role.

The range of arguments against any form of military commitment derives in major part from the experience of the Vietnam war. Prominent themes are the limits of American power, the inability of the United States to understand and successfully interact with Asian peoples in military encounters, and the culpability of the United States in seeking to impose its values as well as its power on other peoples.

Some advocates of strategic withdrawal argue that our economic and political ties to Japan warrant a continued commitment to its defense. But the general mood in the United States, which most minimalists share, is that Japan must play a greater role in its own defense, thus reducing American responsibility in Asia.

Finally, it is asserted that an American military withdrawal is compatible with Asian nationalism and the acceptance of responsibility within and among Asian states for their own future. Indeed, the minimalists frequently argue that only as we depart from Asia militarily will our political, economic, and cultural relations with Asia achieve stability and acceptance.

The strongest arguments for the withdrawal strategy rest on certain objective facts having to do with the current state of U.S. forces and American public opinion. The experiment with a voluntary military force is increasingly acknowledged to be a failure. Despite heavy expenditures, the morale and the quality of the U.S. armed forces today raises the most serious questions about the ability of the United States to field an effective military operation, especially one involving ground forces. Polls indicate, moreover, that the type of consensus among American citizens necessary to sustain such an operation might be exceedingly difficult to obtain, particularly if a limited war became protracted.

Asian leaders have been quick to perceive these problems, and together with other factors, they constitute the principal reasons why recent U.S. actions have not re-established American credibility. Grave doubts about the worth of American commitments and the consistency of American policies continue to exist in Asia. As indicated above, however, strategic withdrawal is no longer the dominant American policy toward Asia. The Carter administration now recognizes that doubts concerning the capacity and will of the United States to uphold existing treaty commitments or to play a strategic role in Asia affect not merely domestic politics and foreign policies within the region, but also all ongoing negotiations involving the United States.

The more vital debate within political and intellectual circles, however, recently has related to the united front versus the equilibrium strategy. Put briefly, the united front strategy would commit the United States to a de facto alliance with Japan and the PRC—together with such other Pacific-Asian states as might be collected—against "Soviet expansionism." Only partly articulated, but influencing policy and mood alike, this debate continues despite the fact that President Carter has proclaimed himself and his administration committed to the policies of equilibrium: "evenhandedness" in dealing with the USSR and the PRC. Given the complexity of present events and attitudes, moreover, the debate will certainly remain alive, with policies of the most vital importance hinging upon its outcome.

Adherents of the united front strategy begin with a premise not dissimilar from that held by some minimalists, namely, that the Soviet Union represents the principal security threat; but they see the USSR as a danger in Asia as well as in Europe and regard meeting the challenge on both fronts as important. Thus, they support an informal entente among the PRC, Japan, and the United States as an Asian counterpart of NATO. Since the United States is unable to play its past security role in the Pacific-Asian theater, they argue, its power must be bolstered by that of the PRC and Japan, each contributing to a strengthened, consolidated resistance to Soviet expansion in Asia.

Another defense of the united front strategy is that by binding the three key Pacific-Asian powers more closely, such issues as Korea can ultimately be resolved peacefully, and in a broader sense, the rigid ideological and political divisions of the past within Asia can be more easily surmounted. Most united front supporters insist that the old dichotomy between Communist and non-Communist Asian states lacks validity and hence there is no need to give priority to the traditional alliance structure.

Few united frontiers would argue for a formal pact cementing a U.S.-Japan-PRC alliance, knowing that this would be unacceptable to all parties concerned. Rather, they have favored a range of economic, political, and strategic policies and "understandings," including rapid recognition of the PRC regardless of the terms required; military assistance to the PRC if requested, together with arrangements conducive to the speedy military and industrial modernization of China; and support for a Japanese tilt toward the PRC combined with a wariness toward any Japanese agreements with the USSR.

The final "pure" alternative, the equilibrium strategy, is premised on the desirability of roughly balancing relations with Russia and China, avoiding any sustained tilt toward either, and negotiating with each on an issue-by-issue basis, keeping in mind U.S. interests and those of our political, economic, and strategic allies. Proponents of the equilibrium strategy do not totally disavow the various propositions underlying the first two strategies. Most would accept the need to avoid the "over-Americanization" of conflicts and to insist on more equitable burden sharing. Most would also regard as reasonable and necessary certain limits on the scope and nature of American strategic commitments; the limits implicit in American culture and the American political system; and the limits imposed by the changing nature of conflict in the late twentieth century.

They submit, however, that the Pacific-Asian region will become an evermore closely inter-related area and should not be treated as a series of separate, isolated parts, susceptible to enclavism. They further argue that this area is of vital and growing importance to the United States. American economic interests in the region now exceed those in any other region, including Europe. The implications of Asian political developments are of equally major consequence to the United States, given the critical role that the nations of this region play on the global stage.

The equilibrium advocates further assert that the natural strategic balance that the minimalists propose be found by the Asians themselves rests upon fallacious reasoning, since both the Soviet Union and the United States have a physical presence, as well as vital interests in the region. An American withdrawal would precipitate an unnatural imbalance, influencing war and peace issues and the outcome of negotiations across a wide range. In an era of protracted, intensive negotiations among all parties, no nation—and particularly a major nation like the United States—can afford to neglect any element of strength needed at negotiations, including that of a strategic presence in one of the world's most important regions.

The equilibriumists view the minimalist argument on alignment with Asian nationalism as simplistic and naive. Which Asian nationalists? Those that went down fighting the communists in Cambodia and Vietnam? The South Korean nationalists or the North Korean nationalists? Not even the Chinese communist nationalists want the American strategic presence in Asia completely removed for reasons connected with their nationalism.

But the equilibriumists diverge sharply with the united fronters on one basic issue, the concept of a de facto alliance with the PRC against the USSR. Such a policy, they believe, would have two very dangerous consequences. First, it would evoke sharp Soviet reaction, making future agreements in such fields as nuclear weapon control or the management of regional crises difficult if not impossible. We would return to the era of the late 1940s and early 1950s, with the enhanced costs and risks that recent advances in military technology have bequeathed to the 1980s. Second, it would be strongly destabilizing for Asia and would cause Chinese hegemony in the region. Recent events in Indochina lend additional credence to this second thesis. The evidence suggests that a militarily strong, economically advancing China is likely to reassert its historic predisposition to exercise its power in East Asia, rather than merely to conserve that power as a strengthened defense against the USSR. Indeed, while there was much talk prior to U.S. recognition of the PRC about Washington playing its China card against Moscow, in fact, it was Peking that played its America card. Armed with recognition largely on its terms, the PRC could undertake its invasion of Vietnam knowing that while the United States did not approve of this embarrassing action, it would not rescind official recognition or take any other action damaging to Chinese interests.

In addition, the exponents of an equilibrium strategy point out that neither Japan nor West Europe favor a united front policy. Although the Japanese government accepted American nudging to approve the Sino-Japanese treaty in the fall of 1978, and subsequently indicated its approval of the December 15 Agreement between the United States and the PRC inaugurating official relations, it has signaled repeatedly that it does not want to be the spearhead of a united front strategy and thus be forced to accept a high-risk foreign policy. Meanwhile, Western European leaders have reacted with similar apprehension to the possibility that American policies might aggravate their relations with the Soviet Union. Both the French and the West German governments have urged that the United States not turn its new relations with China into an anti-Soviet operation. Given these views, ask the equilibriumists, how can the united front strategy be effectuated?

It now seems likely that although the debate over strategy will continue and American policies will be subject to various contortions, a modified equilibrium strategy will ultimately prevail in the 1980s. This strategy, it must be emphasized, will be infused with other strategic strains. An element of withdrawal will continue to be present, its strength depending upon the nature of domestic economic and political trends. The United States is no longer able or willing to play the strategic role in East Asia that it assumed in 1946–1956. It no longer holds preponderant global power. In addition, the relative inertia of Asia is gone, and no single state, however powerful, can hope to guide events or construct an international order largely through its own policies. Meanwhile, the United States itself has evolved into a new and difficult stage at home, with public attention focused upon domestic problems incapable of quick or easy resolution.

These facts now sustain and will continue to sustain some degree of strategic withdrawal. They also dictate the type of strategic presence that will be maintained in the Pacific-Asian region and the type of military response to be expected in the event of a crisis. The one incontrovertible lesson of Vietnam is that the United States cannot become directly involved in a protracted, limited war. Our political culture, the pervasive influence of the modern media, and many other factors doom such a response. Any future American military response will place a premium on speed and hence, in all likelihood, on decisiveness. This does not address the question of indirect involvements through aid to allies or deserving nations. Nor does it necessarily dictate the application of American nuclear power in every instance. But it does indicate that the emphasis will be on the fullest measure of power required to achieve an objective rapidly in the event of the decision to commit American military force. One can assume, therefore, that such a decision will not be taken lightly, especially if it involves a major power.

It is also likely that some elements of the united front strategy will be incorporated into the policies of equilibrium. The relationship between the United States and the Soviet Union is certain to be troubled and complex in the near future. After years of unquestioned military superiority, the United States has been forced to accept reluctantly the principle of Soviet military parity, and many fear that Moscow will aim at military superiority. This concern is understandable. Even among those committed to détente, a gnawing anxiety is often present. The United States has lived with global power for decades. Gradually, the combination of experience and institutional safeguards have made power acceptable, if not entirely comfortable. As the USSR approaches co-equal global power, Americans wonder if Soviet leaders and the

Soviet system can handle great military power without grave danger to the rest of the world.

Against this psychological uneasiness, a policy of collaboration with everyone dedicated to offsetting Soviet power acquires added attractiveness. Short of a full-fledged united front policy, therefore, policies aimed at enhancing Chinese military and economic power are likely to win significant support in the United States despite China's deep involvement in Indochina and the evidence of other Chinese foreign policies contrary to American interests. Abetting this will be the recurrent argument that any swing of the pendulum toward Sino-Soviet rapprochement must be prevented. But the strength of united front sentiment will hinge both on trends in American-Soviet relations and on the domestic and foreign policies of the People's Republic of China.

AMERICAN-JAPANESE RELATIONS

Since the 1950s, both American and Japanese leaders have proclaimed U.S.-Japanese ties as the cornerstone of their respective Pacific-Asian policies. Indeed, the American connection has occupied the central position in Japan's overall foreign policy, both strategically and economically; and for the United States, few if any bilateral relationships of the post-1945 era have been more significant. The U.S.-Japanese alliance has involved not merely security and trade, but cultural relations as well, despite the fact that contacts between our two peoples cannot be described as intimate, a point to which I shall return. Yet in recent years, strains have been recurrent in the alliance, and its future is now problematic. Is the U.S.-Japan entente a cornerstone of policy or a trouble zone?

What are the most probable trends of the 1980s and beyond in the Japanese domestic scene? First, political change is likely to be incremental, but nonetheless meaningful. Since 1945, Japan has had the greatest degree of political stability among advanced industrial nations. Characterized by a one-and-one half party system, Japanese politics have been dominated for over 30 years by a conservative party that currently bears the label Liberal Democratic Party (LDP). In part, this has been possible because the Japanese system of intraparty factionalism has enabled change to take place via the LDP, eliminating the need for intraparty alternation in power. LDP leaders, however, must be given credit for pursuing the type of liberal, pragmatic policies that brought unprecedented prosperity to a war-ravaged, poverty-stricken nation, thus gaining public support, although in gradually diminishing percentages.

Will LDP control of Japanese politics wane in the coming decade and political instability become a new factor, influencing both domestic and foreign policies? In recent national elections, the LDP has obtained less than 50 percent of the vote and has had to depend on the electoral system to preserve its majority in the Diet. It has also benefited from deep divisions in the opposition parties and the high level of ineptitude in the Japan Socialist Party, which would normally have emerged as a formidable challenger.

Two changes appear under way, the combination of which seems certain to affect the future. First, the older political generation running from Yoshida, Kishi, and Sato to Fukuda and Ohira will soon pass from the scene. These men were educated in the prewar era and generally served in the bureaucracy—often in ministries connected with economic policies—before moving laterally into party politics at a high level. It was natural for them to preside over the bureaucratic-conservative party coalition that governed Japan. Shortly, political leadership will gravitate to a generation of men educated in the postwar era, products of more diversified backgrounds, but increasingly coming to power as "pure politicians" and hence more attuned to media, public opinion, and a wider range of interest groups. Under these circumstances, the transition to party-centered coalition politics is logical.

These trends have been under way for several years. Miki (the first postwar "pure politician" prime minister) promoted communications between the LDP and the opposition parties, especially the Komeito and the Democratic Socialist party. Miki's successors—though from a different background—have continued that practice. Japan already has an embryonic coalition politics extending beyond the LDP into the centrist political spectrum. In one sense, therefore, the absolute dominance of the LDP is less consequential than at an earlier point. This combination of new party leadership and coalition politics (even if LDP-dominated) underlies the probabilities of evolutionary change, thus keeping the Japanese polity in rough equilibrium with social change and restraining the extremes of left and right.

This projection, however, is premised on socioeconomic trends reasonably satisfactory to the Japanese people and basically conforming with the broad goals and capacities of the Japanese nation. But if economic problems—recession and protectionism among advanced industrial nations, resource scarcity and costliness, and intensified competition for markets—seriously damages the Japanese economy, U.S.-Japanese relations will become complex and troubled.

Three issues, one relating to procedure and two involving substance, are central to those relations. Since each of these issues will endure into the future, their essence and possible amelioration must be explored. Let us turn to the issue of procedure first. Despite the stake that each government has in close cooperation, meaningful consultation has generally been lacking in spite of various pledges and institutions of the past. As early as the Kennedy administration, bilateral cabinet-level meetings were held, primarily to discuss economic issues. Later, these lapsed. In the private sector, panels have operated with varied agenda, involving businessmen, civic leaders, and scholars. Few, however, have had a sufficient cohesiveness or longevity to make a sustained impact.

It should be admitted that at the policy level, it is the United States that has most frequently pursued unilateralism. On such critical matters as China policy, Washington has not only made major decisions without consulting Tokyo, but has simply notified Japan only hours before public announcement. Economic issues, moreover, have been allowed to reach explosive levels and been thrust into the political arena before task forces have begun tackling them. In belated recognition of procedural defects, the U.S. government has recently revived the concept of a standing bilateral commission of mixed official and private character to review and discuss ongoing economic relations. Also, a joint defense commission has been instituted to coordinate and implement defense policies.

The beginnings in much-needed procedural changes have thus been made. Whether these will develop into thorough consultation across the range of international political, economic, and strategic issues affecting our two nations remains to be seen. Much will depend on the degree of consensus that can be reached regarding current key substantive issues and the skill with which the necessary policies are carried out by both governments. Obviously, effective consultation, even if it is achieved, does not necessarily lead to agreement.

The foremost substantive issue involves economic relations, but it extends beyond bilateral matters into the domestic policies of each country and into those matters of international economic policy and practice affecting many nations. One can predict with assurance, moreover, that the complex questions currently before us will not suddenly be resolved or disappear. Throughout the 1980s and beyond, economic issues will occupy center stage in U.S.-Japanese relations and determine to a considerable degree the general health of the relationship.

Why is equitable resolution of current issues so difficult? First, basic structural changes in both Japan and the United States are required, changes that involve the ongoing system in each nation and hence meet with cultural as well as personal or institutional obstacles. In the future, Japan must restructure its economy to emphasize its domestic market and gradually reduce dependence on export gains. Social services, previously neglected or relegated to the private sector, must in increasing measure become a government responsibility. Meanwhile, the barriers to foreign access to the Japanese market and investment must be removed much more rapidly. And Japanese foreign aid must be less selfish, that is to say, less oriented exclusively to Japanese market interests and gains. Finally, Japanese international market and investment policies must consider the political sensibilities of the nations most heavily involved with Japan, and this requires significant alterations ranging from Japanese behavior overseas to the blitzkrieg technique of rapidly saturating foreign markets.

The obstacles to making these changes thoroughly and swiftly are formidable. The very successes of the past militate against dramatic alterations. Moreover, although it is easy to exaggerate the organic nature of the Japanese economic system by ignoring the intense internal competition and the increasing independence of the private sector, the past role of government as protector of industry and agriculture—in sum, a tightly structured protectionist system vastly different from the relatively loose, often hostile government-business relations of the United States—underscores the difficulties of change and the gap separating the economic systems of our two societies.

Finally, the strengths of modern Japan lie in no small measure in its capacity to utilize aspects of its unique cultural background in the service of modernization. By the same token external economic and social penetration of Japan is more difficult. In essence, the Japanese are a private, introverted people, with exceedingly demanding and hence carefully restricted intimate relations. Indeed, the supreme paradox of Japan is that it is an open society composed of closed units.

As a result of these factors, an economic system that has served Japan extremely well in recent decades has proven highly resistant to change in the face of growing international pressure, to the peril of Japan's relations with the West, including those with the United States. Alterations are now under way, but it remains to be seen whether they will go far enough, fast enough.

Meanwhile, relations between business leaders of both societies have worsened. Many American businessmen consider Japan "the principal enemy" and insist that in addition to protecting its domestic economy unduly, Japan's overseas practices constitute unfair competition. In response, resentment in Japanese business circles to American charges—and the demands of the American government—has risen sharply. The Japanese assert that they are being made the scapegoat for American economic ills and American entrepreneurial defects.

This complaint is not without merit. Like Japan, the United States faces the need for basic structural changes, cultural as well as economic. The need for a meaningful energy policy, for example, grows ever more insistent. Without it, inflation will continue to threaten the American economy and consequently that of the international community. Meanwhile, the extensive reliance of American business upon the domestic market and its lethargy in competing for international markets contrast sharply with its Japanese counterpart. Excerbating the problem, the United States has no international economic policy that might encourage American entrepreneurs in the direction of greater competitiveness abroad. Lagging gains in labor productivity and the obsolescence of certain industrial sectors add further complications.

In the coming decade, the United States should concentrate on taking steps to strengthen its domestic economy. Nothing should have a higher priority than the development of an effective energy policy, control of inflation, and the transformation of obsolescent industries into high-technology industries, thus encouraging increases in labor productivity. Simultaneously, we should devise a set of international economic policies that encourage American enterprises to compete effectively in the international arena and create new international procedures and institutions to facilitate a healthy relationship among the advanced industrial nations and more effective North-South interaction.

It can be predicted, however, that given the complexities of the problems and of democratic policymaking, neither the United States nor Japan will be able to achieve these goals quickly or completely, even if political leaders are strongly committed and there are no serious policy errors. Consequently, U.S.-Japanese economic relations will be marked by friction during the 1980s, with recurrent crises of considerable magnitude. In both societies, nationalism is rising, and although it takes diverse forms, one of its most convenient expressions comes in the economic sphere. Protectionism will be an ever-present issue of the coming decade.

What additional measures can be taken? The recent decision to re-establish a consultative body on economic issues was wise. Care must be taken that this body is broadly representative, is well equipped with staff, and has full access to the policymakers of both nations. In sum, it should be more than a "discussion group." Its policy recommendations should receive serious attention, both from the publics and the governments of the two nations.

Second, it is essential to study and understand the policymaking processes of both societies and to effect such changes as may make them more compatible in the vital area of economic policy. In the past, the situation has been conducive to a gradual, undeterred buildup of tension, leading to a near explosion. Japanese processes have led to initial minimal concessions, followed by procrastination. This leads to increased pressure by the United States, including threats—but the threats are usually not carried out. There follows a temporary reduction of tension after somewhat greater Japanese concessions, but no fundamental change has taken place in the situation. One result of this process is the growing conviction among all governments negotiating with Japan that the Japanese will respond only to "toughness." For Japan, this is likely to become an ever more serious problem unless its negotiation tactics are changed.

American-Japanese relations should be complemented by a multilateral body concerned with the economic issues of the Pacific basin. This organization would not remove the necessity for close bilateral consultation, but it would serve to identify the truly international character of certain economic matters and in addition to dealing with them in the proper perspective, would reduce the sense of exclusiveness that adds to friction in U.S.-Japanese relations.

None of these measures, however, can be effective unless the fundamental changes in the domestic economies of both nations outlined earlier are consummated. Never has there been a closer correlation between domestic and foreign policies than in the field of U.S.-Japanese economic relations.

A second set of issues involving present and future U.S.-Japanese relations concerns security and, more broadly, the most basic questions of global and regional strategy. Since World War II, the security of Japan has been underwritten by the United States. After Vietnam and in the context of mounting economic pressures, various Americans have raised the question of "burden sharing." Should not Japan bear a greater share of the cost for its own security and possibly for that of other nations whose security is vital to Japan's interests?

This issue is made more complex because the official American position appears confused on occasion. There is no U.S. desire to see Japan become a nuclear power, and indeed, it is not clear that current U.S. policy favors an effort by Japan to amend its constitution and accept some responsibility for regional security. To date, the question of burden sharing has related essentially to American base expenses and the development of more adequate Japanese air, naval, and ground defense forces.

In any case, security issues will ultimately be determined by the Japanese themselves. Is Japan destined within the next decade to undertake rapid and extensive rearmament and to remove current barriers to the use of military power as one instrument of national policy, as some observers claim? Although several crucial variables could change the situation, the current answer is no.

A Japanese national defense force is now broadly acceptable to more than four-fifths of the Japanese people. A majority, moreover, while regarding the Mutual Security Treaty as "useful," do not believe that the United States would defend Japan in case of an attack, an illustration of declining American credibility in Asia. Meanwhile, antagonism to the Soviet Union has risen, although a sizable majority of Japanese presently regard the risk of attack from any quarter as low.

It is possible to conjecture that if the perception of external threat rose significantly and the credibility of the United States declined further, the stage would be set for the emergence of a Gaullist Japan committed to an independent, higher-posture foreign policy involving military power. Against this scenerio, however, must be placed a truly formidable array of factors. First, the Japanese sense of geopolitical and economic vulnerability remains high, and current world trends are more likely to increase such feelings. Second, the still recent heritage of a disastrous war combines with the resounding success of a minimal risk and maximal gain post-1945 foreign policy to discourage change, even in the face of shifting conditions. Any dramatic change, particularly one involving increased risk, would turn foreign policy into a liability, rather than an asset, for the government by intensifying Japanese political cleavages.

Thus, the strong likelihood is that Japan will add to its military strength incrementally and relatively modestly, eschewing nuclear weapons and retaining the strictures against security commitments abroad. Although it will seek to increase the political quotient in its foreign policy somewhat, it will retain a low military profile, defensive in nature.

Beyond this, the separation of economics and politics will continue to be a central objective of Japanese foreign policy in most instances, its increased interest in some heightened political role notwithstanding. Japan will seek economic intercourse wherever possible, cutting across ideological lines freely via a "multidimensional" foreign policy. At the same time, Japan will find equidistance in its relations with the major societies neither feasible nor desirable. Its goal will continue to be close ties with the United States, both for economic and security reasons, and a rough balance in its relations with the PRC and the USSR. Recent Soviet policies have made the latter objective impossible to achieve, but despite the tensions involved in Japanese-Soviet relations, Tokyo does not want to play a leading role in an anti-Russian alliance.

This foreign policy will not be fully satisfactory to most of those with whom Japan must interact. To the non-Communist states of Asia, it will be regarded as a policy lacking in political or ethical discrimination, oriented solely toward Japan's economic concerns—a pure market policy. Both China and Russia will continue to exert various pressures on Japan in an effort to influence its future course, China in the direction of an anti-Russian united front, the USSR on behalf of an acceptance of the territorial status quo and involvement in Siberian development on Soviet terms. The United States will have periodic qualms regarding the relatively low level of international responsibility accepted by Japan and the intense competition offered in the international marketplace.

In sum, the future course of U.S.-Japanese relations will involve cooperation and competition, harmony and conflict, satisfaction and frustration—and in more equal portions than in the past. The old patron-client relationship that came so naturally to both parties for several decades can no longer be sustained, although some aspects of it linger on. Yet a new partnership remains more rhetoric than reality, although considerable potential exists if the full measure of attention and ingenuity is directed toward the relationship. It is a relation, however, that will require far more sustained and careful tending than has been given it in recent years.

AMERICAN-KOREAN RELATIONS

The Korean peninsula continues to be one of the more volatile areas of the Pacific-Asian region. Amid conditions of total hostility and minimal communication, South and North Korea have more than one million professional soldiers, augmented by much larger people's militia. Although political stability appears reasonably established in each society at present, a potentially critical succession issue is probable in both south and north within the next decade.

South Korea is a quasi-authoritarian society, with civil liberties restricted and with one-man primacy under President Pak Chong-hi, now 61 years of age. Despite the restrictions carried in the Yushin Constitution, the Republic of Korea (ROK) continues to acknowledge the legitimacy of a political opposition, and such opposition exists, challenging the government party in elections and posing alternative policies—all within legally prescribed limits. The ROK also accepts a pluralistic social order. Commerce, industry, agriculture, education, and religion are possible sources of privatism and separatism. In contrast, North Korea remains a throwback to Stalinism, with as tight a dictatorship and as monolithic a state as exists in the current world. Kim Il-song, now 67, is the last survivor of the first-generation Communist leaders for whom ideology, stern discipline, and full mobilization have assumed consistently high priorities. The Democratic People's Republic of Korea (DPRK) subordinates every individual and group to the party, and although factionalism and jurisdictional struggles cannot be avoided, the omnipresence of party and leader remains the hallmark of the system. The evolutionary potentials of this type of polity would seem much less promising than those of the south, although Kim's passing will open the door to some changes.

The economic differences between south and north are even more striking. With the Japanese model as a guide, the ROK has scored remarkable growth rates in recent years, providing a sizable majority of its people with a comfortable livelihood and raising even the poorest segment to above subsistence level. In contrast, per capita income in North Korea is now substantially lower than that of South Korea. Moreover, the heavy military expenditures of the north and the obsolescence of much of its industrial plant have caused serious economic problems. The DPRK was the first Communist state to default involuntarily on its international debts, and although more technocratically oriented individuals have recently been given greater authority in Pyongyang, the problems are still unresolved. Meanwhile, a south-north dialogue, terminated earlier at northern initiative, was resumed in early 1979 on a precarious off-and-on basis.

What lies ahead? Recurrent political instability over the next decade cannot be ruled out, for either south or north. No viable coalition of forces capable of ousting Pak Chong-hi currently exists, and if economic growth can be sustained, his government seems reasonably secure. But like any system heavily dependent upon one man, uncertainties concerning a post-Pak era abound. Meanwhile, the future of the South Korean economy hinges on controlling inflation and simultaneously responding to labor unrest (a by-product of inflation) and to the more backward rural areas.

The political and economic problems of the north appear more formidable, but here, discipline and control are of much greater magnitude. Although railing against the south for its "country-selling" economic and political policies, the north has given indications of a desire to turn outward economically, importing science and technology, and to move away from the isolationist policies of the past. However, as long as it spends an extraordinarily high percentage of its budget on the military, and relies upon political exhortation first and economic incentives second, the livelihood of its people will be meager.

After Kim Il-song, it appears likely that the military will play a crucial role whoever assumes nominal authority since the ultimate source of power lies here. Within the Korean Workers party a generational struggle may already be under way, with Kim the final arbiter at every turn.

No peaceful reunification of Korea is conceivable now or in the forseeable future. To amalgamate two such different economic, social, and political systems through voluntary agreement and elections is impossible, and those who insist that this is feasible are either naive or involved in an effort at political manipulation. The broad alternatives are relatively few: the gradual development of a network of communications and intercourse, with an agreement upon peaceful coexistence, similar to the experience of the two Germanys; the continuance of minimal contacts and hostility short of war; or the re-emergence of conflict.

Despite the dangers, the latter alternative seems unlikely. Given the two Communist giants to the north, the extensive defensive and offensive preparations of the DPRK, the adamant opposition of the United States, and its own recent economic gains, an ROK thrust northward is a remote possibility. A DPRK thrust southward is more conceivable, but once again, the partly re-established credibility of the U.S.-ROK security ties and the opposition of both China and Russia to a renewal of war on the Korean peninsula make such a gamble a remote possibility under present or foreseeable circumstances.

Continued hostility short of war is a short-term certainty and a longer-term possibility. As long as Kim lives, the DPRK foreign policies of the last 30 years seem frozen, and ancient, unrealistic formulas are put foward repeatedly. In foreign policy, in contrast to certain domestic policies, the Pak government has been remarkably enlightened. The ROK has offered to accept dual south-north recognition both in the United Nations and from states willing to engage in normal diplomatic relations, irrespective of their political-ideological status. It has also proposed a step-by-step entry into south-north relations, commencing with humanitarian measures and progressing to economic relations and then to political matters. The Kim government, on the other hand, denounces cross-recognition as a "plot to create two Koreas" (despite the obvious fact that two Koreas exist, that cross-recognition constitutes no barrier to ultimate reunification should that ever prove feasible, and that North Korea itself earnestly solicits recognition from the United States and Japan).

One can only hope that at some point, North Korea will find global and regional trends so adverse to its rigid position that it will accept accommodation to a realistic formula based essentially upon the German model. In a post-Kim era, this may be possible.

Meanwhile, what are the likely developments in the major power relations of the two Koreas? In recent years, both Koreas have had problems with their key foreign relations. American-ROK ties have been seriously frayed by the American abandonment of South Vietnam, the subsequent retrenchment from political openness in South Korea, the unilateral action of the United States in announcing ground troop withdrawals from Korea, and the so-called Koreagate scandals. Relations with Japan, while less volatile, have been troubled by a heritage of colonialism and ethnic prejudices on both sides, the rapid Japanese penetration of the Korean economy—resented even though its value was acknowledged—and the Korean suspicion—not without foundation—that Japan would like to establish ties with the north roughly equal to those it has with the south.

Currently, U.S.-ROK relations are improving. American credibility has been partially restored, although Korean doubts about it persist, as a result of a reconsideration of troop withdrawal. Recently, the Pak administration has undertaken some liberalization, releasing a number of political prisoners. The scandals have receded amid indications that Korea was scarcely alone in payoffs, with American corporations deeply involved in similar activities in Japan and elsewhere. ROK relations with Japan remain relatively stable. Economic and political issues have been contained, if not resolved. Despite various overtures, however, firm contacts with Russia and China have not developed. The Russians have shown some interest in an ultimate "two Koreas" formula, but they shrink from overt actions beyond the admission of South Koreans into the USSR. China continues its firm commitments to the DPRK, asserting its full support for Kim Il-song's proposals.

North Korea has had problems with the USSR for more than twenty years, and in recent times, USSR-DPRK relations have ranged from cool to near-hostile. The Russians neither like nor trust Kim Il-song, and they correctly perceive that he has long tilted conspicuously toward Peking. But will Peking continue to give full support to Pyongyang, and can that support be translated into meaningful economic, political, and security terms? The DPRK, despite its reservations toward the Soviet Union, remains dependent on it for essential military and industrial equipment. Meanwhile, its efforts to detach the United States and Japan from the ROK have not succeeded, nor have its overall foreign policies attracted significant international support.

In sum, future political changes are inevitable given the relatively high dependency of both political systems upon a single personality; but major shifts from the prevailing political systems are unlikely. Neither Korea is apt to establish and maintain a pure Western-style liberal democracy, although this is clearly more conceivable for the south than the north. Moves in this direction, however, are apt to be contained by many factors: the geopolitical position of the ROK, the probability of continuing ROK-DPRK tension, the political culture of Korean society and the priorities currently accorded economic development, the decline in American influence, and the prevailing trends against Western-style parliamentarism in Asia. The political differences between south and north, however, are and will continue to be important. The north, in all probability, will remain a rigid authoritarian state permitting little or no privatism or legitimate pluralism even after the demise of Kim Il-song. Its comparative disadvantage in size to the south, its contiguity to China and Russia, its culture and recent heritage—all make any significant liberalization improbable, at least during the next decade.

For both Koreas, however, further economic development seems probable. Economic growth in the ROK will and should slow, but the conditions for continued advance are generally good. South Korea is no longer a backward Third World state. It is a middle-sized industrial power of regional and even global significance. The gap between south and north will continue to grow, but the DPRK can remedy its recent economic malaise if some accommodation to the ROK is achieved, promoting a reduction in military expenditures and allowing an accommodation to the advanced industrial world that will enable technology to flow into the country.

Although the path to south-north accommodation is bound to be thorny, there are reasonably good prospects of avoiding another conflict. Much hinges, however, upon the attitudes and actions of the major powers, notwithstanding the primary responsibilities of Seoul and Pyongyang.

Against this background, what is the proper course of action for the United States? First, our continuing security commitment to South Korea is a crucial deterrent to renewed conflict and must be maintained. Further reduction of the American military presence, moreover, should be contingent upon progress in north-south relations and some concrete indication of a DPRK willingness to eschew force.

We should continue to give the Korean issue high priority in our discussions with the Chinese and Russians, and it should serve as one important test of their will to work for peace in the Pacific-Asian region. This issue also demands close consultation with Japan to ensure the maintenance of a common policy, given the importance of the problem to both Japan and the United States.

We should fully support a peaceful settlement of the Korean issue, the interim acceptance of cross-recognition, and the encouragement of step-by-step relations between the two Koreas. We should not weaken the prospects for such developments and further damage our credibility by accepting DPRK demands for bilateral negotiations without South Korea. At the same time, we should continue to make it clear that we are prepared to accept trilateral discussions with North *and* South Korea and would welcome reciprocal recognition of the existing Korean governments by all major states. Finally, we should foster even closer economic, cultural, and political relations with South Korea, lending our continued encouragement to its progress and liberalization without attempting to impose the American system on such a considerably different society.

U.S.-PRC RELATIONS AND THE TAIWAN ISSUE

The establishment of full diplomatic relations with the People's Republic of China and the derecognition of the Republic of China on Taiwan, while underlining a major shift in American policy, have not liquidated a complex problem. There can be no doubt that the United States made the major concessions in the Shanghai Communiqué of 1972 and the December 15 Agreement of 1978 that produced "normalization." Peking obtained American recognition without agreeing to two important principles: the nonuse of force to resolve the Taiwan issue and the right of the United States to furnish defensive arms to Taiwan pending a peaceful settlement of the issue.

In retrospect, it seems clear that the Carter administration was prepared to pay a high price for normalization because the president wanted to settle the issue well before the 1980 elections and to consummate normalization together with a SALT II agreement and an Israeli-Egyptian peace settlement, thus bolstering support for all three actions in Congress and with the American people. Perfect timing proved impossible, and only normalization was delivered on schedule—under conditions of considerable controversy. Armed with American recognition, the PRC proceeded with its plans to punish Vietnam, knowing that the United States, however embarrassed by the southward thrust, would not rescind its action.

The controversy over Taiwan promises to continue, both as a U.S. domestic issue and as a problem between the United States and the PRC, but most Americans have long accepted the establishment of formal relations between the United States and the PRC as desirable, setting aside the question of terms. And at present, the Taiwan issue is not high on the PRC agenda, although some actions have been initiated that will be noted later.

Turning to the broader aspects of U.S.-PRC relations, once again an informed discussion must take PRC domestic trends into account. Yet no task is more hazardous than that of assaying the economic and political future of China. Past judgments by American officials and scholars alike have generally been wrong, often dramatically wrong. Overoptimism regarding China is a disease to which Americans are especially prone (there is no known cure), although Vietnam and the newest evidence regarding Chinese economic planning have had a sobering effect in some quarters.

As for the economic picture, it is now clear that the modernization of China and its one billion people will be a prodigious task even if political stability is maintained, protracted international conflict is avoided, and no further serious errors in economic policy are committed. None of these contingencies can be guaranteed. China possesses some assets, however, that should be catalogued. First, the PRC possesses a truly resourceful people, who have long valued education, had experience in intricate organization, and harbored a work ethic as an integral part of their culture. Each of these legacies has been damaged but not eradicated by the policies of the recent past. Moreover, China now possesses a degree of political control lacking at earlier periods of its modern history, and leaders thus have the capacity to implement policies more effectively. Finally, the present goals are strongly directed toward economic modernization, and there is a seeming willingness to bend if not break ideological barriers and a new commitment to pragmatic, experimental policies that in effect put economics in command.

On the negative side, the problem of scale looms large. Major portions of the society, moreover, remain at marginal subsistence levels, indicating the enormity of the task ahead. The "second generation" problem is also acute. Whether in economic development, political leadership, or culture, the PRC is currently paying a heavy price for the follies of the last two decades, particularly for the so-called Cultural Revolution and its aftermath. Precious years were lost. Thus, industrial managers, like political managers, are generally older military men, and the skills necessary to fuel a scientific-technological revolution are woefully lacking. This gap cannot be made up quickly or easily, whatever the emergency measures employed.

As a manifestation of the heavy hand of the past, a basic paradox runs through the current scene. On the one hand, the commitments are clearly to rapid economic modernization, although a host of concrete issues such as specific priorities, centralization or decentralization, and the extent of economic incentives remain in some dispute. In these respects, Mao—or Maoism—has been turned on its head. But on the other hand, in implementing these policies, Maoism appears to be still in vogue. Extremely ambitious targets are proclaimed, and orders are issued to storm these objectives in the style of a military campaign. The careful coordination and intricate planning necessary to achieve such goals—or even to establish them realistically—are largely lacking.

Presumably these defects can be corrected, although it remains to be seen whether the system of near-complete statism will serve to mobilize and commit the energies and abilities of the Chinese people effectively. Except for removing the systemic restraints, the easier, preliminary tasks involved in modernization have generally been accomplished. The tasks lying ahead will require ever more capital and skill. To some extent, the capital and technology of the advanced world can and will be tapped, but massive infusions of such capital and technology may not be feasible given China's economic weakness. Even if significant infusions take place, their absorption into and impact upon the PRC remain fascinating yet uncertain aspects of the future.

Thus, caution in predicting PRC economic growth appears wise. China will remain a poor country well beyond the end of this century, a nation whose masses, by their sheer numbers, cannot hope to reach the living standards of their smaller neighbors. Growth will probably be significant, although it will not reach the targets established in the ten-year plan scheduled for conclusion in 1985. If agricultural gains average 3 percent and industrial increases average 7–8 percent over the next decade, a combination of stability, effective planning, and good luck (including a reasonable amount of good weather) will be necessary.

Political stability is one of the key variables. What are its prospects? As noted earlier, the problem of the second generation impinges upon Chinese politics at least as much as upon Chinese economics. At the top, China is governed by old men, and no clear succession has been established despite the present titular leadership of Hua Kuo-feng. The death of Teng Hsiao-ping, for example, would create a serious problem since no one, including Hua, is in a position to play his role. Thus, the probabilities are high that in the course of the next decade, recurrent instability will occur in China, with various political changes in the top leadership, some through power struggles. Under such circumstances, the unity of the military is supremely important. Compared with 1969, the political role of the military has been considerably reduced within the party and bureaucracy. However, the professional military are still vastly more involved in politics and play more direct roles in top party and administrative posts than is the case in the USSR. In the event of crisis, moreover, those who control the gun are likely to win, be they civilian or military.

To predict instability is not to predict chaos. The nationalist indoctrination of many decades, the substantial improvements in transport and communications, and the recognition by current leaders of the price to be paid for further disunity all suggest that strenuous efforts will be made to contain differences. The capacity of the police and military to control upheaval, moreover, is infinitely stronger than in the pre-1949 era. These and other factors suggest that periodic instability, even if it is sufficiently serious to harm production, will not produce collapse. A more serious threat is that the movement from belief to cynicism, from élan to boredom, from commitment to lackadaisicalness cannot be reversed among the great masses of the Chinese people.

In foreign policy, Chinese concerns naturally center upon the Soviet Union, and most other aspects of PRC policy are influenced by this fact. In this regard, there has been a relatively slight shift from the Mao to the post-Mao era. With minor revisions, the Chinese leaders continue to divide the world into three parts: the superpowers, the other advanced industrial nations, and the Third World. As a declining power, the United States represents a decreasing threat. Indeed, China promotes a united front strategy remarkably similar to the one pursued by Mao within China after 1936 and seeks American participation in the broadest possible front against Russia. Thus, the PRC attitude toward American power is ambivalent. On the one hand, their policy posits a dependency upon the United States as a countervailing force to the Soviet Union globally. On the other hand, PRC leaders do not want American power to pose obstacles to China's policies for Asia—and despite ardent denials of any desire for hegemony, China does intend to be *the* major power in Asia, with classic security, political, and economic interests prompting a "sphere of influence" approach. The Vietnam conflict of early 1979 illustrated this fact graphically, demonstrating that China is prepared to use military power beyond its borders to further its perceived national interests, and top Chinese spokesmen have made it clear that they intend to continue to oppose Vietnamese hegemony over Indochina.

Meanwhile, the Chinese will continue to employ three instruments—state-to-state, people-to-people, and comrade-to-comrade relations—in advancing their policies, varying these according to specific conditions and opportunities. As China has emerged into the main diplomatic stream, the trend has been toward greater concentration upon state-to-state relations, but Chinese leaders have made it clear that they will not abandon Communist comrades. In such areas as Southeast Asia, the presence of these ties constitutes additional leverage on the governments of the area.

Despite the current bitterness, is a Sino-Soviet rapprochement conceivable? In the broadest terms, four alternatives are possible: full-fledged conflict; continued hostility short of war, but with periodic crises including military incidents; limited détente involving a reduction of tension; and restoration of close ties. Neither an alliance of the 1950 type nor all-out war seems likely. A logical case can be made for the reduction of tension: the type of tactical détente that would decrease costs and allow greater flexibility for both governments. One cannot rule out such a development in the future. Indeed, the first exploratory conversations aimed at normalizing state-to-state relations have gotten under way. For the near term, however, it will be difficult to dissipate the hostility and suspicion between these two highly nationalistic, power-oriented states.

Given these probable trends, what are the alternatives for the United States? As noted earlier, there are advocates of an anti-Soviet united front in the United States, and although the Carter administration has proclaimed evenhandedness in dealing with China and Russia as official policy, not all words or actions have measured up to this phrase.

The common interests of the United States and China presently center on the desire to prevent Russian expansion. This is a legitimate objective, but it would not be in American interests to march against the Soviet Union in order to strengthen China's security, seemingly the foremost desire of current Chinese leaders. The task of the United States is to maintain American credibility globally and to uphold American economic, political, and military strength so that we can negotiate effectively with all parties, with an emphasis on reciprocity and accountability. But these policies must not be confused with policies that in effect would dictate a return to the cold-war atmosphere of an earlier era when U.S.-USSR dialogue was minimal and confrontation was the order of the day. The Soviet Union is a global power, and few major issues can be resolved without its participation or at least its acquiescence. The desire of the PRC to play the role of the proverbial monkey who sits on the mountain and watches two tigers fight is understandable, but it cannot be acceptable to the U.S. government or people.

A de facto alliance with the PRC against the USSR is thus not in the American interest. And although China's interest in modernizing its armed forces is both natural and, within limits, legitimate, the United States should not participate in this effort, both because such participation would produce a swift deterioration in U.S.-Soviet relations, with global consequences, and because it is not clear how a modern Chinese military force will be used. The likely target would not be the Soviet Union, since the United States could not help China achieve military parity with Russia in this century. Even in defensive terms, military modernization would probably be of marginal utility compared with the more historic defense potential involved in a people's war. A venture similar to that recently conducted against Vietnam would be more likely—with consequences not necessarily compatible with American interests.

China's quest for economic development is more susceptible to American support. There is no reason to deny most-favored-nation treatment to Peking, providing similar treatment is accorded Moscow. Once again, our guiding strategy should be that of equilibrium. Our economic relations with China, however, are likely to be of far less significance than some Americans have anticipated, for reasons signaled earlier. China's scarcity of foreign reserves and the natural advantages of Japan and other nations in the China market will largely confine U.S. opportunites to high-technology products and food. While not negligible, U.S.-PRC trade will not equal trade with Taiwan for some time.

Meanwhile, as suggested earlier, Taiwan will continue to be an issue between us. PRC leaders will insist that we have recognized Taiwan as a part of *their* China and that military assistance to Taipei therefore constitutes interference in the internal affairs of a sovereign state. We should stand firm on this matter. Having given away a goodly portion of American credibility in Asia in the recent past, we cannot afford to capitulate further on this issue, with its moral and strategic implications. The United States must uphold two principles frequently enunciated in the past: the Taiwan issue must be settled peacefully, and until such a settlement is achieved, we shall furnish those weapons necessary for the defense of Taiwan. In effecting these policies, various problems may be encountered. Economic and political developments within Taiwan are uncertain, in no small measure because of our diplomatic abandonment of the ROK. Current trends are mixed, and it is too early to make any solid assessments.

We cannot and should not commit ourselves to involvement in the internal politics of Taiwan, but our resolution to stand by a peaceful international settlement is crucial both to our credibility and to the peace and security of the region.

The issue of Korea is of equal importance, and we should take every opportunity to raise this issue in bilateral discussions with the PRC, indicating our desire for cooperation in achieving a peaceful, realistic approach to the problems of the Korean peninsula. Indeed, Korea will be one test of the nature of U.S.-PRC relations. Similarly, consultation should be maintained on other political and strategic issues relating to the Pacific-Asian region, including the thorny problems of Southeast and South Asia. The Vietnam incursion indicates that American influence on Chinese foreign policy is likely to be rather slight, but on some matters, such as acceptance of the Association of Southeast Asian

Nations (ASEAN) and a desire for a strategic balance in southern Asia, a commonality of interests is developing.

Ultimately, it may be possible to bring the PRC into arms control discussions and to interest China in the nuclear proliferation question. In these respects, the past has not been too promising, but there are faint signs that Chinese attitudes are changing. A prelude, however, to the success of future American-Chinese relations is an end to American romanticism about China. The PRC does not intend to carry out *American* policies in Asia; rather it will seek to carry out *its* policies, in some cases, over American objections. This point must be made because of excessive naiveté that has surrounded attitudes toward China, not least of all, regrettably, in the American academic community. American-Chinese relations can serve the purpose of assisting the stabilization of the Pacific-Asian region if they are approached in a realistic fashion, with full cognizance of our differences as well as our common interests and with policies of cordiality combined with firmness on principles to which we are committed.

SOUTHEAST ASIA AND AMERICAN POLICIES

Southeast Asia with its extensive resources, strategic location athwart the passages between southern and eastern Asia, and a population approaching 350 million looms ever larger in the political and economic future of the Pacific-Asian region. This fact has not escaped the attention of the major powers. Despite various setbacks, each maintains a presence, in some cases, a growing presence. Japan's economic involvement throughout the area continues to expand. The United States has just renewed its agreement on bases with the Philippines, and it too has extensive economic interests here. Russian involvement in Indochina continues to rise, together with its interest in improving relations with the ASEAN nations. The PRC has long regarded Southeast Asia as its legitimate sphere of influence and acted accordingly. Its current commitment to prevent the emergence of a Vietnamese empire to its south is coupled with efforts to improve state-to-state relations with most of the non-Communist governments of the area while not abandoning its ties to various Communist guerrilla movements.

The presence of the major powers and the element of hostility that exists among them, especially between China and the Soviet Union, pose additional complexities (and certain advantages) to the indigenous states of Southeast Asia. Some leaders like Lee Kuan Yew have expressed the view that "since we cannot force them all out, it is better to have them all in." Yet the shadow of conflict hangs heavily over the area, as recent developments in Indochina have made strikingly clear. Moreover, it is the type of conflict that threatens to involve the large states, with the danger of expanding a regional struggle into a global one.

Turning first to domestic developments within the Southeast Asian states, one must note the deep cleavage that runs between the northern-tier Communist states of Indochina and the ASEAN states to the south. Not only do domestic trends differ dramatically between these two groups, but continuing efforts to establish a more positive relationship between them have so far yielded meager results. Thus, there are two Southeast Asias at present, or, if one includes isolationist, xenophobic Burma, possibly three.

Current trends within Vietnam, Laos, and Cambodia basically stem from the American abandonment of South Vietnam. At the close of the Vietnam war in 1975, Hanoi could claim not only victory over Saigon, but dominance of Laos. Within Vietnam itself, recent political and economic conditions can be described only as grim. Contrary to the assertions of many outside observers, the Vietnamese Communist leaders showed no interest in a coalition government that would seek reconciliation by including prominent non-Communists. On the contrary, all important non-Communist figures have disappeared—into prison, reeducation camps, or house confinement. From them emanates only a great silence, and many are dead. Hanoi did not even accord the southern Communists a major role in their own governance. Northern dominance of a sullen south has been rigorously maintained, and economic conditions have deteriorated everywhere. Such developments have induced tens of thousands of individuals to undertake the risks of flight, becoming "boat people" and either dying at sea or creating a refugee problem with international repercussions.

These trends, especially in the economic realm, need not be permanent. The capacity of Vietnam to improve its agricultural production radically and to develop a substantial industrial component is sizable, although the losses of managerial, educated, and skilled-labor components of the population have been serious. The richness of the land, the innate capacities of the people, and the potential availability of foreign assistance could be harnessed in a major developmental program in the 1980s.

This, however, will require both a change of leadership and a change of policies. The old, first-generation revolutionaries who dominate the Vietnamese political structure are habituated to Spartanism and war.

Their priorities remain strongly political; internal control through the Vietnam Workers' party; external control through an Indochina federation. Younger leaders will gradually emerge within the next few years, possibly with a different orientation, at least on economic issues. The grimness of Vietnamese life, however, is unlikely to be alleviated in the near term, especially if the tension with China continues, as is probable.

In Laos, Hanoi's hand is omnipresent. Between 250,000 and 300,000 Laotians, ranging from the Meo hill people to many of the former elite, including a sizable number of educated youth, have fled the country. For those remaining, life is generally harsh, but lightened somewhat by the Laotian life-style.

Nearby, Cambodia has presented a pageantry of brutality unparalleled in modern Asia. Deaths at the hands of the Khmer Rouge cannot be calculated accurately, but they appear to have totaled hundreds of thousands, possibly millions. Shortly after the Communists acquired power, moreover, an internecine struggle broke out, and the Chinese-backed forces of Pol Pot and Ieng Sary managing to purge those with strong Vietnamese ties. The stage was set for Vietnamese retaliation, and Hanoi's strike proved highly effective despite Chinese support for the Phnom Penh government. As of mid-1979, a Vietnamese-backed government sits in the capital, and the Pol Pot forces are reduced to guerrilla operations. But Peking will not reconcile itself to Vietnamese hegemony over Indochina without a protracted struggle. Indications are that political instability and recurrent conflict will mark the future as they have the past.

For Thailand, the central issue is whether the Indochina conflict will spill over, providing an added menace to already complicated internal political problems. In recent years the Thai monarchy has perceptibly weakened as a stabilizing force; student-intellectual dissidence has risen; and ethnic, regional, and religious divisions have shown scant indications of closing. Thailand, moreover, shares a long common border with Laos and Cambodia. Thus, when it became apparent that the United States was withdrawing from the area, the Thais turned in classic fashion to another large nation, on this occasion, China, to protect them against a perceived Vietnamese threat. But, like the Vietnamese, the Chinese also have extended ties with the Thai Communist movement, which they do not intend to break. Could another Cambodia lie down the road?

The key problem of neighboring Malaysia is the deep Malay-Chinese ethnic cleavage running through every aspect of the society. Unfortunately, while ethnic animosities have generally been contained, little if any progress has been made in alleviating the basic causes of racial tension. Thus, Islamic extremism and a Sino-Malaysian-dominated communism stand ready in the political wings. Although neither appears close to power, especially the latter, both have the capacity to keep the political waters continuously troubled.

Neither Indonesia nor the Philippines is free from similar problems. In the near term, Indonesia seems likely to retain political stability, primarily because both the Islamic extremists and the Communists suffered devastating blows in the 1960s from which they have not recovered. Corruption and economic difficulties, however, have kindled student-intellectual unrest, and discontent has also been manifested in the military at points in the past. In addition, extensive Javanese control over this vast, disparate country has evoked opposition from the "outer islanders," although this may be lessening. Nevertheless, the process of making a unified nation out of Indonesia remains a truly formidable challenge.

In the Philippines, two revolts continue after years of martial law. Each betokens the still unresolved problems of the society. A so-called New People's Army fights to turn the Philippines into a Communist state, counting on a coalition of student-intellectual dissidents and poor farmers to swell its ranks. A more threatening Islamic revolt keeps much of Mindanao and the Sulu archipelago in turmoil. Both rebel groups have had external assistance at times, reflecting the close ties between civil conflict and international alignments throughout this region. Predictions regarding the future of Philippine politics are hazardous, not merely because of these revolts, but because the Philippine strong man appears to be building no institutional legacy. In the event of the demise of President Ferdinand Marcos, what would occur? A return to full-fledged parliamentary democracy seems unlikely under present conditions. Military rule, at least for an interim period, would seem more probable, but a stable, enduring political structure for this nation of nearly 50 million people remains to be constructed.

Of all the non-Communist states of Southeast Asia, Burma has the most authoritarian political rule at present, one modeled rather closely after the Communist one-party system. Burma, moreover, defies the thesis that military leaders are prone to policies of modernization. No nation of the area has exhibited greater indifference to economic development or displayed such administrative inefficiency. The interests of Burma's numerous ethnic minorities have also been slighted. As a result, conflict has been endemic, and although the Burmese government appears to hold the upper hand at present, the White Flag Communists (with assistance from the neighboring Chinese) have represented a major problem at times in the past, as have separatist groups like the

Karen. And once again, the departure of strong man Ne Win from the political scene will mark Burma's entrance into an uncertain era.

As indicated earlier, some advances with respect to political stability in the Southeast Asian area should be acknowledged. The commitment to economic development is widespread among the newer generation of leaders, and this in turn has resulted in economic gains ranging from satisfactory to extremely good in the ASEAN states in recent years. Gradually, moreover, oncoming generations of citizens are being socialized and are accepting national symbols. Improvements in transport and communications have enhanced the power of the central government and encouraged a sense of national community. With the retreat from the Western parliamentary model has also come the quest for a political structure that will unite traditional cultures with the requirements of the present. In this sense, the thrust has been away from utopianism, toward realism.

Whatever the balance sheet of political trends and probabilities for each state, it is obvious that this area needs a combination of political stability and enlightenment if the economic goals of the 1980s are to be achieved. Most Southeast Asian states aim at growth rates of 7–9 percent per annum over the next decade. These are not unrealistic goals for a number of these states, if adverse political factors do not intervene. Unfortunately, one must predict that such factors will intervene in some cases. Therefore, economic growth and political stability will vary substantially within Southeast Asia over the next decade as a result of the differing impact of four critical and interrelated variables: indigenous human and natural resources; the stage of development already achieved; the geopolitical position of the society and the influence of internal and external forces upon political cohesion and continuity; and the nature of each government's economic and social policies.

Because of the likelihood of uneven development, the progress of a regional organization like ASEAN will be fraught with difficulties. The danger that internal developments in one of the member states will retard or disrupt regional cooperation always exists. ASEAN in some form should survive, however, because closer regional interaction is so eminently logical. Gradually, it will acquire a role beyond a communications network among leaders and extend its economic activities past their present embryonic stage.

In this context, what are the proper policies for the United States? First, it is incumbent upon the United States to make a distinction between those states with which we have considerable common interests and those with which we choose to interact for tactical reasons. Recently, it has appeared to many ASEAN leaders that Washington has altered its priorities and is intrigued with catering to Communist nationalism to exploit intra-Communist divisions, meanwhile allowing traditional relations to deteriorate. This grievance has been exacerbated because to the same leaders it appears that Washington is using the human rights issue as a club to batter them even as it explores closer political and economic ties with the Asian Communist states, being careful in the course of this exploration not to offend Communist sensitivities by dwelling upon human rights. Accompanying and underlining these complaints has been the charge that the United States has become unpredictable and hence that American credibility, especially in matters relating to security, is no longer to be trusted. It is no secret that these views are held in varying degree by all ASEAN states, especially Indonesia, Singapore, and the Philippines.

If the United States is to change its image within the ASEAN community, certain new policies are essential. First, with the ASEAN states as with Japan, the processes of discussion and consultation should be forwarded, not as a means of creating agreement on all matters, but as a means of re-establishing confidence and an indication of desired cooperation.

Second, the United States should establish and maintain a clear distinction between its concern for and commitment to those pluralist societies with mixed economies and some degree of political openness and those societies committed to a one-party dictatorship and a wholly statist economy. Relations with the latter should be conducted with the knowledge that their interest in the United States is largely tactical in nature, with no desire for true reciprocity. Under certain conditions, an American impact is possible, but the range of common interests will continue to be limited. Many of the former states (pluralist societies) will be quasi-authoritarian in nature, but within them the evolutionary potentialities and the opportunities for genuine communication with the United States on a wide front will be much greater. To ignore these facts is to be morally irresponsible, politically naive, and strategically foolish.

Third, while recognizing its limitations, the United States should encourage ASEAN and other regional and bilateral ties within the area that forward the cause of peaceful coexistence and economic advances. At some point soon, moreover, we should take the lead in constructing a Pacific basin community the primary concern of which would be the mutual economic interests of the states of the Pacific region. The time is now ripe for the emergence of such a body, more modest in its initial goals than the European Economic Community but accepting that future economic development and political harmony in the Pacific-Asian region are tied to multilateral cooperation and that such cooperation requires an institutional base.

Finally, within the context of the Guam Declaration and our existing bilateral agreements, we should do whatever is necessary to re-establish our strategic interests in this area. A sense that we will uphold our commitments, maintain a strategic presence, and provide for the legitimate security needs of friendly and aligned states is vitally important to the political and strategic balance in Southeast Asia in the difficult years ahead. To take and hold these positions, moreover, does not mean that we will or should become involved directly in conflict. On the contrary, our purposes should center on being among the existing deterrents that prevent large-scale conflict, especially conflict directly involving the major states. To these ends, the United States, directly or indirectly, must be a party in the protracted multiple negotiations relating to war and peace issues that lie ahead for Southeast Asia. This does not necessarily require—or even make desirable—our direct participation in all such negotiations; but American desires, commitments, and presence should be elements known and properly evaluated by those who sit at the negotiating table. Only if American policies and actions are conducive to these ends can we make a contribution to peaceful coexistence in Southeast Asia that accords with our interests and the interests of those aligned with us.

SOUTH ASIA AND THE UNITED STATES

The South Asian subcontinent represents socioeconomic and political challenges equal to those of any region of the world. More than 800 million people are engaged here in the struggle for deliverance from backwardness. It is all the more remarkable that three of Asia's parliamentary democracies, India, Sri Lanka, and Bangladesh, exist in this area. In many respects, India is the touchstone of South Asia, given its land area, population, and strategic location. After a lengthy, acrimonious struggle with Pakistan, India emerged in the 1970s as the unchallenged leader of the subcontinent. This will not change in the 1980s or beyond unless internal disintegration occurs.

What are the future prospects of this dynamic, volatile, heterogeneous society? Some projections can be advanced with confidence, others only with great trepidation. Once again, in 1979, India was confronted by major political problems, many of which appeared long-term in nature. Morarji Desai's tenure as prime minister came to a stormy end in mid-1979, and in the process the Janata party, which he headed, underwent splits as had the Congress party before it. A new, even more heterogeneous coalition was formed by Charan Singh, another veteran ex-Congress politician who succeeded Desai, but Singh resigned after a mere two months in office. Some observers expect Mrs. Gandhi's Congress faction to make significant gains, but it is doubtful if any political group will obtain a working majority in its own right.

At present, India has no truly national party. Nor does it have any widely acknowledged national leadership. Politics at the center is characterized by struggles for power among rival factions, fitted into loosely knit coalitions by the aged men (and one aging woman) who continue to play the dominant roles on the national stage. The process seems largely devoid of substantive issues and essentially detached from the concerns of the average Indian. Hence, disillusionment with the parliamentary process is growing, and of equal significance, various interest groups (including some sectors of the civil service) are challenging the government over economic or social issues, creating additional instability.

The prospects for recreating a national party or parties seem slight, at least through the electoral process. Indeed, India has had only one national party in its brief history as an independent modern state, namely, the Congress, and while that party as the inheritor of the nationalist revolution, was able to preserve a dominant party system until Mrs. Gandhi's defeat, certain sections of this vast and diverse society were beyond even its reach. To reconstruct the Congress party in its old form would seem virtually impossible, whatever the future political fortunes of Mrs. Gandhi. Nor are the other parties constituting the Janata group likely candidates for truly national status. Each caters to a sectional or regional interest of some type. Finally, while the left, as represented by the major Communist parties and certain smaller elements, shows an indication of closer cooperation with each other, these parties, taken singly or together, have a regional, not a national power base, and that will not change in the foreseeable future.

As long as leadership is determined by elections and political competition, therefore, coalition politics is likely to prevail, and many feel that the prospects under such conditions are for a weak center and stronger, albeit highly diverse states. The difficulties of creating national parties under present circumstances stem largely from the deeply communal nature of Indian society. Communalism, moreover, rather than receding, appears to be advancing at this point. Ethnic, caste, class, and linguistic divisions show no sign of yielding to what might be defined as a "national interest." In its broadest sense, this continuing communalism is exemplified by the north-south cleavage, with the dominant Hindi north represented most forcefully today by the Jana Sangh, while the non-Aryan peoples of the south rally around some Congress faction, the Communists, or a regional party like the Anna Dravida Munnetra Kazhagam of the state of Tamil Nadu and its capital, Madras.

Personality remains of critical importance to Indian politics at every level, and thus, one must seek to look beyond Desai, Singh, and Jagjivan Ram—or even Y.B. Chavan and Mrs. Gandhi—to explore coming generations of potential national leaders. Will their careers center on New Delhi or on state or regional authority? Will they have the same political values as those individuals who emerged under British tutelage? No certain answers can be given to these questions, but when the complexity and depth of the socioeconomic and political problems have been surveyed, one must account it a minor miracle if Indian parliamentarianism and full political openness survive the tests to which they will be put during the remainder of the twentieth century.

Those who are relatively optimistic about the future of Indian democracy point out that Indian politics has always coped more or less successfully with a high quotient of confusion and seeming chaos. They also note that a federal system gives parliamentary democracy its best chance in this setting by enabling regional power to reflect the diversities that exist, while at the same time promoting experience in operating a parliamentary system, often via coalitions, for different political groups. Indian federalism also permits government to function effectively at subnational levels even in the midst of confusion at the top. Optimists further emphasize the thesis that Indian culture (and personality) reject uniformity and rigid controls of the type engendered by authoritarian systems—though it should be noted that this argument was once advanced with respect to the Chinese.

In any case, uncertainties with respect to the political future of India abound. To some extent, populism has taken over in recent years, with parties and politicians promising vastly more than the system could deliver, and being forced to tolerate a rising tide of protest and lawlessness when the promised benefits were not forthcoming. This introduces the issue of economic prospects, a question intimately involved in any soundly based political prediction. Economic prognostication, however, represents a series of complex difficulties in its own right. In drawing up a balance sheet, the positive side of the ledger must be accorded considerable weight. Advances in agriculture in recent years have been substantial. Sizable grain reserves now exist, and India appears to have put the age of recurrent mass famine behind it. In considerable measure, this has been the result of the application of advanced science and technology to Indian agriculture, combined with governmental policies conducive to encouraging rural initiatives. Much stronger groups of middle-class and well-to-do farmers have emerged in certain parts of the country and exercise increased political power. It is asserted, probably correctly, that the poorest segments of rural society have been least benefited by the ongoing revolution, but the individuals who have witnessed no improvement in village conditions or personal livelihood are few.

Nonetheless, any generalization about the Indian economy is certain to be an oversimplification. Sectoral or state-by-state analysis is essential. India has its advanced regions, for example, the Punjab; and it has its dismal cases, with Bihar being one illustration. This is equally true with respect to industrial development. Here, moreover, governmental policies have been subject to some fluctuation, but in general, one central dilemma remains unresolved. Despite recurrent radical rhetoric and the past influence of Russian economic policies, the relation between government and a select number of large private industries is a cozy one and also one that supports neither innovation nor efficiency. At the same time, the state sector is frequently hobbled by the turgid bureaucratism and conservatism characteristic of such operations.

In general, despite various changes in governments and policies, protectionism continues to hold sway in India, providing limited incentive or opportunity for foreign investment apart from a few select fields. At the same time, as noted, policies have not been conducive to genuine competition or rapid growth of modern industry within the Indian private sector. Behind this situation lies one important fact. Gandhism with its emphasis upon rural India and cottage industry and its innate distrust of modern, urban industrialism is by no means dead. While Nehru sought to think and plan in different terms, the ideologies of many of those who now play powerful roles at the center are closer to Gandhi's than to those of his successors. To be sure, the emphasis upon agriculture and small-scale industry has much to commend it, but as currently balanced, Indian economic policies threaten to make the conditions of India's urban centers more complex.

Given recent developments, it is perhaps not surprising that India's economic growth has been uneven. In certain years, increases in the gross national product (GNP) have been good. In 1977–1978, for example, growth exceeded 7 percent, and inflation was held to a remarkable 0.9 percent. Unfortunately, 1978–1979 saw GNP growth decline to 3.6 percent, and inflation rise to 10.2 percent. The prospects are for continued unevenness, both in regional development and for the nation as a whole. Many of the factors needed for successful economic growth are now present in India: improved education; managerial talent on an expanding scale; an industrious and plentiful work force; and an advanced technology in certain fields. The critical variables lie largely in the political realm, and they relate to issues both of stability and of policy.

When all factors are taken into account, three broad alternatives would seem to exist with respect to India's political future. The first, which is ongoing, would be the continuance of weak coalition governments at the center, accompanied by the increased role and authority of the states. Such a development might be conducive to varied experiments—both economic and political—and hence, to new forms of dynamism within the system as a whole. However, it would also put into jeopardy any overall economic planning, or the effective execution of other national programs.

A second possibility would be the return to some form of authoritarian or quasi-authoritarian rule of the type initiated during the so-called Emergency Period. Whether pursued by Mrs. Gandhi or someone else, such a turn might be accompanied by an effort to build a nationwide movement in an attempt to bring heightened unity.

Finally, there is the alternative of military rule, and while that possibility still seems a considerable distance away, it is increasingly and openly discussed. At what point, if political fragmentation and recurrent crises continue, would the military, despite its traditions, feel compelled to intervene? Military involvement in Indian politics has already commenced on a modest scale, with military units called on to quell disturbances, economic and political in nature—including one involving the police. If it comes, military rule may well be initiated as a temporary measure, with the pledge to restore civilian rule—as has been the case in numerous other Asian countries—and with longer-range military governance hinging on developments.

These three alternatives have been presented in pure form, but some mix is not impossible. In any case, current uncertainties and variables are so numerous as to make any firm prediction impossible. Meanwhile, in the realm of foreign relations, Indian ties with the Soviet Union will almost certainly continue. First, because on balance, they have been satisfactory to both parties, and second, because there are no meaningful alternatives. In recent years, Soviet military and economic assistance to India has been substantial, and in this arena, the USSR has operated with circumspection, in part no doubt, because the Indians have been strongly assertive in upholding their position. Despite its insistence, however, the Indian government is not nonaligned today. It is and has for some time been aligned with the Soviet Union, and on some issues (for example, Vietnam) the influence of this alignment is clear. Yet Indian-Soviet ties—now built into both the military and economic structure—have not greatly improved the fortunes of the Indian left, nor is there any evidence that the role these ties will play role in shaping the future structure of Indian politics will be decisive. Even in the economic sphere, various Indian leaders have pursued "an Indian route," a route influenced on occasion by Soviet economic theories, but diverging considerably from the Soviet model. Alignment, in sum, comes in varying degrees and forms in the contemporary world.

A strong Soviet lobby exists in India today, yet top leaders have frequently signaled a desire to reduce dependency on the USSR to some extent, partly by improving relations with China and the United States. Yet obstacles immediately emerge. China's capacities for effective economic interaction, not to mention military assistance, are strictly minimal. Moreover, while Peking has shown some interest in normalizing its relations with New Delhi, the issue is not high on the list of its current priorities. This is partly because it regards India as rather firmly attached to the USSR and partly because of its uncertainties about the Indian political future. The United States, while increasing its economic programs in India somewhat, continues to view South Asia as a region of secondary concern and has no interest in mounting large-scale military or economic assistance programs. On the nuclear question, moreover, differences are deepening. The United States, not without reason, sees the dangers of nuclear proliferation in South Asia as serious, despite denials from Pakistan and India. It senses a rising interest within both nations in the acquisition of nuclear weapons, and it has been frustrated by Indian responses to date.

Meanwhile, the Indian government has not been unconcerned with trends to the west. The collapse of the shah's reign in Iran, the creation of a Marxist, pro-Soviet government in Afghanistan, and the specter of an unstable Pakistan reasserting fundamentalist Islamic values have all made the Indians apprehensive. Despite its ties with Moscow, New Delhi does not desire the growth of Soviet influence throughout western Asia. Nor does it want the further disintegration of Pakistan, a development that might be conducive to the growth of Soviet influence.

Before exploring American policy alternatives with respect to India, let us note briefly the situation elsewhere in South Asia, especially in Pakistan and Bangladesh. Pakistan has lived through troubled times during the past decade, and it is not clear that these troubles have ended. The execution of ex-premier Zulfikar Ali Bhutto is but a symbol of Pakistan's continuing political and regional strife, religious problems, and foreign threats.

Pakistan has never been able to integrate its diverse ethnic groups successfully and the dominance of the Punjabis has been a continuing political problem. It has also been increasingly difficult to find a middle road between the left and the Islamic fundamentalists. The military government of President Zia ul Haq, which came to power in the coup of 1977, currently seeks to ride the Islamic tide, pledging support for a revitalization of Islam and major modifications in the Western democratic system. But Zia faces a combination of growing pressures at home and abroad. The advent of a strongly pro-Soviet government in Kabul has increased the possibility of Afghan support to Pakistan's tribal dissidents in Baluchistan and the North-West Frontier Province. Pakistan harbors thousands of Afghan refugees, some of whom are politically active. Meanwhile, there have been no improvements in relations with India, and disenchantment with the United States remains strong.

Under these conditions, political programs necessarily have a tentative quality. Zia has promised constitutionalism for Pakistan and has suggested that the transition might resemble that which took place in South Korea nearly two decades ago, with the military playing civilian and political roles in the years ahead. At this point, however, it is not clear whether internal and external conditions will permit such a plan.

In Bangladesh, the movement toward constitutionalism and political democracy that culminated in the parliamentary elections of February 1979 is the more extraordinary because of the nature of this society and its problems. The present situation is largely the product of the commitment of President Ziaur Rahman, Bangladesh's military strong man, and thus illustrates that the initiatives of leaders can play a major role in determining institutional experiments. But the future of democracy in Bangladesh remains in considerable doubt.

Like Pakistan, Bangladesh is plagued with serious political divisions running across a wide spectrum, right and left. Unity is preserved because the military remain loyal to Ziaur, providing him with a strength that goes beyond his newly created party and the parliamentary majority it has achieved. Once again, we are witnessing an effort to move from direct military rule to a political system involving considerable political openness, but with military tutelage not totally removed. Another parallel with Pakistan exists, but with important differences. Here too the issue of an Islamic republic has been raised, but in Dacca it lacks official sanction and remains a minority voice.

Bangladesh does not face the same deteriorating situation on its borders as Pakistan or the same threats of foreign involvement—although the shadow of India will always be lengthy. And recent economic gains have moved this nation from the category of an apparent basket case to possible viability, although with multiple problems. As elsewhere in South Asia, the current government has opted for a more open economic system, seeking to energize the private sector and solicit foreign investment through economic incentives.

The latter trend extends to Sri Lanka, indicating that, after several decades of socialist-oriented economic policies, some states of the region are prepared to experiment with programs that may promise more success. Like Bangladesh, Sri Lanka is now seeking to combine parliamentary democracy and economic development through a strong executive system, attempting in some fashion to combine authority and political choice. As one reviews the political experiments in South Asia, one cannot help being impressed with the legacy of British tutelage. In certain settings, for example, Burma, the colonial heritage seems to have had limited impact, perhaps because Burma was long subordinate to the British Indian civil service. In other settings, current experiments may fail. Some argue, moreover, that even a modified parliamentary democracy is not suited to these socioeconomic systems and should be allowed to perish. It is remarkable nonetheless that throughout South Asia the struggle to preserve political openness shows great tenacity against odds far less favorable than in many other regions of the world.

Should American policies with respect to South Asia be reconsidered at this point? For approximately two decades, the United States has regarded South Asia in general and India in particular as an area of relatively low priority. Initially, there was considerable enthusiasm for the newly independent India, and many Americans felt that the global democratic cause could be served if India won the economic competition with China. The political and economic policies of the Nehru era and the anti-American biases of the prime minister himself cooled American ardor. The gap between Nehru's "neutralism" and American-sponsored alliances against Communist expansion grew wider. Only when China attacked India did our two nations come together briefly.

Our sole alliance in the region was with Pakistan, a member of CENTO and long regarded by Washington as a meaningful counterweight to Indian influence, both regionally and internationally. Until the Bangladesh war, U.S. policy was essentially directed toward encouraging a balance between India and Pakistan through military support to Islamabad. Relations with other South Asian states were minimal, although a few programs were directed toward both Nepal and Sri Lanka.

This is a new era, transitional and rife with uncertainties. Indian dominance in South Asia, as noted, has been established, although the future hinges on trends within India itself. Moreover, the possibility of a Pakistan-Indian nuclear contest cannot be ruled out. Meanwhile, a number of South Asian governments are turning away from the ideological rigidities of the past and seeking to fashion pragmatic economic and political policies promising a considerable degree of political openness. Whether India is to be included in such trends and, on a broader front, whether circumstances will work for or against these experiments remains to be seen. In all likelihood, political stability as a prerequisite for economic development will ultimately be given precedence should democracy, South Asian style, be unable to provide it. Yet rigid authoritarianism has thus far failed to implant itself for long in the region.

Under present circumstances, the United States cannot and should not make extensive, unilateral economic or military commitments, governmental in nature. The U.S. stake in East Asia is much greater, but beyond this, current conditions in South Asia are far too fluid to warrant such commitments. In some parts of the region, the American private sector may be able to play a much more significant role than in the past, and this should be encouraged via the creation of new U.S. international economic policies favorable to such activities. In addition, the U.S. should be prepared to make South Asia one of the regions of importance in multilateral assistance programs, conducted in concert with other advanced industrial societies. The opportunity also seems ripe for a wider dialogue with all segments of South Asian societies, especially Indian, and for a broader exchange among politicians, civic leaders, intellectuals, technicians, and the business communities.

Finally, we should seek to cooperate with the Soviet Union in working toward joint policies that will reduce to the greatest extent possible the strong threat of nuclear proliferation in the region. This, indeed, could be an important test of the ability of the United States and the Soviet Union to work effectively together on a problem of mutual interest and deep significance for all peoples of South Asia.

It has been proposed that in view of our concern about the oil lifeline from the Middle East to East Asia we should also increase our strategic presence in South Asia. It has been suggested that an American fleet be stationed in the Indian Ocean, using Diego Garcia as a base. Two serious objections exist to this course. First, none of the nations of South Asia would support such a move, and it could easily redound to the economic and political disadvantage of the United States throughout the region, negating the potentialities for improved political, economic, and cultural relations. Second, it would give the Soviet Union an excellent reason for seeking its own bases and upgraded facilities in the Indian Ocean. For these reasons, a move in this direction is not desirable under present circumstances. Our effort should be to reach an agreement with the Russians to keep military activities in the Indian Ocean minimal. The future of South Asia hinges primarily upon the success or failure of the socioeconomic and political experiments now under way; and although American assistance must and should be subordinate to indigenous efforts, it is to this area that our policies should be directed.

CONCLUSION

The most basic task confronting the United States in the Pacific-Asian region is to construct an Asian policy. Despite various pronouncements made by official spokesmen, we have no comprehensive policy for this vital region, one resting upon certain central principles and established requisite priorities and linkages. Necessarily, such a policy would be subject to alterations as circumstances changed, and at certain points even the fundamental principles underlying it might be reconsidered. The failure to create such a policy, however, results in the type of confusion and "ad hocery" that reduces support at home and abroad and reinforces the image of the United States as a declining, unpredictable power.

Our Asian policy for the 1980s should be based upon two fundamental principles. First, attention and concern should be focused on cultivating relations with those states with which we have the most common interests and the most substantial opportunities for a sustained, meaningful interaction across the entire range of economic, political, cultural, and strategic relations. In no sense does this mean that we should not take our relations with other nations seriously. The recent quest for accommodation with Asian communist states is legitimate *providing* our credibility and principles are not sacrificed in the process and such relations are not advanced at the expense of our other relations. Unfortunately, these conditions have not always been observed recently. As a result, American credibility has suffered in those states with which we have been traditionally aligned. The questions have been raised whether American allies are taken for granted and, at the same time, asked to meet standards wth respect to such matters as human rights not required of those whom Washington is seeking to cultivate. Is it more advantageous to have been an opponent rather than an ally of the United States?

The second fundamental principle that should underlie our Asian policies is that of pursuing a strategy of equilibrium in our relations with China and Russia. The reasons for rejecting the united front strategy are set forth earlier in this essay. Our basic approach to the two major Communist states should be to exhibit willingness to expand economic and cultural relations and to broaden the dialogue by being prepared to enter into negotiations on all matters of common concern. Indeed, continuous dialogue and negotiations should be accepted as a beneficial aspect of our bilateral relations with the PRC and the USSR, indispensable if peaceful coexistence is to be maintained. Negotiations should be conducted on an issue-by-issue basis, with our own interests and those of our close allies kept in mind. We must bring both strength and patience to the negotiations, refusing to be pressured into premature agreement for the sake of political expediency. In reaching understanding, moreover, the maintenance of two principles is crucial: reciprocity and accountability. The former need not be defined mechanistically, but its spirit must permeate such agreements if they are to have acceptability. The latter need not be interpreted as demanding linkage across the entire spectrum of a nation's policies and actions, but it must relate to the issues immediately under consideration. In applying these principles, we should avoid any preordained tilt toward either the PRC or the USSR, cognizant of our current advantage of being able to communicate with both at a time when their mutual communication is minimal, but also aware that Sino-Soviet relations may not be frozen into their present form forever.

NOTE

1. The description of these strategies that follows borrows extensively from two articles of mine, "Approach to Peace and Security in Asia: The Uncertainty Surrounding American Strategic Principles," *Current Scene* August-September 1978, pp. 1–18; and "Les Etats-Unis face á l'Asie: Les embarras du choix," *Politique internationale* no. 2 (Winter 1978–79): 59–80.

Western Europe

Alfred Grosser

XXV

The United States and the nations of Western Europe have seldom before been in such similar circumstances. They enjoy relative prosperity compared with the rest of the world, though it is a prosperity threatened in the short run and even more in the long run. They maintain liberal political systems, while authoritarian regimes hold sway nearly everywhere else—but the governments and political parties of those systems seem less and less able to direct social change. And at the same time, on both sides of the Atlantic, rarely has there been so little awareness of these similarities.

A central requirement of political analysis is that the observer remain conscious of two orders of reality: the material facts, which can be described individually, and the image that players in the political game, be they leaders or citizens, have of these facts. The image in turn becomes a fact that, by virtue of its consequences, can often be more important than the original. To understand French foreign policy, for example, and the attitude of a great majority of the French with respect to the United States, it is more useful to discern the myth according to which the French continue to imagine the events and conclusions of the Yalta Conference in 1945 than to refer to the real events at Yalta, or to (rightly) remind oneself that Yalta no longer relates objectively to today's reality. Then again: the behavior and actions of the French Communist party are, indeed, a fit subject for study. But American policy toward France continues to be based on certain beliefs about the French

For the development of the ideas presented here and for the post-1941 historical background, the author has drawn from his book *Les Occidentaux: Les pays d'Europe et les Etats-Unis* (Paris: Fayard, 1978). There is a German translation, *Das Bündnis: Die westeuropäischen Länder and die USA seit dem Krieg* (Munich: Hanser, 1978), and an American translation will be published by the Seabury Press, New York, in 1980.

Communist party that correspond only remotely to the facts that such study would reveal.

In considering the objective significance of trans-Atlantic relations for the goals of economic balance and the security of the countries of Western Europe and especially the United States, the findings of a 1978 survey that was conducted for the Chicago Council on Foreign Relations are striking.[1] To the question "What are the two or three biggest foreign policy problems facing the United States today?" those interviewed answered as follows:

	Public	Leaders
Middle East	20 percent	47 percent
Reducing foreign aid	18	4
Relations with U.S.S.R.	13	46
Balance of trade	12	19
Staying out of other countries' affairs	11	2
Oil	9	7
[Keeping peace, arms race, decline of dollar, strengthening foreign policy, Africa, Cuba, strengthening defense, and 8 other items followed]		
Western Europe/allies	1	6

These figures, disturbing to Europeans, were balanced somewhat by the answers to other questions, for example: "In your opinion, does the United States have a vital interest in [a particular] country?" The answer was yes, with percentages for the public and the leaders at 80 and 90, respectively, for Saudi Arabia; 78 and 91 for Israel; 67 and 92 for Iran; and, in Western Europe, 69 and 98 for West Germany, 66 and 94 for Great Britain, 54 and 90 for France, and 36 and 80 for Italy. If, in certain situations, those interviewed were confronted with the following alternatives—send troops; do nothing; try to negotiate; refuse to trade; send military supplies; don't know—they replied "Send troops" in the following proportions:

	Public	Leaders
Panama closes canal to United States	58 percent	49 percent
Arabs cut off oil to United States	36	30
Arabs invade Israel	22	31
[other situations followed]		
Soviets invade Western Europe	54	92
Soviets take West Berlin	48	77
Soviets invade Yugoslavia	18	15

Even if the questions were posed in entirety (for example: the USSR could not take West Berlin without first having confronted U.S. troops already there specifically to prevent the USSR from being tempted to take the city), these answers show that European uncertainties about the value of American assurances are not entirely unfounded. This is true largely because the American public, including many leaders, is poorly informed about the realities of the European situation and the extent of trans-Atlantic interdependence.

CONTINUITY AND CHANGE

The first fact about Europe is that there is no Europe. But this assertion is obviously too harsh, for the European Economic Community (EEC) represents a genuine political fact for international relations and even for the internal political life of its member states. With nine members the EEC probably is far less able to act as an entity than it could with six—and with twelve, adding Greece, Spain, and Portugal, the difficulties will increase. But the EEC has passed the stage of being a simple juxtaposition of countries and national policies. It has for some time functioned as an entity, for example, during the Kennedy Round in the sixties and the Tokyo Round in 1979, and during negotiations leading to the signing in 1975 of the Helsinki agreement. And the Nine worked together, as individual states and as the EEC Council, during establishment of the Lomé pacts with 46 African, Caribbean, and Pacific nations. Nevertheless, Europe still does not have much substance in the international sphere; and the United States would be well advised not to fall into the easy habit of treating Europe as a unified instrument, for such a perception is blind to reality and leads to errors of judgment and of politics.

The strongest nations of Western Europe are the German Federal Republic, France, and Great Britain, followed by Italy. But the smaller countries must not be neglected in an attempt to understand the whole. Internal conflicts between the Flemish and the Walloons may soon come to a climax and fragmented Belgium lose its ability to function as a unit. This situation will have numerous effects on the internal development of Western Europe. The Netherlands, and its contradictory politics in the past twenty years, concerns the United States even more. There has been real desire for a European supranationality, but also for EEC expansion to include nations like Great Britain that are firmly opposed to any loss of sovereignty. Why indeed try to realize a strong unified Europe while supporting a trans-Atlantic structure dominated by the United States?

Strangely, the answer to this question can be found in Paris. Since the start of the trend toward European unification, the French interpretation of equality has seemed contradictory. Vis-à-vis the United States,

France continues to maintain a position it has always rejected when put forth at the European level by the Netherlands. According to France, differences in power do not justify inequality; France therefore must be considered the political equal of the United States; but France will not accept Holland as a political equal. The result is that the Netherlands is suspicious of any step toward European unification that seems to favor domination of the small by the big powers and, more especially, any Franco-German domination, may it be led by Adenauer with de Gaulle or Schmidt with Giscard d'Estaing. For the Netherlands, at least, the United States appears as a guarantor against such domination.

France and the Netherlands appear here as cohesive political units. But for most European nations, conflicts over foreign and domestic issues are everyday realities, not just questions that divide the political parties represented in parliament. Churches and trade unions likewise participate in these conflicts.

The wider question of continuity and change in nations and their goals must also be considered. In European-American relations, major changes in the international system have become discontinuities with multiple effects: the 1944–1945 structure (the Great Alliance versus Germany) becoming the 1947–1949 situation (the East-West conflict) that continues to the present; the end of the period of European decolonization in 1960–1962 and the end of the Vietnam war in 1973; and in 1971–1976 profound changes in the international monetary system, beginnings of the oil crisis, and the burgeoning of the economic crisis in the West. Nevertheless, Americans have erred and continue to err in not perceiving clearly the elements of continuity that largely determine the attitudes of Western Europe toward other nations.

Since World War II, Great Britain and France have been the only countries in Western Europe that have never stopped asking a question that perhaps has no answer: How can I continue exercising world influence when I know that I am no longer a world power? Italy and the smaller nations have never seemed to want to exercise worldwide influence. The German Federal Republic has never desired influence outside of Europe, at least not until recently, when its economic and monetary weight have forced it to go beyond the status of political dwarf. The answers to the question above have been quite different for the British and the French. The British have answered: "I will keep or regain influence by exercising a privileged influence over one of the two truly great powers, the United States." And France says: "To retain influence, I can support only a Europe in which France remains the only country that wishes to exercise world influence, which in turn will allow France to speak with all the political weight of European economic power behind it."

But what if your American ally grants you no privileges, from the time of the Lend-Lease Act in 1941 through the pressures you underwent in the sixties in order to join the European group, including the veritable blackmail perpetrated during the Suez expedition? What if your German ally becomes so economically powerful that you feel compelled, by way of counterbalancing this power, to allow the entrance of Great Britain? Both Britain and France have clung to their basic positions, though neither has actually succeeded; and both continue to manifest the will and desire to be recognized as world-oriented powers. This is a fact to which American policy has not in general given sufficient attention. It is of little import whether these desires are justifiable (indeed, who is to judge and in the name of what value system?); they are a reality. Far too seldom have Americans taken into account the fact that obtaining or reinforcing prestige constitutes in itself, for nations and for individuals, a true finality.

Even when there are no tensions between them, France and West Germany remain divided by the fact that the two superpowers do not take the same stand in their policies. As paradoxical as it may sound, the key power for West Germany is the USSR, and West Germany's ties with the United States are a means of satisfying its security obsession; whereas for France, the USSR, as soon as it is not seen as a direct threat, serves in a way as an instrument, for good relations between France and the USSR give more weight to France vis-à-vis the United States.

In the case of France, many American observers committed a grave analytical error while de Gaulle was in power. They believed that the French approved of de Gaulle's foreign policy (not toward Israel, not toward Quebec, but for its general orientation) simply because he was de Gaulle. The truth is that de Gaulle was followed largely *because* of his international stand. His global politics can be defined rather easily: France must attain the highest possible rank as a major Western power. Without the word Western, the key element of de Gaulle's strategy is incomprehensible. For indeed, whenever the Soviet Union exerts some kind of physical threat, France, as a Western power, is firmly on the side of the other Western countries, especially the United States. All recent American experience testifies to this: during the Cuban, Berlin, and U-2 crises, Washington was singularly fortunate in France's loyalty. But when the threats are less precise and direct, France, as a Western power, must win prestige and power in confrontation with the United States. France has few ties with the USSR; it is influenced economically, technologically, culturally, and politically by its ally the United States. General de Gaulle's visits to Moscow in December 1944 and August 1966, and Giscard d'Estaing's in April 1979, were largely to further the recognition of France as an equal partner by one of the two truly Great Powers—which would make it possible to deal with the other one from a better position of power and prestige.

The mythical interpretation of Yalta as an agreement between the USSR and the United States to share the world is partly the cause and partly the justification of a deeply rooted attitude that will not disappear in the foreseeable future. France's perception of Yalta puts the two Big Powers on the same level, so that it can back off from the one that is politically closer but that at the same time exerts pressure on its autonomy; that perception nonetheless recognizes the need for and merits of the Atlantic Alliance, and accepts the reality of trans-Atlantic interdependence.

The tone has changed under Giscard d'Estaing's presidency. But it was not only to capture the votes of Jacques Chirac's party in the European elections of June 10, 1979, that Jean François-Poncet, the new minister of foreign affairs, stated as part of his first speech before the National Assembly on May 3, 1979 that:

> France is not only in Europe. She is in the world. She maintains specific relationships with her Western allies, especially with the United States, but also with the Soviet Union, China, and the African and Arab nations, as well as with her traditional friends on other continents. The original voice of her culture, of her conception of man and society, is heard throughout the world.
>
> . . . Since the war, two powers have shared, if not the world, at least influence upon the world . . . First in confrontation, then, despite many fits and starts, in détente, these two power poles have dominated the entire structure of international relations, each of their confrontations threatening the peace of the whole world.
>
> . . . In taking a firmer hold on their destinies and becoming more capable of solving their problems through regional and world solidarities, the smaller nations will be better able to avoid this Manichean confrontation. France and all of Europe can seize this opportunity.
>
> The cold war and the bipolar structure it has imposed on the world have for a long time rallied our European partners around the American pole. But today we can begin to see the will to affirm their European interests and to free themselves from Atlantic conformism.

As we shall see later, West Germany has backed away from the United States during the seventies. The language and thought of German politics cannot be quite those of France. For three different but connected reasons, despite all her economic and even political power West Germany still is not, and will not be in the foreseeable future, a state like the others. First, Germany is the only Western state with Hitler in its past. Even with the dying off of that portion of the German population who lived as adults under Hitler, and even though more and more individuals outside Germany are answering yes to a French survey question, "Do you believe that a German of your age and your profession has the same problems as yourself?"—still, both the domestic and foreign policies of the Federal Republic are influenced by the events of 1933–1945. And one reason why West Germany wants to be European is that its new power does not allow direct self-expression, for fear of anti-German reaction in Norway, the Netherlands, France, Great Britain, and the United States.

The other two reasons seem contradictory. West Germany is the only Western country that still depends heavily on the international structure of 1944–1945; at the same time the country's reality and beliefs were directly fashioned by the system set up in 1947–1949.

In principle, the government coalition, the Social Democratic party (SPD) and the Free Democratic party (FDP) is, in matters of foreign policy, in conflict with the opposing Christian Democratic Union–Christian Social Union (C.D.U./C.S.U.). But, on May 17, 1972, in the midst of a disagreement over treaties with Moscow, Warsaw, and East Berlin, the three parliamentary groups unanimously adopted a joint resolution (*gemeinsame Resolution*), paragraph 5 of which states: "The powers and responsibilities of the Four Powers regarding both Germany and Berlin will not be affected by the agreements. Since a final settlement of the German question has not yet been effected, the Bundestag regards as essential the continued existence of these powers and responsibilities." And on June 19, 1978, a joint declaration on Berlin by the party presidents said in part: "The Berlin question is inseparable from the German question. Until the German question is solved, Berlin will remain an expression and a symbol of the separation of the Germans entailed by World War II."

Berlin is at issue: documents signed in London in September and November 1944 (even before the first Allied troops entered Germany) by representatives of the United States, the USSR, and Great Britain still constitute the legal foundations of the Western presence in Berlin. Those agreements applied on July 1, 1945, when the American army drew back to allow the Red Army to occupy Thuringia and Saxony (included, in London, in the Soviet zone); they had also been applied when American, French, and British troops entered Berlin, which was destined to be the out-of-zone capital of Germany, jointly governed by the four. It is because of the aerial corridor established in 1945 that Pan American

Airways, British European Airways, and Air France planes, substitutes for the military aircraft of that era, descend from 8,000 to 3,000 meters upon arriving at the vertical of the demarcation between the two Germanys (Lufthansa cannot land in Berlin).

It is not a question only of Berlin, but of the German nation. The greatest paradox is difficult to grasp: Germans want their country to remain deprived of an essential part of its sovereignty. They want the complete takeover of 1945 to be maintained in part, for it is the four occupation powers alone that today embody the unity of the German nation. German unity was proclaimed in the Potsdam accord of August 1945, but it disappeared as a consequence of the new international structure of 1947–1949. The latter at first saw West Berliners and West Germans fear for Berlin in 1948 (a fear not without satisfaction, for the tension gave respectability and morality back to Berlin—the symbol of Nazism became the symbol of liberty); then the German Federal Republic was born alongside the Atlantic alliance, two children of the cold war.

The 1947–1949 system prevailed over that of the Allies versus Germany on two important points, without diminishing the German dependence on all four powers as such. Only West Berlin is protected by the three Western powers, although the whole of Berlin should have come under their common control. But the United States has continuously practiced a policy of containment, despite its many declarations to the contrary: it is understood that the USSR is allowed complete liberty in its zone provided that it respect the demarcation line. This principle was applied to the 1953 revolt in East Berlin, the Hungarian revolution in 1956, and the crushing of Prague in 1968. In Berlin on August 13, 1961, the Germans, including Chancellor Adenauer and Mayor Brandt, did not realize that President Kennedy had given the East permission to construct the Berlin wall through his definition in June of "the three essentials," which concerned only West Berlin and not the separation of the two Berlins or the two Germanys. Even today, the Germans do not recognize the extent to which the cry of the American president—"Ich bin ein Berliner"—which set off an enthusiastic reaction in the Berlin crowd, was deliberately and rather hypocritically ambiguous.

West Germany is the only Western state that must constantly consider the fate of millions of its citizens who live under communist dictatorship; this imposes constraints on its foreign policy. But reunification is not an obsession. On the contrary, the Federal Republic is also the only Western state that has not founded national consensus on the idea of the nation, but rather on a double—liberal and non-national—refusal: rejection of the Nazi dictatorship of the past and rejection of neighboring communism. It has chosen to avoid reunification rather than accept a form of it that might include the slightest communist influence. In domestic politics there has thus emerged a partly admirable, partly disquieting (for the nervous fears it provokes) emphasis on *freiheitliche demokratische Grundordnung*, liberal democratic fundamental order. And in the realm of foreign policy, West Germany is more ready than others (which might create tensions with these others) to establish deeply rooted ties—European or trans-Atlantic—with all who claim the same refusals.

SECURITY PROBLEMS

The basic situation is simple: a purely European security system is impossible. The Soviet Union is the only Great Power on the Continent. In a strictly European security system, it would dominate the whole western portion of the continent, without even raising threats, but by sheer weight. The other Great Power, the United States, thus has to play a role in this system, making it not a European system, but a subsystem of the Soviet-American security structure. This situation leads to two inevitable questions. Are the Soviet leaders certain that the president of the United States would really risk national suicide to protect Western Europe? Wouldn't the United States want Europe to pay a political, economic, or monetary price for protection that, to seem effective, requires the presence of American troops on European soil?

The reasons for this latter requirement have remained unchanged for thirty years. In the case of West Berlin, one could say that the presence of a single American soldier would suffice. His only role is to be killed. If he is there to be killed, he won't be killed. Suppose that there is no American soldier in Berlin and that one day, in a completely spontaneous angry reaction, ten thousand workers from East Berlin, having by chance found weapons, occupy West Berlin. No American president would risk the destruction of the United States to remedy a *fait accompli*, and the risk run by Moscow for the West Berlin stakes would be almost zero. But suppose that the American soldier were present and were killed in the battle. Any American president would be moved to intervene with at least one tank, the Russians would no doubt reply with two tanks, and no one could tell where this escalation would stop: a substantial risk would be run for the West Berlin stakes.

The same reasoning can be applied to all of Western Europe. What ensures its peace and security is that the two Great Powers are in direct contact with each other on European soil. Any attempt at "neutralization" at the center of Europe could create a type of African situation in which the two Great Powers would try to penetrate the so-called neutralized zone, with all the accompanying risks of confrontations and errors in calculation. Thus, since 1948, all the European governments, including the French, have always favored the American presence. De Gaulle, in pulling France out of NATO (while at the same time keeping France in the Alliance), never would have demanded the evacuation of American troops from French soil if fate had not felicitously positioned Germany between France and the Soviet Union.

But if American presence is a necessity, there is perhaps no reason to pay for a counterpart, since the defense of Western Europe is also in the American interest. And this necessary presence is perhaps not enough to ensure security. For both political and strategic reasons, nations other than the United States must have nuclear arms capacity in Europe, if only to be able to threaten the Soviet Union with the escalation to atomic level of any conflict about issues vital to the Europeans but not to the Americans. This reasoning was first put forth in Great Britain, then in France, toward the close of the fifties. It was denounced and opposed by all the U.S. administrations until June 26, 1974, in Brussels, when the heads of government of the member-nations of the Alliance signed a declaration on Atlantic relations that the NATO Council had adopted in Ottawa on June 19. The sixth of fourteen paragraphs concerns two European countries that "have at their disposal nuclear power capable of playing its own deterrent role contributing to the global reinforcement of the deterrent powers of the Alliance," while paragraph 7 contains the American commitment to "maintain its forces in Europe at the level required by the credibility of the strategy of deterrence," and paragraph 9 states that "all members of the Alliance agree that the continued presence of Canadian forces and substantial American forces in Europe plays in irreplaceable role in the defense of North America itself as well as in the defense of Europe." (See the essay by Iklé in this volume.)

No one in France speaks any longer of giving up nuclear power, especially since the Socialist and Communist opposition parties altered their position in the Common Program of 1972, and have become defenders of national nuclear armament. This armament will be developed during the 1980s. The group of strategic missiles buried in the soil of Upper Provence since 1971 is gradually being replaced by fewer but more powerful units, the goal being a total eight times more powerful than the present capacity; the fifth strategic submarine will begin operations in 1980; the sixth, with multiple-head missiles, is planned for 1985, at the same time that the Mirage 2000, a low-altitude penetration plane equipped with newly designed missiles, is to become operative. During this period the British nuclear deterrent force will, in all probability, play an important role in maintaining the security of the

United Kingdom and its European allies, whatever position the United States adopts. The difference between France and Great Britain in the political use of their nuclear forces is another question.

Can we say that the most substantive change has occurred in the German position? The answer is both no and yes. It is no because the permanent German-American entente or, rather, the German submission to American wishes is, at least partially, legendary. Bonn's chronic concerns and criticisms in the face of successive American strategies have at times erupted into genuine crises. In 1956, for example, despite the solid friendship between U.S. Secretary of State Dulles and Chancellor Adenauer, their mutual confidence was seriously shaken by the Radford plan (redeployment of U.S. forces). Nevertheless, the German position has changed, especially in comparison with the situation in the mid-sixties when Erhard's government and the social-democratic opposition rejected all criticism of American politics in Vietnam for fear of seeing the United States lessen its protection of Europe.

The problems and even the tensions between West Germany and the United States are diverse and have varied origins, one of which is simply the economic and monetary power of a less timid Germany. The time is past when Bonn would yield to the slightest American pressure, as, for example, the pressure to increase the German contribution toward the costs of stationing American troops. There was tension concerning the geographic reach of the Alliance. In October 1973, the United States demanded that the European nations help the American assistance efforts in Israel but did not allow them to participate in the American decision-making; without even informing Bonn, Americans used their bases in Germany to speed up the provision of military supplies to Israel. Chancellor Brandt protested and finally asked the U.S. government to stop shipping materiel from German ports. Many German leaders and newspapers began sounding rather Gaullist: was it legitimate that the Atlantic allies had no say in the face of the main Atlantic power, when a crisis—even one outside of the geographic area covered by the 1949 treaty—was of concern for the European nations and could entangle them in a world conflict?

In 1978–1979, the tensions directly involved the defense of Europe. German fears are not essentially different from French fears; above all, they are similar in what may appear as a contradiction: the U.S.-China rapprochement should not go too far, because the predictable Soviet reaction would threaten the desired European détente (a détente wanted, in the case of the Germans, if only to avoid Soviet-created problems in Berlin); but neither should the United States press too much for détente with the Soviet Union, by giving up certain weapons or by accepting certain Soviet conditions of SALT II or of SALT III, if it is to the detriment of European security.

The history of nondecision concerning the neutron bomb exemplifies the difficulties in German-American and in European-American relations.[2] Never before had an American president allowed his decision about the manufacture and the dislocation of a nuclear weapon to depend on a previous agreement with his NATO partners, even though he may well have counted on a refusal that would allow him to make the negative decision he wanted to make in the first place. The dramatization of this incident was quite unexpected, for the way the mass media presented the weapon did not correspond to reality. But the German quandary could have been foreseen. In any event, the chancellor did not wish to answer either concerning the manufacture of this weapon, lest he be accused of violating the German agreement not to participate in nuclear policy, or concerning its possible location, for the Germans were trapped between the desire for better protection and the desire to cease appearing to be the only European nation submitting to the United States and the obvious target in the event of conflict. The location of launching apparatus on West German soil, as desirable as it may have seemed for the security of Europe, was acceptable only if at least one other country had also assented, but no other had.

This happened for political as well as strategic reasons: confidence in the unconditional protection of the "gray zone" by the United States has plummeted. In other words, the United States and the USSR have transformed their national territories into "sanctuaries," implicitly accepting the idea that the European allies of the potential enemy could be destroyed. The title the great liberal daily paper *Süddeutsche Zeitung* gave, on May 13, 1979, to its analysis of reactions at the conclusion of SALT II was, undoubtedly excessive: "Ein Minimum von Vertrauen und ein Maximum von Angst"—a minimum of confidence and a maximum of fear. But, much as they had in the United States, critical reactions to SALT II mounted in Europe, notably in French publications that in principle have traditionally supported the United States. In an editorial of May 14, 1979, Olivier Chevrillon, the editor of the Paris weekly *Le Point*, presented his dramatic analysis of SALT II:

> Even supposing that the agreements on the limitation of strategic arms (SALT II) are as good as Mr. Carter claims, France and her neighbors would be foolish to be appeased. For in the past few months their security has actually been weakened. While Moscow and Washington niggled over their intercontinental missile treaty, Mr. Brezhnev was aiming perfectly designed harquebuses at Western Europe. And anyone can see in his

actions the old Soviet imperial plan. The USSR does not want war, but simply—if I may put it this way—right of inspection over our affairs, that is, suzerainty. By lining up new atomic weapons—the SS-20's—across the European theater, weapons capable of striking any point on the continent (but not of reaching the United States), Moscow has increased its power of political blackmail, and done so with success, for already part of Europe is creeping toward neutrality.

With the SS-20, the Soviets have a means of instantly annihilating all stationary installations and weapons of France and of NATO in Europe. But the new danger arises largely from the precision of these "firing heads." They are capable of the selective destruction, without frightful civilian massacre, of the essential European defense points. The almost surgical appearance of this operation, its "cleanness," and the absence of genocide might relieve Washington of the desire to retaliate.

In short, the probability that the Americans would risk their cities and their lives to safeguard our liberties now seems less strong. But is it really? The issue is at most of secondary importance since deterrence is a psychological battle. We are left with the fact that, on both sides of the Iron Curtain, military and political leaders are having greater and greater doubts about U.S.-Europe solidarity. As a consequence, the Soviets are getting bolder and the Europeans more timid.

One may object that parries are not lacking. For example, NATO envisages the installation of Pershing IIs, and later of long-range Cruise missiles, that is, weapons capable of striking Soviet territory. Reinforcement of these arms would permit retaliation in proportion to the aggression; it would, above all, reaffirm American assurances of security.

Certainly. With the help of the United States, Western Europe could indeed protect itself against possible Soviet blackmail; it could refuse to be "Finlandized." Whether it will have the courage to do so is another question . . .

Leaving aside France, which has quit NATO, we can see that the NATO members are not battling—far from it!—to welcome the Pershing II or similar weapons. The Norwegians refuse them, and the Danes are close to refusing them. The Belgians, the British, the Dutch, and the Germans are divided. In Bonn, M. Wehner, and with him the whole left wing of the Social Democrats, opposes the introduction of missiles like the SS-20 in West Germany, believing that their presence would provoke Moscow's anger. In the face of this pressure, M. Schmidt himself has to be careful. He would not mind having the Pershings but does not want to be the only European head of government to accept them.

What is happening is that by adding the weight of their propaganda to the force of their arms, the Soviets are beginning to exercise a veto power

> over the defense of Western Europe. If this rout continues at all, they will tomorrow choose which weapons we are entitled to own. This would indeed be a singular kind of European "integration."

At the same time, the Europeans are, of course, in favor of any step that might assure détente; that is, they are in favor of SALT II. It is not at all certain that American leaders understand the dual European reaction and the legitimate foundations of this reaction, nor that they understand the contradictions inherent in European perceptions of the Soviet Union and the repercussions of such perceptions on European relations with the United States. It is not likely that Americans comprehend the reasons given by the president of France in May 1979 for the French refusal to take part in SALT III. Since the talks were to include consideration of the reduction of nuclear forces in the "nonessential" European zone in order to guarantee a balance between the two sides, France, whose own atomic weapons, by definition, defend essential objectives, could not let it be believed that it would allow its weapons to become the object of such negotiations.

Tensions over European security are not the only trans-Atlantic military problems. There are at least two others: arms sales and exportation of nuclear materials to third-party nations. The first is specifically a Franco-American clash. During their victorious electoral campaigns of 1974 and 1976 the presidents of both countries asserted their intention to raise the moral standards of arms-export policy, but the exports continued to increase from 1976 to 1978, alongside expanded British efforts in this area. During fiscal 1978, the United States exported $13,600 million worth of military materiel (with about 50 percent of it going to only three countries—Saudi Arabia, Iran, and Israel)—a 20 percent increase over the preceding year. In 1977, France took in orders valued at more than 27 billion francs and delivered materiel worth 14.5 billion francs, which led Socialist deputies who had proposed a bill providing for parliamentary control of the export of war materiel to say: "Total orders received by France in 1977 amount to almost half the total orders received by the United States. Thus, per capita, we sell two times more weapons than the leading arms merchant in the world." Both France and the United States have two reasons for these sales: each wants to improve the trade balance and to better amortize investments made in the weapons industry, thereby helping to ease the national military budget. But their political motives are not always shared and often conflict, as was especially evident in the case of Saudi Arabia immediately after the commercial and political loss of the Iranian market. One can only hope for the coordination of export policies and a decrease in the confrontation—hardly spectacular, but nevertheless real—between France and the United States on this issue.

The nuclear industry poses an ambiguous problem—ambiguous because its different facets are intermingled and one can never tell what the real goals are behind governmental decisions or actions in this area. For example, when in spring 1979 France told West Germany of its need to avoid the slightest risk of broadcasting arms production methods, so as not to have to make immediate delivery of regenerated plutonium, what were its motives? Genuine fear, desire to maintain a political advantage over an economically more powerful German partner, desire to obtain economic advantages during an energy crisis? Or was it the hope of exploiting a technological advantage that would be effective even vis-à-vis the United States, which seems intent on maintaining by any means its lead in research and production? Undoubtedly all these motives were in play simultaneously.

The American side faces a similar situation with respect to the multiple pressures being exerted to undermine Franco-Pakistanian nuclear cooperation—which has in fact suffered a considerable setback—as well as German-Brazilian nuclear cooperation, which is being upheld, according to Chancellor Schmidt's declaration during his visit to Brasilia in early April 1979. The final communiqué on the German-Brazilian talks, published on April 4, 1979, pointed out: "President Figueiredo and Federal Chancellor Schmidt affirm that the relations between the two countries should be further diversified . . . Having given consideration to cooperation in the field of nuclear energy for peaceful purposes, they express their satisfaction with the results already attained and their determination to carry out fully the agreements concluded between the two states."

The last clause is evidently directed against the United States, where the 1975 German-Brazilian nuclear energy agreements had raised intense concerns, both because of the avowed fear of seeing Brazil acquire atomic strength, despite the agreements, and because of German competition in an area where French competition already had to be reckoned with. In any event, the incident showed to what extent France's accusation against Bonn—" In all circumstances and on every occasion you have aligned yourself on the side of the United States"—had become as untrue in the case of nuclear energy as it had been in the case of the monetary issue. Even more than the other European governments, the German government was unhappy about the Nuclear Nonproliferation Act of 1978, which President Carter signed on March 10, 1978. Not only does this law express a deep distrust of the European allies, but it has specific drawbacks: it forces the U.S. government to cancel earlier agreements and may lead the United States to abuse its dominant position in the uranium market, thereby perhaps causing countries with scarce uranium supplies to build breeder reactors, an effect so much in opposition to U.S. wishes that Bonn interpreted the act as primarily a law to prevent the possible construction of a German breeder reactor. Above all, the act reveals the obvious contempt the U.S. Congress has for international solidarity, since several clauses use American legislation to introduce modifications that ought to have remained in the realm of international agreements.

MONETARY DISORDERS AND ECONOMIC CONCERNS

Nuclear problems evolve both from the military and from the economic sphere. The relationship between these two spheres needs closer analysis, for it seems that changes have occurred both in the interpretation and in the reality of the priorities involved. For quite a long time Germany maintained a rather submissive attitude toward the United States for security reasons, while France and Great Britain believed that only the possession of nuclear weapons could confer international status as an influential power. But in 1978, the U.S. government found itself having to seek aid for the dollar and to accept the real conditions established by countries with strong currencies—the yen, the Swiss franc, and the German mark. Yet Japan has no military strength, the Swiss army in no way constitutes a diplomatic force, and West Germany is in a state of total nuclear dependence. What is less novel, but also highly significant, is that all Western governments feel their security threatened more in the economic than in the military sphere. This feeling had already prevailed among European states at the Lisbon conference in 1952 when the consequences of the Atlantic alliance had to be drawn.

Two not unrelated circumstances radically altered the situation that had characterized the fifties and sixties. The first was a change in American attitude in 1969. For twenty years, American priorities with respect to Europe had been largely political. Even though the United States had drawn great advantage from the prevailing monetary system, it rather reluctantly made irresponsible use of this advantage in financing the Vietnam war. Now that irresponsibility was becoming to a certain extent doctrinal: manipulation of the dollar was expected to produce economic advantages independent of political consequences, especially in Europe. Americans scarcely realized that August 15, 1971, the date marking the end of the dollar's convertibility and of the Bretton Woods system, was one of the most critical turning points since World War II. (See the essay by Meier in this volume.)

The second circumstance that abruptly changed the status quo was the oil crisis of 1973. This was in part caused by the collapse of the monetary structure, but it in turn played a powerful role in accelerating the economic crisis, the most spectacular effects of which are still to come.

The Western governments' lack of awareness of the dangers ahead was particularly striking in 1973–1974. Henry Kissinger seems to have been more concerned with taking advantage of the oil crisis to re-establish American political dominance over Europe than to set up a long-term solution to the problem. As for the European governments, rather than show their cohesiveness as they did under the threat of Stalin in 1948, rather than point out to their electorates the need for drastic change, they chose to hide the gravity of the situation and in general to take independent action, France itself becoming the worst example of this attitude. But, over the years, the American monetary structure was revealed as the least justifiable, though its ultimate goals ought to have been obvious to the Europeans: it was aimed exclusively at U.S. national interests and favored international monetary policies that maximized those advantages that might retard the decline of America's relative economic power. To accomplish this end, money and political power had to be separated; the former could no longer be a means of reinforcing the latter.

European criticism of the American attitude reached a peak in 1977. *Le Monde*'s headline called it "irresponsibility"; the *Frankfurter Allgemeine*'s analysis was titled "American Roulette: Seven Cynical Rules of the Game"; while the director of the Swiss National Bank stated that America's economic policies did not live up to its world responsibilities. But the trans-Atlantic monetary conflict had in fact existed since 1968, and, contrary to all appearances, it was not a French-American but a German-American problem. The real attitude of the French did not at all correspond to the publicized one. For ten years, each time Washington and Bonn took opposing stands regarding the floating or the freezing of currencies, Paris took Washington's side because the president of France (especially Georges Pompidou) feared the domination of the mark more than that of the dollar. What is really new about the European monetary system that was prepared in 1978 and implemented in March 1979 is that the European Currency Unit (whose English acronym, ECU, recalls the name of an early French coin and is therefore acceptable in France), is a sign of the Europeans' willingness to act in solidarity, especially in the face of the U.S. dollar and the wild speculations generated by its numerous fluctuations.

The ECU, serving both as a unit of account and as operating currency among central banks, represents an EEC "currency basket," in which the weight of each currency has been established proportional to the weight of the different economies and the strength of their currencies,* including the British pound, even though Great Britain is not now a member nation. Each currency has a pivot price above or below which the exchange rate may generally vary up to 2.25 percent before the central banks must intervene. The two principal initiators of the system, Helmut Schmidt and Valéry Giscard d'Estaing, hoped that the unifying effect of a system with nearly fixed exchange rates would prevail over the destructive effects of greatly differing inflation rates among countries. For the system to work, there must be at least minimal similarities in the economic policies of the member-nations; otherwise the European Monetary Fund, which is to be established at the end of a two-year trial period and is to hold a portion of the dollar and gold reserves of the member-nations, cannot be realized.

Europe cannot become a cohesive unit without close monetary cooperation. But whereas 1948 saw the beginnings of such cooperation with the support and at the request of the United States, this time European solidarity is largely based on the necessity for joint action in confrontation with the United States. For to revive the trans-Atlantic ambiance of the fifties, a sense of solidarity must first be fully reawakened in the United States. But even if the president of the U.S. and his advisers were to move in this direction, wouldn't Congress stand in their way? The manner in which Congress, in May 1979, rejected the president's energy conservation plan suggested to European leaders that the most powerful Western nation had entered a phase of tragic demagogic rejection of cooperative action, by being unwilling to acknowledge the close interdependence of the Western economies, even in the face of the energy shortage.

Historians in the twenty-first century, however, will probably emphasize the similarities between the two sides of the Atlantic: the same mixture of hope and anxiety about nuclear power, the same heedlessness that since 1973 has prevented either side from tackling the oil problem (the government that can most easily be excused is Great Britain, which possesses a new, however temporary, source of oil in the North Sea).

*In percentages, the weights established for the currencies are: German mark, 32.98; French franc, 19.83; British pound sterling, 13.35; Dutch guilder, 10.51; Italian lira, 9.49; Belgian franc, 9.27; Danish crown, 3.06; Irish pound, 1.15; and Luxembourg franc, 0.35.

Not only have governments failed to recognize the consequences of the foreseeable exhaustion of oil resources, but they have behaved as if the available resources would, politically speaking, continue to be at the disposal of the West. It was the Iranian revolution that alerted the industrial nations to what would happen if a political upheaval were to occur in Saudi Arabia, which is not only a close partner of the United States but also furnished France with 36 percent of its supplies of oil in 1978. Since 1973 at least, the absurdity of allowing the automobile industry to remain at the heart of industrial development ought to have been obvious. Yet in 1979 nothing had changed in this regard, especially not in France where the auto industry was even being called upon to help rescue areas suffering economic crisis. No one has wished to recall the fantastic economic reconversion accomplished by the United States for the sake of victory during World War II, and yet the current threat to Western economies is of such magnitude as to justify the most drastic of reconversions.

But rather than take joint, or at least parallel, drastic actions, based on a shared vision of present dangers, the Western nations continue their industrial war. They have not even agreed on the stand to take regarding Japan, which has become the most aggressively "Western" of them all. The allies/adversaries relationship has always existed, but it has not brought about particularly dramatic results during the twenty-year period of general growth. For during a time of threatened production and employment, the "industrial world war" is surely not the solution to the enormous problems that the Western nations must face in common, or at least in a somewhat coordinated fashion, if only to make their citizens cognizant of the realities rather than shower them with myths. Take the case of steel: in the United States there is a tendency to search out the misdeeds of European competition, while in France there is often talk of a German-American effort to bring about the ruin of the French steel industry; but, as statistics show, it is the strength of Japanese competition that must be reckoned with.

The United States certainly must have the impression that it is often the target of conflicting criticisms from Europe and particularly from France. If American firms undertake investments on French soil, that's imperialism. If they take their investments to other countries, that's discrimination against France. If the dollar falters, that's irresponsible manipulation to favor American exports. If it strengthens, that's an attempt to weaken Europe by raising Europe's oil bill. But these contradictions are not entirely unfounded: most American investments in Europe have for quite some time been undertaken with European funds, loans on the Eurodollar market, or reinvestments by European subsidiaries of American companies. As a French expert summarized the changes that occurred in the seventies: "An overvalued fixed dollar, or the conquest of the world by American multinational corporations; an undervalued floating dollar, or a reconquest of the world by American exports."

Must the United States use its relative strength to try to crush European competition by commercial or legal means? A striking example is that of the aeronautics industry, not with respect to the Concorde, a case in which American refusal simply hid the real—French—causes of the commercial failure of the operation, but rather with respect to the Airbus, and twenty years earlier the Caravelle. The manner in which American domination over air traffic over the North Atlantic must be expanded was brought out, with great cynicism, in March 1979 by Michael E. Levine, vice-president of the Civil Aeronautics Bureau.[3]

The struggle on both sides of the Atlantic becomes particularly difficult when it is a question of saving businesses and jobs. The similarities of national interest in this respect are even greater than they were just a few years ago. Profits made from foreign investments allow survival of the parent enterprise, but foreign production brings the risk of unemployment to the parent enterprise. This is as basic a problem for Michelin as it is for Ford and explains the similarities in many trade union concerns as well as certain tensions between France and the United States.

These tensions have been somewhat relieved in the trade sector since the signing in Geneva, on April 12, 1979, of the new GATT (General Agreement on Tariffs and Trade) agreements, ending five and a half years of Tokyo Round negotiations. If complementary negotiations are successful and if the various parliaments authorize ratification of these agreements, gradual reductions in customs duties will take place over a period of eight years, starting January 1, 1980. These agreements seem to have satisfied both sides of the Atlantic, without the measures to be taken being as broad as those upon which the success of the Kennedy Round in 1967 was based. In addition, credit has to be given to the governments for opening up trade channels at a time when, because of the crisis, pressure is increasing to revert to a fair amount of protectionism—a protectionism that, contrary to its sacrosanct doctrine, the United States has never ceased to favor whenever the question has been one of protecting its domestic market but that it has vigorously opposed in the case of its agricultural exports to Europe.[4] The lay observer is apt to be quickly discouraged when trying to unravel the conflicting viewpoints both within the EEC and between Europe as a whole and the

United States. The only certainty is that each side shows an amazing nonacceptance of the other's point of view.

But who is the other? Here, as well as in other areas of political and economic reality, the U.S.-Europe tête-à-tête is gradually being undermined by the passive as well as active presence of other continents, including both the rich and the poor Third World countries. As a result, not only is there a greater complexity of problems, but trans-Atlantic differences and agreements bear less and less upon specifically "Western" problems and more and more upon policies toward other regions.

THE THIRD WORLD AND THE DECLINE OF THE U.S. MODEL IN EUROPE

With the changes in trans-Atlantic relations and the increasing focus on the Third World, the European view of the United States as a political and economic model is slowly disintegrating. Only the more formidable problems spawned by this situation are highlighted here.

In the Middle East, the United States, through Kissinger's and then Carter's initiatives, has played an active role in the search for a settlement, while the successive French governments have kept a critical distance with respect to these attempts and certainly have not taken an impartial stand regarding Israel and the Arab countries. But the separate peace between Israel and Egypt did not noticeably accelerate the global settlement in the Middle East, a settlement that French government declarations have always called for without ever proposing a practicable way to reach it. (See the essay by Duignan and Gann in this volume.)

Recent events in Iran are of a similar nature. Shortly after the fall of the shah's government, it became obvious to Americans that the U.S. government had been practicing blind politics (and, furthermore, completely disregarding analyses provided by American university experts). And this post facto American analysis closely resembled French views at the time of the final crisis of the Iranian regime.[5] But the French government gained nothing by facilitating the movements of the active refugee Ayatollah Khomeini in Neauphle-le-Château, near Paris. The French press evidenced a kind of *Schadenfreude* when faced with the American calamity, before discovering that it was just as much a French calamity, in the case of oil, of investments, and of capital goods export.

With respect to Africa, it is more difficult to know whether true differences exist. The European press most often finds itself expressing absurd contradictions: when the United States intervenes or threatens to intervene, it is proof of expansionism or at least of clumsiness; when the United States refuses to intervene or to threaten, it is proof of weakness and signals a policy of isolationist abdication. But when France intervenes, in Zaire for example, is it because of a desire to set itself apart from the United States, or does it indicate an unexpressed sharing of responsibilities with the United States? The second hypothesis may well be the most plausible, and in that case the failures of French policy in Africa are also American failures. In any event, it is clear that, more than Germany and even more than Great Britain, France plays an important role in Africa, even if its means of action remain limited. In May 1979 the new Franco-African conference at Kigali aroused great interest through the list of African participants alone (Benin, Burundi, Central African Republic, the Comoro Islands, the Congo, the Ivory Coast, Djibouti, Gabon, Upper Volta, Mali, Mauritius, Mauritania, Niger, Rwanda, Senegal, Seychelles, Chad, Togo, Zaire, with Guinea-Bissau, Liberia, and São-Tomé as observers); the limited results obtained remained a sign, however, of the uncertain nature of France's African policy. (See the essay by Gann and Duignan in this volume.)

Politically, but perhaps above all, economically speaking, the EEC, in its role as an active instrument, is more concerned than the United States is with the needs of the poorer Third World countries, especially in Africa. This is in part owing to French influence. It is not purely by chance that one of the two French members, Claude Cheysson, is responsible for the development and cooperation policy at the Commission for European Communities.[6] During recent international meetings, notably in Manila in May 1979, at the fifth U.N. Conference on Trade and Development, there continued to be a certain German-American agreement in the name of the sacred principles of free trade based on price fixing by the market (principles that the United States and West Germany carefully avoid applying to their own agriculture, for which prices are obviously not determined by the market).

The Lomé Agreement takes a completely different course. Signed in 1975 by the EEC and 55 African, Caribbean, and Pacific (ACP) nations, it gives priority to rural development, which accounts for about 45 percent of development aid. The most important innovation of the agreement, whose expanded renewal was negotiated in spring 1979, is clearly the mechanism to stabilize export profits (STABEX), designed to protect the ACP countries from abnormal income fluctuations resulting from unfortuitous weather or market variations. For instance, in July 1978 a STABEX intervention allowed the Senegalese government to save the peanut plantations after a drought by announcing that the losses would be compensated and by distributing aid that kept the peasants from changing their production habits or from taking refuge in the cities. In the case of sugar, Europe guarantees the ACP cane-producing countries what amounts to an indexing based on the prices reserved for European farmers. The guaranteed price is more than double the world price.

Relations between Europe and the ACP countries reflect the overall problem of the joint agricultural policy of the EEC vis-à-vis the rest of the world, a problem whose basis is generally not known in the United States. While the American export-import ratio is at 250 percent ($25 billion worth of agricultural exports versus $10 billion worth of imports), thus permitting American foreign policy to have recourse to a "food weapon," EEC's ratio is only 30 percent. This agricultural problem is in turn tied to the global trade balance of the EEC, which must import 75 percent of its raw materials and for which the Third World represents more than a third of its exports, or three times more than the American market.

Is Latin America part of the Third World? Latin America does not present the same types of problems as Africa, but it fully shares what we might call the intellectual and moral image, or the ideological image, of the Third World, especially because of important developments that occurred within the Catholic church during the sixties, developments that had much to do with showing up the flaws in the image of the United States.

In the forties and fifties Pope Pius XII had considered the defense against atheistic communism as essential. For him, then, the East-West conflict logically constituted the pivotal point of the international system, giving the United States the role of defender of basic values. Pope John XXIII, who succeeded him in 1958, published in July 1961 the encyclical *Mater et Magistra,* in which he said: "Perhaps the most important problem of our era is that of the relations among the economically developed political communities and the developing countries." On December 11, 1962, he opened the Second Vatican Council; and on April 12, 1963, shortly before his death, he published the encyclical *Pacem in Terris,* which denounces the "unjust domination of the least favored peoples." On December 7, 1965, his successor, Paul VI, presented the key conciliary document *Gaudium et spes,* which, in the chapter on economic and social life, reaffirms property rights, but recalls one of the sayings of Saint Thomas: "He who finds himself in extreme need has the right to obtain necessities from the wealth of another." The document also devotes a long, deeply evocative paragraph to the existence of the *latifundia,* "vast, even immense, rural holdings that are barely cultivated . . . while the majority of the population has no land of its own." In March 1967, the encyclical *Populorum Progressio* took up the same theme, adding a clear denunciation of liberal capitalism, producer of "an international imperialism of money."

The Polish pope John Paul II has definitely resumed the emphasis on religious liberty in communist countries, but it was not by chance that he made his first trip to the Latin American Bishops' Conference in Mexico in February 1979. His statements at Puebla echoed the concerns of the earlier popes whose names he bears. The North-South system he described puts the United States in a light completely different from that fostered by the East-West system of relations.

Such a development would have had only limited effects on trans-Atlantic relations if the economic crisis, from 1974 on, had not begun to undermine the positive image of the United States in Europe in yet another fashion. Indeed, until then, in the face of criticism from the left and from the extreme left, a good many Europeans accepted a dual American model. One model was political: not that the American democracy seemed perfect, but its advantages were obvious, in spite of and partly because of Watergate. Many people were more sensitive to the fearless way in which the U.S. press, and later Congress, carried out the inquiry against a president, than to the reprehensible acts of this head of state. But this exemplar is being badly marred by the apparent powerlessness of the American political system in the face of the economic crisis, as evidenced especially by the blockage in Congress of essential energy policies. Moreover, President Carter's hesitations and vacillations in the area of foreign policy present a distinctly less favorable image of the White House than existed in the days of President Nixon, unpopular in his own country, but greatly appreciated on the outside.

The United States also served as an economic model. Its prosperity seemed to justify the conception of liberalism as a harmonious confrontation of forces at the heart of a self-regulating market. This model is now decidedly tottery. Not that liberalism itself is less firmly implanted—far from it. For one thing, Marxism is faltering, in countries like France and Italy, less because of its economic interpretations than because of the political spectacle presented by all the countries whose governments claim kinship with Marxism. Furthermore, the consciousness of global interdependence and the need to export has become so strong that protectionism has become considerably less appealing—even in a country with protectionist traditions like France—than one might have expected at the beginning of the crisis. The explanation for the weakening of the American model in Europe is similar to that given for the general push to the left in Europe in 1945: that is, laissez-faire policies no longer seem acceptable, since it is a question of getting out of a difficult situation. The call for voluntaristic action will no doubt increase, though the motivations for it may well differ. In one country, action will be prompted by a liberal economy, in another, by a more socialistic statism, but the demand for a firm government policy of intervention will gain in intensity, contrary to the European image—truly or falsely conceived—of the American system.

Nevertheless, on both sides of the Atlantic, there exist the same hesitations and perplexities (and the same contradictions: although the crisis is perceived and millions of families are directly affected by unemployment or threats to their jobs, many millions more continue to live just as always, with the same needs and demands as before). These perplexities apply as much to domestic economic policy as they do to foreign policy, trapped as it is between economic constraints and the moral principles that are supposed to establish the superiority of the West over the nonpluralistic regimes of the East and the South. President Carter was strongly criticized in Europe for his hesitant and contradictory policies on foreign civil rights. But the lively European debate about the best course of action has only shown that no one has a rigorously defined program to propose. Iran is a case in point. Should one have pressured the shah to liberalize at the risk of losing power, or should one have foreseen his fall, inasmuch as one had decided not to accept any longer the criminal aspects of his regime? Should an Islamic regime, born of passion, and likewise evidencing so little respect for civil rights, have been allowed to develop?

But one unequivocal trans-Atlantic difference of opinion remains. The feeling persists in Europe that the United States has scarcely changed its stand since its 1954 intervention in Guatemala—namely, that it still tends to label "communistic" any movement that questions a dictatorial regime under U.S. protection, because that regime is providing the United States with economic advantage. As far as the eighties are concerned, it is this attitude above all, that Americans must be encouraged to alter.

RECOMMENDATIONS FOR THE EIGHTIES

Prediction-making, always a risky business, is particularly difficult, if not impossible, as we enter the eighties. Tomorrow the energy crisis could take a dramatic turn, with extremely different political fallouts depending on the countries involved, but it is not inconceivable that the oil-producing nations may begin to acknowledge global interdependence and decide to modulate their pressure; tomorrow a new war may break out in the Middle East, but—who knows?—the Israeli-Egyptian peace settlement may stimulate similar Arab-Israeli agreements; tomorrow the economic crisis may explode Europe, but it is just as probable that a broader consciousness of common dangers will give rise to a spirit of community and spur the creation of a true community.

In any case, there is a general recommendation that can unequivocally be made, and it is one I constantly propose to Europeans, especially my French compatriots: try as hard as possible to understand your trans-Atlantic partner intellectually. European ignorance and misunderstanding about the United States remain enormous. But America is no less ignorant and confused about the political, social, and psychological realities of the European countries. We might even say that European comprehension of the United States is increasing while American understanding of Europe is diminishing. This can be seen at every level. In American secondary schools, foreign-language instruction is being neglected at a time when English is becoming a major European language. In American universities, where some of the most knowledgeable persons on French, German, and Italian subjects are teaching, interest in concrete knowledge about European nations is clearly not on the rise; and this ignorance of facts is accentuated by linguistic ignorance, which is both the cause and the effect of course bibliographies and reading lists that include only English-language texts. The long-term harmful effects of this lack of interest and this ignorance—which are certainly not dissipated by the mass media—cannot be overestimated.

The second recommendation is similar and is aimed at allies on both sides of the Atlantic: you must become more aware not only of trans-Atlantic interdependence but of your joint dependence on the suppliers of raw materials, particularly, of course, the oil-producing nations. This awareness is rapidly increasing in the United States, thanks to the gasoline shortage, but has lagged in Europe, and especially in France, which is preoccupied with its real, but perhaps over-dramatized, dependence on the United States.

During the eighties, the United States will doubtless maintain its international obligations, for only a highly irresponsible administration would dare to abandon them—at the price of catastrophe on all sides. The most obvious obligation is the maintenance of U.S. troops on European soil; the entire defense system depends on it. The United States also has to respond to two seemingly contradictory European concerns: first, the furthering of détente with the USSR, particularly through arms control negotiations; and, second, the maintenance of at least a minimal sense of security in Europe by never negotiating any pact with the Soviets in which the United States makes its territory appear sacrosanct by designating the territory of its European allies as a theater of possible violent conflict between the two Great Powers. Such obligations are not only for the sake of Europe; the United States, too, needs both détente (which, from the economic angle, ensures that the USSR itself has no interest at all in aggravating the Western economic crisis) and a Western Europe that is solidly protected against any Soviet domination.

Contrary to what many Americans, particularly in the agricultural sector, believe, a politically and economically active European community is of definite advantage to the United States in its trans-Atlantic relations as well as in its rapport with other continents. The weakening of America's world image could be somewhat offset (if indeed the salvation of liberal governments truly has high priority among U.S. goals) and the Western world could gain greater organization and harmony, if reasonable negotiations of conflicts of interest in agriculture or in the monetary system were undertaken, in place of masked and primitive—that is, rather anarchistic—confrontations. And if it is truly American policy to favor the development of Europe as a community, the first step must be to convince the Europeans of this, for they are still traumatized by the all-too-obvious ulterior motives of Henry Kissinger's policy, which tended toward reconstituting American hegemony rather than toward establishing trans-Atlantic cooperation in the wake of John Kennedy's "two pillars" principle.

Interdependence must be rationalized and the sharing of tasks with respect to other continents must be organized. But first we must see an end to the type of dual hypocrisy that was particularly glaring in 1973–1974 during the Kissinger-Jobert controversy. The U.S. secretary of state had reproached Europe for remaining blind to all but regional interests and for avoiding responsibilities at the world level. The French foreign minister deplored the fact that Europe had been reduced by the two Great Powers to a virtual nonentity and demanded that Europe play a major role in world affairs. The fact is that Henry Kissinger, like his predecessors and his successors, had no real desire to see a coordinated Europe share in the difficult decisions being made in the Middle East or in Asia. He wanted the Europeans to support American actions but not to share in decision making. Basically, Michel Jobert was not displeased to let the United States carry the real responsibility for Israel's survival, for this would allow France to formulate, without much risk, its own policy toward the Arab states.

Europeans are right to complain of decisions made independently by the United States, which "consults" its allies by informing them at the last minute of decisions already made. But Europeans themselves must be ready to take on real responsibilities, including risky ones. The French certainly seem more willing to do this than the Germans, even though the French, enamored as ever with national prestige, play the roles of Sancho Panza and Don Quixote simultaneously, criticizing the government for every risky gesture. Europe is, however, changing, and we may hope for a greater unity of resolve and action, which the United States would be wrong to try to thwart.

A final recommendation is one that will perhaps be better heeded now than it would have been several years ago: the U.S. government should resolve to control and should succeed in controlling the activities of American firms abroad, especially in Europe. This idea was inconceivable until only recently because liberal noninterventionism was long regarded as sacred. But these days, the necessity, born out of the economic crisis, to gain control of both the domestic and the foreign economy will perhaps make us alive to the great utility of coordinated efforts, mutual limitations, and the establishment of structures that can restore politics to its true rank ahead of economics—but only if politics is properly defined in its highest sense: as all the means that a given community has at its disposal to orient and to master its future. Trans-Atlantic interdependence and similarities of situation are such that there are a fair number of trans-Atlantic problems to be overcome by Americans and Europeans acting in solidarity, once we admit that differences of interest and of situation justify the birth of a European community that has to organize and to take control of a future not necessarily identical with that of the United States.

NOTES

1. Chicago Council on Foreign Relations, *American Public Opinion and U.S. Foreign Policy*, ed. John E. Reilly (Chicago, 1979).

2. Refer to the well-documented analysis by Lothar Ruehl, "Die Nicht-entscheidung über die 'Neutronenwaffe': Ein Beispiel verfehlter Bündnispolitik," *Europa-Archiv* (March 10, 1979): 137–150. For a discussion of German-American problems as a whole, see Alex A. Vardamis, "German-American Military Fissures," *Foreign Policy*, Spring 1979, pp. 87–106.

3. Extracts published in *Le Monde*, March 25, 1979.

4. Cf. the highly critical article by Reinhard Rode, "Die Handelspolitik der USA in den Siebziger Jahren: ein freihändlerisch-protektionistisches Verwirrspiel?" *Politische Vierteljahreschrift*, October 1978, pp. 315–342.

5. Richard Cottam, "The United States and the Iran Revolution," *Foreign Policy*, Spring 1979, pp. 3–34.

6. Cf., for example, his article "L'Europe face au désordre alimentaire mondial," *Politique Internationale* 3 (Spring 1979): 55–66.

Soviet Union
Richard F. Staar

XXVI

Many problems will face the American president in dealing with his Kremlin counterpart during the 1980s. It is assumed that the Soviet collective leadership succeeding Brezhnev probably will continue to utilize such weapons of foreign policy as propaganda, information gathering, trade, and the projection of military power in the same manner as in the past. These instrumentalities will be orchestrated in varying combinations depending on their focus: the confrontational arena of Europe, the less developed countries especially in the Middle East and Africa, and the great power triangle of China–Japan–United States throughout East Asia.

THE SUCCESSION PROBLEM

The current leading Politburo group is comprised almost entirely of individuals who reached the top decision-making level because Stalin's terror machine had cleared the way for their advancement. They participated vigorously in denouncing their superiors from the relative safety of third- and fourth-echelon positions during the bloodletting of the mid-1930s.

One often assumes that others have motives similar to one's own. Such "mirror imaging" can be dangerous, however, when applied to Soviet leaders, whose world outlook has been formed under completely different conditions. Most of them never received a secondary education, having been selected for technical or political training at the college level with only an elementary school background. Many are semieducated, in the conventional sense of the word. Their learning has been narrowed by ideological blinders, and their advancement has depended on ruthless cunning.

The Soviet political system represents the product of Stalin's genius. No substantive change has occurred since the tyrant died in 1953; even though terror remains in suspension, its apparatus has never been dissolved. Somewhat reduced in size, the Gulag archipelago continues to exist as a reminder of the regime's coercive potentials. An "improvement" has been the widespread confinement of prominent dissidents to insane asylums.

Certain Western analysts express the hope that the new generation of Soviet leaders will be different. Such reasoning ignores the fact that those who will succeed the current gerontocracy were recruited into the party machine as local Komsomol (Communist Youth League) secretaries and are totally dedicated to the system. They remain narrow-minded and cynical in their opposition to governments, even communist-ruled ones, that are not under USSR influence. This mentality can be summed up by Lenin's slogan: *kto kogo?* or "Who [will eliminate] whom?"

The immediate succession to Brezhnev probably will take the form of a collective leadership at first. One of the great weaknesses of the Soviet system is that no means exist for any constitutional transfer of power or for the removal of overaged or otherwise disqualified leaders except by conspiracy. Leaders have never even designated successors, and Brezhnev seems determined to prevent any strong replacement from rising by his side. In the past, an apparent successor to the leader has been subject to intrigue by rivals or has been impatient for the mantle. The most recent example was Brezhnev himself, who organized a successful plot against Khrushchev. The most likely next party leader is Konstantin U. Chernenko (born 1911), who became a Central Committee secretary, candidate, and then full Politburo member within a period of two years. A protégé of the general secretary, he accompanied him to the summit meeting with President Carter at Vienna, June 15–18, 1979.

It is most likely that the future succession will consist of two phases. The first transition crisis occurs when the leader is replaced; the second, and more pervasive one, when the new incumbent attempts to affirm his new position and raise himself from primus inter pares to supremacy. The secret police (KGB) and/or the professional military will probably become involved with the succession crisis, especially its second phase, as has happened in the past.

In any event, the period of protracted struggle during an interregnum undoubtedly will weaken the authority of Soviet leaders and their ability to make decisions. Such a period of vulnerability has never been exploited by the United States, although a prime opportunity apparently existed after Stalin's death. Secret police chief Lavrenty P. Beria allegedly proposed to the Politburo that it offer reunification of Germany to the West in return for a commitment not to exploit the Kremlin's succession crisis.

The new Soviet leadership during the 1980s will face many problems: political, economic, structural, social, and cultural. The current and anticipated decline in the rate of industrial growth, a shortage of labor reserves, and an incipient fuel crisis may necessitate a reduction in investments for consumer goods and agriculture. Bureaucratic inefficiency, corruption, favoritism, unequal privileges, and indiscipline permeate the government/party apparatus, with little prospect for improvement. Restive ethnic minorities, Great Russian chauvinism as well as intellectual dissidence, the demographic shift in favor of Central Asian nationalities, and troubles within the client states of Eastern Europe should continue to complicate internal affairs during the post-Brezhnev transitional period.

FOREIGN PROPAGANDA

Despite these domestic or intra-Bloc difficulties, Soviet propaganda almost certainly will continue to glorify alleged USSR achievements while denigrating the West in general and the United States in particular. Magnifying and distributing this message on a worldwide basis are a plethora of international communist front organizations. Although subsidized and controlled by the USSR, they appear to be less obvious tools of Moscow than indigenous communist parties.

These front organizations seldom deviate from the objectives of Soviet foreign policy. They produce and disseminate printed propaganda, organize rallies against the neutron bomb or whatever else the Kremlin happens to oppose, and convince the politically naive to support "national liberation" movements on a worldwide basis. Such are the activities of the so-called World Peace Council, as well as international federations of youth, journalists, women, scientific workers, lawyers, and resistance fighters, to mention a few. Supplementing these groups, many leftist organizations not controlled by the USSR more or less closely follow the Soviet line.

As many front organizations have lost effectiveness, additional innovative techniques have been devised to influence American public opinion, including staged opportunities for elite interaction. Pugwash international conferences follow the line that "science must be used only for the good of mankind and never for its destruction," which benefits Soviet propaganda. While the session at Munich in 1978 advocated a ban on the neutron bomb and cruise missile, it forgot to mention the Backfire bomber or the SS-20 short-range mobile nuclear missile being deployed in East Germany and capable of reaching any Western European target.

Apart from fronts and conferences at the elite level, USSR foreign propaganda attacking the United States floods the world via the printed word and radio. A major theme is the "anti-imperialist struggle." Defensive alliances like the North Atlantic Treaty Organization (NATO) and cooperative regional organizations such as the European Economic Community are regularly denounced, while Soviet proposals for security systems in Europe and Asia are held up as models of dedication to peace.

During 1979, the USSR devoted approximately two thousand hours per week to broadcasting in 83 foreign languages over Radio Moscow alone. Another station called Radio Peace and Progress, although it uses Radio Moscow transmitters, claims to be independent and assumes an even more strident tone. Many clandestine stations are operated by exiled communist party leaders from locations in the USSR and Eastern Europe. In addition, Freiheitssender 904 and Deutscher Soldatensender are directed at the West German armed forces and NATO.

Two government press agencies, Tass and Novosti, disseminate propaganda through correspondents in more than one hundred foreign countries. They skillfully utilize emotional themes, and their calls for peace often strike a responsive chord throughout the world. Communism as the "wave of the future" and USSR leadership in all fields of endeavor are contrasted with the political and economic decline of the United States, whose dollar again was devalued arbitrarily in 1979 by the Soviet government to less than 65 kopeks.

As part of the campaign to discredit the United States, the neutron bomb was described as "the ultimate capitalist weapon, one that killed people but left property intact." Radio Moscow described the Aldo Moro kidnapping and murder in Italy as the work of the Central Intelligence Agency (CIA). Forgeries of an alleged United States Information Agency press release containing a bogus speech by President Carter and even reproductions of a falsified U.S. Army field manual have been circulated. Such propaganda campaigns, estimated to cost over $2 billion per year, portray the American masses opposing preparations by the "military industrial complex" for an attack on the Soviet Union.

INFORMATION GATHERING

Soviet espionage involves professionals, frequently utilizing journalism as a cover; hence, propaganda overlaps with clandestine activities.

Hundreds of Soviet newsmen assigned to foreign posts are in reality intelligence officers who report directly to their own headquarters in Moscow. In addition, it is estimated that at least half of all USSR and Bloc officials abroad work either for the KGB or the GRU, the general intelligence agency and its military counterpart, respectively. To the more than 3,000 Soviet and East European officials (that is, about 1,500 spies) attached to embassies in Washington, D.C., and consulates elsewhere in the United States or the United Nations in New York must be added those wives who also work as agents. This does not include the 65,000 visitors each year from the Bloc, some of whom certainly have intelligence assignments.

The First Directorate at KGB headquarters in Moscow is responsible for all foreign intelligence, including "illegals" (those abroad under deep cover with no apparent USSR connections). In the latter category are those who engage in terrorism, kidnapping, and even assassination of anti-Soviet exiles and defectors. The United States, one of the most open societies in the world, is also the target of massive Soviet industrial espionage. Motives include breaking the already much eroded Western strategic embargo and obtaining advanced technology gratis.

A fire in the American embassy at Moscow in August 1977 led indirectly to discovery in a chimney of sophisticated electronics gear, that could have been placed there before the U.S. government first leased the building in 1952. Surprisingly, the equipment had functioned undisturbed even though at least forty microphones were previously found concealed in walls throughout the embassy. Still publicly unexplained is the reason for low-intensity microwaves beamed at the compound since the early 1960s by Soviet authorities, a practice never admitted, discontinued for three months bracketing the Vienna summit and resumed in mid-July 1979.

American citizens have been recruited by the KGB and GRU in Moscow, other foreign cities, and inside the United States itself. Recent cases included that of a CIA watch officer who stole the manual for the KH-11 reconnaissance satellite and then sold it to a Soviet agent in Athens. Thousands of classified documents found their way to the USSR via an employee who operated a teletype-encoding machine for communication between his private company, CIA headquarters, and the National Security Agency. Moscow thus obtained information on the transmission of intelligence data between American ground stations and satellites. In April 1979 two USSR citizens working at the United Nations in New York, sentenced to prison for buying what they thought was genuine data on the F-14 fighter and antisubmarine warfare, were exchanged for five Soviet dissidents (none of whom had engaged in espionage on behalf of the United States).

High-resolution cameras, mounted on TU-20 long-range reconnaissance aircraft, photograph American military installations overseas. Soviet warships, oceangoing tugs, survey vessels, and trawlers, with electronic gear that includes jamming equipment, remain on permanent station near U.S. naval bases and in the vicinity of fleet operations. Data on defense resources, equipment, operational routines, and possible intentions are obtained by means of orbiting COSMOS satellites, about thirty of which are launched each year at a cost of more than one billion dollars. In Moscow, this information is analyzed and integrated with open materials from thousands of unclassified publications legally obtained from U.S. agencies under the Freedom of Information Act or by purchase from the U.S. Government Printing Office. Other sources include scientific papers picked up at conferences, the American press, journals and books.

Whether the product of this vast information-gathering effort gives Kremlin decision makers an accurate picture of the United States is an important question, the answer to which may be negative. Conversations with several U.S. senators who visited Moscow in 1979 indicated that Politburo members have an ideologically distorted view of basic American governmental processes. This corroborates a statement by former CIA inspector general Lyman B. Kirkpatrick, Jr., who suggested that intelligence information only serves "even more to feed traditional Russian paranoia about everything foreign." Faulty perceptions by USSR decision makers may also be based on slanted reports from their own intelligence apparatus. Deputy CIA director Frank D. Carlucci, during a recent address in San Francisco, while admitting KGB superiority in resources and ability to operate with fewer restraints, claimed that Soviet intelligence remains behind that of America technologically. He also noted that intelligence, in many cases, results in bad news and that nobody would like to be the bearer of such information to the Kremlin. This psychological factor indeed may account in part for the Soviet leaders' distorted picture of the United States.

FOREIGN TRADE

Soviet leaders have always viewed foreign trade as an instrument of economic warfare. To coordinate the economies of its satellites, the USSR has strengthened the Council for Mutual Economic Assistance, which now includes six European members plus Mongolia, Cuba, and Vietnam. Trade with this Bloc constitutes almost three-fifths of the Soviet total. The combined resources of these ten states could provide the basis for autarky, and that may indeed have been Stalin's objective. The tendency, however, has been toward greater dependence on imports from the West. East Bloc indebtedness to the West was $6.5 billion in 1970, about $18 billion four years later, and at the end of 1976 already $40 billion. As of 1979, the Bloc owed the industrialized West more than $60 billion in long- and short-term credits that had been borrowed to finance imports. One-third of that amount comprised loans to the USSR. It is questionable whether such an accumulation of debt is in the national interest of noncommunist Western countries, because it could make economic hostages of business firms as well as official and quasi-official lending agencies.

The United States ranks only sixth in volume (after the Federal Republic of Germany, Japan, Finland, Italy, and France) among noncommunist states in volume of trade with the USSR. One of the reasons for this low level of exchange has been the Jackson-Vanik amendment to the U.S. Trade Act. It prohibited most-favored-nation (MFN) treatment of governments with nonmarket economies that place restrictions on emigration of their own citizens. The president of the United States has authority under this January 1975 legislation to waive provisions of the amendment if he establishes that liberal emigration policies exist.

Although Moscow reacted initially by renouncing its trade agreement with Washington and cracking down on those Soviet citizens who had applied for passports to leave the country, during 1978 it allowed nearly 29,000 Jews to emigrate (approximately 50,000 is the prediction for 1979) in comparison with less than half that number in 1975 (see Table 1). Following oral assurances from the USSR that increased emigration will continue, it has been speculated that an addendum may be added to the next export import bank act that would eliminate

TABLE 1

Emigration from the USSR

Year	Visa to Israel	Direct to U.S.	Direct to West Germany	Total
1973	34,818	758	4,400	39,976
1974	20,376	1,029	6,300	27,705
1975	13,721	1,162	5,800	20,683
1976	14,262	2,574	9,600	26,436
1977	16,738	2,047	9,200	27,985
1978	28,864	1,709	8,500	39,073

Source: Commission on Security and Cooperation in Europe, cited in Susan P. Woodard, "Most Favored Nation Status: Trade with Communist Countries," *Backgrounder*, May 7, 1979, p. 9.

Note: Even if the average monthly rate of 4,000 Jewish emigrants is maintained throughout 1979, the annual total will fall short of the 60,000 discussed in the course of the Jackson-Vanik amendment debate.

emigration requirements from the 1975 Trade Act and change congressional review of MFN status from once a year to once every five years. Furthermore, restrictions on the amount of Export-Import Bank credits for countries with nonmarket economies also may be relaxed.

Despite restrictions, including new provisions for licensing exports to the Soviet Union of all oil and gas-drilling technology by the U.S. government after August 1, 1978, not a single license application has been denied since then. The following month, Dresser Industries of Dallas received approval for a $144 million contract to build a plant north of the Caspian Sea that will produce 100,000 high-quality oil-drilling bits per year. These are extremely difficult to buy outside the United States because other countries have not yet mastered the technology. The package includes computer-controlled electron beam-welding equipment of military significance.

Western technology has made and continues to make substantial contributions to USSR industries producing chemicals, automobiles and trucks, oil-drilling equipment, and computers. About 40 American companies contributed almost one-third of the equipment for the Kama River truck plant. Located about 600 miles east of Moscow, it currently manufactures 15- to 35-ton trucks and before 1982 should achieve its full capacity of 150,000 units per year. The best of these go to the armed forces. Engines produced there are mounted on Soviet armored personnel carriers and assault vehicles.

Only in the electronics field have more stringent U.S. controls been applied in the past because of its undisputed military usefulness. The USSR plans to spend about $18 billion between 1976 and 1980 on this industry in order to compensate for the current five-to-ten-year lag in the development of computer hard- and software. Because of restrictions by the Coordinating Committee of Export Controls in Paris, the Soviet Union has managed to purchase only about 300 computers from the West over the past decade.

The USSR is about to enter the 1980s with an incipient energy crisis, especially because it has provided Eastern Europe in the past with oil and gas at subsidized rates for political reasons. There have been reports of power shortages recently in Soviet industry. In order to alleviate this situation, the USSR needs Western technology and reportedly has strong allies in Washington who argue for dropping all controls on the export of oil and natural gas know-how. These U.S. government officials apparently believe that increased energy production will reduce Soviet pressure on supplies in other parts of the world. In December 1978, several hundred American businessmen negotiated in Moscow about 28 new joint projects in the energy field, valued at more than $10 billion.

If this trend continues, one can anticipate even larger USSR deficit balances in trade with the United States than have occurred over the past seven years (see Table 2). United States agricultural exports to the Soviet Union of corn, wheat, and soybeans accounted for $1.7 billion in value during 1978 alone, which approximated the Soviet deficit.

Although this total may drop, depending on the USSR harvests, Moscow signed a five-year commitment to purchase a minimum of six to eight million tons of wheat and corn per annum beginning in October 1976. Higher amounts may be bought with further U.S. government agreement. This indeed occurred during fiscal 1977–78 and 1978–79 when about fifteen million tons were shipped each year to the Soviet Union. With the predicted winter wheat shortfall, USSR imports could double. A policy question arises regarding future deliveries on such a large scale, which in effect allow the Russians to concentrate on military buildup rather than agriculture and consumer goods.

Despite what happened to an International Harvester company representative (dragged from his car, interrogated by the KGB in prison over a two-week period, charged with currency violations, sentenced to prison, and then allowed to leave the country), none of the other 25 American corporate representatives with offices in Moscow have been withdrawn from the Soviet Union. The U.S.-USSR Trade and Economic Council now has 260 American member companies, which pay a minimum of $1,000 per annum in dues for translation and other services when their representatives are in Moscow to negotiate agreements. The Soviets charge super-capitalist fees and rents; so it costs an average of $0.5 million each year to maintain a single office in Moscow.

U.S.-Soviet deals have included a chemical complex in Odessa; gear-grinding equipment for production of armored vehicles; precision

TABLE 2

United States Trade with the USSR (millions of dollars)

Year	Turnover	Export (to USSR)	Import (from USSR)	Balance (for USSR)
1972	642,055	546,614	95,441	–451,173
1973	1,400,844	1,187,098	213,746	–973,352
1974	957,000	607,000	350,000	–257,000
1975	2,087,000	1,833,000	254,000	–1,579,000
1976	2,526,550	2,305,930	220,620	–2,085,310
1977	1,857,820	1,623,480	234,340	–1,389,140
1978	2,789,410	2,249,020	540,390	–1,708,630
Totals	12,260,679	10,352,142	1,908,537	–8,443,605

Source: Bureau of East-West Trade, U.S. Department of Commerce.

grinding machines that reportedly facilitated the production of multiple independently targetable reentry vehicles (MIRV); wide-bodied jet aircraft technology, resulting from "whipsaw" negotiating tactics vis-à-vis competing American companies; and high-speed electronic computers. It should also be mentioned that several thousand graduate students from the USSR and Eastern Europe have received technical training in the United States.

Brezhnev explained the rationale behind the foregoing in a secret briefing to East European leaders at the height of détente. An excerpt from the speech was reported on September 17, 1973, by the *New York Times*:

> To the Soviet Union, the policy of accommodation does represent a tactical policy shift over the next 15 or so years. The Soviet Union intends to pursue accords with the West and at the same time build up its own economic and military strength.
>
> At the end of this period, in the middle 1980's, the strength of the Soviet Union will have increased to the point at which we, instead of relying on accords, could establish an independent, superior position in dealing with the West.

This, of course, implies that USSR armed forces will be used as an instrument of foreign policy.

MILITARY STRATEGY

The rapid military buildup, as well as projection of power also via surrogates, has played an important role in Soviet relations with the United States. Over the past decade, USSR military expenditures for strategic offensive weapons have totaled about $150 billion in real terms, or three times that of the United States. According to a 1979 CIA study, during the preceding calendar year the Soviet Union allocated $146 billion for military purposes, while the United States defense budget was $102 billion. The CIA predicts that this long-range growth trend will continue into the 1980s.

The USSR has expanded its arsenal of strategic nuclear forces, except for bombers, steadily over the past decade. Meanwhile, the United States maintained the same numbers and thus dropped behind in ICBMs and submarine-launched ballistic missiles. It should be noted that the Soviets have developed a cold-launch, pop-up technique that allows a reload and refire capability. In addition, Soviet ICBMs are located outside silos and are not counted by SALT II. They may number several thousand and can be fired directly from their canisters. America still maintains a comfortable lead in intercontinental bombers and nuclear warheads (see Table 3), although the U.S. advantage in the last category has narrowed since 1963 when it was 4,300 to 1,300 or more than three to one.

During a commencement address at the U.S. Naval Academy on May 30, 1979, Defense Secretary Harold Brown declared that the USSR in 1962–1963 embarked on "a policy of building forces for a preemptive attack against U.S. intercontinental ballistic missiles." He predicted that by the early 1980s, the new SS-18 and SS-19 would provide the Soviet Union the means to destroy "with high assurance" most American land-based ICBMs. According to Brown, "in the past decade the Soviets have added over 1,000 strategic missiles to their inventory and increased the number of deliverable warheads threefold." By the late 1960s, "more

TABLE 3

Key Measures of U.S.-Soviet Military Balance in 1979

Category	United States	Soviet Union	Soviet Advantage(X)
Strategic			
ICBMs (with MIRVs)	1,054 (550)	1,398 (608)	1.3X
SLBMs (with MIRVs)	656 (496)	950 (144)	1.4X
Heavy bombers (excluding Backfire)	573	156	-3.7X
Ballistic missile submarines	41	90	2.2X
Total throw weight	7.8 mil. lb.	14.7 mil. lb.	1.9X
Total megatonnage	2,887 mt.	8,352 mt.	2.9X
Total warheads	8,526	6,132	-1,4X
Interceptors	309	3,200	10.0X
SAMs	36	10,000	278.0X
Ground forces			
Divisions	16 (+3 USMC)	169	10.0X
Tanks	10,500	53,000	5.0X
Artillery	17,500	40,700	2.3X
Air forces			
Medium bombers	66	761	11.5X
Fighter and attack aircraft	3,400	4,690	1.4X
Air defense radar	59	7,000	119.0X
Transports	936	1,305	1.4X
Naval forces			
Active fleet	398	954	2.4X
Carriers	12	3	-4.0X
Naval and marine aircraft	1,464	1,310	-1.1X
Attack submarines	77	270	3.5X

Sources: *Aviation Week & Space Technology,* May 14, 1979, p. 14; U.S. Department of State, *Salt II Agreement* (Washington, D.C., June 18, 1979), p. 49, for figures released by the USSR only on ICBMs, SLBMs, and MIRVs.

Note: Among these twenty indices of military power, the United States has an advantage in only four.

than 200 SS-9's were almost surely targeted against the 100 Minuteman launch control complexes, two missiles to a complex for reliability." The secretary of defense also stated that "the Soviets continue with a policy of building forces that could be used in a preemptive counterforce mode. In particular, the new SS-18 missile, with ten warheads, has the accuracy to destroy most of the American Minuteman missiles in their underground silos."

The danger, of course, is that the USSR in continuing this drive toward overwhelming superiority will place one element of the U.S. strategic triad, the land-based ICBM force, under immediate threat with or without future strategic arms limitation treaties. SALT I in 1972 did not cause any significant pause or restraint on the part of Moscow. Soviet concepts and attitudes differ from those of American strategic thinkers in several critically important ways: belief in a USSR victory and survival after a nuclear war, preparation for such a conflict, surprise attack scenarios, targeting, and input from all command levels. Soviet leaders have never subscribed to the U.S. doctrine of limited war. They do not conceal the objective of total destruction of an enemy's military potential in the journal or monograph literature intended for officers of their own armed forces. On the other hand, when given a forum in the United States, two specialists from the U.S.A. Institute in Moscow claimed that military power does not represent a decisive factor in international relations, strengthening Soviet defense capabilities has no relationship to political intentions, détente has not developed to the extent where they could provide the American reader with statistics on USSR military power, and the "Soviet Union is opposed to any idea of its own strategic superiority" (*Fortune*, February 26, 1979). In reply, former U.S. Arms Control and Disarmament Agency director Fred Charles Iklé, whose own article had precipitated this response, mentioned American proposals for larger strategic arms reductions in November 1974 by President Ford and again in March 1977 by President Carter, both of which were turned down by Moscow.

The SALT II agreement, signed on June 18, 1979, in Vienna limits both sides to a total of 2,400 strategic vehicles through 1981, subsequently dropping to 2,250 each. Since the USSR has 2,504 already, it would dismantle but not necessarily destroy 254 missiles or bombers, whereas the United States will disassemble 33 vehicles since it is only that much above the lower ceiling. However, even with the go-ahead on MX (mobile experimental), the United States could not add this new light missile to the inventory on a replacement basis until after expiration of the treaty on December 31, 1985. Apart from Soviet superiority in missile throw weight, credible verification remains the most critical problem.

The 1972 SALT I agreement already stipulated that neither party would interfere with the other side's national technical means for verification, which includes ground-based sensors and reconnaissance satellites. In July 1978 the USSR conducted an SS-18 test, with much of the missile telemetry transmitted in code, thus violating this commitment. There was a similar occurrence six months later during the test-firing of another SS-18. Moscow did not reply to the protests from Washington. In December at Geneva, Foreign Minister Gromyko verbally assured Secretary of State Vance that the USSR would not encode any missile test data that would hinder American verification of a new accord, presumably meaning SALT II.

Early in 1979, Defense Secretary Brown revealed during an interview that the USSR is spending two and one-half to three times more than the United States on strategic capabilities. The Defense Department's annual posture statement released about the same time indicated that the Soviet Union had begun to surpass the United States in strategic capabilities, a process that SALT II codifies rather than stops. The clearest example of this trend is the SS-18 heavy missile, now numbering almost 200, each equipped with ten MIRVs. During a test in December 1978, the SS-18 had an altered "bus" that could carry twelve or even fourteen warheads rather than the ten later specified in the June 18, 1979 treaty.

Under the SALT II agreement, the Soviet Union will be allowed to produce 308 of these heavy missiles, which have achieved an accuracy between 0.15 and 0.2 of a nautical mile CEP (circular error probable). This would amount to over 3,000 warheads, two of which could be aimed at every American ICBM silo and one each at several hundred other U.S. military targets. That would still leave a large Soviet arsenal of SS-18 warheads in reserve, not to mention such strategic weapons systems as missile-launching submarines. The United States is prohibited from developing any heavy missile under the new treaty.

Evaluation of SALT II must rest on whether the agreement enhances U.S. security and in turn increases world stability. The fact that Soviet delivery vehicles will decline in number during the forthcoming treaty period may not represent the most significant development. Other indices of strategic power reveal the following disparities projected for 1985: three times more USSR warheads (a threefold increase for the United States); growth in Soviet throw weight by one-half (America, one-eighth); a tenfold rise in USSR capability to destroy hardened missile silos (U.S. capacity will quadruple only if cruise missiles are deployed after 1981). It should be noted that neither side will reduce budgets for strategic forces.

Russian leaders fully comprehend the destructiveness of nuclear war.

That is why they continue demanding of their people the sacrifices required to expand military power and fund a civil defense program ten times that of the United States. This probably does not mean that the Soviets will attack when they have achieved a "correlation of forces" to their advantage. However, an overwhelming superiority would allow them to blackmail the West and perhaps obtain their objectives without a mutually destructive nuclear exchange. The potential for massive cheating also could lead to a Soviet "breakout"* that might result in political capitulation by the West.

A buildup of USSR conventional arms also has taken place, roughly since the 1968 invasion of Czechoslovakia, throughout Warsaw Pact territory facing NATO. In terms of general purpose forces, the Soviet Union and its allies in the northern tier alone (East Germany, Poland, Czechoslovakia) have 962,000 ground troops (compared with 791,000 allied personnel in West Germany, Belgium, the Netherlands, and Luxembourg), some 16,000 operational main battle tanks (against 6,000 in these four NATO states), and 3,000 tactical aircraft (opposed to 1,300). The United States would be forced to transport its reserves across the Atlantic, some by air but most by sea, with the Soviet base in Cuba threatening its underbelly, whereas only 500 miles separate the USSR from NATO Europe.

Negotiations on a mutual and balanced force reduction agreement have been under way since November 1973 in Vienna. According to John Lehman, former U.S. Arms Control and Disarmament Agency deputy director, Soviet objectives in these talks have included maintenance of the existing advantageous relationship between the armed forces of East and West; contributing to the climate of détente; and the hope for a reduction of American troops as well as U.S. influence in Europe.

After more than two and one-half years of talks, in June 1976 the Warsaw Pact released figures claiming that it had only 805,000 ground personnel in the area under negotiation—about 155,000 below NATO estimates. Since the American enhanced radiation weapon (mistakenly called a neutron bomb) would have provided a strong defense against tanks, the USSR moved to stop the weapon's deployment in Western Europe. With this purpose, Brezhnev sent threatening letters to all NATO heads of government. Subsequently, in April 1978, President Carter announced postponement of the deployment, but the Soviets

---

*If the USSR covertly develops and deploys significantly more strategic military power than allowed by SALT II, some analysts conclude that such a breakout would be revealed at a critical time during a confrontation. This could radically change the correlation of forces and correspondingly alter American perceptions of the strategic situation.

considered the decision unsatisfactory and officially announced this in a Tass communiqué.

Soviet agreement two months later to the NATO proposal that each side limit its ground forces to 700,000 plus 200,000 air force personnel appears meaningless in the view of the Warsaw Pact contention that it has 155,000 fewer troops than Western estimates. Acceptance of the parity principle by the East must remain suspect under these circumstances. Moscow probably hoped that its ostensibly forthcoming attitude would slow down NATO's long-term defense program, which will cost some $80 billion over the next fifteen years.

THE THIRD WORLD

In contrast with the situation in divided Europe, the Third World remains in a state of flux. Developments there seemingly favor the Soviet Union, at least for the near future. Although few of the postcolonial regimes throughout Asia and Africa have ruling communist parties, some proclaim themselves to be Marxist-Leninist. Others have chosen the "noncapitalist" path of economic development, even though its results have been disappointing. The enormous expansion of the USSR merchant marine and navy is designed to expand trade with the Third World (and curtail that of the United States), bring in hard currency, facilitate penetration of foreign markets, and yield intelligence data.

Much of what the Soviet Union has been doing in Africa also appears to be related directly to its military strategy. Any global projection of power requires overseas bases, access to friendly ports, and ultimately control over some of the world's maritime choke points. The setback in Somalia, where USSR advisers were expelled and the friendship treaty abrogated in November 1977, has been more than compensated by a strengthening of influence in Angola, Mozambique, and most recently Ethiopia. Moscow had decided that Ethiopia is of more politico-strategic importance than Somalia. In addition, more than 50,000 Cuban civilian and military surrogates are stationed in about sixteen African or Middle Eastern countries. The so-called national liberation movements attempting to seize power in Zimbabwe-Rhodesia and South West Africa (Namibia) are supported by the Soviet Union, as well as by its East European client states.

Egypt preceded Somalia in breaking its friendship treaty with the USSR in March 1976, and three years later it signed a peace treaty with

Israel. This action placed President Sadat on a collision course with the Palestine Liberation Organization (PLO), which has the support of the Soviets. The PLO and Syria, Iraq, and Libya are all recipients of arms from Moscow and the East European regimes. Sixteen members of the Arab League voted to break diplomatic relations with and levy economic sanctions against Egypt.

Since the ouster of Mrs. Indira Gandhi, the new government of India has seemed less enthusiastic about the Soviet Union. American influence in India appears to have increased, especially after the coup in Afghanistan, which brought that former buffer state under the control of a pro-Moscow communist regime. Russian support for the recent Vietnamese occupation of Cambodia also may have given Delhi second thoughts about its relations with Moscow. The article in *Pravda* on June 1, 1979, warning Pakistan that the USSR would not stand by indifferently if war broke out with Afghanistan, could have increased India's distrust of the Soviet Union.

In Latin America, apart from a $2 billion annual subsidy for its protégé Cuba, the USSR has fostered economic relations with many noncommunist states. Under an agreement with the Soviet Union, for example, Caracas delivers 20,000 barrels of crude oil a day to Havana. The May 1979 visit by Castro to Mexico included negotiations for petroleum that, if successful, will reduce Moscow's burden. Credits of $700 million over a twenty-year period at 2.5 percent interest to the military dictatorship in Peru is yet another example of how the USSR will sacrifice a local communist party if it can gain influence with the regime in power. By contrast, the United States during 1978 provided to all of Latin America just under 6 percent ($384.6 million) from its total economic aid of $6.5 billion distributed.

China is also a less developed country and, by its own definition, belongs to that category. It clashes ideologically with the USSR, especially in regard to Mao Tse-tung's theory of the three worlds. The so-called hegemonic powers, the Soviet Union and the United States, constitute the first world; developed countries of Australasia, Canada, Europe, and Japan the second; and the less developed states throughout Africa, Asia, and Latin America the third. What Peking would like to see is an alliance between the second and third groups against the first. This theory was endorsed by Chairman Hua Kuo-feng at the party congress in August 1977.

The pragmatic Chinese leadership has modified this theory, perhaps as a tactical maneuver, and accepted a de facto entente with the United States against the Soviet Union. This radical change in policy occurred after American negotiators had accepted all three preconditions demanded by the People's Republic of China (PRC) before relations were normalized on March 1, 1979. These included unilateral abrogation of the U.S.-Taiwan defense treaty. It is of interest to note that Peking has given official notice that the Soviet-PRC treaty signed in 1950 will not be extended automatically for another five years.

Claiming to know the Soviet Union much better than does the United States, the Chinese communists assert that the USSR hopes to become able to strangle Western Europe economically by establishing its control over Middle Eastern oil. This might be achieved through a flanking movement that would include the following: a pro-Soviet regime for Iran in the near future; influence through arms shipments to Iraq and Syria; consolidation of Soviet positions at the Horn of Africa, in South Yemen, and Ethiopia; and control of the large-tanker route around Africa through influence in Mozambique and Angola.

There also appears to be some correlation between the time that certain of the Soviet friendship treaties had been signed (see Table 4) and the outbreak of war. Examples include India's invasion of Pakistan on December 4, 1971; the Ethiopian attack against the Ogaden on December 27, 1978; Vietnam's occupation of Cambodia which started on December 25, 1978; and the cycle of aggressive warfare throughout many parts of southern Africa.

The big Soviet prize in Africa was Ethiopia, to which 10,000 Cubans were transported by Soviet aircraft from Angola and another 15,000 directly from Cuba itself. An additional 10,000 "advisers" arrived from the USSR, Czechoslovakia, East Germany, Hungary, and South Yemen (mostly transferred East Germans). Military equipment and supplies were airlifted by Soviet AN-22 transport planes. This $2 billion in assistance enabled the regime of Lt. Col. Mengistu Haile Mariam, who

TABLE 4

Soviet Friendship Treaties in the Third World

Country	Date signed	Scheduled duration (years)	Abrogated
China	February 14, 1950	30	April 3, 1979
Egypt	May 27, 1971	15	March 14, 1976
India	August 9, 1971	20	
Iraq	April 9, 1972	15	
Somalia	July 11, 1974	20	November 13, 1977
Angola	October 8, 1976	20	
Mozambique	March 31, 1977	20	
Vietnam	November 3, 1978	25	
Ethiopia	November 20, 1978	20	
Afghanistan	December 5, 1978	20	

had seized power in a coup d'etat, to defeat Somalia throughout the Ogaden area and suppress Eritrean insurgents. It also gave USSR military officers an opportunity to gain actual combat experience.

All of these current and possible future developments may provide the USSR armed forces with the potential capability for naval interdiction of operations in the Red Sea and across the Indian Ocean. One of the targets, of course, is South Africa, already cut off from Iranian oil. If Zimbabwe-Rhodesia should fall to the guerrilla front, South Africa would be completely surrounded by hostile states.

POLICY RECOMMENDATIONS

Actions in Washington should be predicated on the clear understanding that future Soviet leaders will continue to differ considerably in both outlook and attitude from their American counterparts. Subterfuge, dissembling, and outright dishonesty cannot be explained away in terms of USSR suspicions or fear of U.S. strategic power, which in fact has been declining since 1956 when President Eisenhower refused to support Britain and France during the Suez crisis and has continued to deteriorate during subsequent administrations. Rather, these characteristics are deeply imbedded in the psychological makeup of Soviet leaders, whose conspiratorial mentality was molded by the Bolshevik Revolution, Leninist neo-Machiavellianism, Stalinist terror, and the unedifying politics of the totalitarian state. They obviously color perceptions of any country not under USSR control.

The struggle for power that will follow Brezhnev's disappearance from the scene may also involve an extended period of disorientation in Moscow. This opportunity could be exploited by a strong American president who has studied past relations with the USSR and decided to place them on a genuine quid pro quo basis. It is self-deluding to hope that a new generation of Soviet leaders voluntarily will change the modus operandi that has proven so successful in their past dealings with the United States. The following are suggested as possible courses of action.

—Without waiting for a change that cannot possibly occur in the USSR unless incentive exists, Washington should establish a small group of experts to analyze Soviet propaganda activities, not only to monitor Russian-language publications and broadcasts over Radio Moscow as well as Radio Peace and Progress, but systematically and persistently to refute them. The anti-American propaganda campaign has continued despite détente. Exposing its themes by the Voice of America/Radio Free Europe/Radio Liberty or even via direct television broadcasting by satellite, as well as through the mass media in the United States, would disabuse the Kremlin of the idea that it can continue the same "cold war" approach toward audiences inside the USSR and elsewhere via international front organizations, without any response or retaliation. There should be a substantial broadening of the effort to increase the amount of information transmitted for the peoples living in the USSR and Eastern Europe as well as to present more effectively the U.S. case throughout the world.

—Espionage capability can be reduced by limiting the Soviet embassy and consulates in the United States to the same number of American diplomatic personnel stationed in the USSR. If a Soviet citizen is caught involved in activities not compatible with his or her status, reciprocal expulsion should not be accepted and no replacement allowed to enter this country. That was the policy of Britain in September 1971 when it declared 105 Soviet officials personae non grata from the embassy, trade mission, Aeroflot office, and Narodny Bank (one-fifth of such persons in London). The same thing occurred in Canada on a more limited basis during spring 1979. The USSR did not retaliate in either case when warned of reciprocal treatment if it attempted to do so. A less passive attitude toward systematic KGB infiltration of United Nations agencies would also help contain espionage.

—Foreign trade with the USSR, which imported about $8.5 billion worth of goods more than it exported to the United States during 1972–1978 and accumulated a huge debt, has not led to improved relations. Helping Moscow solve its economic difficulties by shipments of grain and advanced technology continues to be counterproductive. If these are curtailed, Kremlin decision makers may be forced to reallocate some of their resources from the military to agriculture in order to feed their own population. The United States would strengthen its position by requiring the Soviet Union to balance its accounts periodically and make up the deficit by supplying this country with gold, petroleum, and other materials needed here.

—If an American citizen is roughed up, interrogated by the secret police, and convicted on the basis of falsified evidence, the USSR ambassador to Washington should be told in no uncertain terms that he will be expelled or his counterpart in Moscow recalled if such harassment is not stopped immediately. Accreditation of Soviet journalists should be revoked when their counterparts are harassed by KGB agents provocateur, as happened on several occasions during 1979.

—It is doubtful that SALT II will restrict the USSR in its attempt to attain strategic superiority over the United States if Defense Secretary Brown's assessment is correct. No SALT III may be preferable to having one that again shackles the United States and accepts USSR obligations on faith alone. The same reasoning is applicable to talks on force reduction between NATO and Warsaw Pact representatives. There is, of course, no reason to discontinue negotiations in either area. However, members of American delegations must learn from the experience of their predecessors to anticipate Soviet techniques. Tough bargaining by the USSR must be countered by a similar firmness.

—These same considerations affect the Kremlin's struggle for influence throughout the Third World. In a coordinated effort, the USSR and its dependencies have exploited every opportunity to gain footholds in countries that are located near maritime choke points. The United States is at a disadvantage, unable to send surrogates and unjustly identified with former colonial powers. Positive countermeasures might include limited support for Peking in its own struggle against Moscow throughout the Third World. The Chinese can identify more closely with the populations in the less developed countries because they are in that category themselves and because they are nonwhite. For the time being, at any rate, China shows little interest in acquiring access to foreign ports or other military facilities. This approach might well appeal to Peking, which has much to gain from such cooperation against a common adversary.

—The United States must project itself to the Third World as a revolutionary system that has brought prosperity to the American working class, where skilled laborers often earn more money than professors, and where human rights are strongly upheld by press and courts. The corollary would be a campaign that will expose false USSR propaganda concerning America and tell the truth about Soviet colonialism in Central Asia and Eastern Europe through such forums as the United Nations and the U.S. International Communications Agency externally, as well as through the mass media internally. The USSR suffers from multiple contradictions: between Russians and other nationalities, party elite and masses, the Soviet Union and its dependencies in Eastern

Europe (the latter should be encouraged to act independently). Why is it that spokesmen for the United States rarely if ever mention the fraudulent promise of a classless society or the virulent atheism that persecutes Christianity, Islam, and Judaism? (Encouraging dissidents and émigrés to prepare Russian-language publications for shipment to the USSR would be helpful). It should be pointed out that the American political system enables both groups and individuals to associate freely and allows them to propose policies and programs that are at variance with U.S. government policy. This is the essence of the free way of life and should be projected forcefully on the international scene.

—Special emphasis should be placed on a broad campaign in support of generally accepted human rights. Based upon the 1948 Universal Declaration of Human Rights convention and the more recent 1975 final act at Helsinki, both of which were signed by the Soviet Union, violations of specific provisions should be called to the attention of world public opinion. Complaints by Moscow of interference in domestic affairs can be rejected because the USSR has never hesitated to interfere beyond its own borders to the full extent of capabilities.

—More care should be taken that all exchange programs are reciprocal in nature and not largely channels for transmission of technical information. "Reciprocity in the treatment of participants simply does not exist," according to a recent Twentieth Century Fund task force report. Soviet scholars should not be permitted to travel all over the United States when Americans are restricted largely to a few cities. The frequent denial of access to archives and laboratories in the USSR poses yet another problem.

—Finally, the United States has a weapon that is probably more powerful than oil, namely huge agricultural surpluses. During fiscal year 1978–79, these amounted to $13.4 billion sold to other countries. The government in Washington could purchase all such crops for export and establish a "grain board" on which American farmers would be represented. Canada already has such an organization, and Australia may be willing to coordinate activities in this area. Free market proponents may be against such an agreement, but there is no better way for it to be used as a humanitarian instrument to alleviate famine in the Third World. The potential exists. It should not be difficult to devise a method to use this asset in the interest of national security and that of the West, rather than offer it to an opponent who seeks to destroy the United States.

Middle East

Peter Duignan and L. H. Gann

XXVII

The Middle East is an arbitrary term, for in a narrow sense it includes Egypt, the Arabian Peninsula, Turkey, and Iran, and in a broader sense it extends all the way from the Atlantic coast across North Africa to the eastern border of Iran. The Middle East thus broadly defined is the subject of this essay. Geographically and ethnically, this huge area is extraordinarily varied. There are many subregions, each with its own distinctive historical and cultural traditions.

The numerous sovereign states of the area differ in physical size, armed power, and economic productivity. Many of them are involved in bitter disputes: Turkey with Greece, Algeria with Morocco, Libya with Egypt, Israel with all its Arab neighbors except Egypt. Conflict between the states is often paralleled by struggles between ethnic groups within them. There are discontented Kurdish minorities in Iraq, Iran, and Turkey; Israel contains many discontented Arabs; the Lebanon is split between differing Christian and Muslim sects. In Turkey, Muslim minorities clash with Sunnites; in Syria, an Alawite Shiite minority regime gains much of its legitimacy from the Sunni majority only by standing as a champion of Islam against Israel. Critics of the existing order take courage variously from appeals to Arab nationalism, to Muslim fundamentalism, or to different forms of Marxism that share only two features: hatred of the West and of Israel.

There is, then, the Middle East of great oil wealth and of grinding poverty in the deserts and the urban slums; there is the Middle East of sophisticated trading cities and of lonely mountain settlements. Nevertheless, the Middle Eastern countries have features in common. Their world has been overwhelmingly shaped by Islam. Except for such groups as the Jews in Israel, the Maronite and Greek Orthodox Christians in Lebanon, the Monophysite Copts in Egypt, and Christian minorities in

Syria and Iraq, the region follows Islam.

Most Middle Easterners are farmers, and most of them are poverty-stricken and illiterate. Pastoral nomadism, though romanticized by novelists and film-makers, now involves only a small number of people in remote areas. Agriculture employs men and women also in trading crops or in processing them as packers, canners, driers, and so on.

Farmers must contend with a variety of obstacles. Because the Middle East is primarily desert, cultivated areas are small; only 5–7.5 percent of the land is arable. Summer temperatures are usually high; when the soils become overheated, organic material is destroyed and efficient use of fertilizers is difficult. Water is needed everywhere; oil, in fact, is more available than fresh, clean water.

Farmers also contend with man-made burdens: excessive taxation, governmental inefficiency and corruption, poor marketing facilities, lack of rural credit, deficiencies in transportation. In some regions, holdings are small and scattered; tractors, reaping machines, cattle dips, and other such innovations cannot be introduced easily. The governments of Iran, Iraq, Egypt, and Algeria—others, too—have attempted to introduce land reforms, which have met with varying success. But the redistribution of land to peasant farmers does not of itself usually raise agricultural productivity. Farmers require incentives to improve their methods. They need trucks and roads to transport their crops to the city; they need technical education, banks, and veterinary and agricultural services; they require credit; they may need security of tenure, or a proper handling of water rights—all amounting to a complex physical and organizational infrastructure that cannot be improvised suddenly.

Plagues and pests increase the farmer's woes. Perhaps the greatest curse is mosquito-borne disease: malaria, yellow fever, and other sicknesses remain endemic. The riverine systems of Egypt and Iraq are blighted with schistosomiasis, a severe waterborne disease that spreads with the use of irrigation. Cattle diseases abound; so do locusts, which sometimes swarm into highly cultivated areas and wipe out much of the year's crop.

Most Middle Eastern countries remain economically backward in comparison to the states of Western Europe. The most advanced economy in the Middle East is that of Israel. The oil sheikhdoms on the Persian Gulf have garnered enormous wealth from their exports, and they now number among the world's bankers; Egyptian factories turn out some highly sophisticated products; until recent years, Lebanon had an international reputation as a center of trade and financial services. But, overall, development has been uneven. Each of the most powerful or prosperous Middle Eastern countries—Iran, Turkey, and Saudi

Arabia—has a gross national product (GNP) less than that of Belgium, and but a fraction of that of Great Britain or West Germany (see Table 1). There are striking inequalities in their respective resources. The per capita income of Libya, a major oil-producing country, exceeds that of Japan and that of the USSR (in U.S. dollars at market price, $4,440 as against $4,070 and $2,380, respectively). The per capita income of countries like Turkey and Algeria ranks just below Chile ($750 and $730, as against $830).

The impact of oil has created bizarre discrepancies of wealth and has accentuated social tensions in the Middle East. The GNP of a tiny state like Oman, with fewer than one million people, is almost equal to that of Lebanon, which has almost four times Oman's population. Agriculture has been widely neglected within the oil-producing states. In Iran, for instance, agriculture dropped from 18 percent of the GNP in 1973 to 8 percent in 1977; during the same period food imports rose in value from $32 million to $1.5 billion. Inflation was rampant throughout

TABLE 1

Size and Productivity of Middle Eastern States Compared to West Germany, Great Britain, and Belgium

Country	Population	Estimated GNP in 1977 ($ billions)
Algeria	18,420,000	10.1
Bahrein	345,000	1.7
Egypt	39,760,000	13.3
Iran	36,365,000	72.6
Iraq	12,470,000	16.3
Israel	3,700,000	14.2
Jordan	2,970,000	1.3
Kuwait	1,160,000	12.0
Lebanon	3,060,000	2.9
Libya	2,760,000	18.5
Morocco	18,590,000	9.5
Oman	837,000	2.5
Qatar	205,000	2.4
Saudi Arabia	7,730,000	55.4
Sudan	19,120,000	4.4
Syria	8,110,000	6.5
Turkey	42,110,000	46.6
Tunisia	6,250,000	5.0
United Arab Emirates	875,000	7.7
Yemen Arab Republic (North)	7,270,000	1.2
Yemen, People's Democratic Republic of (South)	1,830,000	0.22
West Germany	63,410,000	508.6
Great Britain	56,700,000	263.6
Belgium	9,930,000	73.4

Source: International Institute of Strategic Studies, *The Military Balance: 1978–1979* (London, 1978).

the Middle East. Many traditional industries and traditional pursuits declined. In Saudi Arabia, the nomadic population now amounts to no more than 700,000 of the seven million people. Within a decade, the nomadic way of life there will probably have disappeared altogether—a serious matter in a kingdom that claims to be built on such traditional Arab values as loyalty to tribal leaders.

There have been great shifts in population. Immigrants do most of the work in the Persian Gulf area. Three million of the seven million people in Saudi Arabia are immigrants: Yemenites, Egyptians, Sudanese, Chadians, Pakistanis, Palestinians, Syrians, Lebanese, and others. The growth of cities has provided new markets for farmers and a labor force for new manufacturing industries. Millions of Turks, Iranians, and Arabs have acquired new skills, so that the sons of peasants and herdsmen now work as financial experts, test pilots, industrial chemists, hydroelectrical engineers, factory managers, computer specialists.

But in social terms, development has entailed a substantial debit column. In all Middle Eastern countries the population has grown extensively. Mortality rates have been lowered. Life expectancy has gone up, and birthrates remain high. In 1975 Cairo had over eight million people; today it has nearly ten million. Tehran and its satellite cities contain five million people; the population of Damascus is approaching two million. Demographic expansion has been accompanied by rapid and often unmanageable urbanization. Many of the urban newcomers live in slums ill provided with water, electricity, and sewage facilities.

In most Middle Eastern countries the population has become more and more youthful. The demographic shifts have contributed to cultural instability, educational problems, crime, lack of jobs for school dropouts, and the radicalization of unemployed or underemployed youngsters. Illiteracy is high; in Egypt it reaches 70 percent. The urban work force has grown, but all too many workers lack skills. Their employment often depends on short-lived construction booms and on a fluctuating demand for menial labor. Agricultural development, on the other hand, has frequently been neglected, an omission all the more regrettable in countries like Iraq and Iran, where farming remains the prime industry.

How will these problems be solved? Middle Easterners overwhelmingly look to the intervention of the state, either in the form of an Islamic republic or in some form of socialist commonwealth. Statist traditions have been strengthened by periods of Western rule. Western colonial officials, like earlier rulers of indigenous origin, created such public works as new irrigation facilities in Egypt, and they interfered in the local economies in a variety of ways. The impact of war further strengthened the powers of the state, and successive governments took over these statist traditions. The expansion of university education created a supply of graduates who looked to public service in state and party bureaucracies and to employment in state-run corporations, with the result that planning, control, interference, and ownership by the state became part of an economic credo that prevails throughout most of the Middle East. To this day, science and technology, business, and banking and management have never commanded the respect accorded to public administration and government.

The bureaucracies draw their candidates from the swollen student population. In countries as diverse as Israel, Egypt, and Iran, the bureaucracies have grown unwieldy, unyielding, interfering, often corrupt, and inefficient. Above all, they have enlarged. In Iran the shah's government supported more than 800,000 civil servants, although no more than 300,000 to 400,000 of their jobs had any social utility. The country employed in addition over a million people in government-owned or government-subsidized industries. These bureaucratic bodies provide a great number of sinecures but leave their incumbents dispirited with useless work and their clients angry at public inefficiency and red tape.

Throughout the Middle East communalism remains strong, not merely in cultural and religious matters, but in economic affairs. Some minority communities, such as the highland Berbers, Maronites, Kurds, Druzes, live in relatively well-defined areas, but others are widely dispersed. Many villages are composed of one predominant ethnic group plus minority groups who often provide specialists in particular occupations. Members of religious minority groups—Jews, Armenians, Copts, Maronites, Bahai, and others—have traditionally supplied a large proportion of the indigenous entrepreneurs; hence, class struggles have often become overlaid with ethno-religious conflicts. The predominance of communal loyalties in countries like Lebanon militates against compromise; politics all too often becomes a zero-sum game, where one community's gain necessarily becomes another's loss. Communal loyalties are so strong that no Middle Eastern state has managed to create a sense of national feeling that transcends them.

The problems of communalism are not by themselves insoluble. Christian and Muslim managed to coexist in the Lebanon for many years. Berber and Arab live side by side in Algeria and Morocco relatively peacefully. But the problems of communalism become aggravated when ethnic divisions coincide with class divisions, and when class divisions are exacerbated by militant ideologies that promise to create a new and better society.

The strength of communalism weakens political legitimacy; the weakness of legitimacy makes for political instability. Israel and Turkey, alone in the Middle East, remain democratic states able to change their rulers through peaceful means. The Israeli army, though influential, is not an independent force in politics, but merely forms the Jewish electorate in arms. Elsewhere, the Middle Eastern regimes are widely subject to the threat of putsches, coups, and plots. Legitimacy remains to be established.

Arab politics suffer further from the weakness of political institutions. There has been an absence of sustained ideological commitment, or real structural change. Many Arab politicians have been socially conservative and have practiced conspiratorial politics or put their trust in military coups. The strength of Arab politics lies in the patron-client and family network, not in political parties or ideology. Arabs seldom have had strong local nationalism, and pan-Arab nationalism resting on the belief that the Arabs are, or should be, a unified people—remains a considerable force.

The Middle East is divided by militant ideologies—Marxism in various forms, Arab nationalism, and a militant Islamic revival that looks to the past and to the pure ideals of the Koran. From Algeria and Egypt across Iran into Afghanistan, Islamic religious movements are on the upswing. Many mullahs, imams, and ayatollahs charge that communists are materialistic and the West is decadent. The Iranian monarchy, once accepted by Western specialists as a modernizing force, fell to such a movement. The kings of Saudi Arabia and Jordan sit uneasily on their respective thrones. Turkey is in political and economic trouble. Libya, ruled by a militant Islamic dictatorship, has become a center of international terrorism.

Of all the conflicts dividing the Middle East, the confrontation between Israel and the Arab states is the most spectacular. Other Middle Eastern states clash over boundaries and oil claims, but Israel is the sole nation whose very survival is at stake. A protégé of the United States, it is regionally regarded as a pariah state whose existence is an affront to its neighbors. Israel and Egypt, the latter until recently its principal adversary, share strikingly similar problems: a large and inefficient bureaucracy, a deficit economy dependent on foreign handouts, and a form of military hypertrophy that induces each combatant to devote a major share of its GNP to defense expenditure. The effects of military hypertrophy are aggravated by the cost of ultramodern weaponry. F15s and MIG aircraft cost a great deal more than World War II Spitfires and Messerschmidts, and they need far more skilled manpower and technical resources for maintenance. The social and economic cost of such military investment is unbearably high for poverty-stricken countries, and it continues to rise.

In theory, the problems of the region should be solved, at least in part, through the enormous infusion of wealth occasioned by the export of oil. Oil has brought unprecedented wealth to Libya, Saudi Arabia, Iran, Iraq, and the Persian Gulf states. All have tended to invest in industrial projects of high cost and prestige value but of little practical use and limited labor utilization. Education and welfare programs are being expanded as urbanization increases.

But a heavy price continues to be paid for rapid change. Inflation and the flight to towns have resulted in slums, overcrowding, and lower living standards. Many farms are deserted, so agricultural productivity is down and food imports have increased. Foreigners are brought in to run the new industries and schools and to service electronic and military equipment. All the oil states devote huge sums to arms. Even with building booms, local services have been outstripped. Inflation and new wealth have led to excessive government spending and imports, and some governments then face considerable deficits.

Rapid development programs combined with this great wealth have weakened traditional values and social systems in the Middle East. The societies in the area stand between two worlds, integrated neither into the old nor into the new. Naturally, rapid change has led to frustrations and resentments, often used as excuses for lashing out at the government or at the foreigner in the nation's midst. The Arab world may have more Khomeini-type revolutions. Although pan-Arabism will not be a major force in the 1980s, pan-Islamism will be, as people turn back to older values and religion.

What can we expect economically for the Middle East in the 1980s? According to a 1978 Rand Corporation study by Arthur Smithies, the oil-rich Arab countries—Saudi Arabia, Kuwait, Iraq, and Libya—will grow rapidly because of increased revenues from oil sales. Saudi Arabia will lead because of its willingness to import foreign labor and technology. By 1985, however, even the Saudis will have balance of payment problems and will have to slow down their development plans. Such oil-poor states as Egypt, Jordan, and Syria will grow only if they continue to receive economic aid.

After 1985 the Arabs will experience trouble in transforming their economies, even with oil wealth. Capital is only one factor in economic growth, and the Arab world is plagued with poor soils, shortages of water, and a lack of material and human resources. Inflation and balance of payments problems will be the most serious handicaps to development. Imports of foreign commodities, labor, and skills will outstrip export revenues. Even if countries like Saudi Arabia were to expand production and increase prices, they would have problems paying for their development plans. The oil-rich then will drop back to moderate growth rates of 5–7 percent. Kuwait is already pursuing a cautious and conservative development program. The oil-poor states will continue through the 1980s to be a drain on the wealthy. But the rich will continue to provide aid because their security depends on friendly neighbors.

In demographic terms, Egypt is the most powerful Arab state; but even if the peace with Israel holds firm, Egypt is likely to face a host of troubles. Diminishing land resources and a growing population must be contended with. Oil resources are modest and there is little in the country to attract foreign investors but much bureaucratic red tape to discourage them. If the government can limit population growth, reduce its foreign exchange deficits by improving exports, end government subsidies, tighten credit, and reduce the money supply, Egypt will have a chance. Above all, Egypt needs to produce more and better managers of its economy. The transportation and marketing systems must be improved also; at present 40 percent of agricultural products never reach the market but rot in the fields or storage bins awaiting transport. If Sadat can put his economic house in order and continue to receive generous foreign aid, Egypt might return to its healthy pre-1967 growth rate. Syria, with Arab aid, grew rapidly (12 percent) from 1973 to 1976 but will fall back to a 5–6 percent growth rate during the 1980s. Jordan is aiming high (12 percent) but, owing to scanty resources, inflation, and labor shortages, will be lucky to reach a 5–6 percent growth rate.

Among the oil-rich states, Iraq may well be the leading Arab country during the 1980s. With a good balance between physical size and population, oil, and agricultural resources, its development plans are more modest and realistic than those of the Saudis. Iraq faces two major challenges to its stability and leadership role in the 1980s. The Ba'athist government, a Sunni minority, rules a Shiite population that knows of events in Iran. The Ba'ath party is essentially an Arab-Marxist secular movement and will have to placate the Shiite religious leaders. (After the fall of the shah and the return of Khomeini, Ba'athist leaders were seen frantically visiting mosques and religious shrines.) The second threat to Iraqi leadership will come from the small but well-organized Communist party, with roots among Kurds and poor Shiites.

Iraq, like all other socialist states, has had a large, inefficient bureaucracy, and its people have been underproductive. Development has been impeded by shortages of labor, expertise, and material. But there are signs of improvement. For one thing, new land reclamation projects promise to end food imports.

Libya, on the other hand, has ceased to grow in economic terms; oil apart, its resources are scanty and its government bad and it may well be condemned to live a hand-to-mouth existence for some time.

For all these oil-producing states, increasing capital will encourage development. Although they are backward technologically, they will be able to buy and use immediately a large amount of advanced technology. If they can learn to manage their resources, or let others manage them, they can reach a high rate of growth. Iran, Iraq, and Algeria have sufficient natural resources—water, fertile land, minerals—and human resources to develop at 9–10 percent a year. This rapid growth depends, of course, on peace in the area, political stability, and reasonable governance. Kuwait, under competent leadership, has done reasonably well. Other oil-producing countries, such as Saudi Arabia, Libya, the United Arab Emirates, and Qatar, face a harder challenge. Even though their capital supply is enormous, their populations are small and they lack water and other natural resources. They have few trained people, backward agricultures, and little or no industry or infrastructure. The harsh climate wears out men, machinery, and structures. Admittedly, as Charles Issawi has observed in *The Middle East: Oil, Conflict and Hope,* capital and technology can overcome these difficulties, if the Islamic religion and poor leadership do not intrude.

For states other than the main oil producers—Morocco, Tunisia, Egypt, Sudan, Israel, Jordan, Syria, the Yemens, and Turkey—the future is likely to be more difficult. These states pay more for imports than they receive for exports. They are dependent on aid and capital from outside. Israel and Turkey may continue to grow at 5–6 percent per annum, but their exports are declining and military costs are rising. Egypt, Morocco, Tunisia, and the Sudan, which have good agricultural sectors, should grow at a reasonable rate if population growth does not consume the increase in productivity and if government mismanagement is reduced.

All Middle Eastern (including the North African) economies can become more viable in the 1980s than they are at present, provided the various countries can live at peace, reduce their oversized armaments, limit their huge bureaucracies, maintain a tolerant policy toward their religious and ethnic minorities, improve their skills, save at a higher rate than at present, and solve their foreign exchange problems. Generally, they need to spend more on their respective agricultural sectors and pay more attention to their farmers' requirements. The big problems of the 1980s in the Middle East will be population and food: more countries will be unable to feed their people or provide work for them.

Statesmanship of a high order will be required. National savings will probably have to reach 20–25 percent of the GNP to finance sufficient investments. (This figure is lower than those attained by many countries in East Asia, where 30–35 percent savings are not uncommon.) Imports must be balanced by exports, or by income from tourism, remittances from citizens working abroad, or financial services rendered to foreigners. Deficit spending is likely to be a prescription for economic disaster.

No one, of course, can predict exactly what will happen; but according to John Waterbury's forecast in *The Middle East in the Coming Decade*, the prospects are grim. In all likelihood, the Middle Eastern countries will fail to evolve a cohesive regional development strategy or collective bargaining position in relation to the "North" (meaning Europe, the United States, and the USSR). The industrialized north will maintain its advantages in terms of trade. Owing to the political differences and economic rivalries among various Middle Eastern states, they will fail to cooperate regionally; instead, bilateral networks will predominate.

Pan-Arab unity has been broken; no individual state is willing to sacrifice its interests for the ideals of pan-Arabism. The rich do not want economic integration, and the weak and divided fear absorption into larger units. Saudi Arabia wants economic clients, not independent, self-reliant allies. The Saudis will try to perpetuate Egypt's and the Sudan's dependence on them; they will not give or lend Egypt large sums to transform its economy. Collective action for economic advancement has proven impossible, except over the issue of oil. The Middle Eastern states, unequal in resources and divided in politics and policies, will not present a united front to the north, but will continue to have to bargain for favors bilaterally.

Given these difficulties, only an optimist would look to a bright future. But the Middle East has confounded many prophets of woe, and the future may yet turn out to be brighter than the past.

FLASH POINTS

The Middle East is in a state of turmoil, and the 1980s are likely to be a troubled period. An exhaustive analysis of Middle Eastern problems would require an entire volume. We shall content ourselves with picking out a few danger spots that are likely to be of major significance, not merely from the local, but also from the international standpoint.

Iran

Until recently the economic development of Iran was one of the success stories of the modern world. Iran is potentially a power with international status because of its size (627,000 square miles, nearly seven times as big as the United Kingdom), its population (33,591,800 in 1976), and its natural resources (especially oil). Remarkable economic development occurred after 1963, when the shah announced his White Revolution, a peaceful revolution imposed from above.

Between 1963 and 1977, the per capita gross national product (GNP) of Iran increased from about $200 to $2,200. New establishments included steel mills, motor car and diesel engine manufacturers, aluminum smelters, and enterprises concerned with textiles, food processing, and handicrafts. The shah made a substantial effort at land reform; cooperative societies were set up, and subsistence farming was starting to give way to cash-crop production. During this period Iran became a military power, equipped with the most modern American weapons. Iran seemed to hold the balance of power in the strategically vital Persian Gulf.

The shah was unable to hold onto power, partly as a result of his own policy failures and partly for reasons beyond his control. Iran, like many other Middle Eastern countries, had to contend with runaway urbanization. Students and urban workers, the most volatile members of the population, grew rapidly in numbers. Unemployment increased in 1978 and 1979, and despite expansion of the country's industries—steel mills, petrochemical complexes, even nuclear power installations—the number of applicants for work exceeded the number of jobs available. The White Revolution had alienated the shah from Iran's traditional aristocracy without gaining peasant support. Iranian smallholders continued to face problems derived from inadequate communications, poor agricultural seeds, and lack of water, modern implements, capital, and other essentials. Even where the reforms were successful, agriculture could not provide an acceptable living for the families engaged in it, nor could it feed Iran's people. Food imports rose sharply, from a cost of only $32 million in 1973 to $1.5 billion four years later. Inflation reached more than 30 percent in 1977. The country had to cope with an overblown and underemployed civil service and with a variety of prestige projects of dubious economic value.

During the last years of the shah's reign, Iran maintained a swollen military establishment of more than 700,000 men, including regular military units and police. The armed forces, like the great state enterprises, prided themselves on possessing some of the world's most modern equipment. But the power of both was often diminished by managerial and technological weaknesses. The lower ranks of the military, especially conscript soldiers, were poorly paid and without social prestige. Middle-class Iranians were disgusted at the brutalities of the secret police (Savak) and by the autocratic nature of royal rule. The great reserve army of students, some poorly qualified technically, looked with apprehension to a future without jobs; urban workers complained because their scanty wages were further diminished by inflation. Shopkeepers were angered by inflation, ill-considered attempts at price control, and by competition from new department stores. Religious leaders, powerful among the lower middle class and the poor, were troubled by the speed of modernization and by its religious and cultural consequences. The shah was increasingly identified with the hated Westerners, supposedly the source of growing social evils. Perhaps most serious, the shah's ruling style precluded the development of any genuinely supportive political institutions, let alone any effective legal opposition. The shah dropped even the pretense of a two-party system. When his position became politically untenable, there was no loyal opposition to take up the reins of government.

Policymakers in the United States, however, had little understanding of Iranian realities. About 1971, cautious support for the shah turned into all-out commitment. State Department officials, military men, and intelligence officers stationed in Iran learned that no one in the White House wanted to hear anything evil about the shah, who received a blank check to purchase the most modern military equipment on a superabundant scale. The Iranian armed forces were often unable to use their new equipment because of deficiencies in training and organization. The blank check issued by the Nixon administration continued to be honored by President Carter, though the shah's power was visibly waning. The United States wanted him to act as its policeman in the troubled but important Persian Gulf area, and as a powerful ally in the Central Treaty Organization (CENTO) to block a Soviet advance into the area.

The Shah did not fall simply because of widespread corruption, a harsh system of governance indifferent to the civil rights of his political opponents, striking social inequalities between the rulers and the ruled, unemployment, and general inefficiency. All these factors were in operation in other countries—including Algeria, a post-revolutionary state. But the Iranian monarchy proved incapable of coping with massive nationwide strikes and accelerating disorder. The economy faltered as oil production was interrupted. By about January 1979, the army had become discouraged and divided within itself, and it lost control of the streets. Even the middle classes, the main beneficiaries of imperial rule, ceased to back up the shah; the urban poor, traditionally a powerful element, became restive. In the end, imperial governance collapsed in a welter of disorder and bloodshed. The assault against the shah's regime was accompanied by a skillfully orchestrated propaganda campaign overseas.

There were three main contenders for power: the army, the Marxists, and the Islamic revolutionaries. The Iranian army, once a strong force, was paralyzed by a breakdown in discipline and by dissensions between opposing factions; many conscripts refused to return to duty, preferring to join the Marxist or Islamic militants. Vast quantities of weapons had fallen into the hands of civilians, and for the time being, the army could not act against armed civilian formations. But the basic structure of the army apparently remained intact, and its potential power remained considerable.

The largest group contending for power was the Islamic revolutionaries headed by Ayatollah Khomeini, an aged religious dignitary. By emphasizing Iran's Islamic legacy, the ayatollah professed a militant form of Iranian nationalism that differed from the secular kind proclaimed by Prime Minister Mosaddeq two decades earlier. The Islamic revolutionaries included technocrats as well as mullahs, poor farmers, and members of the urban middle class. These disparate groups were far from united, but they agreed to form a democratic republic. A comprehensive revolution was begun that would assure freedom to believers and nonbelievers, a radical change in cultural life, and reforms that included an end to liquor stores, gambling casinos, and prostitution. The Islamic revolutionaries stood committed to a neutralist foreign policy, aloof from both the United States and the Soviet Union. They condemned the Marxist ideology of the Tudeh party; but they allied themselves with the Palestine Liberation Organization (PLO), an organization tied in various ways to the pro-Soviet parties of the Middle East and ready to endanger any Islamic government that would refuse to join the struggle against Israel.

The left-wing opposition was less important than the religious dissenting groups; indeed, the USSR appears to have been as surprised as the United States regarding the strength of Islamic radicalism. The left wielded a good deal of influence among students, teachers, academicians, and journalists, and also among industrial workers, especially those in the oil industry. But the left was divided into a number of armed factions that depended on guerrilla warfare. The strongest left-wing group was the Tudeh party, an orthodox Communist movement unswervingly loyal to Moscow, backed by diplomatic, financial, and political aid from the Warsaw Pact countries. The Soviet intelligence services, KGB and GRU, had penetrated the army and Savak (the shah's secret police). Soviet-sponsored publications and radio broadcasts spread "disinformation" (organized lying) designed to discredit the shah's regime.

The Tudeh party used cooperation with Moscow and a new alliance with the Islamic revolutionaries as stepping stones toward a socialist revolution. (Negotiations were facilitated through leftist members of the ayatollah's entourage and through Palestinian exiles with a natural interest in rapprochement between their Communist and Islamic supporters.) In tune with the current line, the Tudeh party's first secretary, Iraj Eskanderi, was replaced early in 1979 by Nueddin Kianuri, who vowed to collaborate with Khomeini in setting up an Islamic revolutionary council.

Iran remains in a precarious position. The economy has weakened through the large-scale exodus of foreign experts, the failure to maintain or to replace industrial equipment, the decline in oil production, the effects of continued strikes in banking, business, and industry. Worst of all has been the seepage of arms into civilian hands. The growth of private armies has been accompanied by administrative disorganization, leaving the revolutionary government with tremendous problems. Iran is made up of many ethnic groups: Arabs, Azerbaijanis, Kurds, and Turkomans. Less than 45 percent of all Iranians speak Persian; the remainder use a variety of other Semitic, Indo-European and Turkic languages. These minorities owed no loyalty to the new republic, and the breakup of the monarchy is likely to open a new era of internal strife. Kurds and Turkoman groups have won some measure of autonomy from the weakened Iranian government. Afghans and Arabs may attempt to link up with their radical brothers in opposition.

At the time of writing, the revolutionary forces are seriously divided, and Iran faces a possible showdown between religious fundamentalists and secularists. The leftists consist of the Tudeh party; a new communist party known as the National Communist party of Iran; and the onetime underground guerrilla organization the Fedayeen-e-Khalq, now well-armed and experienced in clandestine operations. Ranged against them are the religious fundamentalists loyal to Khomeini and the Islamic partisan organization. The moderate republican opposition is in serious straits, faced with the prospect that the extreme left could take over leadership of all secularists discontented with the fundamentalists' bigotry, their use of kangaroo courts, their strident anti-Americanism, and their isolationist policies that threaten to leave Iran without a single friend in an inhospitable world.

Under these circumstances, the options available to the United States are limited. Given Iran's strategic importance in the Persian Gulf, its importance as an oil producer, and its position as a bulwark against the Soviet Union, the United States cannot afford to let the country drift into the Soviet sphere of influence, as has happened in Afghanistan, the People's Republic of Yemen, or Ethiopia. The best chance for the United

States is to reach an arrangement with those very Islamic revolutionaries whom American journalists have described as wild-eyed fanatics out of touch with the modern world. The Carter administration needs to discipline its members to speak with one voice rather than in a discordant chorus. The president and his advisors must resist the temptation to try to be the world's moral arbiters, to comment in public on the real or supposed moral worth of governments—a practice that has alienated each successive ruling Iranian faction from Washington. We have to give up the practice of relying upon a single nation as the "chosen instrument" of U.S. policy. We need a broader diplomatic approach, now that we have to shore up our relations with Turkey, Pakistan, and Saudi Arabia.

The United States has to reorganize its intelligence operations, giving personal responsibility for the quality of local reporting to the ambassador accredited to each foreign government, rather than to some impersonal "country team." Primarily, the United States has to learn how to take up the Soviet Union's ideological challenge. But Americans enjoy potential advantages. The Tudeh party's association with the Soviet Union could be stressed, and we could emphasize the USSR's past territorial claims on Iran. Attention should focus on the bad record of all Marxist radical groups who, when in power, have suppressed civil liberties, attacked religion, and replaced yesterday's rulers with a new privileged class of party functionaries.

Above all, Americans must respect the force of religion in politics, especially in Islamic countries like Iran. We shut our eyes to Savak, to corruption, inefficiency, and the haste in which the shah tried to modernize a feudal society. The United States should have foreseen the dangers of his one-man rule, the too rapid pace of change that alienated students, the middle class, the workers, and the religious leaders. We should have restrained our sales of advanced weaponry, and of industrial equipment that required the presence of 40,000 Americans in a land traditionally wary of foreign domination. We are in danger of making the same mistakes in other parts of the Middle East, such as Saudi Arabia and Egypt.

The Arab-Israeli Dispute

Israel is a small country of few natural resources, but it commands a strategic position at the junction of Asia, southern Europe, and North Africa. Palestine, as the Holy Land sacred to Jews, Christians, and Muslims, overshadowed in religious importance every other country in the world. For four centuries Palestine formed part of the Ottoman

Empire. Then in 1917 the British issued the Balfour Declaration, promising to set up a "national home" in Palestine for the Jewish people; five years later Britain received the area as a mandate from the League of Nations. The British withdrew from the strife-torn country in 1948.

That year the United Nations agreed on a partition plan dividing Palestine into a small Jewish state and a small Arab state, with frontier lines so complex that only a confederal arrangement could have assured their survival. The Zionists accepted the U.N. plan, but the Arabs, seriously underestimating their opponents, decided to fight. The Arab armies were crushed; the Jews extended somewhat the boundaries accorded to them under the U.N. partition, and they would have gained more territory but for an armistice reached under U.N. auspices. But the Arabs refused to conclude peace. A state of latent hostility continued between Israel and her neighbors, with intermittent guerrilla activities.

In 1956, supported by Great Britain and France, Israel struck at Egypt. Egypt was decisively defeated; but under Russo-American pressure, the English and French forces withdrew and Israel was forced to relinquish the Egyptian territory that had been seized. Israel gained a ten-year period of uneasy peace, broken intermittently by guerrilla incursions. In 1967, alarmed by Egypt's threat to close the Gulf of Aqaba to Israeli shipping, Israel struck again. In a lightning campaign, the Israelis seized the Sinai peninsula, as well as the Palestinian West Bank, previously under Jordanian control. In 1973 Egypt and Syria, well-supplied by the Soviet Union with arms and technicians and vastly superior to Israel in numbers, launched a counterattack. Egyptian forces regained control over the Suez Canal, but Syria and Egypt were defeated. Egypt was saved only by U.S. and Soviet pressure. But most of the Sinai, the West Bank, the Gaza Strip, and the Golan Heights remained under Israeli occupation. Israel now had boundaries that seemed relatively defensible.

Despite Israel's military successes, her diplomatic and economic position continued to deteriorate. By the late 1960s the country had become dependent solely on the United States for weapons and diplomatic support. A minor American commitment had turned into an engagement of enormous financial scope. Diplomatically, Israel had become almost a pariah state, exposed to the hostility of the Communist nations, the Arab states, and most Third World countries. Western European countries, once friendly to Israel, preferred to make their peace with the world's principal oil suppliers.

By 1976 the Israeli economy was in a state of disarray, distorted (as was Egypt's economy) by the exigencies of war. Israel's national debt, totaling about $9 billion, began to approach the size of the GNP ($11.4 billion in 1975). Between 1973 and 1978 Israel spent 30–40 percent of its annual budget on defense. Israelis faced a high rate of inflation, a desperate housing shortage, a continuing unfavorable trade balance, sharply reduced domestic consumption, widespread bureaucratic mismanagement, the never-ending hardships of universal military service, and a ruinous rate of taxation—miseries paralleled in many ways in Egypt. Israel was even more dependent on U.S. subsidies than were Egypt, Turkey, Iran, and Jordan—which together had received an even larger subsidy than did Israel from the American taxpayer's pocket (see Table 2).

During the past five years, Israel's dependence on the United States has become even more marked, with U.S. assistance fluctuating between $3 and $5 billion per annum. Israel has become the pensioner of a foreign power—something inconceivable to the Zionist founding fathers.

From the demographic standpoint, Israel's position is equally unenviable. Israel is a tiny country of less than 8,000 square miles, with a population of just under three million Jews and about 600,000 Palestinian Arabs. More than a million Arabs live on the Israeli-occupied West Bank and the Gaza Strip. Israel's birthrate remains relatively low; immigration has been reduced to a trickle. But the Palestinian Arabs' rate of natural increase remains high. Demographers calculate that, unless existing trends are reversed, Palestinian Arabs will constitute 50 percent of Israel's total population within two decades. If Israel insists on retaining

TABLE 2

Major Middle Eastern Beneficiaries of U.S. Aid 1946–1976

Country	U.S. Aid ($ million)
Egypt	
Economic	$2,269.8
Military	
Iran	
Economic	760.0
Military	1,412.5
Israel	
Economic	2,425.6
Military	5,904.2
Jordan	
Economic	1,047.7
Military	551.5
Turkey	
Economic	2,704.2
Military	4,689.9

Source: "The Middle East: U.S. Policy," *Congressional Quarterly* (Washington, D.C., 1977), pp. 82–83. The figures exclude arms purchases.

the West Bank and the Gaza Strip, the Jews will be a minority within Israel by the end of the century.

Another 1.5 million Palestinians have been forced to live in other Arab states and overseas. In the Islamic world, the refugees' position varies sharply. Some are exiles still confined in miserable camps 30 years after the end of the first Arab-Israeli war; others have reached influential positions as managers, technicians, and administrators, especially in Saudi Arabia and Kuwait. But they remain dissatisfied with their condition, a peril to those Arab governments willing to consider compromise with the Zionists. Palestinians have threatened Jordan and ruined Lebanon, and they still provide a reserve army for militants willing to continue guerrilla warfare against Israel and terrorism against the Western powers.

Politically, the Palestinians are championed by the PLO, an alliance of various Marxist and non-Marxist groups. Militarily, the PLO does not amount to much. It cannot conduct conventional operations and it cannot overthrow Israel through terrorism. But diplomatically, backed by the Soviet Union and militant Islamic states like Algeria, Libya, Iraq, and Iran, its position is powerful within the United Nations. No agreement seems possible between the PLO and Israel. The Palestinians see themselves as a new nation, hardened by the miseries of exile—the "new Jews," driven from their rightful soil by Western invaders. To liberate Palestine requires an armed struggle; once Palestine has been freed, only Jews who were living in Palestine before the Zionist invasion will be considered Palestinians.

Israel's position, then, is difficult. Were she to give up the newly conquered regions, her frontiers would be hard to defend. If she were to withdraw to the original armistice line, she would have to give up East Jerusalem, and the Holy City would once more be divided. But if Israel were to hold onto the conquered territories, she would have to contend with a hostile Arab population, endangering her own democratic traditions and alienating public opinion in the United States, whose goodwill has become essential for her survival.

The first sign of a possible breakthrough came with the major shift in Egyptian policy that saw President Sadat in Jerusalem to initiate negotiations for peace. Egypt had borne the brunt of the armed confrontation with Israel. By 1978 her economy was in desperate straits; she needed peace as much as did Israel. In 1978, when Sadat met with Israel's Prime Minister Begin at Camp David, the united Arab front was split; hence Begin achieved a success that had eluded his predecessors for 30 years. As the price for peace, Sadat demanded not only Israel's withdrawal from the Sinai, but, in effect, the creation of an autonomous Palestinian state on the West Bank.

The Israelis were divided. The hawks argued that Israel could not afford to make major territorial concessions that would endanger her military security. A Palestinian rump state would come under PLO domination and become a springboard for continued guerrilla attacks on Israel. Even if the United States were to guarantee the borders of a diminished Israel, such guarantees would not be reliable, given the U.S. record in dealing with allies like South Vietnam and Taiwan. Advocates of a compromise peace, on the other hand, argued that this might be the last chance of a peace treaty with Egypt; continued Israeli occupation of the West Bank, they claimed, is incompatible with Israel's democratic traditions and endangers ties with the United States, Israel's last remaining ally in an increasingly hostile world.

From the standpoint of the United States, the best outcome was the compromise peace reached through genuine understanding between Israel and Egypt. Peace will be costly to Americans, but eventually it will enable them to reduce the enormous commitment of military and economic aid to the region made over the last 30 years. Peace will reduce the danger of confrontation with the Soviet Union and slow down the ruinous arms race in the Middle East. Peace is most likely to be secured if it is guaranteed not by the United States alone, but by the United States and its Western European allies—especially Britain and France, the very powers that the United States spurned during the Suez crisis. The Americans, moreover, cannot afford to abandon Israel. American public opinion remains overwhelmingly pro-Israel and strongly anti-Arab. Abandonment by the United States would go against declared American policy, as well as numerous presidential statements. The credibility of the United States as an ally would be further shaken in the rest of the world. A substantial number of Americans, including such leading defense experts as Admiral Elmo Zumwalt, prefer all-out support for Israel. In any case, the United States has a moral obligation to defend Israel; the destruction of that nation would be a catastrophe for the West.

President Carter, on the other hand, seems to see himself as a global peacemaker, a role that suits both his domestic political interests and his moral convictions. Carter and the State Department originally looked to a comprehensive Middle Eastern settlement in cooperation with the Soviet Union. The Sadat initiative came as a somewhat unwelcome surprise, but subsequently Carter supported it: if Sadat had failed he would probably have fallen from power, and U.S. influence would have suffered yet another serious blow. The United States could not base its Middle Eastern policy on Israel alone. Neither could the United States afford to alienate the entire Muslim world, moderates as well as militants, at a time when the West had become increasingly dependent on Arab oil. The United States should rely, rather, on moderate Arab states like Egypt and Saudi Arabia and, if necessary, should persuade Israel into concessions by threatening to withhold essential military and economic aid.

The Israeli-Egyptian peace treaty concluded in 1979 represented an uneasy compromise that did not fully satisfy either side. Peace entailed a long process of disengagement in which Israel would withdraw in stages from occupied Egyptian territory. Disagreements over the West Bank and Gaza were skillfully masked. Sadat continued to call for Palestinian autonomy on the road to self-determination and statehood, the very objectives that Begin had sworn to oppose. Egypt found itself shunned by the remaining Arab countries, including supposedly "moderate" states like Saudi Arabia; Syria and Iraq took over the role of Israel's principal enemies. The American taxpayer was asked to shoulder large financial obligations for the purpose of giving both military and economic support to Israel and Egypt alike. These new commitments were designed to secure a treaty that, by leaving unresolved the Palestinian issue and the future of the West Bank, might contain the seeds of its own undoing.

Nevertheless, the treaty could conceivably turn out to be President Carter's most singular diplomatic triumph. For the first time in its history, Israel gained formal recognition and acceptance of legitimacy from the most powerful Arab state. Egypt secured time to cope with its desperate internal problems. Unable to fight yet another major war against Israel, it decided to pursue a policy of "Egypt first," dropping out of the Arab alliance.

The future remains hard to foresee. Egypt, cut off from the bulk of the Arab alliance, was subjected to an economic and diplomatic boycott; at the time of writing, even its onetime ally Sudan was likely to move away from Cairo. The Arab boycott could seriously hurt Egypt. Economic sanctions entail the stopping of loans and grants, as well as the expulsion of Egypt from joint Arab companies and possible reprisals against Egyptian labor migrants. The breakup of the Arab Organization for Industrialization will be a particularly serious blow to Egypt's economic well-being. The trade ban will also hurt many foreign companies that were planning to invest in Egypt and to export to Arab markets. Peace, ironically, may reduce the volume of foreign investment owing to the Arab boycott; an increasing weight may be thrown on the West that will be expected to make up the shortfall occasioned by the loss of Arab subsidies.

In spite of these difficulties, Washington should continue its support of Sadat. The PLO and its radical Arab supporters cannot be bought off.

The United States will have to be involved in all future negotiations and may also have to more actively defend itself from threatened guerrilla assaults by PLO supporters abroad. But at least some Palestinians might be satisfied for the time being by the creation of a neutralized Palestinian commonwealth, demilitarized and perhaps joined with Israel in a loose confederacy on the West Bank. The creation of a West Bank state would entail the end of Israeli claims to the historic Jewish lands of Samaria and Judea—a small price for peace. An independent West Bank state can come later.

In the 1980s, Begin, or whoever will then rule Israel, will have to give up the dream of re-establishing the kingdom of Solomon for the ingathering of world Jewry. Unless the Russians should decide to expel the bulk of their Jewish population, or unless there should be an outbreak of anti-Semitism in the Argentine, the sources of Jewish immigration will largely dry up, and few Jews will wish to migrate to Israel. The bulk of the Sinai was never part of Solomon's kingdom; the treaty with Egypt was therefore relatively easy to conclude. A long-term settlement is hardest to reach over the West Bank. In its own interest, the United States should pressure Begin to give up the occupied territories on the West Bank, Gaza, and the Golan Heights in return for political guarantees and continued military aid. Special arrangements will have to be worked out for East Jerusalem to prevent the city from being once more partitioned like Berlin. Should the Palestinians be willing to accept Israel's existence within these borders, they should be brought into future negotiations. Washington will also have to make stronger efforts to woo both Syria and Saudia Arabia as part of a wider settlement.

At present, Egypt and Israel have signed a treaty, but peace may not last. Israel will certainly strike back at a West Bank state willing to become an armed sanctuary for guerrilla operations against Israel. If Jordan, Syria, and Saudi Arabia can be drawn into a settlement, then peace, however precarious, might become a habit, and the new habit might help to quiet the Middle East.

Lebanon

Lebanon has become a major casualty of the Arab-Israeli dispute. Until recently, Lebanese hard work operating within a free enterprise economy had turned the country into one of the most prosperous in the Middle East. (Lebanon's literacy rate is the highest in the Arab world.) For a time, the Lebanese had worked out a political and constitutional modus vivendi between Christian and Muslim. But the presence of armed Palestinian guerrillas added bitterness to Lebanese politics. The Palestinians sided with militant leftist Muslims demanding greater constitutional rights for themselves. A destructive and bloody civil war ensued between Christians and Muslims (often misleadingly referred to abroad as right-wingers and left-wingers). Factional fighting was complicated by private vendettas and gangsterism, which spread as more and more arms fell into the hands of the populace. Many Christians, traditionally hostile to the Zionists, gradually drew closer to the Israelis, who supplied the Christians with instructors and weapons, and who raided across the Lebanese border in retaliation for Palestinian guerrilla assaults on Israel from Lebanese bases.

In the end, the Syrian army intervened in Lebanon, ostensibly to establish peace between warring communities but in fact to tie Lebanon into a greater Syria, controlled from Damascus. At the time of writing, Lebanon had made some progress toward recovery from its civil war. But many Lebanese lost their lives; many more have left the country. Relations between the ethno-religious communities remain strained, and there is some danger that the country could break into segments, since Christians in the south have declared their independence.

In this troubled situation, American interests would be served best by insisting on a neutral Lebanon, independent of Syria, structured on a confederal, perhaps a cantonal basis, that would eliminate the Palestinians as a political and military factor in Lebanon while granting effective self-government to Christians and Muslims alike. This would not be an easy solution to attain, but it is probably the best possible bargain, from our point of view and from that of the Lebanese.

The Persian Gulf

Few areas in the world are as vital to Western Europe and the United States as the Persian Gulf states and Saudi Arabia. By 1976, the Persian Gulf was supplying 38 percent of American oil imports, and this percentage continues to increase. If published predictions by the Central Intelligence Agency are correct, the world's demand for oil will substantially exceed its production capacity by 1985. Saudi Arabia will continue to occupy the key position as a supplier of oil until 1983; thereafter, the Persian Gulf states are likely to become America's principal foreign source of supply.

The transformation of the Persian Gulf states is of relatively recent origin. After World War II, the gulf area became one of the world's principal sources of petroleum. The "oil revolution" occasioned a profound social and economic upheaval; it also had far-reaching political consequences. The oil states were drawn, one by one, into the wider circle of Arab politics during the 1960s and, after 1967, into the Arab-Israeli dispute and the orbit of great-power diplomacy. Great Britain was the traditional ruling power in the region. The British had maintained peace and a local power equilibrium through special treaty relations with Kuwait, Bahrain, Qatar, the Trucial sheikhdoms, and Oman. In 1971 Britain withdrew from the gulf, for it could no longer shape events there; the United States hesitated to step in to fill the vacuum. By a strange quirk of fate, the economic well-being of the United States, and of Western Europe and Japan even more, has come to depend dangerously on a congerie of small, weak, backward, and bitterly divided states whose political future remains in doubt.

Locally, the Persian Gulf states must contend with the ambitions of Saudi Arabia, Iraq, and Iran, all bigger fish than the local sheikhdoms. Above all, the region has become an object of Soviet ambitions, which the gulf sheikhdoms are in no position to resist on their own. They are threatened also by internal subversion, by their own instability, by petty dissensions, and by the possible intervention of Soviet proxy forces—or by a combination of these factors. The menace to Western security is indeed considerable.

The Strait of Hormuz is the strategic key to the area. By mid-1977 about 60 percent of the non-communist world's international waterborne oil traffic was passing through the strait daily aboard some 42 tankers. These ships, vulnerable to precision-guided missiles from the shore throughout the gulf, are even more vulnerable while navigating the narrow channel along the southern shore.

Though they differ in many ways, the Persian Gulf oil states have certain common features. Their populations are small (Kuwait has just over a million people, the United Arab Emirates less than a million, Qatar about 200,000). Their gross national products are vast (Kuwait's in 1975 was $13.9 billion, that of the United Arab Emirates $4 billion). They have few resources other than oil, which dominates local economies throughout the region. They are beset by incredible contrasts between poverty and affluence. Their wealth depends on immigrants, who do most of the productive work. For instance, only about 40 percent of Kuwait's people are natives; the remaining 60 percent are immigrants who do not enjoy Kuwait citizenship. These newcomers include Palestinians, Indians, Pakistanis, Arabs from neighboring countries, and others. Kuwaitis provide only about 20 percent of the labor force, yet more than 70 percent of them are on the government payroll. The proportion of indigenous people in Abu Dhabi is even less, perhaps one-third. Indigenous Arabs predominate only in Bahrain and Oman, but even these countries have large foreign minorities.

Immigrants often perform tasks that natives cannot or will not perform; but the immigrants' rewards sometimes bear little relation to the value of their work. The rulers of Kuwait, Qatar, Abu Dhabi, and Dubai have devoted a considerable proportion of their oil revenue to providing subsidized or free housing, schooling, medical services, cash grants, and jobs for their subjects but not for the foreigners. The result is an elaborate system of financial privileges for locals and discrimination in employment and services for immigrants. Indigenous citizens receive jobs even though they may be barely literate; in consequence, they become privileged state pensioners, while qualified foreigners do the bulk of the work. There is similar discrimination with regard to civil rights. Because the rulers of most gulf states place great obstacles in the way of obtaining citizenship, immigrants often feel bitter resentment toward the governments and subjects of the countries to whose prosperity they have contributed so greatly. Whatever differences may divide them, Palestinians, Egyptians, Iraqis, Syrians—the "northern" Arabs—are united in their resentments and their feelings of superiority to the gulf Arabs.

Not surprisingly, the gulf states, except for Kuwait and Bahrain, are politically unstable. Bahrain is in relatively healthy condition, for it gains substantial revenue from its role as a trading depot and purveyor of mercantile and banking services, as well as from the sale of its oil. Bahrainis are relatively well-educated. The proportion of foreigners there is less than 20 percent. Oman is at the opposite end of the spectrum. The mass of the Omani population has been little affected by the discovery of oil, remaining illiterate, ravaged by disease, suspicious of outsiders and their innovations. A large proportion of the wealth derived from Oman's oil is devoted to armaments.

The future of the gulf states looks unstable. Their peoples are divided by tribes into warring factions; and the immigrant communities are not likely to put up for long with their lot. Development of the oil industry is helping to create a new and discontented proletariat, hence internal unrest is certain to increase. The gulf states have to contend with the ambitions of adjacent Islamic states—Iran, Iraq, and Saudi Arabia—all of whom have in the past striven for increased influence. And the gulf states would form a prize of inestimable value to the Soviet Union.

Faced with this dangerous situation, U.S. policy in the region should be directed toward gradual emancipation of at least the skilled immigrant communities—through civil rights, equal pay and social services—to remove an ever-present irritant. The United States should resist the attempts of Iran or Iraq to establish a hegemony. Washington should seek to preserve the status quo, which is most conducive to American interests; its preservation requires the ability to deploy naval and military power in the area in order to deal with potential threats. At the same time, the Soviet Union and Cuba should be assured that the security of the gulf is a matter of vital interest to the United States and its Western allies; the United States cannot, therefore, tolerate armed intervention through Cuban or other Soviet proxy forces, lest the gulf slip into the Soviet sphere of influence.

The strategic location of the gulf and the control of gulf oil are great prizes, and the political instability of the area offers many opportunities for subversion and conflict. Unfortunately, the area cannot be neutralized at this time. Iran can no longer serve as a policeman for the Persian Gulf, and the United States does not want Iraq to play that role. The greatest barrier to keeping the status quo is the USSR, for it is supporting "liberation" groups and encouraging the advance, for example, of South Yemen into North Yemen and Oman. This drive must be thwarted if peace is to endure.

No Western power is ready yet to establish a protectorate in the gulf; hence maintenance of the status quo is the best policy for the moment. But if instability continues, and if Marxist take-overs threaten to capture the West's oil supply, the United States must be prepared to intervene, or to forge mutual security pacts with local Arab governments. Meanwhile, we can do little to shore up the existing governments except to help in the training of their military and police forces, send engineers to guide their development, and warn the Soviets to leave the area alone. The Arab governments are reluctant to accept American diplomatic advice, and the United States must rewin their confidence.

The recent coalition of Arab states was able to stop, for the time being, the invasion of North Yemen. It is to be hoped that Arab collaboration will continue. Meanwhile, we should encourage the Arabs to form a more structured alliance system to preserve the present governments in power and to defend them, if necessary, with men and materiel. This security system can be loosely organized, but it needs some formal organization that can act quickly to stop war or revolution. Perhaps the Arab League could be reorganized and bolstered.

We in the West must show more firmness. We have to begin to pressure Arab states on oil pricing and on Israel. We should use our technical prowess, our industrial goods, and our food supplies to bargain harder. States taking an anti-Israel stance should receive no aid; radical states should be denied access to our markets and goods.

Saudi Arabia

Saudi Arabia is immense, 873,972 square miles in size, extending over four-fifths of the Arabian Peninsula. Most of the country is wasteland or desert; only a tiny proportion has arable or pasture land. Pastoral farming remains the country's main occupation, although its wealth is derived principally from oil. Saudi Arabia is the greatest oil producer in the Middle East, commanding about one-third of the available oil capacity there and nearly 40 percent of the reserves.

These oil resources were largely developed by the Arabian-American Oil Company (Aramco). During the 1970s the Saudi Arabian government acquired an increasing share in the company's ownership, and in 1977 it started taking over complete control. Nevertheless, Aramco continues to run the industry, which has revolutionized the Saudis' economy.

Saudi Arabia's second development program called for an expenditure of about $140 billion between 1975 and 1980, compared to only $12 billion over the preceding five years. Villages have grown into cities; airfields, roads, and port facilities have been constructed or expanded. A complete welfare program is now in operation, offering free medical care and schooling to most Saudis. The country has become a major source of contracts for foreign, especially American firms; in 1976 alone, U.S. firms received contracts worth more than $27 billion. Revenue derived from the oil industry has provided Saudi Arabia with a vast amount of liquid capital capable of being invested abroad, especially in the United States. From being one of the world's most backward countries, Saudi Arabia has become a great financial power, capable of giving much-needed help to states, like Egypt, that are intrinsically more powerful than it is.

Rapid development, however, has also had the effect of creating tremendous social imbalances; in some respects, though the parallels are not exact, Saudi Arabia compares with pre-revolutionary Iran. Saudi Arabia does not have minority problems comparable to the Kurdish problem in Iran, although there are tribal divisions; most of the population speaks Arabic and practices the Islamic religion. Saudi Arabia's Sunni tradition is less revolutionary in content than the Shi'ite faith of Iran. The rulers have followed a puritanical form of Islam, thereby avoiding hostility from traditional Muslims anxious to defend their faith against the alleged iniquities of the West. But Saudi Arabia nevertheless has problems aplenty. There is widespread criticism of the ruling families for permitting government waste, corruption, and incompetence. While xenophobic Iraq avoided the use of foreign workers in building up its economy, Saudi Arabia became an immigrants' country par excellence. The indigenous population probably numbers no more than five million; there are one and a half to two million foreigners, about half Yemenis and the rest Egyptians, Sudanese, Palestinians, Syrians, Lebanese, and others. Yemenis do most of the heavy unskilled labor; Egyptians, Syrians, Pakistanis, and others do the supervisory and medium-level technical jobs; Americans and Europeans fill the top-level managerial and technical positions; and Saudi Arabians hold the leading posts in defense, administration, public management, and other bureaus.

Like pre-revolutionary Iran, Saudi Arabia has to contend with a rapid rate of urbanization and serious discontent within the labor force. But unlike the case of Iran, educated Saudis who return home share in running the country. A large share of the national wealth has been expended on armaments and prestige projects. The national development plan, designed to diversify the country's economy, has had to be modified. Plans to create a heavy industry have been discarded, partly because of marketing problems, partly because heat, dust, and saline water supplies shorten the life of industrial plants and equipment. Saudi Arabia has to battle serious inflation and the ills that go with a swollen pre-modern bureaucracy.

The Saudi Arabian government might be described as one of despotism softened by paternalism. There is no parliament and no formal constitution. The king serves as both chief of state and head of government. He is his own prime minister and minister of foreign affairs. More than four thousand Saudi princes derive their income from the civil list; they are among the truest supporters of the monarchy, as are the great families, the Sudairis and the al-Sheikhs, who helped the Saudis overrun most of the Arabian Peninsula in the 1920s. The Bedouin population, traditional supporters of the monarchy, is declining numerically and is not the basic population of the state. The regular armed forces, mainly recruited from the cities, are far from loyal. Bedouin units may become subject to the disaffection experienced by uprooted, urbanized Bedouins.

Menaced by unrest within, Saudi Arabia is also threatened by the advance of Marxism in countries as diverse as Ethiopia, Afghanistan, and South Yemen. The United States, in dealing with Saudi Arabia, has made mistakes similar to those committed in its contacts with Iran. For one thing, Saudi Arabia has been armed beyond capacity. The United States has had no interest in the expansion of Saudi power into the gulf, but this policy may have to be changed. We might derive military and diplomatic profit from encouraging the ambitions of Saudi Arabia to become the arbiter of the Middle East, depending not on military might, but on dollar power.

For the present, however, the United States has an essential interest in maintaining the status quo in Saudi Arabia. We should encourage the country to enfranchise at least the educated and skilled of its permanent immigrant population. At the same time, we must help the Saudis to modernize sensibly and to defend their security and their oil production, essential elements in the well-being of the West. We cannot tolerate either an attack on Saudi Arabia through Soviet proxies or a shutdown of the Saudi oil industry. Saudi Arabia, like the Persian Gulf, may have to be assisted militarily and administratively in the case of a foreign invasion or an inner breakdown. This would require an informed and determined public opinion, as well as adequate military forces.

During the 1980s, the West will not be able to do without large supplies of Middle Eastern oil.* If the West is to survive economically and politically, the Middle Eastern oil wells—especially those in the Persian Gulf states and Saudi Arabia—cannot be permitted to pass into communist control. The United States should attempt to protect these oil supplies through strong diplomacy, by strengthening local military forces, and by stabilizing local governments while helping them to modernize. In an extreme emergency, the United States and its Western allies may have to intervene to help Saudi Arabia and the Persian Gulf states. Should the Soviet Union attempt to interfere—directly, through Cuban and East German proxies, or indirectly through radical Arab groups—we and the NATO powers should respond by armed force. Our determination to intervene, in the event of such extreme emergencies, must be stated clearly and unambiguously by the president.

NATO intervention should take place, if possible, in concert with friendly Arab powers like Egypt or Saudi Arabia. Intervention would require expansion of NATO's airlift capacity and highly trained mobile divisions. Military power should also be used if internal subversion is attempted in the Persian Gulf states or Saudi Arabia, or in the eventuality of an oil boycott instituted for political purposes. We must show the will and acquire the means for such intervention in order to blunt radical take-overs or Soviet expansionism.

For this purpose, the United States should develop adequate strategy and contingency plans to move an effective fighting force into the area. (At the time of writing, the United States had at least three airborne divisions ready for takeoff within a matter of hours, but all were light

*For the importance of oil, see essays by Houthakker, Iklé, and Moore in this volume.

divisions, ill-suited for combat against enemy forces equipped with heavy armor like those that foiled Allied operations at Arnheim in World War II.) In order to intervene successfully, our forces require more air transport, a network of pre-positioned bases, fuel and ammunition dumps, spare parts, repair facilities, air strips, and accommodation for troops, all available for use at short notice. These facilities should be located in the Sinai or Saudi Arabia. (The Soviet Union is far advanced in this respect, with extensive stockpiles of weapons light and heavy, ammunition, spare parts, and so forth, distributed as far afield as Libya, Syria, Iraq, Ethiopia, and South Yemen.) American and NATO diplomats would then have the difficult task of persuading Saudi Arabia that a U.S. or NATO promise of support can be relied upon, and that Saudi Arabia should further collaborate with the West lest the Soviets gain a military advantage that could not be undone. The Saudis must be convinced that we intend to stop the Soviet advance and will stand by our friends.

Turkey

Turkey is the most important military power in the Middle East. The country's area is 301,380 square miles, the population about forty million. Ethnically, modern Turkey is fairly homogeneous. More than 90 percent of the population speaks Turkish; the other languages are Arabic, Armenian, and Kurdish. There are, however, several million Kurds in Turkey.

Turkey is rich in a variety of minerals and has a potentially large supply of hydroelectric power, but these resources remain to be developed. Ever since Kemal Atatürk's harsh but competent rule as president from 1923 to 1938, Turkey has opted for westernization, and in economic terms the Turkish achievement has been impressive. The Turkish road and rail network is the best in the Middle East. Turkish agricultural production, dependent almost entirely on peasant enterprise, has increased considerably over the past twenty years. Since the 1950s Turkey has gone through an industrial revolution, and the growth of its GNP has been substantial.

Many economic problems remain, however. Agriculture, accounting for nearly 70 percent of the country's employed population but less than 30 percent of its national income, is still backward and undercapitalized, the stepchild of official planning. Turkey has to contend with a huge bureaucracy and a widely inefficient system of state intervention in economic affairs. The State Planning Organization, set up in 1960, controls all major Turkish private and state investments and wields far-reaching powers regarding foreign investment; the state provides a major share of all fixed capital investments—more than 50 percent in 1970.

Turkey has teetered on the brink of bankruptcy ever since the sudden rise in world oil prices in 1973–1974 intensified existing economic problems. The rate of inflation in 1978 has been variously estimated at 40–60 percent per annum. There have been recurrent deficits in the balance of payments. Since 1970 the foreign debt has tripled, reaching $12 billion early in 1979. Nearly half the country's plant capacity lay unused in early 1979; there were shortages of everything, from light bulbs to traditional Turkish coffee; electrical stoppages were common; industrial unrest was widespread.

Turkey has one of the highest birthrates in the world; nearly two-thirds of the population is under 30 years of age. Migrants from the villages crowd into the cities or try to find work in Western Europe, especially in West Germany and Switzerland. There is a high rate of urbanization, with all its attendant ills, and there are striking contrasts between city and countryside. Unemployment in 1978 supposedly struck 20 percent of the labor force. By 1979 Turkey was divided by bitter violence. Rival gangs of youthful militants carried on savage feuds; political terrorism was widespread. There were clashes between the Sunni Muslims—the majority, who tend toward the right in political orientation—and the Shiite minority, who are apt to sympathize with left-wingers. In 1978 and 1979 rioting led to the imposition of martial law in most provinces.

The riots were suppressed, but Turkey remains potentially unstable. Political order must be regained and economic problems solved: inflation, unemployment, trade deficits, foreign debts. By 1979 Prime Minister Bülent Ecevit's coalition government was under heavy pressure from critics within Parliament and from the extraparliamentary opposition, including militant strikers and terrorists of varying political faiths drawn from the ranks of the intelligentsia. Finally Ecevit resigned.

Turkey's domestic problems are paralleled by difficulties in foreign policy. The country needs to be wary of the Soviet Union, with its traditional claim to Turkish territory in the Caucasus and to control of the Turkish straits (Bosporus and Dardanelles). But Turkey's most immediate foreign problems relate to Greece and Cyprus. A major disagreement, concerning control over the continental shelf in the Aegean Sea, began in 1974 when Greece struck oil in the Aegean and claimed that the continental shelf rights of each island were secured under the Geneva Convention of 1958. Turkey insisted that the Aegean was a special case, in that the continental shelf formed a natural extension of Anatolia.

But the most serious Turko-Greek dispute concerns the island of Cyprus. Both sides can make out a good claim. The majority of Cypriots speak Greek, and many of them would welcome union (*enosis*) with Greece. In the Turkish view, *enosis* would be a gross violation of Turkish minority rights. Cyprus has never been part of Greece. Originally an Ottoman possession, in 1878 Cyprus came under British administration, a domination challenged by Greek partisans in the 1950s. After lengthy negotiations, Turkey, Greece, Great Britain, and the newly formed republic of Cyprus concluded the Treaty of London (1960), which gave special protection to the island's Turkish minority, about one-fifth of the population.

The Turkish minority was exposed to constant harassment during the 1960s and early 1970s. There was bitter intercommunal strife, in which the United States essentially sided with the Greeks. A substantial body of Greek troops infiltrated the island and gradually tried to eliminate the Turkish community. In 1974, in response to the Greek junta's attempt to overthrow President Makarios, Turkish forces landed and enabled the Turkish Cypriots to establish authority over about 40 percent of the island. The Greeks, subject to atrocities, sought refuge in the Greek zone.

In retaliation for Turkey's actions on Cyprus, the Greek-American lobby persuaded Congress to impose an arms embargo against Turkey in 1975. The embargo was later partially rescinded, then lifted altogether; but its consequences to Turko-American relations were disastrous. American military men were evicted from five important intelligence-gathering bases; and the Turkish armed forces, denied additional equipment, suffered in their readiness for war, weakening NATO. In 1977 the Turks began to improve their relations with the Soviet Union, which soon became their principal source of investment capital. In addition, to balance existing commitments to the United States and the European Economic Community, the Turks formed closer ties with Eastern Europe and with the Islamic countries of the Middle East.

From the standpoint of the United States, the embargo was a serious error. For all its present troubles, Turkey is not likely to become another Iran. Turkey is not subject to an absolute monarch, but has an elected parliament and a free press. In constitutional liberties, only Israel can compare with Turkey. There is no mass movement seeking to overthrow the Turkish political system as there was in Iran. Political dissensions are bitter between the ruling socialist-democratic Republican People's party, headed by Bülent Ecevit, and the conservative Justice party, the main oppositional group under Suleiman Demirel. But at this time only small terrorist groups want to overthrow the social order. Compared to Iran, Turkey is more secular and therefore less restricted by Islamic fundamentalism and the influence of conservative ayatollahs or mullahs. The army is not simply a political tool of the ruling government; it will defend the legally elected government and can be relied upon to put down terrorist attacks. Turkey's middle class is much more substantial than Iran's, and modernization has gone a great deal further.

In its international relations, the United States must endeavor to balance its interests in Greece and Turkey. Greco-American ties must take second place to Turko-American relations in the wider calculation of American and overall Western interests. Turkey's strategic position is as important to this country as is Turkish power.

Turkey controls the exit from the Black Sea to the Bosporus, as well as entry to the Aegean Sea through the Dardanelles. The country plays an essential part in NATO by providing a large number of strategic bases for combat, navigation, communications, and intelligence operations. The Turkish armed forces, nearly half a million men, far exceed the Greek forces in numerical strength. Their cooperation is essential for defense of the eastern Mediterranean against the Soviet Union and for NATO's defense of its southern flank.

Even from the Greek standpoint, close U.S.-Turkish relations are essential. Turkey's participation in NATO greatly increases the security of Greece. Turkish control of the Dardanelles blocks the Soviet sea-lanes, making the Soviet Mediterranean fleet vulnerable to NATO air forces and placing difficulties in the way of Soviet naval support to land forces engaged in an attack on Greece. If the Turkish armed forces were neutralized, the Soviets would be able to increase the number of troops stationed on NATO's central front, making the NATO position in Central Europe even more difficult.

Given these elementary military facts, U.S. policy toward Turkey has been offensively moralistic in form, fumbling and inept in content. The United States is no longer trusted by the Turks as a steadfast ally. In 1979, though it remained a member of NATO, Turkey began to move toward the radical Arab camp. Ecevit withdrew from CENTO and asked for its formal dissolution, Iran and Pakistan having already abrogated their membership.

Turkish motives were not hard to fathom. Turkey did not wish to be regarded by the Arab powers as the sole Western outpost in the region. Also, Turkey looks to the Arab countries for economic benefits; Iraq and Libya supply most of its oil and have agreed to extend credits and to buy more Turkish goods. Having experienced diplomatic slights and difficulties in obtaining loans from the West, Turkey has now turned to the radical Arab states and can be counted on to pursue an anti-Israel and pro-Palestine policy. The United States can strengthen Turkey via aid, loans, and military assistance. One of our first tasks in the Middle East must be to restore the Turko-American alliance, which should form the keystone of U.S. policy in the eastern Mediterranean.

Turkey remains strongly nationalist, indeed, xenophobic. Many Turks retain deep pride in the achievements of the Ottoman Empire and continue to feel anger at Europeans for its destruction. Suspicion of foreigners militates against foreign investments. The bureaucracy restricts businessmen's efforts; hence foreigners are apt to go elsewhere. The 1980s will determine whether Turkey can solve its problems under a democratic government or whether it will return to an inefficient form of military rule. The rulers of Turkey face a difficult task; they have to stop internecine violence, improve the economy, limit wasteful and inefficient public enterprise, stimulate exports, encourage tourism, and develop mineral resources. Above all, Turkey must limit its present high rate of population growth. But even if Turkey does not succeed in all these difficult tasks, the United States—in its own interests—should support Turkey by all the means at its command; Turkey is too important for NATO to be allowed to founder or Turkey to drift into revolution.

RUSSIA AND THE UNITED STATES IN THE MIDDLE EAST

Throughout most of its history, the Middle East has been an arena of strife for the great powers. Russia has traditionally sought to extend its boundaries to the south. The British and the French have intervened in the nineteenth and twentieth centuries and the United States (in Lebanon) in 1958.

According to Soviet theoreticians, the Soviet Union represents the interests of the world's working class; the Western powers stand for the power of the bourgeoisie. Conflict between these two contending classes thus is inevitable. Competition for markets, raw materials, or naval bases, along with scholarships, trade, diplomacy, strikes, guerrilla campaigns, and wars of liberation—all must serve as revolutionary tools. Détente, to the Soviets, is but a means of intensifying the global class struggle and assuring the doom of the global bourgeoisie; as they see it, the international balance of forces has shifted in favor of the socialist camp. This balance of power must be tilted further; and in this struggle the Middle East, with its vast oil resources and numerous conflict situations, plays an essential part.

The Soviet Union has used various means to advance toward its ends. In 1945 Moscow called for Soviet control over the Turkish straits; in addition, it laid claim to Turkish territory in the Caucasus and along an extensive stretch of the Turkish Black Sea coast. The Soviets also set up puppet governments in Northern Iran, and communist insurgents attempted to take over Greece. These territorial claims were subsequently abandoned under pressure from the West. The Soviet Union also works through local communist parties. Most of them operate in illegality or semi-legality; their membership remains small; their political power is greatest when they manage to operate as partners within a broader coalition. The Iraqi Communist party, for example, established an alliance with the governing Ba'ath party in 1973; but this alliance did not protect the Communist party from severe persecution later. The Soviet Union, of course, also seeks advantages of a conventional kind by collaborating with incumbent governments, offering them arms and technicians. Through this strategy the USSR has gained many temporary advantages; but there have also been serious reverses, as in Egypt when Sadat turned from Moscow to Washington.

The strategy of a "united front" is likely to be much used during the 1980s. Rather than working on their own or marching under the banner of communists, Marxist-Leninists work by means of militant "fronts" or "liberation movements." Victory having been achieved through a "national democratic revolution," the party's "feudal" or "bourgeois" allies are then destroyed; the formerly allied leaders are suborned, jailed, hanged, or shot. The struggle for "scientific socialism" begins in earnest under the sole guidance of the new ruling party, whose functionaries in theory serve as the self-appointed representatives of the proletariat and in practice form a newly privileged elite.

In Afghanistan, the monarchy was overthrown in 1973 by a militant Islamic movement led by Mohammed Daud, a former prime minister and a relative of the king. The People's Democratic party of Afghanistan, a small Marxist-Leninist body, initially joined Daud in a united front. According to the party's official account, "after the Daud coup, we intensified our work in the armed forces. Our party leadership had always given them much attention. The party had always schooled comrades wearing the uniform, had educated them politically and ideologically." Daud was overthrown by "the vanguard party of the working class," which then set up a pro-Russian dictatorship. Khomeini can expect similar treatment in Iran.

In South Yemen, a National Front for the Liberation of Occupied South Yemen was formed in 1963. Its avowed object was to drive out the British. South Yemen achieved independence in 1967. In their own words, the Marxist-Leninists within the ruling coalition then prepared "the necessary conditions for the transformation of the National Front into a vanguard party of the working class." They sought to achieve this objective through intensifying the class struggle and, above all, through tightening their links with "the socialist community countries headed by the Soviet Union, and with other contingents of the world revolutionary movement." In 1978 the Marxist-Leninists seized control and set up the Yemeni Socialist party (YSP) as the sole repository of power. Yemen then became a military base for Cuban troops and a sanctuary for guerrillas operating against Oman and North Yemen, and it was a point d'appui for Soviet naval units operating in the Indian Ocean. With Cuban instructors, Cuban pilots, and Soviet technicians, and equipped with the most modern arms, the liberation forces have become a formidable menace, not merely to North Yemen and Oman, but also to Saudi Arabia, the linchpin of American oil power in the Middle East. Continued trouble can be expected also in the region of the Horn of Africa until the Soviets are neutralized or countered in Ethiopia.

Seen in a wider context, the Soviet Union and its allies enjoy a number of distinct advantages in the Middle East. Whereas Iranians and Turks have bitter memories of past Russian aggression, the Soviet Union is remote from most Arab countries. The Arabs have experienced only the Western kind of imperialism, not that of the Soviets. Western investments remain popular targets of hostility. The West is widely censured, both as an agent of modernization and as the putative cause of Middle East backwardness. Western propaganda has failed to turn to good advantage the Soviet record as a colonial power in Central Asia, the Caucasus, and Eastern Europe, or Soviet hostility to Islam. Above all, the West is associated with Israel, and Israel, tiny as it is, serves as the scapegoat for all the ills that beset the Arab world.

Fortunately for the West, Soviet policy in the Middle East has evinced serious weaknesses. In Iraq in 1978 and 1979, the ruling Ba'athist party, angered at the Iraqi Communist party's anti-religious stance and disconcerted by developments in Iran, put down the Iraqi communists with a strong hand. Iraq increasingly turned to the West, especially to France, for the supply of new weapons, and it also improved its relations with Saudi Arabia. The Soviets must also contend with numerous other obstacles. Unlike the regimes in power in Prague or East Berlin, the Middle Eastern governments are not creatures of the Kremlin, installed by foreign conquerors. Moreover, Islam remains a potent ideological force, one not easily harnessed to Soviet purposes. Economically, the Middle Eastern countries remain tied to the West, which supplies their principal markets and the bulk of their imports.

The ongoing battle for the region cannot, however, be won by the U.S. alone. The West cannot simply "solve" the problems of the region, military, economic, or political; indeed, the constant search for instant "solutions" has been a bane of America's foreign policy. The United States cannot "teach" Arab governments how better to govern or how to improve the management of their resources. The United States can only step in when its help is requested, and when it can operate with the assistance of local allies like Israel or Egypt. The Palestinian question is likewise too complex to be solved by means of a simple formula, even though it creates many of the problems that allow the Soviets to gain influence and burden the entire region with a wasteful, expensive arms race.

Faced with the Soviet offensive, the United States labors under many disadvantages. The United States is the chief—indeed, the only—great foreign supporter of Israel. We are capitalistic and democratic. Americans own the major share of foreign investment in the Middle East. We have meddled in local politics and we started the arms race in the area. In the eyes of our critics, Americans can do no right. If we invest abroad, we are guilty of exploiting foreign countries. If we do not invest, we incur blame for "boycotting" foreign economies. If we sell modern arms, we are responsible for profiting from the implements of war. If we do not sell up-to-date weapons, we are guilty of imperial selectivity. The list of linked charges never ends. Americans have no instrument comparable to the communist parties' front groups or radical cliques that support Moscow. These cliques are well trained, disciplined, and supported by enormous propaganda, intelligence, and military machines that command the resources of countries as varied as Cuba, the Democratic Republic of Germany, and the Soviet Union and that find fellow travelers in every Western nation.

The Americans have been responsible also for a series of grave tactical mistakes. It is foolish to stake all on the fate of a single ruler, like the former shah of Iran. Nor can Saudi Arabia serve as policeman of the Persian Gulf. The Saudis are too weak to act as policeman anywhere outside their own borders; indeed, they would barely be able to defend themselves against a well-planned "war of liberation" supported by Cuban, Soviet, or East German experts. Given its military and economic deficiencies, even Egypt is hardly in a position to serve as a local proxy for the United States; and Israeli forces, though militarily efficient, cannot be employed in the Arab world for political reasons. The Western alliance thus is in a state of disarray throughout the Middle East, and the West may conceivably have to contend during the 1980s with a radicalized

Middle East controlled by anti-Western Marxist or militant Muslim parties.

What, then, can the United States do? In general, we have many advantages over our Soviet rivals in the area. We are considered the lesser evil compared to the Soviet Union; we are seen as a counterweight to communism, especially in Turkey, Iran, and Israel and in such conservative Arab states as Saudi Arabia. We have important economic assets; American goods are more valued. We can offer food surpluses to areas where food is scarce. American multinational corporations, no matter what leftists say, are efficient producers. American banks and financial institutions, corporations and businesses, goods and technology, then, give us clear advantages in the area if we can sell ourselves and our products. Technological superiority in agriculture, nuclear power, desalination, solar energy, and computers is especially valuable in the Middle East.

The first desideratum remains a stable peace treaty between Israel and Egypt, with American guarantees for both signatories. The advantages of such a treaty to the United States are manifold. Egypt and Israel alike are opposed to the communist camp. An end of hostilities between them diminishes the possibility of future Soviet intervention in the area.

A neutralized Palestinian state is not an ideal solution, but it is the best that can be hoped for. The state could not absorb the majority of Palestinian refugees now living in the Arab world but it would afford them a homeland. They could become citizens of a recognized country, with recognized passports and a possible refuge. "Middle Palestine," the land between Israel and Jordan, could play the same role for the Palestinian diaspora that Israel provides for world Jewry: a focus of national loyalty. At the same time, the United States should encourage other Arab states to provide full civil rights for permanent immigrants of good standing. The conclusion of a peace treaty could split the united Arab front against Israel, thereby persuading Iraq and Syria to recognize Israel.

The United States cannot easily operate in the Middle East without local allies. The Turkish alliance should be rebuilt, if possible. In addition, the United States should continue to sustain both Israel and Egypt. But the Americans would be unwise to overestimate even the collective strength of these two countries. The Western presence in the Middle East must be supported, therefore, by a combined effort on the part of the Western European countries and Japan.

In the past we foolishly diminished British and French influence in the Middle East in the name of "anti-imperialism." We would do better to associate Western Europe with U.S. interests in the Middle East in the 1980s. This objective might best be secured by extending the geographical field of NATO to the South Atlantic and the western Indian Ocean, both vital to the alliance for strategic ports, harbors, air fields, and supply depots, as well as oil resources. The policy of furnishing desert states with vast arsenals of supermodern weapons must cease; countries like Saudi Arabia lack the population to maintain large forces. They would do better to maintain small professional forces capable of dealing with guerrilla incursions and local policing problems, rather than import equipment that they cannot use adequately. We need to provide the Saudis and the gulf states with a protective umbrella such as the British provided until 1971. Forces capable of reacting quickly to threats must be developed by NATO: air transport and mobile elite military divisions that can fly anywhere in the Middle East.

Saudi Arabia wants an air defense system. The U.S. can provide one from aircraft based in the Sinai in one of the bases Israel has left. Prepositioning material and at least laying out the outlines of airfield, repair and supply depots in Israel and in the Sinai would do much to reassure Egypt and the Saudis and remove the Saudis' fears of being attacked by the radical states or the Palestinians. Naval forces in the Persian Gulf area and off the Horn of Africa would also bolster the morale of conservative rulers. At the present time they fear the PLO and Soviet sponsored liberation movements. If we can remove that fear the Saudis are less likely to stay in the radical camp and isolate Egypt.

There is no question that to sustain influence in the Middle East will require increased effort in the 1980s, for internal events in the developing countries will be difficult to control. As a result, unsavory radical regimes are likely to take over from conservative or inept military regimes. We must learn to live with instability. Strong-arm tactics or CIA-orchestrated coups are not an answer; even if we had the will, we would not have the apparatus to carry out such operations. Wherever rapid modernization and Marxist ideology produce turbulence and revolution, we will be handicapped in competing with the Soviet Union for the friendship of various successor governments. Multinational forces provided by the West therefore must protect Israel, Saudi Arabia, and the Persian Gulf. In addition, we should help the Arabs form an effective Arab League force to counter revolutions and invasions.

North Africa threatens to become another trouble spot during the 1980s. At the time of writing, Morocco and Mauritania, having partitioned the former Spanish Sahara between them, are aligned against the Polisario, a so-called liberation front determined to set up an independent Saharan state. Polisario has received support from Libya and Algeria and has succeeded in forcing terms on Mauritania, threatened already on its southern flank by Senegalese claims to Mauritania's most valuable agricultural lands. By 1979, the war against Polisario had reduced Mauritania to near collapse; war had poisoned relations between Algeria and Morocco, imposing heavy military burdens on both, and had split the Organization of African Unity.

In its own interests, the United States should support Morocco against the radicals in Algeria and Libya. But President Carter's policy has remained inconsistent, devoid of strategic coherence. Our present policy regarding Morocco makes no geopolitical sense. Morocco, a moderate monarchy, controls the Straits of Gibraltar, one of the most vital waterways in the world; Morocco has helped to restrain the radical Arab states and has facilitated Egyptian-Israeli peace talks. But the United States does not recognize the take-over by Morocco and Mauritania of the former Spanish Sahara; instead, Washington has bowed to the radical Third World states, led by Algeria, for a Polisario-led independent western Saharan state, a state even less viable from the demographic or economic standpoint than Mauritania. Morocco needs OV-10 counter insurgency aircraft, advanced helicopter gunships, sensors for night fighting, and other military hardware to deal with mechanized Polisario formations. Morocco has the most efficient army in Northwest Africa, and it is a state well worth backing. We should also back the Sudan in its present support of Sadat; in this respect the United States must oppose present Saudi Arabian efforts to use financial might to induce King Hassan of Morocco and President Numayri of Sudan to cut their existing ties with Egypt.

The United States has a good chance to succeed in this objective. Algeria (as well as Libya) needs Western technology and merchandise. Algeria has begun tentatively to encourage Western enterprise and to sell oil to the United States. American diplomacy could help bring about an Algerian-Moroccan compromise. Washington, at the same time, should take a hard line against Libya, a paymaster of international terrorism. If Libya does not stop financing terrorists and if it continues to seek an Islamic nuclear capability, perhaps Egypt would put heavier pressure on Libya, depose President Khadafi, and add Libya to its sphere of influence. Algeria, under present leadership, is likely to be more concerned with domestic programs than with foreign adventures. The rulers of Algeria wish to continue their industrialization program; they are most likely to succeed if they call for Western help. A cartel like the Organization of Petroleum Exporting Countries, of Western exporters of food and industrial equipment, would strengthen our bargaining position with regard to both Algeria and other Arab powers.

WHAT OF THE FUTURE?

The "Vietnam syndrome" has scarred the Carter administration. Watched carefully by Congress, the administration has hesitated to act decisively or plan strategically. Americans at present seem fearful of intervening anywhere in the world, no matter how important our interests are. Faith is put on diplomacy, not in military power, and so Carter has been indecisive and weak. Also, the War Powers Resolution of 1973 severely restricts a president from sending troops to trouble spots, thus the symbolic gesture of sending unarmed F-15s to Saudi Arabia during the Yemen war. The presidency must reassert itself in the 1980s, stopping Congress from interfering in foreign policy matters and returning to secret diplomacy.

Above all, the Western powers must be willing to take up the Soviet ideological and military challenge. As long as the world's communist parties consider themselves at war with all other social systems, the West must resist. Fortunately, the Soviet Union itself is highly vulnerable to ideological assaults carried out through broadcasts, television programs, diplomatic communications, and other such media. Ideological—like military—attacks should be directed against the opponents' points of maximum weakness. The contradictions within the Soviet system are plentiful: the contradiction between the Soviet hegemonial power and its minor allies; contradictions between the great Russian "state nation" and the Soviet nationalities (not merely the Jews); contradictions between the communist great powers; the contradiction between the ruling class of party functionaries and ideologues on the one hand and the masses on the other; the contradiction between Marxism-Leninism and the great religions of mankind, with whom the communists now seek a "historic compromise" for the sake of ultimate victory. If the West will take up the gauntlet, Marxism-Leninism cannot ultimately prevail.

Latin America

Mark Falcoff

XXVIII

The history of U.S. foreign policy is rich in rediscoveries of the importance of Latin America. Will the next decade be such a period? In an international environment that seems increasingly hostile (or at least difficult), it is tempting to fall back to the presumably safer ramparts provided by geographic propinquity and historic interest. The world energy crisis, growing pressures on the dollar, a rudderless Western alliance—all seem to encourage renewed attention to a long-standing sphere of U.S. interest, as a source of markets, raw materials, and perhaps even support in the world forums where monetary and strategic issues are decided.

To take note of a revival of U.S. interest in the area is not to suggest, however, that renewed initiatives will necessarily be well received. During the last fifteen years of benign neglect, Latin American governments have had the freedom to go their own ways on a wide variety of fronts, and the distance between them and the United States has perceptibly widened. Most have opened trade relations with the communist world. New regulations greatly restrict the activities of foreign investors. State monopolies in areas formerly open to major American participation (particularly minerals and hydrocarbons) have become the rule rather than the exception. Dependency explanations, which place most of the blame for Latin America's backwardness on U.S. economic interests, are no longer confined to academic sanctuaries; they are now the common currency of a growing body of generals, bishops, editors, chiefs of state, even Latin American businessmen. Governments resentful of the conservative lending policies of international agencies dominated by the United States have found their way to private money markets in Europe, Japan, and even the Arab world. Although these expedients have not notably improved matters—indeed, some areas, such as international indebtedness, have notably worsened—as a result they have not convinced Latin American governments, publicists, or diplomats that their earlier orientation toward the United States was perhaps the most sensible course after all. Rather, the recriminations have taken on a new and even curious note. The United States is damned for neglecting Latin America and for oppressing and exploiting it—all at the same time!

Hence, the first counsel for anyone contemplating U.S. policy in Latin America during the next decade must be to avoid flights of optimism. No one policy or group of policies, in the short run at least, will reverse trends that have been in the making for a quarter-century or more. One might argue as well that many developments within the region, including the perennial neglect by Washington policymakers, have been due to events beyond anyone's control. It should be kept in mind that the international importance of Latin America has steadily declined since World War II. In 1938 European economic interest in the area was far greater than it is today; as for the United States, Latin America was then its only Third World. Since 1945, European policies of agricultural self-sufficiency and the politics of the European Economic Community have struck hard at Latin America's need for hard currency. And the United States has developed interests in regions of Africa, Asia, and the Middle East formerly conceded to the British, the French, or the Dutch.

It is clear that the agendas of the United States and the Latin American nations have become quite different over the past two decades. Historically, U.S. policy has been dominated by considerations of military and economic security. As defined by Washington, this has meant a desire to prevent the interference of extrahemispheric powers in the affairs of the region, as well as protection of U.S. investments, markets, and sources of supply. In recent years this agenda has been periodically augmented by other political and ideological goals: anti-communism (in the fifties); promotion of democratic regimes and social reform (in the sixties); human rights and nuclear nonproliferation (in the seventies).

At one time many of the southern republics were willing to accept these goals, at least within certain restrictions. But today they reject almost all of them. Moreover, with the dispersal of world industrial capacity and of pretensions to great power status, Latin American demands on the United States have become more difficult to negotiate. Greater access to U.S. markets for certain raw materials and semi-finished goods; greater trade and tariff preferences generally; indexing of raw material prices; postponement of service on, or refinancing of, existing debts; and withdrawal of U.S. political support for U.S.-based multinational corporations—all often counter well-entrenched economic and labor interests within the United States. A few American policies are accepted as applicable to other republics but not to one's own: for example, protection of human rights, which would normally violate the sacred code of nonintervention in the internal affairs of American states.

Finally, the time has probably passed when the United States could have a single Latin American policy applicable to nearly two dozen political communities of unequal size, importance, and potential. Although stratification among Latin American states has always been a fact of life, on an ideological level the United States has been persistently reluctant to admit it (hence such meaningless terms as pan-Americanism and the inter-American system, and such unfortunate devices as the Loeb doctrine and the Hickenlooper Amendment). Rather than promulgate one policy, what the United States must try to do for the next decade is define those clusters of interest and conflict that will dominate its relations with the major states of the region. This survey is intended to provide a model for such discussion.

LATIN AMERICA: THE NEURALGIC POINTS

Mexico

After nearly a quarter-century of continuous economic growth and political stability, Mexico entered the 1970s haunted by serious doubts about her future, doubts that, given her close relationship with the United States, amounted to something approaching a family crisis. In essence, it appeared as if the Mexican Revolution—an extended exercise in populist nationalism, industrialization, patronage networks, and a trickle-down approach to economic development—had exhausted its possibilities. Perhaps it would have been more accurate to say that the revolution was faced with the possibility of being overtaken by Mexico's prodigious rate of human growth.

The facts are these: the country's present rate of population increase is 3.5 percent a year, the fastest among major nations; consequently, its current population of 63 million will have grown by half at the end of the next decade and duplicated itself by the end of the century. Almost one of every two Mexicans is under fifteen years of age, and by 1985 the vast majority of these young people will have entered the labor market. There they will compete with a labor force an astounding 45 percent of which was recently described by the *Wall Street Journal* as unemployed or marginally employed. (According to the same source, 17 percent of the population is earning less than $75 a year.) At the same time, Mexican agriculture has experienced a decline in productivity; and the overall rate of economic growth has slowed from the steady 6 percent a year that has characterized the past three decades.

To meet the undeniable social crisis that these statistics portend, the Mexican government has chosen to borrow abroad rather than to tax the nation's wealthy; thus the long-term debt of the public sector has mushroomed from $3.6 billion (1971) to $25 billion (1977). These obligations now consume nearly a quarter of the country's export earnings; debt service for 1977 exceeded $4 billion. Put simply, Mexico's credit standing cannot endure further welfare spending financed by foreign loans. Yet until recently no alternative seemed possible, given the nation's domestic political and social power structure.

Consequently, it is easy to understand the euphoria that greeted the discovery of new reserves of oil and natural gas in the states of Chiapas and Tabasco in the early and mid-seventies. Those new finds, combined with previously known reserves, have caused PEMEX (Petroleros Mexicanos), the state oil monopoly, to raise its estimate of Mexico's known petroleum holdings to 26 billion barrels. President José López Portillo has set a production target of 2.25 million barrels per day by the end of 1980, of which slightly less than half (1.1 million) will be earmarked for export. These sales, combined with the export of natural gas, should yield nearly $8 billion in annual foreign currency reserves for 1980 and $11 billion by 1983, enough to service the country's long-term foreign public debt and provide the resources to expand imports of capital goods and industrial raw materials.

The implications of this oil bonanza for the United States are too obvious to require extended comment. Although in fact the Mexicans would probably prefer to sell this oil to anyone else, historic animosities have not prevented their leaders from recognizing that the United States is not merely the most logical market for the new surplus, but much the best. Apart from the vast absorptive capacity of the United States, geographical proximity gives Mexico an economic advantage. Vastly lower shipping costs would allow Mexico to compete successfully with oil from the Persian Gulf, and because of contiguous land boundaries with the United States, pipelines could carry natural gas to a market presently consuming twenty trillion cubic feet a year. Neither liquefaction nor burning off the entire amount at the wellhead are satisfactory alternatives, and Mexico lacks the economic capacity to consume locally even a significant part of her natural gas reserves. Further, as her principal foreign customer, the United States would have ample incentive to provide Mexico with the technology and capital necessary to fully exploit her possibilities in the areas of oil and natural gas—particularly the construction of a pipeline network. What capital could not be found in private U.S. banks for such purposes would be forthcoming from agencies like the International Monetary Fund. Development of the American market would also materially improve Mexico's export earnings and general credit standing and would provide some additional domestic employment.

Precisely how much more employment is difficult to say, but the oil industry alone can be expected to provide only 100,000 more jobs. If this figure is multiplied by four or even five, it still falls pitifully short of the nation's true needs. To be sure, the oil boom will have consequences in many areas of the nation's economy, and in fact economists have already noted a quickening in the pace of Mexican private investment, where growth should be facilitated by the easier availability of foreign exchange. However, Mexican leaders are fearful of an unrestrained increase in oil and gas production. They believe—not without foundation—that too much new money plowed too quickly into the Mexican economy will impart a sharper thrust to an already acute inflationary spiral. The oil issue poses to Mexican policymakers the same kinds of painful choices between inflation and employment already familiar to their American counterparts.

Thus, although oil affords Mexico a breathing space in which to face some of her most pressing obligations and domestic needs, it cannot be expected to provide a panacea for her social problems. Nor can the United States remain indifferent to that fact. If the good news for the United States is that her closest southern neighbor has the capacity to release her from dependency on the Organization of Petroleum Exporting Countries (OPEC), the bad news is that even if these energy resources are successfully exploited to mutual advantage, as things stand now they will have little effect on the other most pressing problem in U.S.-Mexican relations: illegal immigration.

The dimensions of this problem have lately become so enormous that they can no longer be ignored in the supposed interests of diplomatic expediency or even domestic civil liberties. It is believed that there are presently between two and three million Mexican workers, legal and illegal, in the United States, with the number of illegals increasing at the rate of 500,000 a year (1977 Immigration and Naturalization Service estimates). As many as 80 percent of all immigrants to the United States may be Mexicans, and probably 8 percent of Mexico's total population and 13 percent of her potential labor force presently lives in this country. Although studies of this migration are few and inexact, it appears that most of its components are young men from low-income rural communities, mainly from the states of central Mexico—precisely those states suffering most acutely from overpopulation and unemployment. Thus Mexico's problems perforce have become those of her northern neighbor as well.

The full implications of this issue for the United States have yet to be fully mapped. At a minimum, it presupposes an enormous additional burden on the welfare, social service, and police agencies of the western United States, a burden that (in the absence of any other measures) is likely to increase geometrically if successive amnesties encourage illegals to declare themselves and make fresh demands upon the U.S. government, now as members of a minority. The issue has already been felt in American domestic politics in two ways: one is the temporizing attitude of the Carter administration, whose Democratic constituency includes an increasingly vocal bilingual (Hispanic) element that favors unconditional amnesty for illegals; the other is a backlash on the part of Western (mostly non-Hispanic) taxpayers and voters, whose most prototypical manifestation to date has been California's Proposition 13.

Unfortunately, the United States cannot solve this problem unilaterally; and to put the matter baldly, Mexico feels that the issue is not nearly her most pressing priority. Mexican responses to the immigration question operate on a number of levels. These range from undisguised glee at the prospect of making good the loss of California in 1848 through a new, invisible invasion force, to shame and regret that the Mexican Revolution has been unable to provide for millions of the nation's potentially most productive citizens, forcing them to abandon their homes and families for an often problematical existence in the United States.

Probably the prevailing attitude within the Mexican government lies somewhere in between: it quietly appreciates the dollar remittances that migrants send home, and above all it recognizes that emigration to the United States presently constitutes a critical safety valve for Mexican society. Were the unemployed of Mexico suddenly denied the prospect of finding work in the United States, the result could conceivably translate overnight into political unrest and social chaos. Mexican leaders also suspect that the U.S. interest in their nation's stability is hardly less palpable than their own—and in this they are not far from the truth. Three billion dollars have been invested in Mexico by American citizens, and private U.S. banks and U.S.–controlled international lending agencies hold 90 percent of the country's foreign debt. Mexico is also an excellent customer, taking well over half her imports from the United States, with whom in recent years she has maintained a consistently unfavorable balance of payments. Serious political unrest would endanger future economic relations, particularly in the critical area of energy production. And, at the very least, the United States could not hope to insulate herself against the consequences of a social upheaval on the other side of a border that in any case is largely imaginary.

Officially, Mexico has long held that most migrants are only temporarily in the United States and will someday return; thus, her only obligation is to ensure that her citizens receive fair treatment while abroad. However, side by side with this somewhat disingenuous posture, Mexican leaders frequently assert that migration is a fundamental human right that the United States cannot abridge (a position that Mexico herself chooses not to observe with respect to Guatemalan migrants on her southern border). Only recently has the Mexican government been willing to publicly acknowledge that the problem is a serious practical one. Pressed to comment during his 1977 visit to the United States, President José López Portillo maintained that emigration could only be stemmed by long-range economic development. Meanwhile, he said, the United States should grant Mexico special commercial status and should continue to absorb her surplus population until she can provide adequately for it.

This response is obviously unsatisfactory to the United States. The migration problem threatens to become far too great in the next decade simply to grant Mexico tariff and trade preferences and hope for the best. For one thing, the performance of the Mexican economy depends upon factors beyond U.S. control. Corruption, jobbery, and nepotism are integral parts of the Mexican economic system, and no amount of aid, direct or indirect, can circumvent the outstretched hands of the bureaucracy and go directly to where it is needed most. To illustrate this point more clearly: from the perspective of U.S. interests, it would be far simpler and more desirable to transfer the present resources expended on a frequently indigent Mexican population in the United States to the poverty-stricken areas from which that population comes. The same funds spent in Mexico would help far more people, and at the same time would relieve the United States of the long-term costs of the problem at home. But such an operation—even if it could win the approval of the U.S. Congress—could never hope to negotiate its way past the shoals of Mexican corruption and an often self-serving nationalism.

Short of such dramatic measures, the United States should do all it can to promote Mexico's economic development. That country's prosperity and well-being (or lack thereof) have come to directly affect our own far more than have those of any other Latin American country. The doctrines of the inter-American system notwithstanding, Mexico should be treated differently from other Latin American nations—differently and more favorably. This said, Mexico must cease to hide behind moralistic slogans and must discuss frankly with the United States the way in which our indirect (but material) relief of her welfare burden can be compensated by concrete agreements in the area of oil and natural gas. Such agreements would necessarily have to provide fixed prices for relatively long terms (for example, three to five years). Those on both sides of the border who deplore such deals, finding them offensive in human terms, should consider that if Mexico is allowed to treat her oil and natural gas as just two more commodities for sale, but refuses to help the United States solve the problem of illegal immigrants, eventually the political and economic system of this country will simply cease to have the capacity to help Mexico at all.

United States-Mexican relations are characterized by a double paradox. On one hand, the interests of the two countries are closely intertwined, but much joint and mutually constructive action is constrained by a fictive nationalism. On the other, in spite of serious problems and (on the Mexican side) much accumulated resentment, relations between the two countries are fundamentally good. During the past decade a number of issues have been successfully resolved: border disputes, the salinity of the Colorado River, drug traffic, prisoner exchanges, and fishing rights. But if these accomplishments afford grounds for optimism, they should lull neither side into complacency. The next decade will probably be the last in which the problems of energy and immigration will remain within the capacity of U.S. and Mexican leaders to manage and satisfactorily resolve.

Cuba

Throughout the early and mid-seventies, all signs pointed to an eventual U.S.-Cuban rapprochement after nearly a generation of undisguised hostility on both sides. In 1973, the two countries reached an agreement on airline hijacking; in 1975, President Gerald Ford partially lifted the U.S. commercial embargo on the island; in 1977, President Jimmy Carter ended U.S. reconnaissance flights over Cuba, lifted travel restrictions, and removed the ban on spending American currency there. Shortly thereafter, the two nations agreed to exchange middle-level diplomats, under the polite fiction of "special interest sections" of the Czech and Swiss embassies in Washington and Havana, respectively. Perhaps of equal significance, at least symbolically, U.S. posture shifted markedly at the Organization of American States (OAS): in the

1975 meeting at San José, Costa Rica, Washington dropped its traditional insistence that other OAS members continue the blockade of the Castro regime.

These brightening prospects were abruptly upset after 1975, however, when Premier Fidel Castro decided to intervene militarily in Africa. First, several thousand well-armed Cuban troops with Soviet weapons tipped the balance in the Angolan civil war, assuring the victory of the leftist Popular Movement for the Liberation of Angola (MPLA) in one of Africa's richest nations. Then Cuban soldiers spread out to other countries: in addition to the 19,000 stationed in Angola in mid-1979, there were 20,000 in Ethiopia and detachments in Mozambique, Congo, Guinea, Guinea-Bissau, Equatorial Guinea, Libya, and Algeria. Cuban military "advisers" have been reported in eight other African nations. In fact, by 1978, a quarter of the island's military establishment was stationed abroad, not including civilian "security advisers" in a number of Third World nations. These overseas adventures have cooled the enthusiasm in Washington for rapprochement, and in the past two years all forward movement seems to have stopped. The Cubans maintain that they are still interested in normalizing relations, but Premier Castro has repeatedly stated that Cuba's role in Africa is not negotiable.

Why is Cuba interested in reopening full diplomatic and commercial relations with the United States? The answer is, simply, that the revolution has failed to yield its expected economic fruits. In spite of much-praised accomplishments in education and health, Cuba is still underdeveloped. The per capita income is one-eighth that of West Germany, the gross national product half that of Portugal. Shortages are ubiquitous; food and other necessities are rationed. The rate of economic growth slowed steadily throughout the seventies, and some estimates predict it will reach but 3 percent in 1980. The regime depends for survival upon Soviet assistance, in the form of a subsidy amounting to nearly $4 million a day with an accumulating debt that by 1986 may reach or even exceed $15 billion. At 3 percent interest, the annual service on this obligation by then would reach $450 million.* World sugar prices have been depressed since 1974; and after years of denouncing earlier reciprocity treaties with the United States, Cubans have decided to try to recapture part of the North American market. Apart from providing the island with hard currency, trade with the United States would restore to

*Obviously, the Soviets can have no reasonable expectation of recovering the principal; perhaps the best they can hope for is a modest annual payment on the service. Much depends upon Cuba's capacity to expand her trade relations and find additional sources of foreign exchange.

it a cheap source of technology, manufactured goods, and certain raw materials—in other words, re-establish the comparative economic advantage that geography always afforded.

What are the prospective rewards for the United States? The Cubans maintain that if this country were willing to remove its present trade embargo, it could expect export sales to the island in the vicinity of $350 million during the first year and perhaps as much as $1 billion annually three or four years after that. Further, a resumption of U.S. purchases of Cuban sugar, tobacco, and other products, they say, would provide the island with funds with which to begin paying the outstanding claims of expropriated U.S. investors that amount presently to $3.5 billion, including interest.

Unfortunately, the state of the Cuban economy simply does not justify these figures; one indication of this, among many, is that the island's current debt to her West European trading partners exceeds $1.5 billion. (Most of her trade with the Soviet bloc is by barter.) Nor is it easy to see how sales of sugar to the United States could ever again reach proportions sufficient to finance payment of a significant portion of the revolutionary debt. The Soviet Union presently buys Cuban sugar at three times the world price, but for the United States there would be no comparable political incentive to follow suit. Further, it is doubtful that the United States could once again find a place for more than a small portion of the Cuban product, since the island's quota (about 25 percent of the total U.S. domestic market before the revolution) was broken up in the 1960s and divided among other foreign producers. At one time Cuba had a special claim to tariff privileges because many of her large-scale producers were North American corporations; obviously, this is not the case today. Finally, even if Cuba could repay her revolutionary debts, one must not assume that she would do so readily. Premier Castro has said that counterclaims for damages inflicted during the Bay of Pigs invasion and for loss of trade during the embargo would have to be balanced against U.S. property losses before any mutually satisfactory figure could be arrived at. (It is worth noting that as of this writing neither France nor Spain—both of whom have maintained continuous, and in the case of France even cordial, relations with Castro—has been able to induce the Cuban regime to compensate expropriated nationals.)

There are some political concessions that the United States might request in exchange for a full resumption of relations, but the Castro regime seems determined to discuss none of them. These include nuclear nonproliferation, the dismantling of Soviet bases, and the abandoning of Cuba's new world role as the foreign legion of Soviet foreign policy. This being the case, if the United States wishes to normalize relations with Cuba, it must content itself with ethereal economic rewards, or even more ethereal compensations in the court of "world opinion."

Some members of Congress have recently argued that any change in our Cuban policy is better than no change at all. They contend 1) that the present policy is inspired by vindictive, spiteful considerations "unworthy of a great nation" (Sen. Frank Church); 2) that since the present policy has not succeeded in isolating Castro or preventing Cuban influence in Africa, "it makes sense to try something different" (Sen. George McGovern); 3) that even though Castro will not presently settle claims or remove troops in Africa in exchange for lifting the trade embargo, unilateral action by the United States would vastly "improve chances of a reasonable and successful resolution of claims . . . and disputes. Without a lifting of the embargo, those disputes will simply continue to fester" (Rep. Jonathan Bingham).

These arguments do not survive closer examination. It is true that there has been a peevish quality to U.S. Cuban policy since the revolution, but policies are not necessarily wrong just because they are inspired by irritation and anger as well as by a concrete reference to national interest. In any case, although our Cuban policy has not changed much in its externals since 1961, the rationale and objectives of that policy assuredly have. In the sixties our goal was to undermine and overthrow Castro; failing that, we aspired to isolate him, particularly from the South American mainland. Today we are ready to accept the Cuban Marxist state as an accomplished fact, and Castro has apparently set aside his commitment to export the revolution to other Latin American countries.* The problem is not U.S. unwillingness to see that the situation has changed so much as it is Castro's refusal to abandon playing a great power role, if not in the western hemisphere, then in the more volatile climes of Africa and the Middle East.

Nor does it make sense to expect that acts of unconditional generosity will encourage a more conciliatory attitude in Havana. As in all communist regimes, "pragmatists" and "ideologists" wage a perpetual struggle in Cuba. To offer something in exchange for nothing would strengthen the hand of those in the Cuban leadership who believe that the regime must operate on strict ideological presumption—specifically, that the United States has lost its nerve and therefore can be challenged

*These lines were written before the fall of Somoza in Nicaragua and the advent there of a revolutionary regime friendly to the Cubans. Obviously, this turn of events had little to do with Cuban intentions, but precisely how it may affect a revision of Castro's estimates of the revolutionary possibilities of other mainland republics remains to be seen.

with impunity. In the case of Angola, for example, Castro's victory was brought about by the U.S. Congress as much as by Soviet arms; but such self-denying acts are not always read accurately by those to whom they are addressed. Instead, they may lead to an exaggerated estimate of one's possibilities and encourage not moderation, but further adventures elsewhere, or greater intractability at international conference tables.

The 1980s will be a critical period in Cuba, replete with difficult economic choices. This is particularly so because in 1986 the island must resume payment on its gargantuan debt to the Soviet Union. Given the lack of American economic interest in today's Cuba, to find a place for the island's sugar in the American market could only be the consequence of a political decision. Cubans must be encouraged to see that, for such consideration, they must be willing to discuss the fundamental political considerations that divide us. To put the present U.S. policy in a holding pattern is not a counsel to inaction as such but a decision to grant the Cubans some additional time in which to ponder the mounting costs of their own intransigence.

Nicaragua

The advent of a revolutionary government in Nicaragua, ending nearly five decades of rule by the Somoza dynasty, was undoubtedly the most dramatic development to occur anywhere in Latin America during 1979. Nicaragua's new international importance, however, rests less on its strategic position, its population, or its economic resources, and more on its symbolic representation as a people-in-arms who successfully defeated one of the last of the region's old-line military tyrants (and by indirection, humiliated his presumed American allies).

The present situation in this Central American republic derives much of its special poignancy from an eerie, if superficial, resemblance to Cuba in the early days of the Castro regime. Like Fulgencio Batista, President Anastasio Somoza had remained in power far too long and resorted to increasingly violent measures to quell his domestic opponents; in both Cuba and Nicaragua, this eventually drove even the conservative business class into the enemy camp. In both countries, the United States had a long record of friendly collaboration with the government and, when the latter chose to pursue a more repressive course, found itself unable, first, to take the government's opponents seriously and, then, when matters worsened, to persuade its client to engage in serious dialogue with them.* In Nicaragua, as in Cuba, the United States finally shut off arms shipments to the government—too late to force it to step down in favor of a moderate alternative, and far too late to win credit with the ascending revolutionary regime. As in Cuba, the new government in Nicaragua was a coalition of moderate reformers and left-wing ideologues, whose precise ideological boundaries remained undefined. (In both countries hatred of a dictator combined with nationalist resentment of the United States to form the real cement that held together a wide range of tendencies.) In Nicaragua, the tendency for history to repeat itself seemed stronger still, not only in the new regime's stated commitment to the construction of socialism (which even the Cubans did not publicly avow in their first moments), but by the new government's anxious self-identification with the Castro regime in international forums. (At the 1979 Havana Conference of Non-Aligned Nations, Nicaragua, practically alone among Latin American participants, supported what was obviously a joint Soviet-Cuban draft of the program-manifesto.)

Happily, these indicators are not the only signs of the times in Nicaragua. The new government, unlike that of Castro, has conspicuously avoided show trials and drumhead executions of defeated opponents and has rigorously prevented wholesale reprisals against officers and members of the discredited National Guard. Many prominent members of the new government, most notably Foreign Minister Miguel D'Escoto, a Maryknoll priest trained in the United States, are political moderates. The new regime appears anxious for American collaboration; it has even asked, irony of ironies, for U.S. military cadres to help mold the San-

*Although for many years critics of the United States roundly condemned it for its relations with the Somoza regime, few showed much awareness of the ambiguities involved. Between the United States and Nicaragua the disparities of economic and military power were so great that mere diplomatic recognition of the Somoza government was regarded, rightly or wrongly, as a concrete political statement. (Somoza himself found it convenient to propagate a version of this argument, however untrue it might have been in its essentials.) Few students of international politics have devoted sufficient study to the phenomenon of policy momentum as it applies to cases such as these: that is, how mere recognition moves imperceptibly to tacit support, and from there to protection and commitment. Nor have they shown much sensitivity to the curious asymmetry that can exist between great powers and client states; the tail sometimes wags the dog. In the case of Nicaragua, the United States, for all of its supposed power, could not force Somoza to act in a fashion consistent with Washington's interests since this would clearly have contravened the interests of the Somoza family. Also, much of Washington's reluctance to deal harshly with Somoza, in recent years at least, was the consequence of the Marxist rhetoric and undisguised sympathy for Cuba articulated by his Sandinista opponents. Perhaps the United States should have been able to look beyond these appearances; yet the degree of reality behind these appearances is still unclear.

dinista irregulars into a disciplined fighting force! Further, in sharp contrast to Cuba, in Nicaragua there are few important U.S. economic interests likely to be affected by postrevolutionary decrees. Most of the modern sectors of the Nicaraguan economy (or at least, the large-scale enterprises) were owned by the Somoza family or its allies; hence, nationalization of these properties should provide no pretext for conflicts between Washington and Managua. For its part, the U.S. government seems anxious to show that it has learned what it regards as the lessons of the Cuban experience. Elaborate steps have been taken to avoid giving the new Nicaraguan government reason to cavil, including massive infusions of economic aid without conditions. (As of September 1979, the Carter administration was sponsoring a bill in Congress that would transfer to Nicaragua more than $100 million in loans and grants during the next two years.) There has been a deliberate attempt to avoid responding to symbolic provocations, such as Nicaraguan conduct at the Havana conference. In a recent statement to the American press, Foreign Minister D'Escoto described U.S. relations with the new regime as off to an excellent start.

It would seem, then, that the United States has survived the Nicaraguan debacle far better than might have been expected. Unfortunately, however, the revolutionary process is far from complete. It is known that the various groupings within the ruling junta have not as yet renounced their separate identities, and it is difficult to imagine that the Marxist component will happily accede to an open political order. (It is not difficult to imagine the advice it is receiving from Havana.) More to the point, some hard decisions lie ahead, particularly in the area of economic policy. Ample Latin American precedent affords grounds for anticipating that the newly nationalized economic enterprises will be run at a loss. This means that two to five years from now, the Nicaraguan government will find it necessary to look abroad for financial aid to make its socialism work. At that point, the United States will be placed in a most difficult and perilous position. If it refuses to subsidize what by then will be an elaborate welfare state, it will have no choice but to accept the blame for whatever political consequences ensue. (Several Nicaraguan officials have already hinted as much.) On the other hand, even if it agrees to what some are already calling ideological blackmail, it may still find it impossible to assure the economic success of Nicaraguan socialism. (One need look no further than Great Britain for a sobering example.) The only certainty one can derive from the present situation is that whatever failures the Nicaraguan regime experiences—for whatever cause—will promptly be blamed on the United States. How long the U.S. Congress will continue to appropriate funds under such conditions (beyond the necessary, logical, and temporary response to the present dislocation of Nicaraguan society) is difficult to say. But an indefinite, unconditional subsidy is surely not a prospect.

These ruminations may, indeed, be too grim; they are intended as an antidote to the overly buoyant optimism currently found in some sectors of the U.S. government and press. The situation in Nicaragua is still extremely fluid. What the Sandinista revolution really "is" and therefore how the United States should respond to it remain to be seen. The responsibility for the outcome depends as much, or more, on Managua, as it does on Washington or New York.

Panama

The next decade will be a critical testing period for the new Panama Canal treaties, concluded in 1977 after more than a decade of negotiations and ratified by the Senate in 1978 after one of the longest and most informed debates in U.S. legislative history. The scenario for the next ten years calls for a gradual phasing out of the symbols of American power in the Canal Zone—postal services, courts, and so forth—and the replacement of the Panama Canal Company by a binational commission whose president, by 1990, will be a Panamanian. By the end of the decade, the transition to full Panamanian sovereignty will be half complete, with a definitive transfer of the territory only in the year 2000.

Despite dire predictions of the chaos that would follow ratification, matters have gone according to schedule so far. But what of the future? For at least the first half of the 1980s, there is little reason to think that the Panamanians will have tired of their nationalistic victory and that they will seek additional satisfactions—especially since the United States agreed to an extremely generous cash settlement ($50 million a year) that in effect makes operating the canal less an economic asset to Panama than is the potential to close or immobilize it.

However, will Panamanians by 1987 or 1988 have grown tired of half ownership and want to take full possession in advance? What seems like a large settlement today may prove inadequate tomorrow or the day after, particularly if world inflationary trends persist. The country's population is expected to grow by half during the next ten years, and economic and social pressures are not likely to lessen. The canal, which has always served as a useful First Cause from which to explain all national ills, conceivably will continue to provide a tempting target.*

Then, too, the treaties contemplate some permanent U.S. military presence in the zone. Whether this will prove as acceptable to Panamanians five or seven years from now as it apparently was in 1977 remains to be seen. It should be noted for cautionary purposes that in the plebiscite staged by President Omar Torrijos, nearly one out of three Panamanians voted against the accords, presumably because they regarded them as excessively solicitous of U.S. interests.

During the treaty debates in the United States, advocates of ratification greatly exaggerated the degree to which the canal had ceased to be important to the economy and security of the United States and the West. Though it is true, for example, that only 17 percent of all U.S. ocean-borne commerce passes through the canal, 70 percent of all the ships transiting its locks have the United States as their destination; and not a few of these ships are oil tankers. Closure of the canal could have a catastrophic effect on fuel supplies and shipping costs within the United States. Further, the canal is a lifeline to Japan, Australia, and New Zealand, which have crucial markets in Europe and the eastern United States, and it is vital for Ecuador, Peru, and Colombia. That the best interests of the United States are served by the fundamental economic health of these nations (particularly the first two) is undeniable. Given the present interdependent nature of Western economic and credit structures, to look only at the canal's direct and immediate impact on U.S. commerce is purposefully myopic. The canal is not negligible to U.S. security—taking "security" in the broadest sense of the word—and political developments in the isthmus must be carefully monitored. It is to be hoped that the experience of increased responsibility in the canal's operation and maintenance will remove the most obvious goads to nationalist resentment and afford Panamanians a sobering education in the true dimensions of their national interest.

Peru

In this troubled Andean republic, the principal challenge to American policymakers in the coming decade will be how to help its gen-

*One response to world inflationary trends is already evident—the announced intention of the Panamanian government to raise transit tolls after the formal transfer of the canal in October 1979. Although this was certainly a predictable outcome, it has led to no small amount of private agonizing on the part of Pacific coast Latin American republics, some of which were really quite vociferous in their support of the Panamanian position during the treaty negotiations.

erals and politicians pick up the pieces from a shipwrecked revolution launched twelve years ago. In 1968 a Nasserist junta led by Gen. Juan Velasco Alvarado seized the banner of reform and set about actualizing programs long articulated by the country's nationalist and Marxist left: nationalization of foreign-owned oil and mining concerns, radical agrarian reform, worker management of industry, expropriation of large corporate properties, and absorption of large-scale enterprises into an expanding public sector. The regime also pursued an independent foreign policy that included recognition of Cuba and alignment with the radical states of the Third World.

By 1975, it was becoming exceedingly difficult for the generals to avoid facing up to the costs of this experiment, and Velasco was pushed out in favor of Gen. Francisco Morales Bermúdez. During the decade of experimentation under Velasco, the country had suffered a crisis of productivity, requiring massive infusions of money to cover losses in publicly owned enterprises and a growing balance-of-payments deficit. The junta's hostile attitude toward private property and foreign investment made it an unattractive risk for conservative lenders; in particular, soft development loans from the World Bank and the International Monetary Fund (IMF) were difficult to come by. On the other hand, General Velasco found a ready source of credit in private banks in Europe, the United States, and Japan. By one estimate, between 1973 and 1977 such institutions lent Peru close to $2.5 billion. The service on this and previous obligations will be about $1.5 billion in 1980, accounting for somewhat more than half the country's foreign exchange earnings. It is not difficult to predict that the moment of hard decisions is close at hand.

Under General Morales Bermúdez, the Peruvian revolution has clearly entered its Thermidor. Radical *velasquista* functionaries, military and civilian, have been quietly eased out of positions of responsibility, and the structure of the revolutionary state is being slowly dismantled. For example, the dormant fishing industry is being denationalized; a nationalistic mining code has been amended to encourage the search for oil; the Law of Industrial Communities (1970) has been changed to reverse worker control of industry; the public sector (Social Property Enterprises) figures low in current government budgets; labor laws have been revised to make it possible to fire employees; expropriated opposition newspapers have been restored to their owners. In addition, the president has announced plans to restore civilian government and convene elections in 1980.

However necessary these measures may be to promote Peruvian economic recovery in the long run, they cannot hope to generate the resources to see the country through the financial crisis that looms ahead in the next five to seven years. Many financial experts believe that Peru's foreign obligations are too closely bunched and favor some form of refinancing. In the last two and a half years the regime has been engaged in enervating discussions with the IMF and has twice broken them off. The generals feel that they have taken enough of IMF's stiff medicine and that it is time for the bankers to do something for them. The latter, however, point to continued budgetary deficits and reckless military spending as proof that the regime has not fully repented of its past financial follies. At present, Peru is subsisting on an emergency IMF loan for $230 million that ensures her capacity to meet some crucial international obligations through January 1981. Negotiations for the overall refinancing of the foreign debt continue. Meanwhile, the government must find a way to implement the austerity plans demanded by its creditors, which are hard to sell to the military and the public.

Much of the difficulty in Peruvian-U.S. relations at this point rests upon a vast misunderstanding: that "Jimmy Carter could save Peru—if he really wanted to." These words, attributed to President Morales Bermúdez, may be apocryphal, but the attitude they represent assuredly is not. This much is true: the United States clearly does have an interest in helping the Peruvian government through the next difficult years. For if that country were to repudiate her foreign debt (a course presently urged upon her by theoreticians of the New International Economic Order and homegrown radicals), this might, apart from its immediate impact upon American bondholders, encourage a rash of similar actions in other Third World countries. But for Jimmy Carter (or possibly his successor) simply to "save" Peru in the manner favored by General Morales Bermúdez would amount to throwing good money after bad—if, that is, on top of the new obligations recently assumed by the United States in connection with the evolving Middle East peace negotiations, the money could be found.

Repudiation or a unilateral moratorium are last-ditch scenarios that even the Peruvian government, for all its desperation, seems hesitant to play out. But there is much talk in both Lima and Washington of the unsettling domestic political consequences of further austerity programs. When the IMF mission arrived in Lima to begin discussions in mid-1977, there was a rash of well-organized protests and riots in the principal cities of provincial Peru that culminated in the first successful strike in the nation's history. Does this mean, as the Peruvian government would have it, that if the United States hews to a hard line on financial matters we may find ourselves facing a new, and far less tractable, negotiating partner in the future?

It is difficult to measure the precise import of such warnings, since they blur the distinction between sporadic protest and long-term revolutionary potential. Austerity is understandably unpopular in an already impoverished country like Peru, and no government that must call for it can expect a peaceful mandate. But public anger and even disorder are not a political program, much less a shadow state. Nor do all the signs of the times point to the increasing radicalization of the Peruvian populace. This is, after all, a country that has had a revolution fresh in the memory of all but small children; it is suffering from acute political fatigue; the slogans of yesteryear have grown thin. In the 1978 elections for a new constituent assembly, the two parties of the center right and right won 68 of 100 seats; the left (divided into half a dozen groups) won only 38. Even more significant, the Revolutionary Socialist party, led by retired Gen. Leonidas Rodriguez Figueroa, one of the "radical" military leaders of the early seventies, made a disappointing showing. It is also known that hard-line officers of the right are waiting in the wings to push the Thermidor considerably beyond its present limits; at its most extreme, this could portend a state resembling Chile or Argentina. Perhaps such a regime could pay its bills, but it might be as incapable of curbing military spending (a principal item on the deficit) as its predecessor.

Not all of Peru's financial problems are her own fault. Some foreign bankers have urged upon Peru loans that they expected to recover from a bonanza oil strike in the Amazon basin; to date the oil has not been found. The fishmeal industry, the country's chief export earner in the sixties, has declined because of overfishing. And the world recession has slackened the market for other Peruvian export lines, particularly sugar, cotton, and some industrial minerals. At this point, distributing the blame for the Peruvian dilemma is less important than mapping a way out of it, and that will require more realism and frankness on both sides than has been evident till now.

The Southern Cone: Chile, Argentina, Uruguay

In these three republics, the issues of human rights and political freedom have become so compelling as to completely overshadow the other kinds of questions—nuclear nonproliferation, treatment of investors, trade and aid policies—that would normally lie at the heart of diplomatic interchange. This state of affairs is surely due in part to the sheer enormity of the repressive apparatus that has been mounted in all three countries, as well as to a sustained campaign by European and U.S. newspapers and church, labor, and university organizations on behalf of *desaparecidos* (missing persons). But much of the concern in North Atlantic liberal circles over the fate of democratic (or, at least, republican) institutions in the Southern Cone arises from a clear recollection that not so very long ago these were precisely the countries that led all Latin America in political maturity, cultural refinement, and general level of civilization. Is today's police state, these observers seem to worry aloud, the future that works for these peoples and ultimately, perhaps, for all of us as well? Many fervently hope not, and to ensure as much have urged upon the United States a policy of ostracism and isolation for Chile and systematic pressure for Argentina and Uruguay. The Carter administration has followed some of these counsels in outline, though often not in detail. There have been some modest results in the case of individual detainees, but the general trend toward liberalization is moving at its own agonizing pace.

Whatever else may be in dispute, it is clear that U.S. policy toward these nations poses political and moral problems of extreme complexity. Perhaps the best way to approach them is to review how these countries arrived at their present state. Since World War II, two characteristics have marked their development: 1) the size and number of groups participating in the political system has increased; 2) the economic surplus to be divided among them has shrunk or disappeared altogether. The economic scene has been dominated by neglect of agriculture, emphasis on what are often wasteful and duplicative import-substitution industries, and above all, unreasonable growth in public sector employment. In Uruguay, the most egregious example, the service sector by the late 1960s accounted for more than half the national product. Low productivity, the need to import foodstuffs (even for former agricultural exporters like Argentina and Uruguay), and wasteful public spending have led to a chronic balance-of-payments deficit and runaway inflation in these countries. To compensate for low or negative economic growth, they have resorted repeatedly to massive foreign borrowing.

The most perfect of political systems could not be expected to survive the scissors of rising demands and declining resources, much less the populist regimes that in these countries latterly attempted the impossible task of aggregating the interests of capital and labor, city and countryside, military and civilian power groups. By its very nature populism presupposes a coalition of class interests, supported by an elaborate system of sectoral allocations. It can work only when there is something to allocate. The welfare state of Uruguay, rather curiously based on the traditional ranching industry, purposely avoided hard economic choices until it had simply devoured the means of its own subsistence. In Argentina, democracy and economic rationality never quite recovered from the Perón experience (1946–1955); what Argentines in the sixties remembered about the forties was merely that the times had been good (as indeed they had, owing to an artificial postwar rise in world commodity prices). The lesson they deduced from this was that a populist restoration would somehow automatically recapture the mix of prosperity and social peace; it took a second, disastrous reign of Perón (1973–1974) to prove otherwise. In Chile, Christian Democrat Eduardo Frei (1964–1970) pursued one brand of populism, his Marxist successor Salvador Allende (1970–1973) another. The accumulated burden compounded of low productivity, costly truces between sectors, mounting foreign indebtedness, and (under Allende) sharpening class conflict led to a devastatingly one-sided civil war in September 1973.

In Argentina and Uruguay during the middle and late 1960s, the shortcomings of populism encouraged many young people, mostly middle-class university graduates, many of them women, to enter into urban guerrilla warfare. In Uruguay, the Tupamaros carried out bank robberies, kidnappings, and assassinations with great skill and verve; their purpose was to expose the impotence of a government dominated by old-line politicos. In this they succeeded. What followed, however, was not the Marxist-nationalist revolution they had anticipated, but a military takeover. In Argentina, partisans of the Trotskyist Ejército Revolucionario del Pueblo (ERP) and the Peronist Montoneros carried on similar attacks against a military government, no doubt encouraging the generals to convoke elections and return to the barracks in 1973. But the restoration of Perón was not sufficient to still rebel guns. Ideological disputes with the aging leader, combined with a disposition to combat that had been wound up to feverish intensity and could not easily be slackened, led to a new fight—first against Perón, then against his helpless, incompetent spouse-successor, encouraging the military to take power once more. In Chile the pattern was somewhat different, but there can be little doubt that the right-wing ultras of Patria y Libertad and their left-wing counterparts in the Trotskyist Movimiento de la Izquierda Revolucionaria (MIR) and Maoist Partido Comunista Revolucionario (PCR) did much to contribute to the erosion of public order that paved the way for the military coup.

Although the struggle of these partisans has been the subject of a romantic film literature (*State of Siege*, for example), in fact such groups have contributed much to the present doleful state of affairs in their countries. Much of their activity was based in the first instance on the assumption that, in densely packed urban settings, they and their allies could operate with near impunity. Failing this, perhaps they could provoke a widespread campaign of repression that would raise public consciousness and kindle a more widespread spirit of rebellion, bringing down the existing regime. None of these expectations were justified by events. Instead, the agencies of order responded by engaging in combat without distinctions. Those suspected of being guerrillas or of sympathizing with them were treated much as if they had been found with arms in hand. The movements were crushed; many innocent civilians were caught in the maw with them; no second wave of rebellion ever emerged.

The advent of right-wing military governments in the Southern Cone has facilitated a degree of economic recovery, since it is now possible to take measures that would have been politically impossible under populist regimes. The rate of inflation has been slowed; foreign currency reserves are being rebuilt; some nationalized industries are beginning to show a profit; foreign capital is returning; and the rate of economic growth has modestly increased. There is no point in denying that these things have been accomplished at considerable cost in the short (and possibly the middle) run to those least able to afford it: the middle and lower classes. Hence, none of these governments rests upon a sure base of popular support, and what support they did have the morning after they came to power has steadily melted away.

This is not to say that the opposition has congealed around a clear and widely accepted alternative. We are continually told that in Chile the challenge to General Pinochet is growing, both inside and outside the government. Perhaps so; but it does not follow, as so many exiles have assured us, that the country is longing to resume the Allende experiment. For many, perhaps most, Chileans the experience of those years was as searing as was the civil war for an earlier generation of Spaniards.

In Argentina, opposition Radicals and Peronists, both inside the country and in exile, are divided into a bewildering multiplicity of groups. Consequently, they are ripe for manipulation and compromise. It is known that the more tractable, including leaders of an always pliable labor movement, are holding quiet discussions with the military. In Uruguay an Institutional Act (1976) clearly copied from the Brazilians deprives an entire generation of politicians of their civic rights, and those who are permitted to function in the future will have to earn and maintain favorable report cards from the military.

Within these admittedly great limitations, some form of civilian rule in both Argentina and Uruguay can be anticipated in the early and middle years of the next decade. The regime in Chile has postponed the date to 1991, and as things stand now there is little reason to think that date will be much advanced, whether General Pinochet or someone else is at the helm.

The choices here for U.S. policy are agonizing. On one hand, since free institutions have declined in these countries precisely as a consequence of economic failure, it may follow that the soundest road to restoring them is economic assistance, particularly to regimes capable of implementing the measures that their troubled economies require. It must be admitted, however, that such a policy could not guarantee economic recovery, since much would depend on the movement of international commodity prices. And, in what may prove to be a long meantime, it abandons the peoples of the Southern Cone to what mercies their military leaders can summon up. There are, in fact, definite signs of a loosening of the repressive apparatus in all three countries. This is probably due less to foreign pressures than to the growing confidence (justified or not) of their governments. It is a trend that, though hopeful in terms of immediate consequences, is certainly reversible.

On the other hand, some argue that free institutions are positive in themselves, regardless of their economic performance, and that everything should be done to make life difficult for the dictators. On the face of it, this argument has undeniable appeal. However, it is not clear that such counsel would necessarily lead to the decline of the dictators; it could do little more than worsen the lot of already afflicted peoples.* Even if successful, at best it could be expected to cancel the modest economic gains of the past three or four years by restoring some variant of the populist coalitions whose policies have already proved ruinous.

The sad truth is that whichever policy the United States adopts (most likely it will be a shamefaced and inadequate compromise between the two), it will not definitively influence the course of events. To put the matter bluntly, these countries have recently passed through a social and political apocalypse the like of which no American except a refugee from 1930s central Europe could conceive. The military leaders of the Southern Cone and American policymakers live in utterly different experiential universes. It can only be hoped that the course of international economic developments, political deflation at home, and quiet, persistent, judicious U.S. pressures can bring these two worlds closer together.

---

*It is legitimate to doubt that tough measures will lead to the result desired so strongly by the exiles and their friends: the voluntary renunciation of power by their victorious enemies. If the precedent of 1940s Franco Spain is any guide, international ostracism can be expected to materially increase the burden upon a people without seriously affecting the regime under which they labor—except, paradoxically, to strengthen it as a symbol of resistance to the hated foreigner. The Pinochet government in Chile has already profited from such a backlash, an unexpected (and much needed) benefit handed to it by the Carter administration.

Brazil

Historically, Brazil has followed a diplomatic line independent of Spanish America in her dealings with the United States, at times playing the role of junior broker between Washington and the more truculent peoples of the hemisphere, particularly the Argentines. The Washington-Rio entente (or unwritten alliance, as one historian aptly put it) reached its peak during World War II, when Brazil alone in Latin America committed combat troops to the European theater. Since 1945 that relationship has approached a similar intimacy only once—during the first years of the present military regime.

If Brazilian politics and foreign policy hold any surprises for U.S. policymakers in the next decade, it will only be because the latter have misunderstood Brazilian motives and goals. Brazil has always had a strong sense of its uniqueness and potential. Hence, even the closest cooperation with the United States has been viewed in terms of the ultimate purpose of Brazilian nationalism: to make Brazil a great power. (This is a point that has been missed as often by spiteful, envious Argentines as by over-sanguine North Americans.)

Contexts change, and so do perceptions of interest. In the mid-1980s Brazil will have a reputable capital goods industry and a creditable nuclear capacity. Her quest for rapid economic growth will require new markets and continued or improved access to established ones. A new generation of officers without personal ties to their American counterparts will be in charge of the defense establishment and probably the government. It is therefore likely that the relationship with the United States, which has always been regarded as special by Brazilian statesmen, will be modified.

Typical of the new sorts of conflicts that will beset Brazilian-U.S. relations in the immediate future is the present chill inspired by differing views on nuclear development. Brazilian interest in this area has always been provoked in large part by the Argentines, who have led the field in South America for a number of years, but its economic desirability was underscored significantly by the rise in world oil prices after 1973. Failing to find a sympathetic hearing in the United States, the Brazilians turned to West Germany and in 1975 concluded an agreement with that country to develop facilities for uranium enrichment in Brazil that should afford her access to the full nuclear fuel cycle in the near future. In addition, West German rocket experts have agreed to help Brazil develop a relatively sophisticated nuclear weapons delivery system by the mid-1980s. The Brazilians claim that their goals in nuclear development are purely peaceful; Washington remains unconvinced. Although

Brazil, unlike Argentina, ratified the Limited Test Ban Treaty of 1963, like her southern rival she has refused to ratify the 1968 Non-Proliferation Treaty or its Latin American version, the Treaty of Tlatelolco. United States pressures on Bonn to refuse to meet Brazilian demands were unpersuasive to the Germans and highly offensive to the Brazilians. At present the United States will not approve further export licenses to Brazil until there are improvements in controls over the fuel. This is inspired by some legitimate concern about whether safeguards are employed, but Brazilians see it as nothing but an excuse to deny them access to a much-needed energy alternative.

What holds true for nuclear questions will likewise apply to other areas: human rights, population policy, trade and tariff considerations, and relations with the Eastern bloc. Pressures, criticisms, or refusals emanating from Washington, whatever their actual motives, are likely to be interpreted as attempts to frustrate Brazil's development objectives. At a minimum, it will be less and less possible for this country to take Brazil for granted as an ally and as a customer. There are already indications that Western Europe and, even more, Japan are making significant incursions into a market that was once the preserve of the United States. This trend has been helped along by U.S. tariff policies, which have prevented the Brazilians from widening their export lines to this country.

It is easy to anticipate that the coming decade will witness a more pluralistic reshaping of Brazilian foreign policy. But precisely what that will mean for the United States is not entirely clear. Contact for Brazil outside the Western alliance might be less nettlesome than some activities within it, such as the recent agreement with West Germany to produce the Leopard tank in Brazil—an exchange for nuclear assistance that allows the Germans to circumvent the existing restriction on arms sales outside the North Atlantic Treaty Organization. Although a full adversary relationship is unlikely, it is possible that by the end of the 1980s Brazil may have assumed the role in hemispheric affairs long played by (but no longer possible for) Argentina: that of a rival pole of attraction and leadership for other Latin American countries. Formerly, Brazil was thought to be inhibited from playing such a role by geographical isolation and linguistic differences; apparently this is no longer the case. Two indications among many are the increasing respectability granted to Brazil's military government by the two leading civilian regimes of the region, Mexico and Venezuela; and the willingness of eight South American nations to follow Brazil's lead in subscribing to the Amazon Pact, which would coordinate joint development of the enormous river basin.

No nation can aspire to great power status if it has not consolidated social peace and political stability at home; hence, all the prospects alluded to above must be balanced against the still vexing challenges to Brazil's domestic order. The economic "miracle" of 1964–1974, characterized by a massive influx of foreign investment and a 10-percent annual growth rate, has clearly come to an end. Since the mid-seventies the country has begun to feel the accumulating weight of debt service; that and higher oil prices have pushed annual inflation rates above 40 percent. The burden on the lower classes, never light, has increased disproportionately. Even the more fortunately placed in Brazilian society have begun to question whether many of the country's economic problems might not have their origins in the government's generous treatment of multinational corporations, particularly with regard to repatriation of profits.

If these economic difficulties did not exist, Brazil's military leaders might be tempted to normalize the political environment and allow a return to civilian rule. But fear of unleashing forces not fully domesticated has caused them to temporize. To be sure, in recent years they have lifted some censorship of the press (but not of the electronic media); they have apparently restrained police torture somewhat; they have allowed exiles to return, though their political rights continue to be denied; and they have permitted more and wider political discussion. The Roman Catholic church is promoting a national movement of conciliation, and a new partial amnesty decreed in the summer of 1979 released many (but not all) political prisoners. The problem remaining is this: every move toward liberalization reveals a new undercurrent threatening long-term stability and encourages the regime to consolidate rather than advance. This explains the victory in the 1978 election of the official candidate, J. B. Figuereido, who during the campaign made no secret of his lack of enthusiasm for a rapid return to full democracy. Even more suggestive, however, was the unusual public response to the official opposition candidate, Gen. Euler Bentes Monteiro—an interest that could never have been provoked by the merits of the man himself.

By the middle of the next decade Figuereido will have completed his term, and the military will be forced to examine once again the question of political normalization. It is hard to see how the matter can be postponed further, that is, if the transition to democracy is to be effected in an orderly and peaceful manner. Whether Brazil can move from military to civilian rule, from authoritarianism to representative institutions, from censorship and proscription to freedom and dignity, hinges partly upon economic developments. But partly, too, it depends upon political imagination. With a large stake in the outcome, the United States cannot but hope that Brazil, so rich in so many things, can find within itself the resources necessary to achieve an open and humane political community.

CONCLUSIONS

This survey, though far from exhaustive, points to four problems that will dominate U.S. Latin American policy in the immediate future.

1) An increasingly burdensome debt service threatens to be the single most important issue facing Latin America in the 1980s. This issue crosses all boundaries—ideological as well as geographic. The situation is critical for Peru and serious for Brazil and Mexico, and it is becoming serious even for oil-rich Venezuela. The Cuban case is unique only in that most of the debt is owed to the Soviet Union. As the region's chief creditor, the United States has a vested interest in helping these governments meet or refinance their obligations. In the case of Peru, this may call for outright recourse to humanitarian aid, including surplus foods, not only to make austerity programs in that country politically palatable, but also to reconcile financial rationality with our own broader national values of helping the unfortunate. However, the capacity of the United States to use its creditor role in a constructive fashion will depend to a large degree on our own financial stability. If we persist in running up large trade deficits that further undermine the dollar, we can expect to wield a diminishing influence—for good or for ill—in Latin American financial circles. Admittedly, there are those in Latin America, and even in some quarters of the United States who would welcome such a turn of events as presaging the "liberation" of these countries from the "neocolonial yoke." But if the United States travels far along the road to insolvency, it is difficult to see where the southern republics would find the liquidity they require for the years ahead.
2) The continuing inability of many Latin American republics to achieve political consensus will make long-range planning very difficult for American policymakers. Critics of the United States often claim that the State Department prefers military dictatorships to civilian governments in Latin America, but it would be closer to the truth to say that Washington prefers stable, predictable (and friendly) governments of whatever coloration. At present, the

regimes that come closest to meeting those requirements are found in Mexico, Venezuela, Costa Rica, and perhaps (stretching definitions a bit), Colombia. All these nations have some measure of civic freedom and some variant of civilian, representative institutions. Military regimes, or regimes with heavy military participation, such as those of Argentina, Brazil, Chile, and Uruguay, are a mixed blessing. Such governments are friendly in the sense that they are anxious to attract American capital and are therefore respectful of existing investment; but they are decidedly hostile when it comes to advice from Washington on how to treat their political opponents. Many believe, for example, that U.S. human rights initiatives have plunged relations with Argentina to their lowest level since World War II—although this is perhaps nothing to be ashamed of.

Moreover, however stable such military governments appear at present, to the degree to which they fail to plan for orderly transition to civilian rule their foundations will be seriously undermined. Precisely how long the machinery of repression and the memory of inept civilian predecessors may shore them up is difficult to say. The fact that they may indeed continue through the next decade (as, by their own pronouncements, it appears they plan to do) tells us little about their capacity to survive beyond that. Hence, beyond the short and middle run, they are not very predictable. The lead time for policy is usually three to five years, often depending on whether special legislation is needed and how long it takes to obtain it from Congress. United States policymakers will have to work through the coming decade with one eye on the agenda, the other on day-to-day developments in some of the major Latin American countries.

3) Although the drive for import-substitution industries seems to have been slowed somewhat in recent years, agriculture continues to be neglected. Even countries that once led in agricultural development (Mexico, Argentina, Uruguay) have been forced to use scarce foreign exchange to purchase foodstuffs. The United States might consider significantly increasing its infrastructure aid—farm-to-market roads, technical assistance, and so forth—as an indirect means of improving Latin America's overall financial situation.

4) The existing tariff structure of the United States is one of the principal barriers to cordial relations with Latin America—at least, this is often said by leading Latin publicists and statesmen. It may

indeed be time for Washington to review existing legislation with a view to widening domestic markets for Latin American exports. However, this cannot be accomplished without resolving two serious problems. One is our own perilous balance-of-payments situation (due largely to oil imports), which must be ameliorated before we can consider providing new markets within the United States for foreign producers. The other is the range of domestic interests—from textile workers to agribusiness lobbies—whose pressures on Congress must be counteracted or neutralized. If the U.S. government were to expend the enormous time and effort that such an undertaking would entail, our Latin trading partners would have to be ready to offer some comparable compensations. These could assume the form of fixed-term price agreements for certain scarce commodities (minerals and hydrocarbons) and possibly a series of commitments to redirect back to the United States purchases that have latterly gone to Western Europe and Japan.

How vigorously and successfully the United States can address itself to these issues will depend to some degree on the level of interest in Latin America that can be elicited in the government, the Congress, and public forums. The somber tone of this essay would seem to suggest that the estrangement of the United States and Latin America is an irreversible process and that both parties should go their separate ways without attempting to revive the illusions of the past. This might in fact be the case if the world order provided acceptable alternatives. But there is a logic to the U.S.-Latin American encounter that endures beyond the serious difficulties of the day. It might be useful, therefore, to conclude by enumerating the elements that continue to bind and engage both ends of the western hemisphere.

As indicated at the start of this essay, during the past fifteen years Latin American countries have considerably widened their commercial and diplomatic horizons without substantially altering the direction of their international life. There has been a modest increase in sales to Western Europe and a significant acceleration in trade with and investment by Japan. However, except for a few areas like arms sales or nuclear energy, the United States remains the region's chief supplier, investor, and creditor. The Europeans—West and East—have interests elsewhere, and the Japanese, who have already felt the full blast of nationalist resentment in Southeast Asia, are determined not to play a major role in the area. Some steps have been taken by the Latin Americans to replace links to countries outside the hemisphere with internal zones of commercial preference, through the Andean Pact and the newly created Latin

American Economic System, for example. But in spite of rhetorical flourish, the accomplishments of such unions have been few. Moreover, member nations (or rather, the governments that have replaced the original signatories) have turned to bickering over such issues as investment policy. Producer cartels have not gone far with most raw materials; and even the most successful example, OPEC, has not been able to recruit Mexico to join Venezuela and Ecuador. The United States thus remains the only major area with both the capacity (however diminished) and the interest (however attenuated) to respond to Latin America's major concerns in the next decade.

For the United States, a turn toward Latin America would have the appeal of returning to familiar ground after a decade of difficulties in Southeast Asia and now in the Middle East. All the links—financial, shipping, communications—are already there. Political and economic intelligence for the region is probably greater than for any other area except parts of Western Europe. And although the cultural ties that bind us are often exaggerated in Pan American rhetoric, Latin America is far closer to the United States in its basic values than to any area of the Third World.

None of this means that the United States should rush to Latin America expecting to be welcomed home as an errant but still loved relation. Too much distance has been traveled in the past ten or fifteen years to make such an approach possible, but neither should it be necessary. There is no better cement between nations than mutual interest. It will be up to the United States to define those areas where complementarity can replace conflict, and slowly work them. This will require patience, which comes hard to Americans, who want instant and dramatic results. It will require as well a willingness to forego slogans and fanfare and, above all, a capacity to ignore frequent brickbats—this on the part of a people whose greatest urge, it has often been said, is to be loved! There will be no spectacular breakthroughs; but the opportunity exists to mend a venerable bridge that has lately fallen into serious disrepair.

Africa

L. H. Gann and Peter Duignan

XXIX

GEOGRAPHY AND POPULATION

Africa is the world's second largest landmass, comprising 11.7 million square miles, or more than three times the size of the United States. The continent measures about 5,000 miles from north to south, a distance comparable to that from London to Beijing, and from east to west—at its broadest—Africa extends over 4,500 miles, equivalent to the span between San Francisco and Yokohama. Africa is not only immense in size, but also diverse in environments and peoples. Its vegetation varies from that on the deserts and alpine pasture lands to tropical jungles and grassy plains. Its people include every racial stock known to the globe. But the continent has certain common features.

Much of Africa is ill-favored by geography. It has been a continent in isolation for most of its history. Its coastline is deficient in natural harbors; most ports are man-made and date only from the recent past. The African continent is shaped by its plateau character. Many parts of the coastal zone are narrow, and the low-lying coastal belt is frequently backed by steep escarpments that make road and railway construction a costly undertaking. The plateau of the continent creates special stream profiles, and African rivers often have rapids near the coast and inland. Cataracts afford magnificent spectacles to tourists and splendid opportunities for hydroelectric engineers. From the transportation standpoint, however, cataracts form impassable obstacles. With some exceptions—the Niger and the Senegal rivers in western Africa and large stretches of the Congo River in Zaïre—most African rivers do not provide natural communication routes.

Africans must also cope with difficult climatic problems. Contrary to the moviemakers' stereotype, less than 9 percent of the continent is covered by jungle or tropical rain forest; even this area is diminishing, as cultivators make inroads on the forest land. Africa's major climatic troubles do not spring so much from excessive rainfall as from sparse or irregular precipitation. Something like 40 percent of the entire continent is covered by dry land or desert; another 40 percent or so consists of savannah; the remainder is covered by forests of different varieties.

Arable land and land under permanent crops occupy but a small proportion of the total—perhaps 7 percent—and even on these selected lands the farmer's lot is usually hard. Most African cultivators must cope with deficient transport and marketing facilities, climatic problems, lack of capital, and with difficulties caused by sharp fluctuations in world prices for African goods or inequitable systems of taxation—the latter sometimes imposed in such a manner as to favor townsmen over countrymen. The farmer also suffers widely from the exactions of incompetent, inefficient, or corrupt administrators. There are, as well, droughts, locust invasions, cattle plagues, plant diseases, tropical sicknesses (malaria, yellow fever, bilharziasis), and a host of other afflictions that strike down men and beasts.

Africa's ethnolinguistic pattern is extraordinarily varied. The number of languages used in sub-Saharan Africa probably exceeds 1,500. Most African states are made up of numerous ethnic groups speaking different languages. In Nigeria, perhaps as many as 150 tongues are spoken, and in South Africa there are twelve major ethnic groups. This has brought problems of unity to all African states, due to linguistic diversity. English, French, and Portuguese were the main languages of European colonization in Africa, and they continue to be spoken throughout the continent. More important, they remain the principal linguistic tools of scholarship, science, higher technology, and international politics; they continue to be used as the official languages in most of the postcolonial states.

Demographically, Africa is an underpopulated continent. Although the continent covers about one-fifth of the world's land surface, it probably contains little more than one-tenth of the world's population. But there are great variations in density. Settlement is scanty in dry bush lands and deserts; people tend to be concentrated in fertile highlands, such as Rwanda and Burundi—among the most closely settled countries on the continent—and along certain river valleys, lake shores, and coastal belts. On the average, one square mile of arable land may have to support 250 people or more, compared with 750 or more in Europe. In some countries, as in Mauritius, or in the urbanized parts of the Transvaal, population densities are much higher. Improved medical services and such boons to human well-being as inexpensive soap, underwear, municipal water purification plants, piped water, and modern sewage facilities have contributed to a tremendous rise in population. The annual rate of increase varies from 2 to more than 3 percent. Demographers estimate that in South Africa, for instance, the population will expand from 25 million in 1970 to 55 million by 2020.

A rapid rise in population invariably engenders social tensions. Unless farmers employ improved methods and grow more crops, pressure on the means of subsistence increases. The rate of urbanization goes up, and urban unemployment increases as more and more school-leavers look for work. High growth rates invariably strain the scanty resources of African governments, especially in terms of education, housing, health services, water supply, and other public necessities. Crime rates grow, as urban youngsters without jobs seek solutions in terms of political radicalism or violence. In most African countries, nearly half the population is under fifteen, compared with about one-quarter of the population in many European countries; hence each working member of the community has to support at least one non-working member in addition to himself or herself. By the end of the century, the population of Africa will increase tremendously, and a much higher proportion will live in cities. Within these cities, the slums will probably be much larger and more unmanageable than they are at present.

THE ECONOMY

In economic terms, Africa is both rich and poor—rich in potential resources, poor when compared with Western Europe or North America. The economic debit balance is depressing. Twenty-one of the 27 so-called less developed countries in the world are in Africa, and about 80 percent of the African population is illiterate. Most Africans are cultivators, dependent primarily on backward methods of agriculture. Much of Africa's wealth derives from a limited number of economic "islands," which cover perhaps 5 percent of the continent's area and produce about 85 percent of the total economic output. Most of these islands are in Nigeria, the Ivory Coast, Kenya, Zaïre, Zimbabwe-Rhodesia, Namibia, Zambia, and, above all, South Africa. The developed regions are usually situated on the coast, along fertile river valleys, in ore-bearing regions, or in fertile highlands. The remainder of the continent consists primarily of desert, semiarid land, or tropical rain forest.

Approximately 75 percent of sub-Saharan Africa experiences but scanty or irregular rainfall; some 90 percent of the surface suffers from major climatic disabilities.

But Africa is rich in potential resources. There is great wealth in hydroelectric power. Africa is a major producer of oil, coal, uranium, copper, iron, gold, diamonds, platinum, chrome, nickel, petroleum, and many other minerals. Much of this wealth has barely been scratched. An enormous amount of geological survey work still needs to be done. This wealth, however, is distributed unevenly. Gold production centers mainly on the Republic of South Africa, while petroleum is found in Nigeria, Libya, and Cabinda; copper comes from Zambia and Zaïre. Foreign skill and foreign capital are essential to the exploration and production of this wealth, and both are in short supply. The importance of mining, however, will continue to grow during the 1980s, especially in southern Africa.

The continent's industrial revolution began in South Africa, which remains the area's industrial giant and accounts for the bulk of Africa's iron and steel production as well as for most of its more sophisticated industries. Alone in sub-Saharan Africa, South Africa commands a great infrastructure, complete with great ports, industrial research facilities, skilled labor, and the ability to turn out a vast range of most complex goods, from rockets to modern mining machinery. In South Africa, as elsewhere in Africa, the state has been the most important factor in industrial development—including such quasi-governmental bodies as the South African Iron and Steel Corporation, the Nuclear Fuels Corporation, and the South African Coal, Oil, and Gas Corporation. South Africa today produces about 40 percent of Africa's industrial output, 60 percent of its electricity, and 80 percent of its steel and will continue to dominate the southern portion of the continent economically. But manufacturing industries have spread to other parts of the continent—starting, as in southern Africa, with agricultural processing, textiles, and light consumer industries that gradually tend to become more sophisticated enterprises. Outside South Africa, Zimbabwe-Rhodesia, and Nigeria, manufacturing as yet is of minor importance, but its role will grow in the future.

Agriculture, however, remains Africa's main resource. Something like one-third of Africa's surface is devoted to agriculture, and 80 percent of its people earn a living by farming or herding. Modern farming, characterized by extensive use of mechanical implements, massive investments of capital, and the applied use of modern science, is confined in the main to southern Africa. Africa's agricultural potential can still be greatly expanded through fencing, improved methods of crop and animal management, the application of artificial fertilizers, agricultural education, the sinking of wells, the construction of dams, and other such measures. Unfortunately, national planners have been inclined to favor townsmen at the farmers' expense. Agricultural production has been disrupted as a result of domestic turmoil followed by the departure of key personnel (Zaïre), by the ravages brought about by guerrilla warfare and counterinsurgency campaigns (Rhodesia, Angola), by enforced collectivization (Tanzania), and by the confiscation of foreign property or the expulsion of foreign-born village traders (Mozambique, Angola, Uganda). Although South Africa manages to export food, countries like Zambia and Zaïre have become net importers. Given the fact that most Africans make their living from agriculture, a rational form of national planning would put the farmers' needs at the top of the priority list in the years ahead.

In terms of international trade, Africa's world position has gained in importance over the last 30 years. Between 1938 and 1970, Africa's total exports increased in value nearly fifteen times, and its exports grew nearly tenfold. African countries, whatever their political complexion, continue to encounter serious obstacles in selling their goods abroad. Exporters have to cope with rapid price fluctuations, with foreign tariffs, growing competition from substitutes—such as aluminum for copper, synthetic fabrics for wool—while the developed countries increasingly trade among themselves in primary as well as manufactured products. There are the perennial problems connected with shortages of skilled manpower and capital, and with lack of entrepreneurial initiative, or its discouragement through bureaucratic graft, and government interference and regulation, or—sometimes—outright confiscation. Instead of supplying foreign aid—much of it to be misapplied or misspent—the Western countries can best assist Africa's economic development by reducing their own tariffs for manufactures as well as primary resources, thereby benefiting both their own consumers and the world at large. (See Bauer's essay in this volume.)

POLITICS

Politically, Africa is organized into a great variety of states that differ enormously in their respective economic, military, and demographic strength. South Africa is by far the most powerful country of sub-Saharan Africa, followed in importance by Nigeria; Ethiopia runs third in military, though not in economic terms. By international standards, however, even the strongest African states are rather insignificant in terms of money or military force. South Africa, for all its economic diversity, has a gross national product (GNP) smaller than Czechoslovakia's ($43.8 and $49.8 billion, respectively); Nigeria's GNP is smaller than Denmark's ($34.2 and $43.8 billion). Admittedly, published GNP figures do not tell the whole story; their value is only illustrative. But the fact remains that even the giants of the continent are only second-rate powers by world standards.

However varied in their respective power, the independent states of sub-Saharan Africa, excepting Liberia and Ethiopia, owe their existence to European empire builders. None of the new states derive from precolonial kingdoms. Europeans drew their boundaries, laid the foundations of their administrative systems, provided the official language, and laid out most existing cities. Towns like Lusaka, Johannesburg, Dakar, Kinshasa, and others are of colonial provenance, as are many of the economic enterprises that helped to sustain urban life.

The new states have become authoritarian. Parliamentary systems survive in only a handful of African states—among them Botswana, South Africa, and Zimbabwe-Rhodesia. The remainder are one-party or military dictatorships. In 1977 only six countries in Africa—Gambia, Kenya, Liberia, Morocco, Rhodesia, and South Africa—had newspapers that were not owned or directly controlled by the government. Few African states pride themselves on having an independent judiciary able to protect their citizens against arbitrary government interference.

With a few possible exceptions like Botswana and Somalia, the new states are ethnic mosaics, and politics hinge to a considerable extent on interethnic relations. Power frequently is concentrated in the hands of dominant ethnic groups—Afrikaners in South Africa, Amhara in Ethiopia, Kikuyu in Kenya, Tutsi in Burundi. Wealthy, or reputedly wealthy, minorities have often received short shrift from their neighbors. Arabs have been largely eliminated from Zanzibar; Ibo have been persecuted in northern Nigeria; Indians have been expelled from Uganda, and harassed in Kenya and Tanzania. The dominant whites in South Africa and Rhodesia have come under fire for the undemocratic nature of their respective regimes. But in terms of civil liberties, dictatorships such as the Central African Empire, Equatorial Guinea, or Uganda have built up records much worse than the more widely criticized record of the white-ruled parliamentary states.

The advocates of decolonization had widely assumed that Africa, freed of the imperial yoke, would march toward a better and more peaceful future. A generation later, these expectations have been disappointed. Since independence, Africa has been torn by wars, civil strife, genocide, expulsions, and so-called liberation struggles. There have been twenty major wars and forty coups since 1958. Twenty-one states are ruled by one-party dictatorships, and nineteen countries are under military rule. In 1979 eight wars involving fifteen states were being fought. There were over 500,000 men under arms and two million or more refugees. Hundreds of thousands had been killed in Rwanda, Burundi, Uganda, in the Sudan, Ethiopia, and Equatorial Guinea. Wars continued in Angola, where the ruling Marxist Movimento Popular de Libertação de Angola (MPLA) was kept in power by 20,000 Cuban troops and hundreds of East German and Russian advisers. Civil war raged in the Cabinda enclave in the north, and especially in the south under Jonas Savimbi's União Nacional para a Indepêndencia Total de Angola (UNITA). In Namibia, South West African People's Organization (SWAPO) guerrillas based in southern Angola battled South African troops. The internal settlement in Rhodesia was being contested by the Patriotic Front of Robert Mugabe and Joshua Nkomo, fighting from Zambia and Mozambique. Retaliatory raids into these countries threatened to widen the war. Amin's regime fell to the Tanzanian army and Ugandan guerrillas in April.

In Eritrea, guerrillas began in 1961 to achieve independence from Ethiopia. As of 1979, about 40,000 Arab-backed guerrillas were battling 200,000 men in the Ethiopian army, which is supported by 20,000 Cuban troops and thousands of Soviet advisers. Somali guerrillas continued to contest the Ogaden region of Ethiopia. Arab states supported the partisans, and Soviet and Cuban personnel guided the Ethiopians. Although the Somali lost the war in 1976, they were reported once again in control of much of the Ogaden. The struggle will probably continue into the 1980s. When Spain retreated from Western Sahara in 1976, Morocco and Mauritania took over; but they have had to resist a rebel group, the Polisario, backed by Algeria. In 1979 about 10,000 irregulars were tying down some 30,000 troops from Morocco and Mauritania.

Wars and coups result from many causes—ethnic rivalry, religious differences, liberation movements, Marxist ideology, irredentism, secessionist movements, military opportunism, or adventurism. Whites clash with blacks in southern Africa. Even more bitter are the less well publicized ethnoreligious conflicts that afflict the southern borderlands of Islam. In Mauritania, blacks ask for increased political representation. In the southern Sudan, discontent against Muslim rule from Khartoum continues to smolder beneath the surface. In Chad, a black government was ousted in 1979 by Muslim rebels supported by Libya. There is a good deal of ethnic discontent, occasioned by arbitrarily drawn colonial boundary lines that continue to divide members of the same ethnic community. These conflicts are likely to continue during the

1980s; conceivably, they might become even more severe.

Africa also suffers from interstate tensions. Although the peacetime armies created by the European colonizers were small in size, Africa has armed rapidly since gaining independence. The Institute for Strategic Studies reported in 1979 that after the Middle East, Africa now accounts for the largest arms expenditure in the Third World.

Instability has thus become endemic to Africa. The parliamentary systems left by European colonial rulers have largely been destroyed. The picture is not universally bleak; countries like Nigeria and Ghana are infinitely freer than states like Angola or Mozambique. Nevertheless, civil liberties barely exist in many African countries, and political opposition groups are widely arrested, imprisoned, banned, or exiled. Many African governments could not stay in power without foreign assistance. Amin in Uganda used Cubans, Palestinians, and Libyans to protect himself; Mobutu of Zaïre depends on Moroccan and Senegalese troops to hold onto Shaba province; Neto in Angola and the Dergue in Ethiopia would be gone, but for Cuban guns.

Unfortunately, these armed establishments commonly rest on a slender economic base. The economic performance of the post-independence regimes has varied widely. Kenya and the Ivory Coast, to mention only two, have made striking progress during the last two decades, as has Liberia. But many other countries now find themselves in a parlous condition. Fiscal mismanagement is rife (as in Zambia and Uganda, for example); so is corruption (for example, in Zaïre, the Central African Empire, and many other states.) Excessive indulgence in prestige projects or the exactions of a parasitical and overgrown bureaucracy may lead to rising indebtedness. The ruling tyrants in countries as varied as Uganda, Equatorial Guinea and the Central African Empire are incapable of running their countries; others, such as Sekou Touré of Guinea and Kaunda of Zambia, have just avoided bankrupting their people. The sense of nationhood and the mantle of legitimacy have not been achieved by most governments, which are dictatorial, incompetent, or corrupt—not because they lack intelligence, but rather because they lack experience and are unrealistic in their aims. Too often the new leaders and their followers care little about efficiency or high standards of probity and dedication in the service of their people. Foreigners must still run the mines and plants, the airlines and technical services, the railways and ports. The presidents of Zambia and Gabon have publicly attacked the laziness of their countrymen. Journalists David Lamb (*New York Times,* February 16, 1979) reported on "national listlessness" in Zambia, where hundreds of government cars rust in lots outside of Lusaka because there is no initiative to fix them. Even countries with exportable minerals are in financial trouble, and many African states exist on the international dole of foreign aid. In a continent still 90 percent agricultural, per capita food production is declining. Zaïre, once a large exporter of agricultural crops, can no longer feed itself. It is only inexpensive maize and canned food from Rhodesia and South Africa that keep Zaïre and Zambia from starvation.

Africa suffers from a shortage of economic entrepreneurs and from an excess of political revolutionaries. Commonly, the state owns too much and regulates too much. Bureaucracies are swollen in size and inept in operation, their despotism muted only by their incompetence. Socialist ideologies abound, reducing material well-being wherever they are in effect. The administrative performance of the new African states has varied widely; ability, competence, and hard work contrast with sordid corruption and mismanagement. In some cases, the new governments might best be described as kleptocracies—the rule of thieves. The ruler of Gabon (with a population of about 600,000 people) built himself a $650 million palace. Mobutu of Zaïre supposedly takes for his own use one out of every five dollars earned by his country. The impoverished Central African Empire had to pay for the monarch's nine palaces, a mansion in France, and a $10 million coronation ceremony. Less well publicized is corruption on the provincial and district levels, corruption of a kind almost unknown during the Pax Britannica.

In our dealings with the so-called less developed countries, we Americans have unfortunately tended to ignore or downplay the problems of political authority and effective rule. Most developing countries in Africa lack a sense of political community and an effective, authoritative, legitimate government. The West widely assumed that through aid and technical assistance we could induce economic growth and thus achieve political stability. In fact, the last decade has seen a widespread decline of political order and legitimacy.

The reasons for this decline are complex. More and more Africans have moved into cities, where men can be organized into parties and trade unions more easily than in villages. Communications have improved. The motor truck, the transistor radio, the cheaply printed newspaper, the school, all have contributed to the growth of political consciousness. At the same time, popular expectations have increased. The advocates of decolonization made far-reaching promises concerning the social and economic benefits to be expected from the demise of the old empires. The successor governments continued to make the most far-reaching promises concerning the future, as did their critics. The growth of the state machinery and the intrusion of the state into economic life have also tended to heighten ethnic tension. As long as the state concerned itself only with raising taxes and arresting criminals, a villager could make a living, no matter who controlled the government. But once the state controlled trade through marketing boards, prices through planning commissions, and credit through state banks, control of the state machinery became a matter of economic survival, and rival ethnic communities acquired a pressing interest in the control of political power. As more and more was expected of the government, the government increasingly became the target of alienated students, intellectuals, and military officers convinced that they had not obtained their due share of political or economic benefits.

Many leaders have opted for Marxist governments, or at least for highly centralized forms of government pledged to state-controlled economies. Despite the claims of Communist and socialist models, they have not proved effective for economic development, but they have given the new rulers tools useful for retaining power. Marxism-Leninism calls for central planning and state monopolies. It offers a model of party organization for gaining popular support and for executing policy. No African state is as yet fully Communist, but countries like Angola and Mozambique are adopting some Communist techniques—an ideology based on scientific socialism, a party structured hierarchically according to Lenin's rule of democratic centralism, autocratic but inefficient planning, secret police, and nationalization of business and industry. The number of Marxist states will probably continue to grow in the 1980s.

THE GROWTH OF SOVIET INFLUENCE

Above all, independent Africa has remained—and will continue to be—a field of international competition. In economics, the European Economic Community (EEC) is by far the most powerful foreign contender. The community of West European states remains Africa's most important trading partner, with the United States, Japan, and the Soviet bloc a long way behind it. France also maintains a military presence in several of the former French territories, a presence that the United States should encourage in its own self-interest. But as conservative leaders die or are replaced, the French presence is likely to be opposed by younger, more radical leaders. South Africa continues to play a major economic role in the affairs of its neighbors—Namibia, Zimbabwe-Rhodesia, Lesotho, Botswana, and Swaziland, and even in countries like Zambia and Mozambique that are officially pledged to the destruction of South Africa's regime.

In addition, Africans must contend with the influence of the Soviet Union. Soviet influence has been exercised through dealings with established non-Marxist governments, through the pressures exercised by orthodox Communist parties (mostly weak and ineffectual), and through liberation movements—originally designed as "fronts" or "movements"—dedicated to bringing about national democratic revolutions as stepping stones to socialism. According to Communist theoreticians, these fronts are to be gradually transformed into Marxist-Leninist vanguard parties dedicated to the pursuit of scientific socialism through democratic centralism and to the global struggle to effect world revolution under Soviet leadership.

The new Soviet imperialism has been sustained by the deployment of Cuban troops in Africa, assisted by Soviet and East German advisers. Early in 1979, the total number of Cubans in Africa exceeded 40,000, nearly one-quarter of Cuba's armed forces. The Organization of African Unity (OAU) has been unable to handle the new threat, any more than they can deal with the supposed white menace from South Africa. The Soviet offensive is supported by diplomacy; by the impressive strength of the Soviet fleet; by the ability of the Soviet air force to transport large numbers of troops, complete with heavy equipment, over thousands of miles; and by an international army of wellwishers—not necessarily Communist—who applaud any move that seems to weaken the West. In the view of Communist theoreticians, the new, military form of proletarian internationalism will alter the international correlation of forces, enabling the Soviet Union to confound imperialism strategically and economically.

According to Communist policymakers, the pursuit of revolution in Africa requires the transformation of progressive movements and fronts into disciplined cadre parties. This process began in Angola, Mozambique, South Yemen, and the People's Republic of the Congo; it is now under way in Ethiopia. The new parties are expected to accept Marxism-Leninism, perhaps as gradually as the Mongolian and Cuban parties and at the same time "cement their solidarity" with the Soviet bloc.

Political infiltration goes with naval expansion and the creation of a great air-transport command. Soviet strategists simultaneously look for control over global "chokepoints." Many American liberals are sceptical of this interpretation, but it makes sense from the Soviet standpoint. Why should the Soviets want to control the Horn of Africa if not for strategic reasons? Why support revolutionaries in Ethiopia and South Yemen when these countries have no valuable minerals and when their foreign trade is insignificant? Why endanger détente by supporting revolution as far afield as South Africa and Afghanistan, but for strategic reasons? The answer is clear. The Soviets seek to combine Russian imperial power with Communist revolution in a bid for global hegemony. The Soviets will, therefore, continue to combine the politics of subversion with an old-fashioned drive for strategic advantage. Since the West is dependent for the time being on Middle Eastern oil and African minerals, the Soviets are in a strong position.

PROBLEM AREAS AND U.S. POLICY

The Horn of Africa, Zaïre, and southern Africa are likely trouble spots for the United States. The Horn is strategically important, dominating, as it does, the major maritime route through the Red Sea and the Suez Canal. It comprises the states of Ethiopia, Djibouti, and Somalia—the most important of which is Ethiopia. With 30 million people, Ethiopia is one of the most ancient and most populous African states; militarily, it is more powerful than all its African neighbors combined.

Ethiopia

Until 1974, Ethiopia was subject to the rule of Emperor Haile Selassie who—like the Shah of Iran—maintained an alliance with the United States and attempted to modernize the country, while preserving much of the traditional social system. The Ethiopian monarchy, however, lacked Iran's oil riches, and its development was slow. The emperor failed to deal with corruption, widespread famines, and a constant trade deficit. He was unable to contain unrest among the new class of intellectuals, the army officers, and the urban poor. There was maladministration and widespread insurgency among the Muslims of Eritrea and the Ogaden. The emperor was overthrown in 1974 by a military coup dedicated, ostensibly, to democratization, to the elimination of feudal and ecclesiastical privileges, and to land reform.

Ethiopia's new rulers, drawn from the ranks of the military, made a clean sweep. They cut the country's existing ties with the United States; they smashed the traditional power of the landed magnates and the church. They set up a self-proclaimed Marxist-Leninist regime, but maintained the Amhara ethnic predominance. In order to do so, they instituted a reign of terror against real or alleged dissenters within and without the revolutionaries' ranks.

In addition, the new government committed itself to a Socialist Resettlement Program, in which scattered farmers were to be relocated, cadres assigned to teach new methods to cultivators, and state farms developed in order to provide surplus capital for industry and to produce raw materials for industrial production. In practice, the new program benefited townsmen at the cultivators' expense and apparently further disrupted agricultural production.

The new authorities were determined to secure Ethiopian power against all external threats. The first of these came from Eritrea, where Ethiopian rule was endangered by a widespread popular rising, backed by the Arab states. Eritrea was not part of the traditional Ethiopian empire; it was linked to Ethiopia in a loose federation in 1952, but was incorporated as a province in 1962. Had the Eritrean revolution succeeded, Ethiopia would have been cut off from direct maritime access, other peoples might also have revolted, and Ethiopia could have been reduced to its highland core.

Even more serious to Ethiopia was the challenge from Somalia. In 1969 General Mohammed Siad Barre staged a coup in Somalia. One of his objectives was to build a Greater Somalia, which would include the former French Somaliland, the Somali areas of Kenya, and—above all—the Somali-speaking parts of Ethiopia in the Ogaden, important to Somalia's Muslim pastoralists for their grazing grounds as well as for national and religious reasons.

The Soviet Union originally had staked everything on Ethiopia's enemies and along with Cuba provided assistance to the Eritrean rebels. More important, a Somali-Soviet Treaty of Friendship and Cooperation, concluded in 1974 against Ethiopia's pro-American government, provided the Soviet Union with many advantages, including the use of valuable port facilities by the Soviet navy. Somalia, a poverty-stricken country, was heavily armed, and by the end of 1977 Somali invaders had seized most of the land claimed from Ethiopia. At the same time, insurgents established effective control over most of Eritrea, thus putting the Ethiopians in a desperate position.

Once the Ethiopian monarchy had been overthrown, the Soviet Union had to make a difficult choice. Initially, the Soviets and Cubans tried to effect a compromise by linking Somalia, Ethiopia, and Djibouti into a federation under Marxist influence. The project failed, and the Soviets switched their allegiance. Ethiopian forces, massively supported by Cuban troops and by Soviet advisers and materiel, inflicted a shattering defeat on the Somalis, driving them out of Ethiopia. The Ethiopians, supported by the Cubans, then turned against the Eritreans, who reverted to guerrilla operations. By the end of 1978, Ethiopia's fortunes had recovered, but at a tremendous cost in money and men.

The Soviet Union, having been forced to withdraw from the Somali port of Berbera, made good its strategic loss in the Red Sea by gaining access to the Eritrean ports of Assab (used for landing Cuban soldiers from Soviet ships), and Massawa (where the Russians set up a floating dry dock previously withdrawn from Berbera). At the same time, the Soviets attempted to reestablish contact with the Eritrean secessionists whom they had previously aided, and Soviet agents again suggested that the Marxist states on the Red Sea should form a pro-Soviet federation.

The growth of Soviet power in the Horn of Africa has placed the United States in a dilemma. America has no conceivable interest in encouraging a socialist Greater Somalia whose claims threaten both Ethiopia and Kenya. The United States' interests are best served by promoting peace and stability in Africa; this object cannot be attained if existing colonial boundaries are challenged. During the 1980s, the United States should thus supply sufficient arms to Somalia to contain Ethiopian expansion at Somalia's expense. Somalia, however, must be persuaded to give up its hopes for a Greater Somalia; perhaps it might be given grazing and watering rights in the Ogaden. The United States should support the Eritreans, which would place additional strains on Ethiopia while helping American-Arab relations. Ethiopian claims to Eritrea are comparatively recent and have neither ethnic nor religious foundations. Moreover, Ethiopian rule has been brutal and repressive.

Above all, the United States can derive no advantage in strengthening the Soviet Union's hold on the southern shores of the Red Sea. Until Ethiopia adopts a more friendly policy toward the United States, the latter should encourage rebellious ethnic groups within the Ethiopian empire and suggest perhaps that Ethiopia be rebuilt as a multiethnic confederation with full rights for Muslims and pagans, who outnumber the Amhara ruling group. As a long-term objective, the United States should seek the withdrawal of Cuban troops and Soviet advisers from the Horn of Africa. The permanent neutralization of the Horn would be in our interests. Neutralization should enable Ethiopia and Somalia to decrease the swollen military budgets that consume large shares of their respective gross national products. Furthermore, it would end the threat to the stability of the Sudan and Kenya, which is fed by Somali ambitions and Eritrean refugees. Primarily, neutralization would deny the Soviet Union one of the strategic prizes of Africa.

Zaïre

The second trouble spot, Zaïre (formerly the Belgian Congo), is potentially one of the richest countries in Africa. It covers 894,348 square miles, more than 75 times the area of Belgium; its mineral wealth is enormous; many areas are fertile; and a great river system facilitates waterborne transport. Before Zaïre achieved independence in 1960, the territory was one of the most prosperous in colonial Africa. The country not only fed itself, it also exported a variety of tropical crops. The Congo was one of the world's major producers of copper, uranium, and industrial diamonds, and had begun to build secondary industries.

Independence in 1960, however, brought political turmoil. Divided into numerous ethnic groups, the country was devoid of inner unity. The army—poorly disciplined, poorly paid, and poorly fed—was a menace more to its own people than to foreign enemies. The economy has continued to decline since independence. Statisticians calculate that between 1974 and 1978 the average Zaïrian's purchasing power had declined by over one-half, and uncontrolled inflation has rendered the currency almost valueless. Zaïre faces a deficit of over $3 billion. Hospitals and health clinics have ceased to operate; the transportation system has broken down for lack of maintenance, fuel, and spare parts; roads have deteriorated; crime is rife; food is short and often beyond the means of average citizens in the big cities. Many rural communities have reverted to subsistence agriculture because there is no way of transporting cash crops to market. The central government's control has ceased in many outlying areas. Agricultural production is now below the level reached at independence, with food imports—then negligible—now exceeding $300 million a year.

The causes of the so-called *mal zaïrois* are many. Between 1974 and 1975, the world price for copper, which accounts for about two-thirds of Zaïre's foreign exchange, dropped from $1.40 to $0.55 a pound, while the costs of imports—especially of food, oil, and spare parts—rose greatly. The country's economic ills were worsened by unwise economic policies, designed primarily to provide jobs for a corrupt, inefficient, and overgrown bureaucracy. In 1973 Zaïre nationalized all foreign-owned agricultural, transport, and commercial enterprises; a year later, it nationalized all firms whose annual turnover exceeded $2 million. A large number of plantations and businesses passed into the hands of party loyalists who managed them poorly and sold much of the existing stock to speculators. Peculation was equally rife in the national treasury; scarce foreign exchange was used for prestige projects or filtered into foreign bank accounts. Economic mismanagement was accompanied by an intense personality cult. Mobutu Sese Seko, a former army sergeant turned dictator, arrogated to himself semidivine status as the country's supreme "guide" and architect of national "authenticity." Mobutu has been accused of accumulating enormous private fortunes for himself and his satraps. The Catholic church, the country's most powerful religious group, continually complains of civil rights violations, corruption, and immorality. There is widespread unrest, especially in Shaba (Katanga) province, the country's main mineral producer.

Zaïre has failed to achieve a workable compromise between its various ethnic components. These ethnic considerations, in turn, play a major part in shaping the country's foreign policy. In the past, the Kongo, a powerful ethnic group within the Zaïre establishment, warmly sympathized with Kongo guerrillas battling against Portuguese rule in neighboring Angola, as well as with UNITA, the Frente Nacional de Libertação de Angola's (FLNA) uncertain ally. In addition, Zaïre has long-established claims on the oil-rich Cabinda enclave that the Portuguese regarded as part of Angola. When Angola achieved independence, Zaïre continued to back Kongo partisans, organized through the FLNA movement, against the new rulers in Luanda. Assisted by Cuban troops, the Kongo guerrillas were put down with a strong hand, but unrest continues. Zaïre paid a heavy price for its policy; the Benguela railway—an important outlet for Zaïre's minerals to the Atlantic—suffered from continuous interruptions and after 1975 ceased to operate altogether.

Katangan refugees in Angola, trained and equipped by East Germans and reinforced by Lunda-speakers from Angola, successively attacked Shaba province in 1977 and again in 1978. The Zaïrian army once again proved helpless; the task of repelling the invaders fell to French and Moroccan troops. Mobutu also received U.S. support; American aircraft assisted a Franco-Belgian airlift that ferried in additional troops from francophone west African states. Mobutu displayed political brilliance by obtaining support from as unlikely a collection of states as South Africa, the People's Republic of China, Egypt, Saudi Arabia, and North Korea. The Angolans then realized that Mobutu was there to stay—at least, for the time being—and in 1978 Angola and Zaïre signed a comprehensive treaty. The signatories agreed to abstain from armed subversion in each other's territory and to reopen the Benguela railway.

Given Zaïre's enormous potential wealth, its strategic position in the heart of Africa, and the absence of an effective challenge to Mobutu's authority, the United States has few options. At present, no viable alternative to Mobutu's rule exists. The division of Zaïre would not be in American interests, and there is no evidence that Mobutu's opponents are less corrupt than he. Therefore, the United States should reluctantly continue to back Mobutu, hoping that a patient policy of persuasion, along with foreign experts to run his government and businesses, may improve the performance of his regime. The United States, with Belgian and French aid, should retrain the army and police and should educate a new class of efficient administrators to reestablish administrative control in the provinces. The transportation system will have to be rebuilt and the peasants guaranteed security so that agricultural production can be restored.

Zaïre's political problems are worsened by its constitutional structure. Belgium unfortunately passed on a centralist and paternalistic tradition even less suited to the multiethnic character of Zaïre than to the former metropole. The Zaïrians learned to look to the central government for all manner of favors and for a great variety of decisions that should have been made locally. Hence, Zaïre would do well to reduce the power of Kinshasa, to give more scope to local authorities, and to reduce the power of the state in the economy. A federal or confederal solution is admittedly difficult in a country where Shaba province, with its mineral wealth, holds most of the economic trumps. An independent Shaba in control of locally raised revenue could function much more easily on its own than Zaïre could exist without Shaba. Nevertheless, Zaïre is unlikely to emerge from the mire unless it adopts a more decentralized form of government. Given the erosion of Kinshasa's control over the outlying provinces, the inefficiency of the central civil service, and the indiscipline of the army, Kinshasa would only be recognizing reality by loosening its constitutional hold over the provinces. A more loosely structured Zaïre is more likely to face the problems of the future successfully than a centralized Zaïre run as a despotism tempered by graft.

Southern Africa

The economic center of gravity in sub-Saharan Africa lies in southern Africa. Its many sovereign states—Angola, Zambia, Malawi, Mozambique, South Africa, Lesotho, Swaziland, Botswana, Rhodesia, and Namibia—are linked in a coherent state system that interacts with the Republic of South Africa. This system is large in size (2 million square miles) and population (4.3 million whites and 40 million blacks). It was once the wealthiest, fastest growing, most powerful, and secure part of the continent, until events in Angola in 1974 destabilized the system. The Republic of South Africa alone accounts for 20 percent of the wealth of Africa, 40 percent of its industrial productivity, including 80 percent of the continent's steel production and 60 percent of its electricity.

South Africa. Economically the system is dominated by South Africa, which has an economic stranglehold over the three enclaves within and along its borders—Swaziland, Lesotho, and Botswana and totally controls Namibia. Rhodesia and Zambia rely heavily on South

Africa. Angola has moved out of the system, at considerable expense to its economy, but Mozambique—for the time being—remains enmeshed within the South African system. Most of the states around or within South Africa depend in varying degrees on it for capital, markets, technology, finance, and business and technical skills. It is also an outlet for migrant workers; 500,000 black laborers reside in South Africa—100,000 from Marxist-Leninist Mozambique alone. Lesotho, Botswana, and Swaziland—all landlocked countries—must import and export their wares through South Africa, which collects customs revenues on their behalf. Many hydroelectric and irrigation schemes in Mozambique and Angola relied heavily on South Africa for financing and construction. No matter what political changes occur in the 1980s, the Republic of South Africa will continue to dominate the wider state system of southern Africa.

South Africa is therefore the economic giant of Africa and its greatest strategic prize. It covers 794,547 square miles and demographically ranks fourth in Africa after Nigeria, Egypt, and Ethiopia, with a population of about 26.7 million (4.4 million whites, 2.4 million Coloureds, 800,000 Asians, and 19.1 million blacks).

These figures, however, give little indication of South Africa's relative economic and military strength; nor do they show the country's extraordinary vitality. South Africa is the only African country with a balanced economy. The country feeds itself and even exports food. It is one of the world's great mineral producers, rich in gold, uranium, coal, iron, nickel, chrome, diamonds, and a host of other minerals, many of them of great strategic value to the Western world. In addition, South Africa is a modern manufacturing country; in certain respects, it is part both of the "First" World and of the "Third" World. It is the most urbanized country in sub-Saharan Africa; 87 percent of the whites and more than 40 percent of the blacks live in cities. South Africa accounts for the bulk of Africa's industrial production and manufactures a variety of sophisticated goods, ranging from mining machinery to ships, planes and rockets.

During World War II and its immediate aftermath, South Africa was respected as an ally of the West; but after 1948 public opinion began to change. According to its critics within and without the U.N., the Pretoria regime is run by a racist clique; its government is a danger to peace and an affront to the dignity of man, and the country is approaching a revolutionary situation that will lead to a racial bloodbath. Hence, the United States has a special responsibility to use its power—diplomatic, economic, moral, perhaps even military—to liberate brown and black people in South Africa. The Carter administration sees the civil rights struggle in South Africa as an extension of the civil rights struggle in the Deep South. The administration therefore considers that the United States must align itself with progressive forces and coerce South Africa into joining the world of racial equality and integration and, through gradual reform, into accepting the U.S. doctrine of one man/one vote.

We dissent from the accepted orthodoxy of academia and international organizations. South Africa, for all its deficiencies, has made extraordinary progress, with a growth rate since World War II second only to Japan's. Despite its authoritarian streak, South Africa is not nearly as repressive as Cambodia, Cuba, or any member of the Warsaw Pact—or indeed, as repressive as numerous African dictatorships with whom the United States enjoys correct relations. White South Africans have often been harsh in their dealings with black people. But there has been nothing like the mass terror characteristic of communist countries and of many African dictatorships. A recent Amnesty International publication bitterly critical of South Africa stated that there are 450 political prisoners; this figure compares most favorably with the thousands and tens of thousands incarcerated in countries like Cuba and Angola, not to mention the Soviet Union and China. South Africa has experienced nothing comparable to the mass expulsions of ethnic minorities that stained the post–World War II history of countries as varied as Burma, Uganda, India, Algeria, Palestine, Poland, Czechoslovakia, Burundi, and Angola. John Vorster or Piet Botha rule more peacefully than potentates like Field Marshal Amin in Uganda, President Nguema in Equatorial Guinea, or Emperor Bokassa in the Central African Empire. Yet no U.N. or OAU resolution has ever dared to condemn these black tyrants in the terms habitually applied to white South Africans.

Critics of South Africa emphasize the numerous economic and educational disabilities that face black South Africans. These critics have a case, but it is exaggerated. Black South Africans do suffer from a variety of discriminatory measures. Nevertheless, they are, on the whole, among the best paid, best educated, and most urbanized blacks in Africa. Black South Africans have a higher average life expectancy than west Africans (50 opposed to 39.2 years). Black wages have gone up steadily; the industrial color bar was recently eliminated; social and educational services available to black South Africans compare favorably with the best available in any part of black Africa.

Given South Africa's economic resilience and strong government, the chances for revolution or military defeat are slender. The army and the administration are neither inefficient, universally corrupt, nor subject to revolutionary infiltration—unlike, say, the former bureaucratic apparatus of South Vietnam or of Cuba under Batista. European morale is good; the Europeans feel they are fighting for their homes and futures. The whites are convinced that their country, despite its deficiencies, has been managed with infinitely less bloodshed than many African countries. The Indians are only too conscious that their lot in white South Africa has been better than the fate of the Indian minorities expelled from black-ruled east Africa.

South African blacks are divided along linguistic, ethnic, and social lines, which makes organizing an effective resistance movement difficult. Employed workers pitted against unemployed youths and students are one factor in the present urban unrest. Moreover, there are no disciplined, cohesive cadres to lead a revolution. The people do not have weapons. The police and an informer system have destroyed all black political organizations that oppose the government, and to date such surveillance has cowed black political movements. Armed intervention by other African states is not feasible at present, given the strength of the South African military establishment and the logistic, organizational, and political weaknesses of the African states.

South Africa's military preparations encompass both counterinsurgency and conventional warfare. The country has a small, mobile regular army and maintains a large active reserve. It has an industrial infrastructure that makes it almost self-sufficient in arms production, and with a five-year oil reserve, it is not vulnerable to an oil boycott. It has stockpiled a great arsenal of weapons, and the recent U.N. arms embargo is unlikely to hurt it. South Africa can deploy armored forces supported by a modern and well-trained air force. It has the technical knowledge and the raw materials to build nuclear weapons and deliver them. It still requires foreign skills and equipment, however, in rocketry, computers, and advanced aircraft. But boycotts are almost impossible to enforce, and as in the past, there will be leaks.

As of 1979, South Africa's peacetime armed forces comprised 38,000 men on active duty in the army, 8,500 in the air force, and 5,000 in the navy. Ninety thousand men are in the commandos—a paramilitary force designed for local defense and counterinsurgency. South Africa can mobilize 250,000 men easily, and including all reserves, its citizen force numbers 450,000. These forces are well-trained, morale is high, and postings to the border areas of Angola, Mozambique, and Rhodesia have given them combat experience. The army is essentially the white electorate in arms; hence, coups are unlikely. Its members are highly motivated, unlike the Portuguese or U.S. draftees of the 1960s and 1970s. Draft resistance and desertion are almost unknown. The South

African navy was originally designed for defense of the Cape route. The international arms boycott has forced South Africa to place its main emphasis on coastal defense, conducted by fast, missile-carrying craft produced domestically.

For internal defense, South Africa has a police force of 54,000 men—about 2.02 per thousand people, a proportion smaller than that of Great Britain or West Germany. Nearly half of this force consists of Africans, Coloureds, and Indians. The police have an extensive intelligence network and great powers of control through the various pass laws and antiterrorism and anticommunist legislation. It is a vital component of South Africa's internal defense. No revolutionary breakdown could occur without the disruption of the police establishment.

War against South Africa by African states in the 1980s is not likely to succeed. Black armies are weak and poorly trained, and even Cuba or East Germany could not defeat South Africa. Only intervention by a major power would bring the nation down. Hopes, then, for a violent overthrow of the South African system, either by foreign invasion or by internal or external guerrilla assaults, belong to the realm of military fantasy for the present.

Furthermore, South Africa plays an essential role in Western defense. The nation's control of the maritime route skirting the Cape of Good Hope, its industrial infrastructure, its command over many vital strategic raw materials, including gold, platinum, uranium, and chrome, make it a valuable asset to the Western world. Western Europe obtains 70 percent of its strategic minerals and 90 percent of its oil from shipping around the Cape. The Soviet plan is to acquire the capability to deny these minerals and oil to the West. Threats to shut off supplies could force Western European states to give in on political issues; the West would therefore be ill-served by exposing itself to future Soviet pressures by losing control over this route, thereby threatening Western Europe with Finlandization.

How, then, should the United States act toward South Africa? A policy of harassment will certainly fail. South Africa generates the bulk of its capital domestically. She can feed herself and is largely independent of imported raw materials. Even a worldwide boycott would not work; South Africa is well placed to resist it. American investments in South Africa occupy too small a place (17 percent of total foreign holdings) to be a major bargaining counter. A U.S. trade embargo is not likely to succeed. Formal trade embargoes, moreover, have been violated by many African states, which do a multi-million dollar business with South Africa every year. Further, it is inconsistent to argue that the Soviet-dominated states can be rendered more amenable to Western values by a policy of détente and by encouraging trade and cultural relations, but that such a policy should not apply to South Africa. There is, in fact, little evidence for convergence between the Soviet system and our own.

The convergence theory is more likely to apply to South Africa than to the Soviet Union. The ruling National (Nationalist) Party in South Africa permits a greater degree of liberty to its citizens than does Frente de Libertação de Moçambique (FRELIMO) in Mozambique or the MPLA in Angola. South African Indians know that they are better off under white rule in South Africa than under black governance in Uganda or Tanzania. Black South Africans have benefited to some extent from the industrial revolution, and they enjoy, on the average, higher living standards than blacks living in neighboring African territories.

The United States should therefore use its diplomatic and commercial position to follow a policy of moderate persuasion designed to bring about reform, not revolutionary change. We should quietly press for improvements in return for economic favors. We should extend, rather than diminish, academic, cultural, athletic, diplomatic, and economic contacts with South Africa. We should be conciliatory in tone and firm in intention. Quiet pressure for change, the gradual ending of apartheid, more education and job opportunities for blacks and Coloureds, more self-government for urban blacks, and more democracy in the Bantu homelands (Bantustans)—these are attainable goals.

American policy is unlikely to succeed, however, if the United States insists that white South Africans surrender political power by introducing a policy of one man/one vote. White South Africans believe, rightly or wrongly, that a powerless white minority would be treated no better by the ruling blacks than the Indians were treated in Uganda and that black rule would entail civil war and economic collapse. The whites may be wrong in their assumptions. But given the experiences of postcolonial Zanzibar (where the Arab minority was destroyed), or Burundi (where the Hutu were cruelly persecuted), or northern Nigeria (where the Ibo were robbed or massacred), or Algeria, Angola, and Mozambique (where most of the European population was compelled to migrate), white fears are not unreasonable.

Can a peaceful South Africa be created in the future? It can, but it will be a difficult task. A successful regime must recognize the diversity of South Africa's ethnic, political, and economic groups and must mediate between them. The striking differences in status and material wealth between blacks, browns, and whites must be gradually reduced. Political power cannot be restricted to whites and to traditional tribal rulers; leadership roles must be shared among the elites of all groups. South

Africa must accept a federal system, but not one based only on the homelands concept. All racially discriminatory legislation and practices must end. Some progress has already been made toward the last goal; segregation, for example, has ended in some hotels, bars, and restaurants. Such legislation as the Group Areas Act and the Mixed Marriages and Immorality Acts, however, must also be repealed. In short, apartheid must be dismantled. Strong efforts need to be made to build a South African consciousness and to stress nationalism based on equality before the law and on human rights.

This complicated, delicate process of accommodation, power sharing, and leveling can succeed only if all groups agree to cooperate. This will not be easy in a multiracial, ethnically diverse society—a society that has long been dominated by whites and is under attack by the South African Communist Party (SACP), the African National Congress (ANC), and the Pan-Africanist Congress (PAC), as well as by radical states and the United Nations. Nevertheless, there are some grounds for hope.

Reform in South Africa in the 1980s will come from within. It will derive from the ruling Nationalist Party, rather than from a divided opposition. The Nationalist Party is not a monolithic bloc, run like a Communist party on the rigid principles of democratic centralism. The party is being transformed by social and economic forces.

South African politicians in recent years have been searching for an alternative to the present Westminster system, where whites rule by parliamentary democracy—for whites only. One man/one vote would destroy white hegemony and would threaten legitimate white interests. So Cabinet Minister Koornhof pushed for a Swiss-cantonal system; Vorster wanted a strong presidential system and a series of parliaments based on race. Others, like C. P. Mulder, outlined a policy of breaking up South Africa into ethnic homelands for each of the races and ethnic groups.

The new Botha plan for sharing power envisages three separate parliaments—for whites, Coloureds, and Indians, respectively—who will look out for their own people. The blacks are not to have their own parliament. The country's affairs are to be run by a cabinet council of seven whites, four Coloureds, and three Asians, under the chairmanship of an "executive state president." The president, who will be elected by a multiracial assembly of fifty whites, twenty-five Coloureds, and fourteen Asians, would have the deciding vote in the cabinet council. Opponents have attacked the plan as unwieldy since the three parliaments could make different laws for each racial group. Critics also fear that the president would have too much power. But the plan at least shows that the white leaders recognize the problem and accept the fact that they cannot rule alone.

The most original proposal is that made by Jordan K. Ngubane, a black South African who described a blueprint for the new South Africa in his book, *An African Explains Apartheid.* He proposed a Swiss-cantonal federation having four types of state: African, Afrikaner, English, and nonracial. These ethnic states would be based in part on traditional living areas. Ngubane recognized the conflicting interests of each racial group and therefore sought a democratic framework that would guarantee that no one group could dominate the others. It will satisfy those who want black majority rule, but will protect legitimate white interests. Unfortunately, few people have read Ngubane's book. Fewer still espouse his ideas.

As we see it, the United States should endeavor to support the *verligtes* (reformists) within the Nationalist Party, rather than the South African opposition, whether liberal or revolutionary. In practice, the United States has done the opposite. We have weakened reform-minded Nationalists by an ineffective combination of sermons and insults that merely serve to consolidate white power. The Nationalist Party wields effective power in South Africa; hence effective change within the country is likely to come from within the system, rather than from outside it.

We realize that our position is hardly popular. Liberal academicians will argue that the right-wingers are bound to win, that even the *verligtes* cannot be trusted to grant justice to the blacks, and that any concessions made by the *verligtes* will count for little and come too late. We are also aware that economic advancement for black and brown South Africans will not necessarily lead to a political transformation of the country. Change will be slow and its pace uncertain.

Nevertheless, we are convinced that our policy provides the best hope for South Africa. The alternatives are worse. The United States has no interest in promoting strife and civil disorder in South Africa, much less in supporting movements that look to the Soviet Union for support in establishing bloodstained tyrannies of the kind now in power in Ethiopia and Angola. Both in the U.S. interest and in that of South Africa, we should, to paraphrase Lenin, call for "all power to the moderates."

Namibia. South Africa's western neighbor is Namibia (South-West Africa), formerly a German colony, subsequently administered by South Africa as a League of Nations and U.N. mandate, and now on the way to formal independence. Namibia covers 318,261 square miles; its population is less than a million—some 12 percent white, 10 percent mixed Afro-European ancestry, and 78 percent black. The black community is divided into eleven ethnic groups, of which the Ovambo are the most important (about 46 percent), followed by the Damara, the Herero, and others.

In more than 70 percent of the country, water is so scarce that even dry-land cropping is out of the question. Except in parts of the well-watered north, grazing is the major form of agriculture. Modern technology has considerably developed the country's natural potential in recent years; extensive South African capital investments, both public and private, in the pastoral industry, up-to-date methods of pasture management, disease control, new techniques of stockbreeding, and new varieties of trees and forage have helped to make farming and ranching somewhat less hazardous occupations than in the past. Port facilities, rail, road, and air services have made the outlying areas more accessible than before in a country where nature failed to provide navigable waterways. Modern vessels exploit the country's fishing grounds along the Atlantic coast. Primarily, Namibia is a major mineral producer.

At the same time, Namibia shares all of South Africa's social problems, as well as problems that accompany rapid urbanization and a high birthrate. There is a striking imbalance between white wealth and black poverty. Whites, for the moment, are by far the best educated and the most prosperous members of the community. South Africa, moreover, continues to maintain a tight economic hold over Namibia. The South Africans have gone to great lengths to subsidize Namibia's budgetary deficits; they have financed much of its development work; and they supply the bulk of Namibia's banking services, its capital, its markets, and its imports.

Given the small size of its population and its large land area, Namibia now has a huge infrastructure, larger than it could have built unaided, with its own resources. No other country could have taken South Africa's place as a supplier of skilled technicians and managers or as a source of capital and as a buyer of Namibia's goods. In subsidizing the Namibian economy, South Africa pursued its enlightened self-interest. South Africa originally hoped to incorporate Namibia as a fifth province. This policy failed, and in 1977 moderates of all races—now united in the Turnhalle Democratic Alliance (TDA)—produced a new constitution, designed to safeguard the interests of each ethnic group. The South African government, in an astonishing about-face, dismantled the administrative machinery of apartheid, agreed to hold free elections, and recognized Namibia as an independent state. The South Africans, however, encountered strong opposition, both from the international community and from SWAPO. The United Nations considered the concessions made by South Africa as inadequate; the TDA became widely, though inaccurately, known as a South African puppet.

The militant opposition, SWAPO (drawn mainly from the ranks of the Ovambo), with support from the United Nations, resisted an election confrontation. SWAPO was by no means a united body. There were splits between the relatively moderate internal wing, allowed to operate legally within Namibia, and the militant external wing, which also suffered from a variety of dissensions. After many twists and turns, SWAPO has become a Marxist-oriented body, allied with the South African ANC, the MPLA, FRELIMO, and ZAPU (Zimbabwe African People's Union), all of them linked by political, ideological, diplomatic, and financial ties to the Soviet Union. SWAPO, as of 1979, considered itself the only legitimate representative of the Namibian people and placed its hopes in the armed struggle waged by small guerrilla bands operating from bases in Angola.

In our view, U.S. interests would be best served in the 1980s by recognizing the new government due to emerge from the planned elections. SWAPO is militarily too weak to take over Namibia on its own. In an ethnically segmented society, SWAPO's base of support is too weak to establish effective governance—unless it is supported by Cuban or possibly East German troops. The United States should resist the creation of a Soviet-dominated, Namibian-Angolan bloc in the South Atlantic. Nor does the West have any interest in supporting a settlement that would lead to the confiscation of foreign enterprise, a voluntary or enforced exodus of Namibian whites, and economic breakdown, leaving Namibia dependent on Soviet and East European help.

Rhodesia. Rhodesia, unlike Namibia, is economically a developed country, with established manufacturing industries, a modern agricultural sector, and considerable mining wealth. Its population is substantial—just under 7 million people, including about a quarter of a million whites. It is a large country, nearly the size of California. Its rate of economic growth during the past thirty years has been one of the most rapid in Africa.

Rhodesia (now known as Zimbabwe-Rhodesia), though part of the British Empire, was never directly administered by Great Britain. It began its political career as the fief of the British South Africa Company, a great chartered concern, and in 1923 became a "self-governing colony"—a quasi-dominion run to all intents and purposes by a minority of white colonists. In 1965 Rhodesia, fearing future intervention from

Great Britain, issued its Unilateral Declaration of Independence (UDI) and subsequently became an unrecognized republic.

The Rhodesians, with South African help, surmounted an international boycott and further expanded their economy. At the same time, they successfully resisted guerrilla incursions from Zambia, and for a time UDI seemed to succeed. When the Portuguese empire collapsed, the position rapidly changed in the guerrilla's favor. A new front opened along the Mozambique border. The Rhodesian security forces were seriously stretched, the South Africans grew convinced that a moderate black government was more likely to cope with the situation than an all-white regime, and—under joint pressure from Washington and Pretoria—Ian Smith in 1976 agreed to a phased hand-over, resulting in a black government.

The "internal settlement," however, has failed to gain international legitimacy. The so-called Patriotic Front (a pro-Marxist alliance of two main parties, ZANU [Zimbabwe African National Union] and ZAPU) vowed to continue guerrilla warfare and establish a one-party regime. The Western powers continued the economic boycott initiated after UDI. American liberals supported this policy and then opposed free elections as long as the Patriotic Front refused to participate. Elections were held and a black prime minister was chosen. The United States, liberals hold, cannot recognize the new constitution that gives special guarantees to whites and protects them against the confiscation of their property and the loss of their jobs. Only negotiations with the Patriotic Front—or surrender to it—on Abel Muzorewa's part can restore peace to a troubled land, for the guerrillas must surely win.

This has put the Salisbury government in a Catch 22 position. Had the Rhodesian authorities excluded foreign observers from the elections, they would have been accused of cheating; but when they invited foreign observers, the proprieties of conducting a free election suddenly became irrelevant. The Salisbury government would have been only too pleased if the Patriotic Front had participated in peaceful elections. But the Patriotic Front has, in fact, excluded itself by insisting that victory must spring from the barrel of a gun and that Zimbabwe must submit to a one-party dictatorship of a Marxist complexion.

What attitude should the United States take toward Rhodesia in the future? As of May 1979, the elections had been completed. Nearly 64 percent of the white and black voters participated—a remarkable result in a strife-torn country. The guerrillas had failed to disrupt the voting, which appears to have been conducted in a reasonably fair manner by African standards. The existing coalition nevertheless has weaknesses. It is divided; it still faces guerrilla warfare; its opponents rely on Soviet help and on assistance offered by the so-called frontline states, especially Mozambique, Tanzania, and Zambia. But the only groups that stand for a form of multiracial, multiparty democracy are made up of Ian Smith, Bishop Muzorewa, and Ndabaningi Sithole, the leaders whom progressive world opinion rejects. Under Margaret Thatcher's Tory government in Great Britain, the internal settlement may secure recognition from Great Britain, Rhodesia's nominal suzerain.

The Patriotic Front is not a viable alternative. It is bitterly divided; it is neither patriotic nor a front—Shona fights Ndebele, Marxist clashes with non-Marxist. A Patriotic Front victory—far from certain at present—would surely be followed by a civil war, economic collapse, and possibly Cuban intervention *à l'angolaise.*

The record of radical movements that have come to power in recent years is so bad as to make all but hard-line Marxists blanch. No sensible or humane person wants radical regimes to come to power—with their confiscation of property, their reeducation centers, the civil wars that such regimes have produced in Angola and Ethiopia, or their purging of the opposition, as in South Yemen and Mozambique. In Angola, civil war reigns and the economy has collapsed; only Cuban guns keep the MPLA in power. Radical parties cooperate in fronts only until they gain power—witness Afghanistan, South Yemen, and Ethiopia. They bring neither peace (witness warfare in Angola and Ethiopia); prosperity (all African Marxist regimes have lowered the well-being of their people); nor democracy (arrests, shootings, reeducation centers, confiscation, and the flight of people mar the records of all radical regimes). It is hard to see how a Patriotic Front takeover in Rhodesia can lead to liberation or democracy.

America's most reasonable course would therefore be to recognize the agreement between Smith and the black leaders and the results of the election and then end our boycott of the regime. The white-black coalition has begun to end racial discrimination and segregation—now officially abolished. Grassroot support is there for Muzorewa and Sithole. The guerrilla war will continue, but a Rhodesia ruled by blacks and whites can contain the guerrillas. If a minority government did so for fourteen years, a majority coalition government unfettered by economic sanctions can do it even better. Eighty percent of the Rhodesian army, which has successfully been fighting the guerrillas, consists of black volunteers. It supports the coalition government. The Patriotic Front, on the other hand, occupies no fixed areas; it does not govern, collect taxes, or hold court in any town or village. The new state of Zimbabwe, ruled by a black majority, would probably perform better against the guerrillas. It is hard to see how American self-interest would be served by helping bring about a Marxist victory.

Liberals object to the guarantees that the new Rhodesian constitution provides for the white minority. Such minority guarantees are, however, not unusual. The Kenya independence constitution, for instance, gave special electoral advantages to whites; the former constitution of Cyprus afforded special protection to the Turkish minority. No American political scientist, however, ever suggested that the United States should therefore withhold recognition from Kenya or Cyprus.

As regards Rhodesia's future, the expropriation of European farms and the expulsion of European administrators, managers, and technicians would not be in black Rhodesia's best interest. The former Belgian Congo, the former Portuguese colonies, and newly independent Algeria all experienced a rapid exodus of their respective white minorities. Their departure was everywhere fraught with serious economic consequences—not just for themselves, but for their adopted countries. It is surely not in anyone's interest, except that of the Communists, to encourage chaos and violent radical rule. The U.S. should therefore recognize the multiracial, democratic regime that resulted from the recent elections.

Angola. Angola is one of the largest African territories—481,351 square miles—with an estimated population of only some 6 million. Its economic potential is great. It is rich in oil, diamonds, and a variety of metals and was formerly an exporter of coffee and other crops. The last decade of Portuguese governance witnessed what in retrospect appears as the golden age of Angolan economic development—the country's agriculture expanded, a beginning was made with secondary industries, new cities grew up in the interior.

The Portuguese, however, proved incapable of maintaining their African empire. Although militarily successful, the Portuguese officer corps was radicalized by an extended guerrilla war that it could not end. The military seized power in Lisbon and then embarked on a rapid course of decolonization. Abrogation of Portuguese rule was followed in Angola by a bitter civil war between contending ethnic groups. In the end, the MPLA, a Marxist body, won through a massive deployment of Cuban troops. But civil war has continued; the MPLA government is unable to control the country, even with Cuban and Soviet assistance.

Angola then moved into the international limelight. American liberals called for U.S. recognition of Angola and were joined in their campaign by liberal politicians who consider that self-interest and equity alike should lead us to recognize the Marxist-Leninist regime at Luanda. But is it in our interest—or indeed, in the interest of the Angolan people—to recognize the MPLA government? We contend that it is not. Neto heads a minority government dominated by Communists and supported by Cuban troops and Russian and East German technicians. Angola has been a bad neighbor, training rebels to attack Shaba province in Zaïre and offering training and sanctuary to SWAPO.

The MPLA, according to its own statements, is not simply a radical African nationalist movement. It is a Marxist-Leninist party, dedicated to the pursuit of scientific socialism and the world revolution. The MPLA does not seek to pursue a neutralist foreign policy, any more than Castro did when he turned Cuba into a revolutionary camp for Communist expansion into Latin America. The MPLA firmly sides with what it calls the socialist camp in the global struggle against the forces of world capitalism. Having started as a popular movement or front, the MPLA—and also FRELIMO—have purged their non-Communist elements and have now advanced from being mass organizations to vanguard parties dedicated to the revolutionary transformation of their respective countries.

The Marxist-Leninist government of Angola draws its support primarily from *mestiços* (people of mixed origin) and from one ethnic group. The MPLA not only is at war with the Ovimbundu and the Bakongo peoples, but has also been forced to crush dissenters within its own ranks who have sought a "black" form of socialism. The MPLA is to all intents and purposes a puppet regime of the Soviets and the Cubans. The United States would derive no benefit from strengthening this regime in the international sphere by according it diplomatic recognition.

There is no analogy between the presence of French troops in Djibouti and Chad, the employment of Moroccans in Zaïre and the presence of Cubans in Angola. First, there is a difference in scale. As of early 1979, some 45,000 Cubans were deployed in Africa—about one-quarter of Cuba's armed forces, a higher proportion than the Americans had in Southeast Asia at the height of the Vietnam war. Second, French troops operated in Chad at the behest of that country's established government. In Angola, on the other hand, the Neto regime is solely the creation of the Cuban invader; without Soviet-Cuban assistance, Neto would not rule in Angola. Third, and most important, France is an ally of the United States and poses no threat to local governments. Cuba is a declared enemy of the United States and has acted aggressively in Angola, Ethiopia, and South Yemen to destabilize the Horn of Africa and southern Africa.

Admittedly, the MPLA permits Gulf Oil to operate on Angolan soil, but that is only common sense since a substantial portion of Angola's revenue derives from Gulf Oil's operations. Similarly, the Soviet Union and its allies have consistently asked for—and received—Western credits and Western infusions of technology and managerial expertise. That does not mean that they are not Communist governments or would not in time of tension stop selling us oil. The Soviet Union itself, however, considers these commercial relations as instruments in the international class struggle, a class struggle of worldwide proportions that the Soviet Union means to win. According to Lenin, the capitalist must be encouraged to sell the very rope by which he will be hanged. But there is no reason for us to encourage the Communists in their policy.

In terms of international morality and civil rights, Angola's record has been deplorable. It is a police state, complete with KGB-trained secret police and reeducation centers. There is widespread persecution of practicing Christians; whites have fled or been forced to leave. The MPLA is a minority party that rules through terror and Cuban troops. The MPLA represents only about one-third of the people; the FLNA and UNITA represent two-thirds of the population and hold large parts of the country. Freedom of speech, freedom of the press, freedom of voting—the very freedoms that we seek to establish in Zimbabwe-Rhodesia through international embargo—are absent in Angola. It is ironic that we refuse to accept an elected, democratic, black-white coalition, majority government in Rhodesia, but want to recognize a nonelected, Marxist, minority government in Angola. The atrocities committed in the course of MPLA's campaigns against UNITA and FLNA have led to a large-scale exodus of refugees to Namibia and Zaïre; there is yet no sign of improvement. Food shortages are everywhere. The Benguela railway has not operated since 1975 because of guerrilla activities; exports have ceased, except from Cabinda.

What of the future? America has been too inclined to structure its foreign policy in Africa to gain the approval of the so-called Third World, the uncommitted nations of Asia and Africa, which are supposed to hold the future world balance of power in their hands. This viewpoint disregards the military realities of power and looks on the present struggle for world supremacy as an ideological beauty competition between East and West, a competition in which the panel of judges is made up of Asians and Africans. Nations are indeed influenced by ideas, but economic and strategic factors play an even larger part in world affairs. It is doubtful that the West is justified in subordinating its interests to the real or imagined demands of neutralists. For when all is said and done, it is only the strength of the West, and nothing but its strength, that has made it possible up to now for Afro-Asian countries to afford the luxury of neutralism. Once the West weakenes, the fates of the new countries are themselves imperiled. To look at the question another way, the friendship of Gabon or Burundi would not help the West in the slightest if we allowed our economic and military defenses to crumble.

Accordingly, there cannot be a simple rule of thumb for the conduct of U.S. foreign policy in Africa as a whole. There are many African countries; the United States accordingly needs many different African policies. We need flexibility, realism, and above all, avoidance of the view that American policy must somehow be ideologically *gleichgeschaltet*. Political and economic warfare against South Africa would not liberalize the Republic nor improve the lot of its black people. On the contrary, we should seek to cooperate with Pretoria, as far as collaboration is in our strategic interest. We should seek to support a moderate form of government in Namibia and Rhodesia, rather than aid our declared enemies. Similarly, we should consider recognition of Angola only after all foreign troops—Cuban, East German, and Soviet military experts—have left. This would force the MPLA to form a coalition government with the two other groups. Such a withdrawal should be a necessary condition for U.S. recognition. We need a new realism in our foreign policy to replace our post-Vietnam timidity. An arc of crisis threatens the stability of the Middle East and Africa. The Soviets, with their Cuban mercenaries, are attempting to overthrow the existing order. We must meet their challenge or risk yet another disastrous defeat for the West.

Fortunately, the Communists also face major problems. Various factors—the diversity of Africa's ethnic composition and the relative weakness of the industrial proletariat in all African countries outside South Africa, the persistence of tribal modes of production in many parts of the continent, the dissension and the lack of trained cadres and discipline within the new ruling parties, and the inability of these parties to deal with the economic disasters engendered by domestic terror, war, and civil strife—make it difficult for the Communists to succeed as easily as their theoreticians assume. Prudence and a respect for historical experience suggest that during the 1980s we make a determined effort to prevent the further spread of Soviet influence in areas where our interests are involved. We should not expect the regimes established by Cuban or Soviet arms to become independent or to sell us strategic minerals or oil in times of stress or conflict. The battle for global supremacy has been joined. It is a battle that we dare not lose.

Index

ABOUT THE HOOVER INSTITUTION

The Hoover Institution at Stanford University consists of a specialized library and archival depository as well as a center devoted to advanced interdisciplinary study on domestic and international affairs in the twentieth century. Since its founding by Herbert Hoover in 1919, the Institution has become an international center for documentation and research on problems of political, economic, and social change throughout most of the world.

Centrally located on the Stanford campus, the Hoover Tower and the Lou Henry and Herbert Hoover Memorial buildings house a library of about 1.5 million volumes and one of the largest private archives in the world, consisting of about four thousand collections. In addition to Stanford students, faculty, and resident staff, users of the library and archives include scholars from all over the world who come to do research in the outstanding area collections on Africa and the Middle East, East Asia, Eastern Europe and Russia, Latin America, North America, and Western Europe.

The Domestic and the International Studies programs publish not only the results of basic research but also current public policy analyses by economists, political scientists, sociologists, and historians. Each year, the National, Peace and Public Affairs Fellows Program provides about fifteen scholars the opportunity to pursue advanced postdoctoral research. The results of this research are disseminated through a variety of channels: seminars, conferences, books published by the Hoover and other presses, journal articles, lectures, and interviews and articles in the news media. In addition, Hoover Institution staff members provide expert congressional testimony, consult for executive agencies, and engage in a wide variety of other public service activities. Some have joint appointments with Stanford University departments and other universities, teach courses, and offer seminars.

ALASKA
GREENLAND
(DEN.)
ICELAND
NORWAY
CANADA
UNITED
KINGDOM
DEN.
R. OF
IRELAND
Manchester
Birmingham
London
NETH.
BEL.
Hamburg
GERMANY
CZECH
Paris
FRANCE
SW.
AUSTR.
Milan
ITALY
Rome
Naples
Montreal
Toronto
Detroit
Boston
Chicago
Cleveland
Pittsburg
New York
Philadelphia
Baltimore
Washington
St. Louis
San Francisco
Los Angeles
UNITED STATES OF AMERICA
Dallas
Houston
AZORES (PORT.)
PORTUGAL
SPAIN
Madrid
GIBRALTER (U.K.)
MALTA
MADEIRA (PORT.)
BERMUDA (U.K.)
MOROCCO
TUNISIA
CANARY IS.
(SPAIN)
ALGERIA
LIBYA
BAHAMAS
Tropic of Cancer
MEXICO
Havana
CUBA
Mexico City
HAITI
DOM. REPUB.
JAMAICA
PUERTO RICO (U.S.A.)
BELIZE (U.K.)
GUATEMALA
HONDURAS
EL SALVADOR
NICARAGUA
COSTA RICA
PANAMA
MAURITANIA
MALI
NIGER
CHAD
SENEGAL
GAMBIA
GUINEA
BISSAU
GUINEA
UPPER VOLTA
BENIN
NIGERIA
S.L.
LIBERIA
IVORY
COAST
GHANA
TOGO
Lagos
CAMEROON
CENTRAL
AFR. EMPIRE
NETHS.
ANTILLES
ST. LUCIA
BARBADOS
GRENADA
TRINIDAD
AND
TOBAGO
Caracas
VENEZUELA
GUYANA
SURINAM
FR. GUIANA
Bogota
COLUMBIA
ECUADOR
EQUAT.
GUINEA
GABON
CONGO
Kinshasa
PERU
BRAZIL
Lima
ANGOLA
BOLIVIA
PARAGUAY
Rio de Janeiro
São Paulo
Tropic of Capricorn
NAMIBIA
(S.W.
AFRICA)
CHILE
URUGUAY
Santiago
Buenos Aires
ARGENTINA
FALKLAND IS.
(U.K.)